INSTRUCTOR'S EDITION

# Operations Management for Competitive Advantage

*ninth edition*

Richard B. Chase
*University of Southern California*

Nicholas J. Aquilano
*University of Arizona*

F. Robert Jacobs
*Indiana University*

McGraw-Hill Irwin

Boston Burr Ridge, IL Dubuque, IA Madison, WI New York San Francisco St. Louis
Bangkok Bogotá Caracas Lisbon London Madrid
Mexico City Milan New Delhi Seoul Singapore Sydney Taipei Toronto

# NOTE TO INSTRUCTORS

First, thank you for using our book in the past and considering this new edition for the future.

Operations management is a dynamic discipline, with new concepts appearing frequently. A critical priority is making this material available quickly. The challenge for a textbook is not only to capture these concepts but to anchor them to the existing body of knowledge in an understandable way. It goes without saying that the basics must be covered effectively as well.

We take pride in our reputation established in the previous eight editions as being the first textbook to introduce and make teachable the latest (and now standard) topics in the field.

We have continued to innovate in this edition. The major revisions to be found are:

- A new organization focuses time and coverage on key operations issues such as Project Management (Chapter 3), Process Analysis (Chapter 4), and Supply Chain Design (Section Three). Consulting and Reengineering are now combined in one chapter. Technical coverage of linear programming and transportation are relocated into a new Supplement at the end of the text called Linear Programming Using Excel Solver. Additional Supplements at text end are Financial Analysis and Operations Technology. These can be covered, or not, at your discretion.
- A new chapter on Process Analysis (Chapter 4) gives students specific tools and methods for analyzing a manufacturing or service process. Students will have a concise yet complete understanding that can then be applied throughout the rest of the course.
- Three hot topics in business today are Electronic Commerce, Supply Chain Management and Enterprise Resource Planning Systems. These topics are studied in the book from the view of the operations function with up-to-date high-level managerial material to clarify the "big picture" of what these topics are and why they are so important to 21st-Century business. In the electronic commerce area for example, we introduce the term "E-Ops" to provide a structure for presenting numerous applications of Electronic Commerce in operations throughout the book.
- Managerial Briefings open two key sections of the text and provide students with an executive-summary style introduction to the concepts of Electronic Commerce (Section 3) and Enterprise Resource Planning (Section 4).
- Technical Notes detail how operations-related problems such as Learning Curves, Waiting Line Management, Layout, and Location are solved. These are concise treatments of the many decisions that need to be made in designing, planning, and managing the operations of a business. Many spreadsheets are included on the student CD to demonstrate how these problems are quickly solved.



- The Student CD has been updated with new electronic tutorials, expanded Excel tools, enhanced quizzes, and greater use of the Internet. Two commercial software packages are also included—TreeAge Decision Analysis and Primavera SureTrak. We are also including Premium Solver from Frontline Systems. A CD icon in the text indicates Excel spreadsheets, simulations, and other assets located on the CD.

- New Internet Research projects provide a medium for Internet research.
- Key terms are now introduced in the chapter outline then defined at the end of each chapter.
- New advanced problems are included in chapters where appropriate.

- Additional cases, classroom exercises, test questions, and updates are available on a website supported by the authors of the book. This website address is *www.mhhe.com/chase.*

In this edition of the book we have continued our emphasis on showing both a manufacturing and services perspective on all of the topics. In addition, we have stressed a global perspective and where appropriate shown how the concepts apply in a global context. A final emphasis of the book has been to show the importance of cross-functional integration of the topics. Special icons are used in the book to highlight services, global, and cross-functional material.

Opening vignettes set the stage for the material in each chapter. Most of these vignettes have been updated with current examples. We believe we have found some real grabbers that can be used as interesting discussion items. Also included within each chapter are operations "Breakthroughs" which provide examples or extensions of the concepts we are presenting.

The book includes 31 interesting cases (11 of which are new this edition), solved problems at the end of chapters, formula summaries, new and revised problems, and updated bibliographies. The four-color design and extensive use of color photos speak for themselves.

Because spreadsheets have become more important as a tool in operations management, we include on the Student CD-ROM templates from problems and cases. These templates are found in the text by the CD icon.

We have included in the **Instructor's Edition** annotations to help teach the course. Titles of video segments from the Irwin Operations Management Video series are noted where they can enhance the text topic. Check answers are placed in the margin next to end-of-chapter problems.

The support package for *Operations Management for Competitive Advantage* includes:

**Student CD** packaged free with the text, includes Excel templates and data files, PowerPoint slides on key concepts for each chapter, practice exams, links to text-referenced websites, electronic tutorials, industry applications software such as Suretrack Project Manager, and video clips of key operations functions for student interest.

**Instructor's CD** (0072392770) places all the supplements, including the Instructor's Solutions Manual, Instructor's Resource Manual, the Test Bank and computerized testing system, PowerPoint slides, 50 video clips, and all the text figures, on one, easy-to-use CD tool. The "Presentation Manager" program allows you to build customized classroom presentations using the resources from the CD.

**Instructor's Solutions Manual** (0072392746) prepared by Ross Fink of Bradley University, contains worked solutions to text problems. A handy grid at the beginning of each chapter indicates what problems correspond to specific topics in the text and their level of difficulty.

**Instructor's Resource Manual** (0072392738) prepared by the authors, includes sample course syllabi, suggested cases, videos, case teaching notes, teaching tips, spreadsheets, and PowerPoint slides for each chapter.

**Test Bank** (0072392754) created by Marc Schniederjans of the University of Nebraska, provides true/false, multiple-choice, and solve-for-the-answer problems. The test bank is also available in a computerized version that allows you to generate, add, and edit questions, save and reload tests, and select questions based on level of difficulty. The computerized version is available on the Instructor's CD.

**Study Guide** (0072392797) prepared by Marilyn Helms of the University of Tennessee at Chattanooga, helps students prepare with an overview of each chapter, key terms, a review quiz, and problems and exercises that parallel text problems.

**Operations Management Video Series** consisting of 27 segments of about 10 minutes each, covers quality, inventory, lean production, CIM, process, and services. These videos show students OM concepts at work in real companies such as United Airlined, Nucor, Honda, and others.

**Internet version of the Beer Distribution Game** that can be played with teams of students in a classroom equipped with Internet access. This game is used to demonstrate Supply Chain System dynamics and is a great exercise for use with the new Chapter 8: Supply Chain Strategy. Details of the game can be found at *http://www.pom.edu/beer/.*

**E-Business Simulator** is a new Internet-based exercise that allows students to experience what it is like to run a business in Internet time. Students take on the role of purchasing, manufacturing, and sales in a fast-paced game where the goal is to make as much money as possible. The game is designed to work with Section Four: Planning and Controlling the Supply Chain. This game can be played in or out of the classroom, and can be played by individual students or by teams of students. Details of the game can be found at *http://www.pom.edu/ebus/.*

Packages available with the text include:

**Mike's Bikes Business Simulation on CD** provides the student with the opportunity to run Mike's Bikes, a bicycle manufacturing company. Through this simulation they'll apply their knowledge of the functional areas of business such as marketing, operations, finance, and accounting to a real business. You can run the game and utilize all these facets of business, or choose which ones you would prefer to focus on. If you'd like more information on Mike's Bikes you can go to *http://smartsims.com/simulations/mikes.bikes/index.asp.* Ask your Irwin/McGraw-Hill Sales Representative how you can package the CD with the text for your students.

**HOM Software for Windows** by Moses, Seshadri, and Yakir offers powerful Windows-based software for solving operations problems such as forecasting, process analysis, waiting line design and analysis, project management, MRP and inventory management, and capacity planning. HOM imports and exports files to and from Excel and each module has a detailed, step-by-step "how to solve" dialog box.

**Multimedia Business Cases** by Kotha/Dunbar. The CD features two cases, one on the Steinway Corporation and one on Starbucks. These cases are dynamic and visually appealing using graphics, animation, and audio components. This can be packaged with the text for student use.

We have written the book to make it more teachable for you with help from reviewers, colleagues, and focus group attendees who are gratefully acknowledged in the preface of the book.

Finally, we have done our best to make the book ineresting reading. We hope you and your students enjoy it.

**Dick Chase**
**Nick Aquilano**
**Bob Jacobs**

# INSTRUCTOR'S WALKTHROUGH

The following section highlights the key features developed to provide you with the best overall teaching text available. We hope these features give you maximum support while allowing you to tailor your course to fit the needs of your students.

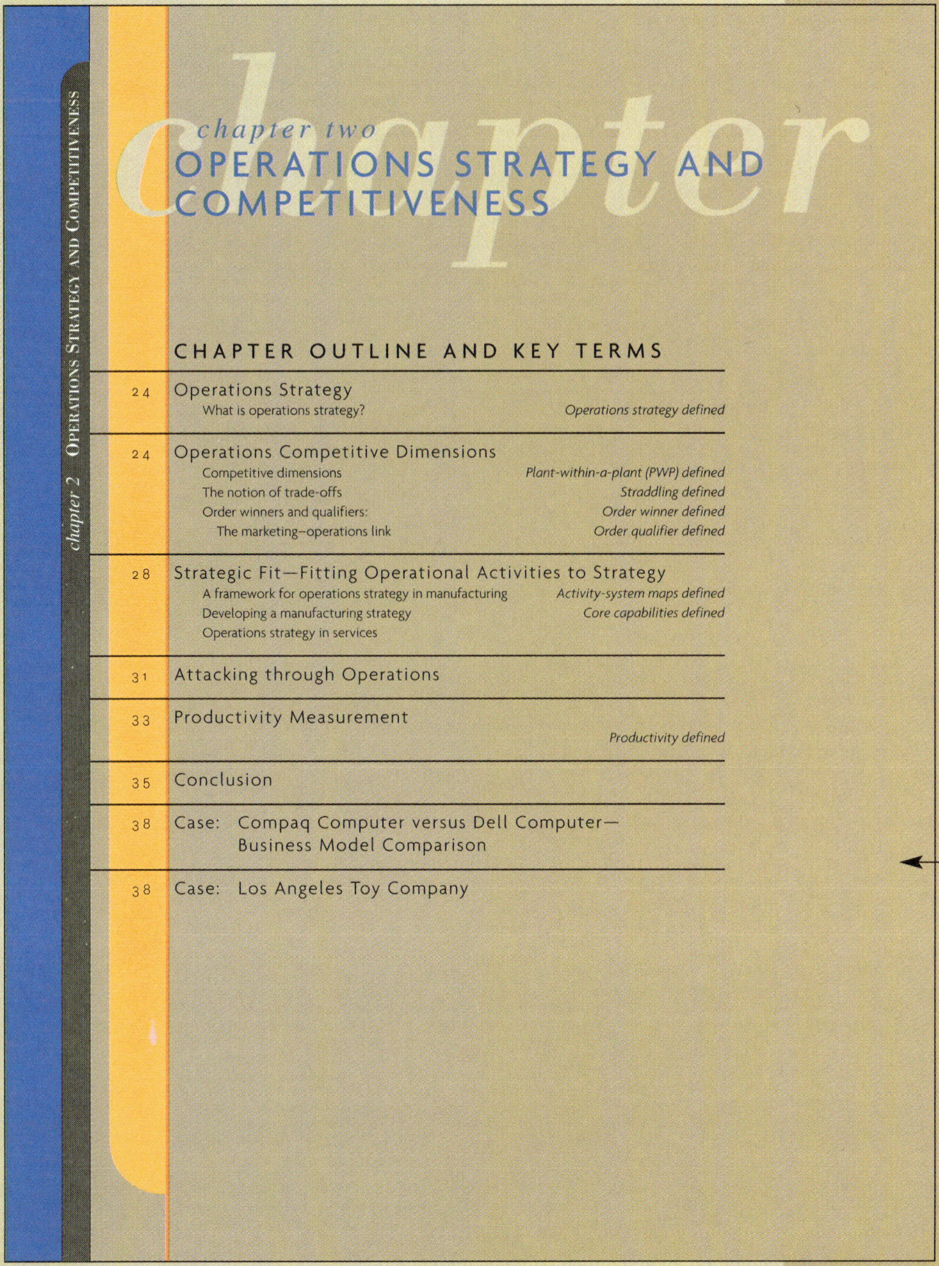

chapter 2 Operations Strategy and Competitiveness

chapter

*chapter two*

OPERATIONS STRATEGY AND COMPETITIVENESS

CHAPTER OUTLINE AND KEY TERMS



## Chapter Outlines and Key Terms

These prepare the student by providing an overview of the chapter material and highlighting key terms that will be introduced.

## Opening Vignettes

Each chapter opens with a short vignette to set the stage and help pique students' interest in the material about to be studied. A few examples include

General Electric and Quality "Black Belts" (Chapter 7)

Dell Computer—New Approach of Going to Market (Chapter 1)

Managing the Value Chain (Chapter 8)

2

Competitive strategy is about being different. It means deliberately choosing a different set of activities to deliver a unique mix of value. Southwest Airlines Company, for example, offers short-haul, low-cost, point-to-point service between midsize cities and secondary airports in large cities. Southwest avoids large airports and does not fly great distances. Southwest's frequent departures and low fares attract price-sensitive customers who otherwise would travel by bus or car, as well as convenience-oriented travelers who would choose a full-service airline on other routes.

Most managers describe strategic positioning in terms of their customers: "Southwest Airlines serves price- and convenience-sensitive travelers," for

example. But the essence of strategy is in business activities—choosing to perform activities differently than rivals. Otherwise, a strategy is nothing more than a marketing slogan that will not withstand competition.

A full-service airline is configured to get passengers from almost any point A to any point B. To reach many destinations and serve passengers with connecting flights, full-service airlines employ a hub-and-spoke system centered on major airports. To attract passengers who desire more comfort, they offer first-class or business-class service. To accommodate passengers who must change planes, they coordinate schedules and check and transfer baggage. And because some passengers will be traveling for many hours, full-service airlines serve meals.

Southwest, in contrast, tailors all its activities to delivering low-cost, convenient service on its particular type of route. Through fast turnarounds at the gate of only 15 minutes, it is able to keep planes flying longer hours than rivals and provide frequent departures with fewer aircraft. Southwest does not offer meals, assigned seats, interline baggage checking, or premium classes of service. Automated ticketing at the gate encourages customers to bypass travel agents, allowing Southwest to avoid their commissions. A standardized fleet of 737 aircraft boosts the efficiency of maintenance.

Southwest has staked out a unique and valuable strategic position based on a tailored set of activities.

**Source:** Reprinted by permission of the *Harvard Business Review*. From "What Is Strategy?" by M. E. Porter, November–December 1996. Copyright © 1996 by the President and Fellows of Harvard College; all rights reserved.

**BREAKTHROUGH**

*Supply Chain Management, Hong Kong Style*

The following are comments by Victor Fung, the Chairman of Li & Fung—the largest export trading company in Hong Kong and an innovator in the development of supply chain management. On behalf of its customers, primarily American and European retailers, Li & Fung works with an ever-expanding network of suppliers around the globe, sourcing clothing and other consumer goods ranging from toys to fashion accessories to luggage.

*Question: How do you define the difference between what Li & Fung does today—supply chain management—and the trading business founded by your grandfather in 1906?*

Fung: When my grandfather started the company in Canton, 90 years ago during the Ching dynasty, his "value added" was that he spoke English. In those days, it took three months to get to China by boat from the West; a letter would take a month. No one at the Chinese factories spoke English, and the American merchants spoke no Chinese. As an interpreter, my grandfather's commission was 15 percent.

Continuing through my father's generation, Li & Fung was basically a broker, charging a fee to put buyers and sellers together. But as an intermediary, the company was squeezed between the growing power of the buyers and the factories. Our margins slipped to 10 percent, then 5 percent, then 3 percent. When I returned to Hong Kong in 1976 my friends warned me that in 10 years buying agents like Li & Fung would be extinct. "Trading is a sunset industry," they all said.

My brother and I felt we could turn the business into something different, and so we took it through several stages of development. In the first stage, we acted as what I would call a regional sourcing agent and extended our geographic reach by establishing offices in Taiwan, Korea, and Singapore. Our knowledge of the region had value for customers. Most big buyers could manage their own sourcing if they needed to deal with only Hong Kong—they'd know which 10 factories to deal with and wouldn't need any help.

But dealing with the whole region was more complex. In textiles, quotas govern world trade. Knowing which quotas have been used up in Hong Kong, for example, tells you when you have to start buying from Taiwan.

Understanding products was also more complex. We knew that in Taiwan the synthetics were better, but that Hong Kong was the place to go for cottons. We could provide a package from the whole region rather than a single product from Hong Kong.

## Breakthrough Boxes

The Breakthroughs provide examples or expansions of the topics presented by highlighting leading companies practicing new, breakthrough ways to run their operations: Breakthroughs include

Project Management Information Systems in Everyday Use (Chapter 3)

The Fun Factor in Safety Incentive Programs (Technical Note 4)

Software Quality in the Information Age (Chapter 7)

*EXAMPLE 3.1: SINGLE TIME ESTIMATE*

Many firms that have tried to enter the notebook computer market have failed. Suppose your firm believes that there is a big demand in this market because existing products have not been designed correctly. They are too heavy, too large, or too small to have standard-size keyboards. Your intended computer will be small enough to carry inside a jacket pocket if need be. The ideal size will be no larger than 5 inches × 9½ inches × 1 inch with a folding keyboard. It should weigh no more than 15 ounces and have an LCD display, a micro disk drive, and an ethernet port. This should appeal to traveling businesspeople, but it could have a much wider market, including students. It should be priced in the $175–$200 range.

The project, then, is to design, develop, and produce a prototype of this small computer. In the rapidly changing computer industry, it is crucial to hit the market with a product of this sort in less than a year. Therefore, the project team has been allowed approximately eight months (35 weeks) to produce the prototype.

*SOLUTION*

The first charge of the project team is to develop a project network chart and estimate the likelihood of completing the prototype computer within the 35 weeks. Let's follow the steps in the development of the network.

1 **Activity identification.** The project team decides that the following activities are the major components of the project: design of the computer, prototype construction, prototype testing, methods specification (summarized in a report), evaluation studies of automatic assembly equipment, an assembly equipment study report, and a final report summarizing all aspects of the design, equipment, and methods.

2 **Activity sequencing and network construction.** On the basis of discussion with staff, the project manager develops the precedence table and sequence network shown in Exhibit 3.4. When constructing a network, take care to ensure that the activities are in the proper order and that the logic of their relationships is maintained. For example, it would be illogical to have a situation where Event A precedes Event B, B precedes C, and C precedes A.

## Examples with Solutions

Examples follow quantitative topics and demonstrate specific procedures and techniques. Clearly set off from the text, they help students understand the computations.

## Service Icons

Icons appear next to service discussions and examples. These emphasize that operations management encompasses services as well as manufacturing.

## Globe Icons

International examples and text discussions are identified by globe icons in the margin.

## Cross-Functional Icons

These icons highlight areas where operations management concepts "link" and integrate with other business functions.

## Internet Icons

These icons highlight exercises that direct students to the Internet for research.

To solve the problem the Excel Solver application needs to be accessed. The Solver is found by selecting Tools and then Solver from the Excel menu. A screen similar to what is shown below should appear. If you cannot find Solver at that location, the required add-in might not have been added when Excel was initially installed on your computer. Solver can easily be added if you have your original Excel installation disk.

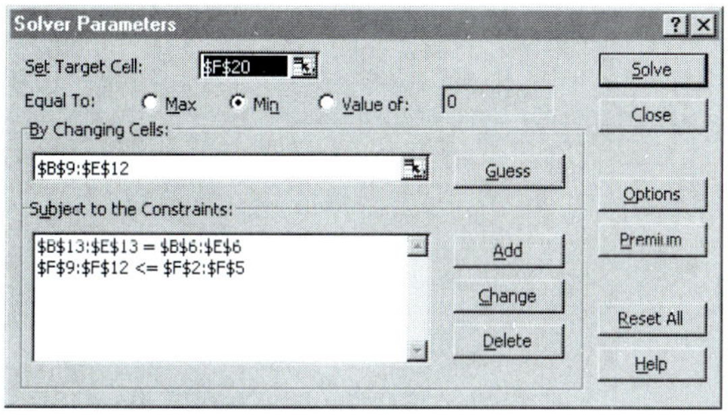


Solver parameters now need to be set. First set the target cell. This is the cell where the total cost associated with the solution is calculated. In our sample problem this is cell F20. Next we need to indicate that we are minimizing this cell. Selecting the "Min" button does this. The location of our solution is indicated in the "Changing Cells." These cells are B9 through E12 in our example.

## Excel Spreadsheet Example

Where applicable, screen captures of an Excel spreadsheet are included. These templates are included on the student CD.

### SOLVED PROBLEM 2

Here are the actual demands for a product for the past six quarters. Using focus forecasting rules 1 through 5, find the best rule to use in predicting the third quarter of this year.

| | Quarter | | | |
|---|---|---|---|---|
| | I | II | III | IV |
| Last year | 1,200 | 700 | 900 | 1,100 |
| This year | 1,400 | 1,000 | | |

#### Solution

*Rule 1:* Next three months' demand = Last three months' demand.

Testing this on the last three months, $F_{II} = A_{I}$; therefore $F_{II} = 1{,}400$.

Actual demand was 1,000, so $\dfrac{1{,}000}{1{,}400} = 71.4\%$.

*Rule 2:* This quarter's demand equals demand in the same quarter last year.
The forecast for the second quarter this year will therefore be 700, the amount for that quarter last year.

Exhibit 8.7

**Product Density Shipping Cost Comparison**

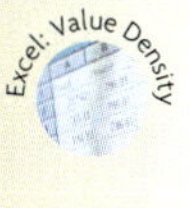


Carrying cost rate = 0.3 Days saved = 6

| Shipping Weight (Pounds) | United Parcel Service: 8-Day Ground Service | Federal Express: 2-Day Air Service | Cost Savings with UPS | Break-Even Product Value | Break-Even Product Value (per Pound) |
|---|---|---|---|---|---|
| 1 | $3.30 | $18.25 | $14.95 | $3,031.53 | $3,031.53 |
| 2 | $3.60 | $20.50 | 16.90 | 3,426.94 | 1,713.47 |
| 3 | $3.85 | $22.50 | 18.65 | 3,781.81 | 1,260.60 |
| 4 | $4.10 | $24.50 | 20.40 | 4,136.67 | 1,034.17 |
| 5 | $4.30 | $26.75 | 22.45 | 4,552.36 | 910.47 |
| 6 | $4.50 | $28.75 | 24.25 | 4,917.36 | 819.56 |
| 7 | $4.65 | $30.75 | 26.10 | 5,292.50 | 756.07 |
| 8 | $4.75 | $32.75 | 28.00 | 5,677.78 | 709.72 |
| 9 | $4.85 | $34.75 | 29.90 | 6,063.06 | 673.67 |
| 10 | $5.00 | $36.75 | 31.75 | 6,438.19 | 643.82 |

An icon in the margin indicates where on the CD the student will find the spreadsheet.

## Photos and Exhibits

The Ninth Edition includes over 100 photos and 280 exhibits to enhance the visual appeal of the text and clarify textual discussions.

Campbell uses a system they call Continuous Product Replenishment. At the food retailer's warehouse, Campbell product arrives from the plant to replenish inventory at the same steady rate as the consumer takes it off the shelf. CPR is driven by an electronic ordering system managed by Campbell, freeing the retailer from this task. Steady production that meets predetermined inventory levels results in cost efficiencies across the entire supply chain.

## Box Inserts

Insights into some of the best current operations management practices are provided here. The inserts come from a variety of newspapers, journals, and business magazines. Examples include

Characteristics of a Well-Designed Service System (Chapter 6)

Studies Find "Quality Stock" Yield Big Payoff (Chapter 7)

Paying the Price—Data Show Damaging Effects of Labor Turnover (Chapter 12)

### Project Managers, Challenges

Despite the fact that 84 percent of project managers are responsible for staying within a project budget, only 15 percent of the time are they faced with direct ramifications for not doing so. In fact, 16 percent of project managers don't always know the budget of their jobs, according to a survey of project managers conducted by Zweig White & Associates, of Natick, Massachusetts.

The survey showed that project managers consider meeting schedules and budgets to be the greatest challenge that they face (19 percent). This may be partially attributed to the areas they rated as their two top complaints—insufficient or inadequate staff support (10 percent) and responsibility without authority (9 percent).

Project managers cited several reasons for not performing their best. Seventeen percent said that all team members are rarely or never allowed to see their own portion of the scope of services for a project. Also, they do not receive much training. Just 26 percent of firms have mandatory formal training for project managers, while 40 percent have optional training, and 29 percent have no training. For the firms that do offer training, the level is inadequate. Few than half of project managers are trained to perform basic tasks such as opening a job number, charging time, and budgeting.

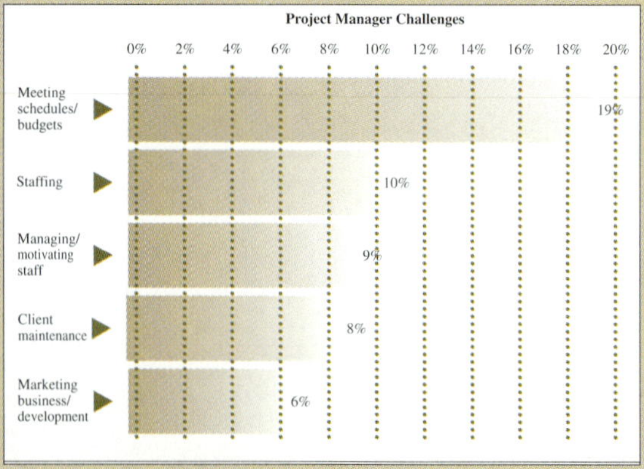


Source: "Project Managers, Challenges," *IIE Solutions*, December 1996, p. 9. Reprinted with permission of the Institute of Industrial Engineers, 25 Technology Park, Norcross, GA 30092, 770-449-0461. Copyright © 1996.

## Key Terms

The unique vocabulary of *Operations* is highlighted in the Key Terms section at the end of the chapter and includes definitions.

### KEY TERMS

**Project** A series of related jobs usually directed toward some major output and requiring a significant period of time to perform.

**Project management** Planning, directing, and controlling resources (people, equipment, material) to meet the technical, cost, and time constraints of a project.

**Pure project** A structure for organizing a project where a self-contained team works full-time on the project.

**Functional project** A structure where team members are assigned from the functional units of the organization. The team members remain a part of their functional units and typically are not dedicated to the project.

**Matrix project** A structure that blends the functional and pure project structures. Each project uses people from different functional areas. A dedicated project manager decides what tasks need to be performed and when, but the functional managers control which people to use.

**Project milestone** A specific event in a project.

**Work breakdown structure** The hierarchy of project tasks, subtasks, and work packages.

**Activities** Pieces of work within a project that consume time. The completion of all the activities of a project marks the end of the project.

**Gantt chart** Shows in a graphic manner the amount of time involved and the sequence in which activities can be performed. Often referred to as a *bar chart.*

**Critical path** The sequence of activities in a project that forms the longest chain in terms of their time to complete. This path contains zero slack time.

**Immediate predecessor** Activity that needs to be completed immediately before another activity.

**Slack time** The time that an activity can be delayed; the difference between the late and early start times of an activity.

**Early start schedule** A project schedule that lists all activities by their early start times.

**Late start schedule** A project schedule that lists all activities by their late start times. This schedule may create savings by postponing purchases of material and other costs associated with the project.

**Time-cost models** Extension of the critical path models that consider the trade-off between the time required to complete an activity and cost.

## Formula Reviews

These lists at the end of chapters summarize formulas in one spot for easy student access and review.

### FORMULA REVIEW

**Expected Time**

[3.1] $$\text{ET} = \frac{a + 4m + b}{6}$$

**Variance ($\sigma^2$) of the activity times**

[3.2] $$\sigma^2 = \left(\frac{b - a}{6}\right)^2$$

## Solved Problems

Representative example problems are placed at the end of appropriate chapters. Each includes a detailed, worked-out solution and provides another level of support for students before they try problems on their own.

### SOLVED PROBLEMS

#### SOLVED PROBLEM 1

A project has been defined to contain the following list of activities, along with their required times for completion:

| Activity | Time (days) | Immediate Predecessors |
|---|---|---|
| A | 1 | — |
| B | 4 | A |
| C | 3 | A |
| D | 7 | A |
| E | 6 | B |
| F | 2 | C, D |
| G | 7 | E, F |
| H | 9 | D |
| I | 4 | G, H |

*a.* Draw the critical path diagram.
*b.* Show the early start and early finish times.
*c.* Show the critical path.
*d.* What would happen if activity F was revised to take four days instead of two?

#### Solution

The answers to *a*, *b*, and *c* are shown in the following diagram.

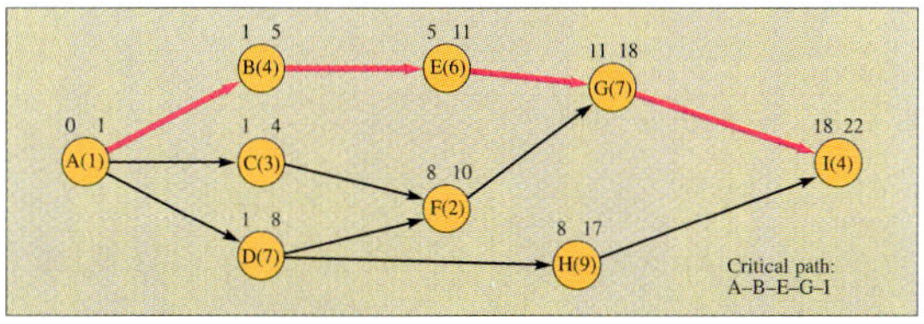


*d.* New critical path: A–D–F–G–I. Time of completion is 23 days.

## Cases

Located at the end of most chapters, 31 cases allow students to think critically about issues discussed in the chapter. Cases include:

Hank Kolb, Director Quality Assurance (Chapter 7)

AOL's move to Flat-Rate Pricing (Chapter 6)

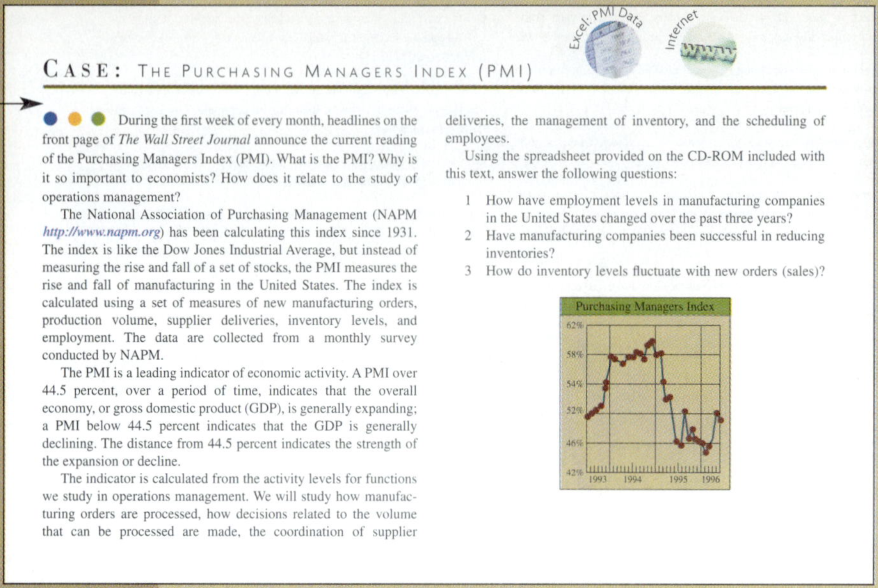

**CASE:** THE PURCHASING MANAGERS INDEX (PMI)

During the first week of every month, headlines on the front page of *The Wall Street Journal* announce the current reading of the Purchasing Managers Index (PMI). What is the PMI? Why is it so important to economists? How does it relate to the study of operations management?

The National Association of Purchasing Management (NAPM *http://www.napm.org*) has been calculating this index since 1931. The index is like the Dow Jones Industrial Average, but instead of measuring the rise and fall of a set of stocks, the PMI measures the rise and fall of manufacturing in the United States. The index is calculated using a set of measures of new manufacturing orders, production volume, supplier deliveries, inventory levels, and employment. The data are collected from a monthly survey conducted by NAPM.

The PMI is a leading indicator of economic activity. A PMI over 44.5 percent, over a period of time, indicates that the overall economy, or gross domestic product (GDP), is generally expanding; a PMI below 44.5 percent indicates that the GDP is generally declining. The distance from 44.5 percent indicates the strength of the expansion or decline.

The indicator is calculated from the activity levels for functions we study in operations management. We will study how manufacturing orders are processed, how decisions related to the volume that can be processed are made, the coordination of supplier deliveries, the management of inventory, and the scheduling of employees.

Using the spreadsheet provided on the CD-ROM included with this text, answer the following questions:

1 How have employment levels in manufacturing companies in the United States changed over the past three years?
2 Have manufacturing companies been successful in reducing inventories?
3 How do inventory levels fluctuate with new orders (sales)?



## Text Website

Visit the website at *www.mhhe.com/chase* for text updates, additional quizzes and cases, *Business Week* articles, and operations tours.

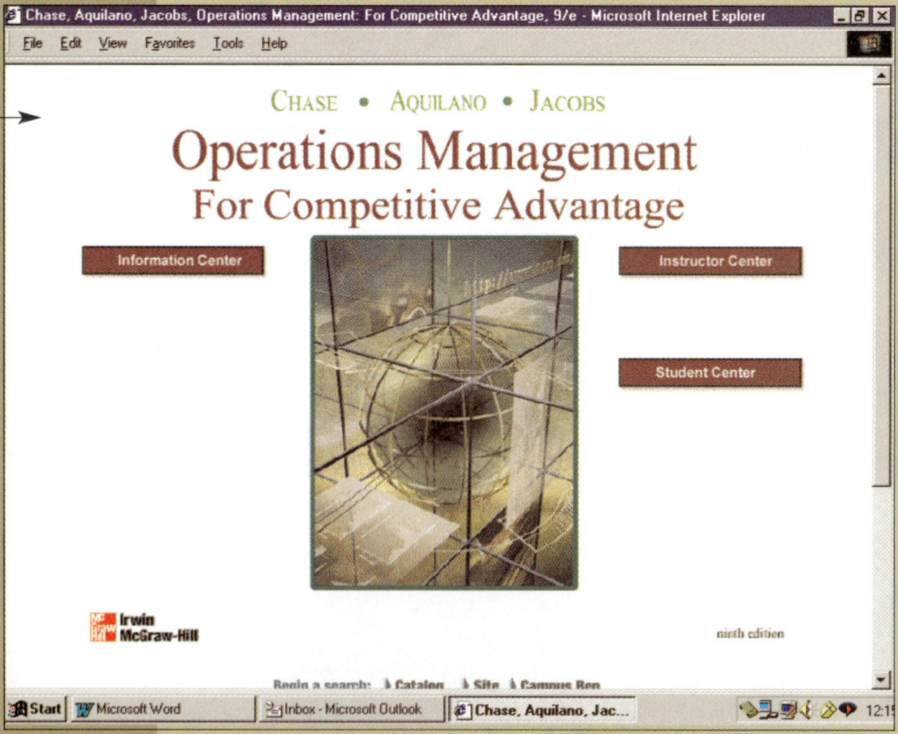

# For the Instructor

The following elements are contained only in the instructor's edition of the text:

## STRATEGIC FIT—FITTING OPERATIONAL ACTIVITIES TO STRATEGY

Vol. VI "Valuation of Operations at ABTco"

All of the activities that make up a firm's operation relate to one another. Making these activities efficient means minimizing their total cost. On the other hand, making them effective means making the combined set of activities support the firm's strategy. Once again, consider Southwest Airlines. Southwest's rapid gate turnaround, which allows frequent departures and greater use of aircraft, is essential to its high-convenience, low-cost positioning. But how does Southwest achieve this? Part of the answer lies in the company's well-paid gate and ground crews, whose productivity in turnarounds is enhanced by flexible union rules. But the bigger part of the answer lies in how Southwest performs (or avoids) other activities. With no meals, no seat assignments, and no interline baggage transfers, Southwest avoids having to perform activities that slow down other airlines. It selects airports and routes to avoid congestion that introduces delays. Southwest's strict limits on the type and length of routes make standardized aircraft possible: Southwest uses only Boeing 737s. Exhibit 2.1 shows how Southwest's strategy is implemented through a set of activities designed to deliver it.[4]

Activity-system maps

**Activity-system maps,** such as the one for Southwest, show how a company's strategy is delivered through a set of tailored activities. In companies with a clear strategy, a number of higher-order strategic themes (in green) can be identified and implemented through

### Video Icons

These margin icons include the title of a segment in the Irwin/McGraw-Hill Operations Management Video Series that enhances the text discussion.

## PROBLEMS

1 The following activities are part of a project to be scheduled using CPM:

| Activity | Immediate Predecessor | Time (weeks) |
|---|---|---|
| A | — | 6 |
| B | A | 3 |
| C | A | 7 |
| D | C | 2 |
| E | B, D | 4 |
| F | D | 3 |
| G | E, F | 7 |

*a.* Draw the network.
*b.* What is the critical path?
*c.* How many weeks will it take to complete the project?
*d.* How much slack does activity B have?

1. *a.* See ISM.
*b.* A–C–D–E–G.
*c.* 26 weeks.
*d.* Six weeks (15 − 9).

2 Schedule the following activities using CPM:

| Activity | Immediate Predecessor | Time (weeks) |
|---|---|---|
| A | — | 1 |
| B | A | 4 |
| C | A | 3 |
| D | B | 2 |
| E | C, D | 5 |
| F | D | 2 |
| G | F | 2 |
| H | E, G | 3 |

*a.* Draw the network.
*b.* What is the critical path?
*c.* How many weeks will it take to complete the project?
*d.* Which activities have slack, and how much?

2. *a.* See ISM.
*b.* A–B–D–E–H.
*c.* 15 weeks.
*d.* C, 3 weeks; F, 1 week; G, 1 week.

### Check Answers

These answers provide instructors with a quick reference in class.

## Operations Management Center

*www.mhhe.com/pom/*

The ultimate Internet resource for faculty looking for pedagogical support or original source referencing, and for students in search of current operations management information, this single site provides support material for all of the Irwin/McGraw-Hill texts. The **OMC** offers a wealth of linkages that complement rather than duplicate the material found in the texts themselves, thereby offering instructors many options for customizing their courses. Created and maintained by Professor Byron Finch of Miami University of Ohio, this site is updated regularly with new features, information, and material.

Besides serving as a virtual electronic library for operations management, the **OMC** provides direct access to individual author-maintained Irwin/McGraw-Hill textbook websites.

To support all of the OM texts, this site offers links to a variety of online OM resources:

Links to OM-related *Business Week* online articles

OM organizations

Online OM Publications

OM Resources, organized by subject or topic

OM Company Tours area with an overview listing of OM topics and a "movie review" for the top 50 real company sites available

Job, Travel, Humor, and College and University resources

Internet Tools, such as search engines, general references, and software sites

General business news and publications

New page devoted to ERP

Descriptions of all segments in the Irwin/McGraw-Hill OM Video Library

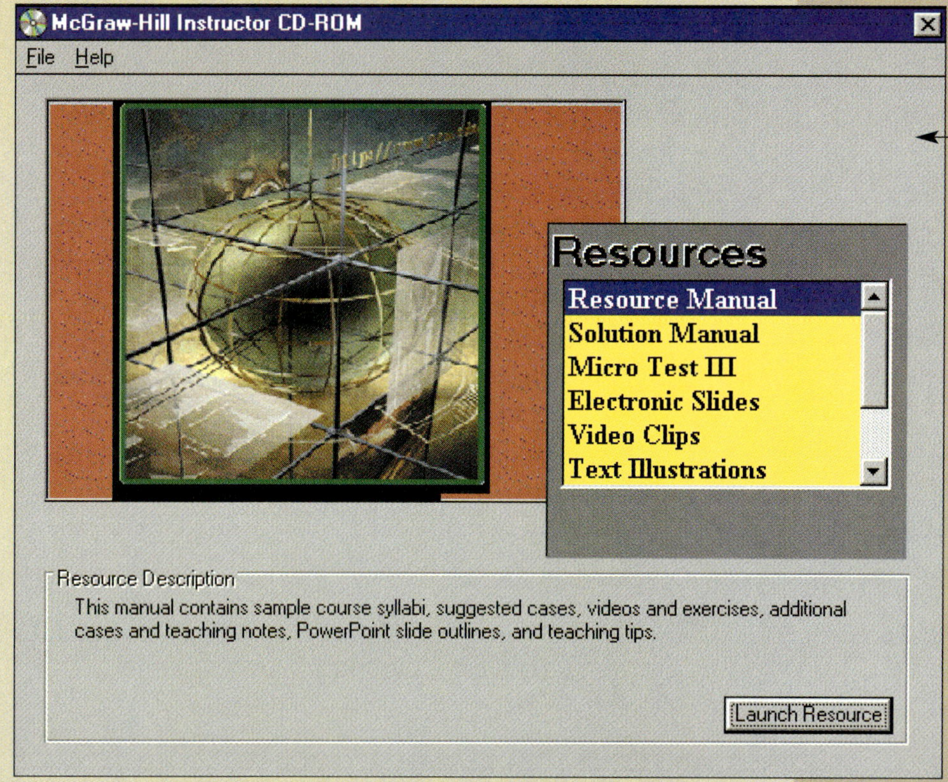


## Instructor Presentation CD-ROM

All of the tools for planning and creating a multimedia lecture presentation are combined in this single Presentation CD-ROM. PowerPoint slides, photos and images, video clips, an Instructor's Manual, and an Electronic Test Bank are a few of the features which allow the instructor to customize lecture notes, select visuals, create tests, and format their presentation using one CD-ROM.

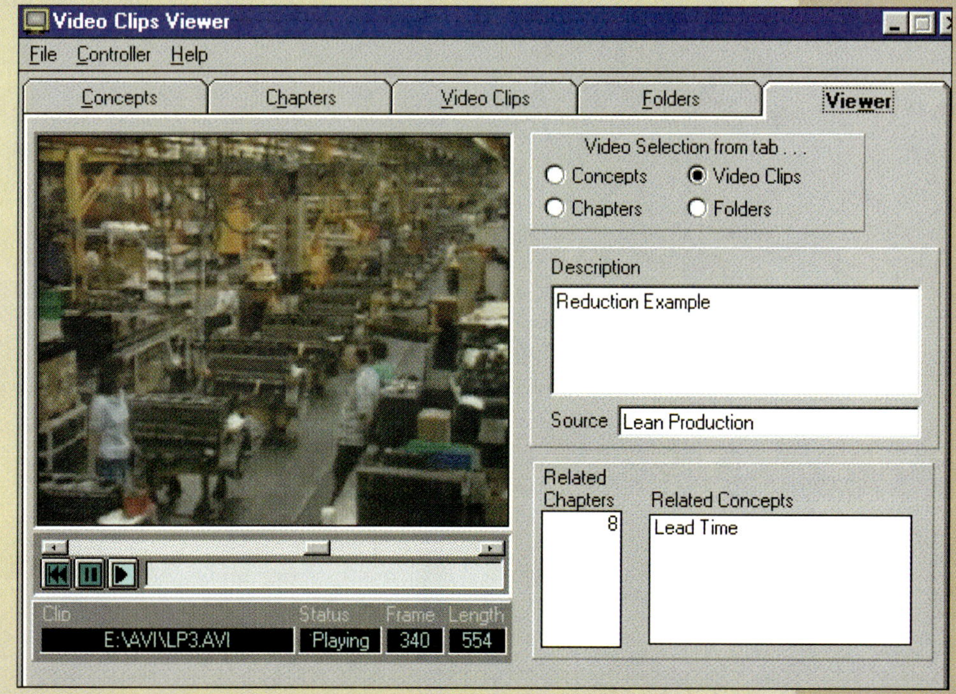


A collection of video clips sorted by concept and chapter can be integrated easily giving ample opportunities to incorporate topic-specific, real-world multimedia material into lectures.

Files can be imported or exported and material on the CD-ROM can be customized to meet the instructor's specific needs.

## HOM Operations Management Software for Windows, by Moses, Seshadri, and Yakir

This new software package developed at NYU offers powerful Windows-based programs for solving real world type operating problems, such as forecasting, process analysis, waiting line design and analysis, project management, MRP and inventory management, and capacity planning and management. All programs include standard edit, file, and help icons and constant "run," "results," and "plot" options. **HOM** imports and exports files to and from Excel and each module has detailed, step-by-step "how to solve" dialog boxes for quick reference or for beginning students.

The **HOM** package also includes data sets drawn from classic Operations cases as well as two integrative cases which utilize all the modules, one from a service company (United Branch Bank) and one from a manufacturer (Ice Queen). The Table of Contents includes Integrative Cases; Process Analysis and Design; Waiting Line Design and Management; Inventory Management and MRP; Forecasting; Aggregate Planning; Project and Time Management; Quality Management.

**HOM** is available as an independent text/software package or at a discount, shrinkwrapped with the text.

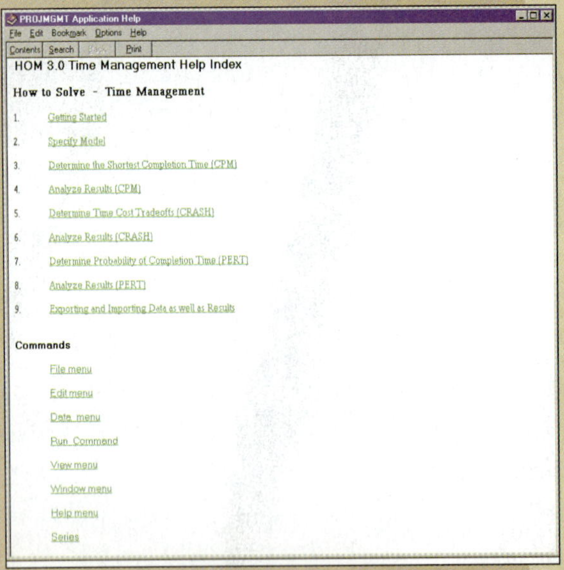


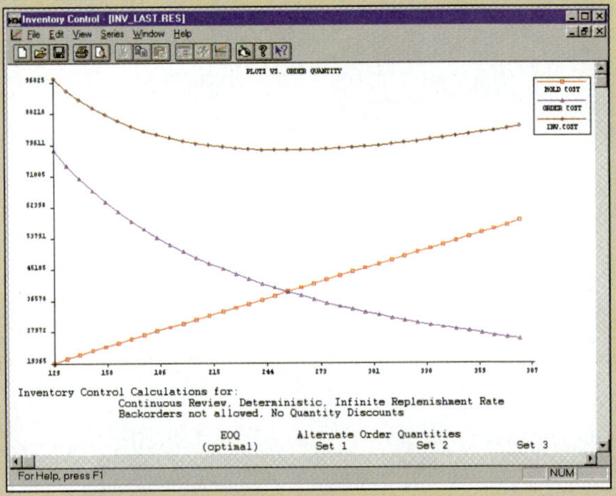


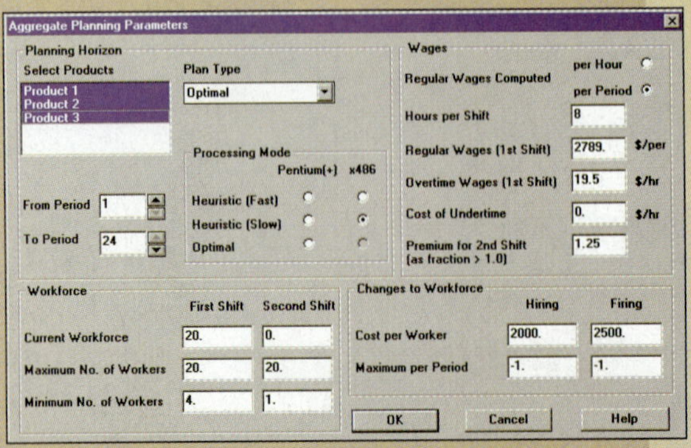


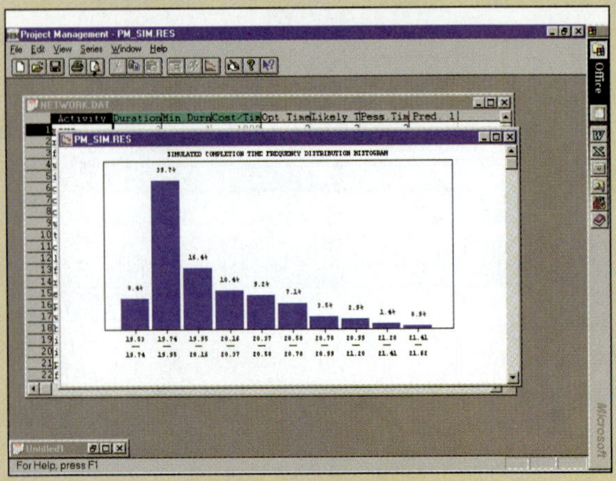

# Operations Management for Competitive Advantage

# THE MCGRAW-HILL/IRWIN SERIES

## Operations and Decision Sciences

### OPERATIONS MANAGEMENT

**Bowersox and Closs**
Logistical Management: The Integrated Supply Chain Process
*First Edition*

**Chase, Aquilano, and Jacobs**
Operations Management for Competitive Advantage
*Ninth Edition*

**Chu, Hottenstein, and Greenlaw**
PROSIM for Windows
*Third Edition*

**Cohen and Apte**
Manufacturing Automation
*First Edition*

**Davis, Aquilano, and Chase**
Fundamentals of Operations Management
*Third Edition*

**Dobler and Burt**
Purchasing and Supply Management
*Sixth Edition*

**Flaherty**
Global Operations Management
*First Edition*

**Fitzsimmons and Fitzsimmons**
Service Management: Operations, Strategy, Information Technology
*Third Edition*

**Gray and Larson**
Project Management: The Managerial Process
*First Edition*

**Hill**
Manufacturing Strategy: Text & Cases
*Third Edition*

**Hopp and Spearman**
Factory Physics
*Second Edition*

**Jacobs and Whybark**
Why ERP: A Primer on SAP Implementaion
*First Edition*

**Lambert and Stock**
Strategic Logistics Management
*Third Edition*

**Leenders and Fearon**
Purchasing and Supply Chain Management
*Eleventh Edition*

**Moses, Seshadri, and Yakir**
HOM Operations Management Software for Windows
*First Edition*

**Nahmias**
Production and Operations Analysis
*Fourth Edition*

**Nicholas**
Competitive Manufacturing Management
*First Edition*

**Olson**
Introduction to Information Systems Project Management
*First Edition*

**Pinedo and Chao**
Operations Scheduling
*First Edition*

**Sanderson and Uzumeri**
Managing Product Families
*First Edition*

**Schroeder**
Operations Management: Contemporary Concepts and Cases
*First Edition*

**Schonberger and Knod**
Operations Management
*Seventh Edition*

**Simchi-Levi, Kaminsky, and Simchi-Levi**
Designing and Managing the Supply Chain: Concepts, Strategies, and Case Studies
*First Edition*

**Sterman**
Business Dynamics: Systems Thinking and Modeling for a Complex World
*First Edition*

**Stevenson**
Production/Operations Management
*Sixth Edition*

**Vollmann, Berry, and Whybark**
Manufacturing Planning & Control Systems
*Fourth Edition*

**Zipkin**
Foundations of Inventory Management
*First Edition*

### QUANTITATIVE METHODS AND MANAGEMENT SCIENCE

**Alwan**
Statistical Process Analysis
*First Edition*

**Bodily, Carraway, Frey, Pfeifer**
Quantitative Business Analysis: Casebook
*First Edition*

**Bodily, Carraway, Frey, Pfeifer**
Quantitative Business Analysis: Text and Cases
*First Edition*

**Bonini, Hausman, and Bierman**
Quantitative Analysis for Business Decisions
*Ninth Edition*

**Hesse**
Managerial Spreadsheet Modeling and Analysis
*First Edition*

**Hillier, Hillier, Lieberman**
Introduction to Management Science: A Modeling and Case Studies Approach with Spreadsheets
*First Edition*

# Operations Management for Competitive Advantage

*ninth edition*


**Richard B. Chase**
*University of Southern California*

**Nicholas J. Aquilano**
*University of Arizona*

**F. Robert Jacobs**
*Indiana University*



McGraw-Hill Irwin

Boston Burr Ridge, IL Dubuque, IA Madison, WI New York San Francisco St. Louis
Bangkok Bogotá Caracas Lisbon London Madrid
Mexico City Milan New Delhi Seoul Singapore Sydney Taipei Toronto

*McGraw-Hill Higher Education*
*A Division of The* ***McGraw-Hill*** *Companies*

OPERATIONS MANAGEMENT FOR COMPETITIVE ADVANTAGE

Published by McGraw-Hill/Irwin, an imprint of The McGraw-Hill Companies, Inc. 1221 Avenue of the Americas, New York, NY, 10020. 

This book is printed on acid-free paper.

domestic 1 2 3 4 5 6 7 8 9 0 VNH/VNH 0 9 8 7 6 5 4 3 2 1 0
international 1 2 3 4 5 6 7 8 9 0 VNH/VNH 0 9 8 7 6 5 4 3 2 1 0

ISBN 0-07-232315-9

Publisher: *Jeffrey J. Shelstad*
Executive editor: *Richard T. Hercher, Jr.*
Senior developmental editor: *Gail Korosa*
Marketing manager: *Zina Craft*
Project manager: *Christine A. Vaughan*
Senior production supervisor: *Heather D. Burbridge*
Freelance design coordinator: *Gino Cieslik*
Senior photo research coordinator: *Keri Johnson*
Senior supplement coordinator: *Becky Szura*
New media developer: *Ed Przyzycki*
Cover design: *Gino Cieslik*
Interior design: *Andrew Curtis*
Cover illustration: *Henk Dawson*
Compositor: *Interactive Composition Corporation*
Typeface: *10/12 Times Roman*
Printer: *Quebecor World*



**Library of Congress Cataloging-in-Publication Data**

Chase, Richard B.
Operations management for competitive advantage / Richard B. Chase, Nicholas J. Aquilano, F. Robert Jacobs.—9th ed.
p. cm.
Rev. ed. of: Production and operations management /R. B. Chase, 8th ed. c1998.
ISBN 0-07-232315-9 (alk. paper)
1. Production management. I. Aquilano, Nicholas J. II. Jacobs, F. Robert. III. Chase, Richard B. Production and operations management. IV. Title.

TS155 .C4237 2001
658.5—dc21

00-038321

INTERNATIONAL EDITION ISBN 0071180303

*To our wives*
*Harriet, Nina, and Jeanne*
*and to our children*
*Laurie, Andy, Glenn, Rob, Christine, and Batsheva*
*Don, Kara, and Mark*
*Jennifer and Suzy*

# PREFACE

Operations management (OM) has been a key element in the improvement in productivity in businesses around the world. Creating a *competitive advantage* through operations requires an understanding of how the operations function contributes to productivity growth. However, our intent in this book is to do more than just show you what companies are doing to create competitive advantage through OM. Our overriding goal is to create a competitive advantage for you in the marketplace by conveying a set of skills and tools that you can actually apply.

Three hot topics in business today are Electronic Commerce, Supply Chain Management, and Enterprise Resource Planning Systems. These topics are studied in the book from the view of the operations function with up-to-date high-level managerial material to clarify the "big picture" of what these topics are and why they are so important to business today. In the electronic commerce area for example, we introduce the term E-Ops to provide a structure for presenting numerous applications of Electronic Commerce in operations throughout the book. Applications that range from high-tech manufacturing to high-touch service are used in the balanced treatment of the traditional topics of the field. Operations management requires a global perspective for many of the topics. Operations management is best done with significant cross-functional integration. Accounting, finance, marketing, human resources management, purchasing, logistics, and engineering impact how firms are run operationally. To highlight our emphasis on services, globalization, and cross-functional integration, we've used the logos you see here in the text margin next to these discussions.

Technical Notes detail how operations related problems are solved. These are concise treatments of the many decisions that need to be made in designing, planning and managing the operations of a business. Many spreadsheets are included on the CD to help clarify how these problems are quickly solved. We've indicated those spreadsheets with the spreadsheet logo shown here in the margin.

There are other instances where we've referenced in the text material that can be found on the CD. For example, in Chapter Four on Process Analysis we've included a slot machine simulation program on the CD and have indicated it with the logo you see in the margin. When you see these logos, check your CD.

Managerial Briefing sections follow Sections Three and Four and provide executive summary-style introductions to concepts of Electronic Commerce and Enterprise Resource Planning.

Operations Management should appeal to individuals who want to be directly involved in making products or providing services. The entry-level operations specialist is the person who determines how best to design, supply, and run the processes. Senior operations managers are responsible for setting the strategic direction of the company from an operations standpoint, deciding what technologies should be used, where facilities should be located, and managing the facilities that make the products or provide the services. Operations Management is an interesting mix of managing people and applying sophisticated technology. The goal is to efficiently create wealth by supplying quality goods and services.

Features to aid in your understanding of the material include the following:

- Solved problems at the end of chapters to serve as models that can be reviewed prior to attempting problems.
- Key terms highlighted in the chapter outline and their definitions at the end of each chapter.
- Answers to selected problems in Appendix A.
- A CD that includes PowerPoint slide outlines of each chapter, Excel® spreadsheets

for many of the solved problems and other examples, practice exams, electronic tutorials, Internet links, and video clips that describe important terminology.
- Breakthrough Boxes to demonstrate leading-edge companies or practices that are innovative and trailblazing.

Our aim is to cover the latest and the most important issues facing OM managers, as well as the basic tools and techniques. We supply many examples of leading-edge companies and practices. We have done our best to make the book interesting reading, and as we said at the outset, give you a competitive advantage in your career.

We hope you enjoy it.

## ACKNOWLEDGMENTS

Several very talented scholars have made major contributions to specific chapters in the book. We are pleased to thank the following individuals:

Clay Whybark of the University of North Carolina for the Process Analysis problems and ideas for the "Bradford Manufacturing" Aggregate Planning case.

Bill Ruch of Arizona State University for his productivity problems.

Doug Blocher of Indiana University for his ideas on Supply Chain Strategy and Inventory Management, and Kurt Bretthauer for his help with the SAP R/3 tutorial.

Ed Silver of Western Ontario for his detailed editing of numerous sections of the book.

Ravi Behara of George Mason University for assistance with Business Process Reengineering.

Louis R. Chase, editor extraordinaire and Shakespeare expert for ideas on several chapters.

Marilyn Helms of the University of Tennessee at Chattanooga for her help with Operations Strategy and Competitiveness and Just-in-Time systems.

Michael Maggard of Northeastern University for his ideas on Service Design.

"Raj" Rajagopalan, Tom Housel, Yahuda Bassok, Jon Yormark, Ram Challappa, and Christoph Langdon of the University of Southern California for their input on E-Ops.

Sriram Dasu, Richard McBride, and Constantin Vaitsos, also at USC, for their suggestions on a variety of topics in the book.

Randy Fernando, a student at Cornell University, for contributing the Java Slot Machine. Of course, Randy is looking for a job, so if you need a great web programmer contact him at prf3@cornell.edu (Web Page: http://www.people.cornell.edu/pages/prf3/index.html). Special thanks to Randy for the contribution.

Special thanks to John McClain of Cornell University for contributing the spreadsheet simulations titled Cell.xls and LineSim.xls.

Special thanks also to Jeffrey Rummel of University of Connecticut who solved all of the examples and problems and checked our answers for accuracy.

Marc Schniederjans of the University of Nebraska prepared the Test Bank and PowerPoint slides, Ross Fink of Bradley University prepared the Instructor's Solutions Manual. Marilyn Helms of the University of Tennessee at Chattanooga revised the Study Guide. Jaideep Motwani of Grand Valley State University wrote the practice quizzes for the student CD. These supplements are a great deal of work to write, and we appreciate their efforts that make teaching the course easier for everyone who uses the text.

We also wish to thank the following reviewers for their many thoughtful suggestions for this edition: Sunil Babar, *Florida Atlantic University;* Paul Bobrowski, *Syracuse University;* Chen Chung, *University of Kentucky;* Dan Heiser, *DePaul University;* Lew Hofman, *College of New Jersey;* Neil Hunt, *Suffolk University;* Shailendra Jha, *Wilfrid Laurier University;* Christer Karlsson, *Stockholm School of Economics;* Debasish Mallick, *Boston College;* Arthur Porter, *Southern Utah*

*University;* Z. Radovilsky, *California State University at Hayward;* William Ruch, *University of Arizona;* Gary Salegna, *Illinois State University;* Glen Schmidt, *Georgetown University;* Marc Schniederjans, *University of Nebraska;* Edward Silver, *University of Calgary;* Charles Watts, *John Carroll University;* Rachel Yang, *University of Illinois;* and Fred Zimmerman, *University of St. Thomas.*

Participants in a text survey shared their ideas about ways to improve teaching the course and what we could do to improve the text. We want to thank Joseph Biggs, *California Polytechnic State University;* Kenneth Boyer, *DePaul University;* Charles Corbett, *UCLA;* James Mike Farrell, *St. Edward University;* Edward A. Genske, *Saginaw Valley State University;* Raymond A. Jacobs, *Ashland University;* Ronald Lau, *University of South Dakota;* Raymond Lutz, *University of Texas-Dallas;* Paul Randolph, *Texas Tech University;* Jim Rappold, *University of Wisconsin;* and John W. Towns III, *Wilmington College.*

We once again thank those individuals whose input over past editions has helped the book evolve to its present form: D. Leblanc, *Vanderbilt University;* Gary Scudder, *Vanderbilt University;* David Cabell, *McNeese State University;* Dilip Chhajed, *University of Illinois;* S. D. Deshmukh, *Northwestern University;* Harry Boer, *University of Twent–Netherlands;* Ashok Rao, *Babson College;* James Lawson, *Mississippi State University;* Y. L. Helio Yang, *San Diego State University;* Keah-Choon Tan, *Mesa State University;* Emre Veral, *Baruch College;* Peter Kelle, *Louisiana State University;* and Bruce Hartman, *University of Arizona.*

We also want to thank former doctoral students who have contributed to the book over the years, including, most recently, Wayne Johannson, *USC;* Douglas Stewart, *Michigan State University;* and Andreas Soteriou, *University of Cyprus;* and earlier on, Arvinder Loomba, *University of Northern Iowa;* Deborah Kellogg, *University of Colorado–Denver;* Blair Berkeley, *California State University–Los Angeles;* and the now grizzled veteran Bill Youngdahl, *Thunderbird American Graduate School of International Management.*

We indeed appreciate the market brilliance and all-out support of our editor, Dick Hercher and the editorial brilliance and selective nudging of our developmental editor, Gail Korosa. Dick and Gail have become part of our families!

Thanks to the McGraw-Hill/Irwin team who make it all possible—Zina Craft, marketing manager; Christine Vaughan, project manager; Gino Cieslik, designer; Heather Burbridge, production supervisor; Keri Johnson, photo research coordinator; Becky Szura, supplements coordinator; and Ed Przyzycki, new media developer.

Last but certainly not least, we thank our families, who for the ninth time let the life cycle of the book disrupt theirs.

**Richard B. Chase**
**Nicholas J. Aquilano**
**F. Robert Jacobs**

# Contents in Brief

## Section One

### Operations Strategy and Managing Change



## Section Two

### Product Design and Process Selection



## Section Three

### Supply Chain Design



## Section Four

### Planning and Controlling the Supply Chain



## Section Five

### Revising the System



### Supplements



### Appendices

# Contents

## Section One

### Operations Strategy and Managing Change

## Section Two

### Product Design and Process Selection

## SECTION THREE

### SUPPLY CHAIN DESIGN

## SECTION FOUR

### PLANNING AND CONTROLLING THE SUPPLY CHAIN

## SECTION FIVE

### REVISING THE SYSTEM

# Operations Management for Competitive Advantage

*section one*

# section 1

# Operations Strategy and Managing Change





## GAINING COMPETITIVE ADVANTAGE

How We Manage Productive Resources Is Critical to strategic growth and competitiveness. Operations management is the managing of these productive resources. It entails the design and control of systems responsible for the productive use of raw materials, human resources, equipment, and facilities in the development of a product or service. This section addresses the issues of operations strategy and competitiveness and how the field of operations management can provide direction in gaining and maintaining competitive advantage. →

chapter

chapter one
# INTRODUCTION TO THE FIELD

## CHAPTER OUTLINE AND KEY TERMS

# 1

"It was Michael's ideas. He's a visionary in our industry," stated Morton Topfer, vice chairman of Dell Computer Corporation, gesturing toward Michael Dell's office across the hallway. "There's no doubt that Dell Online is a huge innovation, just as Dell Direct was a decade ago. But times have changed. We are now a big company, with 1997 revenues of nearly $12 billion and a growth rate of 50 percent over the last three years. We have to be nimble but methodical in how we absorb and build on this new approach of going to market," added Topfer.

Many companies have radically changed how they do business as the Internet has become such a significant tool over the past few years. The Internet, though, is just part of the story, because it only provides a new way to communicate. Other major changes are in the basic structure of how companies operate. These changes in operations are designed to lower cost while providing a product that is in tune with the current market. The key word is *value*. How can a company create the most value for its customers and thus reap the profit growth needed to sustain the company?

www.dell.com

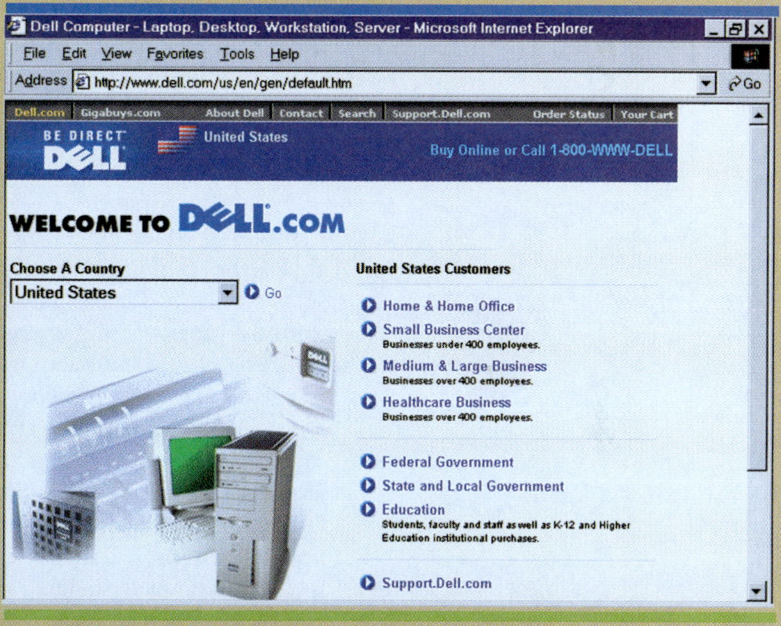


Technology has been a major driver of change in business for over 100 years. At the beginning of the 20th century, some key new technologies were the typewriter and the telephone. It's ironic how dramatically the Internet, another technology focused on communication, is driving change as we move into the 21st century.

**Source:** From "Dell Online," Harvard Business School (9-598-116), p. 1.

## THE FIELD OF OPERATIONS MANAGEMENT

Helping students prepare for their new role in 21st century businesses is the main objective of this book. Our vision is that in the future you will help your organization gain competitive advantage by excelling in meeting the needs of a specific customer segment. Whether you are a marketing, accounting, finance, or operations specialist, effectively serving customers requires knowledge of the topics in this book. Serving a customer *well* invariably means in a timely fashion, with exceptional quality, and at the lowest cost possible. Designing and operating processes that are quick, accurate, and inexpensive are fundamental to all the topics covered in this book.

Efficiency

Effectiveness

Through this book, you will become aware of the concepts and tools that are now being employed by companies around the world as they craft efficient and effective operations. **Efficiency** means doing something at the lowest possible cost. Later in the book we define this more carefully, but roughly speaking the goal of an efficient process is to produce a good or provide a service by using the smallest input of resources. **Effectiveness** means doing the right things to create the most value for the company. Often maximizing effectiveness and efficiency at the same time creates conflict between the two goals. We see this trade-off every day in our lives. At the customer service counter at a local store or bank, being efficient means using the fewest people possible at the counter. Being effective, though, means minimizing the amount of time that customers need to wait in line. Related to efficiency and effectiveness is the concept of **value,** which can be defined as quality divided by price. If you can provide the customer a better car without changing price, value has gone up. If you can give the customer a better car at a *lower* price, value goes way up. A major objective of this book is to show how smart management can achieve high levels of value.

Value

Besides its importance to corporate competitiveness, reasons for studying this field are

1 **A business education is incomplete without an understanding of modern approaches to managing operations.** Every organization produces some product or service, so students must be exposed to modern approaches for doing this effectively. Moreover, hiring organizations now expect business graduates to speak knowledgeably about many issues in the field. While this has long been true in manufacturing, it is becoming equally important in services, both public and private. For example, "reinventing government" initiatives draw heavily on supply chain management, total quality management, business process reengineering, and just-in-time delivery—concepts that fall under the OM umbrella.

2 **Operations management provides a systematic way of looking at organizational processes.** OM uses analytical thinking to deal with real-world problems. It sharpens our understanding of the world around us, whether we are talking about how to compete with Japan or how many lines to have at the bank teller's window.

3 **Operations management presents interesting career opportunities.** These can be in direct supervision of operations or in staff positions in OM specialties such as supply chain management and quality assurance. In addition, consulting firms regularly recruit individuals with strong OM capabilities to work in such areas as process reengineering and enterprise resource planning systems.

4 **The concepts and tools of OM are widely used in managing other functions of a business.** All managers have to plan work, control quality, and ensure productivity of individuals under their supervision. Other employees must know how operations work to effectively perform their jobs.

## WHAT IS OPERATIONS MANAGEMENT?

Operations management

**Operations management (OM)** is defined as the design, operation, and improvement of the systems that create and deliver the firm's primary products and services. Like marketing and finance, OM is a functional field of business with clear line management responsibilities. This point is important because operations management is frequently confused with operations research and management science (OR/MS) and industrial engineering (IE). The essential difference is that OM is a field of management, whereas OR/MS is the application of quantitative methods to decision making in all fields, and IE is an engineering discipline. Thus, while operations managers use the decision making tools of OR/MS (such as critical path scheduling) and are concerned with many of the same issues as IE (such as factory automation), OM's distinct management role distinguishes it from these other disciplines.

Global

As shown in Exhibit 1.1, OM is concerned with the management of the entire system that produces a good or delivers a product. Producing a product such as a cell phone, or providing a service such as a cellular phone account, involves a complex series of transformation processes. Exhibit 1.1 is a supply network for an original equipment manufacturer (OEM), such as Nokia, the Swedish maker of cell phones. To actually produce the phones and get them to the customer, many transformations must take place. For example, the suppliers purchase raw materials and produce the parts for the phone. The Nokia manufacturing plant takes these parts and assembles the various cell phones that have become popular. Orders for the phones are taken over the Internet from all the distributor, dealer, and warehouse sites around the world. Local retailers work directly with customers in setting up and managing the cell phone accounts. OM is concerned with managing all of these individual processes as effectively as possible.

Within the operations function, management decisions can be divided into three broad areas:

Strategic (long-term) decisions.

Tactical (intermediate-term) decisions.

Operational planning and control (short-term) decisions.

EXHIBIT 1.1

## Supply Chain of a Typical Original Equipment Manufacturer

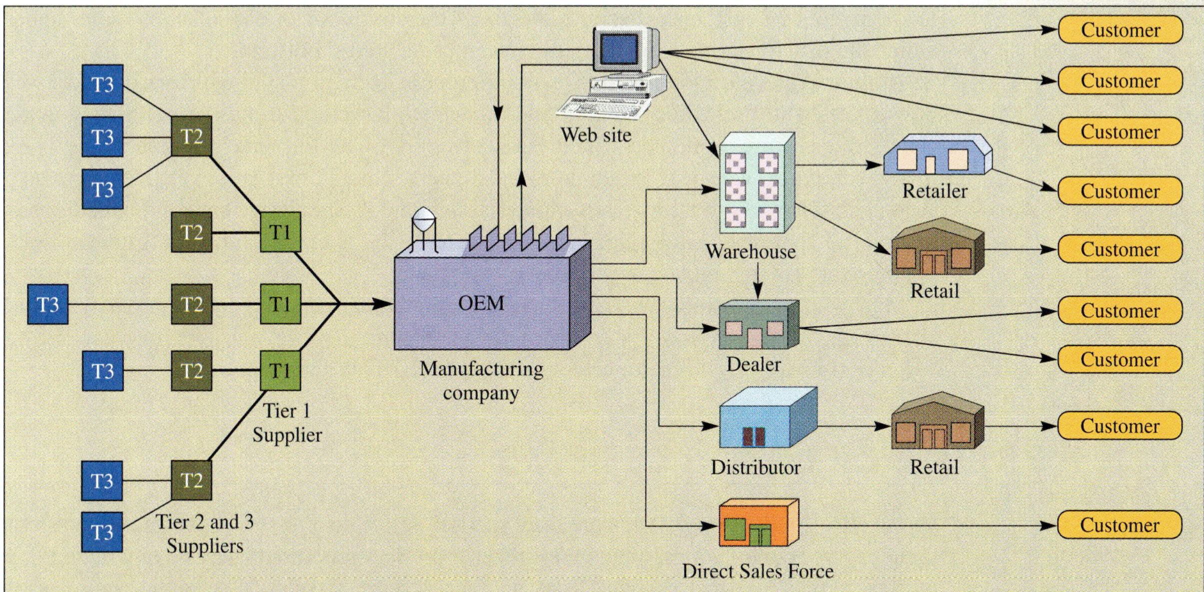


*As this schematic suggests, a value chain is not a simple linear series of connections. It typically involves a complex series of business interactions and channel configurations. Even this graphic, which depicts a handful of links to second- and third-tier suppliers, is relatively simplistic compared to most real-world situations for large OEMs that have to take both upstream and downstream viewpoints.*

SOURCE: J. H. SHERIDAN, "MANAGING THE SUPPLY CHAIN," *INDUSTRY WEEK*, SEPTEMBER 6, 1999, P. 52. REPRINTED WITH PERMISSION FROM *INDUSTRY WEEK*. COPYRIGHT PENTON MEDIA, INC., CLEVELAND, OHIO.

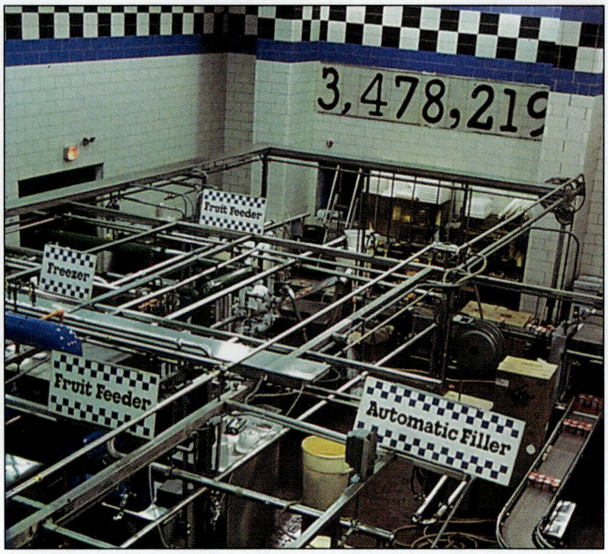


BEN AND JERRY'S MISSION STATEMENT IMPACTS DECISIONS SUCH AS WHERE TO LOCATE, AND HOW TO MAKE THE PRODUCT. THE COMPANY BELIEVES ITS SOCIAL MISSION IS TO IMPROVE THE QUALITY OF LIFE IN ITS LOCAL, NATIONAL, AND INTERNATIONAL COMMUNITIES. ITS SUCCESS, HOWEVER, IS BASED UPON PRODUCING A GREAT ICE CREAM (WITH LARGE CHUNKS OF CHOCOLATE IN EACH QUART OF CHERRY GARCIA).

The strategic issues are usually broad, addressing such questions as these: How will we make the product? Where do we locate the facility or facilities? How much capacity do we need? When should we add more capacity? Thus, by necessity, the time frame for strategic decisions is typically long—usually several years or more, depending on the specific industry. (Chapter 2 discusses operations strategy in depth.)

Operations management decisions at the strategic level impact the company's long-range effectiveness in terms of how it can address its customers' needs. Thus, for the firm to succeed, these decisions must be in alignment with the corporate strategy. Decisions made at the strategic level become the fixed conditions or operating constraints under which the firm must operate in both the intermediate and short term.

At the next level in the decision-making process, tactical planning primarily addresses how to efficiently schedule material and labor within the constraints of previously made strategic decisions. Issues on which OM concentrates on this level include these: How many workers do we need? When do we need them? Should we work overtime or put on a second shift? When should we have material delivered? Should we have a finished goods inventory? These tactical decisions, in turn, become the operating constraints under which operational planning and control decisions are made.

Management decisions with respect to operational planning and control are narrow and short-term by comparison. Issues at this level include these: What jobs do we work on today or this week? Whom do we assign to what tasks? What jobs have priority?

## PRODUCTION SYSTEMS

Production system

Production systems are used in all types of businesses. A **production system** uses resources to transform inputs into some desired output. Inputs may be raw material, a customer, or a finished product from another system. Exhibit 1.2 shows examples of different types of transformation processes in such varied areas as health care, education, and retail stores. In general, transformation processes can be categorized as follows:

- Physical (as in manufacturing).
- Location (as in transportation).

EXHIBIT 1.2

**Input–Transformation–Output Relationships for Typical Systems**

| System | Primary Inputs | Resources | Primary Transformation Function(s) | Typical Desired Output |
|---|---|---|---|---|
| Hospital | Patients | MDs, nurses, medical supplies, equipment | Health care (physiological) | Healthy individuals |
| Restaurant | Hungry customers | Food, chef, wait-staff, environment | Well-prepared, well-served food; agreeable environment (physical and exchange) | Satisfied customers |
| Automobile factory | Sheet steel, engine parts | Tools, equipment, workers | Fabrication and assembly of cars (physical) | High-quality cars |
| College or university | High school graduates | Teachers, books, classrooms | Imparting knowledge and skills (informational) | Educated individuals |
| Department store | Shoppers | Displays, stocks of goods, sales clerks | Attract shoppers, promote products, fill orders (exchange) | Sales to satisfied customers |
| Distribution center | Stockkeeping units (SKUs) | Storage bins, stockpickers | Storage and redistribution | Fast delivery, availability of SKUs |

- Exchange (as in retailing).
- Storage (as in warehousing).
- Physiological (as in health care).
- Informational (as in telecommunications).

These transformations are not mutually exclusive. For example, a department store can (1) allow shoppers to compare prices and quality (informational), (2) hold items in inventory until needed (storage), and (3) sell goods (exchange).

## DIFFERENCES BETWEEN SERVICES AND GOODS PRODUCTION

The essential difference between the two is that service is an intangible process, while a good is the physical output of a process. To put it another way, a service is something that "can be dropped on your foot without hurting you." Other differences are that in services, location of the service facility and direct customer involvement in creating the output are often essential factors; in goods production, they usually are not. There are many shades of gray here. Manufacturers provide many services as part of their product, and many services often manufacture the physical products that they deliver to their customers or consume goods in creating the service. McDonald's manufactures a tangible product, but because it is designed to have some contact with the customer to complete the service production process, the firm is in the service category.

Vol. I. "Services"

Also, from an operations perspective, customers are on the "shop floor" when consuming many services. The shop floor may be called the front office, dining area, operating room, or passenger cabin, depending on the industry. There are also many behind-the-scenes activities with tangible inputs and outputs. For example, major airlines, banks, and insurance companies have large back offices that support customer contact operations. As Chapter 6 on service products and processes relates, such back-office operations process things and information (e.g., tickets, checks, and claims) and so can be run much like a factory. See also the box titled "Linking the Shop-Floor Worker to the Customer."

### LINKING THE SHOP-FLOOR WORKER TO THE CUSTOMER

Tektronix, a manufacturer of electronic equipment, has pioneered direct communication between customers and shop-floor employees. Into the shipping carton of every oscilloscope it sells, the company inserts a postcard listing the names of the workers who built the scope, along with an "800" number to a phone on the shop floor. Every day the factory gets several calls from customers; the six people working in the repair area who answer them have all received telephone training. Customers call for various reasons: to ask questions about the use of their oscilloscopes, to request information about other Tektronix products, and to see if "they can really talk to the person who made their product." Workers and managers meet daily to discuss these calls; if necessary, further conversations with the customer follow up the meetings. In some cases, workers will call customers six months after delivery to find out how well their products are performing.

SOURCE: REPRINTED BY PERMISSION OF THE *HARVARD BUSINESS REVIEW*. EXCERPT FROM "THE SERVICE FACTORY," BY R. B. CHASE AND D. A. GARVIN, JULY–AUGUST 1989. 

## OM IN THE ORGANIZATIONAL CHART

Exhibit 1.3 locates operations activities within a manufacturing organization and two service organizations. Aside from differences in terminology, the service organizations also differ from the manufacturing firm in structure. The manufacturing company typically groups operations activities to produce its products in one department. Service firms scatter operations activities throughout the organization. For example, reservations scheduling in an airline is part of the production process for airline travel, even though it is carried out by a nonoperations department. This is seen even more clearly in banking, where there is often a retail operations department and a check-processing operations department. Note that Chart C, based on Ford's Customer Service Division, reflects the recent trend in many organizations to organize around cross-functional core processes managed by teams. This focuses more directly on the needs of the customer, enriches the work of the employee, and generally enhances coordination. Note also that in both types of organization, it is typical for operations activities to account for the lion's share of capital investment and workforce.

## OPERATIONS AS SERVICE

The emerging model in industry is that every organization is in the service business. This is true whether the organization makes big planes or Big Macs. From this we must recognize that manufacturing operations, as well as every other part of the organization, are also in the service business even if the customer is an internal one. In manufacturing, such services can be divided into core and value-added services that are provided to internal and external customers of the factory.

Core services

The **core services** customers want are products that are made correctly, are customized to their needs, are delivered on time, and are priced competitively. These are commonly summarized as the classic performance objectives of the operations function: *quality, flexibility, speed,* and *price* (or cost of production). Achieving these services is the focus of this book and is discussed in detail in Chapter 2.

Value-added services

**Value-added services** are services that simply make the external customer's life easier or, in the case of internal customers, help them to better carry out their particular function. Value-added factory services can be classified into four broad categories: information, problem solving, sales support, and field support.

1 **Information** is the ability to furnish critical data on product performance, process parameters, and cost to internal groups (such as R&D) and to external customers, who then use the data to improve their own operations or products. For example,

EXHIBIT 1.3

OM in the Organization Chart

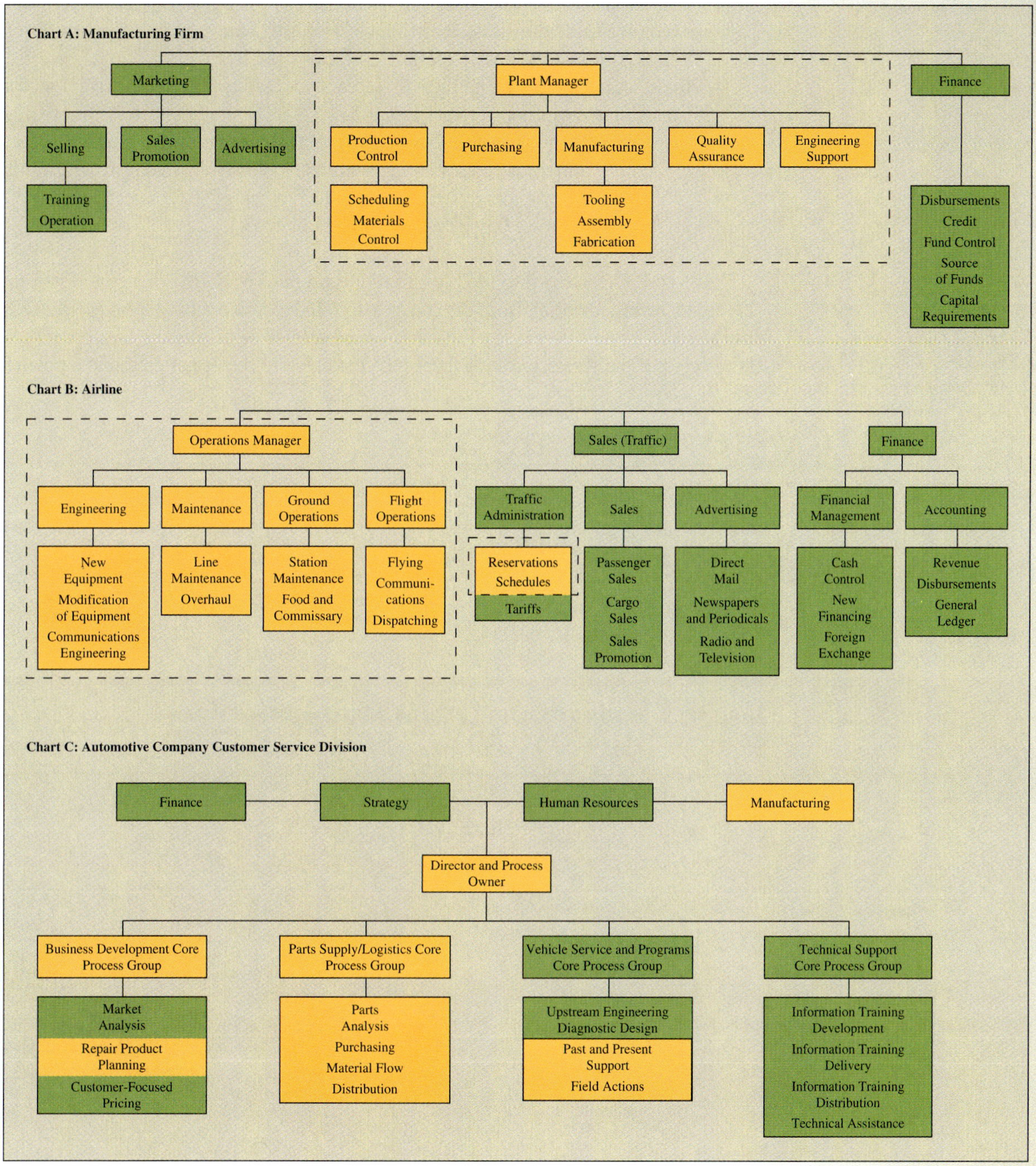


SOURCE FOR CHART C: F. OSTROFF, *THE HORIZONTAL ORGANIZATION* (NEW YORK: OXFORD UNIVERSITY PRESS, 1999), P. 34.

Hewlett-Packard's Fort Collins quality department provides quality data sheets and videotapes documenting actual product testing and field quality performance to field sales and service personnel.

2 **Problem solving** is the ability to help internal and external groups solve problems, especially in quality. For example, Raritan Corporation, a metal rod fabricator, sends factory workers out with salespeople to troubleshoot quality problems. Those factory workers then return to the factory and join with shop-floor personnel on remedial efforts.

3 **Sales support** is the ability to enhance sales and marketing efforts by demonstrating the technology, equipment, or production systems the company is trying to sell. Sometimes sales are enhanced by the factory showing off its workforce's skills. For example, to demonstrate its products' quality, Sara Lee has visitors observe the artistic skills of its "meringue fluffers" on its pie line.

4 **Field support** is the ability to replace defective parts quickly (for example, Caterpillar promises to make repair parts available anywhere in the world within 48 hours) or to replenish stocks quickly to avoid downtime or stockouts (for example, The Limited, a retail chain, is linked to its Hong Kong textile mills via a sophisticated computer system that signals factories to begin producing fast-selling items as soon as weekly sales figures are collected).

Value-added services provided to external customers yield two benefits. First, they differentiate the organization from the competition. Indeed, in many cases it is easier to copy a firm's product than it is to create the value-added service infrastructure to support it. Second, these services build relationships that bind customers to the organization in a positive way.

## PLAN OF THIS BOOK

This book is about methods to effectively produce and distribute the goods and services sold by a company. To give you a better idea of what to expect, we have developed a concept map (see Exhibit 1.4) that shows how the material in this book aligns with top management's view of running a business. To develop a better understanding of the field,

EXHIBIT 1.4

Summary Model of Operations Management for Competitive Advantage

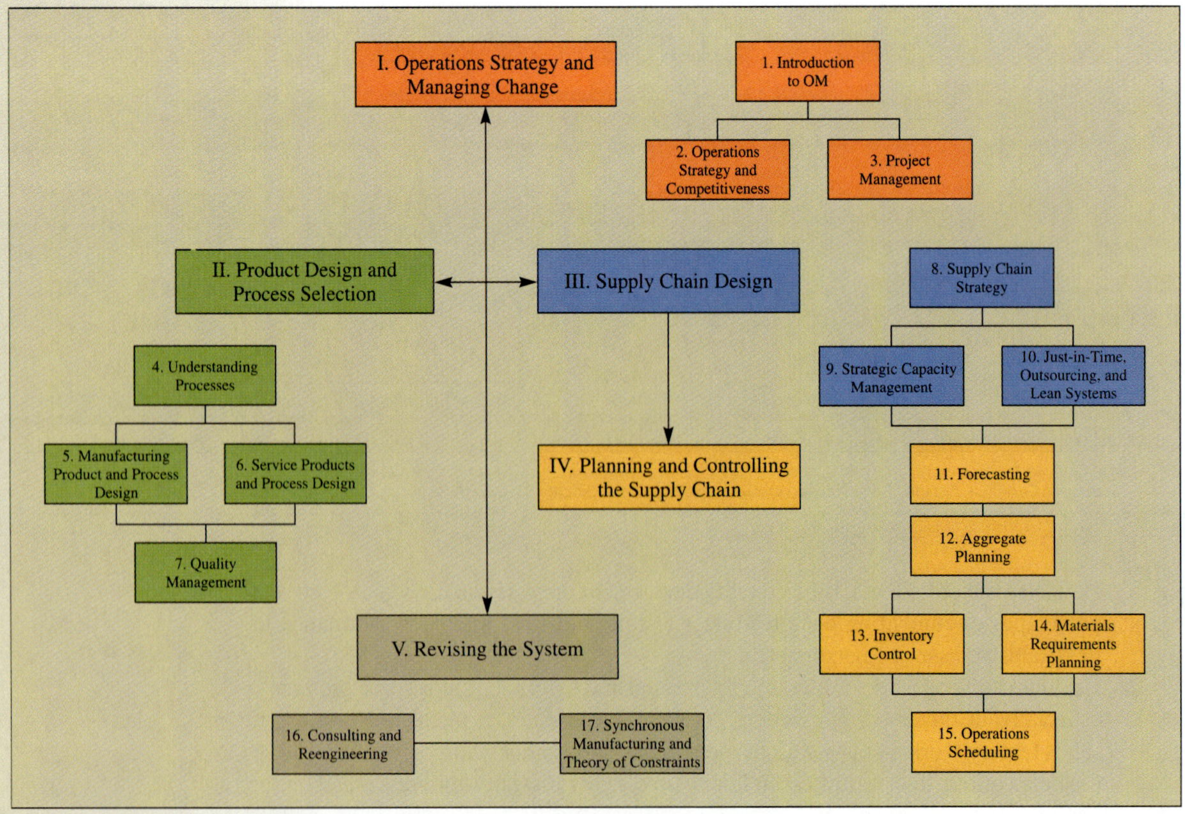

consider the following questions, which are typical of those you might have as you begin your study of operations management.

> **Strategic planning:** Any company must have a comprehensive business plan that is supported by a marketing strategy, operations strategy, and a financial strategy. How does a company ensure that the three strategies support each other?

Strategy is an important and recurring topic in the book. Strategy is covered from a high-level view in Chapter 2 (Operations Strategy) and from a tactical standpoint in three chapters: Chapter 8 (Supply Chain Strategy), Chapter 9 (Strategic Capacity Management), and Chapter 10 (Just-in-Time, Outsourcing, and Lean Systems). Our reason for spreading the strategy material throughout the book is to make things a bit more interesting. In general, we try to give you the "big picture" and then fill in the details with following chapters.

> **Project management:** Working on a project is a common assignment in any company. The success of a project is frequently measured by our ability to complete the project on time and within budget. How can we be confident we will meet these objectives?

Business today, just as in the past, is always changing. The first section of the book is titled "Operations Strategy and Managing Change." The idea is to get you thinking early in your course about how to organize projects that are needed to manage change. As a company's strategy changes in response to market demand and new technology, change is needed. Becoming proficient at managing projects is important to success in operations management.

Section Five of the book (Revising the System) is closely related to this theme of ongoing change. Chapter 16 (Consulting and Reengineering) is designed to show how consultants package the material that is covered in the book. Many students that major in operations end up working for consulting companies, so this insight is valuable. Synchronous Manufactuing and Theory of Constraints, the focus of Chapter 17, is also used by consultants, as well as being very popular among practitioners. The basic idea is to add resources to production bottlenecks that are constraints or obstacles to producing more profit. It is fairly complex material, so we positioned this at the end of the book so that you would have the background needed to better understand the ideas.

> **Decision analysis:** Where should we locate our facility? What equipment should we buy or lease? How many people should we hire? We need the skills to make important financial decisions that relate to the resources that we use. How do we do this?

Making fact-based decisions is what operations management is all about, so this book features extensive coverage of decision-making approaches and tools. One useful way to categorize decisions is by the length of the planning horizon, or the period of time, that the decision maker must consider. For example, building a new plant would be a long-term decision that a firm would need to be happy with for 10 to 15 years into the future. At the other extreme, a decision about how much inventory for a particular item should be ordered for tomorrow typically has a much shorter planning horizon of a few months or in many cases only a few days. Such short-term decisions are usually automated using computer programs. In the intermediate term are decisions that a company needs to live with for only 3 to 12 months. Often these decisions would correspond to yearly model changes or seasonal business cycles.

A typical initial decision is the nature of a firm's operations strategy. This comes from the mission of the firm itself and is tied to the notion of achieving competitive advantage through operations—the broad goal of this book. A key subsequent decision is what type of process a business needs. Design must follow strategy; so, given priorities from the strategic plan, a process can be designed that will support these priorities. Section Two (Product Design and Process Selection) discusses the three-way matching of strategic priorities, product characteristics, and process design. After getting started with some fundamentals in Chapter 4 (Process Analysis), the book covers the details of manufacturing (Chapter 5) and service transformation processes (Chapter 6). The technical notes on job design and work measurement (TN 4), layout (TN 5), and waiting lines (TN6) discuss specific techniques that can help solve problems related to designing these different types of processes.

**Quality:** Can we hope to be a successful business without constantly thinking about quality?

An essential element of process design is building quality into the process, so quality management (Chapter 7) is included in Section Two (Product Design and Process Selection). The technical note on process capability and statistical quality control (TN 7) covers the details.

**Supply chain management and e-commerce:** Supply chain management and e-commerce are big news these days. What are they? Don't I have to be an expert in computers to work in these areas?

Two sections of the book are devoted to this material. Section Three (Supply Chain Design) starts with a discussion of electronic commerce in a managerial briefing. E-commerce uses the Internet to connect directly with customers. Considering the impact of e-commerce on supply chain design is an important topic of the section. The chapters that follow develop the concepts that integrate the transformation processes needed to bring products and services to the customer. Many different transformation processes are needed to put together a supply chain. This chapter discusses the most popular ways to tie suppliers, manufacturers, and customers together. You have probably heard the term "just-in-time"; it is covered in this section.

Section Four (Planning and Controlling the Supply Chain) covers the techniques required to actually run the system. This is at the heart of operations management. The basic building blocks are forecasting (Chapter 11), aggregate (really labor) planning (Chapter 12), inventory control (Chapters 13 and 14) and scheduling (Chapter 15). These daily processes are often partially automated with computer information systems. Coverage of enterprise resource planning systems is included in a managerial briefing that starts this section.

What about the issue of having to be a computer expert to understand these topics? Nothing could be further from the truth. Today the software required to control these processes and to implement e-commerce can be purchased from vendors. There is great value in individuals that can understand how everything in the system should fit together, and then work with the various groups to make the system hum.

As you can see from this discussion, this material is all interrelated. A company's strategy dictates how operations are designed. The design of the operation dictates how it needs to be managed. Finally, because businesses are constantly being presented with new opportunities through new markets, products, and technologies, a business needs to be very good at managing change.

## HISTORICAL DEVELOPMENT OF OM

Exhibit 1.5 gives a timeline of OM's history. Our purpose in this section is not to go through all the details of OM; to do that would require us to recount the entire Industrial Revolution. Rather, the focus will be on major operations-related concepts that have been popular since the 1980s. Where appropriate, how a supposedly new idea relates to an older idea is discussed. (We seem to keep rediscovering the past.)

Historical Summary of OM

EXHIBIT 1.5

| YEAR | CONCEPT | TOOL | ORIGINATOR |
|---|---|---|---|
| 1910s | Principles of scientific management | Formalized time-study and work-study concepts | Frederick W. Taylor (United States) |
| | Industrial psychology | Motion study | Frank and Lillian Gilbreth (United States) |
| | Moving assembly line | Activity scheduling chart | Henry Ford and Henry L. Gantt (United States) |
| | Economic lot size | EOQ applied to inventory control | F. W. Harris (United States) |
| 1930s | Quality control | Sampling inspection and statistical tables for quality control | Walter Shewhart, H. F. Dodge, and H. G. Romig (United States) |
| | Hawthorne studies of worker motivation | Activity sampling for work analysis | Elton Mayo (United States) and L. H. C. Tippett (England) |
| 1940s | Multidisciplinary team approaches to complex system problems | Simplex method of linear programming | Operations research groups (England) and George B. Dantzig (United States) |
| 1950s–60s | Extensive development of operations research tools | Simulation, waiting-line theory, decision theory, mathematical programming, project scheduling techniques of PERT and CPM | Many researchers in the United States and Western Europe |
| 1970s | Widespread use of computers in business | Shop scheduling, inventory control, forecasting, project management, MRP | Led by computer manufacturers, in particular, IBM; Joseph Orlicky and Oliver Wight were the major MRP innovators (United States) |
| | Service quality and productivity | Mass production in the service sector | McDonald's restaurants |
| 1980s | Manufacturing strategy paradigm | Manufacturing as a competitive weapon | Harvard Business School faculty (United States) |
| | JIT, TQC, and factory automation | KANBAN, Poka-yokes, CIM, FMS, CAD/CAM, robots, etc. | Tai-Ichi Ohno of Toyota Motors (Japan), W. E. Deming and J. M. Juran (United States), and engineering disciplines (United States, Germany, and Japan) |
| | Synchronous manufacturing | Bottleneck analysis, OPT, theory of constraints | Eliyahu M. Goldratt (Israel) |
| 1990s | Total quality management | Baldrige quality award, ISO 9000, quality function development, value and concurrent engineering, continuous improvement paradigm | National Institute of Standards and Technology, American Society of Quality Control (United States), and International Organization for Standardization (Europe) |
| | Business process reengineering | Radical change paradigm | Michael Hammer and major consulting firms (United States) |
| | Electronic enterprise | Internet World Wide Web | U.S. government, Netscape Communication Corporation, and Microsoft Corporation |
| | Supply chain management | SAP/R3, client/server software | SAP (Germany), Oracle (United States) |
| 2000s | E-commerce | Internet, World Wide Web | Amazon, e-bay, America Online, Yahoo |

In the late 1950s and early 1960s, scholars began to deal specifically with operations management as opposed to industrial engineering or operations research. Writers such as Edward Bowman and Robert Fetter (*Analysis for Production and Operations Management,* 1957) and Elwood S. Buffa (*Modern Production Management,* 1961) noted the commonality of problems faced by all production systems and emphasized the importance of viewing production operations as a system. They also stressed the useful application of waiting-line theory, simulation, and linear programming, which are now standard topics in the field. In 1973 Chase and Aquilano's first edition of this book stressed the need "to put the management back in operations management." Bob Jacobs joined the book team in 1997.

## JIT AND TQC

The 1980s saw a revolution in the management philosophies and the technologies by which production is carried out. Just-in-time (JIT) production is the major breakthrough

in manufacturing philosophy. Pioneered by the Japanese, JIT is an integrated set of activities designed to achieve high-volume production using minimal inventories of parts that arrive at the workstation exactly when they are needed. The philosophy—coupled with total quality control (TQC), which aggressively seeks to eliminate causes of production defects—is now a cornerstone in many manufacturers' production practices. Chapter 10 covers this topic.

Of course, the Japanese were not the first to develop a highly integrated, efficient production system. In 1913 Henry Ford developed an assembly line to make the Model-T automobile. Ford developed a system for making the Model-T that was constrained only by the capabilities of the workforce and existing technology. Quality was a critical prerequisite for Ford: The line could not run steadily at speed without consistently good components. On-time delivery was also critical for Ford; the desire to keep workers and machines busy with materials flowing constantly made scheduling critical. Product, processes, material, logistics, and people were well integrated and balanced in the design and operation of the plant.[1]

## MANUFACTURING STRATEGY PARADIGM

The late 1970s and early 1980s saw the development of the manufacturing strategy paradigm by researchers at the Harvard Business School. This work by professors William Abernathy, Kim Clark, Robert Hayes, and Steven Wheelwright (built on earlier efforts by Wickham Skinner) emphasized how manufacturing executives could use their factories' capabilities as strategic competitive weapons. Central to their thinking was the notion of factory focus and manufacturing trade-offs. They argued that because a factory cannot excel on all performance measures, its management must devise a focused strategy, creating a focused factory that performs a limited set of tasks extremely well. This required trade-offs among such performance measures as low cost, high quality, and high flexibility in designing and managing factories. Ford seems to have realized this about 60 years before the Harvard professors.

## SERVICE QUALITY AND PRODUCTIVITY

The great diversity of service industries—ranging from airlines to zoos, with many different types in between—precludes identifying any single pioneer or developer that has made a major impact in these areas. However, McDonald's unique approach to quality and productivity has been so successful that it stands as a reference point in thinking about how to deliver high-volume standardized services.

## TOTAL QUALITY MANAGEMENT AND QUALITY CERTIFICATION

Another major development was the focus on total quality management (TQM) in the late 1980s and 1990s. All operations executives are aware of the quality message put forth by the so-called quality gurus—W. Edwards Demming, Joseph M. Juran, and Philip Crosby. It's interesting that these individuals were students of Shewhart, Dodge, and Romig in the 1930s (sometimes it takes a generation for things to catch on). Helping the quality movement along is the Baldrige National Quality Award, which was started in 1987 under the direction of the National Institute of Standards and Technology. The Baldrige Award recognizes companies each year for outstanding quality management systems.

The ISO 9000 certification standards, created by the International Organization for Standardization, now play a major role in setting quality standards for global manufacturers. Many European companies require that their vendors meet these standards as a condition for obtaining contracts.

### BUSINESS PROCESS REENGINEERING

The need to become lean to remain competitive in the global economic recession in the 1990s pushed companies to seek innovations in the processes by which they run their operations. The flavor of business process reengineering (BPR) is conveyed in the title of Michael Hammer's influential article in *Harvard Business Review:* "Reengineering Work: Don't Automate, Obliterate." The approach seeks to make revolutionary changes as opposed to evolutionary changes (which are commonly advocated in TQM). It does this by taking a fresh look at what the organization is trying to do in all its business processes, and then eliminating non–value-added steps and computerizing the remaining ones to achieve the desired outcome.

Hammer actually was not the first consultant to advocate eliminating non–value-added steps and reengineering processes. In the early 1900s, Fredrick W. Taylor developed principles of scientific management which applied scientific analysis to eliminating wasted effort from manual labor. Around the same time, Frank and Lillian Gilbreth used the new technology of the time, motion pictures, to analyze such diverse operations as bricklaying and medical surgery procedures. Many of the innovations that this husband-and-wife team developed, such as time and motion study, are widely used today.

### SUPPLY CHAIN MANAGEMENT

The central idea of supply chain management is to apply a total system approach to managing the flow of information, materials, and services from raw material suppliers through factories and warehouses to the end customer. Recent trends such as outsourcing and mass customization are forcing companies to find flexible ways to meet customer demand. The focus is on optimizing core activities to maximize the speed of response to changes in customer expectations.

### ELECTRONIC COMMERCE

The quick adoption of the Internet and the World Wide Web during the late 1990s is remarkable. The term *electronic commerce* refers to the use of the Internet as an essential element of business activity. The Internet is an outgrowth of a government network called ARPANET, which was created in 1969 by the Defense Department of the U.S. government. The use of Web pages, forms, and interactive search engines is changing the way people collect information, shop, and communicate. It is also changing the way operations managers coordinate and execute production and distribution functions. This new mode of operations is what we refer to as *E-ops*.

## CURRENT ISSUES IN OPERATIONS MANAGEMENT

We conclude our introductory chapter with a summary of current issues facing OM executives. These interrelated issues are interesting points for discussion as we move through the OM topics:

1 **Effectively consolidating the operations resulting from mergers.** There is a growing interest today in mergers, particularly of large companies. Examples include Mercedes Benz and Chrysler, MCI and WorldCom, Compaq Computer and Digital Equipment, and many others. Often these mergers seem to offer great promise for economies of scale and operations efficiency. However, the reality is often different due to differences in culture and technology infrastructure.

2 **Developing flexible supply chains to enable mass customization of products and services.** Virtually every industry is broadening its product lines to provide the variety of choices that customers want. The challenge is not only to produce so many different products but also to distribute the products to a global customer base.

## BREAKTHROUGH

### JAPAN'S PERSONALIZED BIKE PRODUCTION

Does your bike fit you perfectly? Would you like one that does? If you are willing to pay 20 to 30 percent more than you would pay for a mass-produced bike, you can get a Panasonic bike manufactured to exactly match your size, weight, and color preference. You can even get your bike within three weeks of your order (only two weeks if you visit Japan). This is accomplished via a process called the Panasonic Individual Customer System (PICS), which skillfully employs computers, robots, and a small factory workforce to make one-of-a-kind models at the National Bicycle Industrial Company factory in Kokubu, Japan.

The National Bicycle Industrial Company (NBIC), a subsidiary of electronics giant Matsushita, began making the bikes under the Panasonic brand in 1987. With the introduction of its personalized order system (POS) for the Japanese market (PICS was developed for overseas sales), the firm gained international attention as a classic example of **Mass customization**—producing products to order in lot sizes of one.

The factory itself has 21 employees and a computer-aided design system, and is capable of producing any of 8 million variations on 18 models of racing, road, and mountain bikes in 199 color patterns for virtually any size person

The PIC system works in the following way. A customer visits a local Panasonic bicycle store and is measured on a special frame. The storeowner then faxes the specifications to the master control room at the factory. There, an operator punches the specs into a minicomputer, which automatically creates a unique blueprint and produces a bar code. (The CAD blueprint takes about three minutes as opposed to three hours required by company draftspeople prior to computerization.) The bar code is then attached to metal tubes and gears that ultimately become the customer's personal bike. At various stages in the process, line workers access the customer's requirement using the bar code label and a scanner. This information, displayed on a CRT terminal at each station, is fed directly to the computer-controlled machines that are part of a local area computer network. At each step of production, a computer reading the code knows that each part belongs to a specific bike, and it tells a robot where to weld or tells a painter which pattern to follow.

Despite the use of computers and robots, the process is not highly automated. Gears are hand-wired, assembly is manual, and the customer's name is silk-screened by hand with the touch of an artisan. The entire manufacturing and assembly

3 **Managing global supplier, production, and distribution networks.** The implementation of global enterprise resource planning systems, now fairly common in large companies, has challenged managers to use all of this information optimally. This requires a careful understanding of where control should be centralized and where autonomy is important, among other issues.

4 **Increased "commoditization" of suppliers.** Often there are many suppliers that can provide the material needed by a company. Take the case of steel suppliers—in particular, those that supply the auto industry. In the past, the movement was toward long-term contracts between an automobile manufacturing company and its supplier of steel. In order to justify the investment in integrating information systems and other activities, a long-term agreement was forged. Now, with the use of standard Internet communications and with advances in production technology in the steel industry, there is little cost in switching from one supplier to another. Suppliers use a computer term, *plug compatible,* to describe this interchangeability. Steel companies can now be much more aggressive in pursuing different business partners. Internet business-to-business auction sites may dramatically change how business between companies is conducted in the future.

5 **Achieving the "service factory."** This term refers to the growing movement toward developing personalized service for each customer, even though the company may have millions of customers. Retail consumer products companies such as Lands' End and L.L. Bean have been working to develop this type of service while still maintaining a highly efficient operation, much like a high-volume manufacturing plant.

time required to complete a single bike is 150 minutes, and the factory can make about 60 a day. NBIC's mass-production factory (which makes 90 percent of its annual production) can make a standard model in 90 minutes. One might ask why a customer must wait up to three weeks given that it takes less than three hours to make a custom model. According to the general manager of sales, "We could have made the time shorter, but we want people to feel excited about waiting for something special."

To provide a more personal touch to mass customization, the factory is given the responsibility to communicate directly with the customer. Immediately after the factory receives the customer's order, a personalized computer-generated drawing of the bicycle is mailed with a note thanking the customer for choosing the bike. This is followed up with a second personal note, three months later, inquiring about the customer's satisfaction with the bicycle. Finally, a "bicycle birthday card" is sent to commemorate the first anniversary of the bicycle.

CUSTOMERS ARE CUSTOM FITTED IN THE RETAIL STORE WITH OPTIONS FOR 11,231,862 POSSIBLE VARIATIONS OF THE BICYCLE.

SOURCE: S. KOTHA, "THE NATIONAL BICYCLE INDUSTRIAL COMPANY: IMPLEMENTING A STRATEGY OF MASS-CUSTOMIZATION," CASE STUDY FROM THE INTERNATIONAL UNIVERSITY OF JAPAN, 1993; AND S. MOFFAT, "JAPAN'S NEW PERSONALIZED PRODUCTION," *FORTUNE*, OCTOBER 22, 1990, PP. 132–35.

6 **Achieving good service from service firms.** The capability to deliver more services through information technology has not been accompanied by what customers perceive as better service. The value relationship we spoke of earlier in the chapter has perhaps increased slightly because price has dropped for services at a faster rate than has quality. But it's close! Airline customers could certainly attest to this. Meeting this challenge is a complex management problem of workforce management and systems—the essence of what OM is about.

## KEY TERMS

**Efficiency** Doing something at the lowest possible cost.

**Effectiveness** Doing the right things to create the most value for the company.

**Value** Ratio of quality to price paid. Competitive "happiness" is being able to increase quality and reduce price while maintaining or improving profit margins. (This is a way that operations can directly increase customer retention and gain market share.)

**Operations management** Design, operation, and improvement of the systems that create and deliver the firm's primary products and services.

**Production system** System by which resources are used to transform inputs into desired output.

**Core services** Basic things that customers want from the products they purchase. They want them, for example, to be made correctly, customized to their needs, delivered on time, and priced competitively.

**Value-added services** Services that differentiate the organization from competitors and that build relationships that bind customers to the firm in a positive way.

**Mass customization** Producing products to order in lot sizes of one.

## REVIEW AND DISCUSSION QUESTIONS

1 What is the difference between OM and OR/MS? Between OM and IE?
2 How would you distinguish OM from management and organizational behavior as taught at your university?
3 Look at the want ads in *The Wall Street Journal* and evaluate the opportunities for an OM major with several years of experience.
4 What factors account for the resurgence of interest in OM today?
5 Using Exhibit 1.2 as a model, describe the input–transformation–output relationships in the following systems:
   *a.* An airline.
   *b.* A state penitentiary.
   *c.* Branch office of a bank.
   *d.* The home office of a major banking firm.
6 Sketch the production-delivery system used by the National Bicycle Industrial Company in providing the Panasonic bicycle. Could this approach be applied to other consumer goods? Give examples.
7 What are the implications for marketing of Tektronix's "hot line" to the shop-floor worker?
8 Suppose that *Rolling Stone* presented the following headlines relating to OM. To what particular historical events or individuals would they refer?
   - OVER 5 BAZILLION SOLD TO DATE
   - BEANTOWN B-SCHOOL DISCOVERS YOU CAN'T HAVE IT ALL
   - INVENTORY—OH NO!
   - BUSINESSES USE A BIG HAMMER TO FORCE CHANGE
   - FAST HENRY BECOMES MARVEL OF MOTOWN
   - EXECS FOLLOW GURU'S RECIPE FOR BIG Q STEW
   - 10 BILLION FAX MACHINES DUMPED IN THE OCEAN
   - "THE CHAIN GANG" MOVES TO TOP OF THE CHARTS

## CASE: THE PURCHASING MANAGERS INDEX (PMI)

During the first week of every month, headlines on the front page of *The Wall Street Journal* announce the current reading of the Purchasing Managers Index (PMI). What is the PMI? Why is it so important to economists? How does it relate to the study of operations management?

The National Association of Purchasing Management (NAPM *http://www.napm.org*) has been calculating this index since 1931. The index is like the Dow Jones Industrial Average, but instead of measuring the rise and fall of a set of stocks, the PMI measures the rise and fall of manufacturing in the United States. The index is calculated using a set of measures of new manufacturing orders, production volume, supplier deliveries, inventory levels, and employment. The data are collected from a monthly survey conducted by NAPM.

The PMI is a leading indicator of economic activity. A PMI over 44.5 percent, over a period of time, indicates that the overall economy, or gross domestic product (GDP), is generally expanding; a PMI below 44.5 percent indicates that the GDP is generally declining. The distance from 44.5 percent indicates the strength of the expansion or decline.

The indicator is calculated from the activity levels for functions we study in operations management. We will study how manufacturing orders are processed, how decisions related to the volume that can be processed are made, the coordination of supplier deliveries, the management of inventory, and the scheduling of employees.

Using the spreadsheet provided on the CD-ROM included with this text, answer the following questions:

1 How have employment levels in manufacturing companies in the United States changed over the past three years?
2 Have manufacturing companies been successful in reducing inventories?
3 How do inventory levels fluctuate with new orders (sales)?

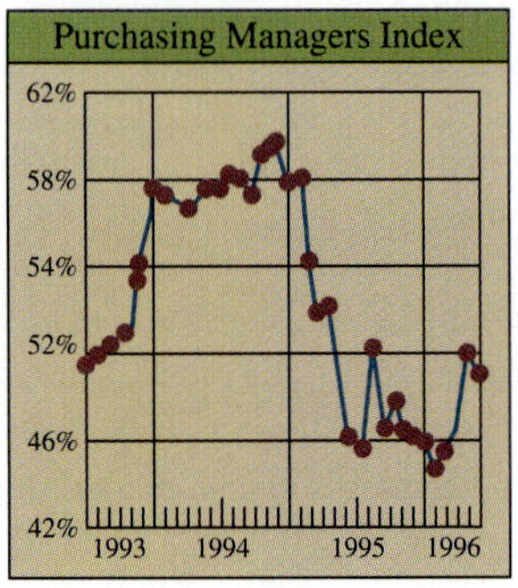

## CASE: FAST-FOOD FEAST

Visit at least two different fast-food restaurants that make hamburgers. For example, in the United States McDonald's, Wendy's, and Burger King are good choices. For some of you fast-food junkies, this will not be difficult; vegans may have to take a friend for product testing. Observe the basic operational differences between these stores. Note the differences in the following processes:

1. How are in-store orders taken?
2. Are the hamburgers prepared to order, or are they prepared ahead of time and delivered from a storage bin?
3. How are special orders handled?
4. How are the hamburgers cooked?
5. How are the hamburgers assembled?
6. Is a microwave oven used in the process?
7. How are other common items, such as french fries and drinks, handled?

## SELECTED BIBLIOGRAPHY

Chase, Richard B., and David A. Garvin. "The Service Factory." *Harvard Business Review* 67, no. 4 (July–August 1989), pp. 61–69.

Cohen, M. A. *Manufacturing Automation*. Chicago: Irwin, 1997.

Hayes, R. H.; S. C. Wheelwright; and K. B. Clark. *Dynamic Manufacturing*. New York: Free Press, 1988.

*Journal of Operations Management*. Washington, DC: American Production and Inventory Control Society, 1980–current.

Kotha, S. "The National Bicycle Industrial Company: Implementing a Strategy of Mass-Customization." Case study from the International University of Japan, 1993.

*Manufacturing & Service Operations Management: M&SOM*. Linthicum, MD: Institute for Operations Research and the Management Sciences, 1999–current.

Moffat, S. "Japan's New Personalized Production." *Fortune*, October 22, 1990, pp. 132–35.

Nersesian, R. L. *Trends and Tools for Operations Management: An Updated Guide for Executives and Managers*. Westport, CT: Quorum, 2000.

*Operations Management Review*. Austin, TX: Operations Management Association, 1982–current.

Pine II, B. J. *Mass Customization: The New Frontier in Business Competition*. Boston: Harvard Business School Press, 1993.

Porter, M., and C. V. Linde. "Green and Competitive: Ending the Stalemate." *Harvard Business Review*, September–October 1995, pp. 120–37.

*Production and Operations Management: An International Journal of the Production and Operations Management Society/POMS*. Baltimore, MD: Production and Operations Management Society, 1992–current.

Slack, N. ed. *The Blackwell Encyclopedia Dictionary of Operations Management*. Cambridge, MA: Blackwell, 1996.

Sower, V. E.; J. Motwani; and M. J. Savoie, eds. *Classic Readings in Operations Management*. Fort Worth: Dryden Press, 1995.

Womak, J. P.; D. T. Jones; and D. Roos. *The Machine That Changed the World*. New York: Rawson Associates, 1990.

Wyzalek J. ed. *Handbook of Enterprise Operations Management, 1999*. Boca Raton, FL: Auerbach, 1999.

## FOOTNOTE

1 See J. Wilson, "Henry Ford: A Just-in-Time Pioneer," *Production & Inventory Management,* Journal 37 (1996), pp. 26–31.

*chapter two*

# OPERATIONS STRATEGY AND COMPETITIVENESS

## CHAPTER OUTLINE AND KEY TERMS

2

Competitive strategy is about being different. It means deliberately choosing a different set of activities to deliver a unique mix of value. Southwest Airlines Company, for example, offers short-haul, low-cost, point-to-point service between midsize cities and secondary airports in large cities. Southwest avoids large airports and does not fly great distances. Southwest's frequent departures and low fares attract price-sensitive customers who otherwise would travel by bus or car, as well as convenience-oriented travelers who would choose a full-service airline on other routes.

Most managers describe strategic positioning in terms of their customers: "Southwest Airlines serves price- and convenience-sensitive travelers," for

example. But the essence of strategy is in business activities—choosing to perform activities differently than rivals. Otherwise, a strategy is nothing more than a marketing slogan that will not withstand competition.

A full-service airline is configured to get passengers from almost any point A to any point B. To reach many destinations and serve passengers with connecting flights, full-service airlines employ a hub-and-spoke system centered on major airports. To attract passengers who desire more comfort, they offer first-class or business-class service. To accommodate passengers who must change planes, they coordinate schedules and check and transfer baggage. And because some passengers will be traveling for many hours, full-service airlines serve meals.

Southwest, in contrast, tailors all its activities to delivering low-cost, convenient service on its particular type of route. Through fast turnarounds at the gate of only 15 minutes, it is able to keep planes flying longer hours than rivals and provide frequent departures with fewer aircraft. Southwest does not offer meals, assigned seats, interline baggage checking, or premium classes of service. Automated ticketing at the gate encourages customers to bypass travel agents, allowing Southwest to avoid their commissions. A standardized fleet of 737 aircraft boosts the efficiency of maintenance.

Southwest has staked out a unique and valuable strategic position based on a tailored set of activities.

**Source:** Reprinted by permission of the *Harvard Business Review*. From "What Is Strategy?" by M. E. Porter, November–December 1996. 

Global

A company that is considered to be world class recognizes that its ability to compete in the marketplace depends on developing an operations strategy that is properly aligned with its mission of serving the customer. A company's *competitiveness* refers to its relative position in comparision to other firms in the local or global marketplace. In this chapter, we first define what operations strategy is and how it relates to competitive priorities. In our discussion of priorities, we explain how priorities change over time for a company. We then address operations strategy in manufacturing and services, how the United States is faring in industrial competitiveness, and how operations performance is measured.

## OPERATIONS STRATEGY

### WHAT IS OPERATIONS STRATEGY?

Operations strategy

**Operations strategy** is concerned with setting broad policies and plans for using the resources of a firm to best support it's long-term competitive strategy. A firm's operations strategy is comprehensive through its integration with corporate strategy. The strategy involves a long-term process that must foster inevitable change. An operations strategy involves decisions that relate to the design of a process and the infrastructure needed to support the process. Process design includes the selection of appropriate technology, sizing the process over time, the role of inventory in the process, and locating the process. The infrastructure decisions involve the logic associated with the planning and control systems, quality assurance and control approaches, work payment structures, and the organization of the operations function.

Operations strategy can be viewed as part of a planning process that coordinates operational goals with those of the larger organization. Since the goals of the larger organization change over time, the operations strategy must be designed to anticipate future needs. The operations capabilities of a firm can be viewed as a portfolio best suited to adapt to the changing product and/or service needs of the firm's customers.

Looking at operations strategy from a historical perspective, U.S. companies, for example in the post–World War II era, experienced tremendous consumer demand that had been pent up during the war. As a result, manufacturing in the United States emphasized turning out high volumes of products to satisfy this demand. In contrast, during the same period, Japanese manufacturing companies focused on the quality of their products. Priorities needed to remain competitive were different for companies in the different countries. Keys to success in operations strategy lie in identifying what the priority choices are, in understanding the consequences of each choice, and in navigating the ensuing trade-offs.

## OPERATIONS COMPETITIVE DIMENSIONS

### COMPETITIVE DIMENSIONS

Vol. IV "Value-Driven Production at Trek"

Given the choices that customers face today, how do they decide which product or service to buy? Different customers are attracted by different attributes. Some customers are primarily interested in the cost of a product or service, and correspondingly some companies attempt to position themselves to offer the lowest price. The major competitive dimensions that form the competitive position of a company include the following.

**Cost—"Make It Cheap"—** Within every industry, there is usually a segment of the market that buys solely on the basis of low cost. To successfully compete in this niche, a firm must be the low-cost producer, but even doing this does not always guarantee profitability and success.

Products sold strictly on the basis of cost are typically commoditylike; in other words, customers cannot distinguish the products of one firm from those of another.

This segment of the market is frequently very large, and many companies are lured by the potential for significant profits, which they associate with the large unit volumes of product. As a consequence, however, competition in this segment is fierce—and so is the failure rate. After all, there can be only one low-cost producer, which usually establishes the selling price in the market.

**Product Quality and Reliability—"Make It Good"—** Quality can be divided into two categories: product quality and process quality. The level of quality in a product's design will vary with the market segment at which it is aimed. Obviously, a child's first two-wheeled bicycle is of significantly different quality than the bicycle of a world-class cyclist. The use of special aluminum alloys and special lightweight sprockets and chains are important to the performance needs of the advanced cyclist. These two types of bicycle are designed for different customers' needs. The higher-quality cyclist product commands a higher price in the marketplace due to its special features.

The goal in establishing the proper level of product quality is to focus on the requirements of the customer. Overdesigned products with too much quality will be viewed as prohibitively expensive. Underdesigned products, on the other hand, will lose customers to products that cost a little more but are perceived by the customers as offering greater value.

Process quality is critical because it relates directly to the reliability of the product. Regardless of whether the product is a child's first two-wheeler or a bicycle for an international cyclist, customers want products without defects. Thus, the goal of process quality is to produce error-free products. Product specifications, given in dimensional tolerances, precisely define how the product is to be made. Adherence to these tolerances is essential to ensure the reliability of the product as defined by its intended use.

**Delivery Speed—"Make It Fast"—** In some markets, a company's ability to deliver more quickly than its competitors may be critical. Take, for example, a company that offers a repair service for computer-networking equipment. A company that can offer on-site repair in only 1 or 2 hours has a significant advantage over a competing firm that guarantees service only within 24 hours.

**Delivery Reliability—"Deliver It When Promised"—** This dimension relates to the ability of the firm to supply the product or service on or before a promised delivery due date. For an automobile manufacturer, it is very important that their supplier of tires provide the needed quantity and types for each day's car production. If the

FEDEX SHIPS NEARLY 5 MILLION PACKAGES DAILY TO OVER 210 COUNTRIES FROM ITS HUBS IN MEMPHIS, INDIANAPOLIS, AND DALLAS. SEEING A NEED FOR SPEEDY, RELIABLE OVERNIGHT DELIVERY, FEDEX BECAME A $14 BILLION COMPANY AND THE WORLD'S LARGEST EXPEDITED DELIVERY SERVICE.

tires needed for a particular car are not available when the car reaches the point on the assembly line where the tires are installed, the whole assembly line may have to be shut down until they arrive. The focus during the 1980s and 1990s on reducing stocks of inventory to lower cost has placed increasing emphasis on delivery reliability as a criterion for evaluating alternative vendors.

**Coping with Changes in Demand—"Change Its Volume"—** In many markets, a company's ability to respond to increases and decreases in demand is an important factor in its ability to compete. It is well known that a company with increasing demand can do little wrong. When demand is strong and increasing, costs are continuously reduced due to economies of scale, and investments in new technologies can be easily justified. But scaling back when demand decreases may require many difficult decisions relating to laying off employees and related reductions in assets. The ability to effectively deal with dynamic market demand over the long term is an essential element of operations strategy.

**Flexibility and New Product Introduction Speed—"Change It"—** Flexibility, from a strategic perspective, refers to the ability of a company to offer a wide variety of products to its customers. An important element of this ability to offer different products is the time required for a company to develop a new product and to convert its processes to offer the new product.

**Other Product-Specific Criteria—"Support It"—** The competitive dimensions just described are certainly the most common. However, often other dimensions relate to specific products or situations. Notice that most of the dimensions listed next are primarily service in nature. Often special services are provided to augment the sales of manufactured products.

1 **Technical liaison and support.** A supplier may be expected to provide technical assistance for product development, particularly during the early stages of design and manufacturing.
2 **Meeting a launch date.** A firm may be required to coordinate with other firms on a complex project. In such cases, manufacturing may take place while development work is still being completed. Coordinating work between firms and working simultaneously on a project will reduce the total time required to complete the project.
3 **Supplier after-sale support.** An important competitive dimension may be the ability of a firm to support its product after the sale. This involves the availability of replacement parts and, possibly, the modification of older, existing products to new performance levels. Speed of response to these after-sale needs is often important as well.
4 **Other dimensions.** These typically include such factors as colors available, size, weight, location of the fabrication site, customization available, and product mix options.

## THE NOTION OF TRADE-OFFS

Central to the concept of operations strategy is the notion of operations focus and trade-offs. The underlying logic is that an operation cannot excel simultaneously on all competitive dimensions. Consequently, management has to decide which parameters of performance are critical to the firm's success, and then concentrate or focus the resources of the firm on these particular characteristics.

For example, if a company wants to focus on speed of delivery, then it cannot be very flexible in terms of its ability to offer a wide range of products. Similarly, a low-cost strategy is not compatible with either speed of delivery or flexibility. High quality is also viewed as a trade-off to low cost. For firms with large existing manufacturing facilities, Skinner suggests

Plant-within-a-plant

the creation of a **plant-within-a-plant (PWP)** concept, in which different locations within the facility are allocated to different product lines, each with their own operations strategy. Under the PWP concept, even the workers are separated to minimize the confusion associated with shifting from one type of strategy to another.[1]

A strategic position is not sustainable unless there are compromises with other positions. Trade-offs occur when activities are incompatible, so that more of one thing necessitates less of another. An airline can choose to serve meals—adding cost and slowing turnaround time at the gate—or it can choose not to, but it cannot do both without bearing major inefficiencies.[2]

Straddling

**Straddling** occurs when a company seeks to match the benefits of a successful position while maintaining its existing position. It adds new features, services, or technologies onto the activities it already performs. A good case study is how Continental Airlines reacted to the strategy of Southwest Airlines, as described at the beginning of this chapter.

While maintaining its position as a full-service airline, Continental set out to match Southwest on a number of point-to-point routes. The airline dubbed the new service Continental Lite. It eliminated meals and first-class service, increased departure frequency, lowered fares, and shortened gate turnaround time. Because Continental remained a full-service airline on other routes, it continued to use travel agents and its mixed fleet of planes and to provide baggage checking and seat assignments.

Trade-offs ultimately grounded Continental Lite. The airline lost hundreds of millions of dollars, and the chief executive officer lost his job. Its planes were delayed leaving congested hub cities or slowed at the gate by baggage transfers. Late flights and cancellations generated a thousand complaints a day. Continental Lite could not afford to compete on price and still pay standard travel agent commissions, but neither could it do without agents for its full-service business. The airline compromised by cutting commissions for all Continental flights. Similarly, it could not afford to offer the same frequent-flier benefits to travelers paying the much lower ticket prices for Lite service. It compromised again by lowering the rewards of Continental's entire frequent-flier program. The results: angry travel agents and full-service customers. Continental tried to compete in two ways at once and paid an enormous straddling penalty.

## ORDER WINNERS AND QUALIFIERS: THE MARKETING–OPERATIONS LINK

Cross Functional

An interface between marketing and operations is necessary to provide a business with an understanding of its markets from both perspectives. Terry Hill, a professor at the London Business School, has coined the terms *order winner* and *order qualifier* to describe marketing-oriented dimensions that are key to competitive success.[3] An **order winner** is a criterion that differentiates the products or services of one firm from another. Depending on the situation, the order-winning criterion may be the cost of the product (price), product quality and reliability, or any of the other dimensions developed earlier. An **order qualifier** is a screening criterion that permits a firm's products to even be considered as possible candidates for purchase. Professor Hill states that a firm must requalify the order qualifiers every day it is in business.

Order winner

Order qualifier

Global

It is important to remember that the order-winning and order-qualifying criteria may change over time. For example, when Japanese companies entered the world automobile markets in the 1970s, they changed the way in which these products won orders, from predominantly price to product quality and reliability. American automobile producers were losing orders through quality to the Japanese companies. By the late 1980s, product quality was raised by Ford, General Motors, and Chrysler (now DaimlerChrysler) so that they are now "qualified" to be in the market. Consumer groups continually monitor the quality and reliability criteria, thus requalifying the top-performing companies. Today the order winners for automobiles vary greatly depending on the model. Customers know the set of features they want (such as reliability, design features, and gas mileage), and they want to purchase a particular combination at the lowest price, thus maximizing value.

## STRATEGIC FIT—FITTING OPERATIONAL ACTIVITIES TO STRATEGY

Vol. VI "Valuation of Operations at ABTco"

All of the activities that make up a firm's operation relate to one another. Making these activities efficient means minimizing their total cost. On the other hand, making them effective means making the combined set of activities support the firm's strategy. Once again, consider Southwest Airlines. Southwest's rapid gate turnaround, which allows frequent departures and greater use of aircraft, is essential to its high-convenience, low-cost positioning. But how does Southwest achieve this? Part of the answer lies in the company's well-paid gate and ground crews, whose productivity in turnarounds is enhanced by flexible union rules. But the bigger part of the answer lies in how Southwest performs (or avoids) other activities. With no meals, no seat assignments, and no interline baggage transfers, Southwest avoids having to perform activities that slow down other airlines. It selects airports and routes to avoid congestion that introduces delays. Southwest's strict limits on the type and length of routes make standardized aircraft possible: Southwest uses only Boeing 737s. Exhibit 2.1 shows how Southwest's strategy is implemented through a set of activities designed to deliver it.[4]

Activity-system maps

**Activity-system maps,** such as the one for Southwest, show how a company's strategy is delivered through a set of tailored activities. In companies with a clear strategy, a number of higher-order strategic themes (in green) can be identified and implemented through

EXHIBIT 2.1

Activity Map Showing How Southwest's Strategy Is Implemented

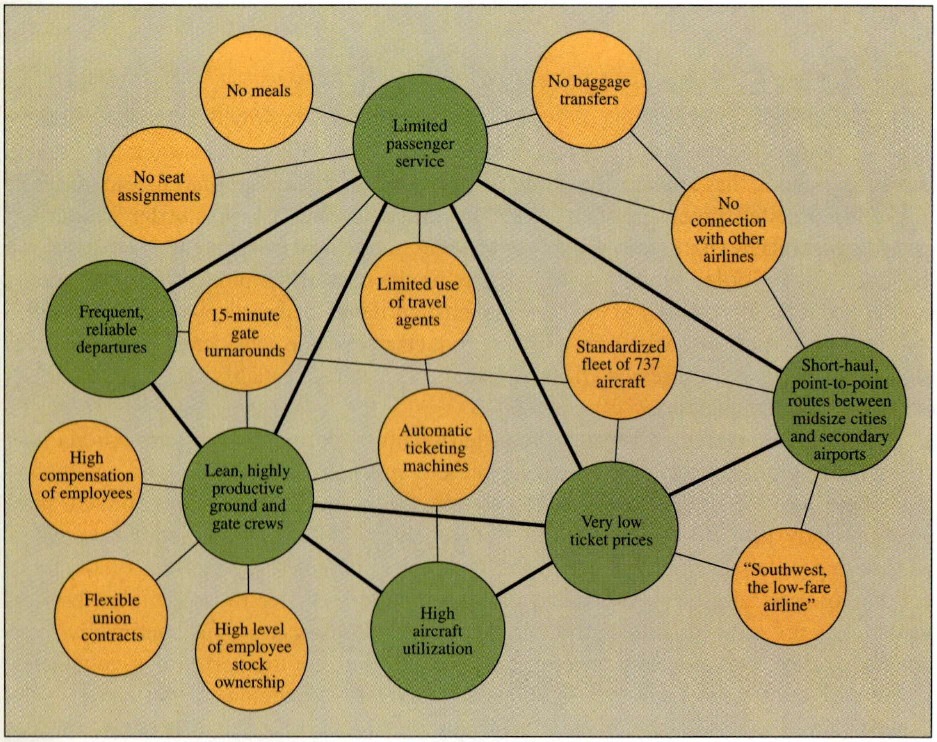


SOURCE: M. E. PORTER, "WHAT IS STRATEGY" *HARVARD BUSINESS REVIEW*, NOVEMBER–DECEMBER 1996, P. 73.

clusters of tightly linked activities. This type of map can be useful in understanding how good the fit is between the system of activities and the company's strategy. Competitive advantage comes from the way a firm's activities fit and reinforce one another.

## A FRAMEWORK FOR OPERATIONS STRATEGY IN MANUFACTURING

Operations strategy cannot be designed in a vacuum. It must be linked vertically to the customer and horizontally to other parts of the enterprise. Exhibit 2.2 shows these linkages between customer needs, their performance priorities and requirements for manufacturing operations, and the operations and related enterprise resource capabilities to satisfy those needs. Overlying this framework is senior management's strategic vision of the firm. The vision identifies, in general terms, the target market, the firm's product line, and its core enterprise and operations capabilities.

The choice of a target market can be difficult, but it must be made. Indeed, it may lead to turning away business—ruling out a customer segment that would simply be unprofitable or too hard to serve given the firm's capabilities. Examples here are U.S. car companies not producing right-hand-drive cars for the Japanese and British markets, as well as clothing manufacturers not making half-sizes in their dress lines. **Core capabilities** (or competencies) are the skills that differentiate the manufacturing (or service firm) from its competitors.

Core capabilities

EXHIBIT 2.2

Operations Strategy Framework: From Customer Needs to Order Fulfillment

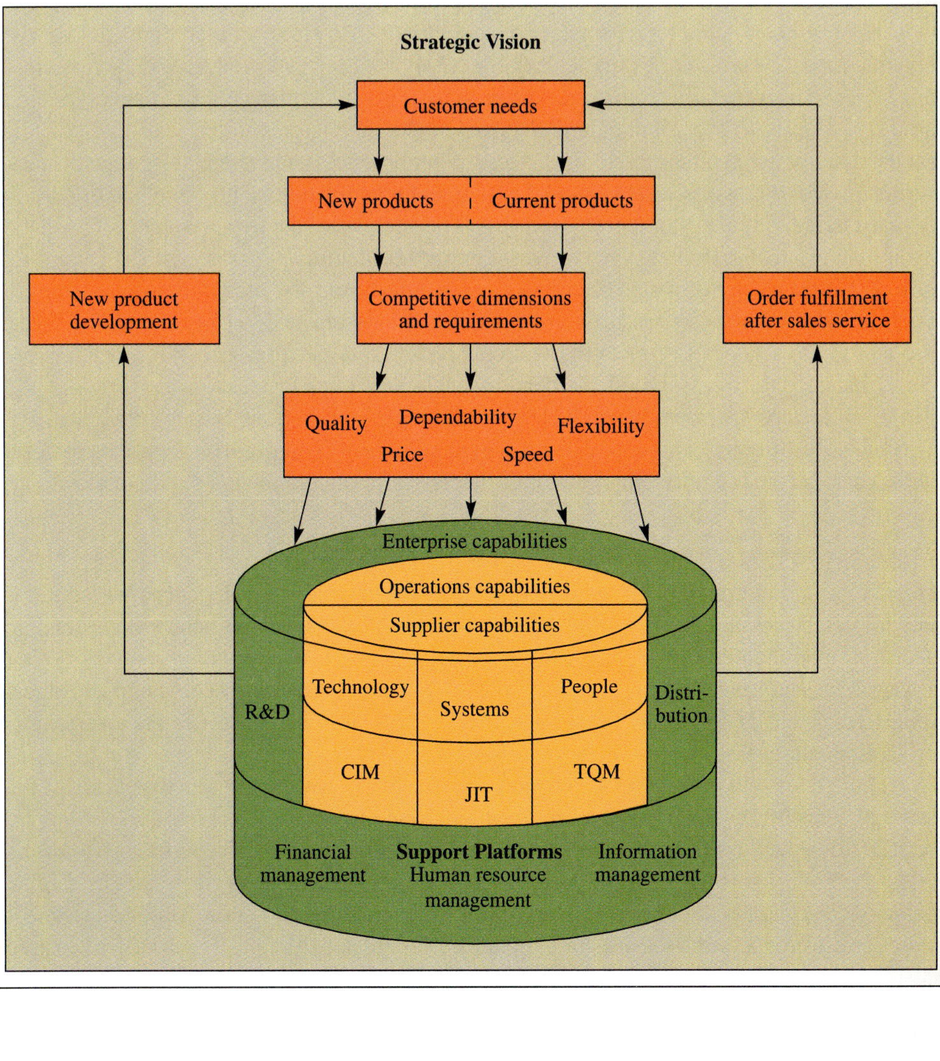

Possibly the most difficult thing for a firm to do is part with tradition. Wickham Skinner argues that managers are often too comfortable with just tinkering with the current system.[5] All the new advanced technologies present themselves as quick fixes. It is easy to patch these technologies into the current system with great enthusiasm. While doing this may be exciting to managers and engineers working for the firm, they may not be creating a distinctive core competence—a competence that wins future customers. Skinner argues that what companies need in this world of intense global competition is not more techniques, but a way to structure a whole new product realization system differently and better than any competitor. In the next section we give guidelines for how that can be done.

## DEVELOPING A MANUFACTURING STRATEGY

The main objectives of manufacturing strategy development are (*a*) to translate required competitive dimensions (typically obtained from marketing) into specific performance requirements for operations, and (*b*) to make the necessary plans to ensure that operations (and enterprise) capabilities are sufficient to accomplish them. The steps for prioritizing these dimensions are

1 Segment the market according to the product group.
2 Identify the product requirements, demand patterns, and profit margins of each group.
3 Determine the order winners and order qualifiers for each group.
4 Convert order winners into specific performance requirements.

The process of achieving a satisfactory manufacturing segmentation that maintains focus is often a matter of deciding which products or product groups fit together in the sense that they have similar market performance characteristics or place similar demands on the manufacturing system. For example, Exhibit 2.3 shows how two product groups manufactured by one instrument manufacturer differ in their manufacturing requirements. The first product group is a range of standard electronic medical equipment that was sold "off the shelf" directly to hospitals and clinics. The second product group is a wider range of measuring devices that were sold to original equipment manufacturers and often had to be customized to individual customer requirements. The analysis of the two product groups in the exhibit shows that they have very different market competitive characteristics. Therefore, different external performance objectives are required from the manufacturing operation. Each product group also has different priorities for its internal performance objectives. Product group 1 needs to concentrate on cost and quality performance. All other internal performance objectives should be bent to achieving this. Product group 2 needs the flexibility to cope with a wide product range and with considerable design turbulence.

Such very different competitive needs will almost certainly require two separate focused units, each devoted to providing the things that are important in their separate markets.

## OPERATIONS STRATEGY IN SERVICES

Operations strategy in service firms is generally inseparable from the corporate strategy. For most services, the service delivery system is the business, and hence, any strategic decision must include operations considerations. However, operations executives do not always have a voice equal to other functions of the firm. A marketing decision to add a new route for an airline or to add new in-flight services may be made despite operations' protests about feasibility (just as in manufacturing).

Although we will discuss service strategy in Chapter 6, we should note that many of the strategy concepts discussed relative to manufacturing also apply to services. For example, service firms may use the plant-within-a-plant (PWP) structure to achieve focus. Hospitals using the PWP focus may have separate units for distinct patient services such as cardiac units, oncology units, labor and delivery units, and rehabilitation units. Major department stores group products and services into separate units or "departments," each with a separate customer focus, ordering, product arrangement, flow, and strategy. Each department—

EXHIBIT 2.3

A Comparison of How Two Product Groups Differ in Their Manufacturing Requirements

| MANUFACTURING REQUIREMENTS DIFFERENCES | PRODUCT GROUP 1 | PRODUCT GROUP 2 |
|---|---|---|
| Products | Standard medical equipment | Electronic measuring devices |
| Customers | Hospitals/clinics | Medical and other OEMs |
| Product specs | Not high-tech, but periodic updates | Varies; some high specs and others less so |
| Product range | Narrow—4 variants | Wide; many types and variants; some customization |
| Design changes | Infrequent | Continuous process |
| Delivery | Customer lead time important—ship directly from stock on hand | On-time delivery important |
| Quality | Conformance/reliability | Performance/conformance |
| Demand variation | Financial year–related but predictable | Lumpy and unpredictable |
| Volume/line | High | Medium to low |
| Margins | Low | Low to very high |
| EXTERNAL PERFORMANCE DIMENSIONS | | |
| Order winners | Price<br>Product reliability | Product specification<br>Product range |
| Qualifiers | Delivery lead time<br>Product specification<br>Quality conformance | Delivery dependability<br>Delivery lead time<br>Price |
| MAIN OPERATIONS PERFORMANCE DIMENSIONS | Cost<br>Quality | New product flexibility<br>Range flexibility<br>Dependability |

SOURCE: N. SLACK, *THE MANUFACTURING ADVANTAGE* (LONDON: MANAGEMENT BOOKS 2000 LTD., 1992), PP. 14–15.

women's sportswear, customer service, children's apparel, housewares, and men's clothing—focuses on specific customer niches with unique needs, particularly if the organization serves a variety of customers and markets with distinct needs. Likewise, order winners and qualifiers have service applications. For a bank, qualifiers might be a good location, availability of tellers and loan officers, and ATMs. Order winners might be relationship banking and customer-oriented banking hours.

## ATTACKING THROUGH OPERATIONS[6]

Consider the following story about how Wal-Mart became the dominant discount retailer in the United States.

Wal-Mart became a public corporation in 1972. At the time it operated 30 discount stores in rural Arkansas, Missouri, and Oklahoma.[7] It had to go public to get the money needed to build its first warehouse. Then, following an unwavering strategy, it steadily expanded from that base. A little over 10 years later it had about 650 stores and almost $4.7 billion in sales. By the 1980s (even though most Americans had never seen a Wal-Mart store or even a Wal-Mart advertisement), one would think that larger rivals like Sears and Kmart would have been aware of its stunning progress and alert to the potential threat it posed. By 1987, only five years later, Wal-Mart had almost 1,200 stores, just over half as many as Kmart (its $16 billion in sales were now about 60 percent of Kmart's); the industry's "country bumpkin" had taken the lead in applying computer technology to track sales and coordinate the replenishment of its stores. Yet, as Wal-Mart steadily approached the large cities where Kmart

THE HANDHELD COMPUTER IS LINKED BY A RADIO FREQUENCY NETWORK TO IN-STORE TERMINALS TO KEEP UP-TO-THE-MINUTE TRACK OF INVENTORY ON HAND AND DELIVERIES. A TYPICAL WAL-MART STORE HAS MORE THAN 70,000 ITEMS IN STOCK AND WAL-MART AS A COMPANY AN ANNUAL TECHNOLOGY BUDGET OF $500 MILLION.

was entrenched, rather than prepare for the predictable head-to-head confrontation, Kmart turned its energies to diversification and building a more upscale image.

By 1993 the battle was essentially over. Wal-Mart's sales had surpassed Kmart's two years earlier and now, with $67 billion, were over half again as large. Over 80 percent of Kmart's stores now faced direct competition from Wal-Mart (while only slightly over half of Wal-Mart's stores competed directly with Kmart), and Kmart—so financially strapped that it could barely cover its annual dividend—was hamstrung in its attempts to renovate its old stores. By then, of course, it was a case of too little, too late. Why didn't it react sooner? What should it have done while it still had a chance to change the course of events?

Kmart did finally attempt to react to Wal-Mart's attack by pouring money into new computerized scanners and new product procurement and inventory control systems. It found that its employees lacked the skills necessary to use the new systems effectively and that the data being entered into them were full of errors. Instilling the organizational discipline required to ensure the accuracy of data and then providing the training required in order to make the most effective use of its sophisticated systems had taken Wal-Mart many years. Kmart could find no shortcut.[8]

In this example we see three different ways that Wal-Mart created a competitive operations advantage that differentiates Wal-Mart from the competition. First, Wal-Mart created significant advantage through the systems that they developed to manage their warehouses and their stores. These systems are the envy of the retailing industry. Next, Wal-Mart created a location advantage. Initially Wal-Mart chose locations without direct competition from the large chains—rural areas in Arkansas, Missouri, and Oklahoma. Once Wal-Mart had developed the infrastructure to compete, Wal-Mart could exploit this great system and compete head-to-head in large urban areas while enjoying a significant operating cost advantage. Finally, in developing their efficient system, Wal-Mart created a culture of supporting values, skills, technologies, supplier–customer relationships, human resources, and approaches to motivation that are neither easily copied nor transferable to other organizations.

Capabilities such as those developed by Wal-Mart are nurtured over a long time. In thinking about how to develop such capabilities, it is useful to break them up into three types:

- *Process-based* capabilities are derived from activities that transform material or information and tend to provide advantages along such standard competitive dimensions as low cost and high quality.
- *Systems (coordination)-based* operating capabilities underpin such competitive advantages as short lead times, a broad range of products or services, the ability to customize on demand, and fast new product development. Such capabilities require broad involvement throughout the entire operating system.

- *Organization-based* operating capabilities involve the ability to master new technologies, design and introduce new products, and bring new plants online significantly faster than one's competitors. Since they are even more difficult to replicate, such capabilities are among the most powerful in the operating arsenal.

For an operations-based competitive advantage to endure over time, operations-based strategies must be dynamic or change over time. Ongoing invention is at the core of today's most effective operations organizations; they cannot stand still while their competitors try to catch up. Those that can consistently create new, more effective ways of delivering value to customers will stay ahead of the pack. Although individuals learn and adapt easily (at least some individuals do this), organizations rarely do. They must be structured and shaped in a way that facilitates learning and change.

The technical note on learning curves that follows this chapter discusses the topics of organizational and individual learning. This is an important topic, and, as you will see, progress in the steady improvement in operating efficiency has been studied over the years. Strategies that combine existing and new operating capabilities in novel ways can be powerful, but the most sustainable advantages are those based on a firm's ability to learn. A company can easily replicate a competitor's equipment and operating policies within a few years. Learning to use them effectively usually takes much longer. A company that continually invents practices that innovatively use new technologies and methods is difficult to catch.

## PRODUCTIVITY MEASUREMENT

Productivity

**Productivity** is a common measure of how well a country, industry, or business unit is using its resources (or factors of production). The Breakthrough Box titled "Internet Gives Competitive Operations Advantage" describes how the Internet has had a major impact on labor productivity in the United States. In its broadest sense, productivity is defined as

$$\text{Productivity} = \frac{\text{Outputs}}{\text{Inputs}}$$

To increase productivity, we want to make this ratio of outputs to inputs as large as practical.

Productivity is what we call a *relative measure.* In other words, to be meaningful, it needs to be compared with something else. For example, what can we learn from the fact that we operate a restaurant, and that its productivity last week was 8.4 customers per labor hour? Nothing!

Productivity comparisons can be made in two ways. First, a company can compare itself with similar operations within its industry, or it can use industry data when such data are available (e.g., comparing productivity among the different stores in a franchise).

Another approach is to measure productivity over time within the same operation. Here we would compare our productivity in one time period with that of the next.

As Exhibit 2.4 shows, productivity may be expressed as partial measures, multifactor measures, or total measures. If we are concerned with the ratio of output to a single input,

EXHIBIT 2.4

**Examples of Productivity Measures**

| | |
|---|---|
| Partial measure | $\frac{\text{Output}}{\text{Labor}}$ or $\frac{\text{Output}}{\text{Capital}}$ or $\frac{\text{Output}}{\text{Materials}}$ or $\frac{\text{Output}}{\text{Energy}}$ |
| Multifactor measure | $\frac{\text{Output}}{\text{Labor} + \text{Capital} + \text{Energy}}$ or $\frac{\text{Output}}{\text{Labor} + \text{Capital} + \text{Materials}}$ |
| Total measure | $\frac{\text{Output}}{\text{Inputs}}$ or $\frac{\text{Goods and services produced}}{\text{All resources used}}$ |

SOURCE: D. J. SUMANTH AND K. TANG, "A REVIEW OF SOME APPROACHES TO THE MANAGEMENT OF TOTAL PRODUCTIVITY IN A COMPANY/ORGANIZATION," *INSTITUTE OF INDUSTRIAL ENGINEERING CONFERENCE PROCEEDINGS*, FALL 1984, P. 305. COPYRIGHT INSTITUTE OF INDUSTRIAL ENGINEERS, 25 TECHNOLOGY PARK/ATLANTA, NORCROSS, GEORGIA 30092.

## BREAKTHROUGH

### INTERNET GIVES COMPETITIVE OPERATIONS ADVANTAGE BY IMPROVING LABOR PRODUCTIVITY

Although technology has been winning increasing credit for its role in the current economic boom, experts are only now beginning to understand how that's happening. By tying hundreds of millions of computers together into a common network, the Internet has turbocharged the U.S. economy and is helping to generate long-elusive improvements in productivity, a critical factor in the country's ability to improve living standards.

A close look at how companies are using the Internet to save billions of dollars in distribution and transaction costs reveals a global productivity revolution in the making. From online self-service systems for employees and customers to direct sales to remote management of far-flung facilities, corporations are changing the way business is done.

Cisco Systems, Inc., for example, has used the Web to convert its expense reporting system to a self-service process that requires only two people to handle 15,000 reports filed each month. The system costs $5 a report, compared with $50 a report for the industry. That's a saving of $675,000 a month. Pete Solvik, Cisco's chief information officer, says the system paid for itself in three months.

New electronic billing schemes are slashing billing cost of such users as utilities and the cost to customers of mailing back payments. IBM figures that these systems will save banks and customers as much as $46 billion a year. Consider the commissions airlines pay to travel agents. These payments cost airlines almost 15 percent of total revenues, third in expenses after labor and fuel. America West, for example, figures it costs the company $6 to sell the average ticket over the Internet, versus $26 through a travel agent.

Or consider IBM. The computer giant saved $300 million in telephone support costs by directing 14 million customer questions to self-service Web sites. The company expects to save an additional $240 million this year by using the Internet to sell $15 billion in products and to buy $12 billion in parts and services. Moreover, the company figures it will save $100 million by training employees online.

Economists used to puzzle over why output per worker in this country had remained almost flat since the early 1970s in spite of hundreds of billions of dollars spent by businesses on computers. The mystery, often referred to as the "productivity paradox," has provided ammunition to critics who say computers have merely wasted the nation's time and money.

But now it seems clear that the Internet, by leveraging the power of computers, is playing a big role in the recent rebound in productivity growth. "Every once in a while, a technology comes along that profoundly changes the way work is done," says Erik Brynjolfson, an expert on productivity at the Massachusetts Institute of Technology's Sloan School of Management. "The Internet is just a better mousetrap."

"Computers weren't able to realize their true potential until they were all connected together," says Ira Magaziner, who recently retired as President Clinton's special adviser on the information economy.

Productivity matters. Only by improving productivity can the nation boost wages without igniting inflation or hurting profitability. The Internet may prove to be to computers what the electric motor was to electricity. Stanford University economist Paul David points out that although electricity became available for lighting in 1881, it wasn't until the 1920s, after the widespread adoption of the electric motor, that electricity boosted productivity in factories.

SOURCE: ADAPTED FROM (AUTHOR NOT CITED), "PRODUCTIVITY JUMPS WITH HELP OF THE NET," *THE WALL STREET JOURNAL*, JUNE 30, 1999.

we have a *partial productivity measure.* If we want to look at the ratio of output to a group of inputs (but not all inputs), we have a *multifactor productivity measure.* If we want to express the ratio of all outputs to all inputs, we have a *total factor measure of productivity* that might be used to describe the productivity of an entire organization or even a nation.

A numerical example of productivity appears in Exhibit 2.5. The data reflect quantitative measures of input and output associated with the production of a certain product. Notice that for the multifactor and partial measures it is not necessary to use total output as the numerator. Often it is desirable to create measures that represent productivity as it relates to some particular output of interest. For example, as in Exhibit 2.5, total units might be

**EXHIBIT 2.5**

**Numerical Example of Productivity Measures**

Excel: Productivity Measures

| INPUT AND OUTPUT PRODUCTION DATA ($) | |
|---|---|
| **OUTPUT** | |
| 1. Finished units | $10,000 |
| 2. Work in process | 2,500 |
| 3. Dividends | 1,000 |
| 4. Bonds | |
| 5. Other income | |
| Total output | $13,500 |
| **INPUT** | |
| 1. Human | $ 3,000 |
| 2. Material | 153 |
| 3. Capital | 10,000 |
| 4. Energy | 540 |
| 5. Other expenses | 1,500 |
| Total input | $15,193 |

**PRODUCTIVITY MEASURE EXAMPLES**

Total measure:

$$\frac{\text{Total output}}{\text{Total input}} = \frac{13{,}500}{15{,}193} = .89$$

Multifactor measures:

$$\frac{\text{Total output}}{\text{Human} + \text{Material}} = \frac{13{,}500}{3{,}153} = 4.28$$

$$\frac{\text{Finished units}}{\text{Human} + \text{Material}} = \frac{10{,}000}{3{,}153} = 3.17$$

Partial measures:

$$\frac{\text{Total output}}{\text{Energy}} = \frac{13{,}500}{540} = 25$$

$$\frac{\text{Finished units}}{\text{Energy}} = \frac{10{,}000}{540} = 18.52$$

NOTE: FIND THE SPREADSHEET ON THE CD INCLUDED WITH THE TEXT.
SOURCE: D. J. SUMANTH AND K. TANG, "A REVIEW OF SOME APPROACHES TO THE MANAGEMENT OF TOTAL PRODUCTIVITY IN A COMPANY/ORGANIZATION," *INSTITUTE OF INDUSTRIAL ENGINEERING CONFERENCE PROCEEDINGS*, FALL 1984, P. 305. COPYRIGHT INSTITUTE OF INDUSTRIAL ENGINEERS, 25 TECHNOLOGY PARK/ATLANTA, NORCROSS, GEORGIA 30092.

**EXHIBIT 2.6**

**Partial Measures of Productivity**

| BUSINESS | PRODUCTIVITY MEASURE |
|---|---|
| Restaurant | Customers (meals) per labor hour |
| Retail store | Sales per square foot |
| Chicken farm | Lb. of meat per lb. of feed |
| Utility plant | Kilowatts per ton of coal |
| Paper mill | Tons of paper per cord of wood |

the output of interest to a production control manager, whereas total output may be of key interest to the plant manager. This process of aggregation and disaggregation of productivity measures provides a means of shifting the level of the analysis to suit a variety of productivity measurement and improvement needs.

Exhibit 2.5 shows all units in dollars. Often, however, management can better understand how the company is performing when units other than dollars are used. In these cases, only partial measures of productivity can be used, as we cannot combine dissimilar units such as labor hours and pounds of material. Some commonly used partial measures of productivity are presented as examples in Exhibit 2.6. Such partial measures of productivity give managers information in familiar units, allowing them to easily relate these measures to the actual operations.

## CONCLUSION

Nonoperations students often view operations strategy and competitiveness, particularly as they pertain to manufacturing, as not being especially relevant to their specialty areas. We hope that this chapter conveys the important link between operations and the competitive success of the firm. The concepts of competitive dimensions, order winners and qualifiers, and capabilities apply to virtually any business and are critical to the ability of the firm to sustain a competitive advantage.

For a firm to remain competitive all of the activities that make up the operations core must buttress the firm's strategy. Many new technologies, and especially the Internet, have an impact on operations capabilities. The firm must actively explore changes in operations strategy to take advantage of these new technologies. Productivity measures provide the benchmarks for how well a company is doing and are useful for measuring improvement. These are important terms that make up the new language of operations strategy—and the language of business.

## KEY TERMS

**Operations strategy** Setting broad policies and plans for using the resources of a firm to best support the firm's long-term competitive strategy.

**Plant-within-a-plant (PWP)** A concept in which different locations within a facility are dedicated to different product lines. Each location is operated according to its own strategy in order to minimize the confusion associated with shifting from one type of strategy to another.

**Straddling** Occurs when a company seeks to match what a competitor is doing by just adding new features, services, or technologies to existing activities. This often creates problems due to the compromises that may need to be made.

**Order winner** A dimension that differentiates the products or services of one firm from another.

**Order qualifier** A dimension that is used to screen a product or service as a candidate for purchase.

**Activity-system map** A diagram that shows how a company's strategy is delivered through a set of supporting activities.

**Core capabilities** Skills that differentiate the manufacturing or service firm from its competitors.

**Productivity** A measure of how well resources are used.

## SOLVED PROBLEM

### SOLVED PROBLEM 1

A furniture manufacturing company has provided the following data. Compare the labor, raw materials and supplies, and total productivity of 1999 and 2000.

| | | 1999 | 2000 |
|---|---|---|---|
| Output: | Sales value of production | $22,000 | $35,000 |
| Input: | Labor | 10,000 | 15,000 |
| | Raw materials and supplies | 8,000 | 12,500 |
| | Capital equipment depreciation | 700 | 1,200 |
| | Other | 2,200 | 4,800 |

### Solution

| | 1999 | 2000 |
|---|---|---|
| Partial productivities | | |
| Labor | 2.20 | 2.33 |
| Raw materials and supplies | 2.75 | 2.80 |
| Total productivity | 1.05 | 1.04 |

## REVIEW AND DISCUSSION QUESTIONS

1 Can a factory be fast, dependable, and flexible, produce high-quality products, and still provide poor service from a customer's perspective?
2 Why should a service organization worry about being world-class if it does not compete outside its own national border? What impact does the Internet have on this?
3 What are the major priorities associated with operations strategy? How has their relationship to each other changed over the years?
4 For each of the different priorities describe the unique characteristics of the market niche with which it is most compatible.

5 A few years ago the dollar showed relative weakness with respect to foreign currencies such as the yen, mark, and pound. This stimulated exports. Why would long-term reliance on a lower-valued dollar be at best a short-term solution to the competitiveness problem?
6 In your opinion, do business schools have competitive priorities?
7 Why does the "proper" operations strategy keep changing for companies that are world-class competitors?
8 What is meant by the expressions *order winners* and *order qualifiers*? What was the order winner(s) for your last major purchase of a product or service?
9 What do we mean when we say productivity is a "relative" measure?
10 What are the typical performance measures for quality, speed of delivery, and flexibility?
11 What should be the criteria for management to adopt a particular performance measure?

## PROBLEMS*

1 Two types of cars (Deluxe and Limited) were produced by a car manufacturer in 1999. Quantities sold, price per unit, and labor hours follow. What is the labor productivity for each car? Explain the problem(s) associated with the labor productivity.

| | QUANTITY | $/UNIT |
|---|---|---|
| Deluxe car | 4,000 units sold | $8,000/car |
| Limited car | 6,000 units sold | $9,500/car |
| Labor, Deluxe | 20,000 hours | $12/hour |
| Labor, Limited | 30,000 hours | $14/hour |

1. 
| Productivity | (hours) |
|---|---|
| Deluxe car | 0.20 |
| Limited car | 0.20 |

| Productivity | (dollars) |
|---|---|
| Deluxe car | 133.33 |
| Limited car | 135.71 |

2 A U.S. manufacturing company operating a subsidiary in an LDC (less developed country) shows the following results:

| | U.S. | LDC |
|---|---|---|
| Sales (units) | 100,000 | 20,000 |
| Labor (hours) | 20,000 | 15,000 |
| Raw materials (currency) | $20,000 | FC 20,000 |
| Capital equipment (hours) | 60,000 | 5,000 |

*a.* Calculate partial labor and capital productivity figures for the parent and subsidiary. Do the results seem misleading?
*b.* Now compute the multifactor productivity figures for labor and capital together. Are the results better?
*c.* Finally, calculate raw material productivity figures (units/$ where $1 = FC 10). Explain why these figures might be greater in the subsidiary.

2. *a.* Yes:

| U.S. | LDC |
|---|---|
| 5.00 | 1.33 |
| 1.67 | 4.00 |

*b.* Yes:

| U.S. | LDC |
|---|---|
| 1.25 | 1.00 |

*c.*

| U.S. | LDC |
|---|---|
| 5 | 10 |

3 Various financial data for 1998 and 1999 follow. Calculate the total productivity measure and the partial measures for labor, capital, and raw materials for this company for both years. What do these measures tell you about this company?

| | | 1998 | 1999 |
|---|---|---|---|
| Output: | Sales | $200,000 | $220,000 |
| Input: | Labor | 30,000 | 40,000 |
| | Raw materials | 35,000 | 45,000 |
| | Energy | 5,000 | 6,000 |
| | Capital | 50,000 | 50,000 |
| | Other | 2,000 | 3,000 |

3. 
| | 1998 | 1999 |
|---|---|---|
| Total productivity | 1.64 | 1.53 |
| Partial labor | 6.67 | 5.50 |
| Partial raw materials | 5.71 | 4.89 |
| Partial capital | 4.00 | 4.40 |

4 An electronics company makes communications devices for military contracts. The company just completed two contracts. The Navy contract was for 2,300 devices and took 25 workers two weeks (40 hours per week) to complete. The Army contract was for 5,500 devices that were produced by 35 workers in three weeks. On which contract were the workers more productive?

4. Army (1.31)

5 A retail store had sales of $45,000 in April and $56,000 in May. The store employs eight full-time workers (they work a 40-hour week). In April the store also had seven part-time workers at 10 hours per week, and in May the store had nine part-timers at 15 hours per week

5. 6.67% increase

* Special thanks to Bill Ruck of Arizona State University for the problems in this section.

6. 4.85% decrease

7. 11.125, 10.675

(assume four weeks in each month). Using sales dollars as the measure of output, what is the percentage change in productivity from April to May?

6 A parcel delivery company delivered 103,000 packages in 1997 when its average employment was 84 drivers. In 1998 the firm handled 112,000 deliveries with 96 drivers. What was the percentage change in productivity from 1997 to 1998?

7 A fast-food restaurant serves hamburgers, cheeseburgers, and chicken sandwiches. The restaurant counts a cheeseburger as equivalent to 1.25 hamburgers and chicken sandwiches as 0.8 hamburgers. Current employment is five full-time employees (who work a 40-hour week). If the restaurant sold 700 hamburgers, 900 cheeseburgers, and 500 chicken sandwiches in one week, what is its productivity? What would its productivity have been if it had sold the same number of sandwiches (2,100) but the mix was 700 of each type?

## CASE: COMPAQ COMPUTER VERSUS DELL COMPUTER—BUSINESS MODEL COMPARISON

Internet WWW

Compaq Computer and Dell Computer have, together with IBM, become the dominant players in the computer industry. For the purposes of this case, focus on the upstarts in the industry, Compaq and Dell. The following table provides a quick comparison of how these two companies do business.

| FEATURE OF THE BUSINESS MODEL | COMPAQ COMPUTER | DELL COMPUTER |
|---|---|---|
| Scope of product line | Full line from very high-end, fault-tolerant servers to inexpensive personal computers. | Personal computers differentiated mainly by speed and configuration details. |
| Sales | Mostly through resellers and channel partners. Recently started an Internet-based "sell direct" capability | Dell's unique direct-to-customer approach eliminates retailers or other resellers. Computers are sold directly to customers via orders taken by phone, fax, or the Internet. |
| Assembly of computers | Most computers are assembled to stock. Off-the-shelf delivery is promised to resellers. | Every computer is built to order. |
| Distribution | Company and reseller run warehouses. | Computers are sent directly to customers using common carriers. |
| Service | Service is provided through the resellers and channel partners. | Most service is provided via free telephone calls and an extensive Internet site. On-site repairs during the warranty period are outsourced to companies such as Unisys and IBM. |

From the table, we see major differences in the business models being used by the two companies. Much more information is available on the web sites of the companies; Compaq is at http://www.compaq.com and Dell is at http://www.dell.com.

### QUESTIONS

1 Compare the two companies based on the major operations priorities: cost, product quality, delivery speed, delivery reliability, coping with changes in demand, flexibility, and new product introduction speed.

2 What are the operations competitive advantages of Compaq compared to Dell?

3 Compare the annual financial statements of Compaq and Dell. The most current statements are available from the web sites of these companies. From an operations standpoint (i.e., look at cost-of-sales data), which company seems stronger? Why?

4 Which company do you think is best positioned to be successful in the first five years of the 21st century? Why do you feel this way?

## CASE: LOS ANGELES TOY COMPANY

The Los Angeles Toy Company (LATC) views its primary task as making for stock a standardized line of high-quality, unique toys that "last from Pablum to puberty." As a rule, LATC introduces one or two new toys a year. In August 2000 the owner and manufacturing manager, Dwight Smith-Daniels, has been informed by his toy inventors that they have designed a Jay Leno doll. This doll will stand two feet high and is capable of telling jokes via an electronic voice synthesizer. One of the company's three manufacturing staff departments, design engineering, states that the product can be made primarily from molded plastic using the firm's new all-purpose molders (now used for making small attachments to the firm's wooden toys). LATC, in its previous initial production of new toys, has relied heavily on its skilled workforce to debug the product design as they make the product and to perform quality inspections on the finished product. Production runs have been short runs to fill customer orders.

If the Jay Leno doll is to go into production, however, the production run size will have to be large, and assembly and testing procedures will have to be more refined. Currently, each toymaker performs almost all of the processing steps at his or her workbench. The production engineering department believes that the assembly of the new toy is well within the skill levels of the current workforce but that the voice synthesizer and battery-operated movement mechanism will have to be subcontracted. LATC has always had good relations with subcontractors, primarily because the firm has placed its orders with sufficient lead time so that its vendors could optimally sequence LATC's orders with those of some larger toy producers in Los Angeles. Dwight Smith-Daniels has always favored long-range production planning so that he can keep his 50 toymakers busy all year. (One of the reasons he set up the factory in Los Angeles was so that he could draw upon the large population of "hip" toymakers who lived there.) Smith-Daniels believes the supervisors of the firm's three production departments—castles, puppets, and novelties—are favorable to the new product. The novelty department supervisor, Tom Callerman, has stated, "My workers can make any toy—you give us an output incentive, and we'll produce around the clock."

The marketing department has forecast a demand of 50,000 Jay Leno dolls for the Christmas rush. The dolls should sell at retail for $29.50. A preliminary cost analysis from the process engineering department is that the dolls will cost no more than $7 each to manufacture. The company is currently operating at 70 percent capacity. Financing is available, and there is no problem with cash flow. Dwight Smith-Daniels is wondering if he should go into production of Jay Leno dolls.

#### QUESTIONS

1. How consistent is the Jay Leno doll order with the current capabilities and focus of LATC?
2. Should LATC (*a*) manufacture the doll itself, (*b*) subcontract the work to a Tijuana, Mexico, manufacturing plant that specializes in high-volume production (at a cost of $8 per doll to LATC), or (*c*) look for another product more in line with its capabilities? The agency that holds the license to Jay Leno products wants a decision right away, as does the Mexican supplier.

## SELECTED BIBLIOGRAPHY

Blackburn, J. D. *Time-Based Competition: The Next Battleground in American Manufacturing.* Homewood, IL: Business One Irwin, 1991.

Chase, R. B., and D. A. Garvin. "The Service Factory." *Harvard Business Review* 67, no. 4 (July–August 1989), pp. 61–69.

Gray, P., and J. Jurison (eds.). *Productivity in the Office and in the Factory.* Danvers, MA: Boyd & Fraser, 1995.

Hart, C. W. L.; J. L. Heskett; and W. E. Sassar, Jr. *Service Breakthroughs: Changing the Rules of the Game.* New York: Free Press, 1990.

Hayes, R. H., and G. P. Pisano. "Beyond World Class: The New Manufacturing Strategy." *Harvard Business Review* 72, no. 1 (January–February 1994), pp. 77–86.

Hayes, R. H.; S. Wheelwright; and K. B. Clark. *Dynamic Manufacturing: Creating the Learning Organization.* New York: Free Press, 1988.

Hill, T. J. *Manufacturing Strategy—Text and Cases,* Burr Ridge; IL: Irwin/McGraw-Hill, 2000.

Hopp, W., and M. Spearman. *Factory Physics: A New Approach to Manufacturing Management.* Burr Ridge, IL: Irwin/McGraw-Hill, 2000.

Skinner, C. W. *Manufacturing: The Formidable Competitive Weapon.* New York: John Wiley & Sons, 1985.

Skinner, W. (ed.). "Special Issue on Manufacturing Strategy." *Production and Operations Management* 5, no. 1 (Spring 1996).

Slack, N. *The Manufacturing Advantage.* London: Management Books 2000 Ltd., 1991.

Stalk, G., Jr. "Time—The Next Source of Competitive Advantage." *Harvard Business Review,* July–August 1988.

## FOOTNOTES

1 C. W. Skinner, "The Focused Factory," *Harvard Business Review* 52, no. 3 (May–June 1974), pp. 113–22.

2 See M. E. Porter, "What Is Strategy?" *Harvard Business Review,* November–December 1996, p. 68.

3 T. Hill, *Manufacturing Strategy—Text and Cases,* 3rd ed. (Burr Ridge, IL: Irwin/McGraw-Hill, 2000).

4 M. E. Porter, "What Is Strategy?" *Harvard Business Review,* November–December 1996, pp. 70–71.

5 W. Skinner, "Three Yards and a Cloud of Dust: Industrial Management at Century End," *Production and Operations Management* 5, no. 1 (Spring 1996), pp. 15–41.

6 This section is adapted from R. H. Hayes and D. M. Upton, "Operations Based Strategy," *California Management Review* 40, no. 4 (Summer 1998), pp. 11–12.

7 "Wal-Mart Stores, Inc.," Harvard Business School Case #9-794-024.

8 From "Operations Based Strategy," *California Management Review* 40, no. 4 (Summer 1998), pp. 11–12.

*technical note two*

# LEARNING CURVES

## OUTLINE AND KEY TERMS



technical note

## APPLICATION OF LEARNING CURVES

A **learning curve** is a line displaying the relationship between unit production time and the cumulative number of units produced. Learning (or experience) curve theory has a wide range of application in the business world. In manufacturing, it can be used to estimate the time for product design and production, as well as costs. Learning curves are important and are sometimes overlooked as one of the trade-offs in just-in-time (JIT) systems, where sequencing and short runs achieve lower inventories by forfeiting some benefits of experience from long product runs. Learning curves are also an integral part in planning corporate strategy, such as decisions concerning pricing, capital investment, and operating costs based on experience curves.

Learning curve

Learning curves can be applied to individuals or organizations. **Individual learning** is improvement that results when people repeat a process and gain skill or efficiency from their own experience. That is, "practice makes perfect." **Organizational learning** results from practice as well, but it also comes from changes in administration, equipment, and product design. In organizational settings, we expect to see both kinds of learning occurring simultaneously and often describe the combined effect with a single learning curve.

Individual learning

Organizational learning

Learning curve theory is based on three assumptions:

1 The amount of time required to complete a given task or unit of a product will be less each time the task is undertaken.
2 The unit time will decrease at a decreasing rate.
3 The reduction in time will follow a predictable pattern.

Each of these assumptions was found to hold true in the airplane industry, where learning curves were first applied.[1] In this application, it was observed that, as output doubled, there was a 20 percent reduction in direct production worker-hours per unit between doubled units. Thus, if it took 100,000 hours for Plane 1, it would take 80,000 hours for Plane 2, 64,000 hours for Plane 4, and so forth. Because the 20 percent reduction meant that, say, Unit 4 took only 80 percent of the production time required for Unit 2, the line connecting the coordinates of output and time was referred to as an "80 percent learning curve." (By convention, the percentage learning rate is used to denote any given exponential learning curve.)

A learning curve may be developed from an arithmetic tabulation, by logarithms, or by some other curve-fitting method, depending on the amount and form of the available data.

There are two ways to think about the improved performance that comes with learning curves: time per unit (as in Exhibit TN2.1A) or units of output per time period (as in TN2.1B). *Time per unit* shows the decrease in time required for each successive unit. *Cumulative average time* shows the cumulative average performance times as the total

EXHIBIT TN2.1

Learning Curves Plotted as Times and Numbers of Units

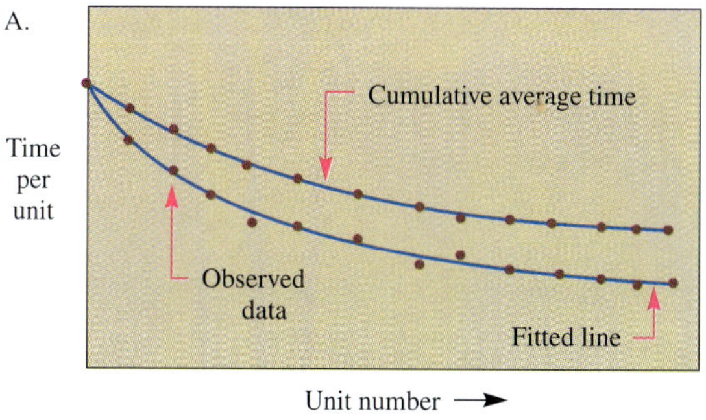


**A Progress Curve**

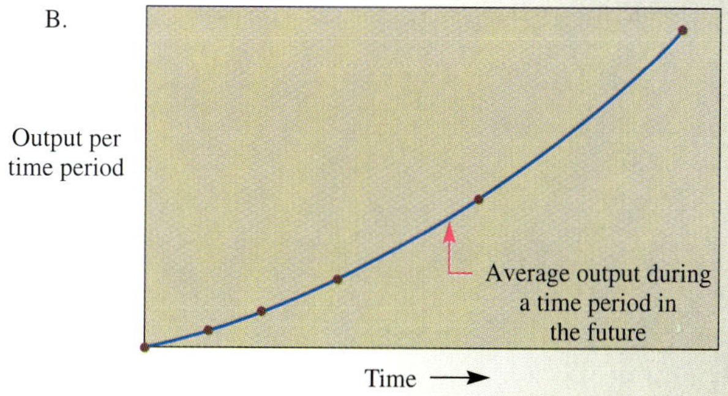


**Industrial Learning**

number of units increases. Time per unit and cumulative average times are also called *progress curves* or *product learning,* and are useful for complex products or products with a longer cycle time. *Units of output per time period* is also called *industry learning* and is generally applied to high-volume production (short cycle time).

Note in Exhibit TN2.1A that the cumulative average curve does not decrease as fast as the time per unit because the time is being averaged. For example, if the time for Units 1, 2, 3, and 4 were 100, 80, 70, and 64, they would be plotted that way on the time per unit graph, but would be plotted as 100, 90, 83.3, and 78.5 on the cumulative average time graph.

## PLOTTING LEARNING CURVES

There are many ways to analyze past data to fit a useful trend line. We will use the simple exponential curve first as an arithmetic procedure and then by a logarithmic analysis. In an arithmetical tabulation approach, a column for units is created by doubling, row by row, as 1, 2, 4, 8, 16. . . . The time for the first unit is multiplied by the learning percentage to obtain the time for the second unit. The second unit is multiplied by the learning percentage for the fourth unit, and so on. Thus, if we are developing an 80 percent learning curve, we would arrive at the figures listed in column 2 of Exhibit TN2.2. Because it is often desirable for planning purposes to know the cumulative direct labor hours, column 4, which lists this information, is also provided. The calculation of these figures is straightforward; for example, for Unit 4, cumulative average direct labor hours would be found by dividing cumulative direct labor hours by 4, yielding the figure given in column 4.

Exhibit TN2.3 shows three curves with different learning rates: 90 percent, 80 percent, and 70 percent. Note that if the cost of the first unit was $100, the 30th unit would cost $59.63 at the 90 percent rate and $17.37 at the 70 percent rate. Differences in learning rates can have dramatic effects.

In practice, learning curves are plotted using a graph with logarithmic scales. The unit curves become linear throughout their entire range and the cumulative curve becomes linear after the first few units. The property of linearity is desirable because it facilitates extrapolation and permits a more accurate reading of the cumulative curve. This type of scale is an option in Microsoft Excel. Simply generate a regular scatter plot in your spreadsheet and then select each axis and format the axis with the logarithmic option. Exhibit TN2.4 shows the 80 percent unit cost curve and average cost curve on a logarithmic scale. Note that the cumulative average cost is essentially linear after the eighth unit.

Although the arithmetic tabulation approach is useful, direct logarithmic analysis of learning curve problems is generally more efficient because it does not require a complete enumeration of successive time–output combinations. Moreover, where such data are not available, an analytical model that uses logarithms may be the most convenient way of obtaining output estimates.

EXHIBIT TN2.2

**Unit, Cumulative, and Cumulative Average Direct Labor Worker-Hours Required for an 80 Percent Learning Curve**

Excel: Learning Curves

| (1) Unit Number | (2) Unit Direct Labor Hours | (3) Cumulative Direct Labor Hours | (4) Cumulative Average Direct Labor Hours |
|---|---|---|---|
| 1 | 100,000 | 100,000 | 100,000 |
| 2 | 80,000 | 180,000 | 90,000 |
| 4 | 64,000 | 314,210 | 78,553 |
| 8 | 51,200 | 534,591 | 66,824 |
| 16 | 40,960 | 892,014 | 55,751 |
| 32 | 32,768 | 1,467,862 | 45,871 |
| 64 | 26,214 | 2,392,453 | 37,382 |
| 128 | 20,972 | 3,874,395 | 30,269 |
| 256 | 16,777 | 6,247,318 | 24,404 |

## LOGARITHMIC ANALYSIS

The normal form of the learning curve equation is[2]

[TN2.1]
$$Y_x = Kx^n$$

where

$x$ = Unit number
$Y_x$ = Number of direct labor hours required to produce the $x$th unit
$K$ = Number of direct labor hours required to produce the first unit
$n = \log b/\log 2$ where $b$ = Learning percentage

We can solve this mathematically or by using a table as shown in the next section. Mathematically, to find the labor-hour requirement for the eighth unit in our example (Exhibit TN2.2), we would substitute as follows:

$$Y_8 = (100{,}000)(8)^n$$

Using logarithms:

$$Y_8 = 100{,}000(8)^{\log 0.8/\log 2}$$
$$= 100{,}000(8)^{-0.322} = \frac{100{,}000}{(8)^{0.322}}$$
$$= \frac{100{,}000}{1.9535} = 51{,}192$$

Therefore, it would take 51,192 hours to make the eighth unit. (See the spreadsheet "Learning Curves.")

## LEARNING CURVE TABLES

When the learning percentage is known, Exhibits TN2.5 and TN2.6 can be easily used to calculate estimated labor hours for a specific unit or for cumulative groups of units. We need only multiply the initial unit labor hour figure by the appropriate tabled value.

To illustrate, suppose we want to double-check the figures in Exhibit TN2.2 for unit and cumulative labor hours for Unit 16. From Exhibit TN2.5, the unit improvement factor for

EXHIBITS TN2.3 & TN2.4

TN2.3—Arithmetic Plot of 70, 80, and 90 Percent Learning Curves

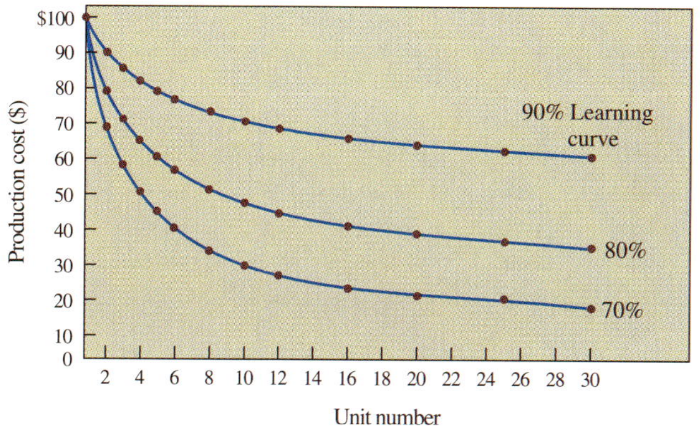


TN2.4—Logarithmic Plot of an 80 Percent Learning Curve

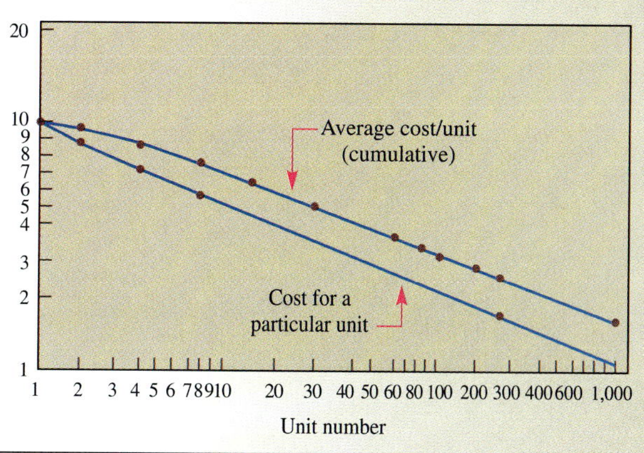

EXHIBIT TN2.5

**Improvement Curves: Table of Unit Values**

Excel: Learning Curves

| UNIT | UNIT IMPROVEMENT FACTOR 60% | 65% | 70% | 75% | 80% | 85% | 90% | 95% |
|---|---|---|---|---|---|---|---|---|
| 1 | 1.0000 | 1.0000 | 1.0000 | 1.0000 | 1.0000 | 1.0000 | 1.0000 | 1.0000 |
| 2 | .6000 | .6500 | .7000 | .7500 | .8000 | .8500 | .9000 | .9500 |
| 3 | .4450 | .5052 | .5682 | .6338 | .7021 | .7729 | .8462 | .9219 |
| 4 | .3600 | .4225 | .4900 | .5625 | .6400 | .7225 | .8100 | .9025 |
| 5 | .3054 | .3678 | .4368 | .5127 | .5956 | .6857 | .7830 | .8877 |
| 6 | .2670 | .3284 | .3977 | .4754 | .5617 | .6570 | .7616 | .8758 |
| 7 | .2383 | .2984 | .3674 | .4459 | .5345 | .6337 | .7439 | .8659 |
| 8 | .2160 | .2746 | .3430 | .4219 | .5120 | .6141 | .7290 | .8574 |
| 9 | .1980 | .2552 | .3228 | .4017 | .4930 | .5974 | .7161 | .8499 |
| 10 | .1832 | .2391 | .3058 | .3846 | .4765 | .5828 | .7047 | .8433 |
| 12 | .1602 | .2135 | .2784 | .3565 | .4493 | .5584 | .6854 | .8320 |
| 14 | .1430 | .1940 | .2572 | .3344 | .4276 | .5386 | .6696 | .8226 |
| 16 | .1290 | .1785 | .2401 | .3164 | .4096 | .5220 | .6561 | .8145 |
| 18 | .1188 | .1659 | .2260 | .3013 | .3944 | .5078 | .6445 | .8074 |
| 20 | .1099 | .1554 | .2141 | .2884 | .3812 | .4954 | .6342 | .8012 |
| 22 | .1025 | .1465 | .2038 | .2772 | .3697 | .4844 | .6251 | .7955 |
| 24 | .0961 | .1387 | .1949 | .2674 | .3595 | .4747 | .6169 | .7904 |
| 25 | .0933 | .1353 | .1908 | .2629 | .3548 | .4701 | .6131 | .7880 |
| 30 | .0815 | .1208 | .1737 | .2437 | .3346 | .4505 | .5963 | .7775 |
| 35 | .0728 | .1097 | .1605 | .2286 | .3184 | .4345 | .5825 | .7687 |
| 40 | .0660 | .1010 | .1498 | .2163 | .3050 | .4211 | .5708 | .7611 |
| 45 | .0605 | .0939 | .1410 | .2060 | .2936 | .4096 | .5607 | .7545 |
| 50 | .0560 | .0879 | .1336 | .1972 | .2838 | .3996 | .5518 | .7486 |
| 60 | .0489 | .0785 | .1216 | .1828 | .2676 | .3829 | .5367 | .7386 |
| 70 | .0437 | .0713 | .1123 | .1715 | .2547 | .3693 | .5243 | .7302 |
| 80 | .0396 | .0657 | .1049 | .1622 | .2440 | .3579 | .5137 | .7231 |
| 90 | .0363 | .0610 | .0987 | .1545 | .2349 | .3482 | .5046 | .7168 |
| 100 | .0336 | .0572 | .0935 | .1479 | .2271 | .3397 | .4966 | .7112 |
| 120 | .0294 | .0510 | .0851 | .1371 | .2141 | .3255 | .4830 | .7017 |
| 140 | .0262 | .0464 | .0786 | .1287 | .2038 | .3139 | .4718 | .6937 |
| 160 | .0237 | .0427 | .0734 | .1217 | .1952 | .3042 | .4623 | .6869 |
| 180 | .0218 | .0397 | .0691 | .1159 | .1879 | .2959 | .4541 | .6809 |
| 200 | .0201 | .0371 | .0655 | .1109 | .1816 | .2887 | .4469 | .6757 |
| 250 | .0171 | .0323 | .0584 | .1011 | .1691 | .2740 | .4320 | .6646 |
| 300 | .0149 | .0289 | .0531 | .0937 | .1594 | .2625 | .4202 | .6557 |
| 350 | .0133 | .0262 | .0491 | .0879 | .1517 | .2532 | .4105 | .6482 |
| 400 | .0121 | .0241 | .0458 | .0832 | .1453 | .2454 | .4022 | .6419 |
| 450 | .0111 | .0224 | .0431 | .0792 | .1399 | .2387 | .3951 | .6363 |
| 500 | .0103 | .0210 | .0408 | .0758 | .1352 | .2329 | .3888 | .6314 |
| 600 | .0090 | .0188 | .0372 | .0703 | .1275 | .2232 | .3782 | .6229 |
| 700 | .0080 | .0171 | .0344 | .0659 | .1214 | .2152 | .3694 | .6158 |
| 800 | .0073 | .0157 | .0321 | .0624 | .1163 | .2086 | .3620 | .6098 |
| 900 | .0067 | .0146 | .0302 | .0594 | .1119 | .2029 | .3556 | .6045 |
| 1,000 | .0062 | .0137 | .0286 | .0569 | .1082 | .1980 | .3499 | .5998 |
| 1,200 | .0054 | .0122 | .0260 | .0527 | .1020 | .1897 | .3404 | .5918 |
| 1,400 | .0048 | .0111 | .0240 | .0495 | .0971 | .1830 | .3325 | .5850 |
| 1,600 | .0044 | .0102 | .0225 | .0468 | .0930 | .1773 | .3258 | .5793 |
| 1,800 | .0040 | .0095 | .0211 | .0446 | .0895 | .1725 | .3200 | .5743 |
| 2,000 | .0037 | .0089 | .0200 | .0427 | .0866 | .1683 | .3149 | .5698 |
| 2,500 | .0031 | .0077 | .0178 | .0389 | .0806 | .1597 | .3044 | .5605 |
| 3,000 | .0027 | .0069 | .0162 | .0360 | .0760 | .1530 | .2961 | .5530 |

EXHIBIT TN2.6

**Improvement Curves: Table of Cumulative Values**

Excel: Learning Curves

CUMULATIVE IMPROVEMENT FACTOR

| UNIT | 60% | 65% | 70% | 75% | 80% | 85% | 90% | 95% |
|---|---|---|---|---|---|---|---|---|
| 1 | 1.000 | 1.000 | 1.000 | 1.000 | 1.000 | 1.000 | 1.000 | 1.000 |
| 2 | 1.600 | 1.650 | 1.700 | 1.750 | 1.800 | 1.850 | 1.900 | 1.950 |
| 3 | 2.045 | 2.155 | 2.268 | 2.384 | 2.502 | 2.623 | 2.746 | 2.872 |
| 4 | 2.405 | 2.578 | 2.758 | 2.946 | 3.142 | 3.345 | 3.556 | 3.774 |
| 5 | 2.710 | 2.946 | 3.195 | 3.459 | 3.738 | 4.031 | 4.339 | 4.662 |
| 6 | 2.977 | 3.274 | 3.593 | 3.934 | 4.299 | 4.688 | 5.101 | 5.538 |
| 7 | 3.216 | 3.572 | 3.960 | 4.380 | 4.834 | 5.322 | 5.845 | 6.404 |
| 8 | 3.432 | 3.847 | 4.303 | 4.802 | 5.346 | 5.936 | 6.574 | 7.261 |
| 9 | 3.630 | 4.102 | 4.626 | 5.204 | 5.839 | 6.533 | 7.290 | 8.111 |
| 10 | 3.813 | 4.341 | 4.931 | 5.589 | 6.315 | 7.116 | 7.994 | 8.955 |
| 12 | 4.144 | 4.780 | 5.501 | 6.315 | 7.227 | 8.244 | 9.374 | 10.62 |
| 14 | 4.438 | 5.177 | 6.026 | 6.994 | 8.092 | 9.331 | 10.72 | 12.27 |
| 16 | 4.704 | 5.541 | 6.514 | 7.635 | 8.920 | 10.38 | 12.04 | 13.91 |
| 18 | 4.946 | 5.879 | 6.972 | 8.245 | 9.716 | 11.41 | 13.33 | 15.52 |
| 20 | 5.171 | 6.195 | 7.407 | 8.828 | 10.48 | 12.40 | 14.61 | 17.13 |
| 22 | 5.379 | 6.492 | 7.819 | 9.388 | 11.23 | 13.38 | 15.86 | 18.72 |
| 24 | 5.574 | 6.773 | 8.213 | 9.928 | 11.95 | 14.33 | 17.10 | 20.31 |
| 25 | 5.668 | 6.909 | 8.404 | 10.19 | 12.31 | 14.80 | 17.71 | 21.10 |
| 30 | 6.097 | 7.540 | 9.305 | 11.45 | 14.02 | 17.09 | 20.73 | 25.00 |
| 35 | 6.478 | 8.109 | 10.13 | 12.72 | 15.64 | 19.29 | 23.67 | 28.86 |
| 40 | 6.821 | 8.631 | 10.90 | 13.72 | 17.19 | 21.43 | 26.54 | 32.68 |
| 45 | 7.134 | 9.114 | 11.62 | 14.77 | 18.68 | 23.50 | 29.37 | 36.47 |
| 50 | 7.422 | 9.565 | 12.31 | 15.78 | 20.12 | 25.51 | 32.14 | 40.22 |
| 60 | 7.941 | 10.39 | 13.57 | 17.67 | 22.87 | 29.41 | 37.57 | 47.65 |
| 70 | 8.401 | 11.13 | 14.74 | 19.43 | 25.47 | 33.17 | 42.87 | 54.99 |
| 80 | 8.814 | 11.82 | 15.82 | 21.09 | 27.96 | 36.80 | 48.05 | 62.25 |
| 90 | 9.191 | 12.45 | 16.83 | 22.67 | 30.35 | 40.32 | 53.14 | 69.45 |
| 100 | 9.539 | 13.03 | 17.79 | 24.18 | 32.65 | 43.75 | 58.14 | 76.59 |
| 120 | 10.16 | 14.11 | 19.57 | 27.02 | 37.05 | 50.39 | 67.93 | 90.71 |
| 140 | 10.72 | 15.08 | 21.20 | 29.67 | 41.22 | 56.78 | 77.46 | 104.7 |
| 160 | 11.21 | 15.97 | 22.72 | 32.17 | 45.20 | 62.95 | 86.80 | 118.5 |
| 180 | 11.67 | 16.79 | 24.14 | 34.54 | 49.03 | 68.95 | 95.96 | 132.1 |
| 200 | 12.09 | 17.55 | 25.48 | 36.80 | 52.72 | 74.79 | 105.0 | 145.7 |
| 250 | 13.01 | 19.28 | 28.56 | 42.05 | 61.47 | 88.83 | 126.9 | 179.2 |
| 300 | 13.81 | 20.81 | 31.34 | 46.94 | 69.66 | 102.2 | 148.2 | 212.2 |
| 350 | 14.51 | 22.18 | 33.89 | 51.48 | 77.43 | 115.1 | 169.0 | 244.8 |
| 400 | 15.14 | 23.44 | 36.26 | 55.75 | 84.85 | 127.6 | 189.3 | 277.0 |
| 450 | 15.72 | 24.60 | 38.48 | 59.80 | 91.97 | 139.7 | 209.2 | 309.0 |
| 500 | 16.26 | 25.68 | 40.58 | 63.68 | 98.85 | 151.5 | 228.8 | 340.6 |
| 600 | 17.21 | 27.67 | 44.47 | 70.97 | 112.0 | 174.2 | 267.1 | 403.3 |
| 700 | 18.06 | 29.45 | 48.04 | 77.77 | 124.4 | 196.1 | 304.5 | 465.3 |
| 800 | 18.82 | 31.09 | 51.36 | 84.18 | 136.3 | 217.3 | 341.0 | 526.5 |
| 900 | 19.51 | 32.60 | 54.46 | 90.26 | 147.7 | 237.9 | 376.9 | 587.2 |
| 1,000 | 20.15 | 31.01 | 57.40 | 96.07 | 158.7 | 257.9 | 412.2 | 647.4 |
| 1,200 | 21.30 | 36.59 | 62.85 | 107.0 | 179.7 | 296.6 | 481.2 | 766.6 |
| 1,400 | 22.32 | 38.92 | 67.85 | 117.2 | 199.6 | 333.9 | 548.4 | 884.2 |
| 1,600 | 23.23 | 41.04 | 72.49 | 126.8 | 218.6 | 369.9 | 614.2 | 1001 |
| 1,800 | 24.06 | 43.00 | 76.85 | 135.9 | 236.8 | 404.9 | 678.8 | 1116 |
| 2,000 | 24.83 | 44.84 | 80.96 | 144.7 | 254.4 | 438.9 | 742.3 | 1230 |
| 2,500 | 26.53 | 48.97 | 90.39 | 165.0 | 296.1 | 520.8 | 897.0 | 1513 |
| 3,000 | 27.99 | 52.62 | 98.90 | 183.7 | 335.2 | 598.9 | 1047 | 1791 |

Unit 16 at 80 percent is .4096. This multiplied by 100,000 (the hours for Unit 1) gives 40,960, the same as in Exhibit TN2.2. From Exhibit TN2.6, the cumulative improvement factor for cumulative hours for the first 16 units is 8.920. When multiplied by 100,000, this gives 892,000, which is reasonably close to the exact value of 892,014 shown in Exhibit TN2.2.

The following is a more involved example of the application of a learning curve to a production problem.

### EXAMPLE TN2.1: SAMPLE LEARNING CURVE PROBLEM

Captain Nemo, owner of the Suboptimum Underwater Boat Company (SUB), is puzzled. He has a contract for 11 boats and has completed 4 of them. He has observed that his production manager, young Mr. Overick, has been reassigning more and more people to torpedo assembly after the construction of the first four boats. The first boat, for example, required 225 workers, each working a 40-hour week, while 45 fewer workers were required for the second boat. Overick has told them that "this is just the beginning" and that he will complete the last boat in the current contract with only 100 workers!

Overick is banking on the learning curve, but has he gone overboard?

### SOLUTION

Because the second boat required 180 workers, a simple exponential curve shows that the learning percentage is 80 percent (180 ÷ 225). To find out how many workers are required for the 11th boat, we look up unit 11 for an 80 percent improvement ratio in Exhibit TN2.5 and multiply this value by the number required for the first sub. By interpolating between Unit 10 and Unit 12 we find the improvement ratio is equal to .4629. This yields 104.15 workers (.4269 interpolated from table × 225). Thus, Overick's estimate missed the boat by four people.

SUB has produced the first unit of a new line of minisubs at a cost of $500,000—$200,000 for materials and $300,000 for labor. It has agreed to accept a 10 percent profit, based on cost, and it is willing to contract on the basis of a 70 percent learning curve. What will be the contract price for three minisubs?

| | | |
|---|---|---|
| Cost of first sub | | $ 500,000 |
| Cost of second sub | | |
| Materials | $200,000 | |
| Labor: $300,000 × .70 | 210,000 | 410,000 |
| Cost of third sub | | |
| Materials | 200,000 | |
| Labor: $300,000 × .5682 | 170,460 | 370,460 |
| Total cost | | 1,280,460 |
| Markup: $1,280,460 × .10 | | 128,046 |
| Selling price | | $1,408,506 |

If the operation is interrupted, then some relearning must occur. How far to go back up the learning curve can be estimated in some cases. ←

## ESTIMATING THE LEARNING PERCENTAGE

If production has been under way for some time, the learning percentage is easily obtained from production records. Generally speaking, the longer the production history, the more accurate the estimate. Because a variety of other problems can occur during the early stages of production, most companies do not begin to collect data for learning curve analysis until some units have been completed.

Statistical analysis should also be used. An exponential learning curve can be fitted to find out how well the curve fits past data. The data can also be plotted on log-log graph paper to check straight-line fit.

If production has not started, estimating the learning percentage becomes enlightened guesswork. In such cases the analyst has these options:

1 Assume that the learning percentage will be the same as it has been for previous applications within the same industry.
2 Assume that it will be the same as it has been for the same or similar products.
3 Analyze the similarities and differences between the proposed startup and previous startups and develop a revised learning percentage that appears to best fit the situation.

There are two reasons for disparities between a firm's learning rate and that of its industry. First, there are the inevitable differences in operating characteristics between any two firms, stemming from the equipment, methods, product design, plant organization, and so forth. Second, procedural differences are manifested in the development of the learning percentage itself, such as whether the industry rate is based on a single product or on a product line, and the manner in which the data were aggregated.

### HOW LONG DOES LEARNING GO ON?

Does output stabilize, or is there continual improvement? Some areas can be shown to improve continually even over decades (radios, computers, and other electronic devices; and, if we allow for the effects of inflation, also automobiles, washing machines, refrigerators, and most other manufactured goods). If the learning curve has been valid for several hundreds or thousands of units, it will probably be valid for several hundreds or thousands more. On the other hand, highly automated systems may have a near zero learning curve because, after installation, they quickly reach a constant volume.

## GENERAL GUIDELINES FOR LEARNING

In this section we offer guidelines for two categories of "learners": individuals and organizations.

### INDIVIDUAL LEARNING

A number of factors affect an individual's performance and rate of learning. Remember that there are two elements involved: the rate of learning and the initial starting level. To explain this more clearly, compare the two learning curves in Exhibit TN2.7. Suppose these

EXHIBIT TN2.7

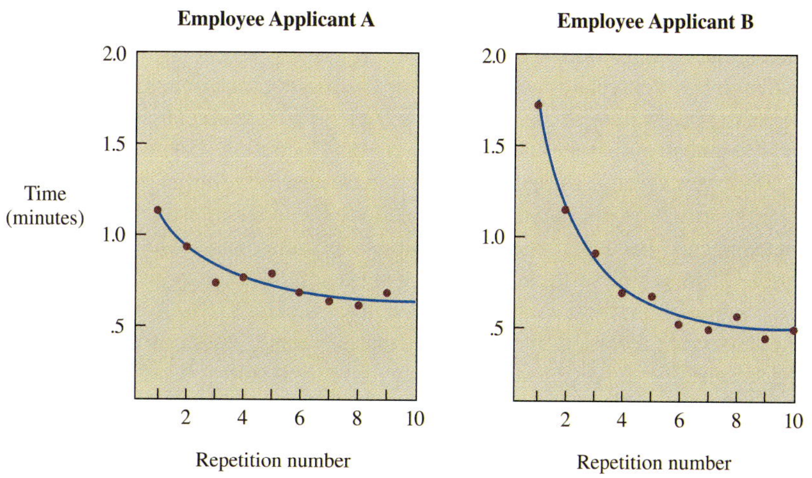


Test Results of Two Job Applicants

were the times for two individuals who performed a simple mechanical test administered by the personnel department as part of their application for employment in the assembly area of manufacturing.

Which applicant would you hire? Applicant A had a much lower starting point but a slower learning rate. Applicant B, although starting at a much higher point, is clearly the better choice. This points out that performance times are important—not just the learning rate by itself.

Some general guidelines to improve individual performance based on learning curves include the following:

1. **Proper selection of workers.** A test should be administered to help choose the workers. These tests should be representative of the planned work: a dexterity test for assembly work, a mental ability test for mental work, tests for interaction with customers for front office work, and so on.
2. **Proper training.** The more effective the training, the faster the learning rate.
3. **Motivation.** Productivity gains based on learning curves are not achieved unless there is a reward. Rewards can be money (individual or group incentive plans) or nonmonetary (employee of the month awards, etc.).
4. **Work specialization.** As a general rule, the simpler the task, the faster the learning. Be careful that boredom doesn't interfere; if it does, redesign the task.
5. **Do one or very few jobs at a time.** Learning is faster on each job if completed one at a time, rather than working on all jobs simultaneously.
6. **Use tools or equipment that assists or supports performance.**
7. **Provide quick and easy access for help.** The benefits from training are realized and continue when assistance is available.
8. **Allow workers to help redesign their tasks.** Taking more performance factors into the scope of the learning curve can, in effect, shift the curve downward.

## ORGANIZATIONAL LEARNING

Organizations learn as well. It has been argued that organizational learning is critical to sustaining a competitive advantage. For the individual, it is easy to conceptualize how knowledge is acquired and retained and how this results in an individual learning effect. Certainly, a main source of organizational learning is the individual learning of the employees. An organization also acquires knowledge in its technology, its structure, documents that it retains, and standard operating procedures.[3] For example, as a manufacturing unit becomes experienced, knowledge is embedded in software and in tooling used for production. Knowledge can also be embedded in the organization's structure. For example, when an organization shifts its industrial engineering group from a functional organization centralized in one area to a decentralized organization where individuals are deployed to particular parts of the plant floor, knowledge about how to become more productive is embedded in the organization's structure.

Knowledge can depreciate if individuals leave the organization. When Lockheed had problems in the production of the L-1011 it was blamed on the fact that the company hired 2,000 inexperienced employees to quickly ramp up production. These employees were put through a four-week training program in aircraft construction. Initial costs rose rather than fell during the initial production of the plane due to the inexperienced workers.

Knowledge can also depreciate if technologies become inaccessible or difficult to use. An example of this is the difficulty in accessing data collected by Landsat, an earth surveillance program. Ninety percent of the data collected before 1979 is now inaccessible because the data were recorded by equipment that no longer exists or cannot be operated. Knowledge can also depreciate if a company's records and routine processes are lost. When Steinway Piano Company decided to put a discontinued piano back into production, the plant discovered it no longer had records or blueprints for the piano.

# LEARNING CURVES APPLIED TO HEART TRANSPLANT MORTALITY

Learning curves provide an excellent means to examine performance. The best comparison for one's performance would be the learning rates for competitors in the industry. Even when a standard or expected level is unknown, much can still be learned by simply using and plotting data in a learning curve fashion. As an illustration of this ability to learn about one's performance, we present the experience of a heart transplant facility in a hospital.[4]

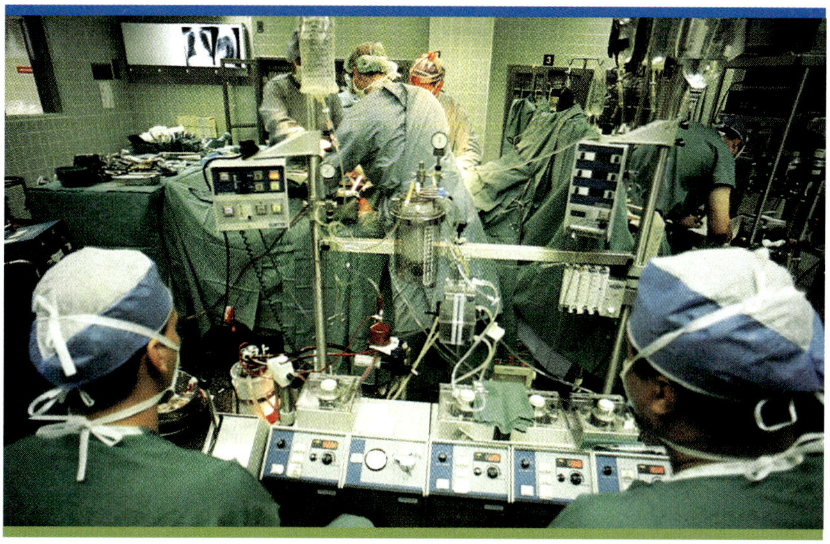

The learning curve model in the heart transplant analysis was of the form

$$Y_i = B_0 + B_1 x^{-B_2}$$

$Y_i$ is the cumulative average resource consumption (the total number of deaths, costs, and so on divided by the number of transplants), $B_0$ is the asymptote (the minimum), $B_1$ is the maximum possible reduction (the difference between the first unit and minimum $B_0$), $x$ is the total number of units produced, and $B_2$ is the rate of change for each successive unit as it moves toward the lower bound.

Exhibit TN2.8 shows the coefficients that were obtained for the model. Exhibit TN2.9 shows the cumulative death rate. This seems to follow an industrial learning curve with a rate just over 80 percent. Seven of the first 23 transplant patients died within a year after transplant surgery. Only 4 of the next 39 patients died within a year. For the cumulative average length of stay, shown in Exhibit TN2.10, the reduction rate is approximately 9 percent.

The least sloping curve (the lowest learning rate) is the cost of heart transplants. Exhibit TN2.11 shows that the initial costs were in the vicinity of \$150,000. After 51 surviving patients (62 procedures, 11 died), the average cost was still close to \$100,000.

EXHIBIT TN2.8

Consumption Coefficients for Heart Transplant Learning Model

| | $B_0$ (ASYMPTOTE) | $B_1$ (RANGE) | $B_2$ (RATE) | PERCENTAGE DECREASE |
|---|---|---|---|---|
| Death rate | .2329 | .8815 | .2362 | 21.04% |
| Length of stay | 28.26 | 23.76 | .0943 | 9.00 |
| Units of service | 1,282.84 | 592.311 | .0763 | 7.35 |
| Adjusted charges | \$96,465.90 | \$53,015.80 | .0667 | 6.45 |

EXHIBIT TN2.9

Death Rates, Less Than One Year Survival

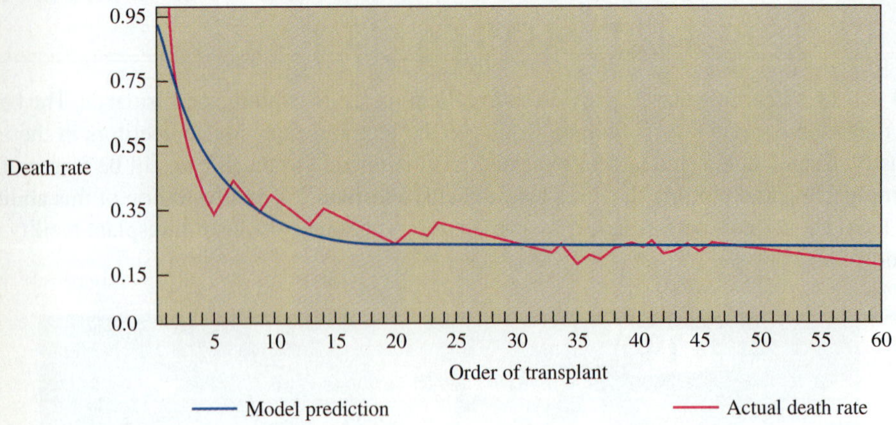


EXHIBIT TN2.10

Average Length of Stay (ALOS) for Heart Transplant Survivors

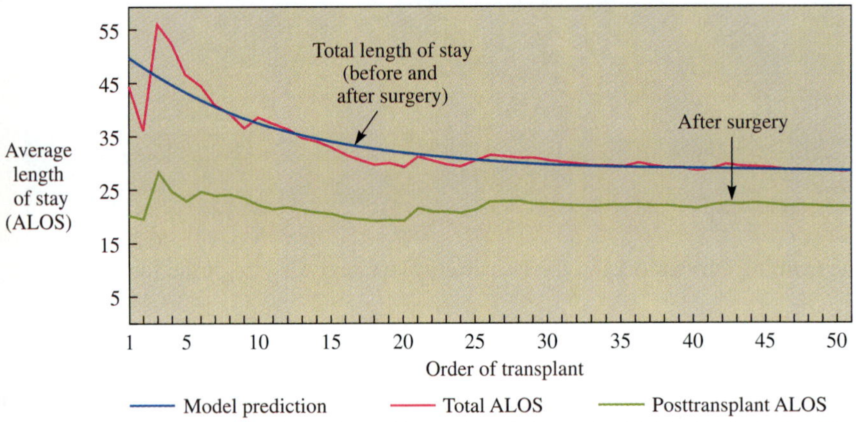


EXHIBIT TN2.11

Cost for Heart Transplant Survivors

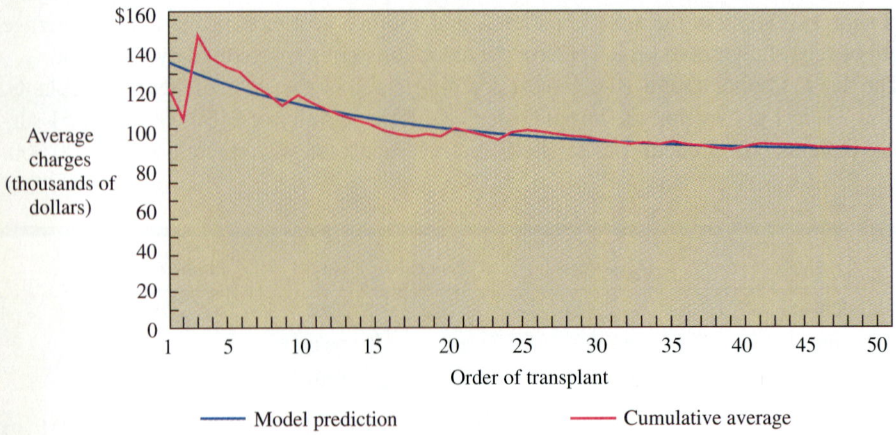


NOTE: FOR TRANSPLANT ADMISSION ONLY, ACTUAL COSTS ARE APPROXIMATELY 50 PERCENT OF CHARGES.

(A learning rate of 80 percent would result in an average cost of \$40,000; a 90 percent rate would result in a cost of \$80,000.)

Why are learning rates high in death rate reduction and low in average length of stay, with the lowest rate in cost reduction? Smith and Larsson question whether the low learning rates may be related to conservatism in dealing with human lives. Or could it be due to the power and insulation of the heart transplant team from pressure to reduce cost? The purpose of this study on learning curves was to make institutions and administrators aware of learning. Institutions need to behave according to learning curve logic—that is, in pricing as well as in motivation for continuous improvement.

## KEY TERMS

**Learning curve** A line displaying the relationship between unit production time and the cumulative number of units produced.

**Individual learning** Improvement that results when people repeat a process and gain skill or efficiency from their own experience.

**Organizational learning** Improvement that comes both from experience and from changes in administration, equipment, and product design.

## FORMULA REVIEW

**Logarithmic curve:**

[TN2.1] $$Y_x = Kx^n$$

## SOLVED PROBLEM

### SOLVED PROBLEM 1

A job applicant is being tested for an assembly line position. Management feels that steady-state times have been approximately reached after 1,000 performances. Regular assembly line workers are expected to perform the task within four minutes.

*a.* If the job applicant performed the first test operation in 10 minutes and the second one in 9 minutes, should this applicant be hired?

*b.* What is the expected time that the job applicant would finish the 10th unit?

*c.* What is a significant limitation of this analysis?

### Solution

*a.* Learning rate = 9 minutes/10 minutes = 90%
From Exhibit TN2.5, the time for the 1,000th unit is .3499 × 10 minutes = 3.499 minutes. Yes, hire the person.

*b.* From Exhibit TN2.5, unit 10 at 90% is .7047. Therefore, the time for the 10th unit = .7047 × 10 = 7.047 minutes.

*c.* More data should be collected on the job applicant's performance.

## REVIEW AND DISCUSSION QUESTIONS

1 If you kept any of your old exam grades from last semester, get them out and write down the grades. Use Exhibits TN2.5 and TN2.6, use log-log graph paper, or use a spreadsheet to find whether the exponential curve fits showing that you experienced learning over the semester (insofar as your exam performance is concerned). If not, can you give some reasons why not?

2 How might the following business specialists use learning curves: accountants, marketers, financial analysts, personnel managers, and computer programmers?

3 As a manager, which learning percentage would you prefer (other things being equal), 110 percent or 60 percent? Explain.

4 What difference does it make if a customer wants a 10,000-unit order produced and delivered all at one time or in 2,500 unit batches?

## PROBLEMS

1 A time standard was set as 0.20 hour per unit after observing 50 cycles. If the task has a 90 percent learning curve, what would be the average time per unit after 100, 200, and 400 cycles?

1. 100th = 0.18 hr.
200th = 0.16 hr.
400th = 0.15 hr.

2. *a.*

1st 10 units = $2,500.00

2nd 10 units = 1,750.00

3rd 10 units = 1,420.50

4th 10 units = 1,225.00

5th 10 units = 1,092.00

*b.* Between max. of $4,250 and min. of $2,645.50.

3. LR parts, 90%, LR labor, 80%

Labor: 11,556 hours.

Parts: $330,876

4. *a.* Labor, $570,150. Materials, 1,356,750 plus something for profit.

*b.* Need to consider forgetting and relearning. Time and cost could be much higher.

5. *a.* From log-log plot, LR = 60%

*b.* About 8,029 hours.

*c.* 6.0 hours.

6. *a.* 70% (see SM for Exhibit 9).

*b.* $145,956,000.

*c.* Cost .0851 × $12 = $1,021,200.

2 You have just received 10 units of a special subassembly from an electronics manufacturer at a price of $250 per unit. A new order has also just come in for your company's product that uses these subassemblies, and you wish to purchase 40 more to be shipped in lots of 10 units each. (The subassemblies are bulky, and you need only 10 a month to fill your new order.)

*a.* Assuming a 70 percent learning curve by your supplier on a similar product last year, how much should you pay for each lot? Assume that the learning rate of 70 percent applies to each lot of 10 units, not each unit.

*b.* Suppose you are the supplier and can produce 20 units now but cannot start production on the second 20 units for two months. What price would you try to negotiate?

3 Johnson Industries received a contract to develop and produce four high-intensity long-distance receiver/transmitters for cellular telephones. The first took 2,000 labor hours and $39,000 worth of purchased and manufactured parts; the second took 1,500 labor hours and $37,000 in parts; the third took 1,450 labor hours and $31,000 in parts; and the fourth took 1,270 labor hours and $31,000 in parts.

Johnson was asked to bid on a follow-on contract for another dozen receiver/transmitter units. Ignoring any forgetting factor effects, what should Johnson estimate time and parts costs to be for the dozen units? Estimate the learning curve using a graph with a log-log scale. This can be easily done with a spreadsheet plot of the data. (Hint: There are two learning curves—one for labor and one for parts.)

4 Lambda Computer Products competed for and won a contract to produce two prototype units of a new type of computer that is based on laser optics rather than on electronic binary bits.

The first unit produced by Lambda took 5,000 hours to produce and required $250,000 worth of material, equipment usage, and supplies. The second unit took 3,500 hours and used $200,000 worth of materials, equipment usage, and supplies. Labor is $30 per hour.

*a.* Lambda was asked to present a bid for 10 additional units as soon as the second unit was completed. Production would start immediately. What would this bid be?

*b.* Suppose there was a significant delay between the contracts. During this time, personnel and equipment were reassigned to other projects. Explain how this would affect the subsequent bid.

5 You've just completed a pilot run of 10 units of a major product and found the processing time for each unit was as follows:

| UNIT NUMBER | TIME (HOURS) |
|---|---|
| 1 | 970 |
| 2 | 640 |
| 3 | 420 |
| 4 | 380 |
| 5 | 320 |
| 6 | 250 |
| 7 | 220 |
| 8 | 240 |
| 9 | 190 |
| 10 | 190 |

*a.* According to the pilot run, what would you estimate the learning rate to be?

*b.* Based on *a*, how much time would it take for the next 190 units, assuming no loss of learning?

*c.* How much time would it take to make the 1,000th unit?

6 Lazer Technologies Inc. (LTI) has produced a total of 20 high-power laser systems that could be used to destroy any approaching enemy missiles or aircraft. The 20 units have been produced, funded in part as private research within the research and development arm of LTI, but the bulk of the funding came from a contract with the U.S. Department of Defense (DOD).

Testing of the laser units has shown that they are effective defense weapons, and through redesign to add portability and easier field maintenance, the units could be truck-mounted.

DOD has asked LTI to submit a bid for 100 units.

The 20 units that LTI has built so far cost the following amounts and are listed in the order in which they were produced:

| UNIT NUMBER | COST ($ MILLIONS) | UNIT NUMBER | COST ($ MILLIONS) |
|---|---|---|---|
| 1 | $12 | 11 | $3.9 |
| 2 | 10 | 12 | 3.5 |
| 3 | 6 | 13 | 3.0 |
| 4 | 6.5 | 14 | 2.8 |
| 5 | 5.8 | 15 | 2.7 |
| 6 | 6 | 16 | 2.6 |
| 7 | 5 | 17 | 2.3 |
| 8 | 3.6 | 18 | 3.0 |
| 9 | 3.6 | 19 | 2.9 |
| 10 | 4.1 | 20 | 2.6 |

*a.* Based on past experience, what is the learning rate? (Hint: You may use a spreadsheet and plot the values using logarithmic scales to make estimates.)

*b.* What bid should LTI submit for the total order of 100 units, assuming that learning continues?

*c.* What is the cost expected to be for the last unit under the learning rate you estimated?

7 Jack Simpson, contract negotiator for Nebula Airframe Company, is currently involved in bidding on a follow-up government contract. In gathering cost data from the first three units, which Nebula produced under a research and development contract, he found that the first unit took 2,000 labor hours, the second took 1,800 labor hours, and the third took 1,692 hours.

In a contract for three more units, how many labor hours should Simpson plan for?

7. 4,710 hours.

8 Honda Motor Company has discovered a problem in the exhaust system of one of its automobile lines and has voluntarily agreed to make the necessary modifications to conform with government safety requirements. Standard procedure is for the firm to pay a flat fee to dealers for each modification completed.

Honda is trying to establish a fair amount of compensation to pay dealers and has decided to choose a number of randomly selected mechanics and observe their performance and learning rate. Analysis demonstrated that the average learning rate was 90 percent, and Honda then decided to pay a $60 fee for each repair (3 hours × $20 per flat-rate hour).

Southwest Honda, Inc., has complained to Honda Motor Company about the fee. Six mechanics, working independently, have completed two modifications each. All took 9 hours on the average to do the first unit and 6.3 hours to do the second. Southwest refuses to do any more unless Honda allows at least 4.5 hours.

What is your opinion of Honda's allowed rate and the mechanics' performance?

8. Learning rate = 70%; unreasonable to ask for 4.5 hours. After 20 repetitions time is about 2 hours.

9 United Research Associates (URA) had received a contract to produce two units of a new cruise missile guidance control. The first unit took 4,000 hours to complete and cost $30,000 in materials and equipment usage. The second took 3,200 hours and cost $21,000 in materials and equipment usage. Labor cost is charged at $18 per hour.

The prime contractor has now approached URA and asked to submit a bid for the cost of producing another 20 guidance controls.

*a.* What will the last unit cost to build?

*b.* What will be the average time for the 20 missile guidance controls?

*c.* What will the average cost be for guidance control for the 20 in the contract?

9. *a.* Cost of 22nd unit = $32,732.40.
*b.* 1,886 hours.
*c.* Average cost = $43,126.50.

10 United Assembly Products (UAP) has a personnel screening process for job applicants to test their ability to perform at the department's long-term average rate. UAP has asked you to modify the test by incorporating learning theory. From the company's data, you discovered that if people can perform a given task in 30 minutes or less on the 20th unit, they achieve the group long-run average. Obviously, all job applicants cannot be subjected to 20 performances of such a task, so you are to determine whether they will likely achieve the desired rate based on only 2 performances.

*a.* Suppose a person took 100 minutes on the first unit and 80 minutes on the second. Should this person be hired?

*b.* What procedure might you establish for hiring (i.e., how to evaluate the job applicant's two performances)?

*c.* What is a significant limitation of this analysis?

10. *a.* If first unit is 100 minutes, the learning rate needs to be 75%, not 80% (80/100). Do not hire
*b.* See ISM.

11. *a.* 3rd = 35.1 hrs.

*b.* Average = 7.9 hrs. each; well worth it.

12. 11th 2.4476/.9 = $2.7196 million

12th 2.3953/.9 = $2.6615 million

$5.3811 million total

13. *a.* 42.165 minutes.

*b.* 35.56 minutes.

14. *a.* 70%

*b.* 501.5 minutes.

*c.* .78 minutes.

11 A potentially large customer offered to subcontract assembly work that is profitable only if you can perform the operations at an average time of less than 20 hours each. The contract is for 1,000 units.

You run a test and do the first one in 50 hours and the second one in 40 hours.

*a.* How long would you expect the third one to take?

*b.* Would you take the contract? Explain.

12 Western Turbine, Inc., has just completed the production of the 10th unit of a new high-efficiency turbine/generator. Its analysis showed that a learning rate of 85 percent existed over the production of the 10 units. If the 10th unit contained labor costs of $2.5 million, what price should Western Turbine charge for labor on the units 11 and 12 to make a profit of 10 percent of the selling price?

13 FES Auto has recently hired Meg the mechanic to specialize in front end alignments. Although she is a trained auto mechanic, she has not used FES's brand of equipment before taking this job. The standard time allocated for a front end alignment is 30 minutes. Her first front end alignment took 50 minutes and her second 47.5 minutes.

*a.* What is the expected time for Meg's 10th front end alignment?

*b.* What is the expected time for Meg's 100th front end alignment?

14 An initial pilot run of 10 units produces the following times:

| Unit Number | Time (Minutes) |
|---|---|
| 1 | 39 |
| 2 | 29 |
| 3 | 23 |
| 4 | 19 |
| 5 | 17 |
| 6 | 16 |
| 7 | 15 |
| 8 | 13 |
| 9 | 13 |
| 10 | 12 |

*a.* According to this pilot run, what is your estimate of the learning rate?

*b.* How much time will it take for the next 90 units?

*c.* How much time will it take to make the 2,000th unit?

## SELECTED BIBLIOGRAPHY

Argote, L., and D. Epple. "Learning Curves in Manufacturing." *Science* 247 (February 1990), pp. 920–24.

Bailey, C. D. "Forgetting and the Learning Curve: A Laboratory Study." *Management Science* 35, no. 3 (March 1989), pp. 340–52.

Globerson, S. "The Influence of Job-Related Variables on the Predictability Power of Three Learning Curve Models." *AIIE Transactions* 12, no. 1 (March 1980), pp. 64–69.

Irving, R. "A Convenient Method for Computing the Learning Curve." *Industrial Engineering* 14, no. 5 (May 1982), pp. 52–54.

Kopsco, D. P., and W. C. Nemitz. "Learning Curves and Lot Sizing for Independent and Dependent Demand." *Journal of Operations Management* 4, no. 1 (November 1983), pp. 73–83.

Kostiuk, P. F., and D. A. Follmann. "Learning Curves, Personal Characteristics, and Job Performance." *Journal of Labor Economics* 7, no. 2 (April 1989), pp. 129–46.

Logan, G. D. "Shapes of Reaction-Time Distribution and Shapes of Learning Curves." *Journal of Experimental Psychology: Learning, Memory, and Cognition* 18, no. 5 (Sept. 1992), pp. 883–915.

Smith, D. B., and J. L. Larsson. "The Impact of Learning on Cost: The Case of Heart Transplantation." *Hospital and Health Services Administration* 34, no. 1 (Spring 1989), pp. 85–97.

Smunt, T. L. "A Comparison of Learning Curve Analysis and Moving Average Ratio Analysis for Detailed Operational Planning." *Decision Sciences* 17, no. 4 (Fall 1986), pp. 475–95.

Towill, D. R. "The Use of Learning Curve Models for Prediction of Batch Production Performance." *International Journal of Operations and Production Management* 5, no. 2 (1985), pp. 13–24.

Weston, M. *Learning Curves: Living Your Life in Full and with Style.* New York: Crown, 2000.

Yelle, L. E. "The Learning Curves: Historical Review and Comprehensive Survey." *Decision Sciences* 10, no. 2 (April 1979), pp. 302–28.

# FOOTNOTES

1 See the classic paper by T. P. Wright, "Factors Affecting the Cost of Airplanes," *Journal of the Aeronautical Sciences,* February 1936, pp. 122–28.

2 This equation says that the number of direct labor hours required for any given unit is reduced exponentially as more units are produced.

3 See L. Argote, "Organizational Learning Curves: Persistence, Transfer and Turnover," *International Journal of Technology Management* 11, no. 7, 8 (1996), pp. 759–69.

4 D. B. Smith, and J. L. Larsson, "The Impact of Learning on Cost: The Case of Heart Transplantation," *Hospital and Health Sciences Administration* 34, no. 1 (Spring 1989), pp. 85–97.

*chapter three*

# PROJECT MANAGEMENT

## CHAPTER OUTLINE AND KEY TERMS

# 3

Microsoft's new Windows 2000 operating system took over five years to develop. With over 30 million lines of code, Windows 2000 was by far the largest and most complicated commercial software project ever undertaken. Microsoft's goal was to produce the first operating system that runs everything from laptops to "dumb" terminals to huge back-office computers. So how did they do it?

Welcome to the software factory. In buildings 9, 10, 26, 27, and 28 on Microsoft's sprawling Redmond, Washington, campus, the company's mammoth Windows 2000 operating system was assembled and torn apart once every 24 hours. The "daily build" began at 6 P.M. That's when engineering managers gathered all of the new features and bug fixes that thousands of programmers produced during the day and bolted them together like so many auto parts. Twelve hours later—if all went well—the build was done, and quality assurance technicians took over. They tested the code on 200 computers and ferreted out anywhere from 250 to 400 new bugs in the program. Teams of managers then reviewed the bug reports and made the daily assignments. Programmers typed away all day on their assignments. Then, at 6 P.M., the whole process began again.

This process started in 1995, and over the length of the project the design goals shifted. Customers began demanding Internet-style software and more simplicity, adding to the time it took to do the project.

So what was it like to lead the Windows 2000 project? Brian Valentine is a hard-driving individual who earned his reputation as a closer by delivering the company's hot-selling Exchange corporate e-mail package in 1996. Valentine said that he had no problem getting fired up for the job. "I have a nice perspective on what it means to be in charge of the most important project in the history of mankind." Now that is dedication!

Adapted from S. Hamm and O. Port, "The Mother of All Software Projects," *Business Week*, February 22, 1999, pp. 69–72. Used with permission from *Business Week*.

Vol. VI "Project Management"

Although most of the material in this chapter focuses on the technical aspects of project management (structuring project networks and calculating the critical path), the management aspects are certainly equally as important. Success in projects is very much a group activity. Paul B. Williams, a teacher of project management for the J. C. Penney Company, stresses how success in working on projects, particularly during the early years, is an important promotion criterion. Williams points out that if you find yourself working in or leading a team, you may be leading or participating in a project and not even recognize it. He argues that the only difference between leading a team and leading a project is that the team focuses on the activity and relationships while the project focuses more on the outcome. Success in leading a team is the quick path to promotion. (See the Breakthrough box titled "Top 10 Reasons Why Project Management Is Important" for more about Williams's ideas.)

## WHAT IS PROJECT MANAGEMENT?

Project

Project management

A **project** may be defined as a series of related jobs usually directed toward some major output and requiring a significant period of time to perform. **Project management** can be defined as planning, directing, and controlling resources (people, equipment, material) to meet the technical, cost, and time constraints of the project.

Although projects are often thought to be one-time occurrences, the fact is that many projects can be repeated or transferred to other settings or products. The result will be another project output. A contractor building houses or a firm producing low-volume products such as supercomputers, locomotives, or linear accelerators can effectively consider these as projects.

## STRUCTURING PROJECTS

Before the project starts, senior management must decide which of three organizational structures will be used to tie the project to the parent firm: pure project, functional project, or matrix project. If the matrix form is chosen, different projects (rows of the matrix) borrow resources from functional areas (columns). Senior management must then decide whether a weak, balanced, or strong form of a matrix is to be used. This establishes whether project managers have little, equal, or more authority than the functional managers with whom they negotiate for resources. Management must also consider the characteristics of the project leader. (See the box titled "Selecting the Right Project Leader.") We next discuss the strengths and weaknesses of the three main forms.

### PURE PROJECT

Cross Functional

Pure project

Tom Peters predicts that most of the world's work will be "brainwork," done in semipermanent networks of small project-oriented teams, each one an autonomous, entrepreneurial center of opportunity; where the necessity for speed and flexibility dooms the hierarchical management structures we and our ancestors grew up with.[1] Thus, out of the three basic project organizational structures, Peters favors the **pure project** (nicknamed *skunk works*), where a self-contained team works full-time on the project.

**ADVANTAGES**

- The project manager has full authority over the project.
- Team members report to one boss. They do not have to worry about dividing loyalty with a functional-area manager.
- Lines of communication are shortened. Decisions are made quickly.
- Team pride, motivation, and commitment are high.

**DISADVANTAGES**

- Duplication of resources. Equipment and people are not shared across projects.
- Organizational goals and policies are ignored, as team members are often both physically and psychologically removed from headquarters.

## BREAKTHROUGH

### Top 10 Reasons Why Project Management Is Important

10 Organizations that are willing to allow hastily planned, poorly led projects weaken themselves and endanger employees by wasting precious resources.

9 Organizations that are flattening (e.g., through reengineering, downsizing, or rightsizing) will depend on projects and project leaders to get work done that was once handled by departments.

8 With rare exceptions, project prime movers believe that project meltdowns are the result of weak project leadership.

7 More than one lumpy project leadership performance can give you a reputation that will repel future project participants.

6 Project work is often disguised by the use of the word *team;* if you find yourself on or leading teams, you're probably working with others to complete a project.

5 The abilities that are required to organize and carry out successful projects will enhance other aspects of your job.

4 Leading successful projects is the best way to prove your promotability to the people who make those decisions.

3 The best way to promote effective project leadership is to set examples that are so powerful and positive that others wouldn't dare do less.

2 Project leaders seldom get better until they know how to do it right.

1 If you're not getting better, you're getting worse as you get older.

SOURCE: REPRINTED FROM *GETTING A PROJECT DONE ON TIME* COPYRIGHT © 1996 P. B. WILLIAMS. REPRINTED BY PERMISSION OF AMACON, A DIVISION OF AMERICAN MANAGEMENT ASSOCIATION INTERNATIONAL, NEW YORK, NY. ALL RIGHTS RESERVED. HTTP://WWW.AMANET.ORG.

### Selecting the Right Project Leader

Senior management must exercise judgment and initiative in finding, selecting, hiring, and training the specific people who will fulfill a project's charter. At Toyota, for example, senior managers explicitly choose a project leader whose personality is consistent with the type of product they intend to introduce. Thus, for a sporty car targeted to a young, aggressive customer, they looked for a "fighter-pilot" type. When the project was to develop a luxurious sedan, they selected an "executive" type. The aim is to select project leaders who, by identifying with both the project and the customer, can internalize much of what counts in the product's total system performance.

SOURCE: S. C. WHEELWRIGHT AND K. B. CLARK, *LEADING PRODUCT DEVELOPMENT* (NEW YORK: THE FREE PRESS, 1995), p. 91.

- The organization falls behind in its knowledge of new technology due to weakened functional divisions.
- Because team members have no functional area home, they worry about life-after-project, and project termination is delayed.

## FUNCTIONAL PROJECT

At the other end of the project organization spectrum is the **functional project,** housing the project within a functional division.

Functional project

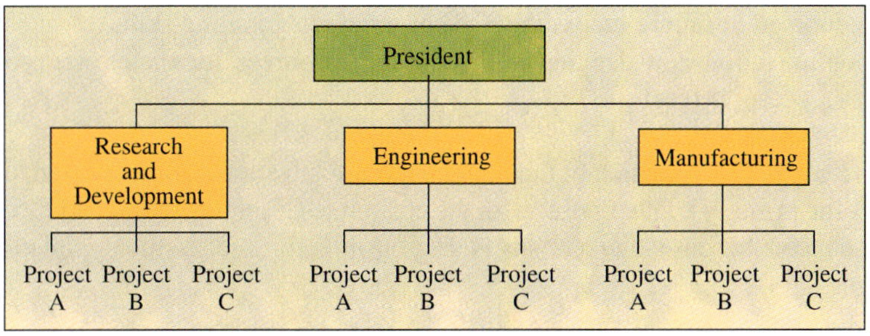

**ADVANTAGES**

- A team member can work on several projects.
- Technical expertise is maintained within the functional area even if individuals leave the project or organization.
- The functional area is a home after the project is completed. Functional specialists can advance vertically.
- A critical mass of specialized functional-area experts creates synergystic solutions to a project's technical problems.

**DISADVANTAGES**

- Aspects of the project that are not directly related to the functional area get short-changed.
- Motivation of team members is often weak.
- Needs of the client are secondary and are responded to slowly.

## MATRIX PROJECT

Matrix project

The classic specialized organizational form "the **matrix project**" attempts to blend properties of functional and pure project structures. Each project utilizes people from different functional areas. The project manager (PM) decides what tasks and when they will be performed, but the functional managers control which people and technologies are used.

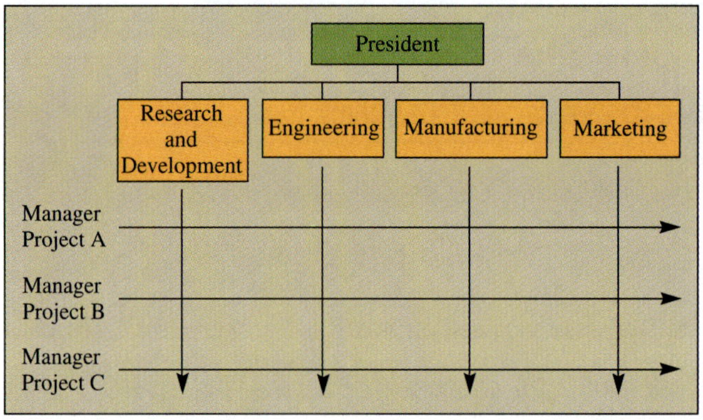


**ADVANTAGES**

- Communication between functional divisions is enhanced.
- A project manager is held responsible for successful completion of the project.
- Duplication of resources is minimized.
- Team members have a functional "home" after project completion, so they are less worried about life-after-project than if they were a pure project organization.
- Policies of the parent organization are followed. This increases support for the project.

**DISADVANTAGES**

- There are two bosses. Often the functional manager will be listened to before the project manager. After all, who can promote you or give you a raise?
- It is doomed to failure unless the PM has strong negotiating skills.
- Suboptimization is a danger, as PMs hoard resources for their own project, thus harming other projects.

Note that regardless of which of the three major organizational forms is used, the project manager is the primary contact point with the customer. Communication and flexibility are greatly enhanced because one person is responsible for successful completion of the project.

# WORK BREAKDOWN STRUCTURE

A project starts out as a *statement of work* (SOW). The SOW may be a written description of the objectives to be achieved, with a brief statement of the work to be done and a proposed schedule specifying the start and completion dates. It could also contain performance measures in terms of budget and completion steps (milestones) and the written reports to be supplied.

A *task* is a further subdivision of a project. It is usually not longer than several months in duration and is performed by one group or organization. A *subtask* may be used if needed to further subdivide the project into more meaningful pieces.

A *work package* is a group of activities combined to be assignable to a single organizational unit. It still falls into the format of all project management; the package provides a description of what is to be done, when it is to be started and completed, the budget, measures of performance, and specific events to be reached at points in time. These specific events are called **project milestones.** Typical milestones might be the completion of the design, the production of a prototype, the completed testing of the prototype, and the approval of a pilot run.

Project milestones

The **work breakdown structure** (WBS) defines the hierarchy of project tasks, subtasks, and work packages. Completion of one or more work packages results in the completion of a subtask; completion of one or more subtasks results in the completion of a task; and finally, the completion of all tasks is required to complete the project. A representation of this structure is shown in Exhibit 3.1.

Work breakdown structure

Exhibit 3.2 shows the WBS for an optical scanner project. The WBS is important in organizing a project because it breaks the project down into manageable pieces. The number of levels will vary depending on the project. How much detail or how many levels to use depends on the following:

- The level at which a single individual or organization can be assigned responsibility and accountability for accomplishing the work package.
- The level at which budget and cost data will be collected during the project.

There is not a single correct WBS for any project, and two different project teams might develop different WBSs for the same project. Some experts have referred to project management as an art rather than a science, because there are so many different ways that a project can be approached. Finding the correct way to organize a project depends on experience with the particular task.

**Activities** are defined within the context of the work breakdown structure and are pieces of work that consume time. Activities do not necessarily require the expenditure of effort by

Activities

EXHIBIT 3.1

An Example of a Work Breakdown Structure

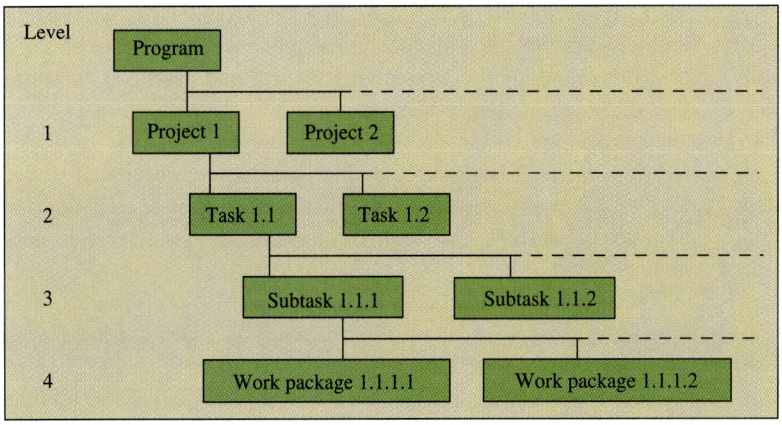

EXHIBIT 3.2

**Work Breakdown Structure, Large Optical Scanner Design**

| Level 1 | 2 | 3 | 4 | | |
|---|---|---|---|---|---|
| x | | | | 1 | Optical simulator design |
| | x | | | 1.1 | Optical design |
| | | x | | 1.1.1 | Telescope design/fab |
| | | x | | 1.1.2 | Telescope/simulator optical interface |
| | | x | | 1.1.3 | Simulator zoom system design |
| | | x | | 1.1.4 | Ancillary simulator optical component specification |
| | x | | | 1.2 | System performance analysis |
| | | x | | 1.2.1 | Overall system firmware and software control |
| | | | x | 1.2.1.1 | Logic flow diagram generation and analysis |
| | | | x | 1.2.1.2 | Basic control algorithm design |
| | | x | | 1.2.2 | Far beam analyzer |
| | | x | | 1.2.3 | System inter- and intra-alignment method design |
| | | x | | 1.2.4 | Data recording and reduction requirements |
| | x | | | 1.3 | System integration |
| | x | | | 1.4 | Cost analysis |
| | | x | | 1.4.1 | Cost/system schedule analysis |
| | | x | | 1.4.2 | Cost/system performance analysis |
| | x | | | 1.5 | Management |
| | | x | | 1.5.1 | System design/engineering management |
| | | x | | 1.5.2 | Program management |
| | x | | | 1.6 | Long lead item procurement |
| | | x | | 1.6.1 | Large optics |
| | | x | | 1.6.2 | Target components |
| | | x | | 1.6.3 | Detectors |

people, although they often do. For example, waiting for paint to dry may be an activity in a project. Activities are identified as part of the WBS. From our sample project in Exhibit 3.2, activities would include telescope design and fabrication (1.1.1), telescope/simulator optical interface (1.1.2), and data recording (1.2.4). Activities need to be defined in such a way that when they are all completed, the project is done.

## PROJECT CONTROL CHARTS

The U.S. Department of Defense (one of the earliest large users of project management) has published a variety of helpful standard forms. Many are used directly or have been modified by firms engaged in project management. Computer programs (such as Primavera Sure Track, which is included on the CD in this book) are available to quickly generate the charts described in this section. Charts are useful because their visual presentation is easily understood. Exhibit 3.3 shows a sample of the available charts.

Gantt chart

Exhibit 3.3A is a sample **Gantt chart,** sometimes referred to as a *bar chart,* showing both the amount of time involved and the sequence in which activities can be performed. The chart is named after Henry L. Gantt, who won a presidential citation for his application of this type of chart to shipbuilding during World War I. In the example in Exhibit 3.3A, "long lead procurement" and "manufacturing schedules" are independent activities and can occur simultaneously. All other activities must be done in the sequence from top to bottom. Exhibit 3.3B graphs the amounts of money spent on labor, material, and overhead. Its value is its clarity in identifying sources and amounts of cost.

Exhibit 3.3C shows the percentage of the project's labor hours that come from the various areas of manufacturing, finance, and so on. These labor hours are related to the proportion of the project's total labor cost. For example, manufacturing is responsible for 50 percent of the project's labor hours, but this 50 percent has been allocated just 40 percent of the total labor dollars charged.

The top half of Exhibit 3.3D shows the degree of completion of these projects. The dotted vertical line signifies today. Project 1, therefore, is already late because it still has work to be done. Project 2 is not being worked on temporarily, so there is a space before the projected work. Project 3 continues to be worked on without interruption. The bottom of Exhibit 3.3D compares actual total costs and projected costs. As we see, two cost overruns occurred, and the current cumulative costs are over projected cumulative costs.

EXHIBIT 3.3

A Sample of Graphic Project Reports

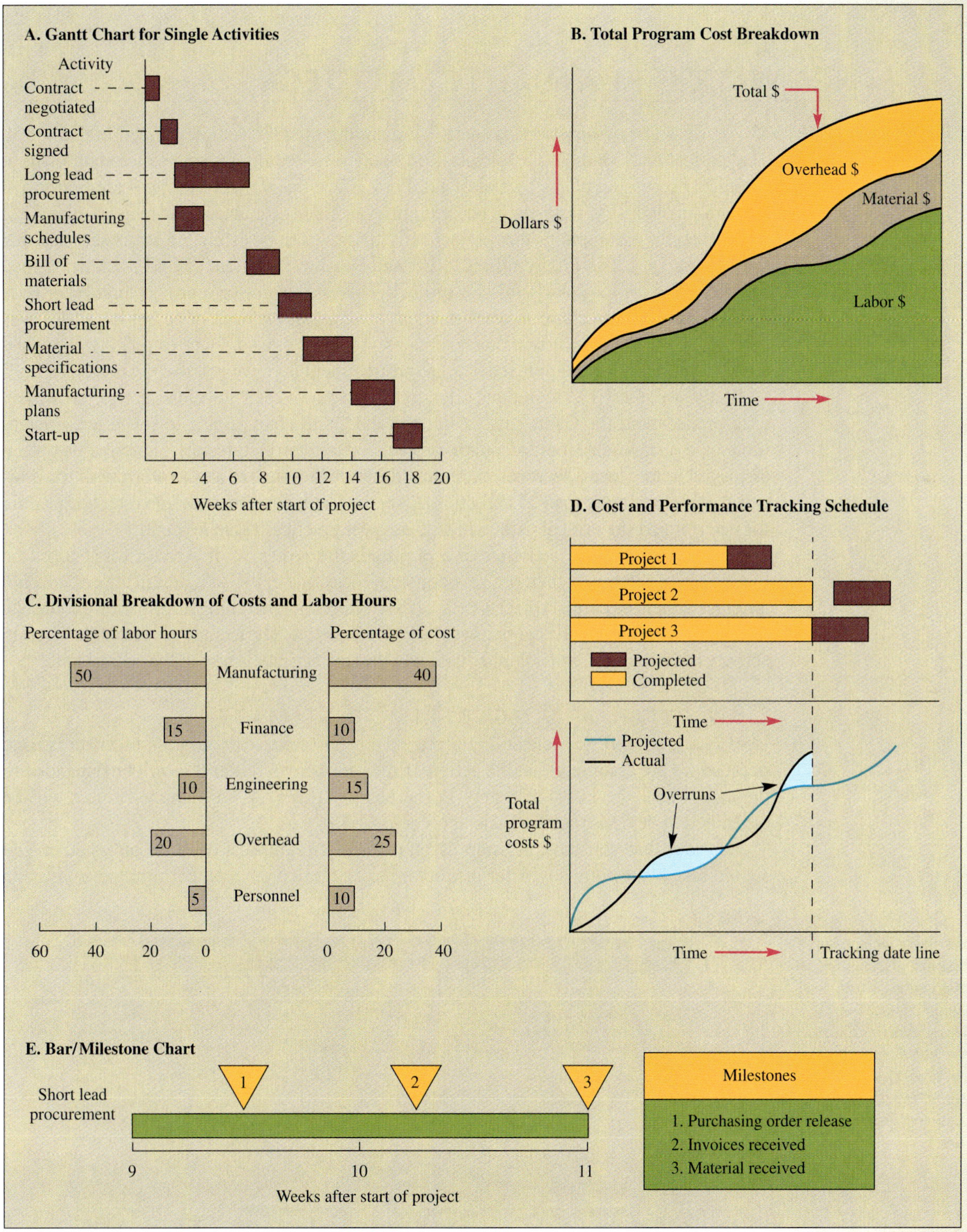


Exhibit 3.3E is a milestone chart. The three milestones mark specific points in the project where checks can be made to see if the project is on time and where it should be. The best place to locate milestones is at the completion of a major activity. In this exhibit, the major activities completed were "purchase order release," "invoices received," and "material received."

Other standard reports can be used for a more detailed presentation comparing cost to progress (such as cost schedule status report—CSSR) or reports providing the basis for partial payment (such as the earned value report).

## NETWORK-PLANNING MODELS

The two best-known network-planning models were developed in the 1950s. The Critical Path Method (CPM) was developed for scheduling maintenance shutdowns at chemical processing plants owned by Du Pont. Since maintenance projects are performed often in this industry, reasonably accurate time estimates for activities are available. CPM is based on the assumptions that project activity times can be estimated accurately and that they do not vary. The Program Evaluation and Review Technique (PERT) was developed for the U.S. Navy's Polaris missile project. This was a massive project involving over 3,000 contractors. Because most of the activities had never been done before, PERT was developed to handle uncertain time estimates. As years passed, features that distinguished CPM from PERT have diminished; so in our treatment here we just use the term CPM.

In a sense, the CPM techniques illustrated here owe their development to the widely used predecessor, the Gantt chart. Although the Gantt chart is able to relate activities to time in a usable fashion for small projects, the interrelationship of activities, when displayed in this form, becomes extremely difficult to visualize and to work with for projects that include more than 25 activities. Also, the Gantt chart provides no direct procedure for determining the critical path, which is of great practical value to identify.

Critical path

The **critical path** of activities in a project is the sequence of activities that form the longest chain in terms of their time to complete. If any one of the activities in the critical path is delayed, then the entire project is delayed. Determining scheduling information about each activity in the project is the major goal of CPM techniques. The techniques calculate when an activity must start and end, together with whether the activity is part of the critical path.

### CPM WITH A SINGLE TIME ESTIMATE

Here is a procedure for scheduling a project. In this case, a single time estimate is used because we are assuming that the activity times are known. Later this will be expanded to the case where there is uncertainty in the activity times. A very simple project will be scheduled to demonstrate the basic approach.

Consider that you have a group assignment that requires a decision on whether you should invest in a company. Your instructor has suggested that you perform the analysis in

AT BOEING, EFFECTIVE PROJECT MANAGEMENT TECHNIQUES WERE ESSENTIAL IN SETTING UP BOTH THE 777 ASSEMBLY SYSTEM AND ITS SCHEDULING AND MANUFACTURING. TWENTY PERCENT OF THE 777 IS BUILT IN JAPAN, ALONG WITH MANUFACTURING HELP FROM AUSTRALIA (RUDDER), NORTHERN IRELAND AND SINGAPORE (NOSE GEAR), KOREAN AIR (WINGTIP), BRAZIL (FIN AND WINGTIP ASSEMBLY), AND ITALY (OUTBOARD WING FLAPS).

the following four steps:

1 Select a company.
2 Obtain the company's annual report and perform a ratio analysis.
3 Collect technical stock price data and construct charts.
4 Individually review the data and make a team decision on whether to buy the stock.

Your group of four people decides that the project can be divided into four activities as suggested by the instructor. You decide that all the team members should be involved in selecting the company and that it should take one week to complete this activity. You will meet at the end of the week to decide what company the group will consider. During this meeting you will divide your group: two people will be responsible for the annual report and ratio analysis, and the other two will collect the technical data and construct the charts. Your group expects it to take two weeks to get the annual report and perform the ratio analysis, and a week to collect the stock price data and generate the charts. You agree that the two groups can work independently. Finally, you agree to meet as a team to make the purchase decision. Before you meet, you want to allow one week for each team member to review all the data.

This is a simple project, but it will serve to demonstrate the approach. The following are the appropriate steps.

1 **Identify each activity to be done in the project, and estimate how long it will take to complete each activity.** This is simple, given the information from your instructor. We identify the activities as follows: A(1), B(2), C(1), D(1). The number is the expected duration of the activity.

2 **Determine the required sequence of activities, and construct a network reflecting the precedence relationships.** An easy way to do this is to first identify the **immediate predecessors** associated with activity. The immediate predecessors are the activities that need to be completed immediately before an activity. Activity A needs to be completed before activities B and C can start. B and C need to be completed before D can start. The following table reflects what we know so far:

Immediate predecessors

| Activity | Designation | Immediate Predecessors | Time (weeks) |
|---|---|---|---|
| Select company | A | None | 1 |
| Obtain annual report and perform ratio analysis | B | A | 2 |
| Collect stock price data and perform technical analysis | C | A | 1 |
| Review data and make a decision | D | B and C | 1 |

Here is a diagram that depicts these precedence relationships:

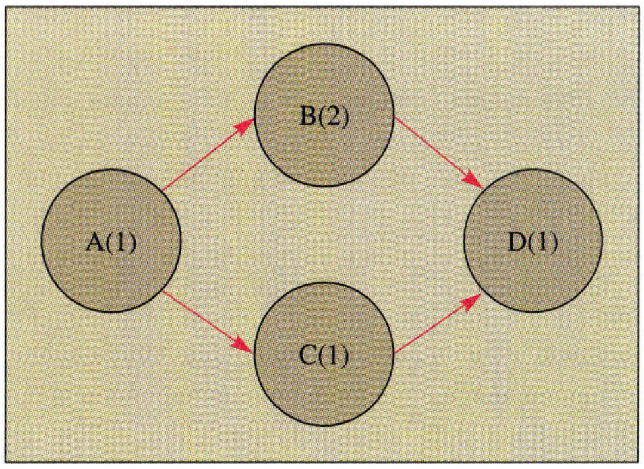

3 **Determine the critical path.** Consider each sequence of activities that runs from the beginning to the end of the project. For our simple project there are two paths: A–B–D and A–C–D. The critical path is the path where the sum of the activity times is the longest. A–B–D has a duration of four weeks, and A–C–D a duration of three weeks. The critical path, therefore, is A–B–D. If any activity along the critical path is delayed, then the entire project will be delayed.

4 **Determine the early start/finish and late start/finish schedule.** To schedule the project, find when each activity needs to start and when it needs to finish. For some activities in a project there may be some leeway in when an activity can start and finish. This is called the **slack time** in an activity. For each activity in the project, we calculate four points in time: the early start, early finish, late start, and late finish times. The early start and early finish are the earliest times that the activity can start and be finished. Similarly, the late start and late finish are the latest times the activities can start and finish. The difference between the late start time and early start time is the slack time. To help keep all of this straight, we place these numbers in special places around the nodes that represent each activity in our network diagram, as shown here.

Slack time

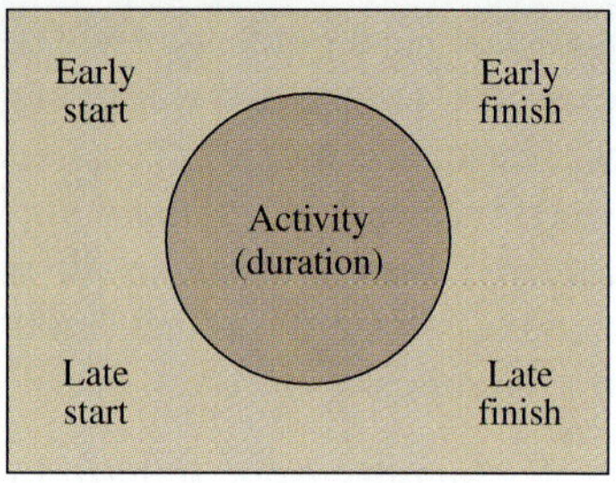


To calculate numbers, start from the beginning of the network and work to the end, calculating the early start and early finish numbers. Start counting with the current period, designated as period 0. Activity A has an early start of 0 and an early finish of 1. Activity B's early start is A's early finish or 1. Similarly, C's early start is 1. The early finish for B is 3, and the early finish for C is 2. Now consider activity D. D cannot start until both B and C are done. Because B cannot be done until 3, D cannot start until that time. The early start for D, therefore, is 3, and the early finish is 4. Our diagram now looks like this.

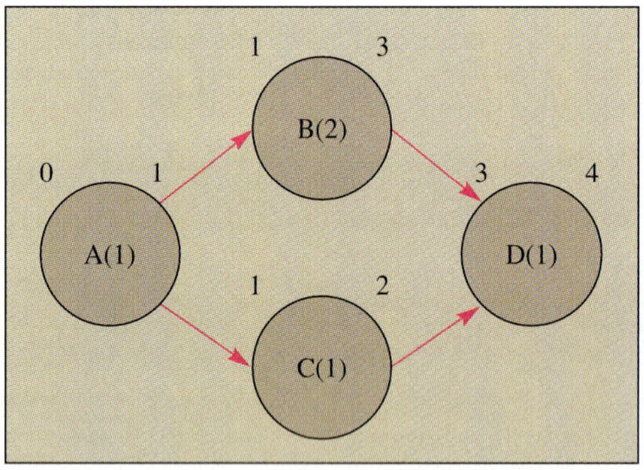


To calculate the late finish and late start times, start from the end of the network and work toward the front. Consider activity D. The earliest that it can be done is at time 4; and if we do not want to delay the completion of the project, the late finish needs to be set to 4. With a duration of 1, the latest that D can start is 3. Now consider activity C. C must be done by time 3 so that D can start, so C's late finish time is 3 and its late start time is 2. Notice the difference between the early and late start and finish times: This activity has 1 week of slack time. Activity B must be done by time 3 so that D can start, so its late finish time is 3 and late start time is 1. There is no slack in B. Finally, activity A must be done so that B and C can start. Because B must start earlier than C, and A must get done in time for B to start, the late finish time for A is 1. Finally, the late start time for A is 0. Notice there is no slack in activities A, B, and D. The final network looks like this. (Hopefully the stock your investment team has chosen is a winner!)

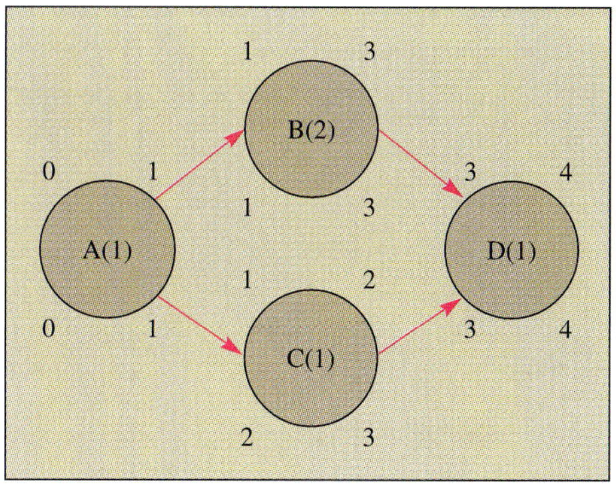


## EXAMPLE 3.1: SINGLE TIME ESTIMATE

Many firms that have tried to enter the notebook computer market have failed. Suppose your firm believes that there is a big demand in this market because existing products have not been designed correctly. They are too heavy, too large, or too small to have standard-size keyboards. Your intended computer will be small enough to carry inside a jacket pocket if need be. The ideal size will be no larger than 5 inches × 9½ inches × 1 inch with a folding keyboard. It should weigh no more than 15 ounces and have an LCD display, a micro disk drive, and an ethernet port. This should appeal to traveling businesspeople, but it could have a much wider market, including students. It should be priced in the $175–$200 range.

The project, then, is to design, develop, and produce a prototype of this small computer. In the rapidly changing computer industry, it is crucial to hit the market with a product of this sort in less than a year. Therefore, the project team has been allowed approximately eight months (35 weeks) to produce the prototype.

## SOLUTION

The first charge of the project team is to develop a project network chart and estimate the likelihood of completing the prototype computer within the 35 weeks. Let's follow the steps in the development of the network.

1 **Activity identification.** The project team decides that the following activities are the major components of the project: design of the computer, prototype construction, prototype testing, methods specification (summarized in a report), evaluation studies of automatic assembly equipment, an assembly equipment study report, and a final report summarizing all aspects of the design, equipment, and methods.

2 **Activity sequencing and network construction.** On the basis of discussion with staff, the project manager develops the precedence table and sequence network shown in Exhibit 3.4. When constructing a network, take care to ensure that the activities are in the proper order and that the logic of their relationships is maintained. For example, it would be illogical to have a situation where Event A precedes Event B, B precedes C, and C precedes A.

3 **Determine the critical path.** The critical path is the longest sequence of connected activities through the network and is defined as the path with zero slack time. This network has four different paths: A–C–F–G, A–C–E–G, A–B–D–F–G, and A–B–D–E–G. The lengths of these paths are 38, 35, 38, and 35 weeks. Note that this project has two different critical paths; this might indicate that this would be a fairly difficult project to manage. Calculating the early start and late start schedules gives additional insight into how difficult this project might be to complete on time. ←

EXHIBIT 3.4

CPM Network for Computer Design Project

CPM ACTIVITY DESIGNATIONS AND TIME ESTIMATES

| ACTIVITY | DESIGNATION | IMMEDIATE PREDECESSORS | TIME (WEEKS) |
|---|---|---|---|
| Design | A | – | 21 |
| Build prototype | B | A | 5 |
| Evaluate equipment | C | A | 7 |
| Test prototype | D | B | 2 |
| Write equipment report | E | C, D | 5 |
| Write methods report | F | C, D | 8 |
| Write final report | G | E, F | 2 |

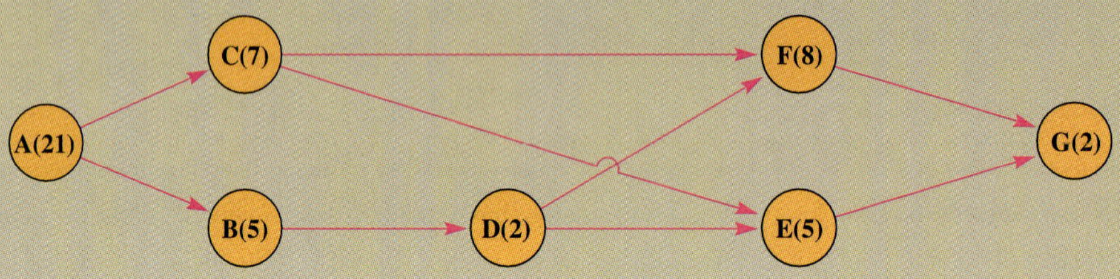


EXHIBIT 3.5

CPM Network for Computer Design Project

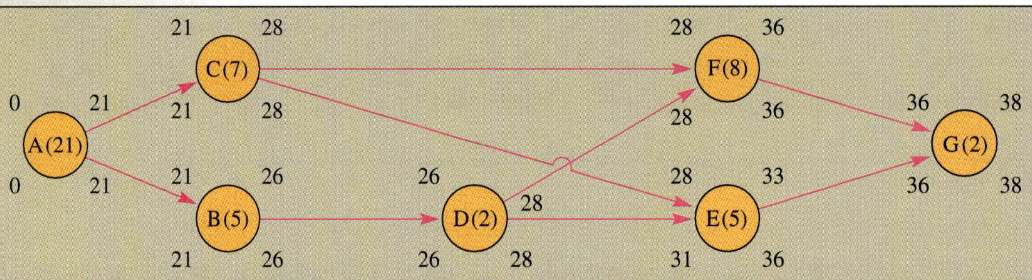


SLACK CALCULATIONS AND CRITICAL PATH DETERMINATIONS

| ACTIVITY | LS–ES | SLACK | ON CRITICAL PATH |
|---|---|---|---|
| A | 0–0 | 0 | ✓ |
| B | 21–21 | 0 | ✓ |
| C | 21–21 | 0 | ✓ |
| D | 26–26 | 0 | ✓ |
| E | 31–28 | 3 | |
| F | 28–28 | 0 | ✓ |
| G | 36–36 | 0 | ✓ |

Early start schedule

Late start schedule

**Early Start and Late Start Schedules** An **early start schedule** is one that lists all of the activities by their early start times. For activities not on the critical path, there is slack time between the completion of each activity and the start of the next activity. The early start schedule completes the project and all its activities as soon as possible.

A **late start schedule** lists the activities to start as late as possible without delaying the completion date of the project. One motivation for using a late start schedule is that savings are realized by postponing purchases of materials, the use of labor, and other costs until necessary. These calculations are shown in Exhibit 3.5. From this we see that the only activity that has slack is activity E. This certainly would be a fairly difficult project to complete on time.

## CPM WITH THREE ACTIVITY TIME ESTIMATES

If a single estimate of the time required to complete an activity is not reliable, the best procedure is to use three time estimates. These three times not only allow us to estimate the activity time but also let us obtain a probability estimate for completion time for the entire network. Briefly, the procedure is as follows: The estimated activity time is calculated using a weighted average of a minimum, maximum, and most likely time estimate. The expected completion time of the network is computed using the procedure described above. Using estimates of variability for the activities on the critical path, the probability of completing the project by particular times can be estimated. (Note that the probability calculations are a distinguishing feature of the classic PERT approach.)

### EXAMPLE 3.2: THREE TIME ESTIMATES

We use the same information as in Example 3.1 with the exception that activities have three time estimates.

### SOLUTION

1 Identify each activity to be done in the project.

2 Determine the sequence of activities and construct a network reflecting the precedence relationships.

3 The three estimates for an activity time are

$a$ = Optimistic time: the minimum reasonable period of time in which the activity can be completed. (There is only a small probability, typically assumed to be 1 percent, that the activity can be completed in less time.)

$m$ = Most likely time: the best guess of the time required. Since $m$ would be the time thought most likely to appear, it is also the mode of the beta distribution discussed in step 4.

$b$ = Pessimistic time: the maximum reasonable period of time the activity would take to be completed. (There is only a small probability, typically assumed to be 1 percent, that it would take longer.)

Typically, this information is gathered from those people who are to perform the activity.

4 Calculate the expected time (ET) for each activity. The formula for this calculation is

[3.1]
$$\text{ET} = \frac{a + 4m + b}{6}$$

This is based on the beta statistical distribution and weights the most likely time ($m$) four times more than either the optimistic time ($a$) or the pessimistic time ($b$). The beta distribution is extremely flexible. It can take on the variety of forms that typically arise; it has finite end points (which limit the possible activity times to the area between $a$ and $b$); and, in the simplified version, it permits straightforward computation of the activity mean and standard deviation.

5 Determine the critical path. Using the expected times, a critical path is calculated in the same way as the single time case.

6 Calculate the variances ($\sigma^2$) of the activity times. Specifically, this is the variance, $\sigma^2$, associated with each ET, and is computed as follows:

[3.2]
$$\sigma^2 = \left(\frac{b - a}{6}\right)^2$$

As you can see, the variance is the square of one-sixth the difference between the two extreme time estimates. Of course, the greater this difference, the larger the variance.

7 Determine the probability of completing the project on a given date, based on the application of the standard normal distribution. A valuable feature of using three time estimates is that it

## PROBABILITY ANALYSIS

The three-time estimate approach introduces the ability to consider the probability that a project will be completed within a particular amount of time. The assumption needed to make this probability estimate is that the activity duration times are independent random variables. If this is true, the central limit theorem can be used to find the mean and the variance of the sequence of activities that forms the critical path. The central limit theorem says that the sum of a group of independent, identically distributed random variables approaches a normal distribution as the number of random variables increases. In the case of project management problems, the random variable is the expected time (ET) for each activity. For this the expected time to complete the critical path activities is the sum of the activity times.

Likewise, because of the assumption of activity time independence, the sum of the variances of the activities along the critical path is the variance of the expected time to complete the path. Recall that the standard deviation is equal to the square root of the variance.

To determine the actual probability of completing the critical path activities within a certain amount of time, we need to find where on our probability distribution the time falls. Appendix E shows the areas of the cumulative standard normal distribution for different values of $Z$. $Z$ measures the number of standard deviations either to the right or to the left of zero in the distribution. Referring to Appendix E, the $G(z)$ values are the area under the curve representing the distribution. The values correspond to the cumulative probability associated with each value of $Z$. For example, the first value in the table, −4.00, has a $G(z)$ equal to .00003. This means that the probability associated with a $Z$ value of −4.0 is only .003 (these decimal values need to be converted to probabilities by multiplying by 100). Similarly, a $Z$ value of 1.50 has a $G(z)$ equal to .93319 or 93.319 percent. The $Z$ values are calculated using Equation (3.3) given in Step 7b of the "Three Time Estimates" example solution. These cumulative probabilities can also be obtained by using the NORMDIST (Z) function built into Microsoft Excel.

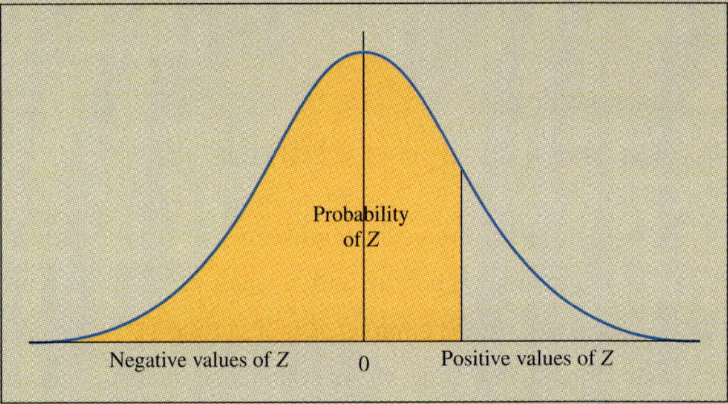


enables the analyst to assess the effect of uncertainty on project completion time. (If you are not familiar with this type of analysis, see the box titled "Probability Analysis.") The mechanics of deriving this probability are as follows:

*a.* Sum the variance values associated with each activity on the critical path.

*b.* Substitute this figure, along with the project due date and the project expected completion time, into the $Z$ transformation formula. This formula is

[3.3]
$$Z = \frac{D - T_E}{\sqrt{\sum \sigma_{cp}^2}}$$

where

$D$ = Desired completion date for the project
$T_E$ = Expected completion time for the project
$\sum \sigma_{cp}^2$ = Sum of the variances along the critical path

*c.* Calculate the value of $Z$, which is the number of standard deviations (of a standard normal distribution) that the project due date is from the expected completion time.

*d.* Using the value of $Z$, find the probability of meeting the project due date (using a table of normal probabilities such as Appendix E). The *expected completion time* is the starting time plus the sum of the activity times on the critical path.

Following the steps just outlined, we developed Exhibit 3.6 showing expected times and variances. The project network was created the same as we did previously. The only difference is that the activity times are weighted averages. We determine the critical path as before, using these values as if they were single numbers. The difference between the single time estimate and the three times

EXHIBIT 3.6

**Activity Expected Times and Variances**

Excel: Project Management

| ACTIVITY | ACTIVITY DESIGNATION | TIME ESTIMATES $a$ | $m$ | $b$ | EXPECTED TIMES (ET) $\frac{a+4m+b}{6}$ | ACTIVITY VARIANCES ($\sigma^2$) $\left(\frac{b-a}{6}\right)^2$ |
|---|---|---|---|---|---|---|
| Design | A | 10 | 22 | 28 | 21 | 9 |
| Build prototype | B | 4 | 4 | 10 | 5 | 1 |
| Evaluate equipment | C | 4 | 6 | 14 | 7 | $2\frac{7}{9}$ |
| Test prototype | D | 1 | 2 | 3 | 2 | $\frac{1}{9}$ |
| Write report | E | 1 | 5 | 9 | 5 | $1\frac{7}{9}$ |
| Write methods report | F | 7 | 8 | 9 | 8 | $\frac{1}{9}$ |
| Write final report | G | 2 | 2 | 2 | 2 | 0 |

EXHIBIT 3.7

**Computer Design Project with Three Time Estimates**

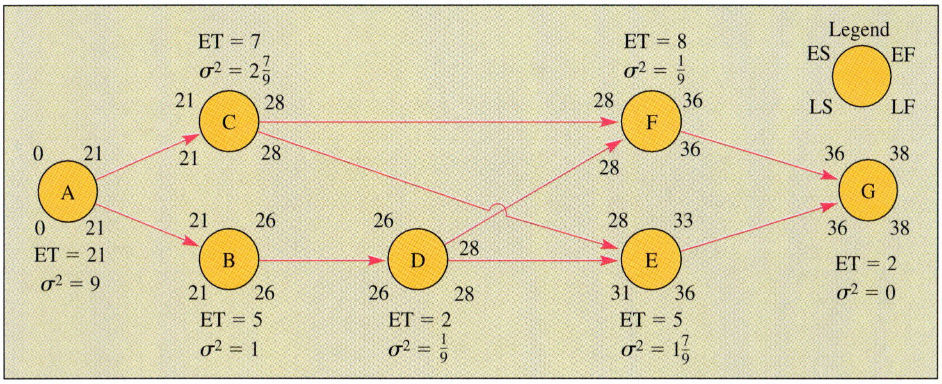


(optimistic, most likely, and pessimistic) is in computing probabilities of completion. Exhibit 3.7 shows the network and critical path.

Because there are two critical paths in the network, we must decide which variances to use in arriving at the probability of meeting the project due date. A conservative approach dictates using the path with the largest total variance to focus management's attention on the activities most likely to exhibit broad variations. On this basis, the variances associated with activities A, C, F, and G would be used to find the probability of completion. Thus $\sum \sigma_{cp}^2 = 9 + 2\frac{7}{9} + \frac{1}{9} + 0 = 11.89$. Suppose management asks for the probability of completing the project in 35 weeks. D, then, is 35. The expected completion time was found to be 38. Substituting into the $Z$ equation and solving, we obtain

$$Z = \frac{D - T_E}{\sqrt{\sum \sigma_{cp}^2}} = \frac{35 - 38}{\sqrt{11.89}} = -0.87$$

Looking at Appendix E we see that a $Z$ value of –0.87 yields a probability of 0.19, which means that the project manager has only about a 19 percent chance of completing the project in 35 weeks. Note that this probability is really the probability of completing the critical path A–C–E–G. Because there is another critical path and other paths that might become critical, the probability of completing the project in 35 weeks is actually less than 0.19. ←

## MAINTAINING ONGOING PROJECT SCHEDULES

It is important to keep a project schedule accurate and current. The schedule tracks progress and identifies problems as they occur while corrective time may still be available. It also monitors the progress of cost and is often the basis for partial payments. Yet schedules are often sloppily kept or even totally abandoned.

## PROJECT MANAGERS, CHALLENGES

Despite the fact that 84 percent of project managers are responsible for staying within a project budget, only 15 percent of the time are they faced with direct ramifications for not doing so. In fact, 16 percent of project managers don't always know the budget of their jobs, according to a survey of project managers conducted by Zweig White & Associates, of Natick, Massachusetts.

The survey showed that project managers consider meeting schedules and budgets to be the greatest challenge that they face (19 percent). This may be partially attributed to the areas they rated as their two top complaints—insufficient or inadequate staff support (10 percent) and responsibility without authority (9 percent).

Project managers cited several reasons for not performing their best. Seventeen percent said that all team members are rarely or never allowed to see their own portion of the scope of services for a project. Also, they do not receive much training. Just 26 percent of firms have mandatory formal training for project managers, while 40 percent have optional training, and 29 percent have no training. For the firms that do offer training, the level is inadequate. Few than half of project managers are trained to perform basic tasks such as opening a job number, charging time, and budgeting.

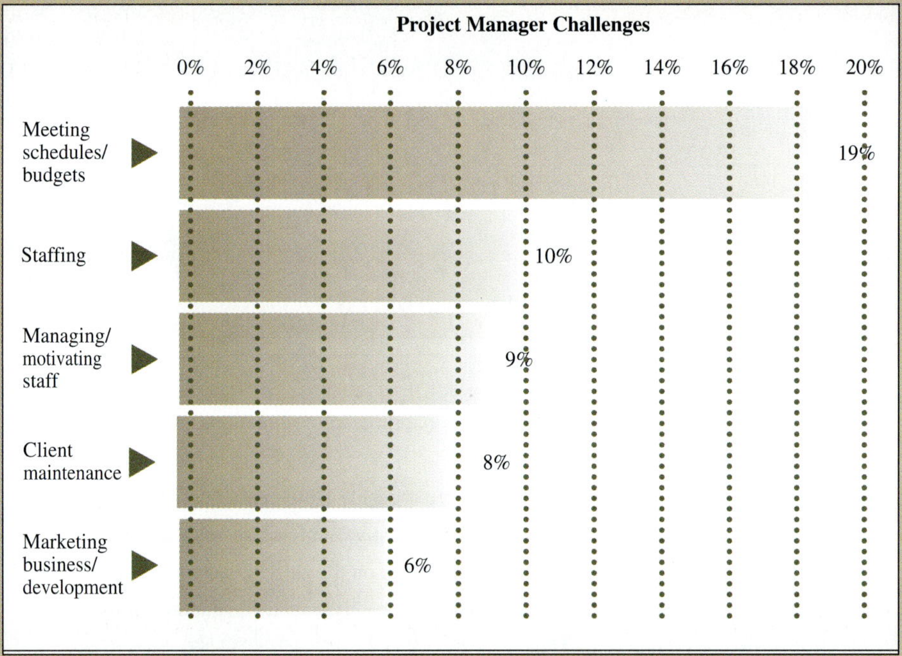


SOURCE: "PROJECT MANAGERS, CHALLENGES," *IIE SOLUTIONS*, DECEMBER 1996, p. 9. REPRINTED WITH PERMISSION OF THE INSTITUTE OF INDUSTRIAL ENGINEERS, 25 TECHNOLOGY PARK, NORCROSS, GA 30092, 770-449-0461. COPYRIGHT © 1996.

A 1996 study that surveyed project managers indicates that there are many potential roadblocks to success. See the box titled "Project Managers, Challenges."

## TIME–COST MODELS

Time–cost models

In practice, project managers are as much concerned with the cost to complete a project as with the time to complete the project. For this reason, **time–cost models** have been devised. These models—extensions of the basic critical path method—attempt to develop a minimum-cost schedule for an entire project and to control expenditures during the project.

EXHIBIT 3.8

Example of Time–Cost Trade-Off Procedure

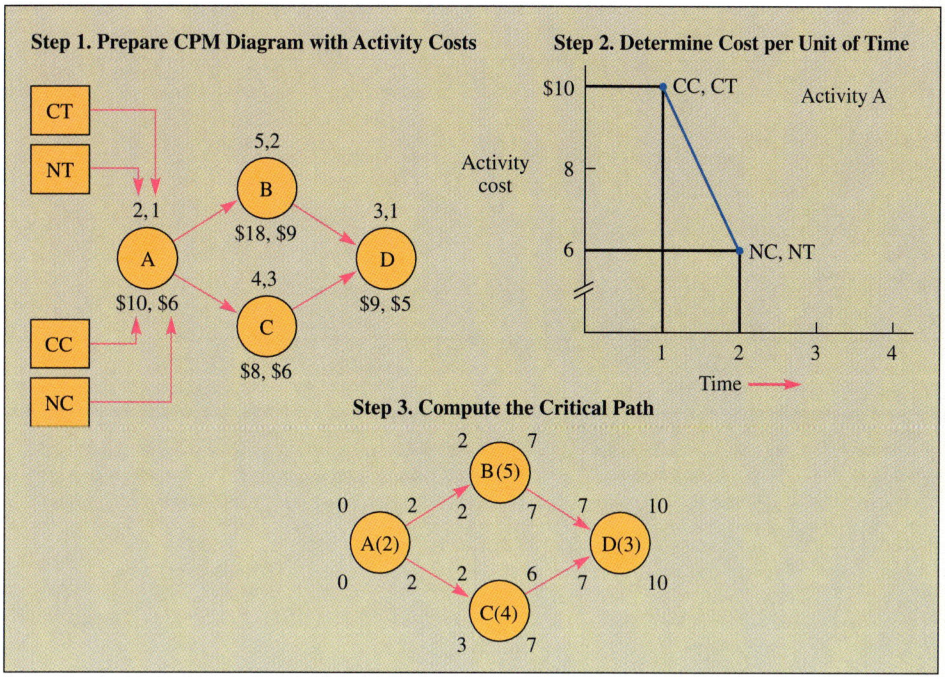


Excel: Project Management

## MINIMUM-COST SCHEDULING (TIME–COST TRADE-OFF)

The basic assumption in minimum-cost scheduling is that there is a relationship between activity completion time and the cost of a project. On one hand, it costs money to expedite an activity; on the other, it costs money to sustain (or lengthen) the project. The costs associated with expediting activities are termed *activity direct costs* and add to the project direct cost. Some may be worker-related, such as overtime work, hiring more workers, and transferring workers from other jobs; others are resource-related, such as buying or leasing additional or more efficient equipment and drawing on additional support facilities.

The costs associated with sustaining the project are termed *project indirect costs:* overhead, facilities, and resource opportunity costs, and, under certain contractual situations, penalty costs or lost incentive payments. Because *activity direct costs* and *project indirect costs* are opposing costs dependent on time, the scheduling problem is essentially one of finding the project duration that minimizes their sum, or in other words, finding the optimum point in a time–cost trade-off.

The procedure for finding this point consists of the following five steps. It is explained by using the simple four-activity network shown in Exhibit 3.8. Assume that the indirect costs remain constant for eight days and then increase at the rate of $5 per day.

1 **Prepare a CPM-type network diagram.** For each activity this diagram should list

*a.* Normal cost (NC): the lowest expected activity costs. (These are the lesser of the cost figures shown under each node in Exhibit 3.8.)
*b.* Normal time (NT): the time associated with each normal cost.
*c.* Crash time (CT): the shortest possible activity time.
*d.* Crash cost (CC): the cost associated with each crash time.

2 **Determine the cost per unit of time (assume days) to expedite each activity.** The relationship between activity time and cost may be shown graphically by plotting CC and CT coordinates and connecting them to the NC and NT coordinates by a concave,

EXHIBIT 3.9

**Calculation of Cost per Day to Expedite Each Activity**

| Activity | CC − NC | NT − CT | $\frac{CC - NC}{NT - CT}$ | Cost per Day to Expedite | Number of Days Activity May Be Shortened |
|---|---|---|---|---|---|
| A | \$10 − \$6 | 2 − 1 | $\frac{\$10 - \$6}{2 - 1}$ | \$4 | 1 |
| B | \$18 − \$9 | 5 − 2 | $\frac{\$18 - \$9}{5 - 2}$ | \$3 | 3 |
| C | \$8 − \$6 | 4 − 3 | $\frac{\$8 - \$6}{4 - 3}$ | \$2 | 1 |
| D | \$9 − \$5 | 3 − 1 | $\frac{\$9 - \$5}{3 - 1}$ | \$2 | 2 |

EXHIBIT 3.10

**Reducing the Project Completion Time One Day at a Time**

| Current Critical Path | Remaining Number of Days Activity May Be Shortened | Cost per Day to Expedite Each Activity | Least-Cost Activity to Expedite | Total Cost of All Activities in Network | Project Completion Time |
|---|---|---|---|---|---|
| ABD | All activity times and costs are normal. | | | \$26 | 10 |
| ABD | A–1, B–3, D–2 | A–4, B–3, D–2 | D | 28 | 9 |
| ABD | A–1, B–3, D–1 | A–4, B–3, D–2 | D | 30 | 8 |
| ABD | A–1, B–3 | A–4, B–3 | B | 33 | 7 |
| ABCD | A–1, B–2, C–1 | A–4, B–3, C–2 | A* | 37 | 6 |
| ABCD | B–2, C–1 | B–3, C–2 | B&C† | 42 | 5 |
| ABCD | B–1 | B–3 | B+ | 45 | 5 |

*To reduce the critical path by one day, reduce either A alone, or B and C together at the same time (either B or C by itself just modifies the critical path without shortening it).

†B&C must be crashed together to reduce the path by one day.

+Crashing activity B does not reduce the length of the project, so this additional cost would not be incurred.

convex, or straight line—or some other form, depending on the actual cost structure of activity performance, as in Exhibit 3.8. For activity A, we assume a linear relationship between time and cost. This assumption is common in practice and helps us derive the cost per day to expedite because this value may be found directly by taking the slope of the line using the formula Slope = (CC − NC) ÷ (NT − CT). (When the assumption of linearity cannot be made, the cost of expediting must be determined graphically for each day the activity may be shortened.)

The calculations needed to obtain the cost of expediting the remaining activities are shown in Exhibit 3.9.

3 **Compute the critical path.** For the simple network we have been using, this schedule would take 10 days. The critical path is A–B–D.

4 **Shorten the critical path at the least cost.** The easiest way to proceed is to start with the normal schedule, find the critical path, and reduce the path time by one day using the lowest-cost activity. Then recompute and find the new critical path and reduce it by one day also. Repeat this procedure until the time of completion is satisfactory, or until there can be no further reduction in the project completion time. Exhibit 3.10 shows the reduction of the network one day at a time.

5 **Plot project direct, indirect, and total-cost curves and find the minimum-cost schedule.** Exhibit 3.11 shows the indirect cost plotted as a constant \$10 per day for eight days and increasing \$5 per day thereafter. The direct costs are plotted from Exhibit 3.10, and the total project cost is shown as the total of the two costs.

Summing the values for direct and indirect costs for each day yields the project total cost curve. As you can see, this curve is at its minimum with an eight-day schedule, which costs \$40 (\$30 direct + \$10 indirect).

EXHIBIT 3.11

Plot of Costs and Minimum Cost Schedule

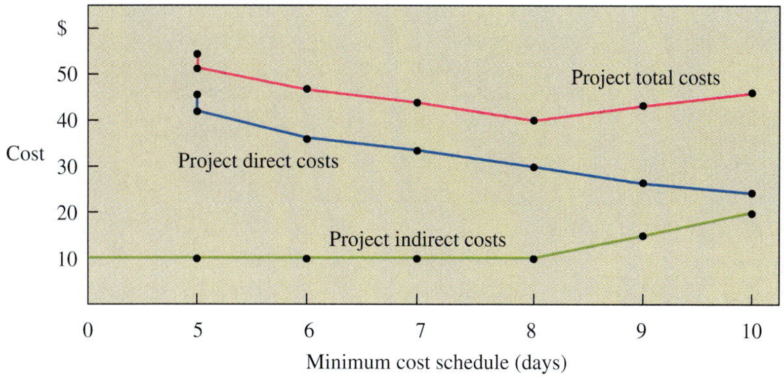


# MANAGING RESOURCES

In addition to scheduling each task, we must assign resources. Modern software quickly highlights overallocations—situations in which allocations exceed resources.

To resolve overallocations manually, you can either add resources or reschedule. Moving a task within its slack can free up resources.

Mid- to high-level project management information systems software (PMIS) can resolve overallocations through a "leveling" feature. Several rules of thumb can be used. You can specify that low-priority tasks should be delayed until higher-priority ones are complete, or that the project should end before or after the original deadline.

## TRACKING PROGRESS

The real action starts after the project gets under way. Actual progress will differ from your original, or baseline, planned progress. Software can hold several different baseline plans, so you can compare monthly snapshots.

A *tracking Gantt chart* superimposes the current schedule onto a baseline plan so deviations are easily noticed. If you prefer, a spreadsheet view of the same information could be output. Deviations between planned start/finish and newly scheduled start/finish also appear, and a "slipping filter" can be applied to highlight or output only those tasks that are scheduled to finish at a later date than the planned baseline.

Management by exception can also be applied to find deviations between budgeted costs and actual costs. (See the Breakthrough box titled "Project Management Information Systems in Everyday Use.")

# CAUTIONS ON CRITICAL PATH ANALYSIS

Several assumptions need to be made to use project critical path analysis. This section summarizes some significant assumptions and their criticisms. One particularly difficult point for operating personnel is understanding the statistics when three time estimates are used. The beta distribution of activity times, the three time estimates, the activity variances, and the use of the normal distribution to arrive at project completion probabilities are all potential sources of misunderstandings, and with misunderstanding comes distrust and obstruction. Thus, management must be sure that the people charged with monitoring and controlling activity performance understand the statistics.

1 **Assumption:** Project activities can be identified as entities. (There is a clear beginning and ending point for each activity.)

# BREAKTHROUGH

## PROJECT MANAGEMENT INFORMATION SYSTEMS IN EVERYDAY USE

The 1990s have seen an explosion of interest in the techniques and concepts of project management with a parallel increase in project management software offerings. A few years ago, there were but a handful of microcomputer-based project management software packages. Now there are over 100 such project management information systems—and the use of these tools is proliferating exponentially. Within our own MBA-level project management classes, about half of the students now enter having had some exposure to such software; all leave knowing at least one package and having been exposed to several others (Microsoft Project for Windows, Primavera Project Planner, Time Line, Project Scheduler, Milestone, Schedule Publisher, Texim Project). As recently as the early 1990s, perhaps one student per class would have prior experience with a PMIS, and our only in-class software was incapable of managing costs, leveling resources, or even displaying a PERT or Gantt chart. Here are examples of three PMISs leading this operations breakthrough.

The Microsoft Project program comes with an excellent online tutorial, which is one reason for its overwhelming popularity with project managers tracking midsized projects. This package aids in scheduling, allocating, and leveling resources, as well as in controlling costs and producing presentation-quality graphics and reports. Exhibit 3.12 shows a Microsoft Project sample output.

If the focus is primarily in scheduling, Kidasa's Milestones, Etc. program produces Gantt charts that can even show dependencies among activities. As the project unfolds and schedules need updating, a Gantt chart's activity start and end dates can easily be modified.

Finally, for managing very large projects or programs having several projects, Primavera Project Planner is often the choice. You will find it interesting to check out Primavera Systems, Inc.'s, website at *http://www.primavera.com* for the latest information on their software products.

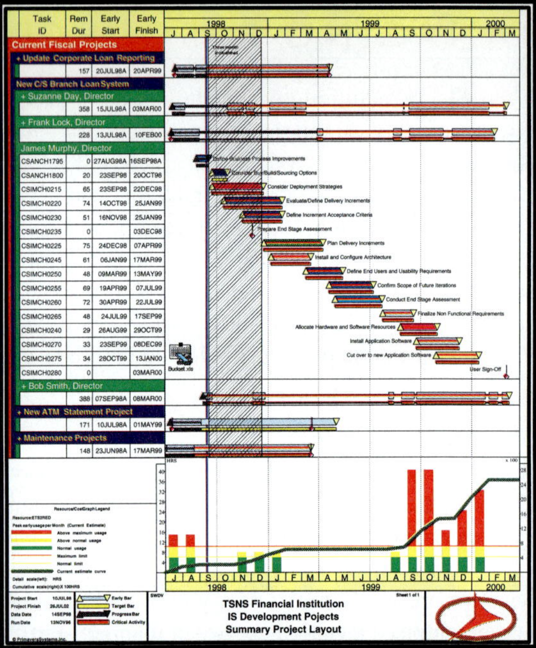


**Criticism:** Projects, especially complex ones, change in content over time, so a network made at the beginning may be highly inaccurate later. Also, the very fact that activities are specified and a network is formalized tends to limit the flexibility that is required to handle changing situations as the project progresses.

2 **Assumption:** Project activity sequence relationships can be specified and networked.

**Criticism:** Sequence relationships cannot always be specified beforehand. In some projects, in fact, ordering certain activities is conditional on previous activities. (Critical path analysis, in the basic form shown here, has no provision for treating this problem, although some other techniques have been proposed that allow the project manager several contingency paths, given different outcomes from each activity.)

3 **Assumption:** Project control should focus on the critical path.

**Criticism:** It is not necessarily true that the longest time-consuming path (or the path with zero slack) obtained from summing activity expected time values ultimately determines project completion time. What often happens as the project progresses is that some activity not on the critical path becomes delayed to such a degree that it extends the entire project. For this reason it has been suggested that a "critical activity" concept replace the critical path concept as the focus of

EXHIBIT 3.12

Microsoft Project Sample Output

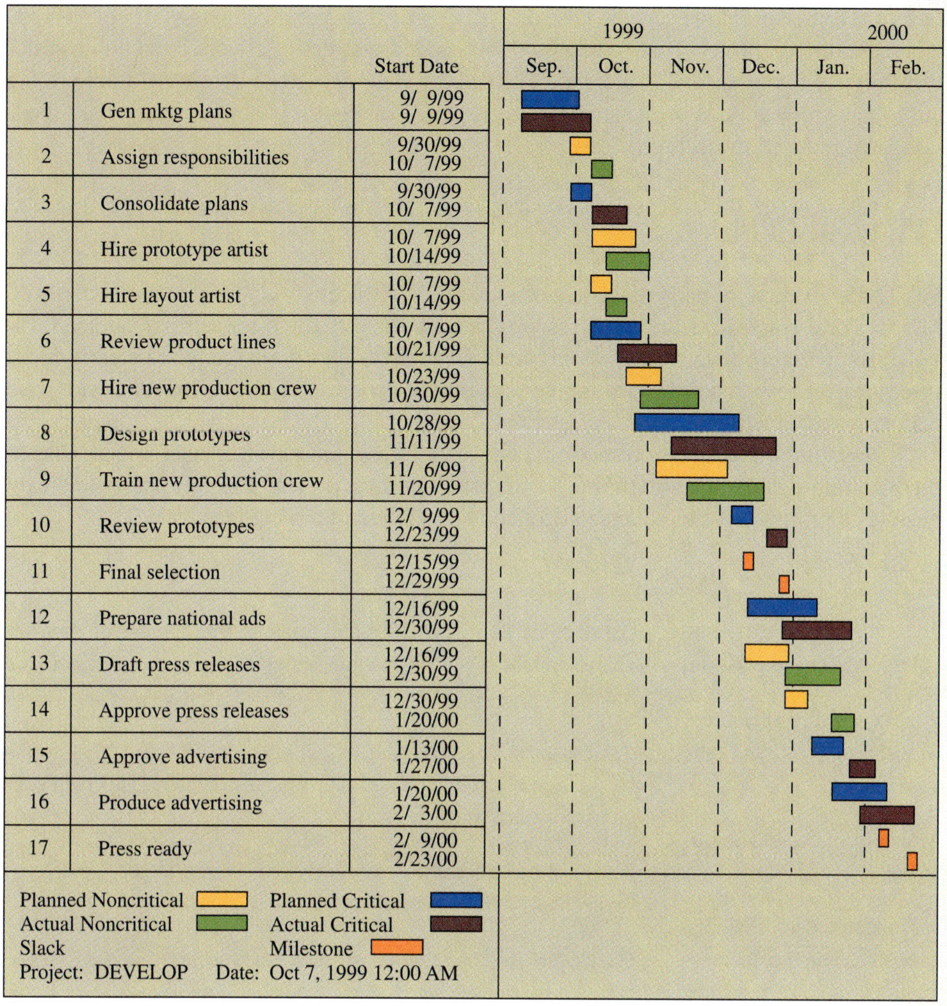


managerial control. Under this approach, attention would center on those activities that have a high potential variation and lie on the critical path or on a "near-critical path." A near-critical path is one that does not share any activities with the critical path and, though it has slack, could become critical if one or a few activities along it become delayed. Obviously, the more parallelism in a network, the more likely that one or more near-critical paths exist. Conversely, the more a network approximates a single series of activities, the less likely it is to have near-critical paths.

4 **Assumption:** The activity time estimates, when using the three time approach, follow the beta distribution, with the variance of the project assumed to equal the sum of the variances along the critical path.

**Criticism:** Although originally the beta distribution was selected for a variety of good reasons, each component of the statistical treatment has been brought into question. First, the formulas are in reality a modification of the beta distribution mean and variance, which, when compared to the basic formulas, could be expected to lead to absolute errors on the order of 10 percent for the entire project and 5 percent for the individual activity variances. Second, given that the activity-time distributions have the properties of unimodality, continuity, and finite positive end points, other distributions with the same properties would yield different means and variances. Third, obtaining three "valid" time estimates to put into the formulas presents operational problems; it is often difficult to arrive at one activity time estimate, let alone three, and the subjective definitions of the optimistic and pessimistic time do not help the matter.

Finally, the cost of applying critical path methods to a project is sometimes used as a basis for criticism. However, the cost of applying critical path techniques rarely exceeds 2 percent of total project cost. When used with added features of a work breakdown structure and various reports, it is more expensive but rarely exceeds 5 percent of total project costs. Thus, this added cost is generally outweighed by the savings from improved scheduling and reduced project time.

## CONCLUSION

Although much of this chapter has dealt with networking techniques, we would like to again emphasize the importance of teamwork. Effective project management involves much more than simply setting up a CPM schedule; it also requires clearly identified project responsibilities, a simple and timely progress reporting system, and good people-management practices.

Projects fail for a number of reasons. The most important reason is insufficient effort in the planning phase. In addition, the implementation of a project will fail unless the team has the commitment of top management and has a talented project manager.

## KEY TERMS

**Project** A series of related jobs usually directed toward some major output and requiring a significant period of time to perform.

**Project management** Planning, directing, and controlling resources (people, equipment, material) to meet the technical, cost, and time constraints of a project.

**Pure project** A structure for organizing a project where a self-contained team works full-time on the project.

**Functional project** A structure where team members are assigned from the functional units of the organization. The team members remain a part of their functional units and typically are not dedicated to the project.

**Matrix project** A structure that blends the functional and pure project structures. Each project uses people from different functional areas. A dedicated project manager decides what tasks need to be performed and when, but the functional managers control which people to use.

**Project milestone** A specific event in a project.

**Work breakdown structure** The hierarchy of project tasks, subtasks, and work packages.

**Activities** Pieces of work within a project that consume time. The completion of all the activities of a project marks the end of the project.

**Gantt chart** Shows in a graphic manner the amount of time involved and the sequence in which activities can be performed. Often referred to as a *bar chart.*

**Critical path** The sequence of activities in a project that forms the longest chain in terms of their time to complete. This path contains zero slack time.

**Immediate predecessor** Activity that needs to be completed immediately before another activity.

**Slack time** The time that an activity can be delayed; the difference between the late and early start times of an activity.

**Early start schedule** A project schedule that lists all activities by their early start times.

**Late start schedule** A project schedule that lists all activities by their late start times. This schedule may create savings by postponing purchases of material and other costs associated with the project.

**Time-cost models** Extension of the critical path models that consider the trade-off between the time required to complete an activity and cost.

## FORMULA REVIEW

**Expected Time**

[3.1] $$\text{ET} = \frac{a + 4m + b}{6}$$

**Variance ($\sigma^2$) of the activity times**

[3.2] $$\sigma^2 = \left(\frac{b - a}{6}\right)^2$$

***Z* transformation formula**

[3.3] $$Z = \frac{D - T_E}{\sqrt{\sum \sigma_{cp}^2}}$$

# SOLVED PROBLEMS

## SOLVED PROBLEM 1

A project has been defined to contain the following list of activities, along with their required times for completion:

| ACTIVITY | TIME (DAYS) | IMMEDIATE PREDECESSORS |
|---|---|---|
| A | 1 | — |
| B | 4 | A |
| C | 3 | A |
| D | 7 | A |
| E | 6 | B |
| F | 2 | C, D |
| G | 7 | E, F |
| H | 9 | D |
| I | 4 | G, H |

*a.* Draw the critical path diagram.
*b.* Show the early start and early finish times.
*c.* Show the critical path.
*d.* What would happen if activity F was revised to take four days instead of two?

### Solution

The answers to *a*, *b*, and *c* are shown in the following diagram.

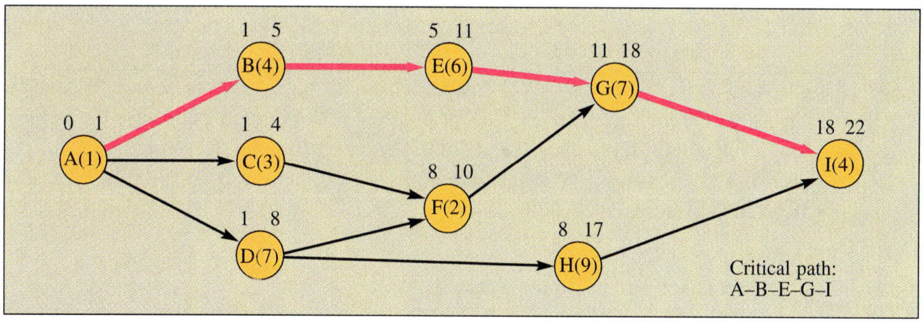


*d.* New critical path: A–D–F–G–I. Time of completion is 23 days.

## SOLVED PROBLEM 2

Here are the precedence requirements, normal and crash activity times, and normal and crash costs for a construction project:

| ACTIVITY | PRECEDING ACTIVITIES | REQUIRED TIME (WEEKS) | | COST | |
|---|---|---|---|---|---|
| | | NORMAL | CRASH | NORMAL | CRASH |
| A | — | 4 | 2 | $10,000 | $11,000 |
| B | A | 3 | 2 | 6,000 | 9,000 |
| C | A | 2 | 1 | 4,000 | 6,000 |
| D | B | 5 | 3 | 14,000 | 18,000 |
| E | B, C | 1 | 1 | 9,000 | 9,000 |
| F | C | 3 | 2 | 7,000 | 8,000 |
| G | E, F | 4 | 2 | 13,000 | 25,000 |
| H | D, E | 4 | 1 | 11,000 | 18,000 |
| I | H, G | 6 | 5 | 20,000 | 29,000 |

*a.* What is the critical path and the estimated completion time?
*b.* To shorten the project by three weeks, which tasks would be shortened and what would the final total project cost be?

## Solution

The construction project network is shown below:

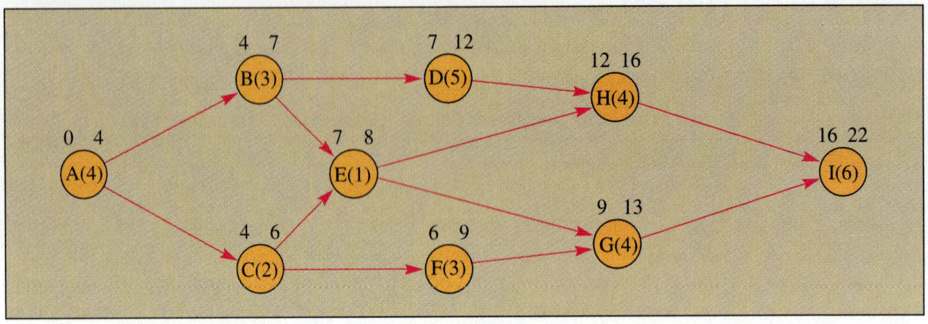


*a.* Critical path A–B–D–H–I.
Normal completion time is 22 weeks.

*b.*

| ACTIVITY | CRASH COST | NORMAL COST | NORMAL TIME | CRASH TIME | COST PER WEEK | WEEKS |
|---|---|---|---|---|---|---|
| A | $11,000 | $10,000 | 4 | 2 | $ 500 | 2 |
| B | 9,000 | 6,000 | 3 | 2 | 3,000 | 1 |
| C | 6,000 | 4,000 | 2 | 1 | 2,000 | 1 |
| D | 18,000 | 14,000 | 5 | 3 | 2,000 | 2 |
| E | 9,000 | 9,000 | 1 | 1 | | 0 |
| F | 8,000 | 7,000 | 3 | 2 | 1,000 | 1 |
| G | 25,000 | 13,000 | 4 | 2 | 6,000 | 2 |
| H | 18,000 | 11,000 | 4 | 1 | 2,333 | 3 |
| I | 29,000 | 20,000 | 6 | 5 | 9,000 | 1 |

(1) 1st week: CP = A–B–D–H–I. Cheapest is A at $500. Critical path stays the same.
(2) 2nd week: A is still the cheapest at $500. Critical path stays the same.
(3) 3rd week: Because A is no longer available, the choices are B (at $3,000), D (at $2,000), H (at $2,333), or I (at $9,000).

Therefore, choose D at $2,000.
Total project cost shortened three weeks is

| | |
|---|---|
| A | $ 11,000 |
| B | 6,000 |
| C | 4,000 |
| D | 16,000 |
| E | 9,000 |
| F | 7,000 |
| G | 13,000 |
| H | 11,000 |
| I | 20,000 |
| | $97,000 |

## REVIEW AND DISCUSSION QUESTIONS

1 What was the strangest project that you have been involved in? Give examples of the following as they pertain to the project: the work breakdown structure, tasks, subtasks, and work package. Were you on the critical path? Did it have a good project manager?
2 What are some reasons project scheduling is not done well?
3 Discuss the graphic presentations in Exhibit 3.3. Are there any other graphic outputs you would like to see if you were project manager?

4 Which characteristics must a project have for critical path scheduling to be applicable? What types of projects have been subjected to critical path analysis?
5 What are the underlying assumptions of minimum-cost scheduling? Are they equally realistic?
6 "Project control should always focus on the critical path." Comment.
7 Why would subcontractors for a government project want their activities on the critical path? Under what conditions would they try to avoid being on the critical path?

## PROBLEMS

1 The following activities are part of a project to be scheduled using CPM:

| ACTIVITY | IMMEDIATE PREDECESSOR | TIME (WEEKS) |
|---|---|---|
| A | — | 6 |
| B | A | 3 |
| C | A | 7 |
| D | C | 2 |
| E | B, D | 4 |
| F | D | 3 |
| G | E, F | 7 |

*a.* Draw the network.
*b.* What is the critical path?
*c.* How many weeks will it take to complete the project?
*d.* How much slack does activity B have?

1. *a.* See ISM.
*b.* A–C–D–E–G.
*c.* 26 weeks.
*d.* Six weeks (15 − 9).

2 Schedule the following activities using CPM:

| ACTIVITY | IMMEDIATE PREDECESSOR | TIME (WEEKS) |
|---|---|---|
| A | — | 1 |
| B | A | 4 |
| C | A | 3 |
| D | B | 2 |
| E | C, D | 5 |
| F | D | 2 |
| G | F | 2 |
| H | E, G | 3 |

*a.* Draw the network.
*b.* What is the critical path?
*c.* How many weeks will it take to complete the project?
*d.* Which activities have slack, and how much?

2. *a.* See ISM.
*b.* A–B–D–E–H.
*c.* 15 weeks.
*d.* C, 3 weeks; F, 1 week; G, 1 week.

3 The R&D department is planning to bid on a large project for the development of a new communication system for commercial planes. The accompanying table shows the activities, times, and sequences required:

| ACTIVITY | IMMEDIATE PREDECESSOR | TIME (WEEKS) |
|---|---|---|
| A | — | 3 |
| B | A | 2 |
| C | A | 4 |
| D | A | 4 |
| E | B | 6 |
| F | C, D | 6 |
| G | D, F | 2 |
| H | D | 3 |
| I | E, G, H | 3 |

3. *a.* See ISM.
*b.* A–C–F–G–I,
+ A–D–F–G–I.
*c.* C: two weeks;
D: two weeks;
G: two weeks.
*d.* Three paths:
A–B–E–I; A–C–F–G–I; and
A–D–F–G–I. 14 weeks.

*a.* Draw the network diagram.
*b.* What is the critical path?
*c.* Suppose you want to shorten the completion time as much as possible, and you have the option of shortening any or all of B, C, D, and G each two weeks. Which would you shorten?
*d.* What is the new critical path and earliest completion time?

4. *a.* See ISM.
*b.* 1–3–6–9–10.
*c.* See ISM.

4 A construction project is broken down into the following 10 activities:

| ACTIVITY | IMMEDIATE PREDECESSOR | TIME (WEEKS) |
|---|---|---|
| 1 | — | 4 |
| 2 | 1 | 2 |
| 3 | 1 | 4 |
| 4 | 1 | 3 |
| 5 | 2, 3 | 5 |
| 6 | 3 | 6 |
| 7 | 4 | 2 |
| 8 | 5 | 3 |
| 9 | 6, 7 | 5 |
| 10 | 8, 9 | 7 |

*a.* Draw the network diagram.
*b.* Find the critical path.
*c.* If activities 1 and 10 cannot be shortened, but activities 2 through 9 can be shortened to a minimum of one week each at a cost of $10,000 per week, which activities would you shorten to cut the project by four weeks?

5. *a.* See ISM.
*b.* B–E–G–H.
*c.* 14.67 days.
*d.* $P(<16) = .7852$.

5 The following represents a project that should be scheduled using CPM:

| | | TIMES (DAYS) | | |
|---|---|---|---|---|
| ACTIVITY | IMMEDIATE PREDECESSORS | *a* | *m* | *b* |
| A | — | 1 | 3 | 5 |
| B | — | 1 | 2 | 3 |
| C | A | 1 | 2 | 3 |
| D | A | 2 | 3 | 4 |
| E | B | 3 | 4 | 11 |
| F | C, D | 3 | 4 | 5 |
| G | D, E | 1 | 4 | 6 |
| H | F, G | 2 | 4 | 5 |

*a.* Draw the network.
*b.* What is the critical path?
*c.* What is the expected project completion time?
*d.* What is the probability of completing this project within 16 days?

6. *a.* Critical path is A–E–G–C–D.
*b.* 26 weeks.
*c.* See ISM. No difference in completion date.

6 Here is a CPM network with activity times in weeks:

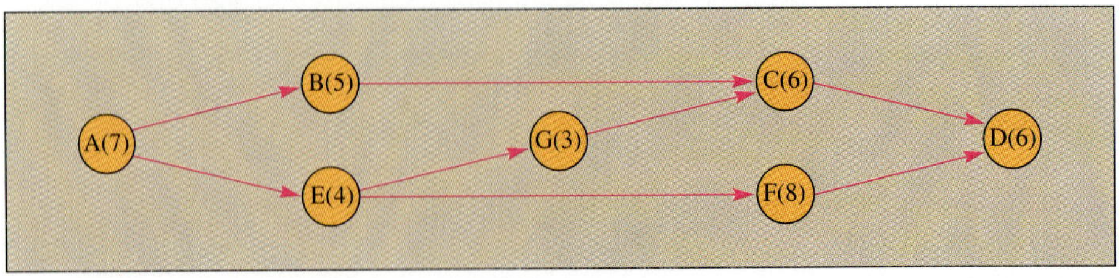


*a.* Determine the critical path.
*b.* How many weeks will the project take to complete?
*c.* Suppose F could be shortened by two weeks and B by one week. How would this affect the completion date?

7 The following table represents a plan for a project:

| JOB NO. | PREDECESSOR JOB(S) | *a* | *m* | *b* |
|---|---|---|---|---|
| 1 | — | 2 | 3 | 4 |
| 2 | 1 | 1 | 2 | 3 |
| 3 | 1 | 4 | 5 | 12 |
| 4 | 1 | 3 | 4 | 11 |
| 5 | 2 | 1 | 3 | 5 |
| 6 | 3 | 1 | 2 | 3 |
| 7 | 4 | 1 | 8 | 9 |
| 8 | 5, 6 | 2 | 4 | 6 |
| 9 | 8 | 2 | 4 | 12 |
| 10 | 7 | 3 | 4 | 5 |
| 11 | 9, 10 | 5 | 7 | 8 |

*a.* Construct the appropriate network diagram.
*b.* Indicate the critical path.
*c.* What is the expected completion time for the project?
*d.* You can accomplish any one of the following at an additional cost of $1,500:
(1) Reduce job 5 by two days.
(2) Reduce job 3 by two days.
(3) Reduce job 7 by two days.
If you will save $1,000 for each day that the earliest completion time is reduced, which action, if any, would you choose?
*e.* What is the probability that the project will take more than 30 days to complete?

7. *a.* See ISM for diagram.
*b.* Critical path is 1–3–6–8–9–11.
*c.* 26.83
*d.* None.
*e.* $P(>30) = .0885$.

8 Here is a network with the activity times shown under the nodes in days:

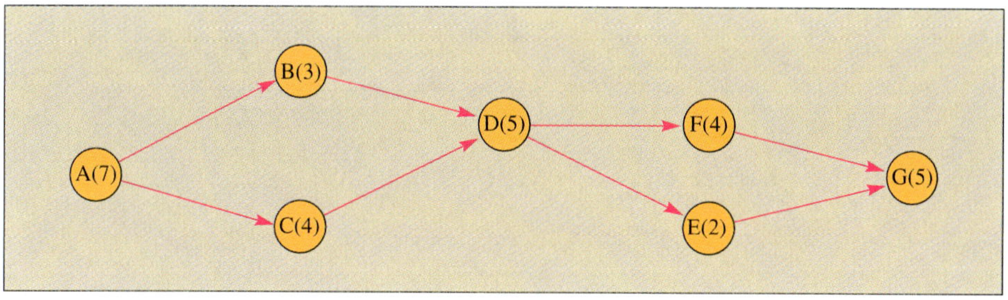


*a.* Find the critical path.
*b.* The following table shows the normal times and the crash times, along with the associated costs for each activity.

| ACTIVITY | NORMAL TIME | CRASH TIME | NORMAL COST | CRASH COST |
|---|---|---|---|---|
| A | 7 | 6 | $7,000 | $ 8,000 |
| B | 3 | 2 | 5,000 | 7,000 |
| C | 4 | 3 | 9,000 | 10,200 |
| D | 5 | 4 | 3,000 | 4,500 |
| E | 2 | 1 | 2,000 | 3,000 |
| F | 4 | 2 | 4,000 | 7,000 |
| G | 5 | 4 | 5,000 | 8,000 |

If the project is to be shortened by four days, show which activities, in order of reduction, would be shortened and the resulting cost.

8. *a.* Critical path is A–C–D–F–G.
*b.*

| DAY | COST | ACTIVITY |
|---|---|---|
| First | $1,000 | A |
| Second | 1,200 | C |
| Third | 1,500 | D (or F) |
| Fourth | 1,500 | F (or D) |
| | $5,200 | |

9 The home office billing department of a chain of department stores prepares monthly inventory reports for use by the stores' purchasing agents. Given the following information, use the critical path method to determine
*a.* How long the total process will take.
*b.* Which jobs can be delayed without delaying the early start of any subsequent activity.

9. *a.* 100 hours.
*b.* Those not on the critical path (i.e., b and d).

| | Job and Description | Immediate Predecessors | Time (hours) |
|---|---|---|---|
| a | Start | — | 0 |
| b | Get computer printouts of customer purchases | a | 10 |
| c | Get stock records for the month | a | 20 |
| d | Reconcile purchase printouts and stock records | b, c | 30 |
| e | Total stock records by department | b, c | 20 |
| f | Determine reorder quantities for coming period | e | 40 |
| g | Prepare stock reports for purchasing agents | d, f | 20 |
| h | Finish | g | 0 |

10. *a.* A–B–D–G, 25 weeks.
*b.* D by one week,
G by one week, and
A by one week.

10 For the network shown:

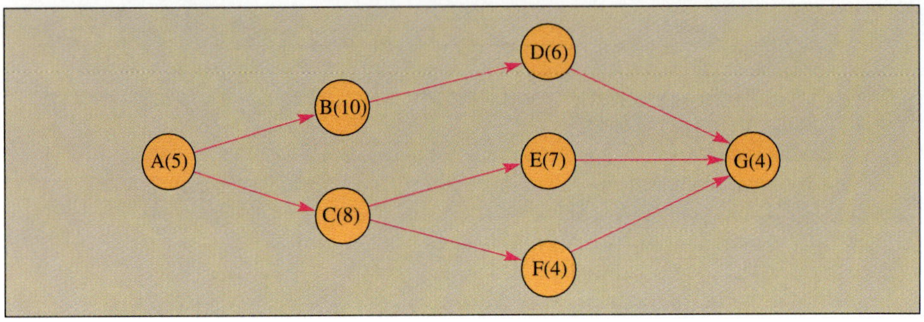


*a.* Determine the critical path and the early completion time for the project.
*b.* For the data shown, reduce the project completion time by three weeks. Assume a linear cost per day shortened, and show, step by step, how you arrived at your schedule.

| Activity | Normal Time | Normal Cost | Crash Time | Crash Cost |
|---|---|---|---|---|
| A | 5 | $ 7,000 | 3 | $13,000 |
| B | 10 | 12,000 | 7 | 18,000 |
| C | 8 | 5,000 | 7 | 7,000 |
| D | 6 | 4,000 | 5 | 5,000 |
| E | 7 | 3,000 | 6 | 6,000 |
| F | 4 | 6,000 | 3 | 7,000 |
| G | 4 | 7,000 | 3 | 9,000 |

11. *a.* A–C–D–F–G.
*b.* 25 weeks.
*c.* E, two weeks;
B, two weeks.
*d.* Shorten A by one week at a cost of $1,000.
Shorten C by one week at a cost of $1,200.
Total cost for two weeks is $2,200.
Critical path is still the same.

11 The following CPM network has estimates of the normal time listed for the activities:

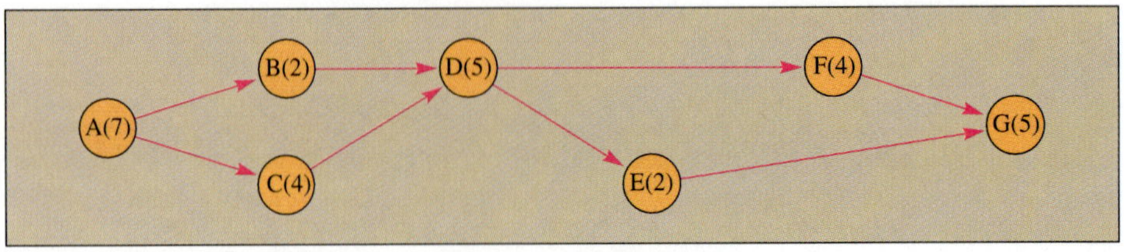


| Activity | Time (weeks) |
|---|---|
| A | 7 |
| B | 2 |
| C | 4 |
| D | 5 |
| E | 2 |
| F | 4 |
| G | 5 |

*a.* Identify the critical path.
*b.* What is the length of time to complete the project?
*c.* Which activities have slack, and how much?
*d.* Here is a table of normal and crash times and costs. Which activities would you shorten to cut two weeks from the schedule in a rational fashion? What would be the incremental cost? Is the critical path changed?

| Activity | Normal Time | Crash Time | Normal Cost | Crash Cost | Possible Number of Weeks Decrease | Cost/Week to Expedite |
|---|---|---|---|---|---|---|
| A | 7 | 6 | $7,000 | $ 8,000 | | |
| B | 2 | 1 | 5,000 | 7,000 | | |
| C | 4 | 3 | 9,000 | 10,200 | | |
| D | 5 | 4 | 3,000 | 4,500 | | |
| E | 2 | 1 | 2,000 | 3,000 | | |
| F | 4 | 2 | 4,000 | 7,000 | | |
| G | 5 | 4 | 5,000 | 8,000 | | |

## ADVANCED PROBLEM

12 Assume the network and data that follow:

| Activity | Normal Time (Weeks) | Normal Cost | Crash Time (Weeks) | Crash Cost | Immediate Predecessors |
|---|---|---|---|---|---|
| A | 2 | $50 | 1 | $70 | — |
| B | 4 | 80 | 2 | 160 | A |
| C | 8 | 70 | 4 | 110 | A |
| D | 6 | 60 | 5 | 80 | A |
| E | 7 | 100 | 6 | 130 | B |
| F | 4 | 40 | 3 | 100 | D |
| G | 5 | 100 | 4 | 150 | E, F |

*a.* Construct the network diagram.
*b.* Indicate the critical path when normal activity times are used.
*c.* Compute the minimum total direct cost for each project duration based on the cost associated with each activity. Consider durations of 13, 14, 15, 16, 17, and 18 weeks.
*d.* If the indirect costs for each project duration are $400 (18 weeks), $350 (17 weeks), $300 (16 weeks), $250 (15 weeks), $200 (14 weeks), and $150 (13 weeks), what is the total project cost for each duration? Indicate the minimum total project cost duration.

12. *a.* See ISM.
*b.* A–B–E–G
*c.* 13 = $760
14 = $660
15 = $600
16 = $550
17 = $520
18 = $500
*d.* 13 = $910
14 = $860
15 = $850
16 = $850
17 = $880
18 = $900
Minimum cost either 15 or 16 days, probably prefer 15

## CASE: THE CAMPUS WEDDING (A)

On March 31 of last year, Mary Jackson burst into the family living room and announced that she and Larry Adams (her college boyfriend) were going to be married. After recovering from the shock, her mother hugged her and asked, "When?" The following conversation resulted:

**Mary:** April 22.

**Mother:** What!

**Father:** The Adams–Jackson wedding will be the social hit of the year. Why so soon?

**Mary:** Because on April 22 the cherry blossoms on campus are always in full bloom! The wedding pictures will be beautiful.

**Mother:** But honey, we can't possibly finish all the things that need to be done by then. Remember all the details that were involved in your sister's wedding? Even if we start tomorrow, it takes a day to reserve the church and reception hall, and they need at least 17 days' notice. That has to be done before we can start decorating the church, which takes three days. An extra $100 contribution on

Sunday would probably cut that 17-day notice to 10 days, though.

**Father:** Ugh!

**Mary:** I want Jane Summers to be my maid of honor.

**Father:** But she's in the Peace Corps, in Guatemala, isn't she? It would take her 10 days to get ready and drive up here.

**Mary:** But we could fly her up in two days, and it would cost only $500. She would have to be here in time to have her dress fitted.

**Father:** Ugh!

**Mother:** And catering! It takes two days to choose the cake and table decorations, and Jack's Catering wants at least 10 days' notice prior to the rehearsal dinner (the night before the wedding).

**Mary:** Can I wear your wedding dress, Mom?

**Mother:** Well, we'd have to replace some lace, but you could wear it, yes. We could order the lace from New York when we order the material for the bridesmaids' dresses. It takes eight days to order and receive the material. The pattern needs to be chosen first, and that would take three days.

**Father:** We could get the material here in five days if we paid an extra $25 to airfreight it.

**Mary:** I want Mrs. Watson to work on the dresses.

**Father:** But she charges $120 a day!

**Mother:** If we did all the sewing, we could finish the dresses in 11 days. If Mrs. Watson helped, we could cut that down to six days, at a cost of $120 for each day less than 11 days.

**Mary:** I don't want anyone but her.

**Mother:** It would take another two days to do the final fitting. It normally takes two days to clean and press the dresses, but that new cleaner downtown could do them in one day if we pay the $30 charge for express service.

**Father:** Everything should be completed by rehearsal night, and that's only 21 days from now. I bet that will be a busy day.

**Mother:** We've forgotten something. The invitations.

**Father:** We should order the invitations from Bob's Printing Shop, and that usually takes 12 days. I'll bet he would do it in five days if we slipped him an extra $35.

**Mother:** It would take us three days to choose the invitation style before we could order them, and we want the envelopes printed with our return address.

**Mary:** Oh! That will be elegant.

**Mother:** The invitations should go out at least 10 days before the wedding. If we let them go any later, some of the relatives would get theirs too late to come, and that would make them mad. I'll bet that if we didn't get them out until eight days before the wedding, Aunt Ethel couldn't make it, and she would reduce her wedding gift by $200.

**Father:** Ugh!

**Mother:** We'll have to take them to the post office to mail them, and that takes a day. Addressing would take four days unless we hired some part-time help, and we can't start until the printer is finished. If we hired someone, we could probably save two days by spending $25 for each day saved.

**Mary:** We need to get gifts to give to the bridesmaids at the rehearsal dinner. I can spend a day and do that.

**Mother:** Before we can even start to write out those invitations, we need a guest list. Heavens, that will take four days to get in order, and only I can understand our address file.

**Mary:** Oh, Mother, I'm so excited. We can start each of the relatives on a different job.

**Mother:** Honey, I don't see how we can do it. Why, we've got to choose the invitations and patterns and reserve the church and . . .

**Father:** Why don't you just take $1500 and elope. Yours sister's wedding cost me $1200, and she didn't have to fly people up from Guatemala, hire extra people, use airfreight, or anything like that.

### QUESTIONS

1 Given the activities and precedence relationships described in the (A) case, develop a network diagram for the wedding plans.
2 Identify the paths. Which are critical?
3 What is the minimum-cost plan that meets the April 22 date?

## CASE: THE CAMPUS WEDDING (B)

Several complications arose during the course of trying to meet the deadline of April 21 for the Adams–Jackson wedding rehearsal. Because Mary Jackson was adamant about having the wedding on April 22 (as was Larry Adams, because he wanted her to be happy), the implications of each of these complications had to be assessed.

1 On April 1 the chairman of the Vestry Committee at the church was left unimpressed by the added donation and said he wouldn't reduce the notice period from 17 to 10 days.
2 A call to Guatemala revealed that the potential bridesmaid had several commitments and could not possibly leave the country until April 10.
3 Mother came down with the four-day flu just as she started on the guest list.
4 The lace and dress materials were lost in transit. Notice of the loss was delivered to the Jackson home early on April 10.
5 There was a small fire at the caterer's shop on April 8. It was estimated that the shop would be closed two or three days for repairs.

Mary Jackson's father, in particular, was concerned about expense and kept offering $1500 to Mary and Larry for them to elope.

QUESTIONS

1 Given your answers to the (A) case, describe the effects on the wedding plans of each incident noted in the (B) case.

SOURCE: ADAPTED FROM A CASE ORIGINALLY WRITTEN BY PROFESSOR D. C. WHYBANK, UNIVERSITY OF NORTH CAROLINA, CHAPEL HILL, NORTH CAROLINA.

## CASE: PROJECT MANAGEMENT AT CPAONE

The auditing division at CPAone (one of the "Big Six" accounting firms) generates financial statements to meet generally accepted accounting principles. In larger audits, the size of the task and the range of problems require the involvement of several people. In the audit of a national corporation, for example, numerous auditors with diverse specialties are required to investigate all aspects of the operation in various geographic areas. Given the number of people and the variety in skills, expertise, and personalities involved, a project manager is needed to oversee and conduct the audit efficiently. Thus, every audit begins by assigning the client to a partner, usually someone who is familiar with the client's business. The partner becomes the project director of the audit and is responsible for writing proposals, staffing the audit, delegating tasks, scheduling, and budgeting.

The project director begins by studying the client's income statement, balance sheet, and other financial statements. If the client has a bad financial reputation, the project director can decide that CPAone will refuse to do the audit. If the client is accepted, the director prepares a proposal outlining the general approach for conducting the audit, the completion date, and the cost estimate.

In determining the general approach for conducting the audit, the project director considers the size of the company and the number of departments. Auditors are then assigned department by department. The audit team is a pure project team, created anew for every audit with people having the skills best suited to the needs of the audit. Generally, each audit has one or two staff accountants, one or two senior accounts, and the project director. Before the proposal is even accepted, the director specifies who will perform each task and the completion dates. Cost estimates are based on estimated labor hours.

During the audit the project director must ensure that all work strictly adheres to the Book of Auditing Standards and is completed on schedule. Each week the client and project director meet to review progress. When problems cannot be solved immediately, the director may call in people from CPAone's tax or consulting divisions. When the team has trouble interpreting financial statements, the project director may request that the client's own personnel be involved. Follow-up service is provided after the audit is completed. The project director sees to it that the client is represented if the IRS requests an examination.

QUESTIONS

1 What are the major milestones associated with this project? What additional information would you need to develop a CPM chart?

2 What are the project director's managerial responsibilities?

SOURCE: *MANAGING BUSINESS AND ENGINEERING PROJECTS*, BY NICHOLAS, © 1990. REPRINTED BY PERMISSION OF PRENTICE HALL, INC., UPPER SADDLE RIVER, NJ.

## SELECTED BIBLIOGRAPHY

Cleland, D. I., and W. R. King. *Project Management Handbook*. New York: Van Nostrand Reinhold, 1983.

Devaux, S. A. *Total Project Control: A Manager's Guide to Integrated Project Planning, Measuring, and Tracking*. New York: Wiley, 1999.

Gray, C. F., and E. W. Larson. *Project Management: The Managerial Process*. Burr Ridge, IL: Irwin/McGraw-Hill, 2000.

Kerzner, H. *Project Management: A Systems Approach to Planning, Scheduling, and Controlling*. 6th ed. New York: Wiley, 1998.

Rogers, T. "Project Management: Emerging as a Requisite for Success." *Industrial Engineering*, June 1993, pp. 42–43.

Smith-Daniels, D. E., and N. J. Aquilano. "Constrained Resource Project Scheduling." *Journal of Operations Management* 4, no. 4 (1984), pp. 369–87.

Smith-Daniels, D. E., and V. Smith-Daniels. "Optimal Project Scheduling with Materials Ordering." *IIE Transactions* 19, no. 2 (June 1987), pp. 122–29.

Williams, P. B. *Getting a Project Done on Time: Managing People, Time, and Results*. New York: The American Management Association, 1996.

## FOOTNOTE

1 T. Peters, *Liberation Management* (New York: Alfred A. Knopf, 1992), p. 5 and cover flyleaf.

*section* ***two***

**section 2**

# Product Design and Process Selection





## How to Become an Efficiency Expert

Maybe becoming an efficiency expert is not your dream, but it is important to learn the fundamentals. Have you ever wondered why you always have to wait in line at one store, but another one seems to be on top of the crowds? A process that works well has been designed properly. This section is about designing efficient processes—all kinds of processes. Companies also need to develop a quality philosophy and integrate it into their processes. This section considers these subjects in both manufacturing and service industries.

chapter

# chapter four
# PROCESS ANALYSIS

## CHAPTER OUTLINE AND KEY TERMS

4

## A HOT MEAL IN 59 SECONDS

Some like it hot. None like it cold.

The difference between selling hot and cold fast food is huge: "The food I throw away today is better than the food I sold five years ago," says Steve Bigari, a McDonald's franchisee here who has tested the new food-preparation technology at his five restaurants for more than a year.

Sales at two of his restaurants are up almost 20 percent since they started selling fresher meals, he says. And the changes haven't even been advertised. Bigari credits the sales boost to the hotter food.

His secret: ultrafast service. Made to order. "It used to be, if you wanted a Filet O' Fish sandwich without the sauce, you were sent to the penalty box," Bigari says. "Not anymore."

Bigari and a *USA Today* reporter randomly tracked the time it took to fill an order placed by two construction workers, Matt Zamba and Howard Ewing, who pulled into the drive-through in a pickup at lunch hour:

12:39:00 P.M.: Taking advantage of a special promotion, the workers order a 2-for-1 Big Mac special. An employee in a headset punches the order into a computer.

12:39:07 P.M.: A sandwich assembler looks up at a monitor and sees the order. He drops two buns into the 10-second toaster, and then begins to assemble the two Big Macs by removing four beef patties from the new, moisture-controlled holding cabinet.

12:39:19 P.M.: The Toyota truck with the construction workers pulls away from the speaker and slowly heads toward the pickup window.

12:39:39 P.M.: The sandwich maker finishes making the two Big Macs and wraps them.

12:39:42 P.M.: Another employee stuffs the Big Macs into a sack and hands it to the cashier at the pickup window.

12:39:48 P.M.: The truck pulls to the pickup window. The driver pays and takes the bag.

12:39:59 P.M.: The order is completed; the truck drives off.

Total time: 59 seconds.

Source: Bruce Horowitz, "A Hot Meal in 59 Seconds," *USA Today*, February 20, 1998, p. 2b. Copyright 1998, USA TODAY. Reprinted with permission.

But wait.

A reporter stops the driver and asks the crucial question: Is the food hot?

"If it wasn't hot, I wouldn't keep coming back," says Zamba, the driver. "It's my third time this week." ←

## PROCESS ANALYSIS

Understanding how processes work is essential to ensuring the competitiveness of a company. A process that does not match the needs of the firm will punish the firm every minute that the firm operates. Take, for example, two fast-food restaurants. If one restaurant can deliver a quarter-pound hamburger to the customer for $.50 in direct costs and a second restaurant costs $.75, no matter what the second restaurant does, it will lose $.25 in profit for every hamburger it sells compared to the first restaurant. Many factors need to be considered when one sets up the process to make those hamburgers. These factors include the cost of the raw materials, the costs associated with how the hamburger is prepared, and the cost of taking the order and delivering it to the customer.

Process

What is a process? A **process** is any part of an organization that takes inputs and transforms them into outputs that, it is hoped, are of greater value to the organization than the original inputs. Consider some examples of processes. Honda Motors assembles the Accord in a plant in Marysville, Ohio. The assembly plant takes in parts and components that have been fabricated for the plant. Using labor, equipment along an assembly line, and energy, these parts and components are transformed into automobiles. McDonald's, at each of its restaurants, uses inputs such as hamburger meat, lettuce, tomatoes, and potatoes. To these inputs, trained labor is added in the form of cooks and order takers, and capital equipment is used to transform the inputs into hamburgers, french fries, and other foods.

Service

In both of these examples, the process produces products as output. However, the outputs of many processes are services. In a hospital, for example, specialized equipment and highly trained doctors, nurses, and technicians are combined with another input, the patient. The patient is transformed through proper treatment and care into a healthy patient. An airline is another example of a service organization. The airline uses airplanes, ground equipment, flight crews, ground crews, reservation personnel, and fuel to transport customers, between locations all over the world.

This chapter describes how to analyze a process. Analyzing a process allows some important questions to be answered, such as these: How many customers can the process handle per hour? How long will it take to serve a customer? What change is needed in the process to expand capacity? How much does the process cost? A difficult, but important, first step in process analysis is to clearly define the purpose of the analysis. Is the purpose to solve a problem? Is it to better understand the impact of a change in how business will be done in the future?

SLOT MACHINES IN A CASINO IN RENO, NEVADA, HAVE A MAJOR IMPACT ON THE CASINO'S PROFITS. AN ELECTRONIC VERSION VERSUS A MECHANICAL VERSION IMPACTS CYCLE TIME WHICH IN TURN AFFECTS REVENUES.

Clearly understanding the purpose of the analysis is critical to setting the level of detail in modeling the process. The analysis must be kept as simple as possible. The following sections of this chapter discuss the details of constructing flowcharts and measures that are appropriate for different types of processes. But first, consider a simple example.

## ANALYZING A LAS VEGAS SLOT MACHINE

The slot machine is common in casinos around the world. Let's use this machine to illustrate how a simple process is analyzed.

Assume that we work for the casino and management is considering a new type of electronic slot machine that is much faster than the current mechanical machine. Management has asked how much we can expect to make from the new electronic machine over a 24-hour period compared to the old mechanical machine.

Begin by analyzing a mechanical slot machine. The slot machine is activated when the customer puts one or more coins in the machine and then pulls the arm on the machine (slot machines are often called "one-armed bandits"). Three wheels spin, and after a time each wheel stops and displays a particular symbol. The machine pays money when certain combinations of symbols simultaneously appear. For those not familiar with how a slot machine works, we have included a slot machine simulation program on the CD included with the book. Sorry, but it does not pay real money.

Slot machines are designed to pay back a certain percentage of what they take in. Typical paybacks would be 90 to 95 percent of what is taken in; the casino keeps 5 to 10 percent. These payback percentages are a function of the number of different symbols that are on each wheel. Each symbol is repeated on each wheel a certain number of times. For example, if a wheel has 10 symbols, one might be a single bar, one a double bar, and one a lemon; two might be cherries, three lucky sevens, and two liberty bells. Because the wheels stop on a random symbol, the probability of lucky sevens coming up on all three wheels is $3/10 \times 3/10 \times 3/10 = 0.027$ or 2.7 percent of the time. The probability of certain combinations of symbols coming up, combined with the payout for each combination, sets the average percentage that the machine is expected to pay out.

Consider a mechanical slot machine that pays out 95 percent of the coins played. With this machine, assume the average player feeds coins into the machine at a pace of one coin each 15 seconds. The 15 seconds is called the *cycle time* of the process. The **cycle time** of a repetitive process is the average time between completions of successive units. In the case of the slot machine, the unit is a silver dollar. With a 15-second cycle time, our mechanical

Cycle time

slot machine can process \$4 (60 seconds/15 seconds) per minute or \$240 (\$4/minute × 60 minutes) per hour. Because our slot machine has a payout of 95 percent, we would expect the machine to give the customer 228 (240 × 0.95) of the silver dollars that it took in and keep \$12 for the casino for each hour that it is in operation. If we started with \$100, we could expect to play for about 8.3 hours (\$100/\$12 per hour) before we would run out of silver dollars. We might be lucky and win the jackpot, or we might be unlucky and lose it all in the first hour; but on average we would expect to lose the entire \$100 in 8.3 hours.

Now consider the new electronic slot machine. It operates in exactly the same manner; the only difference is that it processes coins in 10 seconds. With a 10-second cycle time, the machine processes \$6 (60 seconds/10 seconds) per minute or \$360 (\$6/minute × 60 minutes) per hour. With a 95 percent payout, the machine would give the customer back 342 (360 × 0.95) silver dollars and keep \$18 for the casino each hour. This machine would take our \$100 in only 5.5 hours (\$100/\$18 per hour).

So how much does the electronic slot machine make for the casino in 24 hours compared to the mechanical slot machine? One more critical piece of information is needed to answer this question: How long will the slot machine operate over the 24 hours? The casino feels that the machine will be used 12 out of the 24 hours; this 12 out of 24 hours is the expected utilization of the machine. **Utilization** is the ratio of the time that a resource is actually activated relative to the time that it is available for use. Adjusting for utilization, the expected revenue from the mechanical machine is \$144/day (\$12/hour × 24 hours × 0.5) compared to revenue of \$216/day (\$18/hour × 24 hours × 0.5) for the electronic machine. When an analysis is performed, it is important to qualify the analysis with the assumptions made. In this comparison, we assumed that the operator puts only one silver dollar in the machine at a time and that the utilization would be the same for the mechanical and electronic slot machines.

Utilization

The speed of the slot machine can have a major impact on the casino's revenue. The single slot machine is only a small part of the casino. To really understand how much revenue the casino can generate, we need to consider all of the other revenue-generating processes such as the blackjack and poker tables, keno games, craps, and the other games in the casino. Many times analyzing an enterprise involves evaluating a number of independent activities, like our slot machine. The aggregate performance of each individual activity may be all that is needed to understand the overall process. On the other hand, often there is significant interaction between individual activities or processes that must be considered.

Think about our gambling casino. Many casinos offer great deals on food, which is served right in the casino. What do you think would be the main priority of the food operation manager in one of these casinos? Would great-tasting food be important? How important is the cost of the food? Is speed of service important? Good food certainly is important. If the food is unpleasant, the customer will not even consider eating at the casino. This is bad for the casino because if the customers leave, they take their money with them. Remember, the casino makes money based on how long the customers gamble. The more time spent gambling, the more money the casino makes. What about cost? If the customers think the meals are too expensive, they might leave. So it is important to keep the cost of the meals down so that they can be priced inexpensively. Many casinos even give meals away. How important is it to serve the customer quickly? Think about it this way: Every minute that the customers are sitting in the restaurant, they are not feeding silver dollars into a slot machine. So speed is important because it impacts the revenue generated at the games in the casino.

## PROCESS FLOWCHARTING

Vol. III "Reengineering at Caterpillar"

Often the activities associated with a process affect one another so that it is important to consider the simultaneous performance of a number of activities, all operating at the same time. A good way to start analyzing a process is with a diagram showing the basic elements of a process—typically tasks, flows, and storage areas. Tasks are shown as rectangles, flows as arrows, and the storage of goods or other items as inverted triangles. Sometimes flows through a process can be diverted in multiple directions depending on some condition. Decision points are depicted as a diamond with the different flows running from the points on the diamond. Exhibit 4.1 displays examples of these symbols. It sometimes is useful to separate a diagram into different horizontal or vertical bands. This allows the sepa-

EXHIBIT 4.1

Process Flowchart Example

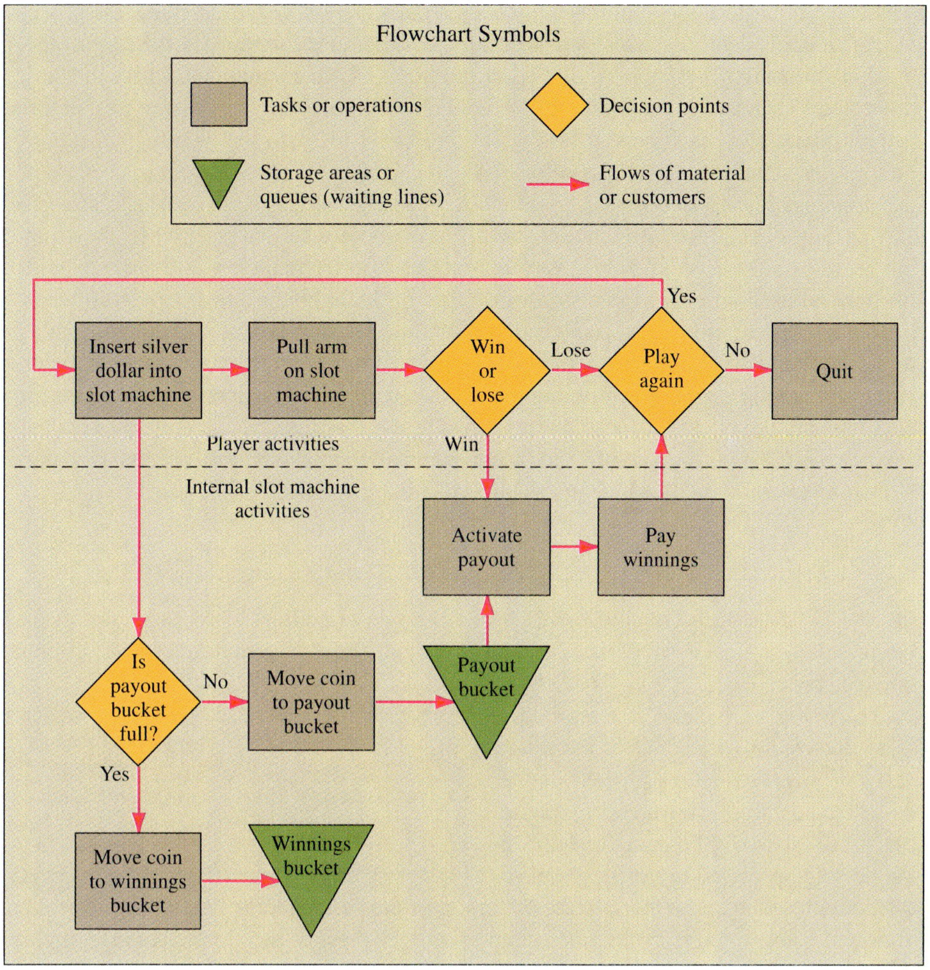


ration of tasks that are part of the process. For example, with the slot machine, the tasks performed by the customer can be separated from the tasks performed by the slot machine.

In the slot machine example, the level of abstraction considers the slot machine as a simple black box that takes in silver dollars and either keeps them or returns some of them during each cycle. Viewing the slot machine as a black box might be fine if the purpose is just to analyze how much the machine is expected to make for the casino each hour. In reality, more activities are required to support the slot machine. Inside the slot machine are two buckets of silver dollars. One bucket stores coins needed for internal use by the slot machine. When a customer wins, the payout comes from this payout bucket. The slot machine is designed to automatically keep this payout bucket filled during play. When the payout bucket is full, the silver dollars are deposited in a second winnings bucket. The winnings bucket must be periodically emptied to claim the winnings for the casino. The flowchart in Exhibit 4.1 depicts the external activities of the player and the internal movement of the coins within the machine.

Probably the most interesting thing about the payout bucket is how big it should be. The slot machine is programmed so that if the payout bucket empties, the machine stops and lights on the top of the machine flash, thus notifying casino personal that a lucky customer has emptied the machine. The payout bucket would be sized to keep this a rare occurrence. Think of the payout bucket as a buffer or intermediate storage area for silver dollars that allows the slot machine to operate on its own. The smaller the payout bucket, the more the casino personnel need to attend to the machine, and the more time the machine is idle for lack of silver dollars. On the other hand, with a larger bucket more money is tied up.

The situation with the winnings bucket in the machine is similar. A small winnings bucket will need to be emptied more often. On the other hand, a large winnings bucket means that the casino does not deposit the money into its bank account as quickly. It is easy to see the advantage of buffering operations with the slot machine. Large buffers allow the process to operate independently, whereas small buffers require more attention. In the case of the slot machine the buffer is composed of the silver dollars. In other situations, where the buffer is other items such as a raw material, these items have a value, so they also represent money.

Consider a slot machine that we expect to deposit $12 into the winnings bucket every hour. If our winnings bucket can hold 1,000 silver dollars, then we expect to need to empty the winnings bucket every 83.3 hours ($1,000/$12 per hour) if the slot machine is used 100 percent of the time. It is interesting to think about what happens when the winnings bucket fills up. If the slot machine is smart enough to know that the winnings bucket is full, it might be programmed to just stop working with its lights flashing as they do when the payout bucket empties. This would cause downtime on the machine and might upset a customer using the machine because the customer would have to move to another slot machine. If the slot machine were not programmed to stop working, the silver dollars would fill the cavity where the bucket is located in the base of the machine. Imagine the mess when the casino worker opens that overflowed machine and all those silver dollars come pouring out. How often would you plan on emptying the winnings bucket?

## TYPES OF PROCESSES

It is useful to categorize processes to describe how a process is designed. By being able to quickly categorize a process, we can show the similarities and differences between processes.

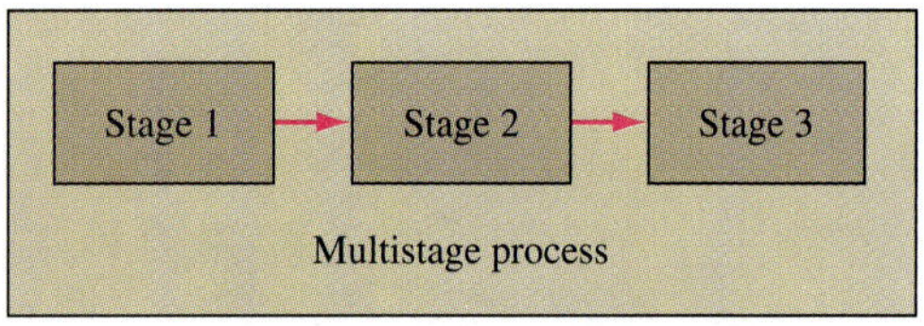


The first way to categorize a process is to determine whether it is a *single-stage* or a *multiple-stage* process. If the slot machine were viewed as a simple black box, it would be categorized as a single-stage process. In this case, all of the activities that are involved in the operation of the slot machine would be collapsed and analyzed using a single cycle time to represent the speed of the slot machine. A multiple-stage process has multiple groups of activities that are linked through flows. The term *stage* is used to indicate that multiple activities have been pulled together for analysis purposes.

Buffering

A multiple-stage process may be buffered internally. **Buffering** refers to a storage area between stages where the output of a stage is placed prior to being used in a downstream stage. Buffering allows the stages to operate independently. If one stage feeds a second stage with no intermediate buffer, then the assumption is that the two stages are directly linked. When a process is designed this way, the most common problems that can happen are blocking and starving. **Blocking** occurs when the activities in the stage must stop because there is no place to deposit the item just completed. **Starving** occurs when the activities in a stage must stop because there is no work.

Blocking

Starving

Consider a two-stage process where the first stage has a cycle time of 30 seconds and the second a cycle time of 45 seconds. If this process needs to produce 100 units, then for each unit produced the first stage would be blocked for 15 seconds.

What would happen if an inventory buffer were placed between the two stages? In this case the first stage would complete the 100 units in 3,000 seconds (30 seconds/unit × 100 units). During these 3,000 seconds the second stage would complete only 66 units ((3,000 − 30) seconds/45 seconds/unit). The 30 seconds are subtracted from the 3,000 seconds because the second stage is starved for the first 30 seconds. This would mean that the inventory would build to 34 units (100 units − 66 units) over that first 3,000 seconds. All of the units would be produced in 4,530 seconds. The second stage in this case is called a **bottleneck** because it limits the capacity of the process.

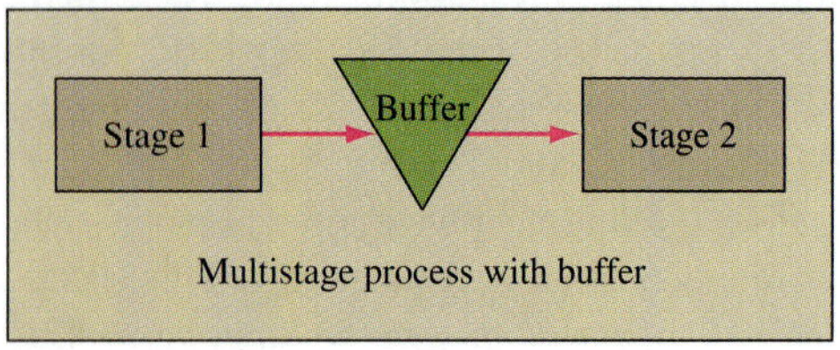


Bottleneck

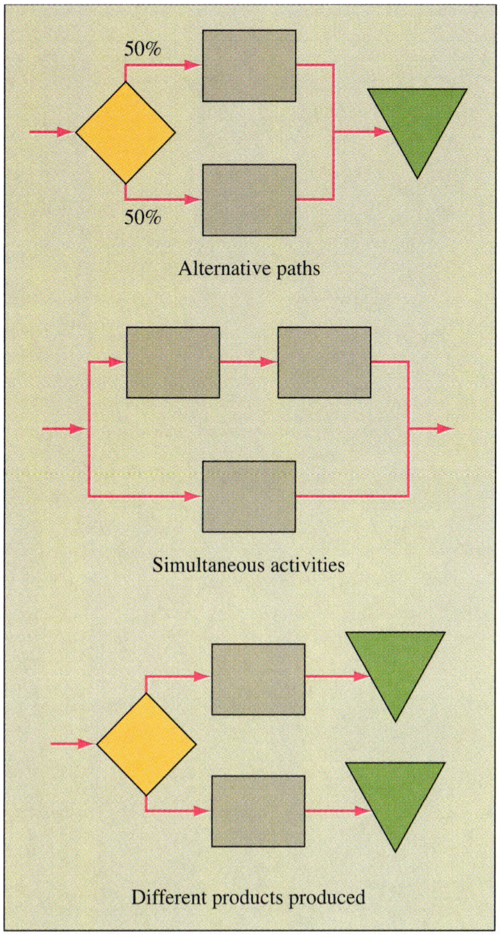


What would happen if the first stage required 45 seconds and the second stage had the 30-second cycle time? In this case the first stage would be the bottleneck, and each unit would go directly from the first stage to the second. The second stage would be starved for 15 seconds waiting for each unit to arrive; however, it would still take 4,530 seconds to complete all 100 units. All of this assumes that there is no variability in the cycle time. With the relatively low 67 percent utilization on the second stage, variability would have little impact on the performance of this system, but if the cycle times were closer some inventory might collect in the buffer.

Often activities, stages, and even entire processes are operated in parallel. For example, operating two identical activities in parallel would theoretically double capacity. Or perhaps two different sets of activities can be done at the same time on the unit being produced. In analyzing a system with parallel activities or stages, it is important to understand the context. In the case where parallel processes represent alternatives, for example, a diamond should show that flows divert and what percentage of the flow moves in each direction. Sometime two or more processes terminate in a common inventory buffer. This normally indicates that the two processes make identical items that are going into this inventory. Separate inventories should be used in the diagram if the outputs of the parallel processes are different.

Another useful way to characterize a process is whether the process *makes to stock* or *makes to order*. To illustrate these concepts, consider the processes used to make hamburgers at the three major fast-food restaurant chains in the United States: McDonald's, Burger King, and Wendy's. In the case of McDonald's, the company recently began converting to a new process that is featured in the chapter opening. We begin our tour of the approaches used by the top fast-food restaurants by first reviewing the traditional approach.

Consider a traditional restaurant making hamburgers. Before the era of fast-food, hamburgers were always made to order. In the traditional process, the customer places an order specifying the degree of doneness (medium or well done) and requests specific condiments (pickles, cheese, mustard, onions, catsup). Using this specification, the cook takes raw hamburger meat from inventory (typically this inventory is refrigerated and the patties have already been made), cooks the hamburger, and warms the bun. The hamburger is then assembled and delivered to the customer. The quality of the hamburger is highly dependent on the skill of the cook.

This **make-to-order** process is activated only in response to an actual order. Inventory (both work-in-process and finished goods) is kept to a minimum. Theoretically, one would expect that response time would be slow because all the activities need to be completed before the product is delivered to the customer. Services by their very nature often use make-to-order processes.

Make-to-order

McDonald's revolutionized the hamburger-making process by developing a high-volume approach. A diagram of McDonald's traditional process is shown in Exhibit 4.2A. Until recently, hamburgers were grilled in batches. Standard hamburgers (for example, the

EXHIBIT 4.2

Making Hamburgers at McDonald's, Burger King, and Wendy's

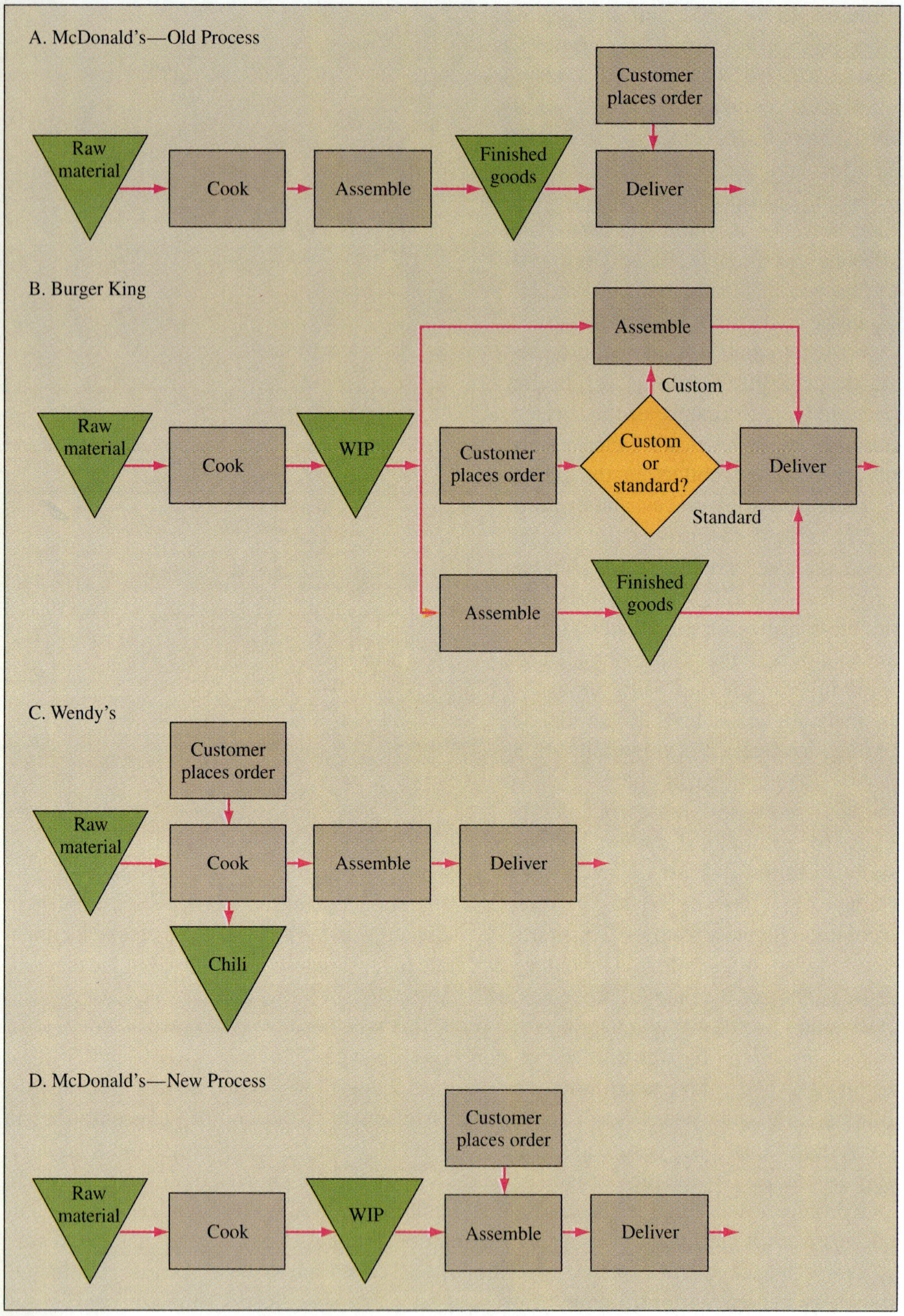


"Big Mac" consists of two beef patties, sauce, lettuce, cheese, pickles, and onion on a sesame seed bun) were then prepared and stored in a holding bin for immediate delivery to the customer. A person that judged current demand and placed orders to keep inventory in the bin at an appropriate level controlled the whole process. This is a highly efficient **make-to-stock** process that produces standard products that can be delivered quickly to the customer. This quick process appeals to families with small children, for whom speed of delivery is important.

Make-to-stock

In general, a make-to-stock process ends with finished goods inventory; customer orders are then served from this inventory. A make-to-stock process can be controlled based on the actual or anticipated amount of finished goods inventory. A target stocking level, for example, might be set, and the process would be periodically activated to maintain that target stocking level. Make-to-stock processes are also used when demand is seasonal. In this case, inventory can be built during the slow season and used during the peak season, thus allowing the process to run at a constant rate throughout the year.

The unique feature of the Burger King process, shown in Exhibit 4.2B, is a highly specialized conveyor–broiler. Raw hamburger patties are placed on a moving conveyor that runs through a flaming broiler. In exactly 90 seconds, the patties are cooked on both sides with a unique broiler taste. Due to the fixed time for a patty to move through the conveyor–broiler, the thickness of the patties must be the same for all the hamburger products. The buns are also warmed on a conveyor. This system results in a unique, highly consistent product. The cooked patties are stored in a warmed storage container. During periods of high demand, some standard hamburgers are prepared and inventoried for immediate delivery. Custom hamburgers with unique combinations of condiments are prepared to order. This *hybrid* process provides flexibility to respond to customer preferences through the assemble-to-order backend process—thus the Burger King "have it your way" slogan. In general, **hybrid** processes combine the features of both make-to-order and make-to-stock. Here two types of process are parallel alternatives at the end of the Burger King process. In the most common hybrid form, a generic product is made and stocked at some point in the process. These generic units are then finished in a final process based on actual orders.

Hybrid

Continuing with our tour, Wendy's uses a make-to-order process (as shown in Exhibit 4.2C) that is in full view of the customer. Hamburger patties are cooked on a grill. During high-volume times, the cook tries to get a little ahead and anticipates the arrival of customers. Patties that are on the grill too long are used in the chili soup. On arrival of a customer order, a patty is taken from the grill and the hamburger is assembled to the exact specifications of the customer. Because the process starts with the cooking of the patty, it is a little slower. The customer can see what is going on, and the perception is a high-quality custom product.

Finally, the new McDonald's process (Exhibit 4.2D) is a hybrid process. Cooked hamburger patties are inventoried in a special storage device that maintains the moistness of the cooked patties for up to 30 minutes. The process makes extensive use of the latest cooking technologies. Hamburger patties are cooked in less than 45 seconds. Buns are toasted in only nine seconds. Individual items on each customer order are transmitted immediately to the area where the hamburgers are assembled using a specially designed computer system. The assembly process that includes toasting the buns is designed to respond to a customer order in only 15 seconds. By combining the latest technology and clever process engineering, McDonald's has developed a very quick response process. The product is fresh, delivered quickly, and made to the exact specifications of the customer.

Each of the processes used by these companies has its strengths and weaknesses. McDonald's is the high-volume leader, catering to families with young children. Burger King has its unique taste. Wendy's appeals to those who want their hamburgers prepared the old-fashioned way. Each company focuses advertising and promotional efforts toward attracting the segment of the market their process characteristics best support.

One final method for categorizing a process is by whether it is paced or nonpaced. Recall that Burger King uses the conveyor–broiler to cook hamburgers in exactly 90 seconds. **Pacing** refers to the fixed timing of the movement of items through the process. In a serial process, the movement of items through each activity (or stage) is often paced in some mechanical way in order to coordinate the line. An assembly line may, for example, move every 45 seconds. Another mechanism used is a clock that counts down the amount of time left in each cycle. When the clock reaches zero, the parts are manually moved to the next activity. Dividing the time available to produce a certain product by customer demand for the product calculates the required cycle time for a process. For example, if an automobile manufacturer needs to produce 1,000 automobiles during a shift where the assembly line operates 420 minutes, the cycle time is 25.2 seconds (420 minutes/1,000 automobiles $\times$ 60 seconds/minute $=$ 25.2 seconds/automobile).

Pacing

# MEASURING PROCESS PERFORMANCE

There is much variation in the way performance metrics are calculated in practice. This section, defines metrics in a manner consistent with the most common use in practice. It is vital, though, to understand exactly how a metric coming from a particular company or industry is calculated prior to making any decisions. It would be easier if metrics were calculated more consistently, but this just is not the case. So if a manager says that his utilization is 90 percent or her efficiency is 115 percent, a standard follow-up question is "How did you calculate that?" Metrics often are calculated in the context of a particular process. Metrics used in cases that you are studying may be defined slightly differently from what is given here. It is important to understand, within the context of the case, how a term is being used.

Comparing the metrics of one company to another, often referred to as *benchmarking,* is an important activity. Metrics tell a firm if progress is being made toward improvement. Similar to the value of financial measures to accountants, process performance metrics give the operations manager a gauge on how productively a process currently is operating and how productivity is changing over time. Often operations managers need to improve the performance of a process or project the impact of a proposed change. The metrics described in this section are important for answering these questions. To help in understanding these calculations, Exhibit 4.3 shows how these metrics relate to one another.

Productivity

Possibly the most common process metric is utilization. As discussed earlier in the chapter, utilization is the ratio of the time that a resource is actually being used relative to the time that it is available for use. Utilization is always measured in reference to some resource—for example, the utilization of direct labor or the utilization of a machine resource. The distinction between productivity and utilization is important. **Productivity** is the ratio of output to input. Total factor productivity is usually measured in monetary units, dollars for example, by taking the dollar value of the output (such as goods and services sold) and dividing by the cost of all the inputs (that is, material, labor, and capital investment). Alternatively, *partial factor productivity* is measured based on an individual input, labor being the most common. Partial factor productivity answers the question of how

EXHIBIT 4.3

Process Performance Metrics

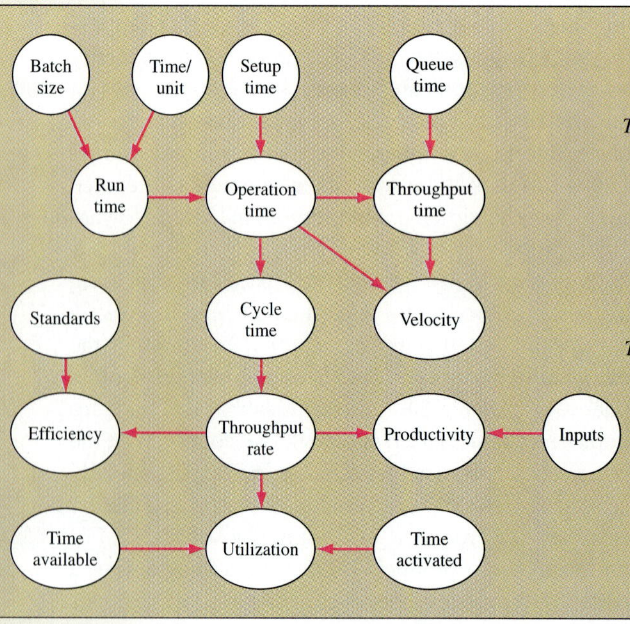


*Operation time* = *Setup time* + *Run time*

*Throughput time* = *Average time for a unit to move through the system*

$$\textit{Velocity} = \frac{\textit{Throughput time}}{\textit{Value-added time}}$$

*Cycle time* = *Average time between completion of units*

$$\textit{Throughput rate} = \frac{1}{\textit{Cycle time}}$$

$$\textit{Efficiency} = \frac{\textit{Actual output}}{\textit{Standard output}}$$

$$\textit{Productivity} = \frac{\textit{Output}}{\textit{Input}}$$

$$\textit{Utilization} = \frac{\textit{Time activated}}{\textit{Time available}}$$

much output we can get from a given level of input; for example, how many computers are made per employee working in the computer manufacturing plant? (See Chapter 2 for additional information about productivity.) Utilization measures the actual activation of the resource. For example, what is the percentage of time that an expensive machine is actually operating?

Efficiency

**Efficiency** is a ratio of the actual output of a process relative to some standard. For example, consider a machine designed to package cereal at a rate of 30 boxes per minute. If during a shift the operators actually produce at a rate of 36 boxes per minute, then the efficiency of the machine is 120 percent (36/30). An alternative way that the term *efficiency* is used is to measure the loss or gain in a process. For example, if 1,000 units of energy are put into a process designed to convert that energy to some alternative form, and the process produces only 800 units of energy in the new form, then the process is 80 percent efficient.

Run time

Setup time

Operation time

**Run time** is the time required to produce a batch of parts. This is calculated by multiplying the time required to produce each unit by the batch size. The **setup time** is the time required to prepare a machine to make a particular item. Machines that have significant setup time will typically run parts in batches. The **operation time** is the sum of the setup time and run time for a batch of parts that are run on a machine. Consider the cereal- boxing machine that is designed to produce at a rate of 30 boxes per minute. The run time for each box is 2 seconds. To switch the machine from 16-ounce boxes to 12-ounce boxes requires a setup time of 30 minutes. The operation time to make a batch of 10,000 12-ounce boxes is 21,800 seconds (30 minutes setup × 60 seconds/minute + 2 seconds/box × 10,000 boxes) or 363.33 minutes.

In practice, often setup time is not included in the utilization of the process. In essence, setup time is categorized like the downtime caused by repair or some other disruption to the process. This assumption can vary from company to company, so it is important when comparing the utilization of a machine or other resource to understand exactly how the company categorizes setup time.

Throughput time

Throughput rate

The cycle time (also defined earlier in this chapter) is the elapsed time between starting and completing a job.* Another related term is **throughput time.** Throughput time includes the time that the unit spends actually being worked on together with the time spent waiting in a queue. As a simple example, consider a paced assembly line that has six stations and runs with a cycle time of 30 seconds. If the stations are located one right after another and every 30 seconds parts move from one station to the next, then the throughput time is three minutes (30 seconds × 6 stations/60 seconds per minute). The **throughput rate** is the output rate that the process is expected to produce over a period of time. The throughput rate of the assembly line is 120 units per hour (60 minutes/hour × 60 seconds/minute ÷ 30 seconds/unit). In this case, the throughput rate is the mathematical inverse of the cycle time.

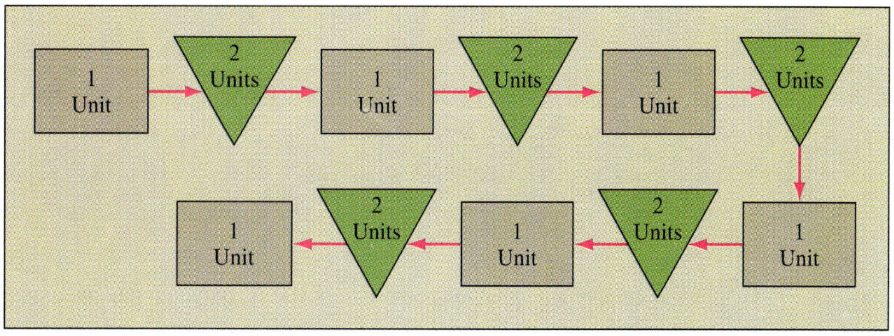


Often units are not worked on 100 percent of the time as they move through a process. Because there often is some variability in the cycle time of a process, buffers are incorporated in the process to allow individual activities to operate independently, at least to some extent. In the six-station assembly line just described, consider the impact of having 10 additional buffer positions along the line. Assume that two of these positions

*Often the term *cycle time* is used to mean *throughput time*. It is important to carefully determine how the term is being used in the context of the process being studied.

are between the first and second workstation, two are between stations 2 and 3, and so forth. If these positions were always occupied, then the throughput time is eight minutes (assuming a total of 16 positions along the assembly line and an average cycle time of 30 seconds).

Process velocity (throughput ratio)

Value-added time

**Process velocity** (also known as **throughput ratio**) is the ratio of the total throughput time to the value-added time. **Value-added time** is the time that useful work is actually being done on the unit. Assuming that all of the activities that are included in the process are value-added activities, value-added time should be the sum of the activity operation times in the process. The process velocity (or throughput ratio) for our assembly line with the 10 additional buffer positions, assuming the positions are used 100 percent of the time, is 2.66 (8 minutes/3 minutes).

Little's Law

**Little's Law**[1] states a mathematical relationship between throughput rate, throughput time, and the amount of work-in-process inventory. Little's Law is useful for estimating the time that an item will spend in work-in-process inventory, which can be useful for calculating the total throughput time for a process. Using the terminology defined in this section, Little's Law is defined as follows:

$$\text{Throughput time} = \frac{\text{Work-in-process}}{\text{Throughput rate}}$$

Notice how this law holds for the example of the assembly line without the buffer inventory. If the assembly line has six stations with one unit of work-in-process at each station, and the throughput rate is two units per minute (60 seconds/30 seconds per unit), then the throughput time is three minutes (6 units/2 units per minute). In general, this equation is useful when two of the three quantities are known. For example, if the throughput time and throughput rate are known, the work-in-process can be calculated. This formula holds for any process that is operating at a steady rate. An example of this is demonstrated in the following section. Little's Law can often help diagnose the performance of a process.

## PROCESS ANALYSIS EXAMPLES

In this section the concepts described thus far in the chapter are illustrated with three examples. These examples are typical of the types of analysis that are performed in manufacturing, services, and logistics businesses. Keep in mind that the analysis used in each example can be applied to many different contexts. Be creative in applying something that you have seen in another context to the problem at hand. The first example analyzes a bread-making process. Following this, a restaurant operation is evaluated. Finally, a typical logistics operation is appraised.

### A BREAD-MAKING OPERATION[2]

*EXAMPLE 4.1: BREAD MAKING*

For the manager of a bakery, a first priority is to understand the products that are made and the process steps required. Exhibit 4.4A is a simplified diagram of the bread-making process. There are two steps required to prepare the bread. The first is preparing the dough and baking the loaves, here referred to as bread making. The second is packaging the loaves. Due to the size of the mixers in the bakery, bread is made in batches of 100 loaves. Bread making completes a batch of 100 loaves every hour, which is the cycle time for the activity. Packaging needs only 0.75 hour to place the 100 loaves in bags.

From this we see that bread making is the bottleneck in the process. A bottleneck is the activity in a process that limits the overall capacity of the process. So if we assume that the bread-making and packaging activities both operate the same amount of time each day, then the bakery has a capacity of 100 loaves per hour. Notice that over the course of the day the packaging operation will be idle for

EXHIBIT 4.4

Bread-Making Processes

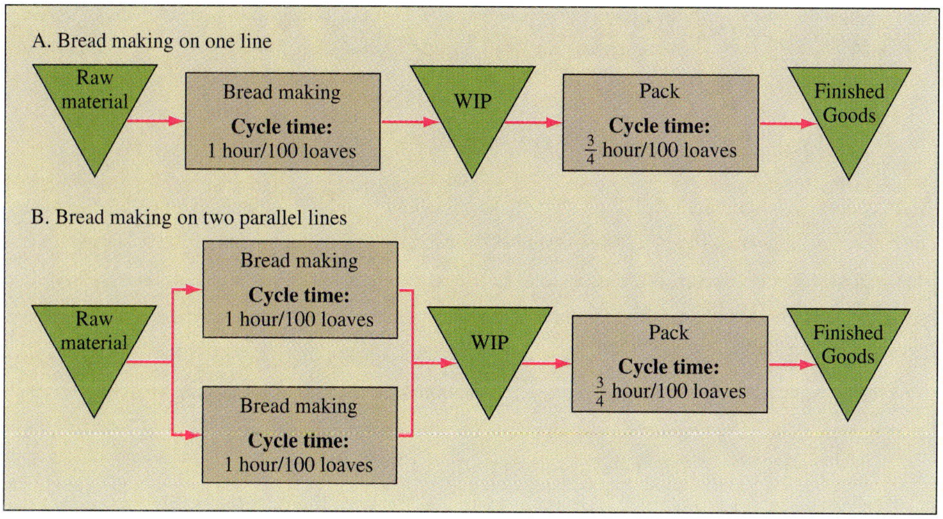


quarter-hour periods in which the next batch of bread is still being made but packaging has already completed bagging the previous batch. One would expect that the packaging operation would be utilized only 75 percent of the time under this scenario.

Suppose that instead of having only one bread-making operation we now have two, as shown in Exhibit 4.4B. The cycle time for each individual bread-making operation is still one hour per 100 loaves. The cycle time for the two bread-making lines operating together is half an hour. Because the packaging operation takes 0.75 hour to bag 100 loaves, the packaging operation now is the bottleneck. If both bread making and packaging were operated the same number of hours each day, it would be necessary to limit how much bread was made because we do not have the capacity to package it. However, if we operated the packaging operation for three shifts and bread making for two shifts each day, then the daily capacity of each would be identical at 3,200 loaves a day (this assumes that the packaging operation starts up one hour after the bread-making operation). Doing this requires building up a shift's worth of inventory each day as work-in-process. Packaging would bag this during the third shift. So what is the throughput time of our bakery?

## SOLUTION

In the original operation with just the single bread-making process, this is easy to calculate because inventory would not build between the bread-making and packaging processes. In this case the throughput time would be 1.75 hours. In the case where we operate the packaging operation for three shifts, the average wait in work-in-process inventory needs to be considered. If both bread-making operations start at the same time, then the first 100 loaves move immediately into packaging while the second 100 loaves wait. The waiting time for each 100-loaf batch increases until the baking is done at the end of the second shift.

This is a case where Little's Law can estimate the time that the bread is sitting in work-in-process. To apply Little's Law we need to estimate the average work-in-process between bread making and packaging. During the first two shifts inventory builds from 0 to 800 loaves. We can estimate the average work-in-process over this 16-hour period to be 400 loaves (half the maximum). Over the last eight-hour shift inventory drops from the 800-loaf maximum down to 0. Again the average work-in-process is 400 loaves. Given this, the overall average over the 24-hour period is simply 400 loaves of bread. The packing process limits the cycle time for the process to 0.75 hour per 100 loaves, and this is equivalent to a throughput rate of 133.3 loaves/hour ($100/0.75 = 133.3$). Little's Law calculates that the average time that loaves are in work-in-process is 3 hours (400 loaves/133.3 loaves/hour).

The total throughput time is the time that the loaves are in work-in-process plus the operations time for the bread-making and packaging processes. The total throughput time then is 4.75 hours (1 hour for bread making + 3 hours in inventory + 0.75 hour packaging). ←

## A RESTAURANT OPERATION

### EXAMPLE 4.2: A RESTAURANT

Our bakery operates in what is referred to as *steady state,* meaning that the operation is started up and runs at a steady rate during the entire time that it is in operation. The output of this steady state process is adjusted by setting the amount of time that the operation is run. In the case of the bakery, we assumed that bread making worked for three shifts and packaging for two shifts.

A restaurant cannot run in this manner. The restaurant must respond to varying customer demand throughout the day. During some peak times, it may be impossible to serve all customers immediately, and some customers may have to wait to be seated. The restaurant, because of this varying demand, is a *non–steady state* process. Keep in mind that many of the menu items in a restaurant can be pre-prepared. The pre-prepared items, salads and desserts for example, help speed the processes that must be performed when customers are at the restaurant being served.

Consider the restaurant in the casino that we discussed earlier. Because it is important that customers be served quickly, the managers have set up a buffet arrangement where customers serve themselves. The buffet is continually replenished to keep items fresh. To further speed service, a fixed amount is charged for the meal, no matter what the customer eats. Assume that we have designed our buffet so customers take an average of 30 minutes to get their food and eat. Further, assume that they typically eat in groups (or customer parties) of two or three to a table. The restaurant has 40 tables. Each table can accommodate four people. What is the maximum capacity of this restaurant?

### SOLUTION

It is easy to see that the restaurant can accommodate 160 people seated at tables at a time. Actually, in this situation it might be more convenient to measure the capacity in terms of customer parties because this is how the capacity will be used. If the average customer party is 2.5 individuals, then the average seat utilization is 62.5 percent (2.5 seats/party ÷ 4 seats/table) when the restaurant is operating at capacity. The cycle time for the restaurant, when operating at capacity, is 0.75 minutes (30 minutes/table ÷ 40 tables). So on average a table would become available every 45 seconds. The restaurant could handle 80 customer parties per hour (60 minutes ÷ 0.75 minutes/party).

The problem with this restaurant is that everyone wants to eat at the same time. Management has collected data and expects the following profile for customer parties arriving during lunch, which runs from 11:30 A.M. until 1:30 P.M. Customers are seated only until 1:00 P.M.

| TIME | PARTIES ARRIVING |
|---|---|
| 11:30–11:45 | 15 |
| 11:45–12:00 | 35 |
| 12:00–12:15 | 30 |
| 12:15–12:30 | 15 |
| 12:30–12:45 | 10 |
| 12:45–1:00 | 5 |
| Total parties | 110 |

Because the restaurant operates for two hours for lunch and the capacity is 80 customer parties per hour, it does not appear that the restaurant has a problem. In reality, though, there is a problem due to the uneven flow of customers into the restaurant. A simple way to analyze the situation is to calculate how we expect the system to look in terms of number of customers being served and number waiting in line at the end of each 15-minute interval. Think of this as taking a snapshot of the restaurant every 15 minutes.

The key to understanding the analysis is to look at the cumulative numbers. The difference between cumulative arrivals and cumulative departures gives the number of customer parties in the restaurant (those seated at tables and those waiting). Because there are only 40 tables, when the cumulative difference through a time interval is greater than 40, a waiting line forms. When all 40 tables are busy, the system is operating at capacity; and, from the previous calculation, we know the cycle time for the entire restaurant is 45 seconds per customer party at this time (this means that on average a table empties every 45 seconds). The last party will need to wait for all of the earlier parties to get a table, so the expected waiting time is the number of parties in line multiplied by the cycle time.

| Time | Parties Arriving (Cumulative) | Parties Departing (Cumulative) | Parties Either at Tables or Waiting to Be Served | Tables Used | Customer Parties Waiting | Expected Waiting Time |
|---|---|---|---|---|---|---|
| 11:30–11:45 | 15 | 0 | 15 | 15 | | |
| 11:45–12:00 | 35 (50) | 0 | 50 | 40 | 10 | 7.5 minutes |
| 12:00–12:15 | 30 (80) | 15 | 65 | 40 | 25 | 18.75 minutes |
| 12:15–12:30 | 15 (95) | 35 (50) | 45 | 40 | 5 | 3.75 minutes |
| 12:30–12:45 | 10 (105) | 30 (80) | 25 | 25 | | |
| 12:45–1:00 | 5 (110) | 15 (95) | 15 | 15 | | |
| 1:00–1:30 | | 15 (110) | 0 | | | |

The analysis shows that by 12 noon, 10 customer parties are waiting in line. This line builds to 25 parties by 12:15. The waiting line shortens to only five parties by 12:30.

So what can we do to solve our waiting line problem? One idea might be to shorten the cycle time for a single table; but customers are unlikely to be rushed through their lunch in less than 30 minutes. Another idea would be to add tables. If the restaurant could add 25 tables, then a wait would not be expected. Of course, this would eat into the space used for slot machines, so this alternative might not be attractive to casino management. A final idea might be to double up parties at the tables, thus getting a higher seat utilization. Doubling up might be the easiest thing to try. If 25 out of the 40 tables were doubled up, our problem would be solved. ←

## PLANNING A TRANSIT BUS OPERATION

### *EXAMPLE 4.3: TRANSIT BUS OPERATION*

The final example involves a *logistics* system. The term *logistics* refers to the movement of things such as materials, people, or finished goods. Our example involves a bus route that would be typical of one used on campus or in a metropolitan area. A similar analysis could be used for analyzing plane routes, truck routes, or ships. Similar to the restaurant, a bus transit route does not operate in steady state. There are definite peaks in demand during the day and evening. A good approach to take, the same as was done with the restaurant, is to analyze distinct periods of time that represent the different types of demand patterns placed on the service. These distinct analyses can be referred to as *scenarios*. Depending on the situation, it might be reasonable to develop either a single solution that covers all the relevant scenarios or a set of solutions for the different scenarios.

A great bus route is the Balabus, or "tourist bus," in Paris. This route loops past all the major attractions in Paris. Some of the sights along the route include Notre-Dame, the Louvre, Concorde, Champs-Elysées, the Arc de Triomphe, the Eiffel Tower, and others.

Consider the problem of planning the number of buses needed to service this route. A number of factors need to be considered. A single bus takes approximately two hours to traverse the route during peak traffic. The route has approximately 60 stops, although the bus stops only when passengers on the bus request a stop or when the driver sees customers waiting to board at a stop. Each bus has seating capacity of about 50 passengers, and another 30 passengers can stand. This route is busy much of the day because visitors to the city tend to start visiting the sites early and continue until dark. Finally, the transit authority wants to give good service and have enough capacity to handle peak customer loads. The following is an analysis of the situation.

## SOLUTION

A key measure of service is how long a customer must wait prior to the arrival of a bus. Consider initially the case of only a single bus serving the route. If a person at a random time comes to a bus stop, we know that the maximum time that the customer needs to wait is two hours. This would be the case when the unlucky customer just missed the bus. If the bus was halfway through the route (relative to where the customer is waiting), then the customer needs to wait one hour. Continuing with this logic, we can estimate the average wait time for the customer to be one hour. In general, we can say that the average wait time would be half the cycle time of the process. If two buses are used, the cycle time is one hour and the average wait is 30 minutes. If we want the average wait to be two minutes, then the required cycle time is four minutes, and 30 buses are needed (120 minutes ÷ 4 minutes/bus = 30 buses).

The next issue relates to the capacity of the system. If we have 30 buses on the route and each bus seats 50 passengers with another 30 standing, we know that we can accommodate 1,500 seated or 2,400 passengers in total at one point in time.

Assume that the following table is an estimate of the number of passengers that travel the route during a typical tourist season day. The table shows calculations of the amount of bus capacity required during each hour. If a customer rides the bus for 45 minutes, then one seat is needed for 45 minutes, or 0.75 hour, to handle that passenger. Of course, 60 minutes, or a full hour's worth, of capacity is available for each seat that we have. At maximum utilization including standing, each bus can handle 80 passenger-hours' worth of load. Dividing the expected passenger load during the hour by the maximum load for a single bus calculates the minimum number of bases needed. Similarly, dividing the expected passenger load by the number of seats on each bus calculates the number of buses needed so that all passengers can be seated.

| Time | Number of Customers | Average Time on Bus | Load (Passenger Hours) | Minimum Number of Buses Needed | Buses Needed for All Passengers to Be Seated |
|---|---|---|---|---|---|
| 8:00–9:00 A.M. | 2,000 | 45 minutes | 1,500 | 18.75 | 30 |
| 9:00–10:00 A.M. | 4,000 | 30 minutes | 2,000 | 25 | 40 |
| 10:00–11:00 A.M. | 6,000 | 30 minutes | 3,000 | 37.5 | 60 |
| 11:00 A.M.–12:00 P.M. | 5,000 | 30 minutes | 2,500 | 31.25 | 50 |
| 12:00–1:00 P.M. | 4,000 | 30 minutes | 2,000 | 25 | 40 |
| 1:00–2:00 P.M. | 3,500 | 30 minutes | 1,750 | 21.875 | 35 |
| 2:00–3:00 P.M. | 3,000 | 45 minutes | 2,250 | 28.125 | 45 |
| 3:00–4:00 P.M. | 3,000 | 45 minutes | 2,250 | 28.125 | 45 |
| 4:00–5:00 P.M. | 3,000 | 45 minutes | 2,250 | 28.125 | 45 |
| 5:00–6:00 P.M. | 4,000 | 45 minutes | 3,000 | 37.5 | 60 |
| 6:00–7:00 P.M. | 3,000 | 45 minutes | 2,250 | 28.125 | 45 |
| 7:00–8:00 P.M. | 1,500 | 45 minutes | 1,125 | 14.0625 | 22.5 |
| TOTALS | 42,000 | | 25,875 | | |

From the analysis, if the Paris transit authority only uses 30 buses throughout the day, many people will need to stand. Further, during the morning rush between 10 and 11 A.M. and the evening rush between 5 and 6 P.M., not all of the customers can be accommodated. It would seem reasonable that at least 40 buses should be used between 9 A.M. and 7 P.M. Even with this number of buses, one would expect passengers to be standing most of the time.

If the transit authority decided to use 40 buses between the extended hours of 8 A.M. through 8 P.M., what would be the average utilization of the buses in terms of seats occupied? Over this 12-hour period, 24,000 seat-hours of capacity would be available (40 buses × 12 hours × 50 seats/bus). The table indicates that 25,875 seat-hours are needed. The utilization would be 107.8 percent (25,875/24,000 × 100). What this means is that on average 7.8 percent of the customers must stand. Of course, this average value significantly understates the severe capacity problem that occurs during the peak times of the day. ←

Consider how useful this type of analysis is to the Paris transit authority. Data can be collected for each day of the week and the analysis performed. Interesting questions concerning the design of the route or the capacity of the buses can be evaluated. Consider, for example, what would happen if the route were split into two parts. What if larger buses that could carry 120 passengers were put into service? The analysis can be extended to include the cost of providing the service by considering the wages paid the operators, the cost to maintain and operate the vehicles, and depreciation of the buses. As seen from this example, designing a transit system involves a trade-off between the convenience of the service, or how frequently buses arrive at each stop, and the capacity utilization of the buses.

## PROCESS THROUGHPUT TIME REDUCTION

Critical processes are subject to the well-known rule that time is money. For example, the longer a customer waits, the more likely it is that the customer will switch to a different vendor. The longer material is kept in inventory, the higher the investment cost. Unfortunately, critical processes often depend on specific limited resources, resulting in bottlenecks. Throughput time can sometimes be reduced without purchasing additional equipment. The following are some suggestions for reducing the throughput time of a process that do not require the purchase of new equipment. Often a combination of ideas is appropriate.[3]

THE SPEED WITH WHICH A COMPANY CAN DESIGN AND DEVELOP NEW PRODUCTS IS A CRITICAL ELEMENT IN ITS ABILITY TO INTRODUCE NEW PRODUCTS INTO THE MARKETPLACE. RAPID PROTOTYPING MACHINES CAN QUICKLY PRODUCE THREE-DIMENSIONAL PROTOTYPES ALLOWING DESIGN, ENGINEERING, AND PRODUCTION PEOPLE TO GIVE THEIR INPUT AND TEST THE DESIGN EARLY IN THE DEVELOPMENT CYCLE. THESE MODELS RESULT IN HIGHER QUALITY PRODUCTS AND LOWER DEVELOPMENT COSTS.

1 **Perform activities in parallel.** Most of the steps in an operations process are performed in sequence. A serial approach results in the throughput time for the entire process being the sum of the individual steps plus transport and waiting time between steps. Using a parallel approach can reduce throughput time by as much as 80 percent and produces a better result.

A classic example is product development, where the current trend is toward concurrent engineering. Instead of forming a concept, making drawings, creating a bill of materials, and mapping processes, all activities are performed in parallel by integrated teams. Development time is reduced dramatically, and the needs of all those involved are addressed during the development process.

2 **Change the sequence of activities.** Documents and products are often transported back and forth between machines, departments, buildings, and so forth. For instance, a document might be transferred between two offices a number of times for inspection and signing. If the sequence of some of these activities can be altered, it may be possible to perform much of the document's processing when it comes to a building the first time.

3 **Reduce interruptions.** Many processes are performed with relatively large time intervals between each activity. For example, purchase orders may be issued only every other day. Individuals preparing reports that result in purchase orders should be aware of deadlines to avoid missing them, because improved timing in these processes can save many days of throughput time.

To illustrate these ideas, consider an electronics manufacturer that has been receiving customer complaints about a long order lead time of 29 days. As assessment of the order-processing system revealed 12 instances where managers had to approve employees' work. It was determined that the first 10 approvals were not needed. This saved an average of seven to eight days in the order processing.

Many subsystems—each performing the same or similar tasks—had interfered with the process. The logical step was to eliminate redundancy, and a detailed flowchart of the process was created. At close inspection, 16 steps proved very similar to one another. Changing the sequence of activities and creating one companywide order document removed 13 of these steps.

Over four months, the order system was totally redesigned to allow information to be entered once and become available to the entire organization. Due to this adjustment, activities could be handled in a parallel manner. After a value-added analysis (focused on eliminating the non–value-adding activities), the manufacturer was able to reduce the customer order lead time from 29 days to 9 days, save cost and employee time per order, and increase customer satisfaction.

## CONCLUSION

Process analysis is a basic skill needed to understand how a business operates. Great insight is obtained by drawing a simple flowchart showing the flow of materials or information through an enterprise. The diagram should include all the operating elements and show how they fit together. Be sure to indicate where material is stored or where orders are queued. Often 90 percent or more of the time that is required to serve a customer is spent just waiting. Hence, merely eliminating the waiting time can dramatically improve the performance of the process.

Remember this fundamental concept when analyzing a process: What goes into the process must come out of the process. A process taken as a whole is like the funnel shown in Exhibit 4.5. The outlet of the funnel restricts the amount that can flow through. In a real business process, certain resources limit output. If too much liquid is poured into the funnel, the level in the funnel will continue to grow. As the level of liquid in the funnel grows, the time that it takes the liquid to flow through the funnel increases. If too much liquid is poured into the funnel, it just spills over the top and never flows through.

EXHIBIT 4.5

What Goes in a Process Must Come out of the Process

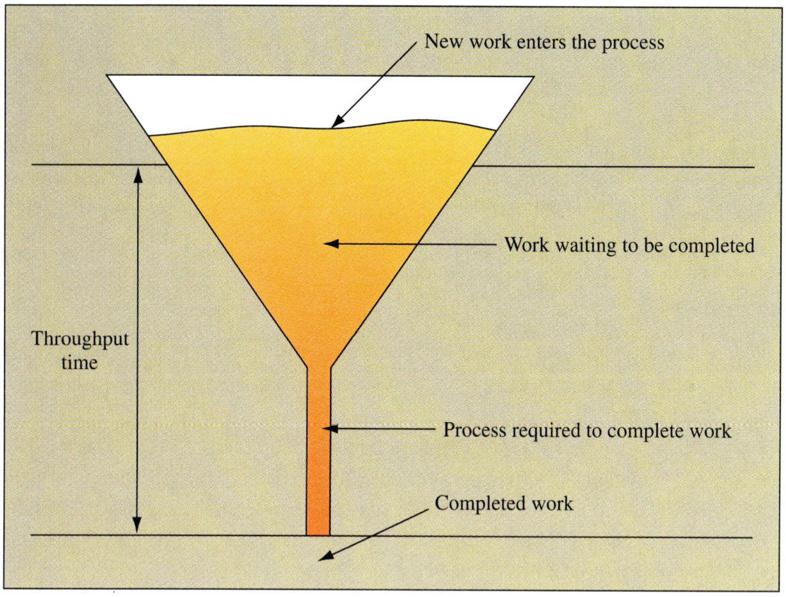


The same is true of a real process. If too many jobs are pumped into the process, the time that it takes to complete a job will increase because the waiting time will increase. At some point, customers will go somewhere else and the business will be lost. When a process is operating at capacity, the only way to take on more work without increasing the waiting time is to add more capacity. This requires finding what activity is limiting the output of the process and increasing the capacity of that activity. In essence, the tube leading out of the funnel needs to be made larger.

## KEY TERMS

**Process** Any set of activities performed by an organization that takes inputs and transforms them into outputs ideally of greater value to the organization than the original inputs.

**Cycle time** The average time between completions of successive units in a process (this is the definition used in this book). The term is sometimes used to mean the elapsed time between starting and completing a job.

**Utilization** The ratio of the time that a resource is actually activated relative to the time that it is available for use.

**Buffering** A storage area between stages where the output of a stage is placed prior to being used in a downstream stage. Buffering allows the stages to operate independently.

**Blocking** The activities in the stage must stop because there is no place to deposit the item just completed.

**Starving** The activities in a stage must stop because there is no work.

**Bottleneck** A resource that limits the capacity or maximum output of the process.

**Make-to-order** A process that is activated only in response to an actual order.

**Make-to-stock** A process that produces standard products that are stored in finished goods inventory. The product is delivered quickly to the customer from the finished goods inventory.

**Hybrid** Combines the features of both make-to-order and make-to-stock. Typically a generic product is made and stocked at some point in the process. These generic units are customized in a final process to meet actual orders.

**Pacing** Movement of items through a process is coordinated through a timing mechanism. Most processes are not paced, but assembly lines usually are paced.

**Productivity** The ratio of output to input. Taking the dollar value of the output and dividing by the dollar value of the inputs usually measures total factor productivity. Alternatively, *partial factor productivity* is measured based on an individual input and often is not calculated using dollar values (an example would be units/person).

**Efficiency** A ratio of the actual output of a process relative to some standard.

**Run time** The time required to produce a batch of parts.

**Setup time** The time required to prepare a machine to make a particular item.

**Operation time** The sum of the setup time and run time for a batch of parts that are run on a machine.

**Throughput time** The average time that it takes a unit to move through an entire process. Usually the term *lead time* is used to refer to the total time that it takes a customer to receive an order (includes time to process the order, throughput time, and delivery time).

**Throughput rate** The output rate that the process is expected to produce over a period of time.

**Process velocity** or **throughput ratio** The ratio of the total throughput time to the value-added time.

**Value-added time** The time in which useful work is actually being done on the unit.

**Little's Law** States a mathematical relationship between throughput rate, throughput time, and the amount of work-in-process inventory. Throughput time is equal to work-in-process divided by the throughput rate.

## Review and Discussion Questions

1 Compare McDonald's old and new processes for making hamburgers. How valid is McDonald's claim that the new process will produce fresher hamburgers for the customer? Comparing McDonald's new process to the processes used by Burger King and Wendy's, which process would appear to produce the freshest hamburgers?

2 State in your own words what Little's Law means. Describe an example that you have observed where Little's Law applies.

3 Explain how having more work-in-process inventory can improve the efficiency of a process. How can this be bad?

4 Recently some operations management experts have begun insisting that simply minimizing process velocity, which actually means minimizing the time that it takes to process something through the system, is the single most important measure for improving a process. Can you think of a situation in which this might not be true?

## Problems[4]

1. Traditional method 20 min. setup + 10 × 2 = 40 min. total scan/retrieve system. 1 min. setup + 10 × 5 = 51 min. total. Traditional method is best.

1 An enterprising student has set up an internship clearinghouse for business students. Each student that uses the service fills out a form and lists up to 10 companies that he or she would like to have contacted. The clearinghouse has a choice of two methods to use for processing the forms. The traditional method requires about 20 minutes to review the form and arrange the information in the proper order for processing. Once this setup is done, it takes only two minutes per company requested to complete the processing. The other alternative uses an optical scan/retrieve system, which takes only a minute to prepare but requires five minutes per company for completing the processing. If it costs about the same amount per minute for processing with either of the two methods, when should each be used?

2. Step 2 is the bottleneck and can process only (40 × 60)/1.5 = 1,600 students per week.

2 Rockness Recycling refurbishes rundown business students. The process uses a moving belt, which carries each student through the five steps of the process in sequence. The five steps are as follows:

| Step | Description | Time Required per Student |
|---|---|---|
| 1 | Unpack and place on belt | 1.0 minutes |
| 2 | Strip off bad habits | 1.5 minutes |
| 3 | Scrub and clean mind | 0.8 minutes |
| 4 | Insert modern methods | 1.0 minutes |
| 5 | Polish and pack | 1.2 minutes |

One faculty member is assigned to each of these steps. Faculty members work a 40-hour week and rotate jobs each week. Mr. Rockness has been working on a contract from General Eclectic, which require delivery of 2,000 refurbished students per week. A representative of the human resources department has just called complaining that the company hasn't been receiving the agreed-upon number of students. A check of finished goods inventory by Mr. Rockness reveals that there is no stock left. What is going on?

3 The bathtub theory of operations management is being promoted as the next breakthrough for global competitiveness. The factory is a bathtub with 50 gallons of capacity. The drain is the outlet to the market and can output three gallons per hour when wide open. The faucet is the raw material input and can let material in at a rate of four gallons per hour. Now, to test your comprehension of the intricacies of operations (assume the bathtub is empty to begin with):

*a.* Draw a diagram of the factory and determine the maximum rate at which the market can be served if all valves are set to maximum. What happens to the system over time?

*b.* Suppose that instead of a faucet, a five-gallon container is used for filling the bathtub (assume a full container is next to the tub to begin with); it takes two hours to refill the container and return it to the bathtub. What happens to the system over time?

3. *a.* Market can be served only 3 gals/hr. In 50 hrs. bathtub will overflow.
*b.* System will be drained every 2 hrs. and only 2.5 gals/hr. demand will be served 0.5 gallons/hr. will be stocked out.

4 A local market research firm has just won a contract for several thousand small projects involving data gathering and statistical analysis. In the past the firm has assigned each project to a single member of its highly trained professional staff. This person would both gather and analyze the data. Using this approach an experienced person can complete an average of 10 such projects in an eight-hour day.

The firm's management is thinking of assigning two people to each project in order to allow them to specialize and become more efficient. The process would require the data gatherer to fill out a matrix on the computer, check it, and transmit it to the statistical analysis program for the analyst to complete. Data can be gathered on one project while the analysis is being completed on another, but the analysis must be complete before the statistical analysis program can accept the new data. After some practice, the new process can be completed with a standard time of 20 minutes for the data gathering and 30 minutes for the analysis.

*a.* What is the production (output per hour) for each alternative? What is the productivity (output per labor hour)?

*b.* How long would it take to complete 1,000 projects with each alternative? What would be the labor content (total number of labor hours) for 1,000 projects for each alternative?

4. *a.* Single operator rate = 10 projects/8 hrs. = 1.25 projects/hr. Productivity = 1.25 projects/hr. 2 operators, 2nd limits to rate of 2 projects/hr. Ist operator would be idle Avg. 10 min. each hour.
*b.* 1,000 projects/1.25 projects/hr = 800 hrs. or 100 days. 2 operators = 1,000 projects/2 projects/hr. = 500 hrs. or 62.5 days.

## ADVANCED PROBLEM

Excel: Bottleneck Simulation

5 Remember Mr. Rockness in Problem 2? He now retrains college professors. It is a much more challenging task but still involves five steps. He has worked hard to balance the line; however, there is a lot of variability. Each stage in the process now handles between one and six faculty members per hour depending on how bad the case is. If there is some inventory available for every position (do not worry about the startup), what is the expected output per hour? (Assume that each stage is independent and that it is equally likely that one, two, three, four, five, or six faculty members get processed each hour at each stage.)*

5. Output = 3.5 students per hour. Actual output per hour is less due to the starving in the system.

## CASE: ANALYZING CASINO MONEY-HANDLING PROCESSES

Retrieving money from a slot machine is referred to as the *drop process.* The drop process begins with a security officer and the slot drop team leader obtaining the slot cabinet keys from the casino cashier's cage. Getting the keys takes about 15 minutes. The slot drop team consists of employees from the hard count coin room, security, and accounting. The slot drop leader, under the observation of a security officer and a person from accounting, actually removes the drop bucket from the slot machine cabinet. When the drop bucket is pulled from the slot cabinet, a tag with the proper slot machine number is placed on top of the coins to identify where that bucket came from when the weigh process begins. Retrieving the drop bucket takes about 10 minutes per slot machine. Once a cart is filled with buckets from 20 different slot machines, the drop team leader and security and accounting people deliver the buckets to the hard count room. The buckets are securely locked in the hard count room to await the start of the hard count process. Delivering and securing the buckets takes about 30 minutes per cart.

The hard count process is performed at a designated time known to gaming regulatory authorities. The hard count team first tests the weigh scale, which takes 10 minutes. The scale determines the dollar value, by denomination, for set weights of 10 and 25 pounds. These results are compared to calibration results, calculated when the scale was last serviced, to determine if a significant variance exists. If one does exist, the hard count supervisor must contact the contractor responsible for maintaining the scale and the controller's office. If no significant variance is found, the weigh process can continue.

Following the scale check, each drop bucket is emptied into the weigh scale holding hopper. Using information from the identification tag, the specific slot machine number from which the bucket

*The idea for this problem came from an exercise developed by Dr. Eli Goldratt titled "The Great Manufacturing Crapshoot."

originated is entered into the weigh scale computer. The weigh scale computer is programmed to convert the weight of coins, by denomination, into specific dollar values, which are recorded in the weigh journal along with the slot machine number. This weighing and recording process takes seven minutes per bucket. Once the scale has weighed the contents of the drop bucket, the coins automatically drop onto a conveyor belt, which transports them to wrapping machines. As the coins are wrapped, the rolls of coins drop onto another conveyor belt, which takes them to a canning station. Twenty-five silver dollars are wrapped in each roll at a rate of 10 rolls per minute.

At the canning station, the coin rolls are placed in metal or plastic cans that hold specific dollar amounts based on coin denomination. The cans are stacked to facilitate counting the wrapped coins. Silver dollar cans hold $1,000, or 40 rolls, and take five minutes to fill and stack. When the weigh process is completed, the weigh scale computer runs a summary report totaling the weight by denomination. These totals are recorded on the weigh/wrap verification report, which takes five minutes to produce.

When the wrap portion of the count is completed and all of the rolled coins have been canned and stacked, they are manually counted by denomination. These totals are also recorded on the weigh/wrap verification report. The variance in both dollar amounts and percentages, for each denomination, is calculated. Variances that exceed plus or minus 2 percent or are $1,000 or greater (whichever is less) must be investigated by the hard count supervisor, who writes an explanatory report. If no significant variances exist, all members of the hard count team sign the weigh/wrap verification report. To complete the hard count process, the casino cashier's cage is then notified that the slot drop is ready to be transferred into cage accountability. Manually counting and verifying the counts takes on average two minutes per can.

In a process separate from the hard count, a cage cashier performs an independent count and verification, by denomination, of the wrap. If everything balances, the main bank cashier signs the weigh/wrap verification report, accepting the slot drop into cage accountability. It is at this point that the actual slot gross gaming revenue is recognized.

#### QUESTIONS

1. Draw a diagram of the drop process. How long should it take to empty 300 silver dollar slot machines?
2. Draw a diagram of the hard count process. How long should this process take to complete for 300 silver dollar slot machines?
3. The casino is considering the purchase of a second coin-wrapping machine. What impact would this have on the hard count process? Is this the most desirable machine to purchase?

## SELECTED BIBLIOGRAPHY

Anupindai, R.; S. Chopra; S. D. Deshmukh; J. A. van Mieghem; and E. Zemel. *Managing Business Process Flows.* Upper Saddle River, NJ: Prentice Hall, 1999.

Gray, A. E., and J. Leonard. "Process Fundamentals." Harvard Business School 9-696-023.

Hopp, J. W., and M. L. Spearman. *Factory Physics: Foundations of Manufacturing Management.* Burr Ridge: Irwin/McGraw-Hill, 2000.

Suri, R. *Quick Response Manufacturing: A Companywide Approach to Reducing Lead Times.* Portland, OR: Productivity Press, 1998.

## FOOTNOTES

1 J. D. C. Little, "A Proof for the Queuing Formula: $L = \lambda W$," *Operations Research* X, no. X (1961), pp. 383–87. Special thanks to J. F. Muth, indiana university.

2 This example is similar to one given by A. E. Gray in "Capacity Analysis: Sample Problems," Harvard Business School (9-696-058).

3 B. Andersen, "Process Cycle Time Reduction," *Quality Progress,* July 1999, p. 120. For some additional guidelines for improving process also see Chapter 16.

4 The authors are indebted to D. Clay. Whybark of the University of North Carolina for contributing these problems.

technical note

TECHNICAL NOTE

*technical note four*

# JOB DESIGN AND WORK MEASUREMENT

## OUTLINE AND KEY TERMS

The operations manager's job, by definition, deals with managing the personnel that create a firm's products and services. To say that this is a challenging job in today's complex environment is an understatement. The diversity of the workforce's cultural and educational background, coupled with frequent organization restructuring, calls for a much higher level of people management skills than has been required in even the recent past.

The objective in managing personnel is to obtain the highest productivity possible without sacrificing quality, service, or responsiveness. The operations manager uses job design techniques to structure the work so that it will meet both the physical and behavioral needs of the human worker. Work measurement methods are used to determine the most efficient means of performing a given task, as well as to set reasonable standards for performing it. People are motivated by many things, only one of which is financial reward. Operations managers can structure such rewards not only to motivate consistently high performance but also to reinforce the most important aspects of the job.

## JOB DESIGN DECISIONS

Job design

**Job design** may be defined as the function of specifying the work activities of an individual or group in an organizational setting. Its objective is to develop job structures that meet the requirements of the organization and its technology and that satisfy the jobholder's personal and individual requirements. Exhibit TN4.1 summarizes the decisions involved. These decisions are affected by the following trends:

1 **Quality control as part of the worker's job.** Now often referred to as "quality at the source" (see Chapter 7), quality control is linked with the concept of empowerment. *Empowerment,* in turn, refers to workers being given authority to stop a production line if there is a quality problem, or to give a customer an on-the-spot refund if service was not satisfactory.

2 **Cross-training workers to perform multiskilled jobs.** As companies downsize, the remaining workforce is expected to do more and different tasks.

3 **Employee involvement and team approaches to designing and organizing work.** This is a central feature in total quality management (TQM) and continuous improvement efforts. In fact, it is safe to say that virtually all TQM programs are team based.

EXHIBIT TN4.1

Job Design Decisions

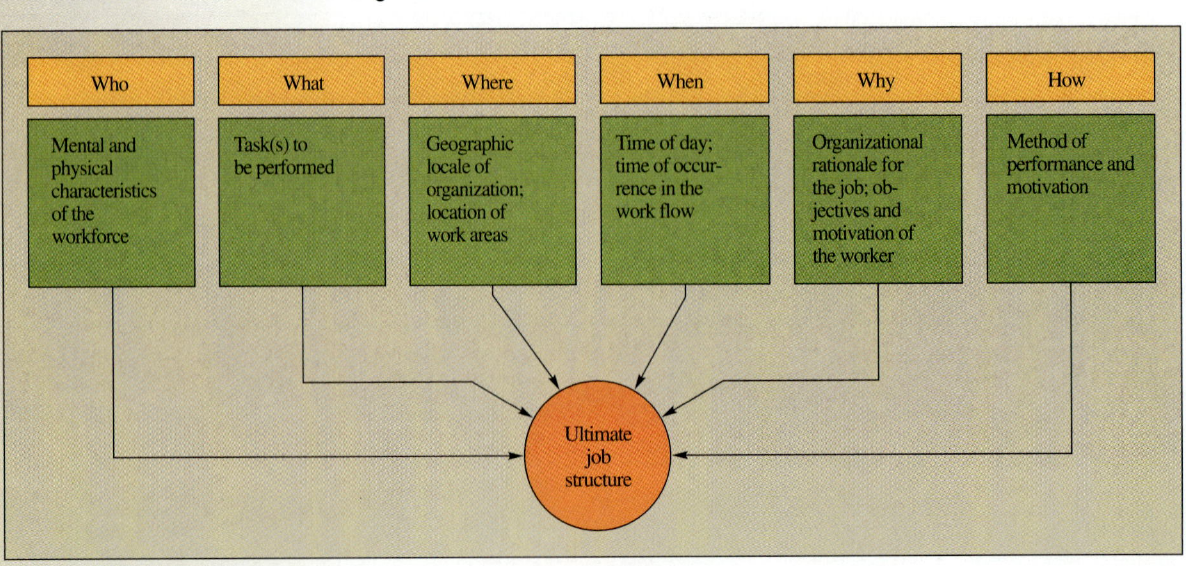

4 **"Informating" ordinary workers through telecommunication networks and computers, thereby expanding the nature of their work and their ability to do it.** In this context, informating is more than just automating work—it is revising work's fundamental structure. Northeast Utilities' computer system, for example, can pinpoint a problem in a service area before the customer service representative answers the phone. The rep uses the computer to troubleshoot serious problems, to weigh probabilities that other customers in the area have been affected, and to dispatch repair crews before other calls are even received.

5 **Extensive use of temporary workers.** Manpower, a company specializing in providing temporary employees, is vying with McDonald's as the largest private employer in the United States with over 500,000 workers on its payroll.

6 **Automation of heavy manual work.** Examples abound in both services (one-person trash pickup trucks) and manufacturing (robot spray painting on auto lines). These changes are driven by safety regulations as well as economics and personnel reasons.

7 **Most important of all, organizational commitment to providing meaningful and rewarding jobs for all employees.** Hewlett-Packard's mission statement lists three "people-related objectives: (1) belief in our people; (2) emphasis on working together and sharing rewards (teamwork and partnership); and (3) a superior working environment that other companies seek but few achieve."

# BEHAVIORAL CONSIDERATIONS IN JOB DESIGN

## DEGREE OF LABOR SPECIALIZATION

Specialization of labor

**Specialization of labor** is the two-edged sword of job design. On one hand, specialization has made possible high-speed, low-cost production, and from a materialistic standpoint, it has greatly enhanced our standard of living. On the other hand, extreme specialization (as we see in mass-production industries) often has serious adverse effects on workers, which in turn are passed on to the production systems. In essence, the problem is to determine how much specialization is enough. At what point do the disadvantages outweigh the advantages? (See Exhibit TN4.2)

EXHIBIT TN4.2

Advantages and Disadvantages of Specialization of Labor

| Advantages of Specialization | |
|---|---|
| **To Management** | **To Labor** |
| 1. Rapid training of the workforce | 1. Little or no education required to obtain work |
| 2. Ease in recruiting new workers | 2. Ease in learning job |
| 3. High output due to simple, repetitive work | |
| 4. Low wages due to ease of substitutability of labor | |
| 5. Close control over work flow and workloads | |

| Disadvantages of Specialization | |
|---|---|
| **To Management** | **To Labor** |
| 1. Difficulty in controlling quality because no one has responsibility for entire product | 1. Boredom stemming from repetitive nature of work |
| 2. Worker dissatisfaction leading to hidden costs arising from turnover, absenteeism, tardiness, grievances, and intentional disruption of production process | 2. Little gratification from work itself because of small contribution to each item |
| 3. Reduced likelihood of improving the process because of workers' limited perspective | 3. Little or no control over the work pace, leading to frustration and fatigue (in assembly line situations) |
| 4. Limited flexibility to change the production process to produce new or improved products | 4. Little opportunity to progress to a better job because significant learning is rarely possible on fractionated work |

Recent research suggests that the disadvantages dominate the advantages much more commonly than was thought in the past. However, simply stating that, for purely humanitarian reasons, specialization should be avoided is risky. The reason, of course, is that people differ in what they want from their work and what they are willing to put into it. Some workers prefer not to make decisions about their work, some like to daydream on the job, and others are simply not capable of performing more complex work. To improve the quality of jobs, leading organizations try different approaches to job design. Two popular contemporary approaches are job enrichment and sociotechnical systems.

## JOB ENRICHMENT

*Job enlargement* generally entails adjusting a specialized job to make it more interesting to the job holder. A job is said to be enlarged *horizontally* if the worker performs a greater number or variety of tasks, and it is said to be enlarged *vertically* if the worker is involved in planning, organizing, and inspecting his or her own work. Horizontal job enlargement is intended to counteract oversimplification and to permit the worker to perform a "whole unit of work." Vertical enlargement (traditionally termed *job enrichment*) attempts to broaden workers' influence in the transformation process by giving them certain managerial powers over their own activities. Today, common practice is to apply both horizontal and vertical enlargement to a given job and refer to the total approach as **job enrichment.**

Job enrichment

The organizational benefits of job enrichment occur in both quality and productivity. Quality in particular improves dramatically because when individuals are responsible for their work output, they take ownership of it and simply do a better job. Also, because they have a broader understanding of the work process, they are more likely to catch errors and make corrections than if the job is narrowly focused. Productivity improvements also occur from job enrichment, but they are not as predictable or as large as the improvements in quality. The reason is that enriched work invaribly contains a mix of tasks that (for manual labor) causes interruptions in rhythm and different motions when switching from one task to the next. Such is not the case for specialized jobs.[1]

## SOCIOTECHNICAL SYSTEMS

Consistent with the job enrichment philosophy but focusing more on the interaction between technology and the work group is the **sociotechnical systems** approach. This approach attempts to develop jobs that adjust the needs of the production process technology to the needs of the worker and work group. The term was developed from studies of weaving mills in India and of coal mines in England in the early 1950s. These studies revealed that work groups could effectively handle many production problems better than management if they were permitted to make their own decisions on scheduling, work allocation among members, bonus sharing, and so forth. This was particularly true when variations in the production process required quick reactions by the group or when one shift's work overlapped with other shifts' work.

Sociotechnical systems

Since those pioneering studies, the sociotechnical approach has been applied in many countries—often under the heading of "autonomous work groups," "Japanese-style work groups," or employee involvement (EI) teams. Most major American manufacturing companies use work teams as the basic building block in so-called high employee involvement plants. They are now becoming common in service organizations as well. The benefits of teams are similar to those of individual job enrichment: They provide higher quality and greater productivity (they often set higher production goals than general management), do their own support work and equipment maintenance, and have increased chances to make meaningful improvements.[2]

One major conclusion from these applications is that the individual or work group requires a logically integrated pattern of work activities that incorporates the following job design principles:

1 **Task variety.** An attempt must be made to provide an optimal variety of tasks within each job. Too much variety can be inefficient for training and frustrating for

the employee. Too little can lead to boredom and fatigue. The optimal level is one that allows the employee to rest from a high level of attention or effort while working on another task or, conversely, to stretch after periods of routine activity.

2 **Skill variety.** Research suggests that employees derive satisfaction from using a number of skill levels.

3 **Feedback.** There should be some means for informing employees quickly when they have achieved their targets. Fast feedback aids the learning process. Ideally, employees should have some responsibility for setting their own standards of quantity and quality.

4 **Task identity.** Sets of tasks should be separated from other sets of tasks by some clear boundary. Whenever possible, a group or individual employee should have responsibility for a set of tasks that is clearly defined, visible, and meaningful. In this way, work is seen as important by the group or individual undertaking it, and others understand and respect its significance.

5 **Task autonomy.** Employees should be able to exercise some control over their work. Areas of discretion and decision making should be available to them.[3]

## PHYSICAL CONSIDERATIONS IN JOB DESIGN

Beyond the behavioral components of job design, another aspect warrants consideration: the physical side. Indeed, while motivation and work group structure strongly influence job performance, they may be of secondary importance if the job is too demanding from a physical (or "human factors") standpoint. One approach to incorporating the physical costs of moderate to heavy work in job design is **work physiology.** Pioneered by Eastman Kodak in the 1960s, work physiology sets work–rest cycles according to the energy expended in various parts of the job. For example, if a job entails caloric expenditure above five calories per minute (the rough baseline for sustainable work), the required rest period must equal or exceed the time spent working. Obviously, the harder the work, the more frequent and longer the rest periods. (Exhibit TN4.3 shows caloric requirements for various activities.)

Work physiology

**Ergonomics** is the term used to describe the study of the physical arrangement of the work space together with the tools used to perform a task. In applying ergonomics, we strive to fit the work to the body rather than forcing the body to conform to the work. As logical as this may sound, it is actually a recent point of view.

Ergonomics

EXHIBIT TN4.3

Calorie Requirements for Various Activities

| TYPE OF ACTIVITY | TYPICAL ENERGY COST IN CALORIES PER MINUTE* | REQUIRED MINUTES OF REST FOR EACH MINUTE OF WORK |
|---|---|---|
| Sitting at rest | 1.7 | — |
| Writing | 2.0 | — |
| Typing on a computer | 2.0 | — |
| Medium assembly work | 2.9 | — |
| Shoe repair | 3.0 | — |
| Machining | 3.3 | — |
| Ironing | 4.4 | — |
| Heavy assembly work | 5.1 | — |
| Chopping wood | 7.5 | 1 |
| Digging | 8.9 | 2 |
| Tending furnace | 12.0 | 3 |
| Walking upstairs | 12.0 | 3 |

*Five calories per minute is generally considered the maximum sustainable level throughout the workday.

OSHKOSH B'GOSH WORKERS WERE PLAGUED BY TENDONITIS AND NUMBNESS. THE COMPANY REDESIGNED THE JOB AND, USING ERGONOMICS, DESIGNED A PULLEY SYSTEM ALLOWING SEWERS TO WORK WITH THEIR ARMS AT REST. IN ADDITION, JOBS WERE ENLARGED THROUGH ROTATION SO PARTS OF THE BODY COULD REST.

## WORK METHODS

In contemporary industry, responsibility for developing work methods in large firms is typically assigned either to a staff department designated *methods analysis* or to an industrial engineering department. In small firms, this activity is often performed by consulting firms that specialize in work methods design.

The principal approach to the study of work methods is the construction of charts, such as operations charts, worker–machine charts, simo (simultaneous motion) charts, and activity charts, in conjunction with time study or standard time data. The choice of which charting method to use depends on the task's activity level—that is, whether the focus is on (1) a production process, (2) the worker at a fixed workplace, (3) a worker interacting with equipment, or (4) a worker interacting with other workers (see Exhibit TN4.4). (These charting techniques were introduced in Chapter 4, where they were used to aid in process analysis. Chapter 6 introduces the service blueprint that accounts for customer interactions.)

### A PRODUCTION PROCESS

The objective in studying a production process is to identify delays, transport distances, processes, and processing time requirements to simplify the entire operation. The underlying philosophy is to eliminate any step in the process that does not add value to the product. The approach is to flowchart the process and then ask the following questions:

What is done? Must it be done? What would happen if it were not done?

Where is the task done? Must it be done at that location or could it be done somewhere else?

When is the task done? Is it critical that it be done then or is there flexibility in time and sequence? Could it be combined with some other step in the process?

How is the task done? Why is it done this way? Is there another way?

Who does the task? Can someone else do it? Should the worker be of a higher or lower skill level?

EXHIBIT TN4.4

**Work Methods Design Aids**

| ACTIVITY | OBJECTIVE OF STUDY | STUDY TECHNIQUES |
|---|---|---|
| Production process | Eliminate or combine steps; shorten transport distance; identify delays | Flow diagram, service blueprint, process chart |
| Worker at fixed workplace | Simplify method; minimize motions | Operations charts, simo charts; apply principles of motion economy |
| Worker's interaction with equipment | Minimize idle time; find number or combination of machines to balance cost of worker and machine idle time | Activity chart, worker–machine charts |
| Worker's interaction with other workers | Maximize productivity; minimize interference | Activity charts, gang process charts |

These thought-provoking questions usually help eliminate much unnecessary work and simplify the remaining work by combining processing steps and changing the order of performance.

The process chart is valuable in studying an overall system, though care must be taken to follow the same item throughout the process. The subject may be a product being manufactured, a service being created, or a person performing a sequence of activities. Exhibit TN4.5 shows a process chart (and flow diagram) for a clerical operation. Exhibit TN4.6 shows common notation in process charting. Can you suggest any ways to improve this process? (See Problem 2.)

## WORKER AT A FIXED WORKPLACE

Many jobs require the worker to remain at a specified workstation. When the nature of the work is primarily manual (such as sorting, inspecting, making entries, or assembly operations), the focus of work design is on simplifying the work method and making the required operator motions as few and as easy as possible.

There are two basic ways to determine the best method when a methods analyst studies a single worker performing an essentially manual task. The first is to search among the workers and find the one who performs the job best. That person's method is then accepted as the standard, and others are trained to perform it in the same way. This was basically F. W. Taylor's approach, though after determining the best method, he searched for "first-class men" to perform according to the method. (A first-class worker possessed the natural ability to do much more productive work in a particular task than the average. Workers who were not first class were transferred to other jobs.) The second way is to observe the performance of a number of workers, analyze in detail each step of their work, and pick out the superior features of each worker's performance. This results in a composite method that combines the best elements of the group studied. Frank Gilbreth, the father of motion study, used this procedure to determine the "one best way" to perform a work task.

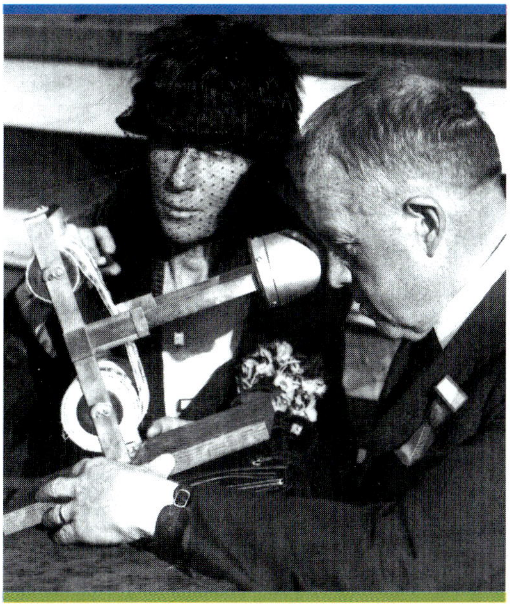

Taylor observed actual performance to find the best method; Frank Gilbreth and his wife Lillian relied on movie film. Through micromotion analysis—observing the filmed work performance frame by frame—the Gilbreths studied work very closely and defined its basic elements, which were termed *therbligs* ("Gilbreth" spelled backward, with the *t* and *h* transposed). Gilbreth is shown holding a wire representation of the path of motion. Their study led to the rules or principles of motion economy, such as "The hands should begin and complete the motions at the same time," and "Work should be arranged to permit natural rhythm."

Once the motions for performing the task have been identified, an *operations chart* may be made, listing the operations and their sequence of

EXHIBIT TN4.5

**Flow Diagram and Process Chart of an Office Procedure—Present Method**

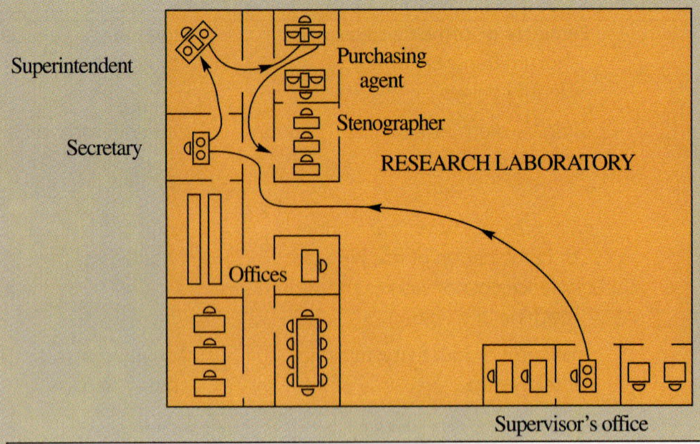


Present Method ☒ PROCESS CHART
Proposed Method ☐

SUBJECT CHARTED Requisition for small tools DATE ________
Chart begins at supervisor's desk and ends at CHART BY J.C.H.
typist's desk in purchasing department CHART NO. R136
DEPARTMENT Research laboratory SHEET NO. 1 OF 1

| DIST. IN FEET | TIME IN MINS. | CHART SYMBOLS | PROCESS DESCRIPTION |
|---|---|---|---|
| | 30 | | Requisitions written by supervisor (one copy) |
| | 180 | | On supervisor's desk (awaiting messenger) |
| 65 | 1 | | By messenger to superintendent's secretary |
| | 120 | | On secretary's desk (awaiting typing) |
| | 30 | | Requisition typed (original requisition copied) |
| 15 | .5 | | By secretary to superintendent |
| | 480 | | On superintendent's desk (awaiting messenger) |
| | 15 | | Examined and approved |
| | 480 | | On superintendent's desk (awaiting approval) |
| 20 | .5 | | To purchasing department |
| | 240 | | On purchasing agent's desk (awaiting approval) |
| | 30 | | Examined and approved |
| | 240 | | On purchasing agent's desk (awaiting messenger) |
| 5 | .25 | | To stenographer's desk |
| | 120 | | On stenographer's desk (awaiting typing of purchase order) |
| | 30 | | Purchase order typed |
| | 240 | | On stenographer's desk (awaiting transfer to main office) |
| | | | |
| | | | |
| 105 | 2241.25 | 3 4 2 8 | Total |

NOTE: REQUISITION IS WRITTEN BY A SUPERVISOR, TYPED BY A SECRETARY, APPROVED BY A SUPERINTENDENT, AND APPROVED BY A PURCHASING AGENT. THEN A PURCHASE ORDER IS PREPARED BY A STENOGRAPHER.

EXHIBIT TN4.6

**Notation for the Process Chart in Exhibit TN4.5**

Operation. Something is actually being done. This may be work on a product, some support activity, or anything that is directly productive in nature.

Transportation. The subject of the study (product, service, or person) moves from one location to another.

Inspection. The subject is observed for quality and correctness.

Delay. The subject of the study must wait before starting the next step in the process.

Storage. The subject is stored, such as finished products in inventory or completed papers in a file. Frequently, a distinction is made between temporary storage and permanent storage by inserting a T or P in the triangle.

performance. For greater detail, a *simo* (simultaneous motion) *chart* may be constructed, listing not only the operations but also the times for both left and right hands. This chart may be assembled from the data collected with a stopwatch, from analysis of a film of the operation, or from predetermined motion—time data (discussed later in the chapter). Many aspects of poor design are immediately obvious: a hand being used as a holding device (rather than a jig or fixture), an idle hand, or an exceptionally long time for positioning.

SOFTWARE FROM DENEB ROBOTICS IS DESIGNED TO HELP COMPANIES PLAN TO MEET PRODUCTION GOALS. WEARING A HARNESS WITH 11 SENSORS, THE WORKER DEMONSTRATES SOFTWARE THAT HELPS ENGINEERS MAXIMIZE EFFICIENCY ON A PRODUCTION LINE BY COORDINATING THE MOVEMENTS OF HUMANS AND ROBOTS WORKING SIDE BY SIDE (SEE THE MONITOR).

## WORKER INTERACTING WITH EQUIPMENT

When a person and equipment operate together to perform a productive process, interest focuses on the efficient use of the person's time and equipment time. When the operator's working time is less than the equipment run time, a worker–machine chart is a useful device in analysis. If the operator can operate several pieces of equipment, the problem is to find the most economical combination of operator and equipment, when the combined cost of the idle time of a particular combination of equipment and the idle time for the worker is at a minimum.

Worker–machine charts are always drawn to scale, the scale being time as measured by length. Exhibit TN4.7 shows a worker–machine chart in a service setting. The question here is, whose utilization use is most important?

### Worker–Machine Chart for a Gourmet Coffee Store

EXHIBIT TN4.7

Time in Seconds: 0, 10, 20, 30, 40, 50, 60, 70

| Person | | | | Machine | |
|---|---|---|---|---|---|
| Customer | Time in sec. | Clerk | Time in sec. | Coffee Grinder | Time in sec. |
| 1. Ask grocer for 1 pound of coffee (brand and grind) | 5 | Listen to order | 5 | Idle | 5 |
| 2. Wait | 15 | Get coffee and put in machine, set grind, and start grinder | 15 | Idle | 15 |
| 3. Wait | 21 | Idle while machine grinds | 21 | Grind coffee | 21 |
| 4. Wait | 12 | Stop grinder, place coffee in package, and close it | 12 | Idle | 12 |
| 5. Receive coffee from grocer, pay grocer, and receive change | 17 | Give coffee to customer, wait for customer to pay for coffee, receive money, and make change | 17 | Idle | 17 |

Summary

| | Customer | Clerk | Coffee Grinder |
|---|---|---|---|
| Idle Time | 48 sec. | 21 sec. | 49 sec. |
| Working Time | 22 | 49 | 21 |
| Total Cycle Time | 70 | 70 | 70 |
| Utilization Percentage | Customer utilization = $\frac{22}{70} = 31\%$ | Clerk utilization = $\frac{49}{70} = 70\%$ | Machine utilization = $\frac{21}{70} = 30\%$ |

The customer, the clerk, and the coffee grinder (machine) are involved in this operation. It required 1 minute 10 seconds for the customer to purchase a pound of coffee in this store. During this time the customer spent 22 seconds, or 31 percent of the time, giving the clerk his order, receiving the ground coffee, and paying the clerk. He was idle the remaining 69 percent of the time. The clerk worked 49 seconds, or 70 percent of the time, and was idle 21 seconds, or 30 percent of the time. The coffee grinder was in operation 21 seconds, or 30 percent of the time, and was idle 70 percent of the time.

EXHIBIT TN4.8

Activity Chart of Emergency Tracheotomy

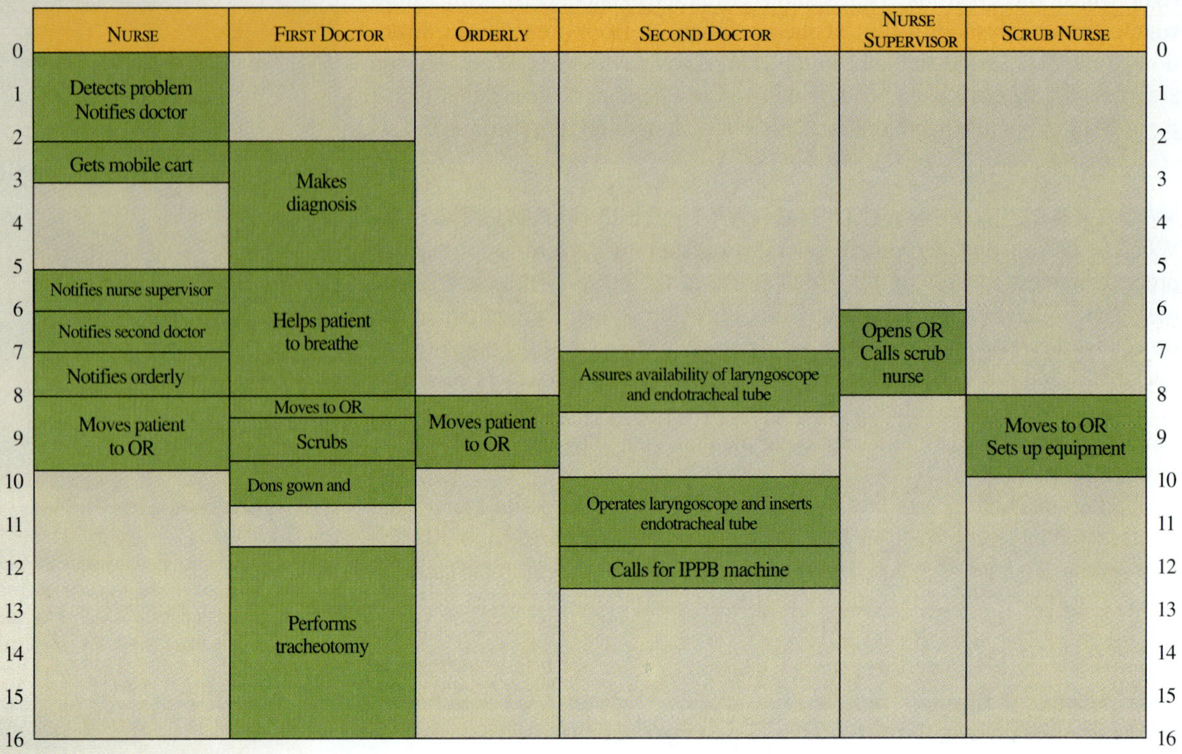


SOURCE: DATA TAKEN FROM H. E. SMALLEY AND J. FREEMAN, *HOSPITAL INDUSTRIAL ENGINEERING* (NEW YORK: REINHOLD, 1966), P. 409.

## WORKERS INTERACTING WITH OTHER WORKERS

The degree of interaction among teams may be as simple as one operator handing a part to another, or as complex as a cardiovascular surgical team of doctors, nurses, anesthesiologist, operator of an artificial heart machine, X-ray technician, standby blood donors, and pathologist (and perhaps a minister to pray a little).

An activity or a gang process chart is useful in plotting each individual's activities on a time scale similar to that of the worker–machine chart. A *gang process chart* is usually employed to trace the interaction of a number of workers with machines in a specified operating cycle to find the best combination of workers and machines. An *activity chart* is less restrictive and may be used to follow the interaction of any group of operators, with or without equipment being involved. Such charts are often used to study and define each operation in an ongoing repetitive process, and they are extremely valuable in developing a standardized procedure for a specific task. Exhibit TN4.8, for example, shows an activity chart for a hospital's emergency routine in performing a tracheotomy (opening a patient's throat surgically to allow the patient to breathe), where detailed activity analysis is critical and any delay could be fatal.

# WORK MEASUREMENT AND STANDARDS

Work measurement

The fundamental purpose of **work measurement** is to set time standards for a job. Such standards are necessary for four reasons:

1 **To schedule work and allocate capacity.** All scheduling approaches require some estimate of how much time it takes to do the work being scheduled.

2 **To provide an objective basis for motivating the workforce and measuring workers' performance.** Measured standards are particularly critical where output-based incentive plans are employed.
3 **To bid for new contracts and to evaluate performance on existing ones.** Questions such as "Can we do it?" and "How are we doing?" presume the existence of standards.
4 **To provide benchmarks for improvement.** In addition to internal evaluation, benchmarking teams regularly compare work standards in their company with those of similar jobs in other organizations.

Work measurement and its resulting work standards have been controversial since Taylor's time. Much of this criticism has come from unions, which argue that management often sets standards that cannot be regularly achieved. (To counter this, in some contracts, the industrial engineer who sets the standard must demonstrate that he or she can do the job over a representative period of time at the rate that was set.) There is also the argument that workers who find a better way of doing the job get penalized by having a revised rate set. (This is commonly called *rate cutting*.)

With the widespread adoption of W. Edwards Deming's ideas, the subject has received renewed criticism. Deming argued that work standards and quotas inhibit process improvement and tend to focus the worker's efforts on speed rather than quality.

Despite these criticisms, work measurement and standards have proved effective. Much depends on sociotechnical aspects of the work. Where the job requires work groups to function as teams and create improvements, worker-set standards often make sense. On the other hand, where the job really boils down to doing the work quickly, with little need for creativity (such as delivering packages for UPS as the box on page 124 relates), tightly engineered, professionally set standards are appropriate.

## WORK MEASUREMENT TECHNIQUES

There are two common techniques for measuring work and setting standards: time study and work sampling. The choice of techniques depends on the level of detail desired and the nature of the work itself. Highly detailed, repetitive work usually calls for time study analysis. When work is infrequent or entails a long cycle time, work sampling is the tool of choice.

A **time study** is generally made with a stopwatch, either on the spot or by analyzing a videotape for the job. The job or task to be studied is separated into measurable parts or elements, and each element is timed individually.

Time study

Some general rules for breaking down the elements are

1 Define each work element to be short in duration but long enough so that it can be timed with a stopwatch and the time can be written down.
2 If the operator works with equipment that runs separately (meaning the operator performs a task and the equipment runs independently), separate the actions of the operator and of the equipment into different elements.
3 Define any delays by the operator or equipment into separate elements.

After a number of repetitions, the collected times are averaged. (The standard deviation may be computed to give a measure of variance in the performance times.) The averaged times for each element are added, yielding the performance time for the operator. However, to make this operator's time usable for all workers, a measure of speed or *performance rating* must be included to "normalize" the job. The application of a rating factor gives what is called *normal time*. For example, if an operator performs a task in two minutes and the time-study analyst estimates her to be performing about 20 percent faster than normal, the operator's performance rating would be 1.2 or 120 percent of normal. The normal time

## WORK MEASUREMENT AT UNITED PARCEL SERVICE

Grabbing a package under his arm, Joseph Polise, a driver for United Parcel Service (UPS), bounds from his brown delivery truck and toward an office building here. A few paces behind him, Marjorie Cusack, a UPS industrial engineer, clutches a digital timer.

Her eyes fixed on Polise, she counts his steps and times his contact with customers. Scribbling on a clipboard, Cusack records every second taken up by stoplights, traffic, detours, doorbells, walkways, stairways, and coffee breaks. "If he goes to the bathroom, we time him," she says.

Seventy-five thousand UPS drivers travel 1.8 billion miles per year and deliver more than 11 million packages a day. On average, UPS drivers move in and out of the truck 200 times a day. An unnecessary step or indirect travel path reduces the effectiveness of the driver and impacts service to the customer. One minute saved each day saves the company $5 million annually. For this reason, UPS spends millions each year to train its drivers in proper, efficient, and safe work methods.

Approximately 3,200 industrial engineers at UPS ensure efficient and reliable customer service by conducting time studies on drivers' routes to provide job method instruction. They have measured even the finest details of the drivers' job, including determining on which finger drivers should consistently carry their key rings to avoid losing them.

In addition to developing specific job methods, UPS provides drivers with custom-built package vehicles with features including

LOADING EFFICIENCY IS STUDIED EXTENSIVELY BY UPS, RESULTING IN UPS TRUCKS THAT CARRY AS MUCH AS 30 PERCENT MORE PACKAGES THAN AN AVERAGE TRUCK.

- Domed seats that allow the driver to slide on and off easily at each delivery stop.
- A drop floor well located behind the rear wheel housing, making the rear of the vehicle only a short step from the ground for easy entry.
- Bulkhead doors that allow easy access to the package compartment and save the driver steps in selecting parcels for delivery.

SOURCE: ABSTRACTED FROM D. MACHALABA, "UP TO SPEED: UNITED PARCEL SERVICE GETS DELIVERIES DONE BY DRIVING ITS WORKERS," *THE WALL STREET JOURNAL*, APRIL 22, 1986, P. 1. INFORMATION PROVIDED BY UPS, 1999.

would be computed as 2 minutes × 1.2, or 2.4 minutes. In equation form,

Normal time

$$\textbf{Normal time} = \text{observed performance time per unit} \times \text{Performance rating}$$

In this example, denoting normal time by *NT*,

$$NT = 2\,(1.2) = 2.4 \text{ minutes}$$

When an operator is observed for a period of time, the number of units produced during this time, along with the performance rating, gives

$$NT = \frac{\text{Time worked}}{\text{Number of units produced}} \times \text{Performance rating}$$

Standard time

**Standard time** is derived by adding to normal time allowances for personal needs (such as washroom and coffee breaks), unavoidable work delays (such as equipment breakdown or lack of materials), and worker fatigue (physical or mental). Two such equations are

$$\text{Standard time} = \text{Normal time} + (\text{Allowances} \times \text{Normal time})$$

or

[TN4.1] $$ST = NT\,(1 + \text{Allowances})$$

and

[TN4.2] $$ST = \frac{NT}{1 - \text{Allowances}}$$

Equation (TN4.1) is most often used in practice. If one presumes that allowances should be applied to the total work period, then equation (TN4.2) is the correct one. To illustrate, suppose that the normal time to perform a task is one minute and that allowances for personal needs, delays, and fatigue total 15 percent; then by equation (TN4.1)

$$ST = 1(1 + 0.15) = 1.15 \text{ minutes}$$

In an eight-hour day, a worker would produce $8 \times 60/1.15$, or 417 units. This implies 417 minutes working and $480 - 417$ (or 63) minutes for allowances.

With equation (TN4.2),

$$ST = \frac{1}{1 - 0.15} = 1.18 \text{ minute}$$

In the same eight-hour day, $8 \times 60/1.18$ (or 408) units are produced with 408 working minutes and 72 minutes for allowances. Depending on which equation is used, there is a difference of nine minutes in the daily allowance time.

*EXAMPLE TN4.1: TIME STUDY FOR A FOUR-ELEMENT JOB*

Exhibit TN4.9 shows a time study of 10 cycles of a four-element job. For each element, there is a space for the watch readings that are recorded in 100ths of a minute. Space is also provided for summarizing the data and applying a performance rating.

*SOLUTION*

The value of $\overline{T}$ is obtained by averaging the observed data. *PR* denotes the performance rating and is multiplied with $\overline{T}$ to obtain the normal time (*NT*) for each element. The normal time for the job is the sum of the element normal times. The standard time, calculated according to equation (TN4.1), is given at the bottom of Exhibit TN4.9. ←

How many observations are enough? Time study is really a sampling process; that is, we take relatively few observations as being representative of many subsequent cycles to be performed by the worker. Based on a great deal of analysis and experience, Benjamin Niebel's table shown in Exhibit TN4.10 indicates that "enough" is a function of cycle length and number of repetitions of the job over a one-year planning period.

Work sampling

A second common technique for measuring a job is called work sampling. As the name suggests, **work sampling** involves observing a portion or sample of the work activity. Then, based on the findings in this sample, statements can be made about the activity. For example, if we were to observe a fire department rescue squad at 100 random times during the day and found it was involved in a rescue mission for 30 of the 100 times (en route, on site, or returning from a call), we would estimate that the rescue squad spends 30 percent of its time directly on rescue mission calls. (The time it takes to make an observation depends on what is being observed. Many times, only a glance is needed to determine the activity, and the majority of studies require only several seconds' observation.)

EXHIBIT TN4.9

**Time-Study Observation Sheet**

Time Study Observation Sheet

Identification of Operation *ASSEMBLE 24" × 36" CHART BLANKS* Date *10/9*

Began Timing: *9:26* Ended Timing: *9:32* | Operator 109 | Approval | Observer

| | Element Description and Breakpoint | 1 (0.00) | 2 | 3 | 4 | 5 | 6 | 7 | 8 | 9 | 10 | ΣT | $\bar{T}$ | PR | NT |
|---|---|---|---|---|---|---|---|---|---|---|---|---|---|---|---|
| 1 | *Fold over end (grasp stapler)* | .07 | .07 | .05 | .07 | .09 | .06 | .05 | .08 | .08 | .06 | .68 | .07 | .90 | .06 |
| | | .07 | .61 | .14 | .67 | .24 | .78 | .33 | .88 | .47 | .09 | | | | |
| 2 | *Staple five times (drop stapler)* | .16 | .14 | .14 | .15 | .16 | .16 | .14 | .17 | .14 | .15 | 1.51 | .15 | 1.05 | .16 |
| | | .23 | .75 | .28 | .82 | .40 | .94 | .47 | .05 | .61 | .24 | | | | |
| 3 | *Bend and insert wire (drop pliers)* | .22 | .25 | .22 | .25 | .23 | .23 | .21 | .26 | .25 | .24 | 2.36 | .24 | 1.00 | .24 |
| | | .45 | .00 | .50 | .07 | .63 | .17 | .68 | .31 | .86 | .48 | | | | |
| 4 | *Dispose of finished chart (touch next sheet)* | .09 | .09 | .10 | .08 | .09 | .11 | .12 | .08 | .17 | .08 | 1.01 | .10 | .90 | .09 |
| | | .54 | .09 | .60 | .15 | .72 | .28 | .80 | .39 | .03 | .56 | | | 0.55 normal minute for cycle | |
| 5 | | | | | | | | | | | | | | | |
| 6 | | | | | | | | | | | | | | | |
| 10 | | | | | | | | | | | | | | | |

Normal cycle time *0.55* + Allowance *(0.55 × 0.143) or 0.08* = Std. time *0.63 min./pc.*

EXHIBIT TN4.10

**Guide to Number of Cycles to Be Observed in a Time Study**

| WHEN TIME PER CYCLE IS MORE THAN | MINIMUM NUMBER OF CYCLES OF STUDY (ACTIVITY): OVER 10,000 PER YEAR | 1,000–10,000 | UNDER 1,000 |
|---|---|---|---|
| 8 hours | 2 | 1 | 1 |
| 3 | 3 | 2 | 1 |
| 2 | 4 | 2 | 1 |
| 1 | 5 | 3 | 2 |
| 48 minutes | 6 | 3 | 2 |
| 30 | 8 | 4 | 3 |
| 20 | 10 | 5 | 4 |
| 12 | 12 | 6 | 5 |
| 8 | 15 | 8 | 6 |
| 5 | 20 | 10 | 8 |
| 3 | 25 | 12 | 10 |
| 2 | 30 | 15 | 12 |
| 1 | 40 | 20 | 15 |
| .7 | 50 | 25 | 20 |
| .5 | 60 | 30 | 25 |
| .3 | 80 | 40 | 30 |
| .2 | 100 | 50 | 40 |
| .1 | 120 | 60 | 50 |
| Under .1 | 140 | 80 | 60 |

SOURCE: B. W. NIEBEL, *MOTION AND TIME STUDY*, 9TH ED. (BURR RIDGE, IL: RICHARD D. IRWIN, 1993), P. 390.

Observing an activity even 100 times may not, however, provide the accuracy desired in the estimate. To refine this estimate, three main issues must be decided. (These points are discussed later in this section, along with an example.)

1 What level of statistical confidence is desired in the results?
2 How many observations are necessary?
3 Precisely when should the observations be made?

The three primary applications for work sampling are

1 Ratio delay to determine the activity-time percentage for personnel or equipment. For example, management may be interested in the amount of time a machine is running or idle.
2 Performance measurement to develop a performance index for workers. When the amount of work time is related to the quantity of output, a measure of performance is developed. This is useful for periodic performance evaluation.
3 Time standards to obtain the standard time for a task. When work sampling is used for this purpose, however, the observer must be experienced because he or she must attach a performance rating to the observations.

The number of observations required in a work-sampling study can be fairly large, ranging from several hundred to several thousand, depending on the activity and desired degree of accuracy. Although the number can be computed from formulas, the easiest way is to refer to a table such as Exhibit TN4.11, which gives the number of observations needed for a 95 percent confidence level in terms of absolute error. *Absolute error* is the actual range of the observations. For example, if a clerk is idle 10 percent of the time and the designer of the study is satisfied with a 2.5 percent range (meaning that the true percentage lies between 7.5 and 12.5 percent), the number of observations required for the work sampling is 576. A 2 percent error (or an interval of 8 to 12 percent) would require 900 observations.

Five steps are involved in making a work-sampling study:

1 Identify the specific activity or activities that are the main purpose for the study. For example, determine the percentage of time that equipment is working, idle, or under repair.
2 Estimate the proportion of time of the activity of interest to the total time (e.g., that the equipment is working 80 percent of the time). These estimates can be made from the analyst's knowledge, past data, reliable guesses from others, or a pilot work-sampling study.
3 State the desired accuracy in the study results.
4 Determine the specific times when each observation is to be made.
5 At two or three intervals during the study period, recompute the required sample size by using the data collected thus far. Adjust the number of observations if appropriate.

The number of observations to be taken in a work-sampling study is usually divided equally over the study period. Thus, if 500 observations are to be made over a 10-day period, observations are usually scheduled at 500/10, or 50 per day. Each day's observations are then assigned a specific time by using a random number table.

## EXAMPLE TN4.2: WORK SAMPLING APPLIED TO NURSING

There has been a long-standing argument that a large amount of nurses' hospital time is spent on nonnursing activities. This, the argument goes, creates an apparent shortage of well-trained nursing personnel, wastes talent, hinders efficiency, and increases hospital costs because nurses' wages are the highest single cost in the operation of a hospital. Further, pressure is growing for hospitals and hospital administrators to contain costs. With that in mind, let us use work sampling to test the hypothesis that a large portion of nurses' time is spent on nonnursing duties.

## SOLUTION

Assume at the outset that we have made a list of all the activities that are part of nursing and will make our observations in only two categories: nursing and nonnursing activities. Actually, there is much debate on what constitutes nursing activity. For instance; is talking to a patient a nursing duty? (An expanded study could list all nursing activities to determine the portion of time spent in each.)

EXHIBIT TN4.11

**Number of Observations Required for a Given Absolute Error at Various Values of *p*, with 95 Percent Confidence Level**

| Percentage of Total Time Occupied by Activity or Delay, *p* | Absolute Error | | | | | |
|---|---|---|---|---|---|---|
| | ±1.0% | ±1.5% | ±2.0% | ±2.5% | ±3.0% | ±3.5% |
| 1 or 99 | 396 | 176 | 99 | 63 | 44 | 32 |
| 2 or 98 | 784 | 348 | 196 | 125 | 87 | 64 |
| 3 or 97 | 1,164 | 517 | 291 | 186 | 129 | 95 |
| 4 or 96 | 1,536 | 683 | 384 | 246 | 171 | 125 |
| 5 or 95 | 1,900 | 844 | 475 | 304 | 211 | 155 |
| 6 or 94 | 2,256 | 1,003 | 564 | 361 | 251 | 184 |
| 7 or 93 | 2,604 | 1,157 | 651 | 417 | 289 | 213 |
| 8 or 92 | 2,944 | 1,308 | 736 | 471 | 327 | 240 |
| 9 or 91 | 3,276 | 1,456 | 819 | 524 | 364 | 267 |
| 10 or 90 | 3,600 | 1,600 | 900 | 576 | 400 | 294 |
| 11 or 89 | 3,916 | 1,740 | 979 | 627 | 435 | 320 |
| 12 or 88 | 4,224 | 1,877 | 1,056 | 676 | 469 | 344 |
| 13 or 87 | 4,524 | 2,011 | 1,131 | 724 | 503 | 369 |
| 14 or 86 | 4,816 | 2,140 | 1,204 | 771 | 535 | 393 |
| 15 or 85 | 5,100 | 2,267 | 1,275 | 816 | 567 | 416 |
| 16 or 84 | 5,376 | 2,389 | 1,344 | 860 | 597 | 439 |
| 17 or 83 | 5,644 | 2,508 | 1,411 | 903 | 627 | 461 |
| 18 or 82 | 5,904 | 2,624 | 1,476 | 945 | 656 | 482 |
| 19 or 81 | 6,156 | 2,736 | 1,539 | 985 | 684 | 502 |
| 20 or 80 | 6,400 | 2,844 | 1,600 | 1,024 | 711 | 522 |
| 21 or 79 | 6,636 | 2,949 | 1,659 | 1,062 | 737 | 542 |
| 22 or 78 | 6,864 | 3,050 | 1,716 | 1,098 | 763 | 560 |
| 23 or 77 | 7,084 | 3,148 | 1,771 | 1,133 | 787 | 578 |
| 24 or 76 | 7,296 | 3,243 | 1,824 | 1,167 | 811 | 596 |
| 25 or 75 | 7,500 | 3,333 | 1,875 | 1,200 | 833 | 612 |
| 26 or 74 | 7,696 | 3,420 | 1,924 | 1,231 | 855 | 628 |
| 27 or 73 | 7,884 | 3,504 | 1,971 | 1,261 | 876 | 644 |
| 28 or 72 | 8,064 | 3,584 | 2,016 | 1,290 | 896 | 658 |
| 29 or 71 | 8,236 | 3,660 | 2,059 | 1,318 | 915 | 672 |
| 30 or 70 | 8,400 | 3,733 | 2,100 | 1,344 | 933 | 686 |
| 31 or 69 | 8,556 | 3,803 | 2,139 | 1,369 | 951 | 698 |
| 32 or 68 | 8,704 | 3,868 | 2,176 | 1,393 | 967 | 710 |
| 33 or 67 | 8,844 | 3,931 | 2,211 | 1,415 | 983 | 722 |
| 34 or 66 | 8,976 | 3,989 | 2,244 | 1,436 | 997 | 733 |
| 35 or 65 | 9,100 | 4,044 | 2,275 | 1,456 | 1,011 | 743 |
| 36 or 64 | 9,216 | 4,096 | 2,304 | 1,475 | 1,024 | 753 |
| 37 or 63 | 9,324 | 4,144 | 2,331 | 1,492 | 1,036 | 761 |
| 38 or 62 | 9,424 | 4,188 | 2,356 | 1,508 | 1,047 | 769 |
| 39 or 61 | 9,516 | 4,229 | 2,379 | 1,523 | 1,057 | 777 |
| 40 or 60 | 9,600 | 4,266 | 2,400 | 1,536 | 1,067 | 784 |
| 41 or 59 | 9,676 | 4,300 | 2,419 | 1,548 | 1,075 | 790 |
| 42 or 58 | 9,744 | 4,330 | 2,436 | 1,559 | 1,083 | 795 |
| 43 or 57 | 9,804 | 4,357 | 2,451 | 1,569 | 1,089 | 800 |
| 44 or 56 | 9,856 | 4,380 | 2,464 | 1,577 | 1,095 | 804 |
| 45 or 55 | 9,900 | 4,400 | 2,475 | 1,584 | 1,099 | 808 |
| 46 or 54 | 9,936 | 4,416 | 2,484 | 1,590 | 1,104 | 811 |
| 47 or 53 | 9,964 | 4,428 | 2,491 | 1,594 | 1,107 | 813 |
| 48 or 52 | 9,984 | 4,437 | 2,496 | 1,597 | 1,109 | 815 |
| 49 or 51 | 9,996 | 4,442 | 2,499 | 1,599 | 1,110 | 816 |
| 50 | 10,000 | 4,444 | 2,500 | 1,600 | 1,111 | 816 |

Note: Number of observations is obtained from the formula $E = Z\sqrt{\frac{p(1-p)}{N}}$ and the required sample ($N$) is $N = \frac{Z^2 p(1-p)}{E^2}$
where $E$ = Absolute error
$p$ = Percentage occurrence of activity or delay being measured
$N$ = Number of random observations (sample size)
$Z$ = Number of standard deviations to give desired confidence level (e.g., for 90 percent confidence, $Z = 1.65$; for 95 percent, $Z = 1.96$; for 99 percent, $Z = 2.23$). In this table $Z = 2$.

Therefore, when we observe during the study and find the nurse performing one of the duties on the nursing list, we simply place a tally mark in the nursing column. If we observe anything besides nursing activities, we place a tally mark in the nonnursing column.

We can now plan the study. Assume that we (or the nursing supervisor) estimate that nurses spend 60 percent of their time in nursing activities. Assume that we would like to be 95 percent confident that findings of our study are within the absolute error range of ±3 percent; that is, if our study shows nurses spend 60 percent of their time on nursing duties, we want to be 95 percent confident that the true percentage lies between 57 and 63 percent. From Exhibit TN4.11, we find that 1,067 observations are required for 60 percent activity time and ±3 percent error. If our study is to take place over 10 days, we start with 107 observations per day.

To determine when each day's observations are to be made, we assign specific numbers to each minute and use a random number table to set up a schedule. If the study extends over an eight-hour shift, we can assign numbers to correspond to each consecutive minute. For this study it is likely the night shift would be run separately because nighttime nursing duties are considerably different from daytime duties. Exhibit TN4.12A shows the assignment of numbers to corresponding minutes. For simplicity, because each number corresponds to one minute, a three-number scheme is used, with the second and third numbers corresponding to the minute of the hour. A number of other schemes would also be appropriate. If a number of studies are planned, a computer program may be used to generate a randomized schedule for the observation times.

If we refer to a random number table and list three-digit numbers, we can assign each number to a time. The random numbers in Exhibit TN4.12B demonstrate the procedure for seven observations.

This procedure is followed to generate 107 observation times, and the times are rearranged chronologically for ease in planning. Rearranging the times determined in Exhibit TN4.12B gives the total observations per day shown in Exhibit TN4.12C (for our sample of seven).

To be perfectly random in this study, we should also "randomize" the nurse we observe each time. (The use of various nurses minimizes the effect of bias.) In the study, our first observation is made

EXHIBIT TN4.12

Sampling Plan for Nurses' Activities
A. Assignment of Numbers to Corresponding Minutes
B. Determination of Observation Times
C. Observation Schedule

A.

| Time | Assigned Numbers |
|---|---|
| 7:00–7:59 A.M. | 100–159 |
| 8:00–8:59 A.M. | 200–259 |
| 9:00–9:59 A.M. | 300–359 |
| 10:00–10:59 A.M. | 400–459 |
| 11:00–11:59 A.M. | 500–559 |
| 12:00–12:59 P.M. | 600–659 |
| 1:00–1:59 P.M. | 700–759 |
| 2:00–2:59 P.M. | 800–859 |

B.

| Random Number | Corresponding Time from the List in 11.13A |
|---|---|
| 669 | Nonexistent |
| 831 | 2:31 P.M. |
| 555 | 11:55 A.M. |
| 470 | Nonexistent |
| 113 | 7:13 A.M. |
| 080 | Nonexistent |
| 520 | 11:20 A.M. |
| 204 | 8:04 A.M. |
| 732 | 1:32 P.M. |
| 420 | 10:20 A.M. |

C.

| Observation | Schedule Time | Nursing Activity(✓) | Nonnursing Activity(✓) |
|---|---|---|---|
| 1 | 7:13 A.M. | | |
| 2 | 8:04 A.M. | | |
| 3 | 10:20 A.M. | | |
| 4 | 11:20 AM | | |
| 5 | 11:55 A.M. | | |
| 6 | 1:32 P.M. | | |
| 7 | 2:31 P.M. | | |

at 7:13 A.M. for Nurse X. We walk into the nurse's area and, on seeing the nurse, check either a nursing or a nonnursing activity. Each observation need be only long enough to determine the class of activity—in most cases only a glance is needed. At 8:04 A.M. we observe Nurse Y. We continue in this way to the end of the day and the 107 observations. At the end of the second day (and 214 observations), we decide to check for the adequacy of our sample size.

Let us say we made 150 observations of nurses working and 64 of them not working, which gives 70.1 percent working. From Exhibit TN4.11, this corresponds to 933 observations. Because we have already taken 214 observations, we need take only 719 over the next eight days, or 90 per day.

When the study is half over, another check should be made. For instance, if days 3, 4, and 5 showed 55, 59, and 64 working observations, the cumulative data would give 328 working observations of a total 484, or a 67.8 percent working activity. For a ±3% error, Exhibit TN4.11 shows the sample size to be about 967, leaving 483 to be made—at 97 per day—for the following five days. Another computation should be made before the last day to see if another adjustment is required. If after the 10th day several more observations are indicated, these can be made on day 11.

If at the end of the study we find that 66 percent of nurses' time is involved with what has been defined as nursing activity, there should be an analysis to identify the remaining 34 percent. Approximately 12 to 15 percent is justifiable for coffee breaks and personal needs, which leaves 20 to 22 percent of the time that must be justified and compared to what the industry considers ideal levels of nursing activity. To identify the nonnursing activities, a more detailed breakdown could have been originally built into the sampling plan. Otherwise, a follow-up study may be in order. ←

As mentioned earlier, work sampling can be used to set time standards. To do this, the analyst must record the subject's performance rate (or index) along with working observations. Exhibit TN4.13 gives a manufacturing example that demonstrates how work sampling can be used for calculating standard time.

## WORK SAMPLING COMPARED TO TIME STUDY

Work sampling offers several advantages:

1. Several work-sampling studies may be conducted simultaneously by one observer.
2. The observer need not be a trained analyst unless the purpose of the study is to determine a time standard.

EXHIBIT TN4.13

**Deriving a Time Standard Using Work Sampling**

| INFORMATION | SOURCE OF DATA | DATA FOR ONE DAY |
|---|---|---|
| Total time expended by operator (working time and idle time) | Computer Payroll system | 480 min. |
| Number of parts produced | Inspection department | 420 pieces |
| Working time in percent | Work sampling | 85% |
| Idle time in percent | Work sampling | 15% |
| Average performance index | Work sampling | 110% |
| Total allowances | Company time-study manual | 15% |

$$\text{Standard time per piece} = \frac{\begin{pmatrix}\text{Total time}\\ \text{in minutes}\end{pmatrix} \times \begin{pmatrix}\text{Working time}\\ \text{proportion}\end{pmatrix} \times \begin{pmatrix}\text{Performance}\\ \text{index}\end{pmatrix}}{\text{Total number of pieces produced}} \times \frac{1}{1 - \text{Allowances}}$$

$$= \left(\frac{480 \times 0.85 \times 1.10}{420}\right) \times \left(\frac{1}{1 - 0.15}\right) = 1.26 \text{ minutes}$$

3 No timing devices are required.
4 Work of a long cycle time may be studied with fewer observer hours.
5 The duration of the study is longer, which minimizes effects of short-period variations.
6 The study may be temporarily delayed at any time with little effect.
7 Because work sampling needs only instantaneous observations (made over a longer period), the operator has less chance to influence the findings by changing his or her work method.

When the cycle time is short, time study is more appropriate than work sampling. One drawback of work sampling is that it does not provide as complete a breakdown of elements as time study. Another difficulty with work sampling is that observers, rather than following a random sequence of observations, tend to develop a repetitive route of travel. This may allow the time of the observations to be predictable and thus invalidate the findings. A third factor—a potential drawback—is that the basic assumption in work sampling is that all observations pertain to the same static system. If the system is in the process of change, work sampling may give misleading results.

# FINANCIAL INCENTIVE PLANS

The third piece of the job design equation is the paycheck. This section briefly reviews common methods for setting financial incentives.

## BASIC COMPENSATION SYSTEMS

The main forms of basic compensation are hourly pay, straight salary, piece rate, and commissions. The first two are based on time spent on the job, with individual performance rewarded by an increase in the base rate. Piece rate plans reward on the basis of direct daily output. (A worker is paid $5 a unit; thus, by producing 10 units per day, the worker earns $50.) Sometimes a guaranteed base is included in a piece-rate plan; a worker would receive this base amount regardless of output, plus a piece-rate bonus. (For example, the worker's hourly base pay is $8, so this coupled with $50 piece-rate earnings gives the worker $114 for an eight-hour day.) Commissions may be thought of as sales-based piece rates and are calculated in the same general way.

The two broad categories of financial incentive plans are individual or small-group incentive plans and organizationwide plans. (See The Breakthrough Box titled "The Fun Factor in Safety Incentive Programs.")

## INDIVIDUAL AND SMALL-GROUP INCENTIVE PLANS

Individual and work group plans traditionally have rewarded performance by using output (often defined by piece rates) and quality measures. Quality is accounted for by a quality adjustment factor, say a percentage of rework.[4] (For example: Incentive pay = Total output × [1 − Percent deduction for rework].) In recent years, skill development has also been rewarded. Sometimes called *pay for knowledge,* this means a worker is compensated for learning new tasks. This is particularly important in job shops using group technology, as well as in banking, where supervisors' jobs require knowledge of new types of financial instruments and selling approaches.

AT&T, for example, instituted incentive programs for its managers—an Individual Incentive Award (IIA) and a Management Team Incentive Award (MTIA). The IIA provides lump-sum bonuses to outstanding performers. These outstanding performers are determined by individual performance ratings accompanied by extensive documentation. The lump-sum bonus can range between 15 and 30 percent of base pay.

## BREAKTHROUGH

### THE FUN FACTOR IN SAFETY INCENTIVE PROGRAMS

Here are the basic ingredients for safety incentive programs that apply to other incentive programs as well.

1 **Choose merchandise.** First things first: get the carrot right. Goodyear Tire ran an extensive study on merchandise versus cash incentives; merchandise won twofold. When you ask your people what they want, the answer will be cash. When you ask the experts what really works, it is merchandise.

2 **A flexible award vehicle.** Traditional programs are structured to give a person who goes a year without an accident an award such as a clock radio. In order to attach incentives to the behavior that prevents the accidents, you must have a flexible delivery vehicle that can be awarded the minute the prevention behavior or observation takes place, yet still building up to the resulting merchandise award. Gamecards that contain points toward merchandise have proved an exciting vehicle. They can be handed out weekly or daily, instantly recognizing employees as they achieve safety behavior acts or observations. If the gamecards are designed right, they should have a trading component where employees are encouraged to trade cards with each other. This further boosts program awareness. Having a flexible award vehicle allows for constant frequent reinforcement, which is a key component to a program's success.

3 **An encompassing campaign.** A campaign that communicates and drives the program, tying it all together, is called for. Southwest Airlines is famous for creating fun campaigns for everything it does. People love games (adults, too). The campaign theme should bring everything together: the award vehicle (gamecard, certificate, or the like), merchandise catalog, program posters, newsletters, communication pieces, behavioral observation reports, and so on. People remember things that are constantly in front of them, things that are fun, and things that benefit them.

4 **Simple administration.** Face it, complexity does not work. If your entire program is not easy for everyone to understand, you are headed in the wrong direction. If the program is tough for you to administer, it could fail as well. Keep it simple and achievable.

5 **Well-thought-out, behavior-based program criteria.** You first must identify the behaviors that will affect the majority of incidents. Your program then must be aimed at gathering information/observations and receiving feedback from employees. Employees must be rewarded for these observations as well as for feedback and, of course, for following the accident prevention criteria. Again, keep it simple.

SOURCE: B. PEAVEY, "THE FUN FACTOR," *OCCUPATIONAL HEALTH & SAFETY* 67, NO. 10. (OCTOBER 1998), P. 163.

MTIAs are granted to members of specific divisions or units. Appropriate division or unit goals are established at the beginning of the year. The goals include department service objectives and interdepartmental goals. A typical MTIA could call for a standard amount equivalent to 1.5 percent of wages plus overtime for the next three years based on performance in the current year.

## ORGANIZATIONWIDE PLANS

Profit sharing and gain sharing are the major types of organizationwide plans. Profit sharing simply distributes a percentage of corporate profits across the workforce. In the United States, at least one-third of all organizations have profit sharing. In Japan, most major companies give profit-based bonuses twice a year to all employees. Such bonuses may range from 50 percent of salaries, in good years, to nothing in bad years.

Gain sharing also involves giving organizationwide bonuses, but it differs from profit sharing in two important respects. First, it typically measures controllable costs or units of output, not profits, in calculating a bonus. Second, gain sharing is always combined with a participative approach to management. The original and best-known gainsharing plan is the Scanlon Plan.

In the late 1930s, the Lapointe Machine and Tool Company was on the verge of bankruptcy, but through the efforts of union president Joseph Scanlon and company management, the Scanlon Plan was devised to save the company by reducing labor costs. In essence, this plan started with the normal labor cost within the firm. Workers as a group were rewarded for any reductions in labor cost below this base cost. The plan's success depended on committees of workers throughout the firm whose purpose was to search out areas for cost saving and to devise ways of improvement. There were many improvements, and the plan did, in fact, save the company.

The basic elements of the Scanlon Plan are

1 **The ratio.** The ratio is the standard that serves as a measure for judging business performance. It can be expressed as

$$\text{Ratio} = \frac{\text{Total labor cost}}{\text{Sales value of production}}$$

2 **The bonus.** The amount of bonus depends on the reduction in costs below the preset ratio.
3 **The production committee.** The production committee is formed to encourage employee suggestions to increase productivity, improve quality, reduce waste, and so forth. The purpose of a production committee is similar to that of a quality circle.
4 **The screening committee.** The screening committee consists of top management and worker representatives who review monthly bonuses, discuss production problems, and consider improvement suggestions.

Gain-sharing plans are now used by more than a thousand firms in the United States and Europe, and are growing in popularity. One survey in the United States indicated that about 13 percent of all firms have them, and that more than 70 percent were started after 1982.[5] Though originally established in small companies such as Lapointe, Lincoln Electric Company, and Herman Miller, gain sharing has been installed by large firms such as TRW, General Electric, Motorola, and Firestone. These companies apply gain sharing to organizational units. Motorola, for example, has virtually all its plant employees covered by gain sharing. These plans are increasing because "they are more than just pay incentive plans; they are a participative approach to management and are often used as a way to install participative management."[6] The typical applications of the plans are discussed, along with merit pay, in Exhibit TN4.14.

## PAY-FOR-PERFORMANCE

*Business Week* magazine ran a survey of compensation for company presidents. Salaries ranged from $350,000 to $8 million. In every case there was an extra "kicker" (a healthy bonus for achievement of certain goals in sales, profits, stock price, or the like). Despite gigantic salaries, every executive was offered an incentive bonus.

The following are more examples of recent incentive pay results:[7]

- At Kaiser Aluminum, located in Jackson, Tennessee, the use of incentive pay contributed to an 80 percent productivity boost over five years. Poor quality costs decreased by 70 percent.
- General Tire's 1,950-employee Mt. Vernon, Illinois, plant used a gain-sharing program to generate $30 million in savings over a five-year period, $20 million of which was paid out to workers in the form of bonuses. The company profited by $10 million.
- General Electric used a merit pay system to reduce its order-to-delivery time from 18 weeks to 5 weeks at its Louisville, Kentucky, appliance plant.
- Wrought Washer Manufacturing Company, located in Milwaukee, Wisconsin, improved productivity by 39 percent with a gain-sharing program in 1993. The workforce earned $165,737 in extra bonuses, and the company saved an additional $110,490.

EXHIBIT TN4.14

Comparison of Common Reward/Incentive Plans

| Type of Plan | Application | Advantages | Disadvantages |
|---|---|---|---|
| Merit pay | Individual | • Allows management to target specific behavior and to easily evolve criteria over time. | • Can be arbitrary and unbiased when incorrectly administered.<br>• Often not clearly tied to business goals. |
| Profit sharing | Group | • Ties business performance to employee reward. | • Often individual or group behavior is not correlated to business performance. |
| Gain sharing | Group | • Specific group performance directly tied to employee reward. | • Often focuses excessively on cost control.<br>• More applicable for tactical improvements than strategic changes. |
| Lump-sum bonuses and individual bonuses | Either | • Allows management to vary criteria and magnitude of reward; able to target specific actions and behavior. | • Often used for and seen as deferred compensation.<br>• Not always a tie to business goals or performance. |
| Pay-for-knowledge | Individual | • Allows management to target specific types of skills and personal growth. | • May not impact business performance unless management targets correct skills and applies new skills effectively. |
| Piece rate | Either | • Allows management to target specific output goals. | • May lead to undesirable competition among workers.<br>• Standards must be kept up to date. |

SOURCE: MODIFIED FROM C. GIFFI, A. ROTH, AND G. SEAL, *COMPETING IN WORLD-CLASS MANUFACTURING, AMERICA'S 21ST CENTURY CHALLENGE* (BURR RIDGE, IL: BUSINESS ONE IRWIN, 1990).

- Whirlpool Corporation's Benton Harbor, Michigan, plant instituted a merit program in 1988. Through 1996, the plant showed productivity gains of about 19 percent annually, with each year building on the previous year. Quality improvements have been substantial, with the number of parts rejected sinking to 4 per million from 837 per million.
- Finally, Jostens, a company that makes quality class rings, instituted a piece-rate system based on the number of good rings produced by each employee. In 1990 the company was producing 16 good rings per employee (deducting rejects and rework). After the program began in 1993, employees began producing 25 good rings per employee—a 56 percent productivity boost—with a lead time of 10 calendar days from work order to shipping. In only a year, productivity increased further to 36 good rings per employee.

The results of these studies are overwhelming. Paying employees based on their performance does work. Many experts, including those at the American Productivity and Quality Center, predict that these systems will become a common part of the strategy that companies employ to improve their performance in the 21st century.

## CONCLUSION

At the outset of this technical note we identified current trends in job design. What will the future hold? One thing is clear: Globalization and the successful application of sophisticated process technologies will make the human element even more important to operations competitiveness than before. Giffi, Roth, and Seal speculate that "the 21st century will be marked by the human resource renaissance." In their view, this renaissance will be characterized by companies actively cultivating their human resources through careful selection and training of the best and brightest employees, implementing innovative team-based employee involvement programs, developing genuinely participative management approaches, and continually retraining their employees.[8] What is the future of the time study techniques also addressed in this technical note? In our opinion, they will always have application to analyzing work methods and, selectively, to setting work standards. Expectations concerning the time required to complete tasks form the basis for calculating capacity requirements and are a key input to labor planning activities.

## KEY TERMS

**Job design** The function of specifying the work activities of an individual or group in an organizational setting.

**Specialization of labor** Simple, repetitive jobs are assigned to each worker.

**Job enrichment** Specialized work is made more interesting by giving the worker a greater variety of tasks or by getting a worker involved in planning, organization, and inspection.

**Sociotechnical systems** A philosophy that focuses more on the interaction between technology and the work group. The approach attempts to develop jobs that adjust the production process technology to the needs of the worker and work group.

**Work physiology** Considers the physical demands of a job. Work–rest cycles are set according to the energy expended on the job.

**Ergonomics** Study of the physical arrangement of the work space together with the tools used to perform a task.

**Work measurement** Job analysis for the purpose of setting time standards.

**Time study** Separation of a job into measurable parts, with each element timed individually. The individual times are then combined, and allowances are added to calculate a standard time.

**Normal time** The time that a normal operator would be expected to take to complete a job without the consideration of allowances.

**Standard time** Calculated by taking the normal time and adding allowances for personal needs, unavoidable work delays, and worker fatigue.

**Work sampling** Analyzing a work activity by observing an activity at random times. Statements about how time is spent during the activity are made from these observations.

## FORMULA REVIEW

**Standard time**

[TN4.1] $$ST = NT(1 + \text{Allowances})$$

[TN4.2] $$ST = \frac{NT}{1 - \text{Allowances}}$$

## SOLVED PROBLEMS

### SOLVED PROBLEM 1

Brandon is very organized and wants to plan his day perfectly. To do this, he has his friend Kelly time his daily activities. Here are the results of her timing Brandon on polishing two pairs of black shoes using the snapback method of timing. What is the standard time for polishing two pairs? (Assume a 5 percent allowance factor for Brandon to put something mellow on the CD player. Account for noncyclically recurring elements by dividing their observed times by the total number of cycles observed.)

| | OBSERVED TIMES | | | | | |
|---|---|---|---|---|---|---|
| ELEMENT | 1 | 2 | 3 | 4 | PERFORMANCE RATING | NT |
| Get shoeshine kit | 0.50 | | | | 125% | |
| Polish shoes | 0.94 | 0.85 | 0.80 | 0.81 | 110 | |
| Put away kit | | | | 0.75 | 80 | |

## Solution

| | $\Sigma T$ | $\bar{T}$ | PERFORMANCE RATING | NT |
|---|---|---|---|---|
| Get shoeshine kit | .50 | .50/2 = .25 | 125% | .31 |
| Polish shoes (2 pairs) | 3.40 | 3.40/2 = 1.70 | 110 | 1.87 |
| Put away kit | .75 | .75/2 = .375 | 80 | .30 |
| Normal time for one pair of shoes | | | | 2.48 |

Standard time for the pair = 2.48 × 1.05 = 2.60 minutes.

## SOLVED PROBLEM 2

A total of 15 observations has been taken on a head baker for a school district. The numerical breakdown of the baker's activities is

| MAKE READY | DO | CLEAN UP | IDLE |
|---|---|---|---|
| 2 | 6 | 3 | 4 |

Based on this information, how many work-sampling observations are required to determine how much of the baker's time is spent in "doing"? Assume a 5 percent desired absolute accuracy and 95 percent confidence level.

## Solution

To calculate the number of observations, use the formula at the bottom of Exhibit TN4.11 because the 95 percent confidence is required (that is, $Z \cong 2$).

$$p = \text{"Doing"} = 6/15 = 40\%$$

$$E = 5\% \text{ (given)}$$

$$N = \frac{4p(1-p)}{E^2} = \frac{4(.4)(1-.4)}{(.05)(.05)} = \frac{.96}{.0025} = 384$$

# REVIEW AND DISCUSSION QUESTIONS

1 Why might practicing managers and industrial engineers be skeptical about job enrichment and sociotechnical approaches to job design?

2 Chase, Aquilano, and Jacobs commonly complain to their families that book writing is hard work and that they should be excused from helping out with the housework so that they can rest. Which exhibit in this chapter should they never let their families see?

3 Is there an inconsistency when a company requires precise time standards and encourages job enlargement?

4 Match the following techniques to their most appropriate application:

| | |
|---|---|
| Worker–machine chart | Washing clothes at laundromat |
| Process chart | Tracing your steps in getting a parking permit |
| Work sampling | Faculty office hours kept |

5 You have timed your friend, Lefty, assembling widgets. His time averaged 12 minutes for the two cycles you timed. He was working very hard, and you believe that none of the nine other

operators doing the same job can beat his time. Are you ready to put forth this time as the standard for making an order of 5,000 widgets? If not, what else should you do?

6 Comment on the following:
*a.* "Work measurement is old hat. We have automated our office, and now we run every bill through our computer (after our 25 clerks have typed the data into our computer database)."
*b.* "It's best that our workers don't know that they are being time studied. That way, they can't complain about us getting in the way when we set time standards."
*c.* "Once we get everybody on an incentive plan, then we will start our work measurement program."
*d.* "Rhythm is fine for dancing, but it has no place on the shop floor."

7 Organizationwide financial incentive plans cover all the workers. Some units or individuals may have contributed more to corporate profits than others. Does this detract from the effectiveness of the incentive plan system? How would your incentive scheme for a small software development firm compare to an established auto manufacturing firm?

## PROBLEMS

1 Use the following form to evaluate a job you have held relative to the five principles of job design given in the chapter. Develop a numerical score by summing the numbers in parentheses.

| | POOR (0) | ADEQUATE (1) | GOOD (2) | OUTSTANDING (3) |
|---|---|---|---|---|
| Task variety | | | | |
| Skill variety | | | | |
| Feedback | | | | |
| Task identity | | | | |
| Task autonomy | | | | |

*a.* Compute the score for your job. Does the score match your subjective feelings about the job as a whole? Explain.
*b.* Compare your score with the scores generated by your classmates. Is there one kind of job that everybody likes and one kind that everybody dislikes?

2 Examine the process chart in Exhibit TN4.5. Can you recommend some improvements to cut down on delays and transportation? (Hint: The research laboratory can suggest changes in the requisition form.)

3 A time study was made of an existing job to develop new time standards. A worker was observed for 45 minutes. During that period, 30 units were produced. The analyst rated the worker as performing at a 90 percent performance rate. Allowances in the firm for rest and personal time are 12 percent.
*a.* What is the normal time for the task?
*b.* What is the standard time for the task?
*c.* If the worker produced 300 units in an eight-hour day, what would be the day's pay if the basic rate was $6 per hour and the premium payment system paid on a 100 percent basis?

4 The Bullington Company wants a time standard established on the painting operation of souvenir horseshoes for the local Pioneer Village. Work sampling is to be used. It is estimated that working time averages 95 percent of total time (working time plus idle time). A co-op student is available to do the work sampling between 8:00 A.M. and 12:00 noon. Sixty working days are to be used for the study. Use Exhibit TN4.11 and an absolute error of 2.5 percent. Use the table of random numbers (Appendix B) to calculate the sampling schedule for the first day (that is, show the times of day that an observation of working/idle should be made). Hint: Start random number selection with the first tour.

5 The final result of the study in Problem 4 estimated working time at 91.0 percent. In a 480-minute shift the best operator painted 1,000 horseshoes. The student's performance index was estimated to be 115 percent. Total allowances for fatigue, personal time, and so on are 10 percent. Calculate the standard time per piece.

1. Correspondence to the guidelines for job design is an accurate predictor of the general level of subjective satisfaction.

2. See ISM

3. *a.* 1.35 minutes.
*b.* 1.51 minutes.
*c.* ST = 1.53 minutes. The worker would not make the bonus.

4.

| | OBSERVATION TIMES |
|---|---|
| (045) | 8:45 |
| (151) | 9:51 |
| (152) | 9:52 |
| (322) | 11:22 |
| (331) | 11:31 |

5. Standard time = .558 minute.

6. ST = .078 min./doughnut.

6 Suppose you want to set a time standard for the baker making her specialty, square doughnuts. A work-sampling study of her on "doughnut day" yielded the following results:

| | |
|---|---|
| Time spent (working and idle) | 32 minutes |
| Number of doughnuts produced | 5,000 |
| Working time | 280 minutes |
| Performance rating | 125% |
| Allowances | 10% |

What is the standard time per doughnut?

7. *a.* NT = .9286 min./part.
*b.* ST = 1.0679 min./part.
*c.* Daily output = 449.50
Day's wages = $44.49.

7 In an attempt to increase productivity and reduce costs, Rho Sigma Corporation is planning to install an incentive pay plan in its manufacturing plant. In developing standards for one operation, time-study analysts observed a worker for 30 minutes. During that time the worker completed 42 parts. The analysts rated the worker as producing at 130 percent. The base wage rate of the worker is $5 per hour. The firm has established 15 percent as a fatigue and personal time allowance.

*a.* What is the normal time for the task?
*b.* What is the standard time for the task?
*c.* If the worker produced 500 units during an eight-hour day, what wages would the worker have earned?

8. *a.* NT = 11.7 min.
*b.* ST = 13.455 min./portfolio.
*c.* Daily output at standard = 35.67: 50 portfolios, day's pay = $134.55.

8 Because new regulations will greatly change the products and services offered by savings and loan associations, time studies must be performed on tellers and other personnel to determine the number and types of personnel needed and incentive wage payment plans that might be installed. As an example of the studies that the various tasks will undergo, consider the following problem and come up with appropriate answers.

A hypothetical case was set up in which the teller (to be retitled later as an *account advisor*) was required to examine a customer's portfolio and determine whether it was more beneficial for the customer to consolidate various CDs into a single issue currently offered, or to leave the portfolio unaltered. A time study made of the teller yielded the following findings:

| | |
|---|---|
| Time of study | 90 minutes |
| Number of portfolios examined | 10 portfolios |
| Performance rating | 130 percent |
| Rest for personal time | 15 percent |
| Teller's proposed new pay rate | $12 per hour |

*a.* What is the normal time for the teller to do a portfolio analysis for the CDs?
*b.* What is the standard time for the analysis?
*c.* If the S&L decides to pay the new tellers on a 100 percent premium payment plan, how much would a teller earn for a day in which he or she analyzed 50 customer portfolios?

9. Sample size = 933. Approximately 16 observations per day. See IM for example of sampling schedule.

9 Based on a manager's observations, a milling machine appears to be idle approximately 30 percent of the time. Develop a work-sampling plan to determine the percentage of idle time, accurate within a 3 percent error (±3%) with a 95 percent confidence level. Use the random numbers from Appendix B to derive the first day's sampling schedule (assume that the sample will take place over 60 days, and that an eight-hour shift is used from 8:00–12:00 and 1:00–5:00).

## CASE: TEAMWORK AT VOLVO

Volvo is trying to determine if the assembly line has become outdated as mass markets disappear. In 1974 the Swedish automaker dismantled the assembly line at its plant in Kalmar, Sweden. The line was replaced with a system in which cars are built by small, decentralized work teams that produce sections of cars. Volvo officials believe strongly that teams, and a return to craftsmanship, will improve quality and increase employees' pride in their work. In fact, Volvo believes so strongly in teamwork that this system is also being put into place at the company's new plant in Uddevalla, Sweden.

The Uddevalla plant was completed in 1990 to build the 740 and 940 models. By the end of 1991, the plant was producing about

22,000 cars annually; at full capacity, it will employ 1,000 workers and produce 40,000 cars annually. At the Uddevalla facility, self-managed teams of 8 to 10 members assemble complete cars from start to finish. Cars being assembled are not moved on a conveyor line from worker to worker but rather are assembled in a stationary position. A special device tilts the car as needed so that workers can perform their tasks. Each team has a high degree of autonomy and responsibility; they set their own break times and vacation schedules and reassign work when a team member is absent. Teams also participate in policy-making decisions and are responsible for a variety of tasks, including quality control, production planning, developing work procedures, servicing equipment, and ordering supplies.

Workers at the Uddevalla plant are paid for performance. In addition to wages, bonuses are paid for maintaining quality and productivity and for meeting weekly delivery targets. There are no supervisors or plant foremen; each of six "production workshops" houses 80 to 100 employees who are divided into assembly teams. Each assembly team has a coordinator (chosen on a rotating basis), who has direct contact with the managers. To make sure the system works, employees are provided with abundant information. Volvo also goes to great lengths to ensure that workers have an in-depth understanding of company history, tradition, and strategy. Free flow of information is encouraged, and workers have input on everything from assembly processes to new-product innovations.

The new system at Uddevalla isn't totally successful. Although morale is up and absenteeism is down, productivity is not as high as at Volvo's plant in Ghent, Belgium, where building a car on the assembly line takes about half the time. Lennert Ericson, president of the metal workers' union at the Uddevalla plant, thinks the approach there will work: "I am convinced that our ways [teams] will be successful and competitive. Our next goal is to be better than Kalmar, and when we get to that, our goal will be to get to Ghent."

Volvo has invested heavily in training workers at the Uddevalla plant. First, employees attend a 16-week initiation course as part of a 16-month training program in which workers learn about auto assembly. Workers are encouraged to share experiences with one another and exchange ideas.

Both union and management feel confident that the new system will improve the organization. But it will take time. The system puts numerous demands on everyone, and there has been some resistance. And like other automakers, Volvo hasn't escaped the current worldwide slump in car sales. But several experts pick Volvo as the company to invest in once the economy rebounds. Stock in the firm climbed from 35 in early 1991 to 60 about a year later, while shares of GM, Ford, and Chrysler were still down from their 1991 highs. Investment firm Bear Stearns thinks the Swedish automaker's profits will boom. In the meantime, striving to become the world's first truly global auto producer, Volvo has developed alliances with French automaker Renault and Japan's Mitsubishi.

Questions

1 What is the difference between teams at the Kalmar plant and self-managed teams at Uddevalla?
2 How important is empowerment in Volvo's Uddevalla facility?
3 Why do you think there is resistance to the team approach at Uddevalla? How can Volvo overcome this resistance?
4 The Uddevalla plant was closed in 1996. Why was it never able to produce cars as inexpensively as the Ghent plant? (Hint: Remember that Uddevalla is in Sweden and Ghent is in Belgium.)

Source: J. M. Ivancevich, P. Lorenzi, and S. Skinner, *Management Quality and Competitiveness* (Burr Ridge, IL: Richard D. Irwin, 1994), pp. 279–80.

## Case: Jeans Therapy—Levi's Factory Workers Are Assigned to Teams, and Morale Takes a Hit

In an industry notorious for low wages and lousy working conditions, Levi's has prided itself on being a grand exception. It offered generous pay plus plenty of charity support in factory towns—all financed by the phenomenal profitability of its brilliantly marketed brand name. It clung to a large U.S. manufacturing base long after other apparel firms began moving offshore, and it often was ranked among the best companies to work for.

But to many of Levi's workers, the company's image has not fit for some time. In 1992 the company directed its U.S. plants to abandon the old piecework system, under which a worker repeatedly performed a single, specialized task (like sewing zippers or attaching belt loops) and was paid according to the amount of work he or she completed. In the new system, groups of 10 to 35 workers would share the tasks and be paid according to the total number of trousers the group completed. Levi's figured that this would cut down on the monotony of the old system and enable stitchers to do different tasks, thus reducing repetitive-stress injuries.

At the time, the team concept was a much-touted movement designed to empower factory workers in many industries, and Levi's unions agreed to the effort. But there was more to it than that for Levi's. Faced with low-cost competitors manufacturing overseas, the San Francisco–based company did not feel it could keep many of its U.S. plants open unless it could raise productivity and reduce costs, particularly those incurred by injured workers pushing to make piecework goals. Teamwork, Levi's felt, would be more humane, safe, and profitable.

Instead, the new system led to a quagmire in which skilled workers found themselves pitted against slower colleagues, damaging morale and triggering corrosive infighting. Many top performers said the first thing they noticed about teams was that their pay shrank—and some of them decided to throttle back. They felt cheated because they were making less. Whenever a team member was absent, inexperienced, or just slow, the rest of the team had to make up for it. That infuriated some team members who felt they were carrying subpar workers. With limited supervision from coaches, groups were forced to resolve most workflow and personality issues themselves.

The fundamental problem arises from the nature of work at Levi's factories. Unlike an assembly line for cars or copiers, speed in garment-making relates directly to a worker's skill and stamina for grueling, repetitive motions of joining and stitching fabric. The workers in Levi's plants operate machines that perform specific tasks: pocket setter, belt looper, and fly stitcher, among others. Some employees work much faster than others.

In 1993 Levi's hired a consulting firm to analyze the problems. Its conclusion was simply that the company should start from scratch and involve all parties in a redesign of pay structures and work processes. As they began discussing the changes, some plant managers complained that the sessions were "at times too touchy-feely and not business-based enough." Some managers just did not like the idea of having sewing machine operators challenge their authority. Costs mounted, and in April 1994 plant managers were warned that they must cut costs by 28 percent on average by the end of 1997 or face an uncertain future.

By early 1997, Levi's share of the domestic men's denim jeans market fell to 26 percent from a high of 48 percent in 1990. Burdened by new debt, Levi's in February 1997 announced plans to cut its salaried workforce by 20 percent over 12 months. Later in November 1997, the firm announced the closing of 11 U.S. plants and layoffs of 6,395 workers. The company said that none of these jobs were transferred overseas. Still, over the years the company shifted much of its work abroad. Industrywide in 1991, approximately 15 percent of the jeans for the U.S. market were manufactured abroad. Approximately 45 percent of the jeans were produced in foreign plants by the end of 1997.

Levi's says the team approach was the company's attempt to ensure long-term survival for as many U.S. plants as possible. Plant closures might have come sooner, and job losses might have been heavier, had teams never been adopted, company officials say. Levi's vows to persevere with the team strategy at its remaining U.S. plants. But unofficially, much of the approach is being scrapped as individual managers seek ways to improve productivity. People in the plants are gradually going back to the old way of doing things.

QUESTIONS

1 What went wrong with Levi's move to teams in their plants?
2 What could Levi's have done differently to avert the problems?
3 Devise a team incentive plan that you think might work.
4 Do you think the need to move jeans production offshore was inevitable? Could Levi's have done anything to avert the problem of increasing labor costs?

SOURCE: R. T. KING, JR., "JEANS THERAPY," *WALL STREET JOURNAL*, MAY 20, 1998, P. A1. REPUBLISHED BY PERMISSION OF DOW JONES, INC. VIA COPYRIGHT CLEARANCE CENTER, INC. 

## SELECTED BIBLIOGRAPHY

Konz, Stephan. *Work Design: Industrial Ergonomics.* 2nd ed. New York: John Wiley & Sons, 1983.

Meyers, F. E. *Time and Motion Study: For Lean Manufacturing.* Upper Saddle River, NJ: Prentice Hall, 1998.

Niebel, B. W., and A. Freiralds. *Methods, Standards, and Work Design.* New York: WCB/McGraw-Hill, 1998.

Parker, S., and T. Hall. *Job and Work Design: Organizing Work to Promote Well-Being and Effectiveness.* Thousand Oaks, CA: Sage, 1998.

Ramsey, G. F. Jr. "Using Self-Administered Work Sampling in a State Agency." *Industrial Engineering,* February 1993, pp. 44–45.

Rutter, R. "Work Sampling: As a Win/Win Management Tool." *Industrial Engineering,* February 1994, pp. 30–31.

Sandberg, ëAke. *Enriching Production: Perspectives on Volvo's Uddevalla Plant as An Alternative to Lean Production.* Brookfield, VT: Avebury, 1995.

Sasser, W. E., and W. E. Fulmer. "Creating Personalized Service Delivery Systems." In *Service Management Effectiveness,* ed. D. Bowen, R. Chase, and T. Cummings. San Francisco: Jossey-Bass, 1990, pp. 213–33.

## FOOTNOTES

1 E. E. Lawler III, *The Ultimate Advantage: Creating the High Involvement Organizations* (San Francisco: Jossey-Bass, 1992), pp. 85–86.

2 Lawler, *The Ultimate Advantage,* pp. 98–99.

3 This summary is taken from E. Mumford and M. Weir, *Computer Systems in Work Design—the ETHICS Method* (New York: Halstead, 1979), p. 42.

4 For a complete discussion of incentive plans, including quality measures, see S. Globerson and R. Parsons, "Multi-Factor Incentive Systems: Current Practices." *Operations Management Review* 3, no. 2 (Winter 1985).

5 C. O'Dell, *People, Performance, and Pay* (Houston: American Productivity Center, 1987).

6 E. E. Lawler III, "Paying for Organizational Performance," Report G87-1(92) (Los Angeles: Center for Effective Organizations, University of Southern California, 1987).

7 These examples are from W. Imberman, "Pay for Performance Boosts Quality Output." *Industrial Engineering,* October 1996, p. 35.

8 C. Giffi, A. Roth, and G. M. Seal, *Competing in World-Class Manufacturing: America's 21st Century Challenge* (Burr Ridge, IL: Richard D. Irwin, 1990), p. 299.

*chapter five*

# PRODUCT DESIGN AND PROCESS SELECTION—MANUFACTURING

## CHAPTER OUTLINE AND KEY TERMS

# AN EFFICIENCY GURU REFITS HONDA TO FIGHT AUTO GIANTS

The car-racing enthusiasts who design its engines have long dominated Honda Motor Company. But lately, a motor for change has been humming at the company, a hard-charging industrial engineer named Masaki Iwai. Iwai, an efficiency expert and cost-cutting fanatic, is betting Honda can reap economies of scale by doubling its speed and efficiency in manufacturing cars. He scoffs at the idea that the company will have to bulk up through a merger or takeover. "Honda will never have to go after volume," says the senior managing director, an influential member of Honda's inner management circle. "We'll be able to make the kind of profits only an industry Goliath can make, with half their volume."

Iwai has set the bar high. He wants to refit Honda's assembly lines so that they can produce any model in the company's lineup, ranging from the minimalist Civic to the luxurious Acura. He aims to make the final assembly line shorter—half the Honda average of 3,300 feet—to slash the time and money required to put new products and models into production. Eventually, he wants each assembly line to have about 20 off-line branches, up from just a few today. One of them would not just install engines but also would actually produce them, work now handled in most cases at specialized plants. Honda's goal is to synchronize engine production and final assembly so that hardly any engines will sit in inventory, representing tied-up money.

Source: "An Efficiency Guru Refits Honda to Fight Auto Giants," *The Wall Street Journal*, September 15, 1999, p. B1. 

In some cases, the changes involve adding labor. Last year the Suzuka, Japan, factory removed a fully automated engine-installation system and replaced it with three workers and some semiautomated equipment. As a result, the station can plop engines into a wider variety of vehicles while doing it in a standardized way, no matter what the mode. Iwai ordered a similar change in seat installation on the Suzuka line, adding two workers. He is often found nosing around the factory before dawn, hours before other managers arrive, looking for equipment being wasted with idle time or uneven flow of parts.

Iwai rarely misses an opportunity to trumpet his less-is-more philosophy. Most manufacturing plants, he says, are "like my Legend," the Honda-built Acura luxury car. "They're equipped with fancy, state-of-the-art, high-tech gadgets nobody uses." Iwai says he recently traded in his Legend for a bare-bones Accord. ←

Vol. VI
"Product Design and Manufacturing at Tri State Industries"

Cross Functional

Designing new products and getting them to market quickly is the challenge facing manufacturers in industries as diverse as computer chips and potato chips. Customers of computer chip manufacturers, such as computer companies, need ever more powerful semiconductors for their evolving product lines. Food producers need to provide their grocery store customers new taste sensations to sustain or enlarge their retail market share.

How manufactured products are designed and how the process to produce them is selected are the topics of this chapter. As shown in Exhibit 5.1, three major functions are involved in these activities: marketing, product development, and manufacturing. Marketing suggests ideas for new products and provides specifications for existing product lines. Product development moves the technical concept for the product to its final design. Manufacturing selects and configures the processes by which the product is to be manufactured.

The product development activity links customer needs and expectations to the activities required to manufacture the product. We will learn about the modern requirement for a speedy development process. Further, the process must be responsive to changing customer expectations and dynamic technological innovations. The process must also cater to diverse local preferences in a global marketplace.

EXHIBIT 5.1

The Major Business Functions Involved in the Product Development Process

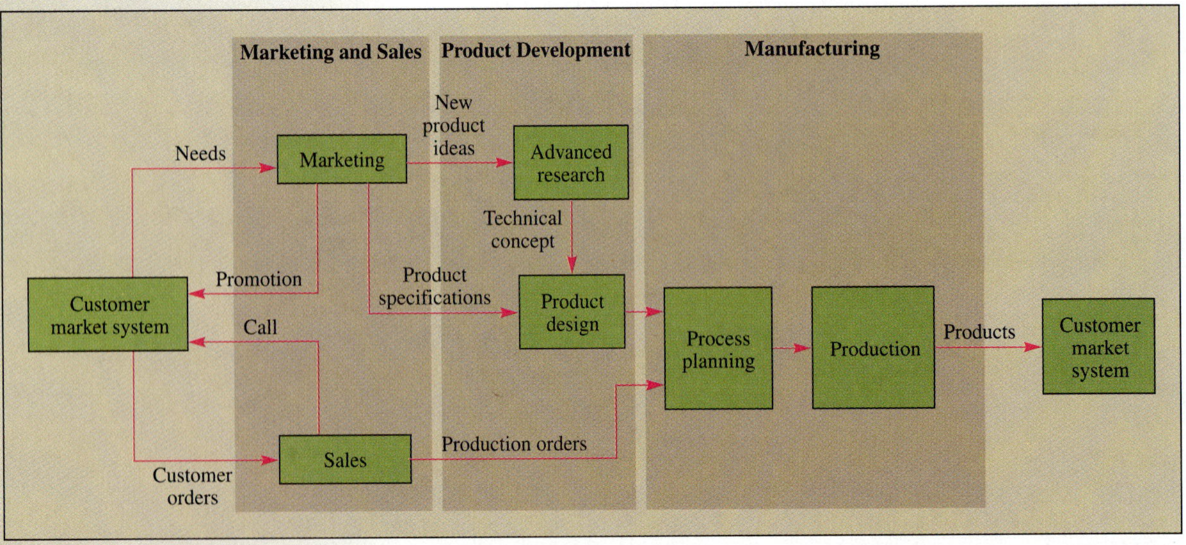


SOURCE: REPRINTED WITH THE PERMISSION OF THE FREE PRESS, AN IMPRINT OF SIMON & SCHUSTER FROM *FAST CYCLE TIME: HOW TO ALIGN PURPOSE, STRATEGY, AND STRUCTURE FOR SPEED* BY C. MEYER. COPYRIGHT © 1993 BY C. MEYER.

## THE PRODUCT DESIGN PROCESS

Although the potential opportunities to be realized in developing new products are exciting, making them happen is a demanding challenge. New product development entails a complex set of activities that cuts across most functions in a business. Exhibit 5.2 lays out the phases of a typical development project.[1] In the first two phases, concept development and product planning, information about market opportunities, competitive moves, technical possibilities, and production requirements must be combined to define the architecture of the new product. This includes its conceptual design, target market, desired level of performance, investment requirements, and financial impact. Before a new-product development program is approved, firms also attempt to prove out the concept through small-scale testing. This test may involve the construction of models and discussions with potential customers.

Cross Functional

Vol. V
"JIT at Tri State" Part 1.

Once approved, a new-product project moves into detailed engineering. The primary activities in this phase are the design and construction of working prototypes and the development of tools and equipment to be used in commercial production. At the heart of detailed product engineering is the "design–build–test" cycle. Both the products and the processes needed are defined in concept, captured in a working model (which may exist on a computer or in physical form), and then subjected to tests that simulate product use. If the model fails to deliver the desired performance characteristics, engineers search for design changes that will close the gap, and the design–build–test cycle is repeated. The conclusion of the detailed engineering phase of development is marked by an engineering "release" or "sign-off" that signifies that the final design meets requirements.

At this time, the firm typically moves development into a pilot manufacturing phase, during which the individual components, built and tested on production equipment, are assembled and tested as a system in the factory. During pilot production, units of the product are produced and the ability of the new or modified manufacturing process to execute at a

EXHIBIT 5.2

**Typical Phases of Product Development**

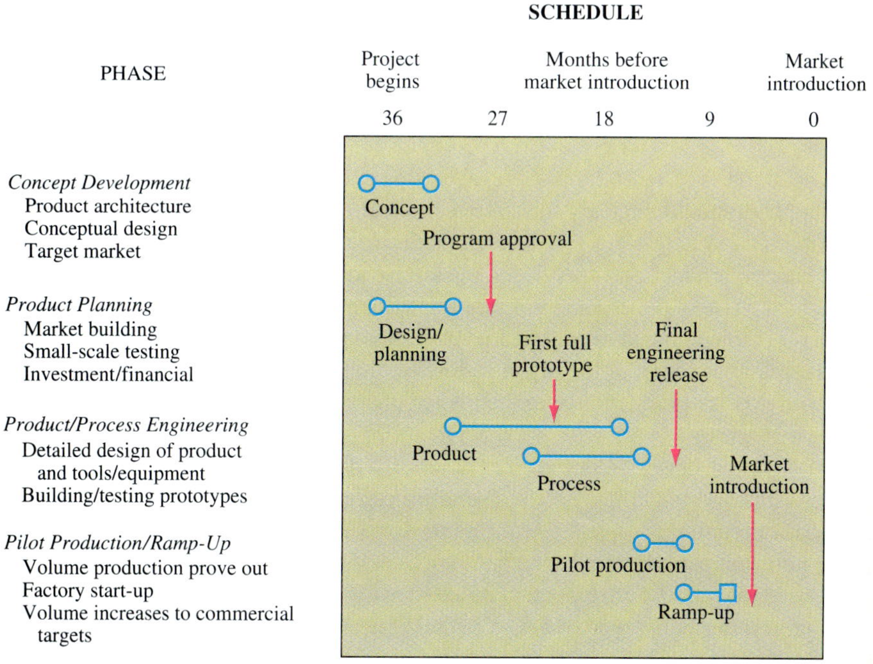


Source: Reprinted with the permission of The Free Press, a Division of Simon & Schuster from *Revolutionizing Product Development: Quantum Leaps in Speed, Efficiency, and Quality* by S. C. Wheelwright and K. B. Clark. Copyright © 1992 by S. C. Wheelwright and K. B. Clark.

EXHIBIT 5.3

**Functional Activities Under Cross-Functional Integration**

| Functional activities | Phases of Development | |
|---|---|---|
| | Concept Development | Product Planning |
| Product Development | Propose new technologies: develop product ideas; build models; conduct simulations. | Choose components and interact with suppliers; build early system prototypes; define product architecture. |
| Marketing | Provide market-based input; propose and investigate product concepts. | Define target customer's parameters; develop estimates of sales and margins; conduct early interaction with customers. |
| Manufacturing | Propose and investigate process concepts. | Develop cost estimates; define process architecture; conduct process simulation; validate suppliers. |
| **Key Milestones** | • Concept for product and process defined. | • Establish product and process architecture. • Define program parameters. |
| **Key Decisions** | Concept approval | Program approval |

commercial rate is tested. At this stage all tooling and equipment should be in place and all parts suppliers should be ready for volume production. This is the point in development at which the total system—design, detailed engineering, tools and equipment, parts, assembly sequences, production supervisors, operators, and technicians—comes together.

The final phase of development is ramp-up. The process has been refined and debugged, but it has yet to operate at a sustained level of production. In ramp-up, production starts at a relatively low volume; as the organization develops confidence in its (and its suppliers') abilities to execute production consistently and marketing's abilities to sell the product, the volume increases.

An individual development project is usually not done in isolation. It interacts with other projects and must fit with the operating organization to be effective. Projects may share critical components and use the same support groups. Additionally, new products may require compatibility in design and function with existing products.

Concurrent engineering

To speed the product development process, many companies have begun using **concurrent engineering** (CE) approaches to organizing the project. Rather than a simple serial approach in which we proceed from one phase to another, CE emphasizes cross-functional integration and concurrent development of a product and its associated processes (see Exhibit 5.3).[2]

Teams provide the primary integration mechanism in CE programs. Three types of teams frequently appear: a program management team, a technical team, and numerous

| Phases of Development | | | |
|---|---|---|---|
| Detailed Product/Process Engineering | | Pilot Production/ Ramp-Up | Market Introduction |
| Phase I | Phase II | | |
| Do detailed design of product and interact with process; build full-scale prototypes; conduct prototype testing. | Refine details of product design; participate in building second-phase prototypes. | Evaluate and test pilot units; solve problems. | Evaluate field experience with product. |
| Conduct customer tests of prototypes; participate in prototyping evaluation. | Conduct second-phase customer tests; evaluate prototypes; plan marketing rollout; establish distribution plan. | Prepare for market rollout; train sales force and field service personnel; prepare order entry/process system. | Fill distribution channels; sell and promote; interact with key customers. |
| Do detailed design of process; design and develop tooling and equipment; participate in building full-scale prototypes. | Test and try out tooling and equipment; build second-phase prototypes; install equipment and bring up new procedures. | Build pilot units in commercial process; refine process based on pilot experience; train personnel and verify supply channel. | Ramp up plant to volume targets; meet targets for quality, yield, and cost. |
| • Build and test complete prototype.<br>• Verify product design. | • Build and refine second-phase prototype.<br>• Verify process tools and design. | • Produce pilot units.<br>• Operate and test complete commercial system. | • Ramp up to volume production.<br>• Meet initial commercial objectives. |
| Detailed design approval | Joint product and process approval | Approval for first commercial sales | Full commercial approval |

THE DESIGN AND DEVELOPMENT OF THE DESKJET PRINTER WAS ONE OF HEWLETT-PACKARD'S FIRST ATTEMPTS TO INTEGRATE MANUFACTURING, MARKETING, QUALITY ASSURANCE, AND FINANCE. WITH GROUPS IN CONSTANT COMMUNICATION WITH EACH OTHER, HP WAS ABLE TO IDENTIFY ACTIVITIES THAT COULD BE PERFORMED CONCURRENTLY WHICH SIGNIFICANTLY REDUCED BOTH DEVELOPMENT TIME AND MANUFACTURING COSTS. AS A RESULT, THE DESKJET PRINTER PROVIDED HP WITH A COMPETITIVE ADVANTAGE IN BOTH COST AND SPEED OF INTRODUCTION.

EXHIBIT 5.4

**Hewlett-Packard Product Development Strategy***

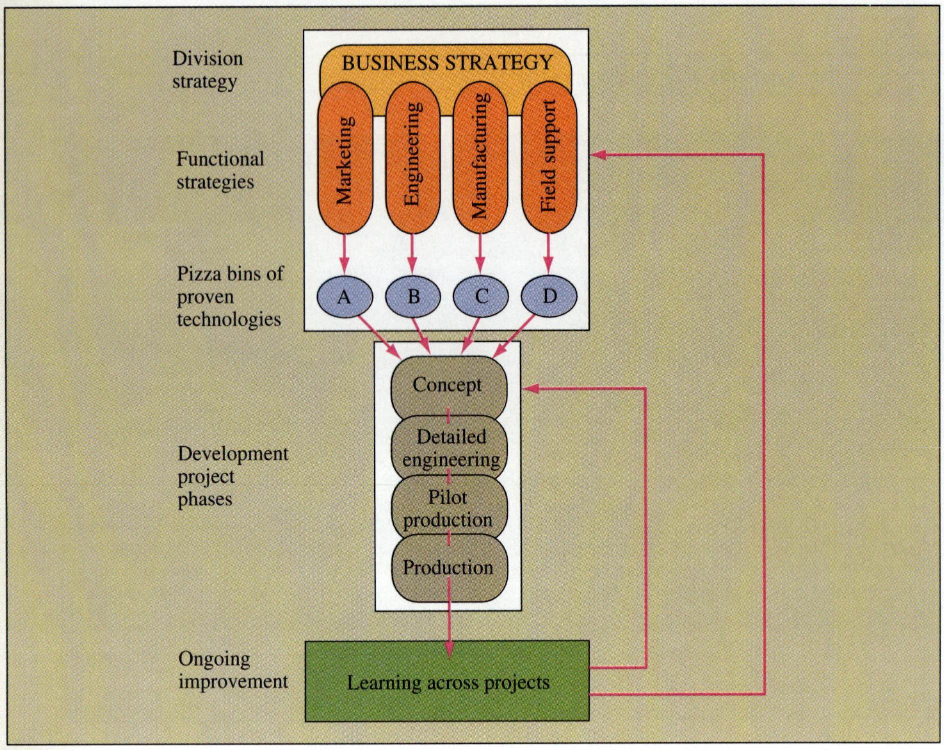


*Hewlett-Packard conceives of the business and functional strategies as key drivers in assessing which technological opportunities hold the greatest promise for a business. Advanced development projects around those technologies then prove technical feasibility *prior* to their application in specific development projects. (Note that HP uses a standard four-phase process in development, followed by efforts to consolidate learning across the set of projects.)

SOURCE: S. C. WHEELWRIGHT AND K. B. CLARK, *REVOLUTIONIZING PRODUCT DEVELOPMENT* (NEW YORK: FREE PRESS, 1992), P. 40.

design–build teams. Depending on the project's complexity, an integration team may be needed to consolidate the efforts of the various design–build teams. Task forces may be formed to address specific problems, such as investigating an emerging technology.

The benefits of the CE approach come mainly from the reduced time to complete a project. Concurrency involves the parallel completion of project phases—for example, simultaneously developing market concepts, product design, manufacturing processes, and product support structure. Frequent information sharing using electronic mail or face-to-face meetings, together with shared integrated design databases, is important to CE success. Hewlett-Packard uses technology-focused teams operating in parallel as part of its strategy. Each team works on a key technology essential to the development of its products (see Exhibit 5.4).

The time saving that results from performing activities in parallel rather than in series can be significant. The saving can come from not only the time overlap but also the reduction in errors that might be made in one phase but not caught until a later stage. We analyzed projects with structures like the product development ones in Chapter 3, "Project Management."

## DESIGNING FOR THE CUSTOMER

Before we detail the hows and whys of designing and producing products, it is useful to reflect (or, perhaps more accurately, to editorialize) on the issue of product design from the user's standpoint. In recent years, companies have been so caught up with

## LEXUS PRODUCT DESIGN IMPROVEMENT—A CONTINUOUS PROCESS

The following example of customer service happened at a Lexus automobile dealership in Louisiana.

A female customer had owned her new Lexus about a week when she returned to the dealership in distress. She wore only one brand of designer shoes, and the heel of the right shoe would get wedged below the accelerator pedal, causing her to have difficulty with the accelerator and, ultimately, to break the heel on the shoe. The service manager at the dealership recorded the problem and offered to make restitution for the shoes.

The woman assumed this would be the last she would hear from the Lexus dealer. A week later, however, a design engineer from the Lexus factory in Japan showed up at her doorstep. He asked to see the shoes, and he made measurements and drew sketches of them. The engineer left without saying a word.

A month later, the woman was contacted by the Lexus dealer and asked to bring her car in. The engineer had redesigned the accelerator pedal to ensure that shoe heels would not get wedged any longer. The dealer replaced the accelerator pedal in her car, and that retrofit pedal is now standard in Lexus production.

SOURCE: T. TAORMINA, *VIRTUAL LEADERSHIP AND THE ISO 9000 IMPERATIVE* (ENGLEWOOD CLIFFS, NJ: PRENTICE HALL, 1996), P. 158.

technological efforts and advances—especially in the field of electronics—that somewhere along the line, consumers were forgotten. (See the box titled "Lexus Product Design Improvement—A Continuous Process.")

Designing for aesthetics and for the user is generally termed *industrial design.* IDEO is one of the most successful industrial design firms in the world. The unique process used at the company is described in the Breakthrough Box titled "IDEO Product Development—Can You Learn Creativity?"

Industrial design is probably the area most abused by manufacturers. When frustrated with products—setting the VCR, working on the car, adjusting a computerized furnace thermostat, or operating a credit card telephone at the airport—most of us have said to ourselves, "The blankety-blank person who designed this should be made to work on it!" Often parts are inaccessible, operation is too complicated, or there is no logic to setting or controlling the unit. Sometimes even worse conditions exist: metal edges are sharp and consumers cut their hands trying to reach for adjustment or repairs. Many products have too many technological features—far more than necessary. Most purchasers of electronic products cannot fully operate them and use only a small number of the available features. This has occurred because computer chips are inexpensive and adding more controls has negligible cost. Including an alarm clock or a calculator on a microwave oven costs little. But do you need it? What happens when you lose the operator's manual to any of these complex devices? Why is it that the "Help" icon on your computer provides so little help? Where is the voice of the customer?

## QUALITY FUNCTION DEPLOYMENT

One approach to getting the voice of the customer into the design specification of a product is **quality function deployment (QFD).**[3] This approach, which uses interfunctional teams from marketing, design engineering, and manufacturing, has been credited by Toyota Motor Corporation for reducing costs on its cars by more than 60 percent by significantly shortening design times.

Quality function deployment (QFD)

The QFD process begins with studying and listening to customers to determine the characteristics of a superior product. Through market research, the consumers' product needs and preferences are defined and broken down into categories called *customer requirements.* One example is an auto manufacturer that would like to improve the design of a car door. Through customer surveys and interviews, it determines that two important customer requirements in a car door are that it "stays open on a hill" and is "easy to close from the

## BREAKTHROUGH

### IDEO PRODUCT DEVELOPMENT—CAN YOU LEARN CREATIVITY?

IDEO Product Development is the world's most celebrated design firm. Its ultimate creation is the process of creativity itself. For founder David M. Kelley and his colleagues, work is play, brainstorming is a science, and the most important rule is to break the rules. (www.ideo.com)

"IDEO is a zoo—oh, lovely metaphor for this age of the nanosecond! Experts of all flavors commingle in 'offices' that look more like cacophonous kindergarten classrooms than home to one of America's (and the world's) most successful design firms. Desks are littered with works-in-progress and the remains of midnight fast food binges. Models of futuristic lamps and movie special-effects devices and high-tech blood-chemistry analyzers, in all stages of development, lie about here and there—and are the cause of nonstop kibitzing. The planet's most advanced software programs, running on the world's most advanced workstations, networked with heaven knows whom from heaven knows where, hum 24 hours a day.

Clients and other outsiders pop in and out without ado. Chatter is ceaseless. Brainstorming sessions, pitting a dozen minds from different disciplines against one another in raucous pursuit of zany ideas, are called on a moment's notice. Bikes line the halls. Joke prizes, along with impressive awards, hang on every wall. The bottom line: IDEO gets the job done on time, on budget, and with exceptional imagination."[1]

IDEO's novel design process centers on two activities that are repeated over and over:

1 **Brainstorming.** IDEO enforces some strict rules during these sessions.
   *a.* Defer judgment so that the flow of ideas is not interrupted.
   *b.* Build on the ideas of others because this is far more productive that hogging the glory for your own insights.
   *c.* Stay focused on the topic; tangents are not allowed.
   *d.* One person at a time so that you do not drown out that quiet, brilliant mumbler in the corner of the room.
   *e.* Go for quantity—150 in 30–45 minutes is good.
   *f.* Encourage wild ideas.
   *g.* Be visual; for example, sketch ideas to help others understand them.

2 **Rapid prototyping.** The idea is that it is easier to discuss a model of something, no matter how primitive, than to talk about a bunch of abstract ideas. Rapid prototyping consists of three R's: rough, rapid, and right. The first two R's are fairly self-explanatory—make your models rough, and make them rapidly. In the early stages, perfecting a model is a waste of time. Right does not mean your model needs to work. Instead, it refers to building lots of small models that focus on specific problems. For example, when a group at IDEO designed a phone, they cut out dozens of pieces of foam and cradled them between their heads and shoulders to find the best shape for a handset.[2]

[1] Excerpt from T. Peters, "Beating the Great Blight of Dullness," *Forbes ASAP* (undated).
[2] E. Brown, "A Day at Innovation U.," *Fortune,* April 12, 1999.

outside." After the customer requirements are defined, they are weighted based on their relative importance to the customer. Next the consumer is asked to compare and rate the company's products with the products of competitors. This process helps the company determine the product characteristics that are important to the consumer and to evaluate its product in relation to others. The end result is a better understanding and focus on product characteristics that require improvement.

House of quality

Customer requirement information forms the basis for a matrix called the **house of quality** (see Exhibit 5.5). By building a house-of-quality matrix, the cross-functional QFD team can use customer feedback to make engineering, marketing, and design decisions. The matrix helps the team to translate customer requirements into concrete operating or engineering goals. The important product characteristics and goals for improvement are jointly agreed on and detailed in the house. This process encourages the different departments to work closely together, and it results in a better understanding of one another's goals and issues. However, the most important benefit of the house of quality is that it helps the team to focus on building a product that satisfies customers.

The first step in building the house of quality is to develop a list of customer requirements for the product. These requirements should be ranked in order of importance. Customers are then asked to compare the company's product to the competition. Next a set

EXHIBIT 5.5

Completed House of Quality Matrix for a Car Door

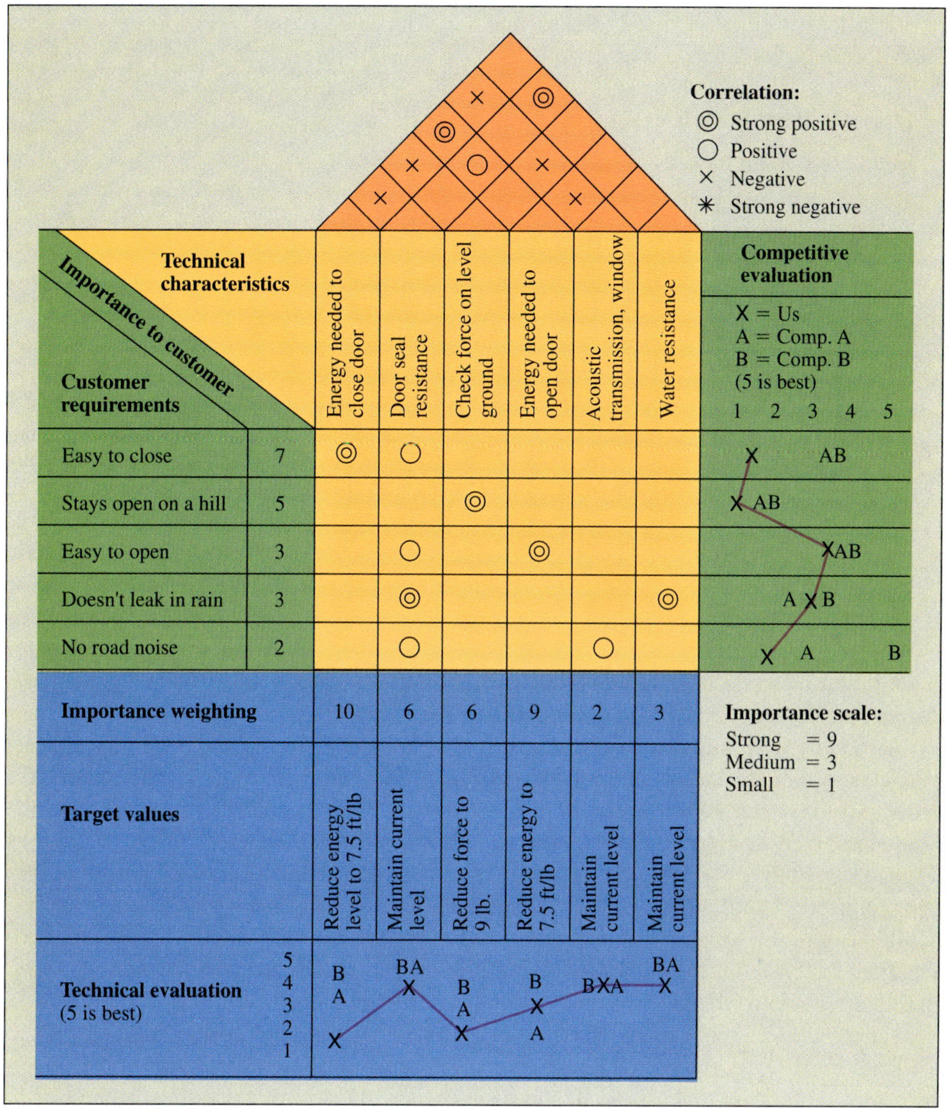


SOURCE: BASED ON J. R. HAUSER AND D. CLAUSING. "THE HOUSE OF QUALITY," *HARVARD BUSINESS REVIEW*, MAY–JUNE 1988, PP. 62–73.

of technical characteristics of the product is developed. These technical characteristics should relate directly to customer requirements. An evaluation of these characteristics should support or refute customer perception of the product. These data are then used to evaluate the strengths and weaknesses of the product in terms of technical characteristics.

## VALUE ANALYSIS/VALUE ENGINEERING

Value analysis/value engineering (VA/VE)

Because it is so important that value be designed into products, we should briefly describe value analysis and value engineering. The purpose of **value analysis/value engineering (VA/VE)** is to simplify products and processes. Its objective is to achieve equivalent or better performance at a lower cost while maintaining all functional requirements defined by the customer. VA/VE does this by identifying and eliminating unnecessary cost. Technically, VA deals with products already in production and is used to analyze product specifications and requirements as shown in production documents and purchase requests. Typically, purchasing departments use VA as a cost reduction technique. Performed before the production stage, value engineering is considered a cost avoidance method. In practice, however, there is a looping back and forth between the two for a given product. This occurs because new materials, processes, and so forth require the application of VA techniques to products that have previously undergone VE. The VA/VE analysis approach involves brainstorming such questions as

Does the item have any design features that are not necessary?

Can two or more parts be combined into one?

How can we cut down the weight?

Are there nonstandard parts that can be eliminated?

In the following section we describe a more formal approach that is often used to guide the process of designing and improving the design of products.

## DESIGNING PRODUCTS FOR MANUFACTURE AND ASSEMBLY

The word *design* has many different meanings. To some it means the aesthetic design of a product, such as the external shape of a car or the color, texture, and shape of the casing of a can opener. In another sense, design can mean establishing the basic parameters of a system. For example, before considering any details, the design of a power plant might mean establishing the characteristics of the various units such as generators, pumps, boilers, connecting pipes, and so forth.

Yet another interpretation of the word *design* is the detailing of the materials, shapes, and tolerance of the individual parts of a product. This is the concern of this section. It is an activity that starts with sketches of parts and assemblies and then progresses to the computer-aided design (CAD) workstation (described in the supplement on Operations Technology at the end of the book), where assembly drawings and detailed part drawings are produced. Traditionally, these drawings are then passed to the manufacturing and assembly engineers, whose job it is to optimize the processes used to produce the final product. Frequently, at this stage manufacturing and assembly problems are encountered and requests are made for design changes. Often these design changes are major and result in considerable additional expense and delays in the final product release.

Traditionally, the attitude of designers has been "We design it, you build it." This has now been termed the "over-the-wall approach," where the designer is sitting on one side of

RAPID PROTOTYPING COMBINED WITH DFMA TOOLS NOT ONLY CAN DETERMINE IF A PRODUCT WILL PERFORM ITS DESIGNED FUNCTIONS, BUT HOW WELL AND FOR HOW LONG. USED EARLY IN THE DESIGN CYCLE, IT LEADS TO MORE ROBUST DESIGNS FOR MANUFACTURE, ASSEMBLY, AND PRODUCT USE, AND ALLOWS CRITICAL CHANGES TO BE MADE BEFORE EXPENSIVE TOOLING IS APPLIED. A PRODUCT'S ESTHETICS AND FUNCTIONALITY ARE CONSIDERED JOINTLY AND RESULT IN PRODUCTS CONSTRUCTED WITH OPTIMAL FUNCTIONALITY, CORRECT MATERIALS, AND EFFICIENT ASSEMBLY.

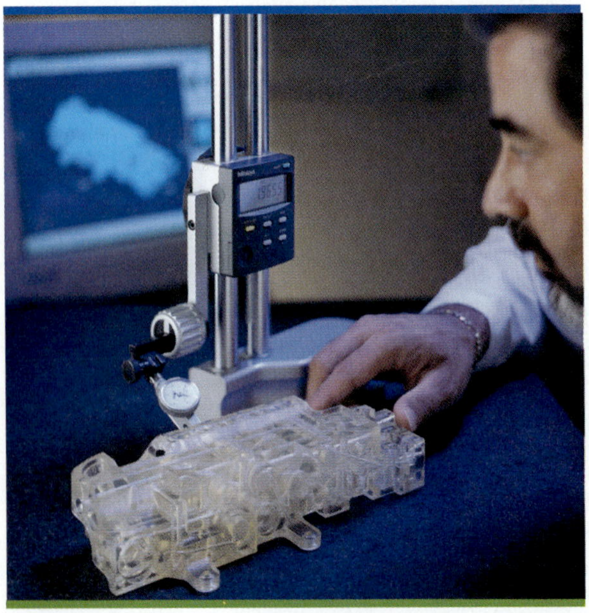

the wall and throwing the design over the wall to the manufacturing engineers. These manufacturing engineers then have to deal with the problems that arise because they were not involved in the design effort. One way to overcome this problem is to consult the manufacturing engineers during the design stage. The resulting teamwork avoids many of the problems that will arise. These concurrent engineering teams require analysis tools to help them study proposed designs and evaluate them from the point of view of manufacturing difficulty and cost.

## HOW DOES DESIGN FOR MANUFACTURING AND ASSEMBLY (DFMA) WORK?

Let's follow an example from the conceptual design stage.[4] Exhibit 5.6 represents a motor drive assembly that is required to sense and control its position on two steel guide rails. This might be the motor that controls a power window in a drive-through window at McDonald's, for example. The motor must be fully enclosed and have a removable cover for access to adjust the position sensor. A major requirement is a rigid base designed to slide up and down the guide rails, which will both support the motor and locate the sensor. The motor and sensor have wires connecting to a power supply and control unit.

A proposed solution is shown in Exhibit 5.7. The base has two bushing inserts so that the holes will not wear out. The motor is secured to the base with two screws and a hole accepts the cylindrical sensor, which is held in place with a set screw. To provide the required covers, an end plate is screwed to two stand-offs, which are screwed into the base. To keep the wires from shorting out on the metal cover, should they become worn, a plastic bushing is fitted to the end plate, through which the wires pass. Finally, a box-shaped cover slides over the whole assembly from below the base and is held in place by four screws, two passing into the base and two passing into the end cover.

The current design has 19 parts that must be assembled to make the motor drive. These parts consist of the two subassemblies—the motor and the sensor—an additional eight main parts (cover, base, two bushings, two stand-offs, a plastic bushing, and the end plate), and nine screws.

The greatest improvements related to DFMA arise from simplification of the product by reducing the number of separate parts. In order to guide the designer in reducing the part count, the methodology provides three criteria against which each part must be examined as it is added to the product during assembly:

1 During the operation of the product, does the part move relative to all other parts already assembled?

EXHIBIT 5.6

Configuration of Required Motor Drive Assembly

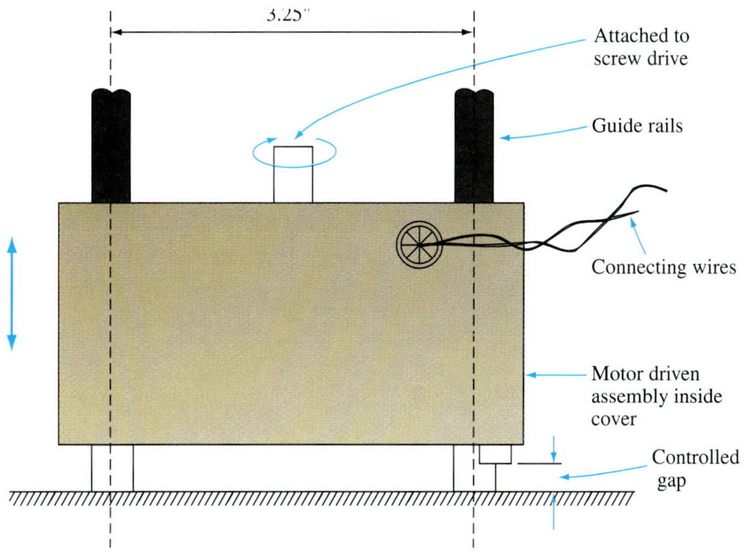

EXHIBIT 5.7

Proposed Motor Drive Design

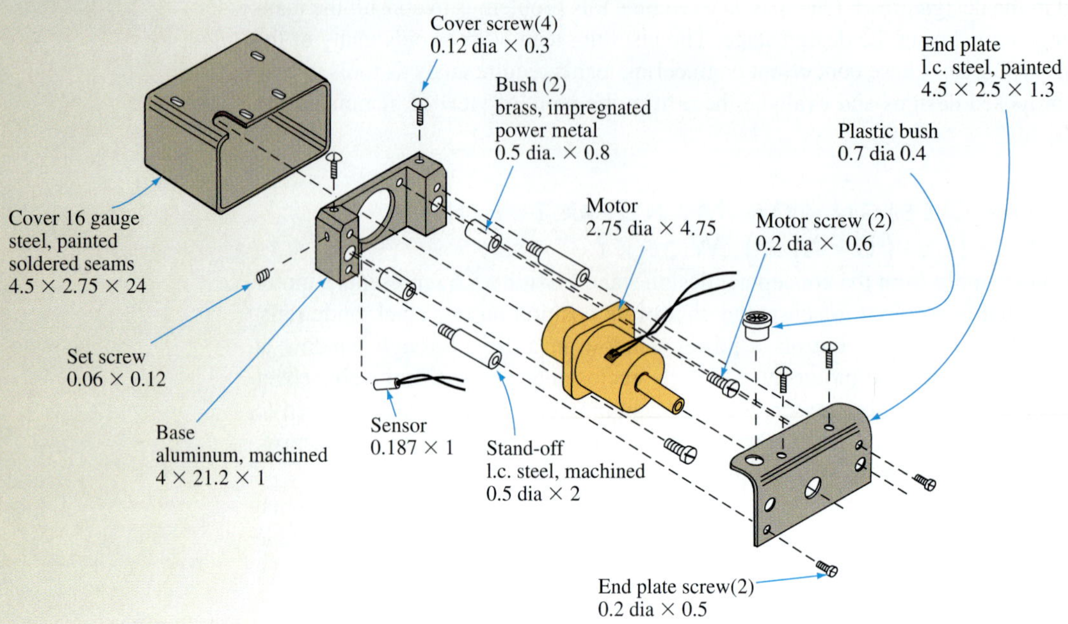


2 Must the part be of a different material than or be isolated from other parts already assembled?

3 Must the part be separate from all other parts to allow the disassembly of the product for adjustment or maintenance?

Application of these criteria to the proposed design would proceed as follows:

1 **Base.** Because this is the first part to be assembled, there are no other parts with which to combine, so it is theoretically a necessary part.

2 **Bushings (2).** These do not satisfy the second criterion. Theoretically, the base and bushings could be of the same material.

3 **Motor.** The motor is a subassembly purchased from a supplier. The criteria do not apply.

4 **Motor screws (2).** In most cases, separate fasteners are not needed, because a fastening arrangement integral to the design (for example, snapping the part into place) is usually possible.

5 **Sensor.** This is another standard subassembly.

6 **Set screw.** Similar to 4, this should not be necessary.

7 **Standoffs (2).** These do not meet the second criterion, they could be incorporated into the base.

8 **End plate.** This must be separate to allow disassembly (apply criterion three).

9 **End plate screws (2).** These should not be necessary.

10 **Plastic bushing.** Could be of the same material, and therefore combined with, the end plate.

11 **Cover.** Could be combined with the end plate.

12 **Cover screws (4).** Not necessary.

From this analysis, it can be seen that if the motor and sensor subassemblies could be arranged to snap or screw into the base, and if a plastic cover could be designed to snap on, only 4 separate items would be needed instead of 19. These four items represent the theoretical minimum number needed to satisfy the constraints of the product design.

At this point, it is up to the design team to justify why the parts above the minimum should be included. Justification may be due to practical, technical, or economic consider-

Exhibit 5.8

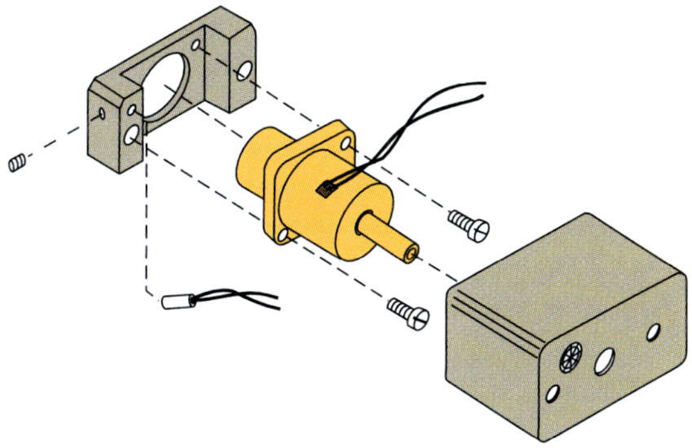

Redesign of Motor Drive Assembly Following Design for Assembly (DFA) Analysis

ations. In this example, it could be argued that two screws are needed to secure the motor and that one set screw is needed to hold the sensor, because any alternatives would be impractical for a low-volume product such as this. However, the design of these screws could be improved by providing them with pilot points to facilitate assembly.

Exhibit 5.8 is a drawing of a redesigned motor drive assembly that uses only seven separate parts. Notice how the parts have been eliminated. The new plastic cover is designed to snap onto the base plate. This new product is much simpler to assemble and should be much less expensive due to the reduced number of parts.

## PROCESS SELECTION

*Process engineering* as used in Exhibit 5.2 refers to the tactical planning activities that regularly occur in manufacturing. *Process selection,* in contrast, refers to the strategic decision of selecting which kind of production processes to have in the plant. For example, in the case of our motor drive, if the volume is very low we might just have a worker sit at a table and produce a small batch of these assemblies. On the other hand, if the volume is very high, setting up an assembly line might be appropriate.

Vol. I
"The Manufacturing Process."

### Types of Processes

Recall from Chapter 4 that processes are categorized based on how they are designed. There we defined terms such as single- and multiple-stage, and make-to-stock and make-to-order processes. Another way to categorize processes is based on what they do.

At the most basic level, the types of processes do the following things:

- Conversion processes include examples such as changing iron ore into steel sheets or making all the ingredients listed on the box of toothpaste into toothpaste.
- Fabrication processes include examples such as changing raw materials into some specific form (for example, making sheet metal into a car fender or forming gold into a crown for a tooth).
- Assembly processes include examples such as assembling a fender to a car, putting toothpaste tubes into a box, or fastening a dental crown in somebody's mouth.
- Testing processes are not, strictly speaking, fundamental processes, are so widely mentioned as a stand-alone major activity that they are included here for completeness.

### Process Flow Structures

A *process flow structure* refers to how a factory organizes material flow using one or more of the process technologies just listed.

Vol. III
"Washburn Guitar"

Hayes and Wheelwright have identified four major process flow structures:

**Job shop.** Production of small batches of a large number of different products, most of which require a different set or sequence of processing steps. Commercial printing

Job shop

firms, airplane manufacturers, machine tool shops, and plants that make custom-designed printed circuit boards are examples of this type of structure.

Batch shop

**Batch shop.** Essentially, a somewhat standardized job shop. Such a structure is generally employed when a business has a relatively stable line of products, each of which is produced in periodic batches, either to customer order or for inventory. Most of these items follow the same flow pattern through the plant. Examples include heavy equipment, electronic devices, and specialty chemicals.

Assembly line

**Assembly line.** Production of discrete parts moving from workstation to workstation at a controlled rate, following the sequence needed to build the product. Examples include manual assembly of toys and appliances, and automatic assembly (called *insertion*) of components on a printed circuit board. When other processes are employed in a line fashion along with assembly, it is commonly referred to as a *production line*. (See Exhibit 5.9.)

Continuous flow

**Continuous flow.** Conversion or further processing of undifferentiated materials such as petroleum, chemicals, or beer, as the photo below shows. As on assembly lines, production follows a predetermined sequence of steps, but the flow is continuous rather than discrete. Such structures are usually highly automated and, in effect, constitute one integrated "machine" that must be operated 24 hours a day to avoid expensive shutdowns and start-ups.

The choice of which flow structure to select, with the exception of continuous flow structures, is generally a function of the volume requirements for each product.

## PRODUCT–PROCESS MATRIX

Product–process matrix

The relationship between process structures and volume requirements is often depicted on a **product–process matrix** (Exhibit 5.10). The way to interpret this matrix is that as volume increases and the product line (the horizontal dimension) narrows, specialized equipment and standardized material flows (the vertical dimension) become economically feasible. Because this evolution in process structure is frequently related to the product's life cycle stage (introduction, growth, or maturity), it is very useful in linking marketing and manufacturing strategies.

The industries listed within the matrix are presented as ideal types that have found their structural niche. (Sample food service systems are included to help readers get a gut feel

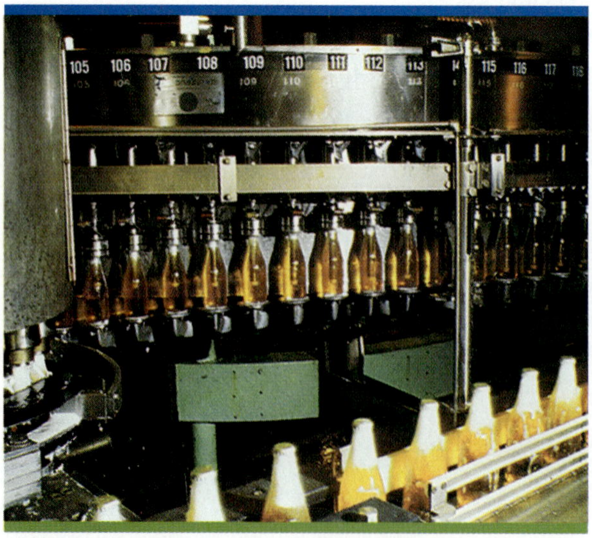

THE MILLER BREWING COMPANY USES A CONTINUOUS PRODUCTION PROCESS. BEER IS BREWED, BOTTLED, PACKAGED, AND SHIPPED ON ONE LONG PRODUCTION LINE WITH SPECIALIZED AUTOMATED EQUIPMENT.

KAWASAKI MOTORS MANUFACTURING USES AN ASSEMBLY PRODUCTION LINE WITH A FIXED SEQUENCE OF ASSEMBLY TASKS AND WORKERS CHECKING QUALITY AT EACH STEP.

EXHIBIT 5.9

*How to Make a Car:* The Production Process in a Modern Car Plant Includes Lots of Checks on Quality and Extensive Treatment to Prevent Corrosion

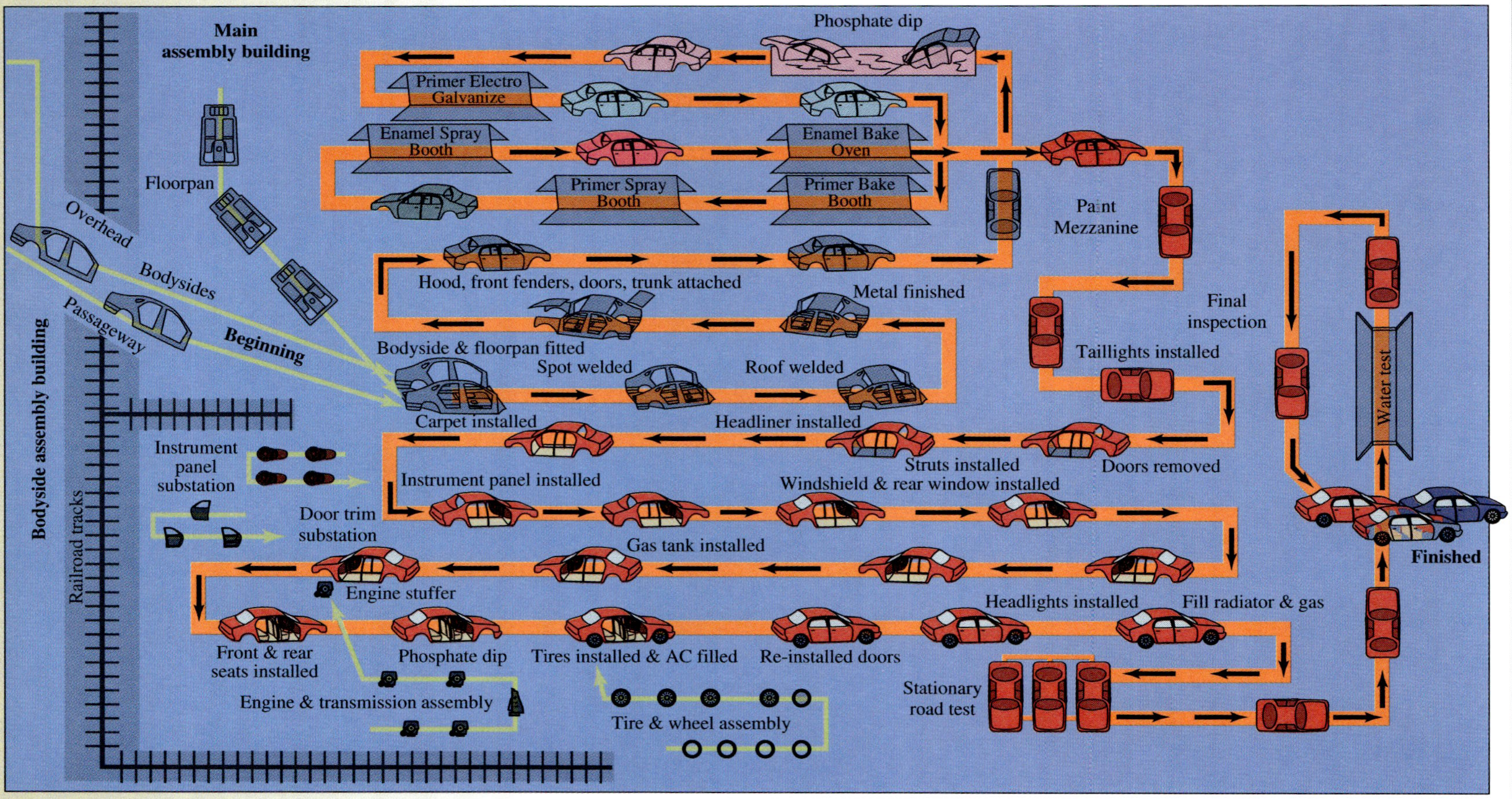


SOURCE: MITCHEL J. FRUMKIN/DRIVE COMMUNICATIONS; *CHICAGO SUN-TIMES*, SEPTEMBER 17, 1999.

EXHIBIT 5.10

Matching Major Stages of Product and Process Life Cycles

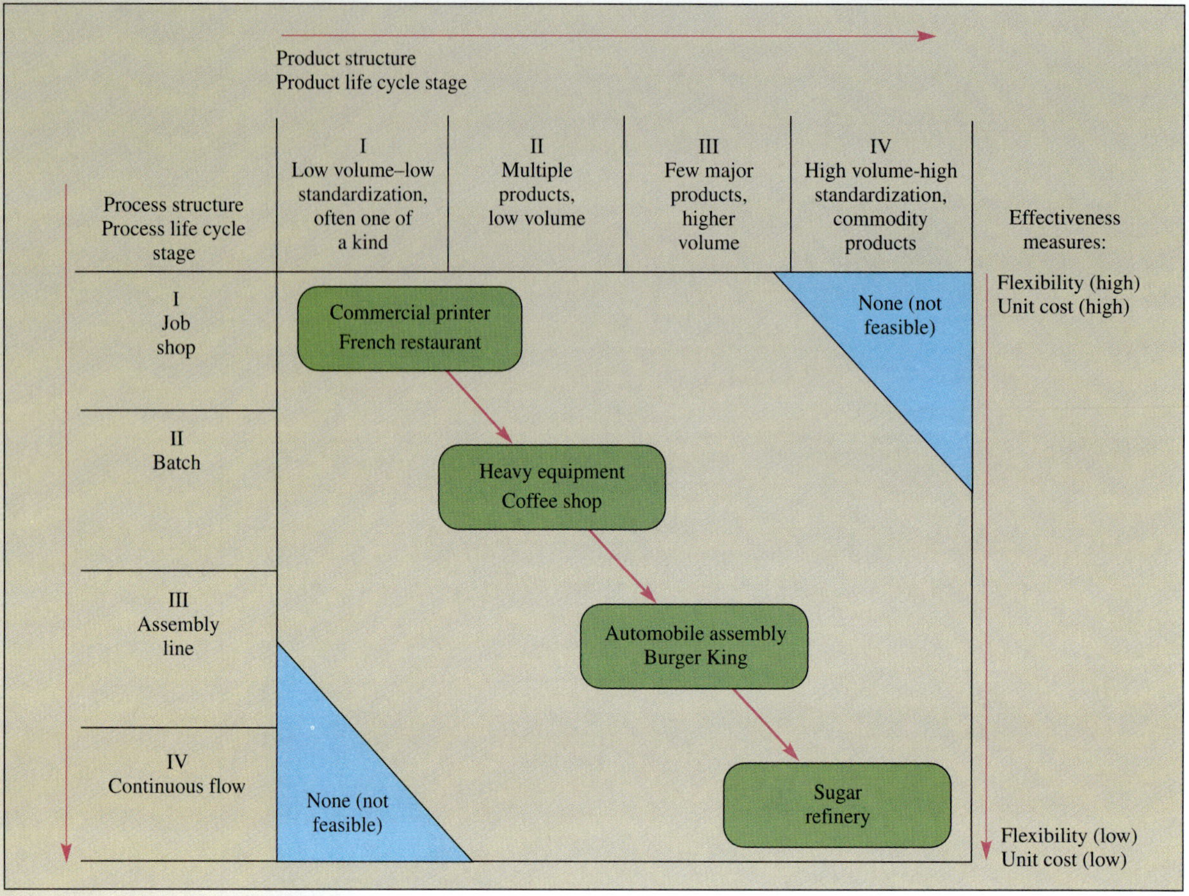


SOURCE: MODIFIED FROM R. HAYES AND S. WHEELWRIGHT, *RESTORING OUR COMPETITIVE EDGE: COMPETING THROUGH MANUFACTURING* (NEW YORK: JOHN WILEY & SONS, 1984), P. 209.

for the dimensions.) It is certainly possible for an industry member to choose another position on the matrix, however. For example, the opening vignette describes Honda Motor Company's redesign of its assembly lines so that any model can be produced. Honda recognizes that with the more flexible lines it will not be able to produce at the high volumes common at Ford or General Motors. This recognition of lower volume paired with the production of a higher variety of products corresponds to a horizontal move from stage III to stage II. From the product–process matrix, one might also think that Honda would move from a pure assembly line to a batch process structure. In the case of Honda, cars will still be made using a modified assembly line structure, but batches of each model will be made; at least that is what our framework would suggest. It will be interesting to learn how successful Honda's new approach is in the future.

## THE VIRTUAL FACTORY

Virtual factory

The new term **virtual factory** refers to manufacturing activities carried out not in one central plant, but rather in multiple locations by suppliers and partner firms as part of a strategic alliance. The role of manufacturing for an auto producer, for example, will shift from solely monitoring activities at one central plant to managing the integration of all steps in the process—no matter where physical production actually takes place. The implications for process planning are profound: The manufacturer must have a deep understanding of the manufacturing capabilities of all parties in the production network and must excel at the difficult task of coordination.

Exhibit 5.11

**Major Decision Variables in Equipment Selection**

| Decision Variable | Factors to Consider |
|---|---|
| Initial investment | Price<br>Manufacturer<br>Availability of used models<br>Space requirements<br>Need for feeder/support equipment |
| Output rate | Actual versus rated capacity |
| Output quality | Consistency in meeting specs<br>Scrap rate |
| Operating requirements | Ease of use<br>Safety<br>Human factors impact |
| Labor requirements | Direct to indirect ratio<br>Skills and training |
| Flexibility | General-purpose versus special-purpose equipment<br>Special tooling |
| Setup requirements | Complexity<br>Changeover speed |
| Maintenance | Complexity<br>Frequency<br>Availability of parts |
| Obsolescence | State of the art<br>Modification for use in other situations |
| In-process inventory | Timing and need for supporting buffer stocks |
| Systemwide impacts | Tie-in with existing or planned systems<br>Control activities<br>Fit with manufacturing strategy |

# BREAK-EVEN ANALYSIS

## Specific Equipment Selection

The choice of specific equipment follows the selection of the general type of process structure. Exhibit 5.11 shows some key factors to consider in the selection decision. Firms may have both general-purpose equipment and special-purpose equipment. For example, a machine shop would have lathes and drill presses (general-purpose) and could have transfer machines (special-purpose). An electronics firm may have a single-function test module to perform only one test at a time (general-purpose) and may have a multifunction test unit to perform multiple tests at the same time (special-purpose). As computer-based technology evolves, however, the general-purpose/special-purpose distinction becomes blurred because a general-purpose machine has the capability to produce just as efficiently as many special-purpose ones.

A standard approach to choosing among alternative processes or equipment is *break-even analysis*. A break-even chart visually presents alternative profits and losses due to the number of units produced or sold. The choice obviously depends on anticipated demand. The method is most suitable when processes and equipment entail a large initial investment and fixed cost, and when variable costs are reasonably proportional to the number of units produced.

### EXAMPLE 5.1: BREAK-EVEN ANALYSIS

Suppose a manufacturer has identified the following options for obtaining a machined part: It can buy the part at $200 per unit (including materials); it can make the part on a numerically controlled semi-automatic lathe at $75 per unit (including materials); or it can make the part on a machining center at $15 per unit (including materials). There is negligible fixed cost if the item is purchased; a semiautomatic lathe costs $80,000; and a machining center costs $200,000.

The total cost for each option is

$$\text{Purchase cost} = \$200 \times \text{Demand}$$
$$\text{Produce using lathe cost} = \$80{,}000 + \$75 \times \text{Demand}$$
$$\text{Produce using machining center cost} = \$200{,}000 + \$15 \times \text{Demand}$$

## SOLUTION

Whether we approach the solution to this problem as cost minimization or profit maximization really makes no difference as long as the relationships remain linear: that is, variable costs and revenue are the same for each incremental unit. Exhibit 5.12 shows the break-even point for each process. If demand is expected to be more than 2,000 units (point A), the machine center is the best choice because this would result in the lowest total cost. If demand is between 640 (point B) and 2,000 units, the semiautomatic lathe is the cheapest. If demand is less than 640 (between 0 and point B), the most economical course is to buy the product.

The break-even point A calculation is

$$\$80{,}000 + \$75 \times \text{Demand} = \$200{,}000 + \$15 \times \text{Demand}$$
$$\text{Demand (point A)} = 120{,}000/60 = 2{,}000 \text{ units}$$

The break-even point B calculation is

$$\$200 \times \text{Demand} = \$80{,}000 + \$75 \times \text{Demand}$$
$$\text{Demand (point B)} = 80{,}000/125 = 640 \text{ units}$$

Consider the effect of revenue, assuming the part sells for \$300 each. As Exhibit 5.12 shows, profit (or loss) is the distance between the revenue line and the alternative process cost. At 1,000 units, for example, maximum profit is the difference between the \$300,000 revenue (point C) and the semiautomatic lathe cost of \$160,000 (point D). For this quantity the semiautomatic lathe is the cheapest alternative available. The optimal choices for both minimizing cost and maximizing profit are the lowest segments of the lines: origin to B, to A, and to the right side of Exhibit 5.12 as shown in red. ←

EXHIBIT 5.12

**Break-Even Chart of Alternative Processes**

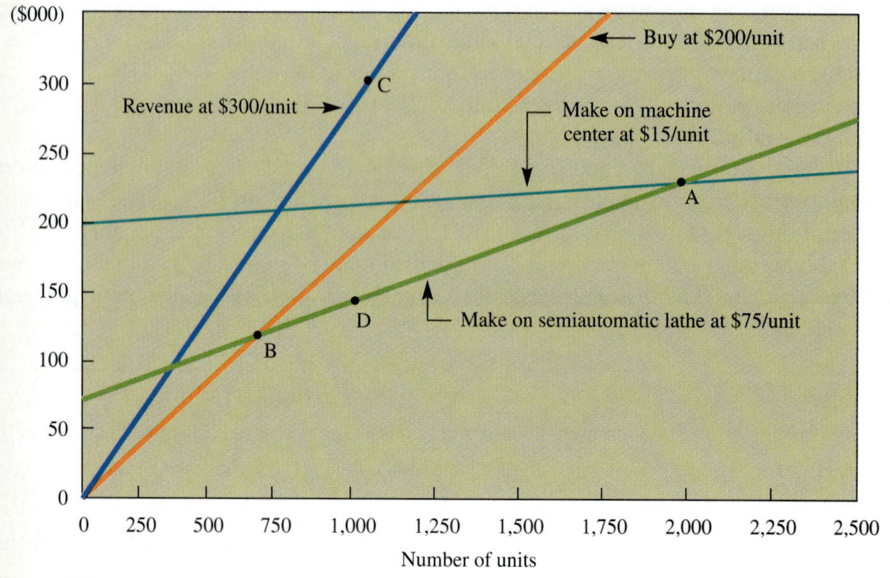

# MANUFACTURING PROCESS FLOW DESIGN

Manufacturing process flow design focuses on the specific processes that raw materials, parts, and subassemblies follow as they move through the plant. The most common production management tools used in planning the process flow are assembly drawings, assembly charts, route sheets, and flow process charts. Each of these charts is a useful diagnostic tool and can be used to improve operations during the steady state of the productive system. Indeed, the standard first step in analyzing any production system is to map the flows and operations using one or more of these techniques. These are the "organization charts" of the manufacturing system.

An *assembly drawing* (Exhibit 5.13) is simply an exploded view of the product showing its component parts. An *assembly chart* (Exhibit 5.14) uses the information presented in the assembly drawing and defines (among other things) how parts go together, their order of assembly, and often the overall material flow pattern.[5] An *operation and route sheet*

EXHIBIT 5.13

Plug Assembly Drawing

EXHIBIT 5.14

Assembly (or Gozinto) Chart for Plug Assembly

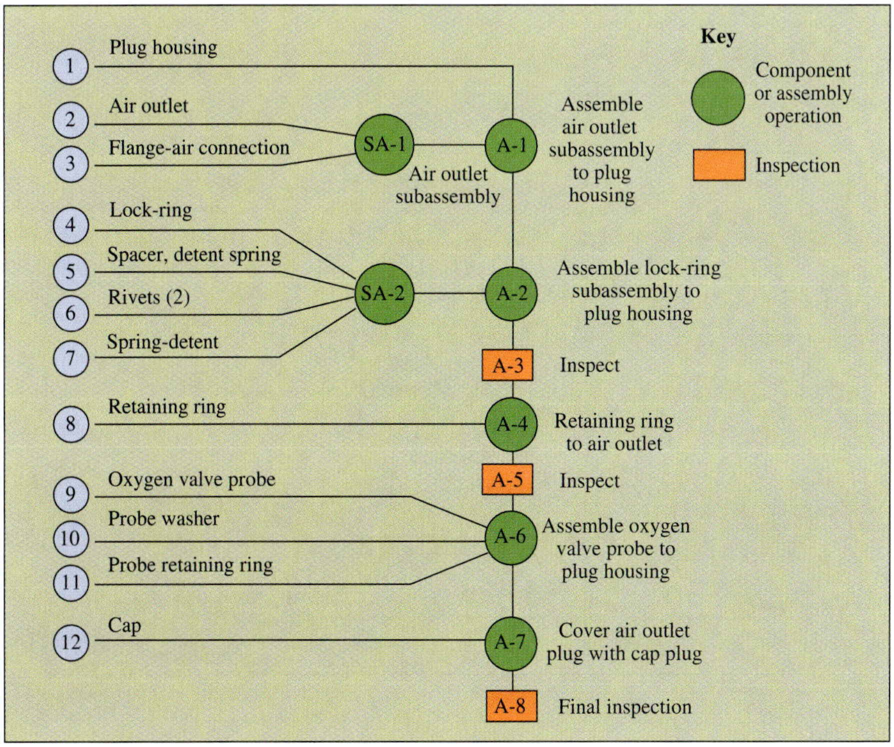

EXHIBIT 5.15

## Operation and Route Sheet for Plug Assembly

| | | |
|---|---|---|
| Material Specs | Part Name: Plug Housing | Part No.: TA 1274 |
| Purchased Stock Size | Usage: Plug Assembly | Date Issued |
| Pcs. Per Pur Size | Assy. No.: TA 1279 | Date Supplied |
| Weight | Sub.Assy. No. | Issued By |

| Oper. No. | Operation Description | Dept. | Machine | Setup Hr. | Rate Pc. Hr. | Tools |
|---|---|---|---|---|---|---|
| 20 | Drill hole .32 $^{+.015}_{-.005}$ | Drill | Mach. 513 Drill | 1.5 | 254 | Drill fixture L-76 Jig # 10393 |
| 30 | Deburr .312 $^{+.015}_{-.005}$ dia. hole | Drill | Mach. 510 Drill | .1 | 424 | Multitooth burring tool |
| 40 | Chamfer .009/875. bore .878/.875 dia (2 passes). bore .7600/7625 (1 pass) | Lathe | Mach. D 109 lathe | 1.0 | 44 | Ramet-1, TPG 221, chamfer tool |
| 50 | Tap hole as designated 1/4 min. full thread | Tap | Mach. 517 drill tap | 2.0 | 180 | Fixture #CR-353 tap. 4 Flute sp. |
| 60 | Bore hole 1.33 to 1.138 dia. | Lathe | H&H E107 | 3.0 | 158 | L44 turret fixture Hartford |
| | | | | | | Superspacer, pl. #45 holder #L46 |
| | | | | | | FDTW-100, insert #21 chk. fixture |
| 70 | Deburr .005 to.010 both sides, hand feed to hard stop | Lathe | E162 lathe | .3 | 175 | Collect CR #179 1327 RPM |
| 80 | Broach keyway to remove thread burrs | Drill | Mach. 507 drill | .4 | 91 | B87 fixture, L59 broach tap. .875120 G-H6 |
| 90 | Hone thread I.D. .822/ .828 | Grind | Grinder | 1.5 | 120 | |
| 95 | Hone .7600/ .7625 | Grind | Grinder | 1.5 | 120 | |
| | | | | | | |
| | | | | | | |

EXHIBIT 5.16

## Process Flowchart for the Plug Housing (partial)

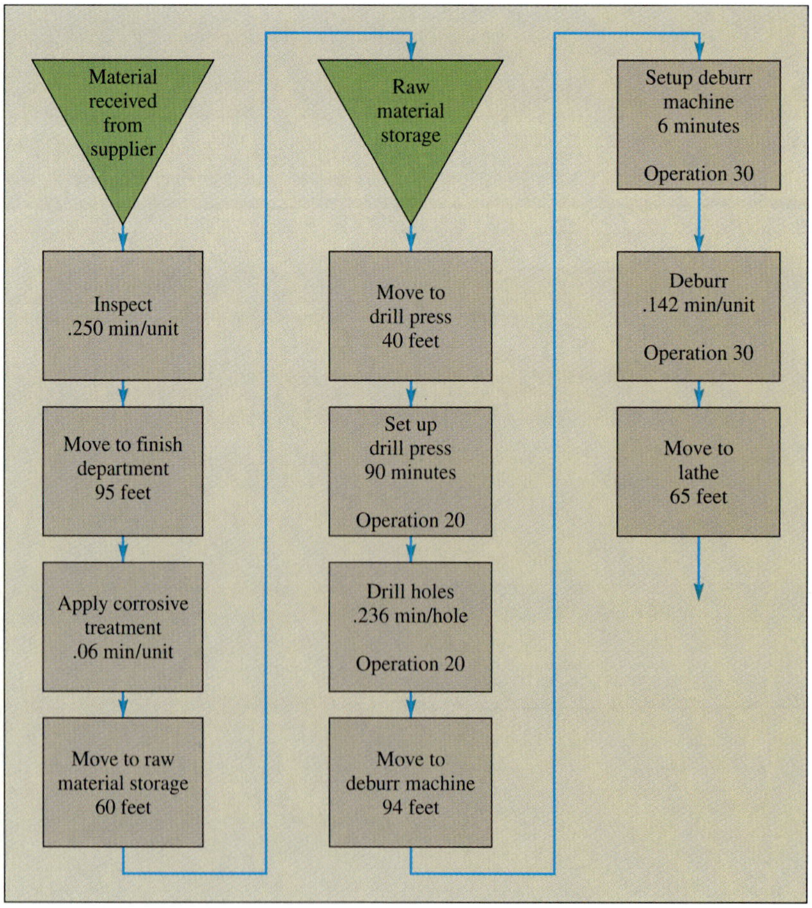

(Exhibit 5.15), as its name implies, specifies operations and process routing for a particular part. It conveys such information as the type of equipment, tooling, and operations required to complete the part.

A *process flowchart* such as Exhibit 5.16 denotes what happens to the product as it progresses through the productive facility. Recall, process flowcharting was covered in Chapter 4. The focus in analyzing a manufacturing operation should be the identification of activities that can be minimized or eliminated, such as movement and storage within the process. As a rule, the fewer the moves, delays, and storages in the process, the better the flow.

### EXAMPLE 5.2: MANUFACTURING PROCESS ANALYSIS

Recall from Chapter 4 that a process usually consists of (1) a set of *tasks,* (2) a *flow* of material and information that connects the set of tasks, and (3) *storage* of material and information.

1 Each task in a process accomplishes, to a certain degree, the transformation of input into the desired output.
2 The flow in a process consists of material flow as well as flow of information. The flow of material transfers a product from one task to its next task. The flow of information helps in determining how much of the transformation has been done in the previous task and what exactly remains to be completed in the present task.
3 When neither a task is being performed nor a part is being transferred, the part has to be stored. Goods in storage, waiting to be processed by the next task, are often called *work-in-process inventory.*

Process analysis involves adjusting the capacities and balance among different parts of the process to maximize output or minimize the costs with available resources. Our company supplies a component to several large auto manufacturers.[6] This component is assembled in a shop by 15 workers working an eight-hour shift on an assembly line that moves at the rate of 150 components per hour. The workers receive their pay in the form of a group incentive amounting to 30 cents per completed good part. This wage is distributed equally among the workers. Management believes that it can hire 15 more workers for a second shift if necessary.

Parts for the final assembly come from two sources. The molding department makes one very critical part and the rest come from outside suppliers. There are 11 machines capable of molding the one part done in-house; but historically, one machine is being overhauled or repaired at any given time. Each machine requires a full-time operator. The machines could each produce 25 parts per hour, and the workers are paid on an individual piece rate of 20 cents per good part. The workers will work overtime at a 50 percent increase in rate, or for 30 cents per good part. The workforce for molding is flexible; currently, only six workers are on this job. Four more are available from a labor pool within the company. The raw materials for each part molded cost 10 cents per part; a detailed analysis by the accounting department has concluded that 2 cents of electricity is used in making each part. The parts purchased from the outside cost 30 cents for each final component produced.

This entire operation is located in a rented building costing $100 per week. Supervision, maintenance, and clerical employees receive $1,000 per week. The accounting department charges depreciation for equipment against this operation at $50 per week.

The accompanying process flow diagram describes the process. The tasks have been shown as rectangles and the storage of goods (inventories) as triangles.

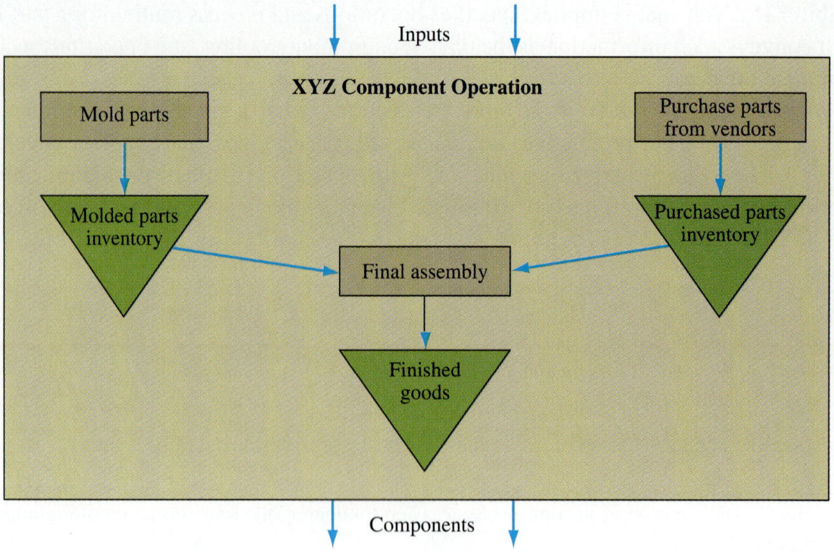


## SOLUTION

***a. Determine the capacity (number of components produced per week) of the entire process. Are the capacities of all the processes balanced?***

*Capacity of the molding process:*

Only six workers are employed for the molding process, each working as a full-time operator for one machine. Thus, only 6 of the 11 machines are operational at present.

$$\text{Molding capacity} = 6 \text{ machines} \times 25 \text{ parts per hour per machine} \times 8 \text{ hours per day} \times 5 \text{ days per week} = 6{,}000 \text{ parts per week}$$

*Capacity of the assembly process:*

$$\text{Assembly capacity} = 150 \text{ components per hour} \times 8 \text{ hours per day} \times 5 \text{ days per week} = 6{,}000 \text{ components per week}$$

Because capacity of both the tasks is 6,000 units per week, they are balanced.

***b. If the molding process were to use 10 machines instead of 6, and no changes were to be made in the final assembly task, what would be the capacity of the entire process?***

*Molding capacity with 10 machines:*

$$\text{Molding capacity} = 10 \text{ machines} \times 25 \text{ parts per hour per machine} \times 8 \text{ hours per day} \times 5 \text{ days per week} = 10{,}000 \text{ parts per week}$$

Because no change has been made in the final assembly task, the capacity of the assembly process remains 6,000 components per week. Thus, even though the molding capacity is 10,000 per week, the capacity of the entire process is only 6,000 per week because in the long run the overall capacity cannot exceed the slowest task.

***c. If our company went to a second shift of eight more hours on the assembly task, what would be the new capacity?***

*A second shift on the assembly task:*

As calculated in the previous section, the molding capacity is 10,000.

$$\text{Assembly capacity} = 150 \text{ components per hour} \times 16 \text{ hours per day} \times 5 \text{ days per week} = 12{,}000 \text{ components per week}$$

Here, even though the assembly capacity is 12,000 per week, the capacity of the entire process remains at 10,000 per week because now the slowest task is the molding process, which has a capacity of 10,000 per week. Thus, we can note here that capacity of a process is not a constant factor; it depends on the availability of inputs and the sequence of tasks. In fact, it depends on several other factors not covered here.

***d. Determine the cost per unit output when the capacity is (1) 6,000 per week or (2) 10,000 per week.***

*(1) Cost per unit when output per week = 6,000*

First, we calculate the cost of producing all the 6,000 parts per week:

| ITEM | CALCULATION | COST |
|---|---|---|
| Raw material for molding | \$0.10 per part × 6,000 = | \$ 600 |
| Parts purchased from outside | \$0.30 per component × 6,000 = | 1,800 |
| Electricity | \$0.02 per part × 6,000 = | 120 |
| Molding labor | \$0.20 per part × 6,000 = | 1,200 |
| Assembly labor | \$0.30 per part × 6,000 = | 1,800 |
| Rent | \$100 per week | 100 |
| Supervision | \$1,000 per week | 1,000 |
| Depreciation | \$50 per week | 50 |
| Total cost | | \$6,670 |

$$\text{Cost per unit} = \frac{\text{Total cost per week}}{\text{Number of units produced per week}} = \frac{\$6,670}{6,000} = \$1.11$$

*(2) Cost per unit when output per week = 10,000*

Next, we calculate the cost of producing all the 10,000 parts per week:

| ITEM | CALCULATION | COST |
|---|---|---|
| Raw material for molding | \$0.10 per part × 10,000 = | \$ 1,000 |
| Parts purchased from outside | \$0.30 per component × 10,000 = | 3,000 |
| Electricity | \$0.02 per part × 10,000 = | 200 |
| Molding labor | \$0.20 per part × 10,000 = | 2,000 |
| Assembly labor | \$0.30 per part × 10,000 = | 3,000 |
| Rent | \$100 per week | 100 |
| Supervision | \$1,000 per week | 1,000 |
| Depreciation | \$50 per week | 50 |
| Total cost | | \$10,350 |

$$\text{Cost per unit} = \frac{\text{Total cost per week}}{\text{Number of units produced per week}} = \frac{\$10,350}{10,000} = \$1.04$$

As you can see, our cost per unit has been reduced by spreading the fixed cost over a greater number of units.

Such process analysis calculations are required for many production decisions discussed throughout this book. ←

## GLOBAL PRODUCT DESIGN AND MANUFACTURING

The globalization of product markets presents a unique challenge to companies today. Globalization relates to a firm's ability to develop and produce products for regions of the world different from its home country. The objective when a company "goes global" is to leverage its size and knowledge to produce additional sales in the new markets. Often, due to the cost of supplying distant locations with product, the company is forced to manufacture locally in the new market area, rather than in its home country.

Joint venture

Typically, it is difficult for a company to globalize on its own. Companies often team up in a joint venture arrangement to facilitate the process. A **joint venture** is an arrangement in which two companies form a third independent company to carry out business. The two companies provide assets and other expertise to the third company and share in its profits.

## THE GLOBAL JOINT VENTURE

Often interesting arrangements are made between companies to facilitate globalization effort. The players would typically involve a parent company, a joint venture partner located in the foreign country, and one or more suppliers working in the foreign country. The parent company actually controls the product. For example, Whirlpool with its "world washer" is known globally for its comprehensive line of home appliances. Whirlpool's excellent design and marketing expertise is an important factor in the successful offering of washers in China. Due to the size of the product, though, it is not economical for Whirlpool to produce the "world washer" in the United States and sell it in China.

Using a joint venture partner with manufacturing expertise in a particular country, Whirlpool is able to produce and deliver the product to the foreign market. The partner is responsible for local customization of the product and for all local production of the product. In identifying a partner, a company such as Whirlpool may seek the low-cost producer of a similar product in the region. In addition to the production capability, the ideal partner might also have a gap in its current product line that is filled by the parent company's product. The parent company can then apply its expertise in product and process design, together with its marketing clout, to augment the current capability of the partner. This can often result in a winning arrangement for both companies.

Just as in the home country, suppliers are important to the foreign arrangement. The ideal supplier would be one that already has operations in the foreign country. Suppliers with operations that match up with the parent company's foreign operations are referred to as *strategic suppliers*. Suppliers provide not only the materials needed to produce the product but also the equipment used in the manufacturing processes. Suppliers often follow the parent company to the foreign country during the globalization effort.

More and more, the supplier is in the position to drive change, particularly technological, in the product or the process. Over the past 10 years, there has been a major shift to more extensive use of suppliers. Often the supplier takes ownership of the process of supplying major groups of items to the joint venture. Supplier choice is based on capability rather than cost.

## GLOBAL PRODUCT DESIGN STRATEGY

Typically, a moderately complex product is structured as a series of modules. The focus is on developing a set of standard modules common to all units sold globally. Standard CAD databases, tolerances, and other design elements are established for these modules. As global requirements, and particularly things like emission standards, become common to the world, more of the product can be standardized.

For these standard modules, common converting processes, which can be easily copied, can be developed. Investment in these common processes can be justified due to the higher volumes. Global sourcing of the equipment for these processes may be an important consideration in selecting suppliers.

The product is customized to local needs through a second set of modules. Unique country characteristics, such as language requirement, styling or design preference, packaging norms, electric power and fuel availability, and local taste preferences are accommodated in these modules. For example, Whirlpool refrigerators, like these sold in Bangkok, come in bright colors because they often are put in living rooms. Often import restrictions or duties may constrain the amount of content not locally produced.

EXHIBIT 5.17

**Performance Measures for Development Projects**

| PERFORMANCE DIMENSION | MEASURES | IMPACT ON COMPETITIVENESS |
|---|---|---|
| Time to market | Frequency of new product introductions | Responsiveness to customers/competitors |
| | Time from initial concept to market introduction | Quality of design—close to market |
| | Number started and number completed | Frequency of projects—model life |
| | Actual versus plan | |
| | Percentage of sales coming from new products | |
| Productivity | Engineering hours per project | Number of projects—freshness and breadth of line |
| | Cost of materials and tooling per project | |
| | Actual versus plan | Frequency of projects—economics of development |
| Quality | Conformance—reliability in use | Reputation—customer loyalty |
| | Design—performance and customer satisfaction | Relative attractiveness to customers—market share |
| | Yield—factory and field | Profitability—cost of ongoing service |

SOURCE: S. C. WHEELWRIGHT AND K. B. CLARK, *REVOLUTIONIZING PRODUCT DEVELOPMENT* (NEW YORK: THE FREE PRESS, 1992), PP. 6–8.

## MEASURING PRODUCT DEVELOPMENT PERFORMANCE

There is strong evidence that generating a steady stream of new products to market is extremely important to competitiveness. To succeed, firms must respond to changing customer needs and the moves of their competitors. The ability to identify opportunities, mount the development effort, and bring to market new products and processes quickly is critical. Firms also must bring new products and processes to market efficiently. Because the number of new products and new process technologies has increased while model lives and life cycles have shrunk, firms must mount more development projects than previously, and these projects must use substantially fewer resources per project.

In the U.S. automobile market, for example, the growth of models and market segments over the last 25 years has meant that an auto firm must initiate close to four times as many development projects simply to maintain its market share position. But smaller volumes per model and shorter design lives mean resource requirements must drop dramatically. Remaining competitive requires efficient engineering, design, and development activities.

Measures of product development success can be categorized into those that relate to the speed and frequency of bringing new products online, to the productivity of the actual development process, and to the quality of the actual products introduced (see Exhibit 5.17). Taken together, time, quality, and productivity define the performance of development, and in combination with other activities—sales, manufacturing, advertising, and customer service—determine the market impact of the project and its profitability.

## CONCLUSION

Designing a customer-pleasing product is an art. Building the product is a science. Moving the product from design to the customer is management. World-class manufacturers excel at the speedy and flexible integration of these processes. A key to this is teamwork, not only on the part of marketing, product development, manufacturing, and distribution, but on the part of the supplier and customer as well.

Vol. IV
"Product and Process Design at Detroit Diesel"

Effective process planning requires clear understanding of what the factory can and cannot do relative to process structures. Many plants use a combination of the structures identified in this chapter—job shops for some parts, batch or assembly operations for others. Frequently a choice exists as to when demand seems likely to favor a switch from one to the other. Making such decisions also requires understanding the nuances of each production process to determine if the process really fits new product specifications. On a day-to-day basis, it requires the ability to systematically analyze capacity capabilities of each processing step, as was done in this chapter.

Finally, there is the issue of technology. Although the details of manufacturing processes constitute the world of the engineer, awareness of modern technologies—particularly computer-integrated manufacturing—is now seen as an essential part of a business education. CIM, along with other operations technologies, is discussed in Supplement C, "Operations Technology."

## KEY TERMS

**Concurrent engineering** Emphasizes cross-functional integration and concurrent development of a product and its associated processes.

**Quality function deployment (QFD)** A process that helps a company determine the product characteristics important to the consumer and to evaluate its own product in relation to others.

**House of quality** A matrix that helps a product design team translate customer requirements into operating and engineering goals.

**Value analysis/value engineering (VA/VE)** Analysis with the purpose of simplifying products and processes by achieving equivalent or better performance at a lower cost.

**Job shop** A process structure suited for low-volume production of a great variety of nonstandard products.

**Batch shop** A process structure that produces a variety of standard products at relatively low volumes. The products are produced periodically in batches to reduce the impact of setup time on equipment.

**Assembly line** A process structure designed to make discrete parts. Parts are moved through a set of specially designed workstations at a controlled rate.

**Continuous flow** An often automated process structure that converts raw materials into finished product in one continuous process.

**Product–process matrix** Shows the relationship between process structures and product volume and variety characteristics.

**Virtual factory** Manufacturing activities carried out in multiple locations by suppliers and partner firms as part of a strategic alliance.

**Joint venture** Two companies form a third independent company to carry out business.

## SOLVED PROBLEMS

### SOLVED PROBLEM 1

A company is considering adding a new feature that will increase unit sales by 6 percent and product cost by 10 percent. Profit is expected to increase by 16 percent of the increased sales. Initially the product cost incurred by the company was 63 percent of the sales price. Should the new feature be added?

#### Solution

Let the sales be \$100 M.

Sales increase by 6% = \$100 M × 6% = \$6 M.

Benefits: Profits increase by 16% of the increased sales = \$6 M × 16% = \$0.96 M.

Cost: Increase product cost by 10% = (\$100 M × 63%) × 10% = \$6.3 M.

Because costs exceed benefits, the new feature should not be added.

### SOLVED PROBLEM 2

An automobile manufacturer is considering a change in an assembly line that should save money due to a reduction in labor and material cost. The change involves the installation of four new robots that will automatically install windshields. The cost of the four robots, including installation and initial programming, is \$400,000. Current practice is to amortize the initial cost of robots over two years on a straight-line basis. The process engineer estimates that one full-time technician will be needed to monitor, maintain, and reprogram the robots on an ongoing basis. This person will cost approximately \$60,000 per year. Currently, the company uses four full-time employees on this job and they each make about \$52,000 per year. One of these employees is a material handler, and this person will still be needed with the new process. To complicate matters, the process engineer estimates that the robots will apply the windshield sealing material in a manner that will result in a savings of \$0.25 per windshield installed. How many automobiles need to be produced over the next two years to make the new robots an attractive investment? Due to the relatively short horizon, do not consider the time value of money.

### Solution

Cost of the current process over the next two years is just the cost of the four full-time employees.

$$\$52{,}000/\text{employee} \times 4 \text{ employees} \times 2 \text{ years} = \$416{,}000$$

The cost of the new process over the next two years, assuming the robot is completely costed over that time, is the following:

$$\$52{,}000/\text{material handler} + \$60{,}000/\text{technician} + \$400{,}000/\text{robots} - \$0.25 \times \text{autos}$$

Equating the two alternatives:

$$\$416{,}000 = \$512{,}000 - \$0.25 \times \text{autos}$$

Solving for the break-even point:

$$-\$96{,}000/-\$0.25 = 384{,}000 \text{ autos}$$

This indicates that to break even, 384,000 autos would need to be produced with the robots over the next two years.

## REVIEW AND DISCUSSION QUESTIONS

1 Discuss the product design philosophy behind industrial design and design for manufacture and assembly. Which one do you think is more important in a customer-focused product development?
2 Discuss design-based incrementalism, which is frequent product redesign throughout the product's life. What are the pros and cons of this idea?
3 What is the primary production document derived from the product design process? What other types of documents does one need to make a product?
4 What factors must be traded off by product development before introducing a new product?
5 How does the QFD approach help? What are some limitations of the QFD approach?
6 What does the product–process matrix tell us? Where would you place a Chinese restaurant on the matrix?
7 It has been noted that during World War II Germany made a critical mistake by having its formidable Tiger tanks produced by locomotive manufacturers, while the less formidable U.S. Sherman tank was produced by American car manufacturers. Use the product–process matrix to explain that mistake and its likely result.
8 What impact does the concept and design stage have on the product's overall cost?
9 Discuss concurrent engineering and how it can benefit a production system.
10 How does the production volume affect break-even analysis?
11 What is meant by a process? Describe its important features.

## PROBLEMS

1 Pick a product and list issues that need to be considered in its design and manufacture. The product can be something like a stereo, telephone, desk, or kitchen appliance. Consider the functional and aesthetic aspects of design as well as the important concerns for manufacturing. 1. See ISM.
2 Consider the construction of a simple 8″ × 10″ wood picture frame. The picture frame consists of four wood pieces that are cut from the wood molding, four staples to hold the frame 2. See ISM.

together, a piece of glass, a backing board made of cardboard, six points to hold the glass and backing board to the frame, and a clip for hanging the picture frame from the wall.

*a.* Construct an assembly chart for the picture frame.

*b.* Construct a flowchart for the entire process from receiving materials to final inspection.

3. See ISM.

3 The following is a partial house of quality for a golf country club. Provide an importance weighting from your perspective (or that of a golfing friend) in the unshaded areas. If you can, using the QFD approach, compare it to a club where you or your friends play.

| WHATs versus HOWs<br>Strong Relationship: ●<br>Medium Relationship: ○<br>Weak Relationship: △ | Physical Aspects | Course location | Grounds maintenance | Landscaping | Pin placement | Course tuning | Tee placement | Service Facilities | Customer-trained attendants | Top-quality food | Highly rated chefs | Attractive restaurant | Tournament Activities | Calloway handicapping | Exciting door prizes | Perception Issues | Invitation only | Types of guests | Income level | Celebrity |
|---|---|---|---|---|---|---|---|---|---|---|---|---|---|---|---|---|---|---|---|---|
| Physical Aspects | | | | | | | | | | | | | | | | | | | | |
| Manicured grounds | | | | | | | | | | | | | | | | | | | | |
| Easy access | | | | | | | | | | | | | | | | | | | | |
| Challenging | | | | | | | | | | | | | | | | | | | | |
| Service Facilities | | | | | | | | | | | | | | | | | | | | |
| Restaurant facilities | | | | | | | | | | | | | | | | | | | | |
| Good food | | | | | | | | | | | | | | | | | | | | |
| Good service | | | | | | | | | | | | | | | | | | | | |
| Good layout | | | | | | | | | | | | | | | | | | | | |
| Plush locker room | | | | | | | | | | | | | | | | | | | | |
| Helpful service attendants | | | | | | | | | | | | | | | | | | | | |
| Tournament Facilities | | | | | | | | | | | | | | | | | | | | |
| Good tournament prize | | | | | | | | | | | | | | | | | | | | |
| Types of players | | | | | | | | | | | | | | | | | | | | |
| Fair handicapping system | | | | | | | | | | | | | | | | | | | | |
| Perception Issues | | | | | | | | | | | | | | | | | | | | |
| Prestigious | | | | | | | | | | | | | | | | | | | | |

4. See ISM.

4 The purpose of this system design exercise is to gain experience in setting up a manufacturing process. (We suggest that this be done as a team project.) Assignment:

*a.* Get one Ping-Pong paddle.

*b.* Specify the type of equipment and raw materials you would need to manufacture that paddle, from the receipt of seasoned wood to packaging for shipment.

*c.* Assume that one unit of each type of equipment is available to you. Further assume that you have a stock of seasoned wood and other materials needed to produce and box 100 paddles. Making reasonable assumptions about times and distances where necessary.

(1) Develop an assembly drawing for the paddle.

(2) Prepare an assembly chart for the paddle.

(3) Develop a process flowchart for the paddle.

(4) Develop a route sheet for the paddle.

5. *a.* See SM for diagram; 5,600 components.
*b.* 8,000; drilling operation.
*c.* 9,600; final assembly operation.
*d.* \$1.81, \$1.79.
*e.* 100, 840.

5 The Goodparts Company produces a component that is subsequently used in the aerospace industry. The component consists of three parts (A, B, and C) that are purchased from outside and cost 40, 35, and 15 cents per piece, respectively. Parts A and B are assembled first on assembly line 1, which produces 140 components per hour. Part C undergoes a drilling operation before being finally assembled with the output from assembly line 1. There are in total six drilling machines, but at present only three of them are operational. Each drilling machine drills part C at a rate of 50 parts per hour. In the final assembly, the output from assembly line 1 is assembled with the drilled part C. The final assembly line produces at a rate of 160 components per hour. At present, components are produced eight hours a day and five days a week. Management believes that if need arises, it can add a second shift of eight hours for the assembly lines.

The cost of assembly labor is 30 cents per part for each assembly line; the cost of drilling labor is 15 cents per part. For drilling, the cost of electricity is 1 cent per part. The total overhead cost has been calculated as $1,200 per week. The depreciation cost for equipment has been calculated as $30 per week.

*a.* Draw a process flow diagram and determine the process capacity (number of components produced per week) of the entire process.

*b.* Suppose a second shift of eight hours is run for assembly line 1 and the same is done for the final assembly line. In addition, four of the six drilling machines are made operational. The drilling machines, however, operate for just eight hours a day. What is the new process capacity (number of components produced per week)? Which of the three operations limits the capacity?

*c.* Management decides to run a second shift of eight hours for assembly line 1 plus a second shift of only four hours for the final assembly line. Five of the six drilling machines operate for eight hours a day. What is the new capacity? Which of the three operations limits the capacity?

*d.* Determine the cost per unit output for questions *b* and *c*.

*e.* The product is sold at $4.00 per unit. Assuming that the cost of a drilling machine (fixed cost) is $30,000 and the company produces 8,000 units per week. Assume that four drilling machines are used for production. If the company had an option to buy the same part at $3.00 per unit, what would be the break-even number of units?

6 A book publisher has fixed costs of $300,000 and variable costs per book of $8.00. The book sells for $23.00 per copy.[7]

*a.* How many books must be sold to break even?

*b.* If the fixed cost increased, would the new break-even point be higher or lower?

*c.* If the variable cost per unit decreased, would the new break-even point be higher or lower?

6. *a.* 20,000 books
*b.* Higher
*c.* Lower

7 A manufacturing process has a fixed cost of $150,000 per month. Each unit of product being produced contains $25 worth of material and takes $45 of labor. How many units are needed to break even if each completed unit has a value of $90?

7. 7500 units

8 Assume a fixed cost of $900, a variable cost of $4.50, and a selling price of $5.50.

*a.* What is the break-even point?

*b.* How many units must be sold to make a profit of $500.00?

*c.* How many units must be sold to average $0.25 profit per unit? $0.50 profit per unit? $1.50 profit per unit?

8. *a.* 900 units
*b.* 1400 units
*c.* 1200 units
1800 units
Impossible

9 Aldo Redondo drives his own car on company business. His employer reimburses him for such travel at the rate of 36 cents per mile. Aldo estimates that his fixed costs per year such as taxes, insurance, and depreciation are $2052. The direct or variable costs such as gas, oil, and maintenance average about 14.4 cents per mile. How many miles must he drive to break even?

9. 9500 miles

10 A firm is selling two products, chairs and bar stools, each at $50 per unit. Chairs have a variable cost of $25 and bar stools $20. Fixed cost for the firm is $20,000.

*a.* If the sales mix is 1:1 (one chair sold for every bar stool sold), what is the break-even point in dollars of sales? In units of chairs and bar stools?

*b.* If the sales mix changes to 1:4 (one chair sold for every four bar stools sold), what is the break-even point in dollars of sales? In units of chairs and bar stools?

10. *a.* $36,400 (364 of each)
*b.* $34,500 (138 chairs, ,552 stools)

## CASE: THE BEST-ENGINEERED PART IS NO PART

Putting together NCR Corp.'s new 2760 electronic cash register is a snap. In fact, William R. Sprague can do it in less than two minutes—blindfolded. To get that kind of easy assembly, Sprague, a senior manufacturing engineer at NCR, insisted that the point-of-sale terminal be designed so that its parts fit together with no screws or bolts.

The entire terminal consists of just 15 vendor-produced components. That's 85 percent fewer parts, from 65 percent fewer suppliers, than in the company's previous low-end model, the 2160. And the terminal takes only 25 percent as much time to assemble. Installation and maintenance are also a breeze, says Sprague. "The simplicity flows through to all of the downstream activities, including field service."

The new NCR product is one of the best examples to date of the payoffs possible from a new engineering approach called *design for manufacturability,* mercifully shortened to DFM. Other DFM enthusiasts include Ford, General Motors, IBM, Motorola, Perkin-Elmer, and Whirlpool. Since 1981, General Electric Co. has used DFM in more than 100 development programs, from major appliances to gearboxes for jet engines. GE figures that the concept has netted $200 million in benefits, either from cost savings or from increased market shares.

### NUTS TO SCREWS

One U.S. champion of DFM is Geoffrey Boothroyd, a professor of industrial and manufacturing engineering at the University of Rhode Island and the cofounder of Boothroyd Dewhurst Inc. This tiny Wakefield, Rhode Island, company has developed several computer programs that analyze designs for ease of manufacturing.

The biggest gains, notes Boothroyd, come from eliminating screws and other fasteners. On a supplier's invoice, screws and bolts may run mere pennies apiece, and collectively they account for only about 5 percent of a typical product's bill of materials. But tack on all of the associated costs, such as the time needed to align components while screws are inserted and tightened, and the price of using those mundane parts can pile up to 75 percent of total assembly costs. "Fasteners should be the first thing to design out of a product," he says.

Had screws been included in the design of NCR's 2760, calculates Sprague, the total cost over the lifetime of the model would have been $12,500—per screw. "The huge impact of little things like screws, primarily on overhead costs, just gets lost," he says. That's understandable, he admits, because for new-product development projects "the overriding factor is hitting the market window. It's better to be on time and over budget than on budget but late."

But NCR got its simplified terminal to market in record time without overlooking the little details. The product was formally introduced last January, just 24 months after development began. Design was a paperless, interdepartmental effort from the very start. The product remained a computer model until all members of the team—from design engineering, manufacturing, purchasing, customer service, and key suppliers—were satisfied.

That way, the printed circuit boards, the molds for its plastic housing, and other elements could all be developed simultaneously. This eliminated the usual lag after designers throw a new product "over the wall" to manufacturing, who then must figure out how to make it. "Breaking down the walls between design and manufacturing to facilitate simultaneous engineering," Sprague declares, "was the real breakthrough."

The design process began with a mechanical computer-aided engineering program that allowed the team to fashion three-dimensional models of each part on a computer screen. The software also analyzed the overall product and its various elements for performance and durability. Then the simulated components were assembled on a computer workstation's screen to assure that they would fit together properly. As the design evolved, it was checked periodically with Boothroyd Dewhurst's DFM software. This prompted several changes that trimmed the parts count from an initial 28 to the final 15.

### NO MOCK-UP

After everyone on the team gave their thumbs-up, the data for the parts were electronically transferred directly into computer-aided manufacturing systems at the various suppliers. The NCR designers were so confident everything would work as intended that they didn't bother making a mock-up.

DFM can be a powerful weapon against foreign competition. Several years ago, IBM used Boothroyd Dewhurst's software to analyze dot-matrix printers it was sourcing from Japan—and found it could do substantially better. Its Proprinter has 65 percent fewer parts and slashed assembly time by 90 percent. "Almost anything made in Japan," insists Professor Boothroyd, "can be improved upon with DFM—often impressively."

### QUESTION

What development problems has the NCR approach overcome?

SOURCE: O. PORT, "THE BEST-ENGINEERED PART IS NO PART AT ALL," *BUSINESS WEEK*, MAY 8, 1989, P. 150. REPRINTED WITH PERMISSION.

## SELECTED BIBLIOGRAPHY

Adler, P. S.; A. Mandelbaum; V. Nguyen; and Elizabeth Schwerer. "Getting the Most out of Your Product Development Process." *Harvard Business Review,* March–April 1996, pp. 134–52.

Adler, P. S.; H. E. Riggs; and S. C. Wheelwright. "Product Development Know-How: Trading Tactics for Strategy." *Sloan Management Review,* Fall 1989, pp. 7–17.

Boothroyd, G.; P. Dewhurt; and W. Knight. *Product Design for Manufacture and Assembly.* New York: Marcel Dekker, Inc., 1994.

Drucker, P. F. "The Emerging Theory of Manufacturing." *Harvard Business Review,* May–June 1990, pp. 94–102.

Edmondson, H. E., and S. C. Wheelwright. "Outstanding Manufacturing in the Coming Decade." *California Management Review,* Summer 1989, pp.70–90.

Hammer, M. "Reengineering Work: Don't Automate, Obliterate." *Harvard Business Review,* July–August 1990, pp. 104–12.

Hayes, R. H., and S. C. Wheelwright. *Restoring Our Competitive Age.* New York: John Wiley & Sons, 1984.

Hill, T. *Manufacturing Strategy.* 3rd ed. Burr Ridge IL.: Irwin/McGraw-Hill, 2000.

Huthwaite, B. *Design for Competitiveness: A Concurrent Engineering Handbook.* Institute for Competitive Design, 530 N. Pine, Rochester, Michigan, 1991.

Meyer, C. *Fast Cycle Time.* New York: Free Press, 1993.

Petroski, H. *Invention by Design: How Engineers Get from Thought to Thing.* Boston, MA: Harvard University Press, 1996.

Roehm, H. A.; D. Klein; and J. F. Castellano. "Springing to World-Class Manufacturing." *Management Accounting,* March 1991, pp. 40–44.

Sakai, K. "The Feudal World of Japanese Manufacturing." *Harvard Business Review,* November–December 1990, pp. 38–49.

Schniederjans, M. J., and J. R. Olsen. *Advanced Topics in Just-in-Time Management,* Westport, CT: Quorum Books, 1999.

Shunk, D. L. *Integrated Process Design and Development.* Burr Ridge, Ill.: Business One Irwin, 1992.

Wheelwright, S. C., and K. B. Clark. *Revolutionizing Product Development.* New York: The Free Press, 1992.

———. *Leading Product Development.* New York: The Free Press, 1995.

Womack, J. P., and D. T. Jones. *Lean Thinking: Banish Waste and Create Wealth in Your Corporation,* New York: Simon and Schuster, 1996.

Ziemke, M. C., and M. S. Spann. "Warning: Don't Be Half-Hearted in Your Efforts to Employ Concurrent Engineering." *Industrial Engineering,* February 1991, pp. 45–49.

## FOOTNOTES

1 S. C. Wheelwright and K. B. Clark, *Revolutionizing Product Development* (New York: The Free Press, 1992), pp. 6–8.

2 M. L. Swink, V. A. Mabert, and J. C. Sandvig describe this approach in "Customizing Concurrent Engineering Processes: Five Case Studies," *Journal of Product Innovation Management* 13 (1996), pp. 229–44.

3 The term quality is actually a mistranslation of the Japanese word for qualities, because QFD is widely used in the context of quality management.

4 Example adapted from G. Boothroyd, P. Dewhurst, and W. Knight, *Product Design for Manufacture and Assembly* (New York: Marcel Dekker, 1994), pp. 5–10.

5 Also called a *Gozinto chart,* named, so the legend goes, after the famous Italian mathematician Zepartzat Gozinto.

6 This section is modified from P. W. Marshall et al., *Operations Management: Text and Cases* (Burr Ridge, IL: Richard D. Irwin, 1975), pp. 12–16.

7 Special thanks to Professor W. Ruch of Arizona State University for his contribution of problems 6 through 10.

TECHNICAL NOTE

*technical note five*

# FACILITY LAYOUT

## OUTLINE AND KEY TERMS



technical note

PLANET EARTH ORBITING THE ASSEMBLY LINE IN A GLOBE FACTORY. THE GLOBES ARE MOVING THROUGH THE FACTORY USING A TRANSPORT SYSTEM SUSPENDED FROM THE CEILING OF THE FACTORY.

Layout decisions entail determining the placement of departments, work groups within the departments, workstations, machines, and stock-holding points within a production facility. The objective is to arrange these elements in a way that ensures a smooth work flow (in a factory) or a particular traffic pattern (in a service organization). In general, the inputs to the layout decision are as follows:

1 Specification of the objectives and corresponding criteria to be used to evaluate the design. The amount of space required, and the distance that must be traveled between elements in the layout, are common basic criteria.
2 Estimates of product or service demand on the system.
3 Processing requirements in terms of number of operations and amount of flow between the elements in the layout.
4 Space requirements for the elements in the layout.
5 Space availability within the facility itself, or if this is a new facility, possible building configurations.

In our treatment of layout, we examine how layouts are developed under various formats (or work-flow structures). Our emphasis is on quantitative techniques, but we also show examples of how qualitative factors are important in the design of the layout. Both manufacturing and service facilities are covered in this technical note.

## BASIC PRODUCTION LAYOUT FORMATS

Vol. I "The Manufacturing Process"

The formats by which departments are arranged in a facility are defined by the general pattern of work flow; there are three basic types (process layout, product layout, and fixed-position layout) and one hybrid type (group technology or cellular layout).

Process layout

A **process layout** (also called a *job-shop* or *functional layout*) is a format in which similar equipment or functions are grouped together, such as all lathes in one area and all stamping machines in another. A part being worked on then travels, according to the established sequence of operations, from area to area, where the proper machines are located for each operation. This type of layout is typical of hospitals, for example, where areas are dedicated to particular types of medical care, such as maternity wards and intensive care units.

Service

Product layout

A **product layout** (also called a *flow-shop layout*) is one in which equipment or work processes are arranged according to the progressive steps by which the product is made. The path for each part is, in effect, a straight line. Production lines for shoes, chemical plants, and car washes are all product layouts.

Group technology (cellular) layout

A **group technology (cellular) layout** groups dissimilar machines into work centers (or cells) to work on products that have similar shapes and processing requirements. A group technology (GT) layout is similar to a process layout in that cells are designed to perform a specific set of processes, and it is similar to a product layout in that the cells are dedicated to a limited range of products. (*Group technology* also refers to the parts classification and coding system used to specify machine types that go into a cell.)

Fixed-position layout

In a **fixed-position layout,** the product (by virtue of its bulk or weight) remains at one location. Manufacturing equipment is moved to the product rather than vice versa. Shipyards, construction sites, and movie lots are examples of this format.

Many manufacturing facilities present a combination of two layout types. For example, a given production area may be laid out by process, while another area may be laid out by product. It is also common to find an entire plant arranged according to product layout—for example, a parts fabrication area followed by a subassembly area, with a final assembly area at the end of the process. Different types of layouts may be used in each area, with a process layout used in fabrication, group technology in subassembly, and a product layout used in final assembly.

## PROCESS LAYOUT

The most common approach to developing a process layout is to arrange departments consisting of like processes in a way that optimizes their relative placement. For example, the departments in a low-volume toy factory might consist of the shipping and receiving department, the plastic molding and stamping department, the metal forming department, the sewing department, and the painting department. Parts for the toys are fabricated in these departments and then sent to assembly departments where they are put together. In many installations, optimal placement often means placing departments with large amounts of interdepartment traffic adjacent to one another.

Suppose that we want to arrange the eight departments of a toy factory to minimize the interdepartmental material handling cost. Initially, let us make the simplifying assumption that all departments have the same amount of space (say, 40 feet by 40 feet) and that the building is 80 feet wide and 160 feet long (and thus compatible with the department dimensions). The first things we would want to know are the nature of the flow between departments and how the material is transported. If the company has another factory that makes similar products, information about flow patterns might be abstracted from the records. On the other hand, if this is a new product line, such information would have to come from routing sheets or from estimates by knowledgeable personnel such as process or industrial engineers. Of course, these data, regardless of their source, will have to be modified to reflect the nature of future orders over the projected life of the proposed layout.

Let us assume that this information is available. We find that all material is transported in a standard-size crate by forklift truck, one crate to a truck (which constitutes one "load"). Now suppose that transportation costs are \$1 to move a load between adjacent departments and \$1 extra for each department in between. The expected loads between departments for the first year of operation are tabulated in Exhibit TN5.1; available plant space is depicted in Exhibit TN5.2. Note that in our example, diagonal moves are permitted so that departments 2 and 3, and 3 and 6, are considered adjacent.

Given this information, our first step is to illustrate the interdepartmental flow by a model, such as Exhibit TN5.3. This provides the basic layout pattern, which we will try to improve.

The second step is to determine the cost of this layout by multiplying the material handling cost by the number of loads moved between each pair of departments. Exhibit TN5.4 presents this information, which is derived as follows: The annual material handling cost between Departments 1 and 2 is \$175 (\$1 × 175 moves), \$60 between Departments 1 and 5 (\$2 × 30 moves), \$60 between Departments 1 and 7 (\$3 × 20 moves), \$240 between diagonal Departments 2 and 7 (\$3 × 80), and so forth. (The "distances" are taken from Exhibit TN5.2 or TN5.3, not Exhibit TN5.4.)

## EXHIBIT TN5.1

### Interdepartmental Flow

**Flow between Departments (Number of Moves)**

| | 1 | 2 | 3 | 4 | 5 | 6 | 7 | 8 |
|---|---|---|---|---|---|---|---|---|
| 1 | | 175 | 50 | 0 | 30 | 200 | 20 | 25 |
| 2 | | | 0 | 100 | 75 | 90 | 80 | 90 |
| 3 | | | | 17 | 88 | 125 | 99 | 180 |
| 4 | | | | | 20 | 5 | 0 | 25 |
| 5 | | | | | | 0 | 180 | 187 |
| 6 | | | | | | | 374 | 103 |
| 7 | | | | | | | | 7 |
| 8 | | | | | | | | |

| Department | Activity |
|---|---|
| 1 | Shipping and receiving |
| 2 | Plastic molding and stamping |
| 3 | Metal forming |
| 4 | Sewing department |
| 5 | Small toy assembly |
| 6 | Large toy assembly |
| 7 | Painting |
| 8 | Mechanism assembly |

## EXHIBIT TN5.2

### Building Dimensions and Departments

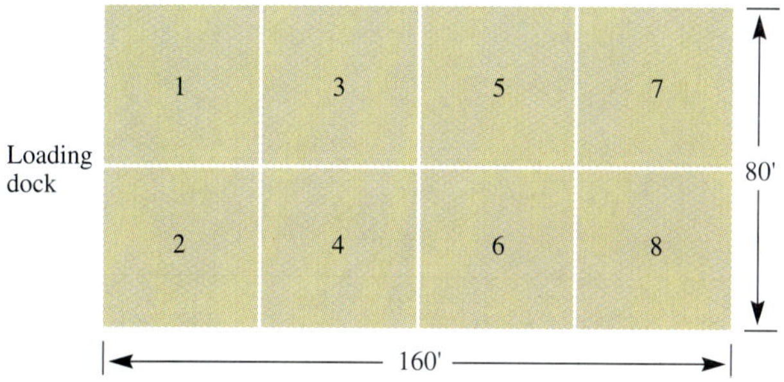


## EXHIBIT TN5.3

### Interdepartmental Flow Graph with Number of Annual Movements

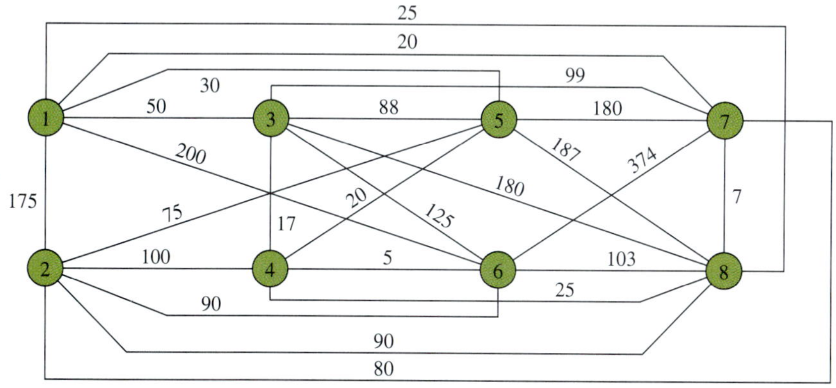


## EXHIBIT TN5.4

### Cost Matrix—First Solution

| $ | 1 | 2 | 3 | 4 | 5 | 6 | 7 | 8 |
|---|---|---|---|---|---|---|---|---|
| 1 | | 175 | 50 | 0 | 60 | 400 | 60 | 75 |
| 2 | | | 0 | 100 | 150 | 180 | 240 | 270 |
| 3 | | | | 17 | 88 | 125 | 198 | 360 |
| 4 | | | | | 20 | 5 | 0 | 50 |
| 5 | | | | | | 0 | 180 | 187 |
| 6 | | | | | | | 374 | 103 |
| 7 | | | | | | | | 7 |
| 8 | | | | | | | | |

Total cost: $3,474

EXHIBIT TN5.5

Revised Interdepartmental Flow Chart (Only interdepartmental flow with effect on cost is depicted.)

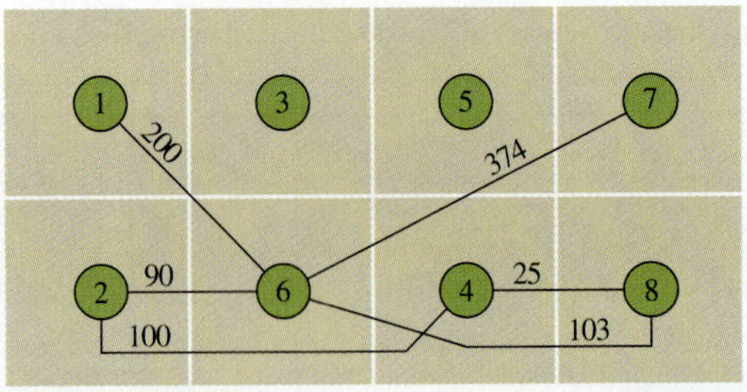


EXHIBIT TN5.6

Cost Matrix—Second Solution

| | 1 | 2 | 3 | 4 | 5 | 6 | 7 | 8 | Net cost change |
|---|---|---|---|---|---|---|---|---|---|
| 1 | | 175 | 50 | 0 | 60 | (200) | 60 | 75 | –$200 |
| 2 | | | 0 | (200) | 150 | (90) | 240 | 270 | + 10 |
| 3 | | | | 17 | 88 | 125 | 198 | 360 | |
| 4 | | | | | 20 | 5 | 0 | (25) | – 25 |
| 5 | | | | | | 0 | 180 | 187 | |
| 6 | | | | | | | (748) | (206) | + $374, + $103 |
| 7 | | | | | | | | 7 | |
| 8 | | | | | | | | | |
| | | | | | | | | | + $262<br>Total cost: $3,736 |

The third step is a search for departmental changes that will reduce costs. On the basis of the graph and the cost matrix, it seems desirable to place Departments 1 and 6 closer together to reduce their high move-distance costs. However, this requires shifting several other departments, thereby affecting their move-distance costs and the total cost of the second solution. Exhibit TN5.5 shows the revised layout resulting from relocating Department 6 and an adjacent department. (Department 4 is arbitrarily selected for this purpose.) The revised cost matrix for the exchange, showing the cost changes, is given in Exhibit TN5.6. Note the total cost is $262 *greater* than in the initial solution. Clearly, doubling the distance between Departments 6 and 7 accounted for the major part of the cost increase. This points out the fact that, even in a small problem, it is rarely easy to decide the correct "obvious move" on the basis of casual inspection.

Thus far, we have shown only one exchange among a large number of potential exchanges; in fact, for an eight-department problem, there are 8! (or 40,320) possible arrangements. Therefore, the procedure we have employed would have only a remote possibility of achieving an optimal combination in a reasonable number of tries. Nor does our problem stop here.

Suppose that we *do* arrive at a good solution solely on the basis of material handling cost, such as that shown in Exhibit TN5.7 (whose total cost is $3,244). We would note, first of all, that our shipping and receiving department is near the center of the factory—an arrangement that probably would not be acceptable. The sewing department is next to the painting department, introducing the hazard that lint, thread, and cloth particles might drift onto painted items. Further, small toy assembly and large toy assembly are located at opposite ends of the plant, which would increase travel time for assemblers (who very likely would be needed in both departments at various times of the day) and for supervisors (who might otherwise supervise both departments simultaneously). Often factors other than material handling cost need to be considered in finalizing a layout.

EXHIBIT TN5.7

**A Feasible Layout**

| | | | |
|---|---|---|---|
| Small toy assembly<br>5 | Mechanism assembly<br>8 | Shipping and receiving<br>1 | Large toy assembly<br>6 |
| Metal forming<br>3 | Plastic molding and stamping<br>2 | Sewing<br>4 | Painting<br>7 |

## COMPUTERIZED LAYOUT TECHNIQUES—CRAFT

A number of computerized layout programs have been developed since the 1970s to help devise good process layouts. Of these, the most widely applied is the Computerized Relative Allocation of Facilities Technique (**CRAFT**).[1]

CRAFT

The CRAFT method follows the same basic idea that we developed in the layout of the toy factory, but with some significant operational differences. Like the toy factory example, it requires a load matrix and a distance matrix as initial inputs, but in addition, it requires a cost per unit distance traveled, say $.10 per foot moved. (Remember, we made the simplifying assumption that cost doubled when material had to jump one department, tripled when it had to jump two departments, and so forth.) With these inputs and an initial layout in the program, CRAFT then tries to improve the relative placement of the departments as measured by total material handling cost for the layout. (Material handling cost between departments = Number of loads × Rectilinear distance between department centroids × Cost per unit distance.) It makes improvements by exchanging pairs of departments iteratively until no further cost reductions are possible. That is, the program calculates the effect on total cost of exchanging departments; if this yields a reduction, the exchange is made, which constitutes an iteration. As we saw in the manual method, the departments are part of a material flow network, so even a simple pairwise exchange generally will affect flow patterns among many other departments.

### *EXAMPLE TN5.1: APPLYING CRAFT TO THE TOY FACTORY*

This example shows how CRAFT is applied to the toy factory problem defined in Exhibits TN5.4–TN5.7.

### *SOLUTION*

A CRAFT layout solution to the toy factory problem is shown in Exhibit TN5.8. It provides a higher-cost layout than the manual one ($3,497 versus $3,244). Note, however, that these costs are not precisely comparable because CRAFT uses rectilinear distances as opposed to Euclidean (straight-line) distances, and links centroids of departments instead of "entrances." Because we

EXHIBIT TN5.8

**CRAFT Solution to Toy Factory Layout**

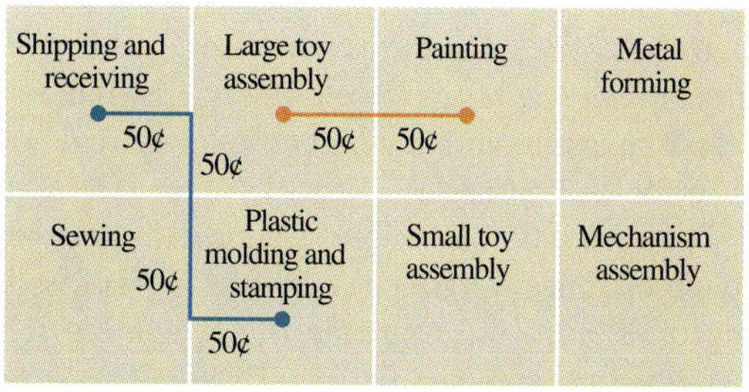


Material handling cost between departments

1 and 2 = $2 × 175 = $350
6 and 7 = $1 × 374 = $374

were not given cost per unit distances in this example, CRAFT simply broke the stated $1-per-unit cost of movement between departments into 50¢ segments. Exhibit TN5.8 shows two example calculations of the CRAFT movement costs. (Having square departments in the toy factory makes this calculation method a reasonable one for example purposes.) Also note that we fixed the location of the shipping and receiving department in the CRAFT solution so that it would be adjacent to the loading dock. ←

Distinguishing features of CRAFT and issues relating to it are as follows:

1 It is a heuristic program. It uses a simple rule of thumb in making evaluations: "Compare two departments at a time and exchange them if it reduces the total cost of the layout." This type of rule is obviously necessary to analyze even a modest-size layout.
2 It does not guarantee an optimal solution.
3 CRAFT is biased by its starting conditions: where you start (that is, the initial layout) will determine the final layout.
4 Starting with a reasonably good solution is more likely to yield a lower-cost final solution, but it does not always. This means that a good strategy for using CRAFT is to generate a variety of different starting layouts to expose the program to different pairwise exchanges.
5 It can handle up to 40 departments and rarely exceeds 10 iterations in arriving at a solution.
6 CRAFT departments consist of combinations of square modules (typically representing floor areas 10 feet by 10 feet). This permits multiple departmental configurations, but often results in strange departmental shapes that have to be modified manually to obtain a realistic layout.
7 A modified version called SPACECRAFT has been developed to handle multistory layout problems.[2]
8 CRAFT assumes the existence of variable-path material handling equipment such as forklift trucks. Therefore, when computerized fixed-path equipment is employed, CRAFT's applicability is greatly reduced.

## SYSTEMATIC LAYOUT PLANNING

Systematic layout planning (SLP)

In certain types of layout problems, numerical flow of items between departments either is impractical to obtain or does not reveal the qualitative factors that may be crucial to the placement decision. In these situations, the venerable technique known as **systematic layout planning (SLP)** can be used.[3] It involves developing a relationship chart showing the degree of importance of having each department located adjacent to every other department. From this chart, an activity relationship diagram, similar to the flow graph used for illustrating material handling between departments, is developed. The activity relationship diagram is then adjusted by trial and error until a satisfactory adjacency pattern is obtained. This pattern, in turn, is modified department by department to meet building space limitations. Exhibit TN5.9 illustrates the technique with a simple five-department problem involving laying out a floor of a department store.

The SLP approach has been quantified for ease of evaluating alternative layouts. This entails assigning numerical weights to the closeness preferences and then trying different layout arrangements. The layout with the highest total closeness score is selected. For example, weights of 16 for "A," 8 for "E," 4 for "I," 2 for "O," 0 for "U," and −80 for "X" could be assigned. The choice of this weight structure is rather ad hoc, but the logic is that the most undesirable preference weighting (−80 for "X") is five times worse than the most desirable weighting of 16 for "A." Applying this weighting scheme using the software gives a score of 40 to the final layout in Exhibit TN5.9. (The score is the summation of the preference scores for each pair—in this case, 10 pairs. Exchanges may be made randomly, by user choice, or by pairs in this software program.)

EXHIBIT TN5.9

Systematic Layout Planning for a Floor of a Department Store

**A. Relationship Chart (based on Tables B and C)**

| From | To 2 | To 3 | To 4 | To 5 | Area (sq. ft.) |
|---|---|---|---|---|---|
| 1. Credit department | I / 6 | U / — | A / 4 | U / — | 100 |
| 2. Toy department | | U / — | I / 1 | A / 1,6 | 400 |
| 3. Wine department | | | U / — | X / 1 | 300 |
| 4. Camera department | | | | X / 1 | 100 |
| 5. Candy department | | | | | 100 |

Letter — Closeness rating
Number — Reason for rating

**B.**

| CODE | REASON* |
|---|---|
| 1 | Type of customer |
| 2 | Ease of supervision |
| 3 | Common personnel |
| 4 | Contact necessary |
| 5 | Share same space |
| 6 | Psychology |

*Others may be used.

**C.**

| VALUE | CLOSENESS | LINE CODE* | NUMERICAL WEIGHTS |
|---|---|---|---|
| A | Absolutely necessary | ≣ | 16 |
| E | Especially important | ≡ | 8 |
| I | Important | = | 4 |
| O | Ordinary closeness OK | — | 2 |
| U | Unimportant | | 0 |
| X | Undesirable | /\/\/\ | 80 |

*Used for example purposes only.

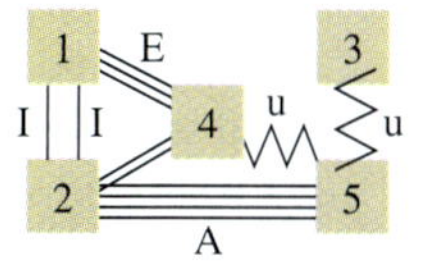

Initial relationship diagram (based on Tables A and C)

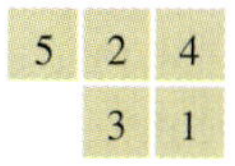

Initial layout based on relationship diagram (ignoring space and building constraints)

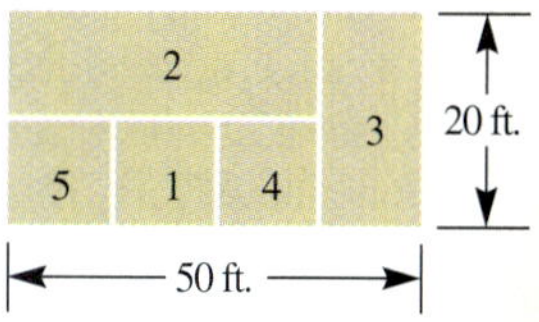

Final layout adjusted by square footage and building size

# PRODUCT LAYOUT

The basic difference between product layout and process layout is the pattern of work flow. As we have seen in process layout, the pattern can be highly variable because material for any given job may have to be routed to the same processing department several times during its production cycle. In product layout, equipment or departments are dedicated to a particular product line, duplicate equipment is employed to avoid backtracking, and a straight-line flow of material movement is achievable. Adopting a product layout makes sense when the batch size of a given product or part is large relative to the number of different products or parts produced.

Vol. II
"Layout Improvements and Equipment Strategies."

## ASSEMBLY LINES

Assembly lines are a special case of product layout. In a general sense, the term *assembly line* refers to progressive assembly linked by some material handling device. The usual assumption is that some form of pacing is present and the allowable processing time is equivalent for all workstations. Within this broad definition, there are important differences among line types. A few of these are material handling devices (belt or roller conveyor, overhead crane); line configuration (U-shape, straight, branching); pacing (mechanical, human); product mix (one product or multiple products); workstation characteristics (workers may

## WHAT'S IT LIKE WORKING ON AN ASSEMBLY LINE?

Ben Hamper, the infamous "Rivethead" working for General Motors, describes his new job on the Chevy Suburban assembly line with the following:

> *The whistle blew and the Rivet Line began to crawl. I took a seat up on the workbench and watched the guy I was replacing tackle his duties. He'd grab one end of a long rail and, with the help of the worker up the line from him, flip it over on its back. CLAAAANNNNNNGGGG! He then raced back to the bench and grabbed a four-wheel-drive spring casting and a muffler hanger. He would rivet the pieces onto the rail. With that completed, he'd jostle the rail back into an upright position and grab a cross member off the overhanging feeder line that curled above the bench. Reaching up with his spare arm, he'd grab a different rivet gun while fidgeting to get the cross member firmly planted so that it aligned with the proper set of holes. He then inserted the rivets and began squashing the cross member into place. Just watching this guy go at it made my head hurt.*
>
> *"How about takin' a stab at it?" the guy asked me after a while. "You're not gonna get the feel of the job sittin' up there on the bench."*
>
> *I politely declined. I didn't want to learn any portion of this monster maze before it was absolutely necessary. Once the bossman thought you had a reasonable grasp of the setup, he was likely to step in and turn you loose on your own. I needed to keep delaying in order to give Art some time to reel me back up to Cab Shop.*
>
> *"Well, you've got three days," the guy replied. "After that, this baby's all yours."*

EXCERPT FROM B. HAMPER'S *RIVETHEAD: TALES FROM THE ASSEMBLY LINE* (NEW YORK: WARNER BOOKS, 1992), P. 90.

sit, stand, walk with the line, or ride the line); and length of the line (few or many workers). For worker insight, see the box titled "What's It Like Working on an Assembly Line?"

The range of products partially or completely assembled on lines includes toys, appliances, autos, planes, guns, garden equipment, clothing, and a wide variety of electronic components. In fact, it is probably safe to say that virtually any product that has multiple parts and is produced in large volume uses assembly lines to some degree. Clearly, lines are an important technology; to really understand their managerial requirements, we should have some familiarity with how a line is balanced.

## ASSEMBLY-LINE BALANCING

Though primarily a scheduling issue, assembly-line balancing often has implications for layout. This would occur when, for balance purposes, workstation size or the number used would have to be physically modified.

Workstation cycle time

The most common assembly line is a moving conveyor that passes a series of workstations in a uniform time interval called the **workstation cycle time** (which is also the time between successive units coming off the end of the line). At each workstation, work is performed on a product either by adding parts or by completing assembly operations. The work performed at each station is made up of many bits of work, termed *tasks, elements,* and *work units*. Such tasks are described by motion–time analysis. Generally, they are groupings that cannot be subdivided on the assembly line without paying a penalty in extra motions.

Assembly-line balancing

Precedence relationship

The total work to be performed at a workstation is equal to the sum of the tasks assigned to that workstation. The **assembly-line balancing** problem is one of assigning all tasks to a series of workstations so that each workstation has no more than can be done in the workstation cycle time, and so that the unassigned (that is, idle) time across all workstations is minimized. The problem is complicated by the relationships among tasks imposed by product design and process technologies. This is called the **precedence relationship,** which specifies the order in which tasks must be performed in the assembly process.

The steps in balancing an assembly line are straightforward:

1 Specify the sequential relationships among tasks using a precedence diagram. The diagram consists of circles and arrows. Circles represent individual tasks; arrows indicate the order of task performance.

2 Determine the required workstation cycle time ($C$), using the formula

$$C = \frac{\text{Production time per day}}{\text{Required output per day (in units)}}$$

3 Determine the theoretical minimum number of workstations ($N_t$) required to satisfy the workstation cycle time constraint using the formula (note that this must be rounded up to the next highest integer).

$$N_t = \frac{\text{Sum of task times } (T)}{\text{Cycle time } (C)}$$

4 Select a primary rule by which tasks are to be assigned to workstations, and a secondary rule to break ties.
5 Assign tasks, one at a time, to the first workstation until the sum of the task times is equal to the workstation cycle time, or no other tasks are feasible because of time or sequence restrictions. Repeat the process for Workstation 2, Workstation 3, and so on until all tasks are assigned.
6 Evaluate the efficiency of the balance derived using the formula[4]

$$\text{Efficiency} = \frac{\text{Sum of task times } (T)}{\text{Actual number of workstations } (N_a) \times \text{Workstation cycle time } (C)}$$

7 If efficiency is unsatisfactory, rebalance using a different decision rule.

### EXAMPLE TN5.2: ASSEMBLY LINE BALANCING

The Model J Wagon is to be assembled on a conveyor belt. Five hundred wagons are required per day. Production time per day is 420 minutes, and the assembly steps and times for the wagon are given in Exhibit TN5.10. Assignment: Find the balance that minimizes the number of workstations, subject to cycle time and precedence constraints.

### SOLUTION

1 Draw a precedence diagram. Exhibit TN5.11 illustrates the sequential relationships identified in Exhibit TN5.10. (The length of the arrows has no meaning.)

EXHIBIT TN5.10

**Assembly Steps and Times for Model J Wagon**

| Task | Task Time (in Seconds) | Description | Tasks That Must Precede |
|---|---|---|---|
| A | 45 | Position rear axle support and hand fasten four screws to nuts. | — |
| B | 11 | Insert rear axle. | A |
| C | 9 | Tighten rear axle support screws to nuts. | B |
| D | 50 | Position front axle assembly and hand fasten with four screws to nuts. | — |
| E | 15 | Tighten front axle assembly screws. | D |
| F | 12 | Position rear wheel #1 and fasten hubcap. | C |
| G | 12 | Position rear wheel #2 and fasten hubcap. | C |
| H | 12 | Position front wheel #1 and fasten hubcap. | E |
| I | 12 | Position front wheel #2 and fasten hubcap. | E |
| J | 8 | Position wagon handle shaft on front axle assembly and hand fasten bolt and nut. | F, G, H, I |
| K | 9 | Tighten bolt and nut. | J |
| | 195 | | |

EXHIBIT TN5.11

**Precedence Graph for Model J Wagon**

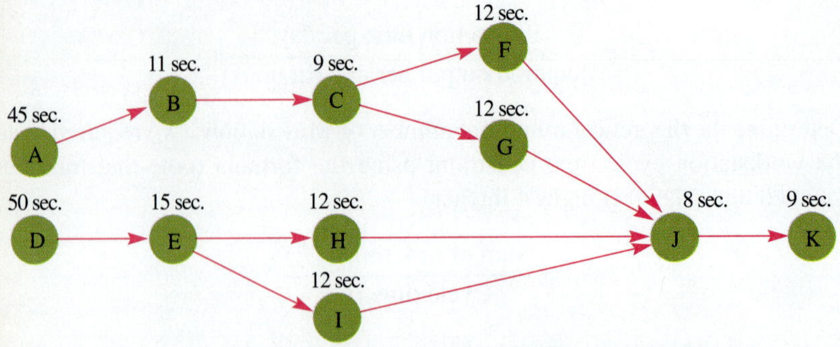


2 Determine workstation cycle time. Here we have to convert to seconds because our task times are in seconds.

$$C = \frac{\text{Production time per day}}{\text{Output per day}} = \frac{60 \text{ sec.} \times 420 \text{ min.}}{500 \text{ wagons}} = \frac{25{,}200}{500} = 50.4$$

3 Determine the theoretical minimum number of workstations required (the actual number may be greater):

$$N_t = \frac{T}{C} = \frac{195 \text{ seconds}}{50.4 \text{ seconds}} = 3.87 = 4 \text{ (rounded up)}$$

4 Select assignment rules. Research has demonstrated that some rules are better than others for certain problem structures. In general, the strategy is to use a rule assigning tasks that either have many followers or are of long duration because they effectively limit the balance achievable. In this case, we use the following as our primary rule:

*a.* Assign tasks in order of the largest number of following tasks.

| Task | Number of Following Tasks |
|---|---|
| A | 6 |
| B or D | 5 |
| C or E | 4 |
| F, G, H, or I | 2 |
| J | 1 |
| K | 0 |

Our secondary rule, to be invoked where ties exist from our primary rule, is

*b.* Assign tasks in order of longest task time (shown in Exhibit TN5.12).

5 Make task assignments to form Workstation 1, Workstation 2, and so forth until all tasks are assigned. The actual assignment is given in Exhibit TN5.12A and is shown graphically in Exhibit TN5.12B.

6 Calculate the efficiency. This is shown in Exhibit TN5.12C.

7 Evaluate the solution. An efficiency of 77 percent indicates an imbalance or idle time of 23 percent (1.0 − .77) across the entire line. From Exhibit TN5.12A we can see that there are 57 total seconds of idle time, and the "choice" job is at Workstation 5.

Is a better balance possible? In this case, yes. Try balancing the line with rule *b* and breaking ties with rule *a*. (This will give you a feasible four-station balance.) ←

EXHIBIT TN5.12

A. Balance Made According to Largest Number of Following Tasks Rule

| | Task | Task Time (in Seconds) | Remaining Unassigned Time (in Seconds) | Feasible Remaining Tasks | Task with Most Followers | Task with Longest Operation Time |
|---|---|---|---|---|---|---|
| Station 1 | A | 45 | 5.4 idle | None | | |
| Station 2 | D | 50 | 0.4 idle | None | | |
| Station 3 | B | 11 | 39.4 | C, E | C, E | E |
| | E | 15 | 24.4 | C, H, I | C | |
| | C | 9 | 15.4 | F, G, H, I | F, G, H, I | F, G, H, I |
| | F* | 12 | 3.4 idle | None | | |
| Station 4 | G | 12 | 38.4 | H, I | H, I | H, I |
| | H* | 12 | 26.4 | I | | |
| | I | 12 | 14.4 | J | | |
| | J | 8 | 6.4 idle | None | | |
| Station 5 | K | 9 | 41.4 idle | None | | |

*Denotes task arbitrarily selected where there is a tie between longest operation times.

B. Precedence Graph for Model J Wagon

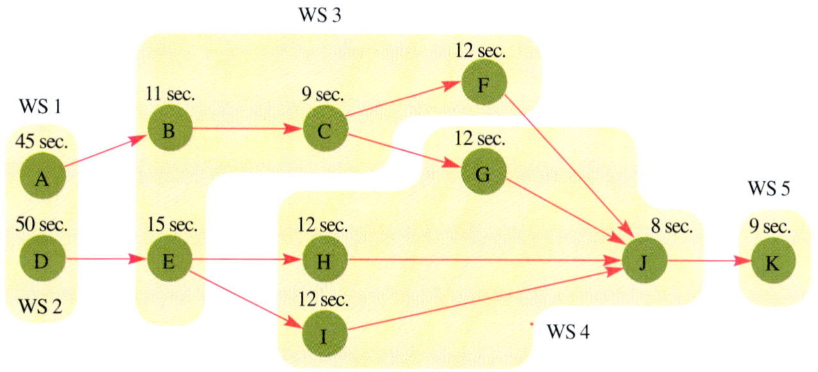


C. Efficiency Calculation

$$\text{Efficiency} = \frac{T}{N_a C} = \frac{195}{(5)(50.4)} = .77, \text{ or } 77\%$$

## SPLITTING TASKS

Often the longest required task time forms the shortest workstation cycle time for the production line. This task time is the lower time bound unless it is possible to split the task into two or more workstations.

Consider the following illustration: Suppose that an assembly line contains the following task times in seconds: 40, 30, 15, 25, 20, 18, 15. The line runs for $7\frac{1}{2}$ hours per day and demand for output is 750 per day.

The workstation cycle time required to produce 750 per day is 36 seconds ($[7\frac{1}{2}$ hours $\times$ 60 minutes $\times$ 60 seconds$]/750$). Our problem is that we have one task that takes 40 seconds. How do we deal with this task?

There are several ways that we may be able to accommodate the 40-second task in a 36-second cycle. Possibilities are

1. **Split the task.** Can we split the task so that complete units are processed in two workstations?
2. **Share the task.** Can the task somehow be shared so an adjacent workstation does part of the work? This differs from the split task in the first option because the adjacent station acts to assist, not to do some units containing the entire task.
3. **Use parallel workstations.** It may be necessary to assign the task to two workstations that would operate in parallel.
4. **Use a more skilled worker.** Because this task exceeds the workstation cycle time by just 11 percent, a faster worker may be able to meet the 36-second time.

5 **Work overtime.** Producing at a rate of one every 40 seconds would create 675 per day, 75 short of the needed 750. The amount of overtime required to produce the additional 75 is 50 minutes (75 × 40 seconds/60 seconds).

6 **Redesign.** It may be possible to redesign the product to reduce the task time slightly.

Other possibilities to reduce the task time include an equipment upgrade, a roaming helper to support the line, a change of materials, and multiskilled workers to operate the line as a team rather than as independent workers.

## FLEXIBLE AND U-SHAPED LINE LAYOUTS

As we saw in the preceding example, assembly line balances frequently result in unequal workstation times. Flexible line layouts such as those shown in Exhibit TN5.13 are a common way of dealing with this problem. In our toy company example, the U-shaped line with work sharing at the bottom of the figure could help resolve the imbalance.

## COMPUTERIZED LINE BALANCING

Companies engaged in assembly methods commonly employ a computer for line balancing. Most develop their own computer programs, but commercial packaged programs are also widely applied. One of these is General Electric Company's *Assembly-Line Configuration (ASYBL$),* which uses the "ranked positional weight" rule in selecting tasks for workstations. Specifically, this rule states that tasks are assigned according to their positional weights, which is the time for a given task plus the task times of all those that follow it. Thus, the task with the highest positional weight would be assigned to the first workstation (subject to time, precedence, and zoning constraints). As is typical with such software, the user has several options for how the problem is to be solved. Exhibit TN5.14 illustrates a portion of program output when a target level of efficiency is used as a basis for deriving and comparing different balances for a 35-task assembly line. (The program can handle up to 450 tasks.) Note the trade-offs that take place as the number of workstations changes. In this case, the larger number of workstations allows for a better balance and, therefore, a higher efficiency.

## MIXED-MODEL LINE BALANCING

This approach is used by JIT manufacturers such as Toyota. Its objective is to meet the demand for a variety of products and to avoid building high inventories. Mixed-model line balancing involves scheduling several different models to be produced over a given day or week on the same line in a cyclical fashion.

THIS ASSEMBLY LINE AT HEWLETT-PACKARD ALLOWS TECHNICIANS THE FLEXIBILITY TO TRADE WORK ELEMENTS, AND ALLOWS MANAGEMENT TO ADD OR SUBTRACT OPERATORS AS NECESSARY.

EXHIBIT TN5.13

**Flexible Line Layouts**

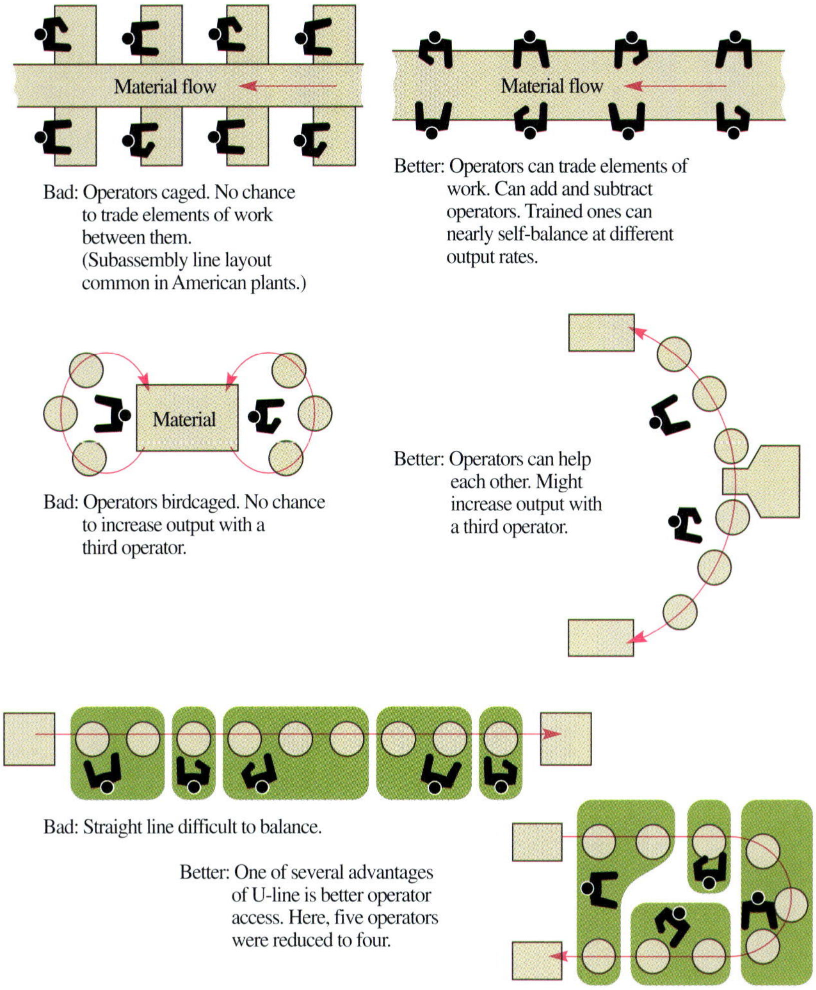


SOURCE: R. W. HALL, *ATTAINING MANUFACTURING EXCELLENCE* (BURR RIDGE, IL: DOW JONES-IRWIN, 1987), P. 125.

EXHIBIT TN5.14

**Sample Computer Output**

```
ENTER OPTION NUMBER? 3
ENTER TARGET EFFICIENCY? .85
TOTAL EFFICIENCY    = 82%
STANDARD DEVIATION =    0.0153
TARGET CYCLE TIME  =   0.347
MINIM. CYCLE TIME  =   0.343
NO. OF STATIONS   = 19
TOTAL EFFICIENCY    = 80%
STANDARD DEVIATION =    0.0175
TARGET CYCLE TIME  =   0.368
MINIM. CYCLE TIME  =   0.368
NO. OF STATIONS   = 18
TOTAL EFFICIENCY    = 75%
STANDARD DEVIATION =    0.0214
TARGET CYCLE TIME  =   0.417
MINIM. CYCLE TIME  =   0.415
NO. OF STATIONS  =   17
```

SOURCE: GENERAL ELECTRIC COMPANY, *ASSEMBLY-LINE CONFIGURATION, ASYBL$ USER'S GUIDE*, REVISED (1985), P. 17.

### EXAMPLE TN5.3: MIXED-MODEL LINE BALANCING

To illustrate how this is done, suppose our toy company has a fabrication line to bore holes in its Model J wagon frame and its Model K wagon frame. The time required to bore the holes is different for each wagon type.

Assume that the final assembly line downstream requires equal numbers of Model J and Model K wagon frames. Assume also that we want to develop a cycle time for the fabrication line that is balanced for the production of equal numbers of J and K frames. Of course, we could produce Model J frames for several days and then produce Model K frames until an equal number of frames have been produced. However, this would build up unnecessary work in process inventory.

If we want to reduce the amount of in-process inventory, we could develop a cycle mix that greatly reduces inventory buildup while keeping within the restrictions of equal numbers of J and K wagon frames.

Process times: 6 minutes per J and 4 minutes per K.
The day consists of 480 minutes (8 hours × 60 minutes).

### SOLUTION

$$6J + 4K = 480$$

Because equal numbers of J and K are to be produced (or J = K), produce 48J and 48K per day, or 6J and 6K per hour.

The following shows one balance of J and K frames.

Balanced Mixed-Model Sequence

| | | | | | | |
|---|---|---|---|---|---|---|
| Model sequence | J J | K K K | J J | J J | K K K | |
| Operation time | 6 6 | 4 4 4 | 6 6 | 6 6 | 4 4 4 | Repeats 8 times per day |
| Minicycle time | 12 | 12 | 12 | 12 | 12 | |
| Total cycle time | | | 60 | | | |

This line is balanced at 6 frames of each type per hour with a minicycle time of 12 minutes.

Another balance is J K K J K J, with times of 6, 4, 4, 6, 4, 6. This balance produces 3J and 3K every 30 minutes with a minicycle time of 10 minutes (JK, KJ, KJ). ←

The simplicity of mixed-model balancing (under conditions of a level production schedule) is seen in Yasuhiro Mondon's description of Toyota Motor Corporation's operations:

> Final assembly lines of Toyota are mixed product lines. The production per day is averaged by taking the number of vehicles in the monthly production schedule classified by specifications, and dividing by the number of working days.
>
> In regard to the production sequence during each day, the cycle time of each different specification vehicle is calculated. To have all specification vehicles appear at their own cycle time, different specification vehicles are ordered to follow each other.[5]

## CURRENT THOUGHTS ON ASSEMBLY LINES

It is true that the widespread use of assembly line methods in manufacturing has dramatically increased output rates. Historically, the focus has almost always been on full utilization of human labor—that is, to design assembly lines minimizing human idle time. Equipment and facility utilization stood in the background as much less important. Past research has tried to find optimal solutions as if the problem stood in a never-changing world.

Newer views of assembly lines take a broader perspective. The intentions are to incorporate greater flexibility in products produced on the line, more variability in workstations (such

## BREAKTHROUGH

### DELL COMPUTER'S SERVER PLANT USES CELLS

The one-person build cells that populate the heart of the plant enhance flexibility—a critical element of Dell Computer's direct build-to-order model. Assisted by Web-based online work instructions, an experienced operator in a standard cell can assemble any of the 10 basic server platforms in various configurations.

"With the old-style progressive-build approach, you pretty much batched your build every day," notes Mark Lozano, senior production control manager. "You couldn't change what was going down the line. But here, you can build whatever you want when you want. In one cell we can have a high-end machine following a low-end machine. That kind of flexibility allows us a much shorter cycle time for all of our platforms."

Server components begin their journey through the plant at one of two locations. In one area, motherboards are prepped and installed into the computer chassis. In the second, a kitting area, other components are pulled from storage racks with the aid of a computerized "pick to light" system and placed into totes. From there, intelligent conveyors—linked to a manufacturing execution system—deliver the materials to an open build cell using a pull process.

In the cell the operator does the rest, including putting in the screws. "The next person who can open it up is the customer," says Kris Vorm, director of server engineering. No downstream quality inspector examines the innards of the unit, unless subsequent electronic tests indicate a pesky quality problem. Under a buddy system, a builder will ask another operator to make a visual inspection before he or she screws the cover onto the box. Next stop is the extended test rack, where detailed diagnostics are conducted prior to downloading and testing the operating system and application software—all based on customer specifications.

ADAPTED FROM J. H. SHERIDAN, "DELL COMPUTER'S SERVER PLANT EMPHASIZES VELOCITY AND FLEXIBILITY, WHILE BALANCING SUPPLY AND DEMAND," *INDUSTRY WEEK*, OCTOBER 18, 1999, PP. 46–48.

as size and number of workers), improved reliability (through routine preventive maintenance), and high-quality output (through improved tooling and training). The Breakthrough Box on Dell Computer describes how a combination of assembly lines and manufacturing cells (the topic of the next section) can be used when product demand changes quickly.

## GROUP TECHNOLOGY (CELLULAR) LAYOUT

Group technology (or cellular) layout allocates dissimilar machines into cells to work on products that have similar shapes and processing requirements. Group technology (GT) layouts are now widely used in metal fabricating, computer chip manufacture, and assembly work. The overall objective is to gain the benefits of product layout in job-shop kinds of production. These benefits include

Vol. IV "The Vision Light System at Federal Signal."

1 **Better human relations.** Cells consist of a few workers who form a small work team; a team turns out complete units of work.
2 **Improved operator expertise.** Workers see only a limited number of different parts in a finite production cycle, so repetition means quick learning.
3 **Less in-process inventory and material handling.** A cell combines several production stages, so fewer parts travel through the shop.

Exhibit TN5.15

Developing a Cell to Produce Wave-Guide Parts

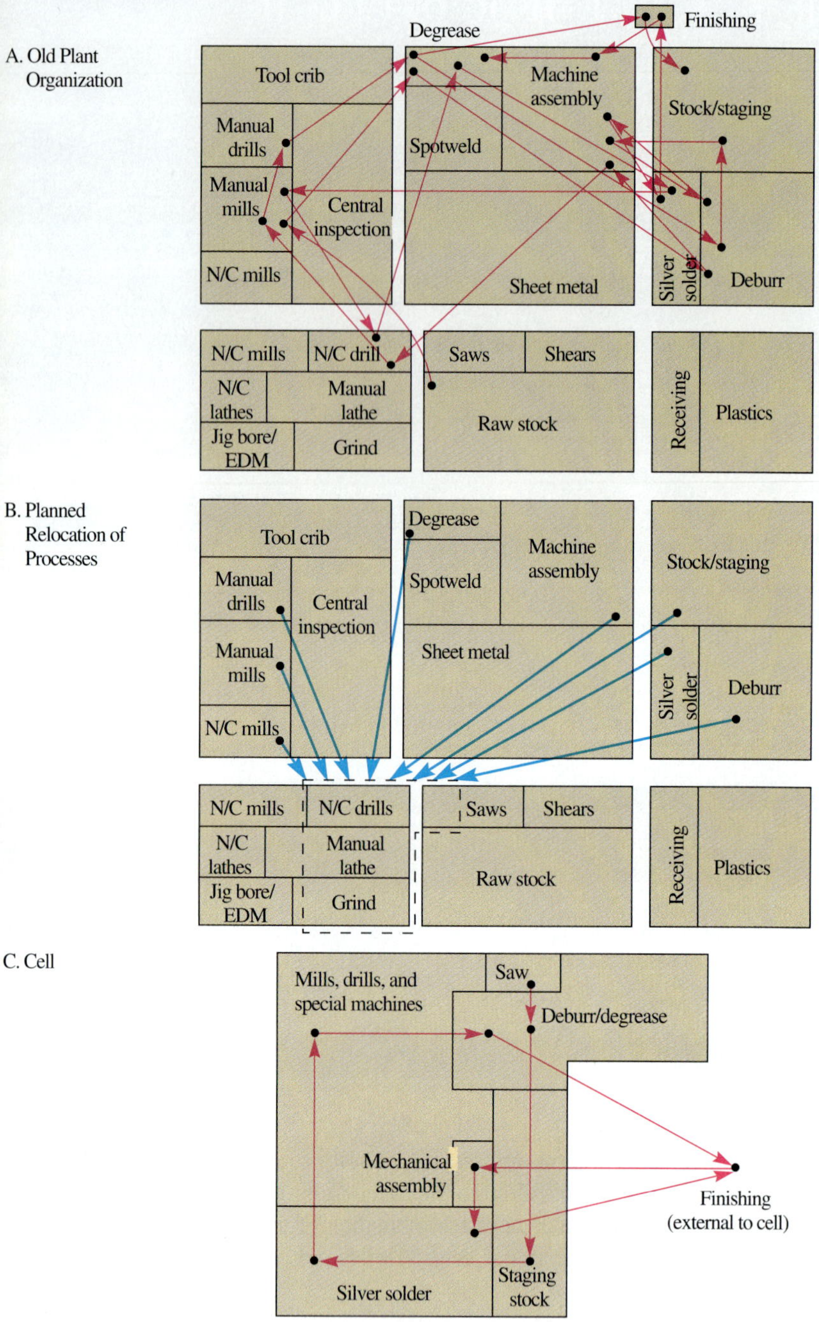


Source: Reprinted with permission of The Free Press, an imprint of Simon and Schuster, from *World Class Manufacturing* by R. J. Schonberger, Copyright © 1986 by Schonberger & Associates.

4 **Faster production setup.** Fewer jobs mean reduced tooling and hence faster tooling changes.

## Developing a GT Layout

Shifting from process layout to a GT cellular layout entails three steps:

1 Grouping parts into families that follow a common sequence of steps. This step requires developing and maintaining a computerized parts classification and coding system. This is often a major expense with such systems, although many companies have developed shortcut procedures for identifying parts families.

2 Identifying dominant flow patterns of parts families as a basis for location or relocation of processes.
3 Physically grouping machines and processes into cells. Often there will be parts that cannot be associated with a family and specialized machinery that cannot be placed in any one cell because of its general use. These unattached parts and machinery are placed in a "remainder cell."

Exhibit TN5.15 illustrates the cell development process followed by Rockwell's Telecommunication Division, maker of wave-guide parts. Part A shows the original process-oriented layout; part B, the planned relocation of process based on parts-family production requirements; and part C, an enlarged layout of the cell designed to perform all but the finishing operation. According to Schonberger, cellular organization was practical here because (1) distinct parts families existed; (2) there were several of each type of machine, so taking a machine out of a cluster did not rob the cluster of all its capacity, leaving no way to produce other products; (3) the work centers were easily movable stand-alone machine tools—heavy, but anchored to the floor rather simply. He adds that these three features represent general guidelines for deciding where cells make sense.[6]

### VIRTUAL GT CELLS

When equipment is not easily movable, many companies dedicate a given machine out of a set of identical machines in a process layout. A virtual GT cell for, say, a two-month production run for the job might consist of Drill 1 in the drills area, Mill 3 in the mill area, and Assembly Area 1 in the machine assembly area. To approximate a GT flow, all work on the particular part family would be done only on these specific machines.

## FIXED-POSITION LAYOUT

Fixed-position layout is characterized by a relatively low number of production units in comparison with process and product layout formats. In developing a fixed-position layout, visualize the product as the hub of a wheel with materials and equipment arranged concentrically around the production point in their order of use and movement difficulty. Thus, in shipbuilding, for example, rivets that are used throughout construction would be placed close to or in the hull; heavy engine parts, which must travel to the hull only once, would be placed at a more distant location; and cranes would be set up close to the hull because of their constant use.

In fixed-position layout, a high degree of task ordering is common, and to the extent that this precedence determines production stages, a fixed-position layout might be developed by arranging materials according to their technological priority. This procedure would be expected in making a layout for a large machine tool, such as a stamping machine, where manufacture follows a rigid sequence; assembly is performed from the ground up, with parts being added to the base in almost a building-block fashion.

As far as quantitative layout techniques are concerned, there is little in the literature devoted to fixed-position formats, even though they have been utilized for thousands of years. In certain situations, however, it may be possible to specify objective criteria and develop a fixed-position layout through quantitative means. For instance, if the material handling cost is significant and the construction site permits more or less straight-line material movement, the CRAFT process layout technique might be advantageously employed.

## RETAIL SERVICE LAYOUT

The objective of a *retail service layout* (as is found in stores, banks, and restaurants) is to maximize net profit per square foot of store space. A company that has been very successful in leveraging every inch of its layout space to achieve this objective is Taco Bell Restaurants. Exhibit TN5.16 illustrates Taco Bell store layouts used in 1986 and from 1991 to the present. The nature of the layout changes reflects actions required to support the

EXHIBIT TN5.16

Taco Bell Restaurant Floor Plans

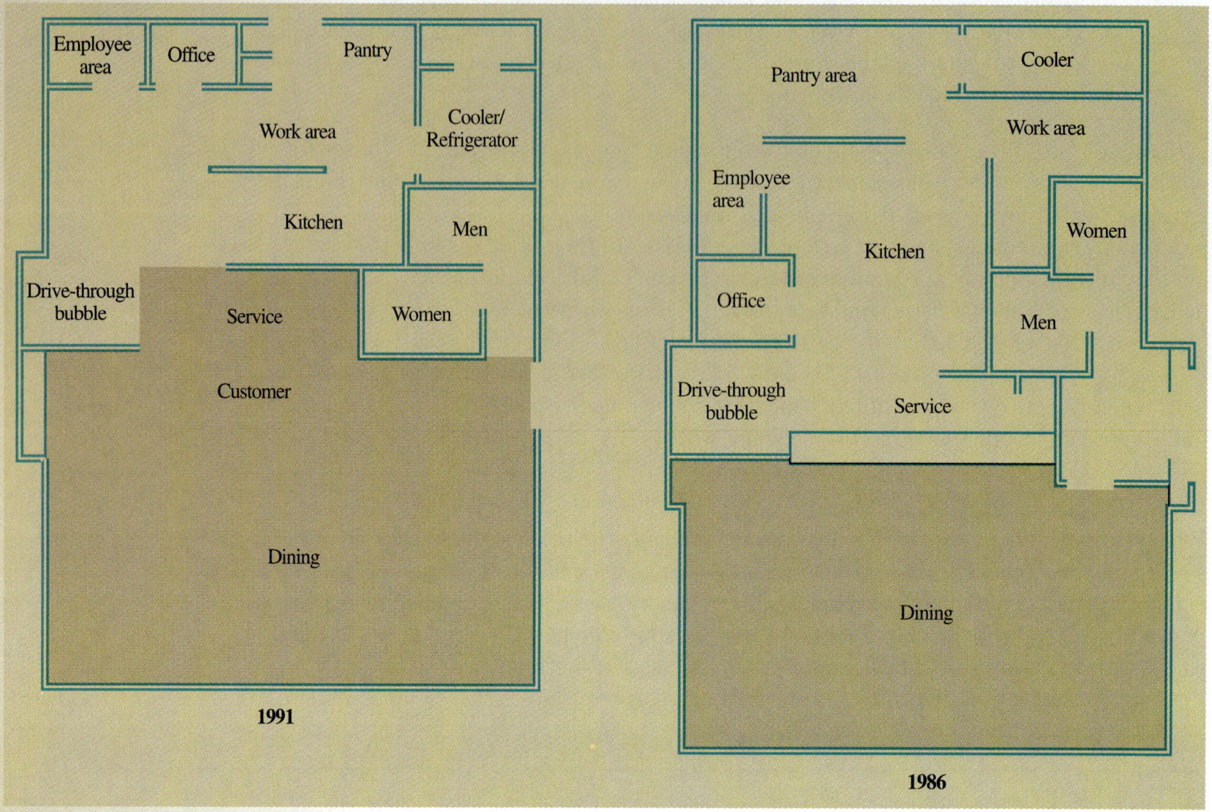


SOURCE: COURTESY OF TACO BELL CORP., LOS ANGELES, CA.

company's value strategy of speed and low prices. Key operational modifications include elimination of many on-site food preparation steps, which simultaneously increased the speed of service while reducing the amount of working space needed. For example, the chopping and bagging of lettuce and the precooking and seasoning of meats, beans, and hard tortilla products are now done at central kitchens or by suppliers. The restaurant kitchens are now heating and assembly units only. In addition to such outsourcing, changes were made in queue structures, such as moving from a single line running parallel to the counter, to a double line running perpendicular to it. This improved product flow facilitated serving drive-through windows, increased capacity, and allowed customers to see assembly workers' faces (as opposed to just their backs, as was the case before).

## SERVICESCAPES

As previously noted, the broad objective of layout in retail services is generally to maximize net profit per square foot of floor space. Operationally, this goal is often translated into such criteria as "minimize handling cost" or "maximize product exposure." However, as Sommers and Kernan observed more than 30 years ago, employing these and similar criteria in service layout planning "results in stores that look like warehouses and requires shoppers to approach the task like order pickers or display case stockers."[7] There are other, more humanistic aspects of the service that must also be considered in the layout.

Bitner coined the term *servicescape* to refer to the physical surroundings in which the service takes place and how these surroundings affect customers and employees. An understanding of the servicescape is necessary to create a good layout for the service firm (or the service-related portions of the manufacturing firm). The servicescape has three

EXHIBIT TN5.17

Alternative Store Layouts

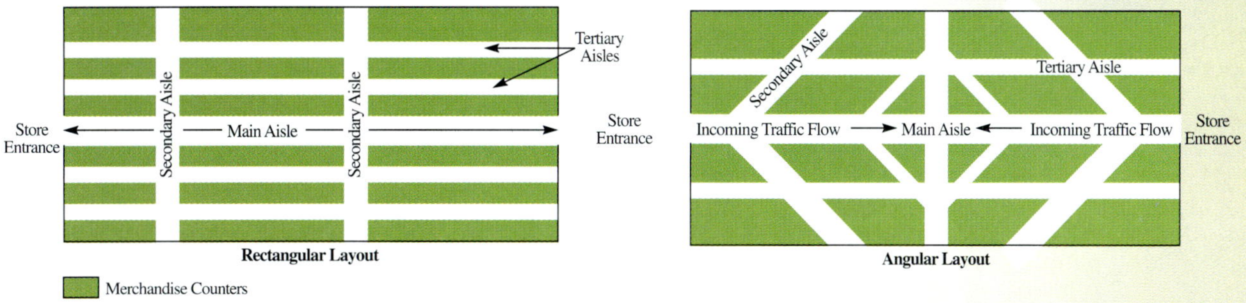


elements that must be considered: the ambient conditions; the spatial layout and functionality; and the signs, symbols, and artifacts.[8]

## AMBIENT CONDITIONS

The term *ambient conditions* refers to background characteristics such as the noise level, music, lighting, temperature, and scent that can affect employee performance and morale as well as customers' perceptions of the service, how long they stay, and how much money they spend. Although many of these characteristics are influenced primarily by the design of the building (such as the placement of light fixtures, acoustic tiles, and exhaust fans), the layout within a building can also have an effect. Areas near food preparation will smell like food, lighting in a hallway outside a theater must be dim, tables near a stage will be noisy, and locations near an entrance will be drafty.

## SPATIAL LAYOUT AND FUNCTIONALITY

Two aspects of the *spatial layout and functionality* are especially important: planning the circulation path of the customers and grouping the merchandise. The goal of circulation planning is to provide a path for the customers that exposes them to as much of the merchandise as possible while placing any needed services along this path in the sequence they will be needed. For example, the photo shows a bank reception area placed where the customer will encounter it immediately upon entering the bank. Aisle characteristics are of particular importance. Aside from determining the number of aisles to be provided, decisions must be made as to the width of the aisles because this is a direct function of expected or desired traffic. Aisle width can also affect the direction of flow through the service. Stu Leonard's Dairy Store in Norwalk, Connecticut, is designed so that it is virtually impossible to turn around a shopping cart once you have entered the shopping flow path. Focal points that catch the customers' attention in the layout can also be used to draw the customers in the desired direction. The famous blue light at Kmart is an example. Another is shown in the photo.

To enhance shoppers' view of merchandise as they proceed down a main aisle, secondary and tertiary aisles may be set at an angle. Consider the two layouts in Exhibit TN5.17. The rectangular layout would probably require less expensive fixtures and contain more display space. If storage considerations are important to the store management, this would be the more desirable layout. On the other hand, the angular layout provides the shopper with a much clearer view of the merchandise and, other things being equal, presents a more desirable selling environment.

It is common practice now to base merchandise groupings on the shopper's view of related items, as opposed to the physical characteristics of the products or shelf space and servicing requirements. This grouping-by-association philosophy is seen in boutiques in department stores and gourmet sections in supermarkets.

WHY ARE THESE PEOPLE SMILING? REMOVABLE, MAGNETIC, LIFE-SIZE CUTOUTS FEATURING "BALLOON" COMMENTS ARE MOUNTED ON THE WALL NEXT TO THE TELLER MACHINES. ALL FIGURES HAVE "FACT TAGS" WITH PRINTED PRODUCT FEATURES. THESE FIGURES MAKE SHOPPING FOR PRODUCT FEATURES ENTERTAINING.

Special mention is in order for a few guidelines derived from marketing research and relating to circulation planning and merchandise grouping:

1 People in supermarkets tend to follow a perimeter pattern in their shopping behavior. Placing high-profit items along the walls of a store will enhance their probability of purchase.
2 Sale merchandise placed at the end of an aisle in supermarkets almost always sells better than the same sale items placed in the interior portion of an aisle.
3 Credit and other nonselling departments that require customers to wait for the completion of their services should be placed either on upper floors or in "dead" areas.
4 In department stores, locations nearest the store entrances and adjacent to front-window displays are most valuable in terms of sales potential.

## SIGNS, SYMBOLS, AND ARTIFACTS

*Signs, symbols, and artifacts* refer to the parts of the service that have social significance. As with the ambiance, these are often a characteristic of the design of the building, although the orientation, location, and size of many objects and areas can carry special meaning. As examples,

- In the old days, bank loan officers were easily identified because their desks were located on a raised section of the bank floor called the platform.
- A person seated at the desk closest to the entrance is usually in charge of greeting customers and directing them to their destination.
- In a department store, the tiled areas indicate the aisles for travel, while carpeted areas indicate departments for browsing.
- Some car salespeople have blackboards installed in their offices because a person writing on a blackboard symbolizes someone who should be listened to and trusted (such as a teacher).

As you might have gathered from these examples, the influence of behavioral factors makes the development of hard and fast rules for servicescape layout rather difficult. Suffice it to say that making the layout choice is not simply a matter of choosing between display space and ease of operation.

## BREAKTHROUGH

### IN NEW DRUG LABS, "PORCHES" AND "HUDDLE ZONES"

"The myths of innovation are always stories about solitary, heroic individuals working on their own who have these sudden leaps of insight. In fact, it's usually much messier than that," Pfizer's Dr. Milne says. "Innovation actually thrives on exchange. It is very social, and you want an environment that speaks to that."

Which is why Dr. Milne and his colleagues junked Pfizer's standard lab model of two parallel hallways—in effect, human traffic lanes—with labs and offices opening off them. In the new buildings, the labs and offices encircle a central core so scientists can gather without being in the way of people passing by. In another departure, office doors are angled into one another so scientists run into each other when leaving. Dr. Milne calls these spots "front porch" interactions.

Extending the togetherness theme, Pfizer groups five to seven scientists in "families," and each family has its own open conference area called a "huddle zone." With huge windows and sweeping views, these spots are the prettiest in the building. Pfizer's "families" are grouped into a "tribe" of 70. Each tribe has its own larger gathering areas. All have coffee carts. Dr. Milne is particularly fond of coffee carts and the interaction they can create.



## OFFICE LAYOUT

The trend in *office layout* is toward more open offices, with personal work spaces separated only by low divider walls. Companies have removed fixed walls to foster greater communication and teamwork. (See, for example, the Breakthrough Box titled "In New Drug Labs, 'Porches' and 'Huddle Zones.'" Signs, symbols, and artifacts, as discussed in the section on service layout, are possibly even more important in office layout than in retailing. For instance, size and orientation of desks can indicate the importance or professionalism of the people behind them.

Service

Central administration offices are often designed and laid out so as to convey the desired image of the company. For example, Scandinavian Airlines System's (SAS) administrative office complex outside Stockholm is a two-story collection of glass-walled pods that provide the feeling of the open communication and flat hierarchy (few levels of organization) that characterize the company's management philosophy.

Global

Service-Master (the highly profitable janitorial management company) positions its "Know-How Room" at the center of its headquarters. This room contains all of the physical products, operations manuals, and pictorial displays of career paths and other symbols for the key knowledge essential to the business. "From this room, the rest of the company can be seen as a big apparatus to bring the knowledge of the marketplace to its employees and potential customers."[9]

## CONCLUSION

Facility layout is where the rubber meets the road in the design and operation of a production system. A good factory (or office) layout can provide real competitive advantage by facilitating material and information flow processes. It can also enhance employees' work life. A good service layout can be an effective "stage" for playing out the service encounter. In conclusion, here are some marks of a good layout in these environments:

**MARKS OF A GOOD LAYOUT FOR MANUFACTURING AND BACK-OFFICE OPERATIONS**

1 Straight-line flow pattern (or adaptation).
2 Backtracking kept to a minimum.
3 Production time predictable.

4 Little interstage storage of materials.
5 Open plant floors so everyone can see what is happening.
6 Bottleneck operations under control.
7 Workstations close together.
8 Orderly handling and storage of materials.
9 No unnecessary rehandling of materials.
10 Easily adjustable to changing conditions.

**MARKS OF A GOOD LAYOUT FOR FACE-TO-FACE SERVICES**

1 Easily understood service flow pattern.
2 Adequate waiting facilities.
3 Easy communication with customers.
4 Easily maintained customer surveillance.
5 Clear exit and entry points with adequate checkout capabilities.
6 Departments and processes arranged so that customers see only what you want them to see.
7 Balance between waiting areas and service areas.
8 Minimum walking and material movement.
9 Lack of clutter.
10 High sales volume per square foot of facility.

## KEY TERMS

**Process layout** Also called a *job-shop* or *functional layout;* a format in which similar equipment or functions are grouped together.

**Product layout** Also called a *flow-shop layout;* equipment or work processes are arranged according to the progressive steps by which the product is made.

**Group technology (cellular) layout** Groups dissimilar machines into work centers (or cells) to work on products that have similar shapes and processing requirements.

**Fixed-position layout** The product remains at one location and equipment is moved to the product.

**CRAFT** (Computerized Relative Allocation of Facilities Technique) A method to help devise good process layouts. The technique is designed to minimize material handling costs in the facility and works by iteratively exchanging pairs of departments until no further cost reductions are possible.

**Systematic Layout Planning (SLP)** A technique for solving process layout problems when the use of numerical flow data between departments is not practical. The technique uses an activity relationship diagram that is adjusted by trial and error until a satisfactory adjacency pattern is obtained.

**Workstation cycle time** The time between successive units coming off the end of an assembly line.

**Assembly-line balancing** The problem of assigning all the tasks to a series of workstations so that each workstation has no more than can be done in the workstation cycle time, and so that idle time across all workstations is minimized.

**Precedence relationship** The order in which tasks must be performed in the assembly process.

## SOLVED PROBLEMS

### SOLVED PROBLEM 1

A university advising office has four rooms, each dedicated to specific problems: petitions (Room A), schedule advising (Room B), grade complaints (Room C), and student counseling (Room D). The office is 80 feet long and 20 feet wide. Each room is 20 feet by 20 feet. The present location of rooms is A, B, C, D—that is, a straight line. The load summary shows the number of contacts that each adviser in a room has with other advisers in the other rooms. Assume that all advisers are equal in this value.

Load summary: $AB = 10, AC = 20, AD = 30,$
$BC = 15, BD = 10, CD = 20.$

*a.* Evaluate this layout according to the material handling cost method.
*b.* Improve the layout by exchanging functions within rooms. Show your amount of improvement using the same method as in *a*.

## Solution

*a.*

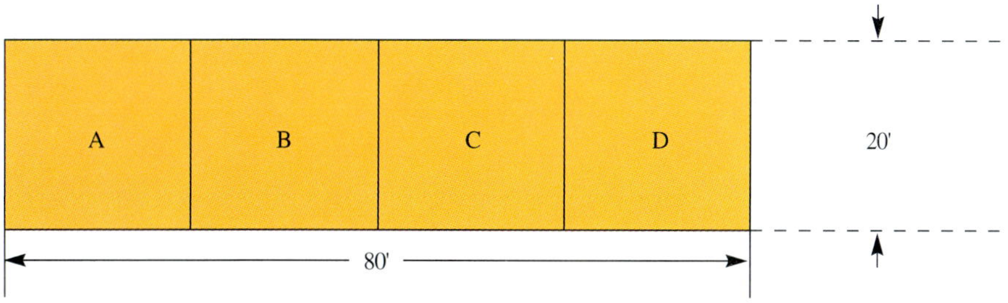


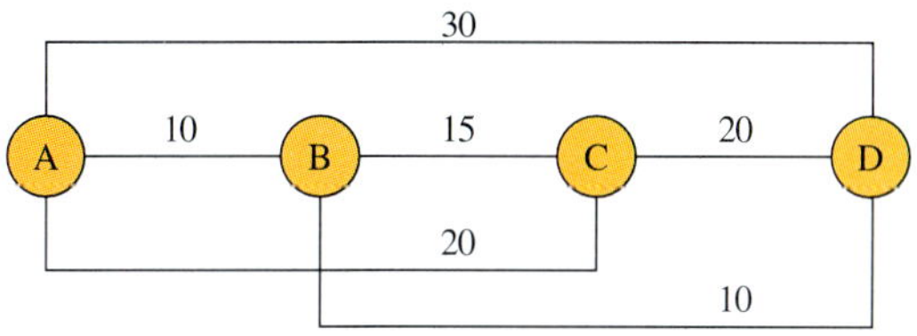


Using the material handling cost method shown in the toy company example, we obtain the following costs, assuming that every nonadjacency doubles the initial cost/unit distance:

$$AB = 10 \times 1 = 10$$
$$AC = 20 \times 2 = 40$$
$$AD = 30 \times 3 = 90$$
$$BC = 15 \times 1 = 15$$
$$BD = 10 \times 2 = 20$$
$$CD = 20 \times 1 = 20$$
$$\text{Current cost} = 195$$

*b.* A better layout would be *BCDA*.

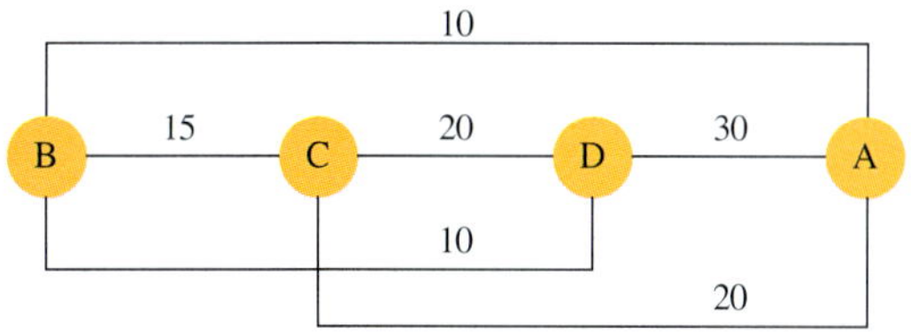


$$AB = 10 \times 3 = 30$$
$$AC = 20 \times 2 = 40$$
$$AD = 30 \times 1 = 30$$
$$BC = 15 \times 1 = 15$$
$$BD = 10 \times 2 = 20$$
$$CD = 20 \times 1 = 20$$
$$\text{Improved cost} = 155$$

## SOLVED PROBLEM 2

The following tasks must be performed on an assembly line in the sequence and times specified:

| TASK | TASK TIME (SECONDS) | TASKS THAT MUST PRECEDE |
|---|---|---|
| A | 50 | — |
| B | 40 | — |
| C | 20 | A |
| D | 45 | C |
| E | 20 | C |
| F | 25 | D |
| G | 10 | E |
| H | 35 | B, F, G |

*a.* Draw the schematic diagram.
*b.* What is the theoretical minimum number of stations required to meet a forecast demand of 400 units per 8-hour day?

*c.* Use the longest task time rule and balance the line in the minimum number of stations to produce 400 units per day.

## Solution

*a.*

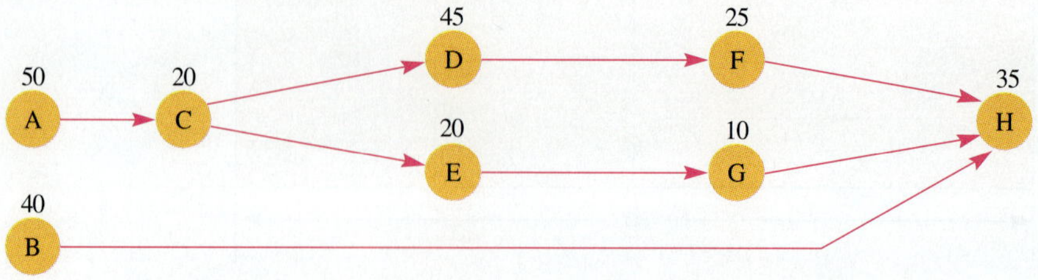


*b.* The theoretical minimum number of stations to meet D = 400 is

$$N_t = \frac{T}{C} = \frac{245 \text{ seconds}}{\left(\dfrac{60 \text{ seconds} \times 480 \text{ minutes}}{400 \text{ units}}\right)} = \frac{245}{72} = 3.4 \text{ stations}$$

*c.*

| | Task | Task Time (Seconds) | Remaining Unassigned Time | Feasible Remaining Task |
|---|---|---|---|---|
| Station 1 | A | 50 | 22 | C |
| | C | 20 | 2 | None |
| Station 2 | D | 45 | 27 | E, F |
| | F | 25 | 2 | None |
| Station 3 | B | 40 | 32 | E |
| | E | 20 | 12 | G |
| | G | 10 | 2 | None |
| Station 4 | H | 35 | 37 | None |

## Review and Discussion Questions

1 What kind of layout is used in a physical fitness center?
2 What is the key difference between SLP and CRAFT?
3 What is the objective of assembly-line balancing? How would you deal with the situation where one worker, although trying hard, is 20 percent slower than the other 10 people on a line?
4 How do you determine the idle time percentage from a given assembly-line balance?
5 What information of particular importance do route sheets and process charts (discussed in Chapter 3) provide to the layout planner?
6 What is the essential requirement for mixed-model lines to be practical?
7 Why might it be difficult to develop a GT layout?
8 In what respects is facility layout a marketing problem in services? Give an example of a service system layout designed to maximize the amount of time the customer is in the system.
9 Consider a department store. Which departments probably should not be located near each other? Would any departments benefit from close proximity?
10 How would a flowchart help in planning the servicescape layout? What sorts of features would act as focal points or otherwise draw customers along certain paths through the service? In a supermarket, what departments should be located first along the customers' path? Which should be located last?

## Problems

1. See ISM.

1 The Cyprus Citrus Cooperative ships a high volume of individual orders for oranges to northern Europe. The paperwork for the shipping notices is done in the accompanying layout. Revise the layout to improve the flow and conserve space if possible.

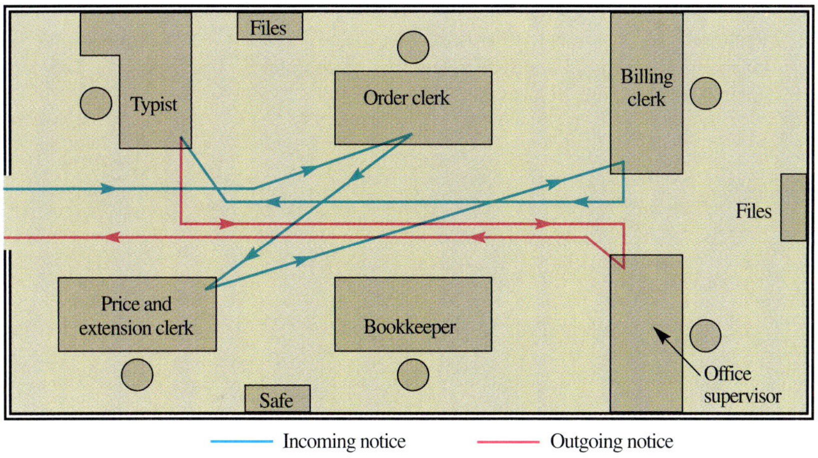


2 An assembly line makes two models of trucks: a Buster and a Duster. Busters take 12 minutes each, and Dusters take 8 minutes each. The daily output requirement is 24 of each per day. Develop a perfectly balanced mixed-model sequence to satisfy demand.

2. See ISM. Output/day: 24B + 24D. Process times: 12 min./B and 8 min./D. BB/DDD BB BB/DDD repetitively.

3 An assembly line is to operate eight hours per day with a desired output of 240 units per day. The following table contains information on this product's task times, and precedence relationships:

3. *a.* See ISM. *b.* 120 seconds. *c.* See ISM. *d.* 87.5%.

| Task | Task Time (Seconds) | Immediate Predecessor |
|---|---|---|
| A | 60 | — |
| B | 80 | A |
| C | 20 | A |
| D | 50 | A |
| E | 90 | B, C |
| F | 30 | C, D |
| G | 30 | E, F |
| H | 60 | G |

*a.* Draw the precedence diagram.
*b.* What is the workstation cycle time?
*c.* Balance this line using the longest task time.
*d.* What is the efficiency of your line balance?

4 The desired daily output for an assembly line is 360 units. This assembly line will operate 450 minutes per day. The following table contains information on this product's task times and precedence relationships:

4. *a.* See ISM. *b.* 75 seconds. *c.* See ISM. *d.* 91.7%

| Task | Task Time (Seconds) | Immediate Predecessor |
|---|---|---|
| A | 30 | — |
| B | 35 | A |
| C | 30 | A |
| D | 35 | B |
| E | 15 | C |
| F | 65 | C |
| G | 40 | E, F |
| H | 25 | D, G |

*a.* Draw the precedence diagram.
*b.* What is the workstation cycle time?
*c.* Balance this line using the largest number of following tasks. Use the longest task time as a secondary criterion.
*d.* What is the efficiency of your line balance?

5. *a.* 27 seconds.
*b.* 6 stations.
*c.* 91.4%
*d.* Work 45 minutes per day overtime.

5 Some tasks and the order in which they must be performed according to their assembly requirements are shown in the following table. These are to be combined into workstations to create an assembly line. The assembly line operates $7\frac{1}{2}$ hours per day. The output requirement is 1,000 units per day.

| Task | Preceding Tasks | Time (Seconds) | Task | Preceding Tasks | Time (Seconds) |
|---|---|---|---|---|---|
| A | — | 15 | G | C | 11 |
| B | A | 24 | H | D | 9 |
| C | A | 6 | I | E | 14 |
| D | B | 12 | J | F, G | 7 |
| E | B | 18 | K | H, I | 15 |
| F | C | 7 | L | J, K | 10 |

*a.* What is the workstation cycle time?
*b.* Balance the line using the longest task time based on the 1,000-unit forecast, stating which tasks would be done in each workstation.
*c.* For *b*, what is the efficiency of your line balance?
*d.* After production was started, Marketing realized that they understated demand and must increase output to 1,100 units. What action would you take? Be specific in quantitative terms, if appropriate.

6. $44,500.

6 An initial solution has been given to the following process layout problem. Given the flows described and a cost of $2.00 per unit per foot, compute the total cost for the layout. Each location is 100 feet long and 50 feet wide as shown on the following figure. Use the centers of departments for distances and measure distance using metropolitan-rectilinear distance.

| Department | | A | B | C | D |
|---|---|---|---|---|---|
| Department | A | 0 | 10 | 25 | 55 |
| | B | | 0 | 10 | 5 |
| | C | | | 0 | 15 |
| | D | | | | 0 |

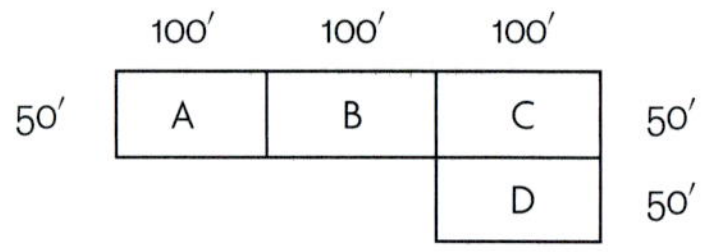


7. *a.* See ISM.
*b.* 90 seconds.
*c.* 4.55, therefore, 5 workstations.

| Station | Tasks |
|---|---|
| 1 | a, d |
| 2 | g, j |
| 3 | c, b |
| 4 | e, h |
| 5 | f, i, k, l |

*d.* See ISM.
*e.* $\frac{410}{5 \times 90} = 91\%$
*f.* Reduce cycle time to 81 seconds or work 45 minutes overtime.

7 An assembly line is to be designed to operate $7\frac{1}{2}$ hours per day and supply a steady demand of 300 units per day. Here are the tasks and their performance times:

| Task | Preceding Tasks | Performance Time (Seconds) | Task | Preceding Tasks | Performance Time (Seconds) |
|---|---|---|---|---|---|
| a | — | 70 | g | d | 60 |
| b | — | 40 | h | e | 50 |
| c | — | 45 | i | f | 15 |
| d | a | 10 | j | g | 25 |
| e | b | 30 | k | h, i | 20 |
| f | c | 20 | l | j, k | 25 |

*a.* Draw the precedence diagram.
*b.* What is the workstation cycle time?
*c.* What is the theoretical minimum number of workstations?
*d.* Assign tasks to workstations using the longest operating time.
*e.* What is the efficiency of your line balance?
*f.* Suppose demand increases by 10 percent. How would you react to this?

8. See ISM for layouts.
Nonadjacency
3–2: 10
6–2: 8
6–5: 3
21

8 S. L. P. Craft would like your help in developing a layout for a new outpatient clinic to be built in California. Based on analysis of another recently built clinic, she obtains the data shown in the following diagram. This includes the number of trips made by patients between departments on a typical day (shown above the diagonal line) and the numbered weights (defined in Exhibit TN5.9) between departments as specified by the new clinic's physicians (below the diagonal). The new building will be 60 feet by 20 feet.

*a.* Develop an interdepartmental flow graph that minimizes patient travel.
*b.* Develop a "good" relationship diagram using systematic layout planning.
*c.* Choose either of the layouts obtained in *a* or *b* and sketch the departments to scale within the building.
*d.* Will this layout be satisfactory to the nursing staff? Explain.

*d.* Doubtful. Station is not centrally located; nurses do a great deal of walking.

| DEPARTMENTS | 2 | 3 | 4 | 5 | 6 | AREA REQUIREMENT (SQ. FT.) |
|---|---|---|---|---|---|---|
| 1 Reception | A 2 | O 5 | E 200 | U 0 | O 10 | 100 |
| 2 X-ray | | E 10 | I 300 | U 0 | O 8 | 100 |
| 3 Surgery | | | I 100 | U 0 | A 4 | 200 |
| 4 Examining rooms (5) | | | | U 0 | I 15 | 500 |
| 5 Lab | | | | | O 3 | 100 |
| 6 Nurses' station | | | | | | 100 |

9 The following tasks are to be performed on an assembly line:

| TASK | SECONDS | TASKS THAT MUST PRECEDE |
|---|---|---|
| A | 20 | — |
| B | 7 | A |
| C | 20 | B |
| D | 22 | B |
| E | 15 | C |
| F | 10 | D |
| G | 16 | E, F |
| H | 8 | G |

The workday is seven hours long. Demand for completed product is 750 per day.
*a.* Find the cycle time.
*b.* What is the theoretical number of workstations?
*c.* Draw the precedence diagram.
*d.* Balance the line using sequential restrictions and the longest operating time rule.
*e.* What is the efficiency of the line balanced as in *d*?
*f.* Suppose that demand rose from 750 to 800 units per day. What would you do? Show any amounts or calculations.
*g.* Suppose that demand rose from 750 to 1,000 units per day. What would you do? Show any amounts or calculations.

9. *a.* 33.6 seconds.
*b.* 3.51, therefore, 4 workstations.
*d.* AB, DF, C, EG, H.
*e.* Efficiency = 70.2%
*f.* Reduce cycle time to 32 seconds and work $6\frac{2}{3}$ minutes overtime.
*g.* 1.89 hours overtime; may be better to rebalance.

10 The Dorton University president has asked the OM department to assign eight biology professors (A, B, C, D, E, F, G, and H) to eight offices (numbered 1 to 8 in the diagram) in the new biology building.

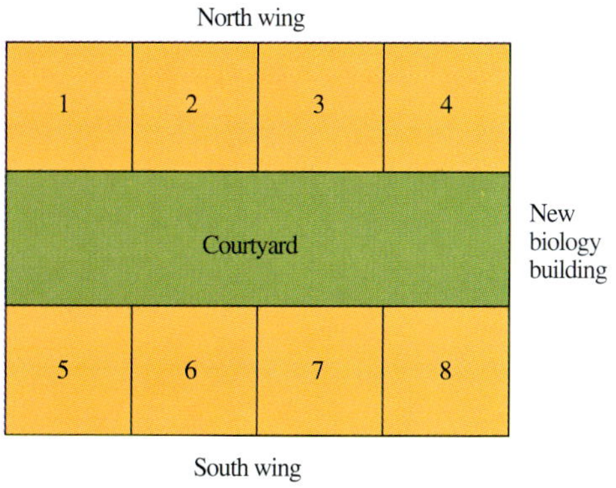


10. *a.* See ISM.
*b.* Layout I:
TMHC = 2(10) + 5(15) + 3(15) + 2(20) + 3(18) + 4(30) + 1(10) + 1(1) + 4(10) = 422
Layout II:
TMHC = 2(25) + 5(15) + 3(10) + 2(18) + 3(20) + 4(30) + 1(10) + 1(18) + 4(10) = 439
Layout I is optimal.

The following distances and two-way flows are given:

**DISTANCES BETWEEN OFFICES (FEET)**

| | 1 | 2 | 3 | 4 | 5 | 6 | 7 | 8 |
|---|---|---|---|---|---|---|---|---|
| 1 | — | 10 | 20 | 30 | 15 | 18 | 25 | 34 |
| 2 | | — | 10 | 20 | 18 | 15 | 18 | 25 |
| 3 | | | — | 10 | 25 | 18 | 15 | 18 |
| 4 | | | | — | 34 | 25 | 18 | 15 |
| 5 | | | | | — | 10 | 20 | 30 |
| 6 | | | | | | — | 10 | 20 |
| 7 | | | | | | | — | 10 |
| 8 | | | | | | | | — |

**TWO-WAY FLOWS (UNITS PER PERIOD)**

| | A | B | C | D | E | F | G | H |
|---|---|---|---|---|---|---|---|---|
| A | — | 2 | 0 | 0 | 5 | 0 | 0 | 0 |
| B | | — | 0 | 0 | 0 | 3 | 0 | 2 |
| C | | | — | 0 | 0 | 0 | 0 | 3 |
| D | | | | — | 4 | 0 | 0 | 0 |
| E | | | | | — | 1 | 0 | 0 |
| F | | | | | | — | 1 | 0 |
| G | | | | | | | — | 4 |
| H | | | | | | | | — |

*a.* If there are no restrictions (constraints) on the assignment of professors to offices, how many alternative assignments are there to evaluate?

*b.* The biology department has sent the following information and requests to the OM department:

Offices 1, 4, 5, and 8 are the only offices with windows.

A must be assigned Office 1.

D and E, the biology department co-chairpeople, must have windows.

H must be directly across the courtyard from D.

A, G, and H must be in the same wing.

F must *not* be next to D or G or directly across from G.

Find the optimal assignment of professors to offices that meets all the requests of the biology department and minimizes total material handling cost. You may use the path flow list as a computational aid.

| PATH | FLOW | PATH | FLOW | PATH | FLOW | PATH | FLOW | PATH | FLOW |
|---|---|---|---|---|---|---|---|---|---|
| A–B | 2 | B–C | 0 | C–D | 0 | D–E | 4 | E–F | 1 |
| A–C | 0 | B–D | 0 | C–E | 0 | D–F | 0 | E–G | 0 |
| A–D | 0 | B–E | 0 | C–F | 0 | D–G | 0 | E–H | 0 |
| A–E | 5 | B–F | 3 | C–G | 0 | D–H | 0 | F–G | 1 |
| A–F | 0 | B–G | 0 | C–H | 3 | | | F–H | 0 |
| A–G | 0 | B–H | 2 | | | | | G–H | 4 |
| A–H | 0 | | | | | | | | |

11 The flow of materials through eight departments is shown in the table below. Even though the table shows flows into and out of the different departments, assume that the direction of flow is not important. In addition, assume that the cost of moving material depends only on the distance moved.

**DEPARTMENTS**

| | 1 | 2 | 3 | 4 | 5 | 6 | 7 | 8 |
|---|---|---|---|---|---|---|---|---|
| 1 | — | 20 | | | | | | |
| 2 | 15 | — | 25 | | | | 4 | |
| 3 | | 5 | — | 40 | 5 | | | |
| 4 | | | 5 | — | 10 | | | |
| 5 | 1 | | | 20 | — | 30 | | |
| 6 | | | | | | — | 20 | |
| 7 | | | | 3 | | | — | 10 |
| 8 | | | | | | | 5 | — |

11. *a.*

| | | | |
|---|---|---|---|
| 1 | 2 | 3 | 4 |
| 8 | 7 | 6 | 5 |

*b.*

| ADJACENCY | FLOW | DISTANCE | FLOW × DISTANCE |
|---|---|---|---|
| 1–2 | 35 | 10 | 350 |
| 1–5 | 1 | 40 | 40 |
| 2–3 | 30 | 10 | 300 |
| 2–7 | 4 | 10 | 40 |
| 3–4 | 45 | 10 | 450 |
| 3–5 | 5 | 20 | 100 |
| 4–5 | 30 | 10 | 300 |
| 4–7 | 3 | 30 | 90 |
| 5–6 | 30 | 10 | 300 |
| 6–7 | 20 | 10 | 200 |
| 7–8 | 15 | 10 | 150 |
| | | Total | 2,320 |

*a.* Construct a schematic layout where the departments are arranged on a 2 × 4 grid with each cell representing a 10 × 10-meter square area.

*b.* Evaluate your layout using a distance times flow measure. Assume that distance is measured rectilinearly (in this case departments that are directly adjacent are 10 meters apart and those that are diagonal to one another are 20 meters apart).

## ADVANCED PROBLEM

12 Elizabeth Johnson's plant needs to design an efficient assembly line to make a new product. The assembly line needs to produce 15 units per hour and there is room for only four workstations. The tasks and the order in which they must be performed are shown in the following table. Tasks cannot be split, and it would be too expensive to duplicate any task.

| Task | Task Time (Minutes) | Immediate Predecessor |
|---|---|---|
| A | 1 | — |
| B | 2 | — |
| C | 3 | — |
| D | 1 | A, B, C |
| E | 3 | C |
| F | 2 | E |
| G | 3 | E |

*a.* Draw the precedence diagram.

*b.* What is the workstation cycle time?

*c.* Balance the line so that only four workstations are required. Use whatever method you feel is appropriate.

*d.* What is the efficiency of your line balance?

12. *a.*

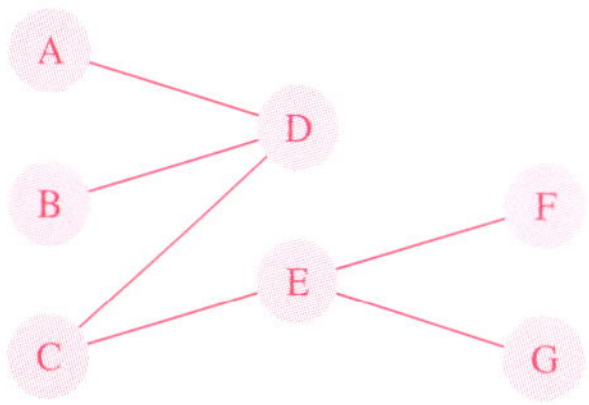


*b.* 4 minutes.

*c.* Station 1 (A and C).
Station 2 (E).
Station 3 (B and F).
Station 4 (D and G).

*d.* 15/16 = .9375.

## CASE: SOTERIOU'S SOUVLAKI

Soteriou looks up from cleaning the floor—the lights are on. This means that the power has finally been hooked up, and soon his restaurant will reopen here in its new location.

Soteriou's Souvlaki is typical of many of the small dining establishments scattered around the perimeter of the university. Specializing in Greek cuisine—souvlaki (lamb kabobs), gyros, tiropita (cheese-filled pastries), and baklava (a honey and pistachio nut dessert)—the restaurant has been very popular with the student body.

The operations are similar to those of most fast food restaurants. Customers enter and queue near the register to place their orders and pay. Food is prepared and given to the customer over the main counter. Drinks are self-serve, and the tables are bused by the customers as they leave. The kitchen is normally run by Soteriou with help from an assistant working the cash register.

Until recently, Soteriou's had been located in a local food court, but earthquake damage, space constraints, and deteriorating sanitary conditions prompted him to move the restaurant to these new quarters. The new facility is a small, free-standing building, formerly a hamburger joint. Although the previous owners have removed all equipment and tables, the large fixed service counter remains, physically marking out the kitchen and dining areas. (See the accompanying figure.)

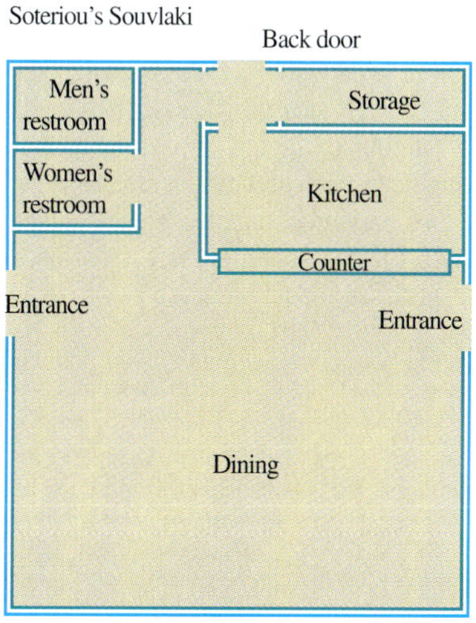


Aware of students' growing health consciousness (and possibly a little heady with the extra floor space in the new building), Soteriou has decided to add a self-service salad bar to the new restaurant. The salad bar will be much like those in other restaurants, but with a more Mediterranean flair.

The new kitchen does not appear to be much larger than the old one, though it is narrower. To prepare his Greek specialties in this new kitchen, Soteriou will need a grill/oven, a storage refrigerator, a preparation table (with hot and cold bins for the condiments, side dishes, and pita bread), a vertical spit broiler for the gyros meat, and

EXHIBIT TN5.18

**The Kitchen**

| | Grill | Prep. Table | Refrig. | Vertical Broiler | Display Case |
|---|---|---|---|---|---|
| Cash register | X | A | X | U | A |
| Grill | — | A | A | U | E |
| Prep. table | — | — | I | A | U |
| Refrigerator | — | — | — | U | X |
| Vertical broiler | — | — | — | — | U |
| Display case | — | — | — | — | — |

EXHIBIT TN5.19

**The Dining Area**

| | No Smoking | Smoking | Drinks | Salad Bar | Waiting Area |
|---|---|---|---|---|---|
| Cash register | U | U | I | I | A |
| No smoking | — | X | E | E | U |
| Smoking | — | — | I | I | U |
| Drinks | — | — | — | U | U |
| Salad bar | — | — | — | — | X |
| Waiting area | — | — | — | — | — |

EXHIBIT TN5.20

**State Automobile License Renewals Process Times**

| Job | Average Time to Perform (Seconds) |
|---|---|
| 1. Review renewal application for correctness | 15 |
| 2. Process and record payment | 30 |
| 3. Check file for violations and restrictions | 60 |
| 4. Conduct eye test | 40 |
| 5. Photograph applicant | 20 |
| 6. Issue temporary license | 30 |

a display case to hold the tiropitas, baklava, and cups for the self-serve drink machines.

The new dining area will include smoking and nonsmoking seating, the salad bar, self-serve drink machines, and an area for the register queues. Of course, the location of the cash register will be important to both the kitchen and dining area layouts.

Leaning against the mop handle, Soteriou looks around the clean, empty floor. Eager to open the new location, he has already ordered all the necessary equipment, but where will he put it? Unfortunately, the equipment will be arriving tomorrow morning. Once it is placed by the delivery crew, it will be hard for Soteriou and his assistant to rearrange it by themselves.

### QUESTION

The matrices in Exhibits TN5.18 and TN5.19 show the importance of proximity for the kitchen equipment and dining area features. Use systematic layout planning (with numerical reference weightings) to develop a floor layout for the kitchen and the dining area of Soteriou's Souvlaki.

SOURCE: THIS CASE WAS PREPARED BY DOUGLAS STEWART. IT IS NOT INTENDED TO SHOW PROPER OR IMPROPER HANDLING OF FOOD.

## CASE: STATE AUTOMOBILE LICENSE RENEWALS

Henry Coupe, manager of a metropolitan branch office of the state department of motor vehicles, attempted to perform an analysis of the driver's license renewal operations. Several steps were to be performed in the process. After examining the license renewal process, he identified the steps and associated times required to perform each step as shown in Exhibit TN5.20.

Coupe found that each step was assigned to a different person. Each application was a separate process in the sequence shown in the exhibit. Coupe determined that his office should be prepared to accommodate the maximum demand of processing 120 renewal applicants per hour.

He observed that the work was unevenly divided among the clerks, and that the clerk who was responsible for checking violations tended to shortcut her task to keep up with the other clerks. Long lines built up during the maximum demand periods.

Coupe also found that jobs 1, 2, 3, and 4 were handled by general clerks who were each paid $6.00 per hour. Job 5 was performed by a photographer paid $8 per hour. Job 6, the issuing of temporary licenses, was required by state policy to be handled by a uniformed motor vehicle officer. Officers were paid $9 per hour, but they could be assigned to any job except photography.

A review of the jobs indicated that job 1, reviewing the application for correctness, had to be performed before any other step. Similarly, job 6, issuing the temporary license, could not be performed until all the other steps were completed. The branch offices were charged $10 per hour for each camera to perform photography.

Coupe was under severe pressure to increase productivity and reduce costs, but he was also told by the regional director of the department of motor vehicles that he had better accommodate the demand for renewals. Otherwise, "heads would roll."

QUESTIONS

1. What is the maximum number of applications per hour that can be handled by the present configuration of the process?
2. How many applications can be processed per hour if a second clerk is added to check for violations?
3. Assuming the addition of one more clerk, what is the maximum number of applications the process can handle?
4. How would you suggest modifying the process to accommodate 120 applications per hour?



## SELECTED BIBLIOGRAPHY

Bitner, M. J. "Servicescapes: The Impact of Physical Surroundings on Customers and Employees." *Journal of Marketing* 56 (April 1992), pp. 57–71.

Bollinger, S. *Fundamentals of Plant Layout.* Society of Manufacturing Engineers in Association with Richard Muther and Associates, 1998.

Bonett, D. G., and R. E. D. Woolsey. "Load-Distance Analysis with Variable Loads." *Production and Inventory Management Journal,* 1st quarter 1993, pp. 32–34.

Choobineh, F. "A Framework for the Design of Cellular Manufacturing Systems." *International Journal of Production Research* 26, no. 7 (1988), pp. 1161–72.

Francis, R. L., and J. A. White. *Facility Layout and Location: An Analytical Approach.* Englewood Cliffs, NJ: Prentice Hall, 1992.

Ghosh, S., and R. Gagnon. "A Comprehensive Literature Review and Analysis of the Design, Balancing and Scheduling of Assembly Systems." *International Journal of Production Research* 27, no. 4 (1989), pp. 637–70.

Green, T. J., and R. P. Sadowski. "A Review of Cellular Manufacturing Assumptions, Advantages and Design Techniques." *Journal of Operations Management* 4, no. 2 (February 1984), pp. 85–97.

Gunther, R. E.; G. D. Johnson; and R. S. Peterson. "Currently Practiced Formulations for the Assembly Line Balance Problem." *Journal of Operations Management* 3, no. 4 (August 1983), pp. 209–21.

Heragu, S. *Facilities Design.* Boston, MA: PWS Publishing Company, 1997.

Hyer, N. L. "The Potential of Group Technology for U.S. Manufacturing." *Journal of Operations Management* 4, no. 3 (May 1984), pp. 183–202.

Johnson, R. "Optimally Balancing Large Assembly Lines with FABLE." *Management Science* 34, no. 2 (February 1988), pp. 240–53.

Love, J. F. *McDonald's: Behind the Arches.* New York: Bantam, 1986.

Meyers, F. E. *Manufacturing Facilities Design and Material Handling,* Upper Saddle River, NJ: Prentice Hall, 2000.

Sule, D. R. *Manufacturing Facilities: Location, Planning, and Design.* Boston: PWS Publishing Company, 1994.

## FOOTNOTES

1 For a discussion of CRAFT and other methods, see R. L. Francis and J. A. White, *Facility Layout and Location: An Analytical Approach* (Englewood Cliffs, NJ: Prentice Hall, 1974).

2 R. Johnson, "Spacecraft for Multi-Floor Layout Planning," *Management Science* 28, no. 4 (April 1982), pp. 407–17.

3 See R. Muther and J. D. Wheeler, "Simplified Systematic Layout Planning," *Factory* 120, nos. 8, 9, 10 (August, September, October 1962), pp. 68–77, 111–19, 101–13.

4 The workstation cycle time used in this calculation should be the actual cycle time used by the assembly line.

5 Y. Monden, *Toyota Production System: Practical Approach to Production Management* (Atlanta, GA: Industrial Engineering and Management Press, Institute of Industrial Engineers, 1983), p. 208.

6 R. J. Schonberger, *World Class Manufacturing* (New York: Free Press, 1986), p. 112.

7 M. S. Sommers and J. B. Kernan, "A Behavioral Approach to Planning, Layout and Display," *Journal of Retailing,* Winter 1965–66, pp. 21–27.

8 M. J. Bitner, "Servicescapes: The Impact of Physical Surroundings on Customers and Employees," *Journal of Marketing* 56 (April 1992), pp. 57–71.

9 R. Norman, *Service Management,* 2nd ed. (New York: John Wiley & Sons, 1991), p. 28.

chapter six

# PRODUCT DESIGN AND PROCESS SELECTION—SERVICES

## CHAPTER OUTLINE AND KEY TERMS

6

## LANDS' END MAKES BIG STRIDES ONLINE

When people talk about shopping on the Internet, names like Amazon.com, eBay, and eToys frequently come to mind. But what about Lands' End? The catalog company best known for its classic clothes is quickly becoming a major player in cyber space. In fact, Lands' End is one of the top sellers of clothes on the Web today and has been lauded for its superb online customer service.

Lands' End already knows how to process an order, operate a warehouse, and ship goods quickly—skills that Web start-ups and many of the brick-and-mortar retailers with online stores are struggling to build. In fact, the

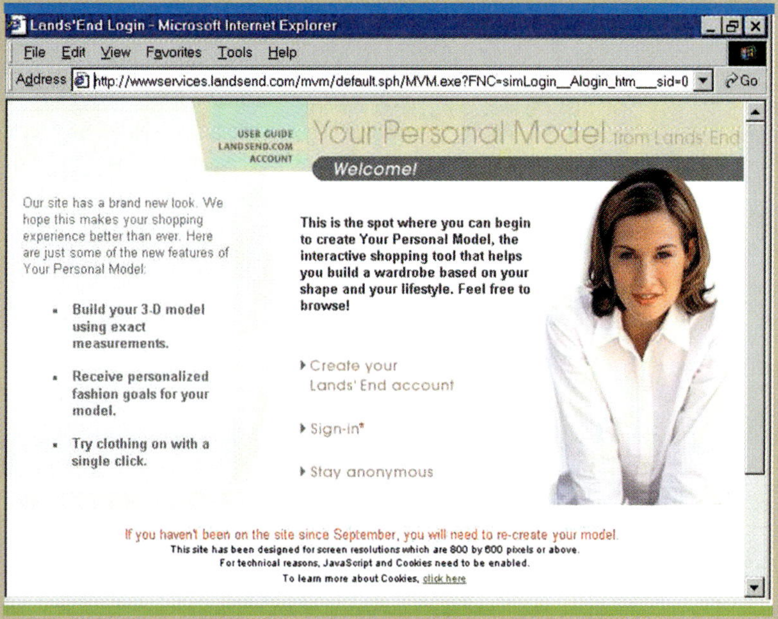


Internet
www.landsend.com

company uses the same warehouses for its online and catalog operations. Inside the massive facility—the size of 16 football fields—workers sort merchandise at a rate of 10,000 pieces an hour. Lands' End ships up to 150,000 orders on its busiest days.

The website provides customers with a shopping experience they cannot get through the catalog. Online, women can "try on" outfits by building an interactive model with their exact measurements. The website also gives style advice and recommends figure-flattering clothes. For men, there's "Oxford Express," where shoppers can selects shirts by color, fabric, cut, sleeve type, and collar. The effect is building a shirt from the ground up, making adjustments as you go along.

The website also uses interactive software that connects a customer service representative to a shopper via on-screen "chat," a two-way dialogue that appears in a tiny box when the shopper clicks on an icon. The agent then synchronizes his or her computer screen with the customer's and can "push" pages of the website with the requested information before the shopper's eyes, in addition to answering questions about sizing, availability, and billing.

Analysts say the website is the company's best shot at significant growth in the coming years. It is attracting new customers, as well as those who are

**Source:** Adapted from Associated Press, "Lands' End Makes Big Strides Online," *Sunday Herald-Times*, December 19, 1999, p. G2..

migrating from the catalog. The Internet also allows the company to reach more international markets.

The Internet opens new approaches for offering high levels of customer service in an efficient manner. Lands' End's novel website described in the opening vignette can quickly respond to the customer that needs a little extra help, yet the site is highly efficient in handling the thousands of orders from customers who do not need special help. Internet technology will probably redefine the meaning of customer service over the next few years. ←

Service

In this chapter, after some preliminary comments about services, we address the issue of service delivery system design, starting with the notion of customer contact as a way of classifying service operations. Next we discuss service organization design, service strategy, and service focus, and describe how marketing and operations interrelate to achieve (or fail to achieve) competitive advantage. We also look at a service-system design matrix that can define the broad features of a service process, and at service blueprints as a way of designing the precise steps of a process. In the latter part of the chapter, we present three service designs used in service industries and discuss how service guarantees can be used as "design drivers." The chapter ends with two case studies of service organizations familiar to many readers of this book—Kinko's Copier Stores and America Online (AOL).

## THE NATURE OF SERVICES

Vol. I "Service"
Vol. III "Shouldice Hospital"

Our study of the nature of services leads to seven generalizations:

1 Everyone is an expert on services. We all think we know what we want from a service organization and, by the very process of living, we have a good deal of experience with the service creation process.
2 Services are idiosyncratic: What works well in providing one kind of service may prove disastrous in another. For example, consuming a restaurant meal in less than half an hour may be exactly what you want at Jack-in-the-Box but be totally unacceptable at an expensive French restaurant.
3 Quality of work is not quality of service. An auto dealership may do good work on your car, but it may take a week to get the job done.
4 Most services contain a mix of tangible and intangible attributes that constitute a *service package*. This package requires different approaches to design and management than the production of goods.
5 High-contact services (described later) are *experienced,* whereas goods are *consumed.*
6 Effective management of services requires an understanding of marketing and personnel, as well as operations.
7 Services often take the form of cycles of encounters involving face-to-face, telephone, electromechanical, and/or mail interactions. (The term *encounter,* by the way, is defined as "meeting in conflict or battle" and hence is often apt as we make our way through the service economy.)

Cross Functional

### SERVICE BUSINESSES AND INTERNAL SERVICES

Service operations management issues exist in two broad organizational contexts:

Facilities-based services

Field-based services

1 **Service business** is the management of organizations whose primary business requires interaction with the customer to produce the service. These include such familiar services as banks, airlines, hospitals, law firms, retail stores, and restaurants. Within this category, we can make a further major distinction: **facilities-based services,** where the customer must go to the service facility; and **field-based services,** where production and consumption of the service take place in the customer's environment (for example, cleaning and home repair services).

Technology has allowed for the transfer of many facility-based services to field-based services. Dental vans bring the dentist to your home; some auto repair services have repair-mobiles; and telemarketing brings the shopping center to your TV screen.

EXHIBIT 6.1

The Service Triangle

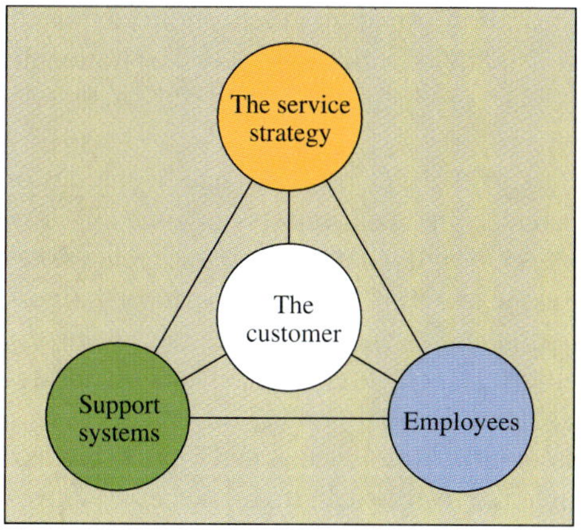


2 **Internal services** is the management of services required to support the activities of the larger organization. These services include such functions as data processing, accounting, engineering, and maintenance. Their customers are the various departments within the organization that require such services. Incidentally, it is not uncommon for an internal service to start marketing its services outside the parent organization and become a service business itself.

Our emphasis in this chapter is on service businesses, but most of the ideas apply equally well to internal services.

### A CONTEMPORARY VIEW OF SERVICE MANAGEMENT

A glance at the management book section in your local bookstore gives ample evidence of the concern for service among practitioners. The way we now view service parallels the way we view quality: The *customer* is (or should be) the focal point of all decisions and actions of the service organization. This philosophy is captured nicely in the service triangle in Exhibit 6.1. Here the customer is the center of things—the service strategy, the systems, and the employees who serve him or her. From this view, the organization exists to serve the customer, and the systems and the employees exist to facilitate the process of service. Some suggest that the service organization also exists to serve the workforce because they generally determine how the service is perceived by the customers. Relative to the latter point, the customer gets the kind of service that management deserves; in other words, how management treats the worker is how the worker will treat the public. If the workforce is well trained and well motivated by management, they will do good jobs for their customers.

The role of operations in the triangle is a major one. Operations is responsible for service systems (procedures, equipment, and facilities) and is responsible for managing the work of the service workforce, who typically comprise the majority of employees in large service organizations. But before we discuss this role in depth, it is useful to classify services to show how the customer affects the operations function.

## AN OPERATIONAL CLASSIFICATION OF SERVICES

Service organizations are generally classified according to the service they provide (financial services, health services, transportation services, and so on). These groupings, though useful in presenting aggregate economic data, are not particularly appropriate for OM purposes because they tell us little about the process. Manufacturing, by contrast, has fairly evocative terms to classify production activities (such as intermittent and continuous production); when applied to a manufacturing setting, they readily convey the essence of the process. Although it is possible to describe services in these same terms, we need one additional item of information to reflect the fact that the customer is involved in the production system. That item, which we believe operationally distinguishes one service system from another in its production function, is the extent of customer contact in the creation of the service.

*Customer contact* refers to the physical presence of the customer in the system, and *creation of the service* refers to the work process involved in providing the service itself. *Extent of contact* here may be roughly defined as the percentage of time the customer must be in the system relative to the total time it takes to perform the customer service. Generally speaking, the greater the percentage of contact time between the service system and the customer, the greater the degree of interaction between the two during the production process.

High and low degree of customer contact

From this conceptualization, it follows that service systems with a **high degree of customer contact** are more difficult to control and more difficult to rationalize than those with a **low degree of customer contact.** In high-contact systems, the customer can affect the time of demand, the exact nature of the service, and the quality, or perceived quality, of service because the customer is involved in the process.

Exhibit 6.2 describes the implications of this distinction. Here we see that each design decision is impacted by whether the customer is present during service delivery. We also see that when work is done behind the scenes (in this case in a bank's processing center), it is performed on customer surrogates—reports, databases, and invoices. We can thus design it according to the same principles we would use in designing a factory—to maximize the amount of items processed during the production day.

EXHIBIT 6.2

Major Differences between High- and Low-Contact Systems in a Bank

| DESIGN DECISION | HIGH-CONTACT SYSTEM (A BRANCH OFFICE) | LOW-CONTACT SYSTEM (A CHECK PROCESSING CENTER) |
|---|---|---|
| Facility location | Operations must be near the customer. | Operations may be placed near supply, transport, or labor. |
| Facility layout | The facility should accommodate the customer's physical and psychological needs and expectations. | The facility should focus on production efficiency. |
| Product design | Environment as well as the physical product define the nature of the service. | The customer is not in the service environment, so the product can be defined by fewer attributes. |
| Process design | Stages of production process have a direct, immediate effect on the customer. | The customer is not involved in majority of processing steps. |
| Scheduling | The customer is in the production schedule and must be accommodated. | The customer is concerned mainly with completion dates. |
| Production planning | Orders cannot be stored, so smoothing production flow will result in loss of business. | Both backlogging and production smoothing are possible. |
| Worker skills | The direct workforce constitutes a major part of the service product and so must be able to interact well with the public. | The direct workforce need only have technical skills. |
| Quality control | Quality standards are often in the eye of the beholder and, thus, are variable. | Quality standards are generally measurable and, thus, fixed. |
| Time standards | Service time depends on customer needs, so time standards are inherently loose. | Work is performed on customer surrogates (such as forms), so time standards can be tight. |
| Wage payment | Variable output requires time-based wage systems. | "Fixable" output permits output-based wage systems. |
| Capacity planning | To avoid lost sales, capacity must be set to match peak demand. | Storable output permits capacity at some average demand level. |

## TIPS ON TIPPING FOR RESTAURANT SERVERS

Research on nonverbal communication has found that more eye contact and greater proximity are associated with great rapport and liking; and because consumers tip friendly servers more than they do less friendly servers, squatting down next to the table increases a server's tip. As shown in the table, such things as introducing oneself, smiling, casually touching customers on the shoulders and palms of their hands, and writing "thank you" on the backs of checks all increase the opportunities for getting tips. An interesting finding is that male waiters should not draw happy faces on the backs of checks because this decreases their tips by about 3 percent!

**Summary of Psychological Studies on Restaurant Tipping**

| Action | Average Tip in Control Treatment | Average Tip in Experimental Treatment | Percentage Increase in Tip |
|---|---|---|---|
| Introducing self | 15%, | 23% | 53% |
| Squatting: | | | |
| Waiter | 15% | 18% | 20 |
| Waitress | 12% | 15% | 25 |
| Smiling | 20% | 48% | 140 |
| Touching | 12% | 17% | 42 |
| Credit-card insignia on tip tray: | | | |
| Restaurant | 16% | 20% | 25 |
| Café | 18% | 22% | 22 |
| Writing "thank you" on check | 16% | 18% | 13 |
| Drawing happy face on check: | | | |
| Waiter | 21% | 18% | −14 |
| Waitress | 28% | 33% | 18 |

SOURCE: M. LYNN, "SEVEN WAYS TO INCREASE SERVERS' TIPS," *THE CORNELL HOTEL AND RESTAURANT ADMINISTRATION QUARTERLY*, JUNE 1996, PP. 24–29.

There can be tremendous diversity of customer influence and, hence, system variability within high-contact service systems. For example, a bank branch offers both simple services such as cash withdrawals that take just a minute or so, and complicated services such as loan application preparation that can take in excess of an hour. Moreover, these activities may range from being self-service through an ATM, to coproduction where bank personnel and the customer work as a team to develop the loan application. The success of high-contact services is often dependent on the nonverbal activities of employees as found in the study described in the "Tips on Tipping for Restaurant Servers" box. Subsequent sections of this chapter say more on ways to configure service activities.

## DESIGNING SERVICE ORGANIZATIONS

In designing service organizations we must remember one distinctive characteristic of services: We cannot inventory services. Unlike manufacturing, where we can build up inventory during slack periods for peak demand and thus maintain a relatively stable level of employment and production planning, in services we must (with a few exceptions) meet demand as it arises. Consequently, in services capacity becomes a dominant issue. Think about the many service situations you find yourself in—for example, eating in a restaurant or going to a Saturday night movie. Generally speaking, if the restaurant or the theater is full, you will decide to go someplace else. So, an important design parameter in services is "What capacity should we aim for?" Too much capacity generates excessive costs. Insufficient capacity leads to lost customers. In these situations, of course, we seek the assistance of marketing. This is one reason we have discount airfares, hotel specials on weekends, and so on. This is also a good illustration of why it is difficult to separate the operations management functions from marketing in services.

Waiting line models, which are discussed in the technical note to this chapter, provide a powerful mathematical tool for analyzing many common service situations. Questions such as how many tellers we should have in a bank or how many telephone lines we need in an Internet service operation can be analyzed with these models. These models can be easily implemented using spreadsheets.

Designing a service organization involves four major elements.[1] The first element is identification of the target market (Who is our customer?); the second is the service concept (How do we differentiate our service in the market?); the third is the service strategy (What is our service package and the operating focus of our service?); and the fourth is the service delivery system (What are the actual processes, staff, and facilities by which the service is created?).

Choosing a target market and developing the service package are top management decisions setting the stage for the direct operating decisions of service strategy and delivery system design.

Several major factors distinguish service design and development from typical manufactured product development. First, the process and the product must be developed simultaneously; indeed, in services, the process is the product. (We say this with the general recognition that many manufacturers are using such concepts as concurrent engineering and DFM [design for manufacture] as approaches to more closely link product design and process design.)

Second, although equipment and software that support a service can be protected by patents and copyrights, a service operation itself lacks the legal protection commonly available to goods production. Third, the service package, rather than a definable good, constitutes the major output of the development process. Fourth, many parts of the service

MARRIOTT REWARDS EMPLOYEES WHO PROVIDE SUPERIOR CUSTOMER SERVICE AND GIVES EMPLOYEES DECISION-MAKING AUTHORITY. THE COMPANY MAILS OUT ONE MILLION QUESTIONNAIRES A YEAR TO KEEP INFORMED ABOUT CUSTOMER SATISFACTION AND SERVICE GAPS.

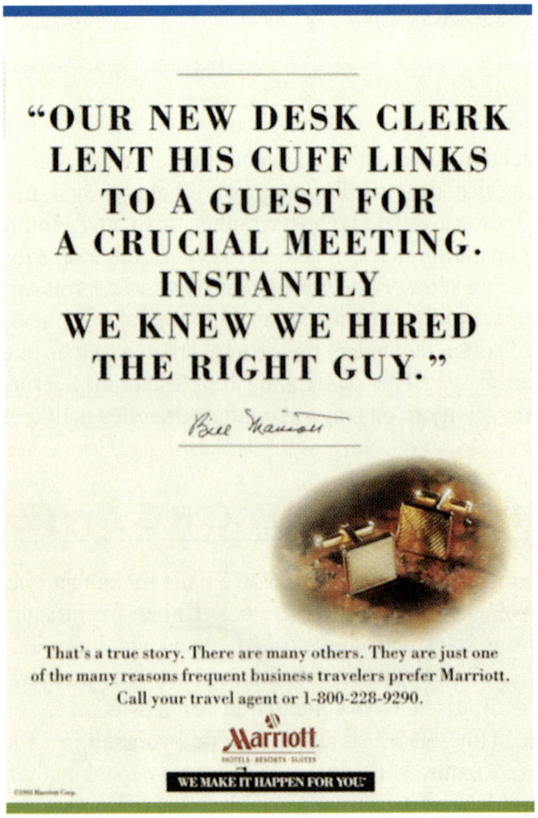

package are often defined by the training individuals receive before they become part of the service organization. In particular, in professional service organizations (PSOs) such as law firms and hospitals, prior certification is necessary for hiring. Fifth, many service organizations can change their service offerings virtually overnight. Routine service organizations (RSOs) such as barbershops, retail stores, and restaurants have this flexibility.

## SERVICE STRATEGY: FOCUS AND ADVANTAGE

Service strategy begins by selecting the operating focus—the performance priorities—by which the service firm will compete. These include

1. Treatment of the customer in terms of friendliness and helpfulness.
2. Speed and convenience of service delivery.
3. Price of the service.
4. Variety of services (essentially a one-stop shopping philosophy).
5. Quality of the tangible goods that are central to or accompany the service. Examples include a "world-class" corned-beef sandwich, eyeglasses made while you wait, or an understandable insurance policy.
6. Unique skills that constitute the service offering, such as hair styling, brain surgery, or piano lessons.

Exhibit 6.3 presents what we view as the operating service focus choices of a number of well-known companies. If our interpretation is correct, it shows that most companies

EXHIBIT 6.3

**Operations Focus of Selected Service Firms**

| | TREATMENT | SPEED/ CONVENIENCE | PRICE | VARIETY | UNIQUE SKILLS/ TANGIBLES |
|---|---|---|---|---|---|
| Nordstrom Department Stores | × | | | | |
| Federal Express Corporation | × | × | | | |
| Merrill Lynch & Company (Cash Management Account) | | × | | ×[a] | |
| Crown Books | | | × | | |
| Wal-Mart Stores | × | | ×[b] | × | |
| Price Club | | | ×[c] | | |
| Disneyland | × | | | | × |
| American Express Company | × | × | | | |
| McDonald's Corporation | | × | × | | |
| Domino's Pizza | | ×[d] | × | | |
| Marriott Corporation | × | | | | |
| Club Med Resorts | ×[e] | | × | | |
| American Airlines | | ×[f] | | × | |
| Singapore Airlines | × | | | | |
| Southwest Airlines | | | ×[g] | | |
| Riverside Methodist Hospital (Columbus, Ohio) | ×[h] | | | | |
| H & R Block | | × | × | | |
| American Automobile Association | | ×[i] | | | |

[a]A cash management account includes checkbook, credit card, money market fund, and other services in one account.
[b]Wal-Mart controls cost of inventory by driving tough bargains with suppliers.
[c]Price Club converts shoppers into warehouse order pickers in exchange for low-priced volume purchases.
[d]First to use the automated pizza maker where an attendant puts a raw pie in one side and pulls out a cooked pie on the other.
[e]All-inclusive, low-cost resorts where staff known as *Gentils Organisateurs* (GOs) coproduce a fun vacation with the guests, *Gentils Membres* (GMs).
[f]Sabre reservation system makes it easy for travel agents to book seats and for the company to instantaneously change prices to counter competitors' rates.
[g]No-frills service (that is, no computerized reservation system, no assigned seating, and no meals) allows lowest prices in the industry.
[h]Riverside Hospital treats patients and their families like customers—gives adult heart patients teddy bears to hold and colorful smocks with hearts imprinted on them. Holding a teddy bear feels good and helps the healing process.
[i]The AAA phone/computer network uses the number of the phone a customer is calling from anywhere in the United States to pinpoint the nearest AAA garage.

choose to compete on relatively few dimensions—that trade-offs have been made. What best practices are being emphasized by service executives? Although most people often think that service quality or service consistency might lead the list, a 1997 survey of executives at 181 service firms showed that accessibility to the service provider was number one. Exhibit 6.4 suggests that accessibility (defined in the study as the ability to get in touch with a service provider, any time, by multiple communication channels) is the "location, location, location" of service industries.

Cross Functional

**Integrating Marketing and Operations to Achieve Competitive Advantage** Achieving competitive advantage in services requires integration of service marketing with service delivery to meet or exceed customer expectations. This holds true no matter which competitive dimensions are emphasized. Companies that do extremely well (or extremely poorly) in this process create legends and nightmares (Exhibit 6.5).

EXHIBIT 6.4

**Best Practices Emphasized by Service Executives**

| ITEMS "MOST" EMPHASIZED | ITEM MEAN* |
|---|---|
| Accessibility | 4.02 |
| Openness to employees. | 3.91 |
| Leadership | 3.87 |
| Listening to the customer | 3.82 |
| Service tangibles | 3.79 |
| Employee handling of service failures | 3.79 |
| Competitive positioning | 3.72 |
| Quality values | 3.68 |
| Consistently meeting customers' needs | 3.68 |
| Customer orientation | 3.66 |
| Management involvement in quality | 3.66 |

Scale: 1 = Little emphasis, 3 = Moderate emphasis, 5 = High emphasis.
*Top 10 most emphasized practices out of 55 best practice items listed in the survey.

SOURCE: A. V. ROTH, R. B. CHASE, AND C. VOSS, "SERVICE IN THE U.S.: A STUDY OF SERVICE PRACTICE AND PERFORMANCE IN THE UNITED STATES," SUPPORTED BY SEVERN TRENT PLC, U.K. GOVERNMENT'S DEPARTMENT OF TRADE AND INDUSTRY, DEPARTMENT OF NATIONAL HERITAGE, 1997.

EXHIBIT 6.5

**Levels of Satisfaction Achieved Due to Service Performance**

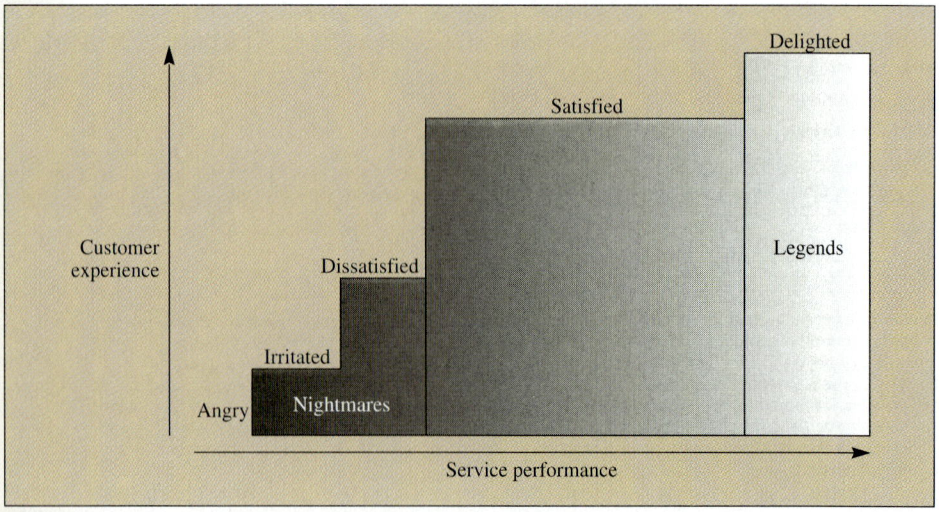


SOURCE: THE MAC GROUP: BUILDING VALUE THROUGH CREATING A SERVICE ADVANTAGE. 1 MONTGOMERY ST., TELESIS TOWER. SUITE 1700, SAN FRANCISCO, CA 94104, JUNE 1990.

EXHIBIT 6.6

Service Measurement Monitoring and Recovery Process

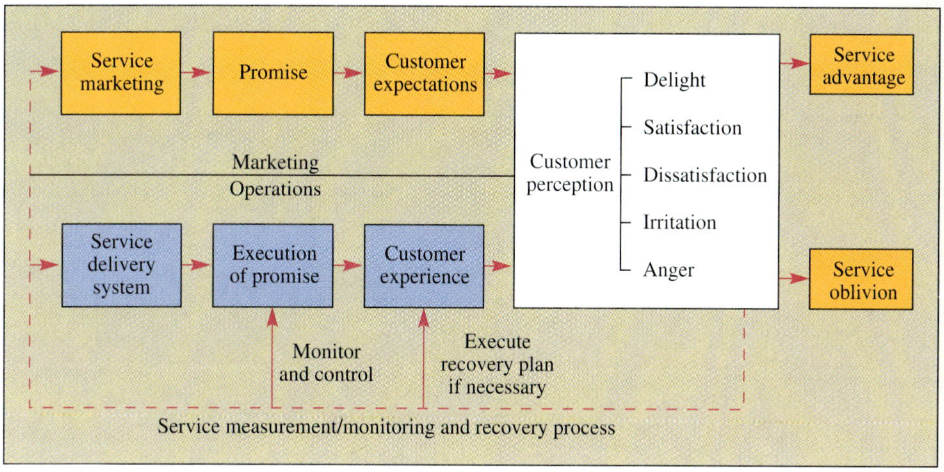


SOURCE: THE MAC GROUP: BUILDING VALUE THROUGH CREATING A SERVICE ADVANTAGE. 1 MONTGOMERY ST., TELESIS TOWER. SUITE 1700, SAN FRANCISCO, CA 94104, JUNE 1990.

Exhibit 6.6 gives an overview of the elements leading to service advantage and service oblivion. As it shows, marketing typically has responsibility for communicating the service promise to the customer and thereby creating customer expectations about service outcomes. Operations is responsible for the actions executing the promise and managing the customer experience. The feedback loop indicates that if outcomes are not satisfactory or do not create service advantage, management may alter either the service marketing strategy or the delivery system. The need to monitor and control the execution phase and have a recovery plan to defuse negative reactions before the customer leaves the system is also indicated.

Monitoring and controlling involve the standard managerial actions of reassigning workers to deal with short-run demand variations (such as Lucky Supermarkets opening up another checkout stand when there are more than three people in line); checking with customers and employees as to how things are going; and, for many services, simply being available to customers. (Customers like the idea that they can talk to the manager . . . and few people want to talk to the assistant manager.)

Recovery planning involves training frontline workers to respond to such situations as overbooking, lost luggage, or a bad meal.

One approach to measuring the economic value of customer satisfaction is to survey your customers. Ask them to rate each of a list of service and quality dimension items on two scales: importance and satisfaction. The point is to focus your attention on factors that are most important to your customers. In particular, focus on factors where their satisfaction rating is below their importance rating. (SERVQUAL, a widely applied questionnaire for measuring customer satisfaction, is discussed in Chapter 7.)

## STRUCTURING THE SERVICE ENCOUNTER: SERVICE-SYSTEM DESIGN MATRIX

Service encounters can be configured in a number of different ways. The service-system design matrix in Exhibit 6.7 identifies six common alternatives.

Vol. II "Service System Design Matrix"

The top of the matrix shows the degree of customer/server contact: the *buffered core,* which is physically separated from the customer; the *permeable system,* which is penetrable by the customer via phone or face-to-face contact; and the *reactive system,* which is both penetrable and reactive to the customer's requirements. The left side of the matrix shows what we believe to be a logical marketing proposition, namely, that the greater the amount of contact, the greater the sales opportunity; the right side shows the impact on production efficiency as the customer exerts more influence on the operation.

EXHIBIT 6.7

**Service-System Design Matrix**

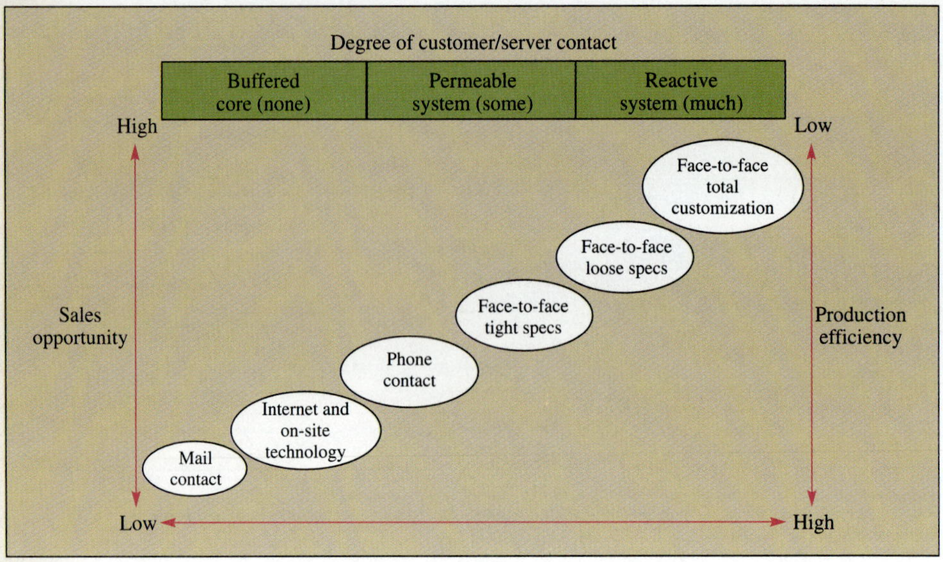


The entries within the matrix list the ways in which service can be delivered. At one extreme, service contact is by mail; customers have little interaction with the system. At the other extreme, customers " have it their way" through face-to-face contact. The remaining four entries in the exhibit contain varying degrees of interaction.

As one would guess, production efficiency decreases as the customer has more contact (and therefore more influence) on the system. To offset this, the face-to-face contact provides high sales opportunity to sell additional products. Conversely, low contact, such as mail, allows the system to work more efficiently because the customer is unable to significantly affect (or disrupt) the system. However, there is relatively little opportunity for additional product sales.

There can be some shifting in the positioning of each entry. For our first example, consider the "Internet and on-site technology" entry in the matrix. The Internet clearly buffers the company from the customer, but interesting opportunities are available to provide relevant information and services to the customer. Because the website can be programmed to intelligently react to the inputs of the customer, significant opportunities for new sales may be possible. In addition, as described in our opening vignette about the Lands' End website, the system can be made to interface with real employees when the customer needs assistance that goes beyond the programming of the website. The Internet is truly a revolutionary technology when applied to the services that need to be provided by a company.

Another example of shifting in the positioning of an entry can be shown with the "face-to-face tight specs" entry in Exhibit 6.7. This entry refers to those situations where there is little variation in the service process—neither customer nor server has much discretion in creating the service. Fast-food restaurants and Disneyland come to mind. Face-to-face loose specs refers to situations where the service process is generally understood but there are options in how it will be performed or in the physical goods that are part of it. A full-service restaurant and a car sales agency are examples. Face-to-face total customization refers to service encounters whose specifications must be developed through some interaction between the customer and server. Legal and medical services are of this type, and the degree to which the resources of the system are mustered for the service determines whether the system is reactive, possibly to the point of even being proactive, or merely permeable. Examples would be the mobilization of an advertising firm's resources in preparation for an office visit by a major client, or an operating team scrambling to prepare for emergency surgery.

Exhibit 6.8 extends the design matrix. It shows the changes in workers, operations, and types of technical innovations as the degree of customer/service system contact changes.

EXHIBIT 6.8

Characteristics of Workers, Operations, and Innovations Relative to the Degree of Customer/Service Contact

Degree of customer/server contact

Low ⟵ ⟶ High

| | | | | | | |
|---|---|---|---|---|---|---|
| Worker requirements | Clerical skills | Helping skills | Verbal skills | Procedural skills | Trade skills | Diagnostic skills |
| Focus of operations | Paper handling | Demand management | Scripting calls | Flow control | Capacity management | Client mix |
| Technological innovations | Office automation | Routing methods | Computer databases | Electronic aids | Self-serve | Client/worker teams |

For worker requirements, the relationships between mail contact and clerical skills, Internet technology and helping skills, and phone contact and verbal skills are self-evident. Face-to-face tight specs require procedural skills in particular, because the worker must follow the routine in conducting a generally standardized, high-volume process. Face-to-face loose specs frequently call for trade skills (shoemaker, draftsperson, maitre d', dental hygienist) to finalize the design for the service. Face-to-face total customization tends to call for diagnostic skills of the professional to ascertain the needs or desires of the client.

### STRATEGIC USES OF THE MATRIX

The matrices in Exhibit 6.7 and Exhibit 6.8 have both operational and strategic uses. The operational uses are reflected in their identification of worker requirements, focus of operations, and innovations previously discussed. The strategic uses include

1 Enabling systematic integration of operations and marketing strategy. Trade-offs become more clear-cut, and more important, at least some of the major design variables are crystallized for analysis purposes. For example, the matrix indicates that it would make little sense relative to sales for a service firm to invest in high-skilled workers if it plans to operate using tight specs.

Cross Functional

2 Clarifying exactly which combination of service delivery the firm is in fact providing. As the company incorporates the delivery options listed on the diagonal, it is becoming diversified in its production process.

3 Permitting comparison with how other firms deliver specific services. This helps to pinpoint a firm's competitive advantage.

4 Indicating evolutionary or life cycle changes that might be in order as the firm grows. Unlike the product–process matrix for manufacturing, however, where natural growth moves in one direction (from job shop to assembly line as volume increases), evolution of service delivery can move in either direction along the diagonal as a function of a sales–efficiency trade-off.

## SERVICE BLUEPRINTING AND FAIL-SAFING

Just as is the case with manufacturing process design, the standard tool for service process design is the flowchart. Recently, the service gurus have begun calling the flowchart a **service blueprint** to emphasize the importance of process design. A unique feature of the service blueprint is the distinction made between the high customer contact aspects of the service (the parts of the process that the customer sees) and those activities that the customer does not see. This distinction is made with a "Line of Visibility" on the flowchart.

Service blueprint

Exhibit 6.9 is a blueprint of a typical automobile service operation. Each activity that makes up a typical service encounter is mapped into the flowchart. To better show the

EXHIBIT 6.9 Fail-Safing an Automotive Service Operation

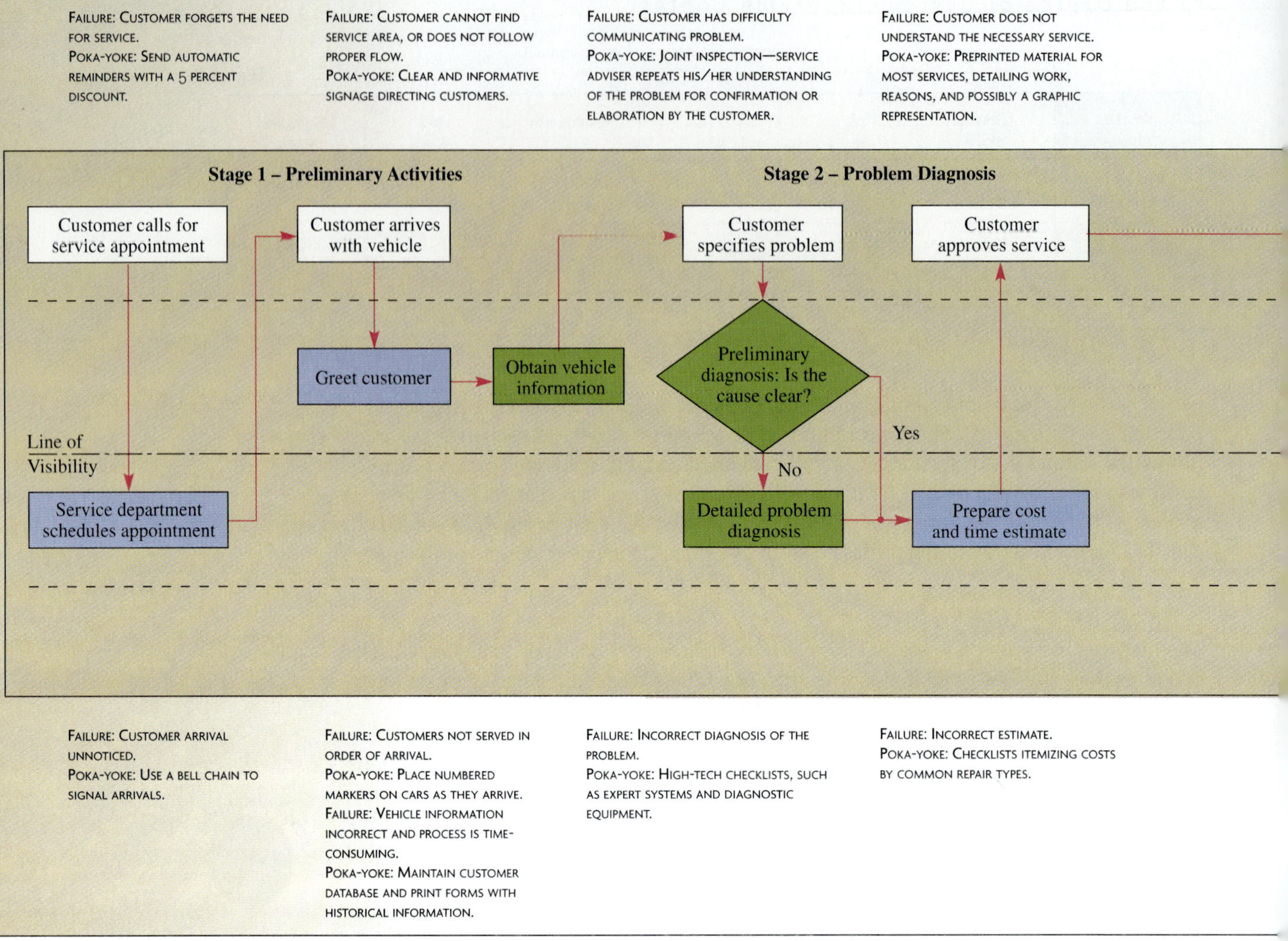


entity that controls the activities, levels are shown in the flowchart. The top level consists of activities that are under the control of the customer. Next are those activities performed by the service manager in handling the customer. The third level is the repair activities performed in the garage; the lowest level is the internal accounting activity.

Basic blueprinting describes the features of the service design but does not provide any direct guidance for how to make the process conform to that design. An approach to this problem is the application of **poka-yokes**—procedures that block the inevitable mistake from becoming a service defect.[2] Poka-yokes (roughly translated from the Japanese as "avoid mistakes") are common in factories (see Chapter 7, "Quality Management," for examples) and consist of such things as fixtures to ensure that parts can be attached only in the right way, electronic switches that automatically shut off equipment if a mistake is made, kitting of parts prior to assembly to make sure the right quantities are used, and checklists to ensure that the right sequence of steps is followed.

Poka-yokes

There are many applications of poka-yokes to services as well. These can be classified into warning methods, physical or visual contact methods, and by what we call the *Three T's*—the Task to be done (Was the car fixed right?); the Treatment accorded to the customer (Was the service manager courteous?); and the Tangible or environmental features of the service facility (Was the waiting area clean and comfortable?). Finally (unlike in manufacturing), service poka-yokes often must be applied to fail-safing the actions of the customer as well as the service worker.

FAILURE: CUSTOMER NOT LOCATED.
POKA-YOKE: ISSUE BEEPERS TO CUSTOMERS WHO WISH TO LEAVE FACILITY.

FAILURE: BILL IS ILLEGIBLE.
POKA-YOKE: TOP COPY TO CUSTOMER, OR PLAIN PAPER BILL.

FAILURE: FEEDBACK NOT OBTAINED.
POKA-YOKE: CUSTOMER SATISFACTION POSTCARD GIVEN TO CUSTOMER WITH KEYS TO VEHICLE.

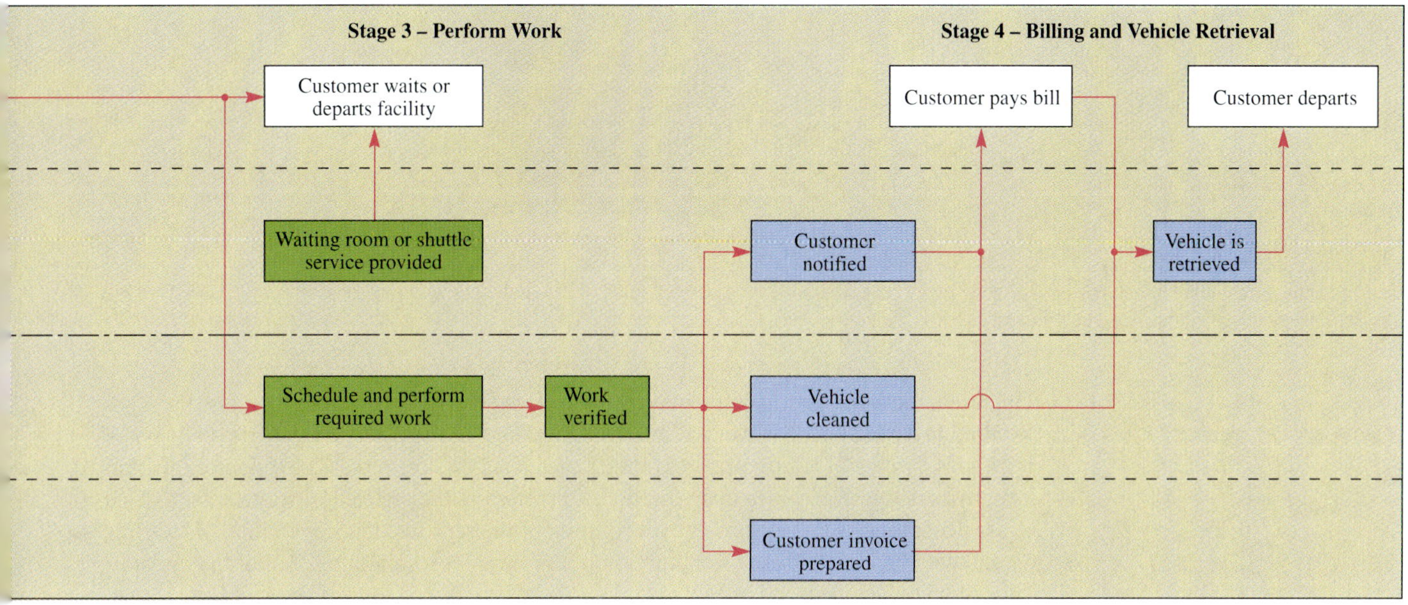


FAILURE: SERVICE SHUTTLE IS INCONVENIENT.
POKA-YOKE: SEATING IN AVAILABLE SHUTTLES IS ALLOCATED WHEN SCHEDULING APPOINTMENTS. LACK OF FREE SPACE INDICATES THAT CUSTOMERS NEEDING SHUTTLE SERVICE SHOULD BE SCHEDULED FOR ANOTHER TIME.
FAILURE: PARTS ARE NOT IN STOCK.
POKA-YOKE: LIMIT SWITCHES ACTIVATE SIGNAL LAMPS WHEN PART LEVEL FALLS BELOW ORDER POINT.

FAILURE: VEHICLE NOT CLEANED CORRECTLY.
POKA-YOKE: PERSON RETRIEVING VEHICLE INSPECTS, ORDERS A TOUCH-UP IF NECESSARY, AND REMOVES FLOOR MAT IN PRESENCE OF CUSTOMER.

FAILURE: VEHICLE TAKES TOO LONG TO ARRIVE.
POKA-YOKE: WHEN CASHIER ENTERS CUSTOMER'S NAME TO PRINT THE BILL, INFORMATION IS ELECTRONICALLY SENT TO RUNNERS WHO RETRIEVE VEHICLE WHILE THE CUSTOMER IS PAYING.

Poka-yoke examples include height bars at amusement parks; indented trays used by surgeons to ensure that no instruments are left in the patient; chains to configure waiting lines; take-a-number systems; turnstiles; beepers on ATMs to warn people to take their cards out of the machine; beepers at restaurants to make sure customers do not miss their table calls; mirrors on telephones to ensure a "smiling voice"; reminder calls for appointments; locks on airline lavatory doors that activate lights inside; small gifts in comment card envelopes to encourage customers to provide feedback about a service; and pictures of what "a clean room" looks like for kindergarten children.

Exhibit 6.9 illustrates how a typical automobile service operation might be fail-safed using poka-yokes. As a final comment, although these procedures cannot guarantee the level of error protection found in the factory, they still can reduce such errors in many service situations.

## THREE CONTRASTING SERVICE DESIGNS

Three contrasting approaches to delivering on-site service are the production line approach, made famous by McDonald's Corporation; the self-service approach, made famous by ATMs and gas stations; and the personal attention approach, made famous by Nordstrom department stores and the Ritz-Carlton Hotel Company.

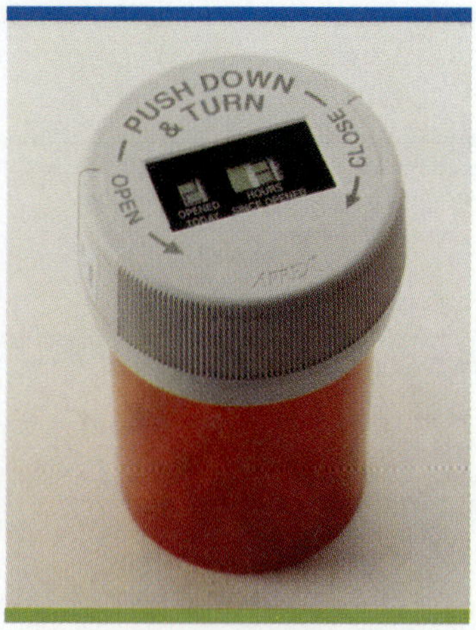


A SUCCESSFUL POKA-YOKE FOR FORGETFUL AND/OR RELUCTANT PATIENTS WHO DON'T TAKE THEIR MEDICINE IS THE "SMART" BOTTLE CAP FROM APREX CORP. IN FREMONT, CALIFORNIA. BUILT WITH A COMPUTER CHIP, ALARM CLOCK AND SMALL DISPLAY PANEL, THE SMART CAP MAINTAINS A RECORD OF HOW FREQUENTLY THE BOTTLE IS OPENED, AND IS EQUIPPED WITH A BEEPER TO REMIND THOSE PATIENTS WHO FORGET TO TAKE THEIR MEDICATIONS.

## THE PRODUCTION LINE APPROACH

The production line approach pioneered by McDonald's refers to more than just the steps required to assemble a Big Mac. Rather, as Theodore Levitt notes, it treats the delivery of fast food as a manufacturing process rather than a service process.[3] The value of this philosophy is that it overcomes many problems inherent in the concept of service itself. That is, service implies subordination or subjugation of the server to the served; manufacturing, on the other hand, avoids this connotation because it focuses on things rather than people. Thus in manufacturing and at McDonald's, "the orientation is toward the efficient production of results not on the attendance on others." Levitt notes that besides McDonald's marketing and financial skills, the company carefully controls "the execution of each outlet's central function—the rapid delivery of a uniform, high-quality mix of prepared foods in an environment of obvious cleanliness, order, and cheerful courtesy. The systematic substitution of equipment for people, combined with the carefully planned use and positioning of technology, enables McDonald's to attract and hold patronage in proportions no predecessor or imitator has managed to duplicate."

Levitt cites several aspects of McDonald's operations to illustrate the concepts. Note the extensive use of what we term poka-yokes.

- The McDonald's french fryer allows cooking of the optimum number of french fries at one time.
- A wide-mouthed scoop is used to pick up the precise amount of french fries for each order size. (The employee never touches the product.)
- Storage space is expressly designed for a predetermined mix of prepackaged and premeasured products.
- Cleanliness is pursued by providing ample trash cans in and outside each facility. (Larger outlets have motorized sweepers for the parking area.)
- Hamburgers are wrapped in color-coded paper.
- Through painstaking attention to total design and facilities planning, everything is built integrally into the (McDonald's) machine itself—into the technology of the system. The only choice available to the attendant is to operate it exactly as the designers intended. Using our service-system design matrix (Exhibit 6.7), we would categorize this as a face-to-face tight spec service.

## THE SELF-SERVICE APPROACH

In contrast to the production line approach, C. H. Lovelock and R. F. Young propose that the service process can be enhanced by having the customer take a greater role in the production of the service.[4] Company websites, automatic teller machines, self-service gas

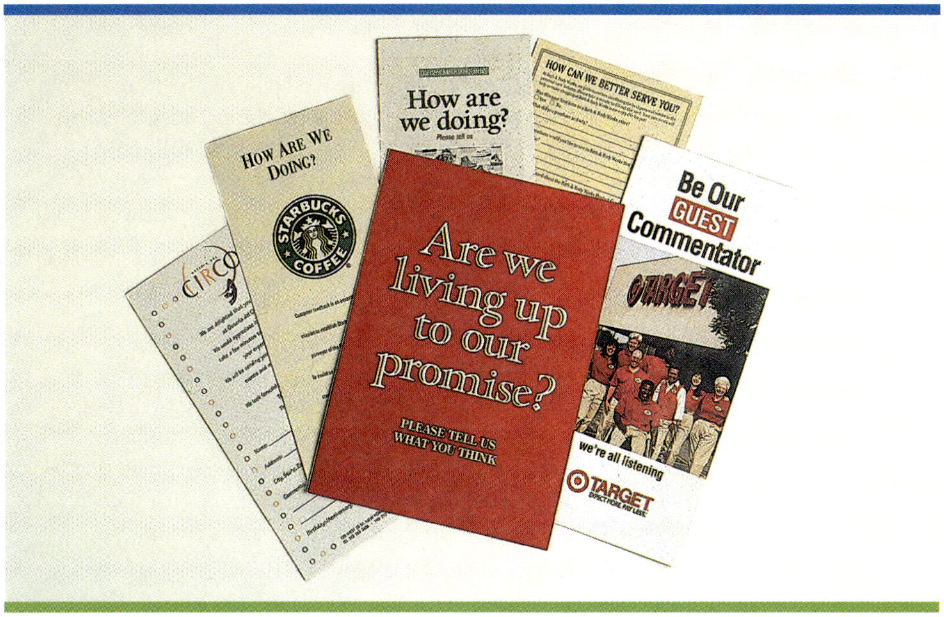


FEEDBACK FROM CUSTOMERS IS INVALUABLE IN HELPING A COMPANY EVALUATE ITSELF. THE RESPONSES TO SURVEY QUESTIONS SUCH AS WHAT NEW SERVICES NEED TO BE OFFERED, AND WHAT WOULD THE CUSTOMER LIKE TO SEE CHANGED, GUIDE COMPANIES IN THEIR GOAL OF "DELIGHTING" CUSTOMERS WITH UNEXPECTEDLY GOOD SERVICES.

stations, salad bars, and in-room coffee-making equipment in motels are approaches that shift the service burden to the consumer. Based on our service-system design matrix, these are great examples of the use of Internet and on-site technology. Many customers like self-service because it puts them in control. For others, this philosophy requires some selling on the part of the service organization to convince customers that it helps them. To this end, Lovelock and Young propose a number of steps, including developing customer trust; promoting the benefits of cost, speed, and convenience; and following up to make sure that the procedures are being effectively used. In essence, this turns customers into "partial employees" who must be trained in what to do and, as noted earlier, be "fail-safed" in case of mistake.

It is often most profitable to provide both full service and self-service at the same facility. As Globerson and Maggard report, "Analysis of gasoline sales after decontrol of the U.S. gasoline market in 1981 shows that cutting prices for self-service gasoline while increasing prices for full service increased dealer profits, in spite of the fact that self-service gas sales increased by from about 22 percent in 1978 to 41 percent in 1984."[5] This certainly is holding true today given the successes of companies with both Internet and local sales stores such as Barnes and Noble and Circuit City.

## THE PERSONAL ATTENTION APPROACH

An interesting contrast in the way personal attention is provided can be seen in Nordstrom Department Stores and the Ritz-Carlton Hotel Company.

At Nordstrom, a rather loose, unstructured process relies on developing a relationship between the individual salesperson and the customer (this is a face-to-face with total customization service). At the Ritz-Carlton, the process is virtually scripted, and the information system rather than the employee keeps track of the guest's (customer's) personal preferences (this is a face-to-face loose spec example). Tom Peters describes Nordstrom's approach here:

> After several visits to a store's men's clothing department, a customer's suit still did not fit. He wrote the company president, who sent a tailor to the customer's office with a new suit for fitting. When the alterations were completed, the suit was delivered to the customer—free of charge.
>
> This incident involved the $1.3 billion, Seattle-based Nordstrom, a specialty clothing retailer. Its sales per square foot are about five times that of a typical department store. Who received the customer's letter and

> urged the extreme (by others' standards) response? Co-chairman John Nordstrom.
>
> The frontline providers of this good service are well paid. Nordstrom's salespersons earn a couple of bucks an hour more than competitors, plus a 6.75 percent commission. Its top salesperson moves over $1 million a year in merchandise. Nordstrom lives for its customers and salespeople. Its only official organization chart puts the customer at the top, followed by sales and sales support people. Next come department managers, then store managers, and the board of directors at the very bottom.
>
> Salespersons religiously carry a "personal book," where they record voluminous information about each of their customers; senior, successful salespeople often have three or four bulging books, which they carry everywhere, according to Betsy Sanders, the vice president who orchestrated the firm's wildly successful penetration of the tough southern California market. "My objective is to get one new personal customer a day," says a budding Nordstrom star. The system helps him do just that. He has a virtually unlimited budget to send cards, flowers, and thank-you notes to customers. He also is encouraged to shepherd his customer to any department in the store to assist in a successful shopping trip.
>
> He also is abetted by what may be the most liberal returns policy in this or any other business: Return *anything,* no questions asked. Sanders says that "trusting customers," or "our bosses" as she repeatedly calls them, is vital to the Nordstrom philosophy. President Jim Nordstrom told the *Los Angeles Times,* "I don't care if they roll a Goodyear tire into the store. If they say they paid $200, give them $200 (in cash) for it." Sanders acknowledges that a few customers rip the store off—"rent hose from us," to use a common insider's line. But this is more than offset by goodwill from the 99 percent-plus who benefit from the "No Problem at Nordstrom" logo that the company lives up to with unmatched zeal.
>
> No bureaucracy gets in the way of serving the customer. Policy? Sanders explains to a dumbfounded group of Silicon Valley executives, "I know this drives the lawyers nuts, but our whole 'policy manual' is just one sentence, 'Use your own best judgment at all times.' " One store manager offers a translation: "Don't chew gum. Don't steal from us."[6]

The Ritz-Carlton approach is described in the following excerpts from the company's Baldrige Award Application Summary and discussions with Scott Long of Ritz-Carlton's Huntington Hotel in Pasadena, California. Exhibit 6.10 shows the formalized service procedure (the Three Steps of Service). Exhibit 6.11 displays the information system used to capture data about guests ("The Ritz-Carlton Repeat Guest History Program"). Note that the three steps of service are integrated into the guest history information system.

> Systems for the collection and utilization of customer reaction and satisfaction are widely deployed and extensively used throughout the organization. Our efforts are centered on various customer segments and product lines.
>
> Our approach is the use of systems which allow every employee to collect and utilize quality-related data on a daily basis. These systems provide critical, responsive data which include:
>
> (1) On-line guest preference information;
> (2) Quantity of error free products and services;
> (3) Opportunities for quality improvement.
>
> Our automated property management systems enable the on-line access and utilization of guest preference information at the individual customer level. All employees collect and input this data, and use the data as part of their service delivery with individual guests.

EXHIBIT 6.10

The Ritz-Carlton Hotel Company (Three Steps of Service)

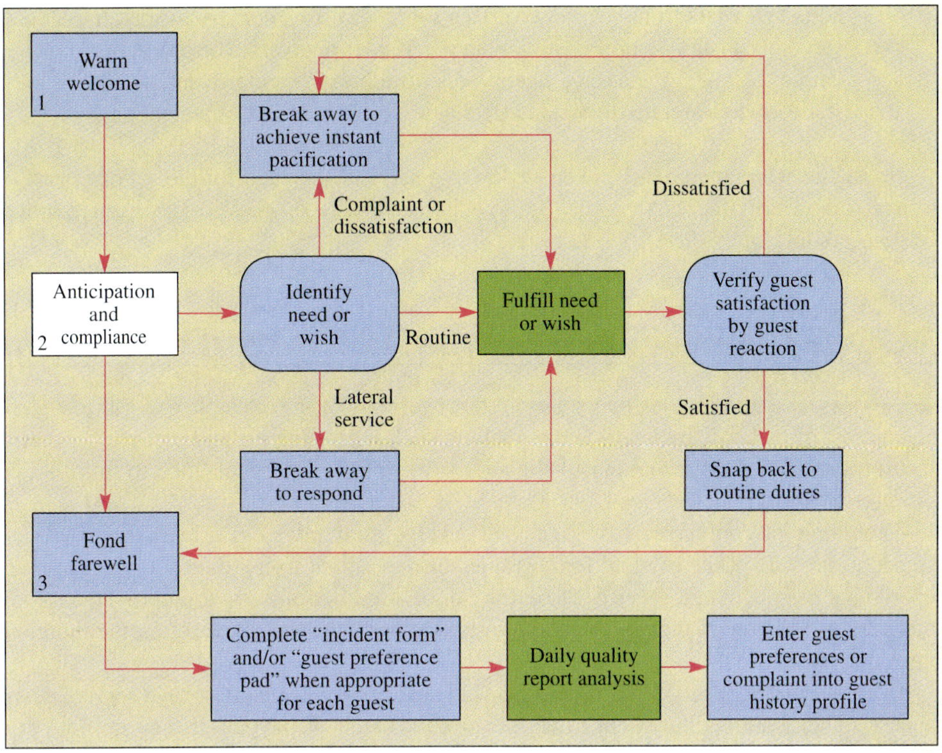


SOURCE: *RITZ-CARLTON MALCOLM BALDRIGE NATIONAL QUALITY AWARD APPLICATION SUMMARY*, 1993, P. 11.

EXHIBIT 6.11

The Ritz-Carlton Repeat Guest History Program (An Aid to Highly Personalized Service Delivery)

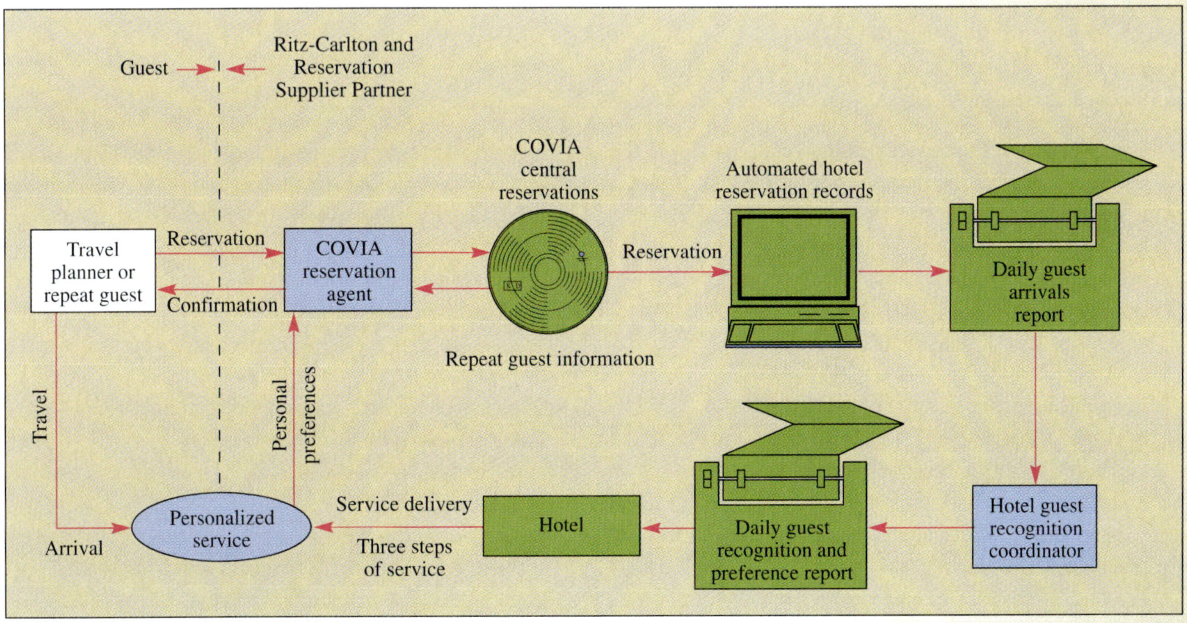


SOURCE: *RITZ-CARLTON MALCOLM BALDRIGE NATIONAL QUALITY AWARD APPLICATION SUMMARY*, 1993, P. 6.

> Our quality production reporting system is a method of aggregating hotel level data from nearly two dozen sources into a summary format. It serves as an early warning system and facilitates analysis. The processes employees use to identify quality opportunities for improvement are standardized in a textbook, and available throughout our organization.[7]

No matter what approach is taken to design a service, the need for the service characteristics shown in the box titled "Seven Characteristics of a Well-Designed Service System" should be evident.

## SERVICE GUARANTEES AS DESIGN DRIVERS

The phrase "Positively, absolutely, overnight" is an example of a service guarantee most of us know by heart. Hiding behind such marketing promises of service satisfaction is a set of actions that must be taken by the operations organization to fulfill these promises.

Service guarantees

Thousands of companies have launched **service guarantees** as a marketing tool designed to provide peace of mind for customers unsure about trying their service. From an operations perspective, a service guarantee can be used not only as an improvement tool but also at the design stage to focus the firm's delivery system squarely on the things it must do well to satisfy the customer.

Even professional service firms such as Rath and Strong Consulting have service guarantees. (Theirs allows the client to choose from a menu of payouts if they do not—for example, cut lead time by $x$ percent. Menu options include refunds and no charge for overtime work to get the job done.)

The elements of a good service guarantee are that it is unconditional (no small print); meaningful to the customer (the payoff fully covers the customer's dissatisfaction); easy to understand and communicate (for employees as well as customers); and painless to invoke (given proactively).[8]

An issue of growing importance in service relates to the ethical and possibly legal responsibility of a company to actually provide the service that is promised. For example, is an airline responsible for transporting a passenger with a guaranteed reservation, even

### SEVEN CHARACTERISTICS OF A WELL-DESIGNED SERVICE SYSTEM

1. **Each element of the service system is consistent with the operating focus of the firm.** For example, when the focus is on speed of delivery, each step in the process should help foster speed.
2. **It is user-friendly.** This means that the customer can interact with it easily—that is, it has good signage, understandable forms, logical steps in the process, and service workers available to answer questions.
3. **It is robust.** That is, it can cope effectively with variations in demand and resource availability. For example, if the computer goes down, effective backup systems are in place to permit service to continue.
4. **It is structured so that consistent performance by its people and systems is easily maintained.** This means the tasks required of the workers are doable, and the supporting technologies are truly supportive and reliable.
5. **It provides effective links between the back office and the front office so that nothing falls between the cracks.** In football parlance, there should be "no fumbled handoffs."
6. **It manages the evidence of service quality in such a way that customers see the value of the service provided.** Many services do a great job behind the scenes but fail to make this visible to the customer. This is particularly true where a service improvement is made. Unless customers are made aware of the improvement through explicit communication about it, the improved performance is unlikely to gain maximum impact.
7. **It is cost-effective.** There is minimum waste of time and resources in delivering the service. Even if the service outcome is satisfactory, customers are often put off by a service company that appears inefficient.

though the flight has been overbooked? Or consider the Internet service provider's responsibility to provide enough telephone lines so that customers do not receive busy signals when they try to connect to the service (see the case study titled "AOL's Move to Flat-Rate Pricing"). These are difficult issues because having excess capacity is expensive. Demand can be nearly impossible to predict with great accuracy, thus making the estimates of needed capacity difficult.

A very powerful tool—waiting line analysis—is available to help better understand the relationships between the factors that drive a service system. These factors include the average number of customers that arrive over a period of time, the average time that it takes to serve each customer, the number of servers, and information about the size of the customer population. Waiting line models have been developed that allow the estimation of expected waiting time and expected resource utilization. This is the topic of the technical note to this chapter.

## CONCLUSION

In this chapter, we have shown how service businesses are in many ways very similar to manufacturing businesses. Likewise is the need for trade-offs in developing a focus. Focus, for example, is important to success, just as it was with the design of manufacturing systems.

The service-system design matrix is in many ways similar to the product–process matrix we used to categorize manufacturing operations. Further, the tools of flow diagrams and capacity analysis are similar as well.

Services are, however, very different compared to manufacturing when we consider the high degree of personalization often required, the speed of delivery needed, the direct customer contact, and the inherent variability of the service encounter. The buffering and scheduling mechanisms that we have available to smooth the demand placed on a manufacturing operation are often not available to the service operation. Services generally require much higher levels of capacity relative to demand. In addition, they place a greater need for flexibility on the part of the workers involved in providing the services.

### KEY TERMS

**Facilities-based services** Customers must go to the place of business.

**Field-based services** Production and consumption take place in the customer's environment.

**High and low degree of customer contact** The physical presence of the customer in the system and the percentage of time the customer must be in the system relative to the total time it takes to perform the service.

**Service blueprint** The flowchart of a service process, emphasizing what is visible and what is not visible to the customer.

**Poka-yokes** Procedures that prevent mistakes from being made. They are commonly found in manufacturing but can also be used in service processes.

**Service guarantee** A promise of service satisfaction backed up by a set of actions that must be taken to fulfill the promise.

### REVIEW AND DISCUSSION QUESTIONS

1 Who is the "customer" in a jail? A cemetery? A summer camp for children?
2 How has price and variety competition changed McDonald's basic formula for success?
3 Could a service firm use a production line approach or self-serve design and still keep a high customer focus (personal attention)? Explain and support your answer with examples.
4 Why should a manager of a bank home office be evaluated differently than a manager of a bank branch?
5 Identify the high-contact and low-contact operations of the following services:
   *a.* A dental office.
   *b.* An airline.
   *c.* An accounting office.
   *d.* An automobile agency.

6 Some suggest that customer expectation is the key to service success. Give an example from your own experience to support or refute this assertion.
7 Where would you place a drive-in church, a campus food vending machine, and a bar's automatic mixed drink machine on the service-system design matrix?
8 Can a manufacturer have a service guarantee in addition to a product guarantee?
9 Suppose you were the manager of a restaurant and you were told honestly that a couple eating dinner had just seen a mouse. What would you say to them? How would you recover from this service crisis?

## PROBLEMS

1. See ISM.

1 Place the following functions of a department store on the service-system design matrix: mail order (that is, catalog), phone order, hardware, stationery, apparel, cosmetics, customer service (such as taking complaints).

2. See ISM.

2 Do the same as in the previous problem for a hospital with the following activities and relationships: physician/patient, nurse/patient, billing, medical records, lab tests, admissions, diagnostic tests (such as X-rays).

3. See ISM.

3 Perform a quick service audit the next time you go shopping at a department store. Evaluate the three T's of service: the Task, the Treatment, and the Tangible features of the service on a scale of 1 (poor), 3 (average), and 5 (excellent). Remember that the tangible features include the environment, layout, and appearance of the store, not the goods you purchased.

4. See ISM.

4 SYSTEM DESCRIPTION EXERCISE
The beginning step in studying a productive system is to develop a description of that system. Once a system is described, we can better determine why the system works well or poorly and recommend production-related improvements. Because most of us are familiar with fast-food restaurants, try your hand at describing the production system employed at, say, a McDonald's. In doing so, answer the following questions:
*a.* What are the important aspects of the service package?
*b.* Which skills and attitudes are needed by the service personnel?
*c.* How can customer demand be altered?
*d.* Provide a rough-cut blueprint of the delivery system. (It is not necessary to provide execution times. Just diagram the basic flow through the system.) Critique the blueprint. Are there any unnecessary steps or can failure points be eliminated?
*e.* Can the customer/provider interface be changed to include more technology? More self-serve?
*f.* Which measures are being used to evaluate the service? Which could be used?
*g.* How does it measure up on the seven characteristics of a well-designed service?

## CASE: KINKO'S COPIER STORES

"We're not your average printer," says Annie Odell, Kinko's regional manager for Louisiana. She's right. She may have the only print shops in town where customers come as much for the company as for the copies. It's a free-wheeling, high-tech operation that marches to the beat of a different drum machine. It looks chaotic; it is chaotic. Yet it produces profit as well as fun.

Odell's copy shop empire has grown from one to seven in six years, including five in the greater New Orleans area.

Kinko's keeps its sales figures a secret, but Odell estimates her New Orleans stores make about 40 million copies a year. At the firm's advertised $4\frac{1}{2}$ cents-per-copy price, that would mean around $1.8 million a year in sales, or an average of over $300,000 per shop. The New Orleans operations rank among Kinko's top 25 percent nationally, reports Becky Barieau of Kinko's of Georgia.

Sales in New Orleans have climbed even while the marketplace has been sinking. At the Carrollton store, revenues increased 10 percent over last year, an excellent showing considering the $4\frac{1}{2}$ cents-per-copy rate has not budged since 1980.

"Depression seems to generate more need for copies," says Wallis Windsor, manager of the Carrollton store. "There are bankruptcies, legal documents, and resumes—hundreds of people who want 50 copies of their resumes on specialty paper."

### PRINTERS SNEER

Kinko's is unique. For one thing, it doesn't do a lick of offset printing. It makes copies, copies, and almost nothing but copies. On the side it binds, folds, staples, collates, makes pads, and takes passport photos.

Kinko's is also unique among quick printing chains in that it doesn't franchise. All 300 or so Kinko's stores are divided among a few closely held corporations, and founder Paul Orfalea holds a piece of virtually all of them. Odell explains that the company avoids franchising to ensure tight control over quality at its outlets.

Others attribute the structure to a desire to avoid the legal restrictions and paperwork demanded by setting up franchises in different states. How it's been kept together is a management feat in itself.

Even the name sticks out. The Yellow Pages list dozens of quick printers with some reference to speed in their names, often intentionally misspelled. "Kinko's" denotes a place that's . . . well, a little kinky. For the record, Orfalea, who plugged in his first photocopier when he was in college, was nicknamed by classmates as "Kinko" for his curly head of hair.

### BROADWAY AND BENIHANA

Kinko's management style draws on both the restaurant business and the stage. Fast copies are like fast food, say the managers. It's not just that every Big Mac is a copy of every other one. Images of eating come up again and again as they try to explain what keeps their customers coming back.

"Making copies is addictive," says Windsor, and points to her clientele of "regulars," who "have made this their office. They will spend four or five hours here although they don't spend more than $5 or $6. People have suggested we open a bar in here."

"Instant gratification is what Kinko's is offering," says another manager.

The last time managers from around the country huddled in Santa Barbara for the company "picnic," they studied looseleaf binders crammed full of floor plans for McDonald's and Benihana of Tokyo—a variation on the acclaimed art of Japanese management.

"You'd find it hard to believe," says Odell, "but Benihana is a lot like Kinko's. They're masters of efficiency. We'll try to set up the floor to get one person operating two copiers, just like Benihana puts one cook between two tables. Our paper is centrally located, just as they have all the chopping prepared ahead of time. Then there's the floater, who floats around and pops in wherever he's needed."

Both Kinko's and Benihana's use theater to attract clients, charging their employees with putting on a good show as well as putting out good service. At the Japanese restaurant, the show is the cook, who sizzles a sukiyaki right in front of your table. At Kinko's it's the clatter of copy machines and the Charlie Chaplin–like spectacle of operators running back and forth between them.

"They do it right in front of you and you get instant quality control," says Odell, "There's no way you're going to drop that document with the customer watching you."

She deliberately displays all her machines and personnel in one big room. "We work out with the public. That's why it's fun," says Odell, "The other guys are behind closed doors."

Windsor enjoys working in a fishbowl. "My personality changes," she says. "I'll be a little more dramatic and louder than I would be in a closed group. I walk quickly. I'll wad up and throw papers a lot."

She believes customers unconsciously get into the act. "Some of the mildest-mannered people get aggressive in here. I've seen a little old lady elbow her way in ahead of people, where if she were in a bank she'd stand in line neatly."

Kinko's does no broadcast and little print advertising, counting on price and word-of-mouth to draw customers; and ambience doesn't hurt. Each Kinko's has its "regulars," who get friendly with particular operators and who favor particular machines. The area in front of the counter is strewn with computers, lettering machines, and light tables, all the better to hook people into making themselves comfortable and coming back.

A recent addition to that mélange is the customer comment form. The customer mails the postage-paid form straight to headquarters in Santa Barbara, where senior managers review it and send a thank-you note to the author before routing it back to the shop manager for action. Odell has several inches of forms on file, along with notes on the follow-up calls she made to the customers.

"We don't choose our market so much as our market chooses us," she says. Each shop keeps a different mix of machines, depending on the needs of its patrons. An operator learns quickly that the Xerox 1000 series picks up blue but not yellow, while the 9000 series picks up yellow and black but not blue. Thus, the store adjoining the Tulane campus does not have a 9000 because students tend to bring in notes and books highlighted with yellow markers.

Another adaptation to the market is "Professor Publishing," a service that lets professors excerpt chapters from several books and print them together as a single textbook. During the first two weeks of every semester, the Broadway office works virtually around-the-clock on this specialty.

Odell maintains that her managers clear all material with publishers before printing a professor's anthology. Indeed, Kinko's says it is one of the most scrupulous of the copy chains about observing copyright laws.

### PRINTING IN A FISHBOWL

If working at the Kinko's shops in New Orleans is like working in a fishbowl, it's a two-way fishbowl where the fish are always peering back at their audience. The crazy-quilt mix of customers provides endless entertainment and a fund of oddball stories to exchange over beers. A sampling:

- One woman insisted that the manager throw away the ribbon on the self-service typewriter she'd just used, fearing that someone might try to use it to recreate her document. Another customer wanted several confidential pages typed, and asked, "Can you get me a typist who won't read them?"
- Some artists enjoy using the photocopiers for the oddest things. One woman brings in stuffed dead birds for reproduction. Another brought in a box of pecans purported to be from the backyard of a house where Tennessee Williams once lived.
- A tipsy woman, about 25 years of age, meandered in from a Mardi Gras parade, curled up next to a window, and fell asleep. There she remained for four hours, while the copiers and binding machines pounded and rattled. Manager Raynell Murphy called the home office. "What should I do?" she asked. "Get a picture," came the word from California, "We can use it as a promotion, you know, to show what a relaxed atmosphere we have at Kinko's."

  Finally, a hulking woman who had just bought some copies walked over to the sleeper, kicked her a couple of times, and asked, "Are you ready yet?" The sleeper arose and groggily headed out the door.

### QUESTIONS

1 Can general operational standards be developed and implemented in all or a majority of Kinko's shops?
2 Discuss the idea of grouping copiers in machine centers so that certain copiers are available for specific tasks.
3 How do the different services offered (private copying versus copying services provided) present separate types of problems for management?

SOURCE: M. BALLARD, "WORKING IN A FISHBOWL," *QUICK PRINTING*, MAY 1987, PP. 30–32. REPRINTED BY PERMISSION.

## CASE: AOL's Move to Flat-Rate Pricing

This case traces the mess that America Online got itself in when it moved to flat-rate pricing in late 1996. The number of people who signed up for AOL's flat-rate service exceeded all expectations. In January 1997 *The Wall Street Journal* article by Thomas Petzinger blasted AOL for not anticipating the customer response. In a second article, about a week later, the government had gotten involved and was forcing AOL to make amends to its customers.

### "Gunning for Growth," AOL's Steve Case Shot Himself in the Foot*

To some people, the customer service crisis at America Online is a technology issue. Others see it as a management issue. Predictably, a few opportunistic lawyers are trying to turn it into a legal issue.

But I think one thing's for sure: The service breakdown at AOL is an ethical issue. Today's topsy-turvy business world does not excuse a company from offering a product it knows it cannot reliably deliver.

Here's the gist of the morality play: Eager for market share as competition heats up in the online world, AOL offered a deep price cut, publicly admitting it would have trouble meeting the added demand. In fact, the strain on the system exceeded the company's worst fears. AOL is now hitting many of its eight million customers—me, for instance—with an unremitting busy signal instead of the instant communication services it assured them they could count on.

Compounding the problem, millions of businesspeople have come to depend on the service to some degree, meaning that AOL's failings reach its customers' customers. It gets worse. Although AOL says it has severely cut back on marketing, at the very moment I was listening to AOL's busy signal the other day my kids were watching the company's pitch for new customers over the Nickelodeon network, complete with a toll-free number. You can get through to sign up, but not to log in.

### AOL to Pay Refunds to Its Customers†

America Online Inc., bowing to pressure from attorneys general in 36 states, reached a preliminary settlement yesterday that will require it to pay refunds of up to $40 per customer to compensate frustrated subscribers who have been unable to gain unlimited access to the crowded online service for the past two months.

The tentative settlement announced yesterday requires AOL to provide customers who used the service less than two hours each month in December and January with a refund of $39.90—twice the monthly fee for unlimited access. AOL also must cease advertising during the month of February, and any advertising after that must disclose that users might encounter problems getting online. The online service also must make it easier for customers to cancel their subscriptions, providing fax numbers and postal addresses to do so, and will have to provide written reports to the state officials updating them on the progress of the refunds.

### Questions

1. Should AOL be held accountable for its inability to provide immediate access to its network?
2. Compare the case of AOL with that of airline companies who regularly oversell their seats.
3. Suggest a policy that AOL should use that relates the capacity of its system to the number of potential users.
4. Should the government get involved in this?

*Adapted from T. Petzinger, Jr., "The Front Lines," *The Wall Street Journal*, January 24, 1997, p. B1.
†Adapted from J. Sandberg, "AOL to Pay Refunds to Its Customers," *The Wall Street Journal*, January 30, 1997, p. A3. © 1997 Dow Jones & Company, Inc. Permission conveyed through the Copyright Clearance Center, Inc.

## SELECTED BIBLIOGRAPHY

Bitran, G. R., and J. Hoech. "The Humanization of Service: Respect at the Moment of Truth." *Sloan Management Review,* Winter 1990, pp. 89–96.

Chase, R. B. *Mistake-Proofing: How to Design Errors Out.* Cambridge, MA: Productivity Press, 1994.

———. "The Customer Contact Approach to Services: Theoretical Bases and Practical Extensions." *Operations Research* 21, no. 4 (1981), pp. 698–705.

———. "The Mall Is My Factory: Reflections of a Service Junkie." *Production and Operations Management,* Winter 1996, pp. 298–308.

Chase, R. B., and D. M. Stewart. "Make Your Service Fail-Safe." *Sloan Management Review,* Spring 1994, pp. 35–44.

Cohen, M. A., and H. L. Lee. "Out of Touch with Customer Needs?" *Sloan Management Review,* Winter 1990, pp. 55–56.

Colley, J. L. *Case Studies in Service Operations.* Duxbury Press: Wadsworth, 1996.

Collier, D. A. *The Service/Quality Solution.* Burr Ridge, IL: Irwin Professional Publishing, 1993.

Finsthal, T. W. "My Employees Are My Service Guarantee." *Harvard Business Review,* July–August 1989, pp. 28–33.

Fitzsimmons, J. A., and M. J. Fitzsimmons. *Service Management: Operations, Strategy, and Information Technology.* New York: Irwin/McGraw-Hill, 1998.

Flint, J., and W. Heuslein. "An Urge to Service." *Forbes,* September 18, 1989, pp. 172–74.

Hackett, G. P. "Investment in Technology: The Service Sector Sinkhole?" *Sloan Management Review,* Winter 1990, pp. 97–103.

Hart, C. W. L. "The Power of Unconditional Service Guarantees." *Harvard Business Review,* July–August 1988, pp. 54–62.

Heskett, J. L. *Managing in the Service Economy.* Cambridge, MA: Harvard University Press, 1986.

Heskett, J. L.; W. E. Sasser, Jr; and C. L. Hart. *Service Breakthroughs: Changing the Rules of the Game.* New York: Free Press, 1990.

Hope, C. *Service Operations Management: Strategy, Design, and Delivery.* New York: Prentice Hall, 1997.

Roth, A. V.; R. B. Chase; and C. Voss. "Service in the U.S.: A Study of Service Practice and Performance in the United States," supported by Severn Trent Plc, U.K. Government's Department of Trade and Industry, Department of National Heritage, 1997.

Schmenner, R. W. *Service Operations Management.* Englewood Cliffs, NJ: Prentice Hall, 1995.

Shapiro, B. P.; V. K. Rangan; R. T. Moriarty; and E. B. Ross. "Manage Customers for Profits, Not Just Sales." *Harvard Business Review,* September–October 1987, pp. 101–8.

Sonnenberg, F. K. "Service Quality: Forethought, Not Afterthought." *Journal of Business Strategy,* September–October 1989, pp. 54–57.

## FOOTNOTES

1 J. Heskett, "Lessons from the Service Sector," *Harvard Business Review,* March–April 1987.

2 R. B. Chase and D. M. Stewart, "Make Your Service Fail-Safe," *Sloan Management Review,* Spring 1994, pp. 35–44.

3 T. Levitt, "Production-Line Approach to Service," *Harvard Business Review* 50, no. 5 (September–October 1972), pp. 41–52.

4 C. H. Lovelock and R. F. Young, "Look to Customers to Increase Productivity," *Harvard Business Review* 57, no. 2, pp. 168–78.

5 S. Globerson and M. J. Maggard, "A Conceptual Model of Self-Service," *International Journal of Production and Operations Management* 11, no. 4 (1991) pp. 33–43.

6 T. Peters, *Quality!* (Palo Alto, CA: TPC Communications, 1986), pp. 10–12.

7 *Ritz-Carlton Malcolm Baldrige National Quality Award Application Summary,* 1993, p. 6.

8 C. W. L. Hart, "The Power of Unconditional Service Guarantees," *Harvard Business Review* 56, no. 4 (July–August 1988), p. 55.

TECHNICAL NOTE

*technical note six*

# WAITING LINE MANAGEMENT

## OUTLINE AND KEY TERMS



technical note

WE'VE ALL HAD TO WAIT IN LINES AND KNOW THAT WHATEVER LINE WE CHOOSE, THE OTHER ONES WILL GO FASTER. HERE PEOPLE LINE UP FOR THE ENTRANCE TO THE LOUVRE IN PARIS, FRANCE.

Queues

Understanding waiting lines or **queues** and learning how to manage them is one of the most important areas in operations management. It is basic to creating schedules, job design, inventory levels, and so on. In our service economy we wait in line every day, from driving to work to checking out at the supermarket. The Breakthrough Box titled "The Largest Mall Landlord in the United States Addresses the Need to Converge Online Space and Offline Space" describes an innovative application of the Internet focused on reducing waiting. We also encounter waiting lines at factories—jobs wait in lines to be worked on at different machines, and machines themselves wait their turn to be overhauled. In short, waiting lines are pervasive.

In this technical note we discuss the basic elements of waiting line problems and provide standard steady-state formulas for solving them. These formulas, arrived at through queuing theory, enable planners to analyze service requirements and establish service facilities appropriate to stated conditions. Queuing theory is broad enough to cover such dissimilar delays as those encountered by customers in a shopping mall or aircraft in a holding pattern awaiting landing slots. Recently, Internet access providers have had problems providing enough modem telephone lines for subscribers dialing into the Internet. This problem can also be analyzed by queuing models.

## ECONOMICS OF THE WAITING LINE PROBLEM

Service

The central problem in virtually every waiting line situation is a trade-off decision. The manager must weigh the added cost of providing more rapid service (more traffic lanes, additional landing strips, more checkout stands) against the inherent cost of waiting.

Frequently, the cost trade-off decision is straightforward. For example, if we find that the total time our employees spend in the line waiting to use a copying machine would otherwise be spent in productive activities, we could compare the cost of installing one additional machine to the value of employee time saved. The decision could then be reduced to dollar terms and the choice easily made.

On the other hand, suppose that our waiting line problem centers on demand for beds in a hospital. We can compute the cost of additional beds by summing the costs for building construction, additional equipment required, and increased maintenance. But what is on the other side of the scale? Here we are confronted with the problem of trying to place a dollar figure on a patient's need for a hospital bed that is unavailable. While we can estimate lost hospital income, what about the human cost arising from this lack of adequate hospital care?

## BREAKTHROUGH

### The Largest Mall Landlord in the United States Addresses the Need to Converge Online Space and Offline Space

As Americans increasingly go online instead of going into shopping centers to make purchases, mall owners are working to make their properties portals to a retail world where websites, catalogs, and offline stores converge. Simon Property Group of Indianapolis, Indiana has launched a Chicago-based Internet venture called clixnmortar.com

Clixnmortar.com recently launched FastFrog.com, an integrated online and offline wish list for teenagers. FastFrog.com gives teenages a way to create electronic gift registries by scanning products at their favorite mall retailers. Teenagers register at a kiosk dubbed the "frog pond" where they receive a handheld zap stick, which enables them to go around the mall and scan the things they want. FastFrog.com then loads the list onto the user's personal Web page, from the user's wish list.

A related clixnmortar.com venture is YourSherpa.com, an integrated online and offline shopping fulfillment service targeted at busy adults who ant to buy things at the mall but do not have time to stand in line to purchase those items. Shoppers register for the service at a kisk known as "base camp," leave a credit card number, and recieve a Palm Pilot equipped with a scanner. Shoppers scan products they want or are considering purchasing. Those items are uploaded on to a user's personal Web page where the user can later decide to purchase them. Once paid for, the user tells YourSherpa.com where and when they want the items delivered.

We suppose that it will not be long before all shopping is done in this new integrated world of online and offline retailing where retailers can leverage their offline assets into the online world and vice versa.

What do you think? Is this the way we will do our Christmas shopping in 2003? At least we will not get any more gifts we have to stand in line to return.

SOURCE: ADAPTED FROM ASSOCIATED PRESS, "INDIANA-BASED MALL GROUP AGGRESSIVE WITH INTERNET." *SUNDAY HERALD-TIMES*, DECEMBER 19, 1999, P. C7.

## COST-EFFECTIVENESS BALANCE

Exhibit TN6.1 shows the essential trade-off relationship under typical (steady-state) customer traffic conditions. Initially, with minimal service capacity, the waiting line cost is at a maximum. As service capacity is increased, there is a reduction in the number of customers in the line and in their waiting times, which decreases waiting line cost. The variation in this function is often represented by the negative exponential curve. The cost of installing service capacity is shown simplistically as a linear rather than step function. The aggregate or total cost is shown as a U-shaped curve, a common approximation in such equilibrium problems. The idealized optimal cost is found at the crossover point between the service capacity and waiting line curves.

## THE PRACTICAL VIEW OF WAITING LINES

Before we proceed with a technical presentation of waiting line theory, it is useful to look at the intuitive side of the issue to see what it means. Exhibit TN6.2 shows arrivals at a service facility (such as a bank) and service requirements at that facility (such as tellers and loan officers). One important variable is the number of arrivals over the hours that the service system is open. From the service delivery viewpoint, customers demand varying amounts of service, often exceeding normal capacity. We can control arrivals in a variety of ways. For example, we can have a short line (such as a drive-in at a fast food restaurant with only several spaces), we can establish specific hours for specific customers, or we can run specials. For the server, we can affect service time by using faster or slower servers, faster or slower machines, different tooling, different material, different layout, faster setup time, and so on.

EXHIBIT TN6.1

Service Capacity versus Waiting Line Trade-Off

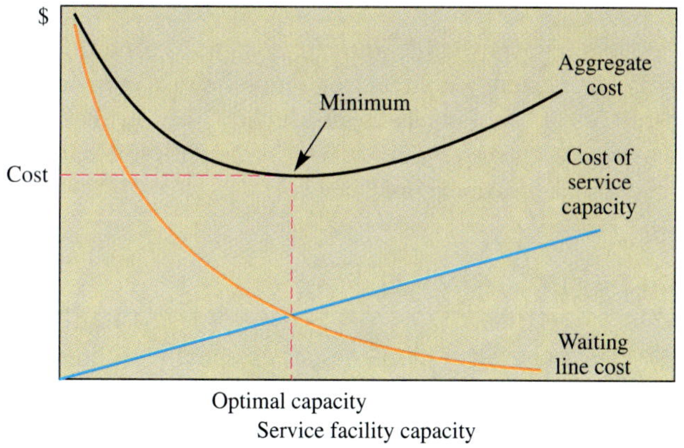


EXHIBIT TN6.2

Arrival and Service Profiles

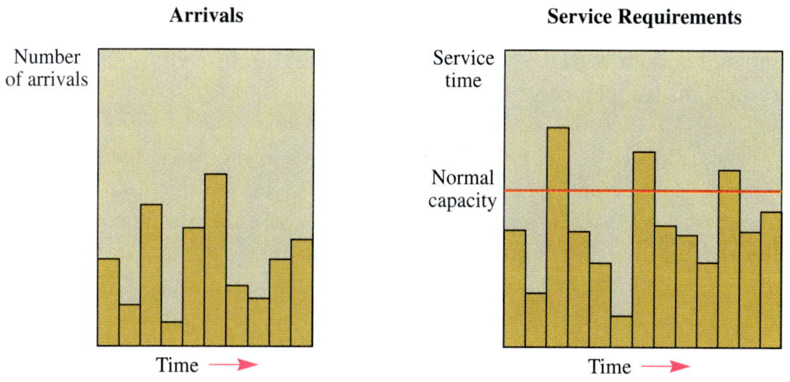

## SUGGESTIONS FOR MANAGING QUEUES

The following are some useful suggestions for managing queues that go beyond the quantitative waiting line models.

1 **Determine an acceptable waiting time for your customers.** How long do your customers expect to wait? Set operational objectives based on what is acceptable.

2 **Try to divert your customer's attention when waiting.** Providing music, a video, or some other form of entertainment may help to distract the customers from the fact they are waiting.

3 **Inform your customers of what to expect.** This is especially important when the waiting time will be longer than normal. Tell them why the waiting time is longer than normal and what you are doing to alleviate the queue.

4 **Keep employees not serving the customers out of sight.** Nothing is more frustrating to someone waiting in line than to see employees, who potentially could be serving those in line, working on other activities.

5 **Segment customers.** If a group of customers needs something that can be done very quickly, give them a special line so they do not have to wait for the slower customers.

6 **Train your servers to be friendly.** Greeting the customer by name, or providing some other special attention, can go a long way toward overcoming the negative feeling of a long wait. (Hint: Rather than telling servers to just "be friendly," psychologists suggest that workers be told when to invoke specific friendly actions such as smiling—when greeting customers, when taking orders, and when giving change (in a convenience store). Tests using such specific behavioral actions have shown significant increases in perceived friendliness of the servers in the eyes of the customer.)

7 **Encourage customers to come during the slack periods.** Inform customers of times when they usually would not have to wait; also tell them when the peak periods are—this may help to smooth the load.

8 **Take a long-term perspective toward getting rid of the queues.** Develop plans for alternative ways to serve your customers. Where appropriate, develop plans for automating or speeding up the process in some manner. This is not to say you want to eliminate personal attention; some customers expect this.

SOURCE: BASED ON K. KATZ, B. M. LARSON, AND R. C. LARSON, "PRESCRIPTION FOR THE WAITING-IN-LINE BLUES," *SLOAN MANAGEMENT REVIEW*, WINTER 1991, PP. 51–52.

The essential point is waiting lines are *not* a fixed condition of a productive system but are to a very large extent within the control of the system management and design. Professor Richard Larson (the famous "wait-watcher") and his colleagues offer useful suggestions for managing queues based on their research in the banking industry. (See the box titled "Suggestions for Managing Queues.")

# THE QUEUING SYSTEM

Queuing system

The **queuing system** consists essentially of three major components: (1) the source population and the way customers arrive at the system, (2) the servicing system, and (3) the condition of the customers exiting the system (back to source population or not?), as seen in Exhibit TN6.3. The following sections discuss each of these areas.

## CUSTOMER ARRIVALS

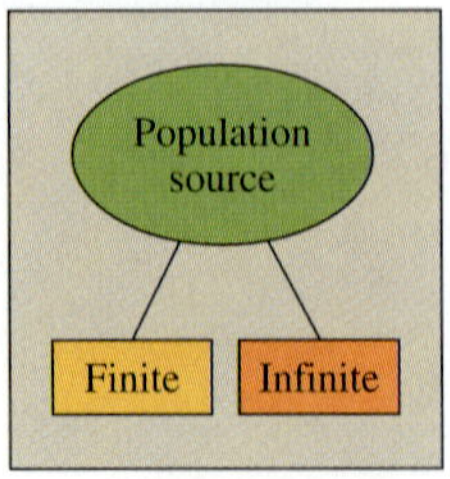


Arrivals at a service system may be drawn from a *finite* or an *infinite* population. The distinction is important because the analyses are based on different premises and require different equations for their solution.

**Finite Population** A *finite population* refers to the limited-size customer pool that will use the service and, at times, form a line. The reason this finite classification is important is that when a customer leaves its position as a member for the population (a machine breaking down and requiring service, for example), the size of the user group is reduced by one, which reduces the probability of the next occurrence. Conversely, when a customer is serviced and returns to the user group, the population increases and the probability of a user requiring service also increases. This finite class of problems requires a separate set of formulas from that of the infinite population case.

EXHIBIT TN6.3

Components of a Queuing System

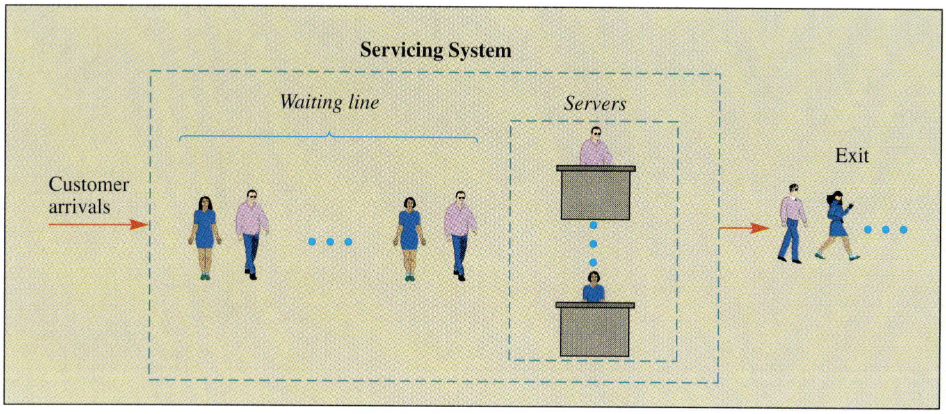


As an example, consider a group of six machines maintained by one repairperson. When one machine breaks down, the source population is reduced to five, and the chance of one of the remaining five breaking down and needing repair is certainly less than when six machines were operating. If two machines are down with only four operating, the probability of another breakdown is again changed. Conversely, when a machine is repaired and returned to service, the machine population increases, thus raising the probability of the next breakdown. A finite population model with one server that can be used in such cases is presented in Exhibits TN6.8 and TN6.10.

**Infinite Population** An *infinite population* is large enough in relation to the service system so that the population size caused by subtractions or additions to the population (a customer needing service or a serviced customer returning to the population) does not significantly affect the system probabilities. If, in the preceding finite explanation, there were 100 machines instead of six, then if one or two machines broke down, the probabilities for the next breakdowns would not be very different and the assumption could be made without a great deal of error that the population (for all practical purposes) was infinite. Nor would the formulas for "infinite" queuing problems cause much error if applied to a physician with 1,000 patients or a department store with 10,000 customers.

## DISTRIBUTION OF ARRIVALS

When describing a waiting system, we need to define the manner in which customers or the waiting units are arranged for service.

Arrival rate

Waiting line formulas generally require an **arrival rate,** or the number of units per period (such as an average of one every six minutes). A *constant* arrival distribution is periodic, with exactly the same time between successive arrivals. In productive systems, the only arrivals that truly approach a constant interval period are those subject to machine control. Much more common are *variable* (random) arrival distributions.

In observing arrivals at a service facility, we can look at them from two viewpoints: First, we can analyze the time between successive arrivals to see if the times follow some statistical distribution. Usually we assume that the time between arrivals is exponentially distributed. Second, we can set some time length ($T$) and try to determine how many arrivals might enter the system within $T$. We typically assume that the number of arrivals per time unit is Poisson distributed.

Exponential distribution

**Exponential Distribution** In the first case, when arrivals at a service facility occur in a purely random fashion, a plot of the interarrival times yields an **exponential distribution** such as that shown in Exhibit TN6.4. The probability function is

[TN6.1] $$f(t) = \lambda e^{-\lambda t}$$

where $\lambda$ is the mean number of arrivals per time period.

EXHIBIT TN6.4

Exponential Distribution

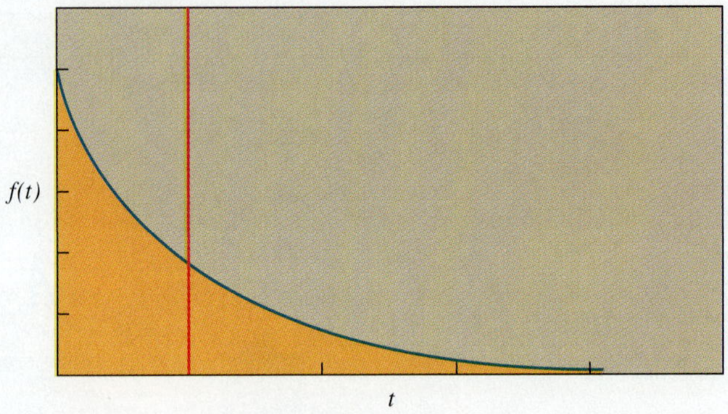


The cumulative area beneath the curve in Exhibit TN6.4 is the summation of Equation TN6.1 over its positive range, which is $e^{-\lambda t}$. This integral allows us to compute the probabilities of arrivals within a specified time. For example, for the case of single arrivals to a waiting line ($\lambda = 1$), the following table can be derived either by solving $e^{-\lambda t}$ or by using Appendix F. Column 2 shows the probability that it will be more than $t$ minutes until the next arrival. Column 3 shows the probability of the next arrival within $t$ minutes (computed as 1 minus column 2)

| (1) $t$ (Minutes) | (2) Probability That the Next Arrival Will Occur in $t$ Minutes or More (from Appendix F or Solving $e^{-t}$) | (3) Probability That the Next Arrival Will Occur in $t$ Minutes or Less [1 − Column (2)] |
|---|---|---|
| 0 | 1.00 | 0 |
| 0.5 | 0.61 | 0.39 |
| 1.0 | 0.37 | 0.63 |
| 1.5 | 0.22 | 0.78 |
| 2.0 | 0.14 | 0.86 |

Poisson distribution

**Poisson Distribution** In the second case, where one is interested in the number of arrivals during some time period $T$, the distribution appears as in Exhibit TN6.5 and is obtained by finding the probability of exactly $n$ arrivals during $T$. If the arrival process is random, the distribution is the **Poisson,** and the formula is

$$P_T(n) = \frac{(\lambda T)^n e^{-\lambda T}}{n!} \quad \text{[TN6.2]}$$

Equation TN6.2 shows the probability of exactly $n$ arrivals in time $T$.[1] For example, if the mean arrival rate of units into a system is three per minute ($\lambda = 3$) and we want to find the probability that exactly five units will arrive within a one-minute period ($n = 5, T = 1$), we have

$$P_1(5) = \frac{(3 \times 1)^5 e^{-3\times 1}}{5!} = \frac{3^5 e^{-3}}{120} = 2.025e^{-3} = 0.101$$

That is, there is a 10.1 percent chance that there will be five arrivals in any one-minute interval.

Although often shown as a smoothed curve, as in Exhibit TN6.5, the Poisson is a discrete distribution. (The curve becomes smoother as $n$ becomes large.) The distribution

EXHIBIT TN6.5

Poisson Distribution for $\lambda T = 3$

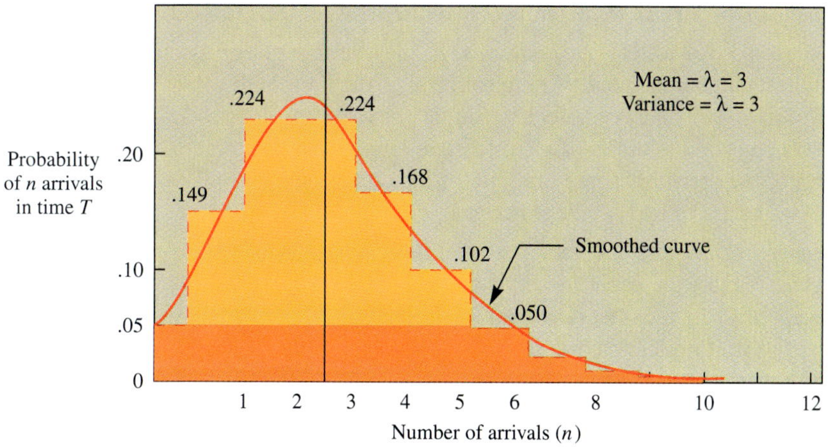


EXHIBIT TN6.6

Customer Arrivals in Queues

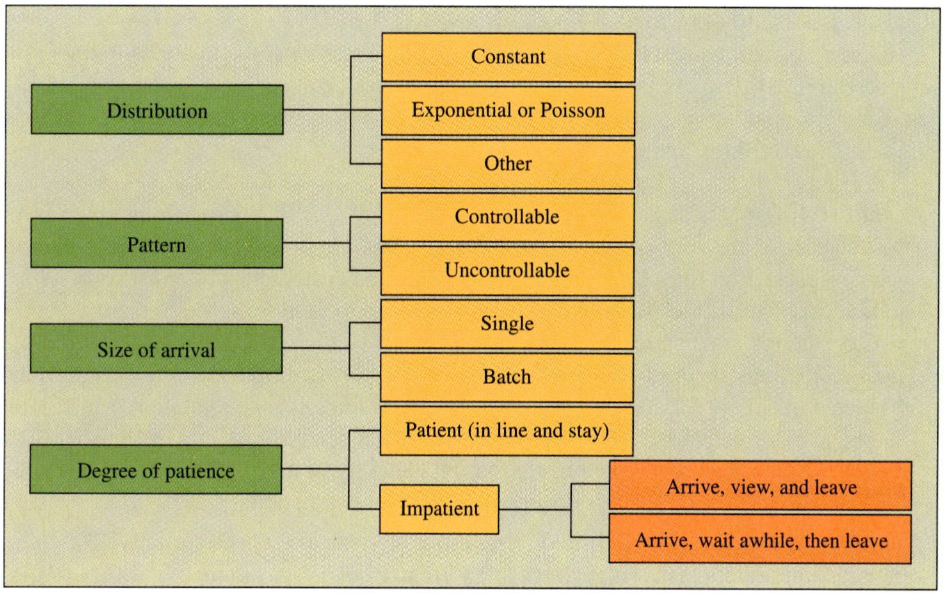


is discrete because $n$ refers, in our example, to the number of arrivals in a system, and this must be an integer. (For example, there cannot be 1.5 arrivals.)

Also note that the exponential and Poisson distributions can be derived from one another. The mean and variance of the Poisson are equal and denoted by $\lambda$. The mean of the exponential is $1/\lambda$ and its variance is $1/\lambda^2$. (Remember that the time between arrivals is exponentially distributed and the number of arrivals per unit of time is Poisson distributed.)

Other arrival characteristics include arrival patterns, size of arrival units, and degree of patience. (See Exhibit TN6.6.)

**Arrival patterns** The arrivals at a system are far more controllable than is generally recognized. Barbers may decrease their Saturday arrival rate (and supposedly shift it to other days of the week) by charging an extra \$1 for adult haircuts or charging adult prices for children's haircuts. Department stores run sales during the off-season or hold one-day-only sales in part for purposes of control. Airlines offer excursion and off-season rates for similar reasons. The simplest of all arrival-control devices is the posting of business hours.

Some service demands are clearly uncontrollable, such as emergency medical demands on a city's hospital facilities. But even in these situations, arrivals at emergency rooms in specific hospitals are controllable to some extent by, say, keeping ambulance drivers in the service region informed of the status of their respective host hospitals.

**Size of arrival units** A *single arrival* may be thought of as one unit. (A unit is the smallest number handled.) A single arrival on the floor of the New York Stock Exchange (NYSE) is 100 shares of stock; a single arrival at an egg-processing plant might be a dozen eggs or a flat of 2½ dozen; a single arrival at a restaurant is a single person.

A *batch arrival* is some multiple of the unit, such as a block of 1,000 shares on the NYSE, a case of eggs at the processing plant, or a party of five at a restaurant.

**Degree of patience** A *patient* arrival is one who waits as long as necessary until the service facility is ready to serve him or her. (Even if arrivals grumble and behave impatiently, the fact that they wait is sufficient to label them as patient arrivals for purposes of waiting line theory.)

There are two classes of *impatient* arrivals. Members of the first class arrive, survey both the service facility and the length of the line, and then decide to leave. Those in the second class arrive, view the situation, join the waiting line, and then, after some period of time, depart. The behavior of the first type is termed *balking,* while the second is termed *reneging*.

## THE QUEUING SYSTEM: FACTORS

The queuing system consists primarily of the waiting line(s) and the available number of servers. Here we discuss issues pertaining to waiting line characteristics and management, line structure, and service rate. Factors to consider with waiting lines include the line length, number of lines, and queue discipline.

**Length** In a practical sense, an infinite line is simply one that is very long in terms of the capacity of the service system. Examples of *infinite potential length* are a line of vehicles backed up for miles at a bridge crossing and customers who must form a line around the block as they wait to purchase tickets at a theater.

Gas stations, loading docks, and parking lots have *limited line capacity* caused by legal restrictions or physical space characteristics. This complicates the waiting line problem not only in service system utilization and waiting line computations but also in the shape of the actual arrival distribution. The arrival denied entry into the line because of lack of space may rejoin the population for a later try or may seek service elsewhere. Either action makes an obvious difference in the finite population case.

**Number of lines** A single line or single file is, of course, one line only. The term multiple lines refers to the single lines that form in front of two or more servers or to single lines that converge at some central redistribution point. The disadvantage of multiple lines in a busy facility is that arrivals often shift lines if several previous services have been of short duration or if those customers currently in other lines appear to require a short service time.

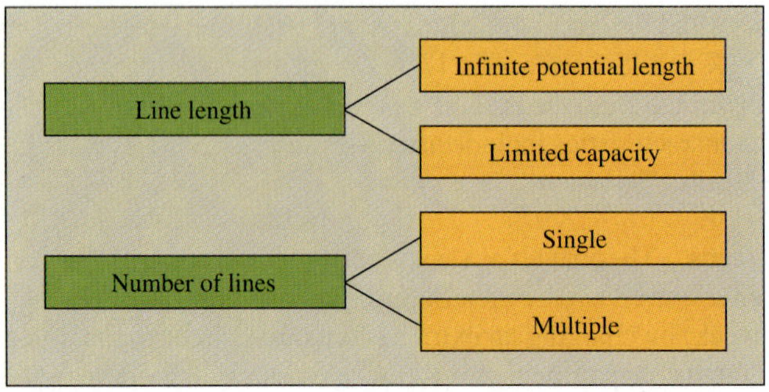


**Queue discipline** A queue discipline is a priority rule or set of rules for determining the order of service to customers in a waiting line. The rules selected can have a dramatic effect on the system's overall performance. The number of customers in line, the average waiting time, the range of variability in waiting time, and the efficiency of the service facility are just a few of the factors affected by the choice of priority rules.

Probably the most common priority rule is first come, first served (FCFS). This rule states that customers in line are served on the basis of their chronological arrival; no other characteristics have any bearing on the selection process. This is popularly accepted as the fairest rule, although in practice it discriminates against the arrival requiring a short service time.

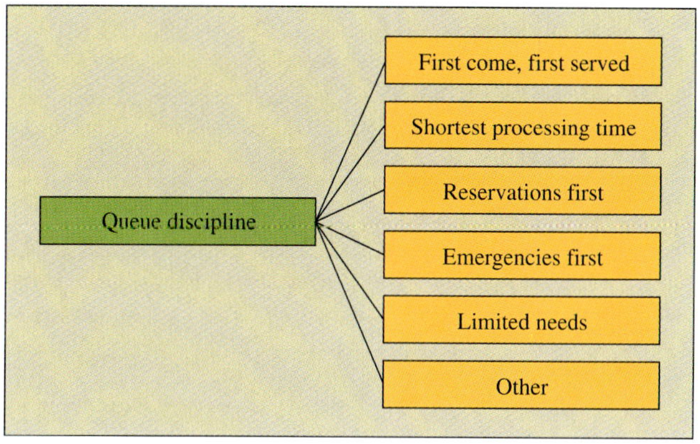


Reservations first, emergencies first, highest-profit customer first, largest orders first, best customers first, longest waiting time in line, and soonest promised date are other examples of priority rules. There are two major practical problems in using any rule: One is ensuring that customers know and follow the rule. The other is ensuring that a system exists to enable employees to manage the line (such as take-a-number systems).

**Service Time Distribution** Another important feature of the waiting structure is the time the customer or unit spends with the server once the service has started. Waiting line formulas generally specify **service rate** as the capacity of the server in number of units per time period (such as 12 completions per hour) and *not* as service time, which might average five minutes each. A constant service time rule states that each service takes exactly the same time. As in constant arrivals, this characteristic is generally limited to machine-controlled operations. Service rate

When service times are random, they can be approximated by the exponential distribution. When using the exponential distribution as an approximation of the service times, we will refer to $\mu$ as the average number of units or customers that can be served per time period.

**Line Structures** As Exhibit TN6.7 shows, the flow of items to be serviced may go through a single line, multiple lines, or some mixtures of the two. The choice of format depends partly on the volume of customers served and partly on the restrictions imposed by sequential requirements governing the order in which service must be performed.

1 **Single channel, single phase** This is the simplest type of waiting line structure, and straightforward formulas are available to solve the problem for standard distribution patterns of arrival and service. When the distributions are nonstandard, the problem is easily solved by computer simulation. A typical example of a single-channel, single-phase situation is the one-person barbershop.

2 **Single channel, multiphase** A car wash is an illustration because a series of services (vacuuming, wetting, washing, rinsing, drying, window cleaning, and parking) is performed in a fairly uniform sequence. A critical factor in the single-channel case with service in series is the amount of buildup of items allowed in front of each service, which in turn constitutes separate waiting lines.

EXHIBIT TN6.7

Line Structures

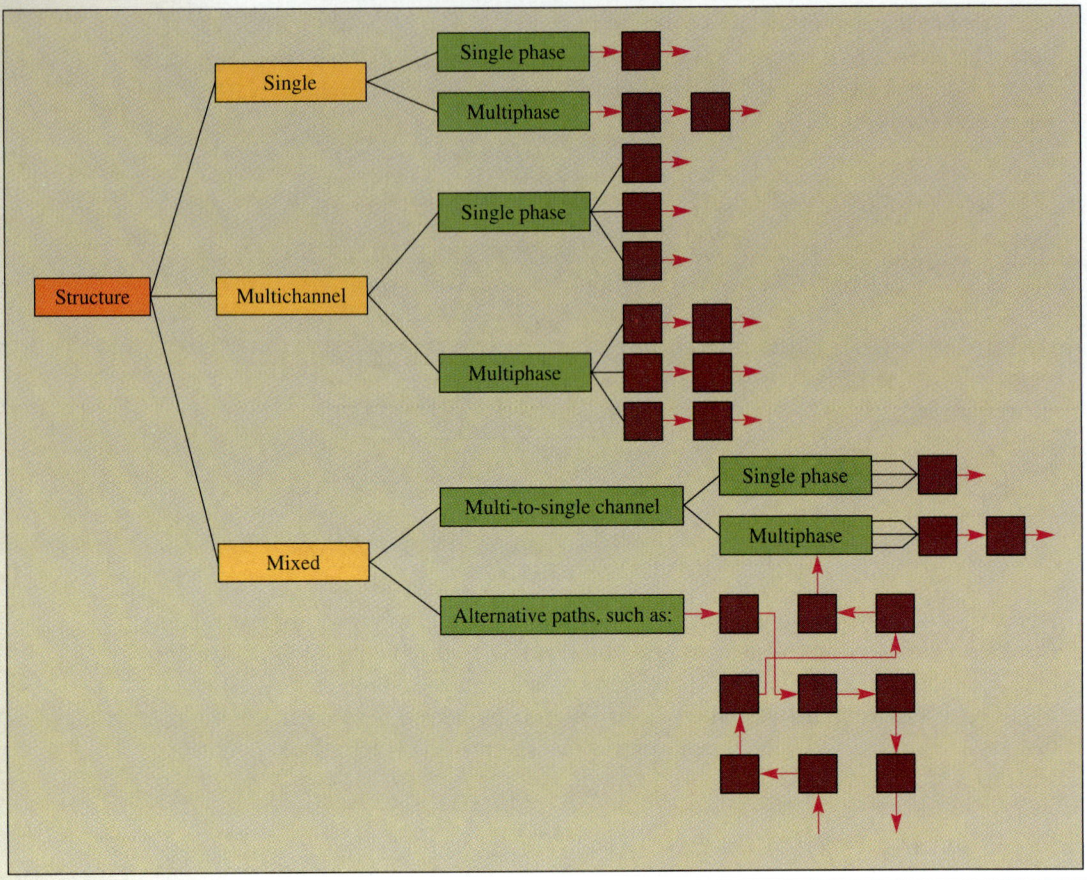


3 **Multichannel, single phase** Tellers' windows in a bank and checkout counters in high-volume department stores exemplify this type of structure. The difficulty with this format is that the uneven service time given each customer results in unequal speed or flow among the lines. This results in some customers being served before others who arrived earlier, as well as in some degree of line shifting. Varying this structure to ensure the servicing of arrivals in chronological order would require forming a single line, from which, as a server becomes available, the next customer in the queue is assigned.

The major problem of this structure is that it requires rigid control of the line to maintain order and to direct customers to available servers. In some instances, assigning numbers to customers in order of their arrival helps alleviate this problem.

4 **Multichannel, multiphase** This case is similar to the preceding one except that two or more services are performed in sequence. The admission of patients in a hospital follows this pattern because a specific sequence of steps is usually followed: initial contact at the admissions desk, filling out forms, making identification tags, obtaining a room assignment, escorting the patient to the room, and so forth. Because several servers are usually available for this procedure, more than one patient at a time may be processed.

5 **Mixed** Under this general heading we consider two subcategories: (1) multiple-to-single channel structures and (2) alternative path structures. Under (1), we find either lines that merge into one for single-phase service, as at a bridge crossing where two lanes merge into one, or lines that merge into one for multiphase service, such as subassembly lines feeding into a main line. Under (2), we encounter two structures that differ in directional flow requirements. The first is similar to the multichannel–multiphase case, except that (a) there may be switching from one channel to the next after the first service has been

rendered, and (b) the number of channels and phases may vary—again—after performance of the first service.

## EXIT

Once a customer is served, two exit fates are possible: (1) The customer may return to the source population and immediately become a competing candidate for service again; or (2) there may be a low probability of reservice. The first case can be illustrated by a machine that has been routinely repaired and returned to duty but may break down again; the second can be illustrated by a machine that has been overhauled or modified and has a low probability of reservice over the near future. In a lighter vein, we might refer to the first as the "recurring-common-cold case" and to the second as the "appendectomy-only-once case."

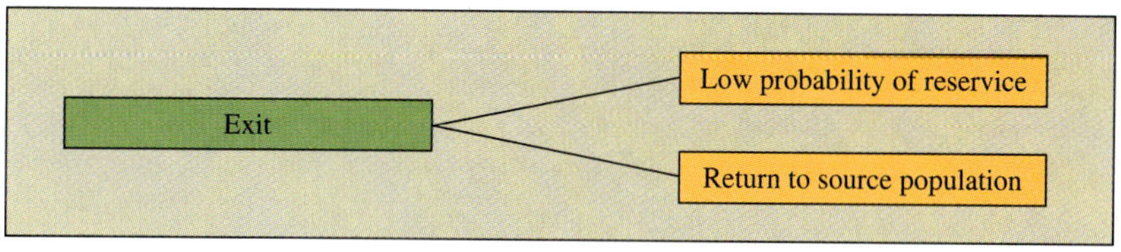


It should be apparent that when the population source is finite, any change in the service performed on customers who return to the population modifies the arrival rate at the service facility. This, of course, alters the characteristics of the waiting line under study and necessitates reanalysis of the problem.

# WAITING LINE MODELS

In this section we present four sample waiting line problems followed by their solutions. Each has a slightly different structure (see Exhibit TN6.8) and solution equation (see Exhibit TN6.10). There are more types of models than these four, but the formulas and solutions become quite complicated, and those problems are generally solved using computer simulation (see Technical Note 15). Also, in using these formulas, keep in mind that they are steady-state formulas derived on the assumption that the process under study is ongoing. Thus, they may provide inaccurate results when applied to processes where the arrival rates and/or service rates change over time. The Excel Spreadsheet Queue.xls, developed by John McClain of Cornell University and included on the CD-Rom, can be used to solve these problems.

EXHIBIT TN6.8

### Properties of Some Specific Waiting Line Models

| MODEL | LAYOUT | SERVICE PHASE | SOURCE POPULATION | ARRIVAL PATTERN | QUEUE DISCIPLINE | SERVICE PATTERN | PERMISSIBLE QUEUE LENGTH | TYPICAL EXAMPLE |
|---|---|---|---|---|---|---|---|---|
| 1 | Single channel | Single | Infinite | Poisson | FCFS | Exponential | Unlimited | Drive-in teller at bank; one-lane toll bridge |
| 2 | Single channel | Single | Infinite | Poisson | FCFS | Constant | Unlimited | Roller coaster rides in amusement park |
| 3 | Multichannel | Single | Infinite | Poisson | FCFS | Exponential | Unlimited | Parts counter in auto agency |
| 4 | Single channel | Single | Finite | Poisson | FCFS | Exponential | Unlimited | Machine breakdown and repair in a factory |

Here is a quick preview of our four problems to illustrate each of the four waiting line models in Exhibits TN6.8 and TN6.10. Exhibit TN6.9 defines the notations used in Exhibit TN6.10.

## EXHIBIT TN6.9 Notations for Equations (Exhibit TN6.10)

**INFINITE QUEUING NOTATION: MODELS 1–3**

$\lambda$ = Arrival rate

$\mu$ = Service rate

$\frac{1}{\mu}$ = Average service time

$\frac{1}{\lambda}$ = Average time between arrivals

$\rho$ = Ratio of total arrival rate to service rate for a single server $\left(\frac{\lambda}{\mu}\right)^*$

$\bar{n}_l$ = Average number waiting in line

$\bar{n}_s$ = Average number in system (including any being served)

$\bar{t}_l$ = Average time waiting in line

$\bar{t}_s$ = Average total time in system (including time to be served)

$n$ = Number of units in the system

$M$ = Number of identical service channels

$P_n$ = Probability of exactly $n$ units in system

$P_w$ = Probability of waiting in line

**FINITE QUEUING NOTATION: MODEL 4**

$D$ = Probability that an arrival must wait in line

$F$ = Efficiency factor, a measure of the effect of having to wait in line

$H$ = Average number of units being serviced

$J$ = Population source less those in queuing system $(N - n)$

$L$ = Average number of units in line

$M$ = Number of service channels

$n$ = Average number of units in queuing system (including the one being served)

$N$ = Number of units in population source

$P_n$ = Probability of exactly $n$ units in queuing system

$T$ = Average time to perform the service

$U$ = Average time between customer service requirements

$W$ = Average waiting time in line

$X$ = Service factor, or proportion of service time required

* For single-server queues this is equivalent to utilization.

## EXHIBIT TN6.10 Equations for Solving Four Model Problems

Model 1

$$\bar{n}_l = \frac{\lambda^2}{\mu(\mu-\lambda)} \qquad \bar{t}_l = \frac{\lambda}{\mu(\mu-\lambda)} \qquad P_n = \left(1-\frac{\lambda}{\mu}\right)\left(\frac{\lambda}{\mu}\right)^n \qquad P_o = \left(1-\frac{\lambda}{\mu}\right) \tag{TN6.3}$$

$$\bar{n}_s = \frac{\lambda}{\mu-\lambda} \qquad \bar{t}_s = \frac{1}{\mu-\lambda} \qquad \rho = \frac{\lambda}{\mu}$$

Model 2

$$\bar{n}_l = \frac{\lambda^2}{2\mu(\mu-\lambda)} \qquad \bar{t}_l = \frac{\lambda}{2\mu(\mu-\lambda)} \tag{TN6.4}$$

$$\bar{n}_s = \bar{n}_l + \frac{\lambda}{\mu} \qquad \bar{t}_s = \bar{t}_l + \frac{1}{\mu}$$

(Exhibit TN6.11 provides the value of $\bar{n}_l$ given $\rho = \lambda/\mu$ and the number of servers $M$.)

Model 3

$$\bar{n}_s = \bar{n}_l + \lambda/\mu \qquad \bar{t}_s = \bar{n}_l/\lambda + 1/\mu \tag{TN6.5}$$

$$\bar{t}_l = \bar{n}_l/\lambda \qquad P_w = \bar{n}_l(M-\rho)/\rho$$

Model 4 is a finite queuing situation that is most easily solved by using finite tables. These tables, in turn, require the manipulation of specific terms.

Model 4

$$X = \frac{T}{T+U} \qquad H = FNX \qquad L = N(1-F) \qquad n = L+H$$

$$P_n = \frac{N!}{(N-n)!}X^n P_0 \qquad J = NF(1-X) \tag{TN6.6}$$

$$W = \frac{L(T-U)}{N-L} = \frac{LT}{H} \qquad F = \frac{T+U}{T+U+W}$$

**Problem 1: Customers in line.** A bank wants to know how many customers are waiting for a drive-in teller, how long they have to wait, the utilization of the teller, and what the service rate would have to be so that 95 percent of the time there will not be more than three cars in the system at any time.

**Problem 2: Equipment selection.** A franchise for Robot Car Wash must decide which equipment to purchase out of a choice of three. Larger units cost more but wash cars faster. To make the decision, costs are related to revenue.

**Problem 3: Determining the number of servers.** An auto agency parts department must decide how many clerks to employ at the counter. More clerks cost more money, but there is a savings because mechanics wait less time.

**Problem 4: Finite population source.** Whereas the previous models assume a large population, finite queuing employs a separate set of equations for those cases where the calling customer population is small. In this last problem, mechanics must service four weaving machines to keep them operating. Based on the costs associated with machines being idle and the costs of mechanics to service them, the problem is to decide how many mechanics to use.

### EXAMPLE TN6.1: CUSTOMERS IN LINE

Western National Bank is considering opening a drive-through window for customer service. Management estimates that customers will arrive at the rate of 15 per hour. The teller who will staff the window can service customers at the rate of one every three minutes.

**Part 1** Assuming Poisson arrivals and exponential service, find

1 Utilization of the teller.
2 Average number in the waiting line.
3 Average number in the system.
4 Average waiting time in line.
5 Average waiting time in the system, including service.

### SOLUTION—Part 1

1 The average utilization of the teller is

$$\rho = \frac{\lambda}{\mu} = \frac{15}{20} = 75 \text{ percent}$$

2 The average number in the waiting line is

$$\bar{n}_l = \frac{\lambda^2}{\mu(\mu - \lambda)} = \frac{(15)^2}{20(20 - 15)} = 2.25 \text{ customers}$$

3 The average number in the system is

$$\bar{n}_s = \frac{\lambda}{\mu - \lambda} = \frac{15}{20 - 15} = 3 \text{ customers}$$

4 Average waiting time in line is

$$\bar{t}_l = \frac{\lambda}{\mu(\mu - \lambda)} = \frac{15}{20(20 - 15)} = 0.15 \text{ hour, or 9 minutes}$$

5 Average waiting time in the system is

$$\bar{t}_s = \frac{1}{\mu - \lambda} = \frac{1}{20 - 15} = 0.2 \text{ hour, or 12 minutes}$$

**Part 2** Because of limited space availability and a desire to provide an acceptable level of service, the bank manager would like to ensure, with 95 percent confidence, that no more than three cars will be in the system at any time. What is the present level of service for the three-car limit? What level of teller use must be attained and what must be the service rate of the teller to ensure the 95 percent level of service? ←

*SOLUTION*—**Part 2**

The present level of service for three or fewer cars is the probability that there are 0, 1, 2, or 3 cars in the system. From Model 1, Exhibit TN6.10.

$$P_n = \left(1 - \frac{\lambda}{\mu}\right)\left(\frac{\lambda}{\mu}\right)^n$$

$$\begin{aligned}
\text{at } n = 0,\ P_0 &= (1 - 15/20)\quad (15/20)^0 = 0.250 \\
\text{at } n = 1,\ P_1 &= (1/4)\quad (15/20)^1 = 0.188 \\
\text{at } n = 2,\ P_2 &= (1/4)\quad (15/20)^2 = 0.141 \\
\text{at } n = 3,\ P_3 &= (1/4)\quad (15/20)^3 = \underline{0.106} \\
& \qquad\qquad 0.685 \quad \text{or} \quad 68.5 \text{ percent}
\end{aligned}$$

The probability of having more than three cars in the system is 1.0 minus the probability of three or fewer cars (1.0 − 0.685 = 31.5 percent).

For a 95 percent service level of three or fewer cars, this states that $P_0 + P_1 + P_2 + P_3 =$ 95 percent.

$$0.95 = \left(1 - \frac{\lambda}{\mu}\right)\left(\frac{\lambda}{\mu}\right)^0 + \left(1 - \frac{\lambda}{\mu}\right)\left(\frac{\lambda}{\mu}\right)^1 + \left(1 - \frac{\lambda}{\mu}\right)\left(\frac{\lambda}{\mu}\right)^2 + \left(1 - \frac{\lambda}{\mu}\right)\left(\frac{\lambda}{\mu}\right)^3$$

$$0.95 = \left(1 - \frac{\lambda}{\mu}\right)\left[1 + \frac{\lambda}{\mu} + \left(\frac{\lambda}{\mu}\right)^2 + \left(\frac{\lambda}{\mu}\right)^3\right]$$

We can solve this by trial and error for values of $\lambda/\mu$. If $\lambda/\mu = 0.50$,

$$0.95 \stackrel{?}{=} 0.5(1 + 0.5 + 0.25 + 0.125)$$

$$0.95 \neq 0.9375$$

With $\lambda/\mu = 0.45$,

$$0.95 \stackrel{?}{=} (1 - 0.45)(1 + 0.45 + 0.203 + 0.091)$$

$$0.95 \neq 0.96$$

With $\lambda/\mu = 0.47$,

$$0.95 \stackrel{?}{=} (1 - 0.47)(1 + 0.47 + 0.221 + 0.104) = 0.9512$$

$$0.95 \approx 0.95135$$

Therefore, with the utilization $\rho = \lambda/\mu$ of 47 percent, the probability of three or fewer cars in the system is 95 percent.

To find the rate of service required to attain this 95 percent service level, we simply solve the equation $\lambda/\mu = 0.47$, where $\lambda$ = number of arrivals per hour. This gives $\mu = 32$ per hour. That is, the teller must serve approximately 32 people per hour (a 60 percent increase over the original 20-per-hour capability) for 95 percent confidence that not more than three cars will be in the system. Perhaps service may be speeded up by modifying the method of service, adding another teller, or limiting the types of transactions available at the drive-through window. Note that with the condition of 95 percent confidence that three or fewer cars will be in the system, the teller will be idle 53 percent of the time. ←

## EXAMPLE TN6.2: EQUIPMENT SELECTION

The Robot Company franchises combination gas and car wash stations throughout the United States. Robot gives a free car wash for a gasoline fill-up or, for a wash alone, charges \$0.50. Past experience shows that the number of customers that have car washes following fill-ups is about the same as for a wash alone. The average profit on a gasoline fill-up is about \$0.70, and the cost of the car wash to Robot is \$0.10. Robot stays open 14 hours per day.

Robot has three power units and drive assemblies, and a franchisee must select the unit preferred. Unit I can wash cars at the rate of one every five minutes and is leased for \$12 per day. Unit II, a larger unit, can wash cars at the rate of one every four minutes but costs \$16 per day. Unit III, the largest, costs \$22 per day and can wash a car in three minutes.

The franchisee estimates that customers will not wait in line more than five minutes for a car wash. A longer time will cause Robot to lose the gasoline sales as well as the car wash sale.

If the estimate of customer arrivals resulting in washes is 10 per hour, which wash unit should be selected?

## SOLUTION

Using unit I, calculate the average waiting time of customers in the wash line ($\mu$ for unit I = 12 per hour). From the Model 2 equations (Exhibit TN6.10),

$$\bar{t}_l = \frac{\lambda}{2\mu(\mu-\lambda)} = \frac{10}{2(12)(12-10)} = 0.208 \text{ hour, or } 12\tfrac{1}{12} \text{ minutes}$$

For unit II at 15 per hour,

$$\bar{t}_l = \frac{10}{2(15)(15-10)} = 0.067 \text{ hour, or 4 minutes}$$

If waiting time is the only criterion, unit II should be purchased. But before we make the final decision, we must look at the profit differential between both units.

With unit I, some customers would balk and renege because of the $12\frac{1}{12}$-minute wait. And, although this greatly complicates the mathematical analysis, we can gain some estimate of lost sales with unit I by increasing $\bar{t}_l = 5$ minutes or $\frac{1}{12}$ hour (the average length of time customers will wait) and solving for $\lambda$. This would be the effective arrival rate of customers:

$$\bar{t}_l = \frac{\lambda}{2\mu(\mu-\lambda)}$$

$$\lambda = \frac{2\bar{t}_l\mu^2}{1+2\bar{t}_l\mu}$$

$$\lambda = \frac{2\left(\frac{1}{12}\right)(12)^2}{1+2\left(\frac{1}{12}\right)(12)} = 8 \text{ per hour}$$

Therefore, because the original estimate of $\lambda$ was 10 per hour, an estimated 2 customers per hour will be lost. Lost profit of 2 customers per hour × 14 hours × $\frac{1}{2}$(\$0.70 fill-up profit + \$0.40 wash profit) = \$15.40 per day. ←

Because the additional cost of unit II over unit I is only $4 per day, the loss of $15.40 profit obviously warrants installing unit II.

The original five-minute maximum wait constraint is satisfied by unit II. Therefore unit III is not considered unless the arrival rate is expected to increase.

## EXAMPLE TN6.3: DETERMINING THE NUMBER OF SERVERS

In the service department of the Glenn-Mark Auto Agency, mechanics requiring parts for auto repair or service present their request forms at the parts department counter. The parts clerk fills a request while the mechanic waits. Mechanics arrive in a random (Poisson) fashion at the rate of 40 per hour, and a clerk can fill requests at the rate of 20 per hour (exponential). If the cost for a parts clerk is $6 per hour and the cost for a mechanic is $12 per hour, determine the optimum number of clerks to staff the counter. (Because of the high arrival rate, an infinite source may be assumed.)

### SOLUTION

First, assume that three clerks will be used because having only one or two clerks would create infinitely long lines (since $\lambda = 40$ and $\mu = 20$). The equations for Model 3 from Exhibit TN6.10 will be used here. But first we need to obtain the average number in line using the table of Exhibit TN6.11. Using the table and values $\lambda/\mu = 2$ and $M = 3$, we obtain $\bar{n}_l = 0.8888$ mechanic.

At this point, we see that we have an average of 0.8888 mechanic waiting all day. For an eight-hour day at $12 per hour, there is a loss of mechanic's time worth 0.8888 mechanic $\times$ $12 per hour $\times$ 8 hours = $85.32.

Our next step is to reobtain the waiting time if we add another parts clerk. We then compare the added cost of the additional employee with the time saved by the mechanics. Again, using the table of Exhibit TN6.11 but with $M = 4$, we obtain

$\bar{n}_l = 0.1730$ mechanic in line

0.1730 $\times$ $12 $\times$ 8 hours = $16.61 cost of a mechanic waiting in line

| | |
|---|---|
| Value of mechanics' time saved is $85.32 − $16.61 | = $68.71 |
| Cost of an additional parts clerk is 8 hours × $6/hour | = 48.00 |
| Cost of reduction by adding fourth clerk | = $20.71 |

This problem could be expanded to consider the addition of runners to deliver parts to mechanics; the problem then would be to determine the optimal number of runners. This, however, would have to include the added cost of lost time caused by errors in parts receipts. For example, a mechanic would recognize a wrong part at the counter and obtain immediate correction, whereas the parts runner might not. ←

## EXAMPLE TN6.4: FINITE POPULATION SOURCE

Studies of a bank of four weaving machines at the Loose Knit textile mill have shown that, on average, each machine needs adjusting every hour and that the current servicer averages $7\frac{1}{2}$ minutes per adjustment. Assuming Poisson arrivals, exponential service, and a machine idle time cost of $40 per hour, determine if a second servicer (who also averages $7\frac{1}{2}$ minutes per adjustment) should be hired at a rate of $7 per hour.

### SOLUTION

This is a finite queuing problem that can be solved by using finite queuing tables. (See Exhibit TN6.12.) The approach in this problem is to compare the cost of machine downtime (either waiting in line or being serviced) and of one repairer, to the cost of machine downtime and two repairers. We

EXHIBIT TN6.11

## Expected Number of People Waiting in Line ($n_l$) for Various Values of $M$ and $\lambda/\mu$

NUMBER OF SERVICE CHANNELS, $M$

| $\lambda/\mu$ | 1 | 2 | 3 | 4 | 5 | 6 | 7 | 8 | 9 | 10 | 11 | 12 | 13 | 14 | 15 |
|---|---|---|---|---|---|---|---|---|---|---|---|---|---|---|---|
| 0.10 | 0.0111 | | | | | | | | | | | | | | |
| 0.15 | 0.0264 | 0.0006 | | | | | | | | | | | | | |
| 0.20 | 0.0500 | 0.0020 | | | | | | | | | | | | | |
| 0.25 | 0.0833 | 0.0039 | | | | | | | | | | | | | |
| 0.30 | 0.1285 | 0.0069 | | | | | | | | | | | | | |
| 0.35 | 0.1884 | 0.0110 | | | | | | | | | | | | | |
| 0.40 | 0.2666 | 0.0166 | | | | | | | | | | | | | |
| 0.45 | 0.3681 | 0.0239 | 0.0019 | | | | | | | | | | | | |
| 0.50 | 0.5000 | 0.0333 | 0.0030 | | | | | | | | | | | | |
| 0.55 | 0.6722 | 0.0149 | 0.0043 | | | | | | | | | | | | |
| 0.60 | 0.9090 | 0.0593 | 0.0061 | | | | | | | | | | | | |
| 0.65 | 1.2071 | 0.0767 | 0.0084 | | | | | | | | | | | | |
| 0.70 | 1.6333 | 0.0976 | 0.0112 | | | | | | | | | | | | |
| 0.75 | 2.2500 | 0.1227 | 0.0147 | | | | | | | | | | | | |
| 0.80 | 3.2000 | 0.1523 | 0.0189 | | | | | | | | | | | | |
| 0.85 | 4.8165 | 0.1873 | 0.0239 | 0.0031 | | | | | | | | | | | |
| 0.90 | 8.1000 | 0.2285 | 0.0300 | 0.0041 | | | | | | | | | | | |
| 0.95 | 18.0500 | 0.2767 | 0.0371 | 0.0053 | | | | | | | | | | | |
| 1.0 | | 0.3333 | 0.0454 | 0.0067 | | | | | | | | | | | |
| 1.2 | | 0.6748 | 0.0940 | 0.0158 | | | | | | | | | | | |
| 1.4 | | 1.3449 | 0.1778 | 0.0324 | 0.0059 | | | | | | | | | | |
| 1.6 | | 2.8441 | 0.3128 | 0.0604 | 0.0121 | | | | | | | | | | |
| 1.8 | | 7.6731 | 0.5320 | 0.1051 | 0.0227 | 0.0047 | | | | | | | | | |
| 2.0 | | | 0.8888 | 0.1730 | 0.0390 | 0.0090 | | | | | | | | | |
| 2.2 | | | 1.4907 | 0.2770 | 0.0059 | 0.0158 | | | | | | | | | |
| 2.4 | | | 2.1261 | 0.4205 | 0.1047 | 0.0266 | 0.0065 | | | | | | | | |
| 2.6 | | | 4.9322 | 0.6581 | 0.1609 | 0.0425 | 0.0110 | | | | | | | | |
| 2.8 | | | 12.2724 | 1.0000 | 0.2411 | 0.0659 | 0.0180 | | | | | | | | |
| 3.0 | | | | 1.5282 | 0.3541 | 0.0991 | 0.0282 | 0.0077 | | | | | | | |
| 3.2 | | | | 2.3855 | 0.5128 | 0.1452 | 0.0427 | 0.0122 | | | | | | | |
| 3.4 | | | | 3.9060 | 0.7365 | 0.2085 | 0.0631 | 0.0189 | | | | | | | |
| 3.6 | | | | 7.0893 | 1.0550 | 0.2947 | 0.0912 | 0.0283 | 0.0084 | | | | | | |
| 3.8 | | | | 16.9366 | 1.5181 | 0.4114 | 0.1292 | 0.0412 | 0.0127 | | | | | | |
| 4.0 | | | | | 2.2164 | 0.5694 | 0.1801 | 0.0590 | 0.0189 | | | | | | |
| 4.2 | | | | | 3.3269 | 0.7837 | 0.2475 | 0.0827 | 0.0273 | 0.0087 | | | | | |
| 4.4 | | | | | 5.2675 | 1.0777 | 0.3364 | 0.1142 | 0.0389 | 0.0128 | | | | | |
| 4.6 | | | | | 9.2885 | 1.4857 | 0.4532 | 0.1555 | 0.0541 | 0.0184 | | | | | |
| 4.8 | | | | | 21.6384 | 2.0708 | 0.6071 | 0.2092 | 0.0742 | 0.0260 | | | | | |
| 5.0 | | | | | | 2.9375 | 0.8102 | 0.2785 | 0.1006 | 0.0361 | 0.0125 | | | | |
| 5.2 | | | | | | 4.3004 | 1.0804 | 0.3680 | 0.1345 | 0.0492 | 0.0175 | | | | |
| 5.4 | | | | | | 6.6609 | 1.4441 | 0.5871 | 0.1779 | 0.0663 | 0.0243 | 0.0085 | | | |
| 5.6 | | | | | | 11.5178 | 1.9436 | 0.6313 | 0.2330 | 0.0683 | 0.0330 | 0.0119 | | | |
| 5.8 | | | | | | 26.3726 | 2.6481 | 0.8225 | 0.3032 | 0.1164 | 0.0443 | 0.0164 | | | |
| 6.0 | | | | | | | 3.6878 | 1.0707 | 0.3918 | 0.1518 | 0.0590 | 0.0224 | | | |
| 6.2 | | | | | | | 5.2979 | 1.3967 | 0.5037 | 0.1964 | 0.0775 | 0.0300 | 0.0113 | | |
| 6.4 | | | | | | | 8.0768 | 1.8040 | 0.6454 | 0.2524 | 0.1008 | 0.0398 | 0.0153 | | |
| 6.6 | | | | | | | 13.7992 | 2.4198 | 0.8247 | 0.3222 | 0.1302 | 0.0523 | 0.0205 | | |
| 6.8 | | | | | | | 31.1270 | 3.2441 | 1.0533 | 0.4090 | 0.1666 | 0.0679 | 0.0271 | 0.0105 | |
| 7.0 | | | | | | | | 4.4471 | 1.3471 | 0.5172 | 0.2119 | 0.0876 | 0.0357 | 0.0141 | |
| 7.2 | | | | | | | | 6.3133 | 1.7288 | 0.6521 | 0.2677 | 0.1119 | 0.0463 | 0.0187 | |
| 7.4 | | | | | | | | 9.5102 | 2.2324 | 0.8202 | 0.3364 | 0.1420 | 0.0595 | 0.0245 | 0.0097 |
| 7.6 | | | | | | | | 16.0379 | 2.9113 | 1.0310 | 0.4211 | 0.1789 | 0.0761 | 0.0318 | 0.0129 |
| 7.8 | | | | | | | | 35.8956 | 3.8558 | 1.2972 | 0.5250 | 0.2243 | 0.0966 | 0.0410 | 0.0168 |
| 8.0 | | | | | | | | | 5.2264 | 1.6364 | 0.6530 | 0.2796 | 0.1214 | 0.0522 | 0.0220 |
| 8.2 | | | | | | | | | 7.3441 | 2.0736 | 0.8109 | 0.3469 | 0.1520 | 0.0663 | 0.0283 |
| 8.4 | | | | | | | | | 10.9592 | 2.6470 | 1.0060 | 0.4288 | 0.1891 | 0.0834 | 0.0361 |
| 8.6 | | | | | | | | | 18.3223 | 3.4160 | 1.2484 | 0.5236 | 0.2341 | 0.1043 | 0.0459 |
| 8.8 | | | | | | | | | 40.6824 | 4.4805 | 1.5524 | 0.6501 | 0.2885 | 0.1208 | 0.0577 |
| 9.0 | | | | | | | | | | 6.0183 | 1.9366 | 0.7980 | 0.3543 | 0.1603 | 0.0723 |
| 9.2 | | | | | | | | | | 8.3869 | 2.4293 | 0.9788 | 0.4333 | 0.1974 | 0.0899 |
| 9.4 | | | | | | | | | | 12.4183 | 3.0732 | 1.2010 | 0.5267 | 0.2419 | 0.1111 |
| 9.6 | | | | | | | | | | 20.6160 | 3.9318 | 1.4752 | 0.5437 | 0.2952 | 0.1367 |
| 9.8 | | | | | | | | | | 45.4769 | 5.1156 | 1.8165 | 0.7827 | 0.3699 | 0.16731 |
| 10 | | | | | | | | | | | 6.8210 | 2.2465 | 0.9506 | 0.4352 | 0.2040 |

EXHIBIT TN6.12

## Finite Queuing Tables

POPULATION 4

| X | M | D | F | X | M | D | F | X | M | D | F |
|---|---|---|---|---|---|---|---|---|---|---|---|
| .015 | 1 | .045 | .999 | | 1 | .479 | .899 | .400 | 3 | .064 | .992 |
| .022 | 1 | .066 | .998 | .180 | 2 | .088 | .991 | | 2 | .372 | .915 |
| .030 | 1 | .090 | .997 | | 1 | .503 | .887 | | 1 | .866 | .595 |
| .034 | 1 | .102 | .996 | .190 | 2 | .098 | .990 | .420 | 3 | .074 | .990 |
| .038 | 1 | .114 | .995 | | 1 | .526 | .874 | | 2 | .403 | .903 |
| .042 | 1 | .126 | .994 | .200 | 3 | .008 | .999 | | 1 | .884 | .572 |
| .046 | 1 | .137 | .993 | | 2 | .108 | .988 | .440 | 3 | .085 | .986 |
| .048 | 1 | .143 | .992 | .200 | 1 | .549 | .862 | | 2 | .435 | .891 |
| .052 | 1 | .155 | .991 | .210 | 3 | .009 | .999 | | 1 | .900 | .551 |
| .054 | 1 | .161 | .990 | | 2 | .118 | .986 | .460 | 3 | .097 | .985 |
| .058 | 1 | .173 | .989 | | 1 | .572 | .849 | | 2 | .466 | .878 |
| .060 | 1 | .179 | .988 | .220 | 3 | .011 | .999 | | 1 | .914 | .530 |
| .062 | 1 | .184 | .987 | | 2 | .129 | .984 | .480 | 3 | .111 | .983 |
| .064 | 1 | .190 | .986 | | 1 | .593 | .835 | | 2 | .498 | .864 |
| .066 | 1 | .196 | .985 | .230 | 3 | .012 | .999 | .480 | 1 | .926 | .511 |
| .070 | 2 | .014 | .999 | | 2 | .140 | .982 | .500 | 3 | .125 | .980 |
| | 1 | .208 | .984 | | 1 | .614 | .822 | | 2 | .529 | .850 |
| .075 | 2 | .016 | .999 | .240 | 3 | .014 | .999 | | 1 | .937 | .492 |
| | 1 | .222 | .981 | | 2 | .151 | .980 | .520 | 3 | .141 | .976 |
| .080 | 2 | .018 | .999 | | 1 | .634 | .808 | | 2 | .561 | .835 |
| | 1 | .237 | .978 | .250 | 3 | .016 | .999 | | 1 | .947 | .475 |
| .085 | 2 | .021 | .999 | | 2 | .163 | .977 | .540 | 3 | .157 | .972 |
| | 1 | .251 | .975 | | 1 | .654 | .794 | | 2 | .592 | .820 |
| .090 | 2 | .023 | .999 | .260 | 3 | .018 | .998 | | 1 | .956 | .459 |
| | 1 | .265 | .972 | | 2 | .175 | .975 | .560 | 3 | .176 | .968 |
| .095 | 2 | .026 | .999 | | 1 | .673 | .780 | | 2 | .623 | .805 |
| | 1 | .280 | .969 | .270 | 3 | .020 | .998 | | 1 | .963 | .443 |
| .100 | 2 | .028 | .999 | | 2 | .187 | .972 | .580 | 3 | .195 | .964 |
| | 1 | .294 | .965 | | 1 | .691 | .766 | | 2 | .653 | .789 |
| .105 | 2 | .031 | .998 | .280 | 3 | .022 | .99s8 | | 1 | .969 | .429 |
| | 1 | .308 | .962 | | 2 | .200 | .968 | .600 | 3 | .216 | .959 |
| .110 | 2 | .034 | .998 | | 1 | .708 | .752 | | 2 | .682 | .774 |
| | 1 | .321 | .958 | .290 | 3 | .024 | .998 | | 1 | .975 | .415 |
| .115 | 2 | .037 | .998 | | 2 | .213 | .965 | .650 | 3 | .275 | .944 |
| | 1 | .335 | .954 | | 1 | .725 | .738 | | 2 | .752 | .734 |
| .120 | 2 | .041 | .997 | .300 | 3 | .027 | .997 | | 1 | .985 | .384 |
| | 1 | .349 | .950 | | 2 | .226 | .962 | .700 | 3 | .343 | .926 |
| .125 | 2 | .044 | .997 | | 1 | .741 | .724 | | 2 | .816 | .695 |
| | 1 | .362 | .945 | .310 | 3 | .030 | .997 | | 1 | .991 | .357 |
| .130 | 2 | .047 | .997 | | 2 | .240 | .958 | .750 | 3 | .422 | .905 |
| | 1 | .376 | .941 | | 1 | .756 | .710 | | 2 | .871 | .657 |
| .135 | 2 | .051 | .996 | .320 | 3 | .033 | .997 | | 1 | .996 | .333 |
| | 1 | .389 | .936 | | 2 | .254 | .954 | .800 | 3 | .512 | .880 |
| .140 | 2 | .055 | .996 | | 1 | .771 | .696 | | 2 | .917 | .621 |
| | 1 | .402 | .931 | .330 | 3 | .036 | .996 | | 1 | .998 | .312 |
| .145 | 2 | .058 | .995 | | 2 | .268 | .950 | .850 | 3 | .614 | .852 |
| | 1 | .415 | .926 | | 1 | .785 | .683 | | 2 | .954 | .587 |
| .150 | 2 | .062 | .995 | .340 | 3 | .039 | .996 | | 1 | .999 | .294 |
| | 1 | .428 | .921 | | 2 | .282 | .945 | .900 | 3 | .729 | .821 |
| .155 | 2 | .066 | .994 | | 1 | .798 | .670 | | 2 | .979 | .555 |
| | 1 | .441 | .916 | .360 | 3 | .047 | .994 | .950 | 3 | .857 | .786 |
| .160 | 2 | .071 | .994 | | 2 | .312 | .936 | | 2 | .995 | .526 |
| | 1 | .454 | .910 | | 1 | .823 | .644 | | | | |
| .165 | 2 | .075 | .993 | .380 | 3 | .055 | .993 | | | | |
| | 1 | .466 | .904 | | 2 | .342 | .926 | | | | |
| .170 | 2 | .079 | .993 | | 1 | .846 | .619 | | | | |

do this by finding the average number of machines that are in the service system and multiply this number by the downtime cost per hour. To this we add the repairers' cost.

Before we proceed, we first define some terms:

$N$ = Number of machines in the population
$M$ = Number of repairers
$T$ = Time required to service a machine
$U$ = Average time a machine runs before requiring service
$X$ = Service factor, or proportion of service time required for each machine ($X = T/(T + U)$)
$L$ = Average number of machines waiting in line to be serviced
$H$ = Average number of machines being serviced

The values to be determined from the finite tables are

$D$ = Probability that a machine needing service will have to wait
$F$ = Efficiency factor, which measures the effect of having to wait in line to be serviced

The tables are arranged according to three variables: $N$, population size; $X$, service factor; and $M$, the number of service channels (repairers in this problem). To look up a value, first find the table for the correct $N$ size, then search the first column for the appropriate $X$, and finally find the line for $M$. Then read off $D$ and $F$. (In addition to these values, other characteristics about a finite queuing system can be found by using the finite formulas.)

To solve the problem, consider Case I with one repairer and Case II with two repairers.

*Case I: One repairer.* From problem statement,

$N = 4$
$M = 1$
$T = 7\frac{1}{2}$ minutes
$U = 60$ minutes

$$X = \frac{T}{T + U} = \frac{7.5}{7.5 + 60} = 0.111$$

From Exhibit TN6.12, which displays the table for $N = 4$, $F$ is interpolated as being approximately 0.957 at $X = 0.111$ and $M = 1$.

The number of machines waiting in line to be serviced is $L$, where

$$L = N(1 - F) = 4(1 - 0.957) = 0.172 \text{ machines}$$

The number of machines being serviced is $H$, where

$$H = FNX = 0.957(4)(0.111) = 0.425 \text{ machines}$$

Exhibit TN6.13 shows the cost resulting from unproductive machine time and the cost of the repairer. ←

EXHIBIT TN6.13

A Comparison of Downtime Costs for Service and Repair of Four Machines

| Number of Repairers | Number of Machines Down $(H + L)$ | Cost per Hour for Machines Down $[(H + L) \times \$40/\text{Hour}]$ | Cost of Repairers ($7/Hour Each) | Total Cost per Hour |
|---|---|---|---|---|
| 1 | 0.597 | $23.88 | $ 7.00 | $30.88 |
| 2 | 0.451 | 18.04 | 14.00 | 32.04 |

*Case II: Two repairers.* From Exhibit TN6.12, at $X = 0.111$ and $M = 2$, $F = 0.998$.

The number of machines waiting in line, $L$, is

$$L = N(1 - F) = 4(1 - 0.998) = 0.008 \text{ machines}$$

The number of machines being serviced, $H$, is

$$H = FNX = 0.998(4)(0.111) = 0.443 \text{ machines}$$

The costs for the machines being idle and for the two repairers are shown in Exhibit TN6.13. The final column of that exhibit shows that retaining just one repairer is the best choice. ←

## COMPUTER SIMULATION OF WAITING LINES

Some waiting line problems that seem simple on first impression turn out to be extremely difficult or impossible to solve. Throughout this supplement we have been treating waiting line situations that are independent; that is, either the entire system consists of a single phase, or else each service that is performed in a series is independent. (This could happen if the output of one service location is allowed to build up in front of the next one so that this, in essence, becomes a calling population for the next service.) When a series of services is performed in sequence where the output rate of one becomes the input rate of the next, we can no longer use the simple formulas. This is also true for any problem where conditions do not meet the requirements of the equations, as specified in Exhibit TN6.9. The technique best suited to solving this type of problem is computer simulation. We treat the topic of modeling and simulation in Technical Note 15.

## CONCLUSION

Waiting line problems both challenge and frustrate those who try to solve them. The basic objective is to balance the cost of waiting with the cost of adding more resources. For a service system this means that the utilization of a server may be quite low to provide a short waiting time to the customer. One main concern in dealing with waiting line problems is which procedure or priority rule to use in selecting the next product or customer to be served.

Many queuing problems appear simple until an attempt is made to solve them. This technical note has dealt with the simpler problems. When the situation becomes more complex, when there are multiple phases or where services are performed only in a particular sequence, computer simulation is necessary to obtain the optimal solution.

## KEY TERMS

**Queue** A line of waiting persons, jobs, things, or the like.

**Queuing system** Consists of three major components: (1) the source population and the way customers arrive at the system, (2) the serving systems, and (3) how customers exit the system.

**Arrival rate** The expected number of customers that arrive each period.

**Exponential distribution** A probability distribution often associated with interarrival times.

**Poisson distribution** Probability distribution often used to describe the number of arrivals during a given time period.

**Service rate** The capacity of a server measured in number of units that can be processed over a given time period.

# FORMULA REVIEW

**Exponential distribution**

[TN6.1] $$f(t) = \lambda e^{-\lambda t}$$

**Poisson distribution**

[TN6.2] $$P_T(n) = \frac{(\lambda T)^n e^{-\lambda T}}{n!}$$

**Model 1 (See Exhibit TN6.7.)**

[TN6.3]
$$\bar{n}_l = \frac{\lambda^2}{\mu(\mu - \lambda)} \qquad \bar{t}_l = \frac{\lambda}{\mu(\mu - \lambda)} \qquad P_n = \left(1 - \frac{\lambda}{\mu}\right)\left(\frac{\lambda}{\mu}\right)^n \qquad P_o = \left(1 - \frac{\lambda}{\mu}\right)$$
$$\bar{n}_s = \frac{\lambda}{\mu - \lambda} \qquad \bar{t}_s = \frac{1}{\mu - \lambda} \qquad \rho = \frac{\lambda}{\mu}$$

**Model 2**

[TN6.4]
$$\bar{n}_l = \frac{\lambda^2}{2\mu(\mu - \lambda)} \qquad \bar{t}_l = \frac{\lambda}{2\mu(\mu - \lambda)}$$
$$\bar{n}_s = \bar{n}_l + \frac{\lambda}{\mu} \qquad \bar{t}_s = \bar{t}_l + \frac{1}{\mu}$$

**Model 3**

[TN6.5]
$$\bar{n}_s = \bar{n}_l + \lambda/\mu$$
$$\bar{t}_l = \bar{n}_l/\lambda$$
$$\bar{t}_s = \bar{n}_l/\lambda + 1/\mu$$
$$P_w = \bar{n}_l(M - \rho)/\rho$$

**Model 4**

[TN6.6]
$$X = \frac{T}{T + U} \qquad H = FNX \qquad L = N(1 - F) \qquad n = L + H$$
$$P_n = \frac{N!}{(N - n)!} X^n P_0 \qquad J = NF(1 - X)$$
$$W = \frac{L(T + U)}{N - L} = \frac{LT}{H} \qquad F = \frac{T + U}{T + U + W}$$

# SOLVED PROBLEMS

## SOLVED PROBLEM 1

Quick Lube Inc. operates a fast lube and oil change garage. On a typical day, customers arrive at the rate of three per hour, and lube jobs are performed at an average rate of one every 15 minutes. The mechanics operate as a team on one car at a time.

Assuming Poisson arrivals and exponential service, find

*a.* Utilization of the lube team.
*b.* The average number of cars in line.
*c.* The average time a car waits before it is lubed.
*d.* The total time it takes to go through the system (that is, waiting in line plus lube time).

## Solution

$\lambda = 3, \mu = 4$

a. Utilization $\rho = \dfrac{\lambda}{\mu} = \dfrac{3}{4} = 75\%.$

b. $\bar{n}_l = \dfrac{\lambda^2}{\mu(\mu - \lambda)} = \dfrac{3^2}{4(4-3)} = \dfrac{9}{4} = 2.25$ cars in line.

c. $\bar{t}_l = \dfrac{\lambda}{\mu(\mu - \lambda)} = \dfrac{3}{4(4-3)} = \dfrac{3}{4} = 45$ minutes in line.

d. $\bar{t}_s = \dfrac{1}{\mu - \lambda} = \dfrac{1}{1} = 1$ hour (waiting + lube).

## SOLVED PROBLEM 2

American Vending Inc. (AVI) supplies vended food to a large university. Because students often kick the machines out of anger and frustration, management has a constant repair problem. The machines break down on an average of three per hour, and the breakdowns are distributed in a Poisson manner. Downtime costs the company \$25/hour per machine, and each maintenance worker gets \$4 per hour. One worker can service machines at an average rate of five per hour, distributed exponentially; two workers working together can service seven per hour, distributed exponentially; and a team of three workers can do eight per hour, distributed exponentially.

What is the optimal maintenance crew size for servicing the machines?

## Solution

*Case I—One worker:*

$\lambda = 3$/hour Poisson, $\mu = 5$/hour exponential

There is an average number of machines in the system of:

$$\bar{n}_s = \frac{\lambda}{\mu - \lambda} = \frac{3}{5-3} = \frac{3}{2} = 1\tfrac{1}{2} \text{ machines}$$

Downtime cost is \$25 × 1.5 = \$37.50 per hour; repair cost is \$4.00 per hour; and total cost per hour for 1 worker is \$37.50 + \$4.00 = \$41.50.

| | |
|---|---|
| Downtime (1.5 × \$25) = | \$37.50 |
| Labor (1 worker × \$4) = | 4.00 |
| | \$41.50 |

*Case II—Two workers:*

$\lambda = 3, \mu = 7$

$$\bar{n}_s = \frac{\lambda}{\mu - \lambda} = \frac{3}{7-3} = .75 \text{ machines}$$

| | |
|---|---|
| Downtime (.75 × \$25) = | \$18.75 |
| Labor (2 workers × \$4.00) = | 8.00 |
| | \$26.75 |

*Case III—Three workers:*

$\lambda = 3, \mu = 8$

$$\bar{n}_s = \frac{\mu}{\mu - \lambda} = \frac{3}{8-3} = \frac{3}{5} = .60 \text{ machines}$$

| | |
|---|---|
| Downtime (.60 × \$25) = | \$15.75 |
| Labor (3 workers × \$4) = | 12.00 |
| | \$27.00 |

Comparing the costs for one, two, or three workers, we see that Case II with two workers is the optimal decision.

## REVIEW AND DISCUSSION QUESTIONS

1 Cultural factors affect waiting lines. For example, fast checkout lines (e.g., 10 items or less) are uncommon in Japan. Why do you think this is so?
2 How many waiting lines did you encounter during your last airline flight?
3 Distinguish between a *channel* and a *phase.*
4 What is the major cost trade-off that must be made in managing waiting line situations?
5 Which assumptions are necessary to employ the formulas given for Model 1?
6 In what way might the first-come, first-served rule be unfair to the customer waiting for service in a bank or hospital?
7 Define, in a practical sense, what is meant by an *exponential service time.*
8 Would you expect the exponential distribution to be a good approximation of service times for
   *a.* Buying an airline ticket at the airport?
   *b.* Riding a merry-go-round at a carnival?
   *c.* Checking out of a hotel?
   *d.* Completing a midterm exam in your OM class?
9 Would you expect the Poisson distribution to be a good approximation of
   *a.* Runners crossing the finish line in the Boston Marathon?
   *b.* Arrival times of the students in your OM class?
   *c.* Arrival times of the bus to your stop at school?

## PROBLEMS

1 Students arrive at the Administrative Services Office at an average of one every 15 minutes, and their requests take on average 10 minutes to be processed. The service counter is staffed by only one clerk, Judy Gumshoes, who works eight hours per day. Assume Poisson arrivals and exponential service times.
   *a.* What percentage of time is Judy idle?
   *b.* How much time, on average, does a student spend waiting in line?
   *c.* How long is the (waiting) line on average?
   *d.* What is the probability that an arriving student (just before entering the Administrative Services Office) will find at least one other student waiting in line?

1. *a.* 33.33%.
*b.* 20 minutes.
*c.* 1.33 students.
*d.* 44.44%.

2 The managers of the Administrative Services Office estimate that the time a student spends waiting in line costs them (due to goodwill loss and so on) $10 per hour. To reduce the time a student spends waiting, they know that they need to improve Judy's processing time (see Problem 1). They are currently considering the following two options:
   *a.* Install a computer system, with which Judy expects to be able to complete a student request 40 percent faster (from 2 minutes per request to 1 minute and 12 seconds, for example).
   *b.* Hire another temporary clerk, who will work at the same rate as Judy.
   If the computer costs $99.50 to operate per day, while the temporary clerk gets paid $75 per day, is Judy right to prefer the hired help? Assume Poisson arrivals and exponential service times.

2. Yes.

3 Sharp Discounts Wholesale Club has two service desks, one at each entrance of the store. Customers arrive at each service desk at an average of one every six minutes. The service rate at each service desk is four minutes per customer.
   *a.* How often (what percentage of time) is each service desk idle?
   *b.* What is the probability that both service clerks are busy?
   *c.* What is the probability that both service clerks are idle?
   *d.* How many customers, on average, are waiting in line in front of each service desk?
   *e.* How much time does a customer spend at the service desk (waiting plus service time)?

3. *a.* 33.33%.
*b.* 44.44%.
*c.* 11.11%.
*d.* 1.33 customers.
*e.* .20 hours or 12 minutes.

4 Sharp Discounts Wholesale Club is considering consolidating its two service desks (see Problem 3) into one location, staffed by two clerks. The clerks will continue to work at the same individual speed of four minutes per customer.
   *a.* What is the probability of waiting in line?
   *b.* How many customers, on average, are waiting in line?
   *c.* How much time does a customer spend at the service desk (waiting plus service time)?
   *d.* Do you think the Sharp Discounts Wholesale Club should consolidate the service desks?

4. *a.* 55%.
*b.* 1.1 customers.
*c.* .12 hours or 7.2 minutes.
*d.* Yes.

5. $\bar{t}_s = 4.125$ minutes.
$\bar{n}_l = 4.05$ cars.
$\bar{n}_s = 4.95$ cars.

5 Burrito King (a new fast-food franchise opening up nationwide) has successfully automated burrito production for its drive-up fast-food establishments. The Burro-Master 9000 requires a constant 45 seconds to produce a batch of burritos. It has been estimated that customers will arrive at the drive-up window according to a Poisson distribution at an average of one every 50 seconds. To help determine the amount of space needed for the line at the drive-up window, Burrito King would like to know the expected average time in the system, the average line length (in cars), and the average number of cars in the system (both in line and at the window).

6. *a.* 3 minutes.
*b.* 45 seconds.
*c.* Yes, about 36 seconds.

6 The Bijou Theater in Hermosa Beach, California, shows vintage movies. Customers arrive at the theater line at the rate of 100 per hour. The ticket seller averages 30 seconds per customer, which includes placing validation stamps on customers' parking lot receipts and punching their frequent watcher cards. (Because of these added services, many customers don't get in until after the feature has started.)

*a.* What is the average customer waiting time in the system?
*b.* What would be the effect on system waiting time of having a second ticket taker doing nothing but validations and card punching, thereby cutting the average service time to 20 seconds?
*c.* Would system waiting time be less than you found in *b* if a second window was opened with each server doing all three tasks?

7. *a.* $2\frac{1}{12}$ people.
*b.* $2\frac{11}{12}$ people.
*c.* 0.208 hour.
*d.* 0.291 hour.
*e.* Infinity.

7 To support National Heart Week, the Heart Association plans to install a free blood pressure testing booth in El Con Mall for the week. Previous experience indicates that, on the average, 10 persons per hour request a test. Assume arrivals are Poisson from an infinite population. Blood pressure measurements can be made at a constant time of five minutes each. Assume the queue length can be infinite with FCFS discipline.

*a.* What average number in line can be expected?
*b.* What average number of persons can be expected to be in the system?
*c.* What is the average amount of time that a person can expect to spend in line?
*d.* On the average, how much time will it take to measure a person's blood pressure, including waiting time?
*e.* On weekends, the arrival rate can be expected to increase to over 12 per hour. What effect will this have on the number in the waiting line?

8. *a.* 3 people.
*b.* 1 minute.
*c.* 75%.
*d.* .4219.
Time reduced by 22 seconds: avg. no. of people reduced by 1.125.

8 A cafeteria serving line has a coffee urn from which customers serve themselves. Arrivals at the urn follow a Poisson distribution at the rate of three per minute. In serving themselves, customers take about 15 seconds, exponentially distributed.

*a.* How many customers would you expect to see on the average at the coffee urn?
*b.* How long would you expect it to take to get a cup of coffee?
*c.* What percentage of time is the urn being used?
*d.* What is the probability that three or more people are in the cafeteria?

If the cafeteria installs an automatic vendor that dispenses a cup of coffee at a constant time of 15 seconds, how does this change your answers to *a* and *b*?

9. *a.* $L = 4(.055) = .22$ waiting.
*b.* $W = .466$ hours.
*c.* $D = .362$.

9 An engineering firm retains a technical specialist to assist four design engineers working on a project. The help that the specialist gives engineers ranges widely in time consumption. The specialist has some answers available in memory; others require computation, and still others require significant search time. On the average, each request for assistance takes the specialist one hour.

The engineers require help from the specialist on the average of once each day. Because each assistance takes about an hour, each engineer can work for seven hours, on the average, without assistance. One further point: Engineers needing help do not interrupt if the specialist is already involved with another problem.

Treat this as a finite queuing problem and answer the following questions:

*a.* How many engineers, on average, are waiting for the technical specialist for help?
*b.* What is the average time that an engineer has to wait for the specialist?
*c.* What is the probability that an engineer will have to wait in line for the specialist?

10. *a.* 2 people.
*b.* 6 minutes.
*c.* .2964.
*d.* 67%.
*e.* 0.03375 hour.

10 L. Winston Martin (an allergist in Tucson) has an excellent system for handling his regular patients who come in just for allergy injections. Patients arrive for an injection and fill out a name slip, which is then placed in an open slot that passes into another room staffed by one or two nurses. The specific injections for a patient are prepared, and the patient is called through a speaker system into the room to receive the injection. At certain times during the day, patient load drops and only one nurse is needed to administer the injections.

Let's focus on the simpler case of the two—namely, when there is one nurse. Also assume that patients arrive in a Poisson fashion and the service rate of the nurse is exponentially distributed. During this slower period, patients arrive with an interarrival time of approximately three minutes. It takes the nurse an average of two minutes to prepare the patients' serum and administer the injection.

*a.* What is the average number you would expect to see in Dr. Martin's facilities?
*b.* How long would it take for a patient to arrive, get an injection, and leave?
*c.* What is the probability that there will be three or more patients on the premises?
*d.* What is the utilization of the nurse?
*e.* Assume three nurses are available. Each takes an average of two minutes to prepare the patients' serum and administer the injection. What is the average total time of a patient in the system?

11 The Judy Gray Income Tax Service is analyzing its customer service operations during the month prior to the April filing deadline. On the basis of past data it has been estimated that customers arrive according to a Poisson process with an average interarrival time of 12 minutes. The time to complete a return for a customer is exponentially distributed with a mean of 10 minutes. Based on this information, answer the following questions:

*a.* If you went to Judy, how much time would you allow for getting your return done?
*b.* On average, how much room should be allowed for the waiting area?
*c.* If Judy stayed in the office 12 hours per day, how many hours on average, per day, would she be busy?
*d.* What is the probability that the system is idle?
*e.* If the arrival rate remained unchanged but the average time in system must be 45 minutes or less, what would need to be changed?

11. *a.* 1 hour.
*b.* 4.17.
*c.* 10.
*d.* .167.
*e.* $\mu \leq 6.33$.

12 A graphics reproduction firm has four units of equipment that are automatic but occasionally become inoperative because of the need for supplies, maintenance, or repair. Each unit requires service roughly twice each hour or, more precisely, each unit of equipment runs an average of 30 minutes before needing service. Service times vary widely, ranging from a simple service (such as pressing a restart switch or repositioning paper) to more involved equipment disassembly. The average service time, however, is five minutes.

Equipment downtime results in a loss of $20 per hour. The one equipment attendant is paid $6 per hour.

Using finite queuing analysis, answer the following questions:

*a.* What is the average number of units in line?
*b.* What is the average number of units still in operation?
*c.* What is the average number of units being serviced?
*d.* The firm is considering adding another attendant at the same $6 rate. Should the firm do it?

12. *a.* Units in line = .288 machines.
*b.* Units in operation = 3.18.
*c.* Units being serviced = .531.
*d.* No. Added cost would be $1.42 per hour.

13 Benny the Barber owns a one-chair shop. At barber college, they told Benny that his customers would exhibit a Poisson arrival distribution and that he would provide an exponential service distribution. His market survey data indicate that customers arrive at a rate of two per hour. It will take Benny an average of 20 minutes to give a haircut. Based on these figures, find the following:

*a.* The average number of customers waiting.
*b.* The average time a customer waits.
*c.* The average time a customer is in the shop.
*d.* The average utilization of Benny's time.

13. *a.* $1\frac{1}{3}$.
*b.* $\frac{2}{3}$ hour.
*c.* 1 hour.
*d.* 67%.

14 Benny the Barber (see Problem 13) is considering the addition of a second chair. Customers would be selected for a haircut on a FCFS basis from those waiting. Benny has assumed that both barbers would take an average of 20 minutes to give a haircut, and that business would remain unchanged with customers arriving at a rate of two per hour. Find the following information to help Benny decide if a second chair should be added:

*a.* The average number of customers waiting.
*b.* The average time a customer waits.
*c.* The average time a customer is in the shop.

14. *a.* .0837.
*b.* 0.0418 hours or 2.51 minutes.
*c.* .3751 hours or 22.51 minutes.

15 Customers enter the camera department of a store at the average rate of six per hour. The department is staffed by one employee, who takes an average of six minutes to serve each arrival. Assume this is a simple Poisson arrival exponentially distributed service time situation.

*a.* As a casual observer, how many people would you expect to see in the camera department (excluding the clerk)? How long would a customer expect to spend in the camera department (total time)?

15. *a.* 1.5 people; 15 minutes.
*b.* 60%.
*c.* 1 − .784 = .216.
*d.* 0.1099 hour.

*b.* What is the utilization of the clerk?
*c.* What is the probability that there are more than two people in the camera department (excluding the clerk)?
*d.* Another clerk has been hired for the camera department who also takes an average of six minutes to serve each arrival. How long would a customer expect to spend in the department now?

16. *a.* 9.167 minutes.
*b.* 9.091 people.
*c.* 0.7513.
*d.* 0.9091; 90.9% of the time.
*e.* 5.0 minutes.

16 Cathy Livingston, bartender at the Tucson Racquet Club, can serve drinks at the rate of one every 50 seconds. During a hot evening recently, the bar was particularly busy and every 55 seconds someone was at the bar asking for a drink.
*a.* Assuming that everyone in the bar drank at the same rate and that Cathy served people on a first-come, first-served basis, how long would you expect to have to wait for a drink?
*b.* How many people would you expect to be waiting for drinks?
*c.* What is the probability that three or more people are waiting for drinks?
*d.* What is the utilization of the bartender (how busy is she)?
*e.* If the bartender is replaced with an automatic drink dispensing machine, how would this change your answer in part *a*?

17. *a.* 0.833.
*b.* 5 documents.
*c.* 0.2 hour.
*d.* 0.4822.
*e.* $\bar{n}_l$ tends to infinity.

17 An office employs several clerks who originate documents and one operator who enters the document information in a word processor. The group originates documents at a rate of 25 per hour. The operator can enter the information with average exponentially distributed time of two minutes. Assume the population is infinite, arrivals are Poisson, and queue length is infinite with FCFS discipline.
*a.* Calculate the percentage utilization of the operator.
*b.* Calculate the average number of documents in the system.
*c.* Calculate the average time in the system.
*d.* Calculate the probability of four or more documents being in the system.
*e.* If another clerk were added, the document origination rate would increase to 30 per hour. What would this do to the word processor workload? Show why.

18. *a.* 0.667.
*b.* 2 students.
*c.* 0.5 hour.
*d.* 0.1976.
*e.* $\bar{n}_l \to \infty$.

18 A study-aid desk staffed by a graduate student has been established to answer students' questions and help in working problems in your OM course. The desk is staffed eight hours per day. The dean wants to know how the facility is working. Statistics show that students arrive at a rate of four per hour, and the distribution is approximately Poisson. Assistance time averages 10 minutes, distributed exponentially. Assume population and line length can be infinite and queue discipline is FCFS.
*a.* Calculate the percentage utilization of the graduate student.
*b.* Calculate the average number of students in the system.
*c.* Calculate the average time in the system.
*d.* Calculate the probability of four or more students being in line or being served.
*e.* Before a test, the arrival of students increases to six per hour on the average. What does this do to the average length of the line?

19. *a.* 4.17 people.
*b.* $\frac{1}{2}$ minute.
*c.* 83.3%.
*d.* $1 - .422 = .578$.

19 At the California border inspection station, vehicles arrive at the rate of 10 per minute in a Poisson distribution. For simplicity in this problem, assume that there is only one lane and one inspector, who can inspect vehicles at the rate of 12 per minute in an exponentially distributed fashion.
*a.* What is the average length of the waiting line?
*b.* What is the average time that a vehicle must wait to get through the system?
*c.* What is the utilization of the inspector?
*d.* What is the probability that when you arrive there will be three or more vehicles ahead of you?

20. *a.* .175.
*b.* .101 minutes or 6.06 seconds.
*c.* .596.
*d.* .143 minutes or 8.58 seconds.

20 The California border inspection station (see Problem 19) is considering the addition of a second inspector. The vehicles would wait in one lane and then be directed to the first available inspector. Arrival rates would remain the same (10 per minute) and the new inspector would process vehicles at the same rate as the first inspector (12 per minute).
*a.* What would be the average length of the waiting line?
*b.* What would be the average time that a vehicle must wait to get through the system? If a second lane was added (one lane for each inspector):
*c.* What would be the average length of the waiting line?
*d.* What would be the average time that a vehicle must wait to get through the system?

21. 1 repairman $\$\infty$/hr.
2 repairmen $120/hr.
3 repairmen $100/hr.

21 During the campus Spring Fling, the bumper car amusement attraction has a problem of cars becoming disabled and in need of repair. Repair personnel can be hired at the rate of $20 per hour, but they only work as one team. Thus, if one person is hired, he or she works alone; two or three people work together on the same repair.

One repairer can fix cars in an average time of 30 minutes. Two repairers take 20 minutes, and three take 15 minutes. While these cars are down, lost income is $40 per hour. Cars tend to break down at the rate of two per hour.

How many repairers should be hired?

22 A toll tunnel has decided to experiment with the use of a debit card for the collection of tolls. Initially, only one lane will be used. Cars are estimated to arrive at this experimental lane at the rate of 750 per hour. It will take exactly four seconds to verify the debit card.

*a.* In how much time would you expect the customer to wait in line, pay with the debit card, and leave?

*b.* How many cars would you expect to see in the system?

22. *a.* 14 seconds.
*b.* 2.92 cars.

## SELECTED BIBLIOGRAPHY

Chase, R. B. "The Mall Is My Factory: Reflections of a Service Junkie." *Productions and Operations Management,* Winter 1996, pp. 298–308.

Cooper, R. B. *Introduction to Queuing Theory.* 2nd ed. New York: Elsevier–North Holland, 1980.

Davis, M. M., and M. J. Maggard, "An Analysis of Customer Satisfaction with Waiting Times in a Two-Stage Service Process." *Journal of Operations Management* 9, no. 3 (August 1990), pp. 324–34.

Fitzsimmons, J. A., and M. J. Fitzsimmons. *Service Management.* Burr Ridge, IL: Irwin/McGraw-Hill, 1998, pp. 318–39.

Hillier, F. S., et al. *Queuing Tables and Graphs.* New York: Elsevier–North Holland, 1981.

Katz, K. L.; B. M. Larson; and R. C. Larson. "Prescription for the Waiting-in-Line Blues: Entertain, Enlighten, and Engage." *Sloan Management Review* 32, no. 2 (Winter 1991), pp. 44–53.

Winston, W. L., and S. C. Albright. *Practical Management Science: Spreadsheet Modeling and Application.* New York: Duxbury, 1997, pp. 537–79.

## FOOTNOTE

1 $n!$ is defined as $n(n-1)(n-2)\cdots(2)(1)$.

chapter

chapter seven

# QUALITY MANAGEMENT

## CHAPTER OUTLINE AND KEY TERMS

# 7

John F. Welch, retiring chairman of General Electric Co., describes how he drives his quality program into GE's far-flung plants: "You can't behave in a calm, rational manner. You've got to be out there on the lunatic fringe. You have to tell your people that quality is critical to survival, you have to demand everybody gets trained, you have to cheerlead, you have to have incentive bonuses, you have to say, 'We must do this.'" The quality control program, Mr. Welch says, is a mammoth undertaking: 40 percent of GE executive bonuses, which run as high as $1 million, now will depend on implementation of the program. Previously bonuses were based only on profit and cash flow.

GE's quality program was borrowed from Motorola, Inc. Six Sigma quality is a disciplined method of eliminating virtually all defects from every one of the company's products, processes, and transactions. GE has spent over half a billion dollars training most of its professional workforce in the concepts. Virtually every professional in the company is now a "Green Belt," which requires three weeks of training and a completed Six Sigma project. To get the coveted "Black Belt" requires a minimum four months of training in statistical and other quality-enhancing measures. The black belts then roam GE plants full-time to set up quality improvement projects. The company has trained over 10,000 black belts. In all, GE has invested hundreds of millions of dollars in training, in specific projects, and in computer systems to analyze and run the quality control program.

The program is producing a variety of benefits, Mr. Welch says. "Your customers are happy with you, you are not firefighting, you are not running a reactive mode." GE expects the program will save $7–10 billion over the next decade. This chapter and the accompanying technical note will get you started on your "Black Belt" and a leadership position within a company like GE.

**Source:** Adapted (and updated) from "Charging Ahead: To Keep GE's Profits Rising, Welch Pushes Quality Control Plan," *The Wall Street Journal*, January 22, 1997, p. A1. 

Vol. I "Quality"
Vol. VII
"Manufacturing Quality at Honda" "A Day In the Life of Quality at Honda" "SPC at Honda"

GE's black belt program is typical of the intense effort that world-class companies are directing to quality management. Today total quality management is taken as a fundamental requirement for any organization to compete, let alone lead its market. The quality movement started in Japan with its Deming Prize for quality. First awarded in 1951, it marked the beginning of an effort that has accelerated over the past 20 years. In the late 1950s the U.S. Department of Defense adopted a series of quality standards that were later adopted by the British Standards Institute and have now evolved into the International Organization for Standardization (ISO) 9000 standards. Formal national recognition of quality in the United States came about with the first Malcolm Baldrige National Quality Award in 1987, and in European countries, with the European Quality Award in 1991.

The quality movement is more than just a series of awards and quality standards—the movement involves a total rethinking of how a business should be run. The term *total quality management (TQM)* has been coined to describe a philosophy that makes quality values the driving force behind leadership, design, planning, and improvement initiatives. The belief is that for long-term financial success, quality is essential. The Baldrige Quality Award provides a template reflecting this philosophy in U.S. organizations.

Global

Quality competition is a global issue. Meeting global quality standards is difficult due to the differences in operating practices in different countries. The International Organization for Standardization (ISO) defined how things should be measured. In one country, a tolerance may be measured in centimeters, while in another, the measurement may be tenths of an inch. ISO specifications go beyond just measurement, however, and include how processes should be documented and what processes are essential to ensuring quality. Using the ISO standards, a company producing a part in China can be compared to a company producing the same part in the United States. These standards, the Baldrige Award, and the quality philosophies of some of the quality gurus are addressed in this chapter. We also discuss the important quality management topics of the cost of quality, continuous improvement, fail-safing, and measuring of service quality.

Returning to the karate analogy, in becoming a black belt you need to know the moves and leveraging techniques for overcoming your opponent. The same is true in quality: statistics are used for leveraging, and our moves include statistical process control, sampling plans, and process capability analysis. The details of these techniques are the topics of the supplement to this chapter. Now, let's break some bricks!

## TOTAL QUALITY MANAGEMENT

Exhibit 7.1 presents a framework summarizing the important elements of TQM discussed in this chapter and its supplement.

Total quality management (TQM)

We define **total quality management (TQM)** as "managing the entire organization so that it excels on all dimensions of products and services that are important to the customer." This definition is more applicable than another commonly used one—"conformance to specifications." Though valid for goods production, the second definition is problematic for many services. Precise specifications for service quality are hard to define and measure. It is possible, however, to find out what's important to the customer and then create the kind of organizational culture that motivates and enables the worker to deliver a quality service.

The philosophical elements of TQM stress the operation of the firm using quality as the integrating element. The generic tools consist of (1) various *statistical process control (SPC)* methods that are used for problem solving and continuous improvement by quality teams and (2) quality function deployment, which is typically used by managers to drive the voice of the customer into the organization. (See Chapter 5 for a discussion of QFD.) Tools of the QC department consist of *statistical quality control (SQC)* methods that are used by the quality professionals working in this department.

EXHIBIT 7.1

**Elements of Total Quality Management**

TQM

Managing the entire organization so that it excels in all dimensions of products and services that are important to the customer.

**Philosophical Element**

- Customer-driven quality
- Leadership
- Continuous improvement
- Employee participation and development
- Quick response
- Design quality and prevention
- Management by fact
- Partnership development
- Corporate responsibility and citizenship

**Generic Tools**

- SPC tools:
  1. Process flowcharts
  2. Check sheets
  3. Pareto analysis and histogram
  4. Cause and effect (or fishbone) diagrams
  5. Run charts
  6. Scatter diagrams
  7. Control charts
- Quality function deployment

**Tools of the QC Department**

- SQC methods:
  1. Sampling plans
  2. Process capability
  3. Taguchi methods

## THE MALCOLM BALDRIGE NATIONAL QUALITY AWARD

In 1987 the Malcolm Baldrige National Quality Improvement Act established the nation's annual award to recognize total quality management in American industry. The Malcolm Baldrige National Quality Award represents the U.S. government's endorsement of quality as an essential part of successful business strategy. The Baldrige Award seeks to improve quality and productivity by

www.quality.nist.gov

1 Helping to stimulate American companies to improve quality and productivity for the pride of recognition while obtaining a competitive edge through decreased costs and increased profits.
2 Establishing guidelines and criteria that can be used by business, industrial, governmental, and other organizations in evaluating quality improvement efforts.
3 Recognizing the achievements of companies that improve the quality of their goods and services and thereby provide an example to others.
4 Providing specific guidance for other American organizations that wish to learn how to manage for high quality by making available detailed information on how winning organizations were able to change their cultures and achieve quality eminence.

Although applications for the Baldrige award have declined over the past few years, quality standards are being reborn in various state-sponsored quality awards. The Baldrige organization sends out over 200,000 criteria packages per year, and in 1999 began to offer awards for health care and for educational institutions. The Baldrige program is clearly meeting its goals of awareness and use of its template. As noted earlier, the Baldrige is a relative newcomer to the quality award business. For over 40 years Japan has recognized its corporate quality leaders by bestowing on them the prestigious **Deming Prize** (see Exhibit 7.2), named after American statistician Dr. W. Edwards Deming, whose quality concepts provided the road map for Japanese success in quality after World War II. The Deming Prize has become so esteemed in Japan that each year, much like America's Academy Awards, millions of Japanese watch the Deming Prize ceremony aired live on television.

Deming Prize

EXHIBIT 7.2

**Comparison of the Deming Prize and the Baldrige Award**

Japan's highly coveted Deming Prize recognizes successful efforts in instituting companywide quality control (CWQC) principles. The Deming Prize is awarded to all companies that meet a standard based on the evaluation process. For those that do not qualify, the examination process is automatically extended (up to two times over three years). Although both the Deming Prize and the Baldrige Award are designed to recognize outstanding business accomplishments, some notable differences follow:

| TOPIC | BALDRIGE AWARD | DEMING PRIZE |
|---|---|---|
| Primary focus | Performance excellence and competitiveness improvement | Statistical quality control |
| Grading criteria | Leadership strategic planning<br>Customer and market focus<br>Information and analysis<br>Human resource development and management<br>Process management<br>Business results | Policy and objectives<br>Organization and operation<br>Education and extension<br>Data gathering/reporting<br>Analysis<br>Standardization<br>Control<br>Quality assurance<br>Effects<br>Future plans |
| Winners | Maximum of two per category | All firms meeting standard |
| Scope | Firms with U.S. operations | Firms from any country |
| First award | 1987 | 1951 |
| Sponsor | National Institute of Standards and Technology | Union of Japanese Scientists and Engineers |

SOURCE: DAVID BUSH AND KEVIN DOOLEY, "THE DEMING PRIZE AND THE BALDRIDGE AWARD: HOW THEY COMPARE," *QUALITY PROGRESS*, JANUARY 1989, PP. 28–30.

## ELIGIBILITY FOR THE BALDRIGE AWARD

There are five categories for the Baldrige Award:

1 Manufacturing companies or subsidiaries that (a) produce and sell manufactured products or manufacturing processes or (b) produce agricultural, mining, or construction products.
2 Service companies or subsidiaries that sell service. Whether a company is classified as manufacturing or service is determined by the larger percentage of sales.
3 Small businesses, which are defined as those that have fewer than 500 employees and that operate independently of any other firm that may have equity ownership.
4 Health care organizations, for profit or not-for-profit.
5 Educational institutions, for profit or not-for-profit.

Up to three awards can be given in each category. Winners are expected to make themselves available to other firms and openly discuss what they did to achieve quality success. Some of the better-known winners include Motorola, Federal Express, and Ritz Carlton Hotels. A list of all recipients is available on the website for the Baldrige Award (www.quality.nist.gov).

## DESCRIPTION OF THE BALDRIGE AWARD CRITERIA

Exhibit 7.3 shows a framework for the award criteria. Note how the Baldrige Award mirrors the broad spectrum of issues necessary for a total quality management system. Scoring for the award falls into seven categories shown in Exhibit 7.4. Note that the greatest scoring weight is on business results.

### Characteristics of Baldrige Winners

One characteristic is that they perform very well as a stock market investment (see the box titled "Study Finds 'Quality

EXHIBIT 7.3

**Baldrige Award Criteria Framework: A Systems Perspective**

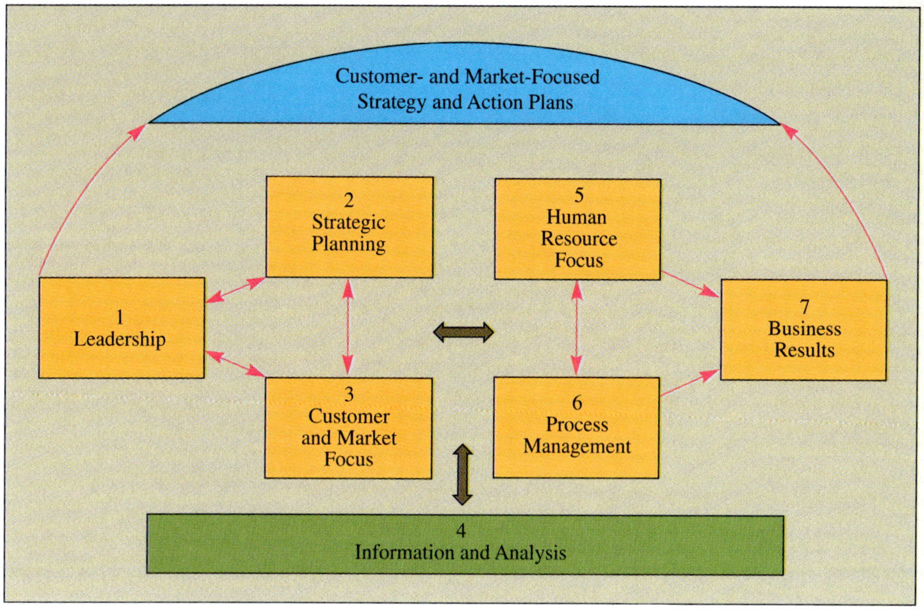


EXHIBIT 7.4

**2000 Criteria for Performance Excellence—Item Listing**

| | 2000 CATEGORIES/ITEMS | | POINT VALUES |
|---|---|---|---|
| 1 | LEADERSHIP | | 125 |
| | 1.1 Organizational Leadership | 85 | |
| | 1.2 Public Responsibility and Citizenship | 40 | |
| 2 | STRATEGIC PLANNING | | 85 |
| | 2.1 Strategy Development | 40 | |
| | 2.2 Strategy Deployment | 45 | |
| 3 | CUSTOMER AND MARKET FOCUS | | 85 |
| | 3.1 Customer and Market Knowledge | 40 | |
| | 3.2 Customer Satisfaction and Relationships | 45 | |
| 4 | INFORMATION AND ANALYSIS | | 85 |
| | 4.1 Measurement of Organizational Performace | 40 | |
| | 4.2 Analysis of Organizational Performance | 45 | |
| 5 | HUMAN RESOURCE FOCUS | | 85 |
| | 5.1 Work Systems | 35 | |
| | 5.2 Employee Education, Training, and Development | 25 | |
| | 5.3 Employee Well-Being and Satisfaction | 25 | |
| 6 | PROCESS MANAGEMENT | | 85 |
| | 6.1 Product and Service Processes | 55 | |
| | 6.2 Support Processes | 15 | |
| | 6.3 Supplier and Partnering Processes | 15 | |
| 7 | BUSINESS RESULTS | | 450 |
| | 7.1 Customer-Focused Results | 115 | |
| | 7.2 Financial and Market Results | 115 | |
| | 7.3 Human Resource Results | 80 | |
| | 7.4 Supplier and Partner Results | 25 | |
| | 7.5 Organizational Effectiveness Results | 115 | |
| Total Points | | | 1000 |

## STUDIES FIND "QUALITY STOCKS" YIELD BIG PAYOFF

A hypothetical sum was invested in each 1990–1997 publicly traded, site-visited applicant's common stock in the year they applied for the Baldrige Award or in the year they became public. The investment was tracked from the first business day of the month following the announcement of the Baldrige Award recipients (or the date when they began public trading, if it was later) through December 1, 1998. In each whole site-visited company, $1,000 was invested. For subsidiaries, the sum invested was $1,000 × the percentage of the parent company's employee base the subunit represented at the time they received a site visit or at the time they became public as a result of a merger or acquisition by a new parent. The same total dollar amount was invested in the S&P 500 on the same day. Here are the results:

| | $INVESTMENT | $VALUE 12/1/98 | % CHANGE |
|---|---|---|---|
| 1990–1997 Site-Visited Applicants | 23,103 | 70,776 | 206% |
| S&P 500 | 23,103 | 53,598 | 32% |

Other studies also are finding that organizations receiving quality awards show long-lasting improvements in their bottom-line results. For example, Singhal and Hendricks studied 600 publicly traded firms that have won quality awards, including the Baldrige, state and private awards, and those given out by major corporations to suppliers. The five-year study showed that, as a whole, these companies had significant improvements in the value of their stock, operating income, sales, return on sales, and employment and asset growth.

SOURCE: K. B. HENDRICKS AND V. R. SINGHAL, "DON'T COUNT TQM OUT," *QUALITY PROGRESS*, APRIL 1999, PP. 35–42. 

Stocks' Yield Big Payoff"). Four common operational elements of all winners are

1 The companies formulated a vision of what they thought quality was and how they would achieve it.
2 Senior management was actively involved.
3 Companies carefully planned and organized their quality effort to be sure it would be effectively initiated.
4 They vigorously controlled the overall process.

## THE EUROPEAN QUALITY AWARD

Global

www.efqm.org

The European Quality Award is similar to the Baldrige Award. (See Exhibit 7.5 for its framework.) It was established in 1988 by the European Foundation for Quality Management, a consortium of 14 leading Western European companies. The EFQM has a membership of over 600 European organizations, all of which are committed to improving efficiency and effectiveness and achieving business excellence. The award is presented annually to the organizations judged to be the most successful exponents of total quality management in Europe. The winners are chosen from among prizewinners in four categories—whole companies, operational units of companies, small and medium-size enterprises (SMEs), and public sector organizations. The model is used as a self-assessment tool; it has nine elements that have been identified as the key components of business excellence. These nine criteria are used to assess an organization's progress toward excellence.

EXHIBIT 7.5

European Quality Award Framework

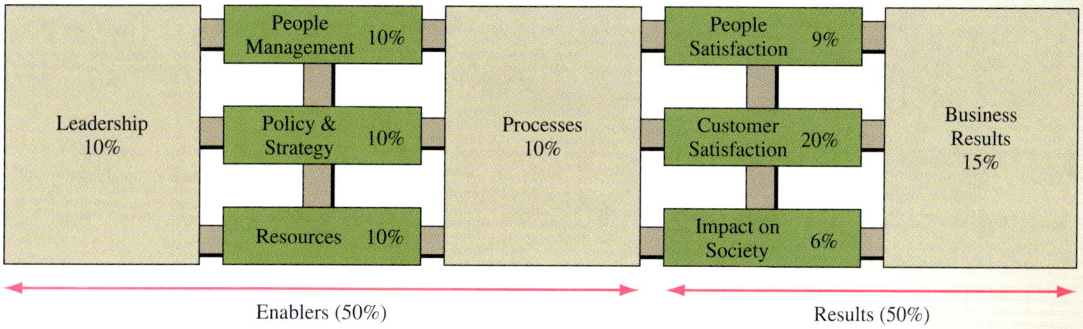


Two of the 1998 winners are TNT United Kingdom and Schindlerhof Hotel and Conference Centre. TNT U.K. employs 10,000 staff and is the market leader in express delivery. It offers time-sensitive delivery of a vast range of commodities, including newspapers, magazines, garments, share certificates, automotive components, office equipment, food and drink, and express parcels. Schindlerhof Hotel and Conference Centre's distinctive feature is that it combines the normal activities of running a conference center with entertainment. They call it the art of playing, which takes place every day: the team managers act as stage directors; the hotel is a stage on which the employees (the cast) perform. Entertainers like the owners create special effects whenever they can.

### THE BALDRIGE AWARD AND THE QUALITY GURUS

One of the intentions of the Baldrige designers was to develop an award that captured the ideas of the leading quality philosophers (or gurus)—Philip Crosby, W. Edwards Deming, and Joseph M. Juran—while at the same time being "nondenominational" with respect to advocating one particular quality view. (See the box titled "W. Edwards Deming" for his famous "14 Points.") Although there are differences in many areas among the three philosophies compared in Exhibit 7.6, it is fair to say that this goal was achieved. The reason lies in the nonprescriptive nature of the Baldrige criteria, the fact that the gurus all advocate generally the same thing, and, in our opinion, the fact that they all emphasize top management leadership in the quality effort. The proof is in the pudding as well—different Baldrige winners have been adherents to Deming, Crosby, or Juran approaches.

## QUALITY SPECIFICATION AND QUALITY COSTS

Fundamental to any quality program is the determination of quality specifications and the costs of achieving (or *not* achieving) those specifications.

Vol. IV "Quality Product and Process Design at Detroit Diesel"

### DEVELOPING QUALITY SPECIFICATIONS

The quality specifications of a product or service derive from decisions and actions made relative to the quality of its design and the quality of its conformance to that design. **Design quality** refers to the inherent value of the product in the marketplace and is thus a strategic decision for the firm. The common dimensions of design quality are listed in Exhibit 7.7.

Design quality

**Conformance quality** refers to the degree to which the product or service design specifications are met. The activities involved in achieving conformance are of a tactical,

Conformance quality

EXHIBIT 7.6

## The Quality Gurus Compared

| | CROSBY | DEMING | JURAN |
|---|---|---|---|
| Definition of quality | Conformance to requirements | A predictable degree of uniformity and dependability at low cost and suited to the market | Fitness for use (satisfies customer's needs) |
| Degree of senior management responsibility | Responsible for quality | Responsible for 94% of quality problems | Less than 20% of quality problems are due to workers |
| Performance standard/ motivation | Zero defects | Quality has many "scales"; use statistics to measure performance in all areas; critical of zero defects | Avoid campaigns to do perfect work |
| General approach | Prevention, not inspection | Reduce variability by continuous improvement; cease mass inspection | General management approach to quality, especially human elements |
| Structure | 14 steps to quality improvement | 14 points for management | 10 steps to quality improvement |
| Statistical process control (SPC) | Rejects statistically acceptable levels of quality [wants 100% perfect quality] | Statistical methods of quality control must be used | Recommends SPC but warns that it can lead to tool-driven approach |
| Improvement basis | A process, not a program; improvement goals | Continuous to reduce variation; eliminate goals without methods | Project-by-project team approach; set goals |
| Teamwork | Quality improvement teams; quality councils | Employee participation in decision making; break down barriers between departments | Team and quality circle approach |
| Costs of quality | Cost of nonconformance; quality is free | No optimum; continuous improvement | Quality is not free; there is not an optimum |
| Purchasing and goods received | State requirements; supplier is extension of business; most faults due to purchasers themselves | Inspection too late; sampling allows defects to enter system; statistical evidence and control charts required | Problems are complex; carry out formal surveys |
| Vendor rating | Yes; quality audits useless | No, critical of most systems | Yes, but help supplier improve |

EXHIBIT 7.7

## The Dimensions of Design Quality

| DIMENSION | MEANING |
|---|---|
| Performance | Primary product or service characteristics |
| Features | Added touches, bells and whistles, secondary characteristics |
| Reliability | Consistency of performance over time, probability of failing |
| Durability | Useful life |
| Serviceability | Ease of repair |
| Response | Characteristics of the human-to-human interface (speed, courtesy, competence) |
| Aesthetics | Sensory characteristics (sound, feel, look, and so on) |
| Reputation | Past performance and other intangibles (perceived quality) |

SOURCE FOR EXHIBITS 7.6 AND 7.7: MODIFIED FROM JOHN S. OAKLAND, *TOTAL QUALITY MANAGEMENT:* LONDON: HEINEMANN PROFESSIONAL PUBLISHING LTD., 1989, PP. 291–92.

day-to-day nature. It should be evident that a product or service can have high design quality but low conformance quality, and vice versa.

Quality at the source

**Quality at the source** is frequently discussed in the context of conformance quality. This means that the person who does the work takes responsibility for making sure that his or her output meets specifications. If this can be accomplished, then in theory, the ultimate

## W. EDWARDS DEMING, 1900–1993

**DEMING'S 14 POINTS:**

1 Create constancy of purpose toward improvement of product and service, with the aim to become competitive, to stay in business, and to provide jobs.

2 Adopt the new philosophy. We are in a new economic age. Western management must awaken to the challenge, must learn their responsibilities and take on leadership for change.

3 Cease dependence on inspection to achieve quality. Eliminate the need for inspection on a mass basis by building quality into the product in the first place.

4 End the practice of awarding business on the basis of price tag. Instead, minimize total cost. Move toward a single supplier for any one item, on a long-term relationship of loyalty and trust.

5 Improve constantly and forever the system of production and service, to improve quality and productivity, and thus constantly decrease costs.

6 Institute training on the job.

7 Institute leadership. The aim of supervision should be to help people and machines and gadgets to do a better job. Supervision of management is in need of overhaul, as well as supervision of production workers.

8 Drive out fear, so that everyone may work effectively for the company.

9 Break down barriers between departments. People in research, design, sales, and production must work as a team, to foresee problems of production and in use that may be encountered with the product or service.

10 Eliminate slogans, exhortations, and targets for the workforce that ask for zero defects and new levels of productivity. Such exhortations only create adversarial relationships because the bulk of the causes of low quality and low productivity belong to the system and thus lie beyond the power of the workforce.

- Eliminate work standards (quotas) on the factory floor. Substitute leadership.
- Eliminate management by objectives. Eliminate management by numbers, numerical goals. Substitute leadership.

11 Remove barriers that rob the hourly worker of his right to pride of workmanship. The responsibility of supervisors must be changed from sheer numbers to quality.

12 Remove barriers that rob people in management and in engineering of their right to pride of workmanship. This means, for example, abolishment of annual or merit rating and of management by objectives.

13 Institute a vigorous program of education and self-improvement.

14 Put everybody in the company to work to accomplish the transformation. The transformation is everyone's job.

SOURCE: DEMING INSTITUTE.

EXHIBIT 7.8

**Examples of Dimensions of Quality**

| | Measures | |
|---|---|---|
| Dimension | Product Example: Stereo Amplifier | Service Example: Checking Account at a Bank |
| Performance | Signal-to-noise ratio, power | Time to process customer requests |
| Features | Remote control | Automatic bill paying |
| Reliability | Mean time to failure | Variability of time to process requests |
| Durability | Useful life (with repair) | Keeping pace with industry trends |
| Serviceability | Modular design | Online reports |
| Response | Courtesy of dealer | Courtesy of teller |
| Aesthetics | Oak-finished cabinet | Appearance of bank lobby |
| Reputation | Market leader for 20 years | Endorsed by community leaders |

SOURCE: MODIFIED FROM PAUL E. PISEK, "DEFINING QUALITY AT THE MARKETING/DEVELOPMENT INTERFACE," *QUALITY PROGRESS*, JUNE 1987, PP. 28–36.

goal of **zero defects** throughout the process is achievable. (Zero defects had been frequently used as the rallying cry for a companywide quality effort. The term has fallen into disrepute because it was often just a slogan, unsupported by quality training and real quality commitment by management.)

Zero defects

Service

Where a product is involved, achieving the quality specifications is typically the responsibility of manufacturing management; in a service industry, it is usually the responsibility of the branch operations management. Exhibit 7.8 shows two examples of the

BREAKTHROUGH

## SOFTWARE QUALITY IN THE INFORMATION AGE

A software application program's quality is determined not only by its ability to perform specified computational or data management functions but also by its ease of use, its flexibility for product innovation, its fit within an existing network, and the ease by which it can be supported by the software provider. In a recent *Harvard Business Review* article, Prahalad and Krishnan suggest that the key to specifying quality features is to understand the software domain. The forces that shape the domain are the interactions that take place between the application software and its end users, and the information technology requirements of the business.

The interactions, or the dialogue between the software and its users, is changing. In the past, retailing application programs established dialogues between, for example, Toys Я Us and the customer for Mattel's Barbie Dolls. Now, with the Internet, customers can link directly to Mattel, and the latter's application programs must be designed to enable information gathering and learning about the purchaser. Prahalad and Krishnan identify four critical dimensions of technology that affect software quality:

1 **Longevity of a technology platform.** A platform is the core technology upon which multiple applications are built. For example, the SAP platform for enterprise resource planning has been around for a number of years and has the advantage of having thousands of users who know if it is operating properly. On the other hand, it has limited flexibility for innovation.
2 **Time to rollout.** Introducing a new application or platform can take an extended period of time. Thus, ease of training and ability to overcome inevitable implementation problems are important measures of software quality.
3 **Legacy systems migration.** Being able to integrate new systems with existing ones is a common problem in large organizations. Disneyland, for example, is currently expending a large amount of money redesigning and centralizing its theme park employee scheduling system.
4 **Evolving technologies.** Many new applications (such as online auctions) and multimedia technologies require companies to experiment before they understand what quality metrics to select for evaluating software performance.

SOURCE: ADAPTED FROM C. K. PRAHALAD AND M. S. KRISHNAN, "THE NEW MEANING OF QUALITY IN THE INFORMATION AGE," *HARVARD BUSINESS REVIEW* 77, NO. 5 (SEPTEMBER–OCTOBER 1999), PP. 109–18.

Dimensions of quality

**dimensions of quality.** One is a stereo amplifier that meets the signal-to-noise ratio standard; the second is a checking account transaction in a bank.

A discussion of the more complex dimensions of software quality is given in the "Software Quality in the Information Age" Breakthrough Box.

Both quality of design and quality of conformance should provide products that meet the customer's objectives for those products. This is often termed the product's *fitness for use,* and it entails identifying the dimensions of the product (or service) that the customer wants (that is, the voice of the customer) and developing a quality control program to ensure that these dimensions are met.

## COST OF QUALITY

Cost of quality

Although few can quarrel with the notion of prevention, management often needs hard numbers to determine how much prevention activities will cost. This issue was recognized by Joseph Juran, who wrote about it in 1951 in his *Quality Control Handbook.* Today, **cost of quality (COQ)** analyses are common in industry and constitute one of the primary functions of QC departments.

There are a number of definitions and interpretations of the term *cost of quality.* From the purist's point of view, it means all of the costs attributable to the production of quality that is not 100 percent perfect. A less stringent definition considers only those costs that are the difference between what can be expected from excellent performance and the current costs that exist.

How significant is the cost of quality? It has been estimated at between 15 and 20 percent of every sales dollar—the cost of reworking, scrapping, repeated service, inspections,

GLOBAL MANUFACTURING FOR MENNEN SPEED STICK DEODORANT AT A SINGLE LOCATION IN MORRISTOWN, NJ SERVES 48 DIFFERENT COUNTRIES. THE TECHNICIAN IS INSPECTING THE MULTI-LANGUAGE LABELING WHICH ENABLES THE SAME PRODUCT TO BE SOLD IN VARIOUS COUNTRIES.

tests, warranties, and other quality-related items. Philip Crosby states that the correct cost for a well-run quality management program should be under 2.5 percent.[1]

Three basic assumptions justify an analysis of the costs of quality: (1) failures are caused, (2) prevention is cheaper, and (3) performance can be measured.

The costs of quality are generally classified into four types:

1 **Appraisal costs.** Costs of the inspection, testing, and other tasks to ensure that the product or process is acceptable.
2 **Prevention costs.** The sum of all the costs to prevent defects, such as the costs to identify the cause of the defect, to implement corrective action to eliminate the cause, to train personnel, to redesign the product or system, and for new equipment or modifications.
3 **Internal failure costs.** Costs for defects incurred within the system: scrap, rework, repair.
4 **External failure costs.** Costs for defects that pass through the system: customer warranty replacements, loss of customers or goodwill, handling complaints, and product repair.

Exhibit 7.9 illustrates the type of report that might be submitted to show the various costs by categories. Prevention is the most important influence. A rule of thumb says that for every dollar you spend in prevention, you can save \$10 in failure and appraisal costs.

Often increases in productivity occur as a by-product of efforts to reduce the cost of quality. A bank, for example, set out to improve quality and reduce the cost of quality and found that it had also boosted productivity. The bank developed this productivity measure for the loan processing area: the number of tickets processed divided by the resources required (labor cost, computer time, ticket forms). Before the quality improvement program, the productivity index was 0.2660 [2,080/(\$11.23 × 640 hours + \$0.05 × 2,600 forms + \$500 for systems costs)]. After the quality improvement project was completed, labor time fell to 546 hours and the number of forms fell to 2,100, for a change in the index to 0.3088, an increase in productivity of 16 percent.

EXHIBIT 7.9

Quality Cost Report

| | Current Month's Cost | Percentage of Total |
|---|---|---|
| Prevention costs | | |
| Quality training | $ 2,000 | 1.3% |
| Reliability consulting | 10,000 | 6.5 |
| Pilot production runs | 5,000 | 3.3 |
| Systems development | 8,000 | 5.2 |
| Total prevention | 25,000 | 16.3 |
| Appraisal costs | | |
| Materials inspection | 6,000 | 3.9 |
| Supplies inspection | 3,000 | 2.0 |
| Reliability testing | 5,000 | 3.3 |
| Laboratory testing | 25,000 | 16.3 |
| Total appraisal | 39,000 | 25.5 |
| Internal failure costs | | |
| Scrap | 15,000 | 9.8 |
| Repair | 18,000 | 11.8 |
| Rework | 12,000 | 7.8 |
| Downtime | 6,000 | 3.9 |
| Total internal failure | 51,000 | 33.3 |
| External failure costs | | |
| Warranty costs | 14,000 | 9.2 |
| Out-of-warranty repairs and replacement | 6,000 | 3.9 |
| Customer complaints | 3,000 | 2.0 |
| Product liability | 10,000 | 6.5 |
| Transportation losses | 5,000 | 3.3 |
| Total external failure | 38,000 | 24.9 |
| Total quality costs | $153,000 | 100.0 |

### GENERIC TOOLS AND TOOLS OF THE QC DEPARTMENT

The generic tools of TQM are those developed for statistical process control (SPC), which we include later in this chapter under "Tools and Procedures of CI" and in the technical note to this chapter.

The typical manufacturing QC department has a variety of functions to perform. These include testing designs for their reliability in the lab and the field; gathering performance data on products in the field and resolving quality problems in the field; planning and budgeting the QC program in the plant; and, finally, designing and overseeing quality control systems and inspection procedures, and actually carrying out inspection activities requiring special technical knowledge to accomplish. The tools of the QC department fall under the heading of statistical quality control (SQC) and consist of two main sections: acceptance sampling and process control. These topics are covered in the technical note to this chapter.

## CONTINUOUS IMPROVEMENT (CI)

Continuous improvement

Continuous improvement (CI) is a management philosophy that approaches the challenge of product and process improvement as a never-ending process of achieving small wins. It is an integral part of a total quality management system. Specifically, **continuous improvement** seeks continual improvement of machinery, materials, labor utilization, and production methods through application of suggestions and ideas of team members. This philosophy is often contrasted with the traditional approach of relying on major technological or theoretical innovations to achieve "big win" improvements. In a survey of 872 North American manufacturing executives, the majority of world-class manufacturers favored continuous improvement over 11 other management enhancement programs.

Vol. I "Improving Operations Methods"

In this section we discuss the key managerial elements of continuous improvement and apply some of the basic tools associated with the CI process. We also discuss its impact on quality improvement.

Although historically CI has been implemented in manufacturing plants, it has become quite common in services as well. Consider the following *Fortune* excerpt about Federal Express:

> At lunch with one team [of back-office employees], this reporter sat impressed as entry-level workers, most with only high school educations, ate their chicken and dropped sophisticated management terms like **kaizen,** the Japanese art of continuous improvement, and *pareto,* a form of problem solving that requires workers to take a logical step-by-step approach. The team described how one day during a weekly meeting, a clerk from quality control pointed out a billing problem. The bigger a package, he explained, the more Fedex charges to deliver it. But the company's wildly busy delivery people sometimes forgot to check whether customers had properly marked the weight of packages on the airbill. That meant that Fedex, whose policy in such cases is to charge customers the lowest rate, was losing money. The team switched on its turbochargers. An employee in billing services found out which field offices in Fedex's labyrinthine 30,000-person courier network were forgetting to check the packages, and then explained the problem to the delivery people. Another worker in billing set up a system to examine the invoices and made sure the solution was working. Last year alone the team's ideas saved the company $2.1 million.[2]

Kaizen

## Tools and Procedures of CI

The approaches companies take to CI as a process range from very structured programs utilizing statistical process control (SPC) tools to simple suggestion systems relying on brainstorming and "back-of-an-envelope" analyses. Exhibit 7.10 shows some common SPC tools used for problem solving and continuous improvement.

Another tool is the **PDCA** (*p*lan-*d*o-*c*heck-*a*ct) **cycle,** often called the Deming Wheel (see Exhibit 7.11), which conveys the sequential and continual nature of the CI process. The *plan* phase of the cycle is where an improvement area (sometimes called a *theme*) and a specific problem with it are identified. It is also where the analysis is done, Exhibit 7.12 is a CI example using the 5W2H method. (5W2H stands for *w*hat, *w*hy, *w*here, *w*hen, *w*ho, *h*ow, and *h*ow much.)

PDCA cycle

The *do* phase of the PDCA cycle deals with implementing the change. Experts usually recommend that the plan be done on a small scale first, and that any changes in the plan be documented. (Check sheets are useful here, too.) The *check* phase deals with evaluating data collected during the implementation. The objective is to see if there is a good fit between the original goal and the actual results. During the *act* phase, the improvement is codified as the new standard procedure and replicated in similar processes throughout the organization.

The group-level CI process is frequently represented as if we were developing a storyboard for a movie. Exhibit 7.13, for example, summarizes the steps just discussed as the "QI (Quality Improvement) Story."

## Benchmarking for CI

The CI approaches described so far are more or less inward looking: They seek to make improvements by analyzing in detail the current practices of the company itself. **External benchmarking,** however, goes outside the organization to examine what industry

External benchmarking

EXHIBIT 7.10

## SPC Tools Commonly Used for Problem Solving and Continuous Improvement

These tools do not substitute for judgment and process knowledge. They help deal with complexity and turn raw data into information that can be used to take action.

**Process Flowchart**

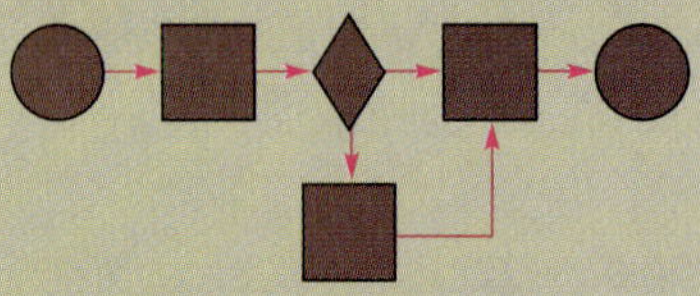

A picture that describes the main steps, branches, and eventual outputs of a process.

**Pareto Analysis**

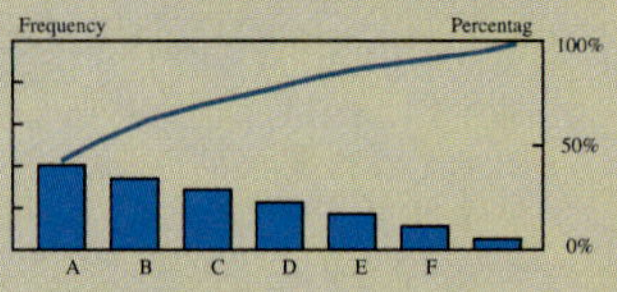


A coordinated approach for identifying, ranking, and working to permanently eliminate defects. Focuses on important error sources. 80/20 rule: 80 percent of the problems are due to 20 percent of the causes.

**Run Chart**

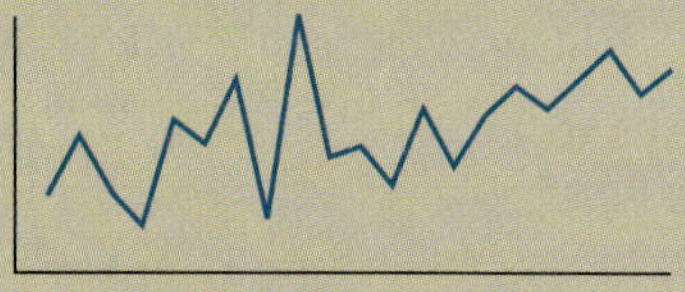

A time sequence chart showing plotted values of a characteristic.

**Data Collection**

Always have an agreed upon and clear reason for any data you collect. Prepare in advance your strategy for both collecting and analyzing the data. Questions that might be asked of data collection: Why? What? Where? How much? When? How? Who? How long?

**Histogram**

A distribution showing the frequency of occurrences between the high and low range of data.

**Scatter Diagram**

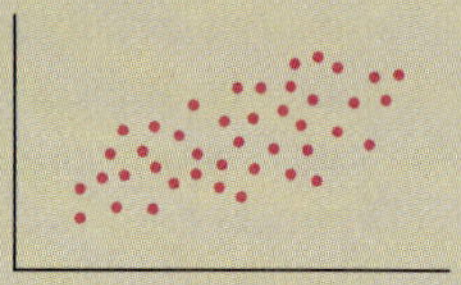

Also known as a correlation chart. A graph of the value of one characteristic versus another characteristic.

**Check Sheet**

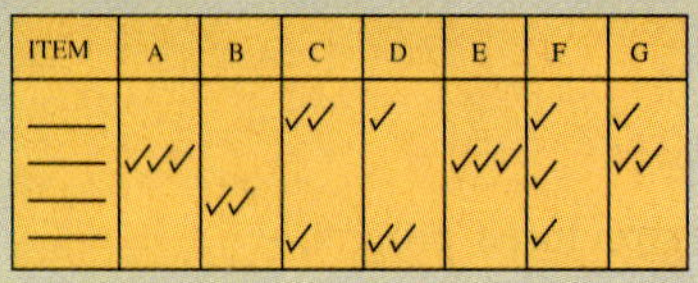


An organized method for recording data.

**Causes and Effect or Fishbone Diagram**

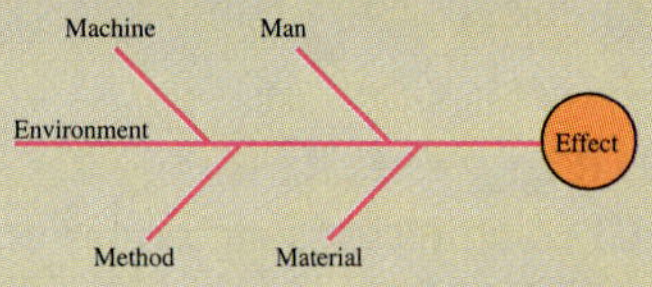


A tool that uses a graphical description of the process elements to analyze potential sources of process variation.

**Control Charts**

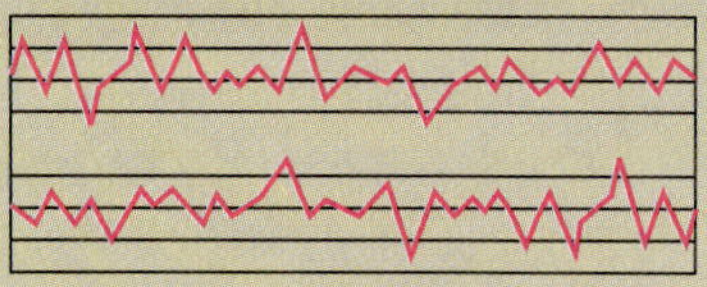

A time sequence chart showing plotted values of a statistic, including a central line and one or more statistically derived control limits.

EXHIBIT 7.11

PDCA Cycle (Deming Wheel)

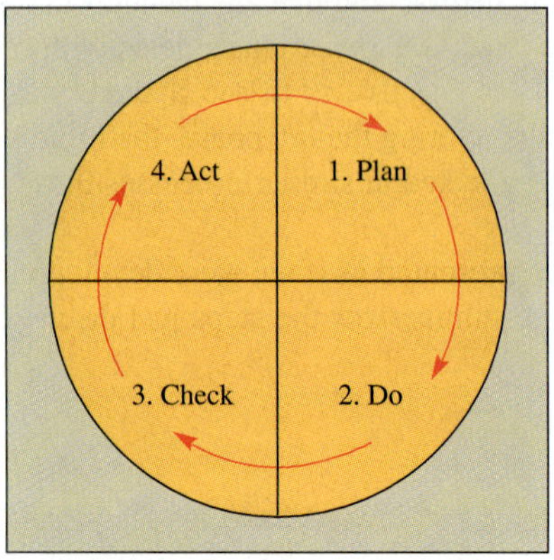

**EXHIBIT 7.12**

**The 5W2H Method**

| TYPE | 5W2H | DESCRIPTION | COUNTERMEASURE |
|---|---|---|---|
| Subject matter | What? | What is being done?<br>Can this task be eliminated? | Eliminate unnecessary tasks. |
| Purpose | Why? | Why is this task necessary?<br>Clarify the purpose. | |
| Location | Where? | Where is it being done?<br>Does it have to be done there? | Change the sequence or combination. |
| Sequence | When? | When is the best time to do it?<br>Does it have to be done then? | |
| People | Who? | Who is doing it?<br>Should someone else do it?<br>Why am I doing it? | |
| Method | How? | How is it being done?<br>Is this the best method?<br>Is there some other way? | Simplify the task. |
| Cost | How much? | How much does it cost now?<br>What will the cost be after improvement? | Select an improvement method. |

A number of simple guidelines have been developed to help people or groups generate new ideas. In general, these guidelines urge you to question everything from every conceivable angle. The figure outlines the 5W2H method. The five "W's" are what, why, where, when, and who; the two "H's" are how and how much.

competitors and excellent performers outside the industry are doing. Its basic objective is simple: Find the best practices that lead to superior performance and see how you can use them. The practice of benchmarking is a hallmark of Malcolm Baldrige National Quality Award winners and is widely used throughout industry in general. Benchmarking typically involves the following steps:

1 **Identify processes needing improvement.** This is equivalent to selecting a theme in CI.

2 **Identify a firm that is the world leader in performing the process.** For many processes, this may be a company that is not in the same industry. Examples include Xerox using L. L. Bean as the benchmark in evaluating its order entry system, or ICL (a major British computer maker) benchmarking Marks and Spenser (a large U.K. clothing retailer) to improve its distribution system. A McKinsey study cited a firm that measured pit stops on a motor racing circuit as a benchmark for worker changes on its assembly line.[3]

Global

3 **Contact the managers of that company and make a personal visit to interview managers and workers.** Many companies select a team of workers from that process to be on a benchmarking team as part of a CI program.

4 **Analyze data.** This entails looking at gaps between what your company is doing and what the benchmark company is doing. There are two aspects of the study: one is comparing the actual processes; the other is comparing the performance of those processes according to some set of measures. The processes are often described using flowcharts or written descriptions. (In some cases, companies permit videotaping, although there is a tendency now for benchmarked companies to keep things under wraps for fear of giving away process secrets.)

Typical performance measures for process comparisons are breakouts of cost, quality, and service, such as cost per order, percentage defectives, and service response time.

EXHIBIT 7.13

The QI Story

| | QI STORY STEP | FUNCTION | TOOLS |
|---|---|---|---|
| | 1. Select theme. | • Decide theme for improvement.<br>• Make clear why the theme is selected. | "Next processes are our customers."<br>• Standardization<br>• Education<br>• Immediate remedy versus recurrence prevention |
| | 2. Grasp the current situation. | • Collect data.<br>• Find the key characteristics of the theme.<br>• Narrow down the problem area.<br>• Establish priorities: serious problems first. | • Check sheet<br>• Histogram<br>• Pareto |
| PLAN | 3. Conduct analysis. | • List all the possible causes of the most serious problem.<br>• Study the relations between possible causes and between causes and problem.<br>• Select some causes and establish hypotheses about possible relations.<br>• Collect data and study cause-and-effect relations. | • Fishbone<br>• Check sheet<br>• Scatter diagram<br>• Stratification |
| | 4. Devise countermeasures. | • Devise countermeasures to eliminate the cause(s) of a problem. | • Intrinsic technology<br>• Experience |
| DO | | • Implement countermeasures. (Experiment.) | |
| CHECK | 5. Confirm the effects of countermeasures. | • Collect data on the effects of the countermeasures.<br>• Do before–after comparison. | • SPC Tools |
| | 6. Standardize the countermeasures. | • Amend the existing standards according to the countermeasures whose effects are confirmed. | |
| ACT | 7. Identify the remaining problems and evaluate the whole procedure. | | |

SOURCE: P. LILLRANK AND N. KANO, *CONTINUOUS IMPROVEMENT: QUALITY CONTROL CIRCLES IN JAPANESE INDUSTRY* (ANN ARBOR: UNIVERSITY OF MICHIGAN, CENTER FOR JAPANESE STUDIES, 1989), P. 26.

## THE SHINGO SYSTEM: FAIL-SAFE DESIGN

The Shingo system developed in parallel and in many ways in conflict with the statistically based approach to quality control. As we discussed in Chapter 6 relating to service applications, this system—or, to be more precise, philosophy of production management—is named after the codeveloper of the Toyota just-in-time system, Shigeo Shingo. Two aspects of the Shingo system in particular have received great attention. One is how to accomplish drastic cuts in equipment setup times by *s*ingle-*m*inute *e*xchange of *d*ie (SMED) procedures. The other, the focus of this section, is the use of source inspection and the poka-yoke system to achieve zero defects.

Shingo has argued that SQC methods do not prevent defects. Although they provide information to tell us probabilistically when a defect will occur, they are after the fact. The way to prevent defects from coming out at the end of a process is to introduce controls within the process. Central to Shingo's approach is the difference between errors and defects. Defects arise because people make errors. Even though errors are inevitable, defects can be prevented if feedback leading to corrective action takes place immediately after the errors are made. Such feedback and action require inspection, which should be done on 100 percent of the items produced. This inspection can be one of three types: successive check, self-check, and source inspection. *Successive check* inspection is performed by the next person in the process or by an objective evaluator such as a group leader. Information on defects is immediate feedback for the worker who produced the product, who then makes the repair. *Self-check* is done by the individual worker and is appropriate by itself on all but items that require sensory judgment (such as existence or severity of scratches, or correct matching of shades of paint). These require successive checks. *Source inspection* is also performed by the individual worker, except instead of checking for defects, the worker checks for the errors that will cause defects. (See Exhibit 7.14 for sources of defects attributable to the worker.) This prevents the defects from ever occurring and, hence, requiring rework. All three types of inspection rely on controls consisting of **fail-safe procedures** or devices (called **poka-yoke**). Poka-yoke includes such things as checklists or special tooling that (1) prevents the worker from making an error that leads to a defect before starting a process or (2) gives rapid feedback of abnormalities in the process to the worker in time to correct them.

Fail-safe procedures

Poka-yoke

There is a wide variety of poka-yokes, ranging from kitting parts from a bin (to ensure that the right number of parts are used in assembly) to sophisticated detection and electronic signaling devices. An example taken from the writings of Shingo is shown in Exhibit 7.15.

There is a good deal more to say about the work of Shingo. Blasting industry's preoccupation with control charts, Shingo states they are nothing but a mirror reflecting current conditions. When a chemical plant QC manager proudly stated that it had 200 charts in a plant of 150 people, Shingo asked him if "they had a control chart for control charts."[4] In addition to his insights into the quality area, his work on SMED is must reading for manufacturing executives.

# ISO 9000

**ISO 9000** is a series of standards agreed upon by the International Organization for Standardization (ISO) and adopted in 1987. More than 100 countries now recognize the 9000 series for quality standards and certification for international trade. ISO 9000 evolved in Europe; in the European Common Market (ECM) alone, almost 50,000 companies have been certified as complying with these standards.

ISO 9000

Global

www.iso.ch

In addition to the ISO 9000 series, there is also the **ISO 14000** series, which was developed to control the impact of an organization's activities and outputs on the environment. The ISO 14000 standards can lead to benefits such as reducing the cost of waste management, conserving energy and materials, lowering distribution costs, and improving corporate image.

ISO 14000

## THE ISO 9000 SERIES

ISO 9000 consists of five primary parts numbered as 9000 through 9004. If we were to display them on a continuum of an operating firm, the series would range from design and development through procurement, production, installation, and servicing (Exhibit 7.16). Whereas ISO 9000 and 9004 only establish guidelines for operation, ISO 9001, 9002, and 9003 are well-defined standards.

Quite a bit of work and expense may be needed to be accredited at the highest level, which is 9001. Furthermore, some firms may not need ISO 9001 accreditation. For example, note that in Exhibit 7.16, ISO 9003 covers quality in production's final inspection and testing. A firm can be accredited at this level of final production only. This would essentially guarantee the firm's quality of final output and be attractive to customers. A broader accreditation would be 9002, which extends from purchasing and production through installation.

## BREAKTHROUGH

### QUALITY 1 ON 1

Even though the Hewlett-Packard Company (HP) has enjoyed financial success and industry kudos, it has not been immune to increasing pressures in today's business world. Pressures such as rising customer expectations, emerging high-growth markets, an increasing dependence on suppliers and other third parties, and accelerating product life cycles have led HP to introduce a new quality campaign: Quality 1 on 1.

"Quality 1 on 1 heralds a shift from quality as a set of beliefs and practices to quality as a purposeful game plan," states Richard LeVitt, director of HP quality, in an internal company document. "Quality 1 on 1 means knowing quality as a customer does and systematically acting on that knowledge to grow a business."

The phrase "Knowing quality as a customer does" means

- Having more awareness of how customers feel about their experiences when they do business with HP.
- Understanding their problems and goals when possible and collaborating on solutions.
- Knowing how customers sum up their experiences and decide whether to do more business with HP.

The phrase "Acting on that knowledge" means more than just fixing problems. It means

- Seeing HP employees and operations as a customer does.
- Creating customer-centered quality systems that span entire value chains.
- Influencing not only an entity's performance, but also the performance of partners, suppliers, and channels that affect the customer experience. Part of the Quality 1 on 1 process asks employees to look at their work not only from a producer's view, but also from a consumer's view.

#### THE PRODUCER'S VIEW

Employees are accustomed to taking the producer's view of quality—a view that is rational and objective. The producer's view of quality has changed over the years at HP, according to LeVitt. "Many ideas have come to represent quality as a *goal* and quality as a *strategy*." The goals have included conforming to requirements, ensuring fitness for use, meeting customer expectations, and providing superior value. The strategies have included tests and inspections, process improvement, and total quality management.

Although these goals and strategies still have an important role in HP today, they don't necessarily lead to customer loyalty. To achieve customer loyalty, the consumer's view is also needed.

#### THE CONSUMER'S VIEW

Consumers don't usually think of quality in terms of conformance to requirements or fitness for use; rather, they have impressions of quality and goals that they hope to fulfill by using a product or service. "Their impressions and goals influence their choices," says LeVitt. "As something is chosen, each consumer begins a sequence of experiences over a span of time. These experiences lead to emotional states, such as satisfaction, delight, anger, or dismay, which influence future choices. Attention to their impressions, goals, experiences, and emotional states can help producers create mutually beneficial relationships with their customers. These relationships are the foundation of Quality 1 on 1."

SOURCE: K. BEMOWSKI, "QUALITY 1 ON 1," *QUALITY PROGRESS*, OCTOBER 1996, P. 33. © 1996 AMERICAN SOCIETY FOR QUALITY. REPRINTED WITH PERMISSION.

There are 20 elements in the ISO 9000 standards that relate to how the system operates and how well it is performing. These are contained in section 4 of the ISO 9000 Guidelines (Exhibit 7.17). Each of these elements applies in varying degrees to the three standards 9001, 9002, and 9003. (ISO 9001 contains all of them.)

ISO 9000 is intentionally vague. A firm interprets the requirements as they relate to its business. From a practical and useful standpoint for businesses, ISO 9000 is valuable to firms because it provides a framework so they can assess where they are and where they would like to be. In its simplest terms, it is sometimes stated that ISO 9000 directs you to "document what you do and then do *as* you documented."

## ISO 9000 CERTIFICATION

Why is it important to become ISO 9000 certified? For one reason, it is essential from a purely competitive standpoint. Consider the situation where you need to purchase parts

There are certain events surrounding the purchase and use of a product or service that become part of a consumer's experience. These events can either increase the person's confidence in the company's product or service or increase the likelihood that he or she will make the next purchase elsewhere.

Although each product or service has its own consumer-experience life cycle, customers generally go through these stages:

1. **Clarifying a purpose and selecting a solution.** The customer becomes aware of his or her needs and selects a product or service that will meet those needs.
2. **Ordering what is chosen at an agreed-on price.** The customer actually buys (or places an order to buy) the product or service. This could be as quick and simple as buying a toothbrush or as time-consuming and complex as buying a new car.
3. **Becoming ready to use the selection.** The customer prepares to use the product or service (for example, setting up a new computer or taking the plastic wrapper off of a new compact disc). Problems and frustrations at this step commonly cause customer dissatisfaction.
4. **Becoming proficient.** The customer learns how to use the product or service. This stage is often more time-consuming with high-technology products, such as computers and videocassette recorders. At this point, a customer discovers whether the product or service meets his or her expectations, so first impressions are important.
5. **Receiving the intended benefits.** The customer receives the anticipated benefits. When no problems arise and the customer's purpose for buying the product or service is met, the customer feels gratified by the good choice he or she made. When problems occur, the customer begins to wonder if he or she should have chosen another product.
6. **Keeping everything going.** If something goes wrong with a product or service, the customer will be at a peak of emotional engagement with the product. The responsiveness of the company at this time is critical. If a situation is not handled well, the customer can develop long-lasting feelings of anger. Conversely, when a situation is effectively handled with an attitude of personal caring and concern, the customer's emotional response can be strongly positive.
7. **Letting go and moving on.** The customer decides to discontinue use of the product or service because it no longer meets his or her needs. By reflecting on his or her interactions, with the product or service and the company that sold it, the customer forms a lasting impression that guides future decisions. These reflections can influence brand loyalty, so attention to the customer relationship at this late stage in the life cycle is also important.

### TWO VIEWS ARE BETTER THAN ONE

Quality 1 on 1 helps employees make a conscious effort to account for the customer's entire experience with the product or service. This is important, says LeVitt, because "Quality isn't just something producers do for consumers. It is a result of the producer's creation of a product and the customer's experience with a product." Thus, taking both the producer's and the consumer's view is necessary in today's marketplace.

for your firm, and several suppliers offer similar parts at similar prices. Assume that one of these firms has been ISO 9000 certified and the others have not. From whom would you purchase? There is no doubt that the ISO 9000–certified company would have the inside track in your decision making. Why? Because ISO 9000 specifies the way the supplier firm operates as well as its quality standards, delivery times, service levels, and so on.

There are three forms of certification:

1. First party: A firm audits itself against ISO 9000 standards.
2. Second party: A customer audits its supplier.
3. Third party: A "qualified" national or international standards or certifying agency serves as auditor.

The best certification of a firm is through a third party. Once passed by the third-party audit, a firm is certified and may be registered and recorded as having achieved ISO 9000 status,

EXHIBIT 7.14

Sources of Defects

*What Are the Sources of Defects?*

There are various types of defects. In order of importance these are

1. Omitted processing
2. Processing errors
3. Errors setting up workpieces
4. Missing parts
5. Wrong parts
6. Processing wrong workpiece
7. Misoperation
8. Adjustment error
9. Equipment not set up properly
10. Tools and jigs improperly prepared

What are the connections between these defects and the mistakes people make?

☆ Causal connections between defects and human errors

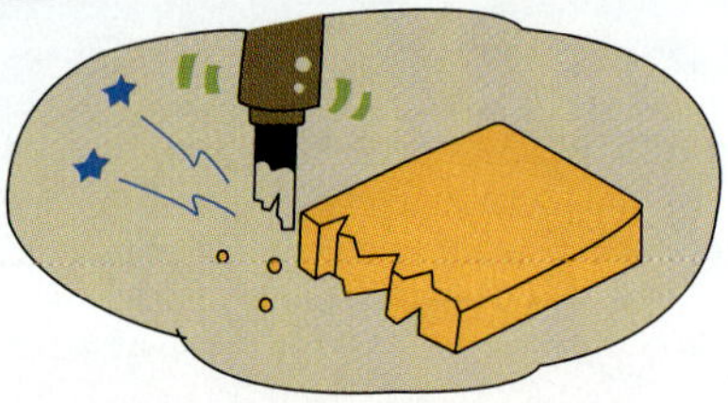

◉ Strongly connected ○ Connected

| Causes of Defects \ Human Errors | Intentional | Mis-understanding | Forgetful | Mis-identification | Amateurs | Willfull | Inadvertent | Slowness | Non-supervision | Surprise |
|---|---|---|---|---|---|---|---|---|---|---|
| Omitted processing | ◉ | ○ | ◉ | ○ | ○ | ○ | ◉ | ○ | ○ | |
| Processing errors | ◉ | ◉ | ○ | ○ | ◉ | ◉ | ◉ | ◉ | ◉ | |
| Errors setting up workpieces | ○ | ○ | ◉ | ○ | ○ | | ◉ | ○ | ○ | |
| Missing parts | ◉ | ○ | ○ | | ○ | ○ | ◉ | | ○ | |
| Wrong parts | ◉ | ◉ | ◉ | ◉ | ◉ | ◉ | ◉ | | ◉ | |
| Processing wrong workpiece | ○ | ◉ | ◉ | ○ | ○ | ◉ | ◉ | | ○ | |
| Misoperation | | | ○ | | | | ○ | | ○ | ◉ |
| Adjustment error | ○ | ○ | ○ | ◉ | ○ | ◉ | ○ | ○ | ○ | ○ |
| Improper equipment setup | | | ○ | | | | ◉ | | | ◉ |
| Improper tools and jigs | | | ○ | | | | ◉ | | | ○ |

SOURCE: N. K. SHIMBUN, LTD./FACTORY MAGAZINE (ED.) *POKA-YOKE: IMPROVING PRODUCT QUALITY BY PREVENTING DEFECTS* (CAMBRIDGE MA: PRODUCTIVITY PRESS, 1989), P. 14. FROM POKA-YOKE: *IMPROVING PRODUCT QUALITY BY PREVENTING DEFECTS* EDITED BY NKS/FACTORY MAGAZINE. COPYRIGHT© 1987 PRODUCTIVITY, INC, PO BOX 13390 PORTLAND, OR 97213. 800-394-6868. *www.productivityinc.com*

and it becomes part of a registry of certified companies. This third-party certification also has legal advantages in the European Community. For example, a manufacturer is liable for injury to a user of the product. The firm, however, can free itself from any liability by showing that it has used the appropriate standards in its production process and carefully selected its suppliers as part of its purchasing requirement. For this reason, there is strong motivation to choose ISO 9000–certified suppliers.

**Before Improvement**

The operation depended on the worker's vigilance.

**After Improvement**

Device to ensure attachment of labels

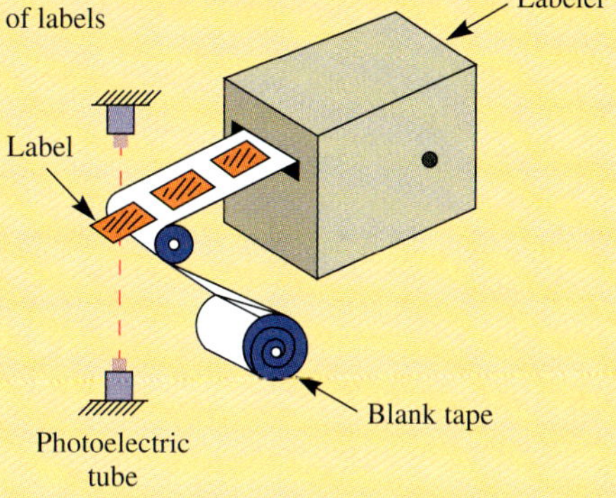


The tape fed out by the labeler turns sharply so that the labels detach and project out from the tape. This is detected by a photoelectric tube and, if the label is not removed and applied to the product within the tact time of 20 seconds, a buzzer sounds and the conveyor stops.

Effect: Label application failures were eliminated.
Cost: ¥15,000 ($75)

EXHIBIT 7.15

Poka-Yoke Example (Placing labels on parts coming down a conveyor)

*Quality System*

9001: Model for Quality Assurance in Design, Production, Installation, and Servicing. (To be used when conformance to specified requirements is to be assured by the supplier during several stages that *may* include design/development, production, installation, and servicing.)

9002: Model for Quality Assurance in Production and Installation. (To be used when conformance to specified requirements is to be assured by the supplier during production and installation.)

9003: Model for Quality Assurance in Final Inspection Test. (To be used when conformance to specified requirements is to be assured by the supplier solely at final inspection and test.)

*Guidelines for Use*

9000: Quality Management and Quality Assurance Standards—Guidelines for Selection and Use.

9004: Quality Management and Quality System Elements—Guidelines.

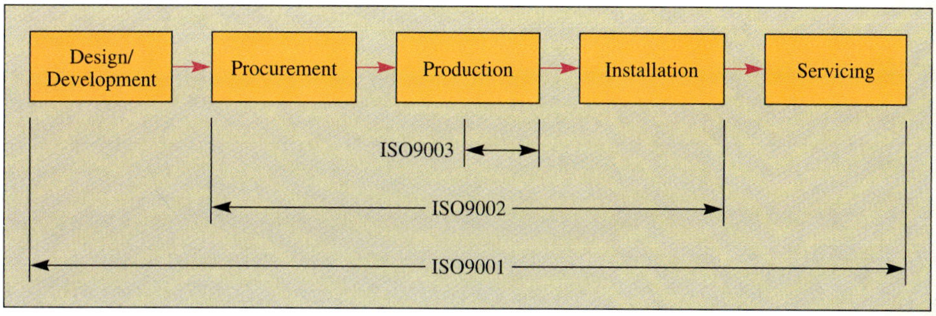


EXHIBIT 7.16

ISO 9000 Standards, Their Areas of Application in Production Flow, and Guidelines for Use

EXHIBIT 7.17

## The 20 Elements to Be Addressed in an ISO 9000 Quality System

1. *Management Responsibility*
   *a.* The quality policy shall be defined, documented, understood, implemented, and maintained.
   *b.* Responsibilities and authorities for all personnel specifying, achieving, and monitoring quality shall be defined. In-house verification resources shall be defined, trained, and funded. A designated management person sees that the Q91 program is implemented and maintained.
2. *Quality System*
   *a.* Procedures shall be prepared.
   *b.* Procedures shall be implemented.
3. *Contract Review*
   *a.* Incoming contracts (and purchase orders) shall be reviewed to see whether the requirements are adequately defined, agree with the bid, and can be implemented.
4. *Design Control*
   *a.* The design project shall be planned.
   *b.* Design input parameters shall be defined.
   *c.* Design output, including crucial product characteristics, shall be documented.
   *d.* Design output shall be verified to meet input requirements.
   *e.* Design changes shall be controlled.
5. *Document Control*
   *a.* Generation of documents shall be controlled.
   *b.* Distribution of documents shall be controlled.
   *c.* Changes to documents shall be controlled.
6. *Purchasing*
   *a.* Potential subcontractors and subsuppliers shall be evaluated for their ability to provide stated requirements.
   *b.* Requirements shall be clearly defined in contracting data.
   *c.* Effectiveness of the subcontractor's quality assurance system shall be assessed.
7. *Customer-Supplied Material*
   *a.* Any customer-supplied material shall be protected against loss or damage.
8. *Product Identification and Traceability*
   *a.* The product shall be identified and traceable by item, batch, or lot during all stages of production, delivery, and installation.
9. *Process Control*
   *a.* Production (and installation) processes shall be defined and planned.
   *b.* Production shall be carried out under controlled conditions: documented instructions, in-process controls, approval of processes and equipment, and criteria for workmanship.
   c. Special processes that cannot be verified after the fact shall be monitored and controlled throughout the processes.
10. *Inspection and Testing*
    *a.* Incoming materials shall be inspected or verified before use.
    *b.* In-process inspection and testing shall be performed.
    *c.* Final inspection and testing shall be performed prior to release of finished product.
    *d.* Records of inspection and test shall be kept.
11. *Inspection, Measuring, and Test Equipment*
    *a.* Equipment used to demonstrate conformance shall be controlled, calibrated, and maintained:
    - Identify measurements to be made.
    - Identify affected instruments.
    - Calibrate instruments (procedures and status indicators).
    - Periodically check calibration.
    - Assess measurement validity if found out of calibration.
    - Control environmental conditions in metrology lab.

    *b.* Measurement uncertainty and equipment capability shall be known.
    *c.* Where test hardware or software is used, it shall be checked before use and rechecked during use.
12. *Inspection and Test Status*
    *a.* Status of inspections and tests shall be maintained for items as they progress through various processing steps.
    *b.* Records shall show who released conforming product.
13. *Control of Nonconforming Product*
    *a.* Nonconforming product shall be controlled to prevent inadvertent use or installation.
    *b.* Review and disposition of nonconforming product shall be accomplished in a formal manner.
14. *Corrective Action*
    *a.* Problem causes shall be identified.
    *b.* Specific problems and their causes shall be corrected.
    *c.* Effectiveness of corrective actions shall be assessed.
15. *Handling, Storage, Packaging, and Delivery*
    *a.* Procedures for handling, storage, packaging, and delivery shall be developed and maintained.
    *b.* Handling controls shall prevent damage and deterioration.
    *c.* Secure storage shall be provided. Product in stock shall be checked for deterioration.
    *d.* Packing, preservation, and marking processes shall be controlled.
    *e.* Quality of the product after final inspection shall be maintained. This might include delivery controls.
16. *Quality Records*
    *a.* Quality records shall be identified, collected, indexed, filed, stored, maintained, and dispositioned.
17. *Internal Quality Audits*
    *a.* Audits shall be planned and performed.
    *b.* Results of audits shall be communicated to management.
    *c.* Any deficiencies found shall be corrected.
18. *Training*
    *a.* Training needs shall be identified.
    *b.* Training shall be provided.
    *c.* Selected tasks might require qualified individuals.
    *d.* Records of training shall be maintained.
19. *Servicing*
    *a.* Servicing activities shall be performed to written procedures.
    *b.* Servicing activities shall meet requirements.
20. *Statistical Techniques*
    *a.* Statistical techniques shall be identified.
    *b.* Statistical techniques shall be used to verify acceptability of process capability and product characteristics.

SOURCE: D. R. ARTER, "DEMYSTIFYING THE ISO 9000/290 SERIES STANDARDS," *QUALITY PROGRESS*, NOVEMBER 1992, P. 66. © 1992 AMERICAN SOCIETY FOR QUALITY CONTROL. REPRINTED WITH PERMISSION.

Certification can take as little as three to six months (if a firm is currently using military standards) or as long as two years (if top management is not fully committed). Certification involves getting the proper documents, initiating the required procedures and practices, and conducting internal audits. This can be followed by a second- or third-party audit as desired.

### ISO 9000 VERSUS THE BALDRIGE CRITERIA

Rabbitt and Bergh nicely answer three questions relating ISO 9000 and the Baldrige award as follows:[5]

1 **Should we go for the Baldrige Award or ISO 9000 certification first?** Go for ISO 9000 compliance first. Achieving certification will help you prepare for the Baldrige. Since 1992 applications for the Baldrige Award have dropped. The Baldrige committee feels that this is in response to companies going for ISO 9000 certification first.

2 **What's the difference between ISO 9000 and the Baldrige Award?** ISO focuses very closely on internal processes, especially manufacturing, sales, administration, and technical support and services. The Baldrige places more emphasis on customer satisfaction and business results.

3 **Do you have to be certified in ISO 9000 before going for the Baldrige?** The Baldrige assumes you have your processes under control and therefore awards relatively few points in this area. The Baldrige addresses the issues of customer satisfaction, business results, and the competitive aspects of gaining increased sales and profitability. ISO 9000 virtually ignores competitive positioning.

## SERVICE QUALITY MEASUREMENT: SERVQUAL

As can be seen in the box titled "Product Quality Is Not Enough," product quality alone will not satisfy the customer. We need to improve the service that supports the products in goods production as well as in "pure service" businesses. Although the approaches to improving product quality are equally applicable to services, identifying what should be improved requires tapping the customer's satisfaction with the service process as well as the outcome from that process. A standard approach to making this determination is to measure the gap between what customers expected and their perceptions of the service provided in a service encounter (see Exhibit 7.18). The size of the gap indicates where improvements should be made. The measurement is done by having customers fill out the **SERVQUAL** questionnaire[6] (contained on the CD that accompanies this book). The questionnaire consists of 22 expectation and matching perception questions relating to the five statistically derived dimensions of service quality listed in Exhibit 7.18. Each item is scored on a 1 to 7 scale, from strongly disagree (1) to strongly agree (7). For example, expectation question 1 states that the company under study "should have up-to-date equipment"; and perception question 1 states that the company "has up-to-date equipment." Thus, if the customer assigns a 6 to expectation and 4 to perception the gap score is −2. (By convention, expectations are subtracted from perceptions.) Typically, tangibles have the lowest gap score because physical features of a service are easier to control.

SERVQUAL

**Weighted SERVQUAL** The SERVQUAL procedure also permits assignment of importance weightings to each of the five dimensions. This is done by allocating 100 points across the dimensions and then multiplying the dimension gap score by points assigned to it. All five weighted dimension scores are then added to derive an overall weighted service

EXHIBIT 7.18

Perceived Service Quality

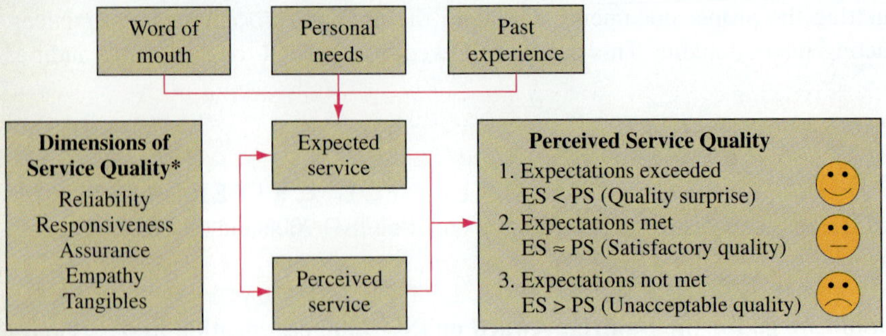


**Reliability:* the ability to perform service as promised, both dependably and accurately.

*Responsiveness:* willingness to help customers promptly.

*Assurance:* knowledge and courtesy of employees, as well as their ability to convey trust.

*Empathy:* caring and individualized attention.

*Tangibles:* the appearance of physical facilities, equipment, and personnel, as well as other factors affecting the senses such as noise and temperature.

SOURCE: ADAPTED WITH PERMISSION FROM THE *JOURNAL OF MARKETING*, PUBLISHED BY THE AMERICAN MARKETING ASSOCIATION, A. PARASURAMAN, V. A. ZEITHAML, AND L. L. BERRY, "A CONCEPTUAL MODEL OF SERVICE QUALITY AND ITS IMPLICATIONS FOR FUTURE RESEARCH," FALL 1985/49, P. 48.

## PRODUCT QUALITY IS NOT ENOUGH

Although the economy is booming and consumers are buying more, in 1999 Americans were less satisfied than ever with their purchases. This was mainly due to a gap between their expectations and their perceptions of quality and service. The American Customer Satisfaction Index (ACSI), which is based on quarterly surveys of current customers of companies that account for 30 to 40 percent of the GDP, continued its overall decline after a slight upturn in 1998. As depicted in the chart below, the overall ACSI index stood at 72 out of 100 midway through 1999. This represented a decline of 3.4 percent since the ACSI debut in 1994.

The zeal for cost cutting by American firms is considered to be a prime suspect in the decline of satisfaction. Although cost cutting may boost earnings in the short term, it may have a significantly adverse impact in the long term. If a company cannot compensate for its cost-cutting measures and maintain its levels of quality and service, it risks alienating customers to such an extent that they curb their future spending. The ACSI has detected such trends.

For example, Compaq Computers' index began falling in 1995 before its financial results began to deteriorate. Compaq's index bottomed out at 67 two years later before recovering to its current score of 71. Subsequently, Compaq's profits have improved. PC makers in general have seen a drop of 8.3 percent since 1994. If prices are falling and PCs are more capable than ever, how can that be? The answer may be that quality alone may not be sufficient to maintain customer satisfaction; acceptable levels of service may be necessary. One PC manufacturer, Dell Computer Corp., has bucked the trend with its index rising 5.6 percent. The keys to Dell's success may be its emphasis on meeting customers' needs and directing repeat customers to similar systems, where product familiarity will be high.

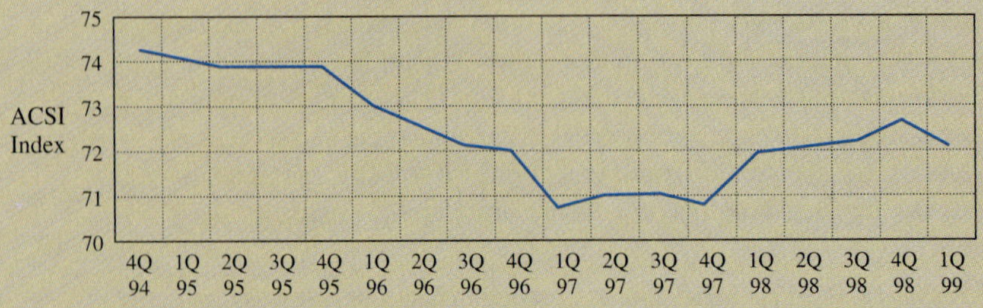


SOURCE: REPUBLISHED WITH PERMISSION OF DOW JONES, INC., FROM *THE WALL STREET JOURNAL*, "QUALITY, SERVICE BARELY PASS MUSTER WITH CONSUMER," AUGUST 16, 1999, P. A2. PERMISSION CONVEYED THROUGH THE COPYRIGHT CLEARANCE CENTER, INC.

quality score. Bank customers, for example, usually weight reliability heavily and tangibles lightly.

**SERVPERF** The customer often has high expectations of service quality in all areas, so a common modification of the approach is to simply use the 22 perceptions score to evaluate the service. This modification is called SERVPERF. Although this loses the "gap" feature, it has been shown to effectively measure the performance of the service company, and it also indicates where the company should improve.

In summary, there is still much debate among service marketing specialists about the SERVQUAL instrument. (One criticism is that it doesn't capture such important service quality dimensions as "fun.") Nevertheless, it is a tool that has been successfully applied in virtually every service business, and service operations specialists should have it as part of their tool kit.

## CONCLUSION

Unless an organization is making such a unique product that it has no real competition—and few are—it had better be a black belt in TQM. The Baldrige Award reflecting the philosophies of the quality gurus has provided a template for all companies to structure and improve their quality practices. We are not alone in seeking competitive national advantage in quality, as evidenced by the European Quality Award and the growing quality skills of many Asian countries. In information technology, developing quality specifications and costs for what is essentially an intangible product is one of the new challenges for quality management. The same can be said for the traditional area of services, where the public is far from satisfied with the level of quality it receives from its service providers. In the technical note that follows this chapter, we provide important statistical tools that management can apply to improve quality in all production environments.

## KEY TERMS

**Total quality management (TQM)** Managing the entire organization so that it excels on all dimensions of products and services that are important to the customer.

**The Deming Prize** An award given by Japan to companies that excel in quality.

**Design quality** The inherent value of the product in the market place.

**Conformance quality** The degree to which the product or service design specifications are met.

**Quality at the source** The person who does the work is responsible for ensuring that specifications are met.

**Zero defects** The goal of a quality program.

**Dimensions of quality** Criteria by which quality is measured.

**Cost of quality** Expenditures related to achieving product or service quality, such as the costs of prevention, appraisal, internal failure, and external failure.

**Continuous improvement** The philosophy of continually seeking improvements in processes through the use of team efforts.

**Kaizen** Japanese term for continuous improvement.

**PDCA cycle** Also called "The Deming wheel"; refers to the *p*lan-*d*o-*c*heck-*a*ct cycle of continuous improvement.

**External benchmarking** Looking outside the company to examine what excellent performers inside and outside the company's industry are doing in the way of quality.

**Fail-safe or poka-yoke procedures** Simple practices that prevent errors or provide feedback in time for the worker to correct errors.

**ISO 9000** Formal standards used for quality certification, developed by the International Organization for Standardization.

**ISO 14000** A series of standards to control the impact of an organization's activities and outputs on the environment.

**SERVQUAL** A service quality questionnaire that measures the gap between customer expectations and perceptions of performance after a service encounter.

## REVIEW AND DISCUSSION QUESTIONS

1 How could you apply the Baldrige Award criteria to your university?
2 Is the goal of zero defects realistic for services such as Blockbuster Video stores?
3 What criteria would you use to evaluate the quality of an Internet website?
4 How is the Baldrige Award process beneficial to companies that do not win?
5 "If line employees are required to assume the quality control function, their productivity will decrease." Discuss this.
6 "You don't inspect quality into a product; you have to build it in." Discuss the implications of this statement.
7 "Before you build quality in, you must think it in." How do the implications of this statement differ from those of Question 6?
8 Business writer Tom Peters has suggested that in making process changes, we should "Try it, test it, and get on with it." How does this philosophy square with the continuous improvement philosophy?
9 Shingo told a story of a poka-yoke he developed to make sure that operators avoided the mistake of putting fewer than the required four springs in a push-button device. The existing method involved assemblers taking individual springs from a box containing several hundred, and then placing two of them behind an ON button and two more behind an OFF button. What was the poka-yoke Shingo created?
10 The typical computerized word processing package is loaded with poka-yokes. List three. Are there any others you wish the packages had?

## PROBLEMS

1. See ISM.
1 Professor Chase is frustrated by his inability to make a good cup of coffee in the morning. Show how you would use a fishbone diagram to analyze the process he uses to make a cup of his evil brew.

2. See ISM.
2 Use the benchmarking process and as many CI tools as you can to show how you can improve your performance in your weakest course in school.

3. See ISM.
3 Consider a simple repair job that you performed that did not turn out particularly well. Analyze the mistakes or defects you made using the Sources of Defects table presented in Exhibit 7.14. Which errors were your fault?

4. See ISM.
4 Evaluate the service quality of your bank using the perceptions of performance portion of the SERVQUAL questionnaire contained on the student CD. Compute the score for each of the five SERVQUAL dimensions. On which dimension does your bank score the highest? Lowest?

## INTERNET ENRICHMENT EXERCISE

www. quality.nist.gov/show.htm

Visit the Baldrige Award website and see who won this year. What quality ideas did the winner demonstrate? What did the winner do that was particularly creative?

## CASE: HANK KOLB, DIRECTOR OF QUALITY ASSURANCE

Hank Kolb was whistling as he walked toward his office, still feeling a bit like a stranger since he had been hired four weeks before as director, of quality assurance. All that week he had been away from the plant at an interesting seminar, entitled "Quality in the 90s," given for quality managers of manufacturing plants by the corporate training department. He was now looking forward to digging into the quality problems at this industrial products plant employing 1,200 people.

Kolb poked his head into the office of Mark Hamler, his immediate subordinate as the quality control manager, and asked him how things had gone during the past week. Hamler's muted smile and an "Oh, fine," stopped Kolb in his tracks. He didn't know Hamler very well and was unsure about pursuing this reply any further. Kolb was still uncertain of how to start building a relationship with him because Hamler had been passed over for the promotion to Kolb's job; Hamler's evaluation form had stated "superb technical knowledge; managerial skills lacking." Kolb decided to inquire a little further and asked Hamler what had happened; he replied, "Oh, just another typical quality snafu. We had a little problem on the Greasex line last week [a specialized degreasing solvent packed in a spray can for the high-technology sector]. A little high pressure was found in some cans on the second shift, but a supervisor vented them so that we could ship them out. We met our delivery schedule!" Because Kolb was still relatively unfamiliar with the plant and its products, he asked Hamler to elaborate; painfully, Hamler continued:

> We've been having some trouble with the new filling equipment and some of the cans were pressurized beyond our AQL [acceptable quality level] on a psi rating scale.
>
> The production rate is still 50 percent of standard, about 14 cases per shift, and we caught it halfway into the shift. Mac Evans [the inspector for that line] picked it up, tagged the cases "hold," and went on about his duties. When he returned at the end of the shift to write up the rejects, Wayne Simmons, first-line supervisor, was by a pallet of finished goods finishing sealing up a carton of the rejected Greasex; the reject "hold" tags had been removed. He told Mac that he had heard about the high pressure from another inspector at coffee break, had come back, taken off the tags, individually turned the cans upside down and vented every one of them in the eight rejected cartons. He told Mac that production planning was really pushing for the stuff and they couldn't delay by having it sent through the rework area. He told Mac that he would get on the operator to run the equipment right next time. Mac didn't write it up but came in about three days ago to tell me about it. Oh, it happens every once in a while and I told him to make sure to check with maintenance to make sure the filling machine was adjusted; and I saw Wayne in the hall and told him that he ought to send the stuff through rework next time.

Kolb was a bit dumbfounded at this and didn't say much—he didn't know if this was a big deal or not. When he got to his office he thought again what Morganthal, general manager, had said when he had hired him. He warned Kolb about the "lack of quality attitude" in the plant, and said that Kolb "should try and do something about this." Morganthal further emphasized the quality problems in the plant: "We have to improve our quality, it's costing us a lot of money, I'm sure of it, but I can't prove it! Hank, you have my full support in this matter; you're in charge of these quality problems. This downward quality–productivity–turnover spiral has to end!"

The incident had happened a week before; the goods were probably out in the customers' hands by now, and everyone had forgotten about it (or wanted to). There seemed to be more pressing problems than this for Kolb to spend his time on, but this continued to nag him. He felt that the quality department was being treated as a joke, and he also felt that this was a personal slap from manufacturing. He didn't want to start a war with the production people, but what could he do? Kolb was troubled enough to cancel his appointments and spend the morning talking to a few people. After a long and very tactful morning, he learned the following information:

1 **From personnel.** The operator for the filling equipment had just been transferred from shipping two weeks ago. He had no formal training in this job but was being trained by Wayne, on the job, to run the equipment. When Mac had tested the high-pressure cans the operator was nowhere to be found and had only learned of the rejected material from Wayne after the shift was over.

2 **From plant maintenance.** This particular piece of automated filling equipment had been purchased two years ago for use on another product. It had been switched to the Greasex line six months ago and maintenance completed 12 work orders during the last month for repairs or adjustments on it. The equipment had been adapted by plant maintenance for handling the lower viscosity of Greasex, which it had not originally been designed for. This included designing a special filling head. There was no scheduled preventive maintenance for this equipment, and the parts for the sensitive filling head, replaced three times in the last six months, had to be made at a nearby machine shop. Nonstandard downtime was 15 percent of actual running time.

3 **From purchasing.** The plastic nozzle heads for the Greasex can, designed by a vendor for this new product on a rush order, were often found to have slight burrs on the inside rim, and this caused some trouble in fitting the top to the can. An increase in application pressure at the filling head by maintenance adjustment had solved the burr application problem or had at least forced the nozzle heads on despite burrs. Purchasing agents said that they were going to talk to the sales representative of the nozzle head supplier about this the next time he came in.

4 **From product design and packaging.** The can, designed especially for Greasex, had been contoured to allow better gripping by the user. This change, instigated by marketing research, set Greasex apart from the appearance of its competitors and was seen as significant by the designers. There had been no test of the effects of the contoured can on filling speed or filling hydrodynamics from a high-pressured filling head. Kolb had a hunch that the new design was acting as a venturi (carrier creating suction) when being filled, but the packaging designer thought that was unlikely.

5 **From the manufacturing manager.** He had heard about the problem; in fact, Simmons had made a joke about it, bragging about how he beat his production quota to the other foremen and shift supervisors. The manufacturing manager thought Simmons was one of the "best foremen we have . . . he always got his production out." His promotion papers were actually on the manufacturing manager's desk when Kolb dropped by. Simmons was being strongly considered for promotion to shift supervisor. The manufacturing manager, under pressure from Morganthal for cost improvements and reduced delivery times, sympathetized with Kolb but said that the rework area would have vented with their pressure gauges what Wayne had done by hand. "But, I'll speak with Wayne about the incident," he said.

6 **From marketing.** The introduction of Greasex had been rushed to market to beat competitors, and a major promotional advertising campaign was under way to increase consumer awareness. A deluge of orders was swamping the order-taking department and putting Greasex high on the back-order list. Production had to turn the stuff out; even being a little off spec was tolerable because "it would be better to have it on the shelf than not there at all. Who cares if the label is a little crooked or the stuff comes out with a little too much pressure? We need market share now in that high-tech segment."

What bothered Kolb most was the safety issue of the high pressure in the cans. He had no way of knowing how much of a hazard the high pressure was or if Simmons had vented them enough to effectively reduce the hazard. The data from the can manufacturer, which Hamler had showed him, indicated that the high pressure found by the inspector was not in the danger area. But, again, the inspector had used only a sample testing procedure to reject the eight cases. Even if he could morally accept that there was no product safety hazard, could Kolb make sure that this would never happen again?

Skipping lunch, Kolb sat in his office and thought about the morning's events. The past week's seminar had talked about the role of quality, productivity and quality, creating a new attitude, and the quality challenge; but where had they told him what to do when this happened? He had left a very good job to come here because he thought the company was serious about the importance of quality, and he wanted a challenge. Kolb had demanded and received a salary equal to the manufacturing, marketing, and R&D directors, and he was one of the direct reports to the general manager. Yet he still didn't know exactly what he should or shouldn't do, or even what he could or couldn't do under these circumstances.

QUESTIONS

1 What are the causes of the quality problems on the Greasex line? Display your answer on a fishbone diagram.
2 What general steps should Hank follow in setting up a continuous improvement program for the company? What problems will he have to overcome to make it work?



## CASE: SHORTENING CUSTOMERS' TELEPHONE WAITING TIME

This case illustrates how a bank applied some of the basic SPC tools shown in Exhibit 7.10 and storyboard concepts to improve customer service. It is the story of a quality circle (QC) program implemented in the main office of a large bank. An average of 500 customers call this office every day. Surveys indicated that callers tended to become irritated if the phone rang more than five times before it was answered, and often would not call the company again. In contrast, a prompt answer after just two rings reassured the customers and made them feel more comfortable doing business by phone.

### SELECTION OF A THEME

Telephone reception was chosen as a QC theme for the following reasons: (1) Telephone reception is the first impression a customer receives from the company; (2) this theme coincided with the company's telephone reception slogan, "Don't make customers wait, and avoid needless switching from extension to extension"; and (3) it also coincided with a companywide campaign being promoted at that time that advocated being friendly to everyone one met.

First, the staff discussed why the present method of answering calls made callers wait. Exhibit 7.19 illustrates a frequent situation in which a call from customer B comes in while the operator is talking with customer A. Let's see why the customer has to wait.

At (1), the operator receives a call from the customer but, due to lack of experience, does not know where to connect the call. At (2), the receiving party cannot answer the phone quickly, perhaps because he or she is unavailable, and no one else can take the call. The result is that the operator must transfer the call to another extension while apologizing for the delay.

### CAUSE-AND-EFFECT (FISHBONE) DIAGRAM AND SITUATION ANALYSIS

To fully understand the situation, the quality circle members decided to conduct a survey regarding callers who waited for more than five rings. Circle members itemized factors at a brainstorming discussion and arranged them in a cause-and-effect diagram. (See Exhibit 7.20.) Operators then kept check sheets on several points to tally the results spanning 12 days from June 4 to 16. (See Exhibit 7.21A.)

### RESULTS OF THE CHECK SHEET SITUATION ANALYSIS

The data recorded on the check sheets unexpectedly revealed that "one operator (partner out of the office)" topped the list by a big margin, occurring a total of 172 times. In this case, the operator on duty had to deal with large numbers of calls when the phones were busy. Customers who had to wait a long time averaged 29.2 daily,

EXHIBIT 7.19

Why Customers Had to Wait

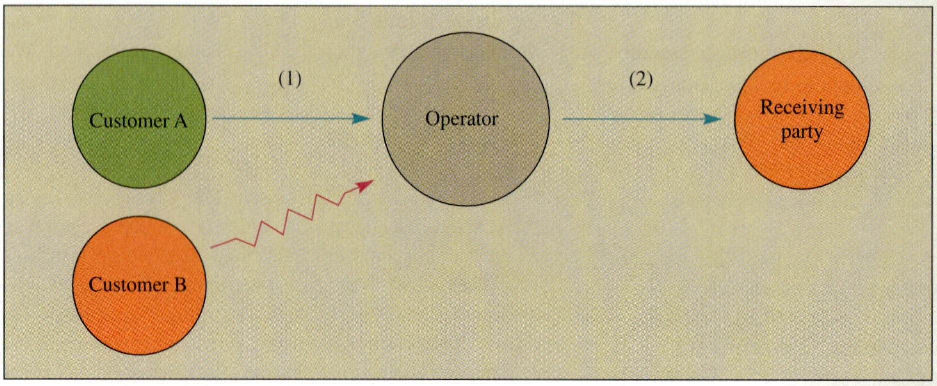

EXHIBIT 7.20

## Cause-and-Effect Diagram

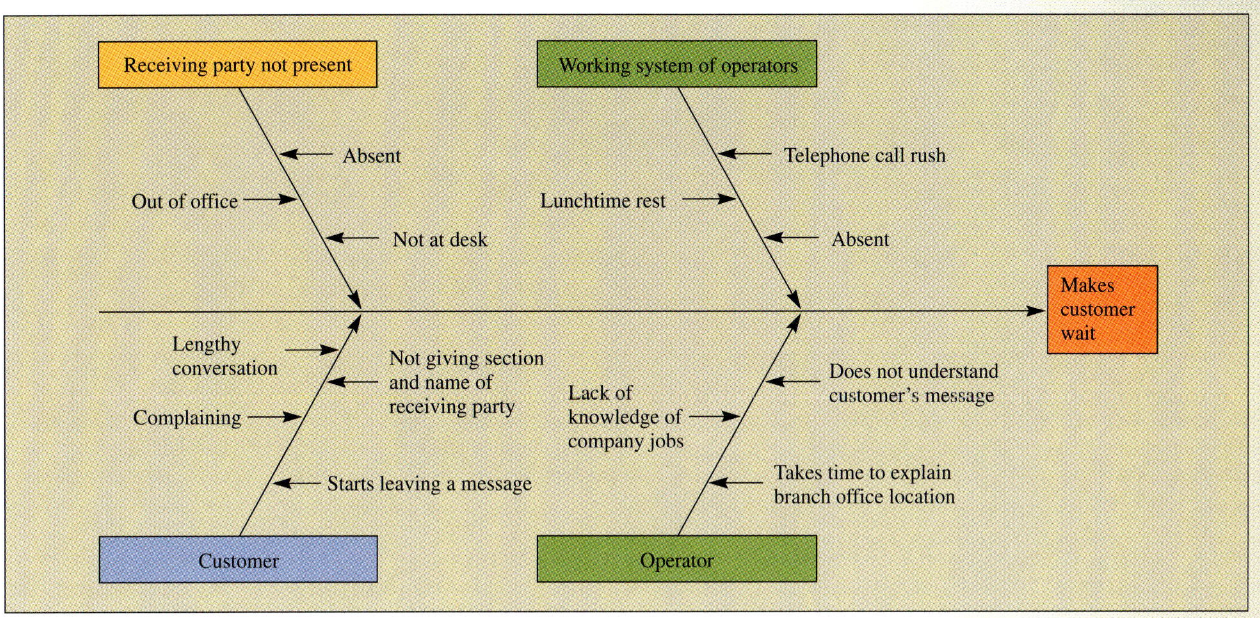


EXHIBIT 7.21

## Causes of Callers' Waits

**. Check Sheet—Designed to Identify the Problems**

| | REASON | | | |
|---|---|---|---|---|
| )ate | NO ONE PRESENT IN SECTION RECEIVING THE CALL | RECEIVING PARTY NOT PRESENT | ONLY ONE OPERATOR (PARTNER OUT OF THE OFFICE) | TOTAL |
| June 4 | \\\\ | 卌 \ | 卌 卌 \ | 24 |
| June 5 | 卌 | 卌 \\\ | 卌 卌 \\\\ | 32 |
| June 6 | 卌 \ | \\\\ | 卌 卌 \\ | 28 |
| June 15 | 卌 | 卌 | 卌 \\\ | 25 |

**. Reasons Why Callers Had to Wait**

| | | DAILY AVERAGE | TOTAL NUMBER |
|---|---|---|---|
| A | One operator (partner out of the office) | 14.3 | 172 |
| B | Receiving party not present | 6.1 | 73 |
| C | No one present in the section receiving the call | 5.1 | 61 |
| D | Section and name of receiving party not given | 1.6 | 19 |
| E | Inquiry about branch office locations | 1.3 | 16 |
| F | Other reasons | 0.8 | 10 |
| | Total | 29.2 | 351 |

Period: 12 days from June 4 to 16, 1980

**C. Reasons Why Callers Had to Wait (Pareto Diagram)**

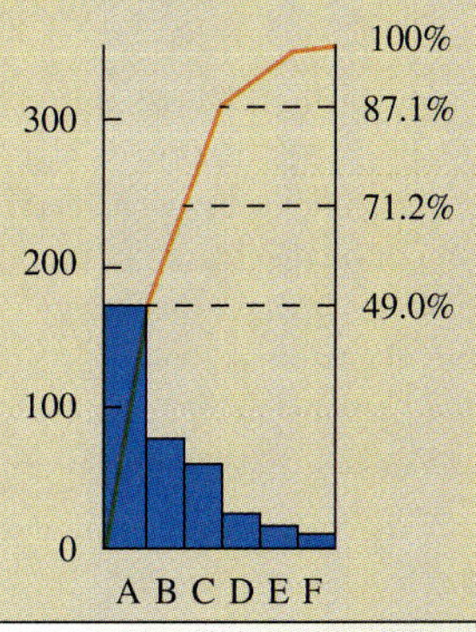

EXHIBIT 7.22

Effects of QC

**A. Effects of QC (Comparison of before and after QC)**

| | REASON WHY CALLERS HAD TO WAIT | TOTAL NUMBER BEFORE | TOTAL NUMBER AFTER | DAILY AVERAGE BEFORE | DAILY AVERAGE AFTER |
|---|---|---|---|---|---|
| A | One operator (partner out of the office) | 172 | 15 | 14.5 | 1.2 |
| B | Receiving party not present | 73 | 17 | 6.1 | 1.4 |
| C | No one present in the section receiving the call | 61 | 20 | 5.1 | 1.7 |
| D | Section and name of receiving party not given | 19 | 4 | 1.6 | 0.3 |
| E | Inquiry about branch office locations | 16 | 3 | 1.3 | 0.2 |
| F | Others | 10 | 0 | 0.8 | 0 |
| | Total | 351 | 59 | 29.2 | 4.8 |

Period: 12 days from Aug. 17 to 30.

Problems are classified according to cause and presented in order of the amount of time consumed. They are illustrated in a bar graph. 100% indicates the total number of time-consuming calls.

**B. Effects of QC (Pareto Diagram)**

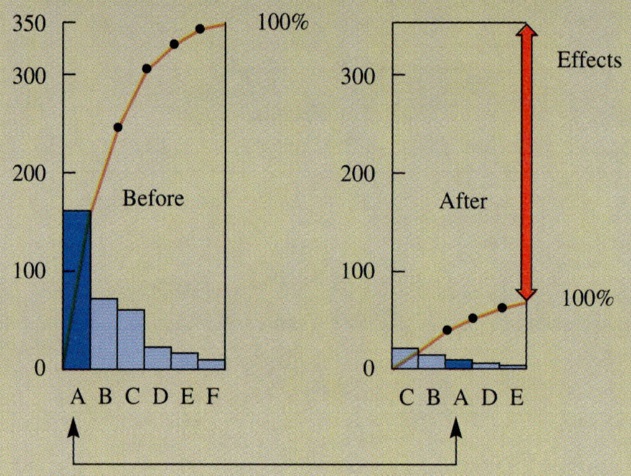


which accounted for 6 percent of the calls received every day. (See Exhibits 7.21B and 7.21C.)

SETTING THE TARGET

After an intense but productive discussion, the staff decided to set a QC program goal of reducing the number of waiting callers to zero. That is to say that all incoming calls would be handled promptly, without inconveniencing the customer.

MEASURES AND EXECUTION

1 **Taking lunches on three different shifts, leaving at least two operators on the job at all times.** Until this resolution was made, a two-shift lunch system had been employed, leaving only one operator on the job while the other was taking a lunch break. However, because the survey revealed that this was a major cause of customers waiting on the line, the company brought in a helper operator from the clerical section.

2 **Asking all employees to leave messages when leaving their desks.** The objective of this rule was to simplify the operator's chores when the receiving party was not at his desk. The new program was explained at the employees' regular morning meetings, and companywide support was requested. To help implement this practice, posters were placed around the office to publicize the new measures.

3 **Compiling a directory listing the personnel and their respective jobs.** The notebook was specially designed to aid the operators, who could not be expected to know the details of every employee's job. The notebook would help properly route calls.

CONFIRMING THE RESULTS

Although the waiting calls could not be reduced to zero, all items presented showed a marked improvement as shown in Exhibits 7.22A and 7.22B. The major cause of delays, "one operator (partner out of the office)," plummeted from 172 incidents during the control period to 15 in the follow-up survey.

SOURCE: FROM "THE QUEST FOR HIGHER QUALITY—THE DEMING PRIZE AND QUALITY CONTROL," RICOH COMPANY, LTD., IN MASAAKI IMAI, *KAIZEN: THE KEY TO JAPAN'S COMPETITIVE SUCCESS* (NEW YORK: RANDOM HOUSE, 1986), PP. 54–58.

## SELECTED BIBLIOGRAPHY

Bemowski, K., and B. Stratton (eds.). *101 Good Ideas: How to Improve Just About Any Process.* Washington D.C.: American Society for Quality, 1999.

Chowdhury, S., and K. Zimmer. *QS-9000 Pioneers—Registered Companies Share Their Strategies for Success.* Burr Ridge, IL: Richard D. Irwin, 1996.

Crosby, P. B. *Quality Is Free.* New York: McGraw-Hill, 1979.

———. *Quality Is Still Free.* New York: McGraw-Hill, 1996.

Deming, W. E. *Quality, Productivity and Competitive Position.* Cambridge, MA: MIT Center for Advanced Engineering Study, 1982.

———. *Out of the Crisis.* Cambridge, MA: MIT Center for Advanced Engineering Study, 1986.

Feigenbaum, A. V. *Total Quality Control.* New York: McGraw-Hill, 1991.

Giffi, C.; A. V. Roth; and G. M. Seal. *Competing in World-Class Manufacturing: America's 21st-Century Challenge.* Burr Ridge, IL: Richard D. Irwin, 1990.

Gitlow, H.; A. Oppenheim; and R. Oppenheim. *Quality Management: Tools and Methods for Improvement.* 2nd ed. New York: Irwin/McGraw Hill, 1995.

Juran, J. M. *Quality Control Handbook.* 3rd ed. New York: McGraw-Hill, 1979.

Juran, J. M., and F. M. Gryna. *Quality Planning and Analysis.* 2nd ed. New York: McGraw-Hill, 1980.

Lampercht, J. L. *Implementing the ISO 9000 Series.* New York: Marcel Dekker, 1993.

Robinson, A. *Modern Approaches to Manufacturing Improvement: The Shingo System.* Cambridge, MA: Productivity Press, 1990.

Shingo, S. *Zero Quality Control: Source Inspection and the Poka-Yoke System.* Stanford, CT: Productivity Press, 1986.

Taormina, T. *Virtual Leadership and the ISO 9000 Imperative.* Englewood Cliffs, NJ: Prentice Hall, 1996.

*1999 Malcolm Baldrige National Quality Award: Criteria and Application Instructions.* Washington, DC: National Institute of Standards and Technology, 1997.

Zemke, R., and J. A. Woods (eds.). *Best Practices in Customer Service.* Amherst, NJ: HRD Press, 1999.

## FOOTNOTES

1 P. B. Crosby, *Quality Is free* (New York: New American Library, 1979), p. 15.

2 B. Dumaine, "Who Needs a Boss?" *Fortune,* May 7, 1990, p. 54.

3 S. Walleck, D. O'Halloran, and C. Leader, "Benchmarking World-Class Performance," *McKinsey Quarterly,* 1991, no. 1, p. 7.

4 A. Robinson, *Modern Approaches to Manufacturing Improvement: The Shingo System* (Cambridge, MA: Productivity Press, 1990), p. 234.

5 J. T. Rabbitt, and P. A. Bergh, *The ISO* 9000 *Book* (White Plains, NY: Quality Resources, 1993), pp. 17–20.

6 A. Parasuraman, V. A. Zeithaml, and L. L. Berry, "SERVQUAL: A Multiple-Item Scale for Measuring Customer Perceptions of Service Quality," *Journal of Retailing* 64, no. 1 (Spring 1988), pp. 12–40.

*technical note seven*

# PROCESS CAPABILITY AND STATISTICAL QUALITY CONTROL

## OUTLINE AND KEY TERMS



technical note

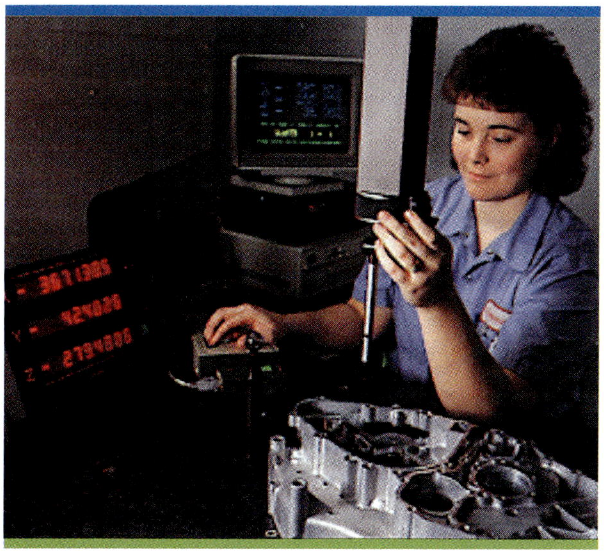

IN MONITORING A PROCESS USING SQC, WORKERS TAKE A SAMPLE WHERE THE DIAMETERS ARE MEASURED AND THE SAMPLE MEAN IS CALCULATED AND PLOTTED. INVESTMENTS IN MACHINERY, TECHNOLOGY, AND EDUCATION ARE DESIGNED TO REDUCE THE NUMBER OF DEFECTS THAT THE PROCESS PRODUCES.

This technical note on statistical quality control (SQC) covers the quantitative aspects of quality management. In general, SQC is a number of different techniques designed to evaluate quality from a conformance view. That is, how well are we doing at meeting the specifications that have been set during the design of the parts or services that we are providing? Managing quality performance using SQC techniques usually involves periodic sampling of a process and analysis of this data using statistically derived performance criteria.

Vol. I
"Quality"
Vol. VII
"Manufacturing Quality at Honda"
"A Day in the Life of Quality at Honda"
"SPC at Honda"

As you will see, SQC can be applied to both manufacturing and service processes. Here are some examples of the types of situations where SQC can be applied:

- How many paint defects are there in the finish of a car? Have we improved our painting process by installating a new sprayer?
- How long does it take to execute market orders in our Web-based trading system? Has the installation of a new server improved the service? Does the performance of the system vary over the trading day?
- How well are we able to maintain the dimensional tolerance on our three-inch ball bearing assembly? Given the variability of our process for making this ball bearing, how many defects would we expect to produce per million bearings that we make?
- How long does it take for customers to be served from our drive-through window during the busy lunch period?

Service

Processes that provide goods and services usually exhibit some variation in their output. This variation can be caused by many factors, some of which we can control and others that are inherent in the process. Variation that is caused by factors that can be clearly identified and possibly even managed is called **assignable variation.** For example, variation caused by workers not being equally trained or by improper machine adjustment is assignable variation. Variation that is inherent in the process itself is called **common variation.** Common variation is often referred to as *random variation* and may be the result of the type of equipment used to complete a process, for example.

Assignable variation

Common variation

As the title of this technical note implies, this material requires an understanding of very basic statistics. Recall from your study of statistics involving numbers that are normally distributed the definition of the mean and standard deviation. The mean is just the average value of a set of numbers. Mathematically this is

[TN7.1]
$$\overline{X} = \sum_{i=1}^{N} x_i / N$$

where:

$x_i$ = Observed value

$N$ = Total number of observed values

The standard deviation is

[TN7.2] $$\sigma = \sqrt{\frac{\sum_{i=1}^{N}(x_i - \overline{X})^2}{N}}$$

In monitoring a process using SQC, samples of the process output would be taken, and sample statistics calculated. The distribution associated with the samples should exhibit the same kind of variability as the actual distribution of the process, although the actual variance of the sampling distribution would be less. This is good because it allows the quick detection of changes in the actual distribution of the process. The purpose of sampling is to find when the process has changed in some nonrandom way, so that the reason for the change can be quickly determined.

In SQC terminology, *sigma* is often used to refer to the sample standard deviation. As you will see in the examples, sigma is calculated in a few different ways, depending on the underlying theoretical distribution (i.e., a normal distribution or a Poisson distribution).

## VARIATION AROUND US

It is generally accepted that, as variation is reduced, quality is improved. Sometimes that knowledge is intuitive. If a train is always on time, schedules can be planned more precisely. If clothing sizes are consistent, time can be saved by ordering from a catalog. But rarely are such things thought about in terms of the value of low variability. With engineers, the knowledge is better defined. Pistons must fit cylinders, doors must fit openings, electrical components must be compatible, and boxes of cereal must have the right amount of raisins—otherwise quality will be unacceptable and customers will be dissatisfied.

However, engineers also know that it is impossible to have zero variability. For this reason, designers establish specifications that define not only the target value of something but also acceptable limits about the target. For example, if the aim value of a dimension is 10 inches, the design specifications might then be 10.00 inches ±0.02 inch. This would tell the manufacturing department that, while it should aim for exactly 10 inches, anything between 9.98 and 10.02 inches is OK. These design limits are often referred to as the **upper and lower specification limits** or the **upper and lower tolerance limits.**

Upper and lower specification or tolerance limits

A traditional way of interpreting such a specification is that any part that falls within the allowed range is equally good, whereas any part falling outside the range is totally bad. This is illustrated in Exhibit TN7.1. (Note that the cost is zero over the entire specification range, and then there is a quantum leap in cost once the limit is violated.)

EXHIBITS TN7.1 & TN7.2

TN 7.1 A Traditional View of the Cost of Variability

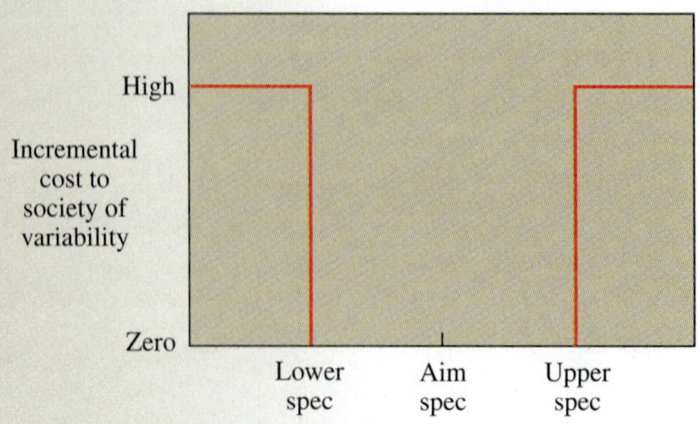


TN 7.2 Taguchi's View of the Cost of Variability

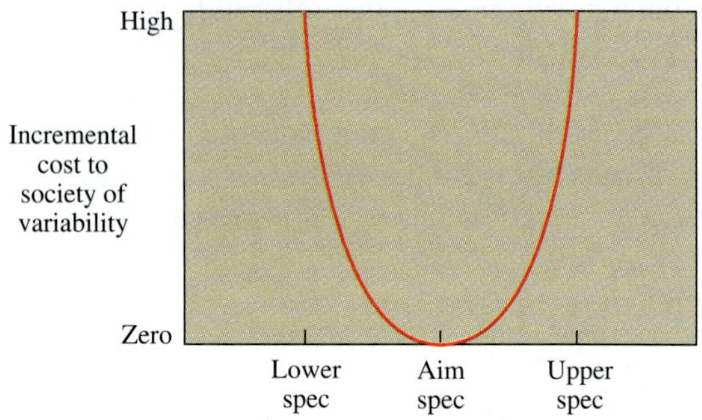

Genichi Taguchi, a noted quality expert from Japan, has pointed out that the traditional view illustrated in Exhibit TN7.1 is nonsense for two reasons:

1 From the customer's view, there is often practically no difference between a product just inside specifications and a product just outside. Conversely, there is a far greater difference in the quality of a product that is the target and the quality of one that is near a limit.
2 As customers get more demanding, there is pressure to reduce variability. However, Exhibit TN7.1 does not reflect this logic.

Taguchi suggests that a more correct picture of the loss is shown in Exhibit TN7.2. Notice that in this graph the cost is represented by a smooth curve. There are dozens of illustrations of this notion: the meshing of gears in a transmission, the speed of photographic film, the temperature in a workplace or department store. In nearly anything that can be measured, the customer sees not a sharp line, but a gradation of acceptability away from the "AIM" specification. Customers see the loss function as Exhibit TN7.2 rather than Exhibit TN7.1.

Of course, if products are consistently scrapped when they are outside specifications, the loss curve flattens out in most cases at a value equivalent to scrap cost in the ranges outside specifications. This is because such products, theoretically at least, will never be sold so there is no external cost to society. However, in many practical situations, either the process is capable of producing a very high percentage of product within specifications and/or 100 percent checking is not done and/or out-of-spec products can be reworked to bring them within specs. In any of these situations, the parabolic loss function is usually a reasonable assumption.

## PROCESS CAPABILITY

Taguchi argues that being within tolerance is not a yes/no decision, but rather a continuous function. The Motorola quality experts, on the other hand, argue that the process used to produce a good or deliver a service should be so good that the probability of generating a defect should be very, very low. Motorola made process capability and product design famous by adopting its now well-known **six-sigma** limits. Six-sigma is a shortcut for saying six standard deviations from the mean. When we design a part, we specify that certain dimensions should be within the upper and lower tolerance limits.

Six-sigma

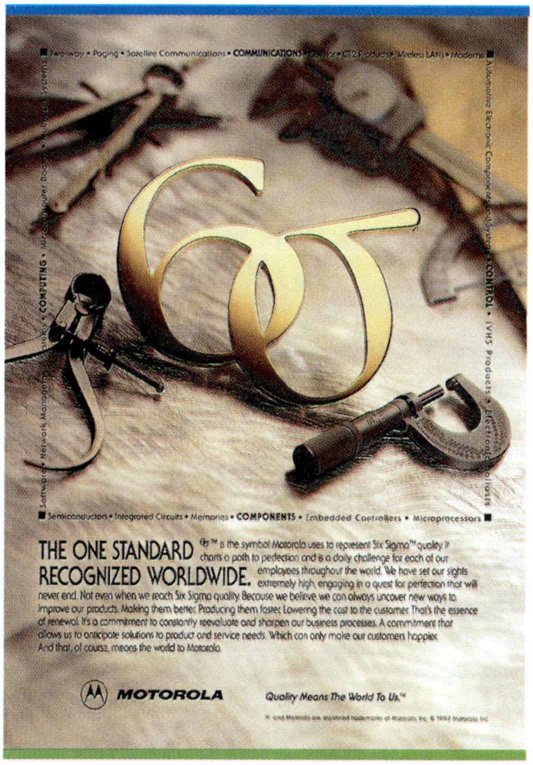


As a simple example, assume that we are designing a bearing for a rotating shaft—say an axle for the wheel of a car. There are many variables involved for both the bearing and the axle—for example, the width of the bearing, the size of the rollers, the size of the axle, the length of the axle, how it is supported, and so on. The designer specifies tolerances for each of these variables to ensure that the parts will fit properly. Suppose that initially a design is selected and the diameter of the bearing is set at 1.250 inches ±0.005 inches. This means that acceptable parts may have a diameter that varies between 1.245 and 1.255 inches (which are the lower and upper tolerance limits).

Next, consider the process in which the bearing will be made. Let's say that by running some tests, we determine the machine output to have a variation of sigma equal to 0.002 inch. If we are using three-sigma control limits on our process, bearings will have a variation of ±0.006 inch. Assuming that the process is centered at 1.250 inches, this means that we will produce parts that vary between 1.244 and 1.256 inches. As we can see, our process limits are greater than the tolerance limits specified by our designer. This is not good, because we will produce many parts that do not meet specifications.

Motorola, with their six-sigma criterion, insists that a process making a part must be capable of operating so that the design tolerances are six standard deviations away from the process mean. For our bearing, this would mean that our process variation would need to be less than or equal to 0.00083 inches (remember our tolerance was ±0.005, which, when divided by 6, is 0.00083). To reduce the variation in the process, we would need to find some better method for controlling the formation of the bearing. Of course, another option would be to redesign the axle assembly so that such perfect bearings are not needed.

We can show the six-sigma limits using an exhibit. Assume that we have changed the process to produce with 0.00083 variation. Now, the design limits and the process limits are acceptable according to Motorola standards. Let's assume that the bearing diameter follows a bell-shaped normal distribution as in Exhibit TN7.3. From our knowledge of the normal distribution, we know that 99.7 percent of the bell-shaped curve falls within ±3 sigma. We would expect only about three parts in 1,000 to fall outside of the three-sigma limits. The tolerance limits are another three sigma out from these control limits! In this case, the actual number of parts we would expect to produce outside the tolerance limits is only two parts per *billion*!

Suppose the central value of the process output shifts away from the mean. Exhibit TN7.4 shows the mean shifted one standard deviation closer to the upper specification limit. This causes a slightly higher number of expected defects, about four parts per million. This is still pretty good, by most people's standards. We use a calculation called the *capability index* to measure how well our process is capable of producing relative to the design tolerances. We describe how to calculate this index in the next section.

## CAPABILITY INDEX ($C_{pk}$)

Capability index ($C_{pk}$)

The **capability index** ($C_{pk}$) shows how well the parts being produced fit into the range specified by the design limits. If the design limits are larger than the three sigma allowed in the process, then the mean of the process can be allowed to drift off-center before readjustment, and a high percentage of good parts will still be produced.

Referring to Exhibits TN7.3 and TN7.4, the capability index ($C_{pk}$) is the position of the mean and tails of the process relative to design specifications. The more off-center, the greater the chance to produce defective parts.

EXHIBITS TN7.3 & TN7.4

TN 7.3 Process Capability

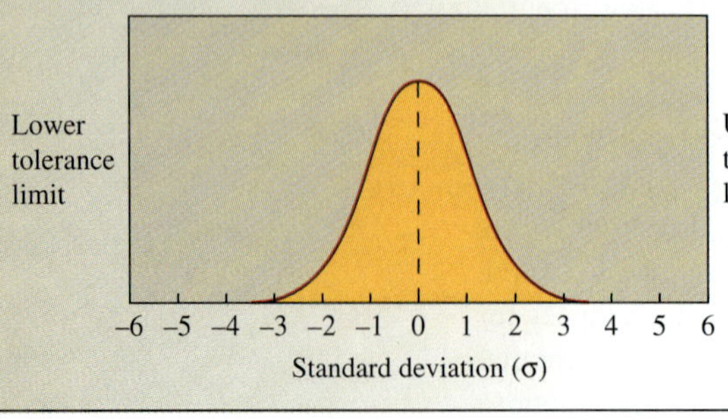


TN 7.4 Process Capability with a Shift in the Process Mean

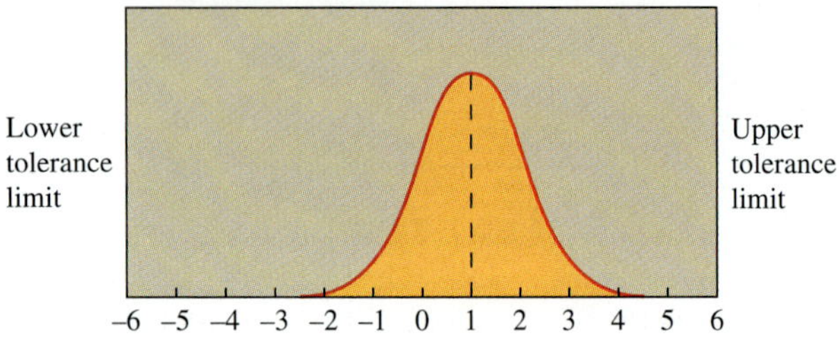

Because the process mean can shift in either direction, the direction of shift and its distance from the design specification set the limit on the process capability. The direction of shift is toward the smaller number.

Formally stated, the capability index ($C_{pk}$) is calculated as the smaller number as follows:

[TN7.3]
$$C_{pk} = \min\left[\frac{\overline{X} - \text{LTL}}{3\sigma} \quad \text{or} \quad \frac{\text{UTL} - \overline{X}}{3\sigma}\right]$$

For simplicity, let's assume our process mean is one inch and $\sigma = .001$. Further, the process mean is exactly in the center as in Exhibit TN7.3. Then for $\overline{X} = 1.000$

$$C_{pk} = \min\left[\frac{1.000 - .994}{3(.001)} \quad \text{or} \quad \frac{1.006 - 1.000}{3(.001)}\right] =$$

$$= \min\left[\frac{.006}{.003} = 2 \quad \text{or} \quad \frac{.006}{.003} = 2\right]$$

Because the mean is in the center, the two calculations are the same and equal to 2. If the mean shifted to $+1.5\sigma$ or 1.0015, then for $\overline{X} = 1.0015$

$$C_{pk} = \min\left[\frac{1.0015 - .994}{3(.001)} \quad \text{or} \quad \frac{1.006 - 1.0015}{3(.001)}\right] =$$

$$= \min\,[2.5 \quad \text{or} \quad 1.5]$$

$C_{pk} = 1.5$, which is the smaller number

This tells us that the process mean has shifted to the right similar to Exhibit TN7.4, but parts are still well within design limits.

Assuming that the process is producing with $\pm 3$ sigma and the process is centered exactly between the design limits, as in Exhibit TN7.3, Birch calculated the fraction of defective units that would fall outside various design limits as follows:[1]

| DESIGN LIMITS | DEFECTIVE PARTS | FRACTION DEFECTIVE |
|---|---|---|
| $\pm 1\sigma$ | 317 per thousand | .3173 |
| $\pm 2\sigma$ | 45 per thousand | .0455 |
| $\pm 3\sigma$ | 2 per thousand | .0027 |
| $\pm 4\sigma$ | 63 per million | .000063 |
| $\pm 5\sigma$ | 574 per billion | .000000574 |
| $\pm 6\sigma$ | 2 per billion | .000000002 |
| $\pm 7\sigma$ | .3 per billion | .0000000000003 |
| $\pm 8\sigma$ | .001 per billion | .0000000000000001 |

Motorola's design limit of six sigma with a shift of the process off the mean by $1.5\sigma$ ($C_{pk} = 1.5$) gives 3.4 defects per million. If the mean is exactly in the center ($C_{pk} = 2$), then 2 defects per *billion* are expected, as the table above shows.

# PROCESS CONTROL PROCEDURES

Process control is concerned with monitoring quality *while the product or service is being produced.* Typical objectives of process control plans are to provide timely information on whether currently produced items are meeting design specifications and to detect shifts in the process that signal that future products may not meet specifications. **Statistical process control (SPC)** involves testing a random sample of output from a process to determine whether the process is producing items within a preselected range.

Statistical process control (SPC)

Attributes

The examples given so far have all been based on quality characteristics (or *variables*) that are measurable, such as the diameter or weight of a part. **Attributes** are quality characteristics that are classified as either conforming or not conforming to specification. Goods or services may be observed to be either good or bad, or functioning or malfunctioning. For example, a lawnmower either runs or it doesn't; it attains a certain level of torque and horsepower or it doesn't. This type of measurement is known as sampling by attributes. Alternatively, a lawnmower's torque and horsepower can be measured as an amount of deviation from a set standard. This type of measurement is known as sampling by variables. The following section describes some standard approaches to controlling processes: first an approach useful for attribute measures and then an approach for variable measures. Both of these techniques result in the construction of control charts. Exhibit TN7.5 shows some examples for how control charts can be analyzed to understand how a process is operating.

EXHIBIT TN7.5

Control Chart Evidence for Investigation

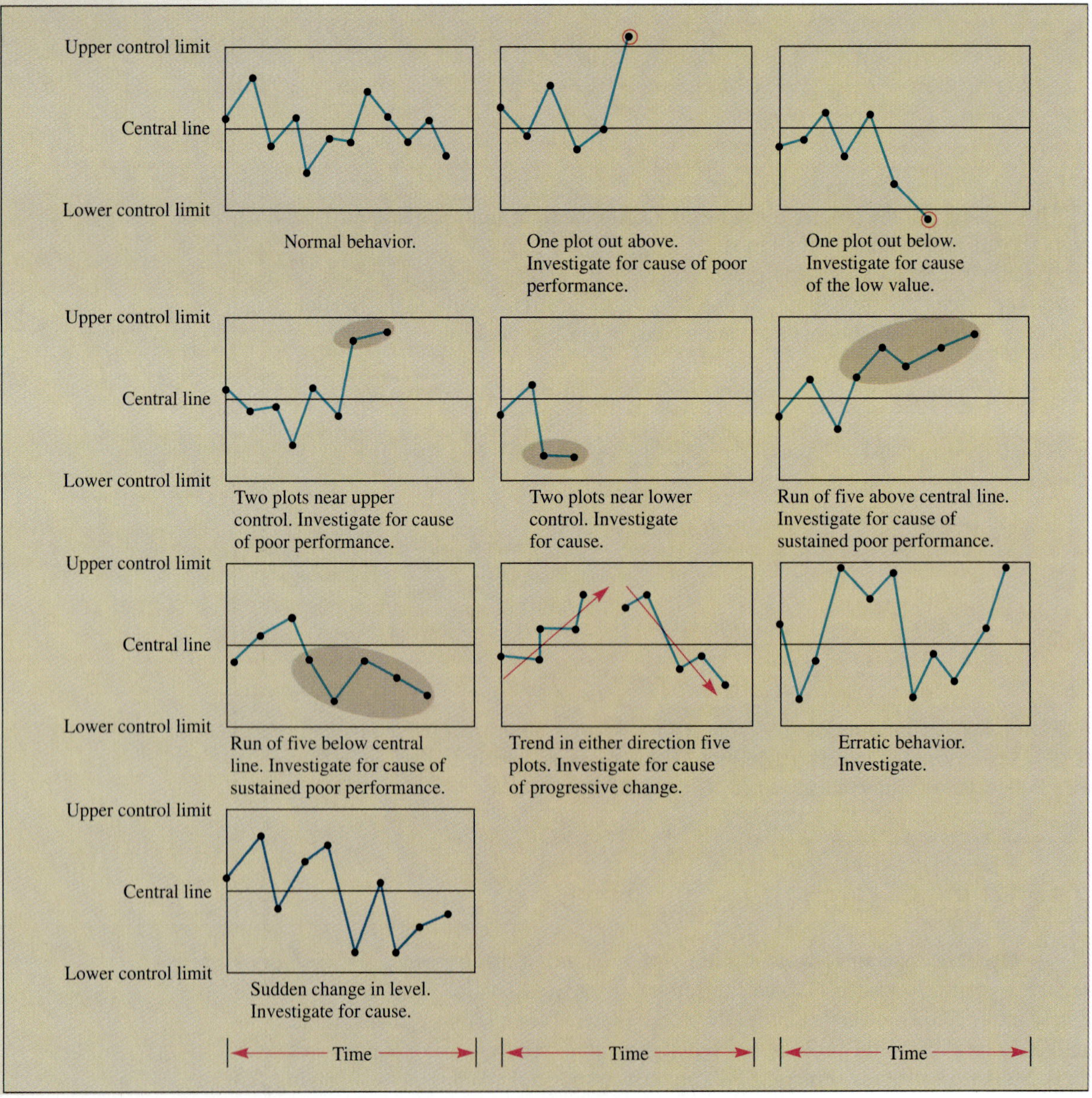

## PROCESS CONTROL WITH ATTRIBUTE MEASUREMENTS: USING *p* CHARTS

Measurement by attributes means taking samples and using a single decision—the item is good, or it is bad. Because it is a yes or no decision, we can use simple statistics to create a *p* chart with an upper control limit (UCL) and a lower control limit (LCL). We can draw these control limits on a graph and then plot the fraction defective of each individual sample tested. The process is assumed to be working correctly when the samples, which are taken periodically during the day, continue to stay between the control limits.

[TN7.4]
$$\bar{p} = \frac{\text{Total number of defects from all samples}}{\text{Number of samples} \times \text{Sample size}}$$

[TN7.5]
$$s_p = \sqrt{\frac{\bar{p}(1-\bar{p})}{n}}$$

[TN7.6]
$$\text{UCL} = \bar{p} + zs_p$$

[TN7.7]
$$\text{LCL} = \bar{p} - zs_p$$

where $\bar{p}$ is the fraction defective, $s_p$ is the standard deviation, $n$ is the sample size, and $z$ is the number of standard deviations for a specific confidence. Typically, $z = 3$ (99.7 percent confidence) or $z = 2.58$ (99 percent confidence) is used.

**Size of the Sample** The size of the sample must be large enough to allow counting of the attribute. For example, if we know that a machine produces 1 percent defects, then a sample size of five would seldom capture a defect. A rule of thumb when setting up a *p* chart is to make the sample large enough to expect to count the attribute twice in each sample. So an appropriate sample size if the defect rate were approximately 1 percent would be 200 units. One final note: In the calculations shown in equations TN7.4–7.7 the assumption is that the sample size is fixed. The calculation of the standard deviation depends on this assumption. If the sample size varies, the standard deviation and upper and lower control limits should be recalculated for each sample.

### EXAMPLE TN7.1: CONTROL CHART DESIGN

An insurance company wants to design a control chart to monitor whether insurance claim forms are being completed correctly. The company intends to use the chart to see if improvements in the design of the form are effective. To start the process the company collected data on the number of incorrectly completed claim forms over the past 10 days. The insurance company processes thousands of these forms each day, and due to the high cost of inspecting each form, only a small representative sample was collected each day. The data and analysis are shown in Exhibit TN7.6.

### SOLUTION

To construct the control chart, first calculate the overall fraction defective from all samples. This sets the centerline for the control chart.

$$\bar{p} = \frac{\text{Total number of defects from all samples}}{\text{Number of sample} \times \text{Sample size}} = \frac{91}{3000} = .03033$$

Next calculate the sample standard deviation:

$$s_p = \sqrt{\frac{\bar{p}(1-\bar{p})}{n}} = \sqrt{\frac{.03033(1-.03033)}{3000}} = .00990$$

Finally, calculate the upper and lower control limits. A $z$-value of 3 gives 99.7 percent confidence that the process is within these limits.

$$\text{UCL} = \bar{p} + 3z = .03033 + 3(.00990) = .06004$$
$$\text{LCL} = \bar{p} - 3z = .03033 - 3(.00990) = .00063$$

EXHIBIT TN7.6

Insurance Company Claim Form

| Sample | Number Inspected | Number of Forms Completed Incorrectly | Fraction Defective |
|---|---|---|---|
| 1 | 300 | 10 | 0.03333 |
| 2 | 300 | 8 | 0.02667 |
| 3 | 300 | 9 | 0.03000 |
| 4 | 300 | 13 | 0.04333 |
| 5 | 300 | 7 | 0.02333 |
| 6 | 300 | 7 | 0.02333 |
| 7 | 300 | 6 | 0.02000 |
| 8 | 300 | 11 | 0.03667 |
| 9 | 300 | 12 | 0.04000 |
| 10 | 300 | 8 | 0.02667 |
| Totals | 3000 | 91 | 0.03033 |
| Sample standard deviation | | | 0.00990 |

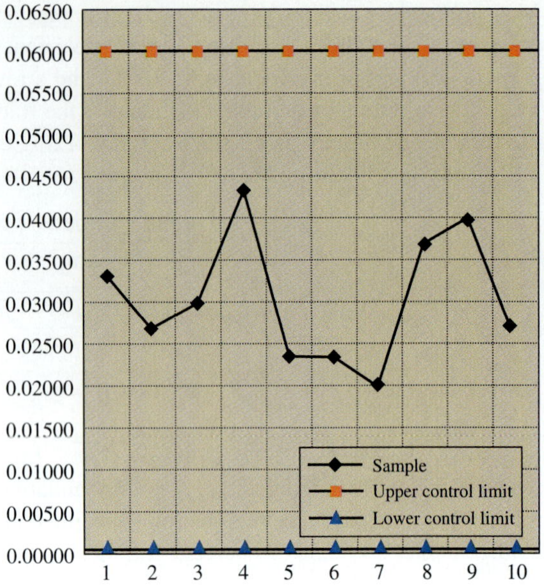


The calculations in Exhibit TN7.6, including the control chart, are included in the spreadsheet SPC.xls. ←

## PROCESS CONTROL WITH VARIABLE MEASUREMENTS: USING $\overline{X}$ AND $R$ CHARTS

$\overline{X}$ and $R$ (range) charts are widely used in statistical process control.

Variables

In attributes sampling, we determine whether something is good or bad, fits or doesn't fit—it is a go/no-go situation. In **variables** sampling, however, we measure the actual weight, volume, number of inches, or other variable measurements, and we develop control charts to determine the acceptability or rejection of the process based on those measurements. For example, in attribute sampling we might decide that if something is over 10 pounds we will reject it and under 10 pounds we will accept it. In variable sampling we measure a sample and may record weights of 9.8 pounds or 10.2 pounds. These values are used to create or modify control charts and to see whether they fall within the acceptable limits.

There are four main issues to address in creating a control chart: the size of the samples, number of samples, frequency of samples, and control limits.

**Size of Samples** For industrial applications in process control involving the measurement of variables, it is preferable to keep the sample size small. There are two main reasons. First, the sample needs to be taken within a reasonable length of time; otherwise, the process might change while the samples are taken. Second, the larger the sample, the more it costs to take.

Sample sizes of four or five units seem to be the preferred numbers. The *means* of samples of this size have an approximately normal distribution, no matter what the distribution of the parent population looks like. Sample sizes greater than five give narrower control limits and thus more sensitivity. For detecting finer variations of a process, it may be necessary, in fact, to use larger sample sizes. However, when sample sizes exceed 15 or so, it would be better to use $\overline{X}$ charts with standard deviation $\sigma$ rather than $\overline{X}$ charts with the range $R$ as we use in Example TN7.2.

**Number of Samples** Once the chart has been set up, each sample taken can be compared to the chart and a decision can be made about whether the process is acceptable.

PROCESS CONTROL CHARTS CAN BE GENERATED WITH COMPUTERS OR MANUALLY. SAMPLES ARE TAKEN FROM THE PROCESS AT STATED TIME INTERVALS AND THEIR AVERAGE PARAMETER VALUES ARE PLOTTED ON THE CHARTS. AS LONG AS THESE VALUES REMAIN WITHIN ESTABLISHED CONTROL LIMITS THE PROCESS IS IN CONTROL.

To set up the charts, however, prudence and statistics suggest that 25 or so samples be taken.

**Frequency of Samples** How often to take a sample is a trade-off between the cost of sampling (along with the cost of the unit if it is destroyed as part of the test) and the benefit of adjusting the system. Usually, it is best to start off with frequent sampling of a process and taper off as confidence in the process builds. For example, one might start with a sample of five units every half hour and end up feeling that one sample per day is adequate.

**Control Limits** Standard practice in statistical process control for variables is to set control limits three standard deviations above the mean and three standard deviations below. This means that 99.7 percent of the sample means are expected to fall within these control limits (that is, within a 99.7 percent confidence interval). Thus, if one sample mean falls outside this obviously wide band, we have strong evidence that the process is out of control.

## How to Construct $\overline{X}$ and $R$ Charts

If the standard deviation of the process distribution is known, the $\overline{X}$ chart may be defined:

[TN7.8]
$$UCL_{\overline{X}} = \overline{\overline{X}} + zs_{\overline{X}} \quad \text{and} \quad LCL_{\overline{X}} = \overline{\overline{X}} - zs_{\overline{X}}$$

where

$s_{\overline{X}} = s/\sqrt{n}$ = Standard deviation of sample means

$s$ = Standard deviation of the process distribution

$n$ = Sample size

$\overline{\overline{X}}$ = Average of sample means or a target value set for the process

$z$ = Number of standard deviations for a specific confidence level (typically, $z = 3$)

An $\overline{X}$ chart is simply a plot of the means of the samples that were taken from a process. $\overline{\overline{X}}$ is the average of the means.

In practice, the standard deviation of the process is not known. For this reason, an approach that uses actual sample data is commonly used. This practical approach is described in the next section.

An $R$ chart is a plot of the range within each sample. The range is the difference between the highest and the lowest numbers in that sample. $R$ values provide an easily calculated measure of variation used like a standard deviation. An $\overline{R}$ chart is the average of the range of each sample. More specifically defined, these are

[Same as TN7.1]
$$\overline{X} = \frac{\sum_{i=1}^{n} X_i}{n}$$

where

$\overline{X}$ = Mean of the sample
$i$ = Item number
$n$ = Total number of items in the sample

[TN7.9]
$$\overline{\overline{X}} = \frac{\sum_{j=1}^{m} \overline{X}_j}{m}$$

where

$\overline{\overline{X}}$ = The average of the means of the samples
$j$ = Sample number
$m$ = Total number of samples
$R_j$ = Difference between the highest and lowest measurement in the sample
$\overline{R}$ = Average of the measurement differences $R$ for all samples, or

[TN7.10]
$$\overline{R} = \frac{\sum_{j=1}^{m} R_j}{m}$$

E. L. Grant and R. Leavenworth computed a table (Exhibit TN7.7) that allows us to easily compute the upper and lower control limits for both the $\overline{X}$ chart and the $R$ chart.[2] These are defined as

[TN7.11] Upper control limit for $\overline{X} = \overline{\overline{X}} + A_2\overline{R}$

[TN7.12] Lower control limit for $\overline{X} = \overline{\overline{X}} - A_2\overline{R}$

[TN7.13] Upper control limit for $R = D_4\overline{R}$

[TN7.14] Lower control limit for $R = D_3\overline{R}$

### EXAMPLE TN7.2: $\overline{X}$ AND R CHARTS

We would like to create $\overline{X}$ and $R$ charts for a process. Exhibit TN7.8 shows measurements for all 25 samples. The last two columns show the average of the sample $\overline{X}$ and the range $R$.

Values for $A_2$, $D_3$, and $D_4$ were obtained from Exhibit TN7.7.

$$\text{Upper control limit for } \overline{X} = \overline{\overline{X}} + A_2\overline{R} = 10.21 + .58(.60) = 10.56$$

$$\text{Lower control limit for } \overline{X} = \overline{\overline{X}} - A_2\overline{R} = 10.21 - .58(.60) = 9.86$$

$$\text{Upper control limit for } R = D_4\overline{R} = 2.11(.60) = 1.27$$

$$\text{Lower control limit for } R = D_3\overline{R} = 0(.60) = 0$$

### SOLUTION

Exhibit TN7.9 shows the $\overline{X}$ chart and $R$ chart with a plot of all the sample means and ranges of the samples. All the points are well within the control limits, although sample 23 is close to the $\overline{X}$ lower control limit. ←

EXHIBIT TN7.7

**Factor for Determining from $\bar{R}$ the Three-Sigma Control Limits for $\bar{X}$ and $R$ Charts**

| Number of Observations in Subgroup $n$ | Factor for $\bar{X}$ Chart $A_2$ | Factors for $R$ Chart: Lower Control Limit $D_3$ | Factors for $R$ Chart: Upper Control Limit $D_4$ |
|---|---|---|---|
| 2 | 1.88 | 0 | 3.27 |
| 3 | 1.02 | 0 | 2.57 |
| 4 | 0.73 | 0 | 2.28 |
| 5 | 0.58 | 0 | 2.11 |
| 6 | 0.48 | 0 | 2.00 |
| 7 | 0.42 | 0.08 | 1.92 |
| 8 | 0.37 | 0.14 | 1.86 |
| 9 | 0.34 | 0.18 | 1.82 |
| 10 | 0.31 | 0.22 | 1.78 |
| 11 | 0.29 | 0.26 | 1.74 |
| 12 | 0.27 | 0.28 | 1.72 |
| 13 | 0.25 | 0.31 | 1.69 |
| 14 | 0.24 | 0.33 | 1.67 |
| 15 | 0.22 | 0.35 | 1.65 |
| 16 | 0.21 | 0.36 | 1.64 |
| 17 | 0.20 | 0.38 | 1.62 |
| 18 | 0.19 | 0.39 | 1.60 |
| 19 | 0.19 | 0.40 | 1.61 |
| 20 | 0.18 | 0.41 | 1.59 |

Upper control limit for $\bar{X} = UCL_{\bar{X}} = \bar{\bar{X}} + A_2\bar{R}$

Lower control limit for $\bar{X} = LCL_{\bar{X}} = \bar{\bar{X}} - A_2\bar{R}$

Upper control limit for $R = UCL_R = D_4\bar{R}$

Lower control limit for $R = LCL_R = D_3\bar{R}$

Note: All factors are based on the normal distribution.

EXHIBIT TN7.8

**Measurements in Samples of Five from a Process**

| Sample Number | Each Unit in Sample | | | | | Average $\bar{X}$ | Range $R$ |
|---|---|---|---|---|---|---|---|
| 1 | 10.60 | 10.40 | 10.30 | 9.90 | 10.20 | 10.28 | .70 |
| 2 | 9.98 | 10.25 | 10.05 | 10.23 | 10.33 | 10.17 | .35 |
| 3 | 9.85 | 9.90 | 10.20 | 10.25 | 10.15 | 10.07 | .40 |
| 4 | 10.20 | 10.10 | 10.30 | 9.90 | 9.95 | 10.09 | .40 |
| 5 | 10.30 | 10.20 | 10.24 | 10.50 | 10.30 | 10.31 | .30 |
| 6 | 10.10 | 10.30 | 10.20 | 10.30 | 9.90 | 10.16 | .40 |
| 7 | 9.98 | 9.90 | 10.20 | 10.40 | 10.10 | 10.12 | .50 |
| 8 | 10.10 | 10.30 | 10.40 | 10.24 | 10.30 | 10.27 | .30 |
| 9 | 10.30 | 10.20 | 10.60 | 10.50 | 10.10 | 10.34 | .50 |
| 10 | 10.30 | 10.40 | 10.50 | 10.10 | 10.20 | 10.30 | .40 |
| 11 | 9.90 | 9.50 | 10.20 | 10.30 | 10.35 | 10.05 | .85 |
| 12 | 10.10 | 10.36 | 10.50 | 9.80 | 9.95 | 10.14 | .70 |
| 13 | 10.20 | 10.50 | 10.70 | 10.10 | 9.90 | 10.28 | .80 |
| 14 | 10.20 | 10.60 | 10.50 | 10.30 | 10.40 | 10.40 | .40 |
| 15 | 10.54 | 10.30 | 10.40 | 10.55 | 10.00 | 10.36 | .55 |
| 16 | 10.20 | 10.60 | 10.15 | 10.00 | 10.50 | 10.29 | .60 |
| 17 | 10.20 | 10.40 | 10.60 | 10.80 | 10.10 | 10.42 | .70 |
| 18 | 9.90 | 9.50 | 9.90 | 10.50 | 10.00 | 9.96 | 1.00 |
| 19 | 10.60 | 10.30 | 10.50 | 9.90 | 9.80 | 10.22 | .80 |
| 20 | 10.60 | 10.40 | 10.30 | 10.40 | 10.20 | 10.38 | .40 |
| 21 | 9.90 | 9.60 | 10.50 | 10.10 | 10.60 | 10.14 | 1.00 |
| 22 | 9.95 | 10.20 | 10.50 | 10.30 | 10.20 | 10.23 | .55 |
| 23 | 10.20 | 9.50 | 9.60 | 9.80 | 10.30 | 9.88 | .80 |
| 24 | 10.30 | 10.60 | 10.30 | 9.90 | 9.80 | 10.18 | .80 |
| 25 | 9.90 | 10.30 | 10.60 | 9.90 | 10.10 | 10.16 | .70 |
| | | | | | | $\bar{\bar{X}} = 10.21$ | |
| | | | | | | | $\bar{R} = .60$ |

EXHIBIT TN7.9 $\bar{X}$ Chart and $R$ Chart

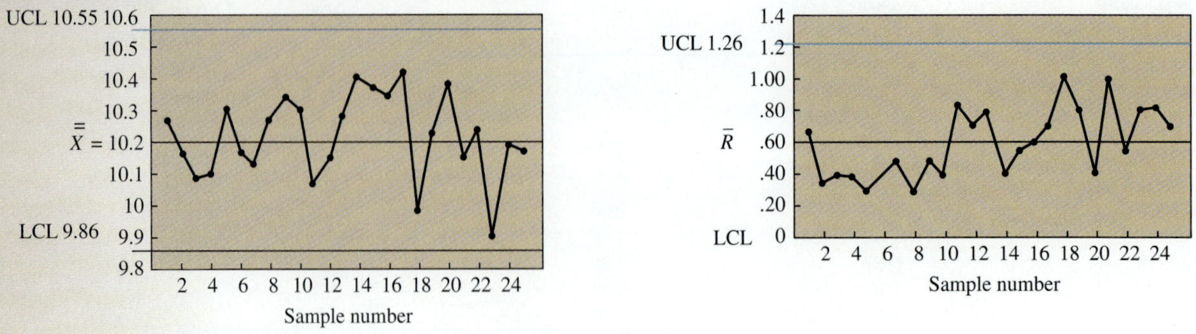


# ACCEPTANCE SAMPLING

## DESIGN OF A SINGLE SAMPLING PLAN FOR ATTRIBUTES

Acceptance sampling is performed on goods that already exist to determine what percentage of products conform to specifications. These products may be items received from another company and evaluated by the receiving department, or they may be components that have passed through a processing step and are evaluated by company personnel either in production or later in the warehousing function. Whether inspection should be done at all is addressed in the following example.

Acceptance sampling is executed through a sampling plan. In this section we illustrate the planning procedures for a single sampling plan—that is, a plan in which the quality is determined from the evaluation of one sample. (Other plans may be developed using two or more samples. See J. M. Juran and F. M. Gryna's *Quality Planning and Analysis* for a discussion of these plans.)

### *EXAMPLE TN7.3: COSTS TO JUSTIFY INSPECTION*

Total (100 percent) inspection is justified when the cost of a loss incurred by not inspecting is greater than the cost of inspection. For example, suppose a faulty item results in a \$10 loss and the average percentage defective of items in the lot is 3 percent.

### *SOLUTION*

If the average percentage of defective items in a lot is 3 percent, the expected cost of faulty items is $0.03 \times \$10$, or \$0.30 each. Therefore, if the cost of inspecting each item is less than \$0.30, the economic decision is to perform 100 percent inspection. Not all defective items will be removed, however, because inspectors will pass some bad items and reject some good ones.

The purpose of a sampling plan is to test the lot to either (1) find its quality or (2) ensure that the quality is what it is supposed to be. Thus, if a quality control supervisor already knows the quality (such as the 0.03 given in the example), he or she does not sample for defects. Either all of them must be inspected to remove the defects or none of them should be inspected, and the rejects pass into the process. The choice simply depends on the cost to inspect and the cost incurred by passing a reject. ←

A single sampling plan is defined by $n$ and $c$, where $n$ is the number of units in the sample and $c$ is the acceptance number. The size of $n$ may vary from one up to all the items in

AN EMPLOYEE INSPECTS THE MANUFACTURE OF REESE'S PEANUT BUTTER CUPS. THIS IS THE LAST STAGE OF FULL QUALITY CONTROL WHERE DEFECTIVE CUPS ARE REMOVED.

the lot (usually denoted as $N$) from which it is drawn. The acceptance number $c$ denotes the maximum number of defective items that can be found in the sample before the lot is rejected. Values for $n$ and $c$ are determined by the interaction of four factors (AQL, $\alpha$, LTPD, and $\beta$) that quantify the objectives of the product's producer and its consumer. The objective of the producer is to ensure that the sampling plan has a low probability of rejecting good lots. Lots are defined as high quality if they contain no more than a specified level of defectives, termed the *acceptable quality level (AQL)*.[3] The objective of the consumer is to ensure that the sampling plan has a low probability of accepting bad lots. Lots are defined as low quality if the percentage of defectives is greater than a specified amount, termed *lot tolerance percent defective (LTPD)*. The probability associated with rejecting a high-quality lot is denoted by the Greek letter alpha ($\alpha$) and is termed the *producer's risk*. The probability associated with accepting a low-quality lot is denoted by the letter beta ($\beta$) and is termed the *consumer's risk*. The selection of particular values for AQL, $\alpha$ LTPD, and $\beta$ is an economic decision based on a cost trade-off or, more typically, on company policy or contractual requirements.

There is a humorous story supposedly about Hewlett-Packard during its first dealings with Japanese vendors, who place great emphasis on high-quality production. HP had insisted on 2 percent AQL in a purchase of 100 cables. During the purchase agreement, some heated discussion took place wherein the Japanese vendor did not want this AQL specification; HP insisted that they would not budge from the 2 percent AQL. The Japanese vendor finally agreed. Later, when the box arrived, there were two packages inside. One contained 100 good cables. The other package had 2 cables with a note stating: "We have sent you 100 good cables. Since you insisted on 2 percent AQL, we have enclosed 2 defective cables in this package, though we do not understand why you want them."

The following example, using an excerpt from a standard acceptance sampling table, illustrates how the four parameters—AQL, $\alpha$, LTPD, and $\beta$—are used in developing a sampling plan.

### EXAMPLE TN7.4: VALUES OF n AND c

Hi-Tech Industries manufactures Z-Band radar scanners used to detect speed traps. The printed circuit boards in the scanners are purchased from an outside vendor. The vendor produces the boards to an AQL of 2 percent defectives and is willing to run a 5 percent risk ($\alpha$) of having lots of this level or fewer defectives rejected. Hi-Tech considers lots of 8 percent or more defectives (LTPD) unacceptable and wants to ensure that it will accept such poor-quality lots no more than 10 percent of the time

EXHIBIT TN7.10

Excerpt from a Sampling Plan Table for $\alpha = 0.05$, $\beta = 0.10$

| c | LTPD ÷ AQL | $n \cdot$ AQL | c | LTPD ÷ AQL | $n \cdot$ AQL |
|---|---|---|---|---|---|
| 0 | 44.890 | 0.052 | 5 | 3.549 | 2.613 |
| 1 | 10.946 | 0.355 | 6 | 3.206 | 3.286 |
| 2 | 6.509 | 0.818 | 7 | 2.957 | 3.981 |
| 3 | 4.890 | 1.366 | 8 | 2.768 | 4.695 |
| 4 | 4.057 | 1.970 | 9 | 2.618 | 5.426 |

($\beta$). A large shipment has just been delivered. What values of $n$ and $c$ should be selected to determine the quality of this lot?

### SOLUTION

The parameters of the problem are AQL $= 0.02$, $\alpha = 0.05$, LTPD $= 0.08$, and $\beta = 0.10$. We can use Exhibit TN7.10 to find $c$ and $n$.

First, divide LTPD by AQL ($0.08 \div 0.02 = 4$). Then, find the ratio in column 2 that is equal to or just greater than that amount (4). This value is 4.057, which is associated with $c = 4$.

Finally, find the value in column 3 that is in the same row as $c = 4$, and divide that quantity by AQL to obtain $n$ ($1.970 \div 0.02 = 98.5$).

The appropriate sampling plan is $c = 4$, $n = 99$. ←

## OPERATING CHARACTERISTIC CURVES

While a sampling plan such as the one just described meets our requirements for the extreme values of good and bad quality, we cannot readily determine how well the plan discriminates between good and bad lots at intermediate values. For this reason, sampling plans are generally displayed graphically through the use of operating characteristic (OC) curves. These curves, which are unique for each combination of $n$ and $c$, simply illustrate the probability of accepting lots with varying percentages of defectives. The procedure we have followed in developing the plan, in fact, specifies two points on an OC curve: one point defined by AQL and $1 - \alpha$, and the other point defined by LTPD and $\beta$. Curves for common values of $n$ and $c$ can be computed or obtained from available tables.[4]

**Shaping the OC Curve** A sampling plan discriminating perfectly between good and bad lots has an infinite slope (vertical) at the selected value of AQL. In Exhibit TN7.11, any percentage defective to the left of 2 percent would always be accepted, and those to the right, always rejected. However, such a curve is possible only with complete inspection of all units and thus is not a possibility with a true sampling plan.

An OC curve should be steep in the region of most interest (between the AQL and the LTPD), which is accomplished by varying $n$ and $c$. If $c$ remains constant, increasing the sample size $n$ causes the OC curve to be more vertical. While holding $n$ constant, decreasing $c$ (the maximum number of defective units) also makes the slope more vertical, moving closer to the origin.

**The Effects of Lot Size** The size of the lot that the sample is taken from has relatively little effect on the quality of protection. Consider, for example, that samples—all of the same size of 20 units—are taken from different lots ranging from a lot size of 200 units to a lot size of infinity. If each lot is known to have 5 percent defectives, the probability of accepting the lot based on the sample of 20 units ranges from about 0.34 to about 0.36. This means that as long as the lot size is several times the sample size, it makes little difference how large the lot is. It seems a bit difficult to accept, but statistically

EXHIBIT TN7.11

Operating Characteristic Curve for AQL $= 0.02$, $\alpha = 0.05$, LTPD $= 0.08$, $\beta = 0.10$

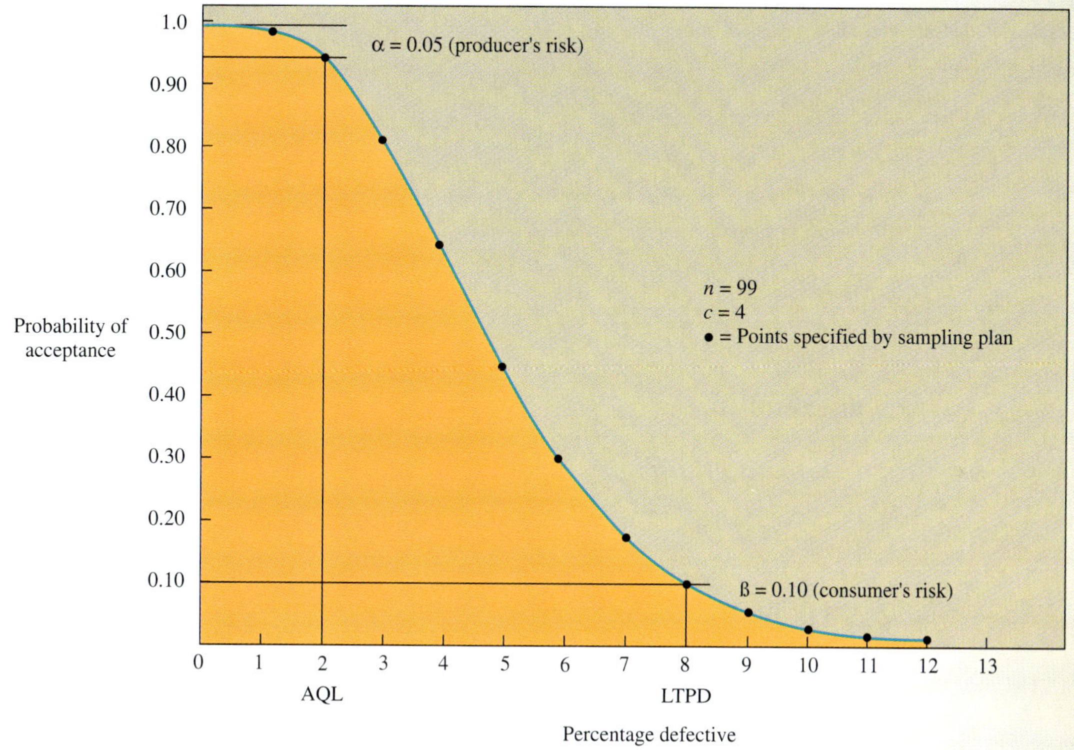


(on the average in the long run) whether we have a carload or box full, we'll get about the same answer. It just seems that a carload should have a larger sample size. Of course, this assumes that the lot is randomly chosen and that defects are randomly spread through the lot.

## CONCLUSION

Statistical quality control is a vital topic. Quality has become so important that statistical quality procedures are *expected* to be part of successful firms. Sampling plans and statistical process control are taken as given with the emphasis shifting to broader aspects (such as eliminating dockside acceptance sampling because of reliable supplier quality, and employee empowerment transforming much of the process control). World-class manufacturing companies expect people to understand the basic concepts of the material presented in this technical note.

## KEY TERMS

**Assignable variation** Deviation in the output of a process that can be clearly identified and managed.

**Common variation** Deviation in the output of a process that is random and inherent in the process itself.

**Upper and lower specification or tolerance limits** The range of values in a measure associated with a process that are allowable given the intended use of the product or service.

**Six-sigma** A shortcut for saying six standard deviations from the mean or average value of a measure.

**Capability index** The ratio of the range of values produced by a process divided by the range of values allowed by the design specification.

**Statistical process control** Techniques for testing a random sample of output from a process to determine whether the process is producing items within a prescribed range.

**Attributes** Quality characteristics that are classified as either conforming or not conforming to specification.

**Variables** Quality characteristics that are measured in actual weight, volume, inches, centimeter, or other measure.

## FORMULA REVIEW

**Mean or average**

[TN7.1] $$\overline{X} = \sum_{i=1}^{N} x_i / N$$

**Standard deviation**

[TN7.2] $$\sigma = \sqrt{\frac{\sum_{i=1}^{N}(x_i - \overline{X})^2}{N}}$$

**Capability index**

[TN7.3] $$C_{pk} = \min\left[\frac{\overline{X} - \text{LTL}}{3\sigma}, \frac{\text{UTL} - \overline{X}}{3\sigma}\right]$$

**Process control charts using attribute measurements**

[TN7.4] $$\overline{p} = \frac{\text{Total number of defects from all samples}}{\text{Number of samples} \times \text{Sample size}}$$

[TN7.5] $$s_p = \sqrt{\frac{\overline{p}(1 - \overline{p})}{n}}$$

[TN7.6] $$\text{UCL} = \overline{p} + z s_p$$

[TN7.7] $$\text{LCL} = \overline{p} - z s_p$$

[TN7.8] $$\text{UCL}_{\overline{X}} = \overline{\overline{X}} + z s_{\overline{x}} \quad \text{and} \quad \text{LCL}_{\overline{X}} = \overline{\overline{X}} - z s_{\overline{X}}$$

**Process control $\overline{X}$ and $R$ charts**

[TN7.9] $$\overline{\overline{X}} = \frac{\sum_{j=1}^{m} \overline{X}_j}{m}$$

[TN7.10] $$\overline{R} = \frac{\sum_{j=1}^{m} R_j}{m}$$

[TN7.11] Upper control limit for $\overline{X} = \overline{\overline{X}} + A_2\overline{R}$

[TN7.12] Lower control limit for $\overline{X} = \overline{\overline{X}} - A_2\overline{R}$

[TN7.13] Upper control limit for $R = D_4\overline{R}$

[TN7.14] Lower control limit for $R = D_3\overline{R}$

# SOLVED PROBLEMS

## SOLVED PROBLEM 1

Completed forms from a particular department of an insurance company were sampled daily to check the performance quality of that department. To establish a tentative norm for the department, one sample of 100 units was collected each day for 15 days, with these results:

| SAMPLE | SAMPLE SIZE | NUMBER OF FORMS WITH ERRORS | SAMPLE | SAMPLE SIZE | NUMBER OF FORMS WITH ERRORS |
|---|---|---|---|---|---|
| 1 | 100 | 4 | 9 | 100 | 4 |
| 2 | 100 | 3 | 10 | 100 | 2 |
| 3 | 100 | 5 | 11 | 100 | 7 |
| 4 | 100 | 0 | 12 | 100 | 2 |
| 5 | 100 | 2 | 13 | 100 | 1 |
| 6 | 100 | 8 | 14 | 100 | 3 |
| 7 | 100 | 1 | 15 | 100 | 1 |
| 8 | 100 | 3 | | | |

*a.* Develop a *p*-chart using a 95 percent confidence interval ($1.96\ s_p$).
*b.* Plot the 15 samples collected.
*c.* What comments can you make about the process?

### Solution

*a.* $$\overline{p} = \frac{46}{15(100)} = .0307$$

$$s_p = \sqrt{\frac{\overline{p}(1-\overline{p})}{n}} = \sqrt{\frac{.0307(1-.0307)}{100}} = \sqrt{.0003} = .017$$

$$\text{UCL} = \overline{p} + 1.96s_p = .031 + 1.96(.017) = .064$$

$$\text{LCL} = \overline{p} - 1.96s_p = .031 - 1.96(.017) = -.003 \text{ or zero}$$

*b.* The defectives are plotted below.

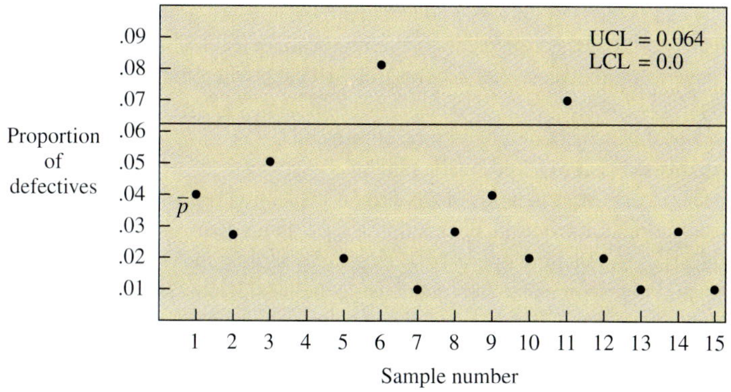


*c.* Of the 15 samples, 2 were out of the control limits. Because the control limits were established as 95 percent, or 1 out of 20, we would say that the process is out of control. It needs to be examined to find the cause of such widespread variation.

## SOLVED PROBLEM 2

Management is trying to decide whether Part A, which is produced with a consistent 3 percent defective rate, should be inspected. If it is not inspected, the 3 percent defectives will go through a product assembly phase and have to be replaced later. If all Part A's are inspected, one-third of the defectives will be found, thus raising the quality to 2 percent defectives.

*a.* Should the inspection be done if the cost of inspecting is \$0.01 per unit and the cost of replacing a defective in the final assembly is \$4.00?

*b.* Suppose the cost of inspecting is \$0.05 per unit rather than \$0.01. Would this change your answer in *a*?

### Solution

Should Part A be inspected?

.03 defective with no inspection.
.02 defective with inspection.

*a.* This problem can be solved simply by looking at the opportunity for 1 percent improvement.

Benefit = .01(\$4.00) = \$0.04
Cost of inspection = \$0.01

Therefore, inspect and save \$0.03 per unit.

*b.* A cost of \$0.05 per unit to inspect would be \$0.01 greater than the savings, so inspection should not be performed.

## REVIEW AND DISCUSSION QUESTIONS

1 The capability index allows for some drifting of the process mean. Discuss what this means in terms of product quality output.

2 Discuss the purposes of and differences between *p*-charts and $\overline{X}$ and *R* charts.

3 In an agreement between a supplier and a customer, the supplier must ensure that all parts are within tolerance before shipment to the customer. What is the effect on the cost of quality to the customer?

4 In the situation described in Question 3, what would be the effect on the cost of quality to the supplier?

5 Discuss the trade-off between achieving a zero AQL (acceptable quality level) and a positive AQL (such as an AQL of 2 percent).

## PROBLEMS

1 A company currently using an inspection process in its material receiving department is trying to install an overall cost reduction program. One possible reduction is the elimination of one inspection position. This position tests material that has a defective content on the average of 0.04. By inspecting all items, the inspector is able to remove all defects. The inspector can inspect 50 units per hour. The hourly rate including fringe benefits for this position is \$9. If the inspection position is eliminated, defects will go into product assembly and will have to be replaced later at a cost of \$10 each when they are detected in final product testing.

*a.* Should this inspection position be eliminated?

*b.* What is the cost to inspect each unit?

*c.* Is there benefit (or loss) from the current inspection process? How much?

1. *a.* Not inspecting cost = \$20/hr. Cost to inspect = \$9/hr. Therefore, inspect.
*b.* \$.18/each.
*c.* \$.22 per unit.

2 A metal fabricator produces connecting rods with an outer diameter that has a 1 ± .01 inch specification. A machine operator takes several sample measurements over time and determines the sample mean outer diameter to be 1.002 inches with a standard deviation of .003 inch.

*a.* Calculate the process capability ratio for this example.

*b.* What does this figure tell you about the process?

2. *a.* $C_{pk}$ = .889.
*b.* The process is capable but needs to adjust the mean downward to achieve the best quality.

3 Ten samples of 15 parts each were taken from an ongoing process to establish a *p*-chart for control. The samples and the number of defectives in each are shown in the following table:

| SAMPLE | n | NUMBER OF DEFECTS IN SAMPLE | SAMPLE | n | NUMBER OF DEFECTS IN SAMPLE |
|---|---|---|---|---|---|
| 1 | 15 | 3 | 6 | 15 | 2 |
| 2 | 15 | 1 | 7 | 15 | 0 |
| 3 | 15 | 0 | 8 | 15 | 3 |
| 4 | 15 | 0 | 9 | 15 | 1 |
| 5 | 15 | 0 | 10 | 15 | 0 |

*a.* Develop a *p*-chart for 95 percent confidence (1.96 standard deviations).

*b.* Based on the plotted data points, what comments can you make?

3. *a.* $\overline{p} = .067$. UCL = .194. LCL = 0.
*b.* Stop the process. Something wrong. There is wide variation and two are out of limits.

4 Output from a process contains 0.02 defective units. Defective units that go undetected into final assemblies cost $25 each to replace. An inspection process, which would detect and remove all defectives, can be established to test these units. However, the inspector, who can test 20 units per hour, is paid $8 per hour, including fringe benefits. Should an inspection station be established to test all units?

*a.* What is the cost to inspect each unit?

*b.* What is the benefit (or loss) from the inspection process?

4. *a.* Cost to inspect = $.40/unit. Cost of defect = $.50/unit. Inspect.
*b.* Benefit is $.10/unit.

5 There is a 3 percent error rate at a specific point in a production process. If an inspector is placed at this point, all the errors can be detected and eliminated. However, the inspector is paid $8 per hour and can inspect units in the process at the rate of 30 per hour.

If no inspector is used and defects are allowed to pass this point, there is a cost of $10 per unit to correct the defect later on.

Should an inspector be hired?

5. Yes, inspecting is cheaper, Cost to inspect is $.267/unit. Cost of defect is $.30/unit.

6 Resistors for electronic circuits are manufactured on a high-speed automated machine. The machine is set up to produce a large run of resistors of 1,000 ohms each.

To set up the machine and to create a control chart to be used throughout the run, 15 samples were taken with four resistors in each sample. The complete list of samples and their measured values are as follows:

6. *a.* $\overline{\overline{X}} = 999.1$; UCL = 1014.965; LCL = 983.235; $\overline{R} = 21.733$; UCL = 49.551 LCL = 0.
See SM for graph.

| SAMPLE NUMBER | READINGS (IN OHMS) | | | |
|---|---|---|---|---|
| 1 | 1010 | 991 | 985 | 986 |
| 2 | 995 | 996 | 1009 | 994 |
| 3 | 990 | 1003 | 1015 | 1008 |
| 4 | 1015 | 1020 | 1009 | 998 |
| 5 | 1013 | 1019 | 1005 | 993 |
| 6 | 994 | 1001 | 994 | 1005 |
| 7 | 989 | 992 | 982 | 1020 |
| 8 | 1001 | 986 | 996 | 996 |
| 9 | 1006 | 989 | 1005 | 1007 |
| 10 | 992 | 1007 | 1006 | 979 |
| 11 | 996 | 1006 | 997 | 989 |
| 12 | 1019 | 996 | 991 | 1011 |
| 13 | 981 | 991 | 989 | 1003 |
| 14 | 999 | 993 | 988 | 984 |
| 15 | 1013 | 1002 | 1005 | 992 |

Develop an $\overline{X}$ chart and an *R* chart and plot the values. From the charts, what comments can you make about the process? (Use three-sigma control limits as in Exhibit TN7.7)

7 In the past, Alpha Corporation has not performed incoming quality control inspections but has taken the word of its vendors. However, Alpha has been having some unsatisfactory experience recently with the quality of purchased items and wants to set up sampling plans for the receiving department to use.

For a particular component, X, Alpha has a lot tolerance percentage defective of 10 percent. Zenon Corporation, from which Alpha purchases this component, has an acceptable quality level in its production facility of 3 percent for component X. Alpha has a consumer's risk of 10 percent and Zenon has a producer's risk of 5 percent.

*a.* When a shipment of Product X is received from Zenon Corporation, what sample size should the receiving department test?

*b.* What is the allowable number of defects in order to accept the shipment?

7. *a.* 87.1 sample size, round to 88.
*b.* c = 5.

8. *a.* $\bar{p} = .06$;
$s_p = .0075$;
UCL = .075;
LCL = .045.
*b.* Process is erratic and out of control.

8 You are the newly appointed assistant administrator at a local hospital, and your first project is to investigate the quality of the patient meals put out by the food-service department. You conducted a 10-day survey by submitting a simple questionnaire to the 400 patients with each meal, asking that they simply check off that the meal was either satisfactory or unsatisfactory. For simplicity in this problem, assume that the response was 1,000 returned questionnaires from the 1,200 meals each day. The results are as follows:

| | Number of Unsatisfactory Meals | Sample Size |
|---|---|---|
| December 1 | 74 | 1,000 |
| December 2 | 42 | 1,000 |
| December 3 | 64 | 1,000 |
| December 4 | 80 | 1,000 |
| December 5 | 40 | 1,000 |
| December 6 | 50 | 1,000 |
| December 7 | 65 | 1,000 |
| December 8 | 70 | 1,000 |
| December 9 | 40 | 1,000 |
| December 10 | 75 | 1,000 |
| | 600 | 10,000 |

*a.* Construct a *p*-chart based on the questionnaire results, using a confidence interval of 95.5 percent, which is two standard deviations.
*b.* What comments can you make about the results of the survey?

9. *a.* $n = 31.3$. (Round sample size to 32).
*b.* Random sample 32; reject if more than 8 are defective.

9 Large-scale integrated (LSI) circuit chips are made in one department of an electronics firm. These chips are incorporated into analog devices that are then encased in epoxy. The yield is not particularly good for LSI manufacture, so the AQL specified by that department is 0.15 while the LTPD acceptable by the assembly department is 0.40.
*a.* Develop a sampling plan.
*b.* Explain what the sampling plan means; that is, how would you tell someone to do the test?

10. $\bar{p} = .0083$;
$s_p = .00287$;
UCL = .01396;
LCL = .00270;
Based on *p*-chart, crime rate has not increased.

10 The state and local police departments are trying to analyze crime rates so they can shift their patrols from decreasing-rate areas to areas where rates are increasing. The city and county have been geographically segmented into areas containing 5,000 residences. The police recognize that not all crimes and offenses are reported: people do not want to become involved, consider the offenses too small to report, are too embarrassed to make a police report, or do not take the time, among other reasons. Every month, because of this, the police are contacting by phone a random sample of 1,000 of the 5,000 residences for data on crime. (Respondents are guaranteed anonymity.) Here are the data collected for the past 12 months for one area:

| Month | Crime Incidence | Sample Size | Crime Rate |
|---|---|---|---|
| January | 7 | 1,000 | 0.007 |
| February | 9 | 1,000 | 0.009 |
| March | 7 | 1,000 | 0.000 |
| April | 7 | 1,000 | 0.007 |
| May | 7 | 1,000 | 0.007 |
| June | 9 | 1,000 | 0.009 |
| July | 7 | 1,000 | 0.007 |
| August | 10 | 1,000 | 0.010 |
| September | 8 | 1,000 | 0.008 |
| October | 11 | 1,000 | 0.011 |
| November | 10 | 1,000 | 0.010 |
| December | 8 | 1,000 | 0.008 |

Construct a $p$-chart for 95 percent confidence (1.96) and plot each of the months. If the next three months show crime incidences in this area as

January = 10 (out of 1,000 sampled)
February = 12 (out of 1,000 sampled)
March = 11 (out of 1,000 sampled)

what comments can you make regarding the crime rate?

11 Some citizens complained to city council members that there should be equal protection under the law against the occurrence of crimes. The citizens argued that this equal protection should be interpreted as indicating that high-crime areas should have more police protection than low-crime areas. Therefore, police patrols and other methods for preventing crime (such as street lighting or cleaning up abandoned areas and buildings) should be used proportionately to crime occurrence.

In a fashion similar to Problem 10, the city has been broken down into 20 geographic areas, each containing 5,000 residences. The 1,000 sampled from each area showed the following incidence of crime during the past month:

11. $\bar{p} = 0.015$; $s_p = 0.00384$; UCL = 0.0225; LCL = 0.0075; Three areas outside UCL warrant further investigation; four areas below LCL warrant investigation.

| AREA | NUMBER OF CRIMES | SAMPLE SIZE | CRIME RATE |
|---|---|---|---|
| 1 | 14 | 1,000 | 0.014 |
| 2 | 3 | 1,000 | 0.003 |
| 3 | 19 | 1,000 | 0.019 |
| 4 | 18 | 1,000 | 0.018 |
| 5 | 14 | 1,000 | 0.014 |
| 6 | 28 | 1,000 | 0.028 |
| 7 | 10 | 1,000 | 0.010 |
| 8 | 18 | 1,000 | 0.018 |
| 9 | 12 | 1,000 | 0.012 |
| 10 | 3 | 1,000 | 0.003 |
| 11 | 20 | 1,000 | 0.020 |
| 12 | 15 | 1,000 | 0.015 |
| 13 | 12 | 1,000 | 0.012 |
| 14 | 14 | 1,000 | 0.014 |
| 15 | 10 | 1,000 | 0.010 |
| 16 | 30 | 1,000 | 0.030 |
| 17 | 4 | 1,000 | 0.004 |
| 18 | 20 | 1,000 | 0.020 |
| 19 | 6 | 1,000 | 0.006 |
| 20 | 30 | 1,000 | 0.030 |
| | 300 | | |

Suggest a reallocation of crime protection effort, if indicated, based on a $p$-chart analysis. To be reasonably certain in your recommendation, select a 95 percent confidence level (that is, $Z = 1.96$).

12 The following table contains the measurements of the key length dimension from a fuel injector. These samples of size five were taken at one-hour intervals.

12. $X = .500$; UCL = .523; LCL = .477; $R = .040$; UCL = .084; LCL = .000; Process is in control.

| | OBSERVATIONS | | | | |
|---|---|---|---|---|---|
| SAMPLE NUMBER | 1 | 2 | 3 | 4 | 5 |
| 1 | .486 | .499 | .493 | .511 | .481 |
| 2 | .499 | .506 | .516 | .494 | .529 |
| 3 | .496 | .500 | .515 | .488 | .521 |
| 4 | .495 | .506 | .483 | .487 | .489 |
| 5 | .472 | .502 | .526 | .469 | .481 |
| 6 | .473 | .495 | .507 | .493 | .506 |
| 7 | .495 | .512 | .490 | .471 | .504 |
| 8 | .525 | .501 | .498 | .474 | .485 |

*continued*

| | Observations | | | | |
|---|---|---|---|---|---|
| Sample Number | 1 | 2 | 3 | 4 | 5 |
| 9 | .497 | .501 | .517 | .506 | .516 |
| 10 | .495 | .505 | .516 | .511 | .497 |
| 11 | .495 | .482 | .468 | .492 | .492 |
| 12 | .483 | .459 | .526 | .506 | .522 |
| 13 | .521 | .512 | .493 | .525 | .510 |
| 14 | .487 | .521 | .507 | .501 | .500 |
| 15 | .493 | .516 | .499 | .511 | .513 |
| 16 | .473 | .506 | .479 | .480 | .523 |
| 17 | .477 | .485 | .513 | .484 | .496 |
| 18 | .515 | .493 | .493 | .485 | .475 |
| 19 | .511 | .536 | .486 | .497 | .491 |
| 20 | .509 | .490 | .470 | .504 | .512 |

Construct a three-sigma $\overline{X}$ chart and $R$ chart (use Exhibit TN7.7) for the length of the fuel injector. What can you say about this process?

13. a. $C_{pk} = .333$
b. No, the machine is not capable of producing this part.

13 C-Spec, Inc., is attempting to determine whether an existing machine is capable of milling an engine part that has a key specification of 4 ± .003 inches. After a trial run on this machine, C-Spec has determined that the machine has a sample mean of 4.001 inches with a standard deviation of .002 inches.
*a.* Calculate the $C_{pk}$ for this machine.
*b.* Should C-Spec use this machine to produce this part? Why?

## ADVANCED PROBLEM

1. a. $C_{pk} = \frac{110 - 100}{3 \times 4} = .8333$
b. $C_{pk} = \frac{92 - 90}{3 \times 4} = .1666$
c. Many defects will be produced. Left tail is a $z = -2/4 = .5$, which corresponds to a probability of 0.1915. Right tail is at $z = 18/4 = 4.5$, which corresponds to a probability of approximately .5. The probability of being inside the limits is $.1915 + .5 = .6915$, and the probability of being outside is $1 - .6915 = .3085$. Approximately 31% of the parts will be defective.

14 Design specifications require that a key dimension on a product measure 100 ± 10 units. A process being considered for producing this product has a standard deviation of four units.
*a.* What can you say (quantitatively) regarding the process capability?
*b.* Suppose the process average shifts to 92. Calculate the new process capability.
*c.* What can you say about the process after the shift? Approximately what percentage of the items produced will be defective?

## SELECTED BIBLIOGRAPHY


Alwan, L. *Statistical Process Analysis.* New York: Irwin/McGraw-Hill, 2000.

Aslup, F., and R. M. Watson. *Practical Statistical Process Control: A Tool for Quality Manufacturing.* New York: Van Nostrand Reinhold, 1993.

Feigenbaum, A. V. *Total Quality Control.* New York: McGraw-Hill, 1991.

Grant, E. L., and R. S. Leavenworth. *Statistical Quality Control.* New York: McGraw-Hill, 1996.

Hardesky, J. L. *Productivity and Quality Improvement: A Practical Guide to Implementing Statistical Process Control.* New York: McGraw-Hill, 1988.

Juran, J. M., and F. M. Gryna. *Quality Planning and Analysis.* 2nd ed. New York: McGraw-Hill, 1980.

Ledolter, J., and C. Burrill. *Statistical Quality Control: Strategies and Tools for Continual Improvement.* New York: Wiley, 1999.

Small, B. B. (with committee). *Statistical Quality Control Handbook.* Western Electric Co., Inc., 1956.

Taguchi, G. *On-Line Quality Control during Production.* Tokyo: Japanese Standards Association, 1987.

Thompson, J. R., and J. Koronacki. *Statistical Process Control for Quality Improvement.* New York: Chapman & Hall, 1993.

Wetherill, G. B., and D. W. Brown. *Statistical Process Control: Theory and Practice.* New York: Chapman & Hall, 1991.

Zimmerman, S. M., and M. L. Icenogel, *Statistical Quality Control; Using Excel.* Milwaukee, WI: ASQ Quality Press, 1999.

# FOOTNOTES

1 D. Birch, "The True Value of 6 Sigma," *Quality Progress,* April 1993. p. 6.

2 E. L. Grant and R. Leavenworth, *Statistical Quality Control* (New York: McGraw-Hill, 1964), p. 562.

3 There is some controversy surrounding AQLs. This is based on the argument that specifying some acceptable percentage of defectives is inconsistent with the philosophical goal of zero defects. In practice, even in the best QC companies, there is an acceptable quality level. The difference is that it may be stated in parts per million rather than in parts per hundred. This is the case in Motorola's six-sigma quality standard, which holds that no more than 3.4 defects per million parts are acceptable.

4 See, for example, H. F. Dodge and H. G. Romig, *Sampling Inspection Tables—Single and Double Sampling* (New York: John Wiley & Sons, 1959); and *Military Standard Sampling Procedures and Tables for Inspection by Attributes* (MIL-STD-105D) (Washington, DC: U.S. Government Printing Office, 1983).

*section* ***three***

# section 3

# Supply Chain Design





## Without Suppliers, Neither a General Nor a Soldier Is Good for Anything

Clerchus of Sparta, in 401 B.C., recognized the value of supply in his speech to the small Greek army he led in a civil war with Artaxerxes II. His army of 14,000 was 1,300 miles from Greece when the Battle of Cunaxa began. The survival of the Greek army depended not only on its discipline, training, and morale but also on its supply chain.

Today the survival of most firms depends on intelligent supply chain decisions. Never have so much technology and brainpower been applied to improving supply chain performance. Point-of-sale scanners, electronic data interchange, and the Internet let all stages of the supply chain hear the customer's voice and react to it.

This section starts with a briefing on electronic commerce showing how firms are taking full advantage of the Internet to become more responsive and to better penetrate customer markets. Chapter 8 is a high-level view of the latest concepts that relate to supply chain strategy. Such ideas as outsourcing, postponement, and global product sourcing are discussed. Capacity management is critical to success in running a global supply chain. Not only must the amount of production, distribution, and other capacity be correct, but it must also be positioned in the right locations to be effective. Capacity management and facility location are the topics of Chapter 9 in this section. We conclude the section with a tactical view of just-in-time systems. Here we discuss the details of working with vendors to coordinate our activities along the supply chain. In addition, we look at how internal processes are designed to support the just-in-time approach while still operating in a lean manner.

*managerial briefing*

# ELECTRONIC COMMERCE AND E-OPS©

## BRIEFING OUTLINE



*In five years' time, all companies will be Internet companies, or they won't be companies at all.*

—Andy Grove, Chairman of Intel

*Operations management has been synonymous with managing tangible assets; with E-Ops, we are moving into managing intangible assets as well, particularly information and knowledge, to create a new paradigm for the field.*

—The authors

managerial briefing

Manufacturing is making stuff; service is making stuff that won't hurt you when you drop it on your foot; and E-Ops is using the Internet to coordinate the making of any kind of stuff. The central tool of electronic commerce, the Internet, is heavily affecting operations, as it does every other facet of business. In this briefing, our purpose is to provide an overview of how the Internet and related concepts of electronic commerce can be used by operations managers to gain competitive advantage. We term this evolving area *E-Operations* or *E-Ops*© for short. We begin with some observations on the nature and impact of electronic commerce.

## THE NATURE OF ELECTRONIC COMMERCE

Electronic commerce (EC)

**Electronic commerce (EC)** is defined as "the use of computer applications communicating over networks to allow buyers and sellers to complete a transaction or part of a transaction."[1] Today, the term *networks* refers to the Internet, a major enabler of change in the business world. Capturing the EC headlines today are "killer apps"—technological breakthroughs that create totally new goods or services.[2]

Researchers have identified two "laws" to explain why EC has flourished. One is Moore's Law, which holds that computing power doubles every 18 to 24 months. An example of this is how the speed of entry-level personal computers continues to increase while the cost of these computers drops. The impact of Moore's Law is that increasing numbers of computers are installed on the Internet, and the cost to support ever-expanding web sites goes down. This forms a solid economic base for the rapid expansion of the capacity and number of participants in EC. In January 1993 there were no web sites; in January 1995 there were 500,000; and as of January 2000 there were over 30,000,000.

The other principle is Metcalfe's Law, which holds that the utility or value of a network equals the square of the number of users. This incredible growth rate is made possible by both the low price of Internet use and the ease of access due to the open standards for sending and receiving multimedia communications over the Web.

The following is a stunning example of a killer app that leveraged the power of Moore's and Metcalfe's laws to grow very quickly.

> The start-up opened its virtual doors to customers on July 4, 1996. The date was a great choice in terms of corporate symbolism, but a terrible one for creating buzz. Most media outlets operate with skeleton crews over Independence Day, so the launch generated almost no press coverage. So much for a virtual "shot heard 'round the world." The launch of the world's first free Web-based email service had more the effect of a wet firecracker. Then a funny thing happened: Customers began signing up. John Fisher, a managing director, was at a trade show with one of the start-up's founders the week of the launch. "His beeper would go off every 30 minutes," Fisher says, "and there would be reports of several thousand more sign-ups. It became immediately clear to us that we had a tiger by the tail."
>
> The first markets to light up were universities—places with ".edu" domains. A user would sign up at, say, Cornell. A day later there'd be a half-dozen users at Cornell. The next day, there'd be 100. By the end of the first week, there'd be 1,000. The service would spread to another university, and the process would repeat itself. Then word of the service began spreading around the world. Within three weeks of the first user from India signing up, 100,000 additional users from that country came on board. "It was like a miracle was unfolding before our eyes," says Jurvetson, a boyish 32-year-old whose voice still conveys the excitement of those early days. "At one board meeting, we'd see, maybe, Sweden show up for the first time. At the next month's meeting, there'd be a huge number of users from that country."

## TRADITIONAL VERSUS ELECTRONIC COMMERCE PURCHASING OF A DESK

Suppose that Tina, an employee at Yormark Inc., wants to buy a new office desk. First Tina generates a request for the desk, including some specifications (two pedestals or one, circular or round, wood or metal), and passes this request on through an approval process involving one or two managers, depending on the cost. That request eventually makes it to the purchasing department, where someone has to check the office supply catalogs to select an appropriate model and vendor. Assume the company doesn't have a single preferred supplier for office furniture, so the purchasing agent has to review several catalogs and call the suppliers to determine the availability and price of the desk. Once the supplier is selected, the agent issues a purchase order and either faxes or mails it to the vendor. (Telephone orders are not accepted because a paper trail is an important part of the process.) After the order has been received, the supplier verifies the credit and sales history of the ordering company, checks the warehouse for inventory, and ascertains when the shipper can pick up the desk from the warehouse and deliver it to Tina's office. Satisfied that the item can be delivered within the time requested, the supplier creates a shipping order, notifies the warehouse, and creates an invoice for the desk. The invoice is mailed, the desk gets delivered, and somewhere along the way, the company pays the bill for the desk. (And quite likely, by this time, Tina has been transferred to a different department!)

Now let's see how this might be done using EC. Tina would visit the web site of either the distributor or the manufacturer and would select the appropriate desk by matching the desired features with data in an online catalog. Tina would then use e-mail to send a digital request (perhaps appending the web page of the selected product) to the manager for approval. The manager would forward the approved e-mail request to purchasing, which could then authorize delivery. The same program could pass an electronic shipping order to the appropriate warehouse and create an invoice. If a shipping agent were used, the warehouse would notify the shipper via e-mail. Once the desk was received, accounts payable would instruct the bank, via e-mail, to transfer payment electronically to the supplier.

The two approaches are compared in the accompanying table. Many of the steps are the same, but the way the information is obtained and transferred through the cycle is different. A wide variety of communication media was needed in the traditional approach, making coordination more difficult and increasing the time required to process the order. But with EC, everything starts out and stays digital; only different applications are needed to transfer the data as they move through the order process. It is this capability that makes EC such a powerful new approach to managing business processes.

| PROCESS STEP | TRADITIONAL COMMERCE (MULTIPLE MEDIA EMPLOYED) | ELECTRONIC COMMERCE (SINGLE MEDIUM EMPLOYED) |
|---|---|---|
| Acquire product information | Magazines, flyers online catalogs | Web pages |
| Request item | Printed forms, letters | E-mail |
| Get order approved | | E-mail |
| Check catalogs, prices | Catalogs | Online catalogs |
| Check product availability and confirm price | Phone, fax | Online catalogs |
| Generate order | Printed form | E-mail, web pages |
| Send order (buyer); receive order (supplier) | Fax, mail | E-mail, EDI, Web |
| Prioritize order | | Online database |
| Check inventory at warehouse | Printed form, phone, fax | Online database, Web pages |
| Schedule delivery | Printed form | E-mail, online database |
| Generate invoice | Printed form | Online database |
| Receive product | Shipper | — |
| Confirm receipt | Printed form | E-mail |
| Send invoice (supplier); receive invoice (buyer) | Mail | E-mail, EDI |
| Schedule payment | Printed form | EDI |
| Send payment (buyer); receive payment (supplier) | Mail | EDI, EFT |

SOURCE: MODIFIED FROM D. KOSIUR, *UNDERSTANDING ELECTRONIC COMMERCE: HOW ONLINE TRANSACTIONS CAN GROW YOUR BUSINESS* (REDMOND WA: STRATEGIC TECHNOLOGY SERIES, MICROSOFT PRESS, 1997, PP. 7–9). REPRODUCED BY PERMISSION OF MICROSOFT PRESS. 

> By Christmas 1996, less than six months after the launch, the new company had 1 million registered users. In the entire history of subscriber-based media, nothing had grown so large, so fast. The company's performance was unprecedented. That it happened with a marketing budget of less than $50,000 was simply unbelievable.
>
> The start-up, of course, was Hotmail, a company that has become a legend among Silicon Valley entrepreneurs for its fast-forward approach to attracting customers and creating value. By Christmas 1997 (less than 18 months after its launch), Hotmail had signed up 12 million subscribers. A few days later, on December 29, founders Sabeer Bhatia and Jack Smith sold the company to Microsoft for $400 million in Microsoft stock. Today, with 50 million registered users, Hotmail is the largest Web-based email service on the planet.[3] (http://www.hotmail.com)

The development of America Online (AOL), the largest Internet service provider, is similar to Hotmail. However, it is not only the AOLs and Hotmails of the world that have developed new EC applications. Consider how two members of the tradition-bound automobile industry, Ford and General Motors, are transforming their operations using the Internet.

> Like a pack of sumo wrestlers bumping bellies, automakers Ford and General Motors, along with Oracle, let loose a series of yelps as they detailed their big e-commerce plans. The world's two biggest carmakers expect to pin their rivals—and no doubt each other—by hosting all of their enormous purchasing operations online, and thereby slashing operating costs. The numbers involved are huge. Ford spends $80 billion a year on parts from 30,000 suppliers. Now, with Oracle's help, it's setting up AutoXchange to put those transactions online. The company will also handle transactions worth another $200 billion in a new way, opening the system to suppliers and partners who will use it to buy and sell auto-related parts. GM is partnering up with Commerce One on GM MarketSite, its own stab at an online ordering system. Like AutoXchange, MarketSite will let GM's suppliers, dealers, and partners do business online.[4]

In addition to killer apps and new megapartnerships, e-commerce has impacts on day-to-day business activities. Consider the box example titled "Traditional versus Electronic Commerce Purchasing of a Desk," describing how the simple process of ordering a desk is affected by the Internet and other information technologies.

## THE CONTEXT OF E-OPS

E-Ops

Cross Functional

**E-Ops** is our term referring to the application of the Internet and its attendant technologies to the field of OM. To understand the organizational context of E-Ops, it is useful to view the infrastructure of a modern organization as consisting of three conceptual levels: the business model level, where the strategy for how a company makes money is defined; the operations level that defines the processes needed to implement the strategy; and the information systems (IS) architecture level that provides computer technology support. This structure is shown in Exhibit MB8.1. Operations' position between the business model and the information systems architecture indicates that it must execute the processes prescribed by the business model and effectively use the tools of the information architecture. The challenge for the organization is that management has to understand how to take advantage of new IS capabilities to better operate existing business models and to enable development of *new* business models. The challenge for operations, in turn, is that it has to implement these business models. As more operations processes are implemented, more

Exhibit MB8.1

The Context of E-Ops

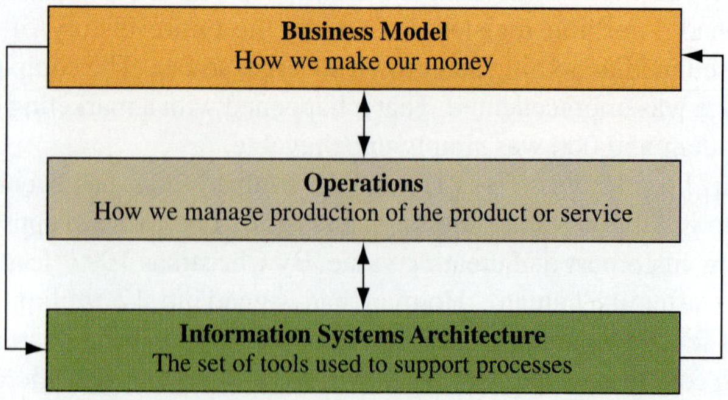


software must be developed, which places pressure on operations to absorb it. With the shortening of product life cycles so common today, the cycle of change is ever faster. And with digital products, where value added is created with software applications, the pressure to quickly implement them is even greater. As we look at the challenges to operations that come from the Internet, it is clear that the management of change must itself become an efficient process.

E-Ops applications can be applied to the internal processes of an organization, such as back office support and common factory processes of ordering, scheduling, product design and development, quality monitoring, and so on. In addition, E-Ops can be used for processes that support the external linkages between a company's suppliers and customers. Certainly the most talked-about applications are these external linkages and the new Internet businesses that have formed to support them. We discuss these businesses next.

## BUSINESS WEB MODELS

In this section, Internet businesses are categorized. These different business models typically involve a fluid collection of businesses. Within such networks, each node or business focuses on a limited number of core competencies to create value. The term **business web** or **B-web** for short has been coined to refer to these types of businesses.

Business web (B-web)

Exhibit MB8.2 summarizes the basic elements of five B-web models—marketplace, aggregator, alliance, value chain, and distributive network. Each of these can be distinguished by their degree of hierarchical economic control and by their degree of value integration. A strong degree of *hierarchical economic control* exists when one organization controls content, pricing, and flow of transactions. *Value integration* relates to how well coordinated the participants are.

Value chain

Aggregators

Marketplace

Companies that set up web sites to manage both customer and suppliers are examples of B-web **value chain** models. Dell Computer and Cisco Systems are good examples: Their products are largely sold over the Internet, and supplier coordination occurs though Internet web sites. **Aggregators,** such as Amazon.com, efficiently offer a variety of similar products to the marketplace. Typically aggregators fix the price of the products to exercise economic control over the market. **Marketplace** B-webs match buyers and sellers and provide a mechanism for negotiating price. Priceline.com is a good example of a marketplace B-web where customers can bid on airline tickets.

Alliance

Distributive network

**Alliance** B-webs support open collaboration and sharing of information between cooperating companies. Twenty-three airlines are banding together to form a new alliance for increasing yields by making it easier for consumers to comparison-shop Web fares online.[5] VerticalNet is another example of a company that has created hundreds of online communities where information can be shared between companies. **Distributive network,** shippers such as United Parcel Service, constitute the linkages among the four other B-web models and provide a common transportation infrastructure to support B-web business.

EXHIBIT MB8.2

## Business Web Models

| | B-WEB MODEL | | | | |
|---|---|---|---|---|---|
| | MARKETPLACE (AGORA) | AGGREGATOR | ALLIANCE | VALUE CHAIN | DISTRIBUTIVE NETWORK |
| DEFINITION | A business web that handles complex exchanges between buyers and sellers. | A company that positions itself as a value-adding intermediary between producers and customers. | Members of a creative community that designs useful things, creates knowledge, or produces shared experiences. | Partnered companies that help produce a highly integrated value proposition through a managed process. Products are custom tailored to match customer needs. | Logistical networks that cut across all business web axes to provide essential transfer services. |
| MAIN THEME | Dynamic pricing | Distribution and delivery | Creative collaboration | Process integration involving partnering companies | Allocation/ distribution |
| KEY PROCESSES | Price discovery by matching buyers and sellers | Needs matching | Information sharing, testing new concepts | Product design, supply chain management | Distribution of cargo |
| OPERATIONS' ROLE | Minimal | Major—lead aggregator takes responsibility for selection, pricing, and order fulfillment | Minimal—the most virtual of all B-webs; basically online communities | Major—primary company manages the entire process using mix of outsourced and internal operations | Major—controls shipping activities that underlie e-commerce |
| OPERATIONS PERFORMANCE CRITERIA | Maintaining information base | Delivery reliability; inventory management; cost control; providing online tools for analysis | Operations reside in the alliance members | Mass customization; JIT delivery; tracking and updating | Delivery reliability; speed; minimizing shipment damage |
| EXAMPLES | Yahoo! Classifieds<br>Ebay<br>Priceline.com<br>E-Steel<br>MetalSite | Amazon.com<br>E-Trade<br>Chemdex.com<br>DongDong.com (the Amazon.com of China) | America Online<br>Open Source Software (Linux) | Dell Computers<br>Cisco Systems<br>Ford Motor Co | Federal Express<br>UPS<br>Transport4 (petroleum shipping) |

SOURCE: MODIFIED FROM D. TAPSCOTT, D. TICOLL, AND A. LOWY, "RISE OF THE BUSINESS WEB," *BUSINESS* 2.0, NOVEMBER 1999, PP. 198–204.

As can be seen in the table, OM's role varies according to the B-web model used. In some instances the only operations that are managed by the focal organization are informational, essentially operating an information exchange and maintaining Web software, such as in the marketplace model. The same is true for the alliance model, although maintaining customer support help lines certainly constitutes operations activities for the members of the alliance. In contrast, the aggregator and value chain have major order fulfillment processes, and hence operations are central to the business. The distributive network is involved in the "heavy lifting" (often literally) of the physical products created by others, and operations, in fact, constitute the business. Obviously, there are gray areas in the classification. Hyperlinks trigger operations activities of organizations within all the B-web models. Also, as we have noted, the Internet is still widely used to supplement processes of non–B-web firms.

## E-OPS APPLICATIONS

In the following sections, we discuss major applications of E-Ops to the topics of this book. These represent common internal processes that can be made more efficient through the application of Internet technology. The primary applications of E-Ops are in supply chain management. Virtually all of the B-web models just described directly support supply chain management.

### SUPPLY CHAIN MANAGEMENT

**Order Fulfillment in Product Provision** Exhibit MB18.3 displays the order fulfillment flows using the Internet for a product manufacturer such as Dell Computers. In this particular example, the product is made to order and the company allocates multiple production orders to factories according to their particular process capabilities. Data are captured at multiple places for data mining and order replenishment.

**Order Fulfillment in Aggregator Businesses** A now-classic application of an Internet-driven order fulfillment process is that of Amazon.com's McDonough, Georgia, distribution center. (See the Breakthrough Box titled "From Your Mouse to Your House.")

EXHIBIT MB8.3 A Make-to-Order Fulfillment Process

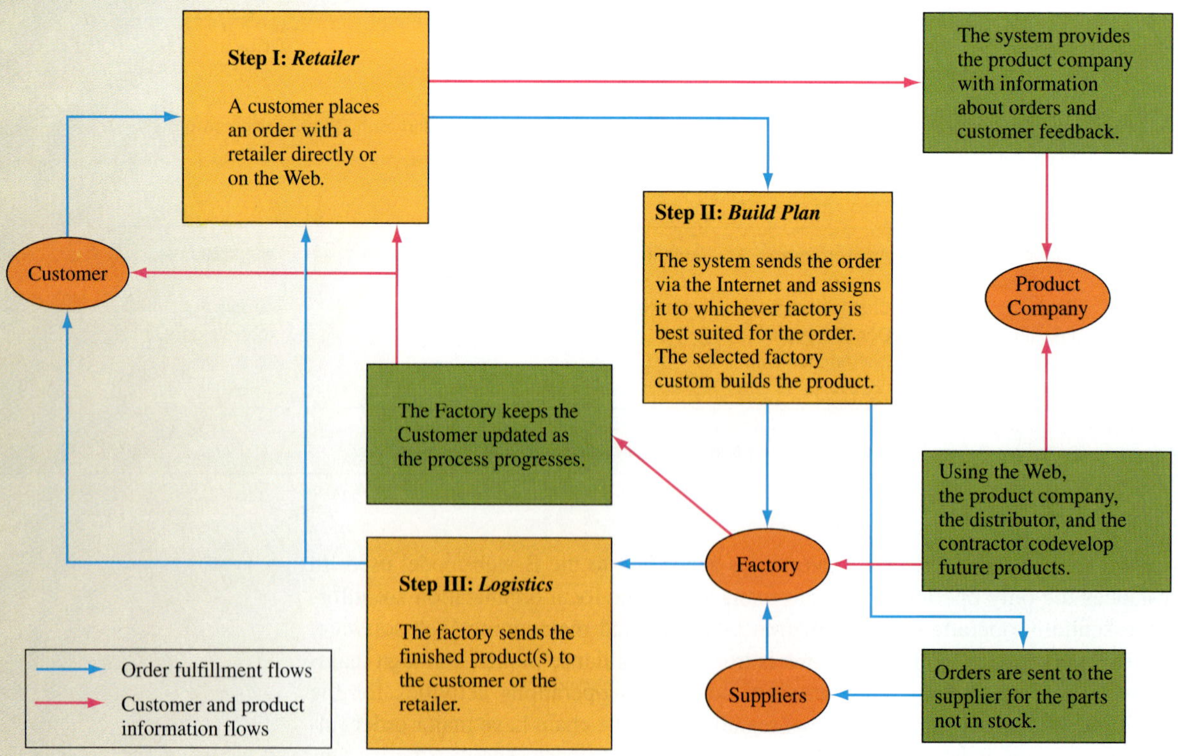


SOURCE: MIKE SHAW, "BUILDING ON E-BUSINESS FROM ENTERPRISE SYSTEMS," *INFORMATION SYSTEMS FRONTIERS*, VOL. 2, NO. 1, 2000.

## Project Management

Information sharing is the key to project management. The Alta Vista Forum Groupware package creates a knowledge repository at an intranet web site to share documents and organize a team's project knowledge. The Livelink Intranet Groupware package allows creation of a document management library at an intranet web site, and lets the user check in and check out project documents.

## Product and Process Design

Cross Functional

Product data management (PDM) systems for designing new products now are able to give any person in an enterprise, from any location, secure access to vital information through a standard Web browser. Users in such markets as electronics, automotive, consumer products, and aerospace can access and view critical enterprise information, such as product designs and workflow. One such system is called the Matrix Web User. At Zenith Electronics Corp., it enables managing the design processes from the marketing concept to industrial design to product assurance. According to one manager, "Only 15 percent of our staff is heavy-duty information creators and require direct access to the Matrix database. We use Matrix Web User to link the remaining 85 percent who need immediate, easy access to the information in the database, but do not need more advanced capabilities".[6]

## Purchasing

National Semiconductor's "My Bill of Materials" is a personalized table for National's registered users that allows them to build a personalized web site for the parts they specify (containing part numbers, package type, part status, pricing and distributor inventory, standard pack method, and a list of user-selected distributors with on-hand available inventory to sell along with hot links into their order forms). Users can create multiple projects and select the information they want to see. Each project becomes an additional link on the user's private web site. All attributes in this selection criteria are updated daily, so you can get the latest information available for the parts you want whenever you want them. Developed product folders include data sheets, simulation results, engineering specifications, and availability and price data for design engineers using specific product packages.

The e-Steel Exchange is an easy-to-use marketplace for both buying and selling steel products. On the e-Steel Exchange a business can either buy or sell by creating offers or inquiries or by simply searching for the products it is interested in. For example, if you are a purchasing agent seeking a particular type of cold-rolled steel, after you submit your inquiry, it will appear in your e-Steel account, where you will be able to track your negotiations. When you reach an agreement, an electronic document is created automatically for both you and the seller. This document contains all the details of the transaction.

## Manufacturing Processes

Flexible manufacturing systems can also be linked to the Internet. One variant of this, called an Intelligent Manufacturing Workstation (IMW), provides a complete "shop in a box" for a given process. It has been successfully implemented in the area of sheet metal bending. Once the design of a typical part is turned over to the prototype Intelligent Manufacturing Workstation, the complete plan is developed in 1 to 10 minutes. The bending machine controller of an IMW is an upgradeable, high-end PC with network connections.[7]

## Inventory Management

Boeing designed a Web front end to its preexisting spare parts inventory system. This site provides current information about availability, location, and prices of spare parts sought by airlines' operations managers. It has become so successful that Boeing is introducing more than 50 customer Web applications in its Boeing Partners' Network.

# BREAKTHROUGH

## FROM YOUR MOUSE TO YOUR HOUSE: WHAT GOES ON BEHIND THE SCENES WHEN YOU PLACE AN ORDER AT AMAZON.COM

### 1: YOU ORDER THREE ITEMS, AND A COMPUTER IN SEATTLE TAKES CHARGE

A computer assigns your order—a book, a game, and a digital camera—to one of Amazon's seven U.S. distribution centers, five of which it opened this year. With 3 million sq. ft., Amazon has 1.5 times the floor space of the Empire State Building.

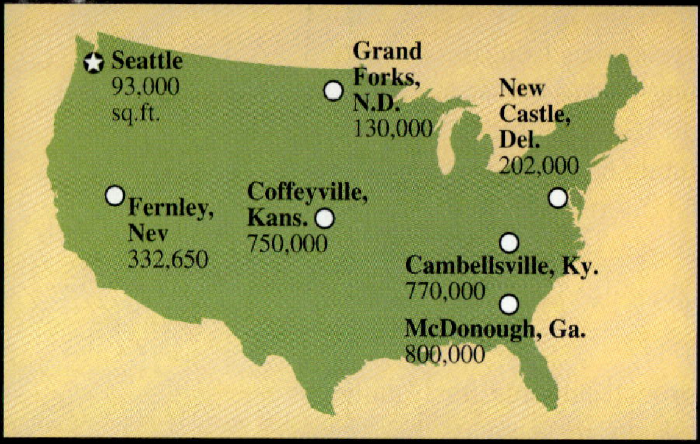


### 2: IN SUBURBAN ATLANTA, THREE RED LIGHTS GO ON

Your order is transmitted to the closest facility that has the products. Amazon's newest, in McDonough, Ga., opened in October and stocks more than a million items. Rows of red lights show which products are ordered. Workers move from bulb to bulb, retrieving an item from the shelf above and pressing a button that resets the light. Computers determine which workers go where.

### 3: YOUR ITEMS ARE PUT INTO CRATES ON MOVING BELTS

Each item goes into a large green crate that contains many customers' orders. When full, the crates ride a series of conveyor belts that winds more than 10 miles through the plant at a constant speed of 2.9 ft. per sec. The bar code on each item is scanned 15 times, by machines and by many of the 600 full-time workers, all of whom get Amazon stock options.

SOURCE: J. ZEFF, "FROM YOUR MOUSE TO YOUR HOUSE", *TIME*, DECEMBER 27, 1999, PP. 72–73. 

4: ALL THREE ITEMS CONVERGE IN A CHUTE, AND THEN INSIDE A BOX

All of the crates arrive at a central point where bar codes are matched with order numbers to determine who gets what. Your three items end up in a 3-ft.-wide chute—one of several thousand—and are placed into a cardboard box with a new bar code that identifies your order.

5: ANY GIFTS YOU'VE CHOSEN ARE WRAPPED BY HAND

Amazon trains an elite group of gift wrappers to "make it look like Mom's". Each worker processes 30 packages an hour (those who fail are reassigned to other jobs). For its busiest season yet, Amazon's warehouses are stocked with 4.4 million yards of ribbon and 7.8 million sq. ft. of wrapping paper—which if laid flat would more than cover Disneyland.

6: THE BOX IS PACKED, TAPED, WEIGHED, AND LABELED BEFORE LEAVING THE WAREHOUSE IN A TRUCK

The McDonough plant was designed to ship as many as 200,000 pieces a day. About 60 percent of orders are shipped via the U.S. Postal Service; nearly everything else goes through United Parcel Service. Both have large facilities within 10 miles of the warehouse. Products that are unusually big or heavy (150 lbs. or more) require special delivery.

7: YOUR ORDER ARRIVES AT YOUR DOORSTEP

Voila! One to seven days later, yet another of Amazon's 13 million customers has been served. (http://www.amazon.com)

EXHIBIT MB8.4

The Internet and Service

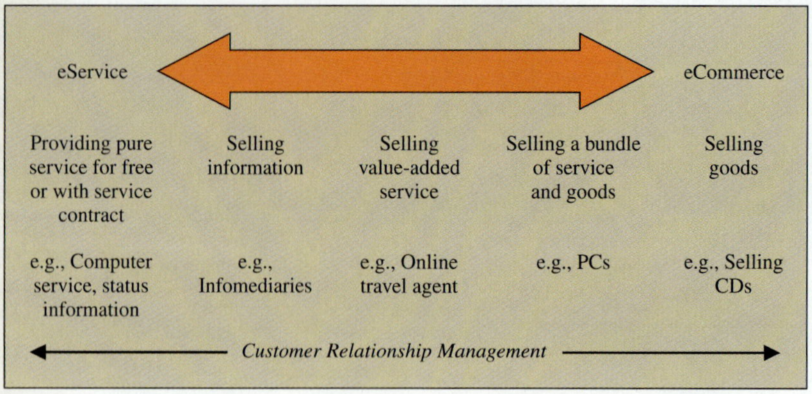


## SERVICES

eService is the delivery of service using new media such as the Web. As Exhibit MB8.4 illustrates, there is a broad spectrum from pure sales on the Web, with little or no service content, to pure service, delivered free, or as part of a service contract. In between there are value-added services such as online travel agents and products sold with a high service content, such as the ability to customize your own computer when ordering it online. Each of these may be linked and supported by Customer Relationship Management (CRM) Systems.[8]

As we discussed in the opening vignette to Chapter 6, on Lands' End, one of the country's largest outsourcers, APAC Customer Services Inc., has launched a service that allows agents to answer questions and communicate with customers live while they're on the Web. Agents literally can control customers' browser screens to help guide them through transactions.

Nordstrom Store's cosmetics department sales personnel record individual customer preferences in an electronic customer book and make this available to stores throughout the United States. This enables a salesperson at any store to quickly find the brand, color, and other features of the cosmetic being sought by the customer, or by another person buying a product for her or him at Nordstrom.

An example of integrated service activities on the Internet is seen in a health care site that provides online services to Humana's 330,000 doctors and 6 million patients. Pharmacy giant CVS is the exclusive online pharmacy for the site. In 2000, the Healtheon/WebMD integrated Medic Computer System's medical practice management system, used by 65,000 doctors, into a co-branded Web site.

## QUALITY MANAGEMENT

The Oracle Corporation has developed Oracle Quality, an enterprisewide repository and data management system that helps to ensure quality standards while maximizing quality-tracking efficiency. It is a closed-loop system that can find root causes, perform ongoing analysis, and take corrective action. It also permits automated corrective actions—controlling machinery, notifying personnel, or placing transactions on hold—without human intervention.

## FORECASTING

Collaborative Forecasting and Replenishment (CFAR) is a formal way for manufacturers and retailers to collaborate on estimates of future demand for products. Organizations post selected data about their sales forecasts on a common Web server, which supply chain partners use to improve their forecasts. CFAR affects forecasting, purchasing, inventory, and logistics planning.[9] An example company is Heineken USA Inc., whose Web-based system takes orders from its 450 distributors and does collaborative forecasting and planning using software from Atlanta-based Logility Inc.

### OPERATIONS SCHEDULING (MANUFACTURING EXECUTION SYSTEMS)

A shop scheduling software suite developed by Realworld Technologies provides schedulers with a window on the whole plant with easy access information from internal networks. Called a *manufacturing execution system (MES),* its capabilities include allowing the user to run "what if" scenarios in real time—using real information from the shop floor—to create schedules. The software also allows for remote access via networks and the Internet, giving outside sales offices real-time production information.

### REENGINEERING AND CONSULTING

Consulting companies such as Andersen Consulting and Ernst & Young use knowledge gained from previous reengineering projects to create standardized methods for follow-on projects. This form of knowledge management is called a *reuse* strategy. Such reused information is stored in data warehouses and shared through the Web.

## E-OPS CHALLENGES AND RECOMMENDATIONS FOR MANAGERS

The growth of e-commerce creates some challenging problems for operations managers. One is that in order to make the Internet's impact as "sticky" as possible, companies are now evaluating their Internet options before making purchasing and production decisions. Another, of course, is integrating the E-Ops into traditionally run production systems and legacy systems. This calls for a different mindset than was necessary when computerization was essentially limited to in-house applications. A third challenge is that an operations managers' ability to oversee their supply chain also allows external members of the supply chain to oversee the manager's domain. Everybody can track everybody else! Finally, there are the raised expectations of customers who are proficient in their interactions with the front end of a supply chain (that is, placing and tracking orders) but are not cognizant of the complex processes that take place in order to fulfill orders on the back end. An article in *Digital Chicago* titled "Desperately Seeking E-Fulfillment" captures the nature of this recurring problem.[10] Excellent back office support and logistics, more than a fancy web site, may well be the new order winners.

We now turn to some suggested requirements for effective E-Ops to cope with these challenges:

- Keep the web site simple. Many ordering web sites are exercises in frustration—they have no logical beginning or end, and they become mazes through which only the brave persevere. Hyperlinks often lead to hypertension. The e-Steel web site mentioned earlier is a good model to follow.
- Become an efficient knowledge provider to customers and other parts of the business. The operations department is often the best source of information regarding implementation problems for customers deploying systems sold by the company. It also is well suited to provide information for suppliers and distributors. Other parts of the business—particularly sales and customer relationship management—need good operations data to help sell and support the product line and identify new products.
- Monitor each third-party fulfillment partner carefully and often. *Third-party fulfillment* can mean anything a retailer outsources: warehouses, site design and hosting, monitoring of site traffic, order processing, and so on. These fulfillment firms usually branch out from whatever originally got them involved with the company. Soon they're acquiring (or being acquired by) other companies and branching into new functions that may not be a central competency.

Cross Functional

# CONCLUSION

We propose that a new specialty of electronic commerce, E-Ops, will become a major aspect of the field of OM. We caution here that although new Internet opportunities may focus management's attention on information technology, it is critical that operations processes be capable of supporting that fancy web site. From a strategic perspective, how one manages E-Ops will depend on the nature of the business web model of which it is a part. We have identified five such B-web models (marketplace, aggregator, alliance, value chain, and distributive network). These can be roughly categorized according to degree of hierarchical control and value integration. Supply chain management is the major application area for E-Ops, and we have presented a general model of order fulfillment for a product company and the actual order fulfillment process used by the bookseller Amazon. com. A variety of other examples of Internet applications that link to operations were discussed as well, and suggestions were made for dealing with the E-Ops challenges facing the operations manager.

## KEY TERMS

**Electronic commerce (EC)** Use of computer applications communicating over networks to allow buyers and sellers to complete a transaction or part of a transaction.

**E-Ops** Application of the Internet and its attendant technologies to the field of OM.

**Business web (B-web) models** Business structures designed around the use of the Internet.

**Value chain** Partnered companies that help produce a highly integrated value proposition through a managed process. Products are custom tailored to match customer needs.

**Aggregator** A company that positions itself as a value-adding intermediary between producers and customers.

**Marketplace** A B-web that handles complex exchanges between buyers and sellers.

**Alliance** Members of a creative community that designs useful things, creates knowledge, or produces shared experiences.

**Distributive network** Logistical networks that cut across all business web axes to provide essential transfer services.

## REVIEW AND DISCUSSION QUESTIONS

1 In their book, *Unleashing the Killer App: Digital Strategies for Market Dominance,* Downes and Chunka suggest that new information technology, such as EC, should be viewed not just as an enabler of change, but also as the driver of change. How does this perspective compare with the continuous improvement philosophy of total quality management and the radical change philosophy of reengineering?
2 What OM tasks are being "created" for the customer by virtue of E-Ops?
3 In what respects have E-Ops impacted global operations management?
4 A bank has set up a telephone system in which it guarantees that a caller will talk to a live person, rather than a computer. What are the pluses and minuses of this approach?
5 Will some products and services forever be immune from EC/E-Ops?
6 At Ford Motors every car and truck model has its own internal web site to track design, production, quality control, and delivery processes. Suppliers and customers also have access to the site, and all parties are expected to provide full supply chain information. How would you expect this to affect the life of a middle manager at a Ford plant?

## INTERNET ENRICHMENT EXERCISE

THE E-OPS GAME

Are you looking for a real challenge? Pit your operations management skills against other students from around the world by playing "The E-Ops Game." Players run a simulated business that sells generic computers over the Internet. The player needs to manage all roles in the e-business. These roles include purchasing material, scheduling production, and selling the product. Your computers are made in an automated factory that can make exactly one computer each second. In Internet time, you need to buy parts for your factory and sell your completed computers. All of these transactions take place in real time in this quick moving Internet game. A great strategy, careful planning, and great execution are keys to high profits in playing the game.

The best players become part of the E-Ops hall of fame with their names listed in the "Top 100." The game is located at http://www.pom.edu/ebus. Create your own private account and join the fun!

## SELECTED BIBLIOGRAPHY


Downes, L., and M. Chunka. *Unleashing the Killer App: Digital Strategies for Market Dominance.* Boston: Harvard Business School Press, 1998.

Kalakota, R., and A. Whinston. *Electronic Commerce: A Manager's Guide.* Boston: Addison Wesley Longman, 1997.

Kosuir, D. *Understanding Electronic Commerce.* Redmond, WA: Microsoft Press, 1997.

Mathieu, R. G. *Manufacturing and the Internet.* Norcross, GA: Institute of Industrial Engineers, 1996.

O'Brien, J. A. *Management Information Systems: Managing Information Technology in the Internetworked Enterprise,* 4th ed. Burr Ridge, IL: Irwin/McGraw-Hill, 1999.

Seybold, P. B., and R. Marshak. *Customers.com: How to Create a Profitable Business Strategy for the Internet and Beyond.* New York: Times Business Random House, 1998.

Tapscott, D., D. Ticoll, and A. Lowy. *Digital Capital: Harnessing the Power of Business Webs.* Boston: Harvard Business School Press, 2000.


## FOOTNOTES

1 PricewaterhouseCoopers, *Technology Forecast: 1999* (10 Anniversary Edition) (Menlo Park, CA: Technology Centre, October 1998), p. 192.

2 L. Downes and M. Chunka, *Unleashing the Killer App: Digital Strntegies for Market Dominance* (Boston: Harvard Business School Press, 1998), p. 61.

3 Adapted from "Network Effects" by E. Ransdell, *Fast Company,* issue 27 (September, 1999). p. 208.

4 "A Review of Press Coverage of the Internet Economy," *The Industry Standard's Media Grok,* November 3, 1999.

5 P. Sullivan, *The Standard,* January 15, 2000.

6 K. Parker, "The Interface of Things to Come," *Manufacturing Systems,* August 1997.

7 D. A. Bourne, "IMW: The Key to Mass Customization," *Robotics World,* Atlanta, Spring 1998.

8 C. A. Voss, "Developing an eService Strategy," *Business Strategy Review,* April 2000, p. 19.

9 PricewaterhouseCoopers, *Technology Forecast: 1999* (10 Anniversary Edition) (Menlo Park, CA: Technology Centre, October 1998), p. 198.

10 J. Siverstein, "Desperately Seeking E-Fulfillment," *Digital Chicago,* November/December 1999, pp. 22–47.

chapter

*chapter eight*
# SUPPLY CHAIN STRATEGY

## CHAPTER OUTLINE AND KEY TERMS

# 8 MANAGING THE VALUE CHAIN

Are you under pressure to control your supply chain? Manufacturers are now looking both upstream and downstream to improve efficiency and deliver value more effectively to customers.

Many manufacturing executives can relate to Deere & Co.'s recent dilemma. The company's Worldwide Commercial & Consumer Equipment Division (WC&CED), like many businesses today, has outsourced a significant portion of its production work. In fact, at the division's Horicon (Wisconsin) Works, purchased parts represent fully 82 percent of the cost of goods sold. As a result, WC&CED—which makes small tractors and commercial mowing equipment—has grown increasingly dependent on its supplier base. Deere WC&CED has found that outsourcing can result in loss of control over key capabilities, which, in turn, can affect a company's ability to introduce changes in response to shifts in the marketplace—or simply to improve its efficiency in serving customers. Consequently, there has been a growing impetus to find ways to manage the "extended enterprise"—to build collaborative relationships and improve the flow of both materials and information throughout the value-creating pipeline. The scope of the challenge extends beyond traditional supply chain management, although this is the key element.

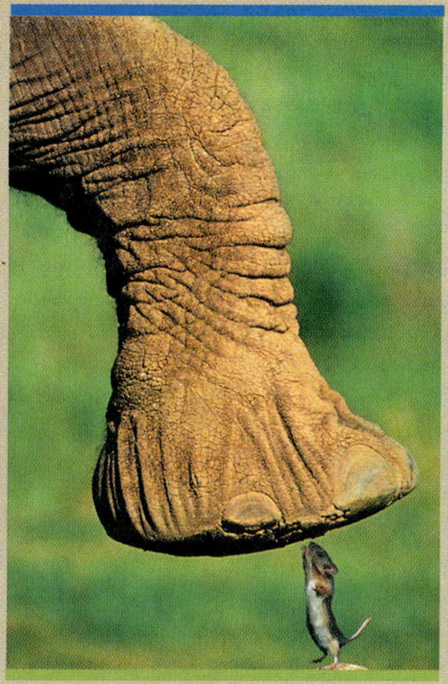

Deere's dilemma demonstrates a larger challenge facing manufacturing executives: How do they position their firms in the *value chain*—the entire series of activities that begins with the processing of raw materials and ends when a finished product is in the hands of the end user? Shaping a strategy that reflects the reality of the downstream marketplace often leads to new approaches to upstream supplier management. A fundamental question in supply chain management is how value is created. If improved efficiency lowers the cost to the end customer, does that increase the perception of value? If so, then strategies such as lean manufacturing, which reduces inventory carrying costs, have a role to play.

So what is the difference between supply chain management and value chain management? Tim Furey, CEO of Oxford Associates, Inc., a marketing

**Source:** Adapted from J. H. Sheridan, "Managing the Value Chain," *Industry Week*, September 6, 1999. Copyright Penton Media, Inc., Cleveland, Ohio.

and sales strategy consulting firm, says that it is where the emphasis is placed. "Supply chain thinking has traditionally been *efficiency*-oriented—a cost reduction and productivity sort of thing—whereas value chain thinking is *effectiveness*-oriented," he says. When companies stress effectiveness, they aren't necessarily trying to reduce costs, but rather "to create the highest value for the customer"—which isn't always the lowest-cost approach. ←

## SUPPLY CHAIN STRATEGY

Supply chain

Supply chain management is a hot topic in business today. The idea is to apply a total systems approach to managing the entire flow of information, materials, and services from raw materials suppliers through factories and warehouses to the end customer. The term **supply chain** comes from a picture of how organizations are linked together as viewed from a particular company. Exhibit 8.1 depicts a global supply chain for both manufacturing and service companies. Note the linkage between suppliers that provide inputs, manufacturing and service support operations that transform the inputs into products and services, and the distribution and local service providers that localize the product. Localization can involve just the delivery of the product or some more involved process that tailors the product or service to the needs of the local market.

So why is supply chain management such a popular topic these days? The answer is that many companies are achieving significant competitive advantage by the way they configure

EXHIBIT 8.1 The Supply Chain Network

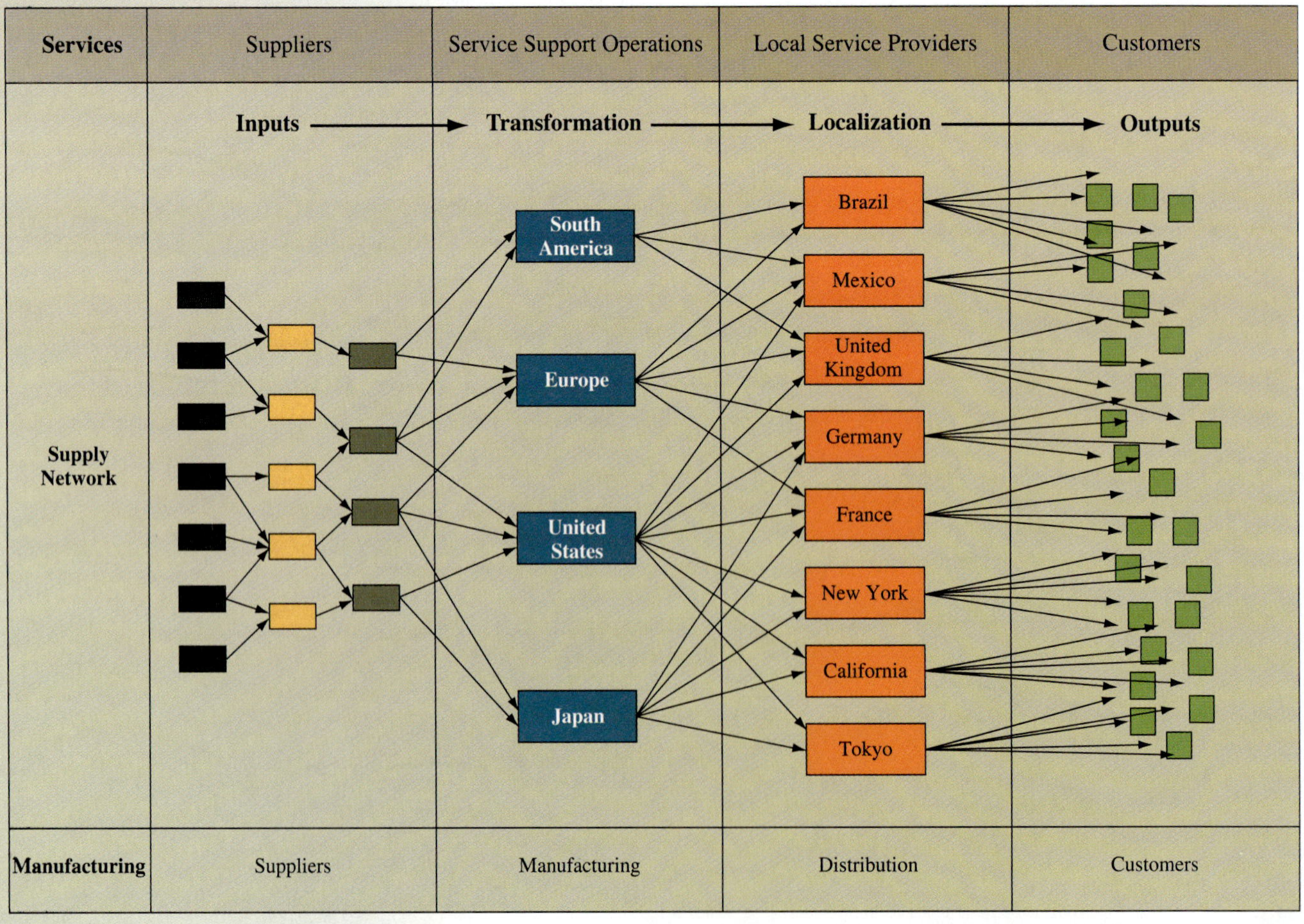

and manage their supply chain operations. Dell Computer, for example, skips the distribution and retail steps typical of a manufacturing company's supply chain. Dell takes orders for its computers from customers over the Internet and manufactures directly to the orders. The computers are never sent to distribution centers and are never displayed in a retail store. Customers are able to get the latest models at very competitive prices in only five or six days using this approach.

Keep in mind that a good supply chain design for Dell may not work for a company like Campbell Soup. If Campbell Soup were to eliminate distribution centers from their supply chain, the costs associated with transporting their products to grocery stores would be excessive. Imagine ordering cans of chicken noodle soup over the Internet directly from the manufacturer. It's an interesting idea, but the cost to transport that individual can of soup is higher than the cost of the soup. The grocery store is needed as the intermediary so that the shipping cost can be reduced through truckload shipments.

Our purpose in this chapter is to show how supply chains should be structured to meet the needs of different products and customer groups. We begin by developing some terminology that will be useful for measuring supply chain performance; then we look strategically at different supply chain designs and the trade-offs involved. Following this, we describe strategies that are important to large companies operating in global markets. These strategies involve outsourcing of work and postponing assembly in the supply chain.

## MEASURING SUPPLY CHAIN PERFORMANCE

One view of the supply chain is centered on the inventories that are positioned in the system. Exhibit 8.2 shows how hamburger meat and potatoes are stored in various locations in a typical fast-food restaurant chain. Here we see the steps that the beef and potatoes move through on their way to the local retail store and then to the customer. At each step inventory is carried, and this inventory has a particular cost to the company. Inventory serves as a buffer, thus allowing each stage to operate independently of the others. For example, the distribution center inventory allows the system that supplies the retail stores to operate independently of the meat and potato packing operations. Because the inventory at each stage ties up money, it is important that the operations at each stage are synchronized to minimize the size of these buffer inventories. The efficiency of the supply chain can be measured based on the size of the inventory investment in the supply chain.

EXHIBIT 8.2

Inventory in the Supply Chain—Fast-Food Restaurant

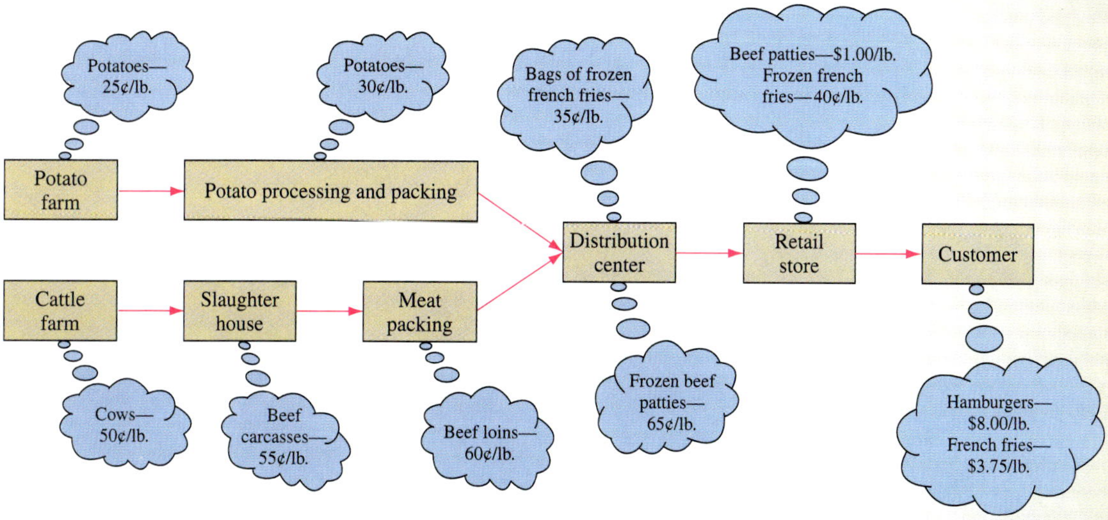

The inventory investment is measured relative to the total cost of the goods that are provided through the supply chain.

Two common measures to evaluate supply chain efficiency are *inventory turnover* and *weeks-of-supply*. These essentially measure the same thing and mathematically are the inverse of one another. **Inventory turnover** is calculated as follows:

Inventory turnover

[8.1]
$$\text{Inventory turnover} = \frac{\text{Cost of goods sold}}{\text{Average aggregate inventory value}}$$

Cost of goods sold

Average aggregate inventory value

The **cost of goods sold** is the annual cost for a company to produce the goods or services provided to customers; it is sometimes referred to as the *cost of revenue*. This does not include the selling and administrative expenses of the company. The **average aggregate inventory value** is the total value of all items held in inventory for the firm valued at cost. It includes the raw material, work-in-process, finished goods, and distribution inventory considered owned by the company.

Good inventory turnover values vary by industry and the type of products being handled. At one extreme, a grocery store chain may turn inventory over 100 times per year. Values of six to seven are more typical.

Weeks of supply

In many situations, particularly when distribution inventory is dominant, **weeks of supply** is the preferred measure. This is a measure of how many weeks' worth of inventory is in the system at a particular point in time. The calculation is as follows:

[8.2]
$$\text{Weeks of supply} = \left(\frac{\text{Average aggregate inventory value}}{\text{Cost of goods sold}}\right) 52 \text{ weeks}$$

When company financial reports cite inventory turnover and weeks of supply, we can assume that the measures are being calculated firmwide. We show an example of this type of calculation in the example that follows using Dell Computer data. These calculations, though, can be done on individual entities within the organization. For example, we might be interested in the production raw materials inventory turnover or the weeks of supply associated with the warehousing operation of a firm. In these cases, the cost would be that associated with the total amount of inventory that runs through the specific inventory. In some very low-inventory operations, days or even hours are a better unit of time for measuring supply.

A firm considers inventory an investment because the intent is for it to be used in the future. Inventory ties up funds that could be used for other purposes, and a firm may have to borrow money to finance the inventory investment. The objective is to have the proper amount of inventory and to have it in the correct locations in the supply chain. Determining the correct amount of inventory to have in each position requires a thorough analysis of the supply chain coupled with the competitive priorities that define the market for the company's products.

### EXAMPLE 8.1: INVENTORY TURNOVER CALCULATION

Dell Computer reported the following information in its 1999 annual report (all amounts are expressed in millions):

| | |
|---|---|
| Net revenue (fiscal year 1999) | $18,243 |
| Cost of revenue (fiscal year 1999) | 14,137 |
| Cost of production materials (fiscal year 1999) | 6,423 |
| Production materials on hand (25 January 1999) | 234 |
| Work-in-process and finished goods on hand (25 January 1999) | 39 |
| Production materials—days of supply | 6 days |

The cost of revenue corresponds to what we call cost of goods sold. One might think that U.S. companies, at least, would use a common accounting terminology, but this is not true. The inventory turnover calculation is

$$\text{Inventory turnover} = \frac{14{,}137}{234 + 39} = 51.78 \text{ turns per year}$$

This is amazing performance for a high-tech company, but it explains much of why the company is such a financial success.

The corresponding weeks of supply calculation is

$$\text{Weeks of supply} = \left(\frac{234 + 39}{14{,}137}\right) 52 = 1 \text{ week} \leftarrow$$

## SUPPLY CHAIN DESIGN STRATEGY

The Dell Company example is unique and interesting. Through a combination of innovative product design, an Internet order-taking process, an innovative assembly system, and amazing cooperation from its suppliers, Dell Computer has been able to create a supply chain that is extremely efficient. Dell Computer now has become the benchmark company for the computer industry.

A key to the success of Dell Computer is the fact that customers order over the Internet and are willing to wait at least a week for the delivery of their computer systems. Most consumers do not buy computers this way; rather, they go to Wal-Mart or Staples or some other discount store and purchase a computer from the available stock in the store. Often the computer is bundled with other services that offer rebates enticing the customer to buy the package, thus reducing the overall cost of the computer and the service.

Marshall Fisher[1] argues that in many cases there are adversarial relations between supply chain partners as well as dysfunctional industry practices such as a reliance on price promotions. Consider the common food industry practice of offering price promotions every January on a product. Retailers respond to the price cut by stocking up, in some cases buying a year's supply—a practice the industry calls *forward buying*. Nobody wins in the deal. Retailers have to pay to carry the year's supply, and the shipment bulge adds cost throughout the supplier's system. For example, the supplier plants must go on overtime starting in October to meet the bulge. Even the vendors that supply the manufacturing plants are affected because they must quickly react to the large surge in raw material requirements.

Vol. II "Supplier Development Outreach Program"

The impact of these types of practices has been studied at companies such as Procter & Gamble. Exhibit 8.3 shows typical order patterns faced by each node in a supply chain that consists of a manufacturer, a distributor, a wholesaler, and a retailer. In this case, the demand is for disposable baby diapers. The retailer's orders to the wholesaler display greater variability than the end-consumer sales; the wholesaler's orders to the manufacturer show even more oscillations; and, finally, the manufacturer's orders to its suppliers are the most volatile. This phenomenon of variability magnification as we move from the customer to the producer in the supply chain is often referred to as the **bullwhip effect.** The effect indicates a lack of synchronization among supply chain members. Even a slight change in consumer sales ripples backward in the form of magnified oscillations upstream, resembling the result of a flick of a bullwhip handle. Because the supply patterns do not match the demand patterns, inventory accumulates at various stages, and shortages and delays occur at others. This bullwhip effect has been observed by many firms in numerous industries, including Campbell Soup and Procter & Gamble in consumer products; Hewlett-Packard, IBM, and Motorola in electronics; General Motors in automobiles; and Eli Lilly in pharmaceuticals.

Bullwhip effect

Campbell Soup has a program called *continuous replenishment* that typifies what many manufacturers are doing to smooth the flow of materials through their supply chain. Here is how the program works. Campbell establishes electronic data interchange (EDI) links with retailers and offers an "everyday low price" that eliminates discounts. Every morning, retailers electronically inform the company of their demand for all Campbell products and of the level of inventories in their distribution centers. Campbell uses that information to forecast future demand and to determine which products require replenishment based on

EXHIBIT 8.3

Increasing Variability of Orders up the Supply Chain

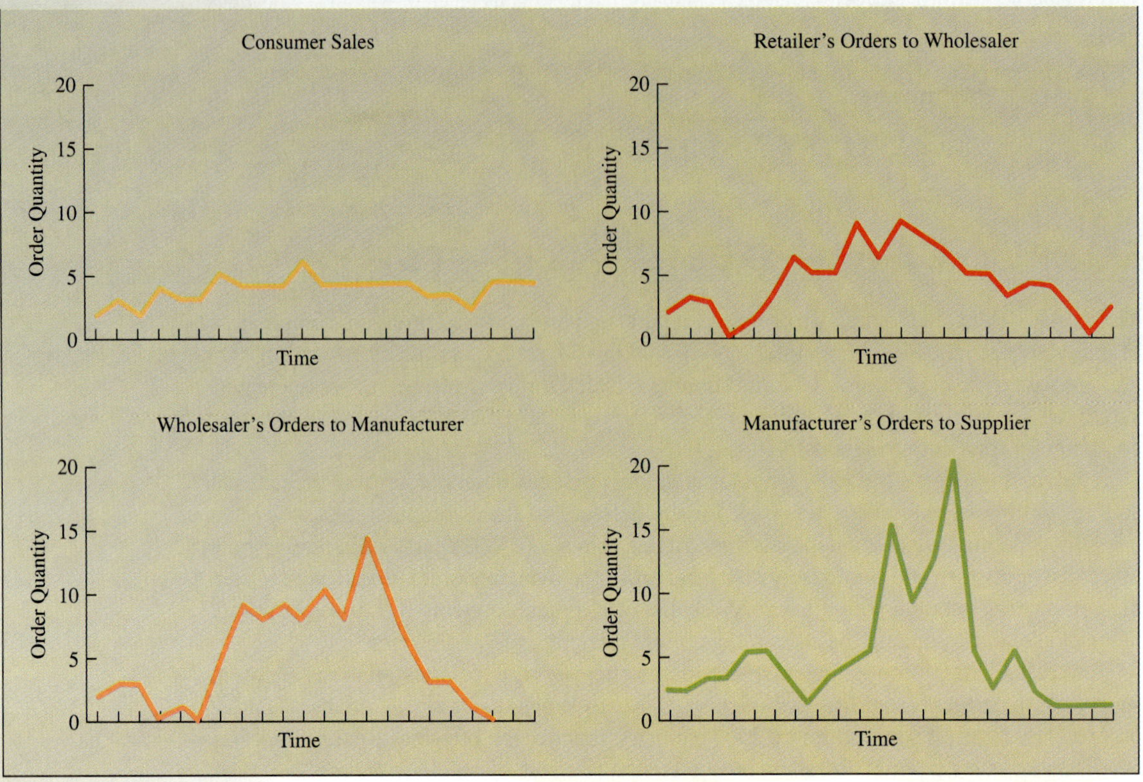


upper and lower inventory limits previously established with each supplier. Trucks leave the Campbell shipping plant that afternoon and arrive at the retailers' distribution centers with the required replenishments the same day. Using this system, Campbell can cut the retailers' inventories, which under the old system averaged four weeks of supply, to about two weeks of supply.

This solves some problems for Campbell Soup, but what are the advantages for the retailer? Most retailers figure that the cost to carry the inventory of a given product for a year equals at least 25 percent of what they paid for the product. A two-week inventory reduction represents a cost savings equal to nearly 1 percent of sales. The average retailer's profits equal about 2 percent of sales, so this saving is enough to increase profits by 50 percent. Because the retailer makes more money on Campbell products delivered through continuous replenishment, it has an incentive to carry a broader line of them and to give them more shelf space. Campbell Soup found that after it introduced the program, sales of its products grew twice as fast through participating retailers as they did through other retailers.

Fisher has developed a framework to help managers understand the nature of demand for their products and then devise the supply chain that can best satisfy that demand. Many aspects of a product's demand are important—for example, product life cycle, demand predictability, product variety, and market standards for lead times and service. Fisher has found that products can be categorized as either primarily functional or primarily innovative. Because each category requires a distinctly different kind of supply chain, the root cause of supply chain problems is a mismatch between the type of product and type of supply chain.

Functional products

**Functional products** include the staples that people buy in a wide range of retail outlets, such as grocery stores and gas stations. Because such products satisfy basic needs, which do not change much over time, they have stable, predictable demand and long life cycles. But

CAMPBELL USES A SYSTEM THEY CALL CONTINUOUS PRODUCT REPLENISHMENT. AT THE FOOD RETAILER'S WAREHOUSE, CAMPBELL PRODUCT ARRIVES FROM THE PLANT TO REPLENISH INVENTORY AT THE SAME STEADY RATE AS THE CONSUMER TAKES IT OFF THE SHELF. CPR IS DRIVEN BY AN ELECTRONIC ORDERING SYSTEM MANAGED BY CAMPBELL, FREEING THE RETAILER FROM THIS TASK. STEADY PRODUCTION THAT MEETS PREDETERMINED INVENTORY LEVELS RESULTS IN COST EFFICIENCIES ACROSS THE ENTIRE SUPPLY CHAIN.

their stability invites competition, which often leads to low profit margins. Specific criteria suggested by Fisher for identifying functional products include the following: product life cycle of more than two years, contribution margin of 5 percent to 20 percent, only 10 to 20 product variations, an average forecast error at time of production of only 10 percent, and a lead time for make-to-order products of from six months to one year.

To avoid low margins, many companies introduce innovations in fashion or technology to give customers an additional reason to buy their products. Fashionable clothes and personal computers are good examples. Although innovation can enable a company to achieve higher profit margins, the very newness of the innovative products makes demand for them unpredictable. These **innovative products** typically have a life cycle of just a few months. Innovative products
Imitators quickly erode the competitive advantage that innovative products enjoy, and companies are forced to introduce a steady stream of newer innovations. The short life cycles and the great variety typical of these products further increase unpredictability.

As Fisher explains, innovative products, with their high profit margins and volatile demand, require a fundamentally different supply chain than stable, low-margin functional products. To understand the difference, one should recognize that a supply chain performs two distinct functions: a physical function and a market mediation function. A supply chain's physical function is to convert raw materials into parts, components, and eventually finished goods and to transport all the goods from one point in the supply chain to the next. Less visible but equally important is market mediation, the purpose of which is ensuring that the variety of products reaching the marketplace matches what consumers want to buy. Each of the two functions incurs distinct costs. Physical costs are the costs of production, transportation, and inventory storage. Market mediation costs arise when supply exceeds demand and a product has to be marked down and sold at a loss or when supply falls short of demand, resulting in lost sales opportunities and dissatisfied customers.

The predictable demand of functional products makes market mediation easy because a good match can be made between supply and demand. Companies that make such products are free to focus on minimizing physical cost—an important goal, given the price sensitivity of most functional products. For these companies, information flow that occurs within the supply chain as suppliers, manufacturers, and retailers coordinate their activities is critical. This information can be used to meet predictable demand at the lowest possible cost.

That approach is exactly wrong for innovative products. The uncertain market reaction to a new, innovative product increases the risk of shortages or excess supplies. High profit margins and the importance of early sales in establishing market share for a new product increase the cost of shortages. Short product life cycles increase the risk of obsolescence and the corresponding cost of excess supplies. Hence, market mediation costs predominate for these products.

Cross Functional

For the innovative product it is most important that early sales numbers or other market signals are read. The company then must react quickly. In this instance, the crucial flow of information occurs not only within the supply chain but also from the marketplace to the chain. The critical decisions to be made about inventory and capacity are not about minimizing cost but about where in the chain to position inventory and available production capacity in order to hedge against uncertain demand. Suppliers should be chosen for their speed and flexibility, not for their low cost. For innovative products the supply chain must be configured to be as responsive to changes as possible to avoid the cost of excess inventory and missed sales opportunities.

Fisher offers the matrix shown in Exhibit 8.4 to help formulate the ideal supply chain strategy. The four cells of the matrix represent the four possible combinations of products and priorities. Efficient processes should be used for functional products and responsive processes for innovative products. Companies that have either an innovative product with an efficient supply chain (upper right-hand cell) or a functional product with a responsive supply chain (lower left-hand cell) tend to be the ones with problems.

Efficient processes are designed to minimize cost. This requires maintaining high average utilization rates on resources, minimizing inventory throughout the supply chain, selecting vendors based primarily on cost and quality, and designing products that can be produced at minimum cost. Market-responsive processes, on the other hand, are designed to minimize lead time so that they can quickly respond to unpredictable demand, thus minimizing stockout costs and obsolete inventory costs. In a market-responsive supply chain, expect excess capacity and higher buffer stocks of parts or finished goods. Vendors would be selected based on speed, flexibility, and quality. Modular product designs would be expected so that product differentiation could be delayed in the supply chain.

It is rare for companies to be in the lower left-hand cell. Most companies that introduce functional products realize that they need efficient chains to supply them. However, companies often find themselves in the upper right-hand cell. The reason a position in this cell does not make sense is that any company with innovative products must realize that the rewards from investments in improving supply chain responsiveness are usually much greater than the rewards from investments in improving the chain's efficiency. For every dollar a company invests in increasing its supply chain's responsiveness, it usually results

EXHIBIT 8.4

Matching Supply Chains with Products

| | Functional Products | Innovative Products |
|---|---|---|
| Efficient Supply Chain | Match | Mismatch |
| Responsive Supply Chain | Mismatch | Match |

in a decrease of more than a dollar in the cost of stockouts and forced markdowns on excess inventory that result from mismatches between supply and demand. Consider a typical innovative product with a contribution margin of 40 percent and an average stockout rate of 25 percent.[2] The lost contribution to profit and overhead resulting from stockouts alone is huge: $40\% \times 25\% = 10$ percent of sales—an amount that should exceed profits before taxes. The logic does not apply to functional products. A contribution margin of 10 percent and average stockout rate of 1 percent mean a lost contribution to profit and overhead of only 0.1 percent of sales—a negligible cost that does not warrant the significant investments required to improve responsiveness.

Global

World Company, a leading Japanese apparel manufacturer, has both innovative and functional products. The company produces its basic styles in a low-cost Chinese plant but keeps production of high-fashion styles in Japan, where the advantage of being able to respond quickly to emerging fashion trends more than offsets the disadvantage of high labor costs.

This alignment of supply chain strategy and product characteristics is extremely important to the operational success of a company. In the remaining sections of this chapter we cover a number of the most popular concepts and technologies that are useful for reducing cost and improving the responsiveness of the supply chain.

## OUTSOURCING

Outsourcing

**Outsourcing** is the act of moving some of a firm's internal activities and decision responsibility to outside providers. The terms of the agreement are established in a contract. Outsourcing goes beyond the more common purchasing and consulting contracts because not only are the activities transferred, but also resources that make the activities occur, including people, facilities, equipment, technology, and other assets, are transferred. The responsibilities for making decisions over certain elements of the activities are transferred, as well. Taking complete responsibility for this is a specialty of contract manufacturers such as Flextronics and Solectron. In the electronics industry, for example, 11 percent of manufacturing is performed by such contract manufacturers many of whom manage the full supply chain, even including distribution and repair.[3]

The reasons why a company decides to outsource can vary greatly. Exhibit 8.5 lists 20 examples of reasons to outsource and the accompanying benefits. Outsourcing allows a firm to focus on activities that represent its core competencies. Thus, the company can create a competitive advantage while reducing cost. An entire function may be outsourced, or some elements of an activity may be outsourced, with the rest kept in-house. For example, some of the elements of information technology may be strategic, some may be critical, and some may be performed less expensively by a third party. Identifying a function as a potential outsourcing target, and then breaking that function into its components, allows decision makers to determine which activities are strategic or critical and should remain in-house and which can be outsourced like commodities. As an example, outsourcing the logistics function will be discussed.

Logistics

Vol. V "International Logistics"

There has been dramatic growth in outsourcing in the logistics area. **Logistics** is a term that refers to the management functions that support the complete cycle of material flow: from the purchase and internal control of production materials; to the planning and control of work-in-process; to the purchasing, shipping, and distribution of the finished product. The emphasis on lean inventory means there is less room for error in deliveries. Trucking companies such as Ryder have started adding the logistics aspect to their businesses—changing from merely moving goods from point A to point B, to managing all or part of all shipments over a longer period, typically three years, and replacing the shipper's employees with their own. Logistics companies now have complex computer tracking technology that reduces the risk in transportation and allows the logistics company to add more value to the firm than it could if the function were performed in-house. Third-party logistics providers track freight using electronic data interchange technology and a satellite system to tell customers exactly where its drivers are and when deliveries will be made. Such technology is critical in some environments where the delivery window may be only 30 minutes long.

EXHIBIT 8.5

**Reasons to Outsource and the Benefits**

ORGANIZATIONALLY DRIVEN REASONS

- Enhance effectiveness by focusing on what you do best.
- Increase flexibility to meet changing business conditions, demand for products and services, and technologies.
- Transform the organization.
- Increase product and service value, customer satisfaction, and shareholder value.

IMPROVEMENT-DRIVEN REASONS

- Improve operating performance (increase quality and productivity, shorten cycle times, and so on).
- Obtain expertise, skills, and technologies that are not otherwise available.
- Improve management and control.
- Improve risk management.
- Acquire innovative ideas.
- Improve credibility and image by associating with superior providers.

FINANCIALLY DRIVEN REASONS

- Reduce investments in assets and free up these resources for other purposes.
- Generate cash by transferring assets to the provider.

REVENUE-DRIVEN REASONS

- Gain market access and business opportunities through the provider's network.
- Accelerate expansion by tapping into the provider's developed capacity, processes, and systems.
- Expand sales and production capacity during periods when such expansion cannot be financed.
- Commercially exploit existing skills.

COST-DRIVEN REASONS

- Reduce costs through superior provider performance and the provider's lower cost structure.
- Turn fixed costs into variable costs.

EMPLOYEE-DRIVEN REASONS

- Give employees a stronger career path.
- Increase commitment and energy in noncore areas.



Federal Express has one of the most advanced systems available for tracking items being sent through its services. The system is available to all customers over the Internet. It tells the exact status of each item currently being carried by the company. Information on the exact time a package is picked up, when it is transferred between hubs in the company's network, and when it is delivered is available on the system. You can access this system at the Fedex website (www.fedex.com). Select your country on the initial screen and then select "tracking" on the menu on the left side of the page. Of course, you will need the actual tracking number for an item currently in the system to get information. Federal Express has integrated its tracking system with many of its customers' in-house information systems.

Another example of innovative outsourcing in logistics involves Hewlett-Packard. Hewlett-Packard turned over its inbound raw materials warehousing in Vancouver, Washington, to Roadway Logistics. Roadway's 140 employees operate the warehouse 24 hours a day, seven days a week, coordinating the delivery of parts to the warehouse and managing storage. Hewlett-Packard's 250 employees were transferred to other company activities. Hewlett-Packard reports savings of 10 percent in warehousing operating costs.

One of the drawbacks to outsourcing is the layoffs that often result. Even in cases where the outsourcing partner hires former employees, they are often hired back at lower wages with fewer benefits. Outsourcing is perceived by many unions as an effort to circumvent union contracts.

EXHIBIT 8.6

Modes of Transportation and Their Advantages and Limitations

- **Highway (trucking)**—flexibility because items can be delivered to almost any location in a continent. Transit times are good, and rates are usually reasonable for small quantities and over short distances.
- **Rail**—low cost, but transit times are long and may be subject to variability.
- **Water**—very high capacity and very low cost; but transit times are very slow, and large areas of the world are not directly accessible to water carriers.
- **Pipeline**—highly specialized and limited to liquids, gases, or solids in slurry form. No packaging is needed, and the costs per mile are low. The initial cost to build the pipeline is very high.
- **Air**—fast but most expensive.

## VALUE DENSITY (VALUE PER UNIT OF WEIGHT)

A common and important decision is how an item should be shipped. The way an item is shipped is referred to as the **transportation mode.** There are five basic modes of transportation: highway, rail, water, pipeline, and air. Each mode has its own advantages and limitations as shown in Exhibit 8.6.

Transportation mode

Although it may seem oversimplified, the value of an item per pound of weight—**value density**—is an important measure when deciding where items should be stocked geographically and how they should be shipped. Consider a company like Intel that makes microprocessor chips for personal computers. The company must decide whether to ship microprocessors to customers by ground or air carrier. Analysis shows that the time saved by air shipment can be justified if the shipping cost is appropriate. The decision involves a trade-off: the reduced transit time and the resulting reduced inventory investment compared to the increase in shipping costs. In the following section, details of the trade-off analysis are provided. Keep in mind that this is just an example of the type of analysis that would be typical in this type of supply chain decision. The basic methodology of building a spreadsheet that allows the trade-off to be studied is sound and can be applied no matter what exact details are needed to explore the alternatives.

Value density

### *EXAMPLE 8.2: EVALUATING THE TRADE-OFF BETWEEN AIR AND GROUND PACKAGE SHIPPING*

We can approach the problem by examining a specific situation. Consider the cost of shipping from Bloomington, Indiana, to Littleton, Massachusetts. Assume that the inventory carrying cost rate is 30 percent per year of the product value. This cost rate captures the cost of capital, insurance, warehouse cost, and so on. We use this cost rate to determine the actual cost to carry an item in inventory for a year given the value of an item. For example, an item that costs $100 would cost $30 to carry in inventory for a year if the carrying cost rate were 30 percent. Our alternative transportation modes are highway service provided by United Parcel Service (UPS), which takes eight days to ship from Bloomington to Littleton, and Federal Express, which offers a two-day air service. Exhibit 8.7 indicates the cost to ship 1 to 10 pounds from Bloomington to Littleton using the alternative services.

### *SOLUTION*

The problem involves equating the cost of transportation via air to the cost of highway shipment plus the cost of carrying inventory for the additional six days. Logically, we can make the general statement that expensive items can be sent by air using Federal Express, whereas lower-value items can be shipped by the less expensive highway service offered by UPS.

$$\text{Shipping cost saving} = \text{Air shipping cost} - \text{Regular highway shipping cost}$$

EXHIBIT 8.7

**Product Density Shipping Cost Comparison**

Excel: Value Density

Carrying cost rate = 0.3 | Days saved = 6

| Shipping Weight (Pounds) | United Parcel Service: 8-Day Ground Service | Federal Express: 2-Day Air Service | Cost Savings with UPS | Break-Even Product Value | Break-Even Product Value (per Pound) |
|---|---|---|---|---|---|
| 1 | $3.30 | $18.25 | $14.95 | $3,031.53 | $3,031.53 |
| 2 | $3.60 | $20.50 | 16.90 | 3,426.94 | 1,713.47 |
| 3 | $3.85 | $22.50 | 18.65 | 3,781.81 | 1,260.60 |
| 4 | $4.10 | $24.50 | 20.40 | 4,136.67 | 1,034.17 |
| 5 | $4.30 | $26.75 | 22.45 | 4,552.36 | 910.47 |
| 6 | $4.50 | $28.75 | 24.25 | 4,917.36 | 819.56 |
| 7 | $4.65 | $30.75 | 26.10 | 5,292.50 | 756.07 |
| 8 | $4.75 | $32.75 | 28.00 | 5,677.78 | 709.72 |
| 9 | $4.85 | $34.75 | 29.90 | 6,063.06 | 673.67 |
| 10 | $5.00 | $36.75 | 31.75 | 6,438.19 | 643.82 |

At break-even, the cost savings are equal to inventory carrying cost.

$$\text{Shipping cost savings} = \text{Inventory carrying cost} = \frac{\text{Item value} \times 0.30 \times 6 \text{ days}}{365 \text{ days per year}}$$

The carrying cost is calculated by multiplying the value of the item (at cost) times the yearly carrying cost percentage (30 percent) times the proportion of the year that the item is being carried—which in this case is 6 out of 365 days.

Solving for item value,

$$\text{Item value} = \frac{365 \times \text{Shipping cost savings}}{0.30 \times 6}$$

The different cost savings in the fourth column of our spreadsheet in Exhibit 8.7 are calculated using our item value equation for each shipping weight. This gives the product value in the fifth column. Dividing by the package weight gives the break-even product value per pound in the last column. The exhibit indicates that any item whose value is greater than that shown in the last column should be shipped by air. For example, a five-pound shipment of integrated circuits whose average value is more than $910.47 per pound should be shipped by Federal Express. ←

## GLOBAL SOURCING

Global

We are in the middle of a major change in the global economy. Great opportunities are available because of the collapse of communism in the Eastern Bloc, the issuance of the Euro currency, and new markets in Turkey, India, South Africa, and so on. We have seen the results of agreements such as the North American Free Trade Agreement and the General Agreement on Tariffs and Trade. China is a huge market and is now a powerful trading partner. The breakthrough box titled "Supply Chain Management, Hong Kong Style" gives great insight into how global sourcing works in the quickly changing and competitive fashion industry.

Managers face an interesting predicament. Let's take the example of Nike, the maker of high-quality tennis shoes. For Nike a key raw material is leather, which is available from many sources around the world. The lowest-cost leather, though, might be available in South America while the least expensive labor is in China, locations that are on the opposite side of the globe. These locations are far removed from the major markets for the shoes in the United States, Europe, and Japan. To make matters worse, those customers in the United States, Europe, and Japan do not even agree on what they want.

Companies that face such diverse sourcing, production, and distribution decisions need to weigh the costs associated with materials, transportation, production, warehousing, and distribution to develop a comprehensive network designed to minimize costs. Of course, this network must be designed with consideration of outsourcing alternatives as described earlier in this chapter. Technical Note 9, Facility Location, describes techniques useful for minimizing these costs.

To further streamline its supply network, in 1999 Apple Computer discontinued building the iMac at its Elk Grove, California, plant, shifting production to LG Electronics, a Korean contract manufacturer that has plants in Seoul and Mexico. As a result, Apple shed 350 workers, including 25 permanent employees and 300 temporary workers at the California plant, which will continue to produce custom-order iMacs and the higher-end G3 computers. LG also has taken over production of iMac units from Apple's plants in Ireland and Singapore.

In the past, parts produced at an Apple supplier in Asia were shipped to the Apple plant in Ireland and later shipped back to Asia. Now, with a partner in Taiwan, the assembly is fully handled in Asia. Apple achieved a dramatic reduction in lead time and a corresponding reduction in cost, plus it is able to get to market faster. Apple has outsourced much of its logistics and transportation planning. Apple does not want to own an airplane or a truck. The company lets someone else negotiate rates and execute the warehousing portion of the business.

Global automobile companies, such as Honda, Toyota, Nissan, General Motor, and Ford, have quickly moved the production of vehicles close to the market where they will be sold. BMW builds the Z3 sports car in South Carolina in the United States; Daimler-Benz builds the Mercedes Benz sports utility vehicle in Alabama; and Honda is building its new Odyssey minivan in Alliston, Ontario, Canada.

## MASS CUSTOMIZATION

Mass customization

The term **mass customization** has been used to describe the ability of a company to deliver highly customized products and services to different customers around the world.[4] The key to mass-customizing effectively is postponing the task of differentiating a product for a specific customer until the latest possible point in the supply network. In order to do this, companies must rethink and integrate the designs of their products, the processes used to make and deliver those products, and the configuration of the entire supply network. By adopting such a comprehensive approach, companies can operate at maximum efficiency and quickly meet customers' orders with a minimum amount of inventory.

Three organization design principles together form the basic building blocks of an effective mass customization program.

**Principle 1:** *A product should be designed so it consists of independent modules that can be assembled into different forms of the product easily and inexpensively.* Hewlett-Packard decided to use a modular product design to allow its DeskJet printers to be easily customized for the European and Asian markets. The company decided to customize the printers at its local distribution centers rather than at its factories. For example, instead of customizing the

## Breakthrough

### Supply Chain Management, Hong Kong Style

The following are comments by Victor Fung, the Chairman of Li & Fung—the largest export trading company in Hong Kong and an innovator in the development of supply chain management. On behalf of its customers, primarily American and European retailers, Li & Fung works with an ever-expanding network of suppliers around the globe, sourcing clothing and other consumer goods ranging from toys to fashion accessories to luggage.

*Question: How do you define the difference between what Li & Fung does today—supply chain management—and the trading business founded by your grandfather in 1906?*

Fung: When my grandfather started the company in Canton, 90 years ago during the Ching dynasty, his "value added" was that he spoke English. In those days, it took three months to get to China by boat from the West; a letter would take a month. No one at the Chinese factories spoke English, and the American merchants spoke no Chinese. As an interpreter, my grandfather's commission was 15 percent.

Continuing through my father's generation, Li & Fung was basically a broker, charging a fee to put buyers and sellers together. But as an intermediary, the company was squeezed between the growing power of the buyers and the factories. Our margins slipped to 10 percent, then 5 percent, then 3 percent. When I returned to Hong Kong in 1976 my friends warned me that in 10 years buying agents like Li & Fung would be extinct. "Trading is a sunset industry," they all said.

My brother and I felt we could turn the business into something different, and so we took it through several stages of development. In the first stage, we acted as what I would call a regional sourcing agent and extended our geographic reach by establishing offices in Taiwan, Korea, and Singapore. Our knowledge of the region had value for customers. Most big buyers could manage their own sourcing if they needed to deal with only Hong Kong—they'd know which 10 factories to deal with and wouldn't need any help.

But dealing with the whole region was more complex. In textiles, quotas govern world trade. Knowing which quotas have been used up in Hong Kong, for example, tells you when you have to start buying from Taiwan.

Understanding products was also more complex. We knew that in Taiwan the synthetics were better, but that Hong Kong was the place to go for cottons. We could provide a package from the whole region rather than a single product from Hong Kong.

DeskJets at its factory in Singapore before shipping them to Europe, Hewlett-Packard has its European distribution center near Stuttgart, Germany, perform this job. The company designed the new printer with a country-specific external power supply that the customer plugs in when setting up the printer. The distribution center not only customizes the product but also purchases the materials that differentiate it (the power supplies, packaging, and manuals). As a result of this redesign, manufacturing costs are slightly higher than when the factories customized the printers, but the total manufacturing, shipping, and inventory costs dropped by 25 percent.

**Principle 2:** *Manufacturing and service processes should be designed so that they consist of independent modules that can be moved or rearranged easily to support different distribution network designs.* The way neighborhood hardware and paint stores match paint colors on their premises is a good example. Instead of making a broad range of different paints to meet customers' specific requirements, factories make generic paint and a variety of color pigments, which hardware and paint stores stock. The stores use

By working with a larger number of countries, we were able to assemble components; we call this "assortment packing." Say I sell a tool kit to a major discount chain. I could buy the spanners from one country and the screwdrivers from another and put together a product package. That has some value in it—not great value, but some.

In the second stage, we took the company's sourcing-agent strategy one step further and became a manager and deliverer of manufacturing programs. In the old model, the customer would say, "This is the item I want. Please go out and find the best place to buy it for me." The new model works this way. The Limited, one of our big customers, comes to us and says, "For next season, this is what we're thinking about—this type of look, these colors, these quantities. Can you come up with a production program?"

Starting with their designers' sketches, we research the market to find the right type of yarn and dye swatches to match the colors. We take product concepts and realize them in prototypes. Buyers can then look at the samples and say, "No, I don't really like that, I like this. Can you do more of this?" We then create an entire program for the season, specifying the product mix and the schedule. We contract for all the resources. We work with factories to plan and monitor production so we can ensure quality and on-time delivery.

This strategy of delivering manufacturing programs carried us through the 1980s, but that decade brought us a new challenge—and led to our third stage. As the Asian tigers emerged, Hong Kong became an increasingly expensive and uncompetitive place to manufacture. For example, we completely lost the low-end transistor radio business to Taiwan and Korea. What saved us was that China began to open up to trade, allowing Hong Kong to fix its cost problem by moving the labor-intensive portion of production across the border into southern China.

So for transistor radios we created little kits—plastic bags filled with all the components needed to build a radio. Then we shipped the kits to China for assembly. After the labor-intensive work was completed, the finished goods came back to Hong Kong for final testing and inspection. If you missed a screw you were in trouble: the whole line stopped cold.

Breaking up the value chain as we did was a novel concept at the time. We call it "dispersed manufacturing." This method of manufacturing soon spread to other industries, giving Hong Kong a new lease on life and also transforming our economy. Between 1979 and 1997, Hong Kong's position as a trading entity moved from number 12 in the world to number 8. All our manufacturing moved into China, and Hong Kong became a huge service economy with 84 percent of its gross domestic product coming from services.

This Hong Kong model of borderless manufacturing has become a new paradigm for the region. Today Asia consists of multiple networks of dispersed manufacturing—high-cost hubs that do the sophisticated planning for regional manufacturing. Bangkok works with the Indochinese peninsula, Taiwan with the Philippines, Seoul, and Northern China. Dispersed manufacturing is what's behind the boom in Asia's trade and investment statistics in the 1990s—companies moving raw materials and semifinished parts around Asia. But the region is still very dependent on the ultimate sources of demand, which are in North America and Western Europe. They start the whole cycle going.

a chromatograph to analyze a customer's paint sample and to determine the paint-and-pigment mixture that will match it. This process provides customers with a virtually unlimited number of consistent choices and, at the same time, significantly reduces the inventory of paint that the stores need to stock in order to match every customer's desired color on demand. **Process postponement** is the term used to describe delay of the process step that differentiates the product to as late in the supply chain as possible. The key to postponement, in this case, was separating the production of the paint and the mixing of the pigment and paint and creating a low-cost chromatograph.

Process postponement

**Principle 3:** *The supply network—the positioning of inventory and the location, number, and structure of service, manufacturing, and distribution facilities—should be designed to provide two capabilities. First, it must be able to supply the basic product to the facilities performing the customization in a cost-effective manner. Second, it must have the flexibility and the responsiveness to take individual customers' orders and deliver the finished, customized good quickly.* To support mass customization an agile supply network is needed. A company with many product options benefits little from having many distribution centers around the world if those centers perform only the tasks of warehousing and distribution. The investments in inventory that are required to support all the options would be enormous. The example of the paint production process just described is ideal because the paint manufacturing company now has a ready source of capacity to handle the final mixing step: the local paint stores. The generic paint can be shipped in bulk and the final product produced while the customer is in the store. The manufacturing economics change radically when a company redesigns its products and processes into modules so that the final customization steps take place on receipt of a customer's order. It becomes cost-effective to have more distribution centers or stores as in the case of the paint example, each of which stocks basic products and performs the final steps in the customization process.

Having distribution centers perform light manufacturing or assembly can help a company both comply with the local-content rules that are prevalent in emerging markets and respond to customers who are unwilling to wait for a customized product to be shipped from a factory in another region. In this way, a company enjoys the best of both worlds: on the one hand, it can concentrate its manufacturing of critical parts in a few sites around the world so that it can achieve economies of scale, and on the other hand, it can maintain a local presence.

Making decisions like these is not easy. It involves people from at least five areas of the company: marketing, research and development, manufacturing, distribution, and finance. These five groups must play the following roles to support an effective mass customization program:

- Marketing must determine the extent to which mass customization is needed to fulfill customers' requirements.
- Research and development must redesign the product so that it can be customized at the most efficient point in the supply network.
- Manufacturing and distribution must coordinate both the supply and redesign of materials and situate manufacturing or assembly processes in the most efficient locations.
- Finance must provide activity-based cost information and financial analyses of the alternatives.

Cross Functional

Each group at any company has its own measures of performance. Marketing, for example, is evaluated on revenue growth, research and development on a product's functionality and the cost of its components, and manufacturing and distribution on the cost of assembling and delivering a product to the customer. The different measures focus the groups on different objectives. Marketing wants to offer as many product options as possible to attract more customers; research and development wants to offer the product with the greatest possible functionality at the lowest possible cost; and manufacturing and distribution want to make one product at a stable volume. If the groups are not properly coordinated, their attempts to optimize their own performance may hurt the company's ability to create the most efficient supply network that can deliver a customized product at the lowest cost. Negotiations among these groups are critical, with the goal being to decide to do what is best for the company as a whole.

A supply chain links all of the stages together from raw materials through production to the consumer. The supply chain is coordinated with an electronic information system. Many options define the logic of these systems; in all cases, the frequency and speed of communicating information through the chain has a great effect on inventory levels, efficiencies, and costs. For large manufacturing companies the new enterprise resource planning systems, discussed in Section Four, are now being used extensively. Electronic commerce, discussed in the managerial briefing in Section Three, is having a dramatic impact on information flow and responsiveness to customer demand.

Managing the supply chain is being shifted, to a large extent, to the vendor. Purchasing contracts are now tied to delivery schedules; we look at the coordination needed to do this when we study just-in-time systems in Chapter 10. Electronic information flow has shifted routine activities to the vendor by allowing direct access to point-of-sales data and giving responsibility for forecasting and delivery of product directly to the vendor. Today such relationships tend to be long-term, but one can speculate whether the relationships will be long-term in the future.

# CONCLUSION

Supply chain management is important in business today. The term *supply chain* comes from a picture of how organizations are linked together as viewed from a particular company. Many companies have enjoyed significant success due to unique ways in which they have organized their supply chains. Dell Computer, for example, skips the distribution and retail steps typical of a manufacturing company's supply chain. However, a good supply chain design for one company may not work for another. This chapter shows how supply chains should be structured to meet the needs of different products and customer groups.

Measures of supply chain efficiency are inventory turnover and weeks of supply. Efficient processes should be used for functional products and responsive processes for innovative products. This alignment of supply chain strategy and product characteristics is extremely important to the operational success of a company.

Companies that face diverse sourcing, production, and distribution decisions need to weigh the costs associated with materials, transportation, production, warehousing, and distribution to develop a comprehensive network designed to minimize costs.

## KEY TERMS

**Supply chain** How organizations are linked together as viewed from a particular company.

**Inventory turnover** and **weeks of supply** Measures of supply chain efficiency that are mathematically the inverse of one another.

**Cost of goods sold** The annual cost for a company to produce the goods or services provided to customers.

**Average aggregate inventory value** The total value of all items held in inventory for the firm valued at cost.

**Weeks of supply** A measure of how many weeks' worth of inventory is in the system at a particular point in time.

**Bullwhip effect** The variability in demand is magnified as we move from the customer to the producer in the supply chain.

**Functional products** Staples that people buy in a wide range of retail outlets, such as grocery stores and gas stations.

**Innovative products** Products like fashionable clothes and personal computers that typically have a life cycle of just a few months.

**Outsourcing** Moving some of a firm's internal activities and decision responsibility to outside providers.

**Logistics** Management functions that support the complete cycle of material flow: from the purchase and internal control of production materials; to the planning and control of work-in-process; to the purchasing, shipping, and distribution of the finished product.

**Transportation mode** How an item is shipped.

**Value density** The value of an item per pound of weight.

**Mass customization** The ability of a company to deliver highly customized products and services to different customers around the world.

**Process postponement** Delay of the process step that differentiates a product to as late in the supply chain as possible.

## FORMULA REVIEW

[8.1]
$$\text{Inventory turnover} = \frac{\text{Cost of goods sold}}{\text{Average aggregate inventory value}}$$

[8.2]
$$\text{Weeks of supply} = \left(\frac{\text{Average aggregate inventory value}}{\text{Cost of goods sold}}\right) 52 \text{ weeks}$$

## REVIEW AND DISCUSSION QUESTIONS

1 What recent changes have caused supply chain management to gain importance?

2 With so much productive capacity and room for expansion in the United States, why would a company based in the United States choose to purchase items from a foreign firm? Discuss the pros and cons.

3 Describe the differences between functional and innovative products.

4 What are characteristics of efficient and responsive supply chains? Can a supply chain be both efficient and responsive? Why or why not?

5 As a supplier, which factors about a buyer (your potential customer) would you consider to be important in setting up a long-term relationship?

6 For the value density problem in Example 8.2, what would the effect be if a competing firm offers you a similar service for 10 percent less than Federal Express's rates?

7 What are the advantages of using the postponement strategy?

8 Describe how outsourcing works. Why would a firm want to outsource?

9 What is so different about Li & Fung's approach to working with their customers? Would this approach work with functional products like toothpaste and basketballs?

10 What are the basic building blocks of an effective mass customization program? What kind of companywide cooperation is required for a successful mass customization program?

## PROBLEMS

1 Calculate the break-even product value of using Express Mail (overnight delivery) versus Parcel Post (three-day delivery) for sending a package from Peoria, Illinois, to Memphis, Tennessee. The following table contains the appropriate costs. Assume that inventory carrying cost is 25 percent per year of the product value and that there are 365 days per year.

1. 2 lbs ($8,854.90), 3 lbs ($10,154.30), 4 lbs ($11,402.60), 5 lbs ($12,738.50), 6 lbs ($15,337.30), 7 lbs ($15,899.40), 8 lbs ($16,563.70), 9 lbs ($17,147.70).

SHIPPING COST: U.S. POSTAL SERVICE; PEORIA, IL, TO MEMPHIS, TN

| WEIGHT (LBS.) | COST (OVERNIGHT) | COST (3-DAY) |
|---|---|---|
| 2 | $15.00 | $2.87 |
| 3 | 17.25 | 3.34 |
| 4 | 19.40 | 3.78 |
| 5 | 21.55 | 4.10 |
| 6 | 25.40 | 4.39 |
| 7 | 26.45 | 4.67 |
| 8 | 27.60 | 4.91 |
| 9 | 28.65 | 5.16 |

2. 6 days' supply of raw materials calculated 234/14,137 = 0.01655, 0.01655 × 365 = 6.04 days
Depends on timing of payments to suppliers. Physical units on hand are higher than this.

3. Inventory turn = (1000 × 52 × 1)/ (350 × 1) = 148.6 turns/year
Days of supply = 365/148.6 = 2.46 days.

2 Using the data from the Dell Computer annual report given in Example 8.1, determine how Dell calculated the six days' supply of raw materials. Do you think six days' supply is a valid representation of the amount of raw material Dell has on hand at the end of the year?

3 The McDonald's fast-food restaurant on campus sells an average of 4,000 quarter-pound hamburgers each week. Hamburger patties are resupplied twice a week, and on average the store has 350 pounds of hamburger in stock. Assume that the hamburger costs $1.00 a pound. What is the inventory turnover for the hamburger patties? On average, how many days of supply are on hand?

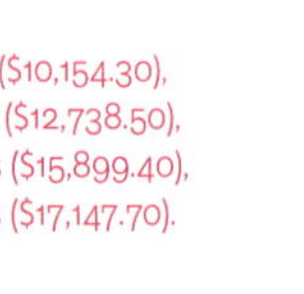


4 The U.S. Airfilter company has hired you as a supply chain consultant. The company makes air filters for residential heating and air conditioning systems. These filters are made in a single plant located in Louisville, Kentucky, in the United States. They are distributed to retailers through wholesale centers in 100 locations in the United States, Canada, and Europe. You have collected the following data relating to the value of inventory in the U.S. Airfilter supply chain:

4. *a.* Average inventory turn = 5.91
*b.* Reduce WIP.
*c.* 5.33 Weeks of raw material.

| | QUARTER 1 (JANUARY THROUGH MARCH) | QUARTER 2 (APRIL THROUGH JUNE) | QUARTER 3 (JULY THROUGH SEPTEMBER) | QUARTER 4 (OCTOBER THROUGH DECEMBER) |
|---|---|---|---|---|
| SALES (TOTAL QUARTER) | | | | |
| UNITED STATES | 300 | 350 | 405 | 375 |
| CANADA | 75 | 60 | 75 | 70 |
| EUROPE | 30 | 33 | 20 | 15 |

| | QUARTER 1 (JANUARY THROUGH MARCH) | QUARTER 2 (APRIL THROUGH JUNE) | QUARTER 3 (JULY THROUGH SEPTEMBER) | QUARTER 4 (OCTOBER THROUGH DECEMBER) |
|---|---|---|---|---|
| COST OF GOODS SOLD (TOTAL QUARTER) | 280 | 295 | 340 | 350 |
| RAW MATERIALS AT THE LOUISVILLE PLANT (END-OF-QUARTER) | 50 | 40 | 55 | 60 |
| WORK-IN-PROCESS AND FINISHED GOODS AT THE LOUISVILLE PLANT (END-OF-QUARTER) | 100 | 105 | 120 | 150 |
| DISTRIBUTION CENTER INVENTORY (END-OF-QUARTER) | | | | |
| UNITED STATES | 25 | 27 | 23 | 30 |
| CANADA | 10 | 11 | 15 | 16 |
| EUROPE | 5 | 4 | 5 | 5 |

All amounts in millions of U.S. dollars

*a.* What is the average inventory turnover for the firm?

*b.* If you were given the assignment to increase inventory turnover, what would you focus on? Why?

*c.* The company reported that it used $500M worth of raw material during the year. On average, how many weeks of supply of raw material are on hand at the factory?

## INTERNET ENRICHMENT EXERCISES

1 Using the United Parcel Service website at *http://www.ups.com* and the Federal Express site at *http://www.fedex.com,* compare rates for shipping a three-pound package, that you will wrap yourself, from New York City to Los Angeles, California. This is a wedding anniversary gift for your parents and is valued at about $100. Your parents' wedding anniversary is in two weeks and you have already purchased and packed the gift. Which service should you use? Why?

2 You are at work in your New York City office and need to send a repair part to a Los Angeles manufacturing plant. The part is a small computer control module weighing only one pound and is valued at about $25. The machine that needs the part is not operating, and it has been estimated that for every hour the machine is not operating, the company loses $150. Which service should you use? Why?

## CASE: PEPE JEANS

Pepe began to produce and sell denim jeans in the early 1970s in the United Kingdom and has achieved enormous growth. Pepe's success was the result of a unique approach in a product market dominated by strong brands and limited variety. Pepe presented a range of jeans styles that offered a better fit than traditional 5-pocket Western jeans (such as those made by Levi Strauss in the United States)—particularly for female customers. The Pepe range of basic styles is modified each season, but each style keeps its identity with a slightly whimsical name featured prominently on the jeans and on the point-of-sale material. Variations such as modified washes, leather trim, and even designer wear marks are applied to respond to changing fashion trends. To learn more about Pepe and its products, visit its web site at *http://www.pepejeans.com.*

Pepe's brand strength is such that the company can demand a retail price that averages about £45 (£1 = $1.6) for its standard products. A high percentage of Pepe sales are through about 1,500 independent outlets throughout the United Kingdom. The company maintains contact with its independent retailers via a group of approximately 10 agents, who are self-employed and work exclusively for Pepe. Each agent is responsible for retailers in a particular area of the country.

Pepe is convinced that a good relationship with the independent retailers is vital to its success. The agent meets with each independent retailer three to four times each year in order to present the new collections and to take sales orders. Because the number of accounts for each agent is so large, contact is often achieved by holding a presentation in a hotel for several retailers. Agents take orders from retailers for six-month delivery. After Pepe receives an order, the retailer has only one week in which to cancel because of the need to place immediate firm orders in Hong Kong to meet the delivery date. The company has had a long-standing policy of not holding any inventory of jeans in the United Kingdom.

After an order is taken and confirmed, the rest of the process up to delivery is administered from the Pepe office in Willesden. The status of orders can be checked from a web site maintained by Pepe. The actual orders are sent to a sourcing agent in Hong Kong who arranges for manufacturing the jeans. The sourcing agent handles all the details associated with materials, fabrication, and shipping the completed jeans to the retailer. Pepe has an outstanding team of young in-house designers who are responsible for developing new styles and the accompanying point-of-sale material. Jeans are made to specifications provided by this team. The team works closely with the Hong Kong sourcing agent to ensure that the jeans are made properly and that the material used is of the highest quality.

A recent survey of the independent retailers indicated some growing problems. The independents praised the fit, quality, and variety of Pepe's jeans, although many thought that they had become much less of a trendsetter than in their early days. It was felt that Pepe's variety of styles and quality were the company's key advantage over the competition. However, the independents were unhappy with Pepe's requirements to place firm orders six months in advance with no possibility of amendment, cancellation, or repeat ordering. Some claimed that the inflexible order system forced them to order less, resulting in stockouts of particular sizes and styles. The retailers estimated that Pepe's sales would increase by about 10 percent with a more flexible ordering system.

The retailers expected to have some slow-moving inventory, but the six-month order lead time made it difficult to accurately order and worsened the problem. Because the fashion market was so impulsive, the current favorites were often not in vogue six months in the future. On the other hand, when demand exceeded expectations, it took a long time to fill the gap. What the retailers wanted was some method of limited returns, exchange, or reordering to overcome the worst of these problems. Pepe was feeling some pressure to respond to these complaints because some of Pepe's smaller competitors offered delivery in only a few days.

Pepe has enjoyed considerable financial success with its current business model. Sales last year were approximately £200M. Cost of sales was approximately 40 percent, operating expenses 28 percent, and profit before taxes nearly 32 percent of sales. The company has no long-term debt and has a very healthy cash position.

Pepe was feeling considerable pressure and felt that a change was going to be needed soon. In evaluating alternatives the company found that the easiest would be to work with the Hong Kong sourcing agent to reduce the lead time associated with orders. The agent agreed that the lead time could be shortened, possibly to as little as six weeks, but costs would increase significantly. Currently, the agent collects orders over a period of time and about every two weeks puts these orders out on bid to about 1,000 potential suppliers. The sourcing agent estimated that costs might go up 30 percent if the lead time were shorted to six weeks. Even with the significant increase in cost, consistent delivery schedules would be difficult to keep.

The sourcing agent suggested that Pepe consider building a finishing operation in the United Kingdom. The agent indicated that a major retail chain in the United States had moved to this type of structure with considerable success. Basically, all the finishing operation did for the U.S. retail chain was apply different washes to the jeans to give them different "worn" looks. The U.S. operation also took orders for the retail stores and shipped the orders. The U.S. firm found that it could give two-day response time to the retail stores.

The sourcing agent indicated that costs for the basic jeans (jeans where the wash has not been applied) could probably be reduced by 10 percent because the volumes would be higher. In addition, lead time for the basic jeans could be reduced to approximately three months because the finishing step would be eliminated and the orders would be larger.

The Pepe designers found this an interesting idea, so they visited the U.S. operation to see how the system worked. They found that they would have to keep about six weeks' supply of basic jeans on hand in the United Kingdom and that they would have to invest in about £1,000,000 worth of equipment. They estimated that it would cost about £500,000 to operate the facility each year. They could locate the facility in the basement of the current Willesden office building, and the renovations would cost about £300,000.

QUESTIONS

1 Acting as an outside consultant, what would you recommend that Pepe do? Given the data in the case, perform a financial analysis to evaluate the alternatives that you have identified. (Assume that the new inventory could be valued at six weeks' worth of the yearly cost of sales. Use a 30 percent inventory carrying cost rate.) Calculate a payback period for each alternative.

2 Are there other alternatives that Pepe should consider?

THE IDEA FOR THIS CASE CAME FROM A CASE TITLED "PEPE JEANS" WRITTEN BY D. BRAMLEY AND C. JOHN OF THE LONDON BUSINESS SCHOOL. PEPE JEANS IS A REAL COMPANY, BUT THE DATA GIVEN IN THE CASE DO NOT REPRESENT ACTUAL COMPANY DATA.

## SELECTED BIBLIOGRAPHY

Dornier, P.; R. Ernst; M. Fender; and P. Kouvelis. *Global Operations and Logistics: Text and Cases.* New York, NY: John Wiley & Sons, 1998.

Greaver II, M. F. *Strategic Outsourcing: A Structured Approach to Outsourcing Decisions and Initiatives.* New York, NY: American Management Association, 1999.

Handfield, R. B., and E. L. Nichols, Jr. *Introduction to Supply Chain Management.* Upper Saddle River, NJ: Prentice Hall, 1999.

Leender, M. R., and H. E. Fearon. *Purchasing and Supply Management.* 11th ed. Burr Ridge, IL: Richard D. Irwin, 1997.

Poirier, C. C., and S. E. Reiter. *Supply Chain Optimization: Building the Strongest Total Business Network.* San Francisco: Berrett-Koehler, 1996.

Simchi-Levi, D.; P. Kaminski; and E. Simchi-Levi. *Supply Chain Management.* Burr Ridge, IL: McGraw-Hill, 2000.

## FOOTNOTES

1 M. L. Fisher, "What is the Right Supply Chain for Your Product?" *Harvard Business Review,* March–April 1997, pp. 105–116.

2 This contribution margin equals price minus variable cost divided by price, expressed as a percentage.

3 "Have Factory Will Travel," *Economist,* February 12–18, 2000, p. 61–62.

4 This section is adapted from E. Feitzinger and H. Lee, "Mass Customization at Hewlett-Packard: The Power of Postponement," *Harvard Business Review,* January–February 1997, pp. 116–121.

chapter nine
# STRATEGIC CAPACITY MANAGEMENT

## CHAPTER OUTLINE AND KEY TERMS

# 9

Once upon a time, in a faraway Paris suburb, a Magic Kingdom was born. The natives were aghast! Minnie and Mickey wouldn't last, they cried! But people now come from far and wide to stand in line for fantasy rides, and the little kingdom grew fast. This modern-day success story has all the makings of a fairy tale, with even the requisite happy ending. With its long lines, hefty profits, and high hotel occupancy rates, Disneyland Paris seems likely to live happily ever after.

Five years after it opened to French insults and widespread skepticism, the American-style theme park 18 miles east of Paris has surpassed the Eiffel Tower and the Louvre as the number one tourist draw in France, even among the French.

Disney's "kick-the-door-down" attitude in the planning, building, and financing of Paris Disney accounts for many of the huge problems that initially faced the resort. In 1994 Euro Disney was renamed Disney Paris and financially restructured. Essentially this restructuring delayed payments to Disney USA and some other financial backers until 1999. In addition to the financial changes, there were also changes in pricing and marketing, drastic cost cutting, and subtle adjustments to the park itself. The following are some of the operational errors related to capacity that contributed to the start-up problems at the park.

1. Disney Paris planners assumed that a visitor's stay at the park would be similar to the four days typically spent at Florida's Disney. Florida's Disney has three theme parks, whereas Disney Paris has only one. Disney Paris is a two-day experience at the most. The excessive checking in and out that resulted required additional computer stations in the park's hotels.

Source: P. Gumbel and R. Turner, "Mouse Trap," *The Wall Street Journal*, March 10, 1994, p A1. Updated from the following articles: Staff Reporter, "The Kingdom Inside a Republic," *Economist*, April 13, 1996, pp. 66–67; and an Associated Press release, "Paris's Mickey Has Better Mousetrap," April 20, 1997.

2 Disney Paris has 5,200 hotel rooms—more than the entire French city of Cannes. Disney priced the rooms more to meet revenue targets than to meet demand. During the first two years, the hotels were just over half full on average. Disney has now changed its approach and announced separate peak, average, and low season rates.

3 Disney thought that Monday would be a light day for visitors and Friday a heavy one, so it allocated staff accordingly; the reality was the reverse. The problem is compounded by the fact that the number of visitors in the high season can be 10 times the number in the low season. Inflexible labor schedules in France also aggravate the problem.

4 Disney built expensive trams along a lake to take guests from the hotels to the park. But people prefer to walk.

5 "We were told that Europeans don't take breakfast, so we downsized the restaurants," recalls one executive. But crowds showed up for a full breakfast. Disney was trying to serve 2,500 breakfasts in 350-seat restaurants at some hotels. Lines were horrendous. Disney reacted quickly with prepackaged breakfast delivery services.

6 The parking space was too small for buses. Restrooms were built for 50 drivers, although there were 200 drivers on peak days.

These problems have all been solved. Thanks to over 50 million visitors, who enjoy the new rides like Space Mountain, Disney Paris is now a great success. Mickey and Minnie, it turns out, are pretty much universal celebrities. ←

Vol. V "JIT at Tri State Industries Part I"

How many customers should a facility be able to serve? How much should a plant be able to produce? What kinds of problems arise as the production system expands? Whether we are talking about Disney near Paris, France, or Clint's Machine Shop in Paris, Texas, such capacity questions are of major concern to their managers. In this chapter we look at capacity strategically—that is, how manufacturing and service firms plan capacity over the long run. We begin by discussing the nature of capacity from an OM perspective.

## CAPACITY MANAGEMENT IN OPERATIONS

Capacity

Service

A dictionary definition of **capacity** is "the ability to hold, receive, store, or accommodate." In a general business sense, it is most frequently viewed as the amount of output that a system is capable of achieving over a specific period of time. In a service setting, this might be the number of customers that can be handled between noon and 1:00 P.M. In manufacturing, this might be the number of automobiles that can be produced in a single shift.

When looking at capacity, operations managers need to look at both resource inputs *and* product outputs. The reason is that, for planning purposes, real (or effective) capacity depends on what is to be produced. For example, a firm that makes multiple products inevitably can produce more of one kind than of another with a given level of resource inputs. Thus, while the managers of an automobile factory may state that their facility has 10,000 labor hours available per year, they are also thinking that these labor hours can be used to make either 50,000 two-door models or 40,000 four-door models (or some mix of the two- and four-door models). This reflects their knowledge of what their current technology and labor force inputs can produce and the product mix that is to be demanded from these resources.

Cross Functional

An operations management view also emphasizes the time dimension of capacity. That is, capacity must also be stated relative to some period of time. This is evidenced in the common distinction drawn between long-range, intermediate-range, and short-range capacity planning. (See the box "Time Horizons for Capacity Planning.")

## TIME HORIZONS FOR CAPACITY PLANNING

Capacity planning is generally viewed in three time durations:

*Long range*—greater than one year. Where productive resources (such as buildings, equipment, or facilities) take a long time to acquire or dispose of, long-range capacity planning requires top management participation and approval.

*Intermediate range*—monthly or quarterly plans for the next 6 to 18 months. Here, capacity may be varied by such alternatives as hiring, layoffs, new tools, minor equipment purchases, and subcontracting.

*Short range*—less than one month. This is tied into the daily or weekly scheduling process and involves making adjustments to eliminate the variance between planned and actual output. This includes alternatives such as overtime, personnel transfers, and alternative production routings.

Finally, capacity planning itself has different meaning to individuals at different levels within the operations management hierarchy. The vice president of manufacturing is concerned with aggregate capacity of all factories within the firm. The vice president's concern relates mainly to the financial resources required to support these factories. You will study this process when you cover capital budgeting during your finance course.

The plant manager (PM) is concerned with the capacity of the individual plant. The PM must decide how best to use this capacity to meet the anticipated demand for products. Because short-term demand may greatly exceed short-term capacity during peak demand periods, the PM must determine when and how much inventory to build in anticipation of these peaks. We will deal with this topic in depth when we cover aggregate planning in Chapter 12.

The first-level supervisor is concerned with capacity of the equipment and staff mix in his or her department. This person will work out detailed schedules to accommodate the daily flow of work. We will study this scheduling process in Chapter 15.

Although there is no one person with the job title "capacity manager," there are several managerial positions charged with the effective use of capacity. *Capacity* is a relative term; in an operations management context, it may be defined as *the amount of resource inputs available relative to output requirements over a particular period of time.* Note that this definition makes no distinction between efficient and inefficient use of capacity. In this respect, it is consistent with how the federal Bureau of Economic Analysis defines *maximum practical capacity* used in its surveys: "That output attained within the normal

THE TELECOMMUNICATIONS SYSTEM OF AT&T PROVIDES LONG-DISTANCE CALLING, 800 NUMBERS, FAXES, VOICE-MESSAGING, AND SERVICES TO 80 MILLION U.S. CONSUMERS. HIGHER USE MEANS A HIGHER RETURN ON THE BILLIONS OF DOLLARS INVESTED IN TELEPHONE NETWORKS. IF CAPACITY IS INADEQUATE, CUSTOMERS CAN BE LOST THROUGH SLOW SERVICE OR BY ALLOWING COMPETITORS TO ENTER THE MARKET. IF CAPACITY IS EXCESSIVE, A COMPANY MAY HAVE TO REDUCE PRICES TO STIMULATE DEMAND OR UNDERUTILIZE ITS WORKFORCE.

## BREAKTHROUGH

### DISRUPTIVE TECHNOLOGIES RESHAPE INDUSTRIES

When the personal computer first began to make a splash in the marketplace, Digital Equipment Corp. (now part of Compaq) and other established minicomputer manufacturers didn't regard it as a serious competitive threat. After all, the early PCs couldn't match the capability of the minis. Over time, however, increasingly powerful microprocessors gave PCs more computing muscle; and, often in networked configurations, they began to displace minicomputers.

It was a classic example of what Clayton Christensen, a professor at Harvard Business School, calls a "disruptive technology"—a phenomenon that tends to reshape entire industries and dislodge the leading companies in those industries. A common thread among disruptive technologies, the Harvard professor explains, is that they typically take root in "undemanding" applications, then move up the performance curve until they threaten more sophisticated market segments. Leading-edge technologies often become vulnerable when lower-cost alternatives—comparatively "trivial" technologies— evolve to the point where they begin to satisfy the bulk of users' performance requirements.

The constant and ongoing change caused by advances in technology makes forecasting future capacity needs extremely difficult.

SOURCE: J. H. SHERIDAN, "DISRUPTIVE TECHNOLOGIES RESHAPE INDUSTRIES," *INDUSTRY WEEK*, JANUARY 10, 2000, PP. 8–9. REPRINTED WITH PERMISSION FROM INDUSTRY WEEK. 

operating schedule of shifts per day and days per week including the use of high-cost inefficient facilities."[1]

Strategic capacity planning

The objective of **strategic capacity planning** is to provide an approach for determining the overall capacity level of capital-intensive resources—facilities, equipment, and overall labor force size—that best supports the company's long-range competitive strategy. The capacity level selected has a critical impact on the firm's response rate, its cost structure, its inventory policies, and its management and staff support requirements. If capacity is inadequate, a company may lose customers through slow service or by allowing competitors to enter the market. If capacity is excessive, a company may have to reduce prices to stimulate demand; underutilize its workforce; carry excess inventory; or seek additional, less profitable products to stay in business.

Anticipating capacity needs today is difficult due to the significant impact of technology on the capacity of a system. The breakthrough box titled "Disruptive Technologies Reshape Industries" includes some insight into the problem. Consider the impact of the Internet on the U.S. economy over the past few years. A significant limit on the growth of business over the Internet is due to the limited speed of the Internet. Recall from our E-Ops Managerial Briefing the definitions of Moore's and Metcalfe's laws. Moore's Law says that semiconductor performance doubles every 18 months. Metcalfe's Law holds that the value of a network grows by the square of the increase in users. The problem is that when a web site becomes saturated with users, all that great e-business just stops. The capacity of the Internet connection and the capacity of the web site servers significantly limit the number of users that can be simultaneously accommodated. The value of a web site is the product of how many millions of users it has and the average speed of its average connection. Faster connections mean sites can offer more services, such as video conferencing, and get extra revenue from TV-like online advertising.

## CAPACITY PLANNING CONCEPTS

Best operating level

The term *capacity* implies an attainable rate of output, for example 300 cars per day, but says nothing about how long that rate can be sustained. Thus, we do not know if this 300 cars per day is a one-day peak or a six-month average. To avoid this problem, the concept of **best operating level** is used. This is the level of capacity for which the process was designed and thus is the volume of output at which average unit cost is minimized. Determining this minimum is difficult because it involves a complex trade-off between the allocation of fixed overhead costs and the cost of overtime, equipment wear, defect rates, and other costs.

An important measure is the **capacity utilization rate,** which reveals how close a firm is to its best operating point (that is, design capacity):

Capacity utilization rate

$$\text{Capacity utilization rate} = \frac{\text{Capacity used}}{\text{Best operating level}}$$

The capacity utilization rate is expressed as a percentage and requires that the numerator and denominator be measured in the same units and time periods (such as machine hour/day, barrels of oil/day, dollar of output/day).

## ECONOMIES AND DISECONOMIES OF SCALE

The basic notion of economies of scale is that as a plant gets larger and volume increases, the average cost per unit of output drops. This is partially due to lower operating and capital cost, because a piece of equipment with twice the capacity of another piece typically does not cost twice as much to purchase or operate. Plants also gain efficiencies when they become large enough to fully utilize dedicated resources for tasks such as material handling, computer equipment, and administrative support personnel.

At some point, the size of a plant becomes too large and diseconomies of scale become a problem. These diseconomies may surface in many different ways. For example, maintaining the demand required to keep the large facility busy may require significant discounting of the product. The U.S. automobile manufacturers continually face this problem. Another typical example involves using a few large-capacity pieces of equipment. Minimizing equipment downtime is essential in this type of operation. M&M Mars, for example, has highly automated, high-volume equipment to make M&Ms. A single packaging line moves 2.6 million M&Ms each hour. Even though direct labor to operate the equipment is very low, the labor required to maintain the equipment is high. (If you would like to tour the M&M factory, check out their web site at http://m-ms.com/factory/tour/.)

In many cases, the size of a plant may be influenced by factors other than the internal equipment, labor, and other capital expenditures. A major factor may be the cost to transport raw materials and finished product to and from the plant. A cement factory, for example, would have a difficult time serving customers more than a few hours from its plant. Analogously, automobile companies such as Ford, Honda, Nissan, and Toyota have found it advantageous to locate plants within specific international markets. The anticipated size of these intended markets will largely dictate the size of the plants.

## THE EXPERIENCE CURVE

A well-known concept is the experience curve. As plants produce more, they gain experience in the best production methods, which reduce their costs of production in a predictable manner. Every time a plant's cumulative production doubles, its production costs decline by a specific percentage depending on the nature of the business. Exhibit 9.1 demonstrates the effect of a 90 percent experience curve on the production costs of hamburgers. (Additional discussion of experience or learning curves is provided in Technical Note 2.)

## WHERE ECONOMIES OF SCALE MEET THE EXPERIENCE CURVE

The astute reader will realize that larger plants can have a two-way cost advantage over their competitors. Not only does a larger plant gain from economies of scale but it will also produce more, giving it experience curve advantages as well. Companies often use this

EXHIBIT 9.1 **The Experience Curve**

*a.* Costs per unit produced fall by a specific percentage each time cumulative production doubles. This relationship can be expressed through a linear scale:

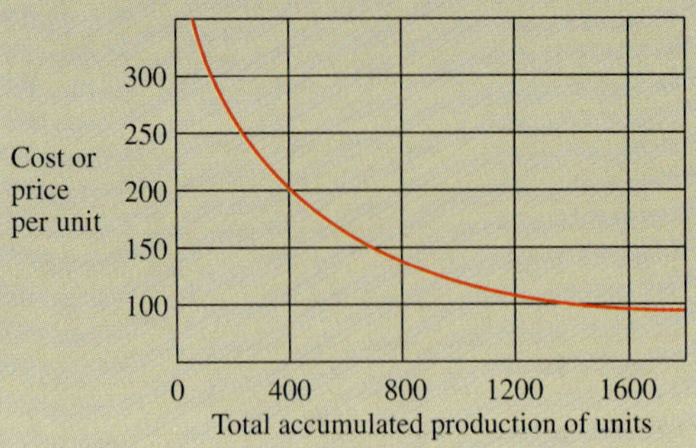


*b.* It can also be expressed through

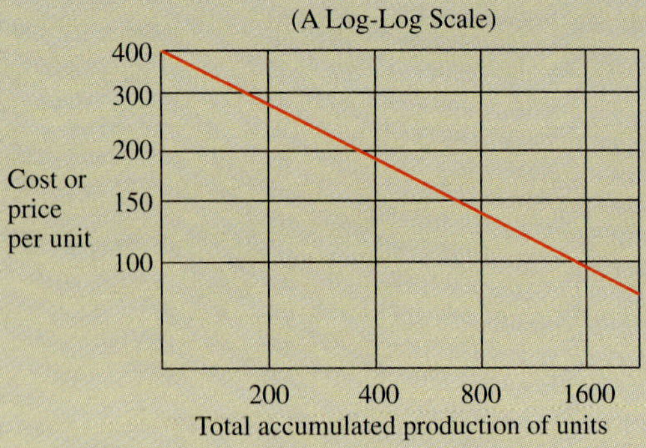


The experience curve percentage varies across industries.

To apply this concept to the restaurant industry, consider a hypothetical fast-food chain that has produced 5 million hamburgers. Given a current variable cost of $0.55 per burger, what will the cost per burger be when cumulative production reaches 10 million burgers? If the firm has a 90 percent experience curve, costs will fall to 90 percent of $0.55, or $0.495, when accumulated production reaches 10 million. At 1 billion hamburgers the variable cost drops to less than $0.25.

Note that sales volume becomes an important issue in achieving cost savings. If firm A serves twice as many hamburgers daily as firm B, it will accumulate "experience" twice as fast.

dual advantage as a competitive strategy by first building a large plant with substantial economies of scale, and then using its lower costs to price aggressively and increase sales volume. The increased volume moves them down the experience curve more quickly than their competitors, allowing the company to lower prices further, gaining still more volume. However, two criteria must be met for this strategy to succeed: (1) The product must fit customers' needs, and (2) the demand must be sufficiently large to support the volume. Consider the case of Chrysler. By the 1970s, economies of scale and experience had given Chrysler the lowest production costs of all the U.S. auto manufacturers. Unfortunately, its cars no longer fit customers' needs, so Chrysler could not sell enough of them to operate its large plants at their design levels, driving their costs up to the highest level among the U.S. producers at that time.

## CAPACITY FOCUS

As noted in Chapter 2, the concept of the focused factory put forth by Wickham Skinner holds that a production facility works best when it focuses on a fairly limited set of production objectives.[2] This means, for example, that a firm should not expect to excel in every aspect of manufacturing performance: cost, quality, flexibility, new product introductions, reliability, short lead times, and low investment. Rather, it should select a limited set of tasks that contributes the most to corporate objectives. However, given the breakthroughs in manufacturing technology, there is an evolution in factory objectives toward trying to do everything well. How do we deal with these apparent contradictions? One way is to say that if the firm does not have the technology to master multiple objectives, then a narrow focus is the logical choice. Another way is to recognize the practical reality that not all firms are in industries that require them to use their full range of capabilities to compete.

Capacity focus

The **capacity focus** concept can also be operationalized through the mechanism of plants within plants—*PWPs* in Skinner's terms. A focused plant may have several PWPs, each of which may have separate suborganizations, equipment and process policies, workforce management policies, production control methods, and so forth for different

THE XEROX FOCUSED FACTORY CREATES A FLEXIBLE AND EFFICIENT WORK ENVIRONMENT WHERE TEAMS OF EMPLOYEES ARE RESPONSIBLE FOR THE END-TO-END MANUFACTURING OF SPECIFIC PRODUCTS. THE FACTORY WAS DESIGNED WITH INPUT FROM THE INDUSTRIAL STAFF, WORKING IN TANDEM WITH ENGINEERS AND MANAGEMENT.

products—even if they are made under the same roof. This, in effect, permits finding the best operating level for each department of the organization and thereby carries the focus concept down to the operating level.

## CAPACITY FLEXIBILITY

Capacity flexibility means having the ability to rapidly increase or decrease production levels, or to shift production capacity quickly from one product or service to another. Such flexibility is achieved through flexible plants, processes, and workers, as well as through strategies that use the capacity of other organizations.

**Flexible Plants** Perhaps the ultimate in plant flexibility is the *zero-changeover-time* plant. Using movable equipment, knockdown walls, and easily accessible and reroutable utilities, such a plant can quickly adapt to change. An analogy to a familiar service business captures the flavor well: a plant with equipment "that is easy to install and easy to tear down and move—like the Ringling Bros.–Barnum and Bailey Circus in the old tent-circus days."[3]

**Flexible Processes** Flexible processes are epitomized by flexible manufacturing systems on the one hand and simple, easily set up equipment on the other. Both of these technological approaches permit rapid low-cost switching from one product line to another, enabling what are sometimes referred to as **economies of scope.** (By definition, economies of scope exist when multiple products can be produced at a lower cost in combination than they can separately.)

Economies of scope

**Flexible Workers** Flexible workers have multiple skills and the ability to switch easily from one kind of task to another. They require broader training than specialized workers and need managers and staff support to facilitate quick changes in their work assignments.

# CAPACITY PLANNING

## CONSIDERATIONS IN ADDING CAPACITY

Many issues must be considered when adding capacity. Three important ones are maintaining system balance, frequency of capacity additions, and the use of external capacity.

**Maintaining System Balance** In a perfectly balanced plant, the output of stage 1 provides the exact input requirement for stage 2. Stage 2's output provides the exact input requirement for stage 3, and so on. In practice, however, achieving such a "perfect" design is usually both impossible and undesirable. One reason is that the best operating levels for each stage generally differ. For instance, department 1 may operate most efficiently over a range of 90 to 110 units per month, whereas department 2, the next stage in the process, is most efficient at 75 to 85 units per month, and department 3 works best over a range of 150 to 200 units per month. Another reason is that variability in product demand and the processes themselves generally leads to imbalance except in automated production lines, which, in essence, are just one big machine.

There are various ways of dealing with imbalance. One is to add capacity to stages that are bottlenecks. This can be done by temporary measures such as scheduling overtime, leasing equipment, or purchasing additional capacity through subcontracting. A second way is through the use of buffer inventories in front of the bottleneck stage to ensure that it always has something to work on. (This is a central feature of the synchronous manufacturing approach detailed in Chapter 17.) A third approach involves duplicating the facilities of one department on which another is dependent.

**Frequency of Capacity Additions** There are two types of costs to consider when adding capacity: the cost of upgrading too frequently and that of upgrading too infrequently. Upgrading capacity too frequently is expensive. Direct costs include removing and replacing old equipment and training employees on the new equipment. In addition, the new equipment must be purchased, often for considerably more than the selling price of the old. Finally, there is the opportunity cost of idling the plant or service site during the changeover period.

Conversely, upgrading capacity too infrequently is also expensive. Infrequent expansion means that capacity is purchased in larger chunks. Any excess capacity that is purchased must be carried as overhead until it is utilized. (Exhibit 9.2 illustrates frequent versus infrequent capacity expansion.)

EXHIBIT 9.2

Frequent versus Infrequent Capacity Expansion

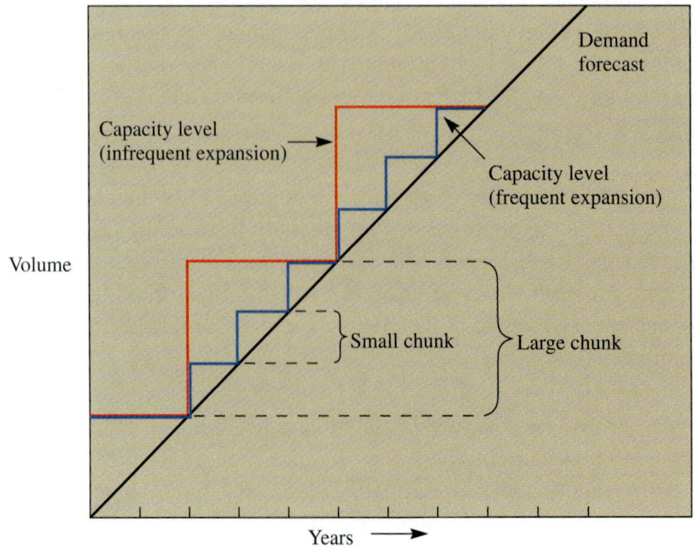

**External Sources of Capacity** In some cases, it may be cheaper to not add capacity at all, but rather to use some existing external source of capacity. Two common strategies used by organizations are subcontracting and sharing capacity. An example of subcontracting is Japanese banks in California subcontracting check-clearing operations. An example of sharing capacity is two domestic airlines flying different routes with different seasonal demands exchanging aircraft (suitably repainted) when one's routes are heavily used and the other's are not. A new twist is airlines sharing routes—using the same flight number even though the airline company may change through the route.

## DETERMINING CAPACITY REQUIREMENTS

In determining capacity requirements, we must address the demands for individual product lines, individual plant capabilities, and allocation of production throughout the plant network. Typically this is done according to the following steps:

1 Use forecasting techniques (see Chapter 11) to predict sales for individual products within each product line.
2 Calculate equipment and labor requirements to meet product line forecasts.
3 Project labor and equipment availabilities over the planning horizon.

Capacity cushion

Often the firm then decides on some **capacity cushion** that will be maintained between the projected requirements and the actual capacity. A capacity cushion is an amount of capacity in excess of expected demand. For example, if the expected annual demand on a facility is $10 million in products per year and the design capacity is $12 million per year, it has a 20 percent capacity cushion. A 20 percent capacity cushion equates to an 83 percent utilization rate (100%/120%).

When a firm's design capacity is less than the capacity required to meet its demand, it is said to have a negative capacity cushion. If, for example, a firm has a demand of $12 million in products per year but can produce only $10 million per year, it has a negative capacity cushion of 16.7 percent.

We now apply these three steps to an example.

### EXAMPLE 9.1: DETERMINING CAPACITY REQUIREMENTS

The Stewart Company produces two flavors of salad dressings: Paul's and Newman's. Each is available in bottles and single-serving plastic bags. Management would like to determine equipment and labor requirements for the next five years.

### SOLUTION

*Step 1. Use forecasting techniques to predict sales for individual products within each product line.* The marketing department, which is now running a promotional campaign for Newman's dressing, provided the following forecast demand values (in thousands) for the next five years. The campaign is expected to continue for the next two years.

| | YEAR | | | | |
|---|---|---|---|---|---|
| | 1 | 2 | 3 | 4 | 5 |
| PAUL'S | | | | | |
| Bottles (000s) | 60 | 100 | 150 | 200 | 250 |
| Plastic bags (000s) | 100 | 200 | 300 | 400 | 500 |
| NEWMAN'S | | | | | |
| Bottles (000s) | 75 | 85 | 95 | 97 | 98 |
| Plastic bags (000s) | 200 | 400 | 600 | 650 | 680 |

*Step 2. Calculate equipment and labor requirements to meet product line forecasts.* Currently, three machines that can package up to 150,000 bottles each per year are available. Each machine requires two operators and can produce bottles of both Newman's and Paul's dressings. Six bottle

machine operators are available. Also, five machines that can package up to 250,000 plastic bags each per year are available. Three operators are required for each machine, which can produce plastic bags of both Newman's and Paul's dressings. Currently, 20 plastic bag machine operators are available.

Total product line forecasts can be calculated from the preceding table by adding the yearly demand for bottles and plastic bags as follows:

| | Year | | | | |
|---|---|---|---|---|---|
| | 1 | 2 | 3 | 4 | 5 |
| Bottles | 135 | 185 | 245 | 297 | 348 |
| Plastic bags | 300 | 600 | 900 | 1,050 | 1,180 |

We can now calculate equipment and labor requirements for the current year (year 1). Because the total available capacity for packaging bottles is 450,000/year (3 machines × 150,000 each), we will be using $135/450 = 0.3$ of the available capacity for the current year, or $0.3 \times 3 = 0.9$ machines. Similarly, we will need $300/1{,}250 = 0.24$ of the available capacity for plastic bags for the current year, or $0.24 \times 5 = 1.2$ machines. The number of crew required to support our forecast demand for the first year will consist of the crew required for the bottle and the plastic bag machines.

The labor requirement for year 1's bottle operation is

$$0.9 \text{ bottle machines} \times 2 \text{ operators} = 1.8 \text{ operators}$$
$$1.2 \text{ bag machines} \times 3 \text{ operators} = 3.6 \text{ operators}$$

*Step 3. Project labor and equipment availabilities over the planning horizon.* We repeat the preceding calculations for the remaining years:

| | Year | | | | |
|---|---|---|---|---|---|
| | 1 | 2 | 3 | 4 | 5 |
| **Plastic Bag Operation** | | | | | |
| Percentage capacity utilized | 24 | 48 | 72 | 84 | 94 |
| Machine requirement | 1.2 | 2.4 | 3.6 | 4.2 | 4.7 |
| Labor requirement | 3.6 | 7.2 | 10.8 | 12.6 | 14.1 |
| **Bottle Operation** | | | | | |
| Percentage capacity utilized | 30 | 41 | 54 | 66 | 77 |
| Machine requirement | .9 | 1.23 | 1.62 | 1.98 | 2.31 |
| Labor requirement | 1.8 | 2.46 | 3.24 | 3.96 | 4.62 |

A positive capacity cushion exists for all five years because the available capacity for both operations always exceeds the expected demand. The Stewart Company can now begin to develop the intermediate-range or aggregate plan for the two production lines. (See Chapter 12 for a discussion of aggregate planning.) ←

## Using Decision Trees to Evaluate Capacity Alternatives

A convenient way to lay out the steps of a capacity problem is through the use of decision trees. The tree format helps not only in understanding the problem but also in finding a solution. A *decision tree* is a schematic model of the sequence of steps in a problem and the conditions and consequences of each step. In recent years, a few commercial software packages have been developed to assist in the construction and analysis of decision trees. These packages make the process quick and easy.

Decision trees are composed of decision nodes with branches to and from them. Usually squares represent decision points, and circles represent chance events. Branches from decision points show the choices available to the decision maker; branches from chance events show the probabilities for their occurrence.

In solving decision tree problems, we work from the end of the tree backward to the start of the tree. As we work back, we calculate the expected values at each step. In calculating the expected value, the time value of money is important if the planning horizon is long.

Once the calculations are made, we prune the tree by eliminating from each decision point all branches except the one with the highest payoff. This process continues to the first decision point, and the decision problem is thereby solved.

We now demonstrate an application to capacity planning for Hackers Computer Store. The exhibits used to solve this problem were generated using a program called DATA by TreeAge Software. (A demonstration version of the software, capable of solving the problems given in this chapter, is included on the book CD.)

## EXAMPLE 9.2: DECISION TREES

The owner of Hackers' Computer Store is considering what to do with his business over the next five years. Sales growth over the past couple of years has been good, but sales could grow substantially if a major electronics firm is built in his area as proposed. Hackers' owner sees three options. The first is to enlarge his current store, the second is to locate at a new site, and the third is to simply wait and do nothing. The decision to expand or move would take little time, and, therefore, the store would not lose revenue. If nothing were done the first year and strong growth occurred, then the decision to expand would be reconsidered. Waiting longer than one year would allow competition to move in and would make expansion no longer feasible.

The assumption and conditions are as follows:

1 Strong growth as a result of the increased population of computer fanatics from the new electronics firm has a 55 percent probability.
2 Strong growth with a new site would give annual returns of $195,000 per year. Weak growth with a new site would mean annual returns of $115,000.
3 Strong growth with an expansion would give annual returns of $190,000 per year. Weak growth with an expansion would mean annual returns of $100,000.
4 At the existing store with no changes, there would be returns of $170,000 per year if there is strong growth and $105,000 per year if growth is weak.
5 Expansion at the current site would cost $87,000.
6 The move to the new site would cost $210,000.
7 If growth is strong and the existing site is enlarged during the second year, the cost would still be $87,000.
8 Operating costs for all options are equal.

## SOLUTION

We construct a decision tree to advise Hackers' owner on the best action. Exhibit 9.3 shows the decision tree for this problem. There are two decision points (shown with the square nodes) and three chance occurrences (round nodes).

The values of each alternative outcome shown on the right of the diagram in Exhibit 9.4 are calculated as follows:

| ALTERNATIVE | REVENUE | | COST | VALUE |
|---|---|---|---|---|
| Move to new location, strong growth | $195,000 × 5 yrs | | $210,000 | $765,000 |
| Move to new location, weak growth | $115,000 × 5 yrs | | $210,000 | $365,000 |
| Expand store, strong growth | $190,000 × 5 yrs | | $87,000 | $863,000 |
| Expand store, weak growth | $100,000 × 5 yrs | | $87,000 | $413,000 |
| Do nothing now, strong growth, expand next year | $170,000 × 1 yr<br>$190,000 × 4 yrs | + | $87,000 | $843,000 |
| Do nothing now, strong growth, do not expand next year | $170,000 × 5 yrs | | $0 | $850,000 |
| Do nothing now, weak growth | $105,000 × 5 yrs | | $0 | $525,000 |

EXHIBIT 9.3

**Decision Tree for Hacker's Computer Store Problem**

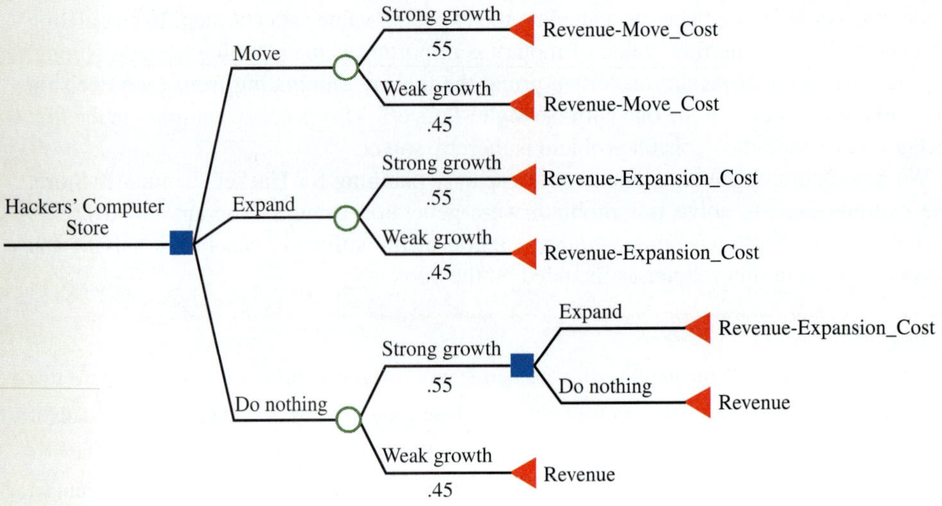


EXHIBIT 9.4

**Decision Tree Analysis Using DATA (TreeAge Software, Inc.)**

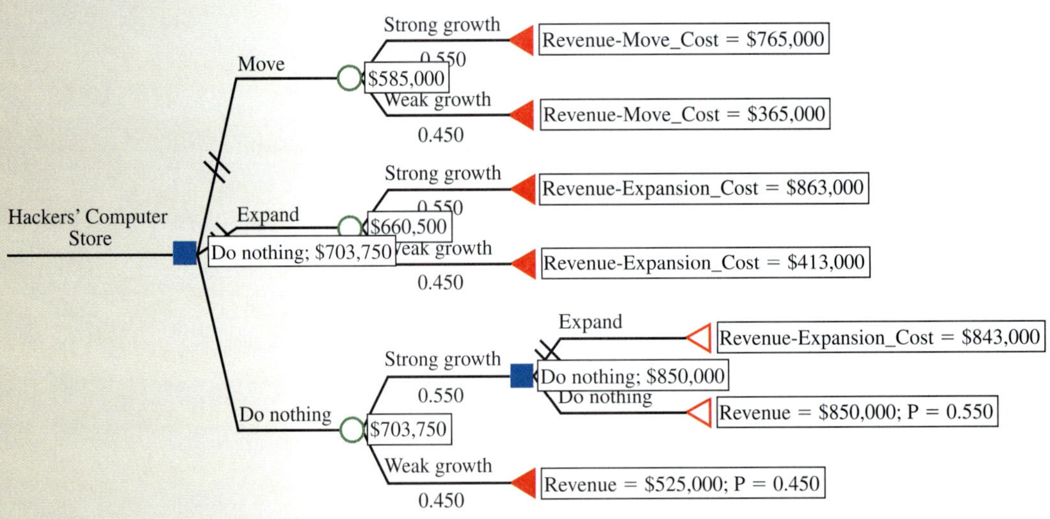


Working from the rightmost alternatives, which are associated with the decision of whether to expand, we see that the alternative of doing nothing has a higher value than the expansion alternative. We therefore eliminate the expansion in the second year alternatives. What this means is that if we do nothing in the first year and we experience strong growth, then in the second year it makes no sense to expand.

Now we can calculate the expected values associated with our current decision alternatives. We simply multiply the value of the alternative by its probability and sum the values. The expected value for the alternative of moving now is $585,000. The expansion alternative has an expected value of $660,500, and doing nothing now has an expected value of $703,750. Our analysis indicates that our best decision is to do nothing (both now and next year)!

Due to the five-year time horizon, it may be useful to consider the time value of the revenue and cost streams when solving this problem. Details concerning the calculation of the discounted monetary values are given in Supplement B ("Financial Analysis"). For example, if we assume a 16 percent interest rate, the first alternative outcome (move now, strong growth) has a discounted revenue valued at $428,487 (195,000 × 3.274293654) minus the $210,000 cost to move immediately.

EXHIBIT 9.5

**Decision Tree Analysis Using Net Present Value Calculations**

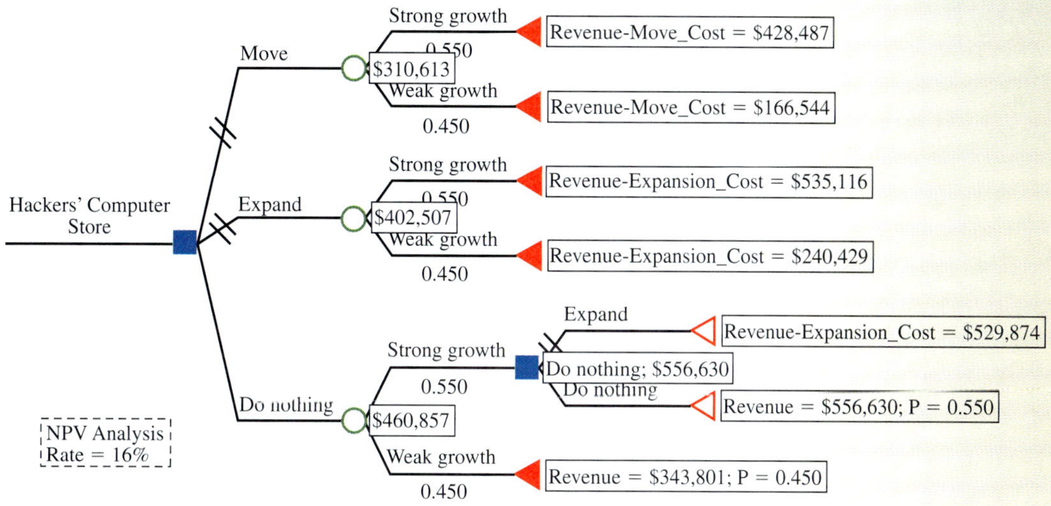


Exhibit 9.5 shows the analysis considering the discounted flows. Details of the calculations are given below. Present value table G.3 (in Appendix G) can be used to look up the discount factors. In order to make our calculations agree with those completed by the computer program, we have used discount factors that are calculated to 10 digits of precision (it is easy to do this with Excel). The only calculation that is a little tricky is the one for revenue when we do nothing now and expand at the beginning of next year. In this case, we have a revenue stream of $170,000 the first year, followed by four years at $190,000. The first part of the calculation (170,000 × .862068966) discounts the first-year revenue to present. The next part (190,000 × 2.798180638) discounts the next four years to the start of year two. We then discount this four-year stream to present value. The computer program used to generate Exhibit 9.5 performed the calculations automatically.

| ALTERNATIVE | REVENUE | COST | VALUE |
|---|---|---|---|
| Move to new location, strong growth | $195,000 × 3.274293654 | $210,000 | $428,487 |
| Move to new location, weak growth | $115,000 × 3.274293654 | $210,000 | $166,544 |
| Expand store, strong growth | $190,000 × 3.274293654 | $87,000 | $535,116 |
| Expand store, weak growth | $100,000 × 3.274203654 | $87,000 | $240,429 |
| Do nothing now, strong growth, expand next year | $170,000 × .862068966 $190,000 × 2.798180638 × .862068966 | $87,000 × .862068966 | $529,874 |
| Do nothing now, strong growth, do not expand next year | $170,000 × 3.274293654 | $0 | $556,630 |
| Do nothing now, weak growth | $105,000 × 3.274293654 | $0 | $343,801 ← |

# PLANNING SERVICE CAPACITY

## CAPACITY PLANNING IN SERVICE VERSUS MANUFACTURING

Although capacity planning in services is subject to many of the same issues as manufacturing capacity planning, and facility sizing can be done in much the same way, there are several important differences. Service capacity is more time- and location-dependent, it is subject to more volatile demand fluctuations, and utilization directly impacts service quality.

**Time** Unlike goods, services cannot be stored for later use. The capacity must be available to produce a service when it is needed. For example, a customer cannot be given a seat that went unoccupied on a previous airline flight if the current flight is full. Nor could the customer purchase a seat on a particular day's flight and take it home to be used at some later date.

**Location** The service capacity must be located near the customer. In manufacturing, production takes place, and then the goods are distributed to the customer. With services, however, the opposite is true. The capacity to deliver the service must first be distributed to the customer (either physically or through some communications medium such as the telephone); then the service can be produced. A hotel room or rental car that is available in another city is not much use to the customer—it must be where the customer is when that customer needs it.

**Volatility of Demand** The volatility of demand on a service delivery system is much higher than that on a manufacturing production system for three reasons. First, as just mentioned, services cannot be stored. This means that inventory cannot smooth the demand as in manufacturing. The second reason is that the customers interact directly with the production system—and these customers often have different needs, will have different levels of experience with the process, and may require different numbers of transactions. This contributes to greater variability in the processing time required for each customer and hence greater variability in the minimum capacity needed. The third reason for the greater volatility in service demand is that it is directly affected by consumer behavior. Influences on customer behavior ranging from the weather to a major event can directly affect demand for different services. Go to any restaurant near your campus during spring break and it will probably be almost empty. Or try to book a room at a local hotel during Homecoming weekend. This behavioral effect can be seen over even shorter time frames such as the lunch-hour rush at a bank's drive-through window or the sudden surge in pizza orders during halftime on Superbowl Sunday. Because of this volatility, service capacity is often planned in increments as small as 10 to 30 minutes, as opposed to the one-week increments more common in manufacturing.

## CAPACITY UTILIZATION AND SERVICE QUALITY

Planning capacity levels for services must consider the day-to-day relationship between service utilization and service quality. Exhibit 9.6 shows a service situation cast in waiting line terms (arrival rates and service rates).[4] As noted by Haywood-Farmer and Nollet, the

EXHIBIT 9.6

**Relationship between the Rate of Service Utilization ($\rho$) and Service Quality**

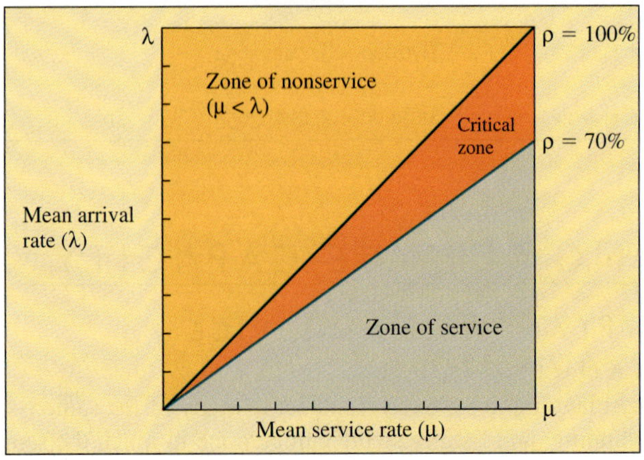


SOURCE: J. HAYWOOD-FARMER AND J. NOLLET, *SERVICES PLUS: EFFECTIVE SERVICE MANAGEMENT* (BOUCHERVILLE, QUEBEC, CANADA: G. MORIN PUBLISHER LTD., 1991). P. 59.

best operating point is near 70 percent of the maximum capacity. This is "enough to keep servers busy but allows enough time to serve customers individually and keep enough capacity in reserve so as not to create too many managerial headaches."[5] In the critical zone, customers are processed through the system, but service quality declines. Above the critical zone, the line builds up and it is likely that many customers may never be served.

Haywood-Farmer and Nollet also note that the optimal utilization rate is very context specific. Low rates are appropriate when both the degree of uncertainty and the stakes are high. For example, hospital emergency rooms and fire departments should aim for low utilization because of the high level of uncertainty and the life-or-death nature of their activities. Relatively predictable services such as commuter trains or service facilities without customer contact, such as postal sorting operations, can plan to operate much nearer 100 percent utilization. Interestingly, there is a third group for which high utilization is desirable. All sports teams like sellouts, not only because of the virtually 100 percent contribution margin of each customer, but because a full house creates an atmosphere that pleases customers, motivates the home team to perform better, and boosts future ticket sales. Stage performances and bars share this phenomenon. On the other hand, many airline passengers feel that a flight is too crowded when the seat next to theirs is occupied. Airlines capitalize on this response to sell more business-class seats.[6]

## CONCLUSION

Strategic capacity planning involves an investment decision that must match resource capabilities to a long-term demand forecast. As discussed in this chapter, factors to be taken into account in selecting capacity additions for both manufacturing and services include

- The likely effects of economies of scale.
- The effects of experience curves.
- The impact of changing facility focus and balance among production stages.
- The degree of flexibility of facilities and the workforce.

For services in particular, a key consideration is the effect of capacity changes on the quality of the service offering. In the next technical note, we discuss the related issue of where to locate the firm's facilities.

Service

## KEY TERMS

**Capacity** The amount of output that a system is capable of achieving over a specific period of time.

**Strategic capacity planning** Determining the overall capacity level of capital-intensive resources that best supports the company's long-range competitive strategy.

**Best operating level** The level of capacity for which the process was designed and the volume of output at which average unit cost is minimized.

**Capacity utilization rate** Measures how close a firm is to its best operating level.

**Capacity focus** Can be operationalized through the plants within plants concept, where a plant has several suborganizations specialized for different products—even though they are under the same roof. This permits finding the best operating level for each suborganization.

**Economies of scope** Exists when multiple products can be produced at a lower cost in combination than they can separately.

**Capacity cushion** Capacity in excess of expected demand.

## SOLVED PROBLEM

### SOLVED PROBLEM 1

E-Education is a new start-up that develops and markets MBA courses offered over the Internet. The company is currently located in Chicago and employs 150 people. Due to strong growth the company needs additional office space. The company has the option of leasing additional space at its current location in Chicago for the next two years, but after that will need to move to a new building. Another option the company is considering is moving the entire operation to a small Midwest town immediately. A third option is for the company to lease a new building in Chicago immediately. If the company chooses the first option and leases new space at its current location, it can at the end of two years either lease a new building in Chicago or move to the small Midwest town.

The following are some additional facts about the alternatives and current situation:

1 The company has a 75 percent chance of surviving the next two years.
2 Leasing the new space for two years at the current location in Chicago would cost \$750,000 per year.
3 Moving the entire operation to a Midwest town would cost \$1 million. Leasing space would run only \$500,000 per year.
4 Moving to a new building in Chicago would cost \$200,000, and leasing the new building's space would cost \$650,000 per year.
5 The company can cancel the lease at any time.
6 The company will build its own building in five years, if it survives.
7 Assume all other costs and revenues are the same no matter where the company is located.

What should E-Education do?

## Solution

Step 1: Construct a decision tree that considers all of E-Education's alternatives. The following shows the tree that has three decision points (with the square nodes) followed by chance occurrences (round nodes). In the case of the first decision point, if the company survives, two additional decision points need consideration.

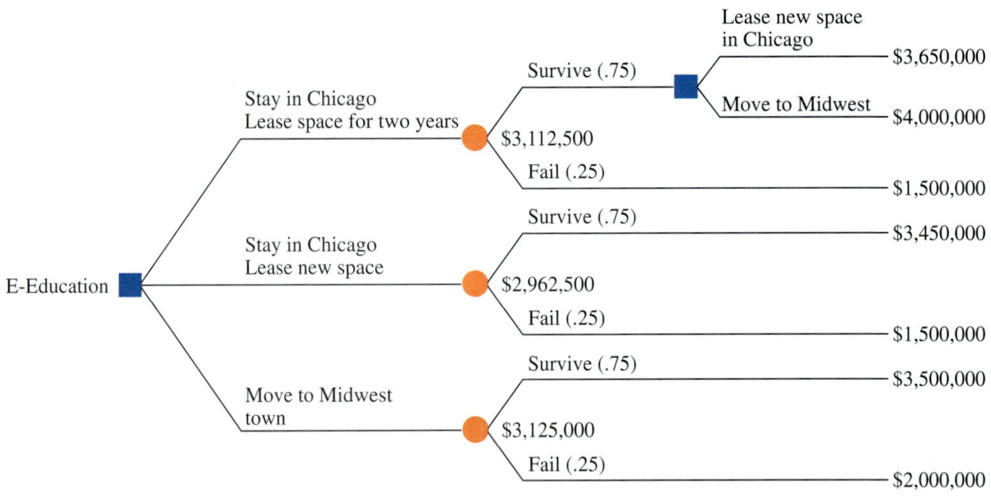


Step 2: Calculate the values of each alternative as follows:

| ALTERNATIVE | CALCULATION | VALUE |
|---|---|---|
| Stay in Chicago, lease space for two years, survive, lease new building in Chicago | (750,000) × 2 + 200,000 + (650,000) × 3 = | \$3,650,000 |
| Stay in Chicago, lease space for two years, survive, move to Midwest | (750,000) × 2 + 1,000,000 + (500,000) × 3 = | \$4,000,000 |
| Stay in Chicago, lease space for two years, fail | (750,000) × 2 = | \$1,500,000 |
| Stay in Chicago, lease new building in Chicago, survive | 200,000 + (650,000) × 5 = | \$3,450,000 |
| Stay in Chicago, lease new building in Chicago, fail | 200,000 + (650,000) × 2 = | \$1,500,000 |
| Move to Midwest, survive | 1,000,000 + (500,000) × 5 = | \$3,500,000 |
| Move to Midwest, fail | 1,000,000 + (500,000) × 2 = | \$2,000,000 |

Working from our rightmost alternatives, the first two alternatives end in decision nodes. Because the first option, staying in Chicago and leasing space for two years, is the lowest cost, this is what we would do if for the first two years we decide to stay in Chicago. If we fail after the first two years, represented by the third alternative, the cost is only $1,500,000. The expected value of the first option of staying in Chicago and leasing space for the first two years is .75 × 3,650,000 + .25 × 1,500,000 = $3,112,500.

The second option, staying in Chicago and leasing a new building now, has an expected value of .75 × 3,450,000 + .25 × 1,500,000 = $2,962,500.

Finally, the third option of moving to the Midwest immediately has an expected value of .75 × 3,500,000 + .25 × 2,000,000 = $3,125,000.

From this, it looks like the best alternative is to stay in Chicago and lease a new building immediately.

## Review and Discussion Questions

1 What capacity problems were encountered at the opening of Paris Disney? What lessons are there for other service companies in planning capacity?
2 List some practical limits to economies of scale; that is, when should a plant stop growing?
3 What are some capacity balance problems faced by the following organizations or facilities?
   *a.* An airline terminal.
   *b.* A university computing center.
   *c.* A clothing manufacturer.
4 What are some major capacity considerations in a hospital? How do they differ from those of a factory?
5 Management may choose to build up capacity in anticipation of demand or in response to developing demand. Cite the advantages and disadvantages of both approaches.
6 What is capacity balance? Why is it hard to achieve? What methods are used to deal with capacity imbalances?
7 What are some reasons for a plant to maintain a capacity cushion? How about a negative capacity cushion?
8 At first glance, the concepts of the focused factory and capacity flexibility may seem to contradict each other. Do they really?

## Problems

1 AlwaysRain Irrigation, Inc., would like to determine capacity requirements for the next four years. Currently two production lines are in place for bronze and plastic sprinklers. Three types of sprinklers are available in both bronze and plastic: 90-degree nozzle sprinklers, 180-degree nozzle sprinklers, and 360-degree nozzle sprinklers. Management has forecast demand for the next four years as follows: 1. See ISM.

| | Yearly Demand | | | |
|---|---|---|---|---|
| | 1 (in 000s) | 2 (in 000s) | 3 (in 000s) | 4 (in 000s) |
| Plastic 90 | 32 | 44 | 55 | 56 |
| Plastic 180 | 15 | 16 | 17 | 18 |
| Plastic 360 | 50 | 55 | 64 | 67 |
| Bronze 90 | 7 | 8 | 9 | 10 |
| Bronze 180 | 3 | 4 | 5 | 6 |
| Bronze 360 | 11 | 12 | 15 | 18 |

Both production lines can produce all the different types of nozzles. Each bronze machine requires two operators and can produce up to 12,000 sprinklers. The plastic injection molding machine requires four operators and can produce up to 200,000 sprinklers. Three bronze machines and only one injection molding machine are available. What are the capacity requirements for the next four years?

2 Suppose that AlwaysRain Irrigation's marketing department will undertake an intense ad campaign for the bronze sprinklers, which are more expensive but also more durable than the 2. Not enough capacity after second year.

plastic ones. Forecast demand for the next four years is

| | YEARLY DEMAND | | | |
|---|---|---|---|---|
| | 1 (IN 000S) | 2 (IN 000S) | 3 (IN 000S) | 4 (IN 000S) |
| Plastic 90 | 32 | 44 | 55 | 56 |
| Plastic 180 | 15 | 16 | 17 | 18 |
| Plastic 360 | 50 | 55 | 64 | 67 |
| Bronze 90 | 11 | 15 | 18 | 23 |
| Bronze 180 | 6 | 5 | 6 | 9 |
| Bronze 360 | 15 | 16 | 17 | 20 |

What are the capacity implications of the marketing campaign?

3 In anticipation of the ad campaign, AlwaysRain bought an additional bronze machine. Will this be enough to ensure that enough capacity is available?

3. No, there is additional need after the third year.

4 Suppose that operators have enough training to operate both the bronze machines and the injection molding machine for the plastic sprinklers. Currently AlwaysRain has 10 such employees. In anticipation of the ad campaign described in Problem 2, management approved the purchase of two additional bronze machines. What are the labor requirement implications?

4. There is a need for additional employees in the fourth year.

5 Expando, Inc. is considering the possibility of building an additional factory that would produce a new addition to their product line. The company is currently considering two options. The first is a small facility that it could build at a cost of $6 million. If demand for new products is low, the company expects to receive $10 million in discounted revenues (present value of future revenues) with the small facility. On the other hand, if demand is high, it expects $12 million in discounted revenues using the small facility. The second option is to build a large factory at a cost of $9 million. Were demand to be low, the company would expect $10 million in discounted revenues with the large plant. If demand is high, the company estimates that the discounted revenues would be $14 million. In either case, the probability of demand being high is .40, and the probability of it being low is .60. Not constructing a new factory would result in no additional revenue being generated because the current factories cannot produce these new products. Construct a decision tree to help Expando make the best decision.

5. Expected NPV—small $4.8 million. Expected NPV—large $2.6 million.

6 A builder has located a piece of property that she would like to buy and eventually build on. The land is currently zoned for four homes per acre, but she is planning to request new zoning. What she builds depends on approval of zoning requests and your analysis of this problem to advise her. With her input and your help, the decision process has been reduced to the following costs, alternatives, and probabilities:

Cost of land: $2 million.

Probability of rezoning: .60.

If the land is rezoned, there will be additional costs for new roads, lighting, and so on, of $1 million.

If the land is rezoned, the contractor must decide whether to build a shopping center or 1,500 apartments that the tentative plan shows would be possible. If she builds a shopping center, there is a 70 percent chance that she can sell the shopping center to a large department chain for $4 million over her construction cost, which excludes the land; and there is a 30 percent chance that she can sell it to an insurance company for $5 million over her construction cost (also excluding the land). If, instead of the shopping center, she decides to build the 1,500 apartments, she places probabilities on the profits as follows: There is a 60 percent chance that she can sell the apartments to a real estate investment corporation for $3,000 each over her construction cost; there is a 40 percent chance that she can get only $2,000 each over her construction cost. (Both exclude the land cost.)

If the land is not rezoned, she will comply with the existing zoning restrictions and simply build 600 homes, on which she expects to make $4,000 over the construction cost on each one (excluding the cost of land).

Draw a decision tree of the problem and determine the best solution and the expected net profit.

6. See ISM. Rezoned shopping center = $4.3 million. Rezoned apartments = $3.9 million. No rezoning = $.4 million. Expected results: .60(1.3) + 0.40(.4) = $.94 million.

## CASE: SHOULDICE HOSPITAL—A CUT ABOVE[7]

Excel: Shouldice Hosp

Vol. III "Shouldice Hospital"

*"Shouldice Hospital, the house that hernias built, is a converted country estate which gives the hospital 'a country club' appeal."*
A quote from *American Medical News*

Shouldice Hospital in Canada is widely known for one thing—hernia repair! In fact, that is the only operation it performs, and it performs a great many of them. Over the past two decades this small 90-bed hospital has averaged 7,000 operations annually. Last year, it had a record year and performed nearly 7,500 operations. Patients' ties to Shouldice do not end when they leave the hospital. Every year the gala Hernia Reunion dinner (with complimentary hernia inspection) draws in excess of 1,000 former patients, some of whom have been attending the event for over 30 years.

A number of notable features in Shouldice's service delivery system contribute to its success. (1) Shouldice accepts only patients with the uncomplicated external hernias, and it uses a superior technique developed for this type of hernia by Dr. Shouldice during World War II. (2) Patients are subject to early ambulation, which promotes healing. (Patients literally walk off the operating table and engage in light exercise throughout their stay, which lasts only three days.) (3) Its country club atmosphere, gregarious nursing staff, and built-in socializing make a surprisingly pleasant experience out of an inherently unpleasant medical problem. Regular times are set aside for tea, cookies, and socializing. All patients are paired up with a roommate with similar background and interests.

### THE PRODUCTION SYSTEM

The medical facilities at Shouldice consist of five operating rooms, a patient recovery room, a laboratory, and six examination rooms. Shouldice performs, on average, 150 operations per week, with patients generally staying at the hospital for three days. Although operations are performed only five days a week, the remainder of the hospital is in operation continuously to attend to recovering patients.

An operation at Shouldice Hospital is performed by one of the 12 full-time surgeons assisted by one of seven part-time assistant surgeons. Surgeons generally take about one hour to prepare for and perform each hernia operation, and they operate on four patients per day. The surgeons' day ends at 4 P.M., although they can expect to be on call every 14th night and every 10th weekend.

### THE SHOULDICE EXPERIENCE

Each patient undergoes a screening exam prior to setting a date for his or her operation. Patients in the Toronto area are encouraged to walk in for the diagnosis. Examinations are done between 9 A.M. and 3:30 P.M. Monday through Friday, and between 10 A.M. and 2 P.M. on Saturday. Out-of-town patients are mailed a medical information questionnaire (also available over the Internet), which is used for the diagnosis. A small percentage of the patients who are overweight or otherwise represent an undue medical risk are refused treatment. The remaining patients receive confirmation cards with the scheduled dates for their operations. A patient's folder is transferred to the reception desk once an arrival date is confirmed.

Patients arrive at the clinic between 1 and 3 P.M. the day before their surgery. After a short wait, they receive a brief preoperative examination. They are then sent to an admissions clerk to complete any necessary paperwork. Patients are next directed to one of the two nurses' stations for blood and urine tests and then are shown to their rooms. They spend the remaining time before orientation getting settled and acquainting themselves with their roommates.

Orientation begins at 5 P.M., followed by dinner in the common dining room. Later in the evening, at 9 P.M., patients gather in the lounge area for tea and cookies. Here new patients can talk with patients who have already had their surgery. Bedtime is between 9:30 and 10 P.M.

On the day of the operation, patients with early operations are awakened at 5:30 A.M. for preoperative sedation. The first operations begin at 7:30 A.M. Shortly before an operation starts, the patient is administered a local anesthetic, leaving him or her alert and fully aware of the proceedings. At the conclusion of the operation, the patient is invited to walk from the operating table to a nearby wheelchair, which is waiting to return the patient to his or her room. After a brief period of rest, the patient is encouraged to get up and start exercising. By 9 P.M. that day, he or she is in the lounge having cookies and tea and talking with new, incoming patients.

The skin clips holding the incision together are loosened, and some are removed, the next day. The remainder are removed the following morning just before the patient is discharged.

When Shouldice Hospital started, the average hospital stay for hernia surgery was three weeks. Today, many institutions push "same day surgery" for a variety of reasons. Shouldice Hospital firmly believes that this is not in the best interests of patients, and is committed to its three-day process. Shouldice's postoperative rehabilitation program is designed to enable the patient to resume normal activities with minimal interruption and discomfort. Shouldice patients frequently return to work in a few days; the average total time off is eight days.

*"It is interesting to note that approximately 1 out of every 100 Shouldice patients is a medical doctor."*

### FUTURE PLANS

The management of Shouldice is thinking of expanding the hospital's capacity to serve considerable unsatisfied demand. To this effect, the vice president is seriously considering two options. The first involves adding one more day of operations (Saturday) to the existing five-day schedule, which would increase capacity by 20 percent. The second option is to add another floor of rooms to the hospital, increasing the number of beds by 50 percent. This would require more aggressive scheduling of the operating rooms.

The administrator of the hospital, however, is concerned about maintaining control over the quality of the service delivered. He thinks the facility is already getting very good utilization. The doctors and the staff are happy with their jobs, and the patients are satisfied with the service. According to him, further expansion of capacity might make it hard to maintain the same kind of working relationships and attitudes.

### QUESTIONS

Exhibit 9.7 is a room-occupancy table for the existing system. Each row in the table follows the patients that checked in on a given day. The columns indicate the number of patients in the hospital on a given day. For example, the first row of the table shows that 30 people checked in on Monday and were in the hospital for Monday, Tuesday, and Wednesday. By summing the columns of the table for Wednesday, we see that there are 90 patients staying in the hospital that day.

EXHIBIT 9.7

**Operations with 90 Beds (30 patients per day)**

| | Beds Required | | | | | | |
|---|---|---|---|---|---|---|---|
| Check-in Day | Monday | Tuesday | Wednesday | Thursday | Friday | Saturday | Sunday |
| Monday | 30 | 30 | 30 | | | | |
| Tuesday | | 30 | 30 | 30 | | | |
| Wednesday | | | 30 | 30 | 30 | | |
| Thursday | | | | 30 | 30 | 30 | |
| Friday | | | | | | | |
| Saturday | | | | | | | |
| Sunday | 30 | 30 | | | | | 30 |
| Total | 60 | 90 | 90 | 90 | 60 | 30 | 30 |

1 How well is the hospital currently utilizing its beds?
2 Develop a similar table to show the effects of adding operations on Saturday. (Assume that 30 operations would still be performed each day.) How would this affect the utilization of the bed capacity? Is this capacity sufficient for the additional patients?
3 Now look at the effect of increasing the number of beds by 50 percent. How many operations could the hospital perform per day before running out of bed capacity? (Assume operations are performed five days per week, with the same number performed on each day.) How well would the new resources be utilized relative to the current operation? Could the hospital really perform this many operations? Why? (Hint: Look at the capacity of the 12 surgeons and the five operating rooms.)
4 Although financial data is sketchy, an estimate from a construction company indicates that adding bed capacity would cost about $100,000 per bed. In addition, the rate charged for the hernia surgery varies between about $900 to $2,000 (U.S. dollars), with an average rate of $1,300 per operation. The surgeons are paid a flat $600 per operation. Due to all the uncertainties in government health care legislation, Shouldice would like to justify any expansion within a five-year time period.

## SELECTED BIBLIOGRAPHY

Amran, M., and N. Kulatilaka. "Disciplined Decisions: Aligning Strategy with the Financial Markets." *Harvard Business Review* (January–February 1999), pp. 95–104.

Bakke, N. A., and R. Hellberg. "The Challenges of Capacity Planning." *International Journal of Production Economics* 31–30 (1993), pp. 243–64.

Hammesfahr, R. D. Jack; J. A. Pope; and A. Ardalan. "Strategic Planning for Production Capacity." *International Journal of Operations and Production Management* 13, no. 5 (1993), pp. 41–53.

Meyer, C. *Fast Cycle Time: How to Align Purpose, Strategy and Structure for Speed.* New York: Free Press, 1993.

Giffi, C.; A. V. Roth; and G. M. Seal, eds. *Competing in World-Class Manufacturing: National Center for Manufacturing Sciences.* Burr Ridge, IL: Business One Irwin, 1990.

## FOOTNOTES

1 In gathering capacity statistics, the Bureau of Economic Analysis asks two questions of surveyed firms: (1) At what percentage of manufacturing capacity did your company operate in (month and year)? (2) At what percentage of (month and year) manufacturing capacity would your company have preferred to operate in order to achieve maximum profits or other objective? See "Survey of Current Business," an annual publication of the *U.S. Department of Commerce Journal.*

2 W. Skinner, "The Focused Factory," *Harvard Business Review,* May–June 1974, pp. 113–21.

3 See R. J. Schonberger, "The Rationalization of Production," *Proceedings of the 50th Anniversary of the Academy of Management* (Chicago: Academy of Management, 1986), pp. 64–70.

4 Waiting lines are discussed in Technical Note 6.

5 J. Haywood-Farmer and J. Nollet, *Services Plus: Effective Service Management* (Boucherville, Quebec, Canada: G. Morin Publisher Ltd., 1991), p. 58.

6 Haywood-Farmer and Nollet, *Services Plus,* p. 58.

7 Shouldice Hospital is at *http://www.shouldice.com.* The website has much additional information concerning the history of the hospital and current hernia operation procedures.

technical note



*technical note nine*

# FACILITY LOCATION

## TECHNICAL NOTE OUTLINE

ARCHER DANIELS MIDLAND (ADM) IS A MAJOR PROCESSOR OF AGRICULTURAL PRODUCTS. ADM'S EUROPORT PLANT IN ROTTERDAM, THE NETHERLANDS, IS THE LARGEST GRAIN-PROCESSING FACILITY IN THE WORLD; IT CAN SHIP BY LAND, RAIL, RIVER, AND SEA.

Where should a plant or service facility be located? This is a top question on the strategic agendas of contemporary manufacturing and service firms, particularly in this age of global markets and global production. Dramatic changes in international trade agreements have made the world truly a "global factory," allowing companies greater flexibility in their location choices. In practice, however, the question of location is very much linked to two competitive imperatives:

1. The need to produce close to the customer due to time-based competition, trade agreements, and shipping costs.
2. The need to locate near the appropriate labor pool to take advantage of low wage costs and/or high technical skills.

This technical note discusses these and other issues in facility location decisions. Examples cover different industries with a global perspective. We present typical techniques involved in facility location analysis and two cases on global location decisions.

## ISSUES IN FACILITY LOCATION

The problem of facility location is faced by both to new and existing businesses, and its solution is critical to a company's eventual success. An important element in designing a company's supply chain is the location of its facilities. For instance, 3M has moved a significant part of its corporate activity, including R&D, to the more temperate climate of Austin, Texas. Toys Я Us has opened a new location in Japan as a part of its global strategy. Disney chose Paris, France, for its European theme park, and BMW assembles the Z3 sports car in South Carolina. Manufacturing and service companies' location decisions are guided by a variety of criteria defined by competitive imperatives. Criteria that influence manufacturing plant and warehouse location planning are discussed next.

**Proximity to Customers** For example, Japan's NatSteel Electronics has built its two largest plants in Mexico and Hungary to be closer to major markets in the United States and Europe—whose buyers want their goods delivered yesterday. Such proximity also helps ensure that customer needs are incorporated into products being developed and built.

**Business Climate** A favorable business climate can include the presence of similar-sized businesses, the presence of companies in the same industry, and, in the case of international locations, the presence of other foreign companies. Probusiness government legislation and local government intervention to facilitate businesses locating in an area via subsidies, tax abatements, and other support are also factors.

**Total Costs** The objective is to select a site with the lowest total cost. This includes regional costs, inbound distribution costs, and outbound distribution costs. Land, construction, labor, taxes, and energy costs comprise the regional costs. In addition, there are hidden costs that are difficult to measure. These involve (1) excessive moving of preproduction material between locations before final delivery to the customers and (2) loss of customer responsiveness arising from locating away from the main customer base.

**Infrastructure** Adequate road, rail, air, and sea transportation is vital. Energy and telecommunications requirements must also be met. In addition, the local government's willingness to invest in upgrading infrastructure to the levels required may be an incentive to select a specific location.

**Quality of Labor** The educational and skill levels of the labor pool must match the company's needs. Even more important are the willingness and ability to learn.

**Suppliers** A high-quality and competitive supplier base makes a given location suitable. The proximity of important suppliers' plants also supports lean production methods.

**Other Facilities** The location of other plants or distribution centers of the same company may influence a new facility's location in the network. Issues of product mix and capacity are strongly interconnected to the location decision in this context.

Free trade zone

Global

**Free Trade Zones** A foreign trade zone or a **free trade zone** is typically a closed facility (under the supervision of the customs department) into which foreign goods can be brought without being subject to the normal customs requirements. There are about 170 such free trade zones in the United States today. Such specialized locations also exist in other countries. Manufacturers in free trade zones can use imported components in the final product and delay payment of customs duties until the product is shipped into the host country.

**Political Risk** The fast-changing geopolitical scenes in numerous nations present exciting, challenging opportunities. But the extended phase of transformation that many countries are undergoing makes the decision to locate in those areas extremely difficult. Political risks in both the country of location and the host country influence location decisions.

**Government Barriers** Barriers to enter and locate in many countries are being removed today through legislation. Yet many nonlegislative and cultural barriers should be considered in location planning.

Trading blocs

**Trading Blocs** The world of **trading blocs** gained a new member with the ratification of the North American Free Trade Agreement (NAFTA). Such agreements influence location decisions, both within and outside trading bloc countries. Firms typically locate, or relocate, within a bloc to take advantage of new market opportunities or lower total costs afforded by the trading agreement. Other companies (those outside the trading bloc countries) decide on locations within the bloc so as not to be disqualified from competing in the new market. Examples include the location of various Japanese auto manufacturing plants in Europe before 1992 as well as recent moves by many communications and financial services companies into Mexico in a post-NAFTA environment.

**Environmental Regulation** The environmental regulations that impact a certain industry in a given location should be included in the location decision. Besides measurable cost implications, these regulations influence the relationship with the local community.

**Host Community** The host community's interest in having the plant in its midst is a necessary part of the evaluation process. Local educational facilities and the broader issue of quality of life are also important.

Global

**Competitive Advantage** An important decision for multinational companies is the nation in which to locate the home base for each distinct business. Porter suggests that a company can have different home bases for distinct businesses or segments.Competitive advantage is created at a home base where strategy is set, the core product and process technology are created, and a critical mass of production takes place. So a company should move its home base to a country that stimulates innovation and provides the best environment for global competitiveness.[1] This concept can also be applied to domestic companies seeking to gain sustainable competitive advantage. It partly explains the southeastern states' recent emergence as the preferred corporate destination within the United States (that is, their business climate fosters innovation and low-cost production).

## PLANT LOCATION METHODS

*"If the boss likes Bakersfield, I like Bakersfield."* Exhibit TN9.1 summarizes the set of decisions that a company must make in choosing a plant location. Although the exhibit implies a step-by-step process, virtually all activities listed take place

EXHIBIT TN9.1

Plant Search: Company XYZ

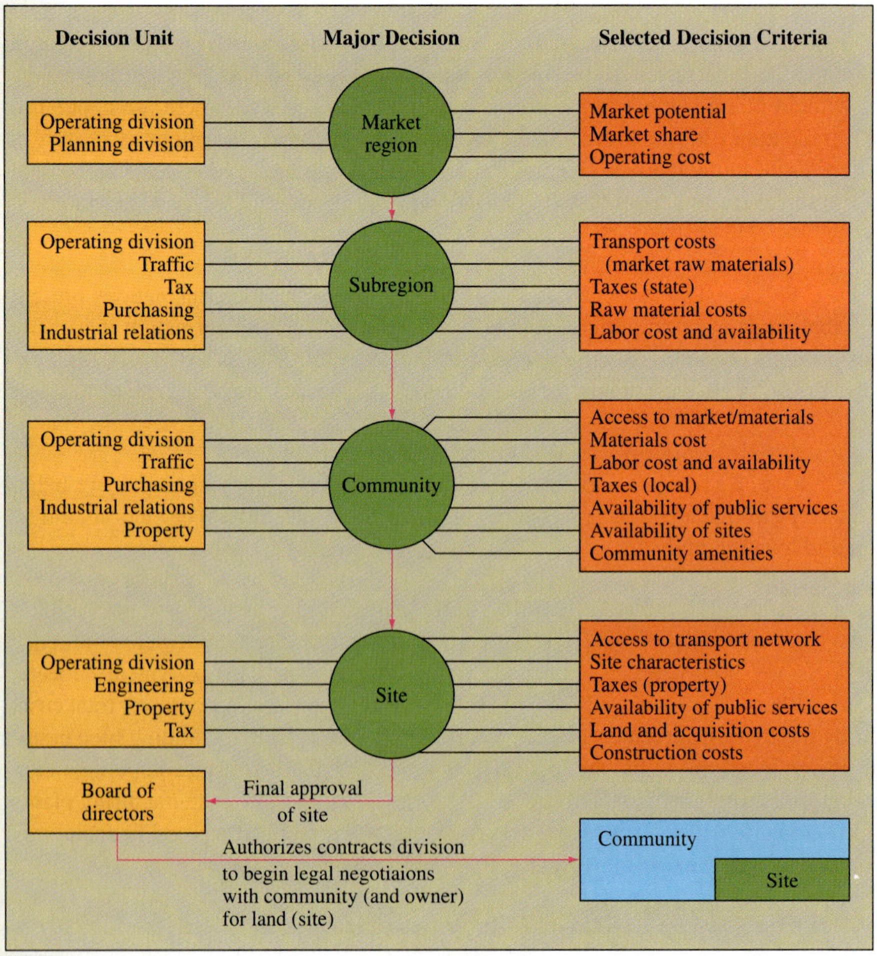


SOURCE: T. M. CARROLL AND R. D. DEAN, "A BAYESIAN APPROACH TO PLANT-LOCATION DECISIONS," *DECISION SCIENCES* 11, NO. 1 (JANUARY 1980), P. 87.

simultaneously. As suggested by the preceding vote for Bakersfield, political decisions may occasionally override systematic analysis.

Evaluation of alternative regions, subregions, and communities is commonly termed *macro analysis*. Evaluation of specific sites in the selected community is termed *micro analysis*. Techniques used to support macro analyses include factor-rating systems, linear programming, and center of gravity. A detailed cost analysis would accompany each of these methods, and they must, of course, be related to business strategy.

## FACTOR-RATING SYSTEMS

**Factor-rating systems** are perhaps the most widely used of the general location techniques because they provide a mechanism to combine diverse factors in an easy-to-understand format.

Factor-rating systems

By way of example, a refinery assigned the following range of point values to major factors affecting a set of possible sites:

| | RANGE |
|---|---|
| Fuels in region | 0 to 330 |
| Power availability and reliability | 0 to 200 |
| Labor climate | 0 to 100 |
| Living conditions | 0 to 100 |
| Transportation | 0 to 50 |
| Water supply | 0 to 10 |
| Climate | 0 to 50 |
| Supplies | 0 to 60 |
| Tax policies and laws | 0 to 20 |

Each site was then rated against each factor, and a point value was selected from its assigned range. The sums of assigned points for each site were then compared. The site with the most points was selected.

A major problem with simple point-rating schemes is that they do not account for the wide range of costs that may occur within each factor. For example, there may be only a few hundred dollars' difference between the best and worst locations on one factor and several thousands of dollars' difference between the best and the worst on another. The first factor may have the most points available to it but provide little help in making the location decision; the second may have few points available but potentially show a real difference in the value of locations. To deal with this problem, it has been suggested that points possible for each factor be derived using a weighting scale based on standard deviations of costs rather than simply total cost amounts. In this way, relative costs can be considered.

## TRANSPORTATION METHOD OF LINEAR PROGRAMMING

The **transportation method** is a special linear programming method. (Note that linear programming is developed in detail in Supplement A.) It gets its name from its application to problems involving transporting products from several sources to several destinations. The two common objectives of such problems are either (1) minimize the cost of shipping $n$ units to $m$ destinations or (2) maximize the profit of shipping $n$ units to $m$ destinations.

Transportation method

### *EXAMPLE TN9.1: U.S. PHARMACEUTICAL COMPANY*

Suppose the U.S. Pharmaceutical Company has four factories supplying the warehouses of four major customers and its management wants to determine the minimum-cost shipping schedule for its monthly output to these customers. Factory supply, warehouse demands, and shipping costs per case for these drugs are shown in Exhibit TN9.2.

EXHIBIT TN9.2

**Data for U.S. Pharmaceutical Transportation Problem**

| | | | | Shipping Costs per Case (in Dollars) | | | | |
|---|---|---|---|---|---|---|---|---|
| Factory | Supply | Warehouse | Demand | From | To Columbus | To St. Louis | To Denver | To Los Angeles |
| Indianapolis | 15 | Columbus | 10 | Indianapolis | $25 | $35 | $36 | $60 |
| Phoenix | 6 | St. Louis | 12 | Phoenix | 55 | 30 | 25 | 25 |
| New York | 14 | Denver | 15 | New York | 40 | 50 | 80 | 90 |
| Atlanta | 11 | Los Angeles | 9 | Atlanta | 30 | 40 | 66 | 75 |

EXHIBIT TN9.3

**Transportation Matrix for U.S. Pharmaceutical Problem**

| From \ To | Columbus | St. Louis | Denver | Los Angeles | Factory supply |
|---|---|---|---|---|---|
| Indianapolis | 25 | 35 | 36 | 60 | 15 |
| Phoenix | 55 | 30 | 25 | 25 | 6 |
| New York | 40 | 50 | 80 | 90 | 14 |
| Atlanta | 30 | 40 | 66 | 75 | 11 |
| Destination requirements | 10 | 12 | 15 | 9 | 46 / 46 |

The transportation matrix for this example appears in Exhibit TN9.3, where supply availability at each factory is shown in the far right column and the warehouse demands are shown in the bottom row. The shipping costs are shown in the small boxes within the cells. For example, the cost to ship one unit from the Indianapolis factory to the customer warehouse in Columbus is $25.

### SOLUTION

This problem can be solved by using Microsoft Excel's Solver function. Exhibit TN9.4 shows how the problem can be set up in the spreadsheet. Cells B6 through E6 contain the requirement for each customer warehouse. Cells F2 through F6 contain the amount that can be supplied from each plant. Cells B2 through E5 are the cost of shipping one unit for each potential plant and warehouse combination.

Cells for the solution of the problem are B9 through E12. These cells can initially be left blank when setting up the spreadsheet. Column cells F9 through F12 are the sum of each row indicating how much is actually being shipped from each factory in the candidate solution. Similarly, row cells B13 through E13 are sums of the amount being shipped to each customer in the candidate solution. The Excel Sum function can be used to calculate these values.

The cost of the candidate solution is calculated in cells B16 through E19. Multiplying the amount shipped in the candidate solution by the cost per unit of shipping over that particular route makes this calculation. For example, multiplying B2 by B9 in cell B16 gives the cost of shipping between Indianapolis and Columbus for the candidate solution. The total cost shown in cell F20 is the sum of all these individual costs.

To solve the problem the Excel Solver application needs to be accessed. The Solver is found by selecting Tools and then Solver from the Excel menu. A screen similar to what is shown below should appear. If you cannot find Solver at that location, the required add-in might not have been added when

EXHIBIT TN9.4

Excel Screen Showing the US Pharmaceutical Problem

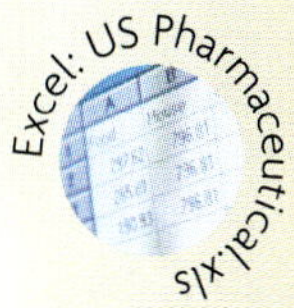


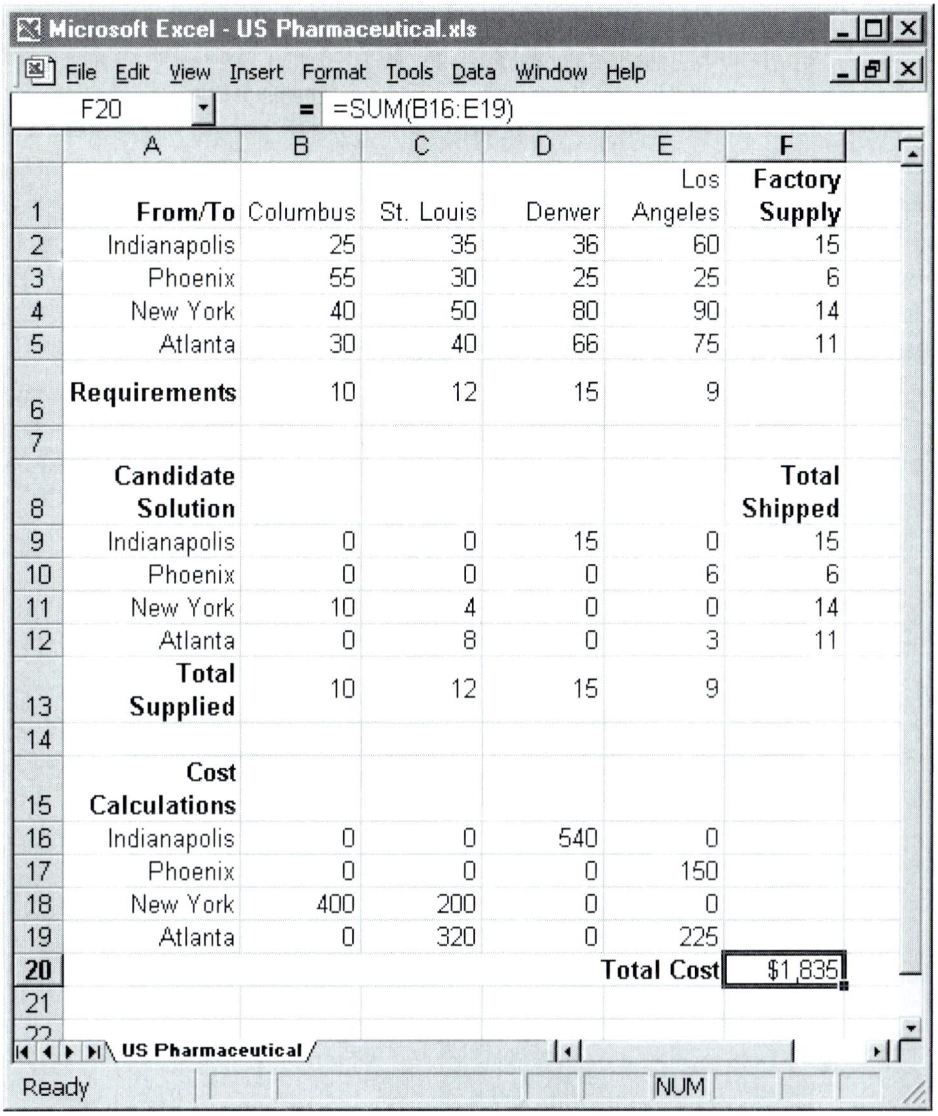


| | A | B | C | D | E | F |
|---|---|---|---|---|---|---|
| 1 | **From/To** | Columbus | St. Louis | Denver | Los Angeles | **Factory Supply** |
| 2 | Indianapolis | 25 | 35 | 36 | 60 | 15 |
| 3 | Phoenix | 55 | 30 | 25 | 25 | 6 |
| 4 | New York | 40 | 50 | 80 | 90 | 14 |
| 5 | Atlanta | 30 | 40 | 66 | 75 | 11 |
| 6 | **Requirements** | 10 | 12 | 15 | 9 | |
| 7 | | | | | | |
| 8 | **Candidate Solution** | | | | | **Total Shipped** |
| 9 | Indianapolis | 0 | 0 | 15 | 0 | 15 |
| 10 | Phoenix | 0 | 0 | 0 | 6 | 6 |
| 11 | New York | 10 | 4 | 0 | 0 | 14 |
| 12 | Atlanta | 0 | 8 | 0 | 3 | 11 |
| 13 | **Total Supplied** | 10 | 12 | 15 | 9 | |
| 14 | | | | | | |
| 15 | **Cost Calculations** | | | | | |
| 16 | Indianapolis | 0 | 0 | 540 | 0 | |
| 17 | Phoenix | 0 | 0 | 0 | 150 | |
| 18 | New York | 400 | 200 | 0 | 0 | |
| 19 | Atlanta | 0 | 320 | 0 | 225 | |
| 20 | | | | | **Total Cost** | $1,835 |
| 21 | | | | | | |

Excel was initially installed on your computer. Solver can easily be added if you have your original Excel installation disk.

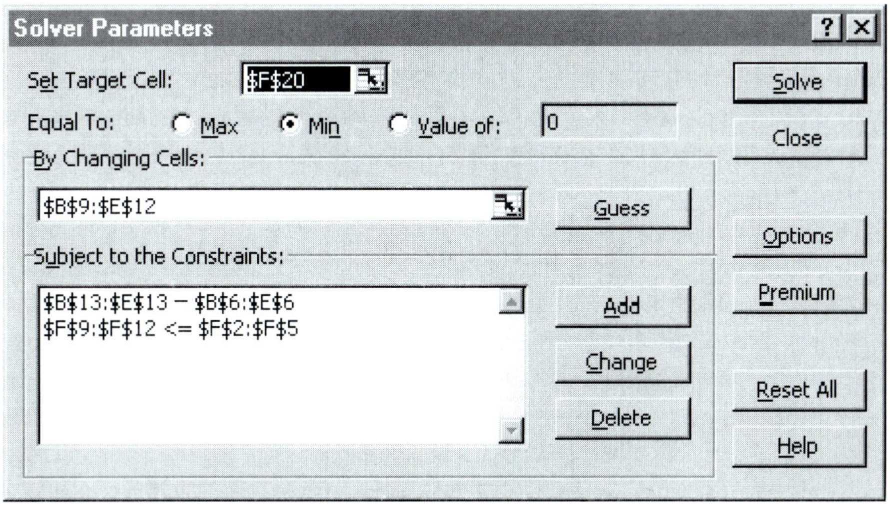

Solver parameters now need to be set. First set the target cell. This is the cell where the total cost associated with the solution is calculated. In our sample problem this is cell F20. Next we need to indicate that we are minimizing this cell. Selecting the "Min" button does this. The location of our solution is indicated in the "Changing Cells." These cells are B9 through E12 in our example.

Next we need to indicate the constraints for our problem. For our transportation problem we need to be sure that customer demand is met and that we do not exceed the capacity of our manufacturing plants. To ensure that demand is met, click on "Add" and highlight the range of cells where we have calculated the total amount being shipped to each customer. This range is B13 to E13 in our example. Next select "=" indicating that we want the amount shipped to equal demand. Finally, on the right side enter the range of cells where the actual customer demand is stated in our spreadsheet. This range is B6 to E6 in our example.

The second set of constraints that ensures that the capacity of our manufacturing plants is not exceeded is entered similarly. The range of cells that indicated how much is being shipped from each factory is F9 to F12. These values need to be less than or equal to (<=) the capacity of each factory, which is in cells F2 to F5. To set up the Solver, a few options need to be set as well. Click on the "Options" button and the following screen should appear:

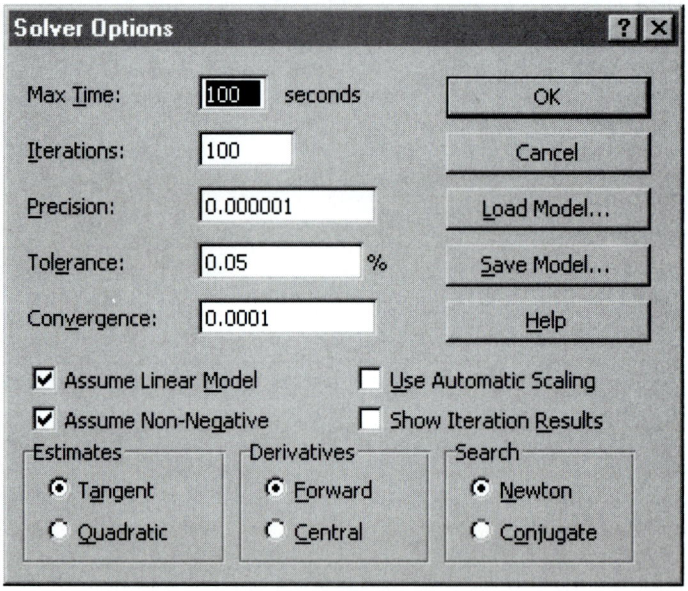


Two options need to be set for solving transportation problems. First we need "Assume Linear Model." This tells the Solver that there are no nonlinear calculations in our spreadsheet. This is important because the Solver can use a very efficient algorithm to calculate the optimal solution to this problem if this condition exists. Next the "Assume Non-Negative" box needs to be checked. This tells Solver that the values in our solution need to be greater than or equal to zero. In transportation problems shipping negative quantities does not make any sense. Click "OK" to return to the main Solver box, and then click "Solve" to actually solve the problem. Solver will notify you that it found a solution. Indicate that you want that solution saved. Finally, click OK to go back to the main spreadsheet. The solution should be in cells B9 to E12.

The transportation method can be used to solve many different types of problems if it is applied innovatively. For example, it can be used to test the cost impact of different candidate locations on the entire production–distribution network. To do this we might add a new row that contains the unit shipping cost from a factory in a new location, say Dallas, to the existing set of customer warehouses, along with the total amount it could supply. We could then solve this particular matrix for minimum total cost. Next we would replace the factory located in Dallas in the same row of the matrix with a factory at a different location, Houston, and again solve for minimum total cost. Assuming the factories in Dallas and Houston would be identical in other important respects, the location resulting in the lowest total cost for the network would be selected.

For additional information about using the Solver, see Supplement A, "Linear Programming with Excel Solver." ←

## CENTER OF GRAVITY METHOD

Center of gravity method

The **center of gravity method** is a technique for locating single facilities that considers the existing facilities, the distances between them, and the volumes of goods to be shipped. The technique is often used to locate intermediate or distribution warehouses. In its simplest form, this method assumes that inbound and outbound transportation costs are equal, and it does not include special shipping costs for less than full loads.

The center of gravity method begins by placing the existing locations on a coordinate grid system. The choice of coordinate systems is entirely arbitrary. The purpose is to establish relative distances between locations. Using longitude and latitude coordinates might be helpful in international decisions. Exhibit TN9.5 shows an example of a grid layout.

The center of gravity is found by calculating the *X* and *Y* coordinates that result in the minimal transportation cost. We use the formulas

$$C_x = \frac{\sum d_{ix} V_i}{\sum V_i}$$

$$C_y = \frac{\sum d_{iy} V_i}{\sum V_i}$$

where

$C_x$ = *X* coordinate of the center of gravity

$C_y$ = *Y* coordinate of the center of gravity

$d_{ix}$ = *X* coordinate of the *i*th location

$d_{iy}$ = *Y* coordinate of the *i*th location

$V_i$ = Volume of goods moved to or from the *i*th location

EXHIBIT TN9.5

Grid Map for Center of Gravity Example

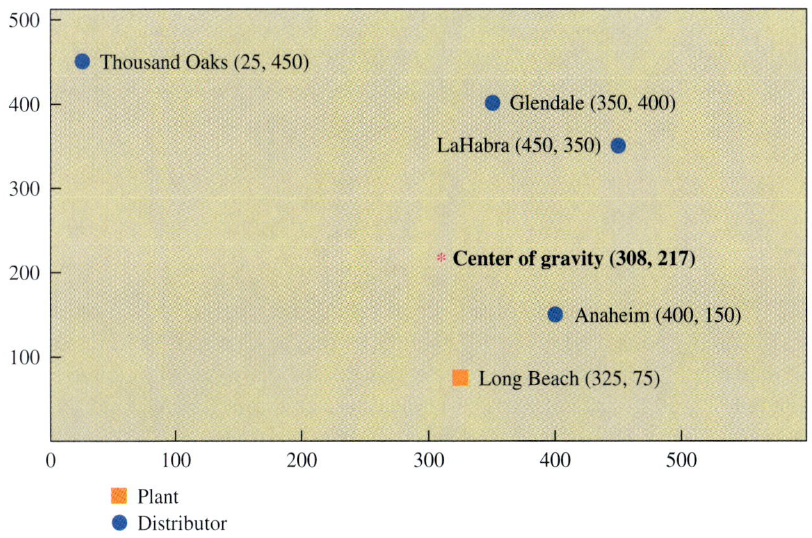

EXHIBIT TN9.6

Shipping Volumes, Center of Gravity Example

| Locations | Gallons of Gasoline per Month (000,000) |
|---|---|
| Long Beach | 1,500 |
| Anaheim | 250 |
| LaHabra | 450 |
| Glendale | 350 |
| Thousand Oaks | 450 |

### EXAMPLE TN9.2: HIOCTANE REFINING COMPANY

The HiOctane Refining Company needs to locate an intermediate holding facility between its refining plant in Long Beach and its major distributors. Exhibit TN9.5 shows the coordinate map. The amount of gasoline shipped to or from the plant and distributors appears in Exhibit TN9.6.

In this example, for the Long Beach location (the first location), $d_{1x} = 325$, $d_{1y} = 75$, and $V_1 = 1{,}500$.

### SOLUTION

Using the information in Exhibits TN9.5 and TN9.6, we can calculate the coordinates of the center of gravity:

$$C_x = \frac{(325 \times 1{,}500) + (400 \times 250) + (450 \times 450) + (350 \times 350) + (25 \times 450)}{1{,}500 + 250 + 450 + 350 + 450}$$

$$= \frac{923{,}750}{3{,}000} = 307.9$$

$$C_y = \frac{(75 \times 1{,}500) + (150 \times 250) + (350 \times 450) + (400 \times 350) + (450 \times 450)}{1{,}500 + 250 + 450 + 350 + 450}$$

$$= \frac{650{,}000}{3{,}000} = 216.7$$

This gives management the $X$ and $Y$ coordinates of approximately 308 and 217, respectively, and provides an initial starting point to search for a new site. By examining the location of the calculated center of gravity on the grid map, we can see that it might be more cost-efficient to ship directly between the Long Beach plant and the Anaheim distributor than to ship via a warehouse near the center of gravity. Before a location decision is made, management would probably recalculate the center of gravity, changing the data to reflect this (that is, decrease the gallons shipped from Long Beach by the amount Anaheim needs and remove Anaheim from the formula). ←

## LOCATING SERVICE FACILITIES

Because of the variety of service firms and the relatively low cost of establishing a service facility compared to one for manufacturing, new service facilities are far more common than new factories and warehouses. Indeed, there are few communities in which rapid population growth has not been paralleled by concurrent rapid growth in retail outlets, restaurants, municipal services, and entertainment facilities.

Services typically have multiple sites to maintain close contact with customers. The location decision is closely tied to the market selection decision. If the target market is

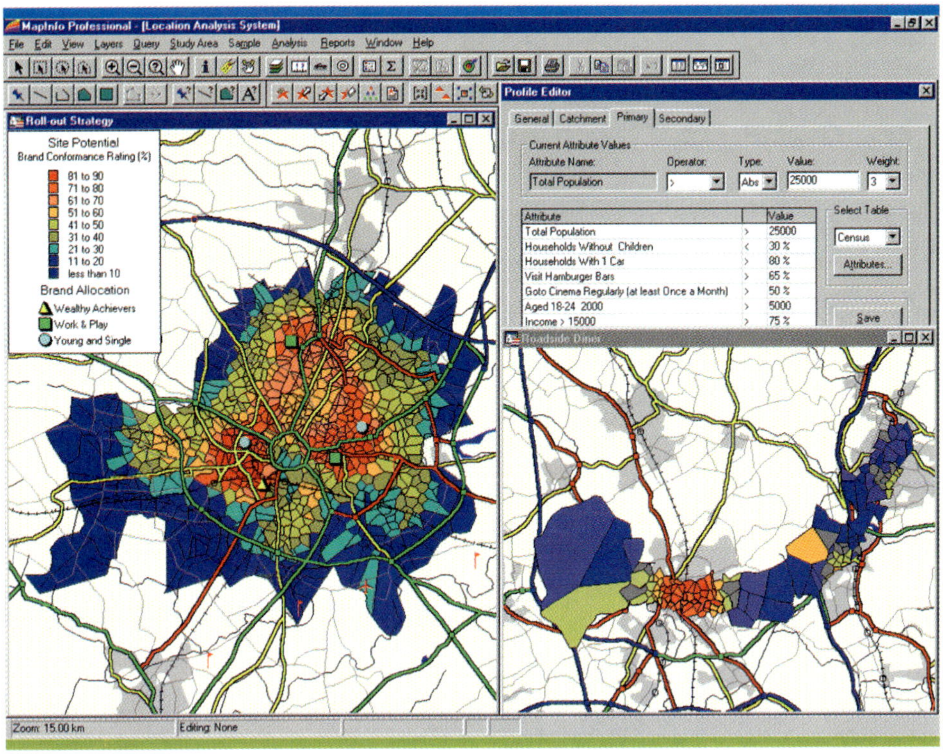


GEOGRAPHIC INFORMATION SYSTEMS (GIS), SHOWN HERE FROM MAPINFO, ARE USED BY RETAILERS, FINANCIAL SERVICES GROUPS, AND OTHERS IN THE SITE SELECTION PROCESS. MAPPING INFORMATION ON POTENTIAL SITES SUCH AS DEMOGRAPHICS, COMPETITORS, AND SO ON ALLOWS INFORMATION TO BE SEEN IN A SINGLE, COMPREHENSIVE VIEW FOR MORE INFORMED DECISION MAKING.

college-age groups, locations in retirement communities—despite desirability in terms of cost, resource availability, and so forth—are not viable alternatives. Market needs also affect the number of sites to be built and the size and characteristics of the sites. Whereas manufacturing location decisions are often made by minimizing costs, many service location decision techniques maximize the profit potential of various sites. Next we present a multiple regression model that can be used to help select good sites.

## EXAMPLE TN9.3: SCREENING LOCATION SITES AT LA QUINTA MOTOR INNS

Selecting good sites is crucial to a hotel chain's success. Of the four major marketing considerations (price, product, promotion, and location), location and product have been shown to be most important for multisite firms. As a result, hotel chain owners who can pick good sites quickly have a distinct competitive advantage.

Exhibit TN9.7 shows the initial list of variables included in a study to help La Quinta Motor Inns screen potential locations for its new hotels.[2] Data were collected on 57 existing La Quinta Inns. Analysis of the data identified the variables that correlated with operating profit in 1983 and 1986. (See Exhibit TN9.8.)

## SOLUTION

A *regression model* (see Chapter 11) was constructed. Its final form was

$$\begin{aligned}\text{Profitability} = {} & 39.05 - 5.41 \times \text{State population per inn } (1{,}000) \\ & + 5.86 \times \text{Price of the inn} \\ & - 3.91 \times \text{Square root of the median income of the area } (1{,}000) \\ & + 1.75 \times \text{College students within four miles}\end{aligned}$$

## EXHIBIT TN9.7

### Independent Variables Collected for the Initial Model-Building Stage

| CATEGORY | NAME | DESCRIPTION |
|---|---|---|
| Competitive | INNRATE | Inn price |
| | PRICE | Room rate for the inn |
| | RATE | Average competitive room rate |
| | RMS 1 | Hotel rooms within 1 mile |
| | RMSTOTAL | Hotel rooms within 3 miles |
| | ROOMSINN | Inn rooms |
| Demand generators | CIVILIAN | Civilian personnel on base |
| | COLLEGE | College enrollment |
| | HOSP1 | Hospital beds within 1 mile |
| | HOSPTOTL | Hospital beds within 4 miles |
| | HVYIND | Heavy industrial employment |
| | LGTIND | Light industrial acreage |
| | MALLS | Shopping mall square footage |
| | MILBLKD | Military base blocked |
| | MILITARY | Military personnel |
| | MILTOT | MILITARY + CIVILIAN |
| | OFC1 | Office space within 1 mile |
| | OFCTOTAL | Office space within 4 miles |
| | OFCCBD | Office space in Central Business District |
| | PASSENGR | Airport passengers enplaned |
| | RETAIL | Scale ranking of retail activity |
| | TOURISTS | Annual tourists |
| | TRAFFIC | Traffic count |
| | VAN | Airport van |
| Demographic | EMPLYPCT | Unemployment percentage |
| | INCOME | Average family income |
| | POPULACE | Residential population |
| Market awareness | AGE | Years inn has been open |
| | NEAREST | Distance to nearest inn |
| | STATE | State population per inn |
| | URBAN | Urban population per inn |
| Physical | ACCESS | Accessibility |
| | ARTERY | Major traffic artery |
| | DISTCBD | Distance to downtown |
| | SIGNVIS | Sign visibility |

## EXHIBIT TN9.8

### A Summary of the Variables That Correlated with Operating Margin in 1983 and 1986

| VARIABLE | 1983 | 1986 |
|---|---|---|
| ACCESS | .20 | |
| AGE | .29 | .49 |
| COLLEGE | | .25 |
| DISTCBD | | −.22 |
| EMPLYPCT | −.22 | −.22 |
| INCOME | | −.23 |
| MILTOT | | .22 |
| NEAREST | −.51 | |
| OFCCBD | .30 | |
| POPULACE | .30 | .35 |
| PRICE | .38 | .58 |
| RATE | | .27 |
| STATE | −.32 | −.33 |
| SIGNVIS | .25 | |
| TRAFFIC | .32 | |
| URBAN | −.22 | −.26 |

The model shows that profitability is affected by market penetration, positively affected by price, negatively affected by higher incomes (the inns do better in lower-median-income areas), and positively affected by colleges nearby.

La Quinta implemented the model on a spreadsheet and routinely uses the spreadsheet to screen potential real estate acquisitions. The founder and president of La Quinta has accepted the model's validity and no longer feels obligated to personally select the sites.

This example shows that a specific model can be obtained from the requirements of service organizations and used to identify the most important features in site selection. ←

# CONCLUSION

Facility location decisions are a key element in any firm's overall strategic plan. Dramatic changes in the global geopolitical environment, coupled with rapid advances in technology, have given decision makers a variety of options and opportunities for locating their businesses. The criteria for selecting appropriate locations have also evolved beyond the singular focus of minimizing cost or distance. Today a number of quantitative and qualitative issues impact location decisions. A company's long-term success depends on its managers' ability to make a comprehensive synthesis of the various dimensions of the multifaceted location problem.

## KEY TERMS

**Free trade zones** A closed facility (under the supervision of government customs officials) into which foreign goods can be brought without being subject to the payment of normal import duties.

**Trading bloc** A group of countries that agrees on a set of special arrangements governing the trading of goods between member countries. Companies may locate in places affected by the agreement to take advantage of new market opportunities.

**Factor-rating system** An approach for selecting a facility location by combining a diverse set of factors. Point scales are developed for each criterion. Each potential site is then evaluated on each criterion and the points are combined to calculate a rating for the site.

**Transportation method** A special linear programming method that is useful for solving problems involving transporting products from several sources to several destinations.

**Center of gravity method** A technique for locating single facilities that considers the existing facilities, the distances between them, and the volumes of goods to be shipped.

## FORMULA REVIEW

**Center of gravity**

$$C_x = \frac{\sum d_{ix} V_i}{\sum V_i}$$

$$C_y = \frac{\sum d_{iy} V_i}{\sum V_i}$$

## SOLVED PROBLEM

### SOLVED PROBLEM 1

Cool Air, a manufacturer of automotive air conditioners, currently produces its XB-300 line at three different locations: Plant A, Plant B, and Plant C. Recently management decided to build all compressors, a major product component, in a separate dedicated facility, Plant D.

Using the center of gravity method and the information displayed in Exhibits TN9.9 and TN9.10, determine the best location for Plant D. Assume a linear relationship between volumes shipped and shipping costs (no premium charges).

EXHIBIT TN9.9

Plant Location Matrix

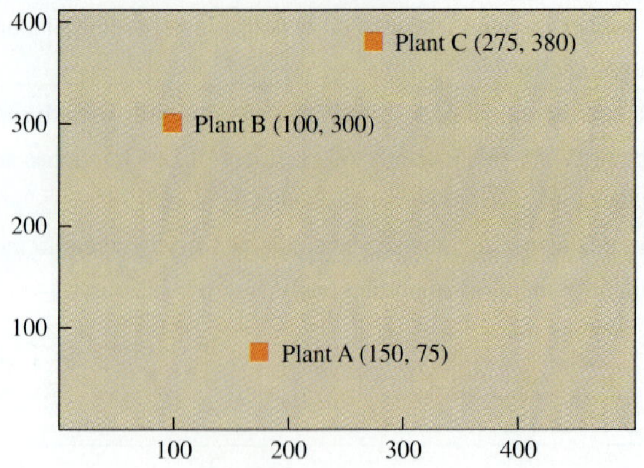


EXHIBIT TN9.10

Quantity of Compressors Required by Each Plant

| PLANT | COMPRESSORS REQUIRED PER YEAR |
|---|---|
| A | 6,000 |
| B | 8,200 |
| C | 7,000 |

## Solution

$d_{1x} = 150 \quad d_{1y} = 75 \quad V_1 = 6{,}000$

$d_{2x} = 100 \quad d_{2y} = 300 \quad V_2 = 8{,}200$

$d_{3x} = 275 \quad d_{3y} = 380 \quad V_3 = 7{,}000$

$$C_x = \frac{\sum d_{ix} V_i}{\sum V_i} = \frac{(150 \times 6{,}000) + (100 \times 8{,}200) + (275 \times 7{,}000)}{6{,}000 + 8{,}200 + 7{,}000} = 172$$

$$C_y = \frac{\sum d_{iy} V_i}{\sum V_i} = \frac{(75 \times 6{,}000) + (300 \times 8{,}200) + (380 \times 7{,}000)}{21{,}200} = 262.7$$

Plant D$[C_x, C_y]$ = D[172, 263]

## REVIEW AND DISCUSSION QUESTIONS

1 What motivations typically cause firms to initiate a facilities location or relocation project?
2 List five major reasons why a new electronic components manufacturing firm should move into your city or town.
3 How do facility location decisions differ for service facilities and manufacturing plants?
4 What are the pros and cons of relocating a small or midsized manufacturing firm (that makes mature products) from the United States to Mexico in the post-NAFTA environment?
5 If you could locate your new software development company anywhere in the world, which place would you choose, and why?

## PROBLEMS

1. $C_x = 176.7$
   $C_y = 241.5$

2. $C_x = 374$
   $C_y = 357$

1 Refer to the information given in the solved problem. Suppose management decides to shift 2,000 units of production from Plant B to Plant A. Does this change the proposed location of Plant D, the compressor production facility? If so, where should Plant D be located?
2 A small manufacturing facility is being planned that will feed parts to three heavy manufacturing facilities. The location of the current plants with their coordinates and volume

requirements is given in the following table:

| PLANT LOCATION | COORDINATES (*x*, *y*) | VOLUME (PARTS PER YEAR) |
|---|---|---|
| Peoria | 300, 320 | 4,000 |
| Decatur | 375, 470 | 6,000 |
| Joliet | 470, 180 | 3,000 |

Use the center of gravity method to determine the best location for this new facility.

3 Bindley Corporation has a one-year contract to supply motors for all washing machines produced by Rinso Ltd. Rinso manufactures the washers at four locations around the country: New York, Fort Worth, San Diego, and Minneapolis. Plans call for the following numbers of washing machines to be produced at each location:

3. See ISM.

Total profit = $4.240.

| | | | |
|---|---|---|---|
| 0 | 0 | 0 | 10 |
| 50 | 0 | 50 | 0 |
| 0 | 70 | 10 | 70 |

or

| | | | |
|---|---|---|---|
| 0 | 0 | 0 | 10 |
| 50 | 50 | 0 | 0 |
| 0 | 20 | 60 | 70 |

Alternate optimal solutions.

| | |
|---|---|
| New York | 50,000 |
| Fort Worth | 70,000 |
| San Diego | 60,000 |
| Minneapolis | 80,000 |

Bindley has three plants that can produce the motors. The plants and production capacities are

| | |
|---|---|
| Boulder | 100,000 |
| Macon | 100,000 |
| Gary | 150,000 |

Due to varying production and transportation costs, the profit Bindley earns on each 1,000 units depends on where they were produced and where they were shipped. The following table gives the accounting department estimates of the dollar profit per unit. (Shipment will be made in lots of 1,000.)

| | SHIPPED TO | | | |
|---|---|---|---|---|
| PRODUCED AT | NEW YORK | FORT WORTH | SAN DIEGO | MINNEAPOLIS |
| Boulder | 7 | 11 | 8 | 13 |
| Macon | 20 | 17 | 12 | 10 |
| Gary | 8 | 18 | 13 | 16 |

Given profit maximization as a criterion, Bindley would like to determine how many motors should be produced at each plant and how many motors should be shipped from each plant to each destination.

*a*. develop a transportation grid for this problem.

*b*. Find the optimal solution using Microsoft Excel.

4 Rent'R Cars is a multisite car rental company in the city. It is trying out a new "return the car to the location most convenient for you" policy to improve customer service. But this means that the company has to constantly move cars around the city to maintain required levels of vehicle availability. The supply and demand for economy cars, and the total cost of moving these vehicles between sites, are shown below.

4. See ISM.

| From \ To | *D* | *E* | *F* | *G* | Supply |
|---|---|---|---|---|---|
| *A* | $9 | $8 | $6 | $5 | 50 |
| *B* | 9 | 8 | 8 | 0 | 40 |
| *C* | 5 | 3 | 3 | 10 | 75 |
| Demand | 50 | 60 | 25 | 30 | 165 / 165 |

a. Find the solution that minimizes moving costs using Microsoft Excel.
b. What would you have to do to the costs to assure that A always sends a car to D as part of the optimal solution?

## CASE: APPLICHEM—THE TRANSPORTATION PROBLEM

Applichem management is faced with the difficult problem of allocating to its customers the capacity of manufacturing plants that are located around the world. Management has long recognized that the manufacturing plants differ greatly in efficiency but has had little success in improving the operations of the inefficient plants. At this time, management has decided to focus on how best to use the capacity of its plants given the differences in manufacturing costs that currently exist. They recognize that this study may result in the significant reduction of output or possibly the shutting down of one or more of the existing plants.

Applichem makes a product called Release-ease. Plastics molding manufacturers use this chemical product. Plastic parts are made by injecting hot plastic into a mold made in the shape of the part. After the plastic has sufficiently cooled, the fresh part is removed from the mold and the mold is then reused to make subsequent parts. Release-ease is a dry powder, applied as part of the manufacturing process, that makes it easy to remove the part from the mold.

Applichem has made the product since the early 1950s, and demand has been consistent over time. A recent study by Applichem's market research team has indicated that demand for Release-ease should be fairly steady for the next five years. Although Applichem does have some competition, particularly in the European markets, management feels that as long as they can provide a quality product at a competitive cost, customers should stick with Applichem. Release-ease sells at an average price of $1.00 per pound.

The company owns plants capable of making Release-ease in the following cities: Gary, Indiana; Windsor Ontario, Canada; Frankfurt, Germany; Mexico City, Mexico; Caracas, Venezuela; and Osaka, Japan. Although the plants are focused on meeting demand for the immediate surrounding regions, there is considerable exporting and importing of product for various reasons. The following table contains data on how demand has been met during the past year:

PRODUCT MADE AND SHIPPED DURING PAST YEAR (×100,000 POUNDS)

| FROM/TO | MEXICO | CANADA | VENEZUELA | EUROPE | UNITED STATES | JAPAN |
|---|---|---|---|---|---|---|
| Mexico City | 3.0 | | 6.3 | | | 7.9 |
| Windsor Ontario | | 2.6 | | | | |
| Caracas | | | 4.1 | | | |
| Frankfort | | | 5.6 | 20.0 | 12.4 | |
| Gary | | | | | 14.0 | |
| Osaka | | | | | | 4.0 |

Differences in the technologies used in the plants and in local raw material and labor costs created significant differences in the cost to produce Release-ease in the various locations. These costs may change dramatically due to currency valuation and labor law changes in some of the countries. This is especially true in Mexico and Venezuela. The capacity of each plant also differs at each location, and management has no interest in increasing capacity anywhere at this time. The following table gives details on the costs to produce and capacity of each plant:

PLANT PRODUCTION COSTS AND CAPACITY

| PLANT | PRODUCTION COST (PER 1,000 LBS) | PLANT CAPACITY (×100,000 LBS) |
|---|---|---|
| Mexico City | 95.01 | 22.0 |
| Windsor Ontario | 97.35 | 3.7 |
| Caracas | 116.34 | 4.5 |
| Frankfurt | 76.69 | 47.0 |
| Gary | 102.93 | 18.5 |
| Osaka | 153.80 | 5.0 |

In considering how best to use the capacity of its plants, Applichem management needs to consider the cost of shipping product from one customer region to another. Applichem now commonly ships product in bulk around the world, but it is expensive. The costs involved are not only the transportation costs but also import duties that are assessed by customs in some countries. Applichem is committed to meeting demand, though, and sometimes this is done even though profit might not be made on all orders.

The following table details the demand in each country, the cost to transport product from each plant to each country, and the current import duty rate levied by each country. (These percentages do not reflect current duties.) Import duty is calculated on the approximate cost of the amount of product brought into the country. (For example, if the cost for 1,000 pounds of Release-ease shipped into Venezuela were $100, the import duty would be $100 × .5 = $50.)

TRANSPORTATION COST (PER 1,000 LBS), IMPORT DUTIES, AND DEMANDS FOR RELEASE-EASE

| PLANT/COUNTRY | MEXICO | CANADA | VENEZUELA | EUROPE | UNITED STATES | JAPAN |
|---|---|---|---|---|---|---|
| Mexico City | 0 | 11.40 | 7.00 | 11.00 | 11.00 | 14.00 |
| Windsor Ontario | 11.00 | 0 | 9.00 | 11.50 | 6.00 | 13.00 |
| Caracas | 7.00 | 10.00 | 0 | 13.00 | 10.40 | 14.30 |
| Frankfurt | 10.00 | 11.50 | 12.50 | 0 | 11.20 | 13.30 |
| Gary | 10.00 | 6.00 | 11.00 | 10.00 | 0 | 12.50 |
| Osaka | 14.00 | 13.00 | 12.50 | 14.20 | 13.00 | 0 |
| Total Demand (×100,000 lbs) | 3.0 | 2.6 | 16.0 | 20.0 | 26.4 | 11.9 |
| Import Duty | 0.0% | 0.0% | 50.0% | 9.5% | 4.5% | 6.0% |

QUESTIONS

Given all this data, set up a spreadsheet (Applichem.xls is a start) and answer the following questions for management:

1 Evaluate the cost associated with the way Applichem's plant capacity is currently being used.
2 Determine the optimal use of Applichem's plant capacity using the Solver in Excel.
3 What would you recommend that Applichem management do? Why?

SOURCE: THIS CASE IS ROUGHLY BASED ON DATA CONTAINED IN "APPLICHEM (A)," HARVARD BUSINESS SCHOOL, 9-685-051.

## CASE: THE PLANT LOCATION PUZZLE[3]

Ann Reardon made her way across the crowded tradeshow floor, deep in thought and oblivious to the noisy activity all around her. As CEO of the Eldora Company (EDC) for the previous 13 years, she had led her organization through a period of extraordinary success. While larger bicycle makers had moved their manufacturing operations overseas to take advantage of lower labor costs, Eldora had stuck with a domestic manufacturing strategy, keeping its plant on the same campus as its corporate offices in Boulder, Colorado. Ann felt that her strategy of keeping all the parts of the company in the same location. Although unconventional, had contributed greatly to cooperation among various departments and, ultimately, to the company's growth: EDC had become the largest and most profitable bicycle company in the United States. Yet her manufacturing vice president, Sean Andrews, was now urging her to build a plant in China.

"Look at the number of companies here," he had said that morning, as they helped several other EDC staffers stack brochures on the exhibit table and position the company's latest models around the perimeter of their area. Manufacturing heads rarely attended trade shows; in fact, this was Sean's first, but he had wanted to attend, and Ann had supported his interest. "There are too many players in this market," he had said. "I've been saying this for two months now, and you know the forecasters' numbers back me up. But if they weren't enough to convince you, just look around. The industry is reaching the saturation point here in the States. We have to break into Asia."

"Leave it alone, Sean," Ann had replied. "I know this is something you're pushing; you've said so in the past. But let's set up a time to talk about it in detail later. This isn't the time or the place."

Now, three hours later, with the show in full swing, Ann understood why Sean had been compelled to speak up again. Having all their competitors in the same room at the same time was a powerful visual reminder of how the industry had changed. She thought about what Sean had said about the U.S. market. In 1992 EDC's sales and earnings had hit record levels. The company now produced almost 30 percent of the bicycles sold in the United States. U.S. mass-market bicycle sales were growing by only 2 percent per year, while the Asian market for those same bikes was nearly doubling annually. And Eldora could not competitively serve those markets from its U.S. manufacturing facility. Two of the largest bike manufacturers in the world, located in rapidly growing Asian markets, enjoyed a significant labor and distribution cost advantage.

She stopped at a mountain bike display set up by a fast-growing young bike company. Mountain bikes with front suspension were the latest trend—the added support and cushion allowed riders to better absorb the shocks inherent in off-road riding without slowing down or losing balance. Most of these bikes were still prohibitively expensive. But Eldora, too, had an entry in this product category, retailing for about $190, and Ann was proud of it. For years, the company had concentrated its efforts on inexpensive bicycles, which retailed through mass merchandisers for between $100 and $200. Eldora's prices were slightly higher than other low-end competitors, but large retailers were willing to pay the premium because EDC had consistently been able to offer many state-of-the-art styles and features with quick, timely deliveries that competitors building overseas couldn't match.

One of the reasons the company had been so successful was that Boulder, Colorado, was a bicyclists' mecca. Eldora employees at all levels shared a genuine love of bicycling and eagerly pursued knowledge of the industry's latest trends and styles. Someone was always suggesting a better way to position the hand brakes or a new toe grip that allowed for better traction and easier dismounts. And Eldora never had a shortage of people willing to test out the latest prototypes.

Another reason was that all marketing staff, engineers, designers, and manufacturing personnel worked on one campus, within a 10-minute walk of one another. Ann had bet big on that strategy, and it had paid off. Communication was easy, and changes in styles, production plans, and the like could be made quickly and efficiently. Mountain bikes, for example, had gone from 0 percent to more than 50 percent of the market volume since 1988, and Eldora had met the increased demand with ease. And when orders for cross-bikes—a mountain/road bike hybrid that had enjoyed a spurt of popularity—began to fall off, Eldora had been able to adjust its production run with minimal disruption.

EDC had also benefited from its foray into the high-end market (bicycles retailing for between $400 and $700) 12 years earlier. One of Ann's first moves as CEO had been to enter into a joint venture with Rinaldi, a high-end Italian bicycle manufacturer that at the time was specializing in racing models. As part of the agreement, EDC had begun importing Rinaldi bikes under the brand name Summit and selling them through specialty bike dealers. Similarly, Rinaldi had begun marketing EDC bikes in Europe. That arrangement had had lasting rewards: Although racing bikes were no longer very popular, EDC's offerings had taken off. About 20 percent of EDC's sales were now made outside the United States (primarily in Europe and Canada) through this and other agreements.

The relationships with Rinaldi and the specialty bike shops also helped keep EDC management aware of the latest industry trends over the years. Most recently, those trends had included a move toward more exotic frame materials like aluminum and carbon fiber and more advanced components, including the new front-fork suspension systems. Ann examined another rival's brochure touting a soon-to-be-released high-end model with these advances. EDC engineers were clearly ahead of the curve.

Her satisfaction was quickly tempered with thoughts of foreign sales performance. Between 1987 and 1991, EDC's foreign sales had grown at an annual rate of over 80 percent. But during the previous two years they had been flat.

Sean appeared at Ann's side, jolting her out of her thoughts and into the reality of her surroundings. "Dale just finished up the first round of retailers' meetings," he said. "We'd like to get some lunch back over at the hotel and talk about our options." Dale Stewart was Eldora's marketing vice president. His views of what was best for the company often differed from Sean's, but the two had an amiable working relationship and enjoyed frequent spirited verbal sparring matches.

"You won't let this go, will you," Ann said, throwing up her hands in a gesture of surrender. "Fine, let's talk. But you know I won't make a decision until we've had a more formal round of discussions back in Boulder next month."

Over sandwiches, Sean made his case. "Our primary markets in North America and western Europe represent less than a quarter of the worldwide demand. Of the 200 million bicycles made in the world last year, 40 million were sold in China, 30 million in India, and 9 million in Japan. Historically, bikes sold in Asia's developing markets were low-end products used as primary modes of transportation. But the economic picture is changing fast. There's a growing middle class. Suddenly people have disposable income. Many consumers there are now seeking higher quality and trendier styles. Mountain bikes with suspension are in. And cross-bikes are still holding their own. In fact, the demand in these markets for the product categories we produce has been doubling annually, and the growth rates seem sustainable.

"If we're going to compete in Asia, though, we need a local plant. My staff has evaluated many locations there. We've looked at wage rates, proximity to markets, and materials costs, and we feel that China is our best bet. We'd like to open a plant there as soon as possible, and start building our position."

Dale jumped in. "Two of our largest competitors, one from China, one from Taiwan, have been filling the demand so far," he said. "In 1990, 97 percent of the volume produced by these companies was for export. In 1994, they are projecting that 45 percent of their production will be for local markets. We can't compete with them from here. About 20 percent of our product cost is labor, and the hourly wages of the manufacturing workforce in these countries are between 5 percent and 15 percent of ours. It also costs us an additional 20 percent in transportation and duties to get our bicycles to these markets."

He glanced at Sean quickly and continued. "But here's where I disagree with Sean. I think we need a short-term solution. These companies have a big lead on us, and the more I think about it, the more I believe we need to put a direct sales operation in Asia first."

"Dale, you're crazy," Sean said, pouring himself some ice water from the pitcher on the table. "What good would an Asian sales operation do without a manufacturing plant? I know we source components in Asia now, but we could save another 10 percent of those parts if we were located there. Then we would really be bringing Eldora to Asia. If we want to compete there, we have to play from our greatest strength—quality. If we did it your way, you wouldn't be selling Eldora bikes. You'd just be selling some product with our label on it. You wouldn't get the quality. You wouldn't build the same kind of reputation we have here. It wouldn't really be Eldora. Over the long term, it couldn't work."

"We're building bicycles, not rocket ships," Dale countered. "There are lots of companies in Asia that could provide us with a product very quickly if we gave them our designs and helped them with their production process. We could outsource production in the short term until we made more permanent arrangements." He turned to Ann. "We could even outsource the product permanently, despite what Sean says. What do we know about building and running a plant in China? All I know is we're losing potential share even as we sit here. The trading companies aren't giving our products the attention they deserve, and they also aren't giving us the information we need on the features that consumers in these markets want. A sales operation would help us learn the market even as we're entering it. Setting up a plant first would take too long. We need to be over there now, and opening a sales operation is the quickest way."

Ann cut in. "Dale has a good point, Sean," she said. "We've been successful here in large part because our entire operation is in Boulder, on one site. We've had complete control over our own flexible manufacturing operation, and that's been a key factor in our ability to meet rapid change in the local market. How would we address the challenges inherent in manufacturing in a facility halfway around the world? Would you consider moving there? And for how long?

"Also, think about our other options. If the biggest issue keeping us out of these markets right now is cost, then both of you are ignoring a few obvious alternatives. Right now, only our frame-building operation is automated. We could cut labor costs significantly by automating more processes. And why are you so bent on China? Frankly, when I was there last month touring facilities, a lot of what I saw worried me. You know, that day I was supposed to tour a production facility, there was a power failure. Judging by the reactions of the personnel in the plant the next day, these outages are common. The roads to the facility are in very poor condition. And wastewater and cleaning solvents are regularly dumped untreated into the waterways. We could operate differently if we located there, but what impact would that have on costs?

"Taiwan has a better-developed infrastructure than China. What about making that our Asian base? And I've heard that Singapore offers attractive tax arrangements to new manufacturing operations. Then there's Mexico. It's closer to home, and aside from distribution costs, the wage rates are similar to Asia's and many of the other risks would be minimized. You both feel strongly about this, I know, but this isn't a decision we can make based on enthusiasm." Ann crumpled up her sandwich wrapper and drank the last of her soda. "Let's get back over to the exhibits. I'm attending the IT seminar at 1:30. We'll schedule a formal meeting on this subject soon. I was going to say next month, but how about bumping it up two weeks?"

Walking back to the convention center with Dale and Sean, Ann realized that she wasn't just frustrated because she didn't know which course EDC should pursue. She was concerned that she really didn't know which aspects of the decision were important and which were irrelevant. Should she establish a division in China? If so, which functions should she start with? Manufacturing? Marketing? And what about engineering? Or should she consider a different location? Would China's low labor costs offset problems caused by a poor infrastructure?

Growth had always been vitally important to Eldora, both in creating value to shareholders and in providing a work environment that could attract and retain the most talented people. Now it appeared that Ann would have to choose between continued growth and a domestic-only manufacturing strategy that had served her well. Ann knew the plant location decision she had made years earlier had been critical to the company's success, and she felt the company's next move would be just as crucial.

QUESTIONS

1 What is the competitive environment facing EDC?
2 What are EDC's strengths in manufacturing?
3 Should EDC establish a manufacturing division in Asia?
4 What plan of action would you recommend to Ann Reardon?



## SELECTED BIBLIOGRAPHY

Ballou, R. H. *Business Logistics Management,* 4th ed. Upper Saddle River, NJ: Prentice Hall, 1998.

Drezner, Z. *Facility Location: A Survey of Applications and Methods.* New York: Springer, 1995.

Francis, R. L., and J. A. White. *Facilities Layout and Location: An Analytical Approach.* Englewood Cliffs, NJ: Prentice Hall, 1992.

Khumawala, B. M., and D. C. Whybark. *The Use of Economic Logic in Facility Location.* West Lafayette, IN: Institute for Research in the Behavioral, Economic, and Management Sciences, Krannert School, Purdue University, 1975.

Skinner, W. "The Focused Factory." *Harvard Business Review.* May–June 1974, pp. 113–21.

Sule, D. R. *Manufacturing Facilities: Location, Planning and Design.* Boston: PWS Publishing Company, 1994.

## FOOTNOTES

1 M. E. Porter, "The Competitive Advantage of Nations." *Harvard Business Review.* March–April 1990.

2 S. E. Kimes and J. A. Fitzsimmons, "Selecting Profitable Hotel Sites at La Quinta Motor Inns." *Interfaces* 20 (March–April 1990), pp. 12–20.

3 This is a broad top-management–oriented strategy case designed to elicit debate.

chapter

*chapter ten*

# JUST-IN-TIME AND LEAN SYSTEMS

## CHAPTER OUTLINE

# 10

## AN AUTOMAKER TRIES THE DELL WAY

Toyota Motor Corp. announced recently that it will begin producing the Camry Solara coupe to customer order in just five days, and it will do the same for other models starting later this year. The announcement surprised an industry that typically requires 30 to 60 days to produce a custom order.

The Toyota announcement raises two questions. First, will the automobile industry, which now predominantly follows a "make to stock" model in North America, change to "make to order," which is more common in Europe and in Japan? Second, will Toyota gain a significant competitive advantage by making this transition first?

For years automakers have made manufacturing decisions by taking an educated guess at consumer demand. This leaves a lot of customers less than fully satisfied. A 1997 Boston Consulting Group study found that nearly half of car buyers couldn't find the configuration or model they wanted. To induce customers to compromise, manufacturers offer rebates and dealers offer deep discounts. It's a lose–lose proposition: Consumers chafe at haggling over price and buying cars they don't really want. Automakers and dealers underwrite billions of dollars of stagnant inventory and see their profits shaved by discounting.

But until now, no major manufacturer was prepared to offer quick custom-order delivery. Some visionaries predicted a 15-day car, but no one thought it was just around the corner. There is plenty of skepticism about whether Toyota can achieve a five-day car without making unacceptable compromises in flexibility and total delivery lead time. Toyota's announcement, however, leaves little doubt about the company's strategy. It was not a trial balloon but a confident statement of intent.

How much competitive advantage can Toyota gain from a five-day car? The Dell success story offers an interesting parallel, although Dell sells directly to customers while Toyota will continue to sell through dealers. Even so, Toyota can derive huge savings from a build-to-order strategy as it helps dealers drive down retail inventories.

Tom Meredith, Dell's chief financial officer, enumerated other benefits of the build-to-order model when he recently spoke to a group of automakers at an industry conference in Troy, Michigan. He explained that building to order leaves customers more satisfied and encourages their loyalty. It also yields a high-velocity supply chain with tight connections to customers and suppliers, dramatically reduced inventories, and increased return on assets. Dell has even put in place a business model in which cash from sales comes in before being paid out to suppliers. Forging a stronger competitive position should also enhance Toyota's relationships with its dealers.

How the industry changes will depend largely on competitive response. In the PC market, Dell's competitors took a beating precisely because they were slow to answer Dell's strategy. Sticking to their entrenched retail channels, they steadily lost market share. Eventually, they came to the inevitable conclusion that the existing approach was no longer competitive. By then they had lost billions of dollars in shareholder value and thousands of jobs.

Automakers could enjoy the benefit of 20/20 hindsight by looking closely at the fallout from failed leadership in the PC industry. With Toyota having made the first move, a competitive build-to-order strategy is now critical for every automaker in the North American marketplace. ←

The most significant production management approach of the post–World War II era is just-in-time (JIT) production. Developed by the Japanese and particularly Toyota, the automaker described in the opening vignette, this approach focuses on streamlining the flow of materials and producing exceptionally high-quality goods and services. Virtually every modern manufacturing organization has used at least some JIT elements in its design. This chapter relates the logic of JIT. It also details approaches to JIT implementation and JIT's application in service organizations. (See the box "Historical Note" for additional information.)

## JIT LOGIC

JIT (Just-in-time)

Vol. IV "JIT at Federal Signal"
Vol. V "Tri State Converting to JIT"

**JIT (just-in-time)** is an integrated set of activities designed to achieve high-volume production using minimal inventories of raw materials, work-in-process, and finished goods. Parts arrive at the next workstation "just in time" and are completed and move through the operation quickly. Just-in-time is also based on the logic that nothing will be produced until it is needed. Exhibit 10.1 illustrates the process. Need is created by actual demand for the product. When an item is sold, in theory, the market pulls a replacement from the last position in the system—final assembly in this case. This triggers an order to the factory production line, where a worker then pulls another unit from an upstream

## HISTORICAL NOTE

JIT gained worldwide prominence in the 1970s, but some of its philosophy can be traced to the early 1900s in the United States. Henry Ford used JIT concepts as he streamlined his moving assembly lines to make automobiles. For example, to eliminate waste, he used the bottom of the packing crates for car seats as the floor board of the car. Although elements of JIT were being used by Japanese industry as early as the 1930s, it was not fully refined until the 1970s, when Tai-ichi Ohno of Toyota Motors used JIT to take Toyota's cars to the forefront of delivery time and quality. Around the same time, quality experts Deming and Juran lectured on the need for American producers to adopt many JIT principles.

EXHIBIT 10.1

JIT Pull System

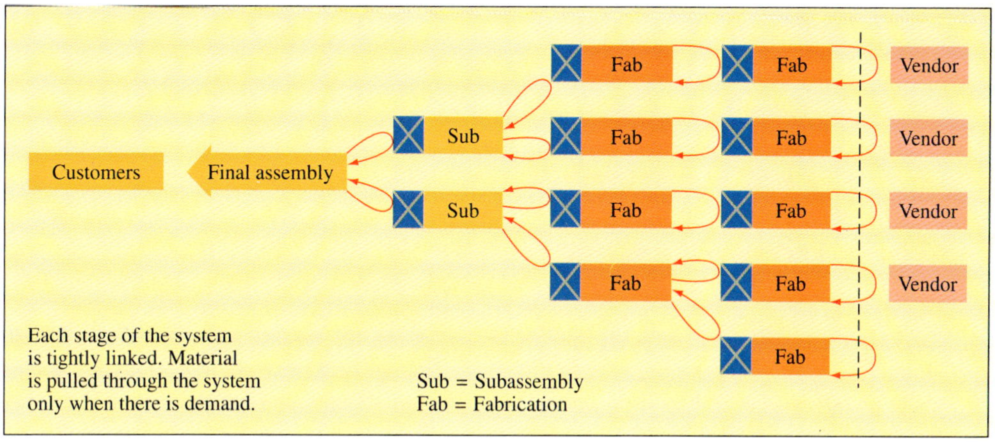


station in the flow to replace the unit taken. This upstream station then pulls from the next station further upstream and so on back to the release of raw materials. To enable this pull process to work smoothly, JIT demands high levels of quality at each stage of the process, strong vendor relations, and a fairly predictable demand for the end product.

JIT can be viewed colloquially as "big JIT" and "little JIT." Big JIT (often termed lean production[1]) is the philosophy of operations management that seeks to eliminate waste in all aspects of a firm's production activities: human relations, vendor relations, technology, and the management of materials and inventories. Little JIT focuses more narrowly on scheduling goods inventories and providing service resources where and when needed.

## THE JAPANESE APPROACH TO PRODUCTIVITY[2]

The Japanese have had a national goal of full employment through industrialization since World War II. The strategy for obtaining market dominance has been targeted to specific product areas—in particular, automotive assembly and consumer electronics. To improve their country's competitive posture, they imported technology. Instead of inventing new technology, they avoided major R&D expenditures and corresponding risks by buying licensing agreements, frequently from U.S. companies. To make these new products, they concentrated their efforts on the factory floor to achieve high productivity and lower unit costs. They directed their best engineering talent to the shop floor, not to product design activities. They also worked to improve product quality and reliability above what competitors could supply. Central to this effort were two philosophies: elimination of waste and respect for people.

## ELIMINATION OF WASTE

The Japanese truly believe in eliminating waste. Waste in Japan, as defined by Toyota's Fujio Cho, is "anything other than the minimum amount of equipment, materials, parts, and workers (working time) which are absolutely essential to production." [An expanded JIT definition advanced by Fujio Cho identifies seven prominent types of waste to be eliminated: (1) waste from overproduction, (2) waste of waiting time, (3) transportation waste, (4) inventory waste, (5) processing waste, (6) waste of motion, and (7) waste from product defects.[3]]

This definition of JIT leaves no room for surplus or safety stock. No safety stocks are allowed because if you cannot use it now, you do not need to make it now; that would be waste. Hidden inventory in storage areas, transit systems, carousels, and conveyors is a key target for inventory reduction.

The seven elements that address elimination of waste are

1. Focused factory networks.
2. Group technology.
3. Quality at the source.
4. JIT production.
5. Uniform plant loading.
6. Kanban production control system.
7. Minimized setup times.

**Focused Factory Networks** The Japanese build small specialized plants rather than large vertically integrated manufacturing facilities. They find large operations and their bureaucracies difficult to manage and not in line with their management styles. Plants designed for one purpose can be constructed and operated more economically. The bulk of Japanese plants, some 60,000, have between 30 and 1,000 workers.

Group technology

**Group Technology** Although invented in the United States, **group technology** was most successfully employed in Japan. This is a philosophy in which similar parts are grouped into families, and the processes required to make the parts are arranged in a specialized work cell. Instead of transferring jobs from one department to another to specialized workers, the Japanese consider all operations required to make a part and group those machines together. Exhibit 10.2 illustrates the difference between the clusters of various machines grouped into work centers for parts versus departmental layouts. The group

EXHIBIT 10.2

**Group Technology versus Departmental Specialty**

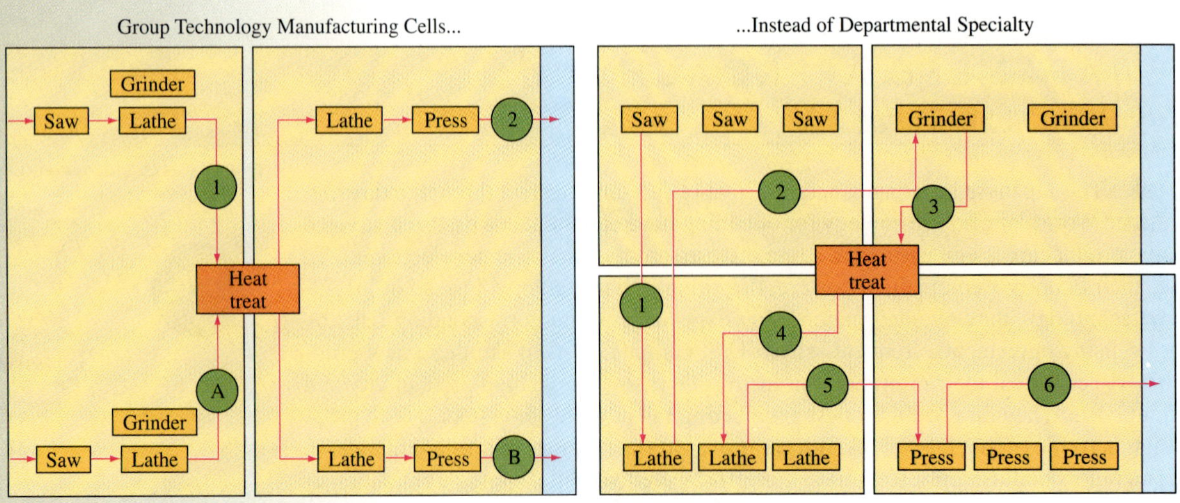

technology cells eliminate movement and queue (waiting) time between operations, reduce inventory, and reduce the number of employees required. Workers, however, must be flexible to run several machines and processes. Due to their advanced skill level, these workers have increased job security. (Group technology cells are described in more depth in Technical Note 5.)

Quality at the source

**Quality at the Source** **Quality at the source** means do it right the first time and, when something goes wrong, stop the process or assembly line immediately. Factory workers become their own inspectors, personally responsible for the quality of their output. Workers concentrate on one part of the job at a time so quality problems are uncovered. If the pace is too fast, if the worker finds a quality problem, or if a safety issue is discovered, the worker is obligated to push a button to stop the line and turn on a visual signal. People from other areas respond to the alarm and the problem. Workers are empowered to do their own maintenance and housekeeping until the problem is fixed.

**JIT Production** JIT means producing what is needed when needed and no more. Anything over the minimum amount necessary is viewed as waste, because effort and material expended for something not needed now cannot be utilized now. This is in contrast to relying on extra material just in case something goes wrong. Exhibit 10.3 shows JIT requirements and assumptions.

JIT is typically applied to repetitive manufacturing, which is when the same or similar items are made one after another. JIT does not require large volumes and can be applied to

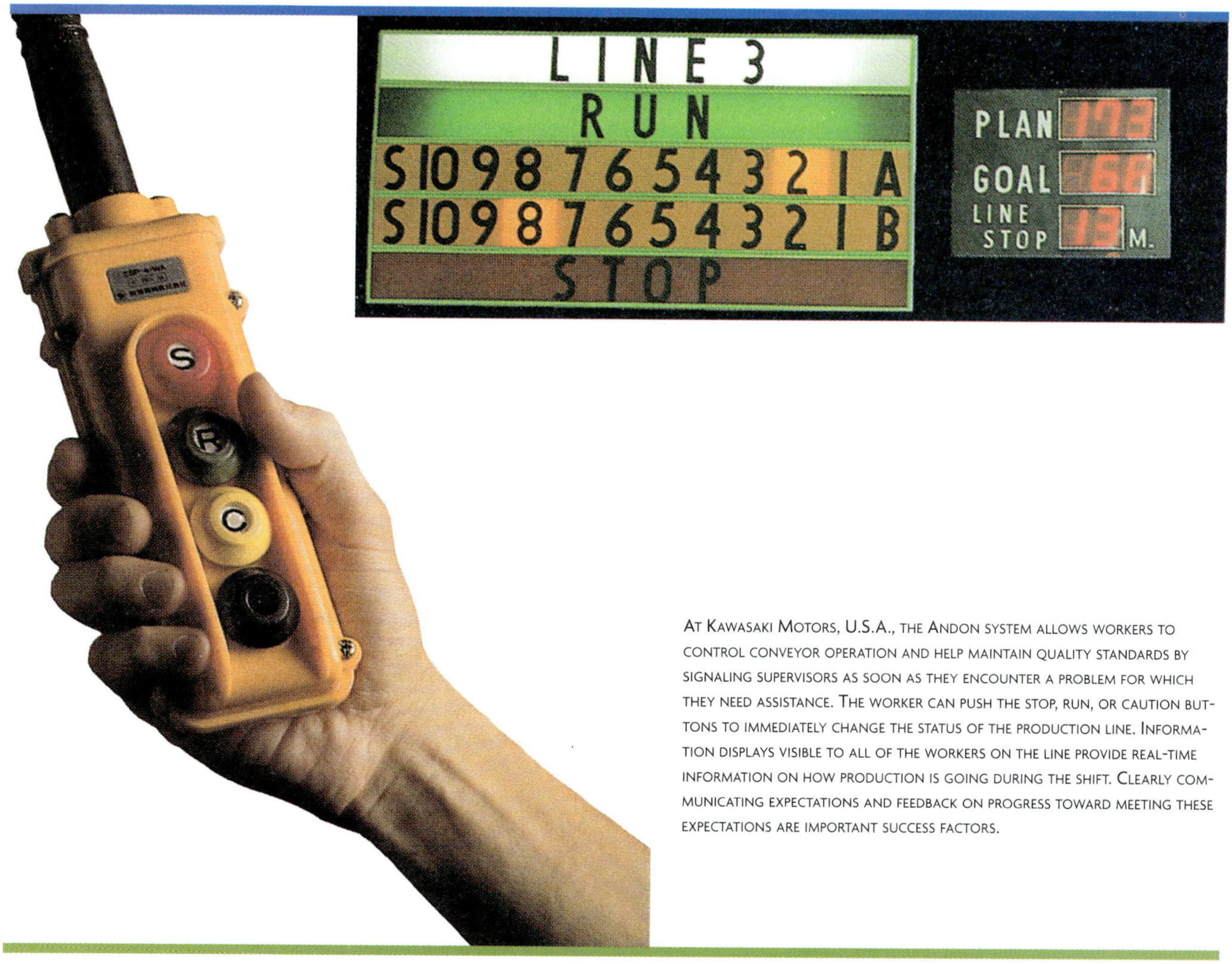


At Kawasaki Motors, U.S.A., the Andon system allows workers to control conveyor operation and help maintain quality standards by signaling supervisors as soon as they encounter a problem for which they need assistance. The worker can push the stop, run, or caution buttons to immediately change the status of the production line. Information displays visible to all of the workers on the line provide real-time information on how production is going during the shift. Clearly communicating expectations and feedback on progress toward meeting these expectations are important success factors.

EXHIBIT 10.3

**Just-in-Time Production**

**WHAT IT IS**
- Management philosophy
- "Pull" system through the plant

**WHAT IT DOES**
- Attacks waste (time, inventory, scrap)
- Exposes problems and bottlenecks
- Achieves streamlined production

**WHAT IT REQUIRES**
- Employee participation
- Industrial engineering/basics
- Continuing improvement
- Total quality control
- Small lot sizes

**WHAT IT ASSUMES**
- Stable environment

EXHIBIT 10.4

**Inventory Hides Problems**

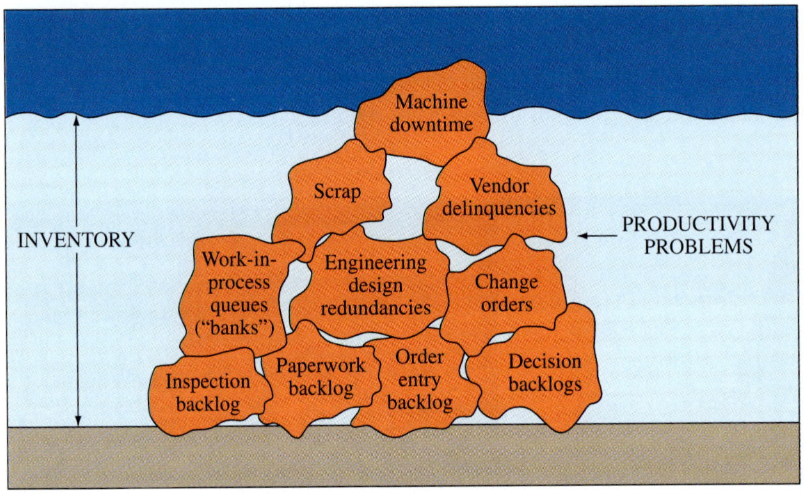


any repetitive segments of a business regardless of where they appear. Under JIT the ideal lot size is one. Although workstations may be geographically dispersed, the Japanese minimize transit time and keep transfer quantities small—typically one-tenth of a day's production. Vendors even ship several times a day to their customers to keep lot sizes small and inventory low. The goal is to drive all inventory queues to zero thus minimizing inventory investment and shortening lead times.

When inventory levels are low, quality problems become very visible. Exhibit 10.4 illustrates this idea. If the water in a pond represents inventory, the rocks represent problems that could occur in a firm. A high level of water hides the problems (rocks). Management assumes everything is fine, but as the water level drops in an economic downturn, problems are presented. If you deliberately force the water level down (particularly in good economic times), you can expose and correct problems before they cause worse problems. JIT manufacturing exposes problems otherwise hidden by excess inventories and staff.

Uniform plant loading

**Uniform Plant Loading** Smoothing the production flow to dampen the reaction waves that normally occur in response to schedule variations is called **uniform plant loading.** When a change is made in a final assembly, the changes are magnified throughout the line and the supply chain. The only way to eliminate the problem is to make adjustments as small as possible by setting a firm monthly production plan for which the output rate is

EXHIBIT 10.5

Toyota Example of Mixed-Model Production Cycle in a Japanese Assembly Plant

| Model | Monthly Quantity | Daily Quantity | Model Cycle Time (Minutes) |
|---|---|---|---|
| Sedan | 5,000 | 250 | 2 |
| Hardtop | 2,500 | 125 | 4 |
| Wagon | 2,500 | 125 | 4 |

Sequence: Sedan, hardtop, sedan, wagon, sedan, hardtop, sedan, wagon, and so on (one minute apart).

EXHIBIT 10.6

Flow of Two Kanbans

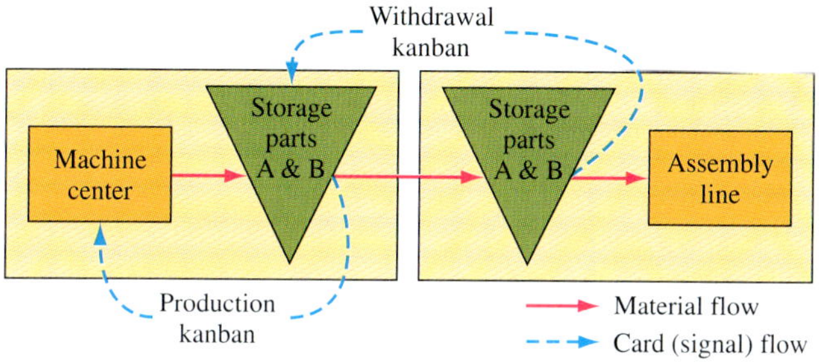


frozen. (This is how a company addresses the need for a stable demand environment noted in Exhibit 10.3.)

The Japanese found they could do this by building the same mix of products every day in small quantities. Thus they always have a total mix available to respond to variations in demand. A Toyota example is shown in Exhibit 10.5. Monthly car style quantities are reduced to daily quantities (assuming a 20-day month) in order to compute a model *cycle time* (defined here as the time between two identical units being completed on the line). The cycle time figure is used to adjust resources to produce the precise quantity needed. The speed of equipment or of the production line is adjusted so only the needed quantity is produced each day. JIT strives to produce on schedule, on cost, and on quality. (Additional discussion of mixed-model assembly is provided in Technical Note 5.)

**Kanban Production Control Systems** A kanban control system uses a signaling device to regulate JIT flows. **Kanban** means "sign" or "instruction card" in Japanese. In a paperless control system, containers can be used instead of cards. The cards or containers make up the **kanban pull system.** The authority to produce or supply additional parts comes from downstream operations. Consider Exhibit 10.6, where we show an assembly line that is supplied with parts by a machine center. The machine center makes two parts, A and B. These two parts are stored in containers that are located next to the assembly line and next to the machine center. Each container next to the assembly line has a withdrawal kanban, and each container next to the machine center has a production kanban. This is often referred to as a two-card kanban system.

Kanban

Kanban pull system

When the assembly line takes the first part A from a full container, a worker takes the withdrawal kanban from the container, and takes the card to the machine center storage area. In the machine center area, the worker finds a container of part A, removes the production kanban, and replaces it with the withdrawal kanban. Placement of this card on the container authorizes the movement of the container to the assembly line. The freed production kanban is placed on a rack by the machine center, which authorizes the production of another lot of material. The cards on the rack become the dispatch list for the machine center. Cards are not the only way to signal the need for production of a part; other visual methods are possible, as shown in Exhibit 10.7.

EXHIBIT 10.7

Diagram of Outbound Stockpoint with Warning Signal Marker

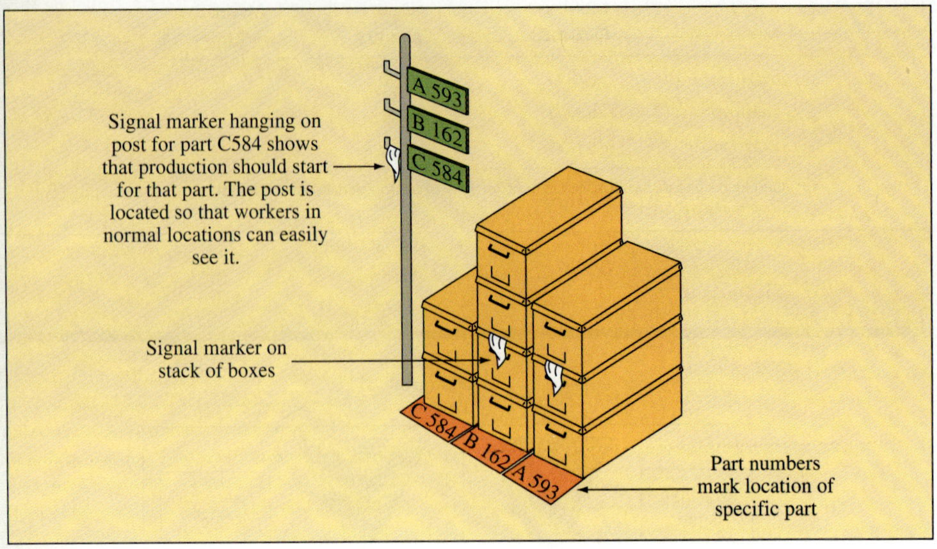


The following are some other possible approaches:

**Container system.** Sometimes the container itself can be used as a signal device. In this case, an empty container on the factory floor visually signals the need to fill it. The amount of inventory is adjusted by simply adding or removing containers.

**Kanban squares.** Some companies use marked spaces on the floor or on a table to identify where material should be stored. When the square is empty, like the one on the left, the supplying operations are authorized to produce; when the square is full, no parts are needed.

**Colored golf balls.** At a Kawasaki engine plant, when a part used in a subassembly is down to its queue limit, the assembler rolls a colored golf ball down a pipe to the replenishment machine center. This tells the operator which part to make next. Many variations have been developed on this approach.

The kanban pull approach can be used not only within a manufacturing facility but also between manufacturing facilities (pulling engines and transmissions into an automobile assembly operation, for example) and between manufacturers and external suppliers.

**Determining the Number of Kanbans Needed** Setting up a kanban control system requires determination of the number of kanban cards (or containers) needed. In a two-card system, we are finding the number of sets of withdrawal and production cards. The kanban cards represent the number of containers of material that flow back and forth between the supplier and the user areas. Each container represents the minimum production lot size to be supplied. The number of containers, therefore, directly controls the amount of work-in-process inventory in the system.

Accurately estimating the lead time needed to produce a container of parts is the key to determining the number of containers. This lead time is a function of the processing time for the container, any waiting time during the production process, and the time required to transport the material to the user. Enough kanbans are needed to cover the expected demand during this lead time plus some additional amount for safety stock. The number of kanban card sets is

$$k = \frac{\text{Expected demand during lead time} + \text{Safety stock}}{\text{Size of the container}}$$

[10.1]
$$= \frac{DL(1+S)}{C}$$

where

$k$ = Number of kanban card sets
$D$ = Average number of units demanded over some time period
$L$ = Lead time to replenish an order (expressed in the same units as demand)
$S$ = Safety stock expressed as a percentage of demand during the lead time (This can be based on a service level and variance as shown in Chapter 13.)
$C$ = Container size

Observe that a kanban system does not produce zero inventory; rather, it controls the amount of material that can be in process at a time—the number of containers of each item. The kanban system can be easily adjusted to fit the current way the system is operating, because card sets can be easily added or removed from the system. If the workers find that they are not able to consistently replenish the item on time, an additional container of material, with the accompanying kanban cards, can be added. If it is found that excess containers of material accumulate, card sets can be easily removed, thus reducing the amount of inventory.

### EXAMPLE 10.1: DETERMINING THE NUMBER OF KANBAN CARD SETS

Arvin Automotive, a company that makes muffler assemblies for the Big Three, is committed to the use of kanban to pull material through its manufacturing cells. Arvin has designed each cell to fabricate a specific family of muffler products. Fabricating a muffler assembly involves cutting and bending pieces of pipe that are welded to a muffler and a catalytic converter. The mufflers and catalytic converters are pulled into the cell based on current demand. The catalytic converters are made in a specialized cell.

Catalytic converters are made in batches of 10 units and are moved in special hand carts to the fabrication cells. The catalytic converter cell is designed so that different types of catalytic converters can be made with virtually no setup loss. The cell can respond to an order for a batch of catalytic converters in approximately four hours. Because the catalytic converter cell is right next to the muffler assembly fabrication cell, transportation time is virtually zero.

The muffler assembly fabrication cell averages approximately eight assemblies per hour. Each assembly uses the same catalytic converter. Due to some variability in the process, management has decided to have safety stock equivalent to 10 percent of the needed inventory.

How many kanban sets are needed to manage the replenishment of the catalytic converters?

### SOLUTION

In this case, the lead time for replenishment of the converters ($L$) is four hours. The demand ($D$) for the catalytic converters is eight per hour. Safety stock ($S$) is 10 percent of the expected demand, and the container size ($C$) is 10 units.

$$k = \frac{8 \times 4(1 + .1)}{10} = \frac{35.2}{10} = 3.52$$

In this case, we would need four kanban card sets, and we would have four containers of converters in the system. In all cases, when we calculate $k$, we will round the number up because we always need to work with full containers of parts. ←

**Minimized Setup Times** Because small lot sizes are the norm, machines must be quickly set up to produce the mixed models on the line. In a widely cited example from the late 1970s, Toyota teams of press operators producing car hoods and fenders were able to change an 800-ton press in 10 minutes, compared with the average of six hours for U.S. workers and four hours for German workers. [Now, however, such speed is common in most U.S. auto plants.] To achieve such setup time reduction, setups are divided into internal and external activities. Internal setups must be done while a machine is stopped. External setups can be done while the machine is running. Other time-saving devices such as duplicate tool holders are also used to speed setups.

### RESPECT FOR PEOPLE

Respect for people is a key to the Japanese improvements. They have traditionally stressed lifetime employment for permanent positions within major firms. Companies try to maintain level payrolls even when business conditions deteriorate. Permanent workers (about one-third of the total workforce) have job security and tend to be more flexible, remain with a company, and do all they can to help a firm achieve its goals. (The recent recession in Japan has caused many Japanese companies to move away from this ideal.)

Global

Company unions in Japan exist to foster a cooperative relationship with management. All employees receive two bonuses a year in good times. Employees know that if the company performs well, they will get a bonus. This encourages workers to improve productivity. Management views workers as assets, not as human machines. Automation and robotics are used extensively to perform dull or routine jobs so employees are free to focus on important improvement tasks.

Subcontractor networks are very important in Japan. More than 90 percent of all Japanese companies are part of the supplier network of small firms. Some suppliers are specialists in a narrow field, usually serving multiple customers. Firms have long-term partnerships with their suppliers and customers. Suppliers consider themselves part of a customer's family.

Bottom-round management

Japanese firms use a **bottom-round management** style made up of consensus management by committees or teams. This decision process is slow but attempts to reach a consensus (not a compromise) by involving all parties, seeking information, and making a decision at the lowest level possible. Unlike in the United States, Japanese top management makes very few operating decisions, but concentrates on strategic planning. This system is effective in the smaller, focused factories of Japan.

Quality circles

**Quality circles** of employees meet weekly to discuss their jobs and problems. These small group improvement activities (SGIA) attempt to devise solutions to problems and share the solutions with management. They are led by a supervisor or production worker and typically include employees from a given production area. Others are multidiscipline teams led by a trained group leader or facilitator.

A recent study by Christer Karlsson of the Stockholm School of Economics points out that the JIT ideas found here are not universally used in all manufacturing companies in Japan. Rather, they are applied situationally and where appropriate. However, the fundamental ideas of elimination of waste and respect for workers are still foundations of the exceptional productivity of most Japanese manufacturing companies.[4]

## NORTH AMERICAN MODIFICATIONS OF JIT

Global

Some of these approaches are difficult to implement in North America. Lifetime employment, company unions, and subcontractor networks are not prevalent in the United States and Canada. Also, U.S. and Canadian companies traditionally use a top-down planning and management structure, which is counter to bottom-round management. In addition, U.S. and Canadian companies are vulnerable to labor strikes over union contracts.

What we can (and have) adopted in the United States and Canada is the Japanese general philosophy and approach to JIT. We have discovered that while the process may take many years to implement, reducing setup times, eliminating inventory, identifying problems, and utilizing the expertise of workers are important, practical guidelines for all organizations. A high percentage of U.S. manufacturers have implemented some form of JIT. Arvin's Total Quality Production System (ATQPS) is a great example of how American companies have implemented JIT (see the box titled "Arvin North American Automotive"). JIT is widely used in Europe as well.

## JIT IMPLEMENTATION REQUIREMENTS

This section is structured around the model shown in Exhibit 10.8. It discusses ways to accomplish JIT production. These suggestions are geared to repetitive production systems—those that make the same products again and again. Also, bear in mind that these elements are linked: Any changes in part of the production system impact other features of the system.

### JIT LAYOUTS AND DESIGN FLOWS

JIT requires the plant layout to be designed to ensure balanced work flow with a minimum of work-in-process inventory. Each workstation is part of a production line, whether or not a physical line actually exists. Capacity is balanced using the same logic for an assembly

How to Accomplish Just-in-Time Production

EXHIBIT 10.8

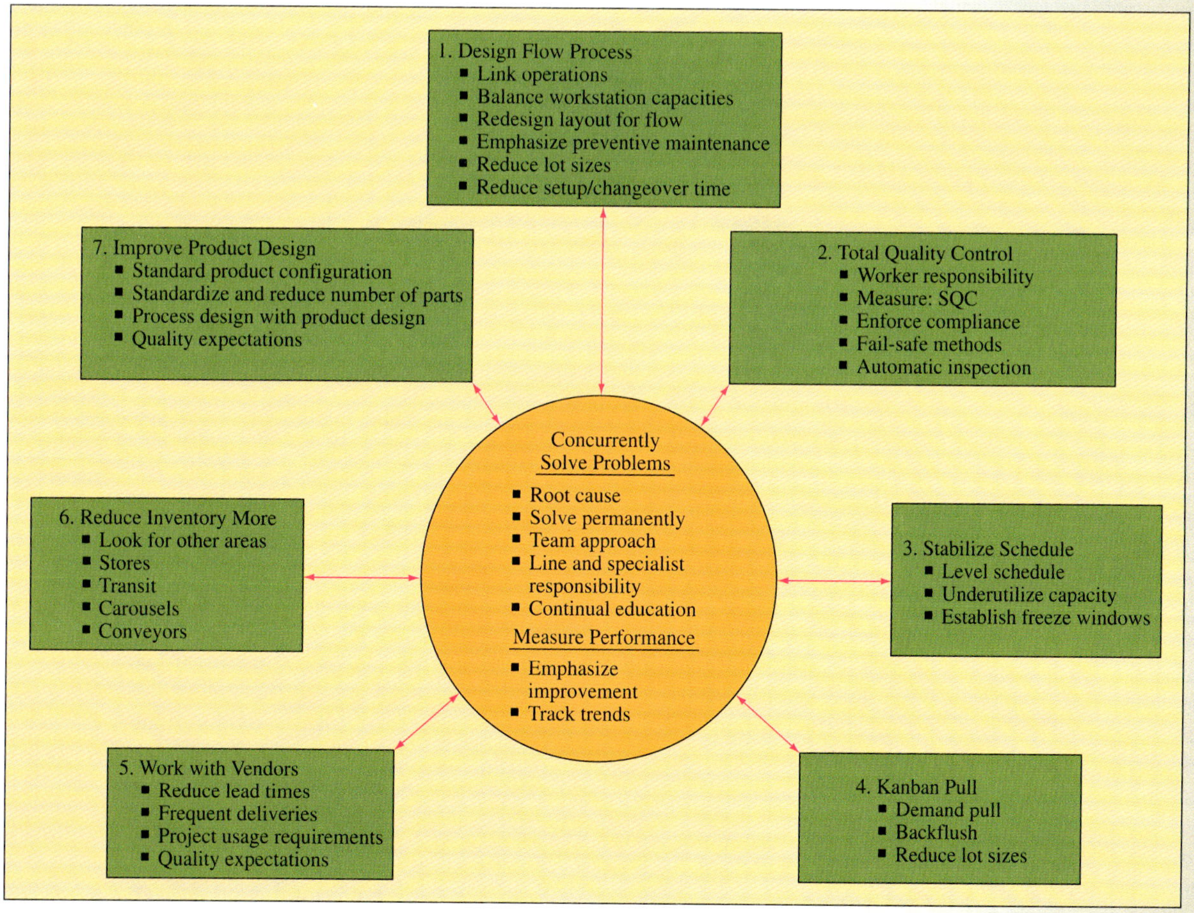


THIS DIAGRAM IS MODELED AFTER THE ONE USED BY HEWLETT-PACKARD'S BOISE PLANT TO ACCOMPLISH ITS JIT PROGRAM.

## PLANT TOUR: ARVIN NORTH AMERICAN AUTOMOTIVE (NAA)

Arvin Automotive was founded in 1919 and has been a supplier of complete exhaust systems for the original equipment market since 1929. Arvin has had great success achieving excellence with its Arvin Total Quality Production System (ATQPS). The JIT production system is just a part of its team approach; Arvin NAA is involved early in the vehicle design with its customers.

Teams meet frequently to assess progress, solve problems, and make decisions. At Arvin, employees work in teams, learn in teams, and succeed in teams. Suggestions and ideas from teams and individuals are the fuel of continuous improvement.

### TEAM PRODUCTION

Each manufacturing cell is laid out to assure visual communications among operators, a smooth flow of materials, timely delivery of components, and responsive shipment of finished products.

line, and operations are linked through a pull system. In addition, the system designer must visualize how all aspects of the internal and external logistics system tie to the layout.

Preventive maintenance

**Preventive maintenance** is emphasized to ensure that flows are not interrupted by downtime or malfunctioning equipment. Preventive maintenance involves periodic inspection and repair designed to keep a machine reliable. Operators perform much of the maintenance because they are most familiar with their machines and because machines are easier to repair, as JIT operations favor several simple machines rather than one large complex one.

The reductions in setup and changeover times previously discussed are necessary to achieve a smooth flow. Exhibit 10.9 shows the relationship between lot size and setup costs. Under a traditional approach, setup cost is treated as a constant, and the optimal order quantity is shown as six. Under the kanban approach of JIT, setup cost is treated as a variable and the optimal order quantity is reduced. In the exhibit, the order quantity has been reduced from six to two under JIT by employing setup-time–saving procedures. This organization will ultimately strive for a lot size of one.

## JIT APPLICATIONS FOR LINE FLOWS

Exhibit 10.10 illustrates a pull system in a simple line flow. In a pure JIT environment, no employee does any work until the product has been pulled from the end of the line by the market. The product could be a final product or a component used in later production.

Team-devised color coding facilitates quick changeover, improving flexibility and quality and promoting production of small lots to meet customer needs precisely. Visual controls remove ambiguity and assure quality at the source.

. . . and to external customers, too.

Arvin NAA's disciplined "pull system" uses production leveling and kanban signals to produce small, efficient lots delivered just in time to internal customers . . .

When a product is pulled, a replenishment unit is pulled from upstream operations. In the exhibit, an item of finished goods is pulled from F, the finished goods inventory. The inventory clerk then goes to processing station E and takes replacement product to fill the void. This pattern continues up the line to worker A, who pulls material from the raw material inventory. The rules of the flow layout require employees to keep completed units at their workstation, and if someone takes the completed work away, the employee must move upstream in the flow to get additional work to complete.

## JIT Applications for Job Shops

JIT is traditionally applied to line flows, but job shop environments also offer JIT benefits. The focus of JIT is product flow. Although job shops are characterized by low volume and high variety, JIT can be used if demand can be stabilized to permit repetitive manufacture. Stabilizing demand is usually easier to accomplish when the demand is from a downstream production stage rather than an end customer. (The logic is that internal customers can smooth their input requirements far more easily than a distributor or individual purchaser.)

Vol. II "Improving Operations Methods"

Factory machining centers, paint shops, and shirt making are examples of job-shop–type operations that process parts and components before they reach final production stages. By way of example, consider the production system in Exhibit 10.11. If a work center produces nine different parts used by several product varieties that are produced just in time, the work center keeps containers of completed output of all nine parts at the center to

EXHIBIT 10.9

**Relationship between Lot Size and Setup Cost**

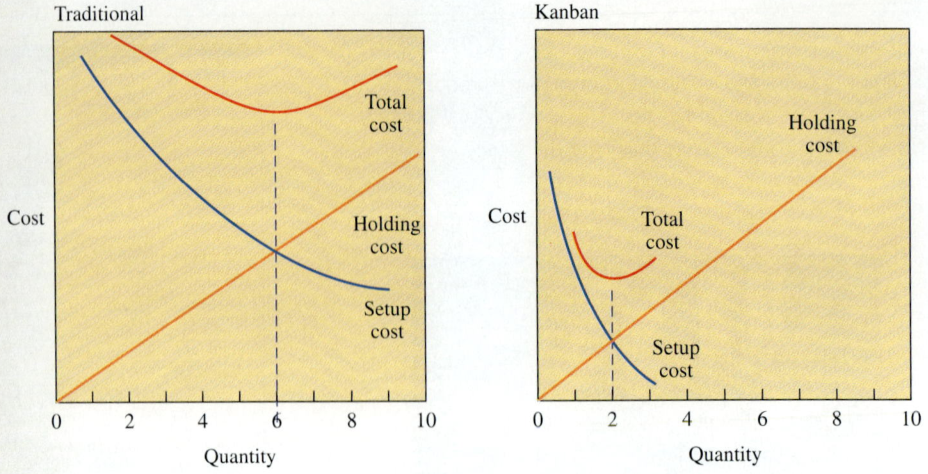


DEFINITIONS: *HOLDING COST* INCLUDES THE COSTS OF STORING INVENTORY AND THE COST OF MONEY TIED UP IN INVENTORY. *SETUP COST* INCLUDES THE WAGE COSTS ATTRIBUTABLE TO WORKERS MAKING THE SETUP, AND VARIOUS ADMINISTRATIVE AND SUPPLIES COSTS. (THESE ARE DEFINED IN TOTAL IN CHAPTER 13, "INVENTORY CONTROL.")

EXHIBIT 10.10

**JIT in a Line Flow Layout**

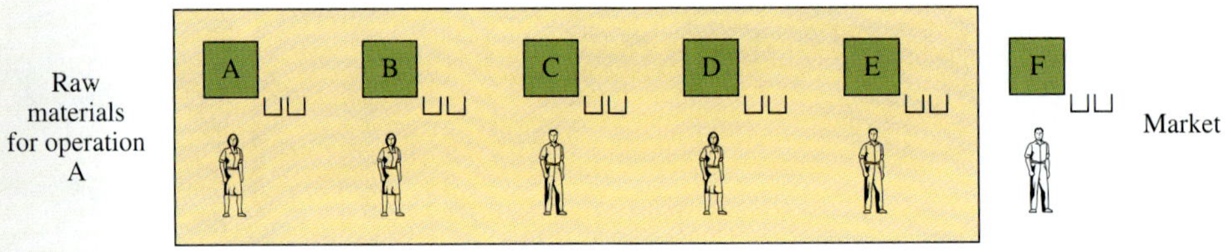


be picked up by users. Operators could make periodic rounds throughout the facility (hourly or more frequently) to pick up empty containers and drop them off at the corresponding upstream work center and to pick up full containers. In Exhibit 10.11, automatic guided vehicles pick up and deliver part numbers $M_5$ and $M_8$ to lines 2 and 3 for processing. These handling procedures can be manual or automated, but either way, these periodic pickups and drop-offs allow the system to operate in a just-in-time mode.

## TQC (TOTAL QUALITY CONTROL)

Total quality control (TQC)

JIT and TQC have merged in theory and practice. **Total quality control (TQC)** is the practice of building quality into the process and not identifying quality by inspection. It also refers to the theory of employees assuming responsibility for the quality of their own work. When employees are responsible for quality, JIT works at its best because only good-quality products are pulled through the system. When all products are good, no "just-in-case" extra inventory is needed. Thus organizations can achieve high quality and high productivity. By using statistical quality control methods and training workers to maintain quality, inspections can be reduced to the first and last units produced. If they are perfect, we can assume the other units between these points are perfect as well.

A foundation of quality is improved product design. Standard product configurations, fewer parts, and standardized parts are important elements in JIT. These design modifications reduce variability in the end item or in the materials that go into the product. Besides improving the producibility of a product, product design activities can facilitate the processing of engineering changes. (Total Quality Management and Statistical Quality Control are described in Chapter 7 and Technical Note 7.)

Exhibit 10.11

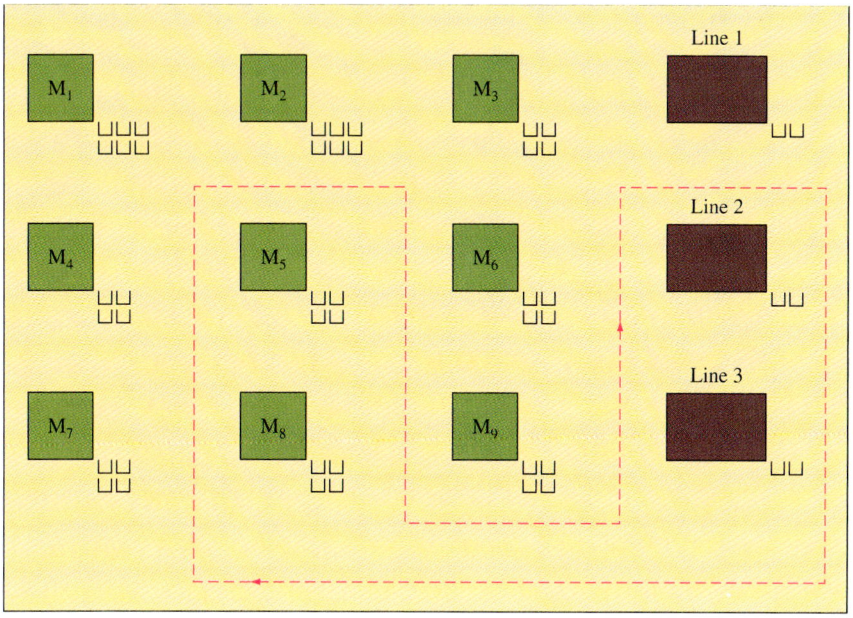


JIT in a Job Shop Layout Showing the Materials Handling Vehicle Route Connecting Machine Centers and Line Operations

## A Stable Schedule

As noted earlier, JIT firms require a stable schedule over a lengthy time horizon. This is accomplished by level scheduling, freeze windows, and underutilization of capacity. A **level schedule** is one that requires material to be pulled into final assembly in a pattern uniform enough to allow the various elements of production to respond to pull signals. It does not necessarily mean that the usage of every part on an assembly line is identified hour by hour for days on end; it does mean that a given production system equipped with flexible setups and a fixed amount of material in the pipelines can respond.[5]

Level schedule

The term **freeze window** refers to that period of time during which the schedule is fixed and no further changes are possible. An added benefit of the stable schedule is seen in how parts and components are accounted for in a pull system. Here, the concept of **backflush** measurement is used to periodically explode an end item's bill of materials (the parts that go into each product) to calculate how many of each part went into the final product(s). This eliminates much of the shop-floor data collection activity, which is required if each part must be tracked and accounted for during production.

Freeze window

Backflush

Underutilization and overutilization of capacity are controversial features of JIT. Conventional approaches use safety stocks and early deliveries as a hedge against production problems like poor quality, machine failures, and unanticipated bottlenecks in traditional manufacturing. Under JIT, excess labor, machines, and overtime provide the hedge. The excess capacity in labor and equipment that results is much cheaper than carrying excess inventory. When demand is greater than expected, overtime must be used. Often part-time labor is used when additional capacity is needed. During idle periods personnel can be put to work on other activities such as special projects, work group activities, and workstation housekeeping.

## Work with Suppliers

Just as customers and employees are key components of the JIT system, vendors are also important to the process. If a firm shares its projected usage requirements with its vendors, they have a long-run picture of the demands that will be placed on their production and distribution systems. Some vendors are linked online with a customer to share production

Vol. II "Supplier Development Outreach Program"

AT FORD MOTOR COMPANY'S VALENCIA, SPAIN, PLANT MORE THAN 20 SUPPLIERS ARE LOCATED IN AN ADJACENT INDUSTRIAL PARK THAT FEEDS PARTS, LIKE THESE BUMPERS, JIT AND IN THE RIGHT ORDER DIRECTLY TO THE ASSEMBLY LINE.

scheduling and input needs data. This permits them to develop level production systems. Confidence in the supplier or vendor's delivery commitment allows reductions of buffer inventories. Maintaining stock at a JIT level requires frequent deliveries during the day. Some suppliers even deliver to a location on the production line and not at a receiving dock. When vendors adopt quality practices, incoming receiving inspections of their products can be bypassed. The breakthrough box titled "Cyberspace Brings Revolution to Purchasing" describes how new Internet companies are streamlining the purchasing process.

A partnership between customers and suppliers has evolved at companies such as Honeywell, Bose, and AT&T. This partnership was conceived by Lance Dixon, director of purchasing at Bose Corporation. His system, titled **JIT II,**[6] brings the vendor into the plant to participate in the customer's purchasing office full-time. Whereas the typical JIT process eliminated inventory and brought the customer and supplier closer, this system adds such benefits as eliminating the buyer and sales representative from the customer–supplier relationship. The vendor replaces the buyer and salesperson. He or she is directed to use the customer's purchase order and to practice concurrent design and engineering. By being in-plant, this empowered employee, or facilitator, can raise the level of communication between the supplier and the customer company employees. Following JIT principles, the practices are customer-focused, cost-effective, quality-driven, and team-based.

JIT II

Having vendor representatives work with Bose engineers on designs has led to substantial improvements in design quality and productivity for the component-quality high-fidelity loudspeakers Bose manufactures. The major advantage is that the customer representative at Bose is empowered to use its system. Bose also applied these concepts to its transportation system and plans material in transit just like its inventory in the warehouse. AT&T and Honeywell have adopted JIT II and have been able to save money and improve productivity by combining the voice of the customer with that of the employee.

## BREAKTHROUGH

### CYBERSPACE BRINGS REVOLUTION TO PURCHASING

For years Arnold Koldenhoven, owner of a small Illinois company that processes leftovers from big steelmakers, bought steel the same way most others in the business did. He picked up the phone, dialed, and hoped the person on the other end not only was available but had enough surplus to sell him, at a decent price. Sometimes he succeeded, but more often he would spend hours playing telephone tag, only to learn the steelmaker didn't have what he needed. Now Koldenhoven flips on his computer, clicks on MetalSite.com and, in less time than he used to spend on hold, checks availability, price, and delivery date. Instead of relying on one or two producers, he compares prices of a half-dozen or so and goes with the best deal. That translates into higher profit for his business, Arrowhead Steel Co.

Until recently, only the car companies, steel's biggest customer, could come close to naming their own price. Everybody else operated under an irregular system of producers, distributors, and brokers charging one customer one price and the next twice as much for the same thing. Now hundreds of small and midsize steel buyers are circumventing all that—and paying less for the steel they buy—by clicking onto MetalSite or its rival e-Steel. Because the steelmaking process is not perfect, a producer often churns out more steel than is necessary to fill particular orders or shipments. The overage traditionally has been warehoused or recycled but either way consumes inventory space and drains company profit. With the web sites, the companies can quickly unload excess and secondary steel, accounting for about 15 percent of the steel sold in the United State. *http://www.e-steel.com; http://www.metalsite.com*

MetalSite and e-Steel are only two of literally hundreds of innovative young companies that have formed in the past few years to support business-to-business commerce. These companies streamline the onerous task of procurement by letting companies connect with suppliers over the Internet.



## JIT IN SERVICES

Many JIT techniques have been successfully applied by service firms. Just as in manufacturing, the suitability of each technique and the corresponding work steps depends on the characteristics of the firm's markets, production and equipment technology, skill sets, and corporate culture. Service firms are not different in this respect. Here are 10 of the more successful applications.[7]

**Organize Problem-Solving Groups** Honeywell is extending its quality circles from manufacturing into its service operations. Other corporations as diverse as First Bank/Dallas, Standard Meat Company, and Miller Brewing Company are using similar approaches to improve service. British Airways used quality circles as a fundamental part of its strategy to implement new service practices.

**Upgrade Housekeeping** Good housekeeping means more than winning the clean broom award. It means that only the necessary items are kept in a work area, that there is a place for everything, and that everything is clean and in a constant state of readiness. The employees clean their own areas.

Service organizations such as McDonald's, Disneyland, and Speedi-Lube have recognized the critical nature of housekeeping. Their dedication to housekeeping has meant that service processes work better, the attitude of continuous improvement is easier to develop, and customers perceive that they are receiving better service.

**Upgrade Quality** The only cost-effective way to improve quality is to develop reliable process capabilities. Process quality is quality at the source—it guarantees first-time production of consistent and uniform products and services.

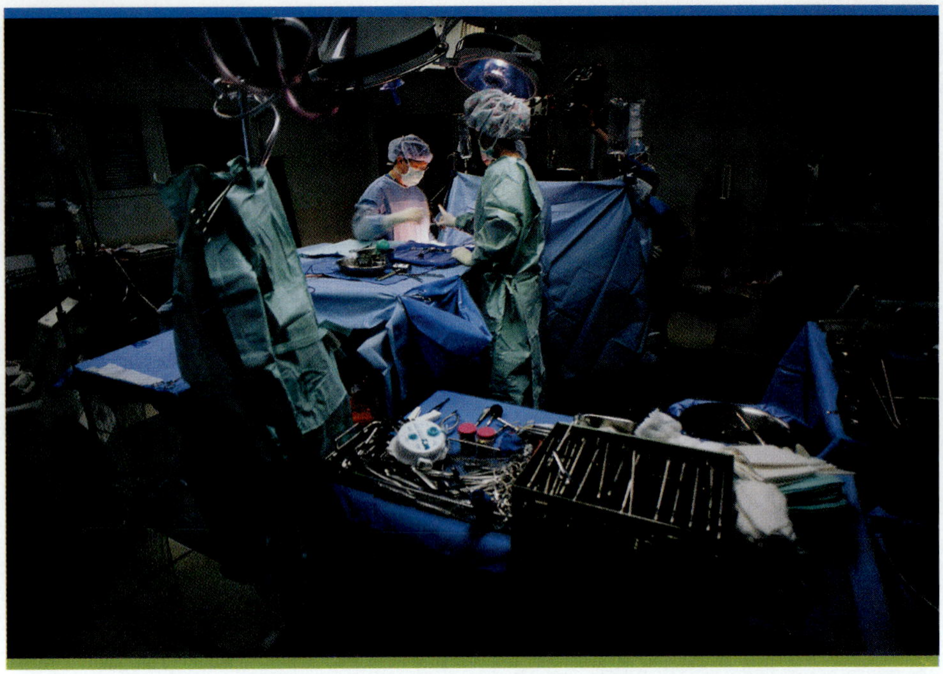

AT DUKE UNIVERSITY MEDICAL CENTER THE SURGICAL TEAM PREPARES FOR A BYPASS OPERATION. SUPPLIES FROM BAXTER INTERNATIONAL PHARMACEUTICALS ARRIVE PACKAGED IN THE ORDER IN WHICH THEY WILL BE USED DURING SURGERY. BAXTER PROVIDES THIS COMPUTER-BASED SERVICE GIVING IT A COMPETITIVE ADVANTAGE IN THE HOSPITAL SUPPLY INDUSTRY.

McDonald's is famous for building quality into its service delivery process. It literally "industrialized" the service delivery system so that part-time, casual workers could provide the same eating experience anywhere in the world. Quality doesn't mean producing the best; it means consistently producing products and services that give the customers their money's worth.

**Clarify Process Flows** Clarification of flows, based on JIT themes, can dramatically improve the process performance. Here are examples.

First, Federal Express Corporation changed air flight patterns from origin-to-destination to origin-to-hub, where the freight is transferred to an outbound plane heading for the destination. This revolutionized the air transport industry. Second, the order-entry department of a manufacturing firm converted from functional subdepartments to customer-centered work groups and reduced the order processing lead time from eight to two days. Third, a county government used the JIT approach to cut the time to record a deed transfer by 50 percent. Finally, Supermaids sends in a team of house cleaners, each with a specific responsibility, to clean each house quickly with parallel processes. Changes in process flows can literally revolutionize service industries.

**Revise Equipment and Process Technologies** Revising technologies involves evaluation of the equipment and processes for their ability to meet the process requirements, to process consistently within tolerance, and to fit the scale and capacity of the work group.

Speedi-Lube converted the standard service station concept to a specialized lubrication and inspection center by changing the service bays from drive-in to drive-through and by eliminating the hoists and instead building pits under the cars where employees have full access to the lubrication areas on the vehicle.

A hospital reduced operating room setup time so that it had the flexibility to perform a wider range of operations without reducing the operating room availability.

**Level the Facility Load** Service firms synchronize production with demand. They have developed unique approaches to leveling demand so they can avoid making customers wait for service. CompuServe sells time for less during the evening. McDonald's offers a special breakfast menu in the morning. Retail stores use take-a-number systems.

The post office charges more for next-day delivery. These are all examples of the service approach for creating uniform facility loads.

**Eliminate Unnecessary Activities** A step that does not add value is a candidate for elimination. A step that does add value may be a candidate for reengineering to improve the process consistency or to reduce the time to perform the tasks.

A hospital discovered that significant time was spent during an operation waiting for an instrument that was not available when the operation began. It developed a checklist of instruments required for each category of operation. Speedi-Lube eliminated steps, but it also added steps that did not improve the lubrication process but did make customers feel more assured about the work being performed.

**Reorganize Physical Configuration** Work area configurations frequently require reorganization during a JIT implementation. Often manufacturers accomplish this by setting up manufacturing cells to produce items in small lots, synchronous to demand. These cells amount to microfactories inside the plant.

Most service firms are far behind manufacturers in this area. However, a few interesting examples do come out of the service sector. Some hospitals—instead of routing patients all over the building for tests, exams, X-rays, and injections—are reorganizing their services into work groups based on the type of problem. Teams that treat only trauma are common, but other work groups have been formed to treat less immediate conditions like hernias. These amount to microclinics within the hospital facility.

**Introduce Demand-Pull Scheduling** Due to the nature of service production and consumption, demand-pull (customer-driven) scheduling is necessary for operating a service business. Moreover, many service firms are separating their operations into "back room" and "customer contact" facilities. This approach creates new problems in coordinating schedules between the facilities. The original Wendy's restaurants were set up so cooks could see cars enter the parking lot. They put a preestablished number of hamburger patties onto the grill for each car. This pull system was designed to have a fresh patty on the grill before the customer even placed an order.

**Develop Supplier Networks** The term *supplier networks* in the JIT context refers to the cooperative association of suppliers and customers working over the long term for mutual benefit. Service firms have not emphasized supplier networks for materials because the service costs are often predominantly labor. Notable exceptions must include service organizations like McDonald's, one of the biggest food products purchasers in the world. A small manufacturer recognized that it needed cooperative relationships for temporary employees as well as for parts. It is considering a campaign to establish JIT-type relationships with a temporary employment service and a trade school to develop a reliable source of trained assemblers.

## CONCLUSION

JIT represents a powerful tool for reducing inventory and improving production and service operations. The Box titled "What Kind of Results Can a Company Expect from Applying Lean Ideas?" shows typical results. Its principles can result in many improvements, but users are cautioned that JIT applications are not universal. Like TQM, JIT implementation faces many problems led by a resistance to change shown by many employees. Education of top management is important. Visible initial pilot programs (rather than a plantwide implementation of JIT all at once) are a good beginning. Management should use care in choosing an implementation team who will be responsible for making the major changes on the plant floor. The team can include 5 to 15 individuals from quality control, engineering, manufacturing, traffic, purchasing, marketing, and other areas. Ongoing team education is important to help employees discard practices that block JIT progress. Again, like TQM, JIT is a series of small improvements that takes time. It requires the patience of all involved parties.

## WHAT KIND OF RESULTS CAN A COMPANY EXPECT FROM APPLYING LEAN IDEAS?

Lantech, a small company based in Louisville, Kentucky, makes machines that are used to stretch-wrap products for shipment. Their machines have been widely adopted by manufacturing companies to stretch-wrap pallets of goods with plastic film so that they can be shipped easily from plant to plant within a manufacturing system and then onward, as finished products, to wholesalers and retailers.

A key element to the change at Lantech was the implementation of manufacturing cells focused on the production of specific models. In the past, Lantech built its four basic models in batches; it fabricated and assembled 10 to 15 machines of a type at a time. However, because customers usually bought only one machine at a time, the company had to store most of the machines in each batch in a finished goods area until they were purchased. Of course, often the machines made in the batch did not have the options the customer wanted, so either the machine had to be reworked or a whole new machine was built. Tracking all the inventory, batches of machines in process, and the custom machine "hot list" led to amazing confusion and waste.

The new Lantech manufacturing cells (a typical one is shown here) allow Lantech to make machines one at a time to customer order. Now no finished goods inventory is kept, and there is virtually no need for complex inventory planning and tracking software. Orders are tracked on a large white board in the sales office, where orders are written as soon as they are confirmed.

The impact of the new approach on performance was remarkable. Although the plant's workforce remained virtually constant at 300, the number of shipped machines doubled between 1991 and 1995. Moreover, Lantech could produce a machine in half the space previously required, the number of defects reported by customers fell from 8 per machine in 1991 to .8 in 1995, and start-to-finish production time for the Q model (which has the highest volume) fell from 16 weeks to 14 hours.

The Q Model Production Cell

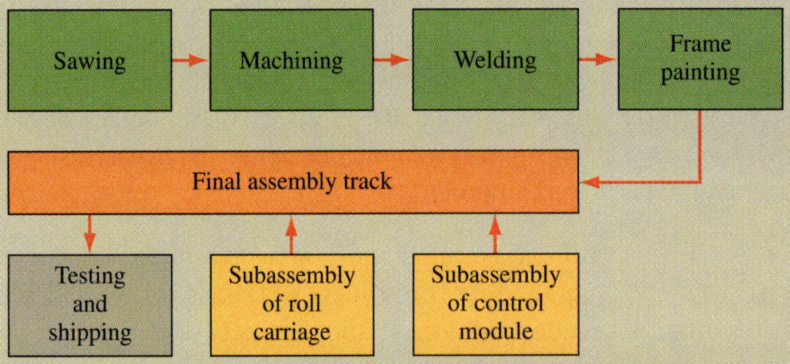


ADAPTED BY PERMISSION FROM JAMES P. WOMACK AND DANIEL T. JONES, *LEAN THINKING: BANISH WASTE AND CREATE WEALTH IN YOUR CORPORATION*, NEW YORK: SIMON & SCHUSTER, 1996, PP. 102–104.

JIT is an encompassing philosophy considering product design, process design, equipment, selection, material management, quality assurance, job design, and productivity improvements. The goal of synchronized, streamlined one-piece-at-a-time production is a world-class standard seldom achieved in practice. Because zero lead time and zero idle time are hard to accomplish, some JIT projects are put quickly in place and later forgotten. Management support, commitment, and training to continue JIT progress are needed.

## KEY TERMS

**JIT (just-in-time)** Integrated activities designed to achieve high-volume production using minimal inventories of raw materials, work-in-process, and finished goods.

**Group technology** A philosophy in which similar parts are grouped into families, and the processes required to make the parts are arranged in a specialized work cell.

**Quality at the source** Philosophy of making factory workers personally responsible for the quality of their output. Workers are expected to make the part correctly the first time and to stop the process immediately if there is a problem.

**Uniform plant loading** Smoothing the production flow to dampen schedule variation.

**Kanban and the kanban pull system** An inventory or production control system that uses a signaling device to regulate flows.

**Bottom-round management** A decision process based on reaching a consensus by involving all parties impacted by the decision.

**Quality circles** Employees meet regularly to discuss their jobs and problems and attempt to devise solutions.

**Preventive maintenance** Periodic inspection and repair designed to keep equipment reliable.

**Total quality control (TQC)** The practice of building quality into the process and not identifying quality by inspection.

**Level schedule** A schedule that pulls material into final assembly at a constant rate.

**Freeze window** The period of time during which the schedule is fixed and no further changes are possible.

**Backflush** Calculating how many of each part were used in production and using these calculations to adjust actual on-hand inventory balances. This eliminates the need to actually track each part used in production.

**JIT II** A concept in which vendors are brought into the plant to participate in the customer's purchasing office full-time.

## FORMULA REVIEW

**Determining the number of kanbans**

[10.1] $$k = \frac{DL(1+S)}{C}$$

## SOLVED PROBLEMS

### SOLVED PROBLEM 1

A local hospital wants to set up a kanban system to manage its supply of blood with the regional blood bank. The regional blood bank delivers blood to the hospital each day with a one-day order lead time (an order placed by 6 P.M. today will be delivered tomorrow afternoon). Internally, the hospital purchasing group places orders for blood each day at 5 P.M. Blood is measured by the pint and is shipped in containers that contain six pints. For a particular blood type, the hospital uses an average of 12 pints per day. Due to the critical nature of a blood shortage, the hospital wants to carry a safety stock of two days' expected supply. How many kanban card sets should the hospital prepare?

#### Solution

This problem is typical of how a real application might look. Using the data given, the variables for this problem are as follows:

$D = 12$ pints per day (average demand)
$L = 1$ day (lead time)
$S = 200$ percent (safety stock, as a fraction this is 2.0)
$C = 6$ pints (container size)

$$k = \frac{DL(1+S)}{C} = \frac{12(1+2)}{6} = 6$$

This indicates that we need to prepare six kanban card sets. Each time a new container of blood (containing six pints) is opened, the card will be sent to purchasing and another six pints of blood will be ordered. When the blood is received the card will be attached to the new container and moved to the blood storage area.

## REVIEW AND DISCUSSION QUESTIONS

1 What JIT principles are being used by Arvin North American Automotive (see the box on pages 404 and 405)? Use the categories in Exhibit 10.8 to develop your answer.
2 Is it possible to achieve zero inventories? Why or why not?
3 Stopping waste is a vital part of JIT. Identify some sources of waste in your home or dorm and discuss how they may be eliminated.
4 Discuss JIT in a job shop layout and in a line layout.
5 Why must JIT have a stable schedule?
6 Will JIT work in service environments? Why or why not?
7 Discuss ways to use JIT to improve one of the following: a pizza restaurant, a hospital, or an auto dealership.

8 What objections might a marketing manager have to uniform plant loading?
9 What are the implications for cost accounting of JIT production?
10 What are the roles of suppliers and customers in a JIT system?
11 Explain how cards are used in a kanban system.
12 In which ways, if any, are the following systems analogous to kanban: returning empty bottles to the supermarket and picking up filled ones; running a hot dog stand at lunchtime; withdrawing money from a checking account; raking leaves into bags?
13 How is a U.S. JIT system different from a Japanese one?
14 Why is JIT hard to implement in practice?
15 Explain the relationship between quality and productivity under the JIT philosophy.

## PROBLEMS

1 5 Kanban card sets.

1 A supplier of instrument gauge clusters uses a kanban system to control material flow. The gauge cluster housings are transported five at a time. A fabrication center produces approximately 10 gauges per hour. It takes approximately two hours for the housing to be replenished. Due to variations in processing times, management has decided to keep 20 percent of the needed inventory as safety stock. How many kanban card sets are needed?

2 2 Kanban card sets.

2 Transmissions are delivered to the fabrication line four at a time. It takes one hour for transmissions to be delivered. Approximately four vehicles are produced each hour, and management has decided that 50 percent of expected demand should be maintained as safety stock. How many kanban card sets are needed?

## CASE: TOYOTA, FORD, GM, AND VOLKSWAGEN—SOME DIFFERING OPINIONS ABOUT WORKING WITH SUPPLIERS

It is interesting to see how the large automobile manufacturers differ in their opinions about working with suppliers and standardization of parts. Consider the following.

### WORKING WITH SUPPLIERS

Tadaaki Jagawa, a Toyota executive vice president, said the number one Japanese automaker "received an invitation" from Ford to join the Ford Internet-based marketplace, tentatively called AutoXchange, where automakers and their suppliers hope to do business more efficiently and cut costs. Ford and GM are in a race to build the largest online marketplace to achieve greater economies of scale, and both are trying to woo other automakers. The two companies have argued that creating a marketplace in which hundreds of billions of dollars in goods and services are traded would give their suppliers access to more business globally, allowing suppliers and manufacturers to slash costs.

Toyota considers the Internet marketplace only a means to efficiency and not an end in itself, Jagawa said. Because the procurement process involves not only the price but also the quality, lead time, and delivery of components, Jagawa said Toyota doesn't want to put competitive components on an open market, such as GM TradeXchange; it would go against Toyota's philosophy of treating suppliers as partners. "We help suppliers cut costs through a guarantee of a long-term contract; putting those parts on the open market pits us against suppliers in an adversary relationship."

Jagawa stressed that Toyota is in discussions with GM "with an open mind." Although it may mean Toyota would trade only raw materials and commonly used parts on either the GM or Ford system, Toyota is interested in making its buying more efficient, he said.

### STANDARDIZING AUTO PARTS

Some of Toyota's talks with GM also involve standardizing components. That would allow the two companies and GM's other participants to share a common electronic procurement infrastructure and maximize the online network's effectiveness.

Toyota and Volkswagen are also trying to hammer out an agreement to standardize select components for vehicles sold in Europe. Jagawa said the two companies launched the talks last summer to identify specific parts they can standardize. He added, however, that the process has been slow because of a "wide gap" between what the two companies consider common components. "VW put on the table 20 to 30 parts as possible targets for standardization; we identified several at most," said Jagawa.

Toyota had said it was considering standardizing components and platforms with the German automaker to cut operating costs in Europe, where the Japanese company has had trouble reducing costs because of its limited sales volume. Toyota sold fewer than 600,000 vehicles in Europe last year.

In Toyota's discussions with both GM and Volkswagen, Jagawa said one problem that could potentially delay an early agreement is their difference over the definition of "competitive" components. Toyota considers a wider range of parts competitive, including steering wheels and in some cases even wire connectors, whereas GM and Volkswagen seem to believe many components can be standardized without hurting competitiveness. "They think we can compete on things like styling and packaging of vehicles; we believe we compete component by component in creating a competitive vehicle," said Jagawa.

### QUESTIONS

1 GM and Ford have quickly pushed the development of large Internet sites to create an environment where suppliers must compete for business. Ford and GM argue that these Internet sites should reduce cost because the negotiations are streamlined. How do you think the suppliers view these sites?

2 Rather than having vendors compete against one another, Toyota is interested in treating suppliers as partners. Is Toyota just being old-fashioned in its views?

3 A major reason for the differences in opinions may be the difference in what Toyota considers "competitive" components. These are the components that would mostly be bought using the Internet trading sites. Who is right? Are steering wheels and wire connectors competitive components?



## CASE: QUALITY PARTS COMPANY

Quality Parts Company supplies gizmos for a computer manufacturer located a few miles away. The company produces two different models of gizmos in production runs ranging from 100 to 300 units.

The production flow of models X and Y is shown in Exhibit 10.12. Model Z requires milling as its first step, but otherwise follows the same flow pattern as X and Y. Skids can hold up to 20 gizmos at a time. Approximate times per unit by operation number and equipment setup times are shown in Exhibit 10.13.

Demand for gizmos from the computer company ranges between 125 and 175 per month, equally divided among X, Y, and Z. Subassembly builds up inventory early in the month to make certain that

EXHIBIT 10.12

Gizmo Production Flow

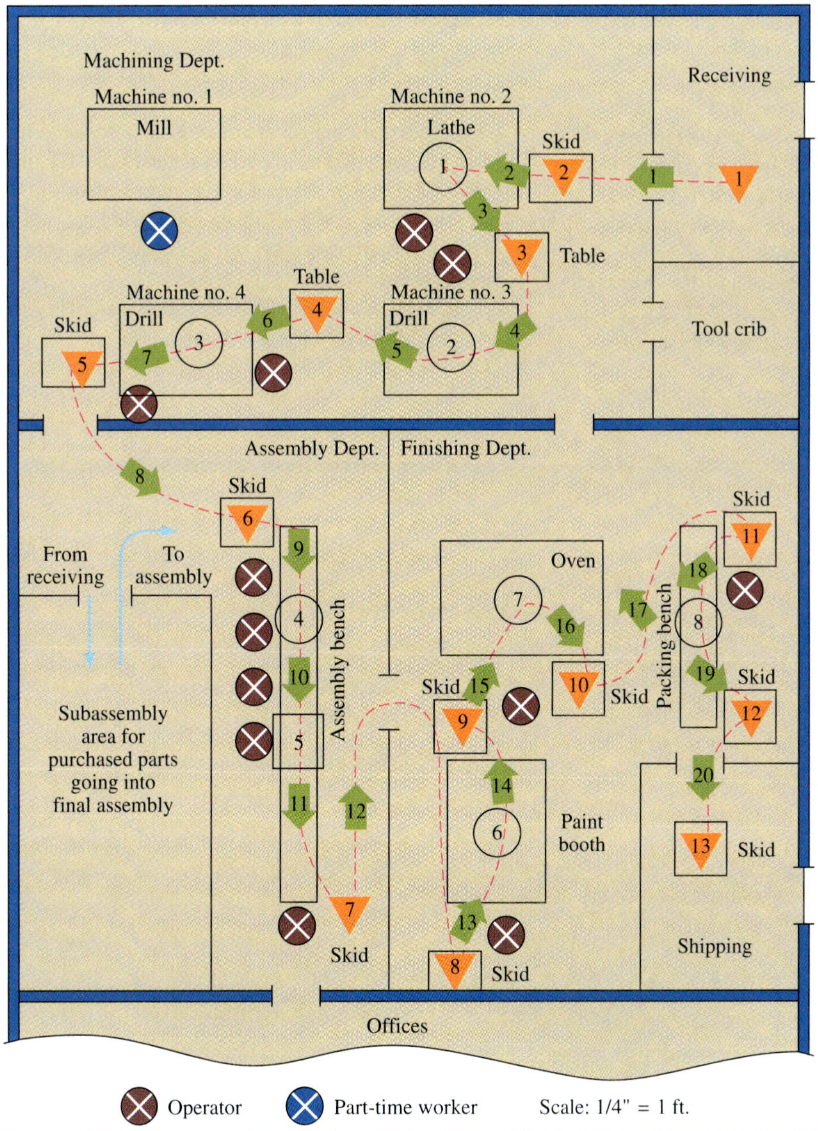

EXHIBIT 10.13

Operations and Setup Time

| Operation Number and Name | Operation Time (Minutes) | Setup Time (Minutes) |
|---|---|---|
| Milling for Model Z | 20 | 60 |
| 1 Lathe | 50 | 30 |
| 2 Mod. 14 drill | 15 | 5 |
| 3 Mod. 14 drill | 40 | 5 |
| 4 Assembly step 1 | 50 | |
| Assembly step 2 | 45 | |
| Assembly step 3 | 50 | |
| 5 Inspection | 30 | |
| 6 Paint | 30 | 20 |
| 7 Oven | 50 | |
| 8 Packing | 5 | |

a buffer stock is always available. Raw materials and purchased parts for subassemblies each constitute 40 percent of the manufacturing cost of a gizmo. Both categories of parts are multiple-sourced from about 80 vendors and are delivered at random times. (Gizmos have 40 different part numbers.)

Scrap rates are about 10 percent at each operation, inventory turns twice yearly, employees are paid on a day rate, employee turnover is 25 percent per year, and net profit from operations is steady at 5 percent per year. Maintenance is performed as needed.

The manager of Quality Parts Company has been contemplating installing an automated ordering system to help control inventories and to "keep the skids filled." (She feels that two days of work in front of a workstation motivates the worker to produce at top speed.) She is also planning to add three inspectors to clean up the quality problem. Further, she is thinking about setting up a rework line to speed repairs. Although she is pleased with the high utilization of most of her equipment and labor, she is concerned about the idle time of the milling machine. Finally, she has asked the industrial engineering department to look into high-rise shelving to store parts coming off machine 4.

QUESTIONS

1 Which of the changes being considered by the manager of Quality Parts Company are counter to the JIT philosophy?
2 Make recommendations for JIT improvements in such areas as scheduling, layout, kanban, task groupings, and inventory. Use quantitative data as much as possible; state necessary assumptions.
3 Sketch the operation of a pull system for quality for Quality Parts Company's current system.
4 Outline a plan for introducing JIT at Quality Parts Company.

## SELECTED BIBLIOGRAPHY


Black, J. T. *The Design of the Factory with a Future.* New York: McGraw-Hill, 1991.

Hall, R. *Attaining Manufacturing Excellence.* Burr Ridge, IL: Dow Jones-Irwin, 1987.

______. *Zero Inventories.* Burr Ridge, IL: Dow Jones-Irwin, 1983.

Karlsson, C. *Japanese Production Management in Sunrise or Sunset.* Stockholm, Sweden: Stockholm School of Economics, EFI/The Economic Research Institute, 1999.

Monden, Y. *The Toyota Management System: Linking the Seven Key Functional Areas.* Cambridge, MA: Productivity Press, 1993.

______. *Toyota Production System. Practical Approach to Production Management.* Atlanta, GA: Industrial Engineering and Management Press, 1983.

Ohno, T. *Toyota Production System: Beyond Large-Scale Production.* Cambridge, MA: Productivity Press, 1988.

Ohno, T., and S. Mito. *Just-in-Time for Today and Tomorrow.* Cambridge, MA: Productivity Press, 1988.

Schonberger, R. J. *Building a Chain of Customers: Linking Business Functions to Create a World-Class Company.* New York: Free Press, 1989.

______. *Japanese Manufacturing Techniques.* New York: Free Press, 1982.

______. *World-Class Manufacturing: The Lessons of Simplicity Applied.* New York: Free Press, 1986.

Schonberger, R. *World Class Manufacturing: The Next Decade: Building Power, Strength, and Value.* New York: Free Press, 1996.

Shingo, S. *A Revolution in Manufacturing: The SMED System.* Tokyo: Japan Management Association, 1983.

______. *A Study of the Toyota Production System from an Industrial Engineering Viewpoint.* Cambridge, MA: Productivity Press, 1989.

Suzaki, K. *The New Manufacturing Challenge: Techniques for Continuous Improvement.* New York: Free Press, 1987.

Womack, J. P.; D. T. Jones; and D. Roos. *The Machine That Changed the World.* New York: R. A. Rawston Associates, 1990.

Womack, J. P. and D. T. Jones. *Lean Thinking: Banish Waste and Create Wealth in Your Corporation.* New York: Simon & Schuster, 1996.

Zipkin, P. H. "Does Manufacturing Need a JIT Revolution?" *Harvard Business Review*, January–February 1991, pp. 40–50.

## FOOTNOTES

1 J. P. Womack, D. T. Jones, and D. Roos, *The Machine That Changed the World* (New York: R. A. Rawston Associates, 1990).

2 K. A. Wantuck, *The Japanese Approach to Productivity* (Southfield, MI: Bendix Corporation, 1983).

3 K. Suzaki, *The New Manufacturing Challenge: Techniques for Continuous Improvement* (New York: Free Press, 1987). pp. 7–25.

4 C. Karlsson (ed.), *Japanese Production Management in Sunrise or Sunset* (Stockholm, Sweden: Stockholm School of Economics, EFI/The Economic Research Institute, 1999).

5 R. H. Hall, *Zero Inventories* (Burr Ridge, IL: Dow Jones-Irwin, 1983), p. 64.

6 L. Dixon and A. M. Porter, *JIT II: Revolution in Buying and Selling* (Newton, MA: Cahners Publishing, 1994).

7 R. J. Benson, "JIT: Not Just For the Factory!" *APICS 29th Annual International Conference Proceedings* (1986), pp. 370–74.

# *section four*

*section* 4

# PLANNING AND CONTROLLING THE SUPPLY CHAIN



## IN RUNNING A BUSINESS, COMPUTERS CAN DO MORE THAN JUST WORD PROCESSING AND E-MAIL

Running a business requires a great planning system. What do we expect to sell in the future? How many people should we hire to handle the Christmas rush? How much inventory do we need? What should we make today? These are all questions that managers need to answer every day. This section discusses different approaches to answering these questions. Computers running comprehensive software packages can help. As a manager, it is important to understand the best way to solve these planning problems, so the right software can be purchased and configured correctly. Often a good spreadsheet is all that is needed.

*managerial briefing*

# ENTERPRISE RESOURCE PLANNING SYSTEMS

## BRIEFING OUTLINE



*managerial briefing*

## INFORMATION CRISIS—THE MISSING DESK

"Okay, Jerry, what's up?"

"I'll tell you what's up! $20,000 is what's up. We've lost the desk for that lawyer in Atlanta. You remember, the one that was supposed to ship a couple of weeks ago. He called me yesterday and said enough is enough. He reminded me of all the delays we had since he first placed the order. I reminded him of all the changes he wanted made. He reminded me that the last notice he got after the final change was that the desk would be there no later than last week. Well, he didn't believe us, so he postponed some big cocktail party until this week so the desk would be there. I stopped reminding him of stuff and said I'd find out what was going on." Jerry was not happy.

"What did you find out?"

"Nothing. I went out in the shop yesterday evening and couldn't find the thing. I tried to call you at home but I guess you didn't get enough vacation."

Source: F. R. Jacobs and D. C. Whybark, *Why ERP? A Primer on SAP Implementation* (Burr Ridge, IL: Irwin/McGraw-Hill, 2000), pp. 10–11.

"Wait a minute, going over to the in-laws to swap the pictures of sand we each took at the beach isn't exactly an extended vacation. How the heck can we lose a lawyer's desk?" Billy was not happy.

"I don't know, and neither did the two guys I talked to from the shop. They said it was still sitting there yesterday. What is going on anyway?" asked Jerry.

"Well, I remember now. There was a delay because of the last-minute change in some of the hardware that the guy wanted. Remember, we found out the vendor couldn't ship that until last week, and then we needed some time to make sure the finish was okay. When we ran the MRP system to check the schedules, I learned that desk wouldn't ship until late last week, but it didn't go. It must have gone yesterday, late. I'll check and let you know."

Back in his office, Billy pulled up the record for the desk and found the order was closed out. He went back to the history file and learned that it indeed had been shipped late yesterday and was off the production books. Why the sales people didn't know it had shipped was a mystery to him. He called the trucking company and asked them where the shipment was. Expecting to be told they would check and call back, he was pleasantly surprised to be told immediately that the shipment was picked up late yesterday, it had gone to Raleigh where another Atlanta-bound shipment was picked up, and the truck was now on the outer beltway of Atlanta. The clerk apologized and said that it might be midday before the delivery could be made. They had to drop off the other shipment first. Finally, the clerk took Billy's number and said he would call if there was any delay in getting the shipment to the customer by noon.

"Why can't we do that?" wondered Billy.

He called Jerry and told him to tell the lawyer to go ahead with his party. Then he asked why the shipment never got picked up in the sales system. Jerry replied, "It looks like it never got entered yesterday. It's probably still on someone's desk. I'll check and see, but I'm really more worried about our not knowing of the delay two weeks ago when you did."

"I wonder if this is a problem that comes from lack of integration," mused Billy as he set about learning about how many forecasts the company had for next month. ←

The missing desk tale depicts a typical situation in a company where information is not integrated. An **Enterprise resource planning (ERP)** system, when implemented correctly, links all the areas of the business. Manufacturing knows about new orders as soon as they are entered in the system. Sales knows the exact status of a customer order. Purchasing knows what manufacturing needs to the minute, and the accounting system is updated as all the relevant transactions occur. The potential benefits are huge. Savings in the redundant posting of information alone can save a company millions of dollars a year. The real value, though, is in the new ways that a company can do business. Many redundant jobs can simply be eliminated. The time taken to do the remaining jobs can be reduced significantly due to the quick availability of information. With a well-designed ERP system, new ways to run the business are possible. Of course, this is not without cost. ERP systems are complex and expensive and may require major changes in processes.

Enterprise resource planning (ERP)

Cross Functional

The purpose of this managerial briefing is to provide an overview of what an ERP system is and why it can benefit a company. The current ERP vendors have set new standards in information integration. In this briefing, we focus on a company called SAP AG and their flagship product R/3. Our intent is not to endorse the SAP R/3 product as the only software product that a firm should consider; rather, this is a good benchmark for comparing other competing products.

Exhibit MB11.1 lists the major developers of ERP software. In a sense, it can be argued that SAP AG was in the right place at the right time.

In the early 1990s, many large companies realized that it was time to update their existing information systems to take advantage of new technologies. Programs written in programming languages such as COBOL, PL1, RPG, and assembler were becoming increasingly expensive to maintain. Further, the mainframe computer technology was not cost-effective compared to the ever more powerful and inexpensive microprocessor-based computers. Change was inevitable, and SAP offered a comprehensive solution.

EXHIBIT MB11.1

**Major Developers of Enterprise Resource Planning Software**

| VENDOR | SPECIAL SOFTWARE FEATURES | WEB SITE |
|---|---|---|
| AIM Computer Solutions | Comprehensive selection of software | *http://www.aimcom.com* |
| American Software | Comprehensive selection; focus on supply chain management | *http://www.amsoftware.com* |
| The Baan Company | Baan IV client/server; dynamic enterprise modeling | *http://www.baan.com* |
| Chesapeake Software Systems | Optimized manufacturing scheduling | *http://www.chessie.com* |
| i2 Technologies | Forecasting, flow manufacturing | *http://www.i2.com* |
| Manugistics | Optimization of logistics functions | *http://www.manugistics.com* |
| Oracle | Comprehensive system; major database vendor | *http://www.oracle.com* |
| PeopleSoft | Comprehensive selection; client/server products | *http://www.peoplesoft.com* |

EXHIBIT MB11.2

**Triple Client Server Configuration**

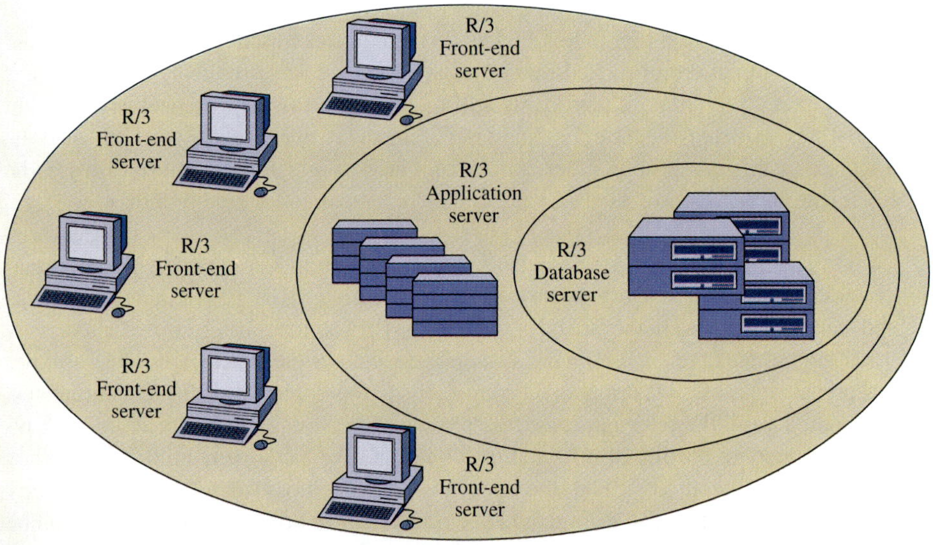


SOURCES: J. BLAIN, *USING SAP R/3* (INDIANAPOLIS, IN: QUE, 1996), P. 42; AND N. H. BANCROFT, *IMPLEMENTING SAP R/3: HOW TO INTRODUCE A LARGE SYSTEM INTO A LARGE ORGANIZATION* (GREENWICH, CT: MANNING PUBLICATIONS, 1996).

## SAP AG'S R/3

Cross Functional

SAP AG, a German firm, is the world leader in providing ERP software. Its flagship product is known as R/3. Many of the world's largest companies use the software, including, in the United States, Baxter Healthcare, Exxon, and even the software giant Microsoft. The software consists of four major modules: Financial Accounting, Human Resources, Manufacturing and Logistics, and Sales and Distribution.

The software is designed to operate in a three-tier client/server configuration. As shown in Exhibit MB11.2, the core of the system is a high-speed network of database servers. These database servers are special computers designed to efficiently handle a large database

EXHIBIT MB11.3

**SAP R/3 and the Applications That Implement Topics Discussed in This Book**

| SAP APPLICATION | PROGRAM | CHAPTER IN BOOK |
|---|---|---|
| Cross application (CA) | Business Process Technology (CA-BPT)<br>CAD Integration (CA-CAD) | Chapters 4, 5 and 16 |
| Project system (PS) | Project Planning (PS-PLN)<br>Project Execution/Integration (PS-EXE) | Chapter 3 |
| Logistics general (LO) | Logistics Information System (LO-LIS)<br>Master Data (LO-MD) | Chapters 5 and 8; Technical Note 9 |
| Human resources (HR) | Workforce Planning (PD-WFP) | Chapters 12 and 15 |
| Personnel administration (HR-PA) | Time Management (PA-TIM)<br>Incentive Wages (PA-INW) | Technical Note 4 |
| Production Planning (PP) | Sales and Operations Planning (PP-SOP)<br>Master Planning (PP-MP)<br>Capacity Requirements Planning (PP-CRP)<br>Material Requirements Planning (PP-MRP)<br>Kanban/Just-in-Time Production (PP-KAB)<br>Repetitive Manufacturing (PP-REM)<br>Assembly Orders (PP-ATO)<br>Production Planning for Process Industries (PP-PI)<br>Plant Data Collection (PP-PDC) | Chapters 10, 11, 12, 14, and 15 |
| Materials management (MM) | Material Requirements Planning (MM-MRP)<br>Purchasing (MM-PUR)<br>Inventory Management (MM-IM)<br>Warehouse Management (MM-WM)<br>Electronic Data Interchange (MM-EDI) | Chapters 12, 13, and 14 |
| Quality management (QM) | Planning Tools (QM-PT)<br>Inspection Processing (QM-IM)<br>Quality Control (QM-QC)<br>Quality Certificates (QM-CA) | Chapters 7 and Technical Note 7 |

of information. The applications, which consist of the modules listed above, can be run on separate computers. The applications are networked around the database cluster and have independent access to it. Users communicate with the applications through the front-end servers, which typically are PCs running Microsoft Windows 2000.

The R/3 applications are fully integrated so that data are shared between all applications. If, for example, an employee posts a shipping transaction in the Sales and Distribution module, the transaction is immediately seen by Accounts Payable in the Financial Accounting module, and by Inventory Management in the Materials Management module. The Manufacturing and Logistics module has applications that support virtually all of the topics discussed in this book, and Exhibit MB11.3 maps these applications into the appropriate chapters. This is an impressive list of features that are packaged with the software. Similar lists could be developed for the accounting, finance, and marketing functional areas.

Much of the success of the product is due to the comprehensive coverage of business applications. In a sense, SAP has changed the face of information technology. We now have the enterprisewide integrated system we only dreamed of a few years ago. Companies can consider the automation of their basic business processes as if it were a utility like electricity or water: Hook it up and get back to the real, challenging business at hand.

Of course, it is not really this simple. The problem is that many of the applications do not line up with the way a company operates. The SAP consultants argue that the modules are designed around industry "best practices." But this, in many cases, means that a firm wishing to use SAP needs to change its practices to those implemented by the SAP programmers.

## R/3 APPLICATION MODULES

Cross Functional

R/3 is built around a comprehensive set of application modules that can be used either alone or in combination. Exhibit MB11.4 shows the major modules of R/3. The modules can be used to support processes that span different functional areas in the firm. Because the modules are integrated and use a common database, transactions processed in one area immediately update all other areas. For example, if an order is received from a customer via the Internet, accounting, production scheduling, and purchasing immediately know about the order and the impact it has on their areas.

Another feature that has been incorporated into the software from the start is the use of a *data warehouse.* See the breakthrough box titled "R/3's Open Information Warehouse" for an example of how this works.

In our review of the application modules that make up R/3 (see Exhibit MB11.4), the emphasis is placed on what these modules actually do, not on the technical aspects of how they communicate with one another. The technical aspects of how SAP has implemented this software are interesting, particularly if you are a student in the information systems area. Much information on the technical aspects of the software is available from the SAP Web page. (*http://www.sap.com*)

SAP organizes the R/3 modules in a variety of ways in its documents. In general, there are four major elements to the organization: financial accounting, human resources, manufacturing and logistics, and sales and distribution. We describe these four elements in terms of functionality, but these descriptions are by no means complete. SAP indicates that modules are updated twice a year, based upon changes in business practices, technological advances, and the requirements of their customers.

EXHIBIT MB11.4

R/3 Application Modules

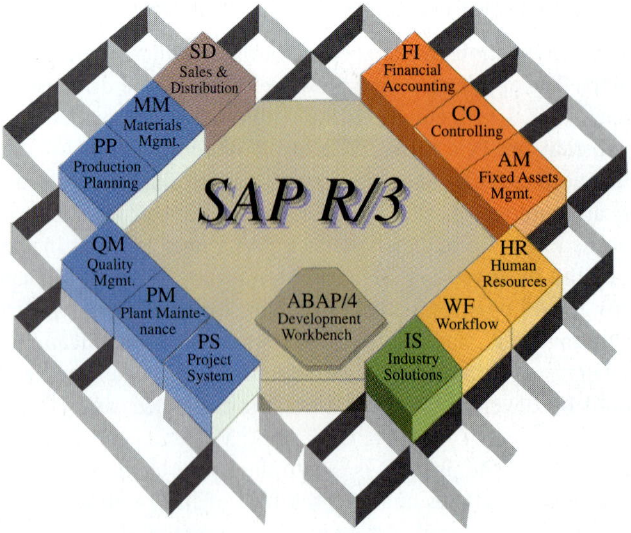


SOURCE: COPYRIGHT BY SAP AG. USED WITH PERMISSION.

## FINANCIAL ACCOUNTING

Financial accounting

The **financial accounting** segment of R/3 includes three major categories of functionality needed to run the financial accounts for a company—financials (FI), controlling (CO), and asset management (AM). FI includes accounts payable, accounts receivable, general ledger, and capital investments. Also included in the FI category are the procedures to post accounts; close the books for the month and year; prepare financial statements, including the balance sheet; and perform planning functions. Naturally, the system provides the capability to document processes, prepare reports, archive certain data, and make additions and changes to the financial data as necessary.

As with all the modules in the R/3 system, the user will find all information current and integrated. Thus, an individual manufacturing plant or sales organization can run a profit-and-loss report at any time during the month and be shown the most up-to-date information. This, of course, depends upon having set up the company hierarchy in such a way that the plant or sales group is designated as a profit-and-loss center.

The controlling category includes costing; cost center, profit center, and enterprise accounting and planning; internal orders; open item management; posting and allocation; profitability analysis; and a variety of reporting functions. It also includes a project system to track activity and costs related to major corporate projects, such as the implementation of an R/3 system. This is not the same thing as a project management system, which can be found in the manufacturing modules.

## BREAKTHROUGH

### R/3's OPEN INFORMATION WAREHOUSE

Any modern database will let you easily formulate an SQL query like "What sales did my company have in Italy in 1997?" A report generated in response to such a query could look like this:

| REGION | Q1 | Q2 | Q3 | Q4 | TOTAL |
|---|---|---|---|---|---|
| Umbria | 1000 | 1200 | 800 | 2000 | 5000 |
| TOSCANA | 2000 | 2600 | 1600 | 2800 | 9000 |
| CALABRIA | 400 | 300 | 150 | 450 | 1300 |
| TOTAL | 3400 | 4100 | 2550 | 5250 | 15300 |

But things get more complex if, for instance, we then want to use this answer as the basis for *drilling down* to look at the sales for different quarters and sales representatives in the various regions. Drilling down means descending through an existing hierarchy to bring out more and more detail.

In the following example, we drill down through the sales hierarchy (sales representatives in Toscana). Signore Corleone's sales do not appear to have been affected by the holiday season in the third quarter.

| SALES | Q1 | Q2 | Q3 | Q4 | TOTAL |
|---|---|---|---|---|---|
| S. Paolo | 500 | 600 | 300 | 500 | 1900 |
| S. Vialli | 700 | 600 | 200 | 700 | 2200 |
| S. Ferrari | 600 | 700 | 400 | 700 | 2400 |
| S. Corleone | 200 | 700 | 700 | 900 | 2500 |
| Total | 2000 | 2600 | 1600 | 2800 | 9000 |

At this point, you can switch to another dimension—for instance, from sales representative to product sold. This is often referred to as *slice and dice.*

| PRODUCT | Q1 | Q2 | Q3 | Q4 | TOTAL |
|---|---|---|---|---|---|
| X-11 | 2000 | 2500 | 1500 | 3550 | 9550 |
| Z-12 | 1400 | 1600 | 1050 | 1700 | 5750 |
| TOTAL | 3400 | 4100 | 2550 | 5250 | 15300 |

From the standpoint of a data analyst, it can now be useful to check sales of particular products in each region. SAP R/3 allows the end user to do this easily using the data warehouse approach implemented within the system.

SOURCE: THIS EXAMPLE WAS TAKEN FROM C. HEINRICH AND M. HOFMANN, "DECISION SUPPORT FROM THE SAP OPEN INFORMATION WAREHOUSE," SAP WEB SITE, MAY 23, 1997, P. 4.

COLGATE COMPANY'S DATA CENTER IN PISCATAWAY, NEW JERSEY HAS REPLACED OVER 25 INDIVIDUAL PROCESSING CENTERS WORLDWIDE. FROM HERE THE COMPANY MANAGES COMMUNICATION NETWORKS AND THE SAP SOFTWARE THAT MONITORS ACTIVITIES ACROSS THE ENTIRE SUPPLY CHAIN. AT COLGATE-U.S. SUPPLY CHIAN INVENTORY HAS BEEN REDUCED TO HALF THAT REQUIRED A FEW YEARS AGO, WHILE CUSTOMER SERVICE LEVELS HAVE IMPROVED TO 99 PERCENT.

Also included is a module to add activity-based costing (ABC) to other types of costing approaches. ABC is recognized as an effective approach to model the flow of costs between cost objects. Activity costs can then be allocated to business processes.

The asset management category includes the ability to manage all types of corporate assets, including fixed assets, leased assets, and real estate. It also includes the capital investment management module, which provides the ability to manage, measure, and oversee capital investment programs. Treasury capabilities are offered, including the ability to manage cash and funds belonging to the corporation.

## HUMAN RESOURCES (HR)

Human resources

The **human resources** (HR) segment contains the full set of capabilities needed to manage, schedule, pay, and hire the people who make a company run. It includes payroll, benefits administration, applicant data administration, personnel development planning, workforce planning, schedule and shift planning, time management, and travel expense accounting.

Because the structure of most companies shifts frequently, one function in the human resources category provides the ability to represent organizational charts, including organizational units, jobs, positions, workplaces, and tasks. Thus, the user can represent and plan matrix organization, split responsibilities, and temporary project groups.

Capturing data from the human resources module, the SAP Business Workflow (WF) system allows management to define and manage the flow of work required in a cross-functional business process. Process owners find this useful for monitoring activities that have deadlines either by individual or by position.

## MANUFACTURING AND LOGISTICS

Manufacturing and logistics

The **manufacturing and logistics** segment is the largest and most complex of the module categories. It can be divided into five major components: materials management (MM), plant maintenance (PM), quality management (QM), production planning and control (PP), and a project management system (PS). Each component is divided into a number of subcomponents. Materials management covers all tasks within the supply chain, including consumption-based planning, purchasing, vendor evaluation, and invoice verification. It also includes inventory and warehouse management to manage stock until usage dictates the cycle should begin again. Electronic kanban/just-in-time delivery is supported.

Plant maintenance supports the activities associated with planning and performing repairs and preventive maintenance. Completion and cost reports are available. Maintenance activities can be managed and measured.

The quality management capability plans and implements procedures for inspection and quality assurance. It is built on the ISO 9001 standard for quality management. It is integrated with the procurement and production processes so that the user can identify inspection points both for incoming materials and for products during the manufacturing process.

Production planning and control supports both discrete and process manufacturing processes. Repetitive and configure-to-order approaches are provided. This set of modules supports all phases of manufacturing, providing capacity leveling and requirements planning, material requirements planning, product costing, bills of material explosion and implosion, CAD dialog interface, and engineering change management. The system allows users to link rework orders to production schedules. Orders can be generated from internal sales orders or from links to a World Wide Web site.

The project management system lets the user set up, manage, and evaluate large, complex projects. Whereas the financial costing project system focuses on costs, the manufacturing project system is used for planning and monitoring dates and resources. The system walks the user through the typical project steps—concept, rough-cut planning, detailed planning, approval, execution, and closing. It manages a sequence of activities, each with its interrelationships to the others. Activities are defined as tasks that take time, are processed without interruption, require resources, and incur costs. Projects are measured based on projected and actual dates and results. The system provides the capability to manage availability, budget, capacity and cost planning, project status, and time scheduling.

## SALES AND DISTRIBUTION (SD)

Sales and distribution

The **sales and distribution** (SD) set of modules provides customer management; sales order management; configuration management; distribution, export controls, shipping, and transportation management; and billing, invoicing, and rebate processing. Because this, like the other modules, can be implemented globally, the user can manage the sales process worldwide. For example, an order may be received in Hong Kong. If the products are not available locally, they may be internally procured from warehouses in other parts of the world and shipped to arrive together at the Hong Kong customer's site.

In sales and distribution, products or services are sold to customers. In implementing the SD module (as in other modules), the company structure must be represented in the system so that, for example, R/3 knows where and when to recognize revenue. It is possible to represent the structure of the firm from the point of view of accounting, materials management, or sales and distribution. These structures can also be combined.

When a sales order is entered, it automatically includes the correct information on pricing, promotions, availability, and shipping options. Batch order processing is available for specialized industries such as food, pharmaceutical, or chemical. Users can reserve inventory for specific customers, request production of subassemblies, or enter orders that are assemble-to-order, build-to-order, or engineer-to-order as well as special customized orders. Exhibit MB11.5 depicts the complex data linkages between modules needed to integrate information managed by the system.

The modules included with the R/3 system are built on what SAP considers best practices. SAP has a research and development group that continually looks for better ways to carry out a particular process or subprocess. System upgrades are designed to reflect the newest best practices.

EXHIBIT MB11.5

Logistics Integration Overview

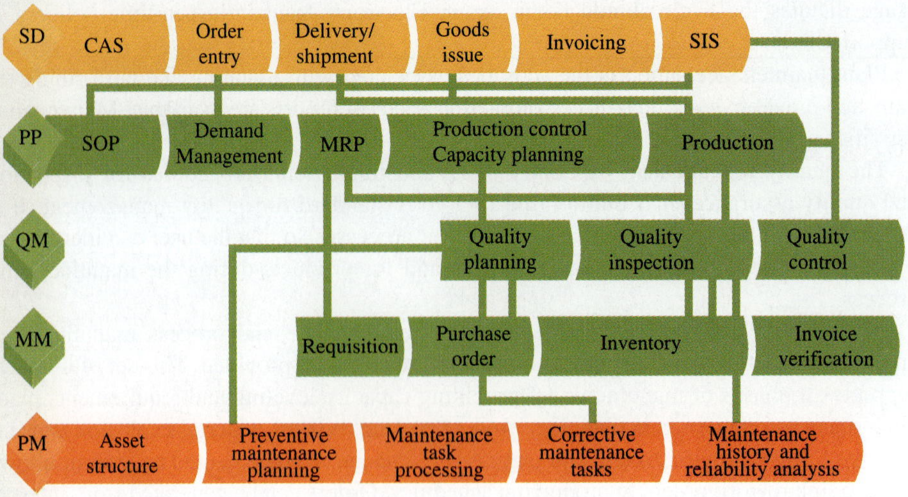


SOURCE: COPYRIGHT BY SAP AG. USED WITH PERMISSION.

In addition to the set of standard modules, SAP also has special add-on modules called Industry Solutions (IS) tailored to specific industries. Included in the current set are modules for the following industries: chemical/petrochemical, oil and gas, public sector, hospital, retailing, printing and publishing, insurance, and banking. These modules add special features that are needed in each industry. SAP expects to develop many more of these types of modules in the future.

## IMPLEMENTING ERP SYSTEMS

SAP has some strong competition. Companies such as Oracle, i2 Technologies, and PeopleSoft have aggressively gone after the market. SAP, though, is the market leader with over 22,000 sites and over 1,000,000 users worldwide. Implementation of ERP is costly, with the actual cost of the software typically one-third or less of the total cost. Large companies, such as Chevron Corp. and Bristol-Myers Squibb, typically earmark $250 million or more to implement an ERP system.

Implementing these systems does not always work out. Allied Waste Industries recently pulled the plug on a brand-new $130 million computer system that used SAP R/3.[1] Allied Waste found SAP too expensive and too complicated to operate. A survey conducted by the Harvard Business School revealed that a large percentage of executives had negative feelings toward ERP software.[2] In particular, they felt that (1) ERP technology could not support their businesses; (2) their organizations could not make changes needed to extract benefits from the new systems; and (3) ERP implementation might actually damage their businesses. The same survey indicated that many companies implementing ERP had overrun cost and schedule targets and had not achieved the benefits sought.

Despite the reservations about ERP, most companies surveyed by Harvard were going ahead with ERP initiatives. The most popular reasons cited included a desire to standardize and improve processes, to improve systems integration, and to improve information quality. Even though there is evidence of many problems with implementing ERP systems, firms continue in their ERP efforts because of the opportunity for substantial reward. A good example of how companies can benefit is in the Breakthrough Box titled "ERP: Some Success Stories."

BREAKTHROUGH

## ERP: Some Success Stories

Like many new technologies, ERP systems have near-magical effects when they work as promised. Consider the following:

- Singapore-based Flextronics International, a $1.1 billion custom manufacturer, has rolled out ERP to its 26 locations around the globe. Based on early implementation, one improvement is increased speed with which the company turns over inventory. Flextronics' managers now shop first in their own internal online store, which contains a dynamic listing of parts and materials available anywhere within the company. Whenever the company needs something, it often finds out that it already owns it. The consolidated supply inventory also helps Flextronics' purchasing managers negotiate better terms with suppliers.
- At Kaasco, an 80-employee furniture maker in Mukilteo, Washington, the company's ERP system prevents production hiccups by linking manufacturing runs to the required bills of materials, so production managers can identify supply defects weeks before they hamper operations. Managers indicate that they used to keep a lot of that in their heads before ERP. An added bonus is that company financials are now always current and on time.
- At IBM's 5,500-employee manufacturing facility in Rochester, Minnesota, the efficiencies generated by an ERP system helped consolidate production of two different hardware lines. In the past, the two lines were run as two totally separate entities, but now they have a single comprehensive overview of the entire factory.

Managers at other companies list dozens of productivity enhancements from ERP systems, including the ability to calculate new prices instantly when a single component in a product is changed; more accurate manufacturing cost comparisons among different facilities; better electronic data interchange (EDI) with vendors and suppliers; more detailed forecasting; rapid delivery of custom quotes for special orders; and the elimination of bottlenecks and duplicate procedures.

SOURCE: "HARVARD MANAGEMENT UPDATE," MARCH 1999, P. 3.

# CONCLUSION

The reason for including this managerial briefing at this point in the book is so you can see that the techniques described in this section are now commonly available and widely implemented in companies. In the following sections we discuss such forecasting tools as moving averages and exponential smoothing, inventory control tools such as material requirements planning, and scheduling using earliest due-date logic. All of these techniques are included in the leading ERP packages. One might think that there is no need to learn how these techniques actually work; all that needs to be done is fire up the ERP system and let it make all the decisions. If it were that simple, we would all be out of work.

In reality, there are many ways to implement these different techniques, and different techniques are applicable to different types of firms. R/3, for example has three ways that forecasts can be calculated (discussed in Chapter 11) and five different lot-sizing rules for batch production (discussed in Chapter 14). So many different decisions need to be made to properly use any system.

To select from the many ERP systems that are available, one needs to evaluate the strengths and weaknesses of each offering. i2 Technologies has a very strong forecasting capability and is known for flow manufacturing scheduling. In Chapter 11 the different types of forecasting systems are discussed in some depth, giving you the ability to evaluate whether the unique characteristics of the i2 offering match what is needed by your firm. Similarly, in Chapter 14, all the different lot-sizing rules are studied, and the flow manufacturing concept is compared to traditional material requirements planning (MRP). Given this information, you can evaluate whether i2 would be good for your company.

In writing this managerial briefing, one temptation was to include an extensive comparison of the various ERP systems available. (A great source of the most current information is the Operations Management Center at *http://mhhe.com/pom.*). The problem with doing this and publishing it in a textbook is that by the time the book is printed the comparison would be out of date. Business software technology is moving at an amazing rate. Every day a new package becomes available with some slick trick that supposedly makes it better than the rest. To make matters worse, each vendor likes to tag names to things to give the appearance of something new. In reality, there are not many new ideas; conventional techniques are typically repackaged in new ways. Sometimes more efficient ways to implement these techniques are developed. Understanding the conventional approaches is an important first step to being able to keep up with this rapidly expanding area of software technology.

## KEY TERMS

**Enterprise resource planning (ERP)** A computer system that integrates application programs in accounting, sales, manufacturing, and the other functions in a firm. This integration is accomplished through a database shared by all the application programs.

**Financial accounting** A segment of R/3 that includes the financials, controlling, and asset management functionality needed to run the financial accounts for a company. Financials include accounts payable, accounts receivable, general ledger, capital investments, and the procedures to close the books for the month and year.

**Human resources** A segment with the capabilities needed to manage, schedule, pay, and hire the people who work for the company. This includes payroll, benefits administration, applicant data administration, personnel development planning, workforce planning, schedule and shift planning, time management, and travel expense accounting.

**Manufacturing and logistics** Contains five major components: materials management, plant maintenance, quality management, production planning and control, and project management.

**Sales and distribution** A segment that includes customer, sales order, and configuration management; distribution export controls; shipping and management; and billing, order, and rebate processing.

## REVIEW AND DISCUSSION QUESTIONS

1 What key technological features of SAP R/3 set it apart from conventional business accounting/planning/control software?

3 SAP R/3 allows the human resources, financial accounting, and manufacturing and logistics modules to be implemented separately. How would this change impact the implementation process?

3 A feature that many companies are considering is taking customer orders via web sites. Put yourself in the place of the person at Ford Motor Company considering this approach to taking customer orders for the Ford Explorer sport utility vehicle. What information would you need to collect from the customer? What information would you give the customer regarding the order? How would the information be used within Ford Motor Company? What major problems would you anticipate need solving prior to implementing the system? If this project is successful—that is, customers find ordering their Explorer over the Web preferable to negotiating with a dealer—what are the long-term implications to Ford Motor Company?

## SELECTED BIBLIOGRAPHY

ASAP World Consultancy, et al. *Using SAP R/3.* Indianapolis, IN: Que, 1996.

Bancroft, N. *Implementing SAP R/3: How to Introduce a Large System into a Large Organization.* Greenwich, CT: Manning, 1996.

Curran, T.; G. Keller; and A. Ladd. *Business Blueprint: Understanding SAP's R/3 Reference Model.* Upper Saddle River, NJ: Prentice Hall PTR, 1998.

Davenport, T. H. "Putting the Enterprise into the System." *Harvard Business Review,* July–August 1998.

Hernâandez, J. A. *The SAP R/3 Handbook.* New York: McGraw-Hill, 1997.

Jacobs, F. R., and D. C. Whybark. *Why ERP? A Primer on SAP Implementation.* Burr Ridge, IL: Irwin/McGraw-Hill, 2000.

Shtub, A. *Enterprise Resource Planning: The Dynamics of Operations Management.* Boston: Klewer Academic Publishers, 1999.

## FOOTNOTES

1 J. Bailey, "Trash Haulers Are Taking Fancy Software to the Dump," *The Wall Street Journal,* June 9, 1999, p. B4.

2 C. X. Escalle and M. Cotteleer, "Enterprise Resource Planning (ERP)" 9-699-020, Harvard Business School, February 11, 1999, p. 3.

chapter

# chapter eleven
# FORECASTING

## CHAPTER OUTLINE AND KEY TERMS

# 11

Wal-Mart's size and power in the retail industry is having a huge influence in the database industry. Wal-Mart manages one of the world's largest data warehouses with more than seven terabytes of data. Now the retailer is about to squeeze even more value from those systems with a new data-mining application that will help it replace inventories in stores. (http://www.walmart.com)

Wal-Mart's formula for success—getting the right product on the appropriate shelf at the lowest price—owes much to the company's multimillion-dollar investment in data warehousing. Wal-Mart has more detail than most of its competitors on what's going on by product, by store, by day.

The systems house data on point of sale, inventory, products in transit, market statistics, customer demographics, finance, product returns, and supplier performance. The data are used for three broad areas of decision support: analyzing trends, managing inventory, and understanding customers. What emerges are "personality traits" for each of Wal-Mart's 3,000 or so outlets, which Wal-Mart managers use to determine product mix and presentation for each store.

Data mining is next. Wal-Mart has developed a demand-forecasting application that looks at individual items for individual stores to decide the seasonal sales profile of each item. The system keeps a year's worth of data on the sales of 100,000 products and predicts which items will be needed in each store.

Wal-Mart is now doing market-basket analysis. Data is collected on items that comprise a shopper's total purchase so that the company can analyze relationships and patterns in customer purchases. The data warehouse is made available over the Web to its store managers and suppliers.

Cross Functional

Forecasts are vital to every business organization and for every significant management decision. Forecasting is the basis of corporate long-run planning. In the functional areas of finance and accounting, forecasts provide the basis for budgetary planning and cost control. Marketing relies on sales forecasting to plan new products, compensate sales personnel, and make other key decisions. Production and operations personnel use forecasts to make periodic decisions involving process selection, capacity planning, and facility layout, as well as for continual decisions about production planning, scheduling, and inventory.

Bear in mind that a perfect forecast is usually impossible. Too many factors in the business environment cannot be predicted with certainty. Therefore, rather than search for the perfect forecast, it is far more important to establish the practice of continual review of forecasts and to learn to live with inaccurate forecasts. This is not to say that we should not try to improve the forecasting model or methodology, but that we should try to find and use the best forecasting method available, *within reason.*

When forecasting, a good strategy is to use two or three methods and look at them for the commonsense view. Will expected changes in the general economy affect the forecast? Are there changes in industrial and private consumer behaviors? Will there be a shortage of essential complementary items? Continual review and updating in light of new data are basic to successful forecasting. In this chapter we look at *qualitative* and *quantitative* forecasting and concentrate primarily on several quantitative time series techniques. We cover in some depth moving averages, linear regression, trends, seasonal ratios (including deseasonalization), and focused forecasting. We also discuss sources and measurement of errors.

## DEMAND MANAGEMENT

The purpose of demand management is to coordinate and control all sources of demand so the productive system can be used efficiently and the product delivered on time.

Where does demand for a firm's product or service come from, and what can a firm do to manage it? There are two basic sources of demand: dependent demand and independent demand. **Dependent demand** is the demand for a product or service caused by the demand for other products or services. For example, if a firm sells 1,000 tricycles, then 1,000 front wheels and 2,000 rear wheels are needed. This type of internal demand needs not a forecast, just a tabulation. As to how many tricycles the firm might sell, this is called **independent demand** because its demand cannot be derived directly from that of other products.[1] We discuss dependence and independence more fully in Chapters 13 and 14.

Dependent demand

Independent demand

There is not much a firm can do about dependent demand. It must be met (although the product or service can be purchased rather than produced internally). But there is a lot a firm can do about independent demand—if it wants to. The firm can

1 **Take an active role to influence demand.** The firm can apply pressure on its sales force, it can offer incentives both to customers and to its own personnel, it can wage campaigns to sell products, and it can cut prices. These actions can increase demand. Conversely, demand can be decreased through price increases or reduced sales efforts.

2 **Take a passive role and simply respond to demand.** There are several reasons a firm may not try to change demand but simply accept what happens. If a firm is running at full capacity, it may not want to do anything about demand. Other reasons are a firm may be powerless to change demand because of the expense to advertise; the market may be fixed in size and static; or demand is beyond

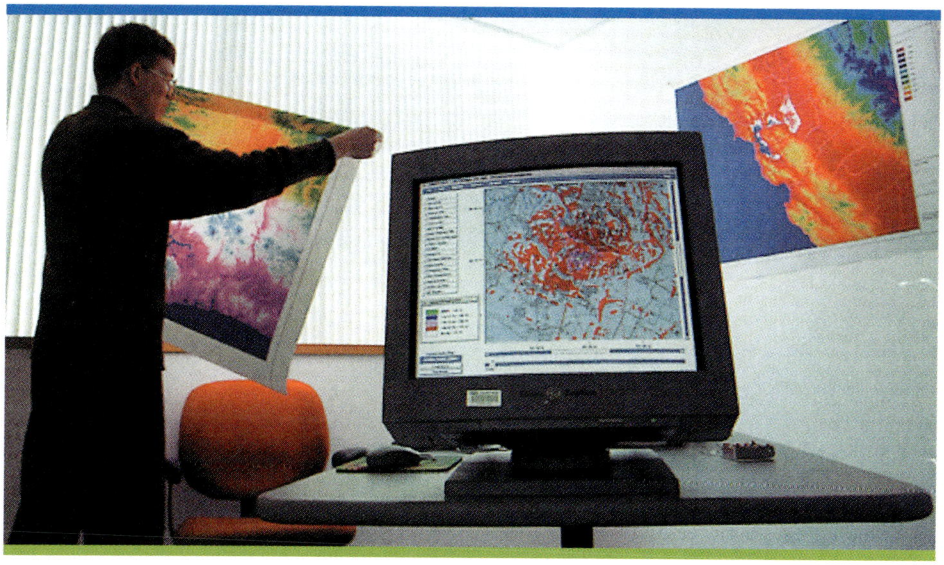

A GTE LABORATORIES ENGINEER EXAMINES A PRINT GENERATED BY GRANET, A GRAPHICS-BASED SOFTWARE TOOL DEVELOPED BY GTE TO HELP ENGINEERS WORLDWIDE PLAN CELLULAR NETWORKS AND FORECAST THEIR PERFORMANCE.

its control (such as in the case of sole supplier). There are other competitive, legal, environmental, ethical, and moral reasons that market demand is passively accepted.

A great deal of coordination is required to manage these dependent, independent, active, and passive demands. These demands originate both internally and externally in the form of new product sales from marketing, repair parts for previously sold products from product service, restocking from the factory warehouses, and supply items for manufacturing. In this chapter, our primary interest is in forecasting for independent items.

## TYPES OF FORECASTING

Forecasting can be classified into four basic types: *qualitative, time series analysis, causal relationships,* and *simulation.*

Qualitative techniques are subjective or judgmental and are based on estimates and opinions. **Time series analysis,** the primary focus of this chapter, is based on the idea that data relating to past demand can be used to predict future demand. Past data may include several components, such as trend, seasonal, or cyclical influences, and are described in the following section. Causal forecasting, which we discuss using the linear regression technique, assumes that demand is related to some underlying factor or factors in the environment. Simulation models allow the forecaster to run through a range of assumptions about the condition of the forecast. Exhibit 11.1 describes a variety of the four basic types of forecasting models. In this chapter we discuss the first four time series analysis methods in the exhibit and the first of the causal techniques.

Time series analysis

## COMPONENTS OF DEMAND

In most cases, demand for products or services can be broken down into six components: average demand for the period, a trend, seasonal element, cyclical elements, random variation, and autocorrelation. Exhibit 11.2 illustrates a demand over a four-year period, showing the average, trend, and seasonal components, and randomness around the smoothed demand curve.

EXHIBIT 11.1

## Forecasting Techniques and Common Models

| | |
|---|---|
| **I. Qualitative** | Subjective; judgmental. Based on estimates and opinions. |
| Grass roots | Derives a forecast by compiling input from those at the end of the hierarchy who deal with what is being forecast. For example, an overall sales forecast may be derived by combining inputs from each salesperson, who is closest to his or her own territory. |
| Market research | Sets out to collect data in a variety of ways (surveys, interviews, and so on) to test hypotheses about the market. This is typically used to forecast long-range and new product sales. |
| Panel consensus | Free open exchange at meetings. The idea is that discussion by the group will produce better forecasts than any one individual. Participants may be executives, salespeople, or customers. |
| Historical analogy | Ties what is being forecast to a similar item. Important in planning new products where a forecast may be derived by using the history of a similar product. |
| Delphi method | Group of experts responds to questionnaire. A moderator compiles results and formulates a new questionnaire that is submitted to the group. Thus, there is a learning process for the group as it receives new information and there is no influence of group pressure or dominating individuals. |
| **II. Time series analysis** | Based on the idea that the history of occurrences over time can be used to predict the future. |
| Simple moving average | A time period containing a number of data points is averaged by dividing the sum of the point values by the number of points. Each, therefore, has equal influence. |
| Weighted moving average | Specific points may be weighted more or less than the others, as seen fit by experience. |
| Exponential smoothing | Recent data points are weighted more with weighting declining exponentially as data become older. |
| Regression analysis | Fits a straight line to past data generally relating the data value to time. Most common fitting technique is least squares. |
| Box Jenkins technique | Very complicated but apparently the most accurate statistical technique available. Relates a class of statistical models to data and fits the model to the time series by using Bayesian posterior distributions. |
| Shiskin time series | (Also called X-11.) Developed by Julius Shiskin of the Census Bureau. An effective method to decompose a time series into seasonals, trends, and irregular. It needs at least three years of history. Very good in identifying turning points, for example, in company sales. |
| Trend projections | Fits a mathematical trend line to the data points and projects it into the future. |
| **III. Causal** | Tries to understand the system underlying and surrounding the item being forecast. For example, sales may be affected by advertising, quality, and competitors. |
| Regression analysis | Similar to least squares method in time series but may contain multiple variables. Basis is that forecast is caused by the occurrence of other events. |
| Econometric models | Attempts to describe some sector of the economy by a series of interdependent equations. |
| Input/output models | Focuses on sales of each industry to other firms and governments. Indicates the changes in sales that a producer industry might expect because of purchasing changes by another industry. |
| Leading indicators | Statistics that move in the same direction as the series being forecast but move before the series, such as an increase in the price of gasoline indicating a future drop in the sale of large cars. |
| **IV. Simulation models** | Dynamic models, usually computer-based, that allow the forecaster to make assumptions about the internal variables and external environment in the model. Depending on the variables in the model, the forecaster may ask such questions as, what would happen to my forecast if price increased by 10 percent? What effect would a mild national recession have on my forecast? |

EXHIBIT 11.2

Historical Product Demand Consisting of a Growth Trend and Seasonal Demand

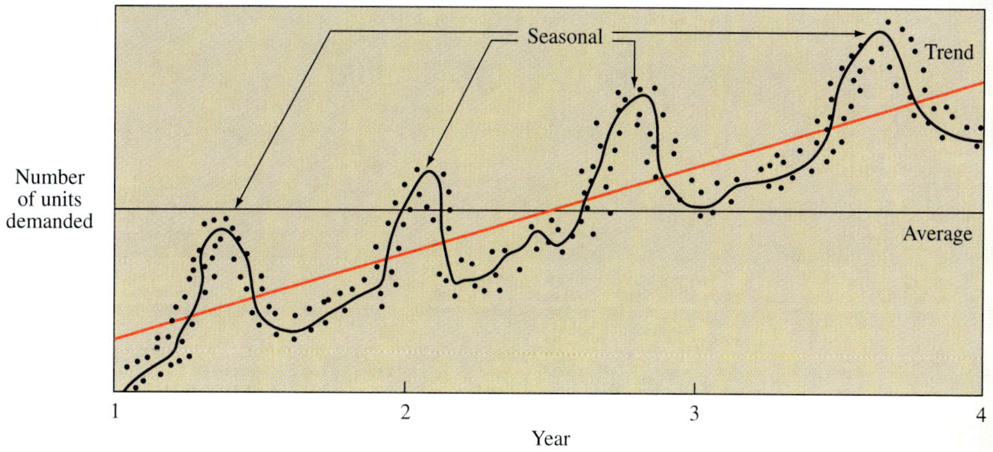


Cyclical factors are more difficult to determine because the time span may be unknown or the cause of the cycle may not be considered. Cyclical influence on demand may come from such occurrences as political elections, war, economic conditions, or sociological pressures.

Random variations are caused by chance events. Statistically, when all the known causes for demand (average, trend, seasonal, cyclical, and autocorrelative) are subtracted from total demand, what remains is the unexplained portion of demand. If we cannot identify the cause of this remainder, it is assumed to be purely random chance.

Autocorrelation denotes the persistence of occurrence. More specifically, the value expected at any point is highly correlated with its own past values. In waiting line theory, the length of a waiting line is highly autocorrelated. That is, if a line is relatively long at one time, then shortly after that time, we would expect the line still to be long.

When demand is random, it may vary widely from one week to another. Where high autocorrelation exists, demand is not expected to change very much from one week to the next.

Trend lines are the usual starting point in developing a forecast. These trend lines are then adjusted for seasonal effects, cyclical elements, and any other expected events that may influence the final forecast. Exhibit 11.3 shows four of the most common types of trends. A linear trend is obviously a straight continuous relationship. An S-curve is typical of a product growth and maturity cycle. The most important point in the S-curve is where the trend changes from slow growth to fast growth, or from fast to slow. An asymptotic trend starts with the highest demand growth at the beginning but then tapers off. Such a curve could happen when a firm enters an existing market with the objective of saturating and capturing a large share of the market. An exponential curve is common in products with explosive growth. The exponential trend suggests that sales will continue to increase—an assumption that may not be safe to make.

A widely used forecasting method plots data and then searches for the standard distribution (such as linear, S-curve, asymptotic, or exponential) that fits best. The attractiveness of this method is that because the mathematics for the curve are known, solving for values for future time periods is easy.

Sometimes our data do not seem to fit any standard curve. This may be due to several causes essentially beating the data from several directions at the same time. For these cases, a simplistic but often effective forecast can be obtained by simply plotting data.

EXHIBIT 11.3

Common Types of Trends

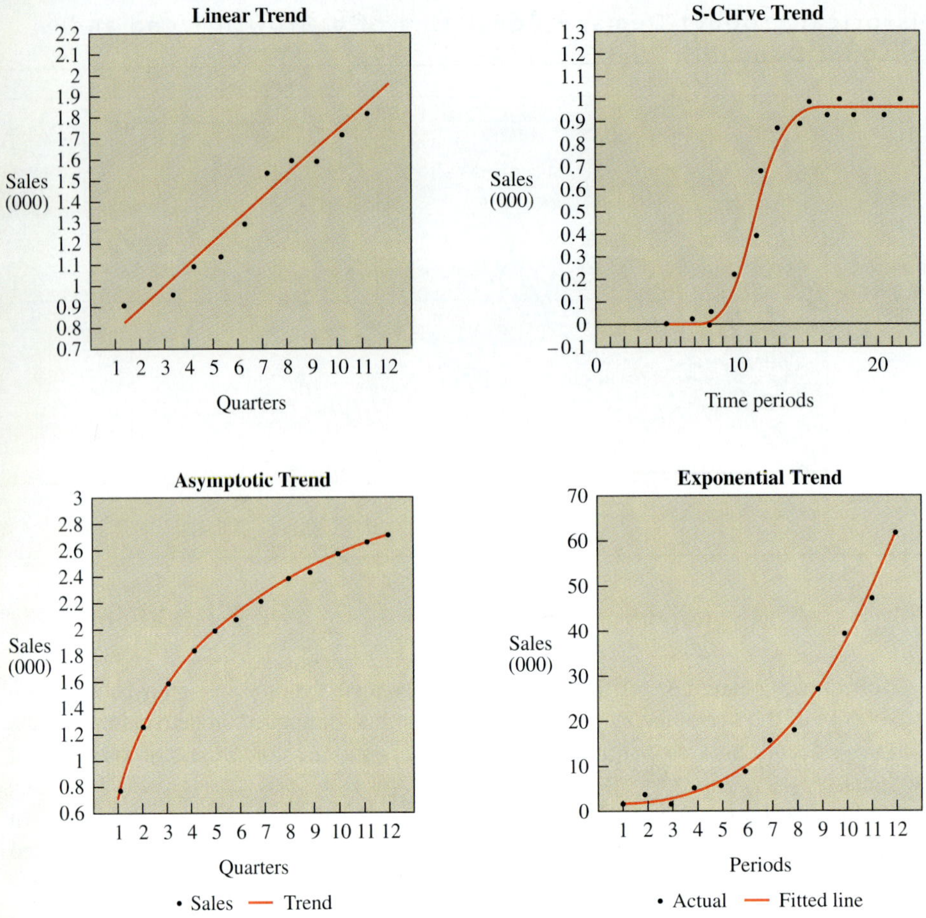


# QUALITATIVE TECHNIQUES IN FORECASTING

## GRASS ROOTS

As stated in Exhibit 11.1, *grass roots* forecasting builds the forecast by adding successively from the bottom. The assumption here is that the person closest to the customer or end use of the product knows its future needs best. Though this is not always true, in many instances it is a valid assumption, and it is the basis for this method.

Forecasts at this bottom level are summed and given to the next higher level. This is usually a district warehouse, which then adds in safety stocks and any effects of ordering quantity sizes. This amount is then fed to the next level, which may be a regional warehouse. The procedure repeats until it becomes an input at the top level, which, in the case of a manufacturing firm, would be the input to the production system.

## MARKET RESEARCH

Firms often hire outside companies that specialize in *market research* to conduct this type of forecasting. You may have been involved in market surveys through a marketing class. Certainly you have not escaped telephone calls asking you about product preferences, your income, habits, and so on.

Market research is used mostly for product research in the sense of looking for new product ideas, likes and dislikes about existing products, which competitive products within a particular class are preferred, and so on. Again, the data collection methods are primarily surveys and interviews.

A NUMBER OF FIRMS, INCLUDING THIRD WAVE RESEARCH GROUP, NOW OFFER MARKETERS SOFTWARE OR DATABASES TO HELP THEM MORE ACCURATELY FORECAST SALES FOR SPECIFIC MARKET AREAS, PRODUCTS, OR SEGMENTS.

## PANEL CONSENSUS

In a *panel consensus,* the idea that two heads are better than one is extrapolated to the idea that a panel of people from a variety of positions can develop a more reliable forecast than a narrower group. Panel forecasts are developed through open meetings with free exchange of ideas from all levels of management and individuals. The difficulty with this open style is that lower employee levels are intimidated by higher levels of management. For example, a salesperson in a particular product line may have a good estimate of future product demand but may not speak up to refute a much different estimate given by the vice president of marketing. The Delphi technique (which we discuss shortly) was developed to try to correct this impairment to free exchange.

When decisions in forecasting are at a broader, higher level (as when introducing a new product line or concerning strategic product decisions such as new marketing areas), the term *executive judgment* is generally used. The term is self-explanatory: a higher level of management is involved.

## HISTORICAL ANALOGY

In trying to forecast demand for a new product, an ideal situation would be where an existing product or generic product could be used as a model. There are many ways to classify such analogies—for example, complementary products, substitutable or competitive products, and products as a function of income. Again, you have surely gotten a deluge of mail advertising products in a category similar to a product purchased via catalog, the Internet, or mail order. If you buy a CD through the mail, you will receive more mail about new CDs and CD players. A causal relationship (listed in Exhibit 11.1, Part III) would be that demand for compact discs is caused by demand for CD players. An analogy would be forecasting the demand for digital videodisc players by analyzing the historical demand for stereo VCRs. The products are in the same general category of electronics and may be bought by consumers at similar rates. A simpler example would be toasters and coffee pots. A firm that already produces toasters and wants to produce coffee pots could use the toaster history as a likely growth model.

## DELPHI METHOD

As we mentioned under panel consensus, a statement or opinion of a higher-level person will likely be weighted more than that of a lower-level person. The worst case is where lower-level people feel threatened and do not contribute their true beliefs. To prevent this problem, the *Delphi method* conceals the identity of the individuals participating in the study. Everyone has the same weight. Procedurally, a moderator creates a questionnaire and distributes it to participants. Their responses are summed and given back to the entire group along with a new set of questions.

The Delphi method was developed by the Rand Corporation in the 1950s. The step-by-step procedure is

1 Choose the experts to participate. There should be a variety of knowledgeable people in different areas.
2 Through a questionnaire (or e-mail), obtain forecasts (and any premises or qualifications for the forecasts) from all participants.
3 Summarize the results and redistribute them to the participants along with appropriate new questions.
4 Summarize again, refining forecasts and conditions, and again develop new questions.
5 Repeat Step 4 if necessary. Distribute the final results to all participants.

The Delphi technique can usually achieve satisfactory results in three rounds. The time required is a function of the number of participants, how much work is involved for them to develop their forecasts, and their speed in responding.

## TIME SERIES ANALYSIS

Time series forecasting models try to predict the future based on past data. For example, sales figures collected for the past six weeks can be used to forecast sales for the seventh week. Quarterly sales figures collected for the past several years can be used to forecast future quarters. Even though both examples contain sales, different forecasting time series models would likely be used.

Exhibit 11.4 shows the time series models and some of their characteristics. The simple moving average forecast is not shown in this table, but it would have the same characteristics as simple exponential smoothing. The weighted moving average can be more tricky if the forecaster includes seasonality or other cyclic influences. Its characteristics would lie somewhere between Holt's exponential smoothing and Winter's exponential smoothing. Though we do not cover the Holt and Winter models in detail, the reader may want to investigate these variations if exponential smoothing seems to apply to the data. Note that the models vary from simple to complex.

Terms such as *short, medium,* and *long* are relative to the context in which they are used. However, in business forecasting *short-term* usually refers to under three months; *medium-term,* three months to two years; and *long-term,* greater than two years. In general, the short-term models compensate for random variation and adjust for short-term changes (such as consumers' responses to a new product). Medium-term forecasts are useful for seasonal effects, and long-term models detect general trends and are especially useful in identifying major turning points.

Which forecasting model a firm should choose depends on

1 Time horizon to forecast.
2 Data availability.
3 Accuracy required.
4 Size of forecasting budget.
5 Availability of qualified personnel.

In selecting a forecasting model, there are other issues such as the firm's degree of flexibility. (The greater the ability to react quickly to changes, the less accurate the forecast needs to be.) Another item is the consequence of a bad forecast. If a large capital investment decision is to be based on a forecast, it should be a good forecast.

EXHIBIT 11.4

## A Guide to Selecting an Appropriate Forecasting Method

| Forecasting Method | Amount of Historical Data | Data Pattern | Forecast Horizon | Preparation Time | Personnel Background |
|---|---|---|---|---|---|
| Simple exponential smoothing | 5 to 10 observations to set the weight | Data should be stationary | Short | Short | Little sophistication |
| Holt's exponential smoothing | 10 to 15 observations to set both weights | Trend but no seasonality | Short to medium | Short | Slight sophistication |
| Winter's exponential smoothing | At least 4 to 5 observations per season | Trend and seasonality | Short to medium | Short | Moderate sophistication |
| Regression trend models | 10 to 20; for seasonality at least 5 per season | Trend and seasonality | Short to medium | Short | Moderate sophistication |
| Causal regression models | 10 observations per independent variable | Can handle complex patterns | Short, medium, or long | Long development time, short time for implementation | Considerable sophistication |
| Time series decomposition | Enough to see 2 peaks and troughs | Handles cyclical and seasonal patterns; may identify turning points | Short to medium | Short to moderate | Little sophistication |
| Box Jenkins | 50 or more observations | Must be stationary or be transformed to stationarity | Short, medium, or long | Long | High sophistication |

SOURCE: J. H. WILSON AND D. ALLISON-KOERBER, "COMBINING SUBJECTIVE AND OBJECTIVE FORECASTS IMPROVES RESULTS," *THE JOURNAL OF BUSINESS FORECASTING*, FALL 1992, P. 4.

## SIMPLE MOVING AVERAGE

When demand for a product is neither growing nor declining rapidly, and if it does not have seasonal characteristics, a moving average can be useful in removing the random fluctuations for forecasting. Although *moving averages* are frequently centered, it is more convenient to use past data to predict the following period directly. To illustrate, a centered five-month average of January, February, March, April, and May gives an average centered on March. However, all five months of data must already exist. If our objective is to forecast for June, we must project our moving average—by some means—from March to June. If the average is not centered but is at the forward end, we can forecast more easily, though we may lose some accuracy. Thus, if we want to forecast June with a five-month moving average, we can take the average of January, February, March, April, and May. When June passes, the forecast for July would be the average of February, March, April, May, and June. This is how Exhibits 11.5 and 11.6 were computed.

Although it is important to select the best period for the moving average, there are several conflicting effects of different period lengths. The longer the moving average period, the more the random elements are smoothed (which may be desirable in many cases). But if there is a trend in the data—either increasing or decreasing—the moving average has the adverse characteristic of lagging the trend. Therefore, while a shorter time span produces more oscillation, there is a closer following of the trend. Conversely, a longer time span gives a smoother response but lags the trend.

The formula for a simple moving average is

[11.1]
$$F_t = \frac{A_{t-1} + A_{t-2} + A_{t-3} + \cdots + A_{t-n}}{n}$$

EXHIBIT 11.5

**Forecast Demand Based on a Three- and a Nine-Week Simple Moving Average**

Excel: Forecasting

| WEEK | DEMAND | 3 WEEK | 9 WEEK | WEEK | DEMAND | 3 WEEK | 9 WEEK |
|---|---|---|---|---|---|---|---|
| 1 | 800 | | | 16 | 1,700 | 2,200 | 1,811 |
| 2 | 1,400 | | | 17 | 1,800 | 2,000 | 1,800 |
| 3 | 1,000 | | | 18 | 2,200 | 1,833 | 1,811 |
| 4 | 1,500 | 1,067 | | 19 | 1,900 | 1,900 | 1,911 |
| 5 | 1,500 | 1,300 | | 20 | 2,400 | 1,967 | 1,933 |
| 6 | 1,300 | 1,333 | | 21 | 2,400 | 2,167 | 2,011 |
| 7 | 1,800 | 1,433 | | 22 | 2,600 | 2,233 | 2,111 |
| 8 | 1,700 | 1,533 | | 23 | 2,000 | 2,467 | 2,144 |
| 9 | 1,300 | 1,600 | | 24 | 2,500 | 2,333 | 2,111 |
| 10 | 1,700 | 1,600 | 1,367 | 25 | 2,600 | 2,367 | 2,167 |
| 11 | 1,700 | 1,567 | 1,467 | 26 | 2,200 | 2,367 | 2,267 |
| 12 | 1,500 | 1,567 | 1,500 | 27 | 2,200 | 2,433 | 2,311 |
| 13 | 2,300 | 1,633 | 1,556 | 28 | 2,500 | 2,333 | 2,311 |
| 14 | 2,300 | 1,833 | 1,644 | 29 | 2,400 | 2,300 | 2,378 |
| 15 | 2,000 | 2,033 | 1,733 | 30 | 2,100 | 2,367 | 2,378 |

EXHIBIT 11.6

**Moving Average Forecast of Three- and Nine-Week Periods versus Actual Demand**

Excel: Forecasting

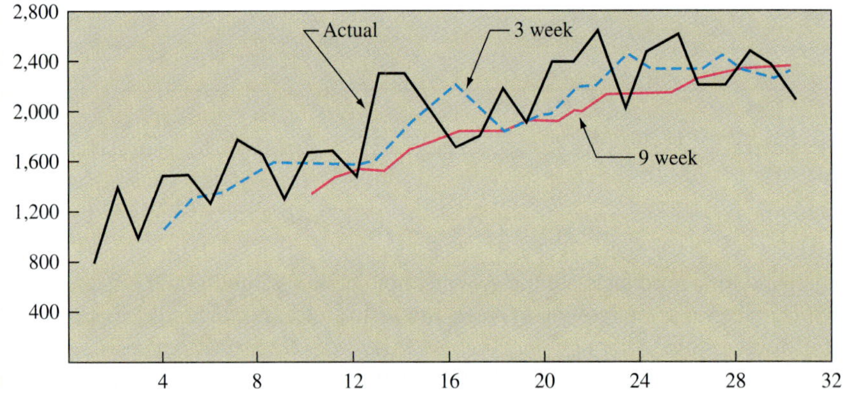


where

$$F_t = \text{Forecast for the coming period}$$
$$n = \text{Number of periods to be averaged}$$
$$A_{t-1} = \text{Actual occurrence in the past period}$$
$$A_{t-2},\ A_{t-3},\ \text{and}\ A_{t-n} = \text{Actual occurrences two periods ago, three periods ago, and so on up to } n \text{ periods ago}$$

Exhibit 11.6, a plot of the data in Exhibit 11.5, shows the effects of various lengths of the period of a moving average. We see that the growth trend levels off at about the 23rd week. The three-week moving average responds better in following this change than the nine-week average, although overall, the nine-week average is smoother.

The main disadvantage in calculating a moving average is that all individual elements must be carried as data because a new forecast period involves adding new data and dropping the earliest data. For a three- or six-period moving average, this is not too severe. But plotting a 60-day moving average for the usage of each of 20,000 items in inventory would involve a significant amount of data.

## WEIGHTED MOVING AVERAGE

Whereas the simple moving average gives equal weight to each component of the moving average database, a weighted moving average allows any weights to be placed on each element, providing, of course, that the sum of all weights equals 1. For example, a department store may find that in a four-month period, the best forecast is derived by using 40 percent of the actual sales for the most recent month, 30 percent of two months ago, 20 percent of three months ago, and 10 percent of four months ago. If actual sales experience was

| MONTH 1 | MONTH 2 | MONTH 3 | MONTH 4 | MONTH 5 |
|---|---|---|---|---|
| 100 | 90 | 105 | 95 | ? |

the forecast for month 5 would be

$$\begin{aligned} F_5 &= 0.40(95) + 0.30(105) + 0.20(90) + 0.10(100) \\ &= 38 + 31.5 + 18 + 10 \\ &= 97.5 \end{aligned}$$

The formula for a weighted moving average is

$$F_t = w_1 A_{t-1} + w_2 A_{t-2} + \cdots + w_n A_{t-n} \tag{11.2}$$

where

$w_1$ = Weight to be given to the actual occurrence for the period $t - 1$
$w_2$ = Weight to be given to the actual occurrence for the period $t - 2$
$w_n$ = Weight to be given to the actual occurrence for the period $t - n$
$n$ = Total number of periods in the forecast

Although many periods may be ignored (that is, their weights are zero) and the weighting scheme may be in any order (for example, more distant data may have greater weights than more recent data), the sum of all the weights must equal 1.

$$\sum_{i=1}^{n} w_i = 1$$

Suppose sales for month 5 actually turned out to be 110. Then the forecast for month 6 would be

$$\begin{aligned} F_6 &= 0.40(110) + 0.30(95) + 0.20(105) + 0.10(90) \\ &= 44 + 28.5 + 21 + 9 \\ &= 102.5 \end{aligned}$$

**Choosing Weights** Experience and trial and error are the simplest ways to choose weights. As a general rule, the most recent past is the most important indicator of what to expect in the future, and therefore, it should get higher weighting. The past month's revenue or plant capacity, for example, would be a better estimate for the coming month than the revenue or plant capacity of several months ago.

However, if the data are seasonal, for example, weights should be established accordingly. Bathing suit sales in July of last year should be weighted more heavily than bathing suit sales in December (in the Northern Hemisphere).

The weighted moving average has a definite advantage over the simple moving average in being able to vary the effects of past data. However, it is more inconvenient and costly to use than the exponential smoothing method, which we examine next.

## EXPONENTIAL SMOOTHING

In the previous methods of forecasting (simple and weighted moving average), the major drawback is the need to continually carry a large amount of historical data. (This is also true for regression analysis techniques, which we soon will cover.) As each new piece of data is added in these methods, the oldest observation is dropped, and the new forecast is calculated. In many applications (perhaps in most), the most recent occurrences are more indicative of the future than those in the more distant past. If this premise is valid—that the importance of data diminishes as the past becomes more distant—then **exponential smoothing** may be the most logical and easiest method to use.

Exponential smoothing

The reason this is called exponential smoothing is because each increment in the past is decreased by $(1 - \alpha)$. If $\alpha$ is 0.05, for example, weights for various periods would be as follows ($\alpha$ is defined below):

| | WEIGHTING AT $\alpha = 0.05$ |
|---|---|
| Most recent weighting $= \alpha(1 - \alpha)^0$ | 0.0500 |
| Data one time period older $= \alpha(1 - \alpha)^1$ | 0.0475 |
| Data two time periods older $= \alpha(1 - \alpha)^2$ | 0.0451 |
| Data three time periods older $= \alpha(1 - \alpha)^3$ | 0.0429 |

Therefore, the exponents 0, 1, 2, 3, . . . , and so on give it its name.

Exponential smoothing is the most used of all forecasting techniques. It is an integral part of virtually all computerized forecasting programs, and it is widely used in ordering inventory in retail firms, wholesale companies, and service agencies.

Exponential smoothing techniques have become well accepted for six major reasons:

1 Exponential models are surprisingly accurate.
2 Formulating an exponential model is relatively easy.
3 The user can understand how the model works.
4 Little computation is required to use the model.
5 Computer storage requirements are small because of the limited use of historical data.
6 Tests for accuracy as to how well the model is performing are easy to compute.

In the exponential smoothing method, only three pieces of data are needed to forecast the future: the most recent forecast, the actual demand that occurred for that forecast period, and a **smoothing constant alpha** ($\alpha$). This smoothing constant determines the level of smoothing and the speed of reaction to differences between forecasts and actual occurrences. The value for the constant is determined both by the nature of the product and by the manager's sense of what constitutes a good response rate. For example, if a firm produced a standard item with relatively stable demand, the reaction rate to differences between actual and forecast demand would tend to be small, perhaps just 5 or 10 percentage points. However, if the firm were experiencing growth, it would be desirable to have a higher reaction rate, perhaps 15 to 30 percentage points, to give greater importance to recent growth experience. The more rapid the growth, the higher the reaction rate should be. Sometimes users of the simple moving average switch to exponential smoothing but like to keep the forecasts about the same as the simple moving average. In this case, $\alpha$ is approximated by $2 \div (n + 1)$, where $n$ is the number of time periods.

Smoothing constant alpha ($\alpha$)

The equation for a single exponential smoothing forecast is simply

$$F_t = F_{t-1} + \alpha(A_{t-1} - F_{t-1}) \quad [11.3]$$

where

$F_t$ = The exponentially smoothed forecast for period $t$
$F_{t-1}$ = The exponentially smoothed forecast made for the prior period
$A_{t-1}$ = The actual demand in the prior period
$\alpha$ = The desired response rate, or smoothing constant

This equation states that the new forecast is equal to the old forecast plus a portion of the error (the difference between the previous forecast and what actually occurred).[2]

To demonstrate the method, assume that the long-run demand for the product under study is relatively stable and a smoothing constant ($\alpha$) of 0.05 is considered appropriate. If the exponential method were used as a continuing policy, a forecast would have been made for last month.[3] Assume that last month's forecast ($F_{t-1}$) was 1,050 units. If 1,000 actually were demanded, rather than 1,050, the forecast for this month would be

$$\begin{aligned} F_t &= F_{t-1} + \alpha(A_{t-1} - F_{t-1}) \\ &= 1{,}050 + 0.05(1{,}000 - 1{,}050) \\ &= 1{,}050 + 0.05(-50) \\ &= 1{,}047.5 \text{ units} \end{aligned}$$

Because the smoothing coefficient is small, the reaction of the new forecast to an error of 50 units is to decrease the next month's forecast by only $2\frac{1}{2}$ units.

Single exponential smoothing has the shortcoming of lagging changes in demand. Exhibit 11.7 presents actual data plotted as a smooth curve to show the lagging effects of the exponential forecasts. The forecast lags during an increase or decrease but overshoots when a change in direction occurs. Note that the higher the value of alpha, the more closely the forecast follows the actual. To more closely track actual demand, a trend factor may be added. Adjusting the value of alpha also helps. This is termed *adaptive forecasting*. Both trend effects and adaptive forecasting are briefly explained in following sections.

EXHIBIT 11.7

**Exponential Forecasts versus Actual Demand for Units of a Product over Time Showing the Forecast Lag**

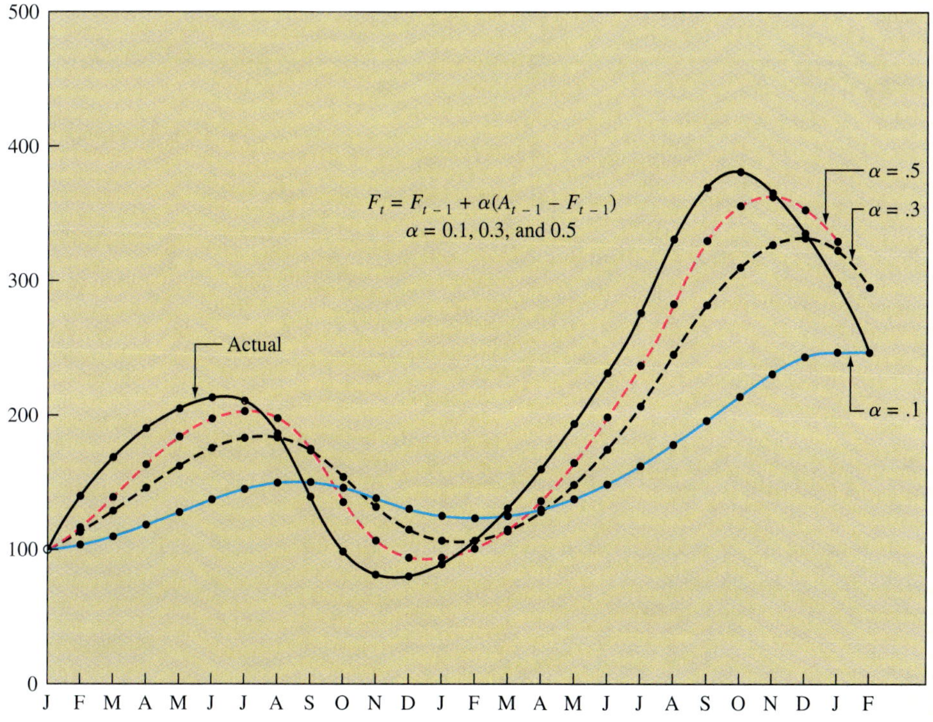

Smoothing constant delta ($\delta$)

**Trend Effects in Exponential Smoothing** Remember that an upward or downward trend in data collected over a sequence of time periods causes the exponential forecast to always lag behind (be above or below) the actual occurrence. Exponentially smoothed forecasts can be corrected somewhat by adding in a trend adjustment. To correct the trend, we need two smoothing constants. Besides the smoothing constant $\alpha$, the trend equation also uses a **smoothing constant delta** ($\delta$). The delta reduces the impact of the error that occurs between the actual and the forecast. If both alpha and delta are not included, the trend overreacts to errors.

To get the trend equation going, the first time it is used the trend value must be entered manually. This initial trend value can be an educated guess or a computation based on observed past data.

The equation to compute the forecast including trend (FIT) is

[11.4] $$\text{FIT}_t = F_t + T_t$$

[11.5] $$F_t = \text{FIT}_{t-1} + \alpha(A_{t-1} - \text{FIT}_{t-1})$$

[11.6] $$T_t = T_{t-1} + \delta(F_t - \text{FIT}_{t-1})$$

where

$F_t$ = The exponentially smoothed forecast for period $t$
$T_t$ = The exponentially smoothed trend for period $t$
$\text{FIT}_t$ = The forecast including trend for period $t$
$\text{FIT}_{t-1}$ = The forecast including trend made for the prior period
$A_{t-1}$ = The actual demand for the prior period
$\alpha$ = Smoothing constant
$\delta$ = Smoothing constant

*EXAMPLE 11.1: FORECAST INCLUDING TREND*

Assume an initial starting $F_t$ of 100 units, a trend of 10 units, an alpha of .20, and a delta of .30. If actual demand turned out to be 115 rather than the forecast 100, calculate the forecast for the next period.

*SOLUTION*

Adding the starting forecast and the trend, we have

$$\text{FIT}_{t-1} = F_{t-1} + T_{t-1} = 100 + 10 = 110$$

The actual $A_{t-1}$ is given as 115. Therefore,

$$\begin{aligned}F_t &= \text{FIT}_{t-1} + \alpha(A_{t-1} - \text{FIT}_{t-1})\\ &= 110 + .2(115 - 110) = 111.0\\ T_t &= T_{t-1} + \delta(F_t - \text{FIT}_{t-1})\\ &= 10 + .3(111 - 110) = 10.3\\ \text{FIT}_t &= F_t + T_t = 111.0 + 10.3 = 121.3\end{aligned}$$

If, instead of 121.3, the actual turned out to be 120, the sequence would be repeated and the forecast for the next period would be

$$\begin{aligned}F_{t+1} &= 121.3 + .2(120 - 121.3) = 121.04\\ T_{t+1} &= 10.3 + .3(121.04 - 121.3) = 10.22\\ \text{FIT}_{t+1} &= 121.04 + 10.22 = 131.26 \leftarrow\end{aligned}$$

**Choosing the Appropriate Value for Alpha** Exponential smoothing requires that the smoothing constant alpha ($\alpha$) be given a value between 0 and 1. If the real demand is stable (such as demand for electricity or food), we would like a small alpha to lessen the effects of short-term or random changes. If the real demand is rapidly increasing or decreasing (such as in fashion items or new small appliances), we would like a large alpha to try to keep up with the change. It would be ideal if we could predict which alpha we should use. Unfortunately, two things work against us. First, it would take some passage of time to determine the alpha that would best fit our actual data. This would be tedious to follow and revise. Second, because demands do change, the alpha we pick this week may need to be revised soon. Therefore, we need some automatic method to track and change our alpha values.

There are two approaches to controlling the value of alpha. One uses various values of alpha. The other uses a tracking signal.

1 **Two or more predetermined values of alpha.** The amount of error between the forecast and the actual demand is measured. Depending on the degree of error, different values of alpha are used. If the error is large, alpha is 0.8; if the error is small, alpha is 0.2.
2 **Computed values for alpha.** A tracking alpha computes whether the forecast is keeping pace with genuine upward or downward changes in demand (as opposed to random changes). In this application, the tracking alpha is defined as the exponentially smoothed actual error divided by the exponentially smoothed absolute error. Alpha changes from period to period within the possible range of 0 to 1.

## FORECAST ERRORS

In using the word *error,* we are referring to the difference between the forecast value and what actually occurred. In statistics, these errors are called *residuals.* As long as the forecast value is within the confidence limits, as we discuss later in "Measurement of Error," this is not really an error. But common usage refers to the difference as an error.

Demand for a product is generated through the interaction of a number of factors too complex to describe accurately in a model. Therefore, all forecasts certainly contain some error. In discussing forecast errors, it is convenient to distinguish between *sources of error* and the *measurement of error.*

## SOURCES OF ERROR

Errors can come from a variety of sources. One common source that many forecasters are unaware of is projecting past trends into the future. For example, when we talk about statistical errors in regression analysis, we are referring to the deviations of observations from our regression line. It is common to attach a confidence band (that is, statistical control limits) to the regression line to reduce the unexplained error. But when we then use this regression line as a forecasting device by projecting it into the future, the error may not be correctly defined by the projected confidence band. This is because the confidence interval is based on past data; it may not hold for projected data points and therefore cannot be used with the same confidence. In fact, experience has shown that the actual errors tend to be greater than those predicted from forecast models.

Errors can be classified as bias or random. *Bias errors* occur when a consistent mistake is made. Sources of bias include failing to include the right variables; using the wrong relationships among variables; employing the wrong trend line; mistakenly shifting the seasonal demand from where it normally occurs; and the existence of some undetected secular trend. *Random errors* can be defined as those that cannot be explained by the forecast model being used.

## MEASUREMENT OF ERROR

Several common terms used to describe the degree of error are *standard error, mean squared error* (or *variance*), and *mean absolute deviation.* In addition, tracking signals may be used to indicate any positive or negative bias in the forecast.

Standard error is discussed in the section on linear regression in this chapter. Because the standard error is the square root of a function, it is often more convenient to use the function itself. This is called the mean square error or variance.

Mean absolute deviation (MAD)

The **mean absolute deviation (MAD)** was in vogue in the past but subsequently was ignored in favor of standard deviation and standard error measures. In recent years, MAD has made a comeback because of its simplicity and usefulness in obtaining tracking signals. MAD is the average error in the forecasts, using absolute values. It is valuable because MAD, like the standard deviation, measures the dispersion of some observed value from some expected value.

MAD is computed using the differences between the actual demand and the forecast demand without regard to sign. It equals the sum of the absolute deviations divided by the number of data points, or, stated in equation form,

[11.7]

$$\text{MAD} = \frac{\sum_{i=1}^{n} |A_t - F_t|}{n}$$

where

$t$ = Period number
$A$ = Actual demand for the period
$F$ = Forecast demand for the period
$n$ = Total number of periods
$|\ |$ = A symbol used to indicate the absolute value disregarding positive and negative signs

When the errors that occur in the forecast are normally distributed (the usual case), the mean absolute deviation relates to the standard deviation as

$$1 \text{ standard deviation} = \sqrt{\frac{\pi}{2}} \times \text{MAD, or approximately } 1.25 \text{ MAD}$$

Conversely,

$$1 \text{ MAD} = 0.8 \text{ standard deviation}$$

The standard deviation is the larger measure. If the MAD of a set of points was found to be 60 units, then the standard deviation would be 75 units. In the usual statistical manner, if control limits were set at plus or minus 3 standard deviations (or ±3.75 MADs), then 99.7 percent of the points would fall within these limits.

Tracking signal

A **tracking signal** is a measurement that indicates whether the forecast average is keeping pace with any genuine upward or downward changes in demand. As used in forecasting, the tracking signal is the *number* of mean absolute deviations that the forecast value is above or below the actual occurrence. Exhibit 11.8 shows a normal distribution with a mean of 0 and a MAD equal to 1. Thus, if we compute the tracking signal and find it equal to minus 2, we can see that the forecast model is providing forecasts that are quite a bit above the mean of the actual occurrences.

A tracking signal (TS) can be calculated using the arithmetic sum of forecast deviations divided by the mean absolute deviation:

[11.8]

$$\text{TS} = \frac{\text{RSFE}}{\text{MAD}}$$

where

RSFE is the running sum of forecast errors, considering the nature of the error. (For example, negative errors cancel positive errors and vice versa.)

EXHIBIT 11.8

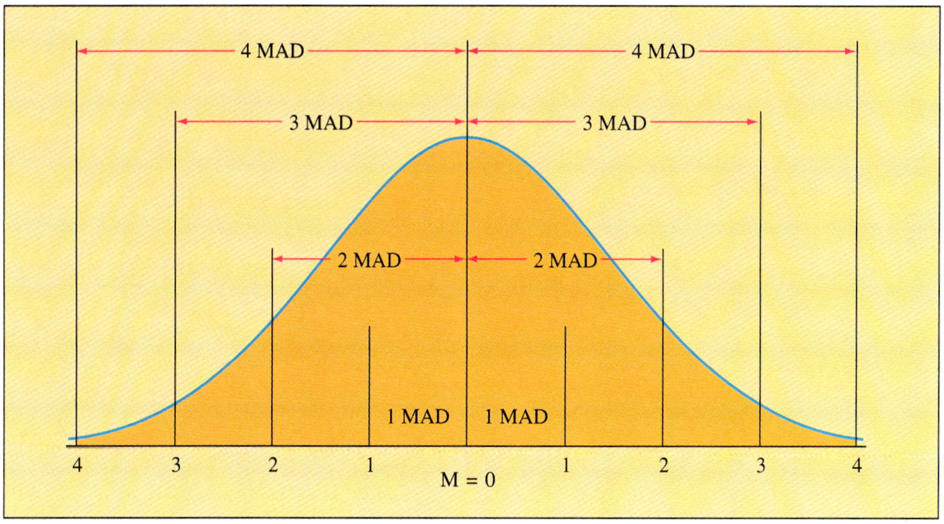


A Normal Distribution with Mean = 0 and MAD = 1

EXHIBIT 11.9

Excel: Forecasting

Computing the Mean Absolute Deviation (MAD), the Running Sum of Forecast Errors (RSFE), and the Tracking Signal (TS) from Forecast and Actual Data

| MONTH | DEMAND FORECAST | ACTUAL | DEVIATION | RSFE | ABS. DEV. | SUM OF ABS. DEV. | MAD* | $TS = \frac{RSFE^{\dagger}}{MAD}$ |
|---|---|---|---|---|---|---|---|---|
| 1 | 1,000 | 950 | −50 | −50 | 50 | 50 | 50 | −1 |
| 2 | 1,000 | 1,070 | +70 | +20 | 70 | 120 | 60 | .33 |
| 3 | 1,000 | 1,100 | +100 | +120 | 100 | 220 | 73.3 | 1.64 |
| 4 | 1,000 | 960 | −40 | +80 | 40 | 260 | 65 | 1.2 |
| 5 | 1,000 | 1,090 | +90 | +170 | 90 | 350 | 70 | 2.4 |
| 6 | 1,000 | 1,050 | +50 | +220 | 50 | 400 | 66.7 | 3.3 |

* For month 6, MAD = 400 ÷ 6 = 66.7.

† For month 6, $TS = \frac{RSFE}{MAD} = \frac{220}{66.7} = 3.3$ MADs.

MAD is the average of all the forecast errors (disregarding whether the deviations are positive or negative). It is the average of the absolute deviations.

Exhibit 11.9 illustrates the procedure for computing MAD and the tracking signal for a six-month period where the forecast had been set at a constant 1,000 and the actual demands that occurred are as shown. In this example, the forecast, on the average, was off by 66.7 units and the tracking signal was equal to 3.3 mean absolute deviations.

We can get a better feel for what the MAD and tracking signal mean by plotting the points on a graph. Though this is not completely legitimate from a sample-size standpoint, we plotted each month in Exhibit 11.10 to show the drift of the tracking signal. Note that it drifted from minus 1 MAD to plus 3.3 MADs. This happened because actual demand was greater than the forecast in four of the six periods. If the actual demand does not fall below the forecast to offset the continual positive RSFE, the tracking signal would continue to rise and we would conclude that assuming a demand of 1,000 is a bad forecast.

Acceptable limits for the tracking signal depend on the size of the demand being forecast (high-volume or high-revenue items should be monitored frequently) and the amount of personnel time available (narrower acceptable limits cause more forecasts to be out of

EXHIBIT 11.10

A Plot of he Tracking Signals Calculated in Exhibit 11.9

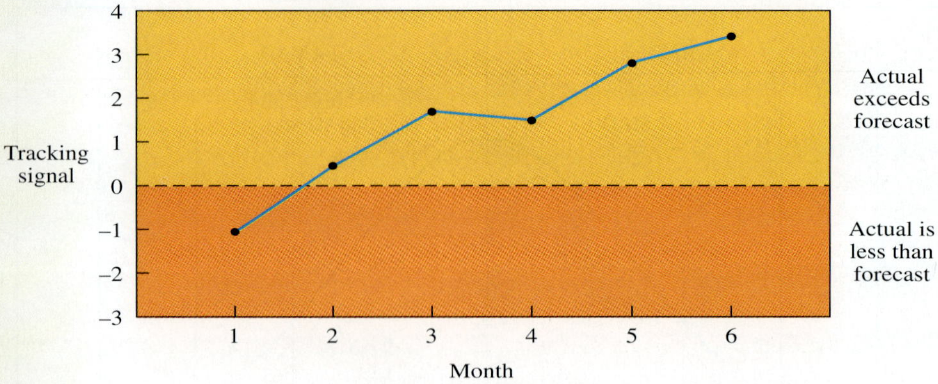


EXHIBIT 11.11

The Percentages of Points Included within the Control Limits for a Range of 1 to 4 MADs

CONTROL LIMITS

| NUMBER OF MADS | RELATED NUMBER OF STANDARD DEVIATIONS | PERCENTAGE OF POINTS LYING WITHIN CONTROL LIMITS |
|---|---|---|
| ±1 | 0.798 | 57.048 |
| ±2 | 1.596 | 88.946 |
| ±3 | 2.394 | 98.334 |
| ±4 | 3.192 | 99.856 |

limits and therefore require more time to investigate). Exhibit 11.11 shows the area within the control limits for a range of 1 to 4 MADs.

In a perfect forecasting model, the sum of the actual forecast errors would be 0; the errors that result in overestimates should be offset by errors that are underestimates. The tracking signal would then also be 0, indicating an unbiased model, neither leading nor lagging the actual demands.

Often MAD is used to forecast errors. It might then be desirable to make the MAD more sensitive to recent data. A useful technique to do this is to compute an exponentially smoothed MAD as a forecast for the next period's error range. The procedure is similar to single exponential smoothing, covered earlier in this chapter. The value of the MAD forecast is to provide a range of error. In the case of inventory control, this is useful in setting safety stock levels.

$$\text{MAD}_t = \alpha|A_{t-1} - F_{t-1}| + (1-\alpha)\text{MAD}_{t-1}$$

where

$\text{MAD}_t$ = Forecast MAD for the $t$th period
$\alpha$ = Smoothing constant (normally in the range of 0.05 to 0.20)
$A_{t-1}$ = Actual demand in the period $t - 1$
$F_{t-1}$ = Forecast demand for period $t - 1$

## LINEAR REGRESSION ANALYSIS

*Regression* can be defined as a functional relationship between two or more correlated variables. It is used to predict one variable given the other. The relationship is usually developed from observed data. The data should be plotted first to see if they appear linear or if at least parts of the data are linear. *Linear regression* refers to the special class of regression where the relationship between variables forms a straight line.

The linear regression line is of the form $Y = a + bX$, where $Y$ is the value of the dependent variable that we are solving for, $a$ is the $Y$ intercept, $b$ is the slope, and $X$ is the independent variable. (In time series analysis, $X$ is units of time.)

Linear regression is useful for long-term forecasting of major occurrences and aggregate planning. For example, linear regression would be very useful to forecast demands for product families. Even though demand for individual products within a family may vary widely during a time period, demand for the total product family is surprisingly smooth.

Linear regression forecasting

The major restriction in using **linear regression forecasting** is, as the name implies, that past data and future projections are assumed to fall about a straight line. Although this does limit its application, sometimes, if we use a shorter period of time, linear regression analysis can still be used. For example, there may be short segments of the longer period that are approximately linear.

Linear regression is used for both time series forecasting and for causal relationship forecasting. When the dependent variable (usually the vertical axis on a graph) changes as a result of time (plotted as the horizontal axis), it is time series analysis. If one variable changes because of the change in another variable, this is a causal relationship (such as the number of deaths from lung cancer increasing with the number of people who smoke).

We use the following example several times in this chapter to compare forecasting models and types of analysis. We use it for hand fitting a line, for the least squares analysis, and for a decomposition example.

## EXAMPLE 11.2: HAND FITTING A TREND LINE

A firm's sales for a product line during the 12 quarters of the past three years were as follows:

| QUARTER | SALES | QUARTER | SALES |
|---|---|---|---|
| 1 | 600 | 7 | 2,600 |
| 2 | 1,550 | 8 | 2,900 |
| 3 | 1,500 | 9 | 3,800 |
| 4 | 1,500 | 10 | 4,500 |
| 5 | 2,400 | 11 | 4,000 |
| 6 | 3,100 | 12 | 4,900 |

The firm wants to forecast each quarter of the fourth year—that is, quarters 13, 14, 15, and 16. In hand fitting a curve, we plot the data and use simple eyeballing or OHA (ocular heuristic approximation).

## SOLUTION

The procedure is quite simple: Lay a straightedge (clear plastic rulers are nice) across the data points until the line seems to fit well, and draw the line. This is the regression line. The next step is to determine the intercept $a$ and slope $b$.

Exhibit 11.12 shows a plot of the data and the straight line we drew through the points. The intercept $a$, where the line cuts the vertical axis, appears to be about 400. The slope $b$ is the "rise" divided by the "run" (the change in the height of some portion of the line divided by the number of units in the horizontal axis). Any two points can be used, but two points some distance apart give the best accuracy because of the errors in reading values from the graph. We use values for the 1st and 12th quarters.

In Exhibit 11.12, by reading from the points on the line the $Y$ values for quarter 1 and quarter 12 are about 750 and 4,950. Therefore,

$$b = (4{,}950 - 750)/(12 - 1) = 382$$

EXHIBIT 11.12

A Hand-Fit Regression

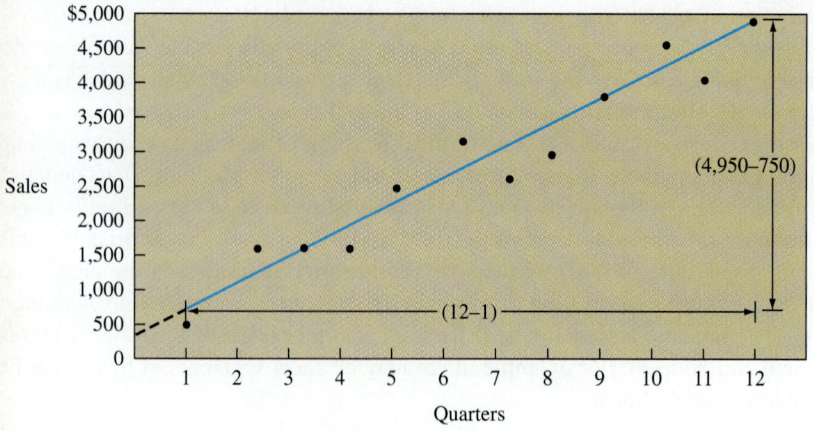


The hand-fit regression equation is therefore

$$Y = 400 + 382x$$

The forecasts for quarters 13 through 16 are

| QUARTER | FORECAST |
|---|---|
| 13 | 400 + 382(13) = 5,366 |
| 14 | 400 + 382(14) = 5,748 |
| 15 | 400 + 382(15) = 6,130 |
| 16 | 400 + 382(16) = 6,512 |

These forecasts are based on the line only and do not identify or adjust for elements such as seasonal or cyclical elements. ←

**Least Squares Method** The least squares equation for linear regression is the same as we used in our hand-fit example:

[11.9] $$Y = a + bx$$

where

$Y$ = Dependent variable computed by the equation
$y$ = The actual dependent variable data point (used below)
$a$ = $Y$ intercept
$b$ = Slope of the line
$x$ = Time period

The least squares method tries to fit the line to the data *that minimizes the sum of the squares of the vertical distance* between each data point and its corresponding point on the line. Exhibit 11.12 showed the 12 data points. If a straight line is drawn through the general area of the points, the difference between the point and the line is $y - Y$. Exhibit 11.13 shows these differences. The sum of the squares of the differences between the plotted data points and the line points is

$$(y_1 - Y_1)^2 + (y_2 - Y_2)^2 + \cdots + (y_{12} - Y_{12})^2$$

The best line to use is the one that minimizes this total.

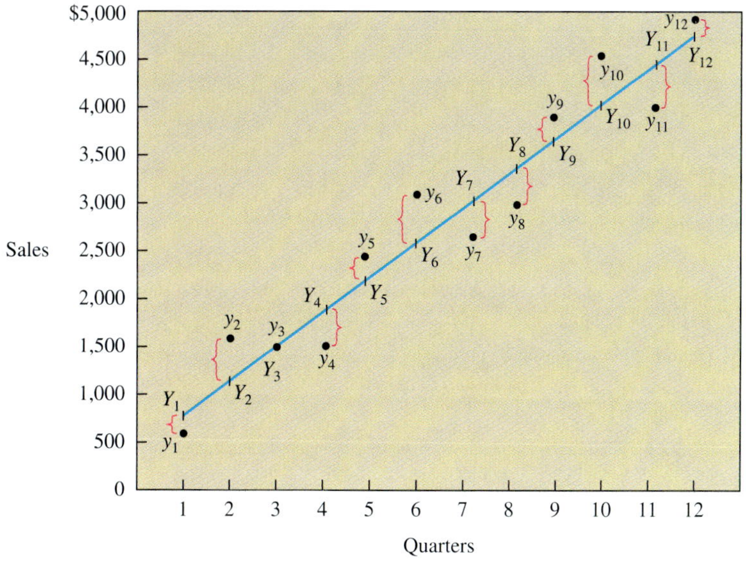


EXHIBIT 11.13

**Least Squares Regression Line**

Excel: Forecasting

As before, the straight line equation is

$$Y = a + bx$$

Previously we determined $a$ and $b$ from the graph. In the least squares method, the equations for $a$ and $b$ are

[11.10] $$a = \bar{y} - b\bar{x}$$

[11.11] $$b = \frac{\sum xy - n\bar{x} \cdot \bar{y}}{\sum x^2 - n\bar{x}^2}$$

where

$a$ = $Y$ intercept
$b$ = Slope of the line
$\bar{y}$ = Average of all $y$s
$\bar{x}$ = Average of all $x$s
$x$ = $x$ value at each data point
$y$ = $y$ value at each data point
$n$ = Number of data points
$Y$ = Value of the dependent variable computed with the regression equation

Exhibit 11.14 shows these computations carried out for the 12 data points in Exhibit 11.12 as part of example 11.2. Note that the final equation for $Y$ shows an intercept of 441.6 and a slope of 359.6. The slope shows that for every unit change in $X$, $Y$ changes by 359.6.

Strictly based on the equation, forecasts for periods 13 through 16 would be

$$Y_{13} = 441.6 + 359.6(13) = 5,116.4$$

$$Y_{14} = 441.6 + 359.6(14) = 5,476.0$$

$$Y_{15} = 441.6 + 359.6(15) = 5,835.6$$

$$Y_{16} = 441.6 + 359.6(16) = 6,195.2$$

EXHIBIT 11.14

**Least Squares Regression Analysis**

Excel: Forecasting

| (1)$x$ | (2)$y$ | (3)$xy$ | (4)$x^2$ | (5)$y^2$ | (6)$Y$ |
|---|---|---|---|---|---|
| 1 | 600 | 600 | 1 | 360,000 | 801.3 |
| 2 | 1,550 | 3,100 | 4 | 2,402,500 | 1,160.9 |
| 3 | 1,500 | 4,500 | 9 | 2,250,000 | 1,520.5 |
| 4 | 1,500 | 6,000 | 16 | 2,250,000 | 1,880.1 |
| 5 | 2,400 | 12,000 | 25 | 5,760,000 | 2,239.7 |
| 6 | 3,100 | 18,600 | 36 | 9,610,000 | 2,599.4 |
| 7 | 2,600 | 18,200 | 49 | 6,760,000 | 2,959.0 |
| 8 | 2,900 | 23,200 | 64 | 8,410,000 | 3,318.6 |
| 9 | 3,800 | 34,200 | 81 | 14,440,000 | 3,678.2 |
| 10 | 4,500 | 45,000 | 100 | 20,250,000 | 4,037.8 |
| 11 | 4,000 | 44,000 | 121 | 16,000,000 | 4,397.4 |
| 12 | 4,900 | 58,800 | 144 | 24,010,000 | 4,757.1 |
| 78 | 33,350 | 268,200 | 650 | 112,502,500 | |

$\bar{x} = 6.5 \quad b = 359.6153$

$\bar{y} = 2{,}779.17 \quad a = 441.6666$

Therefore $Y = 441.66 + 359.6x$

$S_{yx} = 363.9$

The standard error of estimate, or how well the line fits the data, is[4]

[11.12]
$$S_{yx} = \sqrt{\frac{\sum_{i=1}^{n}(y_i - Y_i)^2}{n-2}}$$

The standard error of estimate is computed from the second and last columns of Exhibit 11.14:

$$S_{yx} = \sqrt{\frac{(600 - 801.3)^2 + (1{,}550 - 1{,}160.9)^2 + (1{,}500 - 1{,}520.5)^2 + \cdots + (4{,}900 - 4{,}757.1)^2}{10}}$$
$$= 363.9$$

We discuss the possible existence of seasonal components in the next section on decomposition of a time series.

## DECOMPOSITION OF A TIME SERIES

A *time series* can be defined as chronologically ordered data that may contain one or more components of demand: trend, seasonal, cyclical, autocorrelation, and random. *Decomposition* of a time series means identifying and separating the time series data into these components. In practice, it is relatively easy to identify the trend (even without mathematical analysis, it is usually easy to plot and see the direction of movement) and the seasonal component (by comparing the same period year to year). It is considerably more difficult to identify the cycles (these may be many months or years long), autocorrelation, and random components. (The forecaster usually calls random anything left over that cannot be identified as another component.)

When demand contains both seasonal and trend effects at the same time, the question is how they relate to each other. In this description, we examine two types of seasonal variation: *additive* and *multiplicative*.

EXHIBIT 11.15

Additive and Multiplicative Seasonal Variation Superimposed on Changing Trend

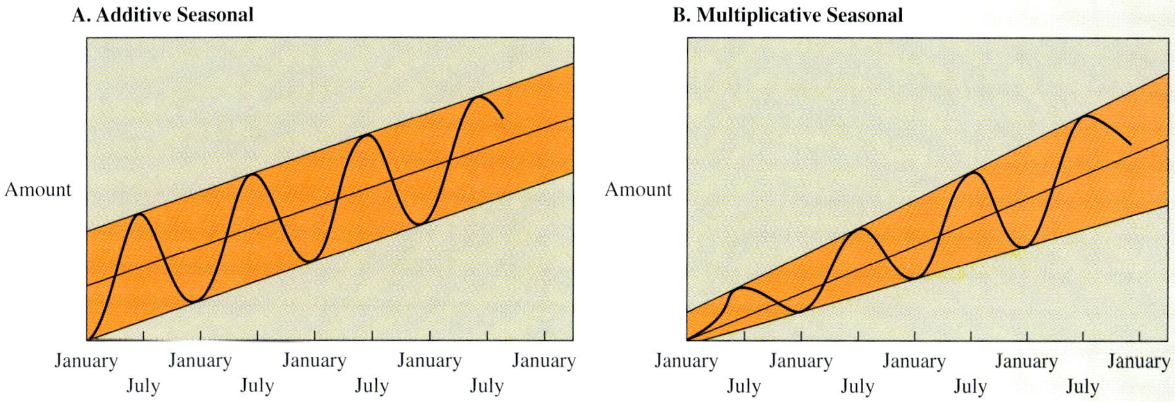


**Additive Seasonal Variation** Additive seasonal variation simply assumes that the seasonal amount is a constant no matter what the trend or average amount is.

$$\text{Forecast including trend and seasonal} = \text{Trend} + \text{Seasonal}$$

Exhibit 11.15A shows an example of increasing trend with constant seasonal amounts.

**Multiplicative Seasonal Variation** In multiplicative seasonal variation, the trend is multiplied by the seasonal factors.

$$\text{Forecast including trend and seasonal} = \text{Trend} \times \text{Seasonal factor}$$

Exhibit 11.15B shows the seasonal variation increasing as the trend increases because its size depends on the trend.

The multiplicative seasonal variation is the usual experience. Essentially, this says that the larger the basic amount projected, the larger the variation around this that we can expect.

**Seasonal Factor (or Index)** A seasonal factor is the amount of correction needed in a time series to adjust for the season of the year.

We usually associate *seasonal* with a period of the year characterized by some particular activity. We use the word *cyclical* to indicate other than annual recurrent periods of repetitive activity.

The following examples show how seasonal indexes are determined and used to forecast (1) a simple calculation based on past seasonal data and (2) the trend and seasonal index from a hand-fit regression line. We follow this with a more formal procedure for the decomposition of data and forecasting using least squares regression.

### *EXAMPLE 11.3: SIMPLE PROPORTION*

Assume that in past years, a firm sold an average of 1,000 units of a particular product line each year. On the average, 200 units were sold in the spring, 350 in the summer, 300 in the fall, and 150 in the winter. The seasonal factor (or index) is the ratio of the amount sold during each season divided by the average for all seasons.

## SOLUTION

In this example, the yearly amount divided equally over all seasons is $1,000 \div 4 = 250$. The seasonal factors therefore are

| | Past Sales | Average Sales for Each Season (1,000/4) | Seasonal Factor |
|---|---|---|---|
| Spring | 200 | 250 | $200/250 = 0.8$ |
| Summer | 350 | 250 | $350/250 = 1.4$ |
| Fall | 300 | 250 | $300/250 = 1.2$ |
| Winter | 150 | 250 | $150/250 = 0.6$ |
| Total | 1,000 | | |

Using these factors, if we expected demand for next year to be 1,100 units, we would forecast the demand to occur as

| | Expected Demand for Next Year | Average Sales for Each Season (1,100/4) | | Seasonal Factor | | Next Year's Seasonal Forecast |
|---|---|---|---|---|---|---|
| Spring | | 275 | × | 0.8 | = | 220 |
| Summer | | 275 | × | 1.4 | = | 385 |
| Fall | | 275 | × | 1.2 | = | 330 |
| Winter | | 275 | × | 0.6 | = | 165 |
| Total | 1,100 | | | | | |

The seasonal factor may be periodically updated as new data are available. The following example shows the seasonal factor and multiplicative seasonal variation.

## EXAMPLE 11.4: COMPUTING TREND AND SEASONAL FACTOR FROM A HAND-FIT STRAIGHT LINE

Here we must compute the trend as well as the seasonal factors.

## SOLUTION

We solve this problem by simply hand fitting a straight line through the data points and measuring the trend and intercept from the graph. Assume the history of data is

| Quarter | Amount | Quarter | Amount |
|---|---|---|---|
| I—1998 | 300 | I—1999 | 520 |
| II—1998 | 200 | II—1999 | 420 |
| III—1998 | 220 | III—1999 | 400 |
| IV—1998 | 530 | IV—1999 | 700 |

First, we plot as in Exhibit 11.16 and then fit a straight line through the data simply by eyeballing. (Naturally, this line and the resulting equation are subject to variation.) The equation for the line is

$$\text{Trend}_t = 170 + 55t$$

Our equation was derived from the intercept 170 plus a rise of $(610 - 170) \div 8$ periods. Next we can derive a seasonal index by comparing the actual data with the trend line as in Exhibit 11.17. The seasonal factor was developed by averaging the same quarters in each year.

EXHIBIT 11.16

A Plot of Quarterly Demand History

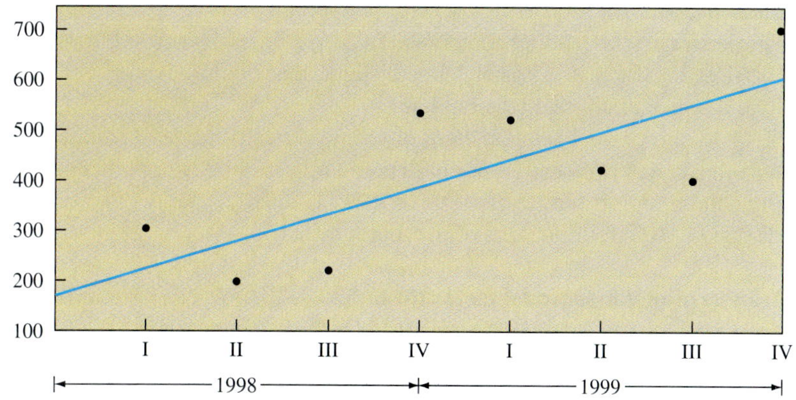


EXHIBIT 11.17

Computing a Seasonal Factor from the Actual Data and Trend Line

| Quarter | Actual Amount | From Trend Equation $T_t = 170 + 55t$ | Ratio of Actual ÷ Trend | Seasonal Factor (Average of Same Quarters in Both Years) |
|---|---|---|---|---|
| 1998 | | | | |
| I | 300 | 225 | 1.33 | |
| II | 200 | 280 | .71 | |
| III | 220 | 335 | .66 | I—1.25 |
| IV | 530 | 390 | 1.36 | II—0.78 |
| 1999 | | | | III—0.69 |
| I | 520 | 445 | 1.17 | IV—1.25 |
| II | 420 | 500 | .84 | |
| III | 400 | 555 | .72 | |
| IV | 700 | 610 | 1.15 | |

We can compute the 2000 forecast including trend and seasonal factors (FITS) as follows:

$$\text{FITS}_t = \text{Trend} \times \text{Seasonal}$$

$$\text{I—2000 FITS}_9 = [170 + 55(9)]1.25 = 831$$

$$\text{II—2000 FITS}_{10} = [170 + 55(10)]0.78 = 562$$

$$\text{III—2000 FITS}_{11} = [170 + 55(11)]0.69 = 535$$

$$\text{IV—2000 FITS}_{12} = [170 + 55(12)]1.25 = 1{,}038 \leftarrow$$

**Decomposition Using Least Squares Regression** Decomposition of a time series means finding the series' basic components of trend, seasonal, and cyclical. Indexes are calculated for seasons and cycles. The forecasting procedure then reverses the process by projecting the trend and adjusting it by the seasonal and cyclical indexes, which were determined in the decomposition process. More formally, the process is

1 Decompose the time series into its components.
   *a.* Find seasonal component.
   *b.* Deseasonalize the demand.
   *c.* Find trend component.
2 Forecast future values of each component.
   *a.* Project trend component into the future.
   *b.* Multiply trend component by seasonal component.

Note that the random component is not included in this list. We implicitly remove the random component from the time series when we average as in Step 1. It is pointless to attempt a projection of the random component in Step 2 unless we have information about some unusual event, such as a major labor dispute, that could adversely affect product demand (and this would not really be random).

Exhibit 11.18 shows the decomposition of a time series using least squares regression and the same basic data we used in our earlier examples. Each data point corresponds to using a single three-month quarter of the three-year (12-quarter) period. Our objective is to forecast demand for the four quarters of the fourth year.

**Step 1. Determine the seasonal factor (or index).** Exhibit 11.18 summarizes the calculations needed. Column 4 develops an average for the same quarters in the three-year period. For example, the first quarters of the three years are added together and divided by three. A seasonal factor is then derived by dividing that average by the general average for all 12 quarters $\left(\frac{33{,}350}{12} \text{ or } 2{,}779\right)$. These are entered in column 5. Note that the seasonal factors are identical for similar quarters in each year.

**Step 2. Deseasonalize the original data.** To remove the seasonal effect on the data, we divide the original data by the seasonal factor. This step is called the deseasonalization of demand and is shown in column 6 of Exhibit 11.18.

EXHIBIT 11.18

## Deseasonalized Demand

| (1) Period $(x)$ | (2) Quarter | (3) Actual Demand $(y)$ | (4) Average of the Same Quarters of Each Year | (5) Seasonal Factor | (6) Deseasonalized Demand $(y_d)$ Col. (3) ÷ Col. (5) | (7) $x^2$ (Col. 1)$^2$ | (8) $x \times y_d$ Col. (1) × Col. (6) |
|---|---|---|---|---|---|---|---|
| 1 | I | 600 | (600 + 2,400 + 3,800)/3 = 2,266.7 | 0.82 | 735.7 | 1 | 735.7 |
| 2 | II | 1,550 | (1,550 + 3,100 + 4,500)/3 = 3,050 | 1.10 | 1,412.4 | 4 | 2,824.7 |
| 3 | III | 1,500 | (1,500 + 2,600 + 4,000)/3 = 2,700 | 0.97 | 1,544.0 | 9 | 4,631.9 |
| 4 | IV | 1,500 | (1,500 + 2,900 + 4,900)/3 = 3,100 | 1.12 | 1,344.8 | 16 | 5,379.0 |
| 5 | I | 2,400 | | 0.82 | 2,942.6 | 25 | 14,713.2 |
| 6 | II | 3,100 | | 1.10 | 2,824.7 | 36 | 16,948.4 |
| 7 | III | 2,600 | | 0.97 | 2,676.2 | 49 | 18,733.6 |
| 8 | IV | 2,900 | | 1.12 | 2,599.9 | 64 | 20,798.9 |
| 9 | I | 3,800 | | 0.82 | 4,659.2 | 81 | 41,932.7 |
| 10 | II | 4,500 | | 1.10 | 4,100.4 | 100 | 41,004.1 |
| 11 | III | 4,000 | | 0.97 | 4,117.3 | 121 | 45,290.1 |
| 12 | IV | 4,900 | | 1.12 | 4,392.9 | 144 | 52,714.5 |
| 78 | | 33,350 | | 12.03 | 33,350.1* | 650 | 265,706.9 |

$\bar{x} = \frac{78}{12} = 6.5 \qquad b = \frac{\sum xy_d - n\bar{x}\bar{y}_d}{\sum x^2 - n\bar{x}^2} = \frac{265{,}706.9 - 12(6.5)2{,}779.2}{650 - 12(6.5)^2} = 342.2$

$\bar{y}_d = 33{,}350/12 = 2{,}779.2 \quad a = \bar{y}_d - b\bar{x} = 2{,}779.2 - 342.2(6.5) = 554.9$

Therefore $Y = a + bx = 554.9 + 342.2x$

* Column 3 and column 6 totals should be equal at 33,350. Differences are due to rounding. Column 5 was rounded to two decimal places.

**Step 3. Develop a least squares regression line for the deseasonalized data.** The purpose here is to develop an equation for the trend line $Y$, which we then modify with the seasonal factor. The procedure is the same as we used before:

$$Y = a + bx$$

where

$y_d$ = Deseasonalized demand (see Exhibit 11.18)
$x$ = Quarter
$Y$ = Demand computed using the regression equation $Y = a + bx$
$a$ = $Y$ intercept
$b$ = Slope of the line

The least squares calculations using columns 1, 7, and 8 of Exhibit 11.18 are shown in the lower section of the exhibit. The final deseasonalized equation for our data is $Y = 554.9 + 342.2x$. This straight line is shown in Exhibit 11.19.

**Step 4. Project the regression line through the period to be forecast.** Our purpose is to forecast periods 13 through 16. We start by solving the equation for $Y$ at each of these periods (shown in step 5, column 3).

**Step 5. Create the final forecast by adjusting the regression line by the seasonal factor.** Recall that the $Y$ equation has been deseasonalized. We now reverse the procedure by multiplying the quarterly data we derived by the seasonal factor for that quarter:

| Period | Quarter | Y from Regression Line | Seasonal Factor | Forecast (Y × Seasonal Factor) |
|---|---|---|---|---|
| 13 | 1 | 5,003.5 | 0.82 | 4,102.87 |
| 14 | 2 | 5,345.7 | 1.10 | 5,880.27 |
| 15 | 3 | 5,687.9 | 0.97 | 5,517.26 |
| 16 | 4 | 6,030.1 | 1.12 | 6,753.71 |

Our forecast is now complete. The procedure is generally the same as what we did in the hand-fit previous example. In the present example, however, we followed a more formal procedure and computed the least squares regression line as well.

**Error Range** When a straight line is fitted through data points and then used for forecasting, errors can come from two sources. First, there are the usual errors similar to the standard deviation of any set of data. Second, there are errors that arise because the line is wrong. Exhibit 11.20 shows this error range. Instead of developing the statistics here, we

EXHIBIT 11.19

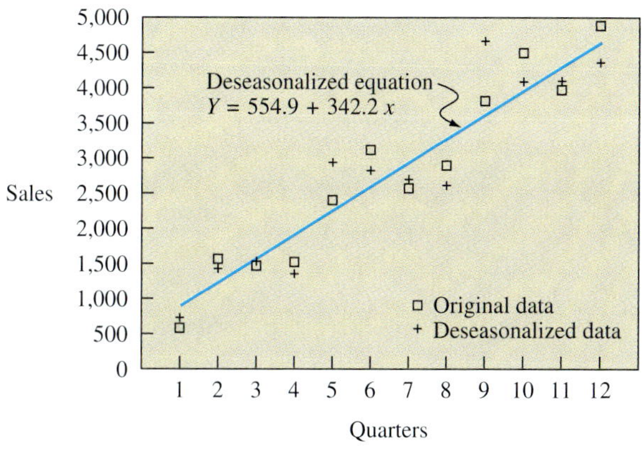


Straight Line Graph of Deseasonalized Equation

EXHIBIT 11.20

Prediction Intervals for Linear Trend

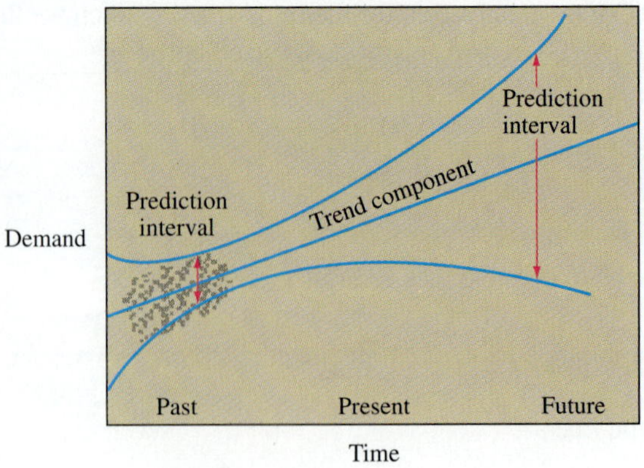


will briefly show why the range broadens. First, visualize that one line is drawn that has some error in that it slants too steeply upward. Standard errors are then calculated for this line. Now visualize another line that slants too steeply downward. It also has a standard error. The total error range, for this analysis, consists of errors resulting from both lines as well as all other possible lines. We included this exhibit to show how the error range widens as we go further into the future.

## CAUSAL RELATIONSHIP FORECASTING

To be of value for the purpose of forecasting, any independent variable must be a leading indicator. For example, we can expect that an extended period of rain will increase sales of umbrellas and raincoats. The rain causes the sale of rain gear. This is a **causal relationship,** where one occurrence causes another. If the causing element is known far enough in advance, it can be used as a basis for forecasting.

Causal relationship

The first step in causal relationship forecasting is to find those occurrences that are really the causes. Often leading indicators are not causal relationships, but in some indirect way, they may suggest that some other things might happen. Other noncausal relationships just seem to exist as a coincidence. One study some years ago showed that the amount of alcohol sold in Sweden was directly proportional to teachers' salaries. Presumably this was a spurious (false) relationship. The following shows one example of a forecast using a causal relationship.

### *EXAMPLE 11.5: FORECASTING USING A CAUSAL RELATIONSHIP*

The Carpet City Store in Carpenteria has kept records of its sales (in square yards) each year, along with the number of permits for new houses in its area.

NUMBER OF HOUSING STARTS

| YEAR | PERMITS | SALES (IN SQ. YDS.) |
|---|---|---|
| 1989 | 18 | 13,000 |
| 1990 | 15 | 12,000 |
| 1991 | 12 | 11,000 |
| 1992 | 10 | 10,000 |
| 1993 | 20 | 14,000 |
| 1994 | 28 | 16,000 |
| 1995 | 35 | 19,000 |
| 1996 | 30 | 17,000 |
| 1997 | 20 | 13,000 |

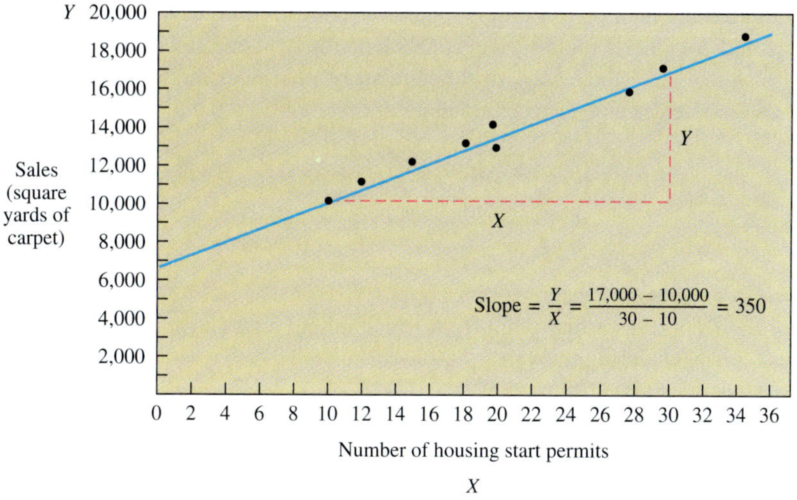


EXHIBIT 11.21

**Causal Relationship: Sales to Housing Starts**

Excel: Forecasting

Carpet City's operations manager believes forecasting sales is possible if housing starts are known for that year. First, the data are plotted in Exhibit 11.21, with

$x$ = Number of housing start permits

$y$ = Sales of carpeting

Because the points appear to be in a straight line, the manager decides to use the linear relationship $Y = a + bx$. We solve this problem by hand fitting a line. We could also solve for this equation using least squares regression as we did earlier.

## SOLUTION

Projecting the hand fit line causes it to intercept the $Y$ axis at about 7,000 yards. This could be interpreted as the demand when no new houses are built; that is, probably as replacement for old carpeting. To estimate the slope, two points are selected, such as

| YEAR | $x$ | $y$ |
|---|---|---|
| 1994 | 10 | 10,000 |
| 1998 | 30 | 17,000 |

From algebra the slope is calculated as

$$b = \frac{y(96) - y(92)}{x(96) - x(92)} = \frac{17{,}000 - 10{,}000}{30 - 10} = \frac{7{,}000}{20} = 350$$

The manager interprets the slope as the average number of square yards of carpet sold for each new house built in the area. The forecasting equation is therefore

$$Y = 7{,}000 + 350x$$

Now suppose that there are 25 permits for houses to be built in 2000. The 2000 sales forecast would therefore be

$$7{,}000 + 350(25) = 15{,}750 \text{ square yards}$$

In this problem, the lag between filing the permit with the appropriate agency and the new homeowner coming to Carpet City to buy carpet makes a causal relationship feasible for forecasting. ←

### MULTIPLE REGRESSION ANALYSIS

Another forecasting method is multiple regression analysis, in which a number of variables are considered, together with the effects of each on the item of interest. For example, in the home furnishings field, the effects of the number of marriages, housing starts, disposable income, and the trend can be expressed in a multiple regression equation, as

$$S = B + B_m(M) + B_h(H) + B_i(I) + B_t(T)$$

where

$S$ = Gross sales for year
$B$ = Base sales, a starting point from which other factors have influence
$M$ = Marriages during the year
$H$ = Housing starts during the year
$I$ = Annual disposable personal income
$T$ = Time trend (first year = 1, second = 2, third = 3, and so forth)

$B_m$, $B_h$, $B_i$, and $B_t$ represent the influence on expected sales of the numbers of marriages and housing starts, income, and trend.

Forecasting by multiple regression is appropriate when a number of factors influence a variable of interest—in this case, sales. Its difficulty lies with the mathematical computation. Fortunately, standard computer programs for multiple regression analysis are available, relieving the need for tedious manual calculation.

Microsoft Excel supports the time series analysis techniques described in this section. These functions are available under the Tools → Data Analysis menu. Analysis tools for exponential smoothing, moving averages, and regression are available.

## FOCUS FORECASTING

Focus forecasting is the creation of Bernie Smith.[5] Smith uses it primarily in finished goods inventory management. Smith substantiates strong arguments that statistical approaches used in forecasting do not give the best results. He states that simple techniques that work well on past data also prove the best in forecasting the future.

### METHODOLOGY OF FOCUS FORECASTING

Focus forecasting

**Focus forecasting** simply tries several rules that seem logical and easy to understand to project past data into the future. Each of these rules is used in a computer simulation program to actually project demand and then measure how well that rule performed when compared to what actually happened. Therefore, the two components of the focus forecasting system are (1) several simple forecasting rules and (2) computer simulation of these rules on past data.

These are simple, commonsense rules made up and then tested to see whether they should be kept. Examples of simple forecasting rules could include

1 Whatever we sold in the past three months is what we will probably sell in the next three months.
2 What we sold in the same three-month period last year, we will probably sell in that three-month period this year. (This would account for seasonal effects.)
3 We will probably sell 10 percent more in the next three months than we sold in the past three months.
4 We will probably sell 50 percent more over the next three months than we did for the same three months of last year.
5 Whatever percentage change we had for the past three months this year compared to the same three months last year will probably be the same percentage change that we will have for the next three months of this year.

These forecasting rules are not hard and fast. If a new rule seems to work well, it is added. If one has not been working well, it is deleted.

The second part of the process is computer simulation. To use the system, a data history should be available—for example, 18 to 24 months of data. The simulation process then uses each forecasting rule to predict some recent past data. The rule that did best in predicting the past is the rule used to predict the future. Example 11.6 is an exercise used by Smith.[6]

## EXAMPLE 11.6: DEMAND IN UNITS FOR A BROILER PAN

The following table shows unit demand for a broiler pan over an 18-month period. (Try to guess what demand might be for July, August, and September this year, and compare your guess to the actual data presented later.)

| | Last Year | This Year | | Last Year | This Year |
|---|---|---|---|---|---|
| January | 6 | 72 | July | 167 | |
| February | 212 | 90 | August | 159 | |
| March | 378 | 108 | September | 201 | |
| April | 129 | 134 | October | 153 | |
| May | 163 | 92 | November | 76 | |
| June | 96 | 137 | December | 30 | |

## SOLUTION

For brevity, we use only two rules to demonstrate the method: 1 and 5. In practice, they would all be used.

Using focus forecasting, we first try forecasting rule 1—whatever we sold in the past three months is what we will probably sell in the next three months. (We are using the terms *demands* and *sales* interchangeably, assuming that demands culminate in actual sales.) We first test this rule on the past three months:

$$\begin{aligned}\text{Forecast (April, May, June)} &= \text{Demand (January + February + March)}\\ &= 72 + 90 + 108 = 270\end{aligned}$$

Because what actually occurred was 363 (134 + 92 + 137), the forecast was 270/363 = 74 percent. In other words, it was 26 percent low.

Let's try another, say rule 5—whatever percentage change we had over last year in the past three months will probably be our percentage change over last year in the next three months.

$$\begin{aligned}&\text{Forecast (April + May + June)}\\ &\quad= \frac{\text{Demand (January + February + March) this year}}{\text{Demand (January + February + March) last year}}\\ &\qquad \times \text{Demand (April + May + June) last year}\\ &\quad= \frac{72 + 90 + 108}{6 + 212 + 378} \times (129 + 163 + 96)\\ &\quad= \frac{270}{596}(388) = 175.77\end{aligned}$$

What actually occurred during April, May, and June this year was 363, so the forecast was 175/363, or only 48 percent of the actual demand.

Because rule 1 was better in predicting the past three months, we use that rule in predicting July, August, and September of this year. Rule 1 says that whatever we sold in the past three months is what we will probably sell in the next three months.

$$\begin{aligned}\text{Forecast (July + August + September)} &= \text{Demand (April + May + June)}\\ &= 134 + 92 + 137 = 363\end{aligned}$$

The actual demand for the period was 357, as seen in the table, which shows the completed demand history for this year and serves as a basis for comparison.

| | LAST YEAR | THIS YEAR | | LAST YEAR | THIS YEAR |
|---|---|---|---|---|---|
| January | 6 | 72 | July | 167 | 120 |
| February | 212 | 90 | August | 159 | 151 |
| March | 378 | 108 | September | 201 | 86 |
| April | 129 | 134 | October | 153 | 113 |
| May | 163 | 92 | November | 76 | 97 |
| June | 96 | 137 | December | 30 | 40 |

Forecasts made using focus forecasting logic are then reviewed and modified (if necessary) by buyers or inventory control personnel who have responsibility over these items. When they see the forecasts made by the computer, they know which method was used and can either accept it or change the forecast if they do not agree. Smith says that about 8 percent of the forecasts are changed by the buyers because they know something that the computer does not (such as the cause of a previous large demand, or that the next forecast is too high because a competitor is introducing a competing product).

Smith states that in all the forecast simulations he has run using variations of exponential smoothing (including adaptive smoothing), focus forecasting gave significantly better results.

### DEVELOPING A FOCUS FORECASTING SYSTEM

Here are suggestions for developing a focus forecasting system:

1. Don't try to add a seasonality index. Let the forecasting system find out seasonality by itself, especially with new items, because seasonality may not apply until the pipeline is filled and the system is stable. The forecasting rules can handle it.
2. When a forecast is unusually high or low (such as two or three times the previous period, or the previous year if there is seasonality), print an indicator such as the letter *R* telling the person affected by this demand to review it. Do not just disregard unusual demands because they may, in fact, be valid changes in the demand pattern.
3. Let the people who will use the forecasts (such as buyers or inventory planners) participate in creating the rules. Smith plays his "can you outguess focus forecasting" game with all the company's buyers. Using two years of data and 2,000 items, focus forecasting makes forecasts for the past six months. Buyers are asked to forecast the past six months using any rule they prefer. If they are consistently better than the existing forecasting rules, their rules are added to the list.
4. Keep the rules simple. That way, they will be easily understood and trusted by users of the forecast.

In summary, it appears that focus forecasting has significant merit when demand is generated outside the system, such as in forecasting end-item demand, spare parts, and materials and supplies used in a variety of products.

Computer time apparently is not very large because Smith forecasts 100,000 items every month using his focus forecasting rules.

## COMPUTER PROGRAMS

Many commercial forecasting programs are available. Most are available for microcomputers and use shared network databases. Major companies, such as Wal-Mart, are now using programs that work over the Internet. In the future, standards will be developed to let manufacturers and merchants work together on forecasts over the Internet.

All but the most sophisticated forecasting formulas are quite easy to understand. Anyone who can use a spreadsheet such as Microsoft Excel® can create a forecasting program on a PC. Depending on one's knowledge of the spreadsheet, a simple program can be written in anywhere from a few minutes to a couple of hours. How this forecast is to be used by the firm could be the bigger challenge. If demand for many items is to be forecast, this becomes a data-handling problem, not a problem in the forecasting logic.

## CONCLUSION

Developing a forecasting system is not easy. However, it must be done because forecasting is fundamental to any planning effort. In the short run, a forecast is needed to predict the requirements for materials, products, services, or other resources to respond to changes in demand. Forecasts permit adjusting schedules and varying labor and materials. In the long run, forecasting is required as a basis for strategic changes, such as developing new markets, developing new products or services, and expanding or creating new facilities.

For long-term forecasts that lead to heavy financial commitments, great care should be taken to derive the forecast. Several approaches should be used. Causal methods such as regression analysis or multiple regression analysis are beneficial. These provide a basis for discussion. Economic factors, product trends, growth factors, and competition, as well as myriad other possible variables, need to be considered and the forecast adjusted to reflect the influence of each.

Short- and intermediate-term forecasting (such as required for inventory control as well as staffing and material scheduling) may be satisfied with simpler models, such as exponential smoothing with perhaps an adaptive feature or a seasonal index. In these applications, thousands of items are usually being forecast. The forecasting routine should therefore be simple and run quickly on a computer. The routines should also detect and respond rapidly to definite short-term changes in demand while at the same time ignoring the occasional spurious demands. Exponential smoothing, when monitored by management to control the value of alpha, is an effective technique.

Focus forecasting appears to offer a reasonable approach to short-term forecasting—say, monthly or quarterly but certainly less than a year. If there is one thing focus forecasting offers, it is close monitoring and rapid response.

In summary, forecasting is tough. A perfect forecast is like a hole in one in golf: great to get but we should be satisfied just to get close to the cup—or, to push the analogy, just to land on the green. The ideal philosophy is to create the best forecast that you reasonably can and then hedge by maintaining flexibility in the system to account for the inevitable forecast error.

## KEY TERMS

**Dependent demand** Requirements for a product or service caused by the demand for other products or services. This type of internal demand does not need a forecast, but can be calculated based on the demand for the other products or services.

**Independent demand** Demand that cannot be directly derived from the demand for other products.

**Time series analysis** A type of forecast in which data relating to past demand are used to predict future demand.

**Exponential smoothing** A time series forecasting technique in which each increment of past demand data is decreased by $(1 - \alpha)$.

**Smoothing constant alpha ($\alpha$)** The parameter in the exponential smoothing equation that controls the speed of reaction to differences between forecasts and actual demand.

**Smoothing constant delta ($\delta$)** An additional parameter used in an exponential smoothing equation that includes an adjustment for trend.

**Mean absolute deviation (MAD)** The average forecast error using absolute values of the error of each past forecast.

**Tracking signal** A measure that indicates whether the forecast average is keeping pace with any genuine upward or downward changes in demand.

**Linear regression forecasting** A forecasting technique that asumes that past data and future projections fall around a straight line.

**Causal relationship** A situation in which one event causes another. If the event is far enough in the future, it can be used as a basis for forecasting.

**Focus forecasting** An approach to forecasting in which several different techniques are tried in a computer simulation and the best technique or combination of techniques is used to make the actual forecast.

## FORMULA REVIEW

**Simple moving average**

[11.1] $$F_t = \frac{A_{t-1} + A_{t-2} + A_{t-3} + \cdots + A_{t-n}}{n}$$

**Weighted moving average**

[11.2] $$F_t = w_1 A_{t-1} + w_2 A_{t-2} + \cdots + w_n A_{t-n}$$

**Single exponential smoothing**

[11.3] $$F_t = F_{t-1} + \alpha(A_{t-1} - F_{t-1})$$

**Exponential smoothing with trend**

[11.4] $$\text{FIT}_t = F_t + T_t$$

[11.5] $$F_t = \text{FIT}_{t-1} + \alpha(A_{t-1} - \text{FIT}_{t-1})$$

[11.6] $$T_t = T_{t-1} + \delta(F_t - \text{FIT}_{t-1})$$

**Mean absolute deviation**

[11.7] $$\text{MAD} = \frac{\sum_{i=1}^{n} |A_t - F_t|}{n}$$

**Tracking signal**

[11.8] $$\text{TS} = \frac{\text{RSFE}}{\text{MAD}}$$

**Least squares regression**

[11.9] $$Y = a + bx$$

[11.10] $$a = \bar{y} - b\bar{x}$$

[11.11] $$b = \frac{\sum xy - n\bar{x} \cdot \bar{y}}{\sum x^2 - n\bar{x}^2}$$

**Standard error of estimate**

[11.12] $$S_{yx} = \sqrt{\frac{\sum_{i=1}^{n} (y_i - Y_i)^2}{n - 2}}$$

## SOLVED PROBLEMS

Excel: Forecasting

### SOLVED PROBLEM 1

Sunrise Baking Company markets doughnuts through a chain of food stores. It has been experiencing over- and underproduction because of forecasting errors. The following data are its demand in dozens of doughnuts for the past four weeks. Doughnuts are made for the following day; for example, Sunday's doughnut production is for Monday's sales, Monday's production is for Tuesday's sales, and so forth. The bakery is closed Saturday, so Friday's production must satisfy demand for both Saturday and Sunday.

| | 4 Weeks Ago | 3 Weeks Ago | 2 Weeks Ago | Last Week |
|---|---|---|---|---|
| Monday | 2,200 | 2,400 | 2,300 | 2,400 |
| Tuesday | 2,000 | 2,100 | 2,200 | 2,200 |
| Wednesday | 2,300 | 2,400 | 2,300 | 2,500 |
| Thursday | 1,800 | 1,900 | 1,800 | 2,000 |
| Friday | 1,900 | 1,800 | 2,100 | 2,000 |
| Saturday | | | | |
| Sunday | 2,800 | 2,700 | 3,000 | 2,900 |

Make a forecast for this week on the following basis:

*a.* Daily, using a simple four-week moving average.
*b.* Daily, using a weighted average of 0.40, 0.30, 0.20, and 0.10 for the past four weeks.
*c.* Sunrise is also planning its purchases of ingredients for bread production. If bread demand had been forecast for last week at 22,000 loaves and only 21,000 loaves were actually demanded, what would Sunrise's forecast be for this week using exponential smoothing with $\alpha = 0.10$?
*d.* Suppose, with the forecast made in *c*, this week's demand actually turns out to be 22,500. What would the new forecast be for the next week?

## Solution

*a.* Simple moving average, four-week.

$$\text{Monday } \frac{2,400 + 2,300 + 2,400 + 2,200}{4} = \frac{9,300}{4} = 2,325 \text{ doz.}$$

$$\text{Tuesday } = \frac{8,500}{4} = 2,125 \text{ doz.}$$

$$\text{Wednesday } = \frac{9,500}{4} = 2,375 \text{ doz.}$$

$$\text{Thursday } = \frac{7,500}{4} = 1,875 \text{ doz.}$$

$$\text{Friday } = \frac{7,800}{4} = 1,950 \text{ doz.}$$

$$\text{Saturday and Sunday } = \frac{11,400}{4} = 2,850 \text{ doz.}$$

*b.* Weighted average with weights of .40, .30, .20, and .10.

| | (.10) | | (.20) | | (.30) | | (.40) | | |
|---|---|---|---|---|---|---|---|---|---|
| Monday | 220 | + | 480 | + | 690 | + | 960 | = | 2,350 |
| Tuesday | 200 | + | 420 | + | 660 | + | 880 | = | 2,160 |
| Wednesday | 230 | + | 480 | + | 690 | + | 1,000 | = | 2,400 |
| Thursday | 180 | + | 380 | + | 540 | + | 800 | = | 1,900 |
| Friday | 190 | + | 360 | + | 630 | + | 800 | = | 1,980 |
| Saturday and Sunday | 280 | + | 540 | + | 900 | + | 1,160 | = | 2,880 |
| | 1,300 | + | 2,660 | + | 4,110 | + | 5,600 | = | 13,670 |

*c.* Exponentially smoothed forecast for bread demand

$$\begin{aligned} F_t &= F_{t-1} + \alpha(A_{t-1} - F_{t-1}) \\ &= 22,000 + 0.10(21,000 - 22,000) \\ &= 22,000 - 100 = 21,900 \text{ loaves} \end{aligned}$$

*d.* Exponentially smoothed forecast

$$F_{t+1} = 21{,}900 + .10(22{,}500 - 21{,}900)$$
$$= 21{,}900 + .10(600) = 21{,}960 \text{ loaves}$$

## SOLVED PROBLEM 2

Excel: Forecasting

Here are the actual demands for a product for the past six quarters. Using focus forecasting rules 1 through 5, find the best rule to use in predicting the third quarter of this year.

| | QUARTER | | | |
|---|---|---|---|---|
| | I | II | III | IV |
| Last year | 1,200 | 700 | 900 | 1,100 |
| This year | 1,400 | 1,000 | | |

### Solution

*Rule 1:* Next three months' demand = Last three months' demand.

Testing this on the last three months, $F_{II} = A_I$; therefore $F_{II} = 1{,}400$.

$$\text{Actual demand was 1,000, so } \frac{1{,}000}{1{,}400} = 71.4\%.$$

*Rule 2:* This quarter's demand equals demand in the same quarter last year.
The forecast for the second quarter this year will therefore be 700, the amount for that quarter last year.

$$\text{Actual demand was 1,000, and } \frac{1{,}000}{700} = 142.9\%.$$

*Rule 3:* 10 percent more than last quarter.

$$F_{II} = 1{,}400 \times 1.10 = 1{,}540$$

$$\text{Actual was 1,000, and } \frac{1{,}000}{1{,}540} = 64.9\%.$$

*Rule 4:* 50 percent more than same quarter last year.

$$F_{II} = 700 \times 1.50 = 1{,}050$$

$$\text{Actual was 1,000, and } \frac{1{,}000}{1{,}050} = 95.2\%.$$

*Rule 5:* Same rate of increase or decrease as last three months.

$$\frac{1{,}400}{1{,}200} = 1.167$$

$$F_{II} = 700 \times 1.167 = 816.7$$

$$\text{Actual was 1,000, so } \frac{1{,}000}{816.7} = 122.4\%.$$

Rule 4 was the closest in predicting the recent quarter—95.2 percent or just 4.8 percent under. Using this rule (50 percent more than the same quarter last year), we would forecast the third quarter this year as 50 percent more than the third quarter last year, or

$$\text{This year } F_{\text{III}} = 1.50\, A_{\text{III}} \quad \text{(last year)}$$

$$F_{\text{III}} = 1.50\,(900) = 1{,}350 \text{ units}$$

## SOLVED PROBLEM 3

A specific forecasting model was used to forecast demand for a product. The forecasts and the corresponding demand that subsequently occurred are shown below. Use the MAD and tracking signal technique to evaluate the accuracy of the forecasting model.

| | ACTUAL | FORECAST |
|---|---|---|
| October | 700 | 660 |
| November | 760 | 840 |
| December | 780 | 750 |
| January | 790 | 835 |
| February | 850 | 910 |
| March | 950 | 890 |

### Solution

Evaluate the forecasting model using MAD and tracking signal.

| | ACTUAL DEMAND | FORECAST DEMAND | ACTUAL DEVIATION | CUMULATIVE DEVIATION (RSFE) | ABSOLUTE DEVIATION |
|---|---|---|---|---|---|
| October | 700 | 660 | 40 | 40 | 40 |
| November | 760 | 840 | −80 | −40 | 80 |
| December | 780 | 750 | 30 | −10 | 30 |
| January | 790 | 835 | −45 | −55 | 45 |
| February | 850 | 910 | −60 | −115 | 60 |
| March | 950 | 890 | 60 | −55 | 60 |
| | | | | | Total dev. = 315 |

$$\text{MAD} = \frac{315}{6} = 52.5$$

$$\text{Tracking signal} = \frac{-55}{52.5} = -1.05$$

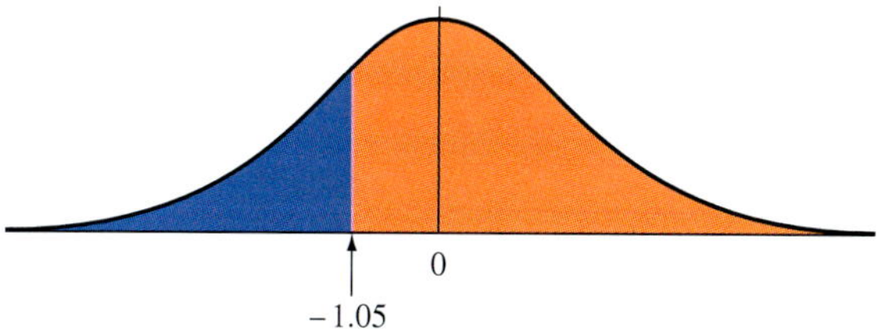


Forecast model is well within the distribution.

## SOLVED PROBLEM 4

Here are quarterly data for the past two years. From these data, prepare a forecast for the upcoming year using decomposition.

| PERIOD | ACTUAL | PERIOD | ACTUAL |
|---|---|---|---|
| 1 | 300 | 5 | 416 |
| 2 | 540 | 6 | 760 |
| 3 | 885 | 7 | 1191 |
| 4 | 580 | 8 | 760 |

## Solution

| (1) PERIOD x | (2) ACTUAL Y | (3) PERIOD AVERAGE | (4) SEASONAL FACTOR | (5) DESEASONALIZED DEMAND |
|---|---|---|---|---|
| 1 | 300 | 358 | 0.527 | 568.99 |
| 2 | 540 | 650 | 0.957 | 564.09 |
| 3 | 885 | 1,038 | 1.529 | 578.92 |
| 4 | 580 | 670 | 0.987 | 587.79 |
| 5 | 416 | | 0.527 | 789.01 |
| 6 | 760 | | 0.957 | 793.91 |
| 7 | 1,191 | | 1.529 | 779.08 |
| 8 | 760 | | 0.987 | 770.21 |
| Total | 5,432 | 2,716 | 8.0 | |
| Average | 679 | 679 | 1 | |

Column 3 is seasonal average. For example, the first-quarter average is

$$\frac{300 + 416}{2} = 358$$

Column 4 is the quarter average (column 3) divided by the overall average (679). Column 5 is the actual data divided by the seasonal index. To determine $x^2$ and $xy$ we can construct a table as follows:

| | PERIOD $x$ | DESEASONALIZED DEMAND ($y_d$) | $x^2$ | $xy$ |
|---|---|---|---|---|
| | 1 | 568.99 | 1 | 569.0 |
| | 2 | 564.09 | 4 | 1128.2 |
| | 3 | 578.92 | 9 | 1736.7 |
| | 4 | 587.79 | 16 | 2351.2 |
| | 5 | 789.01 | 25 | 3945.0 |
| | 6 | 793.91 | 36 | 4763.4 |
| | 7 | 779.08 | 49 | 5453.6 |
| | 8 | 770.21 | 64 | 6161.7 |
| Sums | 36 | 5,432 | 204 | 26,108.8 |
| Average | 4.5 | 679 | | |

Now we calculate regression results for deseasonalized data.

$$b = \frac{(26108) - (8)(4.5)(679)}{(204) - (8)(4.5)^2} = 39.64$$

$$a = \overline{Y} - b\overline{x}$$

$$a = 679 - 39.64(4.5) = 500.6$$

Therefore, the deseasonalized regression results are

$$Y = 500.6 + 39.64x$$

| PERIOD | TREND FORECAST | | SEASONAL FACTOR | | FINAL FORECAST |
|---|---|---|---|---|---|
| 9 | 857.4 | × | 0.527 | = | 452.0 |
| 10 | 897.0 | × | 0.957 | = | 858.7 |
| 11 | 936.7 | × | 1.529 | = | 1431.9 |
| 12 | 976.3 | × | 0.987 | = | 963.4 |

## REVIEW AND DISCUSSION QUESTIONS

1 What is the difference between dependent and independent demand?
2 Examine Exhibit 11.4 and suggest which model you might use for (*a*) bathing suit demand, (*b*) demand for new houses, (*c*) electrical power usage, (*d*) new plant expansion plans.
3 What is the logic in the least squares method of linear regression analysis?
4 Explain the procedure to create a forecast using the decomposition method of least squares regression.
5 Give some very simple rules you might use to manage demand for a firm's product. (An example is "limited to stock on hand.")
6 What strategies are used by supermarkets, airlines, hospitals, banks, and cereal manufacturers to influence demand?
7 All forecasting methods using exponential smoothing, adaptive smoothing, and exponential smoothing including trend require starting values to get the equations going. How would you select the starting value for, say, $F_{t-1}$?
8 From the choice of simple moving average, weighted moving average, exponential smoothing, and linear regression analysis, which forecasting technique would you consider the most accurate? Why?
9 Give some examples that have a multiplicative seasonal trend relationship.
10 What is the main disadvantage of daily forecasting using regression analysis?
11 What are the main problems with using adaptive exponential smoothing in forecasting?
12 How is a seasonal index computed from a regression line analysis?
13 Discuss the basic differences between the mean absolute deviation and the standard deviation.
14 What implications do forecast errors have for the search for ultrasophisticated statistical forecasting models?
15 What are the strongest selling points of focused forecasting?
16 Causal relationships are potentially useful for which component of a time series?

## PROBLEMS

1 Demand for stereo headphones and CD players for joggers has caused Nina Industries to grow almost 50 percent over the past year. The number of joggers continues to expand, so Nina expects demand for headsets to also expand, because, as yet, no safety laws have been passed to prevent joggers from wearing them. Demand for the stereo units for last year was as follows:

1. See ISM.
*a.* $a = 3766.7$
$b = 192.3$
*b.* 810 units

| Month | Demand (Units) | Month | Demand (Units) |
|---|---|---|---|
| January | 4,200 | July | 5,300 |
| February | 4,300 | August | 4,900 |
| March | 4,000 | September | 5,400 |
| April | 4,400 | October | 5,700 |
| May | 5,000 | November | 6,300 |
| June | 4,700 | December | 6,000 |

*a.* Using least squares regression analysis, what would you estimate demand to be for each month next year? Using a spreadsheet, follow the general format in Exhibit 11.14. Compare your results to those obtained by using the forecast spreadsheet function.
*b.* To be reasonably confident of meeting demand, Nina decides to use three standard errors of estimate for safety. How many additional units should be held to meet this level of confidence?

2 Historical demand for a product is:

2. *a.* 15.
*b.* 14.3.
*c.* 13.4.
*d.* $Y = a + bx$
$= 10.8 + .77x.$
*e.* $Y = 10.8 + .77(7)$
$= 16.2.$

| | Demand |
|---|---|
| January | 12 |
| February | 11 |
| March | 15 |
| April | 12 |
| May | 16 |
| June | 15 |

*a.* Using a weighted moving average with weights of 0.60, 0.30, and 0.10, find the July forecast.
*b.* Using a simple three-month moving average, find the July forecast.
*c.* Using single exponential smoothing with $\alpha = 0.2$ and a June forecast = 13, find the July forecast. Make whatever assumptions you wish.
*d.* Using simple linear regression analysis, calculate the regression equation for the preceding demand data.
*e.* Using the regression equation in *d*, calculate the forecast for July.

3. *a.* $F_{t+1} = F_t + .2(A_t - F_t)$. February 84, March 86, April 90, May 88, June 84, *b.* MAD $= \frac{90}{6} = 15$.

3 The following tabulations are actual sales of units for six months and a starting forecast in January.
*a.* Calculate forecasts for the remaining five months using simple exponential smoothing with $\alpha = 0.2$.
*b.* Calculate MAD for the forecasts.

| | ACTUAL | FORECAST |
|---|---|---|
| January | 100 | 80 |
| February | 94 | |
| March | 106 | |
| April | 80 | |
| May | 68 | |
| June | 94 | |

4. See ISM.

4 Zeus Computer Chips, Inc., used to have major contracts to produce the 386- and 486-type chips. The market has been declining during the past three years because of the pentium-type chips, which it cannot produce, so Zeus has the unpleasant task of forecasting next year. The task is unpleasant because the firm has not been able to find replacement chips for its product lines. Here is demand over the past 12 quarters:

| 1997 | | 1998 | | 1999 | |
|---|---|---|---|---|---|
| I | 4,800 | I | 3,500 | I | 3,200 |
| II | 3,500 | II | 2,700 | II | 2,100 |
| III | 4,300 | III | 3,500 | III | 2,700 |
| IV | 3,000 | IV | 2,400 | IV | 1,700 |

Use the decomposition technique to forecast the four quarters of 2000.

5. See ISM.

5 Sales data for two years are as follows. Data are aggregated with two months of sales in each "period."

| MONTHS | SALES | MONTHS | SALES |
|---|---|---|---|
| January–February | 109 | January–February | 115 |
| March–April | 104 | March–April | 112 |
| May–June | 150 | May–June | 159 |
| July–August | 170 | July–August | 182 |
| September–October | 120 | September–October | 126 |
| November–December | 100 | November–December | 106 |

*a.* Plot the data.
*b.* Fit a simple linear regression model to the sales data.
*c.* In addition to the regression model, determine multiplicative seasonal index factors. A full cycle is assumed to be a full year.
*d.* Using the results from parts *b* and *c*, prepare a forecast for the next year.

6 The tracking signals computed using past demand history for three different products are as

follows. Each product used the same forecasting technique.

| | TS 1 | TS 2 | TS 3 |
|---|---|---|---|
| 1 | −2.70 | 1.54 | 0.10 |
| 2 | −2.32 | −0.64 | 0.43 |
| 3 | −1.70 | 2.05 | 1.08 |
| 4 | −1.1 | 2.58 | 1.74 |
| 5 | −0.87 | −0.95 | 1.94 |
| 6 | −0.05 | −1.23 | 2.24 |
| 7 | 0.10 | 0.75 | 2.96 |
| 8 | 0.40 | −1.59 | 3.02 |
| 9 | 1.50 | 0.47 | 3.54 |
| 10 | 2.20 | 2.74 | 3.75 |

Discuss the tracking signals for each and what the implications are.

6. TS 1: Rapid rise in trend. Will shortly be outside limits. Forecast model not good.
TS 2: Forecast OK. Within limits.
TS 3: Rapid rise. Outside limits. Forecast model not good.

7 The following table shows the past two years of quarterly sales information. Assume that there are both trend and seasonal factors and that the season cycle is one year. Use time series decomposition to forecast quarterly sales for the next year.

| QUARTER | SALES | QUARTER | SALES |
|---|---|---|---|
| 1 | 160 | 5 | 215 |
| 2 | 195 | 6 | 240 |
| 3 | 150 | 7 | 205 |
| 4 | 140 | 8 | 190 |

7.

| Quarter | Forecast |
|---|---|
| 9 | 232 |
| 10 | 281 |
| 11 | 239 |
| 12 | 231 |

8 Tucson Machinery, Inc., manufactures numerically controlled machines, which sell for an average price of $0.5 million each. Sales for these NCMs for the past two years were as follows:

| QUARTER | QUANTITY (UNITS) | QUARTER | QUANTITY (UNITS) |
|---|---|---|---|
| 1998 | | 1999 | |
| I | 12 | I | 16 |
| II | 18 | II | 24 |
| III | 26 | III | 28 |
| IV | 16 | IV | 18 |

*a.* Hand fit a line (or do a regression if your calculator has that feature).
*b.* Find the trend and seasonal factors.
*c.* Forecast sales for 2000.

8. *a.* $a = 15.1$;
$= 15.1 + 1.02x$.
*b.* See ISM.
*c.* 2000

| | |
|---|---|
| I | 16.3 |
| II | 25.2 |
| III | 33.4 |
| IV | 21.6 |

9 Not all the items in your office supply store are evenly distributed as far as demand is concerned, so you decide to forecast demand to help plan your stock. Past data for legal-sized yellow tablets for the month of August are

| | | | |
|---|---|---|---|
| Week 1 | 300 | Week 3 | 600 |
| Week 2 | 400 | Week 4 | 700 |

*a.* Using a three-week moving average, what would you forecast the next week to be?
*b.* Using exponential smoothing with $\alpha = 0.20$, if the exponential forecast for week 3 was estimated as the average of the first two weeks [$(300 + 400)/2 = 350$], what would you forecast week 5 to be?

9. *a.* $F_5 = 567$.
*b.* $F_5 = 460$.

10 Given the following history, use focus forecasting to forecast the third quarter of this year. Use three focus forecasting strategies.

| | JAN | FEB | MAR | APR | MAY | JUN | JUL | AUG | SEP | OCT | NOV | DEC |
|---|---|---|---|---|---|---|---|---|---|---|---|---|
| Last year | 100 | 125 | 135 | 175 | 185 | 200 | 150 | 140 | 130 | 200 | 225 | 250 |
| This year | 125 | 135 | 135 | 190 | 200 | 190 | | | | | | |

10. Strategy A: 395, 68%.
Strategy B: 560, 97%.
Strategy C: 434.5, 75%
$F_{III} = 420$

11. *a.* April to September = 130, 150, 160, 170, 160, 150.
*b.* April to September = 136, 146, 150, 159, 153, 146.
*c.* Exponential smoothing performed better.

11 Here are the actual tabulated demands for an item for a nine-month period (January through September). Your supervisor wants to test two forecasting methods to see which method was better over this period.

| MONTH | ACTUAL | MONTH | ACTUAL |
|---|---|---|---|
| January | 110 | June | 180 |
| February | 130 | July | 140 |
| March | 150 | August | 130 |
| April | 170 | September | 140 |
| May | 160 | | |

*a.* Forecast April through September using a three-month moving average.
*b.* Use simple exponential smoothing with an alpha of .3, to estimate April through September.
*c.* Use MAD to decide which method produced the better forecast over the six-month period.

12. MAD = 58.3; TS = −6. Model is giving a poor forecast.

12 A particular forecasting model was used to forecast a six-month period. Here are the forecasts and actual demands that resulted:

| | FORECAST | ACTUAL |
|---|---|---|
| April | 250 | 200 |
| May | 325 | 250 |
| June | 400 | 325 |
| July | 350 | 300 |
| August | 375 | 325 |
| September | 450 | 400 |

Find the tracking signal and state whether you think the model being used is giving acceptable answers.

13. *a.* MAD = 23.75.
*b.* TS = 7.16.
*c.* Tracking signal of 7.16 too large; model is poor.

13 Harlen Industries has a simple forecasting model: Take the actual demand for the same month last year and divide that by the number of fractional weeks in that month. This gives the average weekly demand for that month. This weekly average is used as the weekly forecast for the same month this year. This technique was used to forecast eight weeks for this year, which are shown below along with the actual demand that occurred.

The following eight weeks show the forecast (based on last year) and the demand that actually occurred:

| WEEK | FORECAST DEMAND | ACTUAL DEMAND | WEEK | FORECAST DEMAND | ACTUAL DEMAND |
|---|---|---|---|---|---|
| 1 | 140 | 137 | 5 | 140 | 180 |
| 2 | 140 | 133 | 6 | 150 | 170 |
| 3 | 140 | 150 | 7 | 150 | 185 |
| 4 | 140 | 160 | 8 | 150 | 205 |

*a.* Compute the MAD of forecast errors.
*b.* Using the RSFE, compute the tracking signal.
*c.* Based on your answers to *a* and *b*, comment on Harlen's method of forecasting.

14. *a.* See ISM.
*b.* See ISM.
*c.* Simple MAD = 2.90
With Trend MAD = 0.86.
The Trend model is better.

14 The following table contains the demand from the last 10 months:

| MONTH | ACTUAL DEMAND | MONTH | ACTUAL DEMAND |
|---|---|---|---|
| 1 | 31 | 6 | 36 |
| 2 | 34 | 7 | 38 |
| 3 | 33 | 8 | 40 |
| 4 | 35 | 9 | 40 |
| 5 | 37 | 10 | 41 |

*a.* Calculate the single exponential smoothing forecast for this data using an $\alpha$ of .30 and an initial forecast ($F_1$) of 31.
*b.* Calculate the exponential smoothing with trend forecast for this data using an $\alpha$ of .30 a $\delta$ of .30, an initial trend forecast ($T_1$) of 1, and an initial exponentially smoothed forecast ($F_1$) of 30.
*c.* Calculate the Mean Absolute Deviation (MAD) for each forecast. Which is best?

15 In this problem, you are to test the validity of your forecasting model. Here are the forecasts for a model you have been using and the actual demands that occurred:

15. MAD = 104; TS = 3.1. The TS is 3.1 in week 6. This is a fairly high value, which indicates the model is unacceptable.

| WEEK | FORECAST | ACTUAL |
|---|---|---|
| 1 | 800 | 900 |
| 2 | 850 | 1,000 |
| 3 | 950 | 1,050 |
| 4 | 950 | 900 |
| 5 | 1,000 | 900 |
| 6 | 975 | 1,100 |

Use the method stated in the text to compute the MAD and tracking signal. Then decide whether the forecasting model you have been using is giving reasonable results.

16 Assume that your stock of sales merchandise is maintained based on the forecast demand. If the distributor's sales personnel call on the first day of each month, compute your forecast sales by each of the three methods requested here.

16. *a.* $F_{\text{Sept.}} = 163.3$. *b.* $F_{\text{Sept.}} = 167$. *c.* $F_{\text{Sept.}} = 154$.

| | ACTUAL |
|---|---|
| June | 140 |
| July | 180 |
| August | 170 |

*a.* Using a simple three-month moving average, what is the forecast for September?
*b.* Using a weighted moving average, what is the forecast for September with weights of .20, .30, and .50 for June, July, and August, respectively?
*c.* Using single exponential smoothing and assuming that the forecast for June had been 130, forecast sales for September with a smoothing constant alpha of .30.

17 Historical demand for a product is as follows:

17. *a.* $F_{\text{Oct.}} = 72.5$. *b.* 67. *c.* $Y = 54 + 3.86x$. *d.* 81.

| | DEMAND |
|---|---|
| April | 60 |
| May | 55 |
| June | 75 |
| July | 60 |
| August | 80 |
| September | 75 |

*a.* Using a simple four-month moving average, calculate a forecast for October.
*b.* Using single exponential smoothing with $\alpha = 0.2$ and a September forecast = 65, calculate a forecast for October.
*c.* Using simple linear regression, calculate the trend line for the historical data. Say the $X$ axis is April = 1, May = 2, and so on, while the $Y$ axis is demand.
*d.* Calculate a forecast for October.

18 Sales by quarter for last year and the first three quarters of this year were as follows:

18. Use strategy E to forecast 4th quarter: $F_{\text{IV}} = 7{,}500$.

| | QUARTER | | | |
|---|---|---|---|---|
| | I | II | III | IV |
| Last year | 23,000 | 27,000 | 18,000 | 9,000 |
| This year | 19,000 | 24,000 | 15,000 | |

Using the Focus Forecasting procedure described in the text, forecast expected sales for the fourth quarter of this year.

19. *a.* MAD = 90;
TS = −1.67.
*b.* Model okay because tracking is −1.67.

19 The following table shows predicted product demand using your particular forecasting method along with the actual demand that occurred:

| FORECAST | ACTUAL |
|---|---|
| 1,500 | 1,550 |
| 1,400 | 1,500 |
| 1,700 | 1,600 |
| 1,750 | 1,650 |
| 1,800 | 1,700 |

*a.* Compute the tracking signal using the mean absolute deviation and running sum of forecast errors.
*b.* Discuss whether your forecasting method is giving good predictions.

20. *a.* See ISM.
*b.* See ISM.
*c.* See ISM.
*d.* See ISM.
*e.*

| Forecast | MAD |
|---|---|
| Moving average | 4.07 |
| Weighted moving average | 3.46 |
| Single exponential smoothing | 6.17 |
| Exponential smoothing with trend | 0.89 |

Select the exponential smoothing with trend forecast.

20 Your manager is trying to determine what forecasting method to use. Based upon the following historical data, calculate the following forecast and specify what procedure you would utilize.

| MONTH | ACTUAL DEMAND | MONTH | ACTUAL DEMAND |
|---|---|---|---|
| 1 | 62 | 7 | 76 |
| 2 | 65 | 8 | 78 |
| 3 | 67 | 9 | 78 |
| 4 | 68 | 10 | 80 |
| 5 | 71 | 11 | 84 |
| 6 | 73 | 12 | 85 |

*a.* Calculate the simple three-month moving average forecast for periods 4–12.
*b.* Calculate the weighted three-month moving average using weights of 0.50, 0.30, and 0.20 for periods 4–12.
*c.* Calculate the single exponential smoothing forecast for periods 2–12 using an initial forecast ($F_1$) of 61 and an $\alpha$ of 0.30.
*d.* Calculate the exponential smoothing with trend component forecast for periods 2–12 using an initial trend forecast ($T_1$) of 1.8, an initial exponential smoothing forecast ($F_1$) of 60, an $\alpha$ of 0.30, and a $\delta$ of 0.30.
*e.* Calculate the Mean Absolute Deviation (MAD) for the forecasts made by each technique in periods 4–12. Which forecasting method do you prefer?

21. Forecast (Summer 2000)
$= [210.87 + 55.78(10)] \times 0.45$
$= 768.66 \times 0.45 = 345.$

21 Use regression analysis on deseasonalized demand to forecast demand in summer 2000, given the following historical demand data:

| YEAR | SEASON | ACTUAL DEMAND |
|---|---|---|
| 1998 | Spring | 205 |
| | Summer | 140 |
| | Fall | 375 |
| | Winter | 575 |
| 1999 | Spring | 475 |
| | Summer | 275 |
| | Fall | 685 |
| | Winter | 965 |

22 Here are the data for the past 21 months for actual sales of a particular product:

| | 1998 | 1999 |
|---|---|---|
| January | 300 | 275 |
| February | 400 | 375 |
| March | 425 | 350 |
| April | 450 | 425 |
| May | 400 | 400 |
| June | 460 | 350 |
| July | 400 | 350 |
| August | 300 | 275 |
| September | 375 | 350 |
| October | 500 | |
| November | 550 | |
| December | 500 | |

Develop a forecast for the fourth quarter using three different focus forecasting rules. (Note that to correctly use this procedure, the rules are first tested on the third quarter; the best-performing one is used to forecast the fourth quarter.) Do the problem using quarters, as opposed to forecasting separate months.

22. Each rule is used to predict third quarter of 1999. Strategy B is best. Therefore, $F_{IV,99} = A_{IV,98}$, or 1,550.

23 Actual demand for a product for the past three months was

| | |
|---|---|
| Three months ago | 400 units |
| Two months ago | 350 units |
| Last month | 325 units |

*a.* Using a simple three-month moving average, make a forecast for this month.
*b.* If 300 units were actually demanded this month, what would your forecast be for next month?
*c.* Using simple exponential smoothing, what would your forecast be for this month if the exponentially smoothed forecast for three months ago was 450 units and the smoothing constant was 0.20?

23. *a.* 358.
*b.* 325.
*c.* $F_{\text{two months ago}} = 440$.
$F_{\text{last month}} = 422$.
$F_{\text{this month}} = 403$.

24 After using your forecasting model for six months, you decide to test it using MAD and a tracking signal. Here are the forecast and actual demands for the six-month period:

| Period | Forecast | Actual |
|---|---|---|
| May | 450 | 500 |
| June | 500 | 550 |
| July | 550 | 400 |
| August | 600 | 500 |
| September | 650 | 675 |
| October | 700 | 600 |

*a.* Find the tracking signal.
*b.* Decide whether your forecasting routine is acceptable.

24. *a.* MAD = 79.17; TS = −2.84.
*b.* Forecasts were above the mean of the actual data but acceptable.

25 Goodyear Tire and Rubber Company is the world's largest rubber manufacturer, with automotive products accounting for 82 percent of sales. Cooper Tire and Rubber Company is the ninth largest tire manufacturer in the world, with tires accounting for about 80 percent of sales.

Here are earnings per share for each company by quarter from the first quarter of 1988 through the second quarter of 1991. Forecast earnings per share for the rest of 1991 and 1992. Use exponential smoothing to forecast the third period of 1991, and the time series decomposition method to forecast the last two quarters of 1991 and all four quarters of 1992.

25. See ISM.

(It is much easier to solve this problem on a computer spreadsheet so you can see what is happening.)

EARNINGS PER SHARE

| | QUARTER | GOODYEAR TIRE | COOPER TIRE |
|---|---|---|---|
| 1988 | I | $1.67 | $0.17 |
| | II | 2.35 | 0.24 |
| | III | 1.11 | 0.26 |
| | IV | 1.15 | 0.34 |
| 1989 | I | 1.56 | 0.25 |
| | II | 2.04 | 0.37 |
| | III | 1.14 | 0.36 |
| | IV | 0.38 | 0.44 |
| 1990 | I | 0.29 | 0.33 |
| | II | −0.18 (loss) | 0.40 |
| | III | −0.97 (loss) | 0.41 |
| | IV | 0.20 | 0.47 |
| 1991 | I | −1.54 (loss) | 0.30 |
| | II | 0.38 | 0.47 |

*a.* For the exponential smoothing method, choose the first quarter of 1988 as the beginning forecast. Make two forecasts: one with $\alpha = 0.10$ and one with $\alpha = 0.30$.

*b.* Using the MAD method of testing the forecasting model's performance, plus actual data from 1988 through the second quarter of 1991, how well did the model perform?

*c.* Using the decomposition of a time series method of forecasting, forecast earnings per share for the last two quarters of 1991 and all four quarters of 1992. Is there a seasonal factor in the earnings?

*d.* Using your forecasts, comment on each company: Cooper Tire and Goodyear Tire.

26. See ISM.

26 Consolidated Edison Company of New York, Inc., sells electricity, gas, and steam to New York City and Westchester County. Here are sales revenues for 1981 through 1991. (The last four months of 1991 are estimated.) Forecast revenues for 1992 through 1995. Use your own judgment, intuition, or common sense concerning which model or method to use, as well as the period of data to include.

| | REVENUE (MILLIONS) | | REVENUE (MILLIONS) |
|---|---|---|---|
| 1981 | $4,865.9 | 1987 | $5,094.4 |
| 1982 | 5,067.4 | 1988 | 5,108.8 |
| 1983 | 5,515.6 | 1989 | 5,550.6 |
| 1984 | 5,728.8 | 1990 | 5,738.9 |
| 1985 | 5,497.7 | 1991 | 5,860.0 |
| 1986 | 5,197.7 | | |

## SELECTED BIBLIOGRAPHY


De Lurgio, S. *Forecasting Principles and Applications.* New York: Irwin/McGraw-Hill, 1998.

Diebold, F. X. *Elements of Forecasting.* Cincinnati, Ohio: South-Western College Publishing, 1998.

Hanke, J. E., and A. G. Reitsch. *Business Forecasting.* Upper Saddle River, N.J.: Prentice Hall, 1998.

Makridakis, S; S. C. Wheelwright; and R. J. Hyndman. *Forecasting: Methods for Management.* New York: John Wiley & Sons, 1998.


## FOOTNOTES

1 In addition to dependent and independent demands, other relationships include complementary products and causal relationships where demand for one causes the demand for another.

2 Some writers prefer to call $F_t$ a smoothed average.

3 When exponential smoothing is first introduced, the initial forecast or starting point may be obtained by using a simple estimate or an average of preceding periods such as the average of the first two or three periods.

4 An equation for the standard error that is often easier to compute is $S_{yx} = \sqrt{\dfrac{\sum y^2 - a\sum y - b\sum xy}{n-2}}$

5 B. T. Smith, *Focus Forecasting: Computer Techniques for Inventory Control* (Boston: CBI Publishing, 1984).

6 We use this exercise because it includes real data from the records of American Hardware Supply Company, where Smith was inventory manager. This forecasting exercise has been played by many people: buyers for American Hardware, inventory consultants, and numerous participants at national meetings of the American Production and Inventory Control Society. Further, data for the remainder of the year exist that allow for checking the results.

*chapter twelve*

# AGGREGATE PLANNING

## CHAPTER OUTLINE AND KEY TERMS

# 12

Inventory in the granite business is hard to miss: we make tombstones—a custom product if there ever was one—and when quarry blocks, slabs, bases, and finished stones are hanging around, they're quite visible. It's also pretty dangerous when they pile up (literally) because stones have been known to topple over and fall on people.

It may not be immediately obvious, but tombstone manufacture is a seasonal business; in New England you can't "plant" anything in the winter, so there is a huge demand peak just before Memorial Day. Since quarrying can't be done in the winter either, quarry blocks have to be purchased in the fall. Put this together with the fact that our dealers insist on consolidated shipments to various parts of the country given the weight of the finished product, and you've got the makings of a whopping inventory position during the run-up to the end of May. Add the need for *lots* of overtime for highly skilled craftsmen, and an annual cash flow crisis is going to be part of your life.

My grandmother was president of J. O. Bilodeau & Company, manufacturers of *Paragon Memorials,* in the Granite Center of the World—Barre, Vermont. My uncle and my mother were vice presidents (Sales and Office Administration, respectively), my step-grandfather was general foreman, and my other uncle was plant superintendent. (Our motto: If there's money to be made, for God's sake keep it in the family!) Lunch every day was a working meeting where children knew enough to be quiet; keeping one's mouth shut was a lot better than tangling with Grandma Pinard, so I was in

**Source:** Professor Linda G. Sprague, University of New Hampshire.

high school before I figured out that "Goshdurninventory" was actually three separate words.

When I went off to MIT, Grandma decided I should help pay back my tuition by reporting anything I found out that could help the family business. After hearing about some of systems theorist Jay Forrester's early work, I decided that Grandma should know (and I was just the one to tell her!) that she didn't really have an *inventory* problem. It was just a matter of buying less raw stock so early, insisting that our customers place their Memorial Day orders before Christmas so we could do the work in slack periods and avoid overtime, and telling our dealers that they would just have to pay for more convenient (fewer consolidated) shipments. Fortunately for me, Grandma spoke French-Canadian and hadn't permitted any of my generation to learn it very well, so I didn't fully understand her response. I did, however, grasp its general nature and so got away as quickly as possible.

My mother, of course, took Grandma's side, and there was great hilarity about the wisdom being imparted at the great MIT. Grandma consoled herself with the thought that, in spite of its naive understanding of suppliers, customers, and dealers, MIT was probably giving me enough basic training in engineering that I would "learn a trade"—which would supplement the courses in sewing and tailoring she and my mother had put me through as backup in case MIT wasn't as great as its reputation.

Meanwhile, every year between early April and late May we had a Goshdurninventory problem, and for another month or so beyond that had a cash crisis of epic proportion—as did every other manufacturer in town, to the considerable delight of the local banks. Until the day she died, my grandmother found great humor in what MIT had to say about the Goshdurninventory problem. ←

Aggregate planning

The problems of managing inventory and overtime discussed in the preceding vignette reflect one of the major areas addressed in aggregate planning. **Aggregate planning** involves translating annual and quarterly business plans into broad labor and output plans for the intermediate term (6 to 18 months). Its objective is to minimize the cost of resources required to meet demand over that period.

## OVERVIEW OF OPERATIONS PLANNING ACTIVITIES

Long-range planning
Intermediate-range planning
Short-range planning

Exhibit 12.1 positions aggregate planning relative to other major operations planning activities presented in the text. The time dimension is shown as long, intermediate, and short range. **Long-range planning** is generally done annually, focusing on a horizon greater than one year. **Intermediate-range planning** usually covers a period from 6 to 18 months, with time increments that are monthly or sometimes quarterly. **Short-range planning** covers a period from one day or less to six months, with the time increment usually weekly.

Process planning deals with determining the specific technologies and procedures required to produce a product or service. (See Chapters 5 and 6.) Strategic capacity planning deals with determining the long-term capabilities (such as the size and scope) of the production system. (See Chapter 9.) The aggregate planning process is essentially the same for services and manufacturing, the major exception being manufacturing's use of inventory buildups and cutbacks to smooth production (as we will discuss shortly). After the aggregate planning stage, manufacturing and service planning activities are generally quite different.

Master production shedule (MPS)
Rough-cut capacity planning
Material requirements planning (MRP)

In manufacturing, the planning process can be summarized as follows: The production control group inputs existing or forecast orders into a **master production schedule (MPS).** The MPS generates the amounts and dates of specific items required for each order. **Rough-cut capacity planning** then verifies that production and warehouse facilities, equipment, and labor are available and that key vendors have allocated sufficient capacity to provide materials when needed. As Chapter 14 details, **material requirements planning (MRP)** takes the end product requirements from the MPS and breaks them down into their

EXHIBIT 12.1

Overview of Major Operations Planning Activities

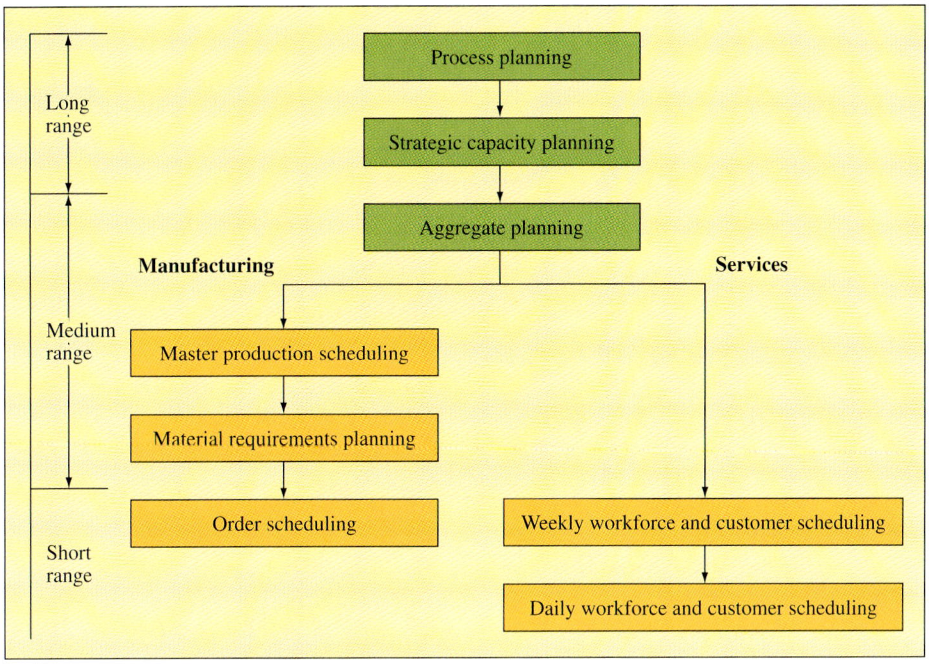


component parts and subassemblies to create a materials plan. This plan specifies when production and purchase orders must be placed for each part and subassembly to complete the products on schedule. Most MRP systems also allocate production capacity to each order. (This is called **capacity requirements planning.**) The final planning activity is daily or weekly **order scheduling** of jobs to specific machines, production lines, or work centers. (See Chapter 15 for details.)

Capacity requirements planning
Order scheduling

In services, once the aggregate staffing level is determined, the focus is on workforce and customer scheduling during the week or even hour by hour during the day. Workforce schedules are a function of the hours the service is available to a customer, the particular skills needed at particular times over the relevant period, and so on. Many service jobs have unique time and legal restrictions affecting scheduling that typical manufacturing work lacks. Airline flight crews are a good example of such constraints that make their scheduling far more complicated than scheduling manufacturing personnel. (Again, see Chapter 15.) Customer (or demand) scheduling deals with setting appointments and reservations for customers to use the service, and assigning priorities when they arrive at the service facility. These obviously range from formal reservation systems to simple sign-up sheets.

Service

Vol. IV "Scheduling Services—the United Solution."

We now turn our attention back to manufacturing.

## HIERARCHICAL PRODUCTION PLANNING

We have looked at manufacturing planning activities within a framework of long range, medium range, and short range. If we were to overlay the organization chart of a firm onto Exhibit 12.1, we would note that higher levels within the organization deal with long-range planning and lower levels deal with short-range planning. In a more formal way, Harlan Meal uses the term *hierarchical production planning (HPP)* to tailor the planning structure to the organization.[1] As Exhibit 12.2 shows, higher levels of management would use aggregate data for top-level decisions, while shop-floor decisions would be made using detailed data. In the extreme case, HPP logically states that top management should not become involved in determining the production lot size at a machine center. By the same token, the production line supervisor should not become involved in planning new product lines.

EXHIBIT 12.2

Hierarchical Planning Process

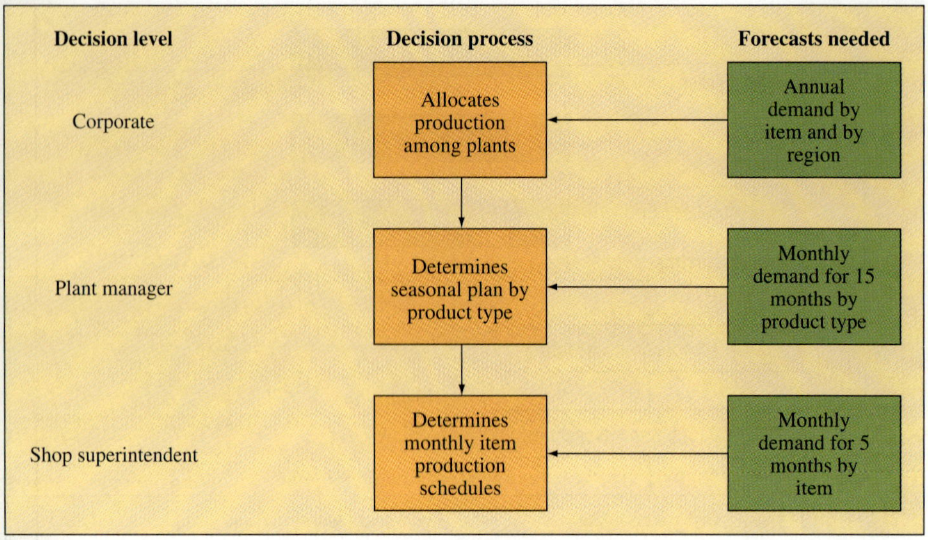




Meal cites as an example a tire manufacturer with several plants. With a *conventional* approach, each plant would tend to build a stock of tires it was confident of selling. An unsatisfactory consequence was that slow-moving items were produced in small quantities during peak season when capacity was scarce.

By centralizing the decision, top managers expected that they could somehow decide which plants would produce which tires in what quantities. This became impossible; not only was the number of detailed variables much too large to review but also it took the decision-making power away from plant management, where it rightly belonged.

The hierarchical procedure divided the decision making, with top management allocating tire production among the plants annually. Plant management would decide on seasonal effects, buildup of inventory, hiring, and so on. Shop management would perform the detailed scheduling of individual items. Shop supervisors, knowing the proportion of time they needed to spend on each product group, could then fill up available capacity.

An advantage of hierarchical planning is that each successive level has a smaller database and a simpler structure.

## AGGREGATE PRODUCTION PLANNING

Again, aggregate production planning is concerned with setting production rates by product group or other broad categories for the intermediate term (6 to 18 months). Note again from Exhibit 12.1 that the aggregate plan precedes the master schedule. *The main purpose of the aggregate plan is to specify the optimal combination of production rate, workforce level, and inventory on hand.* **Production rate** refers to the number of units completed per unit of time (such as per hour or per day). **Workforce level** is the number of workers needed for production (production = production rate × workforce level). **Inventory on hand** is unused inventory carried over from the previous period.

Production rate

Workforce level

Inventory on hand

Here is a formal statement of the aggregate planning problem: Given the demand forecast $F_t$ for each period $t$ in the planning horizon that extends over $T$ periods, determine the production level $P_t$, inventory level $I_t$, and workforce level $W_t$ for periods $t = 1, 2, \ldots, T$ that minimize the relevant costs over the planning horizon.

KAWASAKI MOTORS USA PRODUCES UTILITY VEHICLES, MOTORCYCLES, ALL-TERRAIN VEHICLES, AND JET SKI WATERCRAFT AT ITS PLANT IN LINCOLN, NEBRASKA.

WHILE THE CORPORATE PLAN WOULD SPECIFY HOW MANY UNITS IN EACH PRODUCT LINE, THE AGGREGATE PLAN WOULD DETERMINE HOW TO MEET THIS REQUIREMENT WITH AVAILABLE RESOURCES.

The form of the aggregate plan varies from company to company. In some firms, it is a formalized report containing planning objectives and the planning premises on which it is based. In other companies, particularly smaller ones, the owner may make simple calculations of workforce needs that reflect a general staffing strategy.

The process by which the plan itself is derived also varies. One common approach is to derive it from the corporate annual plan, as shown in Exhibit 12.1. A typical corporate plan contains a section on manufacturing that specifies how many units in each major product line need to be produced over the next 12 months to meet the sales forecast. The planner takes this information and attempts to determine how best to meet these requirements with available resources. Alternatively, some organizations combine output requirements into equivalent units and use this as the basis for aggregate planning. For example, a division of General Motors may be asked to produce a certain number of cars of all types at a particular facility. The production planner would then take the average labor hours required for all models as a basis for the overall aggregate plan. Refinements to this plan, specifically model types to be produced, would be reflected in shorter-term production plans.

Another approach is to develop the aggregate plan by simulating various master production schedules and calculating corresponding capacity requirements to see if adequate labor and equipment exist at each work center. If capacity is inadequate, additional requirements for overtime, subcontracting, extra workers, and so forth are specified for each product line and combined into a rough-cut plan. This plan is then modified by cut-and-try or mathematical methods to derive a final and (one hopes) lower-cost plan.

## PRODUCTION PLANNING ENVIRONMENT

Cross Functional

Exhibit 12.3 illustrates the internal and external factors that constitute the production planning environment. In general, the external environment is outside the production planner's direct control, but in some firms, demand for the product can be managed. Through close cooperation between marketing and operations, promotional activities and price cutting can be used to build demand during slow periods. Conversely, when demand is strong, promotional activities can be curtailed and prices raised to maximize the revenues from those products or services that the firm has the capacity to provide. The current practices in managing demand will be discussed later in the section titled "Yield Management."

EXHIBIT 12.3

Required Inputs to the Production Planning System

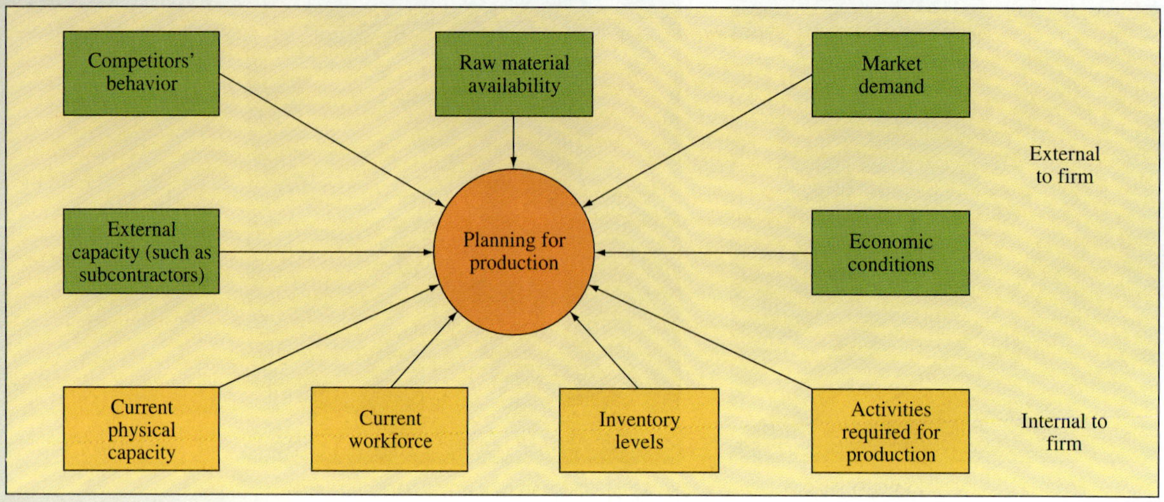

Complementary products may work for firms facing cyclical demand fluctuations. For instance, lawnmower manufacturers will have strong demand for spring and summer, but weak demand during fall and winter. Demands on the production system can be smoothed out by producing a complementary product with high demand during fall and winter, and low demand during spring and summer (for instance, snowmobiles, snowblowers, or leafblowers). With services, cycles are more often measured in hours than months. Restaurants with strong demand during lunch and dinner will often add a breakfast menu to increase demand during the morning hours.

But even so, there are limits to how much demand can be controlled. Ultimately, the production planner must live with the sales projections and orders promised by the marketing function, leaving the internal factors as variables that can be manipulated in deriving a production plan. A new approach to facilitate managing these internal factors is termed *accurate response.* This entails refined measurement of historical demand patterns blended with expert judgment to determine when to begin production of particular items. The key element of the approach is clearly identifying those products for which demand is relatively predictable from those for which demand is relatively unpredictable.[2]

The internal factors themselves differ in their controllability. Current physical capacity (plant and equipment) is usually nearly fixed in the short run; union agreements often constrain what can be done in changing the workforce; physical capacity cannot always be increased; and top management may limit the amount of money that can be tied up in inventories. Still, there is always some flexibility in managing these factors, and production planners can implement one or a combination of the **production planning strategies** discussed here.

Production planning strategies

**Production Planning Strategies** There are essentially three production planning strategies. These strategies involve trade-offs among the workforce size, work hours, inventory, and backlogs.

1 **Chase strategy.*** Match the production rate to the order rate by hiring and laying off employees as the order rate varies. The success of this strategy depends on having a pool of easily trained applicants to draw on as order volumes increase. There are obvious motivational impacts. When order backlogs are low, employees may

*No relation to one of the authors of this text.

feel compelled to slow down out of fear of being laid off as soon as existing orders are completed.

2 **Stable workforce—variable work hours.** Vary the output by varying the number of hours worked through flexible work schedules or overtime. By varying the number of work hours, you can match production quantities to orders. This strategy provides workforce continuity and avoids many of the emotional and tangible costs of hiring and firing associated with the chase strategy.

3 **Level strategy.** Maintain a stable workforce working at a constant output rate. Shortages and surpluses are absorbed by fluctuating inventory levels, order backlogs, and lost sales. Employees benefit from stable work hours at the costs of potentially decreased customer service levels and increased inventory costs. Another concern is the possibility of inventoried products becoming obsolete.

When just one of these variables is used to absorb demand fluctuations, it is termed a **pure strategy;** two or more used in combination constitute a **mixed strategy.** As you might suspect, mixed strategies are more widely applied in industry.

Pure strategy

Mixed strategy

**Subcontracting** In addition to these strategies, managers may also choose to subcontract some portion of production. This strategy is similar to the chase strategy, but hiring and laying off are translated into subcontracting and not subcontracting. Some level of subcontracting can be desirable to accommodate demand fluctuations. However, unless the relationship with the supplier is particularly strong, a manufacturer can lose some control over schedule and quality. For this reason, extensive subcontracting may be viewed as a high-risk strategy.

## RELEVANT COSTS

Four costs are relevant to aggregate production planning. These relate to the production cost itself as well as the cost to hold inventory and to have unfilled orders. More specifically, these are

1 **Basic production costs.** These are the fixed and variable costs incurred in producing a given product type in a given time period. Included are direct and indirect labor costs and regular as well as overtime compensation.

2 **Costs associated with changes in the production rate.** Typical costs in this category are those involved in hiring, training, and laying off personnel. Hiring temporary help is a way of avoiding these costs. See the box titled "Paying the Price" that details the impact on labor productivity of high labor turnover rates.

3 **Inventory holding costs.** A major component is the cost of capital tied up in inventory. Other components are storing, insurance, taxes, spoilage, and obsolescence.

4 **Backordering costs.** Usually these are very hard to measure and include costs of expediting, loss of customer goodwill, and loss of sales revenues resulting from backordering.

**Budgets** To receive funding, operations managers are generally required to submit annual, and sometimes quarterly, budget requests. Aggregate planning activities are key to the success of the budgeting process. Recall that the goal of aggregate planning is to minimize the total production-related costs over the planning horizon by determining the optimal combination of workforce levels and inventory levels. Thus, aggregate planning provides justification for the requested budget amount. Accurate medium-range planning increases the likelihood of (1) receiving the requested budget and (2) operating within the limits of the budget.

In the next section we provide examples of medium-range planning in both manufacturing and service settings. These examples illustrate the trade-offs associated with different production planning strategies.[3]

## PAYING THE PRICE

### DATA SHOW DAMAGING EFFECTS OF LABOR TURNOVER

Does it really matter if your manufacturing plant employs a stable, experienced workforce rather than a workforce whose makeup is constantly changing? That question may be more appropriate today than ever before as a tight labor market allows workers with the right skills to pick and choose their perfect position. Recently compiled data on numerous manufacturing performance measures indicate that the answer to the question is both yes and no. However, if the bottom line is a measure of worker productivity, there is no mixed signal: the higher the labor turnover rate, the more dramatic the dip in worker productivity.

Analysis of data from the Third Annual Industry Week Census of Manufacturers, which compiled data from more than 1,750 U.S. manufacturing plants, showed little to no relationship between annual labor turnover rates and such performance measures as inventory turns, finished-product first-pass quality yields, or on-time delivery rates. However, when the measure examined is productivity—defined as the annual value of plant shipments per employee—the benefit derived from low turnover seems clear: It pays to keep experienced workers on board. While manufacturing plants with annual labor turnover rates of less than 3 percent achieved a median productivity of $200,000, that figure dropped to $120,000 for plants with labor turnover rates of more than 20 percent.

**Productivity in relation to annual labor turnover rate**

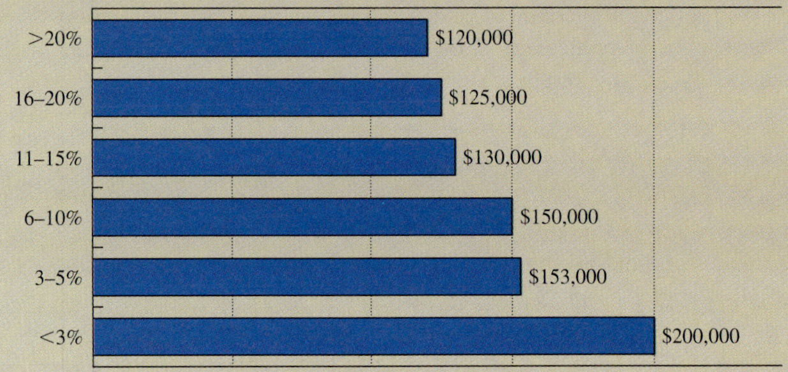


SOURCE: J. JUSKO, "PAYING THE PRICE," *INDUSTRY WEEK*, JANUARY 24, 2000, P. 13. REPRINTED WITH PERMISSION FROM INDUSTRY WEEK. COPYRIGHT PENTON MEDIA, INC., CLEVELAND OHIO.

# AGGREGATE PLANNING TECHNIQUES

Companies commonly use simple cut-and-try charting and graphic methods to develop aggregate plans. A cut-and-try approach involves costing out various production planning alternatives and selecting the one that is best. Elaborate spreadsheets are developed to facilitate the decision process. Sophisticated approaches involving linear programming and simulation are often incorporated into these spreadsheets. In the following, we demonstrate a spreadsheet approach to evaluate four strategies for meeting demand for the CA&J Company. Later we discuss more sophisticated approaches using linear programming.

## A CUT-AND-TRY EXAMPLE: THE CA&J COMPANY

A firm with pronounced seasonal variation normally plans production for a full year to capture the extremes in demand during the busiest and slowest months. But we can illustrate the general principles involved with a shorter horizon. Suppose we wish to set up a production plan for the CA&J Company for the next six months. We are given the following information:

| DEMAND AND WORKING DAYS | | | | | | | |
|---|---|---|---|---|---|---|---|
| | JANUARY | FEBRUARY | MARCH | APRIL | MAY | JUNE | TOTALS |
| Demand forecast | 1,800 | 1,500 | 1,100 | 900 | 1,100 | 1,600 | 8,000 |
| Number of working days | 22 | 19 | 21 | 21 | 22 | 20 | 125 |

| COSTS | |
|---|---|
| Materials | $100.00/unit |
| Inventory holding cost | $1.50/unit/month |
| Marginal cost of stockout | $5.00/unit/month |
| Marginal cost of subcontracting | $20.00/unit ($120 subcontracting cost less $100 material savings) |
| Hiring and training cost | $200.00/worker |
| Layoff cost | $250.00/worker |
| Labor hours required | 5/unit |
| Straight time cost (first eight hours each day) | $4.00/hour |
| Overtime cost (time and a half) | $6.00/hour |

| INVENTORY | |
|---|---|
| Beginning inventory | 400 units |
| Safety stock | 25% of month demand |

In solving this problem, we can exclude the material costs. We could have included this $100 cost in all our calculations, but if we assume that a $100 cost is common to each demanded unit, then we need only concern ourselves with the marginal costs. Because the subcontracting cost is $120, our true cost for subcontracting is just $20 because we save the materials.

Note that many costs are expressed in a different form than typically found in the accounting records of a firm. Therefore, do not expect to obtain all these costs directly from such records, but obtain them indirectly from management personnel, who can help interpret the data.

Cross Functional

Inventory at the beginning of the first period is 400 units. Because the demand forecast is imperfect, the CA&J Company has determined that a *safety stock* (buffer inventory) should be established to reduce the likelihood of stockouts. For this example, assume the safety stock should be one-quarter of the demand forecast. (Chapter 11 covers this topic in more depth.)

Before investigating alternative production plans, it is often useful to convert demand forecasts into *production requirements,* which take into account the safety stock estimates. In Exhibit 12.4, note that these requirements implicitly assume that the safety stock is never actually used, so that the ending inventory each month equals the safety stock for that month. For example, the January safety stock of 450 (25 percent of January demand of 1,800) becomes the inventory at the end of January. The production requirement for

EXHIBIT 12.4

**Aggregate Production Planning Requirements**

| | JANUARY | FEBRUARY | MARCH | APRIL | MAY | JUNE |
|---|---|---|---|---|---|---|
| Beginning inventory | 400 | 450 | 375 | 275 | 225 | 275 |
| Demand forecast | 1,800 | 1,500 | 1,100 | 900 | 1,100 | 1,600 |
| Safety stock (.25 × Demand forecast) | 450 | 375 | 275 | 225 | 275 | 400 |
| Production requirement (Demand forecast + Safety stock − Beginning inventory) | 1,850 | 1,425 | 1,000 | 850 | 1,150 | 1,725 |
| Ending inventory (Beginning inventory + Production requirement − Demand forecast) | 450 | 375 | 275 | 225 | 275 | 400 |

January is demand plus safety stock minus beginning inventory (1,800 + 450 − 400 = 1,850).

Now we must formulate alternative production plans for the CA&J Company. Using a spreadsheet, we investigate four different plans with the objective of finding the one with the lowest total cost.

**Plan 1.** Produce to exact monthly production requirements using a regular eight-hour day by varying workforce size.

**Plan 2.** Produce to meet expected average demand over the next six months by maintaining a constant workforce. This constant number of workers is calculated by finding the average number of workers required each day over the horizon. Take the total production requirements and multiply by the time required for each unit. Then divide by the total time that one person works over the horizon [(8,000 units × 5 hours per unit) ÷ (125 days × 8 hours per day) = 40 workers]. Inventory is allowed to accumulate, with shortages filled from next month's production by backordering. Negative beginning inventory balances indicate that demand is backordered. In some cases, sales may be lost if demand is not met. The lost sales can be shown with a negative ending inventory balance followed by a zero beginning inventory balance in the next period. Notice that in this plan we use our safety stock in January, February, March, and June to meet expected demand.

**Plan 3.** Produce to meet the minimum expected demand (April) using a constant workforce on regular time. Subcontract to meet additional output requirements. The number of workers is calculated by locating the minimum monthly production requirement and determining how many workers would be needed for that month [(850 units × 5 hours per unit) ÷ (21 days × 8 hours per day) = 25 workers] and subcontracting any monthly difference between requirements and production.

**Plan 4.** Produce to meet expected demand for all but the first two months using a constant workforce on regular time. Use overtime to meet additional output requirements. The number of workers is more difficult to compute for this plan, but the goal is to finish June with an ending inventory as close as possible to the June safety stock. By trial and error it can be shown that a constant workforce of 38 workers is the closest approximation.

The next step is to calculate the cost of each plan. This requires the series of simple calculations shown in Exhibit 12.5. Note that the headings in each row are different for each plan because each is a different problem requiring its own data and calculations.

The final step is to tabulate and graph each plan and compare their costs. From Exhibit 12.6 we can see that using subcontractors resulted in the lowest cost (Plan 3). Exhibit 12.7 shows the effects of the four plans. This is a cumulative graph illustrating the expected results on the total production requirement.

Note that we have made one other assumption in this example: The plan can start with any number of workers with no hiring or layoff cost. This usually is the case because an aggregate plan draws on existing personnel, and we can start the plan that way. However, in an actual application, the availability of existing personnel transferable from other areas of the firm may change the assumptions.

Each of these four plans focused on one particular cost, and the first three were simple pure strategies. Obviously, there are many other feasible plans, some of which would use a combination of workforce changes, overtime, and subcontracting. The problems at the end of this chapter include examples of such mixed strategies. In practice, the final plan chosen would come from searching a variety of alternatives and future projections beyond the six-month planning horizon we have used.

Keep in mind that the cut-and-try approach does not guarantee finding the minimum-cost solution. However, spreadsheet programs, such as Microsoft Excel, can perform cut-and-try cost estimates in seconds and have elevated this kind of what-if analysis to a fine art. More sophisticated programs can generate much better solutions without the user having to intercede, as in the cut-and-try method.

## Costs of Four Production Plans

EXHIBIT 12.5

Excel: Aggregate Planning

### PRODUCTION PLAN 1: EXACT PRODUCTION; VARY WORKFORCE

| | JANUARY | FEBRUARY | MARCH | APRIL | MAY | JUNE | TOTAL |
|---|---|---|---|---|---|---|---|
| Production requirement (from Exhibit 12.4) | 1,850 | 1,425 | 1,000 | 850 | 1,150 | 1,725 | |
| Production hours required (Production requirement × 5 hr./unit) | 9,250 | 7,125 | 5,000 | 4,250 | 5,750 | 8,625 | |
| Working days per month | 22 | 19 | 21 | 21 | 22 | 20 | |
| Hours per month per worker (Working days × 8 hrs./day) | 176 | 152 | 168 | 168 | 176 | 160 | |
| Workers required (Production hours required/Hours per month per worker) | 53 | 47 | 30 | 25 | 33 | 54 | |
| New workers hired (assuming opening workforce equal to first month's requirement of 53 workers) | 0 | 0 | 0 | 0 | 8 | 21 | |
| Hiring cost (New workers hired × $200) | $0 | $0 | $0 | $0 | $1,600 | $4,200 | $5,800 |
| Workers laid off | 0 | 6 | 17 | 5 | 0 | 0 | |
| Layoff cost (Workers laid off × $250) | $0 | $1,500 | $4,250 | $1,250 | $0 | $0 | $7,000 |
| Straight time cost (Production hours required × $4) | $37,000 | $28,500 | $20,000 | $17,000 | $23,000 | $34,500 | $160,000 |
| | | | | | | Total cost | $172,800 |

### PRODUCTION PLAN 2: CONSTANT WORKFORCE; VARY INVENTORY AND STOCKOUT

| | JANUARY | FEBRUARY | MARCH | APRIL | MAY | JUNE | TOTAL |
|---|---|---|---|---|---|---|---|
| Beginning inventory | 400 | 8 | −276 | −32 | 412 | 720 | |
| Working days per month | 22 | 19 | 21 | 21 | 22 | 20 | |
| Production hours available (Working days per month × 8 hr./day × 40 workers)* | 7,040 | 6,080 | 6,720 | 6,720 | 7,040 | 6,400 | |
| Actual production (Production hours available/5 hr./unit) | 1,408 | 1,216 | 1,344 | 1,344 | 1,408 | 1,280 | |
| Demand forecast (from Exhibit 12.4) | 1,800 | 1,500 | 1,100 | 900 | 1,100 | 1,600 | |
| Ending inventory (Beginning inventory + Actual production − Demand forecast) | 8 | −276 | −32 | 412 | 720 | 400 | |
| Shortage cost (Units short × $5) | $0 | $1,380 | $160 | $0 | $0 | $0 | $1,540 |
| Safety stock (from Exhibit 12.4) | 450 | 375 | 275 | 225 | 275 | 400 | |
| Units excess (Ending inventory − Safety stock) only if positive amount | 0 | 0 | 0 | 187 | 445 | 0 | |
| Inventory cost (Units excess × $1.50) | $0 | $0 | $0 | $281 | $668 | $0 | $948 |
| Straight time cost (Production hours available × $4) | $28,160 | $24,320 | $26,880 | $26,880 | $28,160 | $25,600 | $160,000 |
| | | | | | | Total cost | $162,488 |

* (Sum of production requirement in Exhibit 12.4 × 5 hr./unit)/(Sum of production hours available × 8 hr./day) = (8,000 × 5)/(125 × 8) = 40.

### PRODUCTION PLAN 3: CONSTANT LOW WORKFORCE; SUBCONTRACT

| | JANUARY | FEBRUARY | MARCH | APRIL | MAY | JUNE | TOTAL |
|---|---|---|---|---|---|---|---|
| Production requirement (from Exhibit 12.4) | 1,850 | 1,425 | 1,000 | 850 | 1,150 | 1,725 | |
| Working days per month | 22 | 19 | 21 | 21 | 22 | 20 | |
| Production hours available (Working days × 8 hrs./day × 25 workers)* | 4,400 | 3,800 | 4,200 | 4,200 | 4,400 | 4,000 | |
| Actual production (Production hours available/5 hr. per unit) | 880 | 760 | 840 | 840 | 880 | 800 | |

(continued)

EXHIBIT 12.5 (Continued)

PRODUCTION PLAN 3: CONSTANT LOW WORKFORCE; SUBCONTRACT (CONTINUED)

| | JANUARY | FEBRUARY | MARCH | APRIL | MAY | JUNE | TOTAL |
|---|---|---|---|---|---|---|---|
| Units subcontracted (Production requirement − Actual production) | 970 | 665 | 160 | 10 | 270 | 925 | |
| Subcontracting cost (Units subcontracted × $20) | $19,400 | $13,300 | $3,200 | $200 | $5,400 | $18,500 | $60,000 |
| Straight time cost (Production hours available × $4) | $17,600 | $15,200 | $16,800 | $16,800 | $17,600 | $16,000 | $100,000 |
| | | | | | | Total cost | $160,000 |

*Minimum production requirement. In this example, April is minimum of 850 units. Number of workers required for April is (850 × 5)/(21 × 8) = 25.

PRODUCTION PLAN 4: CONSTANT WORKFORCE; OVERTIME

| | JANUARY | FEBRUARY | MARCH | APRIL | MAY | JUNE | TOTAL |
|---|---|---|---|---|---|---|---|
| Beginning inventory | 400 | 0 | 0 | 177 | 554 | 792 | |
| Working days per month | 22 | 19 | 21 | 21 | 22 | 20 | |
| Production hours available (Working days × 8 hr./day × 38 workers)* | 6,688 | 5,776 | 6,384 | 6,384 | 6,688 | 6,080 | |
| Regular shift production (Production hours available/5 hrs. per unit) | 1,338 | 1,155 | 1,277 | 1,277 | 1,338 | 1,216 | |
| Demand forecast (from Exhibit 12.4) | 1,800 | 1,500 | 1,100 | 900 | 1,100 | 1,600 | |
| Units available before overtime (Beginning inventory + Regular shift production − Demand forecast). This number has been rounded to the nearest integer. | −62 | −345 | 177 | 554 | 792 | 408 | |
| Units overtime | 62 | 375 | 0 | 0 | 0 | 0 | |
| Overtime cost (Units overtime × 5 hr./unit × $6/hr.) | $1,860 | $10,350 | $0 | $0 | $0 | $0 | $12,210 |
| Safety stock (from Exhibit 12.4) | 450 | 375 | 275 | 225 | 275 | 400 | |
| Units excess (Units available before overtime − Safety stock) only if positive amount | 0 | 0 | 0 | 329 | 517 | 8 | |
| Inventory cost (Units excessive × $1.50) | $0 | $0 | $0 | $494 | $776 | $12 | $1,281 |
| Straight time cost (Production hours available × $4) | $26,752 | $23,104 | $25,536 | $25,536 | $26,752 | $24,320 | $152,000 |
| | | | | | | Total cost | $165,491 |

*Workers determined by trial and error. See text for explanation.

## AGGREGATE PLANNING APPLIED TO SERVICES: TUCSON PARKS AND RECREATION DEPARTMENT

Charting and graphic techniques are also useful for aggregate planning in service applications. The following example shows how a city's parks and recreation department could use the alternatives of full-time employees, part-time employees, and subcontracting to meet its commitment to provide a service to the city.

Tucson Parks and Recreation Department has an operation and maintenance budget of $9,760,000. The department is responsible for developing and maintaining open space, all public recreational programs, adult sports leagues, golf courses, tennis courts, pools, and so

**EXHIBIT 12.6**

**Comparison of Four Plans**

Excel: Aggregate Planning

| Cost | Plan 1: Exact Production; Vary Workforce | Plan 2: Constant Workforce; Vary Inventory and Stockout | Plan 3: Constant Low Workforce; Subcontract | Plan 4: Constant Workforce; Overtime |
|---|---|---|---|---|
| Hiring | $ 5,800 | $ 0 | $ 0 | $ 0 |
| Layoff | 7,000 | 0 | 0 | 0 |
| Excess inventory | 0 | 948 | 0 | 1,281 |
| Shortage | 0 | 1,540 | 0 | 0 |
| Subcontract | 0 | 0 | 60,000 | 0 |
| Overtime | 0 | 0 | 0 | 12,210 |
| Straight time | 160,000 | 160,000 | 100,000 | 152,000 |
| | $172,800 | $162,488 | $160,000 | $165,491 |

**EXHIBIT 12.7**

**Four Plans for Satisfying a Production Requirement over the Number of Production Days Available**

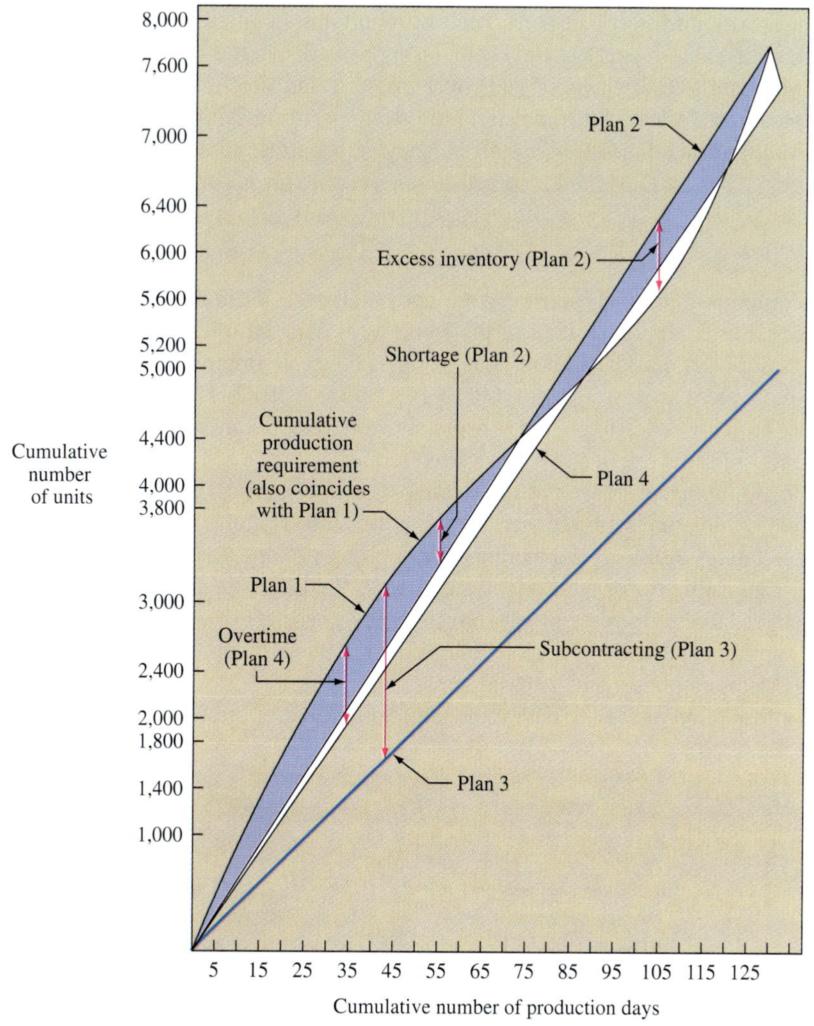

forth. There are 336 full-time-equivalent employees (FTEs). Of these, 216 are full-time permanent personnel who provide the administration and year-round maintenance to all areas. The remaining 120 FTE positions are staffed with part-timers; about three-quarters of them are used during the summer and the remaining quarter in the fall, winter, and spring seasons. The three-fourths (or 90 FTE positions) show up as approximately 800 part-time summer jobs: lifeguards, baseball umpires, and instructors in summer programs for children. Eight hundred part-time jobs came from 90 FTEs because many last only for a month or two, while the FTEs are a year long.

Currently, the only parks and recreation work subcontracted amounts to less than $100,000. This is for the golf and tennis pros and for grounds maintenance at the libraries and veterans' cemetery.

Because of the nature of city employment, the probable bad public image, and civil service rules, the option to hire and fire full-time help daily or weekly to meet seasonal demand is out of the question. However, temporary part-time help is authorized and traditional. Also, it is virtually impossible to have regular (full-time) staff for all the summer jobs. During the summer months, the approximately 800 part-time employees are staffing many programs that occur simultaneously, prohibiting level scheduling over a normal 40-hour week. A wider variety of skills are required (such as umpires, coaches, lifeguards, and teachers of ceramics, guitar, karate, belly dancing, and yoga) than can be expected from full-time employees.

Three options are open to the department in its aggregate planning:

1 The present method, which is to maintain a medium-level full-time staff and schedule work during off-seasons (such as rebuilding baseball fields during the winter months) and to use part-time help during peak demands.
2 Maintain a lower level of staff over the year and subcontract all additional work presently done by full-time staff (still using part-time help).
3 Maintain an administrative staff only and subcontract all work, including part-time help. (This would entail contracts to landscaping firms and pool maintenance companies as well as to newly created private firms to employ and supply part-time help.)

The common unit of measure of work across all areas is full-time equivalent jobs or employees. For example, assume in the same week that 30 lifeguards worked 20 hours each, 40 instructors worked 15 hours each, and 35 baseball umpires worked 10 hours each. This is equivalent to $(30 \times 20) + (40 \times 15) + (35 \times 10) = 1{,}550 \div 40 = 38.75$ FTE positions for that week. Although a considerable amount of workload can be shifted to off-season, most of the work must be done when required.

Full-time employees consist of three groups: (1) the skeleton group of key department personnel coordinating with the city, setting policy, determining budgets, measuring performance, and so forth; (2) the administrative group of supervisory and office personnel who are responsible for or whose jobs are directly linked to the direct-labor workers; and (3) the direct-labor workforce of 116 full-time positions. These workers physically maintain the department's areas of responsibility, such as cleaning up, mowing golf greens and ballfields, trimming trees, and watering grass.

Cost information needed to determine the best alternative strategy is

| | |
|---|---|
| Full-time direct-labor employees | |
| Average wage rate | $4.45 per hour |
| Fringe benefits | 17% of wage rate |
| Administrative costs | 20% of wage rate |
| Part-time employees | |
| Average wage rate | $4.03 per hour |
| Fringe benefits | 11% of wage rate |
| Administrative costs | 25% of wage rate |
| Subcontracting all full-time jobs | $1.6 million |
| Subcontracting all part-time jobs | $1.85 million |

EXHIBIT 12.8

## Actual Demand Requirement for Full-Time Direct Employees and Full-Time Equivalent (FTE) Part-Time Employees

| | JAN. | FEB. | MAR. | APR. | MAY | JUNE | JULY | AUG. | SEPT. | OCT. | NOV. | DEC. | TOTAL |
|---|---|---|---|---|---|---|---|---|---|---|---|---|---|
| Days | 22 | 20 | 21 | 22 | 21 | 20 | 21 | 21 | 21 | 23 | 18 | 22 | 252 |
| Full-time employees | 66 | 28 | 130 | 90 | 195 | 290 | 325 | 92 | 45 | 32 | 29 | 60 | |
| Full-time days* | 1,452 | 560 | 2,730 | 1,980 | 4,095 | 5,800 | 6,825 | 1,932 | 945 | 736 | 522 | 1,320 | 28,897 |
| Full-time equivalent part-time employees | 41 | 75 | 72 | 68 | 72 | 302 | 576 | 72 | 0 | 68 | 84 | 27 | |
| FTE days | 902 | 1,500 | 1,512 | 1,496 | 1,512 | 6,040 | 12,096 | 1,512 | 0 | 1,564 | 1,512 | 594 | 30,240 |

*Full-time days are derived by multiplying the number of days in each month by the number of workers.

EXHIBIT 12.9

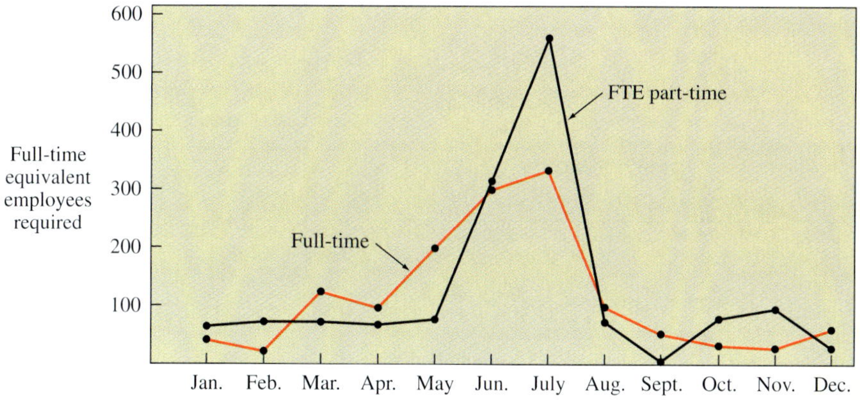


Monthly Requirement for Full-Time Direct-Labor Employees (Other Than Key Personnel) and Full-Time Equivalent Part-Time Employees

June and July are the peak demand seasons in Tucson. Exhibits 12.8 and 12.9 show the high requirements for June and July personnel. The part-time help reaches 576 full-time equivalent positions (although in actual numbers, this is approximately 800 different employees). After a low fall and winter staffing level, the demand shown as "full-time direct" reaches 130 in March (when grounds are reseeded and fertilized) and then increases to a high of 325 in July. The present method levels this uneven demand over the year to an average of 116 full-time year-round employees by early scheduling of work. As previously mentioned, no attempt is made to hire and lay off full-time workers to meet this uneven demand.

Exhibit 12.10 shows the cost calculations for all three alternatives. Exhibit 12.11 compares the total costs for each alternative. From this analysis, it appears that the department is already using the lowest-cost alternative (Alternative 1).

## LEVEL SCHEDULING

In this chapter we looked at four primary strategies for production planning: vary workforce size to meet demand, work overtime and part-time, vary inventory through excesses and shortages, and subcontract.

## EXHIBIT 12.10 Three Possible Plans for the Parks and Recreation Department

**Alternative 1:** Maintain 116 full-time regular direct workers. Schedule work during off-seasons to level workload throughout the year. Continue to use 120 full-time equivalent (FTE) part-time employees to meet high demand periods.

| Costs | Days per Year (Exhibit 12.8) | Hours (Employees × Days × 8 Hours) | Wages (Full-Time, $4.45; Part-Time, $4.03) | Fringe Benefits (Full-Time, 17%; Part-Time, 11%) | Administrative Cost (Full-Time, 20%; Part-Time, 25%) |
|---|---|---|---|---|---|
| 116 full-time regular employees | 252 | 233,856 | $1,040,659 | $176,912 | $208,132 |
| 120 part-time employees | 252 | 241,920 | 974,938 | 107,243 | 243,735 |
| Total cost = $2,751,619 | | | $2,015,597 | $284,155 | $451,867 |

**Alternative 2:** Maintain 50 full-time regular direct workers and the present 120 FTE part-time employees. Subcontract jobs releasing 66 full-time regular employees. Subcontract cost, $1,100,000.

| Cost | Days per Year (Exhibit 12.8) | Hours (Employees × Days × 8 Hours) | Wages (Full-Time, $4.45; Part-Time, $4.03) | Fringe Benefits (Full-Time, 17%; Part-Time, 11%) | Administrative Cost (Full-Time, 20%; Part-Time, 25%) | Subcontract Cost |
|---|---|---|---|---|---|---|
| 50 full-time employees | 252 | 100,800 | $ 448,560 | $ 76,255 | $ 89,712 | $1,100,000 |
| 120 FTE part-time employees Subcontracting cost | 252 | 241,920 | 974,938 | 107,243 | 243,735 | |
| Total cost = $3,040,443 | | | $1,423,498 | $183,498 | $333,447 | $1,100,000 |

**Alternative 3:** Subcontract all jobs previously performed by 116 full-time regular employees. Subcontract cost $1,600,000. Subcontract all jobs previously performed by 120 FTE part-time employees. Subcontract cost $1,850,000.

| Cost | Subcontract Cost |
|---|---|
| 0 full-time employees | |
| 0 part-time employees | |
| Subcontract full-time jobs | $1,600,000 |
| Subcontract part-time jobs | 1,850,000 |
| Total cost | $3,450,000 |

## EXHIBIT 12.11 Comparison of Costs for All Three Alternatives

| | Alternative 1: 116 Full-Time Direct-Labor Employees, 120 Full-Time Equivalent Part-Time Employees | Alternative 2: 50 Full-Time Direct-Labor Employees, 120 Full-Time Equivalent Part-Time Employees, Subcontracting | Alternative 3: Subcontracting Jobs Formerly Performed by 116 Direct-Labor Full-Time Employees and 120 FTE Part-Time Employees |
|---|---|---|---|
| Wages | $2,015,597 | $ 1,423,498 | — |
| Fringe benefits | 284,155 | 183,498 | — |
| Administrative costs | 451,867 | 333,447 | — |
| Subcontracting, full-time jobs | | 1,100,000 | $1,600,000 |
| Subcontracting, part-time jobs | | | 1,850,000 |
| Total | $2,751,619 | $3,040,443 | $3,450,000 |

A level schedule holds production constant over a period of time. It is something of a combination of the strategies we have mentioned here. For each period, it keeps the workforce constant and inventory low, and depends on demand to pull products through. Level production has a number of advantages, which makes it the backbone of JIT production:

1 The entire system can be planned to minimize inventory and work-in-process.
2 Product modifications are up-to-date because of the low amount of work-in-process.
3 There is a smooth flow throughout the production system.
4 Purchased items from vendors can be delivered when needed, and, in fact, often directly to the production line.

Toyota Motor Corporation, for example, creates a yearly production plan that shows the total number of cars to be made and sold. The aggregate production plan creates the system requirements to produce this total number with a level schedule. The secret to success in the Japanese level schedule is *production smoothing*. The aggregate plan is translated into monthly and daily schedules that *sequence* products through the production system. The procedure is essentially this: Two months in advance, the car types and quantities needed are established. This is converted to a detailed plan one month ahead. These quantities are given to subcontractors and vendors so that they can plan on meeting Toyota's needs. The monthly needs of various car types are then translated into daily schedules. For example, if 8,000 units of car type A are needed in one month, along with 6,000 type B, 4,000 type C, and 2,000 type D, and if we assume the line operates 20 days per month, then this would be translated to a daily output of 400, 300, 200, and 100, respectively. Further, this would be sequenced as four units of A, three of B, two of C, and one of D each 9.6 minutes of a two-shift day (960 minutes).

Each worker operates a number of machines, producing a sequence of products. To use this level scheduling technique,

1 Production should be repetitive (assembly-line format).
2 The system must contain excess capacity.
3 Output of the system must be fixed for a period of time (preferably a month).
4 There must be a smooth relationship among purchasing, marketing, and production.
5 The cost of carrying inventory must be high.
6 Equipment costs must be low.
7 The workforce must be multiskilled.

For more about level scheduling, see uniform plant loading in Chapter 10 on just-in-time production systems. Also see the discussion on mixed-model line balancing in Technical Note 5 on layout.

## MATHEMATICAL TECHNIQUES

**Linear Programming** The general model of linear programming is appropriate to aggregate planning if the cost and variable relationships are linear and demand can be treated as deterministic (see Supplement A). For the special case where hiring and firing are not considerations, the more easily formulated transportation model can be applied in a manner similar to the location problem in Technical Note 9.

The application of a transportation matrix to aggregate planning is illustrated by the solved problem in Exhibit 12.12. This formulation is termed a *period model* because it relates production demand to production capacity by periods.[4] In this case, there are four subperiods with demand forecast as 800 units in each. The total capacity available is 3,950 or an excess capacity of 750 (3,950 − 3,200). However, the bottom row of the matrix indicates a desire for 500 units in inventory at the end of the planning period, so unused capacity is reduced to 250. The left side of the matrix indicates the means by which

EXHIBIT 12.12

## Aggregate Planning by the Transportation Method of Linear Programming

| PRODUCTION PERIODS (SOURCES) | | SALES PERIODS 1 | 2 | 3 | 4 | ENDING INVENTORY | UNUSED CAPACITY | TOTAL CAPACITY |
|---|---|---|---|---|---|---|---|---|
| Beginning inventory | | 50 [0] | [5] | [10] | [15] | [20] | [0] | 50 |
| 1 | Regular time | 700 [50] | [55] | [60] | [65] | [70] | [0] | 700 |
| | Overtime | 50 [75] | [80] | [85] | [90] | 50 [95] | 250 [0] | 350 |
| 2 | Regular time | X | 700 [50] | [55] | [60] | [65] | [0] | 700 |
| | Overtime | X | 100 [75] | [80] | [85] | 150 [90] | [0] | 250 |
| 3 | Regular time | X | X | 700 [50] | [55] | [60] | [0] | 700 |
| | Overtime | X | X | 100 [75] | [80] | 150 [85] | [0] | 250 |
| 4 | Regular time | X | X | X | 700 [50] | [55] | [0] | 700 |
| | Overtime | X | X | X | 100 [75] | 150 [80] | [0] | 250 |
| Total requirements | | 800 | 800 | 800 | 800 | 500 | 250 | 3,950 |

EXHIBIT 12.13

## Additional Factors That Can Be Included in the Transportation Method for Aggregate Planning

1. **Multiproduct production.** When more than one product shares common facilities, additional columns are included corresponding to each product. For each month, the number of columns will equal the number of products, and the cost entry in each cell will equal the cost for the corresponding product.
2. **Backordering.** The backorder time and the cost of backordering can be included by treating the assignments marked with an X in Exhibit 12.12 as feasible. If a product demanded in period 1 is delivered in period 2, this is equivalent to meeting period 1's demand with production in period 2. For, say, a $10 unit cost associated with such a backorder, the cost entry in the cell corresponding to period 2 regular time row and period 1 column will be $60 ($10 plus the $50 cost of regular-time production in period 2).
3. **Lost sales.** When stockouts are allowed and a part of the demand is not met, the firm incurs opportunity cost equal to the lost revenue. This can be included in the matrix by adding a "lost sales" row for each period. The cost entry in the cell will be equal to lost revenue per unit.
4. **Perishability.** When perishability does not permit the sale of a product after it has been in stock for a certain period, the corresponding cells in the matrix are treated as infeasible. If the product in Exhibit 12.12 cannot be sold after it has been in stock for two periods, the cells occupying the intersection of period 1 rows and columns beyond period 3 will be infeasible.
5. **Subcontracting.** This can be included by adding a "subcontracting" row for each period. Cost values in each cell would be the unit cost to subcontract plus any inventory holding cost (incremented in the same fashion as regular time and overtime costs).

production is made available over the planning period (that is, beginning inventory and regular and overtime work during each period). An X indicates a period where production cannot be backlogged. That is, you cannot produce in, say, Period 3 to meet demand in Period 2. (This is feasible if the situation allows backorders.) Finally, the costs in each cell are incremented by a holding cost of $5 for each period. Thus, if one produces on regular time in Period 1 to satisfy demand for Period 4, there will be a $15 holding cost. Overtime is, of course, more expensive to start with, but holding costs in this example are not affected by whether production is on regular time or overtime. The solution shown is an optimal one.

The transportation matrix is remarkably versatile and can incorporate a variety of aggregate planning factors as described in Exhibit 12.13.

**Observations on Linear Programming and Mathematical Techniques** Linear programming is appropriate when the cost and variable relation-

Summary Data on Aggregate Planning Methods

EXHIBIT 12.14

| METHODS | ASSUMPTIONS | TECHNIQUES |
|---|---|---|
| 1 Graphic and charting | None | Tests alternative plans through trial and error. Nonoptimal, but simple to develop and easy to understand. |
| 2 Simulation of aggregate plan | Existence of a computer-based production system | Tests aggregate plans developed by other methods. |
| 3 Linear programming—transportation method | Linearity, constant workforce | Useful for the special case where hiring and firing costs are not a consideration. Gives optimal solution. |
| 4 Linear programming—simplex method | Linearity | Can handle any number of variables but often is difficult to formulate. Gives optimal solution. |
| 5 Linear decision rules* | Quadratic cost functions | Uses mathematically derived coefficients to specify production rates and workforce levels in a series of equations. |
| 6 Management coefficients† | That managers are basically good decision makers | Uses statistical analysis of past decisions to make future decisions. Applies, therefore, to just one group of managers; nonoptimal. |
| 7 Search decision rules‡ | Any type of cost structure | Uses pattern search procedure to find minimum points on total cost curves. Complicated to develop; nonoptimal. |

* C. C. HOLT ET. AL., *PLANNING PRODUCTION, INVENTORIES, AND WORK FORCE* (ENGLEWOOD CLIFFS, NJ: PRENTICE HALL, 1960).
† E. H. BOWMAN AND R. B. FETTER, *ANALYSIS FOR PRODUCTION AND OPERATIONS MANAGEMENT*, 3RD ED. (BURR RIDGE, IL: RICHARD D. IRWIN, 1957).
‡ W. H. TAUBERT, "A SEARCH DECISION RULE FOR THE AGGREGATE SCHEDULING PROBLEM," *MANAGEMENT SCIENCE*, FEBRUARY 1978, PP. B343–59.

ships are linear or can be cut into approximately linear segments. Regarding application of sophisticated aggregate planning techniques in industry (see Exhibit 12.14), only linear programming has seen wide usage. Much of this is being done using the Solver Option in Microsoft Excel as described in Supplement A. The basic issue is management's attitude toward models in general. Those companies where modeling is a way of life are likely to try the more sophisticated methods; in those where it is not, we would suspect that graphic and charting approaches would be used. Somewhere in the middle ground lie companies that have substantial experience in data processing and use the computer primarily for detailed scheduling. In these firms, we would expect to see experimentation with alternative cut-and-try plans in developing aggregate plans.

## YIELD MANAGEMENT

Service

Yield management

Why is it that the guy sitting next to you on the plane paid half the price you paid for your ticket? Why was a hotel room you booked more expensive when you booked it six months in advance than when you checked in without a reservation (or vice versa)? The answers lie in the practice known as yield management. **Yield management** can be defined as the process of allocating the right type of capacity to the right type of customer at the right price and time to maximize revenue or yield. Yield management can be a powerful approach to making demand more predictable, which is important to aggregate planning.

Yield management has existed as long as there has been limited capacity for serving customers. However, its widespread scientific application began with American Airlines' computerized reservation system (SABRE), introduced in the mid-1980s. The system allowed the airline to change ticket prices on any routes instantaneously as a function of forecast demand. Peoples' Express, a no-frills, low-cost competitor airline, was one of the most famous victims of American's yield management system. Basically, the system enabled hour-by-hour updating on competing routes so that American could match or better prices wherever Peoples' Express was flying. The president of Peoples' Express realized that the game was lost when his mother flew on American to Peoples' hub for a lower price than Peoples' could offer!

THESE PLANES TAKING OFF REPRESENT THE CULMINATION OF HUNDREDS OF DAILY PRICING DECISIONS MADE BY YIELD MANAGEMENT SYSTEMS. ONE RESULT IS THAT PASSENGERS PAY DIFFERENT FARES FOR THE SAME FLIGHT.

From an operational perspective, yield management is most effective when

1 Demand can be segmented by customer.
2 Fixed costs are high and variable costs are low.
3 Inventory is perishable.
4 Product can be sold in advance.
5 Demand is highly variable.

Hotels illustrate these five characteristics well. They offer one set of rates during the week for the business traveler and another set during the weekend for the vacationer. The variable costs associated with a room (such as cleaning) are low in comparison to the cost of adding rooms to the property. Available rooms cannot be transferred from night to night, and blocks of rooms can be sold to conventions or tours. Finally, potential guests may cut short their stay or not show up at all.

Most organizations (such as airlines, rental car agencies, cruise lines, and hotels) manage yield by establishing decision rules for opening or closing rate classes as a function of expected demand and available supply. The methodologies for doing this can be quite sophisticated. A common approach is to forecast demand over the planning horizon and then use marginal analysis to determine the rates that will be charged if demand is forecast as being above or below set control limits around the forecast mean.

## OPERATING YIELD MANAGEMENT SYSTEMS

A number of interesting issues arise in managing yield. One is that pricing structures must appear logical to the customer and justify the different prices. Such justification, commonly called *rate fences,* may have either a physical basis (such as a room with a view) or a nonphysical basis (like unrestricted access to the Internet). Pricing should also relate to addressing specific capacity problems. If capacity is sufficient for peak demand, price reductions stimulating off-peak demand should be the focus. If capacity is insufficient, offering deals to customers who arrive during nonpeak periods (or creating alternative service locations) may enhance revenue generation.

A second issue is handling variability in arrival or starting times, duration, and time between customers. This entails employing maximally accurate forecasting methods (the greater the accuracy in forecasting demand, the more likely yield management will succeed); coordinated policies on overbooking, deposits, and no-show or cancellation penalties; and well-designed service processes that are reliable and consistent.

EXHIBIT 12.15

**Price/Service Duration Matrix: Positioning of Selected Service Industries**

| | | Price: Fixed | Price: Variable |
|---|---|---|---|
| Duration | Predictable | Quadrant 1:<br>Movies<br>Stadiums/arenas<br>Convention centers | Quadrant 2:<br>Hotels<br>Airlines<br>Rental cars<br>Cruise lines |
| Duration | Unpredictable | Quadrant 3:<br>Restaurants<br>Golf courses<br>Internet service providers | Quadrant 4:<br>Continuing care hospitals |

SOURCE: S. KIMES AND R. B. CHASE, "THE STRATEGIC LEVERS OF YIELD MANAGEMENT," *JOURNAL OF SERVICE RESEARCH* 1, NO. 2, 1998, PP. 298–308.

A third issue relates to managing the service process. Some strategies include scheduling additional personnel to meet peak demand; increased customer coproduction; creating adjustable capacity; utilizing idle capacity for complementary services; and cross-training employees to create reserves for peak periods.

The fourth and perhaps most critical issue is training workers and managers to work in an environment where overbooking and price changes are standard occurrences that directly impact the customer. Companies have developed creative ways for mollifying overbooked customers. A golf course company offers $100 putters to players who have been overbooked at a popular tee time. Airlines, of course, frequently give overbooked passengers free tickets for other flights.

The essence of yield management is the ability to manage demand. In a recent article Kimes and Chase suggest that two strategic levers can be used to accomplish this goal: pricing and duration control. If these two levers are thought of in matrix form (see Exhibit 12.15) with price being either fixed or variable and duration being either predictable or unpredictable, then traditional applications of yield management have been by firms located in the variable price/predictable duration quadrant. This type of matrix provides a framework for a firm to identify its position and the necessary actions to manage yield. For example, an action controlling duration would be to convert the service offering from an event of indeterminate time to an offering that is time-based. This improves reservation planning and hence allocation of resources. An example would be having diners reserve a fixed block of time for dining at a restaurant (e.g., 7–8 PM) rather than an open-ended table reservation for 7 PM.

## CONCLUSION

Aggregate planning translates corporate strategic and capacity plans into broad categories of workforce size, inventory quantity, and production levels. It does not do detailed planning.

Demand variations are a fact of life, so the planning system must include sufficient flexibility to cope with such variations. Flexibility can be achieved by developing alternative sources of supply, cross-training workers to handle a wide variety of orders, and engaging in more frequent replanning during high-demand periods.

Decision rules for production planning should be adhered to once they have been selected. However, they should be carefully analyzed prior to implementation by checks such as simulation of historical data to see what really would have happened if the decision rules had operated in the past.

Yield management is an important tool that can be used to shape demand patterns so a firm can operate more efficiently.

## KEY TERMS

**Aggregate planning** Translating annual and quarterly business plans into labor and production output plans for the intermediate term. The objective is to minimize the cost of resources required to meet demand.

**Long-range planning** Activity typically done annually and focusing on a horizon of a year or more.

**Intermediate-range planning** Activity that usually covers a period from 6 to 18 months with monthly or quarterly time increments.

**Short-range planning** Planning that covers a period less than six months with either daily or weekly increments of time.

**Master production schedule (MPS)** A schedule of the amounts and times when specific items will be manufactured, typically using weekly increments of time.

**Rough-cut capacity planning** Verification that sufficient capacity exists to meet a master production schedule.

**Material requirements planning (MRP)** Given the master production schedule, a procedure that generates specific schedules for component parts and subassemblies.

**Capacity requirements planning** Allocation of production resource capacity to specific orders.

**Order scheduling** Final planning of the use of specific machines, production lines, or work centers to produce orders.

**Production rate** The number of units completed per unit of time.

**Workforce level** The number of production workers needed each period.

**Inventory on hand** Unused inventory carried from a previous period.

**Production planning strategies** Plans that involve trade-offs among workforce size, work hours, inventory, and backlogs.

**Pure strategy** A plan that uses just one of the options available for meeting demand. Typical options include chasing demand, using a stable workforce with overtime or part-time work, and constant production with shortages and overages absorbed by inventory.

**Mixed strategy** A plan that combines options available for meeting demand.

**Yield management** Allocating the right type of capacity to the right type of customer at the right price and time to maximize revenue or yield.

## SOLVED PROBLEM

Excel: Aggregate Planning Solved Problem

Jason Enterprises (JE) produces video telephones for the home market. Quality is not quite as good as it could be at this point, but the selling price is low and Jason can study market response while spending more time on R&D.

At this stage, however, JE needs to develop an aggregate production plan for the six months from January through June. You have been commissioned to create the plan. The following information should help:

DEMAND AND WORKING DAYS

| | JANUARY | FEBRUARY | MARCH | APRIL | MAY | JUNE | TOTALS |
|---|---|---|---|---|---|---|---|
| Demand forecast | 500 | 600 | 650 | 800 | 900 | 800 | 4,250 |
| Number of working days | 22 | 19 | 21 | 21 | 22 | 20 | 125 |

COSTS

| | |
|---|---|
| Materials | $100.00/unit |
| Inventory holding cost | $10.00/unit/month |
| Marginal cost of stockout | $20.00/unit/month |
| Marginal cost of subcontracting | $100.00/unit ($200 subcontracting cost |
| | less $100 material savings) |
| Hiring and training cost | $50.00/worker |
| Layoff cost | $100.00/worker |
| Labor hours required | 4/unit |
| Straight time cost (first eight hours each day) | $12.50/hour |
| Overtime cost (time and a half) | $18.75/hour |

| INVENTORY | |
|---|---|
| Beginning inventory | 200 units |
| Safety stock required | 0% of month demand |

What is the cost of each of the following production strategies?

*a.* Produce exactly to meet demand; vary workforce (assuming opening workforce equal to first month's requirements).
*b.* Constant workforce; vary inventory and allow shortages only (assuming a starting workforce of 10).
*c.* Constant workforce of 10; use subcontracting.

## Solution

AGGREGATE PRODUCTION PLANNING REQUIREMENTS

| | JANUARY | FEBRUARY | MARCH | APRIL | MAY | JUNE | TOTAL |
|---|---|---|---|---|---|---|---|
| Beginning inventory | 200 | 0 | 0 | 0 | 0 | 0 | |
| Demand forecast | 500 | 600 | 650 | 800 | 900 | 800 | |
| Safety stock (0.0 × Demand forecast) | 0 | 0 | 0 | 0 | 0 | 0 | |
| Production requirement (Demand forecast + Safety stock − Beginning inventory) | 300 | 600 | 650 | 800 | 900 | 800 | |
| Ending inventory (Beginning inventory + Production requirement − Demand forecast) | 0 | 0 | 0 | 0 | 0 | 0 | |

PRODUCTION PLAN 1: EXACT PRODUCTION; VARY WORKFORCE

| | JANUARY | FEBRUARY | MARCH | APRIL | MAY | JUNE | TOTAL |
|---|---|---|---|---|---|---|---|
| Production requirement | 300 | 600 | 650 | 800 | 900 | 800 | |
| Production hours required (Production requirement × 4 hr./unit) | 1,200 | 2,400 | 2,600 | 3,200 | 3,600 | 3,200 | |
| Working days per month | 22 | 19 | 21 | 21 | 22 | 20 | |
| Hours per month per worker (Working days × 8 hrs./day) | 176 | 152 | 168 | 168 | 176 | 160 | |
| Workers required (Production hours required/Hours per month per worker) | 7 | 16 | 15 | 19 | 20 | 20 | |
| New workers hired (assuming opening workforce equal to first month's requirement of 7 workers) | 0 | 9 | 0 | 4 | 1 | 0 | |
| Hiring cost (New workers hired × $50) | $0 | $450 | $0 | $200 | $50 | $0 | $700 |
| Workers laid off | 0 | 0 | 1 | 0 | 0 | 0 | |
| Layoff cost (Workers laid off × $100) | $0 | $0 | $100 | $0 | $0 | $0 | $100 |
| Straight time cost (Production hours required × $12.50) | $15,000 | $30,000 | $32,000 | $40,000 | $45,000 | $40,000 | $202,500 |
| | | | | | | | Total cost $203,300 |

**PRODUCTION PLAN 2: CONSTANT WORKFORCE; VARY INVENTORY AND STOCKOUT**

| | JANUARY | FEBRUARY | MARCH | APRIL | MAY | JUNE | TOTAL |
|---|---|---|---|---|---|---|---|
| Beginning inventory | 200 | 140 | −80 | −310 | −690 | −1150 | |
| Working days per month | 22 | 19 | 21 | 21 | 22 | 20 | |
| Production hours available (Working days per month × 8 hr./day × 10 workers)* | 1,760 | 1,520 | 1,680 | 1,680 | 1,760 | 1,600 | |
| Actual production (Production hours available/4 hr./unit) | 440 | 380 | 420 | 420 | 440 | 400 | |
| Demand forecast | 500 | 600 | 650 | 800 | 900 | 800 | |
| Ending inventory (Beginning inventory + Actual production − Demand forecast) | 140 | −80 | −310 | −690 | −1150 | −1550 | |
| Shortage cost (Units short × $20) | $0 | $1,600 | $6,200 | $13,800 | $23,000 | $31,000 | $75,600 |
| Safety stock | 0 | 0 | 0 | 0 | 0 | 0 | |
| Units excess (Ending inventory − Safety stock; only if positive amount) | 140 | 0 | 0 | 0 | 0 | 0 | |
| Inventory cost (Units excess × $10) | $1,400 | $0 | $0 | $0 | $0 | $0 | $1,400 |
| Straight time cost (Production hours available × $12.50) | $22,000 | $19,000 | $21,000 | $21,000 | $22,000 | $20,000 | $125,000 |
| | | | | | | Total cost | $202,000 |

*Assume a constant workforce of 10.

**PRODUCTION PLAN 3: CONSTANT WORKFORCE; SUBCONTRACT**

| | JANUARY | FEBRUARY | MARCH | APRIL | MAY | JUNE | TOTAL |
|---|---|---|---|---|---|---|---|
| Production requirement | 300 | 460† | 650 | 800 | 900 | 800 | |
| Working days per month | 22 | 19 | 21 | 21 | 22 | 20 | |
| Production hours available (Working days × 8 hrs./day × 10 workers)* | 1,760 | 1,520 | 1,680 | 1,680 | 1,760 | 1,600 | |
| Actual production (Production hours available/4 hr. per unit) | 440 | 380 | 420 | 420 | 440 | 400 | |
| Units subcontracted (Production requirements − Actual production) | 0 | 80 | 230 | 380 | 460 | 400 | |
| Subcontracting cost (Units subcontracted × $100) | $0 | $8,000 | $23,000 | $38,000 | $46,000 | $40,000 | $155,000 |
| Straight time cost (Production hours available × $12.50) | $22,000 | $19,000 | $21,000 | $21,000 | $22,000 | $20,000 | $125,000 |
| | | | | | | Total cost | $280,000 |

*Assume a constant workforce of 10.

†600 − 140 units of beginning inventory in February.

**SUMMARY**

| PLAN DESCRIPTION | HIRING | LAYOFF | SUBCONTRACT | STRAIGHT TIME | SHORTAGE | EXCESS INVENTORY | TOTAL COST |
|---|---|---|---|---|---|---|---|
| 1. Exact production; vary workforce | $700 | $100 | | $202,500 | | | $203,300 |
| 2. Constant workforce; vary inventory and shortages | | | | $125,000 | $75,600 | $1,400 | $202,000 |
| 3. Constant workforce; subcontract | | | $155,000 | $125,000 | | | $280,000 |

## Review and Discussion Questions

1 What is the major difference between aggregate planning in manufacturing and aggregate planning in services?

2 What are the basic controllable variables of a production planning problem? What are the four major costs?

3 Distinguish between pure and mixed strategies in production planning.

4 Define level scheduling. How does it differ from the pure strategies in production planning?

5 Compare the best plans in the CA&J Company and the Tucson Parks and Recreation Department. What do they have in common?

6 How does forecast accuracy relate, in general, to the practical application of the aggregate planning models discussed in the chapter?

7 In which way does the time horizon chosen for an aggregate plan determine whether it is the best plan for the firm?

8 In the opening vignette, what did Dr. Sprague's mother and grandmother find so amusing about the wisdom being imparted about inventory "at the great MIT"?

9 How would you apply yield management concepts to a barbershop? A soft drink vending machine?

## Problems

1 For the solved problem, devise the least costly plan you can. You may choose your starting workforce level.

1. See ISM.

2 Assume that Alexandra Industries has purchased Jason Enterprises (see the solved problem) and has instituted Japanese-style management in which workers are guaranteed a job for life (with no layoffs). Based on the data in Problem 1 (and additional information provided here), develop a production plan using the transportation method of linear programming. To keep things simple, plan for the first three months only and convert costs from hours to units in your model. Additional information: overtime is limited to 11 units per month per worker, and up to 5 units per month may be subcontracted at a cost of $100 per unit.

2. See ISM for matrix.

3 Develop a production plan and calculate the annual cost for a firm whose demand forecast is fall, 10,000; winter, 8,000; spring, 7,000; summer, 12,000. Inventory at the beginning of fall is 500 units. At the beginning of fall you currently have 30 workers, but you plan to hire temporary workers at the beginning of summer and lay them off at the end of the summer. In addition, you have negotiated with the union an option to use the regular workforce on overtime during winter or spring if overtime is necessary to prevent stockouts at the end of those quarters. Overtime is *not* available during the fall. Relevant costs are: hiring, $100 for each temp; layoff, $200 for each worker laid off; inventory holding, $5 per unit-quarter; backorder, $10 per unit; straight time, $5 per hour; overtime, $8 per hour. Assume that the productivity is 0.5 units per worker hour, with eight hours per day and 60 days per season.

3. See ISM.
Total cost = $413,600.

4 Plan production for a four-month period: February through May. For February and March, you should produce to exact demand forecast. For April and May, you should use overtime and inventory with a stable workforce; *stable* means that the number of workers needed for March will be held constant through May. However, government constraints put a maximum of 5,000 hours of overtime labor per month in April and May (zero overtime in February and March). If demand exceeds supply, then backorders occur. There are 100 workers on January 1. You are given the following demand forecast: February, 80,000; March, 64,000; April, 100,000; May, 40,000. Productivity is four units per worker hour, eight hours per day, 20 days per month. Assume zero inventory on February 1. Costs are: hiring, $50 per new worker; layoff, $70 per worker laid off; inventory holding, $10 per unit-month; straight-time labor, $10 per hour; overtime, $15 per hour; backorder, $20 per unit. Find the total cost of this plan.

4. See ISM.
Total cost = $1,158,000.

5 Plan production for the next year. The demand forecast is spring, 20,000; summer, 10,000; fall, 15,000; winter, 18,000. At the beginning of spring you have 70 workers and 1,000 units in inventory. The union contract specifies that you may lay off workers only once a year, at the beginning of summer. Also, you may hire new workers only at the end of summer to begin regular work in the fall. The number of workers laid off at the beginning of summer and the number hired at the end of summer should result in planned production levels for summer and fall that equal the demand forecasts for summer and fall, respectively. If demand exceeds supply, use overtime in spring only, which means that backorders could occur in winter. You are given these costs: hiring, $100 per new worker; layoff, $200 per worker laid

5. See ISM.
Total cost = $1,260,500.

off; holding, $20 per unit-quarter, backorder cost, $8 per unit; straight-time labor, $10 per hour; overtime, $15 per hour. Productivity is 0.5 units per worker hour, eight hours per day, 50 days per quarter. Find the total cost.

6. Total cost = $413,750.

6 DAT, Inc. needs to develop an aggregate plan for its product line. Relevant data are

| | | | |
|---|---|---|---|
| Production time: | 1 hour per unit | Beginning inventory: | 500 units |
| Average labor cost: | $10 per hour | Safety stock: | One half-month |
| Workweek: | 5 days, 8 hours each day | Shortage cost: | $20 per unit per month |
| Days per month: | Assume 20 work days per month | Carrying cost: | $5 per unit per month |

The forecast for 1998 is

| JAN. | FEB. | MAR. | APR. | MAY | JUNE | JULY | AUG. | SEPT. | OCT. | NOV. | DEC. |
|---|---|---|---|---|---|---|---|---|---|---|---|
| 2,500 | 3,000 | 4,000 | 3,500 | 3,500 | 3,000 | 3,000 | 4,000 | 4,000 | 4,000 | 3,000 | 3,000 |

Management prefers to keep a constant workforce and production level, absorbing variations in demand through inventory excesses and shortages. Demand not met is carried over to the following month.

Develop an aggregate plan that will meet the demand and other conditions of the problem. Do not try to find the optimum; just find a good solution and state the procedure you might use to test for a better solution. Make any necessary assumptions.

7. See ISM. Total cost = $1,033,000.

7 Old Pueblo Engineering Contractors creates six-month "rolling" schedules, which are recomputed monthly. For competitive reasons (they would need to divulge proprietary design criteria, methods, and so on), Old Pueblo does not subcontract. Therefore, its only options to meet customer requirements are (1) work on regular time; (2) work on overtime, which is limited to 30 percent of regular time; (3) do customers' work early, which would cost an additional $5 per hour per month; and (4) perform customers' work late, which would cost an additional $10 per hour per month penalty, as provided by their contract.

Old Pueblo has 25 engineers on its staff at an hourly rate of $30. Customers' hourly requirements for the six months from January to June are

| JANUARY | FEBRUARY | MARCH | APRIL | MAY | JUNE |
|---|---|---|---|---|---|
| 5,000 | 4,000 | 6,000 | 6,000 | 5,000 | 4,000 |

Develop an aggregate plan using the transportation method of linear programming. Assume 20 working days in each month.

8. See ISM.

8 Alan Industries is expanding its product line to include new models: Model A, Model B, and Model C. These are to be produced on the same production equipment, and the objective is to meet the demands for the three products using overtime where necessary. The demand forecast for the next four months, in required hours, is

| PRODUCT | APRIL | MAY | JUNE | JULY |
|---|---|---|---|---|
| Model A | 800 | 600 | 800 | 1,200 |
| Model B | 600 | 700 | 900 | 1,100 |
| Model C | 700 | 500 | 700 | 850 |

Because the products deteriorate rapidly, there is a high loss in quality and, consequently, a high carryover cost into subsequent periods. Each hour's production carried into future months costs $3 per productive hour of Model A, $4 for Model B, and $5 for Model C.

Production can take place during either regular working hours or overtime. Regular time is paid at $4 when working on Model A, $5 for Model B, and $6 for Model C. Overtime premium is 50 percent.

The available production capacity for regular time and overtime is

| | APRIL | MAY | JUNE | JULY |
|---|---|---|---|---|
| Regular time | 1,500 | 1,300 | 1,800 | 1,700 |
| Overtime | $700 | 650 | 900 | 850 |

*a.* Set up the problem in matrix form and show appropriate costs.
*b.* Show a feasible solution.

9 Shoney Video Concepts produces a line of videodisc players to be linked to personal computers for video games. Videodiscs have much faster access time than tape. With such a computer/video link, the game becomes a very realistic experience. In a simple driving game where the joystick steers the vehicle, for example, rather than seeing computer graphics on the screen, the player is actually viewing a segment of a videodisc shot from a real moving vehicle. Depending on the action of the player (hitting a guard rail, for example), the disc moves virtually instantaneously to that segment and the player becomes part of an actual accident of real vehicles (staged, of course).

9. Workforce required = 10(6700 − 200)/8(249) = 33. Total cost = $34,520.

Shoney is trying to determine a production plan for the next 12 months. The main criterion for this plan is that the employment level is to be held constant over the period. Shoney is continuing in its R&D efforts to develop new applications and prefers not to cause any adverse feeling with the local workforce. For the same reason, all employees should put in full workweeks, even if this is not the lowest-cost alternative. The forecast for the next 12 months is

| MONTH | FORECAST DEMAND | MONTH | FORECAST DEMAND |
|---|---|---|---|
| January | 600 | July | 200 |
| February | 800 | August | 200 |
| March | 900 | September | 300 |
| April | 600 | October | 700 |
| May | 400 | November | 800 |
| June | 300 | December | 900 |

Manufacturing cost is $200 per set, equally divided between materials and labor. Inventory storage cost is $5 per month. A shortage of sets results in lost sales and is estimated to cost an overall $20 per unit short.

The inventory on hand at the beginning of the planning period is 200 units. Ten labor hours are required per videodisc player. The workday is eight hours.

Develop an aggregate production schedule for the year using a constant workforce. For simplicity, assume 22 working days each month except July, when the plant closes down for three weeks' vacation (leaving seven working days). Assume that total production capacity is greater than or equal to total demand.

10 Develop a production schedule to produce the exact production requirements by varying the workforce size for the following problem. Use the example in the chapter as a guide (Plan 1). 10. See ISM.

The monthly forecast for Product X for January, February, and March is 1,000, 1,500, and 1,200, respectively. Safety stock policy recommends that half of the forecast for that month be defined as safety stock. There are 22 working days in January, 19 in February, and 21 in March. Beginning inventory is 500 units.

Manufacturing cost is $200 per unit, storage cost is $3 per unit per month, standard pay rate is $6 per hour, overtime rate is $9 per hour, cost of stockout is $10 per unit per month, marginal cost of subcontracting is $10 per unit, hiring and training cost is $200 per worker, layoff cost is $300 per worker, and worker productivity is 0.1 units per hour. Assume that you start off with 50 workers and that they work 8 hours per day.

Excel: Bradford Manufacturing

## CASE: BRADFORD MANUFACTURING—PLANNING PLANT PRODUCTION

### THE SITUATION

You are the operations manager for a manufacturing plant that produces pudding food products. One of your important responsibilities is to prepare an aggregate plan for the plant. This plan is an important input into the annual budget process. The plan provides information on production rates, manufacturing labor requirements, and projected finished goods inventory levels for the next year.

You make those little boxes of pudding mix on packaging lines in your plant. A packaging line has a number of machines that are linked by conveyors. At the start of the line the pudding is mixed; it is then placed in small packets. These packets are inserted into the small pudding boxes, which are collected and placed in cases that hold 48 boxes of pudding. Finally, 160 cases are collected and put on a pallet. The pallets are staged in a shipping area from which they are sent to four distribution centers. Over the years, the technology of the packaging lines has improved so that all the different flavors can be made in relatively small batches with no setup time to switch between flavors. The plant has 15 of these lines, but currently only 10 are being used. Six employees are required to run each line.

The demand for this product fluctuates from month to month. In addition, there is a seasonal component, with peak sales before Thanksgiving, Christmas, and Easter each year. To complicate matters, at the end of the first quarter of each year the marketing group runs a promotion in which special deals are made for large purchases. Business is going well, and the company has been experiencing a general increase in sales.

The plant sends product to four large distribution warehouses strategically located in the United States. Trucks move product daily. The amounts shipped are based on maintaining target inventory levels at the warehouses. These targets are calculated based on anticipated weeks of supply at each warehouse. Current targets are set at two weeks of supply.

In the past, the company has had a policy of producing very close to what it expects sales to be because of limited capacity for storing finished goods. Production capacity has been adequate to support this policy.

**Forecast Demand by Quarter (1,000 Case Units)**

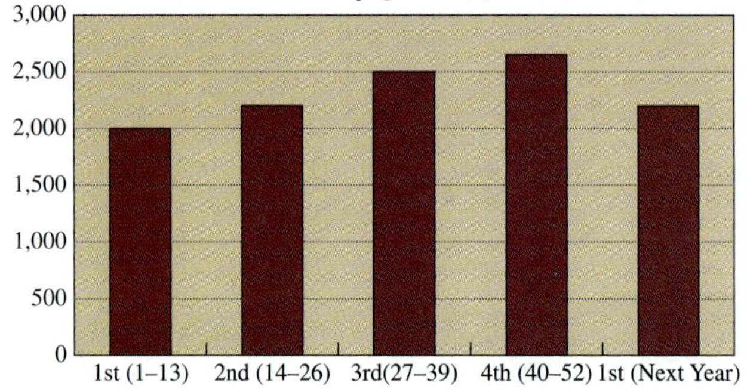


A sales forecast for next year has been prepared by the marketing department. The forecast is based on quarterly sales quotas, which are used to set up an incentive program for the salespeople. Sales are mainly to the large U.S. retail grocers. The pudding is shipped to the grocers from the distribution warehouses based on orders taken by the salespeople.

Your immediate task is to prepare an aggregate plan for the coming year. The technical and economic factors that must be considered in this plan are shown next.

### TECHNICAL AND ECONOMIC INFORMATION

1 Currently the plant is running 10 lines with no overtime. Each line requires six people to run. For planning purposes, the lines are run for 7.5 hours each normal shift. Employees, though, are paid for eight hours work. It is possible to run up to two hours of overtime each day, but it must be scheduled for a week at a time, and all the lines must run overtime when it is scheduled. Workers are paid $20.00/hour during a regular shift and $30.00/hour on overtime. The standard production rate for each line is 450 cases/hour.
2 The marketing forecast for demand is as follows: Q1—2,000; Q2—2,200; Q3—2,500; Q4—2,650; and Q1 (next year)—2,200. These numbers are in 1,000-case units. Each number represents a 13-week forecast.
3 Management has instructed manufacturing to maintain a two-week supply of pudding inventory in the warehouses. The two-week supply should be based on future expected sales. The following are ending inventory target levels for each quarter: Q1—338; Q2—385; Q3—408; Q4—338.
4 Inventory carrying cost is estimated by accounting to be $1.00 per case per year. This means that if a case of pudding is held in inventory for an entire year, the cost to just carry that case in inventory is $1.00. If a case is carried for only one week the cost is $1.00/52 or $.01923. The cost is proportional to the time carried in inventory. There are 200,000 cases in inventory at the beginning of Q1 (this is 200 cases in the 1,000-case units that the forecast is given in).
5 If a stockout occurs, the item is backordered and shipped at a later date. The cost when a backorder occurs is $2.40 per case due to the loss of goodwill and the high cost of emergency shipping.
6 The human resource group estimates that it costs $5,000 to hire and train a new production employee. It costs $3,000 to lay off a production worker.

### QUESTIONS

1 Prepare an aggregate plan for the coming year, assuming that the sales forecast is perfect. Use the spreadsheet "Bradford Manufacturing" from this book's CD. In the spreadsheet an area has been designated for your aggregate plan solution. Supply the number of packaging lines to run and the number of overtime hours for each quarter. You will need to set up the cost calculations in the spreadsheet.

   You may want to try using the Excel Solver to find a solution. You will need to "unprotect" the spreadsheet to run the Solver (Tools > Protection > Unprotect). You will also need to set the "not-negativity" box in the "options" area. Remember that your final solution needs an integer number of lines and an integer number of overtime hours for each quarter. (Solutions that require 8.9134 lines and 1.256 hours of overtime are not feasible.)
2 Review your solution carefully and be prepared to defend it. Bring a printout of your solution to class. If you have a notebook computer, bring it to class with a copy of your completed spreadsheet. Your instructor may run a simulation in class using your solution.

## SELECTED BIBLIOGRAPHY

Brandimarte, P., and A. Villa (eds.). *Modeling Manufacturing Systems: From Aggregate Planning to Real-Time Control.* New York: Springer, 1999.

Fisher, M. L.; J. H. Hammond; W. Obermeyer; and A. Raman. "Making Supply Meet Demand in an Uncertain World." *Harvard Business Review* 72, no. 3 (May–June 1994), pp. 83–93.

Narasimhan, S.; D. W. McLeavey; and P. J. Billington. *Production Planning and Inventory Control.* Englewood Cliffs, NJ: Prentice Hall, 1995.

Silver, E. A.; D. F. Pyke; and R. Peterson. *Inventory Management and Production Planning and Scheduling.* New York: Wiley, 1998.

Smith-Daniels, V.; S. Scheweikhar; and D. Smith-Daniels. "Capacity Management in Health Care Services: Review and Future Research Directions." *Decision Sciences* 19 (1988), pp. 889–919.

Vollmann, T. E.; W. L. Berry; and D. C. Whybark. *Manufacturing Planning and Control Systems.* 4th ed. Burr Ridge, IL: Irwin/McGraw-Hill, 1997.

Whybark, D. C., and G. Vartag. *Global Manufacturing Practices: A Worldwide Survey of Practices in Production Planning and Control.* New York: Elsevier, 1993.

## FOOTNOTES

1 H. C. Meal, "Putting Production Decisions Where They Belong," *Harvard Business Review* 62, no. 2 (March–April 1984), pp. 102–11.

2 M. L. Fisher, J. H. Hammond, W. R. Obermeyer, and A. Raman, "Making Supply Meet Demand in an Uncertain World," *Harvard Business Review* 72, no. 3 (May–June 1994), p. 84.

3 For an interesting application of aggregate planning in nonprofit humanitarian organizations, see C. Sheu and J. G. Wacker, "A Planning and Control Framework for Nonprofit Humanitarian Organizations," *International Journal of Operations and Production Management* 14, no. 4 (1994), pp. 64–77.

4 The analogy used here to the standard transportation problem is that (1) production periods are factories and sales periods are warehouses, (2) wages and holding costs are the transportation costs, and (3) ending inventory and unused capacity are dummy warehouses.

chapter

*chapter thirteen*

# INVENTORY CONTROL

## CHAPTER OUTLINE AND KEY TERMS

13

# THE LONG VIEW OF U.S. INVENTORY PERFORMANCE

Between 1977 and 2000, the typical high-technology company doubled its inventory performance from 2.5 to 5.0 turns. Some firms, such as Apple and Dell, now operate with six to eight days of inventory (61 turns and 46 turns, respectively). This means that the typical company requires 50 percent less inventory to operate its business than it did 20 years ago.

What made this improvement possible? Companies have steadily improved their inventory turns by simultaneously improving their supply chain business processes and the information systems they use to manage their supply chains.

A good example of these types of changes to reduce inventory is the recent alliance of Ford with United Parcel Service (UPS).[1] Ford anticipates cutting the average factory-to-dealer delivery time from two weeks to nine days. The UPS Logistics Group will do this by reorganizing Ford's network of rail and car haulers for faster, more precise delivery of vehicles from assembly to points of purchase. UPS is the world's largest package delivery

company. The fast, precise delivery times should allow Ford to significantly reduce inventory. Dealer online systems that work with the UPS Internet package tracking system are being installed; eventually the tracking will be extended to customers. Ford is counting on its latest e-business initiative to lower its multibillion-dollar transportation and distribution costs, save money through better inventory control, and alleviate longtime distribution problems.

THIS AD FROM GE INFORMATION SERVICES POINTS OUT A MAJOR CONCERN OF COMPANIES—THAT INVENTORY, THOUGH AN ASSET, CAN BE COSTLY IF HELD TOO LONG. IN FINE PRINT GE EXPLAINS ITS SERVICES, WHICH INCLUDE ADVICE IN SETTING UP ELECTRONIC LINKS WITH SUPPLIERS, MANUFACTURERS, AND DISTRIBUTORS TO HELP AVOID COSTLY INVENTORY.

Vol. I "Manufacturing Inventory" and Vol. III "Washburn Guitar"

Ford's alliance with UPS puts it in the vanguard of major manufacturers who are adopting new distribution practices to cut inventories. As we will see when studying the inventory control models in this chapter, if Ford can indeed reduce both its lead time and the variability in that lead time, it should be able to achieve that goal. A key element in reducing inventory is better information. The better the information concerning what we have and what we need, the less inventory needed.

The economic benefit from inventory reduction is evident from the following statistics: The average cost of inventory across all manufacturing in the United States is 30 to 35 percent of its value. For example, if a firm carries an inventory of $20 million, it costs the firm more than $6 million per year. These costs are due to obsolescence, insurance, opportunity costs, and so forth. If the amount of inventory could be reduced to $10 million, for instance, the firm would save over $3 million, which goes directly to the bottom line. That is, the savings from reduced inventory show as increased profit.

In this chapter we present standard inventory models designed to help management keep the cost down while still meeting production and customer service requirements. Also included are special-purpose models, such as price-break, as well as the ABC technique. In addition, we discuss inventory accuracy and show applications of the models in department stores and auto parts supply.

There are conflicting views concerning the teaching of classical inventory models. On one side, articles claim that economic order quantity (EOQ) models are invalid. The other side defends their use. We believe both sides are correct—from within their own arenas. Although you must be careful in their application, there certainly are situations in manufacturing where EOQ models can be successfully used. Just-in-time manufacturing (JIT), for example, is based on the classical production–consumption inventory model discussed here. Classical models are quite valid for the many thousands of companies engaged in product and parts distribution.

Concerning JIT and safety stocks, recall that JIT *does* have safety stock. It shows up as the size of containers and the number of containers between each station in a production sequence. Further, all manufacturers that supply parts cannot have similar JIT schedules. A manufacturer with a JIT system utilizing twice-per-day deliveries by a supplier to the production line might be surprised that the supplier produces those supplies a month's worth at a time using an EOQ formula! How we compute inventory requirements depends on many factors; all methods are valid given the correct set of circumstances. Therefore, we should become familiar with them all.

## DEFINITION OF INVENTORY

**Inventory** is the stock of any item or resource used in an organization. An *inventory system* is the set of policies and controls that monitors levels of inventory and determines what levels should be maintained, when stock should be replenished, and how large orders should be.

Inventory

By convention, *manufacturing inventory* generally refers to items that contribute to or become part of a firm's product output. Manufacturing inventory is typically classified into *raw materials, finished products, component parts, supplies,* and *work-in-process.* In services, *inventory* generally refers to the tangible goods to be sold and the supplies necessary to administer the service.

The basic purpose of inventory analysis in manufacturing and stockkeeping services is to specify (1) when items should be ordered and (2) how large the order should be. Many firms are tending to enter into longer-term relationships with vendors to supply their needs for perhaps the entire year. This changes the "when" and "how many to order" to "when" and "how many to deliver."

## PURPOSES OF INVENTORY

All firms (including JIT operations) keep a supply of inventory for the following reasons:

1 **To maintain independence of operations.** A supply of materials at a work center allows that center flexibility in operations. For example, because there are costs for making each new production setup, this inventory allows management to reduce the number of setups.

Independence of workstations is desirable on assembly lines as well. The time that it takes to do identical operations will naturally vary from one unit to the next. Therefore, it is desirable to have a cushion of several parts within the workstation so that shorter performance times can compensate for longer performance times. This way the average output can be fairly stable.

2 **To meet variation in product demand.** If the demand for the product is known precisely, it may be possible (though not necessarily economical) to produce the product to exactly meet the demand. Usually, however, demand is not completely known, and a safety or buffer stock must be maintained to absorb variation.

3 **To allow flexibility in production scheduling.** A stock of inventory relieves the pressure on the production system to get the goods out. This causes longer lead times, which permit production planning for smoother flow and lower-cost operation through larger lot-size production. High setup costs, for example, favor producing a larger number of units once the setup has been made.

4 **To provide a safeguard for variation in raw material delivery time.** When material is ordered from a vendor, delays can occur for a variety of reasons: a normal variation in shipping time, a shortage of material at the vendor's plant causing backlogs, an unexpected strike at the vendor's plant or at one of the shipping companies, a lost order, or a shipment of incorrect or defective material.

5 **To take advantage of economic purchase order size.** There are costs to place an order: labor, phone calls, typing, postage, and so on. Therefore, the larger each order is, the

fewer the orders that need be written. Also, shipping costs favor larger orders—the larger the shipment, the lower the per-unit cost.

For each of the preceding reasons (especially for items 3, 4, and 5), be aware that inventory is costly and large amounts are generally undesirable. Long cycle times are caused by large amounts of inventory and are undesirable as well.

## INVENTORY COSTS

In making any decision that affects inventory size, the following costs must be considered.

1 **Holding (or carrying) costs.** This broad category includes the costs for storage facilities, handling, insurance, pilferage, breakage, obsolescence, depreciation, taxes, and the opportunity cost of capital. Obviously, high holding costs tend to favor low inventory levels and frequent replenishment.

2 **Setup (or production change) costs.** To make each different product involves obtaining the necessary materials, arranging specific equipment setups, filling out the required papers, appropriately charging time and materials, and moving out the previous stock of material.

If there were no costs or loss of time in changing from one product to another, many small lots would be produced. This would reduce inventory levels, with a resulting savings in cost. One challenge today is to try to reduce these setup costs to permit smaller lot sizes. (This is the goal of a JIT system.)

3 **Ordering costs.** These costs refer to the managerial and clerical costs to prepare the purchase or production order. Ordering costs include all the details, such as counting items and calculating order quantities. The costs associated with maintaining the system needed to track orders are also included in ordering costs.

4 **Shortage costs.** When the stock of an item is depleted, an order for that item must either wait until the stock is replenished or be canceled. There is a trade-off between carrying stock to satisfy demand and the costs resulting from stockout. This balance is sometimes difficult to obtain, because it may not be possible to estimate lost profits, the effects of lost customers, or lateness penalties. Frequently, the assumed shortage cost is little more than a guess, although it is usually possible to specify a range of such costs.

Establishing the correct quantity to order from vendors or the size of lots submitted to the firm's productive facilities involves a search for the minimum total cost resulting from the combined effects of four individual costs: holding costs, setup costs, ordering costs, and shortage costs. Of course, the timing of these orders is a critical factor that may impact inventory cost.

## INDEPENDENT VERSUS DEPENDENT DEMAND

In inventory management, it is important to understand the difference between dependent and independent demand. The reason is that entire inventory systems are predicated on whether demand is derived from an end item or is related to the item itself.

Independent and dependent demand

Briefly, the distinction between **independent and dependent demand** is this: In independent demand, the demands for various items are unrelated to each other. For example, a workstation may produce many parts that are unrelated but meet some external demand requirement. In dependent demand, the need for any one item is a direct result of the need for some other item, usually a higher-level item of which it is part.

In concept, dependent demand is a relatively straightforward computational problem. Needed quantities of a dependent-demand item are simply computed, based on the number needed in each higher-level item in which it is used. For example, if an automobile company plans on producing 500 cars per day, then obviously it will need 2,000 wheels and tires (plus spares). The number of wheels and tires needed is *dependent* on the production levels and is not derived separately. The demand for cars, on the other hand, is *independent*—it comes from many sources external to the automobile firm and is not a part of other products; it is unrelated to the demand for other products.

To determine the quantities of independent items that must be produced, firms usually turn to their sales and market research departments. They use a variety of techniques, including customer surveys, forecasting techniques, and economic and sociological trends, as we discussed in Chapter 11 on forecasting. Because independent demand is uncertain, extra units must be carried in inventory. This chapter presents models to determine how many units need to be ordered, and how many extra units should be carried to reduce the risk of stocking out.

Cross Functional

# INVENTORY SYSTEMS

An inventory system provides the organizational structure and the operating policies for maintaining and controlling goods to be stocked. The system is responsible for ordering and receipt of goods: timing the order placement and keeping track of what has been ordered, how much, and from whom. The system must also follow up to answer such questions as, Has the supplier received the order? Has it been shipped? Are the dates correct? Are the procedures established for reordering or returning undesirable merchandise?

## CLASSIFYING MODELS

There are two general types of inventory systems: **fixed–order quantity models** (also called the *economic order quantity,* EOQ, and **Q-model)** and **fixed–time period models** (also referred to variously as the *periodic* system, *periodic review* system, *fixed–order interval* system, and **P-model**).

Fixed–order quantity models (Q-models)

The basic distinction is that fixed–order quantity models are "event triggered" and fixed–time period models are "time–triggered." That is, a fixed–order quantity model initiates an order when the event of reaching a specified reorder level occurs. This event may take place at any time, depending on the demand for the items considered. In contrast, the fixed–time period model is limited to placing orders at the end of a predetermined time period; only the passage of time triggers the model.

Fixed–time period models (P-models)

To use the fixed–order quantity model (which places an order when the remaining inventory drops to a predetermined order point, *R*), the inventory remaining must be continually monitored. Thus, the fixed–order quantity model is a *perpetual* system, which requires that every time a withdrawal from inventory or an addition to inventory is made, records must be updated to reflect whether the reorder point has been reached. In a fixed–time period model counting takes place only at the review period. (We will discuss some variations of systems that combine features of both.)

Some additional differences tend to influence the choice of systems (also see Exhibit 13.1):

- The fixed–time period model has a larger average inventory because it must also protect against stockout during the review period, *T*; the fixed-quantity model has no review period.
- The fixed–order quantity model favors more expensive items because average inventory is lower.
- The fixed–order quantity model is more appropriate for important items such as critical repair parts because there is closer monitoring and therefore quicker response to potential stockout.
- The fixed–order quantity model requires more time to maintain because every addition or withdrawal is logged.

EXHIBIT 13.1

Fixed–Order Quantity and Fixed–Time Period Differences

| FEATURE | Q-MODEL FIXED–ORDER QUANTITY MODEL | P-MODEL FIXED–TIME PERIOD MODEL |
|---|---|---|
| Order quantity | *Q*—constant (the same amount ordered each time) | *q*—variable (varies each time order is placed) |
| When to place order | *R*—when inventory position drops to the reorder level | *T*—when the review period arrives |
| Recordkeeping | Each time a withdrawal or addition is made | Counted only at review period |
| Size of inventory | Less than fixed–time period model | Larger than fixed–order quantity model |
| Time to maintain | Higher due to perpetual recordkeeping | |
| Type of items | Higher-priced, critical, or important items | |

EXHIBIT 13.2

Comparison of Fixed–Order Quantity and Fixed–Time Period Reordering Inventory Systems

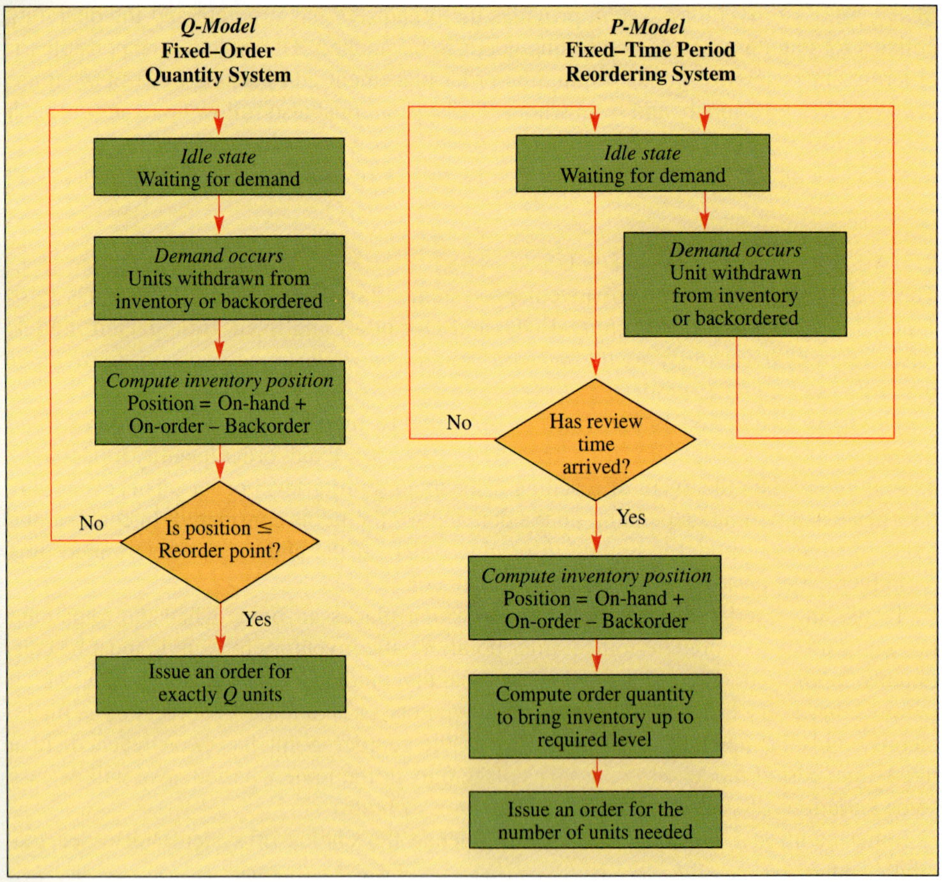


Exhibit 13.2 shows what occurs when each of the two models is put into use and becomes an operating system. As we can see, the fixed–order quantity system focuses on order quantities and reorder points. Procedurally, each time a unit is taken out of stock, the withdrawal is logged and the amount remaining in inventory is immediately compared to the reorder point. If it has dropped to this point, an order for *Q* items is placed. If it has not, the system remains in an idle state until the next withdrawal.

In the fixed–time period system, a decision to place an order is made after the stock has been counted or reviewed. Whether an order is actually placed depends on the inventory position at that time.

# FIXED–ORDER QUANTITY MODELS

Fixed–order quantity models attempt to determine the specific point, $R$, at which an order will be placed and the size of that order, $Q$. The order point, $R$, is always a specified number of units. An order of size $Q$ is placed when the inventory available (currently in stock and on order) reaches the point $R$. **Inventory position** is defined as the on-hand plus on-order minus backordered quantities. The solution to a fixed–order quantity model may stipulate something like this: When the inventory position drops to 36, place an order for 57 more units.

Inventory position

The simplest models in this category occur when all aspects of the situation are known with certainty. If the annual demand for a product is 1,000 units, it is precisely 1,000—not 1,000 plus or minus 10 percent. The same is true for setup costs and holding costs. Although the assumption of complete certainty is rarely valid, it provides a good basis for our coverage of inventory models.

Exhibit 13.3 and the discussion about deriving the optimal order quantity are based on the following characteristics of the model. These assumptions are unrealistic, but they represent a starting point and allow us to use a simple example.

- Demand for the product is constant and uniform throughout the period.
- Lead time (time from ordering to receipt) is constant.
- Price per unit of product is constant.
- Inventory holding cost is based on average inventory.
- Ordering or setup costs are constant.
- All demands for the product will be satisfied. (No backorders are allowed.)

The "sawtooth effect" relating $Q$ and $R$ in Exhibit 13.3 shows that when the inventory position drops to point $R$, a reorder is placed. This order is received at the end of time period $L$, which does not vary in this model.

Tutorial: EOQ

In constructing any inventory model, the first step is to develop a functional relationship between the variables of interest and the measure of effectiveness. In this case, because we are concerned with cost, the following equation pertains:

$$\text{Total annual cost} = \text{Annual purchase cost} + \text{Annual ordering cost} + \text{Annual holding cost}$$

or

[13.1]

$$TC = DC + \frac{D}{Q}S + \frac{Q}{2}H$$

where

$TC$ = Total annual cost
$D$ = Demand (annual)
$C$ = Cost per unit
$Q$ = Quantity to be ordered (the optimal amount is termed the *economic order quantity*—EOQ—or $Q_{\text{opt}}$)
$S$ = Setup cost or cost of placing an order
$R$ = Reorder point
$L$ = Lead time
$H$ = Annual holding and storage cost per unit of average inventory (often holding cost is taken as a percentage of the cost of the item, such as $H = iC$, where $i$ is the percent carrying cost)

On the right side of the equation, $DC$ is the annual purchase cost for the units, $(D/Q)S$ is the annual ordering cost (the actual number of orders placed, $D/Q$, times the cost of each order, $S$), and $(Q/2)H$ is the annual holding cost (the average inventory, $Q/2$, times the cost per unit for holding and storage, $H$). These cost relationships are graphed in Exhibit 13.4.

EXHIBIT 13.3 & 13.4

Basic Fixed–Order Quantity Model

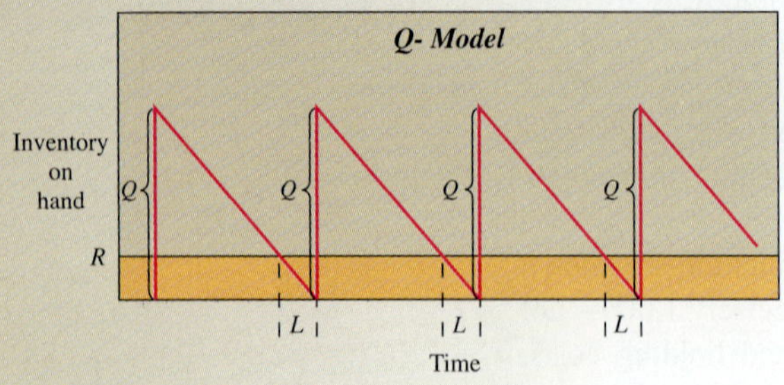


Annual Product Costs, Based on Size of the Order

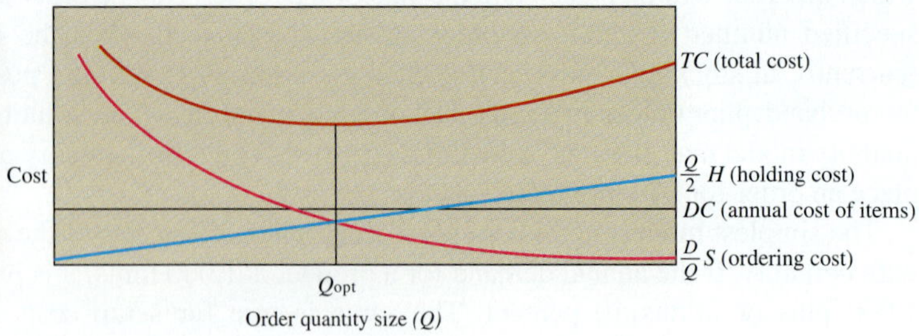


The second step in model development is to find that order quantity $Q_{\text{opt}}$ at which total cost is a minimum. In Exhibit 13.4, the total cost is minimal at the point where the slope of the curve is zero. Using calculus, we take the derivative of total cost with respect to $Q$ and set this equal to zero. For the basic model considered here, the calculations are

$$TC = DC + \frac{D}{Q}S + \frac{Q}{2}H$$

$$\frac{dTC}{dQ} = 0 + \left(\frac{-DS}{Q^2}\right) + \frac{H}{2} = 0$$

[13.2]
$$Q_{\text{opt}} = \sqrt{\frac{2DS}{H}}$$

Because this simple model assumes constant demand and lead time, no safety stock is necessary, and the reorder point, $R$, is simply

[13.3]
$$R = \bar{d}L$$

where

$\bar{d}$ = Average daily demand (constant)
$L$ = Lead time in days (constant)

### EXAMPLE 13.1: ECONOMIC ORDER QUANTITY AND REORDER POINT

Find the economic order quantity and the reorder point, given

Annual demand ($D$) = 1,000 units
Average daily demand ($d$) = 1,000/365
Ordering cost ($S$) = \$5 per order
Holding cost ($H$) = \$1.25 per unit per year
Lead time ($L$) = 5 days
Cost per unit ($C$) = \$12.50

What quantity should be ordered?

### SOLUTION

The optimal order quantity is

$$Q_{\text{opt}} = \sqrt{\frac{2DS}{H}} = \sqrt{\frac{2(1{,}000)5}{1.25}} = \sqrt{8{,}000} = 89.4 \text{ units}$$

The reorder point is

$$R = \bar{d}L = \frac{1{,}000}{365}(5) = 13.7 \text{ units}$$

Rounding to the nearest unit, the inventory policy is as follows: When the inventory position drops to 14, place an order for 89 more.

The total annual cost will be

$$TC = DC + \frac{D}{Q}S + \frac{Q}{2}H$$

$$= 1{,}000(12.50) + \frac{1{,}000}{89}(5) + \frac{89}{2}(1.25)$$

$$= \$12{,}611.81$$

Note that in this example, the purchase cost of the units was not required to determine the order quantity and the reorder point because the cost was constant and unrelated to order size. ←

## Establishing Safety Stock Levels

The previous model assumed that demand was constant and known. In the majority of cases, though, demand is not constant but varies from day to day. Safety stock must therefore be maintained to provide some level of protection against stockouts. **Safety stock** can be defined as the amount of inventory carried in addition to the expected demand. In a normal distribution, this would be the mean. For example, if our average monthly demand is 100 units and we expect next month to be the same, if we carry 120 units, then we have 20 units of safety stock.

Safety stock

Safety stock can be determined based on many different criteria. A common approach is for a company to simply state that a certain number of weeks of supply be kept in safety stock. It is better, though, to use an approach that captures the variability in demand.

For example, an objective may be something like "set the safety stock level so that there will only be a 5 percent chance of stocking out if demand exceeds 300 units." We call this approach to setting safety stock the probability approach.

**The Probability Approach** Using the probability criterion to determine safety stock is pretty simple. With the models described in this chapter, we assume that the demand over a period of time is normally distributed with a mean and a standard deviation. *Again, remember that this approach considers only the probability of running out of stock, not how many units we are short.* To determine the probability of stocking out over the time period, we can simply plot a normal distribution for the expected demand and note where the amount we have on hand lies on the curve.

Let's take a few simple examples to illustrate this. Say we expect demand to be 100 units over the next month, and we know that the standard deviation is 20 units. If we go into the month with just 100 units, we know that our probability of stocking out is 50 percent. Half of the months we would expect demand to be greater than 100 units; half of the months we would expect it to be less than 100 units. Taking this further, if we ordered a month's worth of inventory of 100 units at a time and received it at the beginning of the month, over the long run we would expect to run out of inventory in six months of the year.

If running out this often was not acceptable, we would want to carry extra inventory to reduce this risk of stocking out. One idea might be to carry an extra 20 units of inventory for the item. In this case, we would still order a month's worth of inventory at a time, but we would schedule delivery to arrive when we still have 20 units remaining in inventory. This would give us that little cushion of safety stock to reduce the probability of stocking out. If the standard deviation associated with our demand was 20 units, we would then be carrying one standard deviation worth of safety stock. Looking at the Standard Normal Distribution (Appendix D), and moving one standard deviation to the right of the mean,

AT JOHN DEERE'S DALLAS DEPOT, JOINING A CAROUSEL TO AN ADVANCED COMPUTER SYSTEM RESULTED IN PRODUCTIVITY GAINS. WITH 3,000 FREQUENTLY ORDERED PARTS CONTAINED IN A SIX-STAND CAROUSEL SYSTEM, TWO PEOPLE CAN FILL ORDERS WITHOUT HAVING TO SEARCH THROUGH MILES OF WAREHOUSE SHELVING. WHILE THE ORDER FILLER PULLS A PART FROM ONE OF THE CAROUSELS, THE NEXT PART IS DIRECTED BY COMPUTER TO THE ADJACENT CAROUSEL. THIS ELIMINATES HOURS OF SEARCHING AND SPEEDS PARTS-ORDER SHIPMENTS.

EXHIBIT 13.5

Fixed-Order Quantity Model

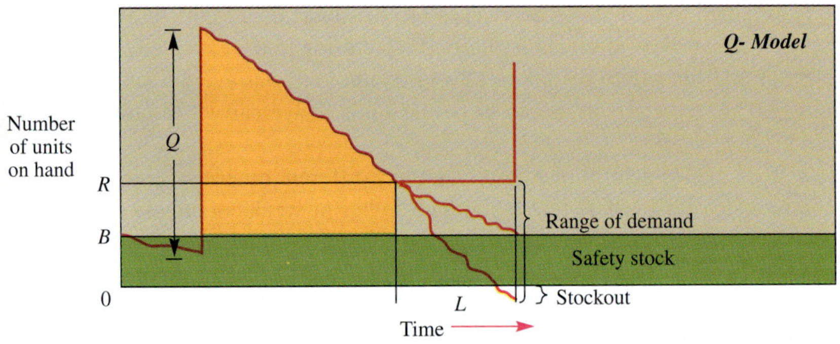


gives a probability of .8413 (from the table we get .3413 and we need to add .5 to this). So approximately 84 percent of the time we would not expect to stock out, and 16 percent of the time we would. Now if we order every month, we would expect to stock out approximately two months per year ($.16 \times 12 = 1.92$). For those using Excel, given a $z$ value, the probability can be obtained with the NORMSINV function.

It is common for companies using this approach to set the probability of not stocking out at 95 percent. This means we would carry about 1.64 standard deviations of safety stock, or 33 units ($1.64 \times 20 = 32.8$) for our example. Once again, keep in mind that this does not mean that we would order 33 units extra each month. Rather, it means that we would still order a month's worth each time, but we would schedule the receipt so that we could expect to have 33 units in inventory when the order arrives. In this case, we would expect to stockout approximately .6 months per year, or that stockouts would occur in 1 of every 20 months.

## FIXED–ORDER QUANTITY MODEL WITH SAFETY STOCK

A fixed–order quantity system perpetually monitors the inventory level and places a new order when stock reaches some level, $R$. The danger of stockout in this model occurs only during the lead time, between the time an order is placed and the time it is received. As shown in Exhibit 13.5, an order is placed when the inventory position drops to the reorder point, $R$. During this lead time $L$, a range of demands is possible. This range is determined either from an analysis of past demand data or from an estimate (if past data are not available).

The amount of safety stock depends on the service level desired, as previously discussed. The quantity to be ordered, $Q$, is calculated in the usual way considering the demand, shortage cost, ordering cost, holding cost, and so forth. A fixed–order quantity model can be used to compute $Q$, such as the simple $Q_{\text{opt}}$ model previously discussed. The reorder point is then set to cover the expected demand during the lead time plus a safety stock determined by the desired service level. Thus, *the key difference between a fixed–order quantity model where demand is known and one where demand is uncertain is in computing the reorder point. The order quantity is the same in both cases.* The uncertainty element is taken into account in the safety stock.

The reorder point is

[13.4] $$R = \bar{d}L + z\sigma_L$$

where

$R$ = Reorder point in units
$\bar{d}$ = Average daily demand
$L$ = Lead time in days (time between placing an order and receiving the items)
$z$ = Number of standard deviations for a specified service probability
$\sigma_L$ = Standard deviation of usage during lead time

The term $z\sigma_L$ is the amount of safety stock. Note that if safety stock is positive, the effect is to place a reorder sooner. That is, $R$ without safety stock is simply the average demand during the lead time. If lead time usage was expected to be 20, for example, and safety stock was computed to be 5 units, then the order would be placed sooner, when 25 units remained. The greater the safety stock, the sooner the order is placed.

**Computing $\bar{d}$, $\sigma_L$, and $z$** Demand during the replenishment lead time is really an estimate or forecast of expected use of inventory from the time an order is placed to when it is received. It may be a single number (for example, if the lead time is a month, the demand may be taken as the previous year's demand divided by 12), or it may be a summation of expected demands over the lead time (such as the sum of daily demands over a 30-day lead time). For the daily demand situation, $d$ can be a forecast demand using any of the models in Chapter 11 on forecasting. For example, if a 30-day period was used to calculate $d$, then a simple average would be

[13.5] $$\bar{d} = \frac{\sum_{i=1}^{n} d_i}{n} = \frac{\sum_{i=1}^{30} d_i}{30}$$

where $n$ is the number of days.

The standard deviation of the daily demand is

[13.6] $$\sigma_d = \sqrt{\frac{\sum_{i=1}^{n} (d_i - \bar{d})^2}{n}} = \sqrt{\frac{\sum_{i=1}^{30} (d_i - \bar{d})^2}{30}}$$

Because $\sigma_d$ refers to one day, if lead time extends over several days we can use the statistical premise that the standard deviation of a series of independent occurrences is equal to the square root of the sum of the variances. That is, in general,

[13.7] $$\sigma_s = \sqrt{\sigma_1^2 + \sigma_2^2 + \cdots + \sigma_i^2}$$

For example, suppose we computed the standard deviation of demand to be 10 units per day. If our lead time to get an order is five days, the standard deviation for the five-day period, because each day can be considered independent, is

$$\sigma_L = \sqrt{(10)^2 + (10)^2 + (10)^2 + (10)^2 + (10)^2} = 22.36$$

Next we need to find $z$, the number of standard deviations of safety stock.

Suppose we wanted our probability of not stocking out during the lead time to be .95. The $z$ value associated with a 95 percent probability of not stocking out is 1.64 (see Appendix D). Given this, safety is calculated as follows:

[13.8] $$\begin{aligned} SS &= z\sigma_L \\ &= 1.64 \times 22.36 \\ &= 36.67 \end{aligned}$$

We now compare two examples. The difference between them is that in the first, the variation in demand is stated in terms of standard deviation over the entire lead time, while in the second, it is stated in terms of standard deviation per day.

### EXAMPLE 13.2: ECONOMIC ORDER QUANTITY

Consider an economic order quantity case where annual demand $D = 1{,}000$ units, economic order quantity $Q = 200$ units, the desired probability of not stocking out $P = .95$, the standard deviation of demand during lead time $\sigma_L = 25$ units, and lead time $L = 15$ days. Determine the reorder point. Assume that demand is over a 250 = workday year.

### SOLUTION

In our example, $\bar{d} = \frac{1000}{250} = 4$, and lead time is 15 days. We use the equation

$$\begin{aligned} R &= \bar{d}L + z\sigma_L \\ &= 4(15) + z(25) \end{aligned}$$

In this case $z$ is 1.64.

Completing the solution for $R$, we have

$$R = 4(15) + 1.64(25) = 60 + 41 = 101 \text{ units}$$

This says that when the stock on hand gets down to 101 units, order 200 more.

### EXAMPLE 13.3: ORDER QUANTITY AND REORDER POINT

Daily demand for a certain product is normally distributed with a mean of 60 and standard deviation of 7. The source of supply is reliable and maintains a constant lead time of six days. The cost of placing the order is $10 and annual holding costs are $0.50 per unit. There are no stockout costs, and unfilled orders are filled as soon as the order arrives. Assume sales occur over the entire 365 days of the year. Find the order quantity and reorder point to satisfy a 95 percent probability of not stocking out during the lead time.

*SOLUTION*

In this problem we need to calculate the order quantity $Q$ as well as the reorder point $R$.

$$\bar{d} = 60 \qquad S = \$10$$
$$\sigma_d = 7 \qquad H = \$0.50$$
$$D = 60(365) \qquad L = 6$$

The optimal order quantity is

$$Q_{\text{opt}} = \sqrt{\frac{2DS}{H}} = \sqrt{\frac{2(60)365(10)}{0.50}} = \sqrt{876{,}000} = 936 \text{ units}$$

To compute the reorder point, we need to calculate the amount of product used during the lead time and add this to the safety stock.

The standard deviation of demand during the lead time of six days is calculated from the variance of the individual days. Because each day's demand is independent[2]

$$\sigma_L = \sqrt{\sum_{i=1}^{L} \sigma_{d_i}^2} = \sqrt{6(7)^2} = 17.15$$

Once again, $z$ is 1.64.

$$R = \bar{d}L + z\sigma_L = 60(6) + 1.64(17.15) = 388 \text{ units}$$

To summarize the policy derived in this example, an order for 936 units is placed whenever the number of units remaining in inventory drops to 388. ←

## FIXED–TIME PERIOD MODELS

In a fixed–time period system, inventory is counted only at particular times, such as every week or every month. Counting inventory and placing orders periodically is desirable in situations such as when vendors make routine visits to customers and take orders for their complete line of products, or when buyers want to combine orders to save transportation costs. Other firms operate on a fixed time period to facilitate planning their inventory count; for example, Distributor X calls every two weeks and employees know that all Distributor X's product must be counted.

Fixed–time period models generate order quantities that vary from period to period, depending on the usage rates. These generally require a higher level of safety stock than a fixed–order quantity system. The fixed–order quantity system assumes continual tracking of inventory on hand, with an order immediately placed when the reorder point is reached. In contrast, the standard fixed–time period models assume that inventory is counted only at the time specified for review. It is possible that some large demand will draw the stock down to zero right after an order is placed. This condition could go unnoticed until the next review period. Then the new order, when placed, still takes time to arrive. Thus, it is possible to be out of stock throughout the entire review period, $T$, and order lead time, $L$. Safety stock, therefore, must protect against stockouts during the review period itself as well as during the lead time from order placement to order receipt.

### FIXED–TIME PERIOD MODEL WITH SAFETY STOCK

In a fixed–time period system, reorders are placed at the time of review ($T$), and the safety stock that must be reordered is

[13.9] $$\text{Safety stock} = z\sigma_{T+L}$$

EXHIBIT 13.6

Fixed-Time Period Inventory Model

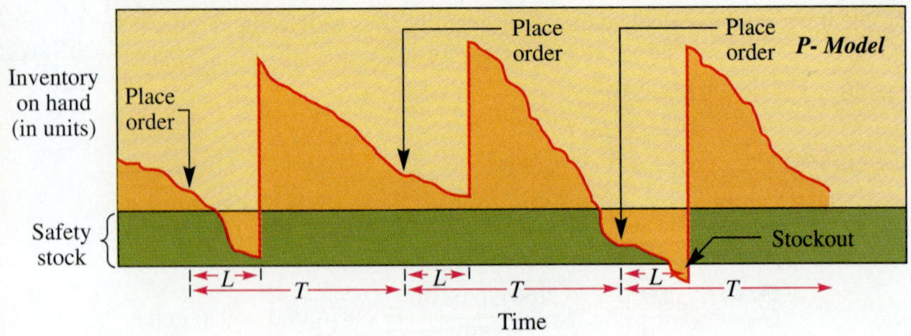


Exhibit 13.6 shows a fixed–time period system with a review cycle of $T$ and a constant lead time of $L$. In this case, demand is randomly distributed about a mean $\bar{d}$. The quantity to order, $q$, is

[13.10]

$$\text{Order quantity} = \begin{array}{c}\text{Average demand}\\ \text{over the}\\ \text{vulnerable period}\end{array} + \begin{array}{c}\text{Safety}\\ \text{stock}\end{array} - \begin{array}{c}\text{Inventory currently}\\ \text{on hand (plus on}\\ \text{order, if any)}\end{array}$$

$$q = \bar{d}(T+L) + z\sigma_{T+L} - I$$

where

$q$ = Quantity to be ordered
$T$ = The number of days between reviews
$L$ = Lead time in days (time between placing an order and receiving it)
$\bar{d}$ = Forecast average daily demand
$z$ = Number of standard deviations for a specified service probability
$\sigma_{T+L}$ = Standard deviation of demand over the review and lead time
$I$ = Current inventory level (includes items on order)

Note: The demand, lead time, review period, and so forth can be any time units such as days, weeks, or years so long as they are consistent throughout the equation.

In this model, demand ($\bar{d}$) can be forecast and revised each review period if desired or the yearly average may be used if appropriate. We assume that demand is normally distributed.

The value of $z$ is dependent on the probability of stocking out and can be found using Appendix D or by using the Excel NORMSINV function.

### EXAMPLE 13.4: QUANTITY TO ORDER

Daily demand for a product is 10 units with a standard deviation of 3 units. The review period is 30 days, and lead time is 14 days. Management has set a policy of satisfying 98 percent of demand from items in stock. At the beginning of this review period, there are 150 units in inventory.

How many units should be ordered?

### SOLUTION

The quantity to order is

$$q = \bar{d}(T+L) + z\sigma_{T+L} - I$$
$$= 10(30+14) + z\sigma_{T+L} - 150$$

Before we can complete the solution, we need to find $\sigma_{T+L}$ and $z$. To find $\sigma_{T+L}$, we use the notion, as before, that the standard deviation of a sequence of independent random variables equals the square root of the sum of the variances. Therefore, the standard deviation during the period $T + L$ is the square root of the sum of the variances for each day:

[13.11]
$$\sigma_{T+L} = \sqrt{\sum_{i=1}^{T+L} \sigma_{d_i}^2}$$

Because each day is independent and $\sigma_d$ is constant,

$$\sigma_{T+L} = \sqrt{(T + L)\sigma_d^2} = \sqrt{(30 + 14)(3)^2} = 19.90$$

The $z$ value for $P = .98$ is 2.05.

The quantity to order, then, is

$$q = \bar{d}(T + L) + z\sigma_{T+L} - I = 10(30 + 14) + 2.05(19.90) - 150 = 331 \text{ units}$$

To ensure a 98 percent probability of not stocking out, order 294 at this review period. ←

## SPECIAL-PURPOSE MODELS

The fixed–order quantity and the fixed–time period models presented thus far differed in their assumptions but had two characteristics in common: (1) The cost of units remained constant for any order size; and (2) the reordering process was continuous—that is, the items were ordered and stocked with the expectation that the need would continue.

This section presents two new models. The first illustrates the effect on order quantity when unit price changes with order size. The second is a single-period model (sometimes called a *static model*) in which ordering and stocking require a cost trade-off each time. This type of model is amenable to solution by marginal analysis.

**Price-Break Models** Price-break models deal with the fact that, generally, the selling price of an item varies with the order size. This is a discrete or step change rather than a per-unit change. For example, wood screws may cost \$0.02 each for 1 to 99 screws, \$1.60 per 100, and \$13.50 per 1,000. To determine the optimal quantity of any item to order, we simply solve for the economic order quantity for each price and at the point of price change. But not all of the economic order quantities determined by the formula are feasible. In the wood screw example, the $Q_{\text{opt}}$ formula might tell us that the optimal decision at the price of 1.6 cents is to order 75 screws. This would be impossible, however, because 75 screws would cost 2 cents each.

The total cost for each feasible economic order quantity and *price-break order quantity* is tabulated, and the $Q$ that leads to the minimum cost is the optimal order size. If holding cost is based on a percentage of unit price, it may not be necessary to compute economic order quantities at each price. Procedurally, the largest order quantity (lowest unit price) is solved first; if the resulting $Q$ is valid, that is the answer. If not, the next largest quantity (second lowest price) is derived. If that is feasible, the cost of this $Q$ is compared to the cost of using the order quantity at the price break above, and the lowest cost determines the optimal $Q$.

Looking at Exhibit 13.7, we see that order quantities are solved from right to left, or from the lowest unit price to the highest, until a valid $Q$ is obtained. Then the order quantity at each *price break* above this $Q$ is used to find which order quantity has the least cost—the computed $Q$, or the $Q$ at one of the price breaks.

EXHIBIT 13.7

**Curves for Three Separate Order Quantity Models in a Three-Price-Break Situation (blue line depicts feasible range of purchases)**

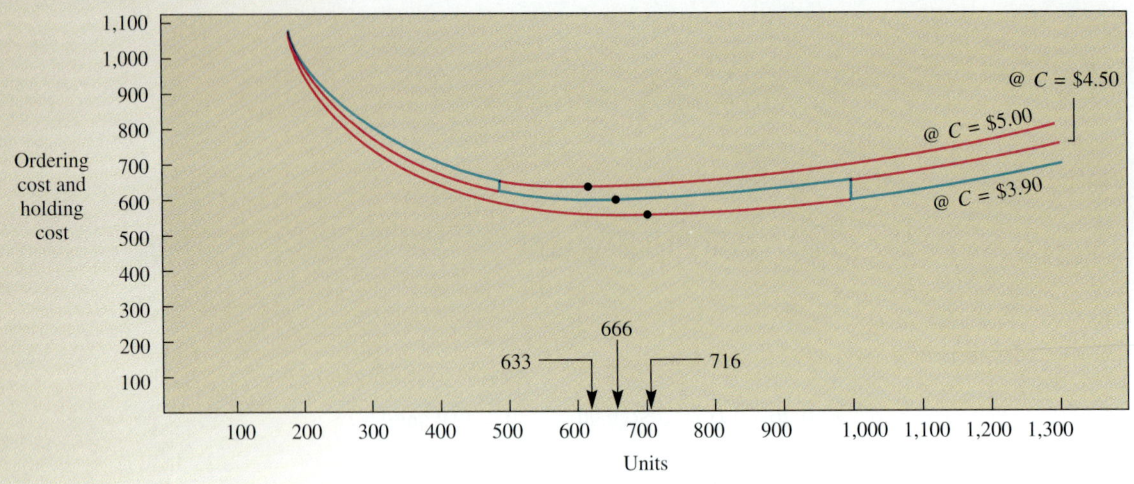


### EXAMPLE 13.5: PRICE BREAK

Consider the following case, where

$D$ = 10,000 units (annual demand)

$S$ = $20 to place each order

$i$ = 20 percent of cost (annual carrying cost, storage, interest, obsolescence, etc.)

$C$ = Cost per unit (according to the order size; orders of 0 to 499 units, $5.00 per unit; 500 to 999, $4.50 per unit; 1,000 and up, $3.90 per unit)

What quantity should be ordered?

### SOLUTION

The appropriate equations from the basic fixed-quantity case are

$$TC = DC + \frac{D}{Q}S + \frac{Q}{2}iC$$

and

[13.12] $$Q = \sqrt{\frac{2DS}{iC}}$$

Solving for the economic order size, we obtain

@ $C$ = $3.90, $Q$ = 716 Not feasible

@ $C$ = $4.50, $Q$ = 666 Feasible, cost = $45,599.70

Check $Q$ = 1,000, Cost = $39,590 Optimal solution

In Exhibit 13.7, which displays the cost relationship and order quantity range, note that most of the order quantity–cost relationships lie outside the feasible range and that only a single, continuous range results. This should be readily apparent because, for example, the first order quantity specifies buying 633 units at $5.00 per unit. However, if 633 units are ordered, the price is $4.50, not $5.00. The same holds true for the third order quantity, which specifies an order of 716 units at $3.90 each. This $3.90 price is not available on orders of less than 1,000 units.

Exhibit 13.8 itemizes the total costs at the economic order quantities and at the price breaks. The optimal order quantity is shown to be 1,000 units. ←

EXHIBIT 13.8

**Relevant Costs in a Three-Price-Break Model**

| | Q = 633 WHERE C = \$5 | Q = 666 WHERE C = \$4.50 | Q = 716 WHERE C = \$3.90 | PRICE BREAK 1,000 |
|---|---|---|---|---|
| Holding cost $\left(\frac{Q}{2}iC\right)$ | | $\frac{666}{2}(0.20)4.50$ = \$299.70 | | $\frac{1{,}000}{2}(0.20)3.90$ = \$390 |
| Ordering cost $\left(\frac{D}{Q}S\right)$ | Not feasible | $\frac{10{,}000(20)}{666}$ = \$300 | Not feasible | $\frac{10{,}000(20)}{1{,}000}$ = \$200 |
| Holding and ordering cost | | \$599.70 | | \$590 |
| Item cost (*DC*) | | 10,000(4.50) | | 10,000(3.90) |
| Total cost | | \$45,599.70 | | \$39,590 |

One practical consideration in price-break problems is that the price reduction from volume purchases frequently makes it seemingly economical to order amounts larger than the $Q_{opt}$. Thus, when applying the model, we must be particularly careful to obtain a valid estimate of product obsolescence and warehousing costs.

**Single-Period Models** Some inventory situations involve placing orders to cover only one demand period or to cover short-lived items at frequent intervals. Sometimes called single-period or "newsboy" problems (for example, how many papers should a newsboy order each day), they are amenable to solution through the classic economic approach of marginal analysis. The optimal stocking level, using marginal analysis, occurs at the point where the benefits derived from carrying the next unit are less than the costs for that unit. Of course, the selection of the specific benefits and costs depends on the problem. For example, we may be looking at costs of holding versus shortage costs or (as we develop further) marginal profit versus marginal loss.

When stocked items are sold, the optimal decision—using marginal analysis—is to stock that quantity where the profit from the sale or use of the last unit is equal to or greater than the losses if the last unit remains unsold. In symbolic terms, this is the condition in which $MP \geq ML$, where

$MP$ = Profit resulting from the $n$th unit if it is sold
$ML$ = Loss resulting from the $n$th unit if it is not sold

Marginal analysis is also valid when we are dealing with probabilities of occurrence. In these situations, we are looking at expected profits and expected losses. By introducing probabilities, the marginal profit–marginal loss equation becomes

$$P(MP) \geq (1 - P)ML$$

where $P$ is the probability of the unit's being sold and $1 - P$ is the probability of it not being sold, because one or the other must occur. (The unit is sold or is not sold.)[3]

Then, solving for $P$, we obtain

$$P \geq \frac{ML}{MP + ML} \tag{13.13}$$

This equation states that we should continue to increase the size of the inventory so long as the probability of selling the last unit added is equal to or greater than the ratio $ML/(MP + ML)$.

Salvage value, or any other benefits derived from unsold goods, can easily be included in the problem. This simply reduces the marginal loss, as the following example shows.

## EXAMPLE 13.6: SALVAGE VALUE

A product is priced to sell at \$100 per unit, and its cost is constant at \$70 per unit. Each unsold unit has a salvage value of \$20. Demand is expected to range between 35 and 40 units for the period; 35 units definitely can be sold and no units over 40 will be sold. The demand probabilities and the associated cumulative probability distribution ($P$) for this situation are shown in Exhibit 13.9.

The marginal profit if a unit is sold is the selling price less the cost, or $MP = \$100 - \$70 = \$30$.

The marginal loss incurred if the unit is not sold is the cost of the unit less the salvage value, or $ML = \$70 - \$20 = \$50$.

How many units should be ordered?

## SOLUTION

The optimal probability of the last unit being sold is

$$P \geq \frac{ML}{MP + ML} = \frac{50}{30 + 50} = 0.625$$

EXHIBIT 13.9

**Demand and Cumulative Probabilities**

| NUMBER OF UNITS DEMANDED | ($p$) PROBABILITY OF THIS DEMAND | THIS UNIT IS | ($P$) PROBABILITY OF SELLING |
|---|---|---|---|
| 35 | 0.10 | 1 to 35 | 1.00 |
| 36 | 0.15 | 36 | 0.90 |
| 37 | 0.25 | 37 | 0.75 |
| 38 | 0.25 | 38 | 0.50 |
| 39 | 0.15 | 39 | 0.25 |
| 40 | 0.10 | 40 | 0.10 |
| 41 | 0 | 41 or more | 0 |

EXHIBIT 13.10

**Marginal Inventory Analysis for Units Having Salvage Value**

| ($N$) UNITS OF DEMAND | ($p$) PROBABILITY OF DEMAND | ($P$) PROBABILITY OF SELLING $n$TH UNIT | ($MP$) EXPECTED MARGINAL PROFIT OF $n$TH UNIT $P(100 - 70)$ | ($ML$) EXPECTED MARGINAL LOSS OF $n$TH UNIT $(1 - P)(70 - 20)$ | (NET) NET PROFIT OF THE $n$TH UNIT $(MP) - (ML)$ |
|---|---|---|---|---|---|
| 35 | 0.10 | 1.00 | \$ 30 | \$ 0 | \$ 30.00 |
| 36 | 0.15 | 0.90 | 27 | 5 | 22 |
| 37 | 0.25 | 0.75 | 22.50 | 12.50 | 10 |
| 38 | 0.25 | 0.50 | 15 | 25 | −10 |
| 39 | 0.15 | 0.25 | 7.50 | 37.50 | −30 |
| 40 | 0.10 | 0.10 | 3 | 45 | |
| 41 | 0 | 0 | | | −42 |

Note: Expected marginal profit is the selling price of \$100 less the unit cost of \$70 times the probability the unit will be sold. Expected marginal loss is the unit cost of \$70 less the salvage value of \$20 times the probability the unit will not be sold.

According to the cumulative probability table (the last column in Exhibit 13.9), the probability of selling the unit must be equal to or greater than 0.625, so 37 units should be stocked. The probability of selling the 37th unit is 0.75. The net benefit from stocking the 37th unit is the expected marginal profit minus the expected marginal loss.

$$\begin{aligned} \text{Net} &= P(MP) - (1 - P)(ML) \\ &= 0.75(\$100 - \$70) - (1 - 0.75)(\$70 - \$20) \\ &= \$22.50 - \$12.50 = \$10 \end{aligned}$$

For the sake of illustration, Exhibit 13.10 shows all possible decisions. From the last column, we can confirm that the optimum decision is 37 units. ←

## MISCELLANEOUS SYSTEMS AND ISSUES

Obtaining actual order, setup, carrying, and shortage costs is difficult—sometimes impossible. Even the assumptions are sometimes unrealistic. For example, Exhibit 13.11 compares ordering costs that are assumed linear to the real case where every addition of a staff person causes a step increase in cost.

All inventory systems are plagued by two major problems: maintaining adequate control over each inventory item, and ensuring that accurate records of stock on hand are kept. In this section we present three simple systems often used in practice (an optional replenishment system, a one-bin system, and a two-bin system), ABC analysis (a method for analyzing inventory based on value), and cycle counting (a technique for improving inventory record accuracy).

### THREE SIMPLE INVENTORY SYSTEMS

**Optional Replenishment System** An optional replenishment system forces reviewing the inventory level at a fixed frequency (such as weekly) and ordering a replenishment supply if the level has dropped below some amount. In Exhibit 13.1, this is a *P* model. For example, the maximum inventory level (which we will call $M$) can be computed based on demand, ordering costs, and shortage costs. Because it takes time and costs money to place an order, a minimum order of size $Q$ can be established. Then, whenever this item is reviewed, the inventory position (we will call it $I$) is subtracted from the replenishment level ($M$). If that number (call it $q$) is equal to or greater than $Q$, order $q$. Otherwise, forget it until the next review period. Stated formally,

$$q = M - I$$

$$\text{If} \quad q \geq Q, \quad \text{order } q.$$

Otherwise, do not order any.

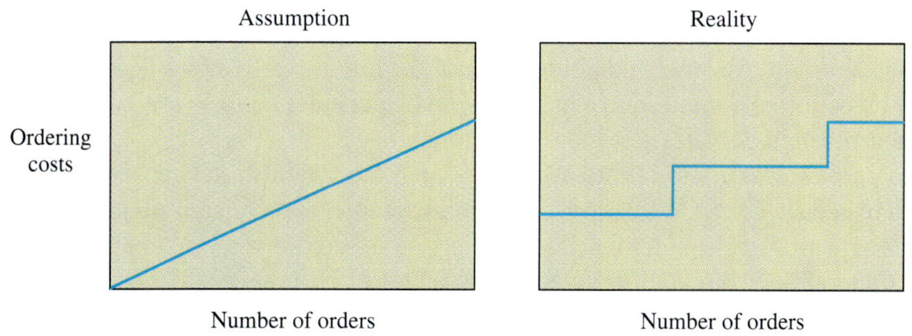


EXHIBIT 13.11

Cost to Place Orders versus the Number of Orders Placed: Linear Assumption and Normal Reality

**Two-Bin System** In a two-bin system, items are used from one bin, and the second bin provides an amount large enough to ensure that the stock can be replenished. In Exhibit 13.1, this is a $Q$ model. Ideally, the second bin would contain an amount equal to the reorder point ($R$) calculated earlier. As soon as the second bin supply is brought to the first bin, an order is placed to replenish the second bin. Actually, these bins can be located together. In fact, there could be just one bin with a divider between. The key to a two-bin operation is to separate the inventory so that part of it is held in reserve until the rest is used first.

**One-Bin System** A one-bin inventory system involves periodic replenishment no matter how few are needed. At fixed periods (such as weekly), the inventory is brought up to its predetermined maximum level. The one bin is always replenished, and it therefore differs from the optional replenishment system, which reorders only when the inventory used is greater than some minimum amount. This is a $P$ model in Exhibit 13.1.

## ABC Inventory Planning

Maintaining inventory through counting, placing orders, receiving stock, and so on takes personnel time and costs money. When there are limits on these resources, the logical move is to try to use the available resources to control inventory in the best way. In other words, focus on the most important items in inventory.

In the nineteenth century Villefredo Pareto, in a study of the distribution of wealth in Milan, found that 20 percent of the people controlled 80 percent of the wealth. This logic of the few having the greatest importance and the many having little importance has been broadened to include many situations and is termed the *Pareto principle.*[4] This is true in our everyday lives (most of our decisions are relatively unimportant, but a few shape our future) and is certainly true in inventory systems (where a few items account for the bulk of our investment).

Any inventory system must specify when an order is to be placed for an item and how many units to order. Most inventory control situations involve so many items that it is not practical to model and give thorough treatment to each item. To get around this problem, the ABC classification scheme divides inventory items into three groupings: high dollar volume (A), moderate dollar volume (B), and low dollar volume (C). Dollar volume is a measure of importance; an item low in cost but high in volume can be more important than a high-cost item with low volume.

**ABC Classification** If the annual usage of items in inventory is listed according to dollar volume, generally, the list shows that a small number of items account for a large dollar volume and that a large number of items account for a small dollar volume. Exhibit 13.12 illustrates the relationship.

The ABC approach divides this list into three groupings by value: A items constitute roughly the top 15 percent of the items, B items the next 35 percent, and C items the last 50 percent. From observation, it appears that the list in Exhibit 13.12 may be meaningfully grouped with A including 20 percent (2 of the 10), B including 30 percent, and C including 50 percent. These points show clear delineations between sections. The result of this segmentation is shown in Exhibit 13.13 and plotted in Exhibit 13.14.

Segmentation may not always occur so neatly. The objective, though, is to try to separate the important from the unimportant. Where the lines actually break depends on the particular inventory under question and on how much personnel time is available. (With more time, a firm could define larger A or B categories.)

The purpose of classifying items into groups is to establish the appropriate degree of control over each item. On a periodic basis, for example, class A items may be more clearly controlled with weekly ordering, B items may be ordered biweekly, and C items may be ordered monthly or bimonthly. Note that the unit cost of items is not related to their classification. An A item may have a high dollar volume through a combination of either low cost and high usage or high cost and low usage. Similarly, C items may have a low dollar

EXHIBIT 13.12

Annual Usage of Inventory by Value

| Item Number | Annual Dollar Usage | Percentage of Total Value |
|---|---|---|
| 22 | $ 95,000 | 40.8% |
| 68 | 75,000 | 32.1 |
| 27 | 25,000 | 10.7 |
| 03 | 15,000 | 6.4 |
| 82 | 13,000 | 5.6 |
| 54 | 7,500 | 3.2 |
| 36 | 1,500 | 0.6 |
| 19 | 800 | 0.3 |
| 23 | 425 | 0.2 |
| 41 | 225 | 0.1 |
| | $233,450 | 100.0% |

EXHIBIT 13.13

ABC Grouping of Inventory Items

| Classification | Item Number | Annual Dollar Usage | Percentage of Total |
|---|---|---|---|
| A | 22, 68 | $170,000 | 72.9% |
| B | 27, 03, 82 | 53,000 | 22.7 |
| C | 54, 36, 19, 23, 41 | 10,450 | 4.4 |
| | | $233,450 | 100.0% |

EXHIBIT 13.14

ABC Inventory Classification (inventory value for each group versus the group's portion of the total list)

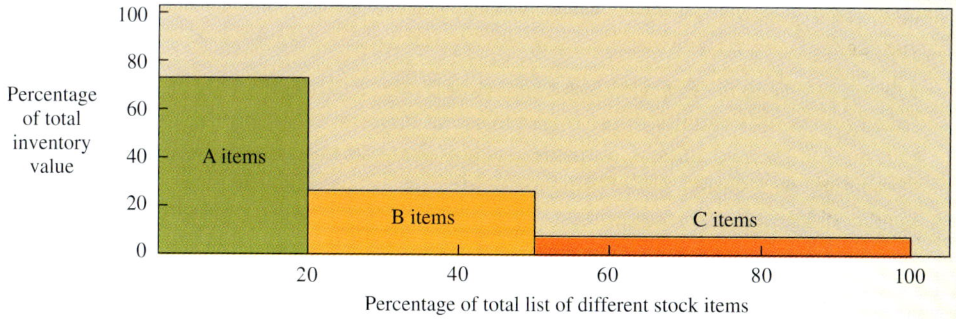


volume because of either low demand or low cost. In an automobile service station, gasoline would be an A item with daily or weekly replenishment; tires, batteries, oil, grease, and transmission fluid may be B items and ordered every two to four weeks; and C items would consist of valve stems, windshield wiper blades, radiator caps, hoses, fan belts, oil and gas additives, car wax, and so forth. C items may be ordered every two or three months or even be allowed to run out before reordering because the penalty for stockout is not serious.

Sometimes an item may be critical to a system if its absence creates a sizable loss. In this case, regardless of the item's classification, sufficiently large stocks should be kept on hand to prevent runout. One way to ensure closer control is to designate this item an A or a B, forcing it into the category even if its dollar volume does not warrant such inclusion.

## BREAKTHROUGH

### INVENTORY ON A GRAND SCALE

Inventory at Wal-Mart is precision on a gargantuan scale, like a maneuver of the Atlantic Fleet or a dam project in the Yangtze River.

In his ruling on Wal-Mart's tax court case, Judge David Laro provided a behind-the-scenes look at the operation. Its effectiveness, he says, has led "many other companies, both domestic and foreign" to seek Wal-Mart's advice on inventory taking.

Preparation alone takes four to six weeks. Forty-five days in advance, the chain's internal audit department sends a preparation kit to each store. It contains detailed instructions, including 13 schedules.

Involved in the inventory are a team of 18 to 40 independent counters and representatives of the company's operations division and departments of loss prevention and internal audit.

At randomly selected stores, employees of Ernst & Young, independent auditors for Wal-Mart, are present to test accuracy by recounting.

An inventory is taken between 8 A.M. and 6 P.M., while the store—some of which are 24-hour operations—is open to customers. Immediately after the inventory is completed, the physical count team reconciles its findings with the book inventory. The results are reviewed later by the internal audit department.

Inventories are taken every 11 to 13 months, and most occur from March through September: inventory is never taken in November or December, when it would interfere with the Christmas season, or in the first week in January, when employees are recuperating and busy with exchanges and returns.

The job can be made no easier by the facts that Wal-Mart's inventory turns over 4.5 times a year (competitors average about 2.8 turns) and its stores carry between 60,000 and 90,000 specific types of merchandise.

Between physical counts, Wal-Mart employs a perpetual system that records, at the time of sale, the cost and quantity of goods sold. This "reveals the cost and/or quantity of goods sold since the beginning of the current period and . . . of goods that are on hand at any given time."

SOURCE: W. RIGGLE. "INVENTORY ON A GRAND SCALE," *SUPERMARKET BUSINESS*, FEBRUARY 1997 P. 45. REPRODUCED WITH PERMISSION FROM SUPERMARKET BUSINESS.

## INVENTORY ACCURACY AND CYCLE COUNTING

Inventory records usually differ from the actual physical count; inventory accuracy refers to how well the two agree. Companies such as Wal-Mart (see the Breakthrough Box titled "Inventory on a Grand Scale") understand the importance of inventory accuracy and expend considerable effort ensuring it. The question is, How much error is acceptable? If the record shows a balance of 683 of part X and an actual count shows 652, is this within reason? Suppose the actual count shows 750, an excess of 67 over the record; is this any better?

Every production system must have agreement, within some specified range, between what the record says is in inventory and what actually is in inventory. There are many reasons why records and inventory may not agree. For example, an open stockroom area allows items to be removed for both legitimate and unauthorized purposes. The legitimate removal may have been done in a hurry and simply not recorded. Sometimes parts are misplaced, turning up months later. Parts are often stored in several locations, but records may be lost or the location recorded incorrectly. Sometimes stock replenishment orders are recorded as received, when in fact they never were. Occasionally, a group of parts is recorded as removed from inventory, but the customer order is canceled and the parts are replaced in inventory without canceling the record. To keep the production system flowing smoothly without parts shortages and efficiently without excess balances, records must be accurate.

How can a firm keep accurate, up-to-date records? The first general rule is to keep the storeroom locked. If only storeroom personnel have access, and one of their measures of performance for personnel evaluation and merit increases is record accuracy, there is a strong motivation to comply. Every location of inventory storage, whether in a locked storeroom or on the production floor, should have a recordkeeping mechanism. A second way is to convey the importance of accurate records to all personnel and depend on them to assist in this effort. (This all boils down to this: Put a fence that goes all the way to the ceiling around the storage area so that workers cannot climb over to get parts; put a lock on the gate and give one person the key. Nobody can pull parts without having the transaction authorized and recorded.)

Another way to ensure accuracy is to count inventory frequently and match this against records. A widely used method is called *cycle counting*.

Cycle counting

**Cycle counting** is a physical inventory-taking technique in which inventory is counted frequently rather than once or twice a year. The key to effective cycle counting and, therefore, to accurate records lies in deciding which items are to be counted, when, and by whom.

Virtually all inventory systems these days are computerized. The computer can be programmed to produce a cycle count notice in the following cases:

1 When the record shows a low or zero balance on hand. (It is easier to count fewer items.)
2 When the record shows a positive balance but a backorder was written (indicating a discrepancy).
3 After some specified level of activity.
4 To signal a review based on the importance of the item (as in the ABC system) such as in the following table:

| ANNUAL DOLLAR USAGE | REVIEW PERIOD |
|---|---|
| $10,000 or more | 30 days or less |
| $3,000–$10,000 | 45 days or less |
| $250–3,000 | 90 days or less |
| Less than $250 | 180 days or less |

The easiest time for stock to be counted is when there is no activity in the stockroom or on the production floor. This means on the weekends or during the second or third shift, when the facility is less busy. If this is not possible, more careful logging and separation of items are required to count inventory while production is going on and transactions are occurring.

The counting cycle depends on the available personnel. Some firms schedule regular stockroom personnel to do the counting during lulls in the regular working day. Other companies hire private firms that come in and count inventory. Still other firms use full-time cycle counters who do nothing but count inventory and resolve differences with the records. Although this last method sounds expensive, many firms believe that it is actually less costly than the usual hectic annual inventory count generally performed during the two- or three-week annual vacation shutdown.

The question of how much error is tolerable between physical inventory and records has been much debated. Some firms strive for 100 percent accuracy, whereas others accept 1, 2, or 3 percent error. The accuracy level often recommended by experts is $\pm 0.2$ percent for A items, $\pm 1$ percent for B items, and $\pm 5$ percent for C items. Regardless of the specific accuracy decided on, the important point is that the level be dependable so that safety stocks may be provided as a cushion. Accuracy is important for a smooth production process so that customer orders can be processed as scheduled and not held up because of unavailable parts.

## INVENTORY CONTROL IN SERVICES

To demonstrate how inventory control is conducted in service organizations, we have selected two areas to describe: a department store and an automobile service agency.

McKESSON, A LEADING DISTRIBUTOR OF PHARMACEUTICALS, USES TECHNOLOGY EFFECTIVELY. THE MACHINE ON THE MAN'S ARM COMBINES A SCANNER, COMPUTER, AND TWO-WAY RADIO TO KEEP TRACK OF INVENTORY AND SPEED ORDER DELIVERY.

Stockkeeping unit (SKU)

**Department Store Inventory Policy** The common term used to identify an inventory item is the **stockkeeping unit (SKU).** The SKU identifies each item, its manufacturer, and its cost. The number of SKUs becomes large even for small departments. For example, if towels carried in a domestic items department are obtained from three manufacturers in three quality levels, three sizes (hand towel, face towel, and bath towel), and four colors, there are 108 different items ($3 \times 3 \times 3 \times 4$). Even if towels are sold only in sets of three pieces (hand towel, face towel, and bath towel), the number of SKUs needed to identify the towel sets is $3 \times 3 \times 1 \times 4 = 36$. Depending on the store, a housewares department may carry 3,000 to 4,000 SKUs, and a linen and domestic items department may carry 5,000 to 6,000.

Such large numbers mean that individual economic order quantities cannot be calculated for each item by hand. How, then, does a department keep tabs on its stock and place orders for replenishment?

Generally, housewares are divided into staple and promotional items. Within these major divisions, further classifications are used, such as cookware and tableware. Also, items are frequently classified by price, as \$5 items, \$4, \$3, and so forth.

The housewares department usually purchases from a distributor rather than directly from a manufacturer. The use of a distributor, who handles products from many manufacturers, has the advantage of fewer orders and faster shipping time (shorter lead time). Further, the distributor's sales personnel may visit the housewares department weekly and count all the items they supply to this department. Then, in line with the replenishment level that has been established by the buyer, the distributor's salesperson places orders for the buyer. This saves the department time in counting inventory and placing orders. The typical lead time for receipt of stock from a housewares distributor is two or three days. The safety stock, therefore, is quite low, and the buyer establishes the replenishment level so as to supply only enough items for the two- to three-day lead time, plus expected demand during the period until the distributor's salesperson's next visit.

Note that a formal method of estimating stockout and establishing safety stock levels is usually not followed because the number of items is too great. Instead, the total value of items in the department is monitored. Thus, replenishment levels are set by dollar allocation.

Through planning, each department has an established monthly value for inventory. By tabulating inventory balance, monthly sales, and items on order, an "open-to-buy" figure is determined. ("Open-to-buy" is the unspent portion of the budget.) This dollar amount is the sum available to the buyer for the following month. When an increase in demand is expected (Christmas, Mother's Day, and so forth), the allocation of funds to the department is increased, resulting in a larger open-to-buy position. Then the replenishment levels are raised in line with the class of goods, responding to the demand increases, thereby creating a higher stock of goods on hand.

In practice, the open-to-buy funds are largely spent during the first days of the month. However, the buyer tries to reserve some funds for special purchases or to restock fast-moving items. Promotional items in housewares are controlled individually (or by class) by the buyer.

**Maintaining an Auto Replacement Parts Inventory** A firm in the automobile service business purchases most of its parts supplies from a small number of distributors. Franchised new-car dealers purchase the great bulk of their supplies from the auto manufacturer. A dealer's demand for auto parts originates primarily from the general public and other departments of the agency, such as the service department or body shop. The problem, in this case, is to determine the order quantities for the several thousand items carried.

A franchised auto agency of medium size may carry a parts inventory valued in the area of $500,000. Because of the nature of this industry, alternate uses of funds are plentiful, so opportunity costs are high. For example, dealers may lease cars, carry their own contracts, stock a larger new-car inventory, or open sidelines such as tire shops, trailer sales, or recreational vehicle sales—all with potentially high returns. This creates pressure to carry a low inventory level of parts and supplies while still meeting an acceptable service level.

Although some dealers still order their inventory by hand, most use computers and software packages provided by car manufacturers. For both manual and computerized systems, an ABC classification works well. Expensive and high-turnover supplies are counted and ordered frequently; low-cost items are ordered in large quantities at infrequent intervals. A common drawback of frequent order placement is the extensive amount of time needed to physically put the items on the shelves and log them in. (However, this restocking procedure does not greatly add to an auto agency's cost because parts department personnel generally do this during slow periods.)

A great variety of computerized systems are currently in use. In a monthly reordering system, for example, the items to be ordered are counted and the number on hand is entered into the computer. By subtracting the number on hand from the previous month's inventory and adding the orders received during the month, the usage rate is determined. Some programs use exponential smoothing forecasts, whereas others use a weighted-average method. For the weighted-average method, the computer program stores the usage rate for, say, four previous months. Then, with the application of a set of weighting factors, a forecast is made in the same manner as described in Chapter11. This works as follows: Suppose usage of a part during January, February, March, and April was 17, 19, 11, and 23, respectively, and the set of corresponding weights was 0.10, 0.20, 0.30, and 0.40. Thus, the forecast for May is $0.10(17) + 0.20(19) + 0.30(11) + 0.40(23)$, or 18 units. If safety stock were included and equal to one-month demand, then 36 units would be ordered (one-month demand plus one-month safety stock) less whatever is on hand at the time of order placement. This simple two-month rule allows for forecast usage during the lead time plus the review period, with the balance providing the safety stock.

The computer output provides a useful reference file, identifying the item, cost, order size, and the number of units on hand. The output itself constitutes the purchase order and is sent to the distributor or factory supply house. The simplicity in this is attractive because, once the forecast weighting is selected, all that needs to be done is to input the number of units of each item on hand. Thus, negligible computation is involved, and very little preparation is needed to send the order out.

## CONCLUSION

This chapter introduced the two main classes of demand: (1) independent demand referring to the external demand for a firm's end product and (2) dependent demand, usually referring—within the firm—to the demand for items created because of the demand for more complex items of which they are a part. Most industries have items in both classes. In manufacturing, for example, independent demand is common for finished products, service and repair parts, and operating supplies; and dependent demand is common for those parts and materials needed to produce the end product. In wholesale and retail sales of consumer goods, most demand is independent—each item is an end item, with the wholesaler or retailer doing no further assembly or fabrication.

Independent demand, the focus of this chapter, is based on statistics. In the fixed–order quantity and fixed–time period models, the influence of service level was shown on safety stock and reorder point determinations. Two special-purpose models—price-break and single-period—were also presented.

To distinguish among item categories for analysis and control, the ABC method was offered. The importance of inventory accuracy was also noted, and cycle counting was described. Finally, brief descriptions of inventory procedures in a department store and an auto parts shop illustrated some of the simpler ways nonmanufacturing firms control their inventory.

In this chapter we also pointed out that inventory reduction requires a knowledge of the operating system. It is not simply a case of selecting an inventory model off the shelf and plugging in some numbers. In the first place, a model might not even be appropriate. In the second case, the numbers might be full of errors or even based on erroneous data. Determining order quantities is often referred to as a trade-off problem; that is, trading off holding costs for setup costs. Note that companies really want to reduce both.

The simple fact is that firms have very large investments in inventory, and the cost to carry this inventory runs from 25 to 35 percent of the inventory's worth annually. Therefore, a major goal of most firms today is to reduce inventory.

A caution is in order, though. The formulas in this chapter try to minimize cost. Bear in mind that a firm's objective should be something like "making money"—so be sure that reducing inventory cost does, in fact, support this. Usually, correctly reducing inventory lowers cost, improves quality and performance, and enhances profit.

## KEY TERMS

**Inventory** The stock of any item or resource used in a organization.

**Independent demand** The demands for various items are unrelated to each other.

**Dependent demand** The need for any one item is a direct result of the need for some other item, usually an item of which it is a part.

**Fixed–order quantity model (or Q model)** An inventory control model where the amount requisitioned is fixed and the actual ordering is triggered by inventory dropping to a specified level of inventory.

**Fixed–time period model (or P model)** An inventory control model that specifies inventory is ordered at the end of a predetermined time period. The interval of time between orders is fixed and the order quantity varies.

**Inventory position** The amount on-hand plus on-order minus backordered quantities. In the case where inventory has been allocated for special purposes, the inventory position is reduced by these allocated amounts.

Safety stock The amount of inventory carried in addition to the expected demand.

Cycle counting A physical inventory-taking technique in which inventory is counted on a frequent basis rather than once or twice a year.

Stockkeeping unit (SKU) A common term used to identify an inventory item.

## FORMULA REVIEW

**$Q$ model. Total annual cost for an ordered $Q$, a per-unit cost $C$, setup cost $S$, and per-unit holding cost $H$.**

[13.1] $$TC = DC + \frac{D}{Q}S + \frac{Q}{2}H$$

**$Q$ model. Optimal (or economic) order quantity.**

[13.2] $$Q_{\text{opt}} = \sqrt{\frac{2DS}{H}}$$

**$Q$ model. Reorder point $R$ based on average daily demand $\bar{d}$ and lead time $L$ in days.**

[13.3] $$R = \bar{d}L$$

**$Q$ model. Reorder point providing a safety stock of $z\sigma_L$.**

[13.4] $$R = \bar{d}L + z\sigma_L$$

**Average daily demand over a period of $n$ days.**

[13.5] $$\bar{d} = \frac{\sum_{i=1}^{n} d_i}{n}$$

**Standard deviation of demand over a period of $n$ days.**

[13.6] $$\sigma_d = \sqrt{\frac{\sum_{i=1}^{n} (d_i - \bar{d})^2}{n}}$$

**Standard deviation of a series of independent demands.**

[13.7] $$\sigma_s = \sqrt{\sigma_1^2 + \sigma_2^2 + \cdots + \sigma_i^2}$$

**$Q$ model. Safety stock calculation.**

[13.8] $$SS = z\sigma_L$$

**$P$ model. Safety stock calculation.**

[13.9] $$SS = z\sigma_{T+L}$$

**$P$ model. Optimal order quantity in a fixed-period system with a review period of $T$ days and lead time of $L$ days.**

[13.10] $$q = \bar{d}(T + L) + z\sigma_{T+L} - I$$

**$P$ model. Standard deviation of a series of independent demands over the review period $T$ and lead time $L$.**

[13.11] $$\sigma_{T+L} = \sqrt{\sum_{i=1}^{T+L} \sigma_{d_i}^2}$$

**$Q$ model. Optimal order quantity based on an order cost $S$, holding cost as a percentage ($i$) of the unit cost ($C$).**

[13.12] $$Q = \sqrt{\frac{2DS}{iC}}$$

**Single-period model. Probability of selling the last unit as a ratio of marginal loss and marginal profit.**

[13.13] $$P \geq \frac{ML}{MP + ML}$$

# SOLVED PROBLEMS

## SOLVED PROBLEM 1

Items purchased from a vendor cost \$20 each, and the forecast for next year's demand is 1,000 units. If it costs \$5 every time an order is placed for more units and the storage cost is \$4 per unit per year, what quantity should be ordered each time?

*a.* What is the total ordering cost for a year?

*b.* What is the total storage cost for a year?

### Solution

The quantity to be ordered each time is

$$Q = \sqrt{\frac{2DS}{H}} = \sqrt{\frac{2(1{,}000)5}{4}} = 50 \text{ units}$$

*a.* The total ordering cost for a year is

$$\frac{D}{Q}S = \frac{1{,}000}{50}(\$5) = \$100$$

*b.* The storage cost for a year is

$$\frac{Q}{2}H = \frac{50}{2}(\$4) = \$100$$

## SOLVED PROBLEM 2

Daily demand for a product is 120 units, with a standard deviation of 30 units. The review period is 14 days and the lead time is 7 days. At the time of review 130 units are in stock. If only a 1 percent risk of stocking out is acceptable, how many units should be ordered?

### Solution

$$\sigma_{T+L} = \sqrt{(14+7)(30)^2} = \sqrt{18{,}900} = 137.5$$

$$z = 2.33$$

$$q = \bar{d}(T+L) + z\sigma_{T+L} - I$$

$$= 120(14+7) + 2.33(137.5) - 130$$

$$= 2{,}710 \text{ units}$$

## SOLVED PROBLEM 3

A company currently has 200 units of a product on hand that it orders every two weeks when the salesperson visits the premises. Demand for the product averages 20 units per day with a standard deviation of 5 units. Lead time for the product to arrive is seven days. Management has a goal of a 95 percent probability of not stocking out for this product.

The salesperson is due to come in late this afternoon when 180 units are left in stock (assuming that 20 are sold today). How many units should be ordered?

### Solution

Given $I = 180$, $T = 14$, $L = 7$, $\bar{d} = 20$

$$\sigma_{T+L} = \sqrt{21(5)^2} = 23$$

$$z = 1.64$$

$$q = \bar{d}(T+L) + z\sigma_{T+L} - I$$

$$= 20(14+7) + 1.64(23) - 180$$

$$q = 278 \text{ units}$$

## REVIEW AND DISCUSSION QUESTIONS

1 Distinguish between dependent and independent demand in a McDonald's restaurant, in an integrated manufacturer of personal copiers, and in a pharmaceutical supply house.
2 Distinguish between in-process inventory, safety stock inventory, and seasonal inventory.
3 Discuss the nature of the costs that affect inventory size.
4 Under which conditions would a plant manager elect to use a fixed–order quantity model as opposed to a fixed–time period model? What are the disadvantages of using a fixed–time period ordering system?
5 Discuss the general procedure for determining the order quantity when price breaks are involved. Would there be any differences in procedure if holding cost were a fixed percentage of price rather than a constant amount?
6 What two basic questions must be answered by an inventory-control decision rule?
7 Discuss the assumptions that are inherent in production setup cost, ordering cost, and carrying costs. How valid are they?
8 "The nice thing about inventory models is that you can pull one off the shelf and apply it so long as your cost estimates are accurate." Comment.
9 Which type of inventory system would you use in the following situations?
*a.* Supplying your kitchen with fresh food.
*b.* Obtaining a daily newspaper.
*c.* Buying gas for your car.
To which of these items do you impute the highest stockout cost?
10 Why is it desirable to classify items into groups, as the ABC classification does?
11 What kind of policy or procedure would you recommend to improve the inventory operation in a department store? What advantages and disadvantages does your system have vis-à-vis the department store inventory operation described in this chapter?

## PROBLEMS

1 Ray's Satellite Emporium wishes to determine the best order size for its best-selling satellite dish (model TS111). Ray has estimated the annual demand for this model at 1,000 units. His cost to carry one unit is $100 per year per unit, and he has estimated that each order costs $25 to place. Using the EOQ model, how many should Ray order each time?

1. Order 22

2 Dunstreet's Department Store would like to develop an inventory ordering policy of a 95 percent probability of not stocking out. To illustrate your recommended procedure, use as an example the ordering policy for white percale sheets.

Demand for white percale sheets is 5,000 per year. The store is open 365 days per year. Every two weeks (14 days) inventory is counted and a new order is placed. It takes 10 days for the sheets to be delivered. Standard deviation of demand for the sheets is five per day. There are currently 150 sheets on hand.

How many sheets should you order?

2. $z = 1.64$
$q = 219$

3 Charlie's Pizza orders all of its pepperoni, olives, anchovies, and mozzarella cheese to be shipped directly from Italy. An American distributor stops by every four weeks to take orders. Because the orders are shipped directly from Italy, they take three weeks to arrive.

Charlie's Pizza uses an average of 150 pounds of pepperoni each week, with a standard deviation of 30 pounds. Charlie's prides itself on offering only the best-quality ingredients and a high level of service, so it wants to ensure a 98 percent probability of not stocking out on pepperoni.

Assume that the sales representative just walked in the door and there are currently 500 pounds of pepperoni in the walk-in cooler. How many pounds of pepperoni would you order?

3. $q = 713$

4 Given the following information, formulate an inventory management system. The item is demanded 50 weeks a year.

| | | | |
|---|---|---|---|
| Item cost | $10.00 | Standard deviation of weekly demand | 25 per week |
| Order cost | $250.00 | | |
| Annual holding cost (%) | 33% of item cost | Lead time | 1 week |
| Annual demand | 25,750 | Service probability | 95% |
| Average demand | 515 per week | | |

*a.* State the order quantity and reorder point.
*b.* Determine the annual holding and order costs.

4. *a.* R = 556; Q = 1975
*b.* Holding cost = $3,258.75
Ordering cost = $3,259.49
*c.* Holding cost = $3,300.00
Ordering cost = $3,218.75
Savings = $643.24

*c.* If a price break of $50 per order was offered for purchase quantities of over 2,000, would you take advantage of it? How much would you save annually?

5. $q = 137$ chips
max $q = 172$ chips

5 Lieutenant Commander Data is planning to make his monthly (every 30 days) trek to Gamma Hydra City to pick up a supply of isolinear chips. The trip will take Data about two days. Before he leaves, he calls in the order to the GHC Supply Store. He uses chips at an average rate of five per day (seven days per week) with a standard deviation of demand of one per day. He needs a 98 percent service probability. If he currently has 35 chips in inventory, how many should he order? What is the most he will ever have to order?

6. *a.* $Q = 1{,}225$.
$R = 824$.
*b.* $q = 390 -$ (Inventory on hand)

6 Jill's Job Shop buys two parts (Tegdiws and Widgets) for use in its production system from two different suppliers. The parts are needed throughout the entire 52-week year. Tegdiws are used at a relatively constant rate and are ordered whenever the remaining quantity drops to the reorder level. Widgets are ordered from a supplier who stops by every three weeks. Data for both products are as follows:

| ITEM | TEGDIW | WIDGET |
|---|---|---|
| Annual demand | 10,000 | 5,000 |
| Holding cost (% of item cost) | 20% | 20% |
| Setup or order cost | $150.00 | $25.00 |
| Lead time | 4 weeks | 1 week |
| Safety stock | 55 units | 5 units |
| Item cost | $10.00 | $2.00 |

*a.* What is the inventory control system for Tegdiws? That is, what is the reorder quantity and what is the reorder point?
*b.* What is the inventory control system for Widgets?

7. *a.* $Q = 100$ units.
*b.* Order 100 each time.

7 Demand for an item is 1,000 units per year. Each order placed costs $10; the annual cost to carry items in inventory is $2 each.
*a.* In what quantities should the item be ordered?
*b.* Supposing a $100 discount on each order is given if orders are placed in quantities of 500 or more. Should orders be placed in quantities of 500, or should you stick to the decision you made in *a*?

8. $Q = 3120$
$R = 1569$
Service probability = 84.8%

8 The annual demand for a product is 15,600 units. The weekly demand is 300 units with a standard deviation of 90 units. The cost to place an order is $31.20, and the time from ordering to receipt is four weeks. The annual inventory carrying cost is $0.10 per unit. Find the reorder point necessary to provide a 98 percent service probability.

Suppose the production manager is asked to reduce the safety stock of this item by 50 percent. If she does so, what will the new service probability be?

9. $q = 1755$

9 Daily demand for a product is 100 units, with a standard deviation of 25 units. The review period is 10 days and the lead time is 6 days. At the time of review there are 50 units in stock. If 98 percent service probability is desired, how many units should be ordered?

10. *a.* $Q = 89$
*b.* $223.61
*c.* $223.61

10 Item X is a standard item stocked in a company's inventory of component parts. Each year the firm, on a random basis, uses about 2,000 of item X, which costs $25 each. Storage costs, which include insurance and cost of capital, amount to $5 per unit of average inventory. Every time an order is placed for more item X, it costs $10.
*a.* Whenever item X is ordered, what should the order size be?
*b.* What is the annual cost for ordering item X?
*c.* What is the annual cost for storing item X?

11. $Q = 2000$
$R = 1082$
Service probability = 84%

11 Annual demand for a product is 13,000 units; weekly demand is 250 units with a standard deviation of 40 units. The cost of placing an order is $100, and the time from ordering to receipt is four weeks. The annual inventory carrying cost is $0.65 per unit. To provide a 98 percent service probability, what must the reorder point be?

Suppose the production manager is told to reduce the safety stock of this item by 100 units. If this is done, what will the new service probability be?

12. $TC = \$56{,}370$; 1,000 at a time.

12 A particular raw material is available to a company at three different prices, depending on the size of the order:

| | |
|---|---|
| Less than 100 pounds | $20 per pound |
| 100 pounds to 999 pounds | $19 per pound |
| More than 1,000 pounds | $18 per pound |

The cost to place an order is $40. Annual demand is 3,000 units. Holding (or carrying) cost is 25 percent of the material price.

What is the economic order quantity to buy each time?

13 In the past, Taylor Industries has used a fixed–time period inventory system that involved taking a complete inventory count of all items each month. However, increasing labor costs are forcing Taylor Industries to examine alternative ways to reduce the amount of labor involved in inventory stockrooms, yet without increasing other costs, such as shortage costs. Here is a random sample of 20 of Taylor's items.

| ITEM NUMBER | ANNUAL USAGE | ITEM NUMBER | ANNUAL USAGE |
|---|---|---|---|
| 1 | $ 1,500 | 11 | $13,000 |
| 2 | 12,000 | 12 | 600 |
| 3 | 2,200 | 13 | 42,000 |
| 4 | 50,000 | 14 | 9,900 |
| 5 | 9,600 | 15 | 1,200 |
| 6 | 750 | 16 | 10,200 |
| 7 | 2,000 | 17 | 4,000 |
| 8 | 11,000 | 18 | 61,000 |
| 9 | 800 | 19 | 3,500 |
| 10 | 15,000 | 20 | 2,900 |

*a.* What would you recommend Taylor do to cut back its labor cost? (Illustrate using an ABC plan.)

*b.* Item 15 is critical to continued operations. How would you recommend it be classified?

13. *a.* Cut costs using an ABC inventory plan. A items (4, 13, 18); B items (2, 5, 8, 10, 11, 14, 16); C items (remainder).
*b.* Item 15 is critical and should be classified as an A item.

14 Gentle Ben's Bar and Restaurant uses 5,000 quart bottles of an imported wine each year. The effervescent wine costs $3 per bottle and is served only in whole bottles because it loses its bubbles quickly. Ben figures that it costs $10 each time an order is placed, and holding costs are 20 percent of the purchase price. It takes three weeks for an order to arrive. Weekly demand is 100 bottles (closed two weeks per year) with a standard deviation of 30 bottles.

Ben would like to use an inventory system that minimizes inventory cost and will provide a 95 percent service probability.

*a.* What is the economic quantity for Ben to order?

*b.* At what inventory level should he place an order?

14. *a.* 408 bottles.
*b.* $R = 385$ bottles.

15 Retailers Warehouse (RW) is an independent supplier of household items to department stores. RW attempts to stock enough items for a 98 percent service probability.

A stainless steel knife set is one item it stocks. Demand (2,400 sets per year) is relatively stable over the entire year. Whenever new stock is ordered, a buyer must assure that numbers are correct for stock on hand and then phone in a new order. The total cost involved to place an order is about $5. RW figures that holding inventory in stock and paying for interest on borrowed capital, insurance, and so on adds up to about $4 holding cost per unit per year.

Analysis of the past data shows that the standard deviation of demand from retailers is about four units per day for a 365-day year. Lead time to get the order is seven days.

*a.* What is the economic order quantity?

*b.* What is the reorder point?

15. *a.* $Q = 77$.
*b.* $R = 68$.

16 Daily demand for a product is 60 units with a standard deviation of 10 units. The review period is 10 days, and lead time is 2 days. At the time of review there are 100 units in stock. If 98 percent service probability is desired, how many units should be ordered?

16. $q = 691$

17 University Drug Pharmaceuticals orders its antibiotics every two weeks (14 days) when a salesperson visits from one of the pharmaceutical companies. Tetracycline is one of its most prescribed antibiotics, with average daily demand of 2,000 capsules. The standard deviation of daily demand was derived from examining prescriptions filled over the past three months and was found to be 800 capsules. It takes five days for the order to arrive. University Drug would like to satisfy 99 percent of the prescriptions. The salesperson just arrived, and there are currently 25,000 capsules in stock.

How many capsules should be ordered?

17. $\sigma_{T+L} = 3487$
$q = 21{,}112$

18 Sally's Silk Screening produces specialty T-shirts that are primarily sold at special events. She is trying to decide how many to produce for an upcoming event. During the event itself, which lasts one day, Sally can sell T-shirts for $20 apiece. However, when the event ends,

18. Produce 600 T-shirts.

any unsold T-shirts are sold for $4 apiece. It costs Sally $8 to make a specialty T-shirt. Using Sally's estimate of demand that follows, how many T-shirts should she produce for the upcoming event?

| DEMAND | PROBABILITY |
|---|---|
| 300 | .05 |
| 400 | .10 |
| 500 | .40 |
| 600 | .30 |
| 700 | .10 |
| 800 | .05 |

19. *a.* Similar to Exhibit 13.10
*b.* 2,400 dozen.
*c.* $P = .50$

19 Famous Albert prides himself on being the Cookie King of the West. Small, freshly baked cookies are the specialty of his shop. Famous Albert has asked for help to determine the number of cookies he should make each day. From an analysis of past demand he estimates demand for cookies as

| DEMAND | PROBABILITY OF DEMAND |
|---|---|
| 1,800 dozen | 0.05 |
| 2,000 | 0.10 |
| 2,200 | 0.20 |
| 2,400 | 0.30 |
| 2,600 | 0.20 |
| 2,800 | 0.10 |
| 3,000 | 0.05 |

Each dozen sells for $0.69 and costs $0.49, which includes handling and transportation. Cookies that are not sold at the end of the day are reduced to $0.29 and sold the following day as day-old merchandise.

*a.* Construct a table showing the profits or losses for each possible quantity.
*b.* What is the optimal number of cookies to make?
*c.* Solve this problem by using marginal analysis.

20. $Q = 216$
$R = 34$

20 Sarah's Muffler Shop has one standard muffler that fits a large variety of cars. Sarah wishes to establish a reorder point system to manage inventory of this standard muffler. Use the following information to determine the best order size and the reorder point:

| | | | |
|---|---|---|---|
| Annual demand | 3,500 mufflers | Ordering cost | $50 per order |
| Standard deviation of daily demand | 6 mufflers per working day | Service probability | 90% |
| Item cost | $30 per muffler | Lead time | 2 working days |
| Annual holding cost | 25% of item value | Working days | 300 per year |

21. *a.* ABC
*b.* A items (f, k, q);
B items (c, e, g, n, r, t);
C items (remainder)

21 Alpha Products, Inc., is having a problem trying to control inventory. There is insufficient time to devote to all its items equally. Here is a sample of some items stocked, along with the annual usage of each item expressed in dollar volume.

| ITEM | ANNUAL DOLLAR USAGE | ITEM | ANNUAL DOLLAR USAGE |
|---|---|---|---|
| a | $ 7,000 | k | $80,000 |
| b | 1,000 | l | 400 |
| c | 14,000 | m | 1,100 |
| d | 2,000 | n | 30,000 |
| e | 24,000 | o | 1,900 |
| f | 68,000 | p | 800 |
| g | 17,000 | q | 90,000 |
| h | 900 | r | 12,000 |
| i | 1,700 | s | 3,000 |
| j | 2,300 | t | 32,000 |

*a.* Can you suggest a system for allocating control time?
*b.* Specify where each item from the list would be placed.

22 After graduation, you decide to go into a partnership in an office supply store that has existed for a number of years. Walking through the store and stockrooms, you find a great discrepancy in service levels. Some spaces and bins for items are completely empty; others have supplies that are covered with dust and have obviously been there a long time. You decide to take on the project of establishing consistent levels of inventory to meet customer demands. Most of your supplies are purchased from just a few distributors that call on your store once every two weeks. 22. $\bar{d} = \frac{5000}{365}$ $q = 257$

You choose, as your first item for study, computer printer paper. You examine the sales records and purchase orders and find that demand for the past 12 months was 5,000 boxes. Using your calculator you sample some days' demands and estimate that the standard deviation of daily demand is 10 boxes. You also search out these figures:

Cost per box of paper: $11.

Desired service probability: 98 percent.

Store is open every day.

Salesperson visits every two weeks.

Delivery time following visit is three days.

Using your procedure, how many boxes of paper would be ordered if, on the day the salesperson calls, 60 boxes are on hand?

23 A distributor of large appliances needs to determine the order quantities and reorder points for the various products it carries. The following data refer to a specific refrigerator in its product line: 23. *a.* $Q = 32$. *b.* $R = 28$

| | |
|---|---|
| Cost to place an order | $100 |
| Holding cost | 20 percent of product cost per year |
| Cost of refrigerator | $500 each |
| Annual demand | 500 refrigerators |
| Standard deviation during lead time | 10 refrigerators |
| Lead time | 7 days |

Consider an even daily demand and a 365-day year.
*a.* What is the economic order quantity?
*b.* If the distributor wants a 97 percent service probability, what reorder point, $R$, should be used?

24 It is your responsibility, as the new head of the automotive section of Nichols Department Store, to ensure that reorder quantities for the various items have been correctly established. You decide to test one item and choose Michelin tires, XW size 185 × 14 BSW. A perpetual inventory system has been used, so you examine this as well as other records and come up with the following data: 24. *a.* $Q = 76$ *b.* $R = 25$

| | |
|---|---|
| Cost per tire | $35 each |
| Holding cost | 20 percent of tire cost per year |
| Demand | 1,000 per year |
| Ordering cost | $20 per order |
| Standard deviation of daily demand | 3 tires |
| Delivery lead time | 4 days |

Because customers generally do not wait for tires but go elsewhere, you decide on a service probability of 98 percent. Assume the demand occurs 365 days per year.
*a.* Determine the order quantity.
*b.* Determine the reorder point.

25 UA Hamburger Hamlet (UAHH) places a daily order for its high-volume items (hamburger patties, buns, milk, and so on). UAHH counts its current inventory on hand once per day and phones in its order for delivery 24 hours later. Determine the number of hamburgers UAHH 25. 729 hamburgers.

should order for the following conditions:

| | |
|---|---|
| Average daily demand | 600 |
| Standard deviation of demand | 100 |
| Desired service probability | 99% |
| Hamburger inventory | 800 |

26. 5,000 pounds.

26 CU, Incorporated, (CUI) produces copper contacts that it uses in switches and relays. CUI needs to determine the order quantity, $Q$, to meet the annual demand at the lowest cost. The price of copper depends on the quantity ordered. Here are price-break and other data for the problem:

| | |
|---|---|
| Price of copper: | $0.82 per pound up to 2,499 pounds |
| | $0.81 per pound for orders between 2,500 and 4,999 pounds |
| | $0.80 per pound for orders greater than 5,000 pounds |
| Annual demand: | 50,000 pounds per year |
| Holding cost: | 20 percent per unit per year of the price of the copper |
| Ordering cost: | $30 |

Which quantity should be ordered?

27. A items (5, 3);
B items (4, 7, 9);
C items (remainder).

27 DAT, Inc., produces digital audiotapes to be used in the consumer audio division. DAT lacks sufficient personnel in its inventory supply section to closely control each item stocked, so it has asked you to determine an ABC classification. Here is a sample from the inventory records:

| Item | Average Monthly Demand | Price per Unit | Item | Average Monthly Demand | Price per Unit |
|---|---|---|---|---|---|
| 1 | 700 | $6.00 | 6 | 100 | 10.00 |
| 2 | 200 | 4.00 | 7 | 3,000 | 2.00 |
| 3 | 2,000 | 12.00 | 8 | 2,500 | 1.00 |
| 4 | 1,100 | 20.00 | 9 | 500 | 10.00 |
| 5 | 4,000 | 21.00 | 10 | 1,000 | 2.00 |

Develop an ABC classification for these 10 items.

28. *a.* $Q = 540$
$R = 280$
*b.* $R = 339$

28 A local service station is open 7 days per week, 365 days per year. Sales of 10W40 grade premium oil average 20 cans per day. Inventory holding costs are $0.50 per can per year. Ordering costs are $10 per order. Lead time is two weeks. Backorders are not practical—the motorist drives away.

*a.* Based on these data, choose the appropriate inventory model and calculate the economic order quantity and reorder point. Describe in a sentence how the plan would work. Hint: Assume demand is deterministic.

*b.* The boss is concerned about this model because demand really varies. The standard deviation of demand was determined from a data sample to be 6.15 cans per day. The manager wants a 99.5 percent service probability. Determine a new inventory plan based on this information and the data in *a*. Use $Q_{opt}$ from *a*.

29. $q = 23.41 \sim 24$.

29 Dave's Auto Supply custom mixes paint for its customers. The shop performs a weekly inventory count of the main colors that are used for mixing paint. Determine the amount of white paint that should be ordered using the following information:

| | |
|---|---|
| Average weekly demand | 20 gallons |
| Standard deviation of demand | 5 gallons/week |
| Desired service probability | 98% |
| Current inventory | 25 gallons |
| Lead time | 1 week |

## CASE: HEWLETT-PACKARD—SUPPLYING THE DESKJET PRINTER IN EUROPE

The DeskJet printer was introduced in 1988 and has become one of Hewlett–Packard's (HP's) most successful products. Sales have grown steadily, reaching a level of over 600,000 units in 1990. Unfortunately, inventory growth has tracked sales growth closely. HP's distribution centers are filled with pallets of the DeskJet printer. Worse yet, the organization in Europe claims that inventory levels there need to be raised even further to maintain satisfactory product availability.

### THE DESKJET SUPPLY CHAIN

The network of suppliers, manufacturing sites, distribution centers (DCs), dealers, and customers for the DeskJet product comprise the DeskJet supply chain (see Exhibit 13.15). HP in Vancouver does manufacturing. There are two key stages in the manufacturing process: (1) printed circuit assembly and test (PCAT) and (2) final assembly and test (FAT). PCAT involves the assembly and testing of electronic components (like integrated circuits, read-only memories, and raw printed circuit boards) to make logic boards used in the printer. FAT involves the assembly of other subassemblies (like motors, cables, keypads, plastic chassis, gears, and the printed circuit assemblies from PCAT) to produce a working printer, as well as the final testing of the printer. The components needed for PCAT and FAT are sourced from other HP divisions as well as from external suppliers worldwide.

Selling the DeskJet in Europe requires customizing the printer to meet the language and power supply requirements of the local countries, a process known as "localization." Specifically, the localization of the DeskJet of different countries involves assembling the appropriate power supply module, which reflects the correct voltage requirements (110 or 220) and power cord plug, and packaging it with the working printer and a manual written in the appropriate language. Currently, the final test is done with the actual power supply module included with the printer. Hence, the finished products of the factory are "localized" versions of the printer destined for all the different countries. For the European Market six different versions are currently produced. These are designated A, AA, AB, AQ, AU, and AY as indicated in the Bills of Materials shown in Exhibit 13.16.

The total factory throughput time through the PCAT and FAT stages is about one week. The transportation time from Vancouver to the European DC is five weeks. The long shipment time to Europe is due to ocean transit and the time to clear customs and duties at port of entry. The plant sends a weekly shipment of printers to the DC in Europe.

The printer industry is highly competitive. Resellers want to carry as little inventory as possible. Consequently there has been increasing pressure for HP as a manufacturer to provide high levels of availability at the DC. In response, management has decided to stock the DCs so that a high level of availability is maintained.

EXHIBIT 13.15

HP DeskJet Supply Chain

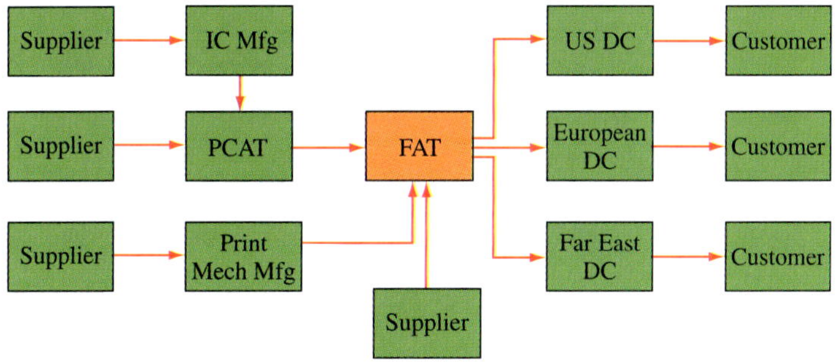


Key: IC Mfg—Integrated Circuit Manufacturing
PCAT—Printed Circuit Assembly and Test
FAT—Final Assembly and Test
Print Mech Mfg—Print Mechanism Manufacturing

EXHIBIT 13.16

HP DeskJet Bill of Materials

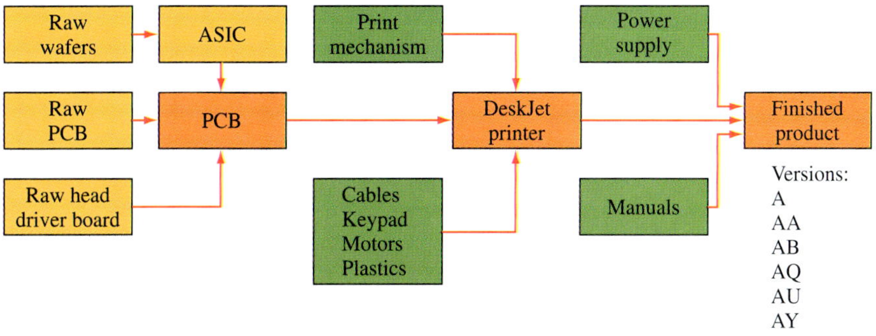

EXHIBIT 13.17

## DeskJet Demand Data from Europe

Excel: HP DeskJet

| EUROPE OPTIONS | NOV. | DEC. | JAN. | FEB. | MAR. | APR. | MAY. | JUN. | JUL. | AUG. | SEP. | OCT. |
|---|---|---|---|---|---|---|---|---|---|---|---|---|
| A | 80 | – | 60 | 90 | 21 | 48 | – | 9 | 20 | 54 | 84 | 42 |
| AB | 20,572 | 20,895 | 19,252 | 11,052 | 19,864 | 20,316 | 13,336 | 10,578 | 6,095 | 14,496 | 23,712 | 9,792 |
| AU | 4,564 | 3,207 | 7,485 | 4,908 | 5,295 | 90 | – | 5,004 | 4,385 | 5,103 | 4,302 | 6,153 |
| AA | 400 | 255 | 408 | 645 | 210 | 87 | 432 | 816 | 430 | 630 | 456 | 273 |
| AQ | 4,008 | 2,196 | 4,761 | 1,953 | 1,008 | 2,358 | 1,676 | 540 | 2,310 | 2,046 | 1,797 | 2,961 |
| AY | 248 | 450 | 378 | 306 | 219 | 204 | 248 | 484 | 164 | 363 | 384 | 234 |
| Total | 29,872 | 27,003 | 32,344 | 18,954 | 26,617 | 23,103 | 15,692 | 17,431 | 13,405 | 22,692 | 30,735 | 19,455 |

### THE INVENTORY SERVICE CRISIS

To limit the amount of inventory throughout the DeskJet supply chain and at the same time provide the high level of service needed has been quite a challenge to Vancouver's management. The manufacturing group has been very successful in reducing the uncertainties caused by delivery to the European DC. Forecasting demand in Europe, though, is a significant problem. It has become common to have product shortages for model demands from some countries, while inventory of other models keeps piling up. In the past, the target inventory levels at the DCs were based on safety stocks that were a result of some judgmental rule of thumb. Specifically, target inventory levels, equal to one-month average sales, were set for each model carried in the DC. Now, however, if seems that the increasing difficulty of getting accurate forecasts means the safety stock rules should be revisited.

HP has put together a team of employees to help implement a scientifically based safety stock system that will be responsive to forecast errors and replenishment lead times. They are to recommend a method for calculating appropriate safety stock levels for the various DeskJet models carried in the European DC. The team has a good sample of demand data that can be used for developing the safety stock methodology (see Exhibit 13.17). HP hopes this new methodology will solve the inventory and service problem.

One issue that continually comes up is the choice of inventory carrying cost to be used in safety stock analyses. Estimates within the company range from 12 percent (HP's cost of debt plus some warehousing expenses) to 60 percent (based on the ROI expected of new product development projects). Management has decided to use 25 percent for this study. Assume that all printers cost an average of approximately $250 each to produce and ship to Europe. Another issue is the choice of safety stock probability for the model. The company has decided to use a probability of 98 percent, a number that marketing feels is appropriate.

### THE DISTRIBUTION PROCESS

The DCs have traditionally envisioned their process as a simple, straight-line, standardized process. There are four process stops:

1. Receive (complete) products from various suppliers and stock them.
2. Pick the various products needed to fill a customer order.
3. Shrink-wrap the complete order and label it.
4. Ship the order via the appropriate carrier.

The DeskJet printer fits well into the standard process. In contrast, other products, such as personal computers and monitors, require special processing called "integration," which includes addition of an appropriate keyboard and manual for the destination country. Although this extra processing does not require much extra labor, it is difficult to accommodate in the standard process and disrupts the material flow. There is considerable frustration within DC management regarding the support of assembly processes. In general, DC management stresses the DCs' role as warehouses and the need to continue to do what they are best at—distribution.

Top management, though, feels that integration of the product at the warehouse is extremely valuable because it allows generic products to be sent to the DC with final configuration of the product done just prior to shipment to the customer. Rather than the factory making products specific to a country, generic products could be produced and shipped to Europe. Management is very interested in studying the value of this approach as it could be applied to the DeskJet printers.

### QUESTIONS

1. Develop an inventory model for managing the DeskJet printers in Europe assuming that the Vancouver plant continues to produce the 6 models sold in Europe. Using the data in Exhibit 13.17, apply your model and calculate the expected yearly investment in DeskJet printer inventory in the Europe DC.
2. Compare your results from question 1 to the current policy of carrying one month's average inventory at the DC.
3. Evaluate the idea of supplying generic printers to the Europe DC and integrating the product by packaging the power supply and the instruction manual at the DC just prior to delivery to the European resellers. Focus on the impact on DC inventory investment in this analysis.
4. What is your recommendation to HP?

## SELECTED BIBLIOGRAPHY

Brooks, R. B., and L. W. Wilson. *Inventory Record Accuracy: Unleashing the Power of Cycle Counting*. Essex Junction, VT: Oliver Wight, 1993.

Silver, E., D. Pyke, and R. Peterson. *Decision Systems for Inventory Management and Production Planning and Control.* 3rd ed. New York: Wiley, 1998.

Sipper, D., and R. L. Bulfin, Jr. *Production Planning, Control, and Integration.* New York: McGraw-Hill, 1997.

Tersine, R. J. *Principles of Inventory and Materials Management.* 4th ed. New York: North-Holland, 1994.

Vollmann, T. E.; W. L. Berry; and D. C. Whybark. *Manufacturing Planning and Control Systems.* 4th ed. Burr Ridge, IL: Richard D. Irwin, 1997.

Wild, T. *Best Practices in Inventory Management.* New York: Wiley, 1998.

Zipkin, P. H. *Foundations of Inventory Management.* Chicago: Irwin/McGraw-Hill, 2000.

## FOOTNOTES

1 M. Truby, *The Detroit News,* February 3, 2000, p. B1.

2 As previously discussed, the standard deviation of a sum of independent variables equals the square root of the sum of the variances.

3 $P$ is actually a cumulative probability because the sale of the $n$th unit depends not only on exactly $n$ being demanded but also on the demand for any number greater than $n$.

4 The Pareto principle is also widely applied in quality problems through the use of Pareto charts. (See Chapter 7.)

*chapter fourteen*

# MATERIAL REQUIREMENTS PLANNING

## CHAPTER OUTLINE AND KEY TERMS

14

# FROM PUSH TO PULL

In the 1980s manufacturing led the national economy in the move from batch-oriented data processing systems to online transaction processing systems. The focus was MRP (initially material requirements planning, evolving to manufacturing resource planning), which later evolved into enterprise resource planning (ERP). It has been a long ride, and anyone who has been there for the duration deserves a rest.

However, the winds of change are blowing again as yet another new paradigm comes roaring through manufacturing. Specifically, we are speaking of the change in our economy from a build-to-stock to a build-to-order model of doing business.

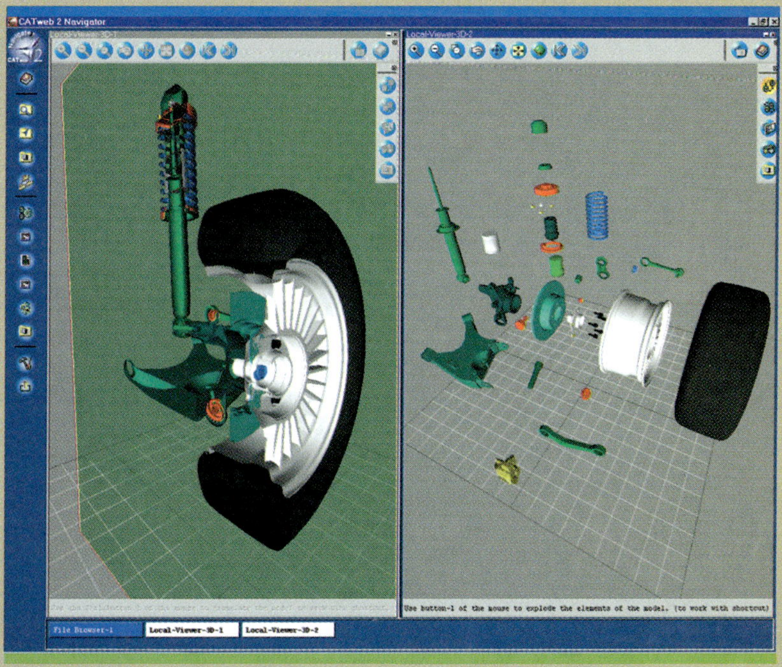


The weak link in the build-to-stock model is inventory management, and this can be traced to an even weaker link, reliance upon sales forecasts. A build-to-order model begins with the order, not the forecast. The old problem of coordinating the procurement of parts, production of the product, and shipping the product still exists.

Today the term *flow management* is used to describe new hybrid production planning systems that combine the information integration and planning capability of MRP with the response of a JIT kanban system. Major ERP software vendors such as Oracle, SAP, and i2 Technologies are selling these new systems.

Essentially, the idea with flow management is to produce a constantly changing mix of products, a mix that is based on current orders, using a stream of parts that are supplied just-in-time. It's important not to be tricked into thinking that all these new words really represent something new. Actually, flow manufacturing just combines things that have been used for years. In this case the combination is JIT kanban logic, MRP logic for planning material requirements, and client–server ERP.

As Virginia Slims ads used to say, "You've come a long way, baby." So has material requirements planning (MRP) come a long way. From humble beginnings computing the schedules and amounts of materials required, MRP has grown to become fully integrated, interactive, real-time systems capable of multisite global applications. In this chapter we go back to the beginning and introduce the basic MRP system and take you through the logic and calculations of scheduling and materials ordering.

Material requirements planning (MRP)

**Material requirements planning (MRP)** systems have been installed almost universally in manufacturing firms, even those considered small. The reason is that MRP is a logical, easily understandable approach to the problem of determining the number of parts, components, and materials needed to produce each end item. MRP also provides the schedule specifying when each of these materials, parts, and components should be ordered or produced.

Manufacturing resource planning (MRP II)

The original MRP planned only materials. However, as computer power grew and applications expanded, so did the breadth of MRP. Soon it considered resources as well as materials and was called **MRP II,** standing for **manufacturing resource planning.** A complete MRP program included 20 or so modules controlling the entire system from order entry through scheduling, inventory control, finance, accounting, accounts payable, and so on. Today MRP impacts the entire system and includes just-in-time, kanban, and computer-integrated manufacturing (CIM).

Cross Functional

All firms maintain a bill of materials file (BOM), which is simply the sequence of everything that goes into the final product. It can be called a *product structure tree,* a *schematic,* or a *flow diagram,* which shows the order of creating the item. Also maintained by all firms is an inventory file. This database contains specifications about each item, where it is purchased or produced, and how long it takes. MRP in its basic form is a computer program determining how much of each item is needed and when it is needed to complete a specified number of units in a specific time period. MRP does this by reaching into the bill of materials file and inventory records file to create a time schedule and the number of units needed at each step in the process.

MRP is based on dependent demand. Dependent demand is caused by the demand for a higher-level item. Tires, wheels, and engines are dependent demand items based on the demand for automobiles.

Determining the number of dependent demand items needed is essentially a straightforward multiplication process. If one Part A takes five parts of B to make, then five parts of

THE ABILITY OF MANUFACTURERS TO KEEP TRACK OF INVENTORY, DUE DATES, PRODUCTION SCHEDULES, WORK LOADS, AND CAPACITY ARE VITAL AND MRP SYSTEMS OFFER A NUMBER OF BENEFITS FOR ASSEMBLY-TYPE OPERATIONS. MRP IS ESPECIALLY USEFUL IN INDUSTRIES WITH COMPLEX PRODUCTS, VARYING DUE DATES, AND FLUCTUATING DEMAND.

A require 25 parts of B. The basic difference in independent demand covered in the previous chapter and dependent demand covered in this chapter is as follows: If Part A is sold outside the firm, the amount of Part A that we sell is uncertain. We need to create a forecast using past data or do something like a market analysis. Part A is an independent item. However, Part B is a dependent part and its use depends on Part A. The number of B needed is simply the number of A times five. As a result of this type of multiplication, the requirements of other dependent demand items tend to become more and more lumpy as we go farther down into the product creation sequence. Lumpiness means that the requirements tend to bunch or lump rather than having an even dispersal. This is also caused by the way manufacturing is done. When manufacturing occurs in lots, items needed to produce the lot are withdrawn from inventory in quantities (perhaps all at once) rather than one at a time.

The main purpose of this chapter is to explain MRP more thoroughly and to demonstrate its use. We show that just-in-time (JIT) systems and MRP are not necessarily competing ways for production but can work effectively together.

## WHERE MRP CAN BE USED

MRP is being used in a variety of industries with a job-shop environment (meaning that a number of products are made in batches using the same productive equipment). The list in Exhibit 14.1 includes process industries, but note that the processes mentioned are confined to job runs that alternate output product and do not include continuous processes such as petroleum or steel.

As you can see in the exhibit, MRP is most valuable to companies involved in assembly operations and least valuable to those in fabrication.

One more point to note: MRP does not work well in companies that produce a low number of units annually. Especially for companies producing complex, expensive products requiring advanced research and design, experience has shown that lead times tend to be too long and too uncertain, and the product configuration too complex, for MRP to

EXHIBIT 14.1

Industry Applications and Expected Benefits of MRP

| INDUSTRY TYPE | EXAMPLES | EXPECTED BENEFITS |
|---|---|---|
| Assemble-to-stock | Combines multiple component parts into a finished product, which is then stocked in inventory to satisfy customer demand. Examples: watches, tools, appliances. | High |
| Fabricate-to-stock | Items are manufactured by machine rather than assembled from parts. These are standard stock items carried in anticipation of customer demand. Examples: piston rings, electrical switches. | Low |
| Assemble-to-order | A final assembly is made from standard options that the customer chooses. Examples: trucks, generators, motors. | High |
| Fabricate-to-order | Items are manufactured by machine to customer order. These are generally industrial orders. Examples: bearings, gears, fasteners. | Low |
| Manufacture-to-order | Items are fabricated or assembled completely to customer specification. Examples: turbine generators, heavy machine tools. | High |
| Process | Includes industries such as foundries, rubber and plastics, specialty paper, chemicals, paint, drug, food processors. | Medium |

handle. Such companies need the control features that network scheduling techniques offer; they would be better off using project scheduling methods (covered previously in Chapter 3).

## A SIMPLE MRP EXAMPLE

Before discussing details of an MRP system, we briefly explain how quantities are calculated, lead times are offset, and order releases and receipts are established.

Suppose that we are to produce Product T, which is made of two parts U and three parts V. Part U, in turn, is made of one part W and two parts X. Part V is made of two parts W and two parts Y. Exhibit 14.2 shows the product structure tree of Product T. By simple computation, we calculate that if 100 units of T are required, we need

$$
\begin{array}{lll}
\text{Part U:} & 2 \times \text{number of Ts} = \quad 2 \times 100 & = 200 \\
\text{Part V:} & 3 \times \text{number of Ts} = \quad 3 \times 100 & = 300 \\
\text{Part W:} & \left\{ \begin{array}{l} 1 \times \text{number of Us} = \quad 1 \times 200 \\ +2 \times \text{number of Vs} = \quad +2 \times 300 \end{array} \right\} & = 800 \\
\text{Part X:} & 2 \times \text{number of Us} = \quad 2 \times 200 & = 400 \\
\text{Part Y:} & 2 \times \text{number of Vs} = \quad 2 \times 300 & = 600
\end{array}
$$

Now consider the time needed to obtain these items, either to produce the part internally or to obtain it from an outside vendor. Assume, now, that T takes one week to make; U, 2 weeks; V, 2 weeks; W, 3 weeks; X, 1 week; and Y, 1 week. If we know when Product T is required, we can create a schedule chart specifying when all materials must be ordered and received to meet the demand for T. Exhibit 14.3 shows which items are needed and when. We have thus created a material requirements plan based on the demand for Product T, the knowledge of how T is made, and the time needed to obtain each part.

From this simple illustration, it is apparent that developing a material requirements plan manually for thousands or even hundreds of items would be impractical—a great deal of computation is needed, and a tremendous amount of data must be available about the inventory status (number of units on hand, on order, and so forth) and about the product structure (how the product is made and how many units of each material are required). Because we are compelled to use a computer, our emphasis from here on in this chapter is to discuss the files needed for a computer program and the general makeup of the system. However, the basic logic of the program is essentially the same as that for our simple example.

EXHIBIT 14.2

Product Structure Tree for Product T

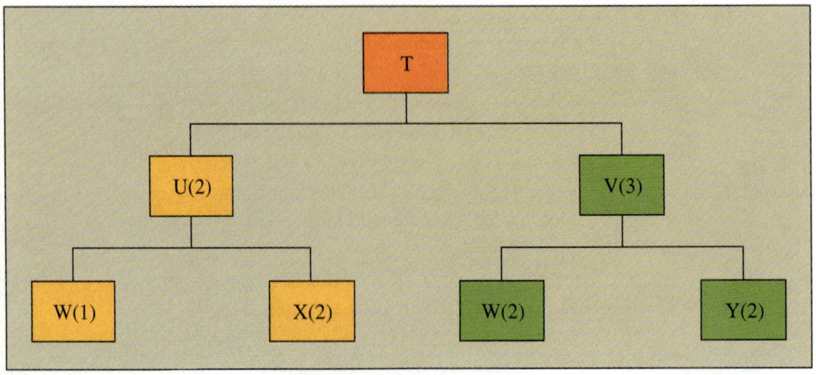

EXHIBIT 14.3

Material Requirements Plan for Completing 100 Units of Product T in Period 7

| | | Week | | | | | | | |
|---|---|---|---|---|---|---|---|---|---|
| | | 1 | 2 | 3 | 4 | 5 | 6 | 7 | |
| T | Required date | | | | | | | 100 | T lead time = 1 week |
| | Order placement | | | | | | 100 | | |
| U | Required date | | | | | | 200 | | U lead time = 2 weeks |
| | Order placement | | | | 200 | | | | |
| V | Required date | | | | | | 300 | | V lead time = 2 weeks |
| | Order placement | | | | 300 | | | | |
| W | Required date | | | | 800 | | | | W lead time = 3 weeks |
| | Order placement | 800 | | | | | | | |
| X | Required date | | | | 400 | | | | X lead time = 1 week |
| | Order placement | | | 400 | | | | | |
| Y | Required date | | | | 600 | | | | Y lead time = 1 week |
| | Order placement | | | 600 | | | | | |

## MASTER PRODUCTION SCHEDULE

Generally, the master schedule deals with end items. If the end item is quite large or quite expensive, however, the master schedule may schedule major subassemblies or components instead.

All production systems have limited capacity and limited resources. This presents a challenging job for the master scheduler. Although the aggregate plan provides the general range of operation, the master scheduler must specify exactly what is to be produced. These decisions are made while responding to pressures from various functional areas, such as the sales department (meet the customer's promised due date), finance (minimize inventory), management (maximize productivity and customer service, minimize resource needs), and manufacturing (have level schedules and minimize setup time).

To determine an acceptable feasible schedule to be released to the shop, trial master production schedules are run through the MRP program. The resulting planned order releases (the detailed production schedules) are checked to make sure that resources are available and that the completion times are reasonable. What appears to be a feasible master schedule may turn out to require excessive resources once the product explosion has taken place and materials, parts, and components from lower levels are determined. If this does happen (the usual case), the master production schedule is then modified with these limitations and the MRP program is run again. To ensure good master scheduling, the master scheduler (the human being) must

- Include all demands from product sales, warehouse replenishment, spares, and interplant requirements.
- Never lose sight of the aggregate plan.
- Be involved with customer order promising.
- Be visible to all levels of management.
- Objectively trade off manufacturing, marketing, and engineering conflicts.
- Identify and communicate all problems.

Cross Functional

The upper portion of Exhibit 14.4 shows an aggregate plan for the total number of mattresses planned per month, without regard for mattress type. The lower portion shows a master production schedule specifying the exact type of mattress and the quantity planned for production by week. The next level down (not shown) would be the MRP program that develops detailed schedules showing when cotton batting, springs, and hardwood are needed to make the mattresses.

EXHIBIT 14.4

The Aggregate Plan and the Master Production Schedule for Mattresses

Aggregate Production Plan for Mattresses

| Month | 1 | 2 |
|---|---|---|
| Mattress production | 900 | 950 |

Master Production Schedule for Mattress Models

| | 1 | 2 | 3 | 4 | 5 | 6 | 7 | 8 |
|---|---|---|---|---|---|---|---|---|
| Model 327 | 200 | | | 400 | | 200 | 100 | |
| Model 538 | | 100 | 100 | | 150 | | 100 | |
| Model 749 | | | 100 | | | 200 | | 200 |

EXHIBIT 14.5

Master Production Schedule Time Fences

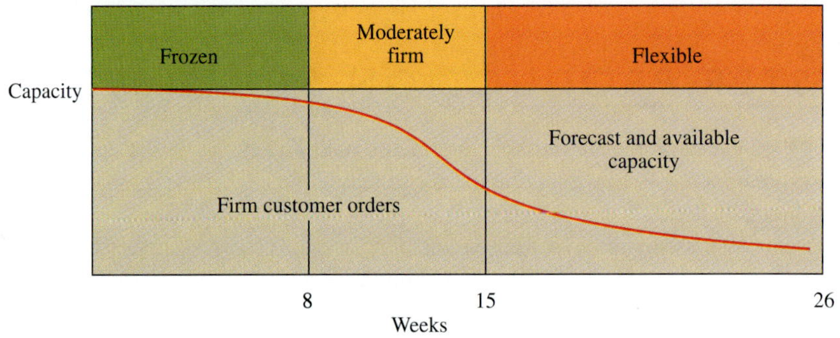


Master production schedule (MPS)

To again summarize the planning sequence, the aggregate production plan, discussed in Chapter 12, specifies product groups. It does not specify exact items. The next level down in the planning process is the master production schedule. The **master production schedule (MPS)** is the time-phased plan specifying how many and when the firm plans to build each end item. For example, the aggregate plan for a furniture company may specify the total volume of mattresses it plans to produce over the next month or next quarter. The MPS goes the next step down and identifies the exact size mattresses and their qualities and styles. All of the mattresses sold by the company would be specified by the MPS. The MPS also states period by period (usually weekly) how many and when each of these mattress types is needed.

Still further down the disaggregation process is the MRP program, which calculates and schedules all raw materials, parts, and supplies needed to make the mattress specified by the MPS.

## TIME FENCES

The question of flexibility within a master production schedule depends on several factors: production lead time, commitment of parts and components to a specific end item, relationship between the customer and vendor, amount of excess capacity, and the reluctance or willingness of management to make changes.

The purpose of time fences is to maintain a reasonably controlled flow through the production system. Unless some operating rules are established and adhered to, the system could be chaotic and filled with overdue orders and constant expediting.

Exhibit 14.5 shows an example of a master production schedule time fence. Management defines *time fences* as periods of time having some specified level of opportunity for the customer to make changes. (The customer may be the firm's own marketing department, which may be considering product promotions, broadening variety, or the like.) Note in the exhibit that for the next eight weeks, this particular master schedule is frozen. Each firm has its own time fences and operating rules. Under these rules, *frozen* could be defined as anything from absolutely no changes in one company to only the most minor of changes in another. *Moderately firm* may allow changes in specific products within a product group so long as parts are available. *Flexible* may allow almost any variations in products, with the provisions that capacity remains about the same and that there are no long lead time items involved.

## MATERIAL REQUIREMENTS PLANNING (MRP) SYSTEMS

As we stated previously, based on a *master schedule* derived from a *production plan,* a *material requirements planning (MRP) system* creates schedules identifying the specific parts and materials required to produce end items, the exact numbers needed, and the dates when orders for these materials should be released and be received or completed within the production cycle. MRP systems use a computer program to carry out these operations. Most firms have used computerized inventory systems for years, but they were independent of the scheduling system; MRP links them together.

### PURPOSES OF MRP

The main purposes of a basic MRP system are to control inventory levels, assign operating priorities for items, and plan capacity to load the production system. The *theme* of MRP is "getting the right materials to the right place at the right time."

The *objectives* of inventory management under an MRP system are the same as under any inventory management system: to improve customer service, minimize inventory investment, and maximize production operating efficiency.

The *philosophy* of material requirements planning is that materials should be expedited (hurried) when their lack would delay the overall production schedule, and de-expedited (delayed) when the schedule falls behind and postpones their need. Traditionally, and perhaps still typically, when an order is behind schedule, significant effort is spent trying to get it back on schedule. However, the opposite is not always true; when an order, for whatever reason, has its completion date delayed, the appropriate adjustments are not made in the schedule. This results in a one-sided effort—later orders are hurried, but early orders are not rescheduled for later. Aside from perhaps using scarce capacity, it is preferable not to have raw materials and work-in-process before the actual need because inventories tie up finances, clutter up stockrooms, prohibit design changes, and prevent the cancellation or delay of orders.

## MATERIAL REQUIREMENTS PLANNING SYSTEM STRUCTURE

The material requirements planning portion of manufacturing activities most closely interacts with the master schedule, bill of materials file, inventory records file, and the output reports as shown in Exhibit 14.6.

Each facet of Exhibit 14.6 is detailed in the following sections, but essentially, the MRP system works as follows: Orders for products are used to create a master production schedule, which states the number of items to be produced during specific time periods. A bill of materials file identifies the specific materials used to make each item and the correct quantities of each. The inventory records file contains data such as the number of units on hand and on order. These three sources—master production schedule, bill of materials file, and

EXHIBIT 14.6

Overall View of the Inputs to a Standard Material Requirements Planning Program and the Reports Generated by the Program

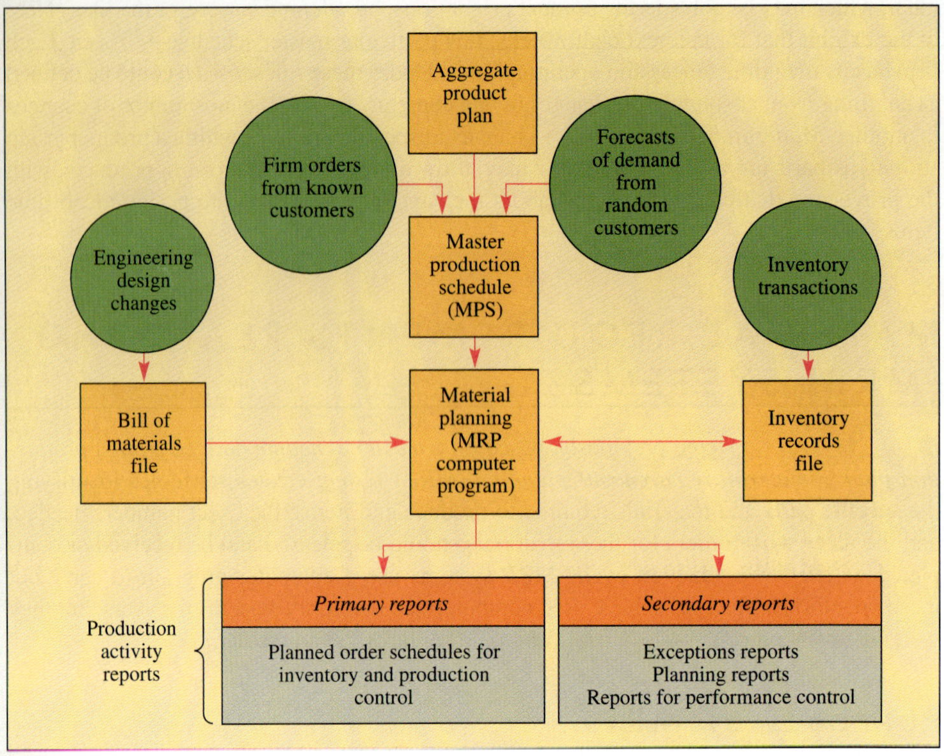


inventory records file—become the data sources for the material requirements program, which expands the production schedule into a detailed order scheduling plan for the entire production sequence.

## DEMAND FOR PRODUCTS

Product demand for end items comes primarily from two main sources. The first is known customers who have placed specific orders, such as those generated by sales personnel, or from interdepartment transactions. These orders usually carry promised delivery dates. There is no forecasting involved in these orders—simply add them up. The second source is forecast demand. These are the normal independent-demand orders; the forecasting models presented in Chapter 11 can be used to predict the quantities. The demand from the known customers and the forecast demand are combined and become the input for the master production schedule.

In addition to the demand for end products, customers also order specific parts and components either as spares, or for service and repair. These demands are not usually part of the master production schedule; instead, they are fed directly into the material requirements planning program at the appropriate levels. That is, they are added in as a gross requirement for that part or component.

## BILL OF MATERIALS FILE

Bill of materials (BOM)

The **bill of materials (BOM)** file contains the complete product description, listing not only the materials, parts, and components but also the sequence in which the product is created. This BOM file is one of the three main inputs to the MRP program. (The other two are the master schedule and the inventory records file.)

Vol. IV "Production Tour of Vision Light System at Federal Signal"

The BOM file is often called the *product structure file* or *product tree* because it shows how a product is put together. It contains the information to identify each item and the quantity used per unit of the item of which it is a part. To illustrate this, consider Product A

Exhibit 14.7

Bill of Materials (Product Structure Tree) for Product A

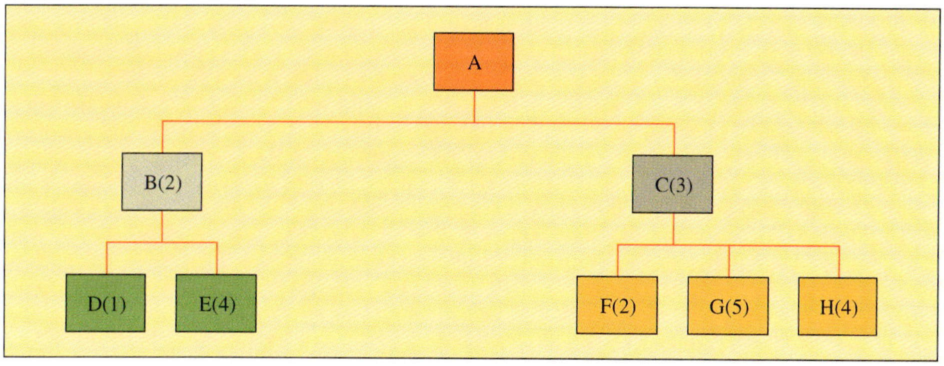


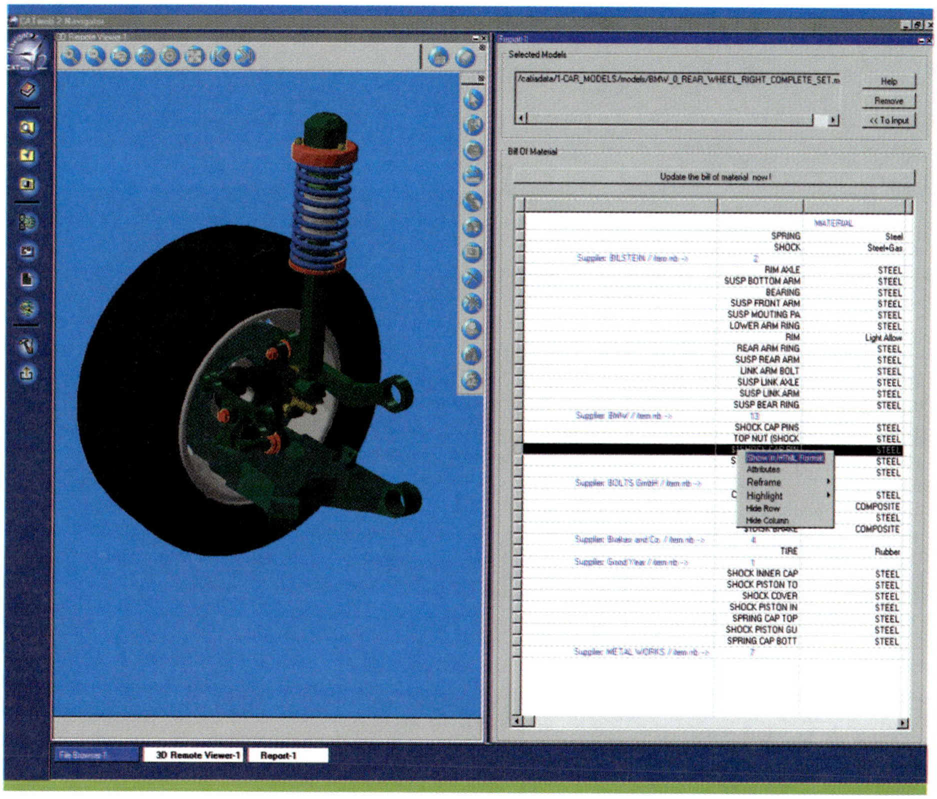


The chapter opening vignette shows the exploded parts view of a wheel assembly. The CATWeb Navigator from IBM gives users the ability to generate in real time the assembled bill of materials of the displayed 3D model.

shown in Exhibit 14.7. Product A is made of two units of Part B and three units of Part C. Part B is made of one unit of Part D and four units of Part E. Part C is made of two units of Part F, five units of Part G, and four units of Part H.

Bill of materials often list parts using an indented structure. This clearly identifies each item and the manner in which it is assembled because each indentation signifies the components of the item. A comparison of the indented parts in Exhibit 14.8 with the item structure in Exhibit 14.7 shows the ease of relating the two displays. From a computer standpoint, however, storing items in indented parts lists is very inefficient. To compute the amount of each item needed at the lower levels, each item would need to be expanded ("exploded") and summed. A more efficient procedure is to store parts data in simple single-level lists. That is, each item and component is listed showing only its parent and the number of units needed per unit of its parent. This avoids duplication because it includes each assembly only once. Exhibit 14.8 shows both the indented parts list and the single-level parts list for Product A.

EXHIBIT 14.8

Parts List in an Indented Format and in a Single-Level List

| Indented Parts List | | | Single-Level Parts List | |
|---|---|---|---|---|
| A | | | A | |
| | B(2) | | | B(2) |
| | | D(1) | | C(3) |
| | | E(4) | B | |
| | C(3) | | | D(1) |
| | | F(2) | | E(4) |
| | | G(5) | C | |
| | | H(4) | | F(2) |
| | | | | G(5) |
| | | | | H(4) |

EXHIBIT 14.9

Product L Hierarchy in (a) Expanded to the Lowest Level of Each Item in (b)

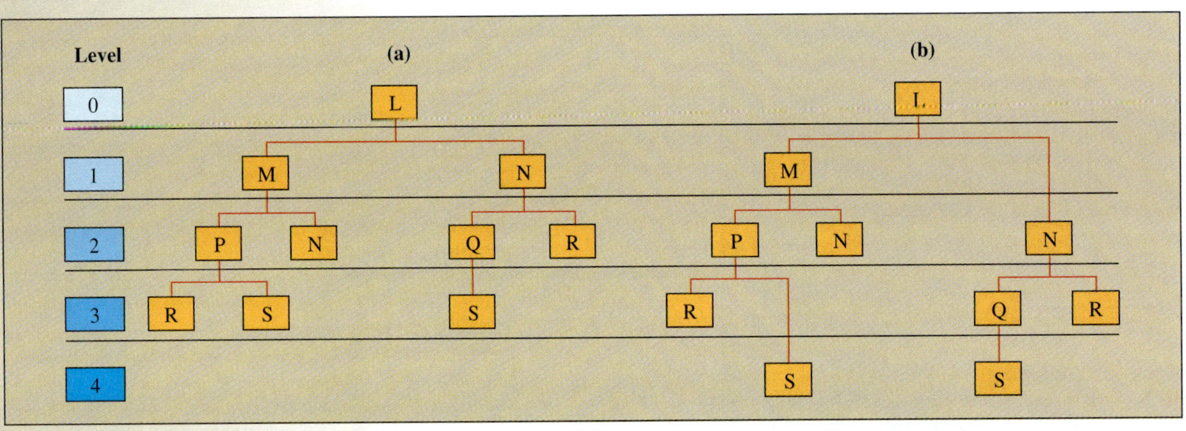


A *modular* bill of materials is the term for a buildable item that can be produced and stocked as a subassembly. It is also a standard item with no options within the module. Many end items that are large and expensive are better scheduled and controlled as modules (or subassemblies). It is particularly advantageous to schedule subassembly modules when the same subassemblies appear in different end items. For example, a manufacturer of cranes can combine booms, transmissions, and engines in a variety of ways to meet a customer's needs. Using a modular bill of materials simplifies the scheduling and control and also makes it easier to forecast the use of different modules. Another benefit in using modular bills is that if the same item is used in a number of products, then the total inventory investment can be minimized.

A *planning* bill of materials includes items with fractional options. (A planning bill can specify, for example, 0.3 of a part. What that means is that 30 percent of the units produced contain that part and 70 percent do not.)

**Low-Level Coding** If all identical parts occur at the same level for each end product, the total number of parts and materials needed for a product can be computed easily. Consider Product L shown in Exhibit 14.9a. Notice that Item N, for example, occurs both as an input to L and as an input to M. Item N, therefore, needs to be lowered to level 2 (Exhibit 14.9b) to bring all Ns to the same level. If all identical items are placed at the same

Exhibit 14.10

The Inventory Status Record for an Item in Inventory

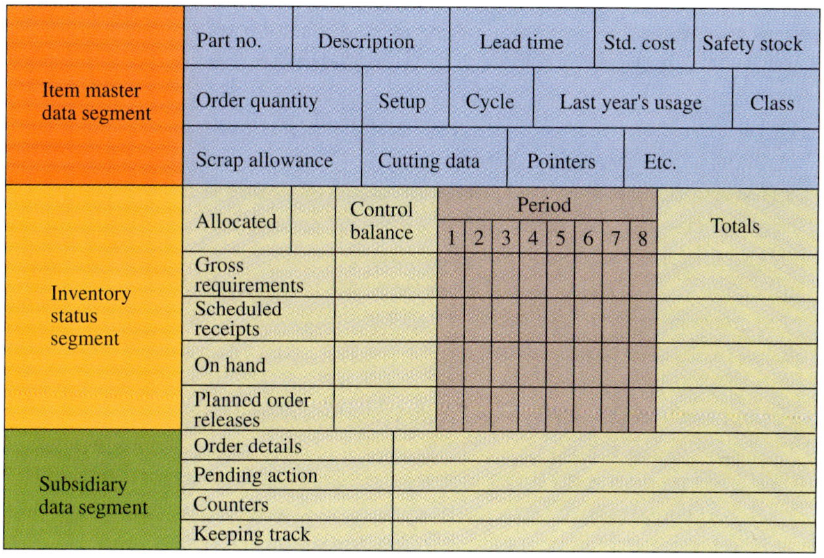


level, it becomes a simple matter for the computer to scan across each level and summarize the number of units of each item required.

## Inventory Records File

The inventory records file can be quite lengthy. Exhibit 14.10 shows the variety of information contained in the inventory records. The MRP program accesses the *status* segment of the record according to specific time periods (called *time buckets* in MRP slang). These records are accessed as needed during the program run.

As we will see, the MRP program performs its analysis from the top of the product structure downward, calculating requirements level by level. There are times, however, when it is desirable to identify the parent item that caused the material requirement. The MRP program allows the creation of a *peg record* file either separately or as part of the inventory record file. Pegging requirements allows us to retrace a material requirement upward in the product structure through each level, identifying each parent item that created the demand.

**Inventory Transactions File** The inventory status file is kept up to date by posting inventory transactions as they occur. These changes occur because of stock receipts and disbursements, scrap losses, wrong parts, canceled orders, and so forth.

## MRP Computer Program

The material requirements planning program operates using information from the inventory records, the master schedule, and the bill of materials. The process of calculating the exact requirements for each item managed by the system is often referred to as the "explosion" process. Working from the top level downward in the bill of materials, requirements from parent items are used to calculate the requirements for component items. Consideration is taken of current on-hand balances, and orders that are scheduled for receipt in the future.

The following is a general description of the MRP explosion process:

1 The requirements for level 0 items, typically referred to as "end items," are retrieved from the master schedule. These requirements are referred to as "gross requirements" by the MRP program. Typically, the gross requirements are scheduled in weekly time buckets.

2 Next, the program uses the current on-hand balance, together with the schedule of orders that will be received in the future to calculate the "net requirements." Net requirements are the amounts that are needed week by week in the future over and above what is currently on hand or committed to through an order already released and scheduled.
3 Using net requirements the program calculates when orders should be received to meet these requirements. This can be a simple process of just scheduling orders to arrive according to the exact net requirements or a more complicated process where requirements are combined for multiple periods. This schedule of when orders should arrive is referred to as "planned-order receipts."
4 Since there is typically a lead time associated with each order, the next step is to find a schedule for when orders are actually released. Offsetting the "planned-order receipts" by the required lead time does this. This schedule is referred to as the "planned-order release."
5 After these four steps have been completed for all the level zero items, the program moves to level 1 items.
6 The gross requirements for each level 1 item are calculated from the planned-order release schedule for the parents of each level 1 item. Any additional independent demand also needs to be included in the gross requirements.
7 After the gross requirements have been determined, net requirements, planned-order receipts, and planned-order releases are calculated as described in steps 2–4 above.
8 This process is then repeated for each level in the bill of materials.

Net change systems

The process of doing these calculations is much simpler than the description as you will see in the example that follows. Typically, the explosion calculations are performed each week or whenever changes have been made to the master schedule. Some MRP programs have the option of generating immediate schedules, called *net change* schedules. **Net change systems** are "activity" driven and requirements and schedules are updated whenever a transaction is processed that has an impact on the item. Net change enables the system to reflect in "real time" the exact status of each item managed by the system.

## AN EXAMPLE USING MRP

Ampere, Inc., produces a line of electric meters installed in residential buildings by electric utility companies to measure power consumption. Meters used on single-family homes are of two basic types for different voltage and amperage ranges. In addition to complete meters, some parts and subassemblies are sold separately for repair or for changeovers to a different voltage or power load. The problem for the MRP system is to determine a production schedule to identify each item, the period it is needed, and the appropriate quantities. This schedule is then checked for feasibility, and the schedule is modified if necessary.

### FORECASTING DEMAND

Demand for the meters and components originates from two sources: regular customers that place firm orders, and unidentified customers that make the normal random demands for these items. The random requirements were forecast using one of the usual techniques described in Chapter 11 and past demand data. Exhibit 14.11 shows the requirement for Meters A and B, Subassembly D, and Part E for a six-month period (months three through eight).

### DEVELOPING A MASTER PRODUCTION SCHEDULE

For the meter and component requirements specified in Exhibit 14.11, assume that the quantities to satisfy the known demands are to be delivered according to customers' delivery

EXHIBIT 14.11

Future Requirements for Meters A and B, Subassembly D, and Part E Stemming from Specific Customer Orders and from Random Sources

| | Meter A | | Meter B | | Subassembly D | | Part E | |
|---|---|---|---|---|---|---|---|---|
| Month | Known | Random | Known | Random | Known | Random | Known | Random |
| 3 | 1,000 | 250 | 400 | 60 | 200 | 70 | 300 | 80 |
| 4 | 600 | 250 | 300 | 60 | 180 | 70 | 350 | 80 |
| 5 | 300 | 250 | 500 | 60 | 250 | 70 | 300 | 80 |
| 6 | 700 | 250 | 400 | 60 | 200 | 70 | 250 | 80 |
| 7 | 600 | 250 | 300 | 60 | 150 | 70 | 200 | 80 |
| 8 | 700 | 250 | 700 | 60 | 160 | 70 | 200 | 80 |

EXHIBIT 14.12

A Master Schedule to Satisfy Demand Requirements as Specified in Exhibit 14.11

| | Week | | | | | | | | |
|---|---|---|---|---|---|---|---|---|---|
| | 9 | 10 | 11 | 12 | 13 | 14 | 15 | 16 | 17 |
| Meter A | 1,250 | | | | 850 | | | | 550 |
| Meter B | 460 | | | | 360 | | | | 560 |
| Subassembly D | 270 | | | | 250 | | | | 320 |
| Part E | 380 | | | | 430 | | | | 380 |

schedules throughout the month, but that the items to satisfy random demands must be available during the first week of the month.

Our schedule assumes that *all* items are to be available the first week of the month. This assumption trial is reasonable because management (in our example) prefers to produce meters in one single lot each month rather than a number of lots throughout the month.

Exhibit 14.12 shows the trial master schedule that we use under these conditions, with demands for months 3 and 4 listed in the first week of each month, or as weeks 9 and 13. For brevity, we will work with only these two demand periods. The schedule we develop should be examined for resource availability, capacity availability, and so on, and then revised and run again. We will stop with our example at the end of this one schedule, however.

## Bill of Materials (Product Structure) File

The product structure for Meters A and B is shown in Exhibit 14.13 in the typical way using low-level coding, in which each item is placed at the lowest level at which it appears in the structure hierarchy. Meters A and B consist of two subassemblies, C and D, and two parts, E and F. Quantities in parentheses indicate the number of units required per unit of the parent item.

Exhibit 14.14 shows an indented parts list for the structure of Meters A and B. As mentioned earlier in the chapter, the BOM file carries all items without indentation for computational ease, but the indented printout clearly shows the manner of product assembly.

## Inventory Records (Item Master) File

The inventory records file would be similar to the one shown in Exhibit 14.10. The difference, as we saw earlier in this chapter, is that the inventory records file also contains much additional data, such as vendor identity, cost, and lead times. For this example, the pertinent

EXHIBIT 14.13

## Product Structure for Meters A and B

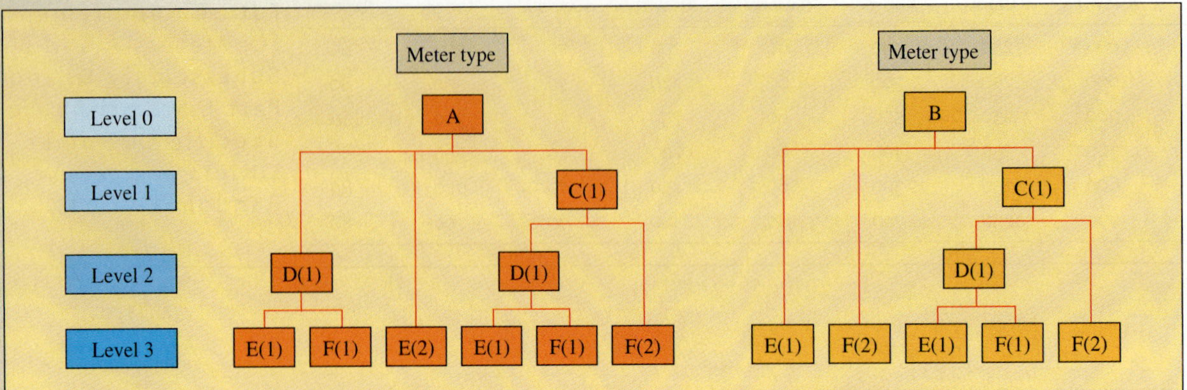


Exhibit shows the subassemblies and parts that make up the meters and shows the numbers of units required per unit of parent in parentheses.

EXHIBIT 14.14

## Indented Parts List for Meter A and Meter B, with the Required Number of Items per Unit of Parent Listed in Parentheses

| METER A | | | | METER B | | | |
|---|---|---|---|---|---|---|---|
| A | | | | B | | | |
| | D(1) | | | | E(1) | | |
| | | E(1) | | | F(2) | | |
| | | F(1) | | | C(1) | | |
| | E(2) | | | | | D(1) | |
| | C(1) | | | | | | E(1) |
| | | D(1) | | | | | F(1) |
| | | | E(1) | | | F(2) | |
| | | | F(1) | | | | |
| | | F(2) | | | | | |

EXHIBIT 14.15

## Number of Units on Hand and Lead Time Data That Would Appear on the Inventory Record File

| ITEM | ON-HAND INVENTORY | LEAD TIME (WEEKS) |
|---|---|---|
| A | 50 | 2 |
| B | 60 | 2 |
| C | 40 | 1 |
| D | 30 | 1 |
| E | 30 | 1 |
| F | 40 | 1 |

data contained in the inventory records file are the on-hand inventory at the start of the program run and the lead times. Taken from the inventory records file, these data are shown in Exhibit 14.15.

## RUNNING THE MRP PROGRAM

The correct conditions are now set to run the MRP computer program: End-item requirements have been established through the master production schedule, while the status of

EXHIBIT 14.16

Material Requirements Planning Schedule for Meters A and B, Subassemblies C and D, and Parts E and F

| Item | | Week 4 | 5 | 6 | 7 | 8 | 9 | 10 | 11 | 12 | 13 |
|---|---|---|---|---|---|---|---|---|---|---|---|
| A | Gross requirements | | | | | | 1,250 | | | | 850 |
| | On hand 50 | | | | | | 50 | | | | |
| | Net requirements | | | | | | 1,200 | | | | |
| (LT = 2) | Planned order receipt | | | | | | 1,200 | | | | |
| | Planned order release | | | | 1,200 | | | | | | |
| B | Gross requirements | | | | | | 460 | | | | 360 |
| | On hand 60 | | | | | | 60 | | | | |
| | Net requirements | | | | | | 400 | | | | |
| (LT = 2) | Planned order receipt | | | | | | 400 | | | | |
| | Planned order release | | | | 400 | | | | | | |
| C | Gross requirements | | | | 400<br>1,200 | | | | | | |
| | On hand 40 | | | | 40 | | | | | | |
| | Net requirements | | | | 1,560 | | | | | | |
| (LT = 1) | Planned order receipt | | | | 1,560 | | | | | | |
| | Planned order release | | | 1,560 | | | | | | | |
| D | Gross requirements | | | 1,560 | 1,200 | | 270 | | | | 250 |
| | On hand 30 | | | 30 | 0 | | 0 | | | | |
| | Net requirements | | | 1,530 | 1,200 | | 270 | | | | |
| (LT = 1) | Planned order receipt | | | 1,530 | 1,200 | | 270 | | | | |
| | Planned order release | | 1,530 | 1,200 | | 270 | | | | | |
| E | Gross requirements | | 1,530 | 1,200 | 2,400<br>400 | 270 | 380 | | | | 430 |
| | On hand 30 | | 30 | 0 | 0 | 0 | 0 | | | | |
| | Net requirements | | 1,500 | 1,200 | 2,800 | 270 | 380 | | | | |
| (LT = 1) | Planned order receipt | | 1,500 | 1,200 | 2,800 | 270 | 380 | | | | |
| | Planned order release | 1,500 | 1,200 | 2,800 | 270 | 380 | | | | | |
| F | Gross requirements | | 1,530 | 3,120<br>1,200 | 800 | 270 | | | | | |
| | On hand 40 | | 40 | 0 | 0 | 0 | | | | | |
| | Net requirements | | 1,490 | 4,320 | 800 | 270 | | | | | |
| (LT = 1) | Planned order receipt | | 1,490 | 4,320 | 800 | 270 | | | | | |
| | Planned order release | 1,490 | 4,320 | 800 | 270 | | | | | | |

inventory and the order lead times are contained in the inventory item master file, and the bill of materials file contains the product structure data. The MRP program now explodes the item requirements according to the BOM file, level by level, in conjunction with the inventory records file. A release date for the net requirements order is offset to an earlier time period to account for the lead time. Orders for parts and subassemblies are added through the inventory file, bypassing the master production schedule, which, ordinarily, does not schedule at a low enough level to include spares and repair parts.

Exhibit 14.16 shows the planned order release dates for this particular run. The following analysis explains the program logic. (We will confine our analysis to the problem of meeting the gross requirements for 1,250 units of Meter A, 460 units of Meter B, 270 units of Subassembly D, and 380 units of Part E, all in Week 9.)

The 50 units of A on hand result in a net requirement of 1,200 units of A. To receive Meter A in Week 9, the order must be placed in Week 7 to account for the two-week lead time. The same procedure follows for Item B, resulting in a planned 400-unit order released in Period 7.

EXHIBIT 14.17

The Identification of the Parent of Items C, D, E, and F and Item Gross Requirements Stated by Specific Weeks

| ITEM | PARENT | NUMBER OF UNITS PER PARENT | RESULTANT GROSS REQUIREMENT | GROSS REQUIREMENT WEEK |
|---|---|---|---|---|
| C | A | 1 | 1,200 | 7 |
| C | B | 1 | 400 | 7 |
| D | A | 1 | 1,200 | 7 |
| D | C | 1 | 1,560 | 6 |
| E | A | 2 | 2,400 | 7 |
| E | B | 1 | 400 | 7 |
| E | D | 1 | 1,530 | 5 |
| E | D | 1 | 1,200 | 6 |
| F | B | 2 | 800 | 7 |
| F | C | 2 | 3,120 | 6 |
| F | D | 1 | 1,200 | 6 |
| F | D | 1 | 1,530 | 5 |

The rationale for these steps is that for an item to be released for processing, all of its components must be available. The planned order release date for the parent item therefore becomes the same gross requirement period for the subitems.

Referring to Exhibit 14.13, level 1, one unit of C is required for each A and each B. Therefore, the gross requirements for C in Week 7 are 1,600 units (1,200 for A and 400 for B.) Taking into account the 40 units on hand and the one-week lead time, 1,560 units of C must be ordered in Week 6.

Level 2 of Exhibit 14.13 shows that one unit of D is required for each A and each C. The 1,200 units of D required for A are gross requirements in Week 7, and the 1,560 units of D for item C are the gross requirements for Week 6. Using the on-hand inventory first and the one-week lead time results in the planned order releases for 1,530 units in Week 5 and 1,200 units in Week 6.

Level 3 contains Items E and F. Because E and F are each used in several places, Exhibit 14.17 is presented to identify more clearly the parent item, the number of units required for each parent item, and the week in which it is required. Two units of Item E are used in each Item A. The 1,200-unit planned order release for A in Period 7 becomes the gross requirement for 2,400 units of E in the same period. One unit of E is used in each B, so the planned order release for 400 units of B in Period 7 becomes the gross requirement for 400 units of E in week 7. Item E is also used in Item D at the rate of one per unit. The 1,530-unit planned order release for D in Period 5 becomes the gross requirement for 1,530 units of E in Period 5 and a 1,500-unit planned order release in Period 4 after accounting for the 30 units on hand and the one-week lead time. The 1,200-unit planned order release for D in Period 6 results in gross requirements for 1,200 units of E in Week 6 and a planned order release for 1,200 units in Week 5.

Item F is used in B, C, and D. The planned order releases for B, C, and D become the gross requirements for F for the same week, except that the planned order releases for 400 units of B and 1,560 of C become gross requirements for 800 and 3,120 units of F because the usage rate is two per unit.

The independent order for 270 units of Subassembly D in Week 9 is handled as an input to D's gross requirements for that week. This is then exploded into the derived requirements for 270 units of E and F. The 380-unit requirement for Part E to meet an independent repair part demand is fed directly into the gross requirements for Part E.

The independent demands for Week 13 have not been expanded as yet.

The bottom line of each item in Exhibit 14.16 is taken as a proposed load on the productive system. The final production schedule is developed manually or with the firm's computerized production package. If the schedule is infeasible or the loading unacceptable, the master production schedule is revised and the MRP package is run again with the new master schedule.

# IMPROVEMENTS IN THE MRP SYSTEM

MRP, as it was originally introduced and as we have discussed it so far in this chapter, considered only materials. Revising the schedule because of capacity considerations was done external to the MRP software program. The schedule was revised because of the capacity constraints and the MRP program was run again. (The Nichols case at the end of this chapter requires that the schedule be revised manually in Question 2 of the case.) The response to all other elements and resource requirements were not part of the system. Later refinements included the capacity of the work centers as part of the software program. Feedback of information was also introduced. We give an example of capacity planning at a work center and a closed-loop system. Following that we discuss MRP II systems.

## COMPUTING WORK CENTER LOAD

The place to start in computing capacity requirements is right from the routing sheets for the jobs scheduled to be processed. Exhibit 5.15 in Chapter 5 shows the routing sheet for a plug assembly. Note that the routing sheet specifies where a job is to be sent, the particular operations involved, and the standard setup time and run time per piece. These are the types of figures used to compute the total work at each work center.

While the routing sheet is a "job view" that follows a particular job around the productive facility, a work center file is the view seen from a work center. Each work center is generally a functionally defined center so that jobs routed to it require the same type of work and the same equipment. From the work center view, if there is adequate capacity, the issue is just sequencing because all jobs will be done on time. (We discuss priority scheduling rules in Chapter 15.) If there is insufficient capacity, however, the problem must be resolved because some jobs will be late unless the schedule is adjusted.

Exhibit 14.18 shows a work center that has various jobs assigned to it. Note that the capacity per week was computed at the bottom of the exhibit at 161.5 hours. The jobs

EXHIBIT 14.18

**Workload for Work Center A**

| Week | Job No. | Units | Setup Time | Run Time per Unit | Total Job Time | Total for Week |
|---|---|---|---|---|---|---|
| 10 | 145 | 100 | 3.5 | .23 | 26.5 | |
| | 167 | 160 | 2.4 | .26 | 44.0 | |
| | 158 | 70 | 1.2 | .13 | 10.3 | |
| | 193 | 300 | 6.0 | .17 | 57.0 | 137.8 |
| 11 | 132 | 80 | 5.0 | .36 | 33.8 | |
| | 126 | 150 | 3.0 | .22 | 36.0 | |
| | 180 | 180 | 2.5 | .30 | 56.5 | |
| | 178 | 120 | 4.0 | .50 | 64.0 | 190.3 |
| 12 | 147 | 90 | 3.0 | .18 | 19.2 | |
| | 156 | 200 | 3.5 | .14 | 31.5 | |
| | 198 | 250 | 1.5 | .16 | 41.5 | |
| | 172 | 100 | 2.0 | .12 | 14.0 | |
| | 139 | 120 | 2.2 | .17 | 22.6 | 128.8 |

**Computing Work Center Capacity**

The available capacity in standard hours is 161.5 hours per five-day week, calculated as (2 machines) × (2 shifts) (10 hours/shift) (85% machine utilization) (95% efficiency).

EXHIBIT 14.19

Scheduled Workload for Work Center A

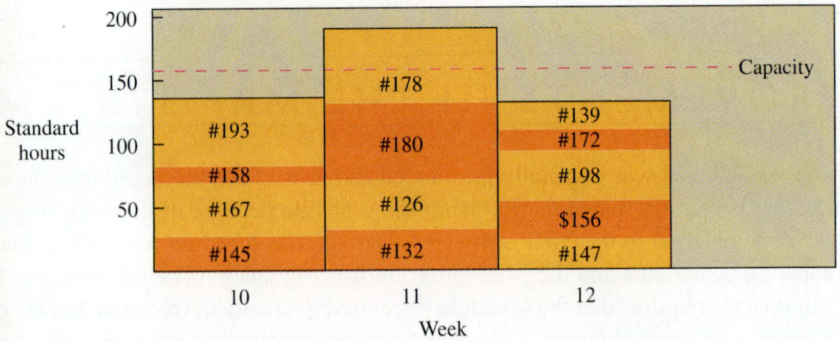


scheduled for the three weeks result in two weeks planned under work center capacity, and one week over capacity.

Exhibit 14.18 uses the terms *utilization* and *efficiency*. In this exhibit, utilization refers to the actual time that the machines are used. Efficiency refers to how well the machine is performing while it is being used. Efficiency is usually defined as a comparison to a defined standard output or an engineering design rate. For instance, a machine used for six hours of an eight-hour shift is utilized 6/8, or 75 percent. If the standard output for that machine is defined as 200 parts per hour and an average of 250 parts are made, then efficiency is 125 percent. Note that in these definitions, efficiency can be more than 100 percent, but utilization cannot.

Exhibit 14.19 shows a loading representation of Work Center A for the three weeks. The scheduled work exceeds capacity for Week 11. There are several options available:

1 Work overtime.
2 Select an alternative work center that could perform the task.
3 Subcontract to an outside shop.
4 Try to schedule part of the work of Week 11 earlier into Week 10, and delay part of the work into Week 12.
5 Renegotiate the due date and reschedule.

An MRP program with a capacity requirements planning module allows rescheduling to try to level capacity. Two techniques used are backward scheduling and forward scheduling—the fourth option on the preceding list. The objective of the master scheduler is to try to spread the load in Exhibit 14.19 more evenly to remain within the available capacity.

## CLOSED-LOOP MRP

Closed-loop MRP

When the material requirements planning (MRP) system has information feedback from its module outputs, this is termed **closed-loop MRP.** Closed-loop MRP is defined as

> A system built around material requirements that includes the additional planning functions of sales and operations (production planning, master production scheduling, and capacity requirements planning). Once this planning phase is complete and the plans have been accepted as realistic and attainable, the execution functions come into play. These include the manufacturing control functions of input-output (capacity) measurement, detailed scheduling and dispatching, as well as anticipated delay reports from both the plant and suppliers, supplier scheduling, etc. The term "closed-loop" implies that not only is each of these elements included in the overall system, but also that feedback is provided by the execution functions so that the planning can be kept valid at all times.[1]

EXHIBIT 14.20

Closed-Loop MRP System Showing Feedback

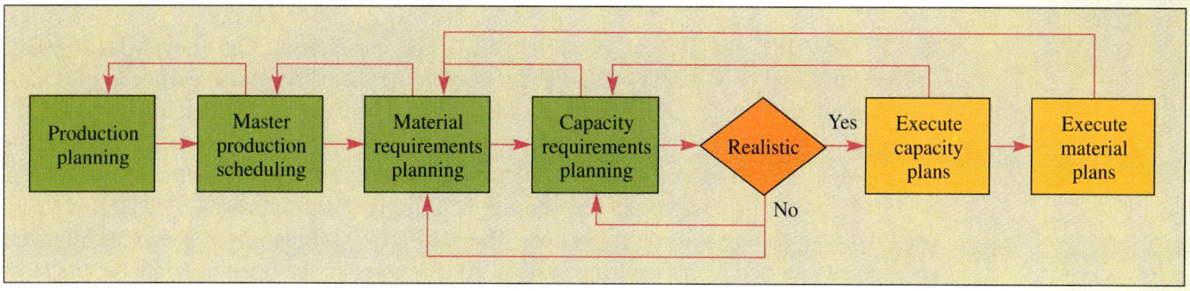


Exhibit 14.20 shows a closed-loop MRP system. The closed loop means that questions and output data are looped back up the system for verification and, if necessary, modification. Recognize that the input to the MRP system is the master production schedule, as was stated earlier in the chapter. The MRP program does an explosion of all the parts, components, and other resources needed to meet this schedule. The capacity requirements planning module then checks the MRP output to see if sufficient capacity exists. If it does not, feedback to the MRP module indicates that the schedule needs to be modified. Continuing through the MRP system, orders are released to the production system by executing the capacity and material plans. From that point on, it is a matter of monitoring, data collection, completing the order, and evaluating results. Any changes in production, capacity, or material are fed back into the system.

## MRP II (MANUFACTURING RESOURCE PLANNING)

Vol. I "Lean Production"

An expansion of the material requirements planning system to include other portions of the productive system was natural and to be expected. One of the first to be included was the purchasing function. At the same time, there was a more detailed inclusion of the production system itself—on the shop floor, in dispatching, and in the detailed scheduling control. MRP had already included work center capacity limitations, so it was obvious that the name *material requirements planning* was no longer adequate to describe the expanded system. Someone (probably Ollie Wight) introduced the name *manufacturing resource planning (MRP II)* to reflect the idea that more and more of the firm was becoming involved in the program. To quote Wight,

> The fundamental manufacturing equation is:
>
> What are we going to make?
> What does it take to make it?
> What do we have?
> What do we have to get?[2]

The initial intent for MRP II was to plan and monitor all of the resources of a manufacturing firm—manufacturing, marketing, finance, and engineering—through a closed-loop system generating financial figures. The second important intent of the MRP II concept was that it simulate the manufacturing system.

# FLOW MANUFACTURING: EMBEDDING JIT INTO MRP

MRP and JIT each have benefits. The question is, Can they work together successfully, and how would one go about combining them? As stated earlier in the chapter, most major manufacturing firms use MRP. Of the firms using MRP, many in repetitive manufacturing also use JIT techniques. Although JIT is best suited to repetitive manufacturing, MRP is used in everything from custom job shops to assembly-line production. A challenge arises in integrating the shop-floor improvement approaches of JIT with an MRP-based planning and control system. The MRP/JIT combination creates what might be considered a hybrid manufacturing system. As discussed in the opening vignette, the term **flow manufacturing** is now being used by many software vendors to describe new software modules that combine MRP and JIT logic.

Flow manufacturing

Exhibit 14.21 shows a master production schedule with an MRP system on the left. MRP systems can help create the master production schedule. From that point on, it

EXHIBIT 14.21

Controlling Production Processes with MRP Alone and MRP/JIT Combined

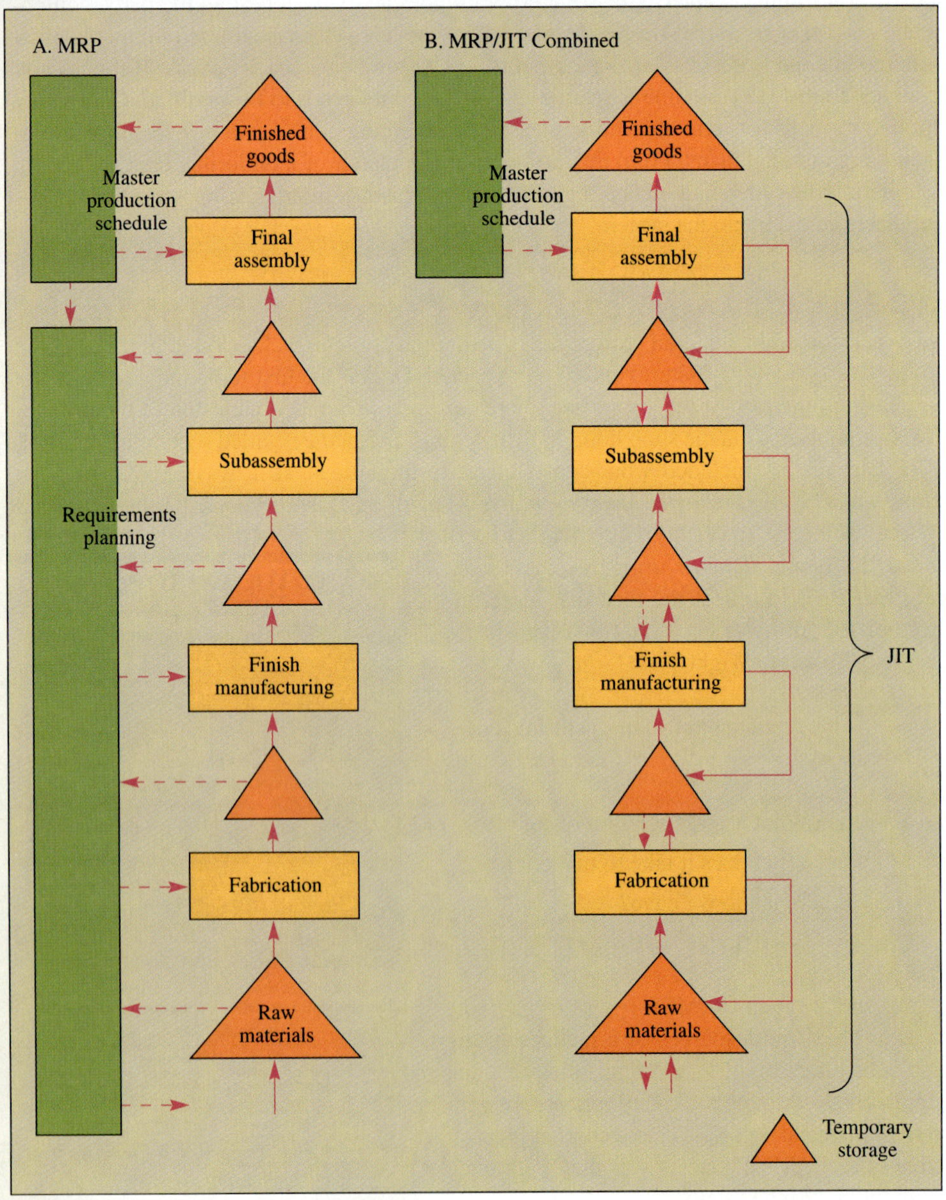

remains a pure MRP system. Scheduling resources such as inventory are continuously controlled and monitored.

The right side of Exhibit 14.21 shows a master production schedule at the top feeding a JIT system. Computer control has been severed, and the JIT portion operates as its own separate pull method drawing from preceding stages. MRP may well be used to help create the master production schedule, but MRP's involvement stops there.

Exhibit 14.22 shows a hybrid MRP/JIT system. The top half shows a conventional MRP system with its standard inputs such as forecast demand, inventory status, and bills of materials. It produces a plan. The system in the bottom of the exhibit, in a JIT manner, controls when vendors should deliver material, when product is to be produced, and when completed product is to be distributed. The middle section—the shop schedule and kanban system—is the interface coupling the MRP and JIT systems along with the capacity control and group technology planning.

EXHIBIT 14.22

An MRP Planning System with JIT Production and Distribution

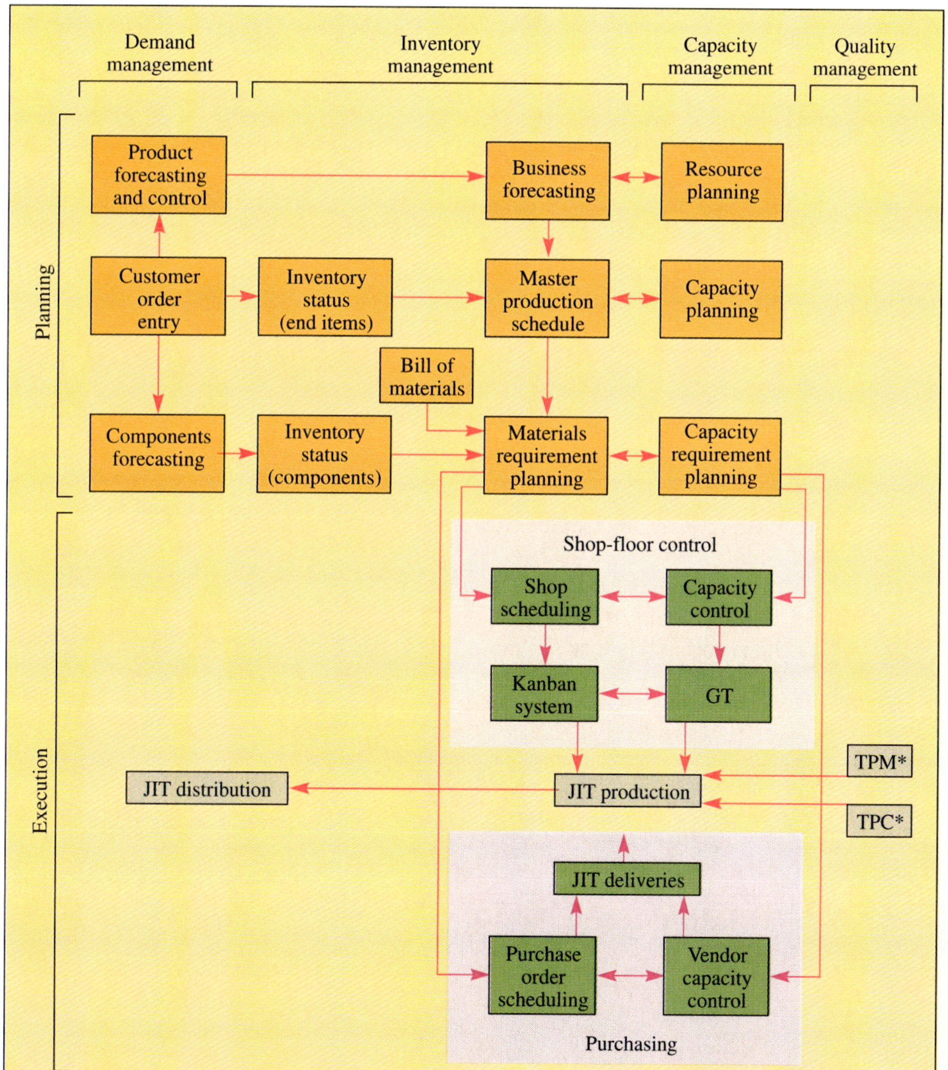


*TPC = total process control; TPM = total preventive maintenance.

SOURCE: C. Y. LEE, "A RECENT DEVELOPMENT OF THE INTEGRATED MANUFACTURING SYSTEM: A HYBRID OF MRP AND JIT," *INTERNATIONAL JOURNAL OF OPERATIONS AND PRODUCTION MANAGEMENT* 13, NO. 4 (1993), P. 9.

# LOT SIZING IN MRP SYSTEMS

The determination of lot sizes in an MRP system is a complicated and difficult problem. Lot sizes are the part quantities issued in the planned order receipt and planned order release sections of an MRP schedule. For parts produced in-house, lot sizes are the production quantities of batch sizes. For purchased parts, these are the quantities ordered from the supplier. Lot sizes generally meet part requirements for one or more periods.

Most lot-sizing techniques deal with how to balance the setup or order costs and holding costs associated with meeting the net requirements generated by the MRP planning process. Many MRP systems have options for computing lot sizes based on some of the more commonly used techniques. It should be obvious, though, that the use of lot-sizing techniques increases the complexity in generating MRP schedules. When fully exploded, the numbers of parts scheduled can be enormous.

Next we explain four lot-sizing techniques using a common example. The lot-sizing techniques presented are lot-for-lot (L4L), economic order quantity (EOQ), least total cost (LTC), and least unit cost (LUC).

Consider the following MRP lot-sizing problem; the net requirements are shown for eight scheduling weeks:

| | | | | | | | |
|---|---|---|---|---|---|---|---|
| Cost per item | | | | | $10.00 | | |
| Order or setup cost | | | | | $47.00 | | |
| Inventory carrying cost/week | | | | | 0.5% | | |
| Weekly net requirements: | | | | | | | |
| 1 | 2 | 3 | 4 | 5 | 6 | 7 | 8 |
| 50 | 60 | 70 | 60 | 95 | 75 | 60 | 55 |

## LOT-FOR-LOT

Lot-for-lot (L4L) is the most common technique. It

- Sets planned orders to exactly match the net requirements.
- Produces exactly what is needed each week with none carried over into future periods.
- Minimizes carrying cost.
- Does not take into account setup costs or capacity limitations.

Exhibit 14.23 shows the lot-for-lot calculations. The net requirements are given in column 2. Because the logic of lot-for-lot says the production quantity (column 3) will exactly match the required quantity (column 2), there will be no inventory left at the end

EXHIBIT 14.23 Lot-for-Lot Run Size for an MRP Schedule

| (1) Week | (2) Net Requirements | (3) Production Quantity | (4) Ending Inventory | (5) Holding Cost | (6) Setup Cost | (7) Total Cost |
|---|---|---|---|---|---|---|
| 1 | 50 | 50 | 0 | $0.00 | $47.00 | $ 47.00 |
| 2 | 60 | 60 | 0 | 0.00 | 47.00 | 94.00 |
| 3 | 70 | 70 | 0 | 0.00 | 47.00 | 141.00 |
| 4 | 60 | 60 | 0 | 0.00 | 47.00 | 188.00 |
| 5 | 95 | 95 | 0 | 0.00 | 47.00 | 235.00 |
| 6 | 75 | 75 | 0 | 0.00 | 47.00 | 282.00 |
| 7 | 60 | 60 | 0 | 0.00 | 47.00 | 329.00 |
| 8 | 55 | 55 | 0 | 0.00 | 47.00 | 376.00 |

(column 4). Without any inventory to carry over into the next week, there is zero holding cost (column 5). However, lot-for-lot requires a setup cost each week (column 6). Incidentally, there is a setup cost each week because this is a work center where a variety of items are worked on each week. This is not a case where the work center is committed to one product and sits idle when it is not working on that product (in which case only one setup would result). Lot-for-lot causes high setup costs.

## ECONOMIC ORDER QUANTITY

In Chapter 13 we already discussed the EOQ model that explicitly balances setup and holding costs. In an EOQ model, either fairly constant demand must exist or safety stock must be kept to provide for demand variability. The EOQ model uses an estimate of total annual demand, the setup or order cost, and the annual holding cost. EOQ was not designed for a system with discrete time periods such as MRP. The lot-sizing techniques used for MRP assume that part requirements are satisfied at the start of the period. Holding costs are then charged only to the ending inventory for the period, not to the average inventory as in the case of the EOQ model. EOQ assumes that parts are used continuously during the period. The lot sizes generated by EOQ do not always cover the entire number of periods. For example, the EOQ might provide the requirements for 4.6 periods. Using the same data as in the lot-for-lot example, the economic order quantity is calculated as follows:

$$\text{Annual demand based on the 8 weeks} = D = \frac{525}{8} \times 52 = 3{,}412.5 \text{ units}$$

$$\text{Annual holding cost} = H = 0.5\% \times \$10 \times 52 \text{ weeks} = \$2.60 \text{ per unit}$$

$$\text{Setup cost} = S = \$47 \text{ (given)}$$

$$\therefore \text{ EOQ} = \sqrt{\frac{2DS}{H}} = \sqrt{\frac{2(3{,}412.5)(\$47)}{\$2.60}} = 351 \text{ units}$$

Exhibit 14.24 shows the MRP schedule using an EOQ of 351 units. The EOQ lot size in Week 1 is enough to meet requirements for Weeks 1 through 5 and a portion of Week 6. Then, in Week 6 another EOQ lot is planned to meet the requirements for Weeks 6 through 8. Notice that the EOQ plan leaves some inventory at the end of Week 8 to carry forward into Week 9.

## LEAST TOTAL COST

The least total cost method (LTC) is a dynamic lot-sizing technique that calculates the order quantity by comparing the carrying cost and the setup (or ordering) costs for various lot sizes and then selects the lot in which these are most nearly equal.

EXHIBIT 14.24

**Economic Order Quantity Run Size for an MRP Schedule**

| WEEK | NET REQUIREMENTS | PRODUCTION QUANTITY | ENDING INVENTORY | HOLDING COST | SETUP COST | TOTAL COST |
|---|---|---|---|---|---|---|
| 1 | 50 | 351 | 301 | $15.05 | $47.00 | $ 62.05 |
| 2 | 60 | 0 | 241 | 12.05 | 0.00 | 74.10 |
| 3 | 70 | 0 | 171 | 8.55 | 0.00 | 82.65 |
| 4 | 60 | 0 | 111 | 5.55 | 0.00 | 88.20 |
| 5 | 95 | 0 | 16 | 0.80 | 0.00 | 89.00 |
| 6 | 75 | 351 | 292 | 14.60 | 47.00 | 150.60 |
| 7 | 60 | 0 | 232 | 11.60 | 0.00 | 162.20 |
| 8 | 55 | 0 | 177 | 8.85 | 0.00 | 171.05 |

EXHIBIT 14.25

Least Total Cost Run Size for an MRP Schedule

| WEEKS | QUANTITY ORDERED | CARRYING COST | ORDER COST | TOTAL COST | |
|---|---|---|---|---|---|
| 1 | 50 | $ 0.00 | $ 47.00 | $ 47.00 | |
| 1–2 | 110 | 3.00 | 47.00 | 50.00 | |
| 1–3 | 180 | 10.00 | 47.00 | 57.00 | |
| 1–4 | 240 | 19.00 | 47.00 | 66.00 | |
| 1–5 | 335 | 38.00 | 47.00 | 85.00 | ← Least total cost |
| 1–6 | 410 | 56.75 | 47.00 | 103.75 | |
| 1–7 | 470 | 74.75 | 47.00 | 121.75 | |
| 1–8 | 525 | 94.00 | 47.00 | 141.00 | |
| 6 | 75 | 0.00 | 47.00 | 47.00 | |
| 6–7 | 135 | 3.00 | 47.00 | 50.00 | |
| 6–8 | 190 | 8.50 | 47.00 | 55.50 | ← Least total cost |

| WEEKS | NET REQUIREMENTS | PRODUCTION QUANTITY | ENDING INVENTORY | HOLDING COST | SETUP COST | TOTAL COST |
|---|---|---|---|---|---|---|
| 1 | 50 | 335 | 285 | $14.25 | $47.00 | $ 61.25 |
| 2 | 60 | 0 | 225 | 11.25 | 0.00 | 72.50 |
| 3 | 70 | 0 | 155 | 7.75 | 0.00 | 80.25 |
| 4 | 60 | 0 | 95 | 4.75 | 0.00 | 85.00 |
| 5 | 95 | 0 | 0 | 0.00 | 0.00 | 85.00 |
| 6 | 75 | 190 | 115 | 5.75 | 47.00 | 137.75 |
| 7 | 60 | 0 | 55 | 2.75 | 0.00 | 140.50 |
| 8 | 55 | 0 | 0 | 0.00 | 0.00 | 140.05 |

The top half of Exhibit 14.25 shows the least cost lot size results. The procedure to compute least total cost lot sizes is to compare order costs and holding costs for various numbers of weeks. For example, costs are compared for producing in Week 1 to cover the requirements for Week 1; producing in Week 1 for Weeks 1 and 2; producing in Week 1 to cover Weeks 1, 2, and 3, and so on. The correct selection is the lot size where the ordering costs and holding costs are approximately equal. In Exhibit 14.25 the best lot size is 335 because a $38 carrying cost and a $47 ordering cost are closer than $56.25 and $47 ($9 versus $9.25). This lot size covers requirements for Weeks 1 through 5. Unlike EOQ, the lot size covers only whole numbers of periods.

Based on the Week 1 decision to place an order to cover five weeks, we are now located in Week 6, and our problem is to determine how many weeks into the future we can provide for from here. Exhibit 14.25 shows that holding and ordering costs are closest in the quantity that covers requirements for Weeks 6 through 8. Notice that the holding and ordering costs here are far apart. This is because our example extends only to Week 8. If the planning horizon were longer, the lot size planned for Week 6 would likely cover more weeks into the future beyond Week 8. This brings up one of the limitations of both LTC and LUC (discussed below). Both techniques are influenced by the length of the planning horizon. The bottom half of Exhibit 14.25 shows the final run size and total cost.

## LEAST UNIT COST

The least unit cost method is a dynamic lot-sizing technique that adds ordering and inventory carrying cost for each trial lot size and divides by the number of units in each lot size, picking the lot size with the lowest unit cost. The top half of Exhibit 14.26 calculates

EXHIBIT 14.26

Least Unit Cost Run Size for an MRP Schedule

| WEEKS | QUANTITY ORDERED | CARRYING COST | ORDER COST | TOTAL COST | UNIT COST |
|---|---|---|---|---|---|
| 1 | 50 | $ 0.00 | $ 47.00 | $ 47.00 | $0.9400 |
| 1–2 | 110 | 3.00 | 47.00 | 50.00 | 0.4545 |
| 1–3 | 180 | 10.00 | 47.00 | 57.00 | 0.3167 |
| 1–4 | 240 | 19.00 | 47.00 | 66.00 | 0.2750 |
| 1–5 | 335 | 38.00 | 47.00 | 85.00 | 0.2537 |
| 1–6 | 410 | 56.75 | 47.00 | 103.75 | 0.2530 ← Least unit cost |
| 1–7 | 470 | 74.75 | 47.00 | 121.75 | 0.2590 |
| 1–8 | 525 | 94.00 | 47.00 | 141.00 | 0.2686 |
| 7 | 60 | 0.00 | 47.00 | 47.00 | 0.7833 |
| 7–8 | 115 | 2.75 | 47.00 | 49.75 | 0.4326 ← Least unit cost |

| WEEK | NET REQUIREMENTS | PRODUCTION QUANTITY | ENDING INVENTORY | HOLDING COST | SETUP COST | TOTAL COST |
|---|---|---|---|---|---|---|
| 1 | 50 | 410 | 360 | $18.00 | $ 47.00 | $ 65.00 |
| 2 | 60 | 0 | 300 | 15.00 | 0.00 | 80.00 |
| 3 | 70 | 0 | 230 | 11.50 | 0.00 | 91.50 |
| 4 | 60 | 0 | 170 | 8.50 | 0.00 | 100.00 |
| 5 | 95 | 0 | 75 | 3.75 | 0.00 | 103.75 |
| 6 | 75 | 0 | 0 | 0 | 0 | 103.75 |
| 7 | 60 | 115 | 55 | 2.75 | 47.00 | 153.50 |
| 8 | 55 | 0 | 0 | 0 | 0 | $153.50 |

the unit cost for ordering lots to meet the needs of Weeks 1 through 8. Note that the minimum occurred when the quantity 410, ordered in Week 1, was sufficient to cover Weeks 1 through 6. The lot size planned for Week 7 covers through the end of the planning horizon.

The least unit cost run size and total cost are shown in the bottom half of Exhibit 14.26.

## CHOOSING THE BEST LOT SIZE

Using the lot-for-lot method, the total cost for the eight weeks is $376; the EOQ total cost is $171.05; the least total cost method is $140.50; and the least unit cost is $153.50. The lowest cost was obtained using the least total cost method of $140.50. If there were more than eight weeks, the lowest cost could differ.

The advantage of the least unit cost method is that it is a more complete analysis and would take into account ordering or setup costs that might change as the order size increases. If the ordering or setup costs remain constant, the lowest total cost method is more attractive because it is simpler and easier to compute; yet it would be just as accurate under that restriction.

# CONCLUSION

Since the 1970s, MRP has grown from its purpose of determining simple time schedules, to its present advanced types that tie together all major functions of an organization. During its growth and its application, MRP's disadvantages as a scheduling mechanism have been well recognized. This is largely because MRP tries to do too much in light of the dynamic, often jumpy system in which it is trying to operate.

MRP is recognized, however, for its excellent databases and linkages within the firm. MRP also does a good job in helping to produce master schedules. Many firms in repetitive manufacturing are installing JIT systems to link with the MRP system. JIT takes the master production schedule as its pulling force but does not use MRP's generated schedule. Results indicate that this is working very well.

Many newer MRP-type software programs have been developed since the early 1990s. These allow more open exchange of data than the earlier systems, embrace a larger part of the firm's operation (such as multiple sites, global customers, languages, and currency rates), and operate in real time.

Over the longer term, experts predict that e-business will force manufacturers to abandon the MRP or work order business model, a model that depends on accurate forecasts. Flow manufacturing, in which a company aims to minimize its working inventory and drive production by actual demand, rather than forecasts, is starting to take root.[3]

MRP's service applications have not fared well, even though it seems that they should have. The MRP approach would appear to be valuable in producing services because service scheduling consists of identifying the final service and then tracing back to the resources needed, such as equipment, space, and personnel. Consider, for example, a hospital operating room planning an open-heart surgery. The master schedule can establish a time for the surgery (or surgeries, if several are scheduled). The BOM could specify all required equipment and personnel—MDs, nurses, anesthesiologist, operating room, heart/lung machine, defibrillator, and so forth. The inventory status file would show the availability of the resources and commit them to the project. The MRP program could then produce a schedule showing when various parts of the operation are to be started, expected completion time, required materials, and so forth. Checking this schedule would allow "capacity planning" in answering such questions as "Are all the materials and personnel available?" and "Does the system produce a feasible schedule?"

We still believe that MRP systems will eventually find their way into service applications. But after a number of years of believing this, we have not seen development and implementation. One reason is that even service managers who are aware of it believe that MRP is just a manufacturing tool. Also, service managers tend to be people-oriented and skeptical of tools from outside their industry.

## KEY TERMS

**Material requirements planning (MRP)** The logic for determining the number of parts, components, and materials needed to produce a product. MRP also provides the schedule specifying when each of these materials, parts, and components should be ordered or produced.

**Manufacturing resource planning (MRP II)** An expanded version of MRP that integrates finance, accounting, accounts payable, and other business processes into the production scheduling and inventory control functions that are part of a basic MRP system.

**Master production schedule (MPS)** A time-phased plan specifying how many and when the firm plans to build each end item.

**Bill of materials (BOM)** A computer file that contains the complete product description, listing the materials, parts, and components and the sequence in which the product is created.

**Net change system** An MRP system that calculates the impact of a change in the MRP data (the inventory status, BOM, or master schedule) immediately. This is a common feature in current systems.

**Closed-loop MRP** The use of actual data from the production system to continually update the MRP system. This feedback is provided so that planning can be kept valid at all times.

**Flow manufacturing** Hybrid production planning systems that combine the information integration and planning capabilities of MRP with the response of a JIT kanban system.

# SOLVED PROBLEMS

## SOLVED PROBLEM 1

Product X is made of two units of Y and three of Z. Y is made of one unit of A and two units of B. Z is made of two units of A and four units of C.

Lead time for X is one week; Y, two weeks; Z, three weeks; A, two weeks; B, one week; and C, three weeks.

*a.* Draw the bill of materials (product structure tree).

*b.* If 100 units of X are needed in week 10, develop a planning schedule showing when each item should be ordered and in what quantity.

### Solution

*a.*

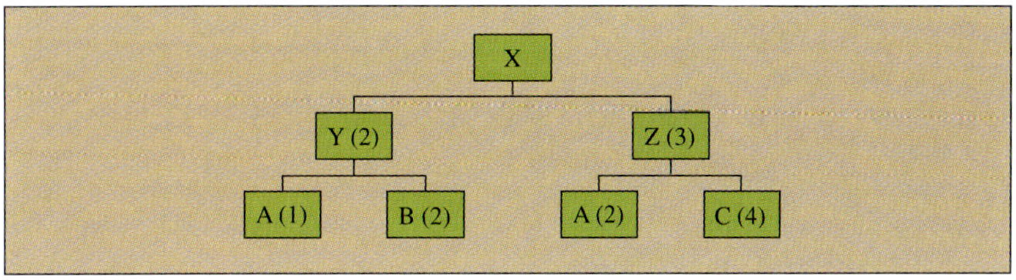


*b.*

| | | 3 | 4 | 5 | 6 | 7 | 8 | 9 | 10 |
|---|---|---|---|---|---|---|---|---|---|
| X | LT = 1 | | | | | | | 100 | 100 |
| Y | LT = 2 | | | | | 200 | | 200 | |
| Z | LT = 3 | | | | 300 | | | 300 | |
| A | LT = 2 | | 600 | 200 | 600 | 200 | | | |
| B | LT = 1 | | | | 400 | 400 | | | |
| C | LT = 3 | 1200 | | | 1200 | | | | |

## SOLVED PROBLEM 2

Product M is made of two units of N and three of P. N is made of two units of R and four units of S. R is made of one unit of S and three units of T. P is made of two units of T and four units of U.

*a.* Show the bill of materials (product structure tree).

*b.* If 100 M are required, how many units of each component are needed?

*c.* Show both a single-level parts list and an indented parts list.

### Solution

*a.*

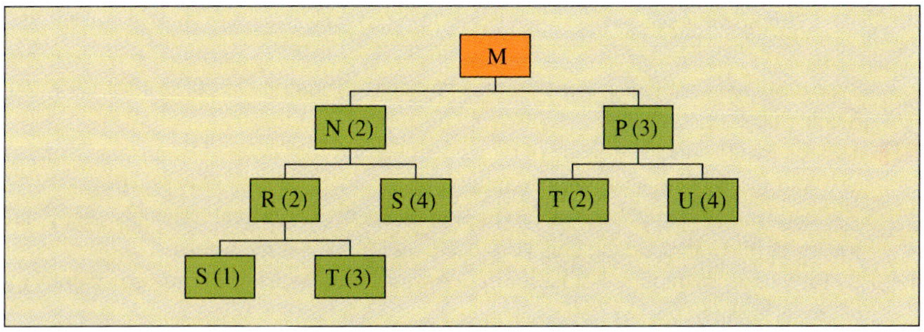


*b.* M = 100
N = 200
P = 300
R = 400

S = 800 + 400 = 1,200
T = 600 + 1,200 = 1,800
U = 1,200

*c.*

| SINGLE-LEVEL PARTS LIST | | INDENTED PARTS LIST | | | |
|---|---|---|---|---|---|
| M | | M | | | |
| | N (2) | | N(2) | | |
| | P (3) | | | R(2) | |
| N | | | | | S (1) |
| | R (2) | | | | T (3) |
| | S (4) | | | S (4) | |
| R | | | P (3) | | |
| | S (1) | | | T (2) | |
| | T (3) | | | U (4) | |
| P | | | | | |
| | T (2) | | | | |
| | U (4) | | | | |

## REVIEW AND DISCUSSION QUESTIONS

1 Discuss the meaning of MRP terms such as *planned order release* and *scheduled order receipts.*

2 Many practitioners currently update MRP weekly or biweekly. Would it be more valuable if it were updated daily? Discuss.

3 What is the role of safety stock in an MRP system?

4 How does MRP relate to CIM? (See Supplement C.)

5 Contrast the significance of the term *lead time* in the traditional EOQ context and in an MRP system.

6 Discuss the importance of the master production schedule in an MRP system.

7 "MRP just prepares shopping lists. It does not do the shopping or cook the dinner." Comment.

8 What are the sources of demand in an MRP system? Are these dependent or independent, and how are they used as inputs to the system?

9 State the types of data that would be carried in the bill of materials file and the inventory record file.

## PROBLEMS

1. See table.

1 In the following MRP planning schedule for Item J, indicate the correct net requirements, planned order receipts, and planned order releases to meet the gross requirements. Lead time is one week.

| | WEEK NUMBER | | | | | |
|---|---|---|---|---|---|---|
| ITEM J | 0 | 1 | 2 | 3 | 4 | 5 |
| Gross requirements | | | 75 | | 50 | 70 |
| On-hand 40 | | | 40 | | 0 | 0 |
| Net requirements | | | 35 | | 50 | 70 |
| Planned order receipt | | | 35 | | 50 | 70 |
| Planned order release | | 35 | | 50 | 70 | |

2. See ISM.

2 Repeat Solved Problem 1 using current on-hand inventories of 20 X, 40 Y, 30 Z, 50 A, 100 B, and 900 C.

3. *a.*

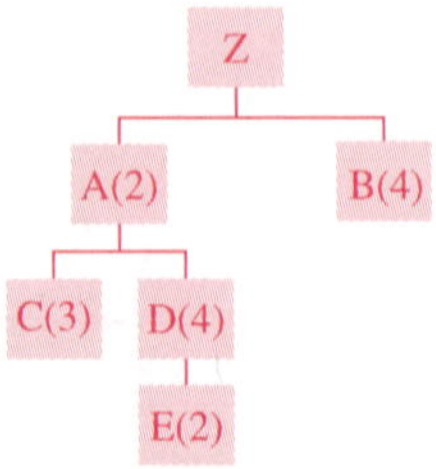


3 Assume that Product Z is made of two units of A and four units of B. A is made of three units of C and four D. D is made of two units of E.

Lead times for purchase or fabrication of each unit to final assembly are: Z takes two weeks; A, B, C, and D take one week each; and E takes three weeks.

Fifty units are required in Period 10. (Assume that there is currently no inventory on hand of any of these items.)

*a.* Show the bill of materials (product structure tree).

*b.* Develop an MRP planning schedule showing gross and net requirements and order release and order receipt dates.

3. *b.* See ISM.

4. See ISM.

4 *Note:* For Problems 4 through 9, to simplify data handling to include the receipt of orders that have actually been placed in previous periods, the following six-level scheme can be

used. (A number of different techniques are used in practice, but the important issue is to keep track of what is on hand, what is expected to arrive, what is needed, and what size orders should be placed.) One way to calculate the numbers is as follows:

| | WEEK |
|---|---|
| Gross requirements | |
| Scheduled receipts | |
| On hand from prior period | |
| Net requirements | |
| Planned order receipt | |
| Planned order release | |

One unit of A is made of three units of B, one unit of C, and two units of D. B is composed of two units of E and one unit of D. C is made of one unit of B and two units of E. E is made of one unit of F.

Items B, C, E, and F have one-week lead times; A and D have lead times of two weeks.

Assume that lot-for-lot (L4L) lot sizing is used for Items A, B, and F; lots of size 50, 50, and 200 are used for Items C, D, and E, respectively. Items C, E, and F have on-hand (beginning) inventories of 10, 50, and 150, respectively; all other items have zero beginning inventory. We are scheduled to receive 10 units of A in Week 2, 50 units of E in Week 1, and also 50 units of F in Week 1. There are no other scheduled receipts. If 30 units of A are required in Week 8, use the low-level-coded bill of materials to find the necessary planned order releases for all components.

5 One unit of A is made of two units of B, three units of C, and two units of D. B is composed of one unit of E and two units of F. C is made of two units of F and one unit of D. E is made of two units of D. Items A, C, D, and F have one-week lead times; B and E have lead times of two weeks. Lot-for-lot (L4L) lot sizing is used for Items A, B, C, and D; lots of size 50 and 180 are used for Items E and F, respectively. Item C has an on-hand (beginning) inventory of 15; D has an on-hand inventory of 50; all other items have zero beginning inventory. We are scheduled to receive 20 units of Item E in Week 2; there are no other scheduled receipts.

Construct simple and low-level-coded bills of materials (product structure tree) and indented and summarized parts list.

If 20 units of A are required in Week 8, use the low-level-coded bill of materials to find the necessary planned order releases for all components. (See the note in Problem 4.)

5. See ISM.

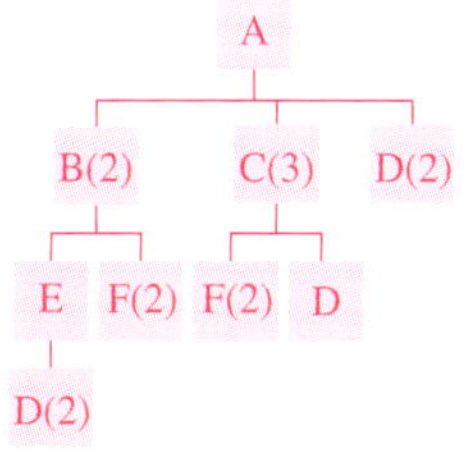


6 One unit of A is made of one unit of B and one unit of C. B is made of four units of C and one unit of E and F. C is made of two units of D and one unit of E. E is made of three units of F. Item C has a lead time of one week; Items A, B, E, and F have two-week lead times; and Item D has a lead time of three weeks. Lot-for-lot lot sizing is used for Items A, D, and E; lots of size 50, 100, and 50 are used for Items B, C, and F, respectively. Items A, C, D, and E have on-hand (beginning) inventories of 20, 50, 100, and 10, respectively; all other items have zero beginning inventory. We are scheduled to receive 10 units of A in Week 1, 100 units of C in Week 1, and 100 units of D in Week 3; there are no other scheduled receipts. If 50 units of A are required in Week 10, use the low-level-coded bill of materials (product structure tree) to find the necessary planned order releases for all components. (See the note in Problem 4.)

6. See ISM.

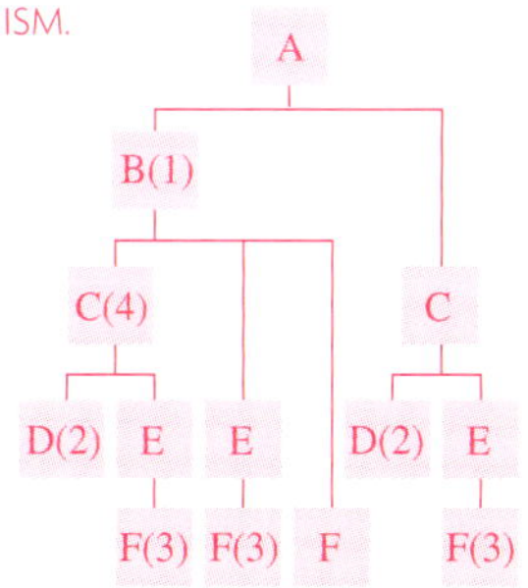


7 One unit of A is made of two units of B and one unit of C. B is made of three units of D and one unit of F. C is composed of three units of B, one unit of D, and four units of E. D is made of one unit of E. Item C has a lead time of one week; Items A, B, E, and F have two-week lead times; and Item D has a lead time of three weeks. Lot-for-lot lot sizing is used for Items C, E, and F; lots of size 20, 40, and 160 are used for Items A, B, and D, respectively. Items A, B, D, and E have on-hand (beginning) inventories of 5, 10, 100, and 100, respectively; all other items have zero beginning inventories. We are scheduled to receive 10 units of A in Week 3, 20 units of B in Week 7, 40 units of F in Week 5, and 60 units of E in Week 2; there are no other schedule receipts. If 20 units of A are required in Week 10, use the low-level-coded bill of materials (product structure tree) to find the necessary planned order releases for all components. (See the note in Problem 4.)

7. See ISM.

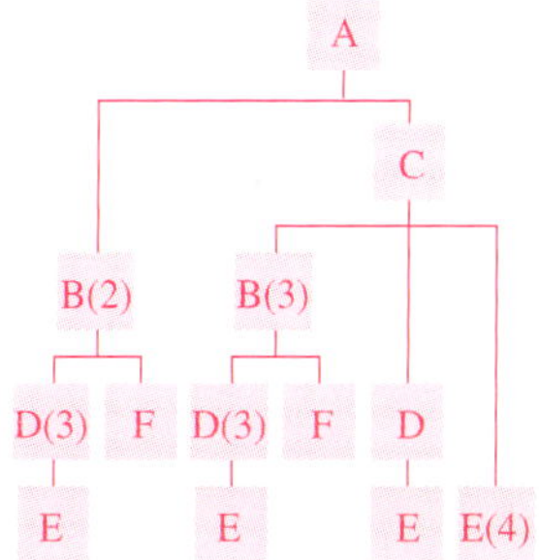


8 One unit of A is composed of 2 units of B and three units of C. Each B is composed of one unit of F. C is made of one unit of D, one unit of E, and two units of F. Items A, B, C, and

8. See ISM.

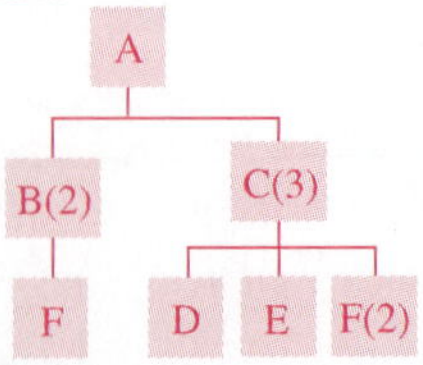


D have 20, 50, 60, and 25 units of on-hand inventory. Items A, B, and C use lot-for-lot (L4L) as their lot-sizing technique, while D, E, and F require multiples of 50, 100, and 100, respectively, to be purchased. B has scheduled receipts of 30 units in Period 1. No other scheduled receipts exist. Lead times are one period for Items A, B, and D, and two periods for Items C, E, and F. Gross requirements for A are 20 units in Period 1, 20 units in Period 2, 60 units in Period 6, and 50 units in Period 8. Find the planned order releases for all items.

9. See ISM.

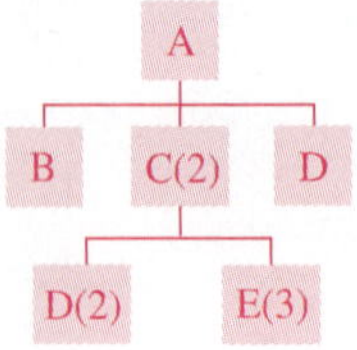


9 Each unit of A is composed of one unit of B, two units of C, and one unit of D. C is composed of two units of D and three units of E. Items A, C, D, and E have on-hand inventories of 20, 10, 20, and 10 units, respectively. Item B has a scheduled receipt of 10 units in Period 1, and C has a scheduled receipt of 50 units in Period 1. Lot-for-lot (L4L) is used for Items A and B. Item C requires a minimum lot size of 50 units. D and E are required to be purchased in multiples of 100 and 50, respectively. Lead times are one period for Items A, B, and C, and two periods for Items D and E. The gross requirements for A are 30 in Period 2, 30 in Period 5, and 40 in Period 8. Find the planned order releases for all items.

10. Using least total cost method, order 250 units. The least unit cost method indicates order of 450 units.

10 The MRP gross requirements for Item A are shown here for the next 10 weeks. Lead time for A is three weeks and setup cost is $10. There is a carrying cost of $0.01 per unit per week. Beginning inventory is 90 units.

| | Week | | | | | | | | | |
|---|---|---|---|---|---|---|---|---|---|---|
| | 1 | 2 | 3 | 4 | 5 | 6 | 7 | 8 | 9 | 10 |
| Gross Requirements | 30 | 50 | 10 | 20 | 70 | 80 | 20 | 60 | 200 | 50 |

Use the least total cost or the least unit cost lot-sizing method to determine when and for what quantity the first order should be released.

11. See ISM.

11 (This problem is intended as a very simple exercise to go from the aggregate plan to the master schedule to the MRP.) Gigamemory Storage Devices, Inc., produces CD-ROMs (read only memory) and WORMs (write once read many) for the computer market. Aggregate demand for the WORMs for the next two quarters is 2,100 units and 2,700 units. Assume that demand is distributed evenly for each month of the quarter.

There are two models of the WORM: an internal model and an external model. The drive assemblies in both are the same, but the electronics and housing are different. Demand is higher for the external model and currently is 70 percent of aggregate demand.

The bill of materials and the lead times follow. One drive assembly and one electronic and housing unit go into each WORM.

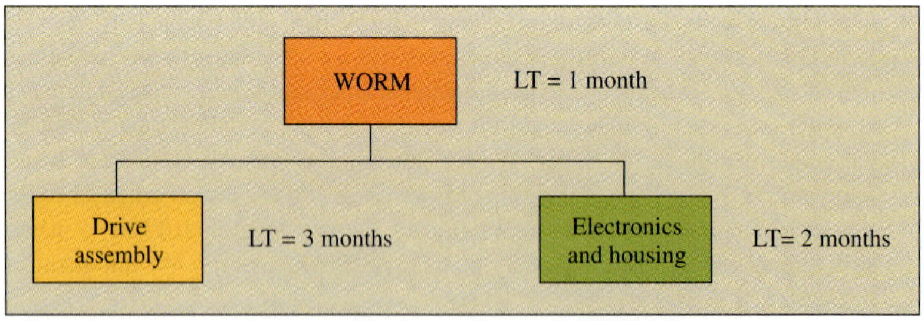


The MRP system is run monthly. Currently, 200 external WORMs and 100 internal WORMs are in stock. Also in stock are 250 drive assemblies, 50 internal electronic and housing units, and 125 external electronic and housing units.

Problem: Show the aggregate plan, the master production schedule, and the full MRP with the gross and net requirements and planned order releases.

12.

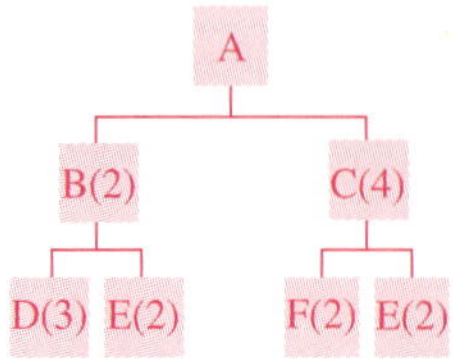


12 Product A is an end item and is made from two units of B and four of C. B is made of three units of D and two of E. C is made of two units of F and two of E.

A has a lead time of one week. B, C, and E have lead times of two weeks, and D and F have lead times of three weeks.

*a.* Show the bill of materials (product structure tree).

*b.* If 100 units of A are required in Week 10, develop the MRP planning schedule, specifying when items are to be ordered and received. There are currently no units of inventory on hand.

13 Product A consists of two units of Subassembly B, three units of C, and one unit of D. B is composed of four units of E and three units of F. C is made of two units of H and three units of D. H is made of five units of E and two units of G.

*a.* Construct a simple bill of materials (product structure tree).
*b.* Construct a product structure tree using low-level coding.
*c.* Construct an indented parts list.
*d.* To produce 100 units of A, determine the numbers of units of B, C, D, E, F, G, and H required.

13. See ISM.

14 The MRP gross requirements for Item X are shown here for the next 10 weeks. Lead time for A is two weeks, and setup cost is $9. There is a carrying cost of $0.02 per unit per week. Beginning inventory is 70 units.

14. Using least total cost method, order 180 units. Using least unit cost method, order either 180 units or 220 units.

| | Week | | | | | | | | | |
|---|---|---|---|---|---|---|---|---|---|---|
| | 1 | 2 | 3 | 4 | 5 | 6 | 7 | 8 | 9 | 10 |
| Gross Requirements | 20 | 10 | 15 | 45 | 10 | 30 | 100 | 20 | 40 | 150 |

Use the least total cost or the least unit cost lot-sizing method to determine when and for what quantity the first order should be released.

15 Audio Products, Inc., produces two AM/FM/CD players for cars. The radio/CD units are identical, but the mounting hardware and finish trim differ. The standard model fits intermediate and full-size cars, and the sports model fits small sports cars.

15. See ISM.

Audio Products handles the production in the following way. The chassis (radio/CD unit) is assembled in Mexico and has a manufacturing lead time of two weeks. The mounting hardware is purchased from a sheet steel company and has a three-week lead time. The finish trim is purchased from a Taiwan electronics company with offices in Los Angeles as prepackaged units consisting of knobs and various trim pieces. Trim packages have a two-week lead time. Final assembly time may be disregarded because adding the trim package and mounting are performed by the customer.

Audio Products supplies wholesalers and retailers, who place specific orders for both models up to eight weeks in advance. These orders, together with enough additional units to satisfy the small number of individual sales, are summarized in the following demand schedule:

| | Week | | | | | | | |
|---|---|---|---|---|---|---|---|---|
| Model | 1 | 2 | 3 | 4 | 5 | 6 | 7 | 8 |
| Standard Model | | | | 300 | | | | 400 |
| Sports Model | | | | | 200 | | | 100 |

There are currently 50 radio/CD units on hand but no trim packages or mounting hardware.

Prepare a material requirements plan to meet the demand schedule exactly. Specify the gross and net requirements, on-hand amounts, and the planned order release and receipt periods for the radio/CD chassis, the standard trim and sports car model trim, and the standard mounting hardware and the sports car mounting hardware.

16 An item has a setup cost of $100 and a weekly holding cost of $0.50 per unit. Given the following net requirements, what should the lot sizes be using lot-for-lot (L4L), economic order quantity (EOQ), and least total cost (LTC)? Also, what is the total cost associated with each lot-sizing technique?

16. L4L: place 8 orders equal to net requirements, total cost $800. EOQ: place 3 orders of size 110 in periods 1, 5, & 8, total cost $550. LTC: place an order of size 100 in Week 1, and an order of size 140 in Week 5, total cost $415.

| Week | Net Requirements | Week | Net Requirements |
|---|---|---|---|
| 1 | 10 | 5 | 20 |
| 2 | 30 | 6 | 40 |
| 3 | 10 | 7 | 50 |
| 4 | 50 | 8 | 30 |

17 Brown and Brown Electronics manufactures a line of digital videodisc (DVD) players. Although there are differences among the various products, there are a number of common

17. See ISM.

parts within each player. The bill of materials, showing the number of each item required, lead times, and the current inventory on hand for the parts and components, follows:

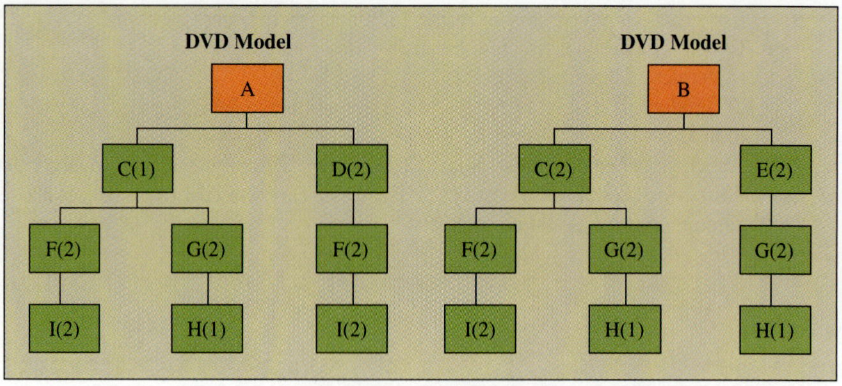


| ITEM | NUMBER CURRENTLY IN STOCK | LEAD TIME (WEEKS) |
|---|---|---|
| DVD Model A | 30 | 1 |
| DVD Model B | 50 | 2 |
| Subassembly C | 75 | 1 |
| Subassembly D | 80 | 2 |
| Subassembly E | 100 | 1 |
| Part F | 150 | 1 |
| Part G | 40 | 1 |
| Raw Material H | 200 | 2 |
| Raw Material I | 300 | 2 |

Brown and Brown created a forecast that it plans to use as its master production schedule, producing exactly to schedule. Part of the MPS shows a demand for 700 units of Model A and 1,200 units of Model B in Week 10.

Develop an MRP schedule to meet the demand.

## CASE: NICHOLS COMPANY

This particular December day seemed bleak to Joe Williams, president of Nichols Company (NCO). He sat in his office watching the dying embers in his fireplace, hoping to clear his mind. Suddenly there came a tapping by someone gently rapping, rapping at his office door. "Another headache," he muttered, "tapping at my office door. Only that and nothing more."*

The intruder was Barney Thompson, director of marketing. "A major account has just canceled a large purchase of A units because we are backordered on tubing. This can't continue. My sales force is out beating the bushes for customers, and our production manager can't provide the product."

For the past several months, operations at NCO have been unsteady. Inventory levels have been high, while at the same time, there have been stockouts. This has resulted in late deliveries, complaints, and cancellations. To compound the problem, overtime has been excessive.

### HISTORY

Nichols Company was started by Joe Williams and Susan Schaap, both with MBAs from the University of Arizona. Much has happened since Williams and Schaap formed the company. Schaap has left the company and is working in real estate development in Queensland, Australia. Under the direction of Williams, NCO has diversified to include a number of other products.

NCO currently has 355 full-time employees directly involved in manufacturing the three primary products: A, B, and C. Final assembly takes place in a converted warehouse adjacent to NCO's main plant.

### THE MEETING

Williams called a meeting the next day to get input on the problems facing NCO and to lay the groundwork for some solutions. Attending the meeting, besides himself and Barney Thompson, were

*With Apologies to E. A. P. (Edgar Allen Poe).

Allison Bright of production and inventory control, Trevor Hansen of purchasing, and Margaret Wu of accounting.

The meeting lasted all morning. Participation was vocal and intense.

Bright said, "The forecasts that marketing sends us are always way off. We are constantly having to expedite one product or another to meet current demand. This runs up our overtime."

Thompson said, "Production tries to run too lean. We need a large inventory of finished goods. If I had the merchandise, my salespeople could sell 20 percent more product."

Wu said, "No way! Our inventory is already uncomfortably high. We can't afford the holding costs, not to mention how fast technology changes around here causing even more inventory, much of it obsolete."

Bright said, "The only way I can meet our stringent cost requirement is to buy in volume."

At the end of the meeting, Williams had lots of input but no specific plan. What do you think he should do? Use Exhibits 14.27 through 14.30 showing relevant data to answer the specific questions at the end of the case.

EXHIBIT 14.27

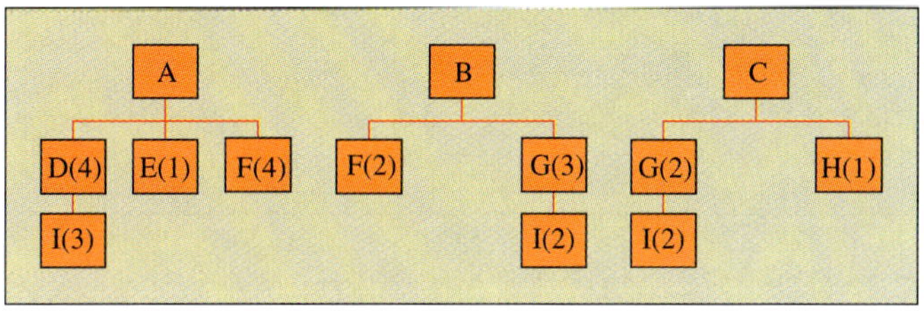


Bills of Materials for Products A, B, and C

EXHIBIT 14.28

Work Center Routings for Products and Components

| Item | Work Center Number | Standard Time (Hours per Unit) | Item | Work Center Number | Standard Time (Hours per Unit) |
|---|---|---|---|---|---|
| Product A | 1 | 0.20 | Component E | 2 | 0.15 |
| | 4 | 0.10 | | 4 | 0.05 |
| Product B | 2 | 0.30 | Component F | 2 | 0.15 |
| | 4 | 0.08 | | 3 | 0.20 |
| Product C | 3 | 0.10 | Component G | 1 | 0.30 |
| | 4 | 0.05 | | 2 | 0.10 |
| Component D | 1 | 0.15 | Component H | 1 | 0.05 |
| | 4 | 0.10 | | 3 | 0.10 |

EXHIBIT 14.29

Inventory Levels and Lead Times for Each Item on the Bill of Materials at the Beginning of Week 1

| Product/Component | On Hand (Units) | Lead Time (Weeks) |
|---|---|---|
| Product A | 100 | 1 |
| Product B | 200 | 1 |
| Product C | 175 | 1 |
| Component D | 200 | 1 |
| Component E | 195 | 1 |
| Component F | 120 | 1 |
| Component G | 200 | 1 |
| Component H | 200 | 1 |
| Raw Material I | 300 | 1 |

EXHIBIT 14.30

Forecast Demand for Weeks 4 to 27

| WEEK | PRODUCT A | PRODUCT B | PRODUCT C | WEEK | PRODUCT A | PRODUCT B | PRODUCT C |
|---|---|---|---|---|---|---|---|
| 1 | | | | 15 | 1,900 | 1,900 | 1,500 |
| 2 | | | | 16 | 2,200 | 2,300 | 2,300 |
| 3 | | | | 17 | 2,000 | 2,300 | 2,300 |
| 4 | 1,500 | 2,200 | 1,200 | 18 | 1,700 | 2,100 | 2,000 |
| 5 | 1,700 | 2,100 | 1,400 | 19 | 1,600 | 1,900 | 1,700 |
| 6 | 1,150 | 1,900 | 1,000 | 20 | 1,400 | 1,800 | 1,800 |
| 7 | 1,100 | 1,800 | 1,500 | 21 | 1,100 | 1,800 | 2,200 |
| 8 | 1,000 | 1,800 | 1,400 | 22 | 1,000 | 1,900 | 1,900 |
| 9 | 1,100 | 1,600 | 1,100 | 23 | 1,400 | 1,700 | 2,400 |
| 10 | 1,400 | 1,600 | 1,800 | 24 | 1,400 | 1,700 | 2,400 |
| 11 | 1,400 | 1,700 | 1,700 | 25 | 1,500 | 1,700 | 2,600 |
| 12 | 1,700 | 1,700 | 1,300 | 26 | 1,600 | 1,800 | 2,400 |
| 13 | 1,700 | 1,700 | 1,700 | 27 | 1,500 | 1,900 | 2,500 |
| 14 | 1,800 | 1,700 | 1,700 | | | | |

QUESTIONS

Use Microsoft Excel to solve the Nichols Company case. (Note that if you start from scratch, it will take several hours to answer Question 1, about the same for Question 2, and perhaps double that for Question 3. A spreadsheet is on the CD included with this book to help with this problem.)

*Simplifying assumption:* To get the program started, some time is needed at the beginning because MRP backloads the system. For simplicity, assume that the forecasts (and therefore demands) are zero for Periods 1 through 3. Also assume that the starting inventory specified in Exhibit 14.29 is available from Week 1. For the master production schedule, use only End Items A, B, and C.

To modify production quantities, adjust only Products A, B, and C. Do not adjust the quantities of D, E, F, G, H, and I. These should be linked so that changes in A, B, and C automatically adjust them.

1 Disregarding machine center limitations, develop an MRP schedule and also capacity profiles for the four machine centers.

2 Work center capacities and costs follow. Repeat (1) creating a *feasible* schedule (within the capacities of the machine centers) and compute the relevant costs. Do this by adjusting the MPS only. Try to minimize the total cost of operation for the 27 weeks.

3 Suppose end items had to be ordered in multiples of 100 units, components in multiples of 500 units, and raw materials in multiples of 1,000 units. How would this change your schedule?

| | CAPACITY | COST |
|---|---|---|
| Work Center 1 | 6,000 hours available | $20 per hour |
| Work Center 2 | 4,500 hours available | $25 per hour |
| Work Center 3 | 2,400 hours available | $35 per hour |
| Work Center 4 | 1,200 hours available | $65 per hour |
| Inventory carrying cost | | |
| End Items A, B, and C | $2.00 per unit | |
| Components D, E, F, G, and H | $1.50 per unit | |
| Raw Material I | $1.00 per unit | |
| Backorder cost | | |
| End Items A, B, and C | $20 per unit | |
| Components D, E, F, G, and H | $14 per unit | |
| Raw Material I | $8 per unit | |

## SELECTED BIBLIOGRAPHY

Drexl, A., and E. Kimms (eds.). *Beyond Manufacturing Resource Planning (MRP II): Advanced Models and Methods for Production Planning.* New York: Springer, 1998.

Lee, C. Y. "A Recent Development of the Integrated Manufacturing System: A Hybrid of MRP and JIT." *International Journal of Operations and Production Management* 13, no. 4 (1993), pp. 3–17.

Orlicky, J. *Materials Requirements Planning.* New York: McGraw-Hill, 1975. (This is the classic book on MRP.)

Sipper, D., and R. Bulfin. *Production: Planning, Control, and Integration.* New York: McGraw-Hill, 1997.

Turbide, D. A. *MRP+: The Adaptation, Enhancement, and Application of MRP.* New York: Industrial Press, 1993.

Vollmann, T. E.; W. L. Berry; and D. C. Whybark. *Manufacturing Planning and Control Systems.* 4th ed. Burr Ridge, IL: Richard D. Irwin, 1997.

Wallace, T. F. "MRP II & JIT Work Together in Plan and Practice." *Automation.* March 1990, pp. 40–42.

Wight, O. *MRP II: Making It Happen.* 2nd ed. Essex Junction, VT: Oliver Wight, 1990.

———. *The Executive Guide to Successful MRP II.* Williston, VT: Oliver Wight, 1982.

## FOOTNOTES

1 Dictionary definitions are reprinted with the permission of APICS, Inc., *APICS Dictionary,* 8th ed., 1995.

2 O. Wight. The *Executive's Guide to Successful MRP II* (Williston, VT: Oliver Wight, 1982), pp. 6, 17.

3. Martin Lamonica, "Life After ERP," *InfoWorld,* Vol. 21, No. 33, August 16, 1999, p. 35.

chapter

*chapter fifteen*

# OPERATIONS SCHEDULING

## CHAPTER OUTLINE AND KEY TERMS

# 15

Why should accounting and finance types worry about the nitty-gritty problems of scheduling, such as long queue times? Answer: Work flow equals cash flow, and work flow is driven by the schedule!

Consider the figure below. In poorly scheduled job shops, it is not at all uncommon for jobs to wait for 95 percent of their total production cycle (a). This results in a long work flow cycle (b). Add inventory time and receivables collection time to this and you get a long cash flow cycle (c). But if you can do a good job of scheduling, you can eliminate, say, 75 percent of the queue time (d, e) and cut your cash flow cycle by the same amount of time.

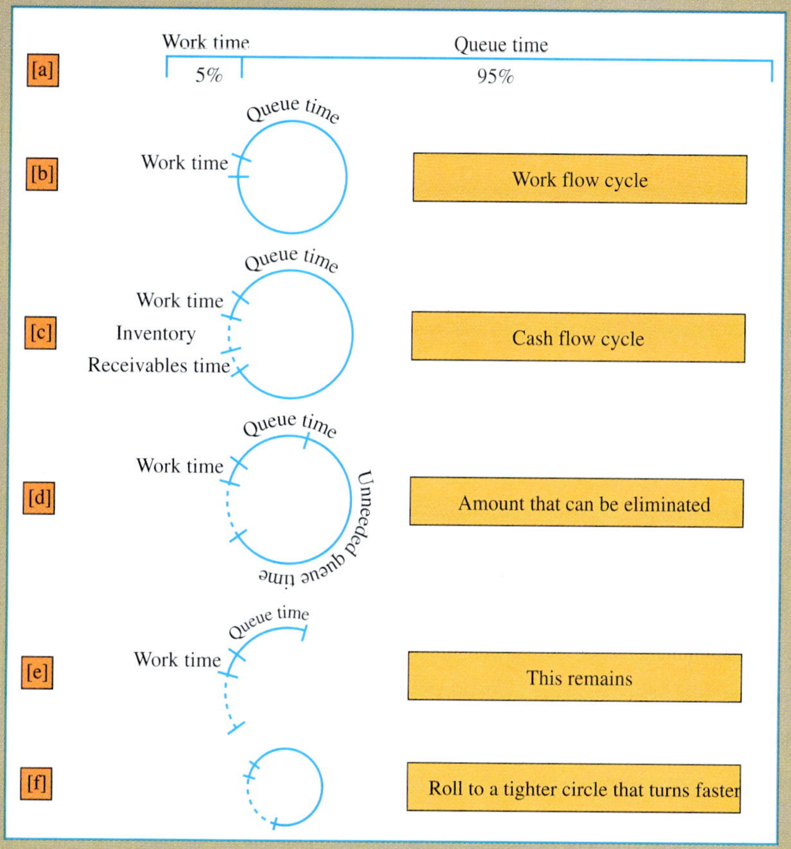


Source: Modified from W. E. Sandman with J. P. Hayes, *How to Win Productivity in Manufacturing* (Dresher, PA: Yellow Book of Pennsylvania, 1980), p. 57.

THIS WORK CENTER AT DANA CORPORATION'S WARNER ELECTRIC FACILITY IN CHIHUAHUA, MEXICO, MANUFACTURES CRUISE CONTROL MOTORS FOR FORD MOTOR COMPANY. THE FACILITY USES THE LATEST IN WELDING AND MACHINING TECHNOLOGY AND REPORTED LESS THAN SIX DEFECTS PER MILLION UNITS DELIVERED.

Vol. III "Washburn Guitars"

Again, work flow equals cash flow, and scheduling lies at the heart of the process. A schedule is a timetable for performing activities, utilizing resources, or allocating facilities. In this chapter we discuss short-run scheduling and control of orders with an emphasis on work centers. We also introduce some basic approaches to short-term scheduling of workers in services.

## MANUFACTURING EXECUTION SYSTEMS

Operations scheduling is at the heart of what is currently referred to as Manufacturing Execution Systems (MES). An MES is an information system that schedules, dispatches, tracks, monitors, and controls production on the factory floor. Such systems also provide real-time linkages to MRP systems, product and process planning, as well as systems that extend beyond the factory including supply chain management, ERP, sales, and service management. There are a number of software specialty houses that develop and implement MESs as part of a suite of software tools. (See for example, Ontrack, www.ontrack-mes.com/.)

## THE NATURE AND IMPORTANCE OF WORK CENTERS

Work center

A **work center** is an area in a business in which productive resources are organized and work is completed. The work center may be a single machine, a group of machines, or an area where a particular type of work is done. These work centers can be organized according to function in a job-shop configuration; or by product in a flow, assembly line, or group technology cell (GT cell) configuration. Recall from the discussion in Technical Note 5 that many firms have moved from the job-shop configuration to GT cells. Exhibit TN5.15 showed an example of job-shop and GT cell configurations from Rockwell Telecommunications Division.

In the case of the job shop, jobs need to be routed between functionally organized work centers to complete the work. When a job arrives at a work center—for example, the drilling department in a factory that makes custom-printed circuit boards—it enters a queue to wait for a drilling machine that can drill the required holes. Scheduling, in this case, involves determining the order for running the jobs, and also assigning a machine that can be used to make the holes.

A characteristic that distinguishes one scheduling system from another is how capacity is considered in determining the schedule. Scheduling systems can use either infinite or finite loading. **Infinite loading** occurs when work is assigned to a work center simply based on what is needed over time. No consideration is given directly to whether there is sufficient capacity at the resources required to complete the work, nor is the actual sequence of the work as done by each resource in the work center considered. Often, a simple check is made of key resources to see if they are overloaded in an aggregate sense, as demonstrated in Chapter 14 in Exhibit 14.19. This is done by calculating the amount of work required over a period (usually a week) using setup and run time standards for each order. When using an infinite loading system, lead time is estimated by taking a multiple of the expected operation time (setup and run time) plus an expected queuing delay caused by material movement and waiting for the order to be worked on.

Infinite loading

A **finite loading** approach actually schedules in detail each resource using the setup and run time required for each order. In essence, the system determines exactly what will be done by each resource at every moment during the working day. If an operation is delayed due to a part(s) shortage, the order will sit in queue and wait until the part is available from a preceding operation. Theoretically, all schedules are feasible when finite loading is used.

Finite loading

Another characteristic that distinguishes scheduling systems is whether the schedule is generated forward or backward in time. For this forward–backward dimension, the most common is forward scheduling. **Forward scheduling** refers to the situation in which the system takes an order and then schedules each operation that must be completed forward in time. A system that forward schedules can tell the earliest date that an order can be completed. Conversely, **backward scheduling** starts from some date in the future (possibly a due date) and schedules the required operations in reverse sequence. The backward schedule tells when an order must be started in order to be done by a specific date.

Forward scheduling

Backward scheduling

A material requirements planning (MRP) system is an example of an infinite, backward scheduling system for materials. With simple MRP, each order has a due date sometime in the future. In this case, the system calculates parts needs by backward scheduling the time that the operations will be run to complete the orders. The time required to make each part (or batch of parts) is estimated based on historical data. The scheduling systems addressed in this chapter are intended for the processes required to actually make those parts and subassemblies.

Thus far, the term *resources* has been used in a generic sense. In practice, we need to decide what we are going to actually schedule. Commonly, processes are referred to as either machine limited or labor limited. In a **machine-limited process,** equipment is the critical resource that is scheduled. Similarly, in a **labor-limited process,** people are the key resource that is scheduled. Most actual processes are either labor limited or machine limited but, luckily, not both.

Machine-limited process

Labor-limited process

Exhibit 15.1 describes the scheduling approaches typically used for different manufacturing processes. Whether capacity is considered depends on the actual process. Available computer technology allows generation of very detailed schedules, such as scheduling each job on each machine and assigning a specific worker to the machine at a specific point in time. Systems that capture the exact state of each job and each resource are also available. Using bar-coding technology, these systems can efficiently capture all of this detailed information. The Breakthrough Box on the Optimax system describes a typical example of the innovative new scheduling systems that are being developed to interface with enterprise resource planning software such as SAP R/3.

## TYPICAL SCHEDULING AND CONTROL FUNCTIONS

The following functions must be performed in scheduling and controlling an operation:

1 Allocating orders, equipment, and personnel to work centers or other specified locations. Essentially, this is short-run capacity planning.
2 Determining the sequence of order performance (that is, establishing job priorities).
3 Initiating performance of the scheduled work. This is commonly termed **dispatching** of orders.

Dispatching

EXHIBIT 15.1

## Types of Manufacturing Processes and Scheduling Approaches

| Type | Product | Characteristics | Typical Scheduling Approach |
|---|---|---|---|
| Pure process | Chemicals, steel, wire and cables, liquids (beer, soda), canned goods | Full automation, low labor content in product costs, facilities dedicated to one product | Finite forward scheduling of the process; machine limited |
| High-volume manufacturing | Automobiles, telephones, fasteners, textiles, motors, household, fixtures | Automated equipment, partial automated handling, moving assembly lines, most equipment in line | Finite forward scheduling of the line (a production rate is typical); machine limited; parts are pulled to the line using just-in-time (kanban) system |
| Mid-volume manufacturing | Industrial parts, high-end consumer products | GT cells, focused minifactories | Infinite forward scheduling typical: priority control; typically labor limited, but often machine limited; often responding to just-in-time orders from customers or MRP due dates |
| Low-volume Job shops | Custom or prototype equipment, specialized instruments, low-volume industrial products | Machining centers organized by manufacturing function (not in line), high labor content in product cost, general-purpose machinery with significant changeover time, little automation of material handling, large variety of product | Infinite, forward scheduling of jobs: usually labor limited, but certain functions may be machine limited (a heat-treating process or a precision machining center, for example); priorities determined by MRP due dates |

## BREAKTHROUGH

### OPTIMAX INTELLIGENT SCHEDULING AND PLANNING

One of the newer wrinkles in the scheduling arena is "order promising," observes Jeff Herrman, president and CEO of Optimax Systems Corp., a Cambridge, Massachusetts, provider of intelligent scheduling and planning systems. Optimax offers real-time available-to-promise (ATP) functionality in its latest offering, OptiFlex ATP, which it began offering in early 1997. "It doesn't simply match orders to preplanned production slots, but actually determines the factory's ability to fulfill an order by checking detailed constraints such as machine capacity, material availability, labor, and logistics," Herrman says. "It does this in real time, while the customer is on the line. I like to call it 'The customer schedules the factory.' " The approach: A user connects to a Web page, then clicks on order entry, then selects order configuration and requests a shipment date—and receives an "instant" reply as to whether the order can be fulfilled by the requested date.

More likely, the analysis of the factory's ability to produce and ship an order by a given date would occur in response to a query from a dealer or a salesperson in the field, he notes. "But ultimately, the customer could bypass sales," Herrman predicts. "For routine orders, this is very possible."

Although the OptiMax product is designed to supplement ERP systems (it will work with SAP), some vendors of broad-based packages are talking about offering sophisticated Internet-compatible scheduling systems as integral parts of the ERP software.

SOURCE: BASED ON INFORMATION CONTAINED IN J. H. SHERIDAN, "GEARING UP FOR E-COMMERCE," *INDUSTRY WEEK*, NOVEMBER 18, 1996, P. 43.

EXHIBIT 15.2

Typical Scheduling Process

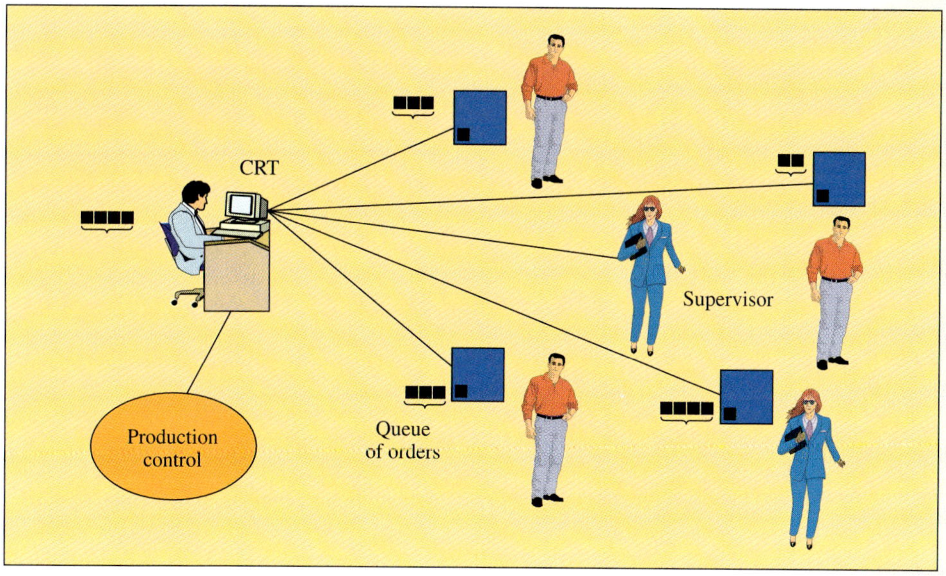


4 Shop-floor control (or production activity control) involving
   a. Reviewing the status and controlling the progress of orders as they are being worked on.
   b. Expediting late and critical orders.[1]

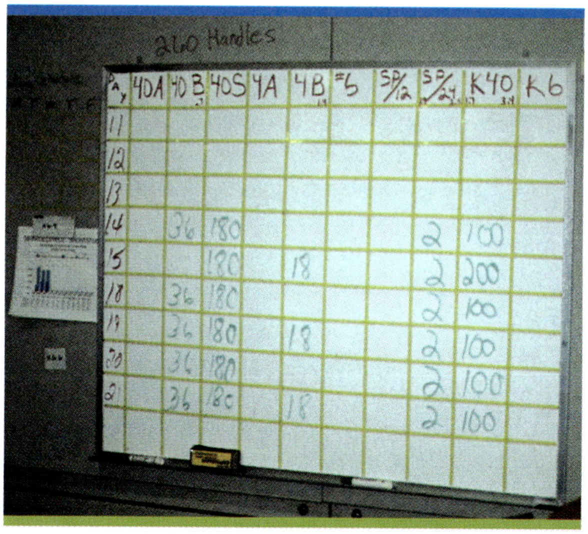

A simple work-center scheduling process is shown in Exhibit 15.2. At the start of the day, the scheduler (in this case, a production control person assigned to this department) selects and sequences available jobs to be run at individual workstations. The scheduler's decisions would be based on the operations and routing requirements of each job, the status of existing jobs at each work center, the queue of work before each work center, job priorities, material availability, anticipated job orders to be released later in the day, and work-center resource capabilities (labor and/or machines).

To help organize the schedule, the scheduler would draw on job status information from the previous day, external information provided by central production control, process engineering, and so on. The scheduler would also confer with the supervisor of the department about the feasibility of the schedule, especially workforce considerations and potential bottlenecks. The details of the schedule are communicated to workers via dispatch lists shown on computer terminals, in hard-copy printouts, or by posting a list of what should be worked on in central areas. Visible schedule boards, such as that depicted above in the

## TEN PRIORITY RULES FOR JOB SEQUENCING

1 FCFS (first-come, first-served). Orders are run in the order they arrive in the department.
2 SOT (shortest operating time). Run the job with the shortest completion time first, next shortest second, and so on. This is identical to SPT (shortest processing time).
3 Due date—earliest due date first: run the job with the earliest due date first. DDate—when referring to the entire job; OPNDD—when referring to the next operation.
4 Start date—due date minus normal lead time. Run the job with the earliest start date first.
5 STR (slack time remaining). This is calculated as the time remaining before the due date minus the processing time remaining. Orders with the shortest STR are run first.
6 STR/OP (slack time remaining per operation). Orders with the shortest STR/OP are run first. STR/OP is calculated as follows:

$$\text{STR/OP} = \frac{\text{Time remaining before due date} - \text{Remaining processing time}}{\text{Number of remaining operations}}$$

7 CR (critical ratio). This is calculated as the difference between the due date and the current date divided by the number of work days remaining. Orders with the smallest CR are run first.
8 QR (queue ratio). This is calculated as the slack time remaining in the schedule divided by the planned remaining queue time. Orders with the smallest QR are run first.
9 LCFS (last-come, first-served). This rule occurs frequently by default. As orders arrive they are placed on the top of the stack; the operator usually picks up the order on top to run first.
10 Random order or whim. The supervisors or the operators usually select whichever job they feel like running.

SOURCE: LIST MODIFIED FROM D. W. FOGARTY, J. H. BLACKSTONE, JR., AND T. R. HOFFMANN, *PRODUCTION AND INVENTORY MANAGEMENT* (CINCINNATI: SOUTH-WESTERN PUBLISHING, 1991), PP. 452–53.

picture of Bernard Welding, are highly effective ways to communicate the priority and current status of work.

## OBJECTIVES OF WORK-CENTER SCHEDULING

The objectives of work-center scheduling are (1) to meet due dates, (2) to minimize lead time, (3) to minimize setup time or cost, (4) to minimize work-in-process inventory, and (5) to maximize machine or labor utilization. (The last objective is controversial because simply keeping all equipment and/or employees busy may not be the most effective way to manage flow through the process.)

## JOB SEQUENCING

Sequencing

Priority rules

The process of determining which job to start first on some machine or in some work center is know as **sequencing** or priority sequencing. **Priority rules** are the rules used in obtaining a job sequence. These can be very simple, requiring only that jobs be sequenced according to one piece of data, such as processing time, due date, or order of arrival. Other rules, though equally simple, may require several pieces of information, typically to derive an index number such as the least-slack rule and the critical-ratio rule (both defined later). Still others, such as Johnson's rule (also discussed later), apply to job scheduling on a sequence of machines and require a computational procedure to specify the order of performance. Ten of the more common priority rules are shown in the box titled "Ten Priority Rules for Job Sequencing."

The following standard measures of schedule performance are used to evaluate priority rules:

1 Meeting due dates of customers or downstream operations.
2 Minimizing the flow time (the time a job spends in the process).

3 Minimizing work-in-process inventory.
4 Minimizing idle time of machines or workers.

# PRIORITY RULES AND TECHNIQUES

## SCHEDULING *n* JOBS ON ONE MACHINE

Let's look at some of the 10 priority rules compared in a static scheduling situation involving four jobs on one machine. (In scheduling terminology, this class of problems is referred to as an "$n$ job—one-machine problem" or simply "$n/1$.") The theoretical difficulty of scheduling problems increases as more machines are considered rather than as more jobs must be processed; therefore, the only restriction on $n$ is that it be a specified, finite number. Consider the following example.

### EXAMPLE 15.1: n JOBS ON ONE MACHINE

Mike Morales is the supervisor of Legal Copy-Express, which provides copy services for downtown Los Angeles law firms. Five customers submitted their orders at the beginning of the week. Specific scheduling data are as follows:

| Job (in Order of Arrival) | Processing Time (Days) | Due Date (Days Hence) |
|---|---|---|
| A | 3 | 5 |
| B | 4 | 6 |
| C | 2 | 7 |
| D | 6 | 9 |
| E | 1 | 2 |

All orders require the use of the only color copy machine available; Morales must decide on the processing sequence for the five orders. The evaluation criterion is minimum flow time. Suppose that Morales decides to use the FCFS rule in an attempt to make Legal Copy-Express appear fair to its customers.

### SOLUTION

FCFS RULE: The FCFS rule results in the following flow times:

FCFS SCHEDULE

| Job Sequence | Processing Time (Days) | Due Date (Days Hence) | Flow Time (Days) |
|---|---|---|---|
| A | 3 | 5 | $0 + 3 = 3$ |
| B | 4 | 6 | $3 + 4 = 7$ |
| C | 2 | 7 | $7 + 2 = 9$ |
| D | 6 | 9 | $9 + 6 = 15$ |
| E | 1 | 2 | $15 + 1 = 16$ |

Total flow time $= 3 + 7 + 9 + 15 + 16 = 50$ days

Mean flow time $= \frac{50}{5} = 10$ days

Comparing the due date of each job with its flow time, we observe that only Job A will be on time. Jobs B, C, D, and E will be late by 1, 2, 6, and 14 days, respectively. On average, a job will be late by $(0 + 1 + 2 + 6 + 14)/5 = 4.6$ days.

### SOLUTION

SOT RULE: Let's now consider the SOT rule. Here Morales gives the highest priority to the order that has the shortest processing time. The resulting flow times are

SOT SCHEDULE

| JOB SEQUENCE | PROCESSING TIME (DAYS) | DUE DATE (DAYS HENCE) | FLOW TIME (DAYS) |
|---|---|---|---|
| E | 1 | 2 | 0 + 1 = 1 |
| C | 2 | 7 | 1 + 2 = 3 |
| A | 3 | 5 | 3 + 3 = 6 |
| B | 4 | 6 | 6 + 4 = 10 |
| D | 6 | 9 | 10 + 6 = 16 |

Total flow time = 1 + 3 + 6 + 10 + 16 = 36 days

Mean flow time = $\frac{36}{5}$ = 7.2 days

SOT results in a lower average flow time than the FCFS rule. In addition, Jobs E and C will be ready before the due date, and Job A is late by only one day. On average, a job will be late by (0 + 0 + 1 + 4 + 7)/5 = 2.4 days.

### SOLUTION

DDATE RULE: If Morales decides to use the DDate rule, the resulting schedule is

DDATE SCHEDULE

| JOB SEQUENCE | PROCESSING TIME (DAYS) | DUE DATE (DAYS HENCE) | FLOW TIME (DAYS) |
|---|---|---|---|
| E | 1 | 2 | 0 + 1 = 1 |
| A | 3 | 5 | 1 + 3 = 4 |
| B | 4 | 6 | 4 + 4 = 8 |
| C | 2 | 7 | 8 + 2 = 10 |
| D | 6 | 9 | 10 + 6 = 16 |

Total completion time = 1 + 4 + 8 + 10 + 16 = 39 days
Mean flow time = 7.8 days

In this case Jobs B, C, and D will be late. On average, a job will be late by (0 + 0 + 2 + 3 + 7)/ 5 = 2.4 days.

### SOLUTION

LCFS, RANDOM, and STR RULES: Here are the resulting flow times of the LCFS, random, and STR rules:

| JOB SEQUENCE | PROCESSING TIME (DAYS) | DUE DATE (DAYS HENCE) | FLOW TIME (DAYS) |
|---|---|---|---|
| LCFS Schedule | | | |
| E | 1 | 2 | 0 + 1 = 1 |
| D | 6 | 9 | 1 + 6 = 7 |
| C | 2 | 7 | 7 + 2 = 9 |
| B | 4 | 6 | 9 + 4 = 13 |
| A | 3 | 5 | 13 + 3 = 16 |

Total flow time = 46 days

Mean flow time = 9.2 days

Average lateness = 4.0 days

*(Continued)*

| Job Sequence | Processing Time (Days) | Due Date (Days Hence) | Flow Time (Days) |
|---|---|---|---|
| Random Schedule | | | |
| D | 6 | 9 | 0 + 6 = 6 |
| C | 2 | 7 | 6 + 2 = 8 |
| A | 3 | 5 | 8 + 3 = 11 |
| E | 1 | 2 | 11 + 1 = 12 |
| B | 4 | 6 | 12 + 4 = 16 |
| Total flow time = 53 days | | | |
| Mean flow time = 10.6 days | | | |
| Average lateness = 5.4 days | | | |
| STR Schedule | | | |
| E | 1 | 2 | 0 + 1 = 1 |
| A | 3 | 5 | 1 + 3 – 4 |
| B | 4 | 6 | 4 + 4 = 8 |
| D | 6 | 9 | 8 + 6 = 14 |
| C | 2 | 7 | 14 + 2 = 16 |
| Total flow time = 43 days | | | |
| Mean flow time = 8.6 days | | | |
| Average lateness = 3.2 days | | | ← |

## Comparison of Priority Rules

Here are some of the results summarized for the rules that Morales examined:

| Rule | Total Completion Time (Days) | Average Completion Time (Days) | Average Lateness (Days) |
|---|---|---|---|
| FCFS | 50 | 10 | 4.6 |
| SOT | 36 | 7.2 | 2.4 |
| DDate | 39 | 7.8 | 2.4 |
| LCFS | 46 | 9.2 | 4.0 |
| Random | 53 | 10.6 | 5.4 |
| STR | 43 | 8.6 | 3.2 |

Obviously, here SOT is better than the rest of the rules, but is this always the case? The answer is yes. Moreover, it can be shown mathematically that the SOT rule yields an optimal solution for the $n/1$ case in such other evaluation criteria as mean waiting time and mean completion time. In fact, so powerful is this simple rule that it has been termed "the most important concept in the entire subject of sequencing."[2]

## Scheduling *n* Jobs on Two Machines

The next step up in complexity is the $n/2$ flow-shop case, where two or more jobs must be processed on two machines in a common sequence. As in the $n/1$ case, there is an approach that leads to an optimal solution according to certain criteria. The objective of this approach, termed **Johnson's rule** or *Johnson's method* (after its developer), is to minimize the flow time from the beginning of the first job until the finish of the last. Johnson's rule consists of the following steps:

Johnson's rule

1. List the operation time for each job on both machines.
2. Select the shortest operation time.
3. If the shortest time is for the first machine, do the job first; if it is for the second machine, do the job last.
4. Repeat Steps 2 and 3 for each remaining job until the schedule is complete.

### EXAMPLE 15.2: n JOBS ON TWO MACHINES

We can illustrate this procedure by scheduling four jobs through two machines.

### SOLUTION

*Step 1:* List operation times.

| JOB | OPERATION TIME ON MACHINE 1 | OPERATION TIME ON MACHINE 2 |
|---|---|---|
| A | 3 | 2 |
| B | 6 | 8 |
| C | 5 | 6 |
| D | 7 | 4 |

*Steps 2 and 3:* Select the shortest operation time and assign. Job A is shortest on Machine 2 and is assigned first and performed last. (Once assigned, Job A is no longer available to be scheduled.)

*Step 4:* Repeat Steps 2 and 3 until completion of the schedule. Select the shortest operation time among the remaining jobs. Job D is second shortest on Machine 2, so it is performed second to last. (Remember, Job A is last.) Now Jobs A and D are not available for scheduling. Job C is the shortest on Machine 1 among the remaining jobs. Job C is performed first. Now only Job B is left with the shortest operation time on Machine 1. Thus, according to Step 3, it is performed first among the remaining, or second overall. (Job C was already scheduled first.)

In summary, the solution sequence is C → B → D → A, and the flow time is 25 days, which is a minimum. Also minimized are total idle time and mean idle time. The final schedule appears in Exhibit 15.3.

These steps result in scheduling the jobs having the shortest time in the beginning and end of the schedule. As a result, the concurrent operating time for the two machines is maximized, thus minimizing the total operating time required to complete the jobs. ←

Johnson's method has been extended to yield an optimal solution for the $n/3$ case. When flow–shop scheduling problems larger than $n/3$ arise (and they generally do), analytical solution procedures leading to optimality are not available. The reason for this is that even though the jobs may arrive in static fashion at the first machine, the scheduling problem becomes dynamic, and waiting lines start to form in front of machines downstream.

## SCHEDULING A SET NUMBER OF JOBS ON THE SAME NUMBER OF MACHINES

Some job shops have enough of the right kinds of machines to start all jobs at the same time. Here the problem is not which job to do first, but rather which particular assignment of individual jobs to individual machines will result in the best overall schedule. In such cases, we can use the assignment method.

EXHIBIT 15.3

Optimal Schedule of Jobs Using Johnson's Rule

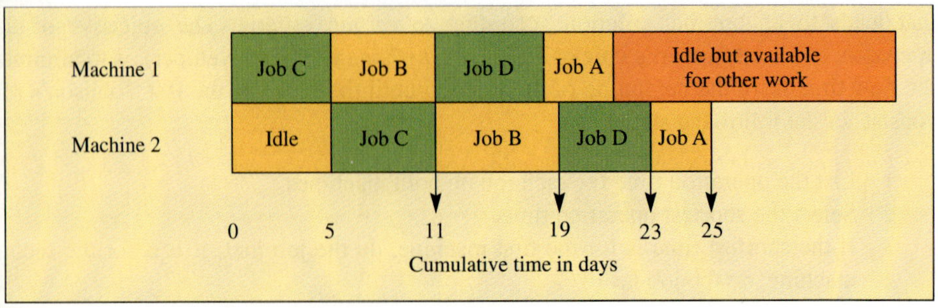

The **assignment method** is a special case of the transportation method of linear programming. It can be applied to situations where there are *n* supply sources and *n* demand uses (such as five jobs on five machines) and the objective is to minimize or maximize some measure of effectiveness. This technique is convenient in applications involving allocation of jobs to work centers, people to jobs, and so on. The assignment method is appropriate in solving problems that have the following characteristics:

Assignment method

1 There are *n* "things" to be distributed to *n* "destinations."
2 Each thing must be assigned to one and only one destination.
3 Only one criterion can be used (minimum cost, maximum profit, or minimum completion time, for example).

## EXAMPLE 15.3: ASSIGNMENT METHOD

Suppose that a scheduler has five jobs that can be performed on any of five machines ($n = 5$). The cost of completing each job–machine combination is shown in Exhibit 15.4. The scheduler would like to devise a minimum-cost assignment. (There are 5!, or 120, possible assignments.)

## SOLUTION

This problem may be solved by the assignment method, which consists of four steps (Note that this can also be solved using the Excel Solver):

1 Subtract the smallest number in each *row* from itself and all other numbers in that row. (There will then be at least one zero in each row.)
2 Subtract the smallest number in each *column* from all other numbers in that column. (There will then be at least one zero in each column.)
3 Determine if the *minimum* number of lines required to cover each zero is equal to *n*. If so, an optimal solution has been found, because job machine assignments must be made at the zero entries, and this test proves that this is possible. If the minimum number of lines required is less than *n*, go to Step 4.
4 Draw the least possible number of lines through all the zeros. (These may be the same lines used in Step 3.) Subtract the smallest number not covered by lines from itself and all other uncovered numbers, and add it to the number at each intersection of lines. Repeat Step 3.

For the example problem, the steps listed in Exhibit 15.5 would be followed.

Note that even though there are two zeros in three rows and three columns, the solution shown in Exhibit 15.5 is the only one possible for this problem because Job III must be assigned to Machine C to meet the "assign to zero" requirement. Other problems may have more than one optimal solution, depending, of course, on the costs involved. ←

The nonmathematical rationale of the assignment method is one of minimizing opportunity costs.[3] For example, if we decided to assign Job I to Machine A instead of to Machine E,

EXHIBIT 15.4

**Assignment Matrix Showing Machine Processing Costs for Each Job**

| | MACHINE | | | | |
|---|---|---|---|---|---|
| JOB | A | B | C | D | E |
| I | $5 | $6 | $4 | $8 | $3 |
| II | 6 | 4 | 9 | 8 | 5 |
| III | 4 | 3 | 2 | 5 | 4 |
| IV | 7 | 2 | 4 | 5 | 3 |
| V | 3 | 6 | 4 | 5 | 5 |

EXHIBIT 15.5

**Procedure to Solve an Assignment Matrix**

Step 1: Row reduction—the smallest number is subtracted from each row.

| | Machine | | | | |
|---|---|---|---|---|---|
| **Job** | **A** | **B** | **C** | **D** | **E** |
| I | 2 | 3 | 1 | 5 | 0 |
| II | 2 | 0 | 5 | 4 | 1 |
| III | 2 | 1 | 0 | 3 | 2 |
| IV | 5 | 0 | 2 | 3 | 1 |
| V | 0 | 3 | 1 | 2 | 2 |

Step 2: Column reduction—the smallest number is subtracted from each column.

| | Machine | | | | |
|---|---|---|---|---|---|
| **Job** | **A** | **B** | **C** | **D** | **E** |
| I | 2 | 3 | 1 | 3 | 0 |
| II | 2 | 0 | 5 | 2 | 1 |
| III | 2 | 1 | 0 | 1 | 2 |
| IV | 5 | 0 | 2 | 1 | 1 |
| V | 0 | 3 | 1 | 0 | 2 |

Step 3: Apply line test—the number of lines to cover all zeros is 4; because 5 are required, go to step 4.

| | Machine | | | | |
|---|---|---|---|---|---|
| **Job** | **A** | **B** | **C** | **D** | **E** |
| I | 2 | 3 | 1 | 3 | 0 |
| II | 2 | 0 | 5 | 2 | 1 |
| III | 2 | 1 | 0 | 1 | 2 |
| IV | 5 | 0 | 2 | 1 | 1 |
| V | 0 | 3 | 1 | 0 | 2 |

Step 4: Subtract smallest uncovered number and add to intersection of lines. Using lines drawn in Step 3, smallest uncovered number is 1.

| | Machine | | | | |
|---|---|---|---|---|---|
| **Job** | **A** | **B** | **C** | **D** | **E** |
| I | 1 | 3 | 0 | 2 | 0 |
| II | 1 | 0 | 4 | 1 | 1 |
| III | 2 | 2 | 0 | 1 | 3 |
| IV | 4 | 0 | 1 | 0 | 1 |
| V | 0 | 4 | 1 | 0 | 3 |

Optimal solution—by "line test."

| | Machine | | | | |
|---|---|---|---|---|---|
| **Job** | **A** | **B** | **C** | **D** | **E** |
| I | 1 | 3 | 0 | 2 | 0 |
| II | 1 | 0 | 4 | 1 | 1 |
| III | 2 | 2 | 0 | 1 | 3 |
| IV | 4 | 0 | 1 | 0 | 1 |
| V | 0 | 4 | 1 | 0 | 3 |

Optimal assignments and their costs.

| | |
|---|---|
| Job I to Machine E | $ 3 |
| Job II to Machine B | 4 |
| Job III to Machine C | 2 |
| Job IV to Machine D | 5 |
| Job V to Machine A | 3 |
| Total cost | $17 |

we would be sacrificing the opportunity to save $2($5 − $3). The assignment algorithm in effect performs such comparisons for the entire set of alternative assignments by means of row and column reduction, as described in Steps 1 and 2. It makes similar comparisons in Step 4. Obviously, if assignments are made to zero cells, no opportunity cost, with respect to the entire matrix, occurs.

## SCHEDULING *n* JOBS ON *m* MACHINES

Complex job shops are characterized by multiple machine centers processing a variety of different jobs arriving at the machine centers intermittently throughout the day. If there are $n$ jobs to be processed on $m$ machines and all jobs are processed on all machines, then there are $(n!)^m$ alternative schedules for this job set. Because of the large number of schedules that exist for even small job shops, computer simulation (see Technical Note 15) is the only practical way to determine the relative merits of different priority rules in such situations. As in the case of $n$ jobs on one machine, the 10 priority rules (and more) have been compared relative to their performance on the evaluation criteria previously mentioned. By way of example, John Kanet and Jack Hayya focused on due date–oriented priority rules to see which one was best. Their simulation of a complex job shop led to the finding that total job competition rules of "DDATE, STR, and CR were outperformed by their 'operation' counterparts OPNDD, STR/OP, and OPCR" for all seven of the performance criteria used.[4]

**Which Priority Rule Should Be Used?** We believe that the needs of most manufacturers are reasonably satisfied by a relatively simple priority scheme that embodies the following principles:

1 It should be dynamic, that is, computed frequently during a job to reflect changing conditions.
2 It should be based in one way or another on slack (the difference between the work remaining to be done on a job and the time remaining to do it). This embodies the due date features suggested by Kanet and Hayya.

Newer approaches combine simulation with human schedulers to create schedules.

## SHOP-FLOOR CONTROL

Scheduling job priorities is just one aspect of **shop-floor control** (now often called *production activity control*). The *APICS Dictionary* defines a *shop-floor control system* as

Shop-floor control

> A system for utilizing data from the shop floor as well as data processing files to maintain and communicate status information on shop orders and work centers.

The major functions of shop-floor control are:

1 Assigning priority of each shop order.
2 Maintaining work-in-process quantity information.
3 Conveying shop-order status information to the office.
4 Providing actual output data for capacity control purposes.
5 Providing quantity by location by shop order for WIP inventory and accounting purposes.
6 Measuring efficiency, utilization, and productivity of manpower and machines.

### GANTT CHARTS

Smaller job shops and individual departments of large ones employ the venerable Gantt chart to help plan and track jobs. As described in Chapter 3, the Gantt Chart is a type of bar chart that plots tasks against time. Gantt charts are used for project planning as well as to coordinate a number of scheduled activities. The example in Exhibit 15.6 indicates that Job A is behind schedule by about four hours, Job B is ahead of schedule, and Job C has been completed, after a delayed start for equipment maintenance. Note that whether the job is ahead of schedule or behind schedule is based on where it stands compared to where we are

EXHIBIT 15.6

Gantt Chart

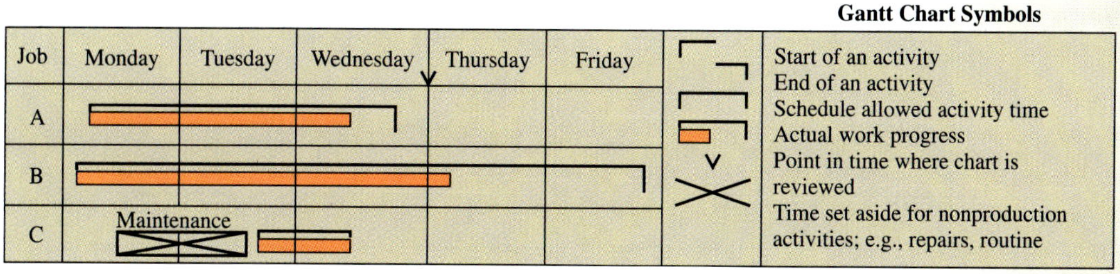

now. In Exhibit 15.6 we are at the end of Wednesday, and Job A should have been completed. Job B has already had some of Thursday's work completed.

## TOOLS OF SHOP-FLOOR CONTROL

The basic tools of shop-floor control are

1 The *daily dispatch list,* which tells the supervisor which jobs are to be run, their priority, and how long each will take. (See Exhibit 15.7a.)

2 Various *status and exception reports,* including
   a. The anticipated delay report, made out by the shop planner once or twice a week and reviewed by the chief shop planner to see if there are any serious delays that could affect the master schedule. (See Exhibit 15.7b.)
   b. Scrap reports.
   c. Rework reports.
   d. Performance summary reports giving the number and percentage of orders completed on schedule, lateness of unfilled orders, volume of output, and so on.
   e. Shortage list.

EXHIBIT 15.7

Some Basic Tools of Shop-Floor Control

**A. Dispatch List**

Work center 1501—Day 205

| Start date | Job # | Description | Run time |
|---|---|---|---|
| 201 | 15131 | Shaft | 11.4 |
| 203 | 15143 | Stud | 20.6 |
| 205 | 15145 | Spindle | 4.3 |
| 205 | 15712 | Spindle | 8.6 |
| 207 | 15340 | Metering rod | 6.5 |
| 208 | 15312 | Shaft | 4.6 |

**B. Anticipated Delay Report**

Dept. 24 April 8

| Part # | Sched. date | New date | Cause of delay | Action |
|---|---|---|---|---|
| 17125 | 4/10 | 4/15 | Fixture broke | Toolroom will return on 4/15 |
| 13044 | 4/11 | 5/1 | Out for plating—plater on strike | New lot started |
| 17653 | 4/11 | 4/14 | New part holes don't align | Engineering laying out new jig |

**C. Input/Output Control Report**

Work center 0162

| Week ending | 505 | 512 | 519 | 526 |
|---|---|---|---|---|
| Planned input | 210 | 210 | 210 | 210 |
| Actual input | 110 | 150 | 140 | 130 |
| Cumulative deviation | –100 | –160 | –230 | –310 |
| Planned output | 210 | 210 | 210 | 210 |
| Actual output | 140 | 120 | 160 | 120 |
| Cumulative deviation | –70 | –160 | –210 | –300 |

3 An *input/output control report,* which is used by the supervisor to monitor the workload–capacity relationship for each workstation. (See Exhibit 15.7c.)

## INPUT/OUTPUT CONTROL

Input/output (I/O) control

**Input/output (I/O) control** is a major feature of a manufacturing planning and control system. Its major precept is that the planned work input to a work center should never exceed the planned work output. When the input exceeds the output, backlogs build up at the work center, which in turn increases the lead time estimates for jobs upstream. Moreover, when jobs pile up at the work center, congestion occurs, processing becomes inefficient, and the flow of work to downstream work centers becomes sporadic. (The water flow analogy to shop capacity control in Exhibit 15.8 illustrates the general phenomenon.) Exhibit 15.7c shows an I/O report for a downstream work center. Looking first at the lower or output half of the report, we see that output is far below plan. It would seem that a serious capacity problem exists for this work center. However, looking at the input part of the plan, it becomes apparent that the serious capacity problem exists at an upstream work center feeding this work center. The control process would entail finding the cause of upstream problems and adjusting capacity and inputs accordingly. The basic solution is simple: Either increase capacity at the bottleneck station, or reduce the input to it. (Input reduction at bottleneck work centers, incidentally, is usually the first step recommended by production control consultants when job shops get into trouble.)

## DATA INTEGRITY

Shop-floor control systems in most modern plants are now computerized, with job status information entered directly into a computer as the job enters and leaves a work center. Many plants have gone heavily into bar coding and optical scanners to speed up the reporting process and to cut down on data entry errors.[5] As you might guess, the key problems in

EXHIBIT 15.8

Shop Capacity Control Load Flow

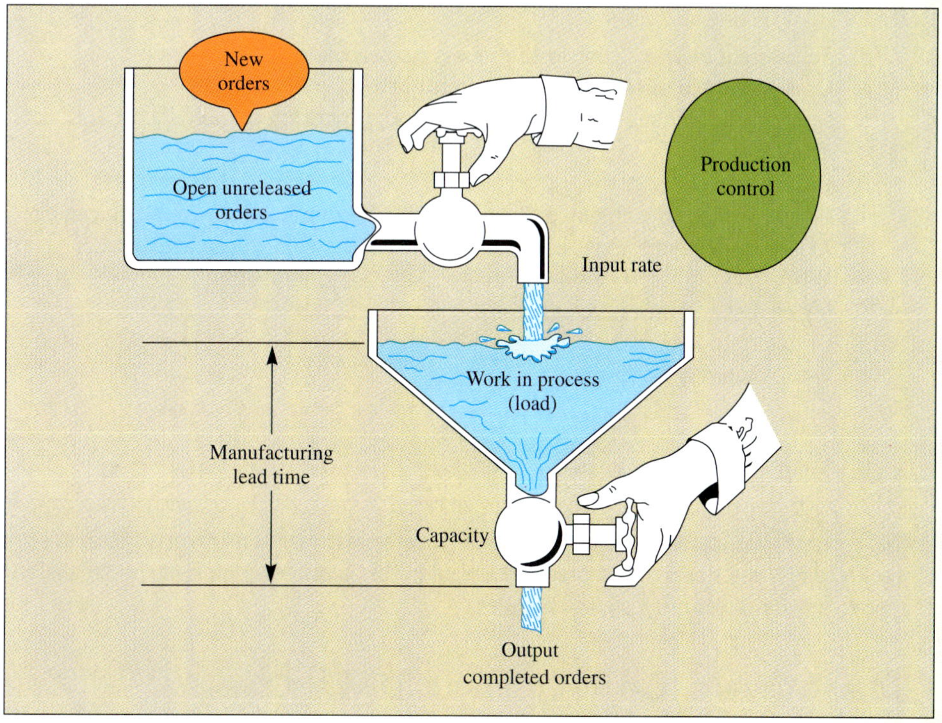


SOURCE: "TRAINING AID—SHOP FLOOR CONTROL," UNDATED. REPRINTED WITH PERMISSION OF APICS—THE EDUCATIONAL SOCIETY FOR RESOURCE MANAGEMENT, FALLS CHURCH, VA.

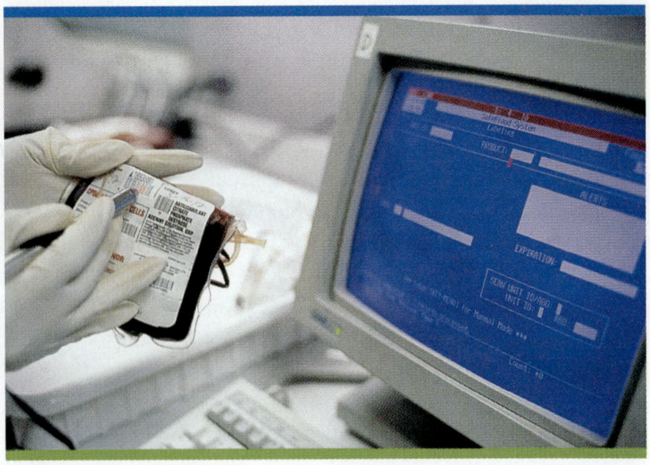

shop-floor control are data inaccuracy and lack of timeliness. When these occur, data fed back to the overall planning system are wrong, and incorrect production decisions are made. Typical results are excess inventory, stockout problems, or both; missed due dates; and inaccuracies in job costing.

Of course, maintaining data integrity requires that a sound data-gathering system be in place; but more important, it requires adherence to the system by everybody interacting with it. Most firms recognize this, but maintaining what is variously referred to as *shop discipline, data integrity,* or *data responsibility* is not always easy. And despite periodic drives to publicize the importance of careful shop-floor reporting by creating data integrity task forces, inaccuracies can still creep into the system in many ways: A line worker drops a part under the workbench and pulls a replacement from stock without recording either transaction. An inventory clerk makes an error in a cycle count. A manufacturing engineer fails to note a change in the routing of a part. A department supervisor decides to work jobs in a different order than specified in the dispatch list.

### PRINCIPLES OF WORK-CENTER SCHEDULING

Much of our discussion of work-center scheduling systems can be summarized in the following principles:

1. There is a direct equivalence between work flow and cash flow.
2. The effectiveness of any shop should be measured by speed of flow through the shop.
3. Schedule jobs as a string, with process steps back to back.
4. Once started, a job should not be interrupted.
5. Speed of flow is most efficiently achieved by focusing on bottleneck work centers and jobs.
6. Reschedule every day.
7. Obtain feedback each day on jobs that are not completed at each work center.
8. Match work-center input information to what the worker can actually do.
9. When seeking improvement in output, look for incompatibility between engineering design and process execution.
10. Certainty of standards, routings, and so forth is not possible in a shop, but always work toward achieving it.

## PERSONNEL SCHEDULING IN SERVICES

Service

The scheduling problem in most service organizations revolves around setting weekly, daily, and hourly personnel schedules. In this section we present simple analytical approaches for developing such schedules.

### SCHEDULING CONSECUTIVE DAYS OFF

Vol. IV "Scheduling Services—the United Solution"

A practical problem encountered in many services is setting schedules so that employees can have two consecutive days off. The importance of the problem stems from the fact that the Fair Labor Standards Act requires overtime pay for any work hours (by hourly workers) in excess of 40 hours per week. Obviously, if two consecutive days off cannot be scheduled each week for each employee, the likelihood of unnecessary overtime is quite high. In addition, most people probably prefer two consecutive days off per week. The following heuristic procedure was modified from that developed by James Browne and Rajen Tibrewala to deal with this problem.[6]

**Objective** Find the schedule that minimizes the number of five-day workers with two consecutive days off, subject to the demands of the daily staffing schedule.

**Procedure** Starting with the total number of workers required for each day of the week, create a schedule by adding one worker at a time. This is a two-step procedure:

*Step 1.* Assign the first worker to all of the days that require staffing. Do this by simply recopying the total requirements for each day. (This gives us an easy way to keep track of the number of workers needed each day.) A positive number means that the worker has been assigned to work that day.

Because the first worker may have been assigned to all seven days, circle the two consecutive days with the lowest numbers. These will be considered for days off. The lowest pair is the one where the highest number in the pair is equal to or lower than the highest number in any other pair. This ensures that the days with the highest requirements are covered by staff. (Monday and Sunday may be chosen even though they are at opposite ends of the array of days.) In case of ties, choose the days-off pair with the lowest requirement on an adjacent day. This day may be before or after the pair. If a tie still remains, choose the first of the available tied pairs. (Do not bother using further tie-breaking rules, such as second lowest adjacent days.)

*Step 2.* For Worker 2, subtract 1 from each of the days not circled with positive numbers and enter this in the Worker 2 row. This indicates that one less worker is required on these days because the first worker has just been assigned to them.

The two steps are repeated for the second worker, the third worker, and so forth, until no more workers are required to satisfy the schedule.

## EXAMPLE 15.4: SCHEDULING DAYS OFF

| | NUMBER OF WORKERS REQUIRED | | | | | | |
|---|---|---|---|---|---|---|---|
| | M | TU | W | TH | F | S | SU |
| | 4 | 3 | 4 | 2 | 3 | 1 | 2 |
| Worker 1 | 4 | 3 | 4 | 2 | 3 | (1 | 2) |
| Worker 2 | 3 | 2 | 3 | 1 | (2 | 1) | 2 |
| Worker 3 | 2 | 1 | 2 | 0 | 2 | (1 | 1) |
| Worker 4 | 1 | (0 | 1) | 0 | 1 | 1 | 1 |
| Worker 5 | 0 | 0 | 1 | 0 | 0 | 0 | 0 |

## SOLUTION

This solution consists of five workers covering 19 worker days, although slightly different assignments may be equally satisfactory.

The schedule is Worker 1 assigned S–Su off, Worker 2 F–S off, Worker 3 S–Su off, Worker 4 Tu–W off, and Worker 5 works only on Wednesday because there are no further requirements for the other days. Note that Workers 3 and 4 are also off on Thursday. ←

## SCHEDULING DAILY WORK TIMES

We now show how bank clearinghouses and back-office operations of large bank branches establish daily work times. Basically, management wants to derive a staffing plan that (1) requires the fewest workers to accomplish the daily workload and (2) minimizes the variance between actual and planned output.

EXHIBIT 15.9

### Daily Staff Hours Required to Schedule Daily Work Times

| | | Function | | | | | | | | |
|---|---|---|---|---|---|---|---|---|---|---|
| | | Receive | | Preprocess | | Microfilm | | Verify | | Totals |
| Product | Daily Volume | *P/H* | $H_{std}$ | *P/H* | $H_{std}$ | *P/H* | $H_{std}$ | *P/H* | $H_{std}$ | $H_{std}$ |
| Checks | 2,000 | 1,000 | 2.0 | 600 | 3.3 | 240 | 8.3 | 640 | 3.1 | 16.7 |
| Statements | 1,000 | — | — | 600 | 1.7 | 250 | 4.0 | 150 | 6.7 | 12.4 |
| Notes | 200 | 30 | 6.7 | 15 | 13.3 | | — | | | 20.0 |
| Investments | 400 | 100 | 4.0 | 50 | 8.0 | 200 | 2.0 | 150 | 2.7 | 16.7 |
| Collections | 500 | 300 | 1.7 | | | 300 | 1.7 | 60 | 8.4 | 11.8 |
| Total hours required | | | 14.4 | | 26.3 | | 16.0 | | 20.9 | 77.6 |
| Times 1.25 (absences and vacations) | | | 18.0 | | 32.9 | | 20.0 | | 26.1 | |
| Divided by 8 hours equals staff required | | | 2.3 | | 4.1 | | 2.5 | | 3.3 | 12.2 |

Note: *P/H* indicates production rate per hour: $H_{std}$ indicates required hours.

EXHIBIT 15.10

### Staffing Plan

| Function | Staff Required | Staff Available | Variance (±) | Management Actions |
|---|---|---|---|---|
| Receive | 2.3 | 2.0 | −0.3 | Use overtime. |
| Preprocess | 4.1 | 4.0 | −0.1 | Use overtime. |
| Microfilm | 2.5 | 3.0 | +0.5 | Use excess to verify. |
| Verify | 3.3 | 3.0 | −0.3 | Get 0.3 from microfilm. |

In structuring the problem, bank management defines inputs (checks, statements, investment documents, and so forth) as *products,* which are routed through different processes or *functions* (receiving, sorting, encoding, and so forth).

To solve the problem, a daily demand forecast is made by product for each function. This is converted to labor hours required per function, which in turn is converted to workers required per function. These figures are then tabled, summed, and adjusted by an absence and vacation factor to give planned hours. Then they are divided by the number of hours in the workday to yield the number of workers required. This yields the daily staff hours required. (See Exhibit 15.9.) This becomes the basis for a departmental staffing plan that lists the workers required, workers available, variance, and managerial action in light of variance. (See Exhibit 15.10.)

## SCHEDULING HOURLY WORK TIMES

Services such as restaurants face changing requirements from hour to hour. More workers are needed for peak hours, and fewer are needed in between. Management must continuously adjust to this changing requirement. This kind of personnel scheduling situation can be approached by applying a simple rule, the *"first-hour" principle.*[7] This procedure can be best explained using the following example. Assume that each worker works continuously for an eight-hour shift. The first-hour rule says that for the first hour, we assign a number of workers equal to the requirement in that period. For each subsequent period, assign the exact number of additional workers to meet the requirements. When in a period one or more workers come to the end of their shifts, add more workers only if they are needed

# BREAKTHROUGH

## AUTOMATED SYSTEMS FOR CALL CENTER MANAGEMENT

The trend in call centers is, in a word, growth. An increased volume of calls, coupled with the growing complexity of staff scheduling (longer operating hours, weekend shifts, mixture of full- and part-time staff, etc.) make workforce management problems ideally suited for the computer. Workforce management software, combined with the historical and real-time statistics of the Automated Call Distributor (a software program sold by Call Center Solutions), is an essential tool for a professionally managed call center in today's world.

The basic functions associated with a workforce management software system are as follows:

Call volume forecasting. A workforce management system uses the ACD's historical and current call information to predict future call volume based on overall calling trends, seasonal factors and other predictable calling patterns. To incorporate any changes in calling patterns, forecasts are automatically updated with new information through a direct ACD interface.

Staffing calculations. A telephone traffic engineering technique is used to determine the required number of staff based on the forecast workload. This technique, called Erlang C, takes into account the random arrival of calls into the center, as well as the "hold for the first agent" queuing that typically takes place.

Staff scheduling. "Bodies in chairs" staff requirements along with nonproductive time estimates (for breaks, training, meetings, etc.) are used to determine a schedule requirement for each half-hour or quarter-hour period. A set of optimal schedules is then created based on these requirements and a call center's unique scheduling rules and constraints. These schedules are then assigned to staff based on shift bid rules and employee preferences.

Day-to-day performance tracking. Perhaps the most critical component of a workforce management system is the intra-day comparison of actual performance against the plan. Call center management must actively compare the actual number of calls by half-hour to the call forecast, actual call handle time against estimated handle time and actual number of staff on the phones to the schedule plan. The call center manager needs to see these changes as they are happening to make necessary adjustments as quickly as possible.

An automated workforce management system generally produces measurable improvements in the following areas:

More efficient scheduling. The savings associated with more efficient scheduling can take many forms, including reduced overall staff hours, reduced need for overtime and identification of overstaffed periods to offer time off without pay. Workforce management system users generally experience a minimum reduction of staff hours of 2 percent and average potential is in the 5 to 10 percent range.

Automation of workforce management tasks. Depending on how often forecasting and scheduling tasks are performed and to what degree they are currently automated, a wide range of savings in staff time may result from automating them with a full-featured workforce management system. It is generally expected that at least 25 percent of administrative and managerial time currently devoted to the manual performance of these tasks can be saved.

Reduction in workforce shrinkage. Many hours of staff time are lost in most call centers due to excessive amounts of nonproductive time (time spent not handling calls). An automated workforce management system can provide historical and real-time information on schedule adherence and schedule exceptions for better management and control of staff, reducing workforce shrinkage from 1 to 5 percent in most call centers.

Reduction in network costs. A more consistent level of service to callers and a reduction in queue time and toll-free network costs can be achieved with the workforce management software's creation of a set of schedules that minimizes understaffing as well as overstaffing.

Increased revenues. For call centers that realize revenue by answering calls (catalogs, reservations centers, etc.), workforce management automation can help reduce queue times and improve service, thereby reducing the number of abandons and increasing the number of revenue calls completed.

In addition to these measurable cost savings, there are many intangible benefits. Perhaps the biggest of these is the addition of a sophisticated "what-if" planning capability that allows management to forecast and plan staff needs for the short-term to respond to unexpected changes, as well as to address long-term budgeting and planning.

SOURCE: MODIFIED FROM PENNY REYNOLDS, "AUTOMATING FOR BETTER WORKFORCE MANAGEMENT," *CALL CENTER SOLUTIONS*, NORWALK, VOL. 17, NO. 9, MAR 1999, PP. 74–80.

to meet the requirement. The following table shows the worker requirements for the first 12 hours in a 24-hour restaurant:

| | Period | | | | | | | | | | | |
|---|---|---|---|---|---|---|---|---|---|---|---|---|
| | 10 A.M. | 11 A.M. | Noon | 1 P.M. | 2 P.M. | 3 P.M. | 4 P.M. | 5 P.M. | 6 P.M. | 7 P.M. | 8 P.M. | 9 P.M. |
| Requirement | 4 | 6 | 8 | 8 | 6 | 4 | 4 | 6 | 8 | 10 | 10 | 6 |

The schedule shows that four workers are assigned at 10 A.M., two are added at 11 A.M., and another two are added at noon to meet the requirement. From noon to 5 P.M. we have eight workers on duty. Note the overstaffing between 2 P.M. and 6 P.M. The four workers assigned at 10 A.M. finish their eight-hour shifts by 6 P.M., and four more workers are added to start their shifts. The two workers starting at 11 A.M. leave by 7 P.M., and the number of workers available drops to six. Therefore, four new workers are assigned at 7 P.M. At 9 P.M., there are 10 workers on duty, which is more than the requirement, so no worker is added. This procedure continues as new requirements are given.

| | Period | | | | | | | | | | | |
|---|---|---|---|---|---|---|---|---|---|---|---|---|
| | 10 A.M. | 11 A.M. | Noon | 1 P.M. | 2 P.M. | 3 P.M. | 4 P.M. | 5 P.M. | 6 P.M. | 7 P.M. | 8 P.M. | 9 P.M. |
| Requirement | 4 | 6 | 8 | 8 | 6 | 4 | 4 | 6 | 8 | 10 | 10 | 6 |
| Assigned | 4 | 2 | 2 | 0 | 0 | 0 | 0 | 0 | 4 | 4 | 2 | 0 |
| On Duty | 4 | 6 | 8 | 8 | 8 | 8 | 8 | 8 | 8 | 10 | 10 | 10 |

Another option is splitting shifts. For example, the worker can come in, work for four hours, then come back two hours later for another four hours. The impact of this option in scheduling is essentially similar to that of changing lot size in production. When workers start working, they have to log in, change uniforms, and probably get necessary information from workers in the previous shift. This preparation can be considered as the "setup cost" in a production scenario. Splitting shifts is like having smaller production lot sizes and thus more preparation (more setups). This problem can be solved by linear programming methods described in the Nanda and Browne bibliographic reference.

A major application area for service scheduling is call centers. The Breakthrough Box titled "Automated Systems for Call Center Management" describes the problems involved and the benefits provided by a representative automated system for call center management.

## CONCLUSION

In manufacturing job shops, scheduling now relies heavily on simulation to estimate the flow of work through the system to determine bottlenecks and adjust job priorities. Various software packages are available to do this. In services, the focus is typically on employee scheduling using mathematical tools that can be used to set work schedules in light of expected customer demand. No matter what the scheduling situation is, it is important to avoid suboptimization—a schedule that works well for one part of the organization but creates problems for other parts or, most importantly, for the customer.

## KEY TERMS

**Work center** An area in a business in which productive resources are organized and work is completed.

**Infinite loading** Work is assigned to a work center based on what is needed over time. Capacity is not considered.

**Finite loading** Each resource is scheduled in detail using the setup and run time required for each order. The system determines exactly what will be done by each resource at every moment during the working day.

**Forward scheduling** Schedules from now into the future to tell the earliest that an order can be completed.

**Backward scheduling** Starts from some date in the future (typically the due date) and schedules the required operations in reverse sequence. Tells the latest time when an order can be started so that it is completed by a specific date.

**Machine-limited process** Equipment is the critical resource that is scheduled.

**Labor-limited process** People are the key resource that is scheduled.

**Dispatching** The activity of initiating scheduled work.

**Sequencing** The process of determining which job to start first on a machine or work center.

**Priority rules** The logic used to determine the sequence of jobs in a queue.

**Johnson's rule** A sequencing rule used for scheduling any number of jobs on two machines. The rule is designed to minimize the time required to complete all the jobs.

**Assignment method** A special case of the transportation method of linear programming that is used to allocate a specific number of jobs to the same number of machines.

**Shop-floor (production activity) control** A system for utilizing data from the shop floor to maintain and communicate status information on shop orders and work centers.

**Input/output (I/O) control** Work being released into a work center should never exceed the planned work output. When the input exceeds the output, backlogs build up at the work center that increase the lead time.

# SOLVED PROBLEM

## SOLVED PROBLEM 1

Nancy's Auto Seat Cover and Paint Shop is bidding on a contract to do all the custom work for Smiling Ed's used car dealership. One of the main requirements in obtaining this contract is rapid delivery time, because Ed—for reasons we shall not go into here—wants the cars facelifted and back on his lot in a hurry. Ed has said that if Nancy can refit and repaint five cars that Ed has just received in 24 hours or less, the contract will be hers. Following is the time (in hours) required in the refitting shop and the paint shop for each of the five cars. Assuming that cars go through the refitting operations before they are repainted, can Nancy meet the time requirements and get the contract?

| Car | Refitting Time (Hours) | Repainting Time (Hours) |
|---|---|---|
| A | 6 | 3 |
| B | 0 | 4 |
| C | 5 | 2 |
| D | 8 | 6 |
| E | 2 | 1 |

### Solution

This problem can be viewed as a two-machine flow shop and can be easily solved using Johnson's rule. The final schedule is B-D-A-C-E.

| | Original Data | | Johnson Rule | |
|---|---|---|---|---|
| Car | Refitting Time (Hours) | Repainting Time (Hours) | Order of Selection | Position in Sequence |
| A | 6 | 3 | 4 | 3 |
| B | 0 | 4 | 1 | 1 |
| C | 5 | 2 | 3 | 4 |
| D | 8 | 6 | 5 | 2 |
| E | 2 | 1 | 2 | 5 |

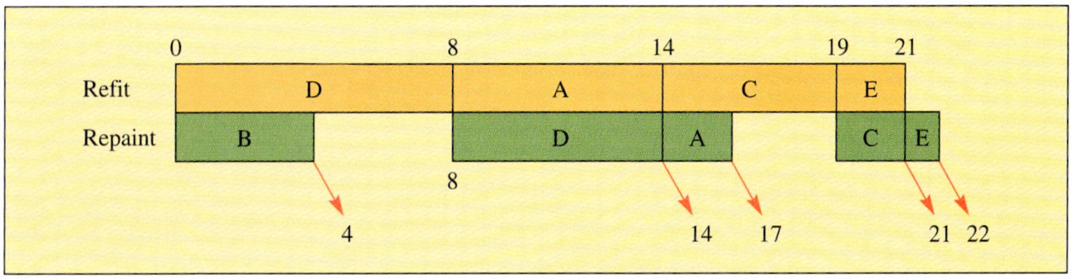

## REVIEW AND DISCUSSION QUESTIONS

1 What are the objectives of work-center scheduling?
2 Distinguish between a job shop, a GT cell, and a flow shop.
3 What practical considerations are deterrents to using the SOT rule?
4 What priority rule do you use in scheduling your study time for midterm examinations? If you have five exams to study for, how many alternative schedules exist?
5 The SOT rule provides an optimal solution in a number of evaluation criteria. Should the manager of a bank use the SOT rule as a priority rule? Why?
6 Data integrity is a big deal in industry. Why?
7 Why does batching cause so much trouble in job shops?
8 What job characteristics would lead you to schedule jobs according to "longest processing time first"?
9 Why is managing bottlenecks so important in job-shop scheduling?
10 Under what conditions is the assignment method appropriate?
11 How might planning for a special customer affect the personnel schedule in a service?

## PROBLEMS

1. 

| Car | Priority |
|---|---|
| C | First |
| A | Tie for second |
| B | Tie for second |

1 Christine has three cars that must be overhauled by her ace mechanic, Megan. Given the following data about the cars, use least slack per remaining operation to determine Megan's scheduling priority for each:

| Car | Customer Pick-Up Time (Hours Hence) | Remaining Overhaul Time (Hours) | Remaining Operation |
|---|---|---|---|
| A | 10 | 4 | Painting |
| B | 17 | 5 | Wheel alignment, painting |
| C | 15 | 1 | Chrome plating, painting, seat repair |

2. See table

2 A hotel has to schedule its receptionists according to hourly loads. Management has identified the number of receptionists needed to meet the hourly requirement, which changes from day to day. Assume each receptionist works a four-hour shift. Given the following staffing requirement in a certain day, use the first-hour principle to find the personnel schedule:

| | Period | | | | | | | | | | | |
|---|---|---|---|---|---|---|---|---|---|---|---|---|
| | 8 A.M. | 9 A.M. | 10 A.M. | 11 A.M. | Noon | 1 P.M. | 2 P.M. | 3 P.M. | 4 P.M. | 5 P.M. | 6 P.M. | 7 P.M. |
| Requirement | 2 | 3 | 5 | 8 | 8 | 6 | 5 | 8 | 8 | 6 | 4 | 3 |
| Assigned | 2 | 1 | 2 | 3 | 2 | | | 6 | 2 | | | 1 |
| On duty | 2 | 3 | 5 | 8 | 8 | 7 | 5 | 8 | 8 | 8 | 8 | 3 |

3. Job order
5
6
7
3
1
2
4

3 Seven jobs must be processed in two operations: A and B. All seven jobs must go through A and B in that sequence—A first, then B. Determine the optimal order in which the jobs should be sequenced through the process using these times:

| Job | Process A Time | Process B Time |
|---|---|---|
| 1 | 9 | 6 |
| 2 | 8 | 5 |
| 3 | 7 | 7 |
| 4 | 6 | 3 |
| 5 | 1 | 2 |
| 6 | 2 | 6 |
| 7 | 4 | 7 |

4. 4 workers: 2—TuW, 1—SuM, 1—WTh, answer may vary.

4 Jumbo's Restaurant is trying to create a consecutive days off schedule that uses the fewest workers. Use the following information to create a consecutive days off schedule:

| | Day | | | | | | |
|---|---|---|---|---|---|---|---|
| | M | Tu | W | Th | F | S | Su |
| Requirements | 2 | 2 | 1 | 3 | 3 | 4 | 2 |

5 The following list of jobs in a critical department includes estimates of their required times:

| JOB | REQUIRED TIME (DAYS) | DAYS TO DELIVERY PROMISE | SLACK |
|---|---|---|---|
| A | 8 | 12 | 4 |
| B | 3 | 9 | 6 |
| C | 7 | 8 | 1 |
| D | 1 | 11 | 10 |
| E | 10 | −10 | — |
| F | 6 | 10 | 4 |
| G | 5 | −8 | — |
| H | 4 | 6 | 2 |

*a.* Use the shortest operation time rule to schedule these jobs.

What is the schedule?

What is the mean flow time?

*b.* The boss does not like the schedule in *a*. Jobs E and G must be done first, for obvious reasons. (They are already late.) Reschedule and do the best you can while scheduling Jobs E and G first and second, respectively.

What is the new schedule?

What is the new mean flow time?

5. *a.* Schedule: DBHGFCAE.
Total flow time = 149.
Mean flow time = 149/8 = 18.625 days.
*b.* E 10 days.
G 5
C 7
H 4
F 6
A 8
B 3
D 1
Mean flow time = 232/8 = 29 days.

6 The following matrix shows the costs in thousands of dollars for assigning Individuals A, B, C, and D to Jobs 1, 2, 3, and 4. Solve the problem showing your final assignments in order to minimize cost.

| | JOBS | | | |
|---|---|---|---|---|
| INDIVIDUALS | 1 | 2 | 3 | 4 |
| A | 7 | 9 | 3 | 5 |
| B | 3 | 11 | 7 | 6 |
| C | 4 | 5 | 6 | 2 |
| D | 5 | 9 | 10 | 12 |

6. Worker A—Job 3;
Worker B—Job 1;
Worker C—Job 4;
Worker D—Job 2;
Cost = $17,000.

7 A manufacturing facility has five jobs to be scheduled into production. The following table gives the processing times plus the necessary wait times and other necessary delays for each of the jobs. Assume that today is April 3 and the jobs are due on the dates shown:

| JOB | DAYS OF ACTUAL PROCESSING TIME REQUIRED | DAYS OF NECESSARY DELAY TIME | TOTAL TIME REQUIRED | DATE JOB DUE |
|---|---|---|---|---|
| 1 | 2 | 12 | 14 | April 30 |
| 2 | 5 | 8 | 13 | April 21 |
| 3 | 9 | 15 | 24 | April 28 |
| 4 | 7 | 9 | 16 | April 29 |
| 5 | 4 | 22 | 26 | April 27 |

Determine *two* schedules, stating the order in which the jobs are to be done. Use the critical ratio priority rule for one. You may use any other rule for the second schedule as long as you state what it is.

7. Critical ratio schedule: 5, 3, 2, 4, 1. Earliest due date, job priority: 2, 5, 3, 4, 1. Shortest processing time (including delay time): 2, 1, 4, 3, 5.

8 An accounting firm, Debits 'R Us, would like to keep its auditing staff to a maximum of five people and still satisfy the staffing needs and the policy of two days off per week. Given the following requirements, is this possible? What should the schedule be?

Requirements (Monday through Sunday): 3, 2, 3, 5, 4, 3, 4.

8. Worker 1, MT off
Worker 2, TW off
Worker 3, SSu off
Worker 4, MT off
Worker 5, FS off
Answers may vary

9 Jobs A, B, C, D, and E must go through Processes I and II in that sequence (Process I first, then Process II). Use Johnson's rule to determine the optimal sequence in which to schedule the jobs to minimize the total required time.

9. Johnson's rule:
E
A
B
D
C

| Job | Required Processing Time on I | Required Processing Time on II |
|---|---|---|
| A | 4 | 5 |
| B | 16 | 14 |
| C | 8 | 7 |
| D | 12 | 11 |
| E | 3 | 9 |

10. A does no work
B uses 1
C uses 5
D uses 2
E uses 3
F uses 4
Total cost $200

10 In a job shop, six machinists were uniquely qualified to operate any one of the five machines in the shop. The job shop had considerable backlog, and all five machines were kept busy at all times. The one machinist not operating a machine was usually occupied doing clerical or routine maintenance work. Given the value schedule below for each machinist on each of the five machines, develop an optimal assignment. (Hint: Add a dummy column with zero cost values, and solve using the assignment method.)

| | Machine | | | | |
|---|---|---|---|---|---|
| Machinist | 1 | 2 | 3 | 4 | 5 |
| A | 65 | 50 | 60 | 55 | 80 |
| B | 30 | 75 | 125 | 50 | 40 |
| C | 75 | 35 | 85 | 95 | 45 |
| D | 60 | 40 | 115 | 130 | 110 |
| E | 90 | 85 | 40 | 80 | 95 |
| F | 145 | 60 | 55 | 45 | 85 |

11.
| Area | Cost |
|---|---|
| BB 3 | $ 700 |
| DD 1 | 600 |
| BFN 4 | 500 |
| TD 2 | 1,800 |
| | $ 3,600 |

11 Joe has achieved a position of some power in the institution in which he currently resides and works. In fact, things have gone so well that he has decided to divide the day-to-day operations of his business activities among four trusted subordinates: Big Bob, Dirty Dave, Baby Face Nick, and Tricky Dick. The question is how he should do this in order to take advantage of his associates' unique skills and to minimize the costs from running all areas for the next year. The following matrix summarizes the costs that arise under each possible combination of men and areas:

| | Area | | | |
|---|---|---|---|---|
| Associate | 1 | 2 | 3 | 4 |
| Big Bob | $1,400 | $1,800 | $ 700 | $1,000 |
| Dirty Dave | 600 | 2,200 | 1,500 | 1,300 |
| Baby Face Nick | 800 | 1,100 | 1,200 | 500 |
| Tricky Dick | 1,000 | 1,800 | 2,100 | 1,500 |

12. Order of performance
8, 9, 5, 7, 3, 1, 2, 6, 10, 4.

12 Joe has now been released from his government job. Based on his excellent performance, he was able to land a job as production scheduler in a brand-new custom refinishing auto service shop located near the border. Techniques have improved in the several years he was out of circulation, so processing times are considerably faster. This system is capable of handling 10 cars per day. The sequence now is customizing first, followed by repainting.

| Car | Customizing Time (Hours) | Painting (Hours) | Car | Customizing Time (Hours) | Painting (Hours) |
|---|---|---|---|---|---|
| 1 | 3.0 | 1.2 | 6 | 2.1 | 0.8 |
| 2 | 2.0 | 0.9 | 7 | 3.2 | 1.4 |
| 3 | 2.5 | 1.3 | 8 | 0.6 | 1.8 |
| 4 | 0.7 | 0.5 | 9 | 1.1 | 1.5 |
| 5 | 1.6 | 1.7 | 10 | 1.8 | 0.7 |

In what sequence should Joe schedule the cars?

13 The following table contains information regarding jobs that are to be scheduled through one machine:

| Job | Processing Time (Days) | Due Date |
|---|---|---|
| A | 4 | 20 |
| B | 12 | 30 |
| C | 2 | 15 |
| D | 11 | 16 |
| E | 10 | 18 |
| F | 3 | 5 |
| G | 6 | 9 |

*a.* What is the First Come, First Served (FCFS) schedule?
*b.* What is the Shortest Operating Time (SOT) schedule?
*c.* What is the Slack Time Remaining (STR) schedule?
*d.* What is the earliest Due Date (DD) schedule?
*e.* What are the mean flow times for each of the schedules above?

13. *a.* A, B, C, D, E, F, G.
*b.* C, F, A, G, E, D, B.
*c.* F, G, D, E, C, A, B.
*d.* F, G, C, D, E, A, B.
*e.* FCFS 28.0; SOT 20.0; STR 25.4; DD 23.0 days.

14 Schedule the following six jobs through two machines in sequence to minimize the flow time using Johnson's rule:

| Job | Operations Time: Machine 1 | Operations Time: Machine 2 |
|---|---|---|
| A | 5 | 2 |
| B | 16 | 15 |
| C | 1 | 9 |
| D | 13 | 11 |
| E | 17 | 3 |
| F | 18 | 7 |

14. C, B, D, F, E, A.

15 Martina's Bar and Grill wishes to create a consecutive days off schedule for its waitering staff. Even though business is heaviest on Friday and Saturday, part-time workers are difficult to find in this area. Create a consecutive days off schedule using the fewest workers possible given the following wait staff requirements for each day of the week:

| | Day: M | Tu | W | Th | F | S | Su |
|---|---|---|---|---|---|---|---|
| Requirements | 5 | 2 | 3 | 4 | 8 | 9 | 3 |

15. 9 workers: 5—TW, 3—SuM, 1—WTh.

16 The following wait staff are needed at a restaurant. Use the first-hour principle to generate a personnel schedule. Assume a four-hour shift.

| Period | 11 A.M. | Noon | 1 P.M. | 2 P.M. | 3 P.M. | 4 P.M. | 5 P.M. | 6 P.M. | 7 P.M. | 8 P.M. | 9 P.M. |
|---|---|---|---|---|---|---|---|---|---|---|---|
| Requirements | 4 | 8 | 5 | 3 | 2 | 3 | 5 | 7 | 5 | 4 | 2 |
| Assigned | 4 | 4 | | | | 3 | 2 | 2 | | | |
| On-Duty | 4 | 8 | 8 | 8 | 4 | 3 | 5 | 7 | 7 | 4 | 2 |

16. See table.

17 The following matrix contains the costs (in dollars) associated with assigning Jobs A, B, C, D, and E to Machines 1, 2, 3, 4, and 5. Assign jobs to machines to minimize costs.

| Jobs | Machines: 1 | 2 | 3 | 4 | 5 |
|---|---|---|---|---|---|
| A | 6 | 11 | 12 | 3 | 10 |
| B | 5 | 12 | 10 | 7 | 9 |
| C | 7 | 14 | 13 | 8 | 12 |
| D | 4 | 15 | 16 | 7 | 9 |
| E | 5 | 13 | 17 | 11 | 12 |

17. A to 4
B to 3
C to 2
D to 5
E to 1
Cost is $41

## CASE: KEEP PATIENTS WAITING? NOT IN MY OFFICE

Good doctor-patient relations begin with both parties being punctual for appointments. This is particularly important in my specialty—pediatrics. Mothers whose children have only minor problems don't like them to sit in the waiting room with really sick ones, and the sick kids become fussy if they have to wait long.

But lateness—no matter who's responsible for it—can cause problems in any practice. Once you've fallen more than slightly behind, it may be impossible to catch up that day. And although it's unfair to keep someone waiting who may have other appointments, the average office patient cools his heels for almost 20 minutes, according to one recent survey. Patients may tolerate this, but they don't like it.

I don't tolerate that in my office, and I don't believe you have to in yours. I see patients *exactly* at the appointed hour more than 99 times out of 100. So there are many GPs (grateful patients) in my busy solo practice. Parents often remark to me, "We really appreciate your being on time. Why can't other doctors do that too?" My answer is "I don't know, but I'm willing to tell them how I do it."

### BOOKING APPOINTMENTS REALISTICALLY

The key to successful scheduling is to allot the proper amount of time for each visit, depending on the services required, and then stick to it. This means that the physician must pace himself carefully, receptionists must be corrected if they stray from the plan, and patients must be taught to respect their appointment times.

By actually timing a number of patient visits, I found that they break down into several categories. We allow half an hour for any new patient, 15 minutes for a well-baby checkup or an important illness, and either 5 or 10 minutes for a recheck on an illness or injury, an immunization, or a minor problem like warts. You can, of course, work out your own time allocations, geared to the way you practice.

When appointments are made, every patient is given a specific time, such as 10:30 or 2:40. It's an absolute no-no for anyone in my office to say to a patient, "Come in 10 minutes" or "Come in a half-hour." People often interpret such instructions differently, and nobody knows just when they'll arrive.

There are three examining rooms that I use routinely, a fourth that I reserve for teenagers, and a fifth for emergencies. With that many rooms, I don't waste time waiting for patients, and they rarely have to sit in the reception area. In fact, some of the younger children complain that they don't get time to play with the toys and puzzles in the waiting room before being examined, and their mothers have to let them play awhile on the way out.

On a light day I see 20 to 30 patients between 9 A.M. and 5 P.M. But our appointment system is flexible enough to let me see 40 to 50 patients in the same number of hours if I have to. Here's how we tighten the schedule:

My two assistants (three on the busiest days) have standing orders to keep a number of slots open throughout each day for patients with acute illnesses. We try to reserve more such openings in the winter months and on the days following weekends and holidays, when we're busier than usual.

Initial visits, for which we allow 30 minutes, are always scheduled on the hour or the half-hour. If I finish such a visit sooner than planned, we may be able to squeeze in a patient who needs to be seen immediately. And, if necessary, we can book two or three visits in 15 minutes between well checks. With these cushions to fall back on, I'm free to spend an extra 10 minutes or so on a serious case, knowing that the lost time can be made up quickly.

Parents of new patients are asked to arrive in the office a few minutes before they're scheduled in order to get the preliminary paperwork done. At that time the receptionist informs them, "The doctor always keeps an accurate appointment schedule." Some already know this and have chosen me for that very reason. Others, however, don't even know that there *are* doctors who honor appointment times, so we feel that it's best to warn them on the first visit.

### FITTING IN EMERGENCIES

Emergencies are the excuse doctors most often give for failing to stick to their appointment schedules. Well, when a child comes in with a broken arm or the hospital calls with an emergency Caesarean section, naturally I drop everything else. If the interruption is brief, I may just scramble to catch up. If it's likely to be longer, the next few patients are given the choice of waiting or making new appointments. Occasionally my assistants have to reschedule all appointments for the next hour or two. Most such interruptions, though, take no more than 10 to 20 minutes, and the patients usually choose to wait. I then try to fit them into the spaces we've reserved for acute cases that require last-minute appointments.

The important thing is that emergencies are never allowed to spoil my schedule for the whole day. Once a delay has been adjusted for, I'm on time for all later appointments. The only situation I can imagine that would really wreck my schedule is simultaneous emergencies in the office and at the hospital—but that has never occurred.

When I return to the patient I've left, I say, "Sorry to have kept you waiting, I had an emergency—a bad cut" (or whatever). A typical reply from the parent: "No problem, Doctor. In all the years I've been coming here, you've never made me wait before. And I'd surely want you to leave the room if *my* kid were hurt."

Emergencies aside, I get few walk-ins, because it's generally known in the community that I see patients only by appointment except in urgent circumstances. A nonemergency walk-in is handled as a phone call would be. The receptionist asks whether the visitor wants advice or an appointment. If the latter, he or she is offered the earliest time available for nonacute cases.

### TAMING THE TELEPHONE

Phone calls from patients can sabotage an appointment schedule if you let them. I don't. Unlike some pediatricians, I don't have a regular telephone hour, but my assistants will handle calls from parents at any time during office hours. If the question is a simple one, such as "How much aspirin do you give a one-year-old?" the assistant will answer it. If the question requires an answer from me, the assistant writes it in the patient's chart and brings it to me while I'm seeing another child. I write the answer in—or she enters it in the chart. Then she relays it to the caller.

What if the caller insists on talking with me directly? The standard reply is "The doctor will talk with you personally if it won't take more than one minute. Otherwise you'll have to make an appointment and come in." I'm rarely called to the phone in such cases, but if the mother is very upset, I prefer to talk with her. I don't always limit her to one minute; I may let the conversation run two or three. But the caller knows I've left a patient to talk with her, so she tends to keep it brief.

DEALING WITH LATECOMERS

Some people are habitually late; others have legitimate reasons for occasional tardiness, such as a flat tire or "He threw up on me." Either way, I'm hard-nosed enough not to see them immediately if they arrive at my office more than 10 minutes behind schedule, because to do so would delay patients who arrived on time. Anyone who is less than 10 minutes late is seen right away, but is reminded of what the appointment time was.

When it's exactly 10 minutes past the time reserved for a patient and he hasn't appeared at the office, a receptionist phones his home to arrange a later appointment. If there's no answer and the patient arrives at the office a few minutes later, the receptionist says pleasantly, "Hey, we were looking for you. The doctor's had to go ahead with his other appointments, but we'll squeeze you in as soon as we can." A note is then made in the patient's chart showing the date, how late he was, and whether he was seen that day or given another appointment. This helps us identify the rare chronic offender and take stronger measures if necessary.

Most people appear not to mind waiting if they know they themselves have caused the delay. And I'd rather incur the anger of the rare person who *does* mind than risk the ill will of the many patients who would otherwise have to wait after coming in on schedule. Although I'm prepared to be firm with parents, this is rarely necessary. My office in no way resembles an army camp. On the contrary, most people are happy with the way we run it, and tell us so frequently.

COPING WITH NO-SHOWS

What about the patient who has an appointment, doesn't turn up at all, and can't be reached by telephone? Those facts, too, are noted in the chart. Usually there's a simple explanation, such as being out of town and forgetting about the appointment. If it happens a second time, we follow the same procedure. A third-time offender, though, receives a letter reminding him that time was set aside for him and he failed to keep three appointments. In the future, he's told, he'll be billed for such wasted time.

That's about as tough as we ever get with the few people who foul up our scheduling. I've never dropped a patient for doing so. In fact, I can't recall actually billing a no-show; the letter threatening to do so seems to cure them. And when they come back—as nearly all of them do—they enjoy the same respect and convenience as my other patients.

QUESTIONS

1 What features of the appointment scheduling system were crucial in capturing "many grateful patients"?
2 What procedures were followed to keep the appointment system flexible enough to accommodate the emergency cases, and yet be able to keep up with the other patients' appointments?
3 How were the special cases such as latecomers and no-shows handled?

SOURCE: W. B. SCHAFER, "KEEP PATIENTS WAITING? NOT IN MY OFFICE," *MEDICAL ECONOMICS*, MAY 12, 1986, PP. 137–141. 

## SELECTED BIBLIOGRAPHY

Baker, K. R. *Introduction to Sequencing and Scheduling.* New York: Wiley, 1974. (Current edition is available from author.)

Berry, W. L.; R. Penlesky; and T. E. Vollmann. "Critical Ratio Scheduling: Dynamic Due-Date Procedures under Demand Uncertainty." *IIE Transactions* 16, no. 1 (March 1984), pp. 81–89.

Conway, R. W.; W. L. Maxwell; and L. W. Miller. *Theory of Scheduling.* Reading, MA: Addison-Wesley, 1967.

Goldratt, E. M., and J. Cox. *The Goal: A Process of Ongoing Improvement.* Great Barrington, MA: North River Press, 1992.

Johnson, S. M. "Optimal Two Stage and Three Stage Production Schedules with Setup Time Included." *Naval Logistics Quarterly* 1, no. 1 (March 1954), pp. 61–68.

Nanda, R., and J. Browne. *Introduction to Employee Scheduling.* New York: Van Nostrand Reinhold, 1992.

Pinedo, M., and X. Chao. *Operations Scheduling with Applications in Manufacturing and Services.* Boston, MA: Irwin/McGraw-Hill, 1998.

Sandman, W. E., with J. P. Hayes. *How to Win Productivity in Manufacturing.* Dresher, PA: Yellow Book of Pennsylvania, 1980.

Sule, D. R. *Industrial Scheduling.* Boston: PWS Publishing Company, 1997.

## FOOTNOTES

1 Despite the fact that expediting is frowned on by production control specialists, it is nevertheless a reality of life. In fact, a typical entry-level job in production control is that of expeditor or "stock chaser." In some companies, a good expeditor—one who can negotiate a critical job through the system or can scrounge up materials that nobody thought were available—is a prized possession.

2 R. W. Conway, W. L. Maxwell, and L. W. Miller, *Theory of Scheduling* (Reading, MA: Addison-Wesley, 1967), p. 26. A classic book on the subject.

3 The underlying rationale of the procedure of adding and subtracting the smallest cell values is as follows: Additional zeros are entered into the matrix by subtracting an amount equal to one of the cells from all cells. Negative numbers, which are not permissible, occur in the matrix. To get rid of the negative numbers, an amount equal to the maximum negative number must be added to each element of the row or column in which it occurs. This results in adding this amount twice to any cell that lies at the intersection of a row and a column that were both changed. The net result is that the lined rows and columns revert to their

original amounts, and the intersections increase by the amount subtracted from the uncovered cells. (The reader may wish to prove this by solving the example without using lines.)

4 J. K. Kanet and J. C. Hayya, "Priority Dispatching with Operation Due Dates in a Job Shop," *Journal of Operations Management* 2, no. 3 (May 1982), p. 170.

5 Some companies also use "smartshelves" (inventory bins with weight sensors beneath each shelf). When an item is removed from inventory, a signal is sent to a central computer that notes the time, date, quantity, and location of the transaction.

6 J. J. Browne and R. K. Tibrewala, "Manpower Scheduling," *Industrial Engineering* 7, no. 8 (August 1975), pp. 22–23.

7 Browne and Tibrewala, "Manpower Scheduling." Also see the Nanda and Browne text on employee scheduling listed in the bibliography for a discussion of this as well as many other techniques and software.

technical note



# technical note fifteen SIMULATION

## OUTLINE AND KEY TERMS

Service

Simulation has become a standard tool in business. In manufacturing, simulation is used to determine production schedules, inventory levels, and maintenance procedures; to plan capacity, resource requirements, and processes; and more. In services, simulation is widely used to analyze waiting lines and scheduling operations. Often, when a mathematical technique fails, we turn to simulation.

## DEFINITION OF SIMULATION

Although the term *simulation* can have various meanings depending on its application, in business, it generally refers to using a computer to perform experiments on a model of a real system. Examples of other types of simulation are airplane flight simulators, video games, and virtual reality animation. Simulation experiments may be undertaken before a real system is operational, to aid in its design, to see how the system might react to changes in its operating rules, or to evaluate the system's response to changes in its structure. Simulation is particularly appropriate to situations in which the size or complexity of the problem makes the use of optimizing techniques difficult or impossible. Thus, job shops, which are characterized by complex queuing problems, have been studied extensively via simulation, as have certain types of inventory, layout, and maintenance problems (to name but a few). Simulation can also be used in conjunction with traditional statistical and management science techniques.

In addition, simulation is useful in training managers and workers in how the real system operates, in demonstrating the effects of changes in system variables, in real-time control, and in developing new ideas about how to run the business.

## SIMULATION METHODOLOGY

Exhibit TN15.1 is a flowchart of the major phases in a simulation study. In this section, we develop each phase with particular reference to the key factors noted at the right of the chart.

EXHIBIT TN15.1

Major Phases in a Simulation Study

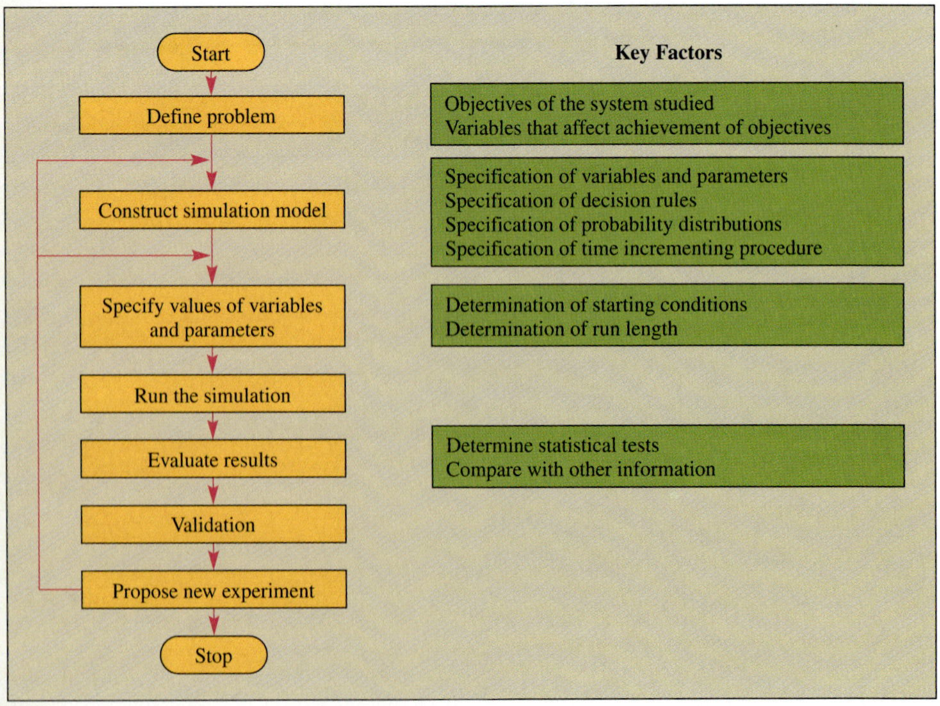

## PROBLEM DEFINITION

Problem definition for purposes of simulation differs little from problem definition for any other tool of analysis. Essentially, it entails specifying the objectives and identifying the relevant controllable and uncontrollable variables of the system to be studied. Consider the example of a fish market. The objective of the market's owner is maximizing the profit on sales of fish. The relevant controllable variable (that is, under the control of the decision maker) is the ordering rule; the relevant uncontrollable variables are the daily demand levels for fish and the amount of fish sold. Other possible objectives could also be specified, such as to maximize profit from the sale of lobsters or to maximize sales revenue.

## CONSTRUCTING A SIMULATION MODEL

A feature that distinguishes simulation from techniques such as linear programming or queuing theory is the fact that a simulation model must be custom built for each problem situation. (A linear programming model, in contrast, can be used in a variety of situations with only a restatement of the values for the objective function and constraint equations.) There are simulation languages that make the model building easier, however. We discuss this subject later in this technical note. The unique nature of each simulation model means that the procedures discussed later for building and executing a model represent a synthesis of various approaches to simulation and are guidelines rather than rigid rules.

**Specification of Variables and Parameters** The first step in constructing a simulation model is determining which properties of the real system should be fixed (called **parameters** and which should be allowed to vary throughout the simulation run (called **variables**). In a fish market, the variables are the amount of fish ordered, the amount demanded, and the amount sold; the parameters are the cost of the fish and the selling price of the fish. In most simulations, the focus is on the status of the variables at different points in time, such as the number of pounds of fish demanded and sold each day.

Parameters

Variables

**Specification of Decision Rules** **Decision rules** (or operating rules) are sets of conditions under which the behavior of the simulation model is observed. These rules are either directly or indirectly the focus of most simulation studies. In many simulations, decision rules are priority rules (for example, which customer to serve first, which job to process first). In certain situations these can be quite involved, taking into account a large number of variables in the system. For example, an inventory ordering rule could be stated in such a way that the amount to order would depend on the amount in inventory, the amount previously ordered but not received, the amount backordered, and the desired safety stock.

Decision rules

**Specification of Probability Distributions** Two categories of **distributions** can be used for simulation: empirical frequency distributions and standard mathematical distributions. An empirical distribution is derived from observing the relative frequencies of some event such as arrivals in a line or demand for a product. In other words, it is a custom-built demand distribution that is relevant only to a particular situation. It might appear like the one shown on the left side of Exhibit TN15.2. Such distributions have to be determined by direct observation or detailed analysis of records. (We show how to use these later in the waiting line simulation example.) But often demand, for example, can reasonably be assumed to closely approximate a standard mathematical distribution such as the normal or Poisson. This greatly simplifies data collection and computerization.

Distributions

### *EXAMPLE TN15.1: RELATING RANDOM NUMBERS TO A STANDARD DISTRIBUTION*

To illustrate how to relate random numbers to a standard distribution, suppose that daily demand for newspapers from a vending machine is normally distributed with a mean of 55 and standard deviation of 10. (This distribution is shown on the right side of Exhibit TN15.2.) Under this assumption, the generation of daily demand would employ a table of randomly distributed normal numbers (or deviates) in conjunction with the statistical formula $D_n = \bar{x} + Z_n\sigma$ (terms defined later).[1]

EXHIBIT TN15.2

**Actual Distribution of Demand and Normal Distribution with the Same Mean**

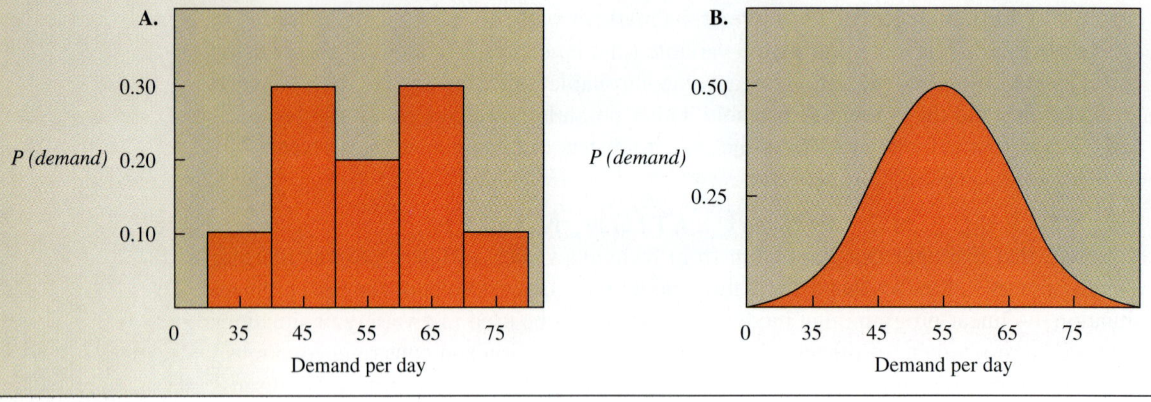


EXHIBIT TN15.3

**Randomly Distributed Normal Numbers**

| | | | | | |
|---|---|---|---|---|---|
| 1.23481 | −1.66161 | 1.49673 | −.26990 | −.23812 | .34506 |
| 1.54221 | .02629 | 1.22318 | .52304 | .18124 | .20790 |
| .19126 | 1.18250 | 1.00826 | .24826 | −1.35882 | .70691 |
| −.54929 | −.87214 | −2.75470 | −1.19941 | −1.45402 | .16760 |
| 1.14463 | −.23153 | 1.11241 | 1.08497 | −.28185 | −.17022 |
| −.63248 | −.04776 | −.55806 | .04496 | 1.16515 | 2.24938 |
| −.29988 | .31052 | −.49094 | −.00926 | −.28278 | −.95339 |
| −.32855 | −.93166 | −.04187 | −.94171 | 1.64410 | −.96893 |
| .35331 | .56176 | −.98726 | .82752 | .32468 | .36915 |
| .72576 | | | | | |
| .04406 | | | | | |

## SOLUTION

1 Draw a five- or six-digit number from Exhibit TN15.3. The entries in this table are randomly developed deviate values that pertain to a normal distribution having a mean of 0 and a standard deviation of 1. The term *deviate* refers to the number of standard deviations some value is from the mean and, in this case, represents the number of standard deviations that any day's demand is from the mean demand. In the preceding formula for $D_n$, it would be the value for $Z$ on day $n$. If we are simulating Day 1 and using the first entry in Exhibit TN15.3, then $Z_1 = 1.23481$. A negative deviate value means simply that the particular level of demand will be less than the mean, not that demand will be a negative value.

2 Substitute the value of $Z_1$, along with the predetermined values for $x$ and $\sigma$, into the formula

$$D_n = \overline{x} + Z_n\sigma$$

where

$D$ = Demand on day $n$

$\overline{x}$ = Mean demand (55 in this example)

$\sigma$ = Estimated standard deviation (10 in this example)

$Z_n$ = Number of standard deviations from the mean on day $n$

Thus $D_n = 55 + (1.23481)(10)$.

3 Solve for $D_n$:

$$D_n = 55 + 12.3481$$
$$D_n = 67.3481$$

4 Repeat Steps 1 to 3, using different normal deviates from the table until the desired number of days have been simulated. ←

**Specification of Time-Incrementing Procedure** In a simulation model, time can be advanced by one of two methods: (1) fixed-time increments or (2) variable-time increments. Under both methods of **time incrementing,** the concept of a simulated clock is important. In the fixed-time increment method, uniform clock-time increments (such as minutes, hours, or days) are specified, and the simulation proceeds by fixed intervals from one time period to the next. At each point in clock time, the system is scanned to determine if any events are to occur. If they are, the events are simulated, and time is advanced; if they are not, time is still advanced by one unit.

Time incrementing

In the variable-time increment method, clock time is advanced by the amount required to initiate the next event.

Which method is most appropriate? Experience suggests that the fixed-time increment is desirable when events of interest occur with regularity or when the number of events is large, with several commonly occurring in the same time period. The variable-time increment method is generally desirable, taking less computer run time when there are relatively few events occurring within a considerable amount of time. It ignores time intervals where nothing happens and immediately advances to the next point when some event does take place.

## SPECIFYING VALUES OF VARIABLES AND PARAMETERS

A variable, by definition, changes in value as the simulation progresses, but it must be given an initial starting value. The value of a parameter, remember, stays constant; however, it may be changed as different alternatives are studied in other simulations.

**Determining Starting Conditions** Determining starting conditions for variables is a major tactical decision in simulation. This is because the model is biased by the set of initial starting values until the model has settled down to a steady state. To cope with this problem, analysts have followed various approaches, such as (1) discarding data generated during the early parts of the run, (2) selecting starting conditions that reduce the duration of the warm-up period, or (3) selecting starting conditions that eliminate bias. To employ any of these alternatives, however, the analyst must have some idea of the range of output data expected. Therefore, in one sense, the analyst biases results. On the other hand, one of the unique features of simulation is that it allows judgment to enter into the design and analysis of the simulation; so if the analyst has some information that bears on the problem, it should be included.

**Determining Run Length** The length of the simulation run (**run length** or **run time**) depends on the purpose of the simulation. Perhaps the most common approach is to continue the simulation until it has achieved equilibrium. In the fish market example, this would mean that simulated fish sales correspond to their historical relative frequencies. Another approach is to run the simulation for a set period, such as a month, a year, or a decade, and see if the conditions at the end of the period appear reasonable. A third approach is to set run length so that a sufficiently large sample is gathered for purposes of statistical hypothesis testing. This alternative is considered further in the next section.

Run length (run time)

## EVALUATING RESULTS

The types of conclusions that can be drawn from a simulation depend, of course, on the degree to which the model reflects the real system, but they also depend on the design of the simulation in a statistical sense. Indeed, many analysts view simulation as a form of hypothesis testing, with each simulation run providing one or more pieces of sample data that are amenable to formal analysis through inferential statistical methods. Statistical procedures commonly used in evaluating simulation results include analysis of variance, regression analysis, and *t* tests.

In most situations, the analyst has other information available with which to compare the simulation results: past operating data from the real system, operating data from the performance of similar systems, and the analyst's own intuitive understanding of the real system's operation. Admittedly, however, information obtained from these sources is probably not sufficient to validate the conclusions derived from the simulation. Thus, the only true test of a simulation is how well the real system performs after the results of the study have been implemented.

## VALIDATION

In this context, *validation* refers to testing the computer program to ensure that the simulation is correct. Specifically, it is a check to see whether the computer code is a valid translation of the flowchart model and whether the simulation adequately represents the real system. Errors may arise in the program from mistakes in the coding or from mistakes in logic. Mistakes in coding are usually easily found because the program is most likely not executed by the computer. Mistakes in logic, however, present more of a challenge. In these cases, the program runs but fails to yield correct results.

To deal with this problem, the analyst has three alternatives: (1) have the program print out all calculations and verify these calculations by separate computation, (2) simulate present conditions and compare the results with the existing system, or (3) pick some point in the simulation run and compare its output to the answer obtained from solving a relevant mathematical model of the situation at that point. Even though the first two approaches have obvious drawbacks, they are more likely to be employed than the third, because if we had a relevant mathematical model in mind, we would probably be able to solve the problem without the aid of simulation.

## PROPOSING A NEW EXPERIMENT

Based on the simulation results, a new simulation experiment may be in order. We might like to change many of the factors: parameters, variables, decision rules, starting conditions, and run length. As for parameters, we might be interested in replicating the simulation with several different costs or prices of a product to see what changes would occur. Trying different decision rules would obviously be in order if the initial rules led to poor results or if these runs yielded new insights into the problem. (The procedure of using the same stream of random numbers is a good general approach in that it sharpens the differences among alternatives and permits shorter runs.) Also, the values from the previous experiment may be useful starting conditions for subsequent simulations.

Finally, whether trying different run lengths constitutes a new experiment rather than a replication of a previous experiment depends on the types of events that occur in the system operation over time. It might happen, for example, that the system has more than one stable level of operation and that reaching the second level is time dependent. Thus, while the first series of runs of, say, 100 periods shows stable conditions, doubling the length of the series may provide new and distinctly different but equally stable conditions. In this case, running the simulation over 200 time periods could be thought of as a new experiment.

## COMPUTERIZATION

When using a computer model, we reduce the system to be studied to a symbolic representation to be run on a computer. Although it is beyond this book's scope to detail the technical aspects of computer modeling, some that bear directly on simulation are

1 Computer language selection.
2 Flowcharting.

3 Coding.
4 Data generation.
5 Output reports.
6 Validation.

We say more about simulation programs and languages at the end of this technical note.

**Output Reports** General-purpose languages permit the analyst to specify any type of output report (or data) desired, providing one is willing to pay the price in programming effort. Special-purpose languages have standard routines that can be activated by one or two program statements to print out such data as means, variances, and standard deviations. Regardless of language, however, our experience has been that too much data from a simulation can be as dysfunctional to problem solving as too little data; both situations tend to obscure important, truly meaningful information about the system under study.

## SIMULATING WAITING LINES

Waiting lines that occur in series and parallel (such as in assembly lines and job shops) usually cannot be solved mathematically. However, because waiting lines are often easily simulated on a computer, we have chosen a two-stage assembly line as our second simulation example.

### Example: A Two-Stage Assembly Line

Consider an assembly line that makes a product of significant physical size, such as a refrigerator, stove, car, boat, TV, or furniture. Exhibit TN15.4 shows two workstations on such a line.

The size of the product is an important consideration in assembly-line analysis and design because the number of products that can exist at each workstation affects worker performance. If the product is large, then the workstations are dependent on each other. Exhibit TN15.4, for example, shows Bob and Ray working on a two-stage line where Bob's output in Station 1 is fed to Ray in Station 2. If the workstations are adjacent so that there is no room for items in between, then Bob, by working slowly, would cause Ray to wait. Conversely, if Bob completes a product quickly (or if Ray takes longer to finish the task), then Bob must wait for Ray.

In this simulation, assume that Bob, the first worker on the line, can pull over a new item to work on whenever needed. We concentrate our analysis on the interaction between Bob and Ray.

EXHIBIT TN15.4

Two Workstations on an Assembly Line

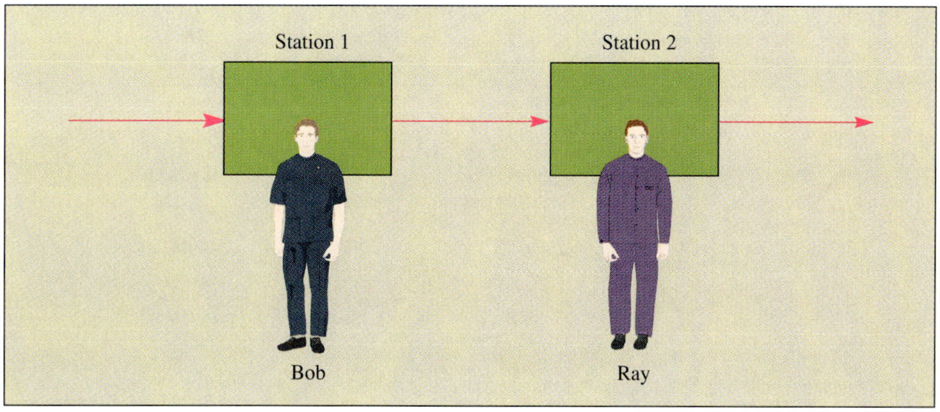

**Objective of the Study** We would like to answer a number of questions about the assembly line from this study. A partial list would be

- What is the average performance time of each worker?
- What is the output rate of product through this line?
- How much time does Bob wait for Ray?
- How much time does Ray wait for Bob?
- If the space between the two stations were increased so that items could be stored there and give workers some independence, how would this affect output rates, wait times, and so on?

**Data Collection** To simulate this system, we need the performance times of Bob and Ray. One way to collect these data is to divide the range of performance times into segments, and then observe each worker. A simple check or tally mark in each of these segments results in a useful histogram of data.

Exhibit TN15.5 shows the data collection form used to observe the performances of Bob and Ray. To simplify the procedure, performance time was divided into 10-second intervals. Bob was observed for 100 repetitions of the work task, and Ray was observed just 50 times. The number of observations does not have to be the same, but the more there are and the smaller the size of the time segments, the more accurate the study will be. The trade-off is that more observations and smaller segments take more time and more people (as well as more time to program and run a simulation).

Exhibit TN15.6 contains the random number intervals assigned that correspond to the same ratio as the actual observed data. For example, Bob had 4 out of 100 times at

EXHIBIT TN15.5

Data Collection Form for Worker Observation

| | Bob | | Ray | |
|---|---|---|---|---|
| Seconds | | Totals | | Totals |
| 5–14.99 | IIII | 4 | IIII | 4 |
| 15–24.99 | 卌 I | 6 | 卌 | 5 |
| 25–34.99 | 卌 卌 | 10 | 卌 I | 6 |
| 35–44.99 | 卌卌卌卌 | 20 | 卌 II | 7 |
| 45–54.99 | 卌卌卌卌卌卌卌卌 | 40 | 卌卌 | 10 |
| 55–64.99 | 卌 卌 I | 11 | 卌 III | 8 |
| 65–74.99 | 卌 | 5 | 卌 I | 6 |
| 75–84.99 | IIII | 4 | IIII | 4 |
| | | 100 | | 50 |

EXHIBIT TN15.6

Random Number Intervals for Bob and Ray

| Seconds | Time Frequencies for Bob (Operation 1) | RN Intervals | Time Frequencies for Ray (Operation 2) | RN Intervals |
|---|---|---|---|---|
| 10 | 4 | 00–03 | 4 | 00–07 |
| 20 | 6 | 04–09 | 5 | 08–17 |
| 30 | 10 | 10–19 | 6 | 18–29 |
| 40 | 20 | 20–39 | 7 | 30–43 |
| 50 | 40 | 40–79 | 10 | 44–63 |
| 60 | 11 | 80–90 | 8 | 64–79 |
| 70 | 5 | 91–95 | 6 | 80–91 |
| 80 | 4 | 96–99 | 4 | 92–99 |
| | 100 | | 50 | |

10 seconds. Therefore, if we used 100 numbers, we would assign 4 of those numbers as corresponding to 10 seconds. We could have assigned any four numbers, for example, 42, 18, 12, and 93. However, these would be a nuisance to search for, so we assign consecutive numbers, such as 00, 01, 02, and 03.

There were 50 observations of Ray. There are two ways we could assign random numbers. First, we could use just 50 numbers (say 00–49) and ignore any numbers over that. However, this is wasteful because we would discard 50 percent of all the numbers from the list. Another choice would be to double the frequency number. For example, rather than assign, say, numbers 0–03 to account for the 4 observations out of 50 that took 10 seconds, we could assign numbers 00–07 to represent 8 observations out of 100, which is double the observed number but the same frequency. Actually, for this example and the speed of computers, the savings of time by doubling is insignificant.

Exhibit TN15.7 shows a hand simulation of 10 items processed by Bob and Ray. The random numbers used were from Appendix B, starting at the first column of two numbers and working downward.

Assume that we start out at time 00 and run it in continuous seconds (not bothering to convert this to hours and minutes). The first random number is 56 and corresponds to Bob's performance at 50 seconds on the first item. The item is passed to Ray, who starts at 50 seconds. Relating the next random number, 83, to Exhibit TN15.6, we find that Ray takes 70 seconds to complete the item. In the meantime, Bob starts on the next item at time 50 and takes 50 seconds (random number 55), finishing at time 100. However, Bob cannot start on the third item until Ray gets through with the first item at time 120. Bob, therefore, has a wait time of 20 seconds. (If there was storage space between Bob and Ray, this item could have been moved out of Bob's workstation, and Bob could have started the next item at time 100.) The remainder of the exhibit was calculated following the same pattern: obtaining a random number, finding the corresponding processing time, noting the wait time (if any), and computing the finish time. Note that with no storage space between Bob and Ray, there was considerable waiting time for both workers.

We can now answer some questions and make some statements about the system. For example,

The output time averages 60 seconds per unit (the complete time 600 for Ray divided by 10 units).

Utilization of Bob is $\frac{470}{530} = 88.7$ percent.

EXHIBIT TN15.7

## Simulation of Bob and Ray—Two-Stage Assembly Line

| | Bob | | | | | | Ray | | | | |
|---|---|---|---|---|---|---|---|---|---|---|---|
| Item Number | Random Number | Start Time | Performance Time | Finish Time | Wait Time | Storage Space | Random Number | Start Time | Performance Time | Finish Time | Wait Time |
| 1 | 56 | 00 | 50 | 50 | | 0 | 83 | 50 | 70 | 120 | 50 |
| 2 | 55 | 50 | 50 | 100 | 20 | 0 | 47 | 120 | 50 | 170 | |
| 3 | 84 | 120 | 60 | 180 | | 0 | 08 | 180 | 20 | 200 | 10 |
| 4 | 36 | 180 | 40 | 220 | | 0 | 05 | 220 | 10 | 230 | 20 |
| 5 | 26 | 220 | 40 | 260 | | 0 | 42 | 260 | 40 | 300 | 30 |
| 6 | 95 | 260 | 70 | 330 | | 0 | 95 | 330 | 80 | 410 | 30 |
| 7 | 66 | 330 | 50 | 380 | 30 | 0 | 17 | 410 | 20 | 430 | |
| 8 | 03 | 410 | 10 | 420 | 10 | 0 | 21 | 430 | 30 | 460 | |
| 9 | 57 | 430 | 50 | 480 | | 0 | 31 | 480 | 40 | 520 | 20 |
| 10 | 69 | 480 | 50 | 530 | | 0 | 90 | 530 | 70 | 600 | 10 |
| | | | 470 | | 60 | | | | 430 | | 170 |

Utilization of Ray is $\frac{430}{550}$ = 78.2 percent (disregarding the initial startup wait for the first item of 50 seconds).

The average performance time for Bob is $\frac{470}{10}$ = 47 seconds.

The average performance time for Ray is $\frac{430}{10}$ = 43 seconds.

We have demonstrated how this problem would be solved in a simple manual simulation. A sample of 10 is really too small to place much confidence in, so this problem should be run on a computer for several thousand iterations. (We extend this same problem further in the next section of this technical note.)

It is also vital to study the effect of item storage space between workers. The problem would be run to see what the throughput time and worker utilization times are with no storage space between workers. A second run should increase this storage space to one unit, with the corresponding changes noted. Repeating the runs for two, three, four, and so on offers management a chance to compute the additional cost of space compared with the increased use. Such increased space between workers may require a larger building, more materials and parts in the system, material handling equipment, and a transfer machine, plus added heat, light, building maintenance, and so on.

These would also be useful data for management to see what changes in the system would occur if one worker position was automated. The assembly line could be simulated using data from the automated process to see if such a change would be cost justified.

## SPREADSHEET SIMULATION

As we have stated throughout this book, spreadsheets such as Microsoft Excel are very useful for a variety of problems. Exhibit TN15.8 shows Bob and Ray's two-stage assembly line on an Excel spreadsheet. The procedure follows the same pattern as our manual display in Exhibit TN15.7.

The total simulation on Excel passed through 1,200 iterations (shown in Exhibits TN15.10 and TN15.11); that is, 1,200 parts were finished by Ray. Simulation, as an analytic tool, has an advantage over quantitative methods in that it is dynamic, whereas analytic methods show long-run average performance. As you can see in Exhibits TN15.9 and TN15.10, there is an unmistakable startup (or transient) phase. We could even raise some questions about the long-term operation of the line because it does not seem to have settled to a constant (steady state) value, even after the 1,200 items. Exhibit TN15.9 shows 100 items that pass through the Bob and Ray two-stage system. Notice the wide variation in time for the first units completed. These figures are the average time that units take. It is a cumulative number; that is, the first unit takes the time generated by the random numbers. The average time for two units is the average time of the sum of the first and second units. The average time for three units is the average time for the sum of the first three units, and so on. This display could have almost any starting shape, not necessarily what we have shown. It all depends on the stream of random numbers. What we can be sure of is that the times do oscillate for a while until they settle down as units are finished and smooth the average.

Exhibit TN15.10 shows the average time that parts spend in the system. At the start, the display shows an increasing amount of time in the system. This can be expected because the system started empty and there are no interruptions for parts passing from Bob to Ray. Often parts enter the system and may have to wait between stages as work-in-process; this causes delays for subsequent parts and adds to the waiting time. As time goes on, however, stability should occur unless the capacity of the second stage is less than the first stage's. In our present case, we did not allow space between them. Therefore, if Bob finished first, he had to wait for Ray. If Ray finished first, he had to wait for Bob.

Exhibit TN15.11 shows the results of simulating Bob and Ray completing 1,200 units of product. Compare these figures to those that we obtained simulating 10 items by hand. Not too

EXHIBIT TN15.8

## Bob and Ray Two-Stage Assembly Line on Microsoft Excel

Excel: Two-Stage Assembly.xls

| | | Bob | | | | | Ray | | | | | | |
|---|---|---|---|---|---|---|---|---|---|---|---|---|---|
| Item | RN | Start Time | Perf. Time | Finish Time | Wait Time | RN | Start Time | Perf. Time | Finish Time | Wait Time | Average Time/Unit | Total Time | Average Time in System |
| 1 | 93 | 0 | 70 | 70 | 0 | 0 | 70 | 10 | 80 | 70 | 80.0 | 80 | 80.0 |
| 2 | 52 | 70 | 50 | 120 | 0 | 44 | 120 | 50 | 170 | 40 | 85.0 | 100 | 90.0 |
| 3 | 15 | 120 | 30 | 150 | 20 | 72 | 170 | 60 | 230 | 0 | 76.7 | 110 | 96.7 |
| 4 | 64 | 170 | 50 | 220 | 10 | 35 | 230 | 40 | 270 | 0 | 67.5 | 100 | 97.5 |
| 5 | 86 | 230 | 60 | 290 | 0 | 2 | 290 | 10 | 300 | 20 | 60.0 | 70 | 92.0 |
| 6 | 20 | 290 | 40 | 330 | 0 | 82 | 330 | 70 | 400 | 30 | 66.7 | 110 | 95.0 |
| 7 | 83 | 330 | 60 | 390 | 10 | 31 | 400 | 40 | 440 | 0 | 62.9 | 110 | 97.1 |
| 8 | 89 | 400 | 60 | 460 | 0 | 13 | 460 | 20 | 480 | 20 | 60.0 | 80 | 95.0 |
| 9 | 69 | 460 | 50 | 510 | 0 | 53 | 510 | 50 | 560 | 30 | 62.2 | 100 | 95.6 |
| 10 | 41 | 510 | 50 | 560 | 0 | 48 | 560 | 50 | 610 | 0 | 61.0 | 100 | 96.0 |
| 11 | 32 | 560 | 40 | 600 | 10 | 13 | 610 | 20 | 630 | 0 | 57.3 | 70 | 93.6 |
| 12 | 1 | 610 | 10 | 620 | 10 | 67 | 630 | 60 | 690 | 0 | 57.5 | 80 | 92.5 |
| 13 | 11 | 630 | 30 | 660 | 30 | 91 | 690 | 70 | 760 | 0 | 58.5 | 130 | 95.4 |
| 14 | 2 | 690 | 10 | 700 | 60 | 76 | 760 | 60 | 820 | 0 | 58.6 | 130 | 97.9 |
| 15 | 11 | 760 | 30 | 790 | 30 | 41 | 820 | 40 | 860 | 0 | 57.3 | 100 | 98.0 |
| 16 | 55 | 820 | 50 | 870 | 0 | 34 | 870 | 40 | 910 | 10 | 56.9 | 90 | 97.5 |
| 17 | 18 | 870 | 30 | 900 | 10 | 28 | 910 | 30 | 940 | 0 | 55.3 | 70 | 95.9 |
| 18 | 39 | 910 | 40 | 950 | 0 | 53 | 950 | 50 | 1000 | 10 | 55.6 | 90 | 95.6 |
| 19 | 13 | 950 | 30 | 980 | 20 | 41 | 1000 | 40 | 1040 | 0 | 54.7 | 90 | 95.3 |
| 20 | 7 | 1000 | 20 | 1020 | 20 | 21 | 1040 | 30 | 1070 | 0 | 53.5 | 70 | 94.0 |
| 21 | 29 | 1040 | 40 | 1080 | 0 | 54 | 1080 | 50 | 1130 | 10 | 53.8 | 90 | 93.8 |
| 22 | 58 | 1080 | 50 | 1130 | 0 | 39 | 1130 | 40 | 1170 | 0 | 53.2 | 90 | 93.6 |
| 23 | 95 | 1130 | 70 | 1200 | 0 | 70 | 1200 | 60 | 1260 | 30 | 54.8 | 130 | 95.2 |
| 24 | 27 | 1200 | 40 | 1240 | 20 | 60 | 1260 | 50 | 1310 | 0 | 54.6 | 110 | 95.8 |
| 25 | 59 | 1260 | 50 | 1310 | 0 | 93 | 1310 | 80 | 1390 | 0 | 55.6 | 130 | 97.2 |
| 26 | 85 | 1310 | 60 | 1370 | 20 | 51 | 1390 | 50 | 1440 | 0 | 55.4 | 130 | 98.5 |
| 27 | 12 | 1390 | 30 | 1420 | 20 | 35 | 1440 | 40 | 1480 | 0 | 54.8 | 90 | 98.1 |
| 28 | 34 | 1440 | 40 | 1480 | 0 | 51 | 1480 | 50 | 1530 | 0 | 54.6 | 90 | 97.9 |
| 29 | 60 | 1480 | 50 | 1530 | 0 | 87 | 1530 | 70 | 1600 | 0 | 55.2 | 120 | 98.6 |
| 30 | 97 | 1530 | 80 | 1610 | 0 | 29 | 1610 | 30 | 1640 | 10 | 54.7 | 110 | 99.0 |

bad, is it? The average performance time for Bob is shown as 46.48 seconds. This is close to the weighted average of what you would expect in the long run. For Bob it is $(10 \times 4 + 20 \times 6 + 30 \times 10$ etc.$)/100 = 45.9$ seconds. Ray's expected time is $(10 \times 4 + 20 \times 5 + 30 \times 6$ etc.$)/50 = 46.4$ seconds.

The two-stage assembly line simulation is a good example of a specially designed spreadsheet for analyzing this problem. More general simulation programs built within Excel are available. John McClain, professor of operations management at Cornell University, has developed two simulation spreadsheets that can be used to demonstrate a variety of common systems. These spreadsheets have been included on this book's CD-ROM.

Excel: LineSim.xls

The first spreadsheet, titled "LineSim.xls," is designed to analyze a simple serial production line. This is a system with a series of machines; the output of one machine goes to a storage area, which is the input to the next machine. The spreadsheet can be easily configured for different numbers of machines, different buffer sizes, and numerous processing time distributions. In addition, machine breakdowns and repairs can be modeled. The second spreadsheet,

Excel: CellSim.xls

EXHIBIT TN15.9 & 10

TN15.9—Average Time per Unit of Output (Finish Time/Number of Units)

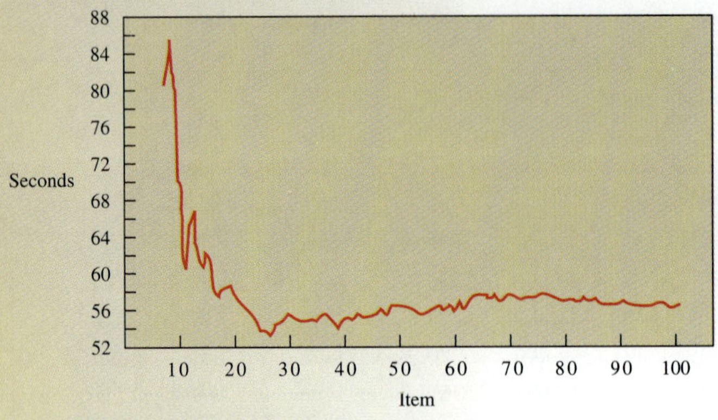


TN15.10—Average Time the Product Spends in the System

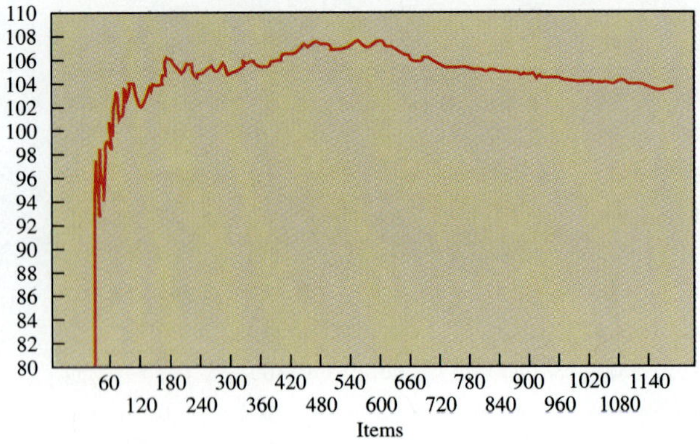


EXHIBIT TN15.11

Results of Simulating 1,200 Units Processed by Bob and Ray

| | BOB | RAY | UNIT |
|---|---|---|---|
| Utilization | 0.81 | 0.85 | |
| Average wait time | 10.02 | 9.63 | |
| Average performance time | 46.48 | 46.88 | |
| Average time per unit | | | 57.65 |
| Average time in system | | | 103.38 |

"CellSim.xls," is similar but allows machines to be arranged more generally. We thank Professor McClain for making these spreadsheets available.

## SIMULATION PROGRAMS AND LANGUAGES

Simulation models can be classified as *continuous* or *discrete*. Continuous models are based on mathematical equations and therefore are continuous, with values for all points in time. In contrast, discrete simulation occurs only at specific points. For example, customers arriving at a bank teller's window would be discrete simulation. The simulation jumps from point to point; the arrival of a customer, the start of a service, the ending of service, the arrival of the next customer, and so on. Discrete simulation can also be triggered to run by units of time (daily, hourly, minute by minute). This is called *event simulation;* points in between either have no value to our simulation or cannot be computed because of the lack of some sort of mathematical relationship to link the succeeding events. Operations management applications almost exclusively use discrete (event) simulation.

Simulation programs also can be categorized as general-purpose and special-purpose. General-purpose software is really language that allows programmers to build their own models. Examples are SLAM II, SIMSCRIPT II.5, SIMAN, GPSS/H, GPSS/PC, PC-MODEL, and RESQ. Special-purpose software simulation programs are specially built to simulate specific applications, such as MAP/1 and SIMFACTORY. In a specialized simulation for manufacturing, for example, provisions in the model allow for specifying the number of work centers, their description, arrival rates, processing time, batch sizes, quantities of work in process, available resources including labor, sequences, and so on. Additionally, the program may allow the observer to watch the animated operation and see the quantities and flows throughout the system as the simulation is running. Data are collected, analyzed, and presented in a form most suitable for that type of application.

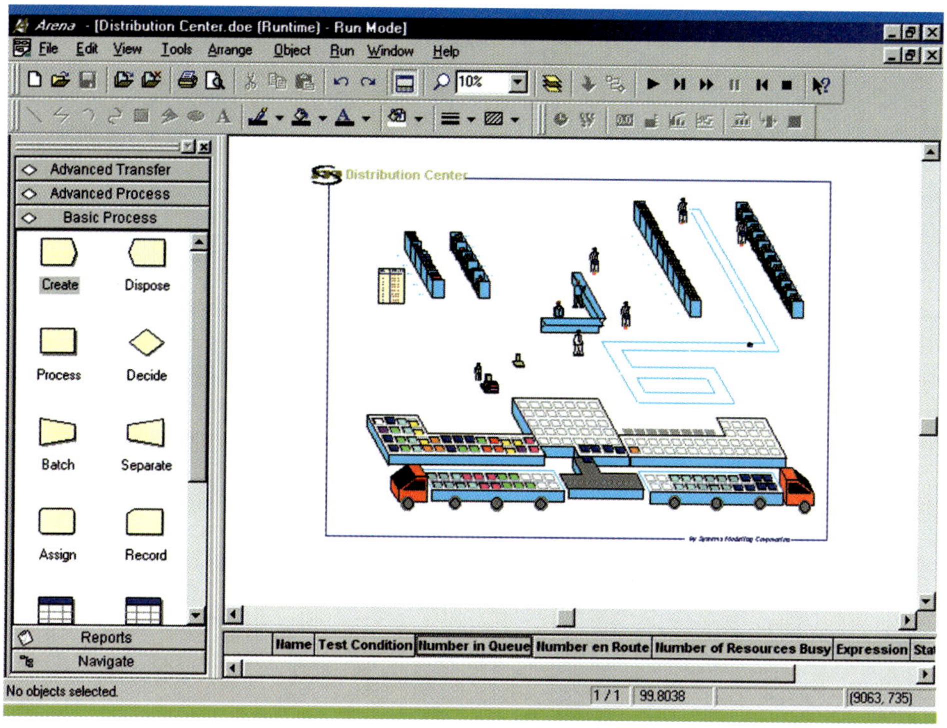


SYSTEMS MODELING CORPORATION MAKES SOFTWARE FOR SYSTEMS FROM MANUFACTURING OPERATIONS TO FAST FOOD RESTAURANTS. MODELS DEVELOPED WITH THEIR ARENA® PRODUCT CAN BE USED TO HELP ENGINEERS AND MANAGERS LOOK FOR BOTTLENECKS AND PROBLEMS IN AN EXISTING SYSTEM OR GAUGE THE CAPACITY FLOW OF A PROPOSED SYSTEM SUCH AS THE DISTRIBUTION CENTER SHOWN HERE.

Many software simulation programs are available. How, then, do you choose a program from a long list? The first step is to understand the different types of simulation. Then it becomes a matter of reviewing programs on the market to find one that fits your specific needs. (See the Breakthrough Box titled "Hospital Overcrowding Solutions Are Found with Simulation" for a successful application of a commercial program.)

As a last comment on simulation programs, do not rule out spreadsheets for simulation. As you noticed, we simulated Bob and Ray on a spreadsheet in the preceding section. Spreadsheets are becoming quite user-friendly and are adding many features, such as allowing random number generation and asking what-if questions. The simplicity in using a spreadsheet for simulation may well compensate for any needed reduction in the complexity of the problem in order to use the spreadsheet.

@RISK is an add-in program that works with Microsoft Excel. The program adds many useful simulation-related functions to the spreadsheet. Using @RISK automates the process of taking random values from a specified distribution function, automates the recalculation of the spreadsheet with the new random values, and captures output values and statistics. @RISK simplifies the process of building and running spreadsheet simulations.[2]

## DESIRABLE FEATURES OF SIMULATION SOFTWARE

Simulation software takes a while to learn to use. Once specific software is learned, the tendency is to stay with it for a long time, so the choice must be made carefully. Simulation software should

1 Be capable of being used interactively as well as allowing complete runs.
2 Be user-friendly and easy to understand.
3 Allow modules to be built and then connected. In this way models can be worked on separately without affecting the rest of the system.
4 Allow users to write and incorporate their own routines; no simulation program can provide for all needs.
5 Have building blocks that contain built-in commands (such as statistical analysis or decision rules for where to go next).
6 Have macro capability, such as the ability to develop machining cells.
7 Have material flow capability. Operations involve the movement of material and people; the program should be able to model trucks, cranes, conveyers, and so on.

# BREAKTHROUGH

## HOSPITAL OVERCROWDING SOLUTIONS ARE FOUND WITH SIMULATION

Thanks to increased life expectancy through improved health care coupled with shifting population demographics, hospitals everywhere are becoming increasingly overcrowded. Limited health care budgets are forcing hospitals to explore creative solutions. But creative solutions can be risky, so they need to be carefully evaluated. From the standpoint of cost, the earlier a solution can be evaluated and either accepted or rejected, the better.

Along these lines, the outpatient laboratory at Bay Medical Center was experiencing serious capacity constraints. Adding to its difficulties, a renovation designed to improve efficiency actually added to the overcrowding problem. Dave Nall, a management engineer for Bay Medical Center, ran a study to evaluate several alternatives and make recommendations designed to reduce bottlenecks and improve patient flow through the outpatient laboratory. The objective of this study was to develop and evaluate alternative ways of reducing overcrowding at the outpatient laboratory.

### SOLUTION

The key technology employed by Dave in conducting this analysis was computer simulation. Dave had used computer simulation numerous times in the past and had found that it was an efficient way to both gain insight into the problem and evaluate the solutions.

Through discussions with managers responsible for the outpatient laboratory, Dave built a network describing the patient's flow through the laboratory as it was currently configured. Then data were collected on the times required for patients to receive the various services they might need as well as the travel time between rooms where the services were provided. From this information, Dave constructed a computer simulation of the baseline laboratory configuration.

Dave then modified the computer simulation and used it to study issues relating to three categories of solutions to outpatient laboratory overcrowding: (1) changing staff, including both medical and administrative staff; (2) utilizing another clinic as an overflow laboratory; and (3) possible redesign of the laboratory facility itself.

With respect to staffing, the computer simulation verified that the medical staff currently employed was indeed the optimal number. However, Dave found that the administrative functions, if anything, were overstaffed and that a staff reduction could take place with no appreciable reduction in patient service. Staffing was not the key problem. With respect to the option of utilizing another laboratory for overflow, there were significant opportunities for improving throughput if other patients could be enticed to use another laboratory. Although the simulation did not tell him how to get the patients to use an alternative laboratory, it did allow Dave to quantify the

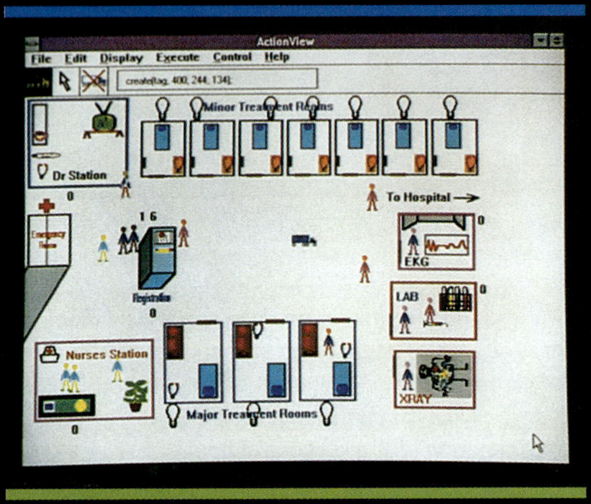


benefits of implementing policies that would increase alternative laboratory usage by 5 percent, 10 percent, and so on. With respect to redesign of the existing outpatient laboratory, Dave determined that, with a relatively minor redesign of the facility and a procedural change, the laboratory would become significantly more productive. Increased productivity would, of course, lead to better patient service.

### BENEFITS

Individually, no one could have accurately guessed the impact of the different ways of addressing overcrowding at the outpatient laboratory at Bay Medical Center. Through the results of the simulation analysis and the insights gained. Dave was able to assess the relative merits of each alternative as well as predict their impact. With a small investment in Dave's time, Bay Medical Center was able to make informed decisions with an understanding of both costs and benefits. As a result, the right decisions were made, money was saved, and patients were better served.

SOURCE: MICRO ANALYSIS AND DESIGN SIMULATION SOFTWARE, INC., BOULDER, CO.

8 Output standard statistics such as cycle times, utilizations, and wait times.
9 Allow a variety of data analysis alternatives for both input and output data.
10 Have animation capabilities to display graphically the product flow through the system.
11 Permit interactive debugging of the model so the user can trace flows through the model and more easily find errors.[3]

## ADVANTAGES AND DISADVANTAGES OF SIMULATION

The following is not intended as a comprehensive list of reasons why one should elect to use or not use simulation as a technique. Rather, we state some of the generally accepted advantages and disadvantages.

### ADVANTAGES

1 Developing the model of a system often leads to a better understanding of the real system.
2 Time can be compressed in simulation; years of experience in the real system can be compressed into seconds or minutes.
3 Simulation does not disrupt ongoing activities of the real system.
4 Simulation is far more general than mathematical models and can be used where conditions are not suitable for standard mathematical analysis.
5 Simulation can be used as a game for training experience.
6 Simulation provides a more realistic replication of a system than mathematical analysis.
7 Simulation can be used to analyze transient conditions, whereas mathematical techniques usually cannot.
8 Many standard packaged models, covering a wide range of topics, are available commercially.
9 Simulation answers what-if questions.

### DISADVANTAGES

1 Although a great deal of time and effort may be spent to develop a model for simulation, there is no guarantee that the model will, in fact, provide good answers.
2 There is no way to prove that a simulation model's performance is completely reliable. Simulation involves numerous repetitions of sequences that are based on randomly generated occurrences. An apparently stable system can, with the right combination of events—however unlikely—explode.
3 Depending on the system to be simulated, building a simulation model can take anywhere from an hour to 100 worker years. Complicated systems can be very costly and take a long time.
4 Simulation may be less accurate than mathematical analysis because it is randomly based. If a given system can be represented by a mathematical model, it may be better to use than simulation.
5 A significant amount of computer time may be needed to run complex models.
6 The technique of simulation, while making progress, still lacks a standardized approach. Therefore, models of the same system built by different individuals may differ widely.

## CONCLUSION

We could make the statement that anything that can be done mathematically can be done with simulation. However, simulation is not always the best choice. Mathematical analysis, when appropriate to a specific problem, is usually faster and less expensive. Also, it is usually provable as far as the technique is concerned, and the only real question is whether the system is adequately represented by the mathematical model.

Simulation, however, has nothing fixed; there are no boundaries to building a model or making assumptions about the system. Expanding computer power and memory have pushed out the limits of what can be simulated. Further, the continued development of simulation languages and programs—both general-purpose programs (SIMAN, SLAM) and special-purpose programs (Process Model SIMFACTORY, Optima!)—have made the entire process of creating simulation models much easier.

## KEY TERMS

**Parameters** Properties of a simulation model that are fixed.

**Variables** Properties of a simulation model that are allowed to vary throughout the simulation run. The results of the simulation are analyzed through these variables.

**Decision rules** Logic that controls the behavior of a simulation.

**Distributions** The probability distributions that are used to model the random events in a simulation.

**Time incrementing** The process of moving through time in a simulation.

**Run length (or run time)** The duration of a simulation in simulated time or number of events.

## SOLVED PROBLEMS

### SOLVED PROBLEM 1

To use an old statistical example for simulation, if an urn contains 100 balls, of which 10 percent are green, 40 percent are red, and 50 percent are spotted, develop a simulation model of the process of drawing balls at random from the urn. Each time a ball is drawn and its color noted, it is replaced. Use the following random numbers as you desire.

Simulate drawing 10 balls from the urn. Show which numbers you have used.

| | | | |
|---|---|---|---|
| 26768 | 66954 | 83125 | 08021 |
| 42613 | 17457 | 55503 | 36458 |
| 95457 | 03704 | 47019 | 05752 |
| 95276 | 56970 | 84828 | 05752 |

#### Solution

Assign random numbers to the balls to correspond to the percentage present in the urn.

| | RANDOM NUMBER |
|---|---|
| 10 green balls | 00–09 |
| 40 red balls | 10–49 |
| 50 spotted balls | 50–99 |

Many possible answers exist, depending on how the random numbers were assigned and which numbers were used from the list provided in the problem.

For the random number sequence above and using the first two numbers of those given, we obtain

| RN | COLOR | RN | COLOR |
|---|---|---|---|
| 26 | Red | 17 | Red |
| 42 | Red | 3 | Green |
| 95 | Spotted | 56 | Spotted |
| 95 | Spotted | 83 | Spotted |
| 66 | Spotted | 55 | Spotted |

For the 10 there were 1 green, 3 red, and 6 spotted balls—a good estimate based on a sample of only 10!

### SOLVED PROBLEM 2

A rural clinic receives a delivery of fresh plasma once each week from a central blood bank. The supply varies according to demand from other clinics and hospitals in the region but ranges between four and nine pints of the most widely used blood type, type O. The number of patients per week requiring this blood varies from zero to four, and each patient may need from one to four pints. Given the following delivery quantities, patient distribution, and demand per patient, what would be the number of pints in excess or short for a six-week period? Use simulation to derive your answer. Consider that plasma is storable and there is currently none on hand.

| Delivery Quantities | | Patient Distribution | | Demand per Patient | |
|---|---|---|---|---|---|
| Pints per Week | Probability | Patients per Week Requiring Blood | Probability | Pints | Probability |
| 4 | 0.15 | 0 | 0.25 | 1 | 0.40 |
| 5 | 0.20 | 1 | 0.25 | 2 | 0.30 |
| 6 | 0.25 | 2 | 0.30 | 3 | 0.20 |
| 7 | 0.15 | 3 | 0.15 | 4 | 0.10 |
| 8 | 0.15 | 4 | 0.05 | | |
| 9 | 0.10 | | | | |

## Solution

First develop a random number sequence; then simulate.

| Delivery | | | Number of Patients | | | Patient Demand | | |
|---|---|---|---|---|---|---|---|---|
| Pints | Probability | Random Number | Blood | Probability | Random Number | Pints | Probability | Random Number |
| 4 | .15 | 00–14 | 0 | .25 | 00–24 | 1 | .40 | 00–39 |
| 5 | .20 | 15–34 | 1 | .25 | 25–49 | 2 | .30 | 40–69 |
| 6 | .25 | 35–59 | 2 | .30 | 50–79 | 3 | .20 | 70–89 |
| 7 | .15 | 60–74 | 3 | .15 | 80–94 | 4 | .10 | 90–99 |
| 8 | .15 | 75–89 | 4 | .05 | 95–99 | | | |
| 9 | .10 | 90–99 | | | | | | |

| | | Quantity Delivered | | | Patients Needing Blood | | Quantity Needed | | | |
|---|---|---|---|---|---|---|---|---|---|---|
| Week No. | Beginning Inventory | RN | Pints | Total Blood on Hand | RN | Patients | Patient | RN | Pints | Number of Pints Remaining |
| 1 | 0 | 74 | 7 | 7 | 85 | 3 | First | 21 | 1 | 6 |
| | | | | | | | Second | 06 | 1 | 5 |
| | | | | | | | Third | 71 | 3 | 2 |
| 2 | 2 | 31 | 5 | 7 | 28 | 1 | | 96 | 4 | 3 |
| 3 | 3 | 02 | 4 | 7 | 72 | 2 | First | 12 | 1 | 6 |
| | | | | | | | Second | 67 | 2 | 4 |
| 4 | 4 | 53 | 6 | 10 | 44 | 1 | | 23 | 1 | 9 |
| 5 | 9 | 16 | 5 | 14 | 16 | 0 | | | | 14 |
| 6 | 14 | 40 | 6 | 20 | 83 | 3 | First | 65 | 2 | 18 |
| | | | | | | | Second | 34 | 1 | 17 |
| | | | | | | | Third | 82 | 3 | 14 |
| 7 | 14 | | | | | | | | | |

At the end of six weeks, there were 14 pints on hand.

## REVIEW AND DISCUSSION QUESTIONS

1 Why is simulation often called a technique of last resort?
2 What roles does statistical hypothesis testing play in simulation?
3 What determines whether a simulation model is valid?
4 Must you use a computer to get good information from a simulation? Explain.
5 What methods are used to increment time in a simulation model? How do they work?

6 What are the pros and cons of starting a simulation with the system empty? With the system in equilibrium?

7 Distinguish between known mathematical distributions and empirical distributions. What information is needed to simulate using a known mathematical distribution?

8 What is the importance of run length in simulation? Is a run of 100 observations twice as valid as a run of 50? Explain.

## PROBLEMS

1. See ISM.

1 CLASSROOM SIMULATION: FISH FORWARDERS

This is a competitive exercise designed to test players' skills at setting inventory ordering rules over a 10-week planning horizon. Maximum profit at the end determines the winner.

Fish Forwarders supplies fresh shrimp to a variety of customers in the New Orleans area. It orders cases of shrimp from fleet representatives at the beginning of each week to meet a demand from its customers at the middle of the week. Shrimp are subsequently delivered to Fish Forwarders and then, at the end of the week, to its customers.

Both the supply of shrimp and the demand for shrimp are uncertain. The supply may vary as much as ±10 percent from the amount ordered, and by contract, Fish Forwarders must purchase this supply. The probability associated with this variation is −10 percent, 30 percent of the time; 0 percent, 50 percent of the time; and +10 percent, 20 percent of the time. Weekly demand for shrimp is normally distributed with a mean of 800 cases and standard deviation of 100 cases.

A case of shrimp costs Fish Forwarders $30 and sells for $50. Any shrimp not sold at the end of the week are sold to a cat-food company at $4 per case. Fish Forwarders may, if it chooses, order the shrimp flash-frozen by the supplier at dockside, but this raises the cost of a case by $4 and, hence, costs Fish Forwarders $34 per case.

*Procedure for play.* The game requires that each week a decision be made as to how many cases to order of regular shrimp and of flash-frozen shrimp. The number ordered may be any amount. The instructor plays the role of referee and supplies the random numbers. The steps in playing the game are as follows:

*a.* Decide on the order amount of regular shrimp or flash-frozen shrimp and enter the figures in column 3 of the worksheet. (See Exhibit TN15.12.) Assume that there is no opening inventory of flash-frozen shrimp.

*b.* Determine the amount that arrives and enter it under "Orders received." To accomplish this, the referee draws a random number from a uniform random number table (such as that in Appendix B) and finds its associated level of variation from the following random

EXHIBIT TN15.12

Simulation Worksheet

| (1) | (2) | (3) | | (4) | | (5) | (6) | (7) | (8) | | (9) |
|---|---|---|---|---|---|---|---|---|---|---|---|
| Week | Flash-frozen inventory | Orders placed | | Orders received | | Available (regular and flash-frozen) | Demand (800 + 100Z) | Sales (minimum of demand or available) | Excess | | Shortages |
| | | Regular | Flash-frozen | Regular | Flash-frozen | | | | Regular | Flash | |
| 1 | | | | | | | | | | | |
| 2 | | | | | | | | | | | |
| 3 | | | | | | | | | | | |
| 4 | | | | | | | | | | | |
| 5 | | | | | | | | | | | |
| 6 | | | | | | | | | | | |
| 7 | | MARDI GRAS | | | | * | | | | | |
| 8 | | | | | | | | | | | |
| 9 | | | | | | | | | | | |
| 10 | | | | | | | | | | | |
| Total | | | | | | | | | | | |

*Flash-frozen only.

number intervals: 00 to 29 = −10 percent, 30 to 70 = 0 percent, and 80 to 99 = +10 percent. If the random number is, say, 13, the amount of variation will be −10 percent. Thus if you decide to order 1,000 regular cases of shrimp and 100 flash-frozen cases, the amount you would actually receive would be 1,000 − 0.10(1,000), or 900 regular cases, and 100 − 0.10(100), or 90 flash-frozen cases. (Note that the variation is the same for both regular and flash-frozen shrimp.) These amounts are then entered in column 4.

*c.* Add the amount of flash-frozen shrimp in inventory (if any) to the quantity of regular and flash-frozen shrimp just received and enter this amount in column 5. This would be 990, using the figures provided earlier.

*d.* Determine the demand for shrimp. To accomplish this, the referee draws a random normal deviate value from Exhibit TN15.3 or Appendix C and enters it into the equation at the top of column 6. Thus if the deviate value is −1.76, demand for the week is 800 + 100(−1.76), or 624.

*e.* Determine the amount sold. This will be the lesser of the amount demanded (column 6) and the amount available (column 5). Thus, if a player has received 990 and demand is 624, the quantity entered will be 624 (with 990 − 624, or 366 left over).

*f.* Determine the excess. The amount of excess is simply that quantity remaining after demand for a given week is filled. Always assume that regular shrimp are sold before the flash-frozen. Thus if we use the 366 figure obtained in *e*, the excess would include all the original 90 cases of flash-frozen shrimp.

*g.* Determine shortages. This is simply the amount of unsatisfied demand each period, and it occurs only when demand is greater than sales. (Because all customers use the shrimp within the week in which they are delivered, backorders are not relevant.) The amount of shortage (in cases of shrimp) is entered in column 9.

*Profit determination.* Exhibit TN15.13 is provided for determining the profit achieved at the end of play. The values to be entered in the table are obtained by summing the relevant columns of Exhibit TN15.12 and making the calculations.

*Assignment.* Simulate operations for a total of 10 weeks. It is suggested that a 10-minute break be taken at the end of Week 5, allowing the players to evaluate how they may improve their performance. They might also wish to plan an ordering strategy for the week of Mardi Gras, when no shrimp will be supplied.

2 The manager of a small post office is concerned that the growing township is overloading the one-window service being offered. Sample data are collected on 100 individuals who arrive for service:

2. Average customer waiting time = 1/6 min. Average teller idle time = 4/6 min.

| Time Between Arrivals (Minutes) | Frequency |
|---|---|
| 1 | 8 |
| 2 | 35 |
| 3 | 34 |
| 4 | 17 |
| 5 | 6 |
| | 100 |

| Service Time (Minutes) | Frequency |
|---|---|
| 1.0 | 12 |
| 1.5 | 21 |
| 2.0 | 36 |
| 2.5 | 19 |
| 3.0 | 7 |
| 3.5 | 5 |
| | 100 |

EXHIBIT TN15.13

**Profit from Fish Forwarders' Operations**

| | | |
|---|---|---|
| Revenue from sales ($50 × Col. 7) | $______ | |
| Revenue from salvage ($4 × Col. 8 reg.) | $______ | |
| Total revenue | | $______ |
| Cost of regular purchases ($30 × Col. 4 reg.) | $______ | |
| Cost of flash-frozen purchases ($34 × Col. 4 flash) | $______ | |
| Cost of holding flash-frozen shrimp ($2 × Col. 8 flash) | $______ | |
| Cost of shortages ($20 × Col. 9) | $______ | |
| Total cost | | $______ |
| Profit | | $______ |

Using the following random number sequence, simulate six arrivals; estimate the average customer waiting time and the average idle time for clerks.

RN: 08, 74, 24, 34, 45, 86, 31, 32, 45, 21, 10, 67, 60, 17, 60, 87, 74, 96

3. Option *a*:

| Total Pay | Total Time |
|---|---|
| $6 | 7 |
| $9 | 7 |

Option *b*:

| Total Time |
|---|
| 6.5 |
| 7.5 |

Option *c*.

| Total Time |
|---|
| 5 |
| 4 |

Average trip time:

Option *a* = 7

Option *b* = 7

option *c* = 4.5

3 Thomas Magnus, a private investigator, has been contacted by a potential client in Kamalo, Molokai. The call came just in time because Magnus is down to his last $10. Employment, however, is conditional on Magnus meeting the client at Kamalo within eight hours. Magnus, presently at the Masters' residence in Kipahulu, Maui, has three alternative ways to get to Kamalo. Magnus may

*a.* Drive to the native village of Honokahua and take an outrigger to Kamalo.
*b.* Drive to Honokahua and swim the 10 miles across Pailolo Channel to Kamalo.
*c.* Drive to Hana and ask his friend T. C. to fly him by helicopter to Kamalo.

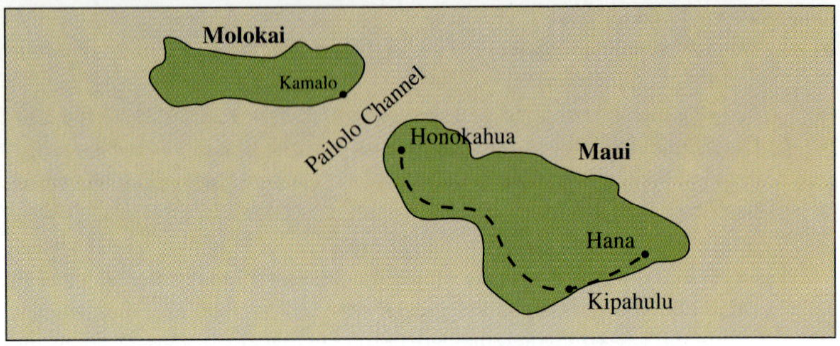


If option *a* is chosen, driving times to Honokahua are given in Distribution 1. Once at Honokahua, Magnus must negotiate with the friendly Tai natives. Negotiations always include a few Mai Tais, so if Magnus begins to negotiate, swimming becomes impossible. Negotiations center on how much each of the three outrigger crew members will be paid. Negotiation time, crew pay, and outrigger travel time are in Distributions 3, 4, and 5, respectively. You may assume each crew member is paid the same amount. If crew pay totals more than $10, Magnus is out of luck—trip time may then be taken to be infinity.

If option *b* is chosen, driving times to Honokahua and swimming times are given in Distributions 1 and 6.

If option *c* is chosen, driving times to Hana are given in Distribution 2. T. C., however, is at the airport only 10 percent of the time. If T. C. is not at the airport, Magnus will wait for him to arrive. Magnus's waiting time is given by Distribution 8. T. C. may refuse to fly for the $10 Magnus has available; Magnus puts the probability of T. C. refusing to fly for $10 at 30 percent. You may assume negotiation time is zero. If T. C. refuses, Magnus will drive to Honokahua via Kipahulu and swim to Kamalo. Helicopter flying times are given in Distribution 7.

Simulate each of the three alternative transportation plans *twice* and, based on your simulation results, calculate the average trip time for each plan. Use the following random numbers in the order they appear; do not skip any random numbers.

RN: 7, 3, 0, 4, 0, 5, 3, 5, 6, 1, 6, 6, 4, 8, 4, 9, 0, 7, 7, 1, 7, 0, 6, 8, 8, 7, 9, 0, 1, 2, 9, 7, 3, 2, 3, 8, 6, 0, 6, 0, 5, 9, 7, 9, 6, 4, 7, 2, 8, 7, 8, 1, 7, 0, 5

**Distribution 1: Time to drive from Kipahulu to Honokahua (hours)**

| Time | Probability | RN |
|---|---|---|
| 1 | .2 | 0–1 |
| 1.5 | .6 | 2–7 |
| 2 | .2 | 8–9 |

**Distribution 2: Time to drive from Kipahulu to Hana and vice versa (hours)**

| Time | Probability | RN |
|---|---|---|
| .5 | .2 | 0–1 |
| 1 | .7 | 2–8 |
| 1.5 | .1 | 9 |

**Distribution 3: Negotiation time (hours)**

| Time | Probability | RN |
|---|---|---|
| 1 | .2 | 0–1 |
| 1.5 | .3 | 2–4 |
| 2 | .3 | 5–7 |
| 2.5 | .2 | 8–9 |

**Distribution 4: Outrigger pay per crew member**

| Pay | Probability | RN |
|---|---|---|
| $2 | .3 | 0–2 |
| 3 | .3 | 3–5 |
| 4 | .4 | 6–9 |

**Distribution 5: Outrigger travel time from Honokahua to Kamalo (hours)**

| TIME | PROBABILITY | RN |
|---|---|---|
| 3 | .1 | 0 |
| 4 | .5 | 1–5 |
| 5 | .4 | 6–9 |

**Distribution 6: Time to swim from Honokahua to Kamalo (hours)**

| TIME | PROBABILITY | RN |
|---|---|---|
| 5 | .2 | 0–1 |
| 6 | .6 | 2–7 |
| 7 | .2 | 8–9 |

**Distribution 7: Time to fly from Hana to Kamalo (hours)**

| TIME | PROBABILITY | RN |
|---|---|---|
| 1 | .1 | 0 |
| 1.5 | .7 | 1–7 |
| 2 | .2 | 8–9 |

**Distribution 8: Magnus's waiting time at airport (hours)**

| TIME | PROBABILITY | RN |
|---|---|---|
| 1 | .1 | 0 |
| 2 | .2 | 1–2 |
| 3 | .4 | 3–6 |
| 4 | .3 | 7–9 |

4 A bank of machines in a manufacturing shop breaks down according to the following interarrival time distribution. The time it takes one repairperson to complete the repair of a machine is given in the service time distribution:

4. Average downtime = 14.5/5 or 2.9 hours.

| INTERARRIVAL TIME (HOURS) | $P(X)$ | RN |
|---|---|---|
| .5 | .30 | 0–29 |
| 1.0 | .22 | 30–51 |
| 1.5 | .16 | 52–67 |
| 2.0 | .10 | 68–77 |
| 3.0 | .14 | 78–91 |
| 4.0 | .08 | 92–99 |
| | 1.00 | |

| SERVICE TIME (HOURS) | $P(X)$ | RN |
|---|---|---|
| .5 | .25 | 0–24 |
| 1.0 | .20 | 25–44 |
| 2.0 | .25 | 45–69 |
| 3.0 | .15 | 70–84 |
| 4.0 | .10 | 85–94 |
| 5.0 | .05 | 95–99 |
| | 1.00 | |

Simulate the breakdown of five machines. Calculate the average machine downtime using two repairpersons and the following random number sequence. (Both repairpersons cannot work on the same machine.)

RN: 30, 81, 02, 91, 51, 08, 28, 44, 86, 84, 29, 08, 37, 34, 99

5 Jennifer Jones owns a small candy store she operates herself. A study was made observing the time between customers coming into the store and the time that Jones took to serve them. The following data were collected from 100 customers observed:

5. See ISM.

| INTERARRIVAL TIME (MINUTES) | NUMBER OF OBSERVATIONS |
|---|---|
| 1 | 5 |
| 2 | 10 |
| 3 | 10 |
| 4 | 15 |
| 5 | 15 |
| 6 | 20 |
| 7 | 10 |
| 8 | 8 |
| 9 | 5 |
| 10 | 2 |

| SERVICE TIME (MINUTES) | NUMBER OF OBSERVATIONS |
|---|---|
| 1 | 10 |
| 2 | 15 |
| 3 | 15 |
| 4 | 20 |
| 5 | 15 |
| 6 | 10 |
| 7 | 8 |
| 8 | 4 |
| 9 | 2 |
| 10 | 1 |

Simulate the system (all of the arrivals and services) until 10 customers pass through the system and are serviced.

How long does the average customer spend in the system? Use Appendix B to obtain random numbers.

6. See ISM.

6 A professional football coach has six running backs on his squad. He wants to evaluate how injuries might affect his stock of running backs. A minor injury causes a player to be removed from the game and miss only the next game. A major injury puts the player out of action for the rest of the season. The probability of a major injury in a game is 0.05. There is at most one major injury per game. The probability distribution of minor injuries per game is

| NUMBER OF INJURIES | PROBABILITY |
|---|---|
| 0 | .2 |
| 1 | .5 |
| 2 | .22 |
| 3 | .05 |
| 4 | .025 |
| 5 | .005 |
| | 1.000 |

Injuries seem to happen in a completely random manner, with no discernible pattern over the season. A season is 10 games.

Using the following random numbers, simulate the fluctuations in the coach's stock of running backs over the season. Assume that he hires no additional running backs during the season.

RN: 044, 392, 898, 615, 986, 959, 558, 353, 577, 866, 305, 813, 024, 189, 878, 023, 285, 442, 862, 848, 060, 131, 963, 874, 805, 105, 452

7. Condition 1 Condition 2
a. (1) Idle 18 min. 76 + 134 = 210 min.
(2) Delay 87 min. 0 min.
b. Cost of repairperson
$ 38.80 $ 77.20
Cost of machine down time
$175.33 $117.33
Total cost
$214.13 $194.53
Lowest cost is Condition 2.

7 At Tucson Mills, minor breakdowns of machines occur frequently. The occurrence of breakdowns and the service time to fix the machines are randomly distributed. Management is concerned with minimizing the cost of breakdowns. The cost per hour for the machines to be down is $40. The cost of service repairpersons is $12 per hour. A preliminary study has produced the following data on times between successive breakdowns and their service times:

RELATIVE FREQUENCY OF BREAKDOWNS

| | | | | | | |
|---|---|---|---|---|---|---|
| Time between breakdowns (in minutes) | 4 | 5 | 6 | 7 | 8 | 9 |
| Relative frequency | .10 | .30 | .25 | .20 | .10 | .05 |

RELATIVE FREQUENCY OF SERVICE TIMES

| | | | | | | |
|---|---|---|---|---|---|---|
| Service time (in minutes) | 4 | 5 | 6 | 7 | 8 | 9 |
| Relative frequency | .10 | .40 | .20 | .15 | .10 | .05 |

Simulate 30 breakdowns under two conditions: with one service repairperson and with two service repairpersons.

Use the following random number sequence to determine time between breakdowns:

RN: 85, 16, 65, 76, 93, 99, 65, 70, 58, 44, 02, 85, 01, 97, 63, 52, 53, 11, 62, 28, 84, 82, 27, 20, 39, 70, 26, 21, 41, 81

Use the following random number sequence to determine service times:

RN: 68, 26, 85, 11, 16, 26, 95, 67, 97, 73, 75, 64, 26, 45, 01, 87, 20, 01, 19, 36, 69, 89, 81, 81, 02, 05, 10, 51, 24, 36

*a.* Using the results of the simulations, calculate
(1) The total idle time for the service repairpersons under each condition.
(2) The total delay caused by waiting for a service repairperson to begin working on a breakdown.

*b.* Determine the lowest-cost approach.

8 Jethro's service station has one gasoline pump. Because everyone in Kornfield County drives big cars, there is room at the station for only three cars, including the car at the pump. Cars arriving when three cars are already at the station drive on to another station. Use the following probability distributions to simulate the arrival of four cars to Jethro's station:

8. Avg. time in system is 35/4 or 8.75 minutes.

| Interarrival Time (Minutes) | P(X) | RN | Service Time (Minutes) | P(X) | RN |
|---|---|---|---|---|---|
| 10 | .40 | 0–39 | 5 | .45 | 0–44 |
| 20 | .35 | 40–74 | 10 | .30 | 45–74 |
| 30 | .20 | 75–94 | 15 | .20 | 75–94 |
| 40 | .05 | 95–99 | 20 | .05 | 95–99 |

Use the following random numbers sequence:

RN: 99, 00, 73, 09, 38, 53, 72, 91

How many cars go to another station?
What is the average time a car spends at the station?

9 You have been hired as a consultant by a supermarket chain to answer a basic question: How many items per customer should be permitted in the fast checkout line? This is no trivial question for the chain's management; your findings will be the basis for corporate policy for all 2,000 stores. The vice president of operations has given you one month to do the study and two assistants to help you gather the data.

9. See ISM.

In starting this study, you decide to avoid queuing theory as the tool for analysis (because of your concern about the reliability of its assumptions) and instead opt for simulation. Given the following data, explain in detail how you would go about your analysis stating (1) the criteria you would use in making your recommendation, (2) what additional data you would need to set up your simulation, (3) how you would gather the preliminary data, (4) how you would set up the problem for simulation, and (5) which factors would affect the applicability of your findings to all of the stores.

| | |
|---|---|
| Store locations: | The United States and Canada |
| Hours of operation: | 16 per day |
| Average store size: | 9 checkout stands including fast checkout |
| Available checkers: | 7 to 10 (some engage in stocking activities when not at a checkout stand) |

10 The saga of Joe from Chapter 15 (Problem 12, page 608) continues. Joe has the opportunity to do a big repair job for a local motorcycle club. (Their cycles were accidentally run over by a garbage truck.) The compensation for the job is good, but it is vital that the total repair time for the five cycles be less than 40 hours. (The leader of the club has stated that he would be very distressed if the cycles were not available for a planned rally.) Joe knows from experience that repairs of this type often entail several trips between processes for a given cycle, so estimates of time are difficult to provide. Still, Joe has the following historical data about the probability that a job will start in each process, processing time in each process, and transitional probabilities between each pair of processes:

10. See ISM.
Joe can finish the job in 15 hours according to the simulation and schedule.

| Process | Probability of Job Starting in Process | Processing Time Probability (Hours) 1 | 2 | 3 | Probability of Going from Process to Other Processes or Completion (Out): Frame | Engine Work | Painting | Out |
|---|---|---|---|---|---|---|---|---|
| Frame repair | 0.5 | 0.2 | 0.4 | 0.4 | — | 0.4 | 0.4 | 0.2 |
| Engine work | 0.3 | 0.6 | 0.1 | 0.3 | 0.3 | — | 0.4 | 0.3 |
| Painting | 0.2 | 0.3 | 0.3 | 0.4 | 0.1 | 0.1 | — | 0.8 |

Given this information, use simulation to determine the repair times for each cycle. Display your results on a Gantt chart showing an FCFS schedule. (Assume that only one cycle can be worked on at a time in each process.) Based on your simulation, what do you recommend Joe do next?

11. One car bypasses.

11 "Eat at Helen's" has decided to add a drive-up window to the restaurant. Due to limited capital, there is enough space for only two cars in the drive-up window lane (one being served and one waiting). Helen would like to know how many customers are bypassing her restaurant due to the limited space in the drive-up window lane. Simulate 10 cars as they attempt to use the drive-up window using the following distributions and random numbers:

| Time Between Arrivals (Minutes) | Probability |
|---|---|
| 1 | 0.40 |
| 2 | 0.30 |
| 3 | 0.15 |
| 4 | 0.15 |

| Service Time (Minutes) | Probability |
|---|---|
| 1 | 0.20 |
| 2 | 0.40 |
| 3 | 0.40 |

Use the following two-digit random numbers for this problem:

Arrivals: 37, 60, 79, 21, 85, 71, 48, 39, 31, 35
Service: 66, 74, 90, 95, 29, 72, 17, 55, 15, 36

12. See ISM.

12. Jane's Auto World has a policy of placing an order for 27 of the most popular model whenever inventory reaches 20. Lead time on delivery is two weeks, and 25 automobiles are currently on hand. Simulate 15 weeks' worth of sales using the following probabilities that were derived from historical information:

| Sales per Week | Probability | Sales per Week | Probability |
|---|---|---|---|
| 5 | .05 | 10 | .20 |
| 6 | .05 | 11 | .20 |
| 7 | .10 | 12 | .10 |
| 8 | .10 | 13 | .05 |
| 9 | .10 | 14 | .05 |

Use the following random numbers for sales: 23, 59, 82, 83, 61, 00, 48, 33, 06, 32, 82, 51, 54, 66, 55.
Does this policy appear to be appropriate? Explain.

## ADVANCED CASE: UNDERSTANDING THE IMPACT OF VARIABILITY ON THE CAPACITY OF A PRODUCTION SYSTEM

This exercise, which uses LineSim.xls, is an opportunity to study the impact that variability in processing time has on the capacity of a simple serial production system. Much more complex systems could be studied, but our hope is that by studying this simple system, you will gain insight that can be applied to more complex systems.

The system we are studying is similar to the two-stage assembly line discussed in this technical note; here we look at a three-stage assembly line. In practice, assembly lines have many more workstations, but completing an exercise with more workstations would take considerably longer. If you do not believe that your results can be generalized to a larger system, feel free to expand your study.

For this study we use the Serial Line Simulator (LineSim.xls) that is included on this book's CD-ROM. This Microsoft Excel spreadsheet simulates a simple serial production line. We are indebted to John McClain at the Johnson Graduate School of Management, Cornell University, for allowing us to use his innovative spreadsheet.

### GOAL OF THIS EXERCISE

Our goal in this exercise is that you learn firsthand how variability can impact the performance of multistage production systems. A common approach used to reduce the impact of variability is through some type of buffering mechanism. To be more specific, in our system variability exists in the amount of time that it takes to perform work at a workstation. In analyzing the system we use the average time to complete each unit, so sometimes it takes longer and sometime less time. It probably seldom takes exactly the average time.

When there is variability, production engineers put buffer stations between each workstation. These buffers allow the variability to be smoothed so that the variability in one workstation has less impact on the other workstations. An interesting question to study with simulation is if these buffers are eliminated, or if there are 100 units between each workstation, how would this change the performance of the system?

### DETAILS OF THE EXERCISE

Start with the spreadsheet as Professor McClain configures it initially. Click the "Design" tab, and note that we have a three-station assembly line. The stations are named "Joe," "Next's," and "M2." There is a buffer area downstream from "Joe" with a capacity of one unit, and another downstream from "Next's" with a capacity of one unit. The way this simulation is designed, "Joe" will always have something to work on, and "M2" can always deposit finished work in a storage area.

Notice that the processing time distribution is Shifted Exponential with a mean of 5 and a standard deviation of 5. The shape of this distribution, described in the "Instructions" tab, shows that there is much process time variation. Answer the following question before going on to the next part of the exercise:

Question 1: How many units would you expect to be able to produce over 100 time periods?

Click the "Run" tab and, using the default values for "Run-In Time," "Run Length," and "Repetitions," run the simulation. Tabulate the average utilization at each machine based on the five repetitions, and tabulate the mean and standard deviation of the output of the system (these data are in the "Machine" worksheet).

Question 2: How many units did you actually produce per 100 time periods? Explain any difference between your simulation result and your estimate made in Question 1.

Next map the impact that increased buffer inventory has on the output of the system. You can change the buffer behind "Joe" and "Next" by changing the inventory cell designated "Joe's Inventory" (this is on the "Design" worksheet) and then clicking "Make Storage Areas Like #1."

Question 3: Create a graph that shows the impact of changing the buffer stock on the output of the system. Consider buffer levels that vary from 0 to a maximum of 20 units. What can you conclude from your experiment?

Finally, experiment with the impact of a bottleneck in the system.

Question 4: What would be the impact on system performance if "M2" had a processing time that averaged 6 time units? (Assume that "Joe" and "Next" still run at an average of 5.) What happens to the inventory after "Joe" and "Next"? Does varying the size of these inventories have any impact?

Question 5: What happens if instead of "M2" being the bottleneck, "Joe" is the bottleneck? Do the buffers at "Joe" and "Next" have any impact?

Keep your answers brief; your entire report, including graphs, should be no longer than two double-spaced pages.

## SELECTED BIBLIOGRAPHY


Evans, J. R., and D. L. Olson. *Introduction to Simulation and Risk Analysis.* Upper Saddle River, N.J.: Prentice Hall, 1998.

Harrington, H. J., and K. Tumay. *Simulation Modeling Methods.* New York: McGraw-Hill, 1999.

MicroAnalysis and Design Software Inc. "Hospital Overcrowding Solutions Are Found with Simulation." *Industrial Engineering,* December 1993, p. 557.

Law, A. M., and W. D. Kelton. *Simulation Modeling and Analysis.* New York: McGraw-Hill, 2000.

Pritsker, A. A. *Introduction to Simulation and SLAM II.* New York: Wiley, 1995.

Winston, W. L. *Simulation Modeling Using @RISK.* Belmont, CA: Wadsworth, 1996.


## FOOTNOTES

1 The basis formula is $Z = \frac{x-\mu}{\sigma}$, which when restated in terms of $x$, appears as $x = \mu + Z\sigma$. We then substituted $D_n$ for $x$ and $\bar{x}$ for $\mu$ to relate the method more directly to the sample problem.

2 See W. L. Winston, *Simulation Modeling Using @RISK* (Belmont, CA: Wadsworth, 1996). @RISK is a product of Palisade Corporation (http://www.palisade.com).

3 S. W. Haider and J. Banks, "Simulation Software Products for Analyzing Manufacturing Systems," *Industrial Engineering* 18, no. 7 (July 1986), pp. 98–103.

# section 5

# Revising the System





## "There Is Nothing Permanent Except Change." —Greek Philosopher Heraclitus, 500 B.C.

"If it ain't broke, don't fix it" is a questionable maxim in the business world of today. If a company is not improving its operations, its managers just aren't doing their jobs. The reality is that competing companies must continually improve to keep up. Improved business practices, improved technology, and better products make change inevitable.

Chapter 16, "Operations Consulting and Reengineering," describes the actual business of change management—key to the success of operations consulting practices around the world. Here you will see how many of the ideas described in the book are fundamental to the services provided by these companies. Many students majoring in operations management find employment with consulting companies.

Finally, Chapter 17 covers the innovative "Synchronous Manufacturing and Theory of Constraints" ideas of Dr. Eliyahu M. Goldratt. Dr. Goldratt's ideas have forced both practitioners and academics to rethink many conventional business and engineering practices. His framework for identifying and exploiting constraints that limit the profitability of the firm has been widely adopted.

*chapter sixteen*

# OPERATIONS CONSULTING AND REENGINEERING

## CHAPTER OUTLINE AND KEY TERMS

16

## CONSULTING'S NEW ERA

Reengineering and automation of business processes are well developed. So, although early on the enterprise–application consulting community had more business than it could handle, supply has caught demand. The question becomes, What new value-added services will consultants offer to manufacturers during the next few years? The answer rests with manufacturers themselves and with the new questions they are raising about how to operate their businesses and leverage their IT investments. "The buying factor in the consulting marketplace has changed," says Robert McIlhattan, vice chairman of U.S. consulting services in Ernst & Young LLP's (E&Y) Chicago

office. "In the recent past, the client knew what the agenda was . . . to implement a particular package for a specific reason. The key buying determinant was how to do that, get it done in a specific time frame, in a cost-effective manner, and minimize risk associated with the solution. Now the client is asking the fundamental questions, 'What do I do to get the value out of the investment, to continue to drive growth in my organization, to increase efficiencies, to leverage my investments?' These are very different questions from how to do it." Manufacturers are looking at information technology to support contemporary objectives such as increasing collaboration, linking businesses, driving decision making into the organization, improving management decision making and increasing agility and velocity, and capturing new revenue streams.

**Source:** T. Stevens, "Consulting's New Era," *Industry Week*, August 16, 1999, pp. 24–25. Reprinted with permission from *Industry Week*, August 16, 1999. 

Up to the challenge, the consulting community has new offerings to capitalize on these opportunities, with services in three basic categories: realizing new benefits from systems already in place; adding value with the ever-increasing list of new bolt-on applications that enterprise resource planning (ERP) and specialty vendors are offering; and outsourcing—from applications maintenance, to business process, to entire supply chains and retail sales channels. ←

Consulting has become one of the major areas of employment for business graduates. However, as the opening vignette suggests, consulting clients now are seeking more than just implementation of packaged programs (such as for ERP): they now seek ways of leveraging such programs to get "more bang for the consulting buck." This means that students becoming consultants must understand the full range of operations concepts presented in this book.

This chapter discusses some specifics of how one goes about consulting for operations, as well as the nature of the consulting business in general. A secondary purpose is to provide a brief overview of business process reengineering because much consulting work falls under this heading.

## WHAT IS OPERATIONS CONSULTING?

Operations consulting

**Operations consulting** deals with assisting clients in developing operations strategies and improving production processes. In strategy development, the focus is on analyzing the capabilities of operations in light of the firm's competitive strategy. By way of example, Treacy and Wiersema suggest that market leadership can be attained in one of three ways: through product leadership, through operational excellence, or through customer intimacy.[1] Each of these strategies may well call for different operations capabilities and focus. The operations consultant must be able to assist management in understanding these differences and be able to define the most effective combination of technology and systems to execute the strategy. In process improvement, the focus is on employing analytical tools and methods to help operating managers enhance performance of their departments. Deloitte & Touche Consulting lists the actions to improve processes as follows: refine/revise processes, revise activities, reconfigure flows, revise policies/procedures, change outputs, and realign structure. We say more about both strategy issues and tools later. Regardless of where one focuses, *an effective job of operations consulting results in an alignment between strategy and process dimensions that enhances the business performance of the client.*

## THE NATURE OF THE MANAGEMENT CONSULTING INDUSTRY

Fredrick W. Taylor, "the father of scientific management," is also credited as "the father of management consulting." Taylor, a young engineer, devised a philosophy and system of production management at the turn of the century. His book, *The Principles of Scientific Management,* converted what had been an art into a systematic, teachable approach to the study of work. Since Taylor's time, management consulting has reached far beyond the shop floor. Today management consulting is booming, as can be seen by the revenue figures from *Consultants News* given in Exhibit 16.1A. The reasons for this boom include the following: market pressures on clients to reengineer their core processes and eliminate their noncore processes; globalization requiring companies to seek expert advice on entering foreign markets and defending local ones against new competitors; and the need to better manage information technology, including systems integration, packaged software solutions, and, of course, Internet applications.

The management consulting industry can be categorized in three ways: by size, by specialization, and by in-house and external consultants. Most consulting firms are small,

Exhibit 16.1

**Consulting Industry Data**

**A. *Consultants News* Largest 10**

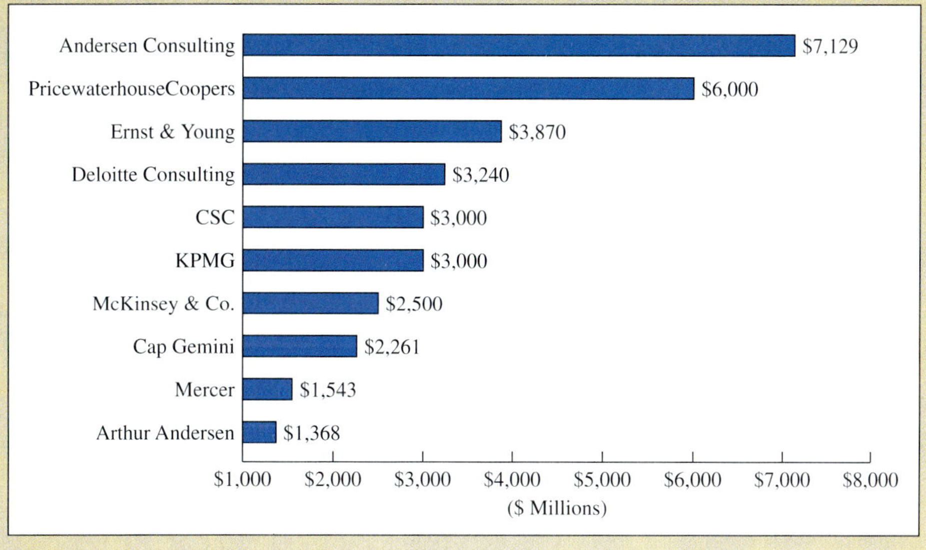


**B. Size of Sector and Major Firms by Sector**

*Strategy* (18%)
- McKinsey & Co.
- Bain & Co.
- Boston Consulting Group

*Operations Management* (24%)
- Booz-Allen & Hamilton
- Arthur D. Little

*Information Technology* (48%)
- Andersen Consulting
- Big Five accounting firms
- CSC

*Human Resources* (10%)
- Mercer
- Towers Perrin
- Hewitt

**C. Manufacturing, Financial Services Largest Markets**

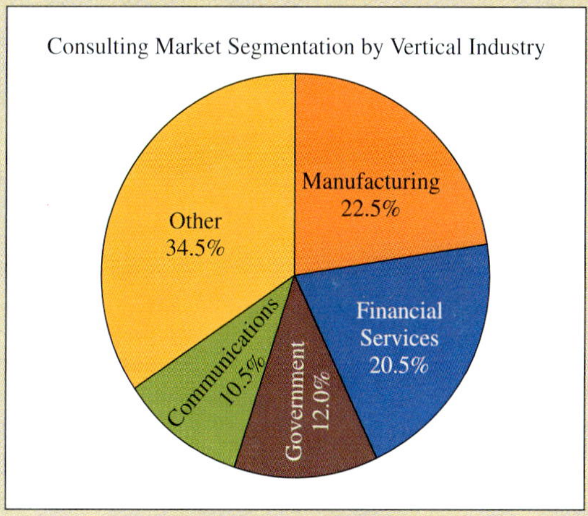


Source: Kennedy Information/www.kennedyinfo.com.

generating less than $500,000 in annual billings. But as David J. Collis notes in his article, "The Management Consulting Industry," the typical consultant works for a large firm, with three-quarters working for firms employing more than 100 professionals.[2] Relative to specialization, although all large firms provide a variety of services, they may also specialize by function, such as operations management, or by industry, such as manufacturing (see Exhibit 16.1B and 16.1C). Most large consulting companies are built on information technology (IT) and accounting work. The third basis for segmentation, in-house versus external, refers to whether a company maintains its own consulting organization or buys consulting services from the outside. Collis observes that internal consulting arms are common in large companies and are often affiliated with planning departments.

Cross Functional

Consulting firms are also frequently characterized according to whether their primary skill is in strategic planning or in tactical analysis and implementation. McKinsey and Company and the Boston Consulting Group are standard examples of strategy-type companies, whereas Gemini Consulting and the Hay Group focus rather extensively on tactical and implementation projects. The big accounting firms and Andersen Consulting are known for providing a wide range of services. The major new players in the consulting business are the large information technology firms such as Computer Sciences Corporation (CSC), Electronic Data Systems (EDS), and IBM. Consultancies are faced with problems similar to those of their clients: the need to provide a global presence, the need to computerize to coordinate activities, and the need to continually recruit and train their workers. This has led consultancies to make the hard choice of being very large or being a boutique firm. Being in the middle creates problems of lack of scale economies on the one hand and lack of focus and flexibility on the other.

"Finders"

"Minders"

"Grinders"

The hierarchy of the typical consulting firm can be viewed as a pyramid. At the top of the pyramid are the partners or seniors, whose primary function is sales and client relations. In the middle are managers, who manage consulting projects or "engagements." At the bottom are juniors, who carry out the consulting work as part of a consulting team. There are gradations in rank within each of these categories (such as senior partners). The three categories are frequently referred to colloquially as the **"finders"** (of new business), the **"minders"** (or managers) of the project teams, and the **"grinders"** (the consultants who do the work). Consulting firms typically work in project teams, selected according to client needs and the preferences of the project managers and the first-line consultants themselves. Getting oneself assigned to interesting, high-visibility projects with good coworkers is an important career strategy of most junior consultants. Being in demand for team membership and obtaining quality consulting experiences are critical for achieving long-term success with a consulting firm (or being attractive to another firm within or outside of consulting).

## ECONOMICS OF CONSULTING FIRMS

The economics of consulting firms have been written about extensively by David H. Maister. In his classic article, "Balancing the Professional Service Firm,"[3] he draws the analogy of the consulting firm as a job shop, where the right kinds of "machines" (professional staff) must be correctly allocated to the right kinds of jobs (consulting projects). As in any job shop, the degree of job customization and attendant complexity is critical. The most complex projects, which Maister calls *brain surgery* projects, require innovation and creativity. Next come *gray hair* projects, which require a great deal of experience but little in the way of innovation. A third type of project is the *procedures* project, where the general nature of the problem is well known and the activities necessary to complete it are similar to those performed on other projects.

Because consulting firms are typically partnerships, the goal is to maximize profits for the partners. This, in turn, is achieved by leveraging the skills of the partners through the effective use of midlevel and junior consultants. This is often presented as a ratio of partners to midlevel to junior consultants for the average project. (See Exhibit 16.2 for a numerical example of how profitability is calculated for a hypothetical consulting firm, Guru Associates.) Because most consulting firms are engaged in multiple projects simultaneously, the percentage of billable employee hours assigned to all projects (target utilization) will be less than 100 percent. A practice that specializes in cutting-edge, high-client risk (brain surgery) work must be staffed with a high partner-to-junior ratio because lower-level people will not be able to deliver the quality of services required. In contrast, practices that deal with more procedural, low-risk work will be inefficient if they do not have a lower ratio of partners to juniors because high-priced staff should not be doing low-value tasks.

The most common method for improving efficiency is the use of uniform approaches to each aspect of a consulting job. Andersen Consulting, the company most famous for this approach, sends its new consultants through a boot camp at its St. Charles, Illinois, training facility. At this boot camp, it provides highly refined, standardized methods for such common operations work as systems design, process reengineering, and continuous

EXHIBIT 16.2

The Economics of Guru Associates

| Level | No. | Target Utilization | Target Billable Hours @ 2,000 Hours per Person per Year | Billing Rate | Fees | Salary per Individual | Total Salaries |
|---|---|---|---|---|---|---|---|
| Partner (senior) | 4 | 75% | 6,000 | $200 | $1,200,000 | (see calculations below) | |
| Middle | 8 | 75% | 12,000 | $100 | $1,200,000 | $75,000 | $600,000 |
| Junior | 20 | 90% | 36,000 | $50 | $1,800,000 | $32,000 | $640,000 |
| Totals | | | | | $4,200,000 | | $1,240,000 |

| | |
|---|---|
| Fees | $4,200,000 |
| Salaries | (1,240,000) |
| Contributions | $2,960,000 |
| Overhead* | $1,280,000 |
| Partner profits | $1,680,000 |
| Per partner | $ 420,000 |

* Assume overhead costs of $40,000 per professional.

SOURCE: D. H. MAISTER, *MANAGING THE PROFESSIONAL SERVICE FIRM* (NEW YORK: THE FREE PRESS, 1993), P. 11. 

improvement, and for the project management and reporting procedures by which such work is carried out. Of course, other large consulting firms have their own training methods and step-by-step procedures for selling, designing, and executing consulting projects.

## WHEN OPERATIONS CONSULTING IS NEEDED

The following are some of the major strategic and tactical areas where companies typically seek operations consulting. Looking first at manufacturing consulting areas (grouped under what could be called *the 5 Ps of production*), we have

- *Plant:* Adding and locating new plants; expanding, contracting, or refocusing existing facilities.
- *People:* Quality improvement, setting/revising work standards, learning curve analysis.
- *Parts:* Make or buy decisions, vendor selection decisions.
- *Processes:* Technology evaluation, process improvement, reengineering.
- *Planning and control systems:* Supply chain management, MRP, shop-floor control, warehousing, distribution.

Obviously, many of these issues are interrelated, calling for systemwide solutions. Examples of common themes reflecting this are developing manufacturing strategy; designing and implementing JIT systems; implementing MRP or proprietary ERP software such as SAP and Baan IV; and systems integration involving client–server technology. Typical questions addressed are "How can the client cut lead times? How can inventory be reduced? How can better control be maintained over the shop floor?" Among the hot areas of manufacturing strategy consulting are developing factory focus; the factory of the future (although much of this requires engineering expertise); supply chain management; and, of course, global manufacturing networks. At the tactical level, there is a huge market for

REENGINEERING AND RESTRUCTURING HAVE INCREASED THE DEMAND FOR CONSULTING SERVICES, SUCH AS THOSE ADVERTISED HERE BY ANDERSEN CONSULTING, THAT PROMOTE THEIR ABILITY TO HELP BIG ORGANIZATIONS BECOME MORE AGILE.

consulting in ISO 9000 quality certification, TQM training, and designing and implementing decentralized production control systems.

Turning to services, while consulting firms in manufacturing may have broad specialties in process industries on the one hand and assembly or discrete product manufacture on the other, service operations consulting typically has a strong industry or sector focus. A common consulting portfolio of specialties in services (and areas of consulting need) would include the following:

Financial services (staffing, automation, quality studies).

Health care (staffing, billing, office procedures, phone answering, layout).

Transportation (route scheduling and shipping logistics for goods haulers, reservation systems and baggage handling for airlines).

Hospitality (reservations, staffing, cost containment, quality programs).

Without question, however, the major area of operations consulting emphasis in most service industries is reengineering.

## WHEN ARE OPERATIONS CONSULTANTS NEEDED?

Companies typically seek out operations consultants when they are faced with major investment decisions or when they believe that they are not getting maximum effectiveness from their productive capacity. As an example of the first type of situation, consider the following:

> A national pie restaurant chain retained consultants to determine if a major addition to its freezer storage capacity was needed at its pie-making plant. Its lease had run out on a nearby freezer warehouse, so the firm had to make a decision rather quickly. The pie plant manager wanted a $500,000 increase in capacity. After analysis of the demand for various

types of pies, the distribution system, and the contractual arrangement with the shipper, the consultant concluded that management could avoid all but a $30,000 investment in capacity if they did the following: Run a mixed-model production schedule for pies according to a forecast for each of 10 kinds of pies (for example, 20 percent strawberry, 30 percent cherry, 30 percent apple, and 20 percent other pies each two-day pie production cycle). To do this, more timely information about pie demand at each of the chain restaurants had to be obtained. This in turn required that information links for pie requirements go directly to the factory. (Previously the distributor bought the pies and resold them to the restaurants.) Finally, the company renegotiated pickup times from the pie plant to enable just-in-time delivery at the restaurants. The company was in a much stronger bargaining situation than they were five years previously, and the distributor was willing to make reasonable adjustments.

The lesson from this is that few investment decisions in operations are all or nothing, and good solutions can be obtained by simply applying standard OM concepts of production planning, forecasting, and scheduling. The solution recognized that the problem must be viewed at a systemwide level to see how better planning and distribution could substitute for brick and mortar capacity.

## THE OPERATIONS CONSULTING PROCESS

The broad steps in the operations consulting process (see Exhibit 16.3) are roughly the same as for any type of management consulting. The major differences exist in the nature of the problem to be analyzed and the kinds of analytical methods to be employed. Like general management consulting, operations consulting may focus on the strategic level or tactical level, and the process itself generally requires extensive interviewing of employees, managers, and, frequently, customers. If there is one large difference, it is that operations consulting leads to changes in physical or information processes whose results are measurable immediately. General management consulting usually calls

EXHIBIT 16.3

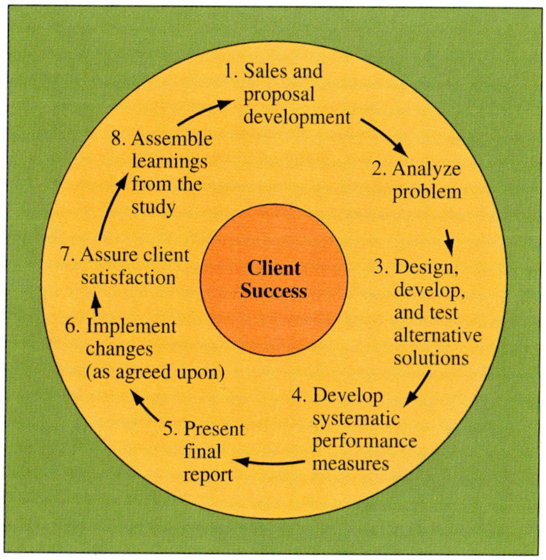


Stages in the Operations Consulting Process

## BREAKTHROUGH

### ASK ERNIE

Customized consulting is offered on the Ernie website. According to the home page description, "When you access the Ernie private website, you are asked to type in a question, assign a title to it, and offer some background information to help us understand your needs. Then you simply select a topic area that best matches your inquiry and your message is ready to go. When you've submitted your question to Ernie, it's automatically routed to the appropriate professional, who receives an e-mail saying he or she has a question from Ernie. You'll hear back from Ernie with a personalized, online consultation to help you make decisions or, perhaps, keep the dialogue going to make sure you've had all your questions answered on that hot business concern. Large cost savings have been reported. For example, Ernie can take a company's product attributes, and for $4,000 will recommend appropriate ERP software—a service that costs more than $100,000 when provided by traditional consultants.

SOURCE: W. MOUGAYAR, *BUSINESS 2.0*, JANUARY 2000, P. 179.

for changes in attitudes and culture, which take longer to yield measurable results. The roles in which consultants find themselves range from an *expert,* to a *pair of hands,* to a *collaborative or process consultant.* Generally, the collaborative or process consultation role is most effective in operations management consulting projects. Some consulting firms now provide the expert role online. (See the "Ask Ernie" Breakthrough Box.)

The steps in a typical operations consulting process are summarized in Exhibit 16.3. A recent book by Ethan M. Rasiel on the McKinsey & Company approach[4] offers some practical guidelines for conducting consulting projects:

- Be careful what you promise in structuring an engagement. *Underpromise and overdeliver* is a good maxim.
- Get the team mix right. You can't just throw four random people at a problem and expect them to solve it. Think about what sorts of skill and personalities work best for the project at hand, and choose your teammates accordingly.
- The 80–20 rule is a management truth. Eighty percent of sales come from 20 percent of the sales force; 80 percent of your time is taken up with 20 percent of your job; and so on.
- Don't boil the ocean. Don't try to analyze everything—be selective in what you investigate.
- Use the elevator test. If you know your solution so well that you can explain it clearly and precisely to your client in a 30-second elevator ride, you are doing well enough to sell it to the client.
- Pluck the low-hanging fruit. If you can make an immediate improvement even though you are in the middle of a project, do it. It boosts morale and gives credibility to your analysis.
- Make a chart every day. Commit your learning to paper; it will help push your thinking and assure that you won't forget it.
- Hit singles. You can't do everything, so don't try. It's better to get to first base consistently than to try to hit a home run and strike out 9 times out of 10.
- Don't accept "I have no idea." Clients and their staff always know something, so probe them for some educated guesses.
- Engage the client in the process. If the client doesn't support you, the project will stall. Keep your clients engaged by keeping them involved.
- Get buy-in throughout the organization. If your solution is to have lasting impact on your client, you have to get support for it throughout the organization.
- Be rigorous about implementation. Making change happen takes a lot of work. Be rigorous and thorough. Make sure someone takes responsibility for getting the job done.

# OPERATIONS CONSULTING TOOL KIT

Operations consulting tools can be categorized as tools for *problem definition, data gathering, data analysis and solution development, cost impact and payoff analysis,* and *implementation.* These—along with some tools from strategic management, marketing, and information systems that are commonly used in OM consulting—are noted in Exhibit 16.4 and are described next. (Note that several of these tools are used in more than one stage of a project.)

## PROBLEM DEFINITION TOOLS

**Issue Trees** Issue trees are used by McKinsey to structure or map the key problems to be investigated and provide a working initial hypothesis as to the likely solution to these problems. As can be seen in Exhibit 16.5, a tree starts with the general problem (increase widget sales) and then goes level by level until potential sources of the problem are identified. Once the tree is laid out, the relationships it proposes and possible solutions are debated, and the project plan is then specified.

**Customer Surveys** Frequently OM consultants are called in to address problems identified by customer surveys performed by marketing consultants or marketing staff. Often, however, these are out of date or are in a form that does not separate process issues

EXHIBIT 16.4

Operations Consulting Tool Kit

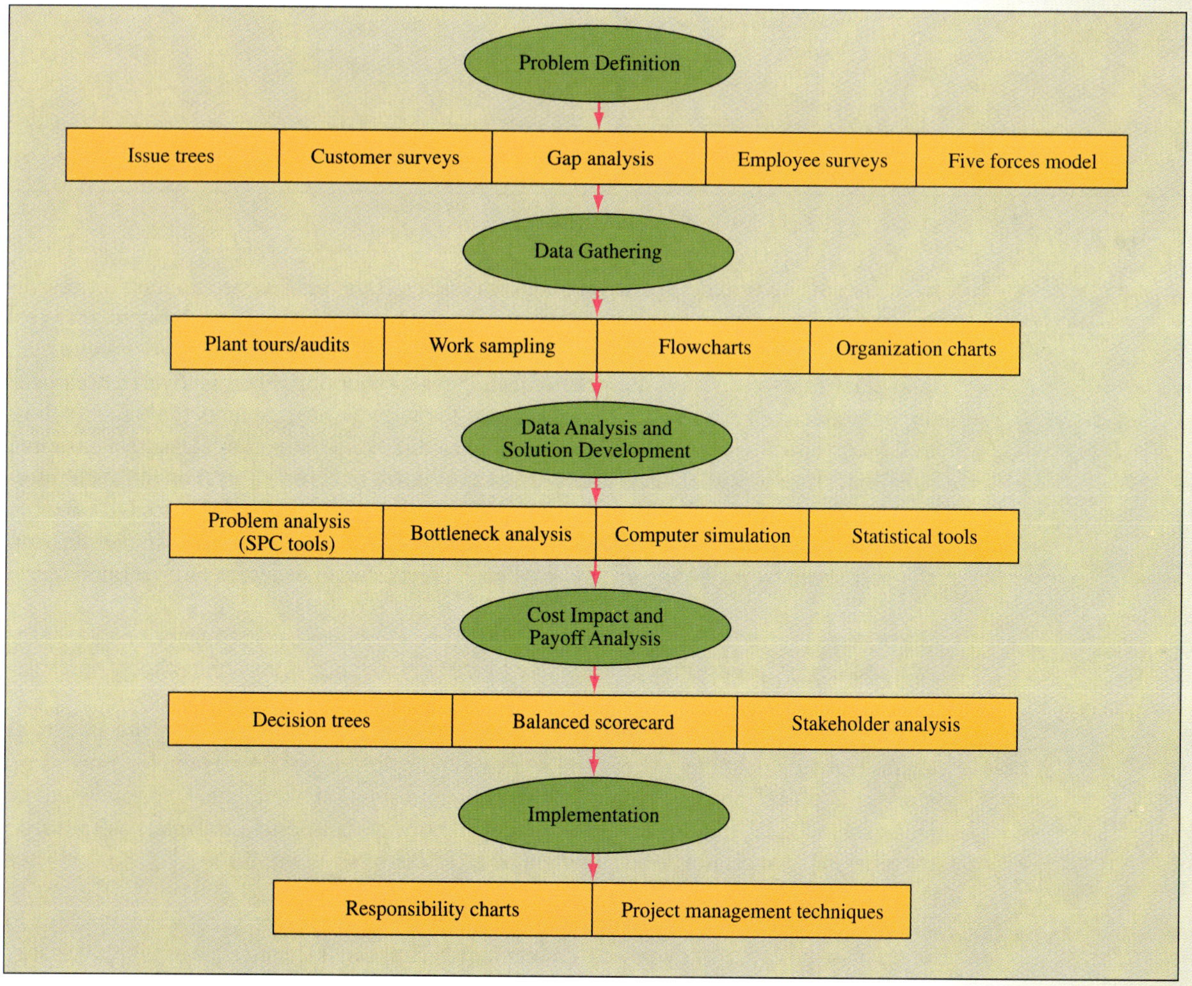

EXHIBIT 16.5

Issue Tree for Acme Widgets

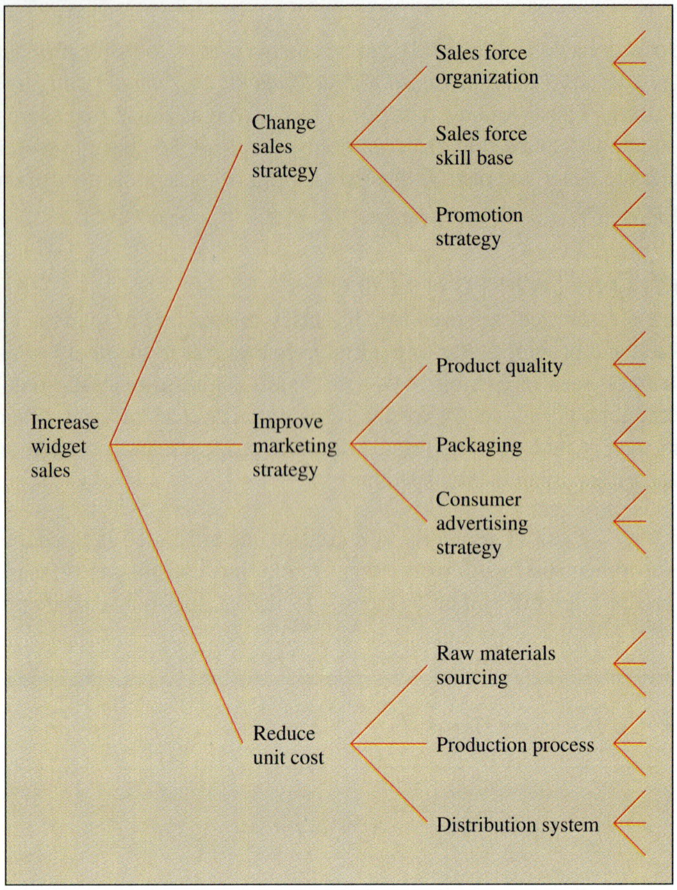


SOURCE: E. M. RASIEL, *THE MCKINSEY WAY*, (NEW YORK, MCGRAW-HILL, 1998), P. 12.

from advertising or other marketing concerns. Even if the surveys are in good form, calling customers and soliciting their experience with the company is a good way to get a feel for process performance. A key use of customer surveys is *customer loyalty analysis,* although in reality customers are not so much "loyal" (your dog, Spot, is loyal) as "earned" through effective performance. Nevertheless, the term *loyalty* captures the flavor of how well an organization is performing according to three critical market measures: customer retention, share of wallet, and price sensitivity relative to competitors. Having such information available helps the OM consultant drill down into the organization to find what operational factors are directly linked to customer retention. Although loyalty studies are usually performed by marketing groups, OM consultants should be aware of their importance.

**Gap Analysis** Gap analysis is used to assess the client's performance relative to the expectations of its customers, or relative to the performance of its competitors. An example is shown in Exhibit 16.6.

Another form of gap analysis is benchmarking particular client company processes against exemplars in the process and measuring the differences. For example, if one is interested in billing process accuracy and problem resolution, American Express would be the benchmark; for timeliness and efficiency in railway transportation, Japanese Railways; for order entry in catalog sales, it would be L. L. Bean.

**Employee Surveys** Such surveys range from employee satisfaction surveys to suggestion surveys. A key point to remember is if the consultant requests employee suggestions, such information must be carefully evaluated and acted upon by management. A

EXHIBIT 16.6

Gap Analysis

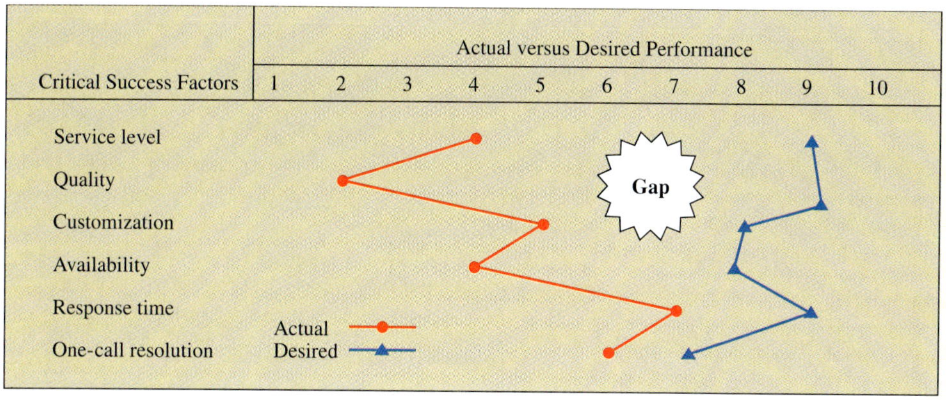


SOURCE: DELOITTE & TOUCHE CONSULTING GROUP.

EXHIBIT 16.7

Value Chain

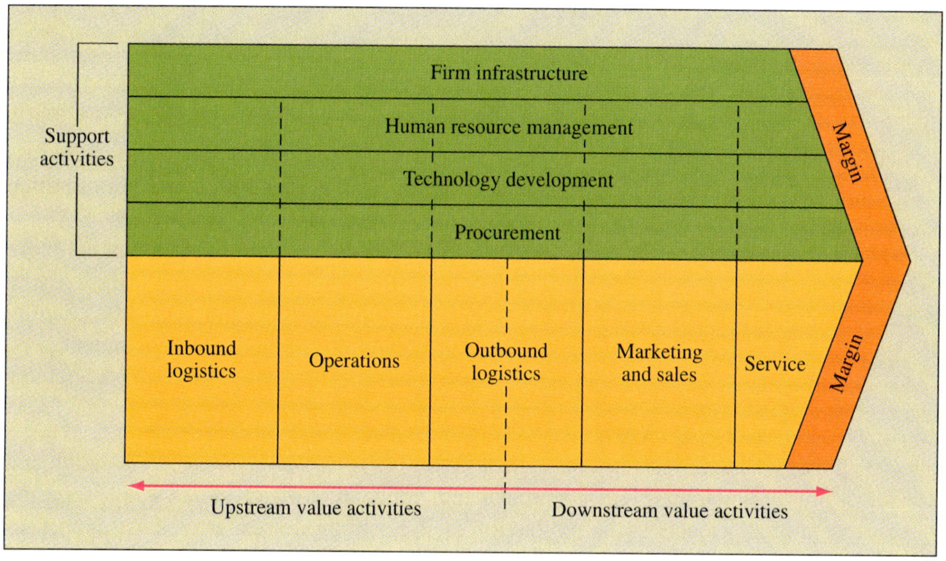




few years ago, Singapore Airlines distributed a questionnaire to its flight personnel, but made the mistake of not following through to address their concerns. As a result, the employees were more critical of the company than if the survey had not been taken, and to this day the company does not use this form of evaluation.

**Five Forces Model** This is one of the better-known approaches to evaluating a company's competitive position in light of the structure of its industry. The five forces are buyer power, potential entrants, suppliers, substitute products, and industry rivals. The consultant applies the model by developing a list of factors that fit under each of these headings. Some examples of where a client's competitive position might be strong are when buyers have limited information, there are major barriers to potential entrants, there are many alternative suppliers, there are few substitute products (or services), and there are few industry rivals.

Often used with the five forces model is the *value chain,* such as shown in Exhibit 16.7. The value chain provides a structure to capture the linkage of organizational activities that

### FIELD GUIDE TO PLANTS (FOR PLANT TOURS)

**PLANT**

1. What is the overall capacity of the plant? ($ or units)
2. What are the bottleneck resource(s) in the plant?
3. How is productivity measured?

**PEOPLE**

1. Is there clear evidence of employee involvement and a positive attitude?
2. Is this a good place to work? (incentives, bonuses)
3. Are the employees well-informed and knowledgeable?

**PARTS**

1. Do you see any major inventory buildup? (raw mtls., WIP, finished goods)
2. Are parts storage areas isolated with limited access?
3. Are defects (scrap, rework) clearly identified and quarantined?

**PROCESSES**

1. What is the process flow? (job shop, batch, assembly line, continuous flow)
2. What are the major processing departments of the plant? Sketch the process flow for the major products manufactured at the plant.
3. Is the plant active at reducing setup times and improving quality?

**PLANNING AND CONTROL SYSTEMS**

1. How does the company plan operations? (make to order, make to forecast)
2. Does the plant use pull or push systems?
3. Does the plant measure on-time delivery, inventory turns, backorder, backlog, and the like?

create value for the customer and profit for the firm. It is particularly useful to get across the notion that operations and the other activities must work cross-functionally for optimal organizational performance (and avoid the dreaded "functional silo" syndrome).

A tool similar to the five forces model is *SWOT analysis.* This is a somewhat more general method of evaluating an organization, and has the advantage of being easy to remember: *S*trengths of the client, *W*eaknesses of the client, *O*pportunities for the client in the industry, and *T*hreats from competitors or the economic and market environment.

## DATA GATHERING

**Plant Tours/Audits** These can be classified as manufacturing tours/audits and service facility tours/audits. Full manufacturing audits are a major undertaking, entailing measurement of all aspects of the production facility and processes, as well as support activities such as maintenance and inventory stockkeeping. Frequently these require several weeks, utilizing checklists developed explicitly for the client's industry. Plant tours, on the other hand, are usually much less detailed and can be done in a half day. The purpose of the tour is to get a general understanding of the manufacturing process before focusing on a particular problem area. Tours use generic checklists or general questions such as given in the box "Field Guide to Plants" developed for our classes.[5]

Complete service facility audits are also a major undertaking, but they differ from manufacturing audits in that, when properly done, they focus on the customer's experience as much as on the utilization of resources. Typical questions in a service audit address time to get service, the cleanliness of the facility, staff sizing, and customer satisfaction. A service facility tour or walk-through can often be done as a mystery shopper, where the consultant actually partakes of the service and records his or her experiences. (In consulting with the Peninsula Hotel in Beverly Hills 90210, one of the authors went through the grueling ordeal of staying the night in a $2,500-per-night villa and reporting to management on the quality of the experience.)

**Work Sampling** Work sampling entails random sampling observations of work activities, designed to give a statistically valid picture of how time is spent by a worker or the utilization of equipment. Diary studies are another way to collect activity data. These are used by consultants to get an understanding of very specific tasks being performed by the

WORKER PARTICIPATION AND EMPOWERMENT ARE IMPORTANT ISSUES IN REENGINEERING AND IN TOTAL QUALITY MANAGEMENT. HERE AT THE TRW PLANT IN MARSHALL, ILLINOIS, THAT MANUFACTURES AIR BAG CRASH SENSORS, WORKERS BECOME THEIR OWN INSPECTORS, PERSONALLY RESPONSIBLE FOR THE QUALITY OF THEIR OUTPUTS.

workforce. In these, the employee simply writes down the activities he or she performs during the week as they occur. This avoids the problem of having analysts look over a worker's shoulder to gather data. Examples of where these studies are used include library front desks, nursing, and knowledge work.

**Flowcharts** Flowcharts can be used in both manufacturing and services to track materials, information, and people flows. Workflow software, such as Optima! and BPR Capture, are widely used for process analysis. In addition to providing capabilities for defining a process, most workflow software provides four other basic functions: work assignment and routing, scheduling, work list management, and automatic status and process metrics. Flowcharts used in services—service blueprints—are basically the same thing, but add the important distinction of the line of visibility to clearly differentiate activities that take place with the customer versus those that are behind the scenes. In our opinion, the service blueprint is not used to its full potential by consulting firms, perhaps because relatively few consultants are exposed to them in their training.

Service

**Organization Charts** Organization charts are often subject to change, so care must be taken to see who really reports to whom. Some companies are loath to share organization charts externally. Several years ago a senior manager from a large electronics firm told us that a detailed organization chart gives free information to the competition.

## DATA ANALYSIS AND SOLUTION DEVELOPMENT

**Problem Analysis (SPC Tools)** Pareto analysis, fishbone diagrams, run charts, scatter diagrams, and control charts are fundamental tools in virtually every continuous improvement project. *Pareto analysis* is applied to inventory management under the heading of ABC analysis. Such ABC analysis is still the standard starting point of production control consultants when examining inventory management problems. *Fishbone diagrams* (or cause-and-effect diagrams) are a great way to organize one's first cut at a consulting problem (and they make a great impression when used to analyze, for example, a case study as part of the employment selection process for a consulting firm). *Run charts, scatter diagrams,* and *control charts* are tools that one is simply expected to know when doing operations consulting.

**Bottleneck Analysis** Resource bottlenecks appear in most OM consulting projects. In such cases the consultant has to specify how available capacity is related to required capacity for some product or service in order to identify and eliminate the bottleneck. This isn't always evident, and abstracting the relationships calls for the same kind of logical analysis used in the classic "word problems" you loved in high school algebra.

**Computer Simulation** Computer simulation analysis has become a very common tool in OM consulting. For example, Arthur Andersen supplies Optima!, a process charting package with simulation capability, in the CD-ROM packages they supply to their analysts. Other general-purpose simulation packages used by consultants, as well as in many business schools, are Extend and Crystal Ball. SimFactory and ProModel (manufacturing systems), MedModel (hospital simulation), and ServiceModel are examples of specialized packages. For smaller and less complex simulations, consultants often use Excel.

Some of the new simulation packages include causal loop diagrams. These are a form of systems diagram that is particularly useful when modeling the factors that enhance or degrade system performance. Causal loops are of two types: reinforcing loops and balancing loops. *Reinforcing loops* generate exponential growth and collapse, in which the growth or collapse continues at an ever-increasing rate. *Balancing loops* reflect the mechanisms that counter reinforcing loops, thereby driving the system toward equilibrium. By way of example, with reference to Exhibit 16.8, suppose you have a quality goal that is reflected in a quality standard. The reinforcing loop (R) indicates that the standard, if left unmodified, would yield an ever-increasing (or decreasing) level of actual quality. In reality, what happens is that the balancing loop (B) comes into play. Effective time required to meet the standard determines time pressure (on the workers), which, in turn, modifies the actual quality achieved and ultimately achievement of the quality standard itself. An obvious use of the system shown here would be to hypothesize the consequences of raising the quality goal, or raising or lowering the values of the other variables in the system. In addition to its use in problem analysis, consultants often use causal loop analysis simulations to help client companies become more effective learning organizations.[6]

**Statistical Tools** *Correlation analysis* and *regression analysis* are expected skills for consulting in OM. The good news is that these types of analyses are easily performed with spreadsheets. *Hypothesis testing* is mentioned frequently in the consulting firm methodology manuals, and one should certainly be able to perform Chi-square and *t*-tests in analyzing data. Two other widely used tools that use statistical analysis are *queuing theory* and *forecasting*. Consultants frequently use queuing theory to investigate how many service channels are needed to handle customers in person or on the phone. Forecasting problems likewise arise continually in OM consulting (such as forecasting the incoming calls to a call center).

A newly emerging tool (not shown on our exhibit) is *data envelopment analysis*. DEA is a linear programming technique used to measure the relative performance of branches of multisite service organizations such as banks, franchise outlets, and public agencies. A DEA model compares each branch with all other branches and computes an efficiency

EXHIBIT 16.8

Causal Loop Analysis

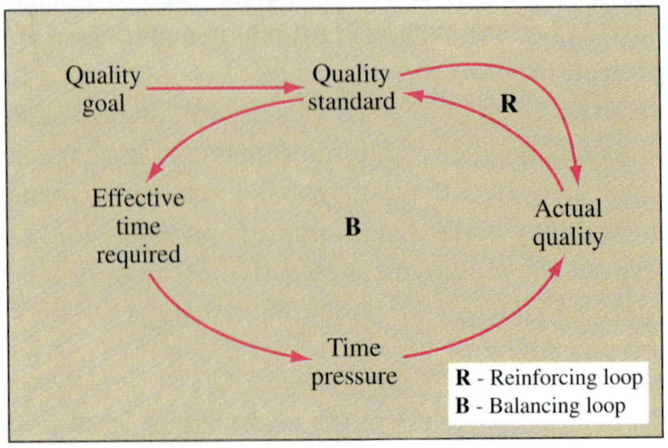

rating based on the ratio of resource inputs to product or service outputs. The key feature of the approach is that it permits using multiple inputs such as materials and labor hours, and multiple outputs such as products sold and repeat customers, to get an efficiency ratio. This feature provides a more comprehensive and reliable measure of efficiency that a set of operating ratios or profit measures.[7]

### COST IMPACT AND PAYOFF ANALYSIS

**Decision Trees** Decision trees represent a fundamental tool from the broad area of risk analysis. They are widely used in examining plant and equipment investments and R&D projects. Decision trees are built into various software packages such as @ Risk (*Risk Analysis for Spreadsheets,* Palisade Publications, 1995), which in addition to tree-type analysis has simulation capability.

**Stakeholder Analysis** Most consulting projects impact in some way each of five types of stakeholders: customers, stockholders, employees, suppliers, and the community. The importance of considering the interest of all stakeholders is reflected in the mission statements of virtually all major corporations and, as such, provides guidance for consultants in formulating their recommendations.

**Balanced Scorecard** In an attempt to reflect the particular needs of each stakeholder group in a performance measurement system, accountants have developed what is termed a *balanced scorecard.* (Balance refers to the fact that the scorecard looks at more than just the bottom line or one or two other performance measures.) Atkinson et al. note how the Bank of Montreal has used the balanced scorecard notion in setting specific goals and measures for customer service, employee relations, return to owners, and community relations. A key feature of the system is that it is tailored to what senior management and branch-level management can control.[8]

### IMPLEMENTATION

**Responsibility Charts** A responsibility chart is used in planning the task responsibilities for a project. It usually takes the form of a matrix with tasks listed across the top and project team members down the side. The goal is to make sure that a checkmark exists in each cell to assure that a person is assigned to each task.

**Project Management Techniques** Consulting firms use the project management techniques of CPM/PERT and Gantt charts to plan and monitor the entire portfolio of consulting engagements of the firm, as well as individual consulting projects. Microsoft Project and Primavera Project Planner are examples of commonly used software to automate such tools. Evolve Software has developed a software suite for professional service firms, modeled on ERP for manufacturing, that allows management to integrate opportunity management (the selling process), resource management, and delivery management. It should be emphasized that these planning tools are very much secondary to the people management skills needed to successfully execute a consulting project. This admonition is likewise true for all of the tools we have discussed in this section.

## BUSINESS PROCESS REENGINEERING (BPR)

Reengineering

Michael Hammer, the management expert who initiated the reengineering movement, defines **reengineering** as "the fundamental rethinking and radical redesign of business processes to achieve dramatic improvements in critical, contemporary measures of performance, such as cost, quality, service, and speed."[9] It uses many of the tools just discussed to achieve these goals.

Vol. III "Reengineering at Caterpillar"

The concept of reengineering has been around for nearly two decades and was implemented in a piecemeal fashion in organizations. Production organizations have been in the

Vol. VI "Valuation of Operations at ABTco"

vanguard without knowing it. They have undertaken reengineering by implementing concurrent engineering, lean production, cellular manufacturing, group technology, and pull-type production systems. These represent fundamental rethinking of the manufacturing process.

Reengineering is often compared to total quality management (TQM), a topic covered in depth in Chapter 7. Some people have said that the two are, in fact, the same, while others have even argued that they are incompatible. Michael Hammer says that the two concepts are compatible and actually complement one another. Both concepts are centered on a customer focus. The concepts of teamwork, worker participation and empowerment, cross-functionality, process analysis and measurement, supplier involvement, and benchmarking are significant contributions from quality management. In addition, the need for a "total" view of the organization has been reemphasized by quality management in an era of extensive functionalization of business. Quality management has also influenced company culture and values by exposing organizations to the need for change. The basic difference between the two is that quality management has emphasized continuous and incremental improvement of processes that are in control, whereas reengineering is about radical, discontinuous change through process innovation. Thus a given process is enhanced by TQM until its useful lifetime is over, at which point it is reengineered. Then enhancement is resumed and the entire cycle starts again. Hammer points out that this is not a once-in-a-lifetime endeavor. As business circumstances change in major ways, so must process designs.

## PRINCIPLES OF REENGINEERING

Reengineering is about achieving a significant improvement in processes so that contemporary customer requirements of quality, speed, innovation, customization, and service are met. Hammer has proposed seven principles or rules for reengineering and integration.[10]

**Rule 1. Organize around Outcomes, Not Tasks** Several specialized tasks previously performed by different people should be combined into a single job. This could be performed by an individual "case worker" or by a "case team." The new job created should involve all the steps in a process that creates a well-defined outcome. Organizing around outcomes eliminates the need for handoffs, resulting in greater speed, productivity, and customer responsiveness. It also provides a single knowledgeable point of contact for the customer.

Cross Functional

**Rule 2. Have Those Who Use the Output of the Process Perform the Process** In other words, work should be carried out where it is makes the most sense to do it. This results in people closest to the process actually performing the work, which shifts work across traditional intra- and interorganizational boundaries. For instance, employees can make some of their own purchases without going through purchasing, customers can perform simply repairs themselves, and suppliers can be asked to manage parts inventory. Relocating work in this fashion eliminates the need to coordinate the performers and users of a process.

**Rule 3. Merge Information-Processing Work into the Real Work That Produces the Information** This means that people who collect information should also be responsible for processing it. It minimizes the need for another group to reconcile and process that information, and greatly reduces errors by cutting the number of external contact points for a process. A typical accounts payable department that reconciles purchase orders, receiving notices, and supplier invoices is a case in point. By eliminating the need for invoices by processing orders and receiving information online, much of the work done in the traditional accounts payable function becomes unnecessary.

**Rule 4. Treat Geographically Dispersed Resources as Though They Were Centralized** Information technology now makes the concept of

THIS TEAM OF MAINTENANCE AND OPERATING WORKERS AT UNION CARBIDE'S FACTORY IN TAFT, LOUISIANA, TORE UP THEIR OLD PROCESS MAP, CREATED A NEW ONE, AND FOUND SAVINGS WORTH MORE THAN $20 MILLION—50 PERCENT MORE THAN WHAT MANAGEMENT EXPECTED.

hybrid centralized/decentralized operations a reality. It facilitates the parallel processing of work by separate organizational units that perform the same job, while improving the company's overall control. For instance, centralized databases and telecommunication networks now allow companies to link with separate units or individual field personnel, providing them with economies of scale while maintaining their individual flexibility and responsiveness to customers.

**Rule 5. Link Parallel Activities Instead of Integrating Their Results** The concept of integrating only the outcomes of parallel activities that must eventually come together is the primary cause for rework, high costs, and delays in the final outcome of the overall process. Such parallel activities should be linked continually and coordinated during the process.

**Rule 6. Put the Decision Point Where the Work Is Performed, and Build Control into the Process** Decision making should be made part of the work performed. This is possible today with a more educated and knowledgeable workforce plus decision-aiding technology. Controls are now made part of the process. The vertical compression that results produces flatter, more responsive organizations.

**Rule 7. Capture Information Once—at the Source** Information should be collected and captured in the company's online information system only once—at the source where it was created. This approach avoids erroneous data entries and costly reentries.

## GUIDELINES FOR IMPLEMENTATION

The principles of business process reengineering just enumerated are based on a common platform of the innovative use of information technology. But creating a new process and sustaining the improvement requires more than a creative application of information technology. A recent study of reengineering applications in 765 hospitals[11] yielded the following three managerial guidelines that apply to almost every organization contemplating reengineering:

1 **Codification of reengineering:** Organizationwide change programs such as reengineering are complex processes whose implementation may be separated by space and time. Middle managers are often left to implement significant portions of reengineering proposals. Codifying provides guidance and direction for consistent, efficient implementation.

2 **Clear goals and consistent feedback:** Goals and expectations must be clearly established, preapplication baseline data gathered, and the results monitored and fed back to employees. Without clear feedback employees often became dissatisfied, and their perceptions of reengineering success can be quite different from actual outcomes. For example, the hospital researchers found that at 10 hospitals they studied in depth, most employees in 4 of them felt that the reengineering program had done little to change costs, even though their costs had actually dropped 2 to 12 percent relative to their competitors'. On the other hand, four hospitals in which most felt that reengineering had lowered costs actually experienced an increase in relative costs and a deterioration of their cost position.

3 **High executive involvement in clinical changes:** A high level of involvement by the chief executive officer in major process changes (clinical changes in hospitals) improves reengineering outcomes. Bogue et al. found that CEOs in unsuccessful applications tended to be more involved in reductions of managers and employees and less engaged in activities surrounding clinical changes.

## CONCLUSION

Consulting opportunities abound for individuals with OM skills. This is true not only for the major consulting firms but also for the smaller niche firms, particularly those with capabilities in supply chain management and Internet applications. The profitability to partners of a consulting firm depends on their being able to effectively leverage their time with that of their junior consultants. For beginning consultants the goal is to get involved in high-visibility projects where they can demonstrate their skills and increase their skill sets. Companies such as Andersen Consulting and McKinsey & Company have developed special approaches to consulting that are part art and part procedure. Much of the success of a consulting engagement depends on the people-handling skills of the consultant. This is especially true for reengineering, where changing not just practices and procedures but also work cultures is often necessary if the reengineering is to succeed.

## KEY TERMS

**Operations consulting** Assisting clients in developing operations strategies and improving production processes.

**"Finders"** Partners or senior consultants whose primary function is sales and client relations.

**"Minders"** Managers of a consulting firm whose primary function is managing consulting projects.

**"Grinders"** Junior consultants whose primary function is to do the work.

**Reengineering (or business process reengineering)** The fundamental rethinking and radical redesign of business processes to achieve dramatic improvements in cost, quality, service, and speed.

## REVIEW AND DISCUSSION QUESTIONS

Internet WWW

1 Check the websites of the consulting companies listed in the chapter. Which ones impressed you most as a potential client and as a potential employee?
Boston Consulting Group (www.bcg.com)
Deloitte & Touche (www.dttus.com)
Ernst & Young (ernie.ey.com)
McKinsey & Co. (www.McKinsey.com)

2 What does it take to be a good consultant? Is this the career for you?

3 Think about the registration process at your university. Develop a flowchart to understand it. How would you radically redesign this process?
4 Have you driven any car lately? Try not to think of the insurance claim settlement process while you drive! How would you reengineer your insurance company's claim process?
5 Identify the typical processes in manufacturing firms. Discuss how the new product development process interacts with the traditional functions in the firm.

## PROBLEMS

1 You have been asked to bid on a consulting job to increase the profitability of a golf course company. It owns three courses in Cleveland, Ohio. Prepare a proposal to find out why other companies are more profitable and what to do about it.
2 Work with two other students to develop a two-page prospectus describing the particular features of an OM consulting practice you would start after graduation. (Hint: Identify a target market and unique skills your team possesses that fit that market.)
3 Sketch a typical materials procurement process that exists in functional organizations. Using reengineering principles, challenge the status quo and redesign this process.
4 An equipment manufacturer has the following steps in its order entry process:
*a.* Take the order and fax it to order entry.
*b.* Enter the order into the system (10 percent unclear or incorrect).
*c.* Check stock availability (stock not available for 15 percent of orders).
*d.* Check customer credit (10 percent of orders have credit questions).
*e.* Send bill of materials to warehouse.
The order receipt to warehouse cycle time is typically 48 hours; 80 percent of the orders are handled without error; and order handling costs are 6 percent of order revenue. Should you reengineer this process, or is continuous improvement the appropriate approach? If you choose to reengineer, how would you go about it?

## CASE: A CALIFORNIA AUTO CLUB REENGINEERS CUSTOMER SERVICE

For the 3 million members who count on its services, the California State Automobile Association (CSAA) often seems like a trusted member of the family.

Yet CSAA is no mom-and-pop operation. Were it a publicly traded corporation, CSAA, with its $3.2 billion in assets, would rank on the *Fortune* 500 list of America's largest diversified financial companies. Its 5,700 employees operate in a network of 72 district offices throughout its membership territory in Northern California and Nevada. CSAA's diversified operations range from tour books and emergency road services to airline ticketing, auto and homeowner's insurance, and traveler's checks.

Two years ago CSAA embarked on a long-term reengineering effort. From an operations center on the 23rd floor of its San Francisco headquarters, teams of employees have been putting every business process under a microscope. They are seeking ways to make operations better and more efficient while rekindling the close relationship with members that had been CSAA's trademark.

"It was obvious that the old ways of doing business wouldn't work in the future, and that we needed to make some fundamental changes," says Gregory A. Smith, vice president and general manager of insurance operations. The goals are to improve customer service threefold; to reduce baseline expenses by as much as 20 percent; and to enrich jobs and enhance career growth for employees. For the daily transactions that are the bread and butter of the organization, the targeted process time reductions are also ambitious: 2 days to renew an automobile policy instead of 25; 2 days for a new homeowner's policy instead of 21; 7 minutes for hotel reservations instead of 13.

### A REENGINEERED JOB

Through its reengineering effort, CSAA has designed a new system for serving customers centering around a new position called "member service consultant." The people in this job will be capable of handling 80 percent of a member's needs, from renting a car to making an insurance claim. Specialists will field the remaining calls or visits that require additional expertise.

Supporting the service consultant will be a new information system that links data that currently reside in three separate systems. This technology will enable a service consultant to respond to most members on the spot.

Business reengineering at CSAA is very much a work in progress, with pilot programs and tests scheduled for rollout through 1993. Before the reengineering effort was launched in February 1991, however, a preliminary phase was designed to find "quick hits"—immediate, tangible steps to streamline operations.

### THREE QUICKIES

One quick hit was to authorize field offices to give insured members a proof of coverage form that previously had to be routed through CSAA headquarters. Another streamlining step was to expand the expiration time for membership cards to two years instead of one, resulting in savings of about $500,000. Average turnaround time for processing new business applications was reduced from six days to three days; and the proportion of new auto policies that had to be "reworked" (processed more than once) dropped from 50 percent to 16 percent. In total, the quick hits resulted in estimated savings of nearly $4 million.

### A COMPREHENSIVE SURVEY

Four employee teams, reflecting the range of CSAA's operations—sales and underwriting, claims, service delivery (representing the main functional areas)—were formed along with a strategic marketing team to focus on broader issues. These teams undertook the most comprehensive survey of CSAA members and employees in the organization's history. Members were asked about CSAA services and products in focus groups and during visits to district offices. Employees were asked a range of questions about their work, including "What would you do if you were president of CSAA for a day?"

The surveys showed remarkable coherence between the issues cited by members and employees. Most of the frustrations for both groups concerned the highly segmented way that CSAA's services were provided. A member visiting a typical office had to go to one window for an insurance claim, another for a road map, and still others for registration renewals, traveler's checks, and additional services. As James P. Molinelli, executive vice president described it, "That's not service—that's a pinball effect." If a member phoned in for help, the CSAA staffer answering questions about underwriting couldn't handle a question about travel or claims, and had to refer callers to another phone number.

### TELEPHONE GRIDLOCK

The whole issue of telephone service emerged as a headache for members and employees alike. Members spoke of confusing recorded messages and long waiting periods in limbo while on hold. By one estimate, up to 30 percent of callers were hanging up before being helped. Rather than battle the telephone logjam, some members were making personal visits to district offices for their transactions. However, increasing personnel at the offices not only was expensive, it didn't solve the long-term problem.

Furthermore, members and employees alike said that CSAA's activities had become so varied that it was difficult to understand the range of services. For example, many holders of automobile insurance policies said they were unaware that CSAA also offered homeowner's insurance.

In addition to the internal issues, the reengineering effort also had to address an operating environment that was increasingly difficult and complex. New competition is entering every arena of CSAA's business, from car manufacturers offering their own emergency road services to companies providing computer systems that let travelers book airline flights from their homes.

### GET CRAZY

The reengineering teams are tackling these and other issues in a series of meetings that the service-delivery team describes as "Get Smart—Get Crazy—Get Serious—Get Going."

"The ground rules for the meetings were—no hidden agendas, be open and honest, and have a sense of urgency," says Phyllis M. Love, manager of mail and records processing, who serves on the teams. "At meetings there's a lot of back and forth, negotiation, and compromise."

The central issue that emerged was the fragmented way that CSAA services were dispensed—insurance underwriting here, travel services there. The member service consultant was a key innovation, but making it work required intensive cross-training for employees on the range of CSAA services, and a computer system that would pull all the vital information together and make it readily available. In the fall of 1991, three employees from field offices went to headquarters for an intensive, three-week cross-training program. They also helped design, develop, and test a prototype system that would support the new service consultant.

The acid test for the new business model came when the group began acting out scenarios simulating work in the CSAA office of the future. "Members" played by employees would interact with an employee playing the role of the service consultant. Needed modifications in the business model were identified, and within two months simulations were being conducted for senior CSAA management.

Meanwhile, the teams adhered to a policy of "communicate, communicate, communicate" to the entire CSAA workforce. Workshops and meetings in the field, posters and newsletters, and a series of videotapes called *New Directions* explained the rationale for the program and helped prepare the workforce for the transition.

### SELL WITH SCENARIOS

The powerful new information system will liberate the service consultants from a paper-intensive, error-prone work environment. Onscreen prompts will announce changes in regulations and procedures, replacing stacks of thumbtacked memos that now fill up bulletin boards. The system will also allow the running of rapid "what-if" scenarios for a member who wants to know, for example, how changing the deductible will affect her insurance premium.

The reengineering effort is now being carried forward by five interdisciplinary teams whose focus includes workforce retraining, reward and performance measurement, and information technology.

"We're trying to create a learning environment for the future, for all levels of employees from clerical to management," says John Clark, a regional claims manager who has served on two reengineering teams.

### A ONE-STOP SHOP

There's a "back to the future" aspect to the reengineering effort. "In the past, when district offices were smaller, a member could walk in and talk to anybody on the staff about any problem. Everyone in the office had to know something about everything, and members could get complete service with just one stop," says James P. Molinelli, executive vice president. Now, CSAA's best practices of the past are about to reemerge with a distinctly contemporary look.

### QUESTIONS

1 Describe the customer service process at CSAA and discuss the different phases of the reengineering effort.
2 What tools from the operations consulting tool kit were applied here? Which other ones would be of value here? Explain.
3 Discuss process enablers' role developing the new design.

SOURCE: REPRINTED FROM R. S. BUDAY, "REENGINEERING ONE FIRM'S PRODUCT DEVELOPMENT AND ANOTHER'S SERVICE DELIVERY," *PLANNING REVIEW*, MARCH–APRIL 1993, PP. 17–19. REPRINTED WITH PERMISSION FROM THE PLANNING FORUM, THE INTERNATIONAL SOCIETY FOR STRATEGIC MANAGEMENT AND PLANNING.

## Selected Bibliography


Bartlett, C. A., and S. Ghoshal. "Rebuilding Behavioral Context: Turn Process Reengineering into People Rejuvenation." *Sloan Management Review,* Fall 1995, pp. 11–23.

Bogue, E. M.; M. J. Schwartz; and S. L. Watson. "The Effects of Reengineering: Fad or Competitive Factor?" *Journal of Healthcare Management* 44, no. 6 (November–December 1999), pp. 456–76.

Davenport, T. H. *Process Innovation: Reengineering Work through Information Technology.* Boston: Harvard Business School Press, 1993.

Davenport, T. H., and J. E. Short. "The New Industrial Engineering: Information Technology and Business Process Redesign." *Sloan Management Review* 31, no. 4 (Summer 1990), pp. 11–27.

Greiner, L., and R. Savich. *Consulting to Management.* New York: Prentice Hall, 1998.

Hammer, M. *Beyond Reengineering.* New York: Harper Collins, 1996.

———. "Reengineering Work: Don't Automate, Obliterate." *Harvard Business Review* 90, no. 4 (July–August 1990), pp. 104–12.

Hammer, M., and J. Champy. *Reengineering the Corporation: A Manifesto for Business Revolution.* New York: Harper Business, 1993.

Hammer, M., and S. Stanton. "How Process Enterprises Really Work." *Harvard Business Review* 99, no. 6 (November–December 1999), pp. 108–18.

Heygate, R., and G. Brebach. "Corporate Reengineering." *The McKinsey Quarterly,* Spring 1991, pp. 44–55.

Maister, D. H. *Managing the Professional Service Firm.* The Free Press, 1993.

Rasiel, E. M. *The McKinsey Way: Using the Techniques of the World's Top Strategic Consultants to Help You and Your Business.* New York: McGraw-Hill, 1998.

Rohleder, T. R., and E. A. Silver. "A Tutorial on Business Process Improvement." *Journal of Operations Management* 15, no. 2 (May 1997), pp. 139–54.

Upton, D., and S. Macadam. "Why (and How) to Take a Plant Tour." *Harvard Business Review,* May–June 1997, pp. 97–106.


## Footnotes

1 M. Treacy and F. Wiersema, *The Discipline of Market Leaders* (Reading, MA: Addison Wesley, 1997).

2 D. J. Collis, "The Management Consulting Industry," *Internet Class Notes,* Harvard Business School, 1996.

3 D. H. Maister, "Balancing the Professional Service Firm," *Sloan Management Review* 24, no. 1 (Fall 1982), pp. 15–29.

4 E. M. Rasiel, *The McKinsey Way: Using the Techniques of the World's Top Strategic Consultants to Help You and Your Business* (New York: McGraw-Hill, 1998).

5 For more information on plant tours, see D. Upton and S. Macadam, "Why (and How) to Take a Plant Tour," *Harvard Business Review,* May–June 1997, pp. 97–106.

6 See P. Senge, *The Fifth Discipline: The Art and Practice of the Learning Organization* (New York: Doubleday Currency, 1990).

7 J. Fitzsimmons and M. Fitzsimmons, *Service Management, Operations, Strategy, and Information Technology,* 2nd ed. (New York: Irwin/McGraw-Hill, 1998), p. 74.

8 A. Atkinson, R. Banker, R. Kaplan, and M. Young, *Management Accounting* (Englewood Cliffs, NJ: Prentice Hall, 1995), p. 446.

9 M. Hammer and J. Champy, *Reengineering the Corporation: A Manifesto for Business Revolution* (New York: Harper Business, 1993), p. 30.

10 M. Hammer, "Reengineering Work: Don't Automate, Obliterate," *Harvard Business Review* 90, no. 4 (July–August 1990), pp. 104–12.

11 E. M. Bogue, M. J. Schwartz, and S. L. Watson, "The Effects of Reengineering: Fad or Competitive Factor?" *Journal of Healthcare Management* 44, no. 6 (November–December 1999), pp. 456–76.

chapter seventeen

# SYNCHRONOUS MANUFACTURING AND THEORY OF CONSTRAINTS

## CHAPTER OUTLINE AND KEY TERMS

# 17

Scene: Alex Rogo is the plant manager at the Barrington Plant of UniWare, a Division of UniCo. He has had a lot of trouble with his plant in keeping schedules, reducing inventory, improving quality, and cutting costs, among other problems. Bill Peach, division vice president, just visited him and gave him three months to improve, or else the plant will be closed.

Alex's son Dave and his Boy Scout troop are taking a 20-mile overnight hike (10 miles to Devil's Gulch where they will camp for the night, returning the following morning). Alex had been coaxed by his wife and son to accompany the troop. They are now on the hike and way behind schedule. The line of scouts is spread way out with the fastest kids in front; Herbie, the

slowest, lags way behind in the rear. Alex is trying to figure out how he can make the Boy Scouts stay together and move faster.

Up front, you've got Andy, who wants to set a speed record. And here you are stuck behind Fat Herbie, the slowest kid in the woods. After an hour, the kid in front—if he's really moving at three miles per hour—is going to be two miles ahead, which means you're going to have to run two miles to catch up with him.

Alex is thinking, "If this were my plant, Peach wouldn't even give me three months. I'd already be on the street by now. The demand was for us to cover 10 miles in five hours, and we've only done half of that. Inventory is racing out of sight. The carrying costs on that inventory would be rising. We'd be ruining the company."

"Okay," I say. "Everybody join hands."

They all look at each other.

"Come on! Just do it!" I tell them. "And don't let go."

**Source:** E. M. Goldratt and J. Cox, *The Goal: A Process of Ongoing Improvement*, 2nd rev. ed. (Great Barrington, MA: North River Press, 1992), pp. 114–18.

Then I take Herbie by the hand and, as if I'm dragging a chain, I go up the trail, snaking past the entire line. Hand in hand, the rest of the troop follows. I pass Andy and keep walking. When I'm twice the distance of the lineup, I stop. What I've done is turn the entire troop around so that the boys have exactly the opposite order they had before.

"Now listen up!" I say. "This is the order you're going to stay in until we reach where we're going. Understood? Nobody passes anybody.

"The idea of this hike is not to see who can get there the fastest. The idea is to get there together. We're not a bunch of individuals out here. We're a team."

So we start off again. And it works. No kidding. Everybody stays together behind Herbie. I've gone to the back of the line so I can keep tabs, and I keep waiting for the gaps to appear, but they don't.

"Mr. Rogo, can't we put somebody faster up front?" asks a kid ahead of me.

"Listen, if you guys want to go faster, then you have to figure out a way to let Herbie go faster," I tell them.

One of the kids in the rear says, "Hey, Herbie, what have you got in your pack?"

Herbie stops and turns around. I tell him to come to the back of the line and take off his pack. As he does, I take the pack from him—and nearly drop it.

"Herbie, this thing weighs a ton," I say. "What have you got in here?"

"Nothing much," says Herbie.

I open it up and reach in. Out comes a six-pack of soda. Next are some cans of spaghetti. Then come a box of candy bars, a jar of pickles, and two cans of tuna fish. Beneath a raincoat and rubber boots and a bag of tent stakes, I pull out a large iron skillet.

"Herbie, look, you've done a great job of lugging this stuff so far. But we have to make you able to move faster," I say. "If we take some of the load off you, you'll be able to do a better job at the front of the line."

Herbie finally seems to understand.

Again we start walking. But this time, Herbie can really move. Relieved of most of the weight in his pack, it's as if he's walking on air. We're flying now, doing twice the speed as a troop that we did before. And we still stay together. Inventory is down. Throughput is up.

Dave and I share the same tent that night. We're lying inside it, both of us tired. Dave is quiet for a while. Then he speaks up.

He says, "You know, Dad, I was really proud of you today."

"You were? How come?"

"The way you figured out what was going on and kept everyone together, and put Herbie in front."

"Thanks," I tell him. "Actually, I learned a lot of things today."

"You did?"

"Yeah, stuff that I think is going to help me straighten out the plant," I say.

"Really? Like what?"

"Are you sure you want to hear about it?"

"Sure I am," he claims.

This is the beginning of Alex's successful turnaround of his plant—applying simple principles to the plant's operation. ←

The story of Herbie is an analogy to the problems facing plant manager Alex Rogo and comes from a best-selling novel, *The Goal,* by Dr. Eli Goldratt.[1] Around 1980, Goldratt contended that manufacturers were not doing a good job in scheduling and in controlling their resources and inventories. To solve this problem, Goldratt and his associates at a company named Creative Output developed software that scheduled jobs through manufacturing processes, taking into account limited facilities, machines, personnel, tools, materials, and any other constraints that would affect a firm's ability to adhere to a schedule.

This was called *optimized production technology (OPT).* The schedules were feasible and accurate and could be run on a computer in a fraction of the time needed by an MRP system. This was because the scheduling logic was based on the separation of bottleneck and nonbottleneck operations. To explain the principles behind the OPT scheduling logic, Goldratt described nine production scheduling rules (see Exhibit 17.1). After approximately 100

EXHIBIT 17.1

**Goldratt's Rules of Production Scheduling**

1. Do not balance capacity—balance the flow.
2. The level of utilization of a nonbottleneck resource is determined not by its own potential but by some other constraint in the system.
3. Utilization and activation of a resource are not the same.
4. An hour lost at a bottleneck is an hour lost for the entire system.
5. An hour saved at a nonbottleneck is a mirage.
6. Bottlenecks govern both throughput and inventory in the system.
7. The transfer batch may not and many times should not be equal to the process batch.
8. A process batch should be variable both along its route and in time.
9. Priorities can be set only by examining the system's constraints. Lead time is a derivative of the schedule.

EXHIBIT 17.2

**Goldratt's Theory of Constraints (TOC)**

1. Identify the system constraints. (No improvement is possible unless the constraint or weakest link is found.)
2. Decide how to exploit the system constraints. (Make the constraints as effective as possible.)
3. Subordinate everything else to that decision. (Align every other part of the system to support the constraints even if this reduces the efficiency of nonconstraint resources.)
4. Elevate the system constraints. (If output is still inadequate, acquire more of this resource so it no longer is a constraint.)
5. If, in the previous steps, the constraints have been broken, go back to Step 1, but do not let inertia become the system constraint. (After this constraint problem is solved, go back to the beginning and start over. This is a continuous process of improvement: identifying constraints, breaking them, and then identifying the new ones that result.)

large firms had installed this software, Goldratt went on to promote the logic of the approach rather than the software. The software is still being developed and sold by Software Technology Limited (www.stg.co.uk).

In broadening his scope, Goldratt has developed his "Theory of Constraints" (TOC), which has become popular as a problem-solving approach that can be applied to many business areas (see Exhibit 17.2). His Goldratt Institute teaches courses in improving production, distribution, and project management. The common thread through all of these courses is Goldratt's TOC concepts. The Breakthrough Box titled "U.S. Air Force Medical Group Applies Theory of Constraints" describes an interesting application of the concept.

In this chapter we focus on Goldratt's approach to manufacturing. To correctly treat the topic, we decided to approach it in the same way that Goldratt did: that is, first defining some basic issues about firms—purposes, goals, and performance measures—and then dealing with scheduling, providing buffer inventories, the influences of quality, and the interactions with marketing and accounting.

Synchronous manufacturing

Underlying Goldratt's work is the notion of **synchronous manufacturing,** which refers to the entire production process working in harmony to achieve the profit goal of the firm. When manufacturing is truly synchronized, its emphasis is on total system performance, not on localized measures such as labor or machine utilization.

## GOAL OF THE FIRM

Although many people disagree with him, Goldratt has a very straightforward idea of the goal of a firm:

THE GOAL OF A FIRM IS TO MAKE MONEY

Goldratt argues that although an organization may have many purposes—providing jobs, consuming raw materials, increasing sales, increasing share of the market, developing

## BREAKTHROUGH

### U.S. AIR FORCE MEDICAL GROUP APPLIES THEORY OF CONSTRAINTS

Health care providers operating in today's managed care environment are between a rock and a hard place. If their goal is to increase profits and stay in business, systems must increase revenue and at the same time control costs. To increase revenue, the system must enroll more lives. Of course this obligates the system to provide more care, which drives more resource needs and increases cost. However, controlling costs requires that resources not be added. Resolving this conflict is a key survival issue for the health care provider.

The 366th Medical Group, a U.S. Air Force unit located on Mountain Home Air Force Base in rural Idaho, applied the five-step TOC process to improve patient access to their service and reduce costs. The team evaluated key processes by flowcharting them and identifying the constraint in each process. Changes in the patient scheduling process were key to major improvements.

In the scheduling process, the constraint was the availability of routine appointment times (TOC step one, identify the system constraints). By analyzing the process, the team recognized a fundamental assumption underlying the way the scheduling was managed. Once schedule templates, which allocated appointment slots to different types of appointments, were created, they were not changed. This assumed that the demand for all the different types of appointments remained constant. Of course, no one believed that demand was constant, but the schedules were managed as if it was. By scheduling to the "expected average" for each type of appointment, the system was wrong most of the time.

The team acted to exploit the routine appointment constraint (TOC step two) by ensuring that all routine appointments were scheduled. They discovered a high no-show rate and designed interventions to decrease it.

Next the team subordinated other types of appointments to routine appointments (TOC step three) by creating a "dynamic appointment template" concept. An appointment manager was designated and given the responsibility to adjust the proportions of appointments dedicated to each type. Appointments allocated to types that were not filled were quickly switched on an ongoing basis. The appointment manager needed to spend only about 15 minutes per day adjusting the schedule template. This simple change was enough to relieve the routine appointment constraint and dramatically improve the capacity of the process.

SOURCE: ADAPTED FROM D. E. WOMACK AND S. FLOWERS, "IMPROVING SYSTEM PERFORMANCE: A CASE STUDY IN THE APPLICATION OF THE THEORY OF CONSTRAINTS," *JOURNAL OF HEALTHCARE MANAGEMENT,* SEPTEMBER–OCTOBER 1999, PP. 397–405.

technology, or producing high-quality products—these do not guarantee long-term survival of the firm. They are means to achieve the goal, not the goal itself. If the firm makes money—and only then—it will prosper. When a firm has money, it can place more emphasis on other objectives.

## PERFORMANCE MEASUREMENTS

To adequately measure a firm's performance, two sets of measurements must be used: one from the financial point of view and the other from the operations point of view.

Cross Functional

### FINANCIAL MEASUREMENTS

We have three measures of the firm's ability to make money:

1 *Net profit*—an absolute measurement in dollars.
2 *Return on investment*—a relative measure based on investment.
3 *Cash flow*—a survival measurement.

All three measurements must be used together. For example, a *net profit* of $10 million is important as one measurement, but it has no real meaning until we know how much investment it took to generate that $10 million. If the investment was $100 million, this is a 10 percent *return on investment. Cash flow* is important because cash is necessary to pay bills for day-to-day operations; without cash, a firm can go bankrupt even though it is very sound in normal accounting terms. A firm can have a high profit and a high return on investment but still be short on cash if, for example, profit is invested in new equipment or tied up in inventory.

## OPERATIONAL MEASUREMENTS

Financial measurements work well at the higher level, but they cannot be used at the operational level. We need another set of measurements that will give us guidance:

1 **Throughput**—the rate at which money is generated by the system through sales.
2 **Inventory**—all the money that the system has invested in purchasing things it intends to sell.
3 **Operating expenses**—all the money that the system spends to turn inventory into throughput.

Throughput

Inventory

Operating expenses

Throughput is specifically defined as goods *sold.* An inventory of finished goods is not throughput, but inventory. Actual sales must occur. It is specifically defined this way to prevent the system from continuing to produce under the illusion that the goods *might* be sold. Such action simply increases costs, builds inventory, and consumes cash. Inventory that is carried (whether work-in-process or finished goods) is valued only at the cost of the materials it contains. Labor cost and machine hours are ignored. (In traditional accounting terms, money spent is called *value added.*)

Although this is often an arguable point, using only the raw material cost is a conservative view. When using the value-added method (which includes all costs of production), inventory is inflated and presents some serious income and balance sheet problems. Consider, for example, work-in-process or finished-goods inventory that has become obsolete, or for which a contract was canceled. It is a difficult management decision to declare large amounts of inventory as scrap because it is often carried on the books as an asset even though it may really have no value. Using just raw materials cost also avoids the problem of determining which costs are direct and which are indirect.

Operating expenses include production costs (such as direct labor, indirect labor, inventory carrying costs, equipment depreciation, and materials and supplies used in production) and administrative costs. The key difference here is that there is no need to separate direct and indirect labor.

As shown in Exhibit 17.3, the objective of a firm is to treat all three measurements simultaneously and continually; this achieves the goal of making money.

From an operations standpoint, the goal of the firm is to

INCREASE THROUGHPUT WHILE SIMULTANEOUSLY REDUCING INVENTORY AND REDUCING OPERATING EXPENSE.

EXHIBIT 17.3

Operational Goal

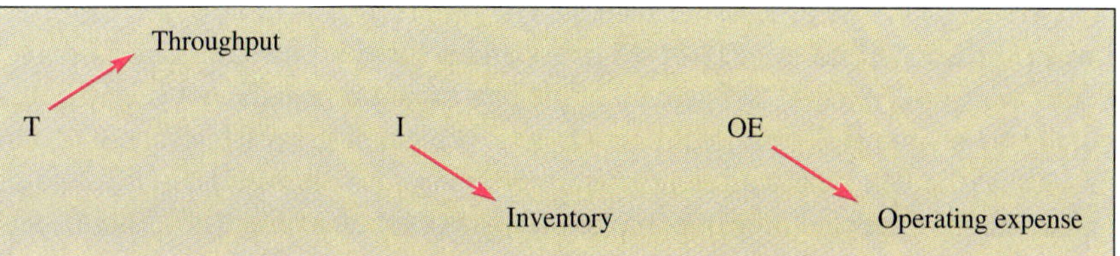


The operational goal of a firm is to increase throughput while reducing inventory and operating expense.

Productivity

## PRODUCTIVITY

Typically, **productivity** is measured in terms of output per labor hour. However, this measurement does not ensure that the firm will make money (for example, when extra output is not sold but accumulates as inventory). To test whether productivity has increased, we should ask these questions: Has the action taken increased throughput? Has it decreased inventory? Has it decreased operational expense? This leads us to a new definition:

PRODUCTIVITY IS ALL THE ACTIONS THAT BRING A COMPANY CLOSER TO ITS GOALS.

# UNBALANCED CAPACITY

Historically (and still typically in most firms) manufacturers have tried to balance capacity across a sequence of processes in an attempt to match capacity with market demand. However, this is the wrong thing to do—*unbalanced capacity* is better. The vignette at the beginning of this chapter is an example of unbalanced capacity. Some Boy Scouts were fast walkers, whereas Herbie was very slow. The challenge is to use this difference advantageously.

Consider a simple process line with several stations, for example. Once the output rate of the line has been established, production people try to make the capacities of all stations the same. This is done by adjusting machines or equipment used, workloads, skill and type of labor assigned, tools used, overtime budgeted, and so on.

In synchronous manufacturing thinking, however, making all capacities the same is viewed as a bad decision. Such a balance would be possible only if the output times of all stations were constant or had a very narrow distribution. A normal variation in output times causes downstream stations to have idle time when upstream stations take longer to process. Conversely, when upstream stations process in a shorter time, inventory builds up between the stations. The effect of the statistical variation is cumulative. The only way that this variation can be smoothed is by increasing work-in-process to absorb the variation (a bad choice because we should be trying to reduce work-in-process) or increasing capacities downstream to be able to make up for the longer upstream times. The rule here is that capacities within the process sequence should not be balanced to the same levels. Rather, attempts should be made to balance the flow of product through the system. When flow is balanced, capacities are unbalanced. This idea is further explained in the next section.

## DEPENDENT EVENTS AND STATISTICAL FLUCTUATIONS

The term *dependent events* refers to a process sequence. If a process flows from A to B to C to D, and each process must be completed before passing on to the next step, then B, C, and D are dependent events. The ability to do the next process is dependent on the preceding one.

*Statistical fluctuation* refers to the normal variation about a mean or average. When statistical fluctuations occur in a dependent sequence without any inventory between workstations, there is no opportunity to achieve the average output. When one process takes longer than the average, the next process cannot make up the time. We follow through an example of this to show what could happen.

Suppose that we wanted to process five items that could come from the two distributions in Exhibit 17.4. The processing sequence is from A to B with no space for inventory in between. Process A has a mean of 10 hours and a standard deviation of 2 hours. This means that we would expect 95.5 percent of the processing time to be between 6 hours and 14 hours (plus or minus 2 sigma). Process B has a constant processing time of 10 hours.

We see that the last item was completed in 66 hours, for an average of 13.2 hours per item, although the expected time of completion was 60, for an average of 12 hours per item (taking into account the waiting time for the first unit by Process B).

Suppose we reverse the processes—B feeds A. To illustrate the possible delays, we also reverse A's performance times. (See Exhibit 17.5.) Again, the completion time of the last

EXHIBIT 17.4

### Processing and Completion Times, Process A to Process B

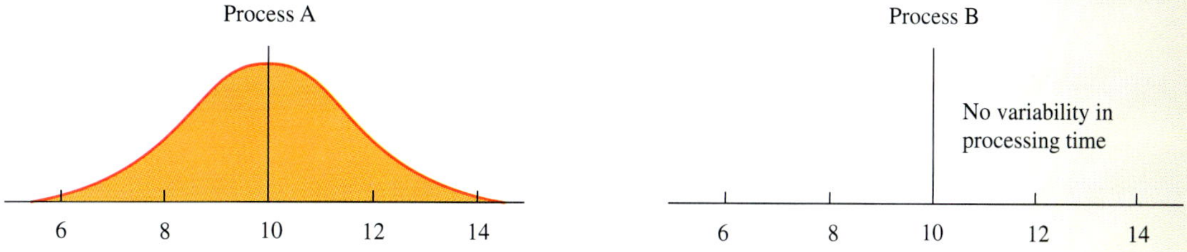


| ITEM NUMBER | START TIME | PROCESSING TIME | FINISH TIME |
|---|---|---|---|
| 1 | 0 hrs | 14 hrs | 14 hrs |
| 2 | 14 | 12 | 26 |
| 3 | 26 | 10 | 36 |
| 4 | 36 | 8 | 44 |
| 5 | 44 | 6 | 50 |
| | Average = 10 hours | | |

| ITEM NUMBER | START TIME | PROCESSING TIME | FINISH TIME |
|---|---|---|---|
| 1 | 14 hrs | 10 hrs | 24 hrs |
| 2 | 26 | 10 | 36 |
| 3 | 36 | 10 | 46 |
| 4 | 46 | 10 | 56 |
| 5 | 56 | 10 | 66 |
| | Average = 10 hours | | |

Here the flow is from Process A to Process B. Process A has a mean of 10 hours and a standard deviation of 2 hours; Process B has a constant 10-hour processing time.

EXHIBIT 17.5

### Processing and Completion Times, Process B to Process A

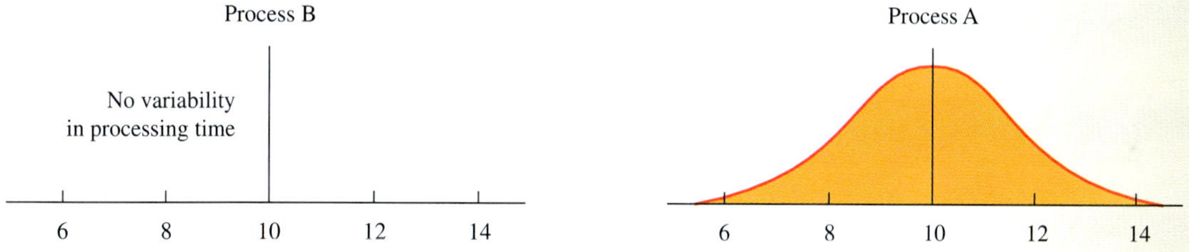


| ITEM NUMBER | START TIME | PROCESSING TIME | FINISH TIME |
|---|---|---|---|
| 1 | 0 hrs | 10 hrs | 10 hrs |
| 2 | 10 | 10 | 20 |
| 3 | 20 | 10 | 30 |
| 4 | 30 | 10 | 40 |
| 5 | 40 | 10 | 50 |
| | Average = 10 hours | | |

| ITEM NUMBER | START TIME | PROCESSING TIME | FINISH TIME |
|---|---|---|---|
| 1 | 10 hrs | 6 hrs | 16 hrs |
| 2 | 20 | 8 | 28 |
| 3 | 30 | 10 | 40 |
| 4 | 40 | 12 | 52 |
| 5 | 52 | 14 | 66 |
| | Average = 10 hours | | |

This is similar to Exhibit 17.4. However, the processing sequence has been reversed as well as the order of Process A's times.

item is greater than the average (13.2 hours rather than 12 hours). Process A and Process B have the same average performance time of 10 hours, and yet performance is late. In neither case could we achieve the expected average output rate. Why? Because the time lost when the second process is idle cannot be made up.

This example is intended to challenge the theory that capacities should be balanced to an average time. *Rather than balancing capacities, the flow of product through the system should be balanced.*

# BOTTLENECKS AND CAPACITY-CONSTRAINED RESOURCES

Bottleneck

A **bottleneck** is defined as any resource whose capacity is less than the demand placed upon it. A bottleneck is a constraint within the system that limits throughput. It is that point in the manufacturing process where flow thins to a narrow stream. A bottleneck may be a machine, scarce or highly skilled labor, or a specialized tool. Observations in industry have shown that most plants have very few bottleneck operations.

If there is no bottleneck, then excess capacity exists and the system should be changed to create a bottleneck (such as more setups or reduced capacity), which we will discuss later.

Nonbottleneck

*Capacity* is defined as the available time for production. This excludes maintenance and other downtime. A **nonbottleneck** is any resource whose capacity is greater than the demand placed on it. A nonbottleneck, therefore, should not be working constantly because it can produce more than is needed. A nonbottleneck contains idle time.

Capacity-constrained resource (CCR)

A **capacity-constrained resource (CCR)** is one whose utilization is close to capacity and could be a bottleneck if it is not scheduled carefully. For example, a CCR may be receiving work in a job-shop environment from several sources. If these sources schedule their flow in a way that causes occasional idle time for the CCR in excess of its unused capacity time, the CCR becomes a bottleneck when the surge of work arrives at a later time. This can happen if batch sizes are changed or if one of the upstream operations is not working for some reason and does not feed enough work to the CCR.

# BASIC MANUFACTURING BUILDING BLOCKS

All manufacturing processes and flows can be simplified to four basic configurations, as shown in Exhibit 17.6. In Exhibit 17.6A, product that flows through Process X feeds into Process Y. In B, Y is feeding X. In C, Process X and Process Y are creating

EXHIBIT 17.6

**The Basic Building Blocks of Manufacturing Derived by Grouping Process Flows**

| Description | Basic Building Blocks Simplified by Grouping Nonbottlenecks |
|---|---|
| A. Bottleneck feeding nonbottleneck | X → Y → Market |
| B. Nonbottleneck feeding bottleneck | Y → X → Market |
| C. Output of bottleneck and nonbottleneck assembled into a product | X → Final Assembly; Y → Final Assembly; Final Assembly → Market |
| D. Bottleneck and nonbottleneck have independent markets for their output | X → Market; Y → Market |

Original Representation

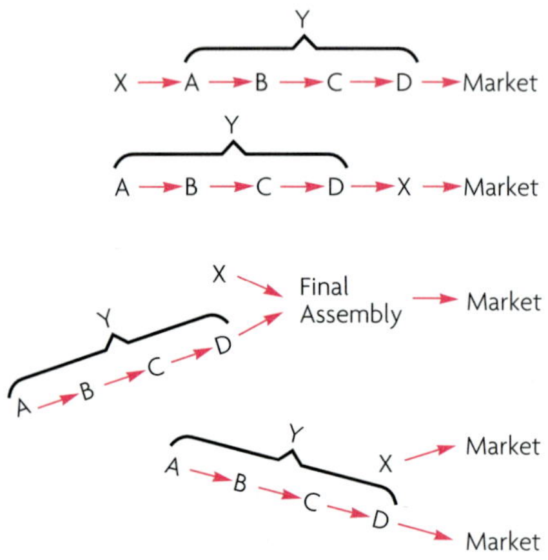


X is a bottleneck.
Y is a nonbottleneck (has excess capacity).

subassemblies, which are then combined, say to feed the market demand. In D, Process X and Process Y are independent of each other and are supplying their own markets. The last column in the exhibit shows possible sequences of nonbottleneck resources, which can be grouped and displayed as Y to simplify the representation.

The value in using these basic building blocks is that a production process can be greatly simplified for analysis and control. Rather than track and schedule all of the steps in a production sequence through nonbottleneck operations, for example, attention can be placed at the beginning and end points of the building block groupings.

## METHODS FOR CONTROL

Exhibit 17.7 shows how bottleneck and nonbottleneck resources should be managed.

Resource X and Resource Y are work centers that can produce a variety of products. Each of these work centers has 200 hours available per month. For simplicity, assume that we are dealing with only one product and we will alter the conditions and makeup for four different situations. Each unit of X takes one hour of production time and the market demand is 200 units per month. Each unit of Y takes 45 minutes of production time and the market demand is also 200 units per month.

Exhibit 17.7A shows a bottleneck feeding a nonbottleneck. Product flows from Work Center X to Work Center Y. X is the bottleneck because it has a capacity of 200 units (200 hours/1 hour per unit) and Y has a capacity of 267 units (200 hours/45 minutes per unit). Because Y has to wait for X and Y has a higher capacity than X, no extra product accumulates in the system. It all flows through to the market.

Exhibit 17.7B is the reverse of A, with Y feeding X. This is a nonbottleneck feeding a bottleneck. Because Y has a capacity of 267 units and X has a capacity of only 200 units, we should produce only 200 units of Y (75 percent of capacity) or else work-in-process will accumulate in front of X.

EXHIBIT 17.7

Product Flow through Bottlenecks and Nonbottlenecks

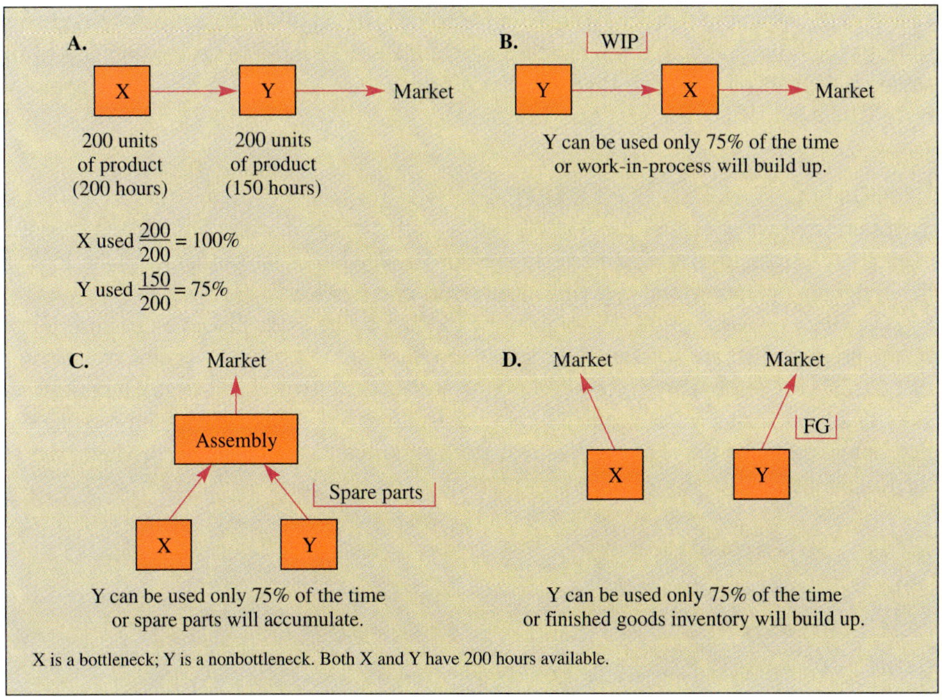

Exhibit 17.7C shows that the products produced by X and Y are assembled and then sold to the market. Because one unit from X and one unit from Y form an assembly, X is the bottleneck with 200 units of capacity and, therefore, Y should not work more than 75 percent or else extra parts will accumulate.

In Exhibit 17.7D, equal quantities of product from X and Y are demanded by the market. In this case we can call these products "finished goods" because they face independent demands. Here Y has access to material independent of X and, with a higher capacity than needed to satisfy the market, it can produce more product than the market will take. However, this would create an inventory of unneeded finished goods.

The four situations just discussed demonstrate bottleneck and nonbottleneck resources and their relationships to production and market demand. They show that the industry practice of using resource utilization as a measure of performance can encourage the overuse of nonbottlenecks and result in excess inventories.

## Time Components

The following kinds of time make up production cycle time:

1 *Setup time*—the time that a part spends waiting for a resource to be set up to work on this same part.
2 *Processing time*—the time that the part is being processed.
3 *Queue time*—the time that a part waits for a resource while the resource is busy with something else.
4 *Wait time*—the time that a part waits not for a resource but for another part so that they can be assembled together.
5 *Idle time*—the unused time; that is, the cycle time less the sum of the setup time, processing time, queue time, and wait time.

For a part waiting to go through a bottleneck, queue time is the greatest. As we discuss later in this chapter, this is because the bottleneck has a fairly large amount of work to do in front of it (to make sure that it is always working). For a nonbottleneck, wait time is the greatest. The part is just sitting there waiting for the arrival of other parts so that an assembly can take place.

Schedulers are tempted to save setup times. Suppose that the batch sizes are doubled to save half the setup times. Then, with a double batch size, all of the other times (processing time, queue time, and wait time) increase twofold. Because these times are doubled while saving only half of the setup time, the net result is that the work-in-process is approximately doubled, as is the investment in inventory.

## Finding the Bottleneck

There are two ways to find the bottleneck (or bottlenecks) in a system. One is to run a capacity resource profile; the other is to use our knowledge of the particular plant, look at the system in operation, and talk with supervisors and workers.

A capacity resource profile is obtained by looking at the loads placed on each resource by the products that are scheduled through them. In running a capacity profile, we assume that the data are reasonably accurate, although not necessarily perfect. As an example, consider that products have been routed through Resources M1 through M5. Suppose that our first computation of the resource loads on each resource caused by these products shows the following:

| | |
|---|---|
| M1 | 130 percent of capacity |
| M2 | 120 percent of capacity |
| M3 | 105 percent of capacity |
| M4 | 95 percent of capacity |
| M5 | 85 percent of capacity |

For this first analysis, we can disregard any resources at lower percentages because they are nonbottlenecks and should not be a problem. With this list in hand, we should physically go to the facility and check all five operations. Note that M1, M2, and M3 are overloaded; that is, they are scheduled above their capacities. We would expect to see large quantities of inventory in front of M1. If this is not the case, errors must exist somewhere—perhaps in the bill of materials or in the routing sheets. Let's say that our observations and discussions with shop personnel showed that there were errors in M1, M2, M3, and M4. We tracked them down, made the appropriate corrections, and ran the capacity profile again:

| | |
|---|---|
| M2 | 115 percent of capacity |
| M1 | 110 percent of capacity |
| M3 | 105 percent of capacity |
| M4 | 90 percent of capacity |
| M5 | 85 percent of capacity |

M1, M2, and M3 are still showing a lack of sufficient capacity, but M2 is the most serious. If we now have confidence in our numbers, we use M2 as our bottleneck. If the data contain too many errors for a reliable data analysis, it may not be worth spending time (it could take months) making all the corrections.

## SAVING TIME

Recall that a bottleneck is a resource whose capacity is less than the demand placed on it. Because we focus on bottlenecks as restricting *throughput* (defined as *sales*), a bottleneck's capacity is less than the market demand. There are a number of ways we can save time on a bottleneck (better tooling, higher-quality labor, larger batch sizes, reducing setup times, and so forth), but how valuable is the extra time? Very, very valuable!

AN HOUR SAVED AT THE BOTTLENECK ADDS AN EXTRA HOUR TO THE ENTIRE PRODUCTION SYSTEM.

How about time saved on a nonbottleneck resource?

AN HOUR SAVED AT A NONBOTTLENECK IS A MIRAGE AND ONLY ADDS AN HOUR TO ITS IDLE TIME.

Because a nonbottleneck has more capacity than the system needs for its current throughput, it already contains idle time. Implementing any measures to save more time does not increase throughput but only serves to increase its idle time.

## AVOID CHANGING A NONBOTTLENECK INTO A BOTTLENECK

When nonbottleneck resources are scheduled with larger batch sizes, this action could create a bottleneck that we certainly would want to avoid. Consider the case in Exhibit 17.8, where $Y_1$, $Y_2$, and $Y_3$ are nonbottleneck resources. $Y_1$ currently produces Part A, which is routed to $Y_3$, and Part B, which is routed to $Y_2$. To produce Part A, $Y_1$ has a 200-minute setup time and a processing time of 1 minute per part. Part A is currently produced in batches of 500 units. To produce Part B, $Y_1$ has a setup time of 150 minutes and 2 minutes' processing time per part. Part B is currently produced in batches of 200 units. With this sequence, $Y_2$ is utilized 70 percent of the time and $Y_3$ is utilized 80 percent of the time.

Because setup time is 200 minutes for $Y_1$ on Part A, both worker and supervisor mistakenly believe that more production can be gained if fewer setups are made. Let's assume that the batch size is increased to 1,500 units and see what happens. The illusion is that we

EXHIBIT 17.8

Nonbottleneck Resources

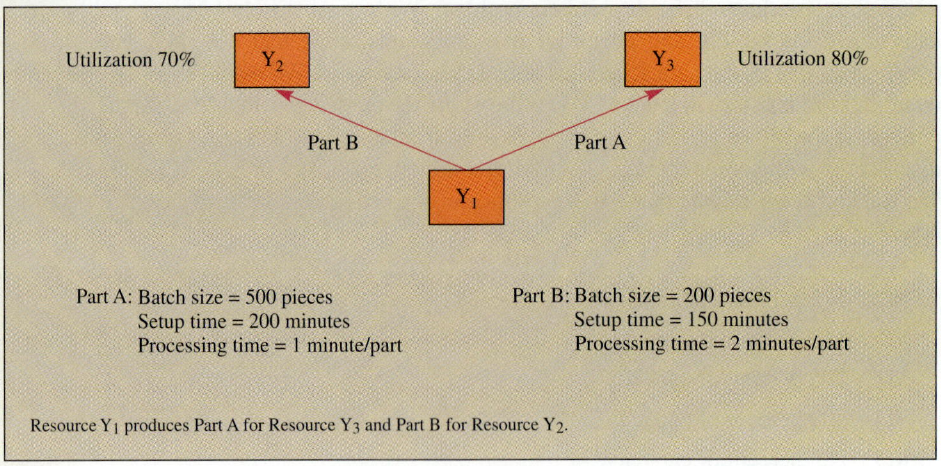


have saved 400 minutes of setup. (Instead of three setups taking 600 minutes to produce three batches of 500 units each, there is just one setup with a 1,500-unit batch.)

The problem is that the 400 minutes saved served no purpose, but this delay did interfere with the production of Part B because $Y_1$ produces Part B for $Y_2$. The sequence before any changes were made was Part A (700 minutes), Part B (550 minutes), Part A (700 minutes), Part B (550 minutes), and so on. Now, however, when the Part A batch is increased to 1,500 units (1,700 minutes), $Y_2$ and $Y_3$ could well be starved for work and have to wait more time than they have available (30 percent idle time for $Y_2$ and 20 percent for $Y_3$). The new sequence would be Part A (1,700 minutes), Part B (1,350 minutes), and so on. Such an extended wait for $Y_2$ and $Y_3$ could be disruptive. $Y_2$ and $Y_3$ could become temporary bottlenecks and lose throughput for the system.

## DRUM, BUFFER, ROPE

Every production system needs some control point or points to control the flow of product through the system. If the system contains a bottleneck, the bottleneck is the best place for control. This control point is called the *drum* because it strikes the beat that the rest of the system (or those parts that it influences) uses to function. Recall that a *bottleneck* is defined as a resource that does not have the capacity to meet demand. Therefore, a bottleneck is working all the time, and one reason for using it as a control point is to make sure that the operations upstream do not overproduce and build up excess work-in-process inventory that the bottleneck cannot handle.

If there is no bottleneck, the next best place to set the drum would be a capacity-constrained resource (CCR). A capacity-constrained resource, remember, is one that is operating near capacity but, on the average, has adequate capability as long as it is not incorrectly scheduled (for example, with too many setups, causing it to run short of capacity, or producing too large a lot size, thereby starving downstream operations).

If neither a bottleneck nor a CCR is present, the control point can be designated anywhere. The best position would generally be at some divergent point where the output of the resource is used in several downstream operations.

Dealing with the bottleneck is most critical, and our discussion focuses on ensuring that the bottleneck always has work to do. Exhibit 17.9 shows a simple linear flow A through G. Suppose that Resource D, which is a machine center, is a bottleneck. This means that the capacities are greater both upstream and downstream from it. If this sequence is not controlled, we would expect to see a large amount of inventory in front of Work Center D and very little anywhere else. There would be little finished goods inventory because (by the definition of the term *bottleneck*) all the product produced would be taken by the market.

Exhibit 17.9

Linear Flow of Product with a Bottleneck

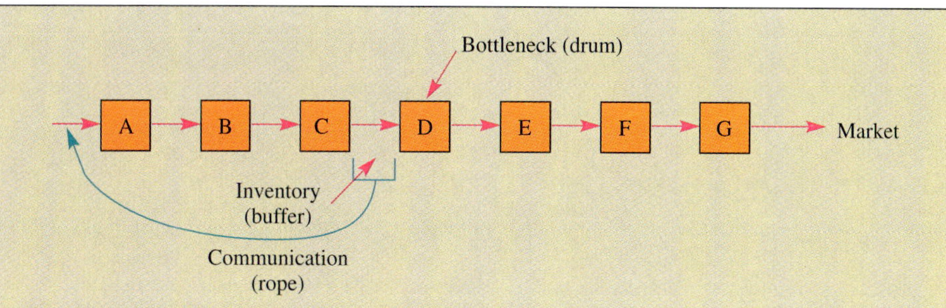


Product flows from Work Centers A through G. Work Center D is a bottleneck.

Exhibit 17.10

Capacity Profile of Work Center D (Showing Assigned Jobs A through P over a Period of Four 24-Hour Days)

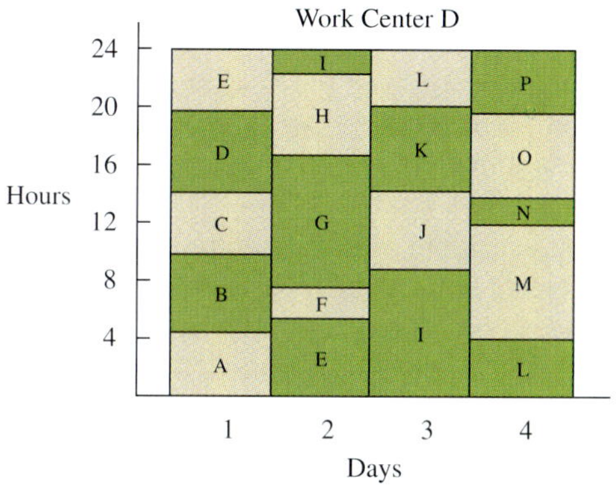


There are two things that we must do with this bottleneck:

1. Keep a *buffer* inventory in front of it to make sure that it always has something to work on. Because it is a bottleneck, its output determines the throughput of the system.
2. Communicate back upstream to A what D has produced so that A provides only that amount. This keeps inventory from building up. This communication is called the *rope.* It can be formal (such as a schedule) or informal (such as daily discussion).

The buffer inventory in front of a bottleneck operation is a *time buffer.* We want to make sure that Work Center D always has work to do, and it does not matter which of the scheduled products are worked on. We might, for example, provide 96 hours of inventory in the buffer as shown in the sequence A through P in Exhibit 17.10. Jobs A through about half of E are scheduled during the 24 hours of Day 1; Jobs E through a portion of Job I are scheduled during the second 24-hour day; Jobs I through part of L are scheduled during the third 24-hour day; and Jobs L through P are scheduled during the fourth 24-hour day, for a total of 96 hours. This means that through normal variation, or if something happens upstream and the output has been temporarily stalled, D can work for another 96 hours, protecting the throughput. (The 96 hours of work, incidentally, include setups and processing times contained in the job sheets, which usually are based on engineering standard times.)

We might ask, How large should the time buffer be? The answer: As large as it needs to be to ensure that the bottleneck continues to work. By examining the variation of each operation, we can make a guess. Theoretically, the size of the buffer can be computed statistically by examining past performance data, or the sequence can be simulated. In any event, precision is not critical. We could start with an estimate of the time buffer as

EXHIBIT 17.11

Linear Flow of Product with a Capacity-Constrained Resource

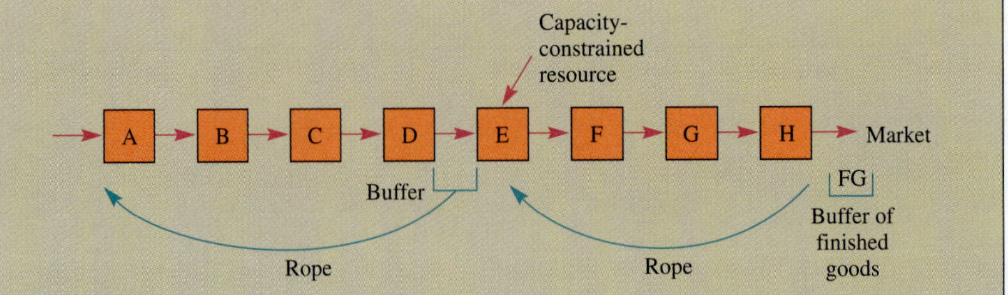

Product flows through Work Centers A through H. Work Center E is capacity constrained.

one-fourth of the total lead time of the system. Say the sequence A to G in our example (Exhibit 17.9) took a total of 16 days. We could start with a buffer of four days in front of D. If during the next few days or weeks the buffer runs out, we need to increase the buffer size. We do this by releasing extra material to the first operation, A. On the other hand, if we find that our buffer never drops below three days, we might want to hold back releases to A and reduce the time buffer to three days. Experience is the best determination of the final buffer size.

If the drum is not a bottleneck but a CCR (and thus it can have a small amount of idle time), we might want to create two buffer inventories—one in front of the CCR and the second at the end as finished goods. (See Exhibit 17.11.) The finished-goods inventory protects the market, and the time buffer in front of the CCR protects throughput. For this CCR case, the market cannot take all that we can produce, so we want to ensure that finished goods are available when the market does decide to purchase.

We need two ropes in this case: (1) a rope communicating from finished-goods inventory back to the drum to increase or decrease output, and (2) a rope from the drum back to the material release point, specifying how much material is needed.

Exhibit 17.12 is a more detailed network flow showing one bottleneck. Inventory is provided not only in front of that bottleneck but also after the nonbottleneck assembly to which it is assembled. This ensures that the flow of product is not slowed down by having to wait after it leaves the bottleneck.

## IMPORTANCE OF QUALITY

An MRP system allows for rejects by building a larger batch than actually needed. A JIT system cannot tolerate poor quality because JIT success is based on a balanced capacity. A defective part or component can cause a JIT system to shut down, thereby losing throughput of the total system. Synchronous manufacturing, however, has excess capacity throughout the system, except for the bottleneck. If a bad part is produced upstream of the bottleneck, the result is that there is a loss of material only. Because of the excess capacity, there is still time to do another operation to replace the one just scrapped. For the bottleneck, however, extra time does not exist, so there should be a quality control inspection just prior to the bottleneck to ensure that the bottleneck works only on good product. Also, there needs to be assurance downstream from the bottleneck that the passing product is not scrapped—that would mean lost throughput.

## BATCH SIZES

In an assembly line, what is the batch size? Some would say "one" because one unit is moved at a time; others would say "infinity" because the line continues to produce the same item. Both answers are correct, but they differ in their point of view. The first answer, "one," in an assembly line focuses on the *part* transferred one unit at a time. The second focuses on the *process*. From the point of view of the resource, the process batch is infinity because it is continuing to run the same units. Thus, in an assembly line, we have a *process*

EXHIBIT 17.12

Network Flow with One Bottleneck

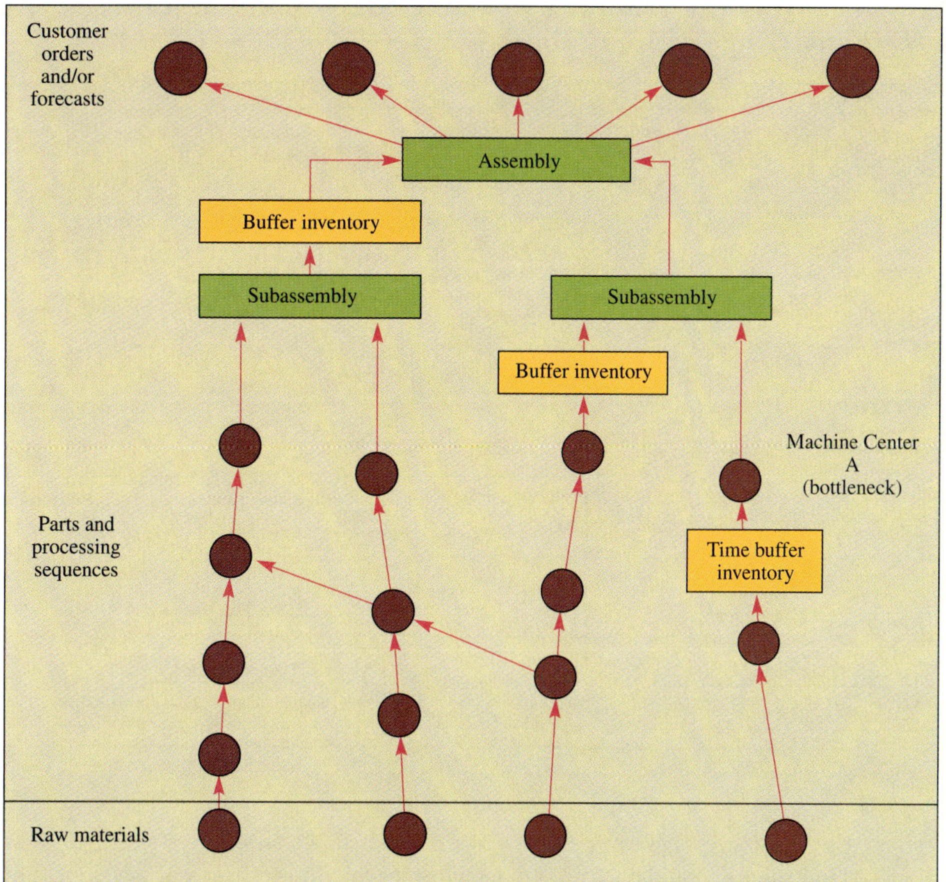


Product flows from raw materials through processing to the market. Inventory buffers protect throughput.

*batch* of infinity (or all the units until we change to another process setup) and a *transfer batch* of one unit.

Setup costs and carrying costs were treated in depth in Chapter 13 ("Inventory Control"). In the present context, setup costs relate to the process batch and carrying costs relate to the transfer batch.

A process batch is of a size large enough or small enough to be processed in a particular length of time. From the point of view of a resource, two times are involved: setup time and processing run time (ignoring downtime for maintenance or repair). Larger process batch sizes require fewer setups and therefore can generate more processing time and more output. For bottleneck resources, larger batch sizes are desirable. For nonbottleneck resources, smaller process batch sizes are desirable (by using up the existing idle time), thereby reducing work-in-process inventory.

Transfer batches refer to the movement of part of the process batch. Rather than wait for the entire batch to be finished, work that has been completed by that operation can be moved to the next downstream workstation so that it can begin working on that batch. A transfer batch can be equal to a process batch, but it should not be larger under a properly designed system. This could occur only if a completed process batch was held until sometime later when a second batch was processed. If this later time was acceptable in the beginning, then both jobs should be combined and processed together at the later time.

The advantage of using transfer batches that are smaller than the process batch quantity is that the total production time is shorter so the amount of work-in-process is smaller. Exhibit 17.13 shows a situation where the total production lead time was reduced from 2,100 to 1,310 minutes by (1) using a transfer batch size of 100 rather than 1,000 and (2) reducing the process batch sizes of Operation 2.

EXHIBIT 17.13

**Effect of Changing the Process Batch Sizes on Production Lead Time for a Job Order of 1,000 Units**

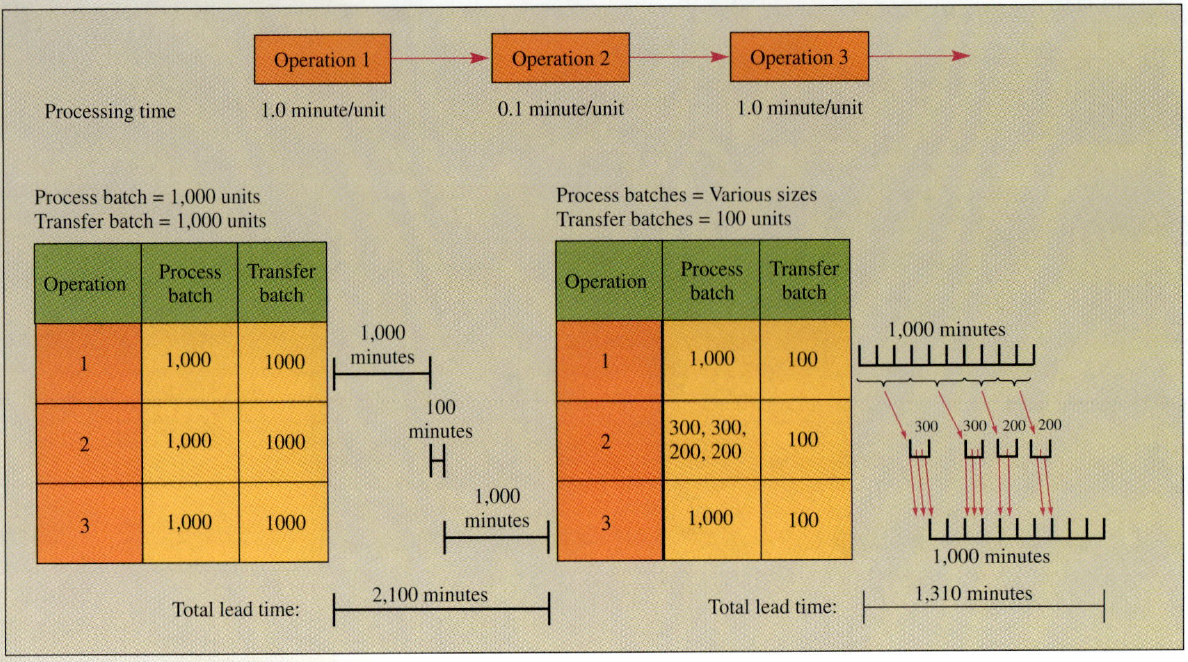


## How to Determine Process Batch and Transfer Batch Sizes

Logic would suggest that the master production schedule (however it was developed) be analyzed as to its effect on various work centers. In an MRP system, this means that the master production schedule should be run through the MRP and the CRP (capacity requirements planning program) to generate a detailed load on each work center. Srikanth states that from his experience, there are too many errors in the manufacturing database to do this.[2] He suggests using the alternative procedure of first identifying the probable CCRs and bottlenecks. There should be only one (or a few), and they should be reviewed by managers so that they understand which resources are actually controlling their plant. These resources set the drumbeat.

Rather than try to adjust the master production schedule to change resource loads, it is more practical to control the flow at each bottleneck or CCR to bring the capacities in line. The process batch sizes and transfer batch sizes are changed after comparing past performances in meeting due dates.

Smaller transfer batches give lower work-in-process inventory but faster product flow (and consequently shorter lead time). More material handling is required, however. Larger transfer batches give longer lead times and higher inventories, but there is less material handling. Therefore, the transfer batch size is determined by a trade-off of production lead times, inventory reduction benefits, and costs of material movement.

When trying to control the flow at CCRs and bottlenecks, there are four possible situations:

1. A bottleneck (no idle time) with no setup time required when changing from one product to another.
2. A bottleneck with setup time required to change from one product to another.
3. A capacity-constrained resource (CCR with a small amount of idle time) with no setup time required to change from one product to another.
4. A CCR with setup time required when changing from one product to another.

In the first case (a bottleneck with no setup time to change products), jobs should be processed in the order of the schedule so that delivery is on time. Without setups, only the sequence is important. In the second case, when setups are required, larger batch sizes combine separate similar jobs in the sequence. This means reaching ahead into future time periods. Some jobs will therefore be done early. Because this is a bottleneck resource, larger batches save setups and thereby increase throughput. (The setup time saved is used for processing.) The larger process batches may cause the early-scheduled jobs to be late. Therefore, frequent small transfer batches are necessary to try to shorten the lead time.

Situations 3 and 4 include a CCR without a setup and a CCR with setup time requirements. Handling the CCR would be similar to handling a nonbottleneck, though more carefully. That is, a CCR has some idle time. It would be appropriate here to cut the size of some of the process batches so that there can be more frequent changes of product. This would decrease lead time, and jobs would be more likely to be done on time. In a make-to-stock situation, cutting process batch sizes has a much more profound effect than increasing the number of transfer batches. This is because the resulting product mix is much greater, leading to reduced WIP and production lead time.

## How to Treat Inventory

The traditional view of inventory is that its only negative impact on a firm's performance is its carrying cost. We now realize inventory's negative impact also comes from lengthening lead times and creating problems with engineering changes. (When an engineering change on a product comes through, which commonly occurs, product still within the production system often must be modified to include the changes. Therefore, less work-in-process reduces the number of engineering changes to be made.)

Fox and Goldratt propose to treat inventory as a loan given to the manufacturing unit. The value of the loan is based only on the purchased items that are part of the inventory. As we stated earlier, inventory is treated in this chapter as material cost only, without any accounting-type value added from production. If inventory is carried as a loan to manufacturing, we need a way to measure how long the loan is carried. One measurement is dollar days.

**Dollar Days** A useful performance measurement is the concept of *dollar days,* a measurement of the value of inventory and the time it stays within an area. To use this measure, we could simply multiply the total value of inventory by the number of days inventory spends within a department.

Suppose Department X carries an average inventory of $40,000, and, on the average, the inventory stays within the department five days. In dollar days, Department X is charged with $40,000 times five days, or $200,000 dollar days of inventory. At this point, we cannot say the $200,000 is high or low, but it does show where the inventory is located. Management can then see where it should focus attention and determine acceptable levels. Techniques can be instituted to try to reduce the number of dollar days while being careful that such a measure does not become a local objective (that is, minimizing dollar days) and hurt the global objectives (such as increasing ROI, cash flow, and net profit).

Dollar days could be beneficial in a variety of ways. Consider the current practice of using efficiencies or equipment utilization as a performance measurement. To get high utilization, large amounts of inventory are held to keep everything working. However, high inventories would result in a high number of dollar days, which would discourage high levels of work-in-process. Dollar day measurements could also be used in other areas:

- Marketing—to discourage holding large amounts of finished-goods inventory. The net result would be to encourage sale of finished products.
- Purchasing—to discourage placing large purchase orders that on the surface appear to take advantage of quantity discounts. This would encourage just-in-time purchasing.

Cross Functional

- Manufacturing—to discourage large work-in-process and producing earlier than needed. This would promote rapid flow of material within the plant.
- Project management—to quantify a project's limited resource investments as a function of time. This promotes the proper allocation of resources to competing projects.

## COMPARING SYNCHRONOUS MANUFACTURING TO MRP AND JIT

MRP uses *backward scheduling* after having been fed a master production schedule. MRP schedules production through a bill of materials explosion in a backward manner—working backward in time from the desired completion date. As a secondary procedure, MRP, through its capacity resource planning module, develops capacity utilization profiles of work centers. When work centers are overloaded, either the master production schedule must be adjusted or enough slack capacity must be left unscheduled in the system so that work can be smoothed at the local level (by work center supervisors or the workers themselves). Trying to smooth capacity using MRP is so difficult and would require so many computer runs that capacity overloads and underloads are best left to local decisions, such as at the machine centers. An MRP schedule becomes invalid just days after it was created.

The synchronous manufacturing approach uses *forward scheduling* because it focuses on the critical resources. These are scheduled forward in time, ensuring that loads placed on them are within capacity. The noncritical (or nonbottleneck) resources are then scheduled to support the critical resources. (This can be done backward to minimize the length of time that inventories are held.) This procedure ensures a feasible schedule. To help reduce lead time and work-in-process, in synchronous manufacturing the process batch size and transfer batch size are varied—a procedure that MRP is not able to do.

Comparing JIT to synchronous manufacturing, JIT does an excellent job in reducing lead times and work-in-process, but it has several drawbacks:

1 JIT is limited to repetitive manufacturing.
2 JIT requires a stable production level (usually about a month long).
3 JIT does not allow very much flexibility in the products produced. (Products must be similar with a limited number of options.)
4 JIT still requires work-in-process when used with kanban so that there is "something to pull." This means that completed work must be stored on the downstream side of each workstation to be pulled by the next workstation.
5 Vendors need to be located nearby because the system depends on smaller, more frequent deliveries.

Because synchronous manufacturing uses a schedule to assign work to each workstation, there is no need for more work-in-process other than that being worked on. The exception is for inventory specifically placed in front of a bottleneck to ensure continual work, or at specific points downstream from a bottleneck to ensure flow of product.

Concerning continual improvements to the system, JIT is a trial-and-error procedure applied to a real system. In synchronous manufacturing, the system can be programmed and simulated on a computer because the schedules are realistic (can be accomplished) and computer run time is short.

## RELATIONSHIP WITH OTHER FUNCTIONAL AREAS

Cross Functional

The production system must work closely with other functional areas to achieve the best operating system. This section briefly discusses accounting and marketing—areas where conflicts can occur, and where cooperation and joint planning should occur.

## ACCOUNTING'S INFLUENCE

Sometimes we are led into making decisions to suit the measurement system rather than to follow the firm's goals. Consider the following example: Suppose that two old machines are currently being used to produce a product. The processing time for each is 20 minutes per part and, because each has the capacity of three parts per hour, they have the combined capacity of six per hour, which exactly meets the market demand of six parts per hour. Suppose that engineering finds a new machine that produces parts in 12 minutes rather than 20. However, the capacity of this one machine is only five per hour, which does not meet the market demand. Logic would seem to dictate that the supervisor should use an old machine to make up the lacking one unit per hour. However, the system does not allow this. The standard has been changed from the 20 minutes each to 12 minutes each and performance would look very bad on paper because the variance would be 67 percent [20 − 12)/12] for units made on the old machines. The supervisor, therefore, would work the new machine on overtime.

**Problems in Cost Accounting Measurements** Cost accounting is used for performance measurement, cost determinations, investment justification, and inventory valuation. Two sets of accounting performance measurements are used for evaluation: (1) global measurements, which are financial statements showing net profit, return on investment, and cash flow (with which we agree); and (2) local cost accounting measurements showing efficiencies (as variances from standard) or utilization rate (hours worked/hours present).

From the cost accounting (local measurement) viewpoint, then, performance has traditionally been based on cost and full utilization. This logic forces supervisors to activate their workers all the time, which leads to excessive inventory. The cost accounting measurement system can also instigate other problems. For example, attempting to use the idle time to increase utilization can create a bottleneck, as we discussed earlier in this chapter. Any measurement system should support the objectives of the firm and not stand in the way. Fortunately, the cost accounting measurement philosophy is changing.

## MARKETING AND PRODUCTION

Marketing and production should communicate and conduct their activities in close harmony. In practice, however, they act very independently. There are many reasons for this. The difficulties range from differences in personalities and cultures to unlike systems of merits and rewards in the two functions. Marketing people are judged on the growth of the company in terms of sales, market share, and new products introduced. Marketing is sales oriented. Manufacturing people are evaluated on cost and utilization. Therefore, marketing wants a variety of products to increase the company's position, whereas manufacturing is trying to reduce cost.

Data used for evaluating marketing and manufacturing are also quite different. Marketing data are "soft" (qualitative); manufacturing data are "hard" (quantitative). The orientation and experiences of marketing and production people also differ. Those in marketing management have likely come up through sales and a close association with customers. Top manufacturing managers have likely progressed through production operations and therefore have plant performance as a top objective.

Cultural differences can also be important in contrasting marketing and manufacturing personnel. Marketing people tend to have a greater ego drive and are more outgoing. Manufacturing personnel tend to be more meticulous and perhaps more introverted (at least less extroverted than their marketing counterparts).

The solution to coping with these differences is to develop an equitable set of measurements to evaluate performance in each area, and to promote strong lines of communication so that they both contribute to reaching the firm's goals.

We now present two examples to show that different objectives and measurement criteria can lead to the wrong decisions. These examples also show that, even though you may have all the data required, you still may not be able to solve the problem—unless you know how!

### EXAMPLE 17.1: WHAT TO PRODUCE?

In this first example, three products (A, B, and C) are sold in the market at $50, $75, and $60 per unit, respectively. The market will take all that can be supplied.

Three work centers (X, Y, and Z) process the three products as shown in Exhibit 17.14. Processing times for each work center are also shown. Note that each work center works on all three products. Raw materials, parts, and components are added at each work center to produce each product. The per unit cost of these materials is shown as RM.

Which product or products should be produced?

### SOLUTION

Three different objectives could exist that lead to different conclusions:

1 Maximize sales revenue because marketing personnel are paid commissions based on total revenue.
2 Maximize per unit gross profit.
3 Maximize total gross profit.

In this example we use gross profit as selling price less materials. We could also include other expenses such as operating expenses, but we left them out for simplicity. (We include operating expenses in our next example.)

*Objective 1: Maximize sales commission.* Sales personnel in this case are unaware of the processing time required so, therefore, they will try to sell only B at $75 per unit and none of A or C. Maximum

EXHIBIT 17.14

Prices and Production Requirements for Three Products and Three Work Centers

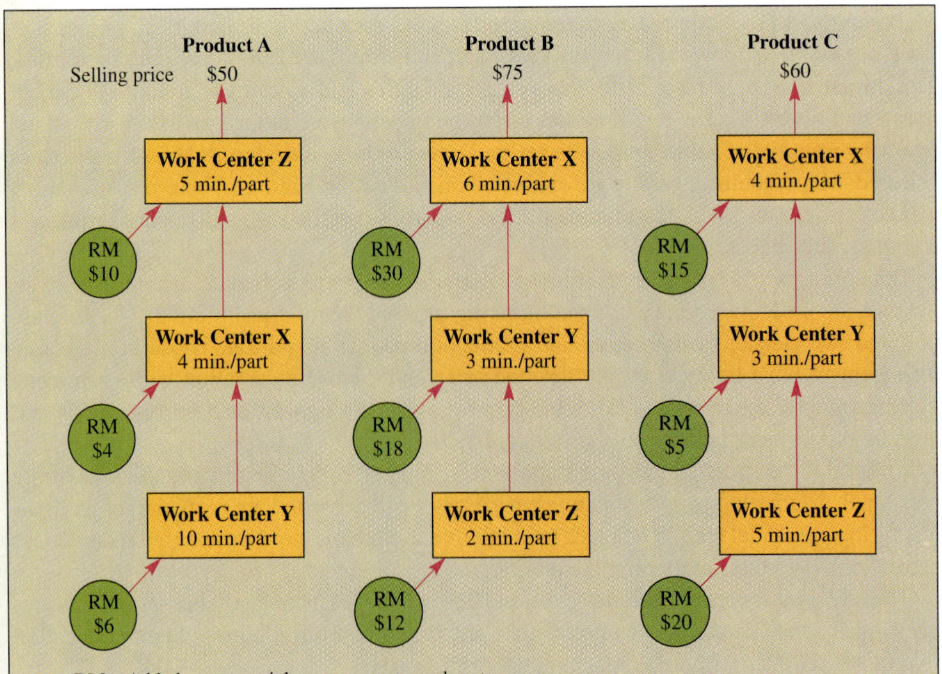


RM = Added raw materials, components, and parts
There is only one of each work center X, Y, and Z.

revenue is determined by the limiting resource as follows:

| PRODUCT | LIMITING RESOURCE | TIME REQUIRED | NUMBER PRODUCED PER HOUR | SELLING PRICE | SALES REVENUE PER HOUR |
|---|---|---|---|---|---|
| A | Y | 10 min | 6 | $50 | $300 |
| B | X | 6 min | 10 | 75 | 750 |
| C | Z | 5 min | 12 | 60 | 720 |

*Objective 2: Maximize per unit gross profit.*

| (1) PRODUCT | (2) SELLING PRICE | (3) RAW MATERIAL COST | (4) GROSS PROFIT PER UNIT (2) − (3) |
|---|---|---|---|
| A | $50 | $20 | $30 |
| B | $75 | $60 | $15 |
| C | $60 | $40 | $20 |

The decision would be to sell only Product A, which has a $30 per unit gross profit.

*Objective 3: Maximize total gross profit.* We can solve this problem by finding either total gross profit for the period or the rate at which profit is generated. We use rate to solve the problem both because it is easier and because it is a more appropriate measure. We use profit per hour as the rate.

Note that each product has a different work center that limits its output. The rate at which the product is made is then based on this bottleneck work center.

| (1) PRODUCT | (2) LIMITING WORK CENTER | (3) PROCESSING TIME PER UNIT (MINUTES) | (4) PRODUCT OUTPUT RATE (PER HOUR) | (5) SELLING PRICE | (6) RAW MATERIAL COST | (7) PROFIT PER UNIT | (8) PROFIT PER HOUR (4) × (7) |
|---|---|---|---|---|---|---|---|
| A | Y | 10 | 6 | $50 | $20 | $30 | $180 |
| B | X | 6 | 10 | 75 | 60 | 15 | 150 |
| C | Z | 5 | 12 | 60 | 40 | 20 | 240 |

From our calculations, Product C provides the highest profit of $240 per hour. Note that we get three different answers:

1 We choose B to maximize sales revenue.
2 We choose A to maximize profit per unit.
3 We choose C to maximize total profit.

Choosing Product C is obviously the correct answer for the firm.

In this example, all work centers were required for each product and each product had a different work center as a constraint. We did this to simplify the problem and to ensure that only one product would surface as the answer. If there were more work centers or the same work center constraint in different products, the problem could still easily be solved using linear programming (as in Supplement A).

## EXAMPLE 17.2: HOW MUCH TO PRODUCE?

In this example, shown in Exhibit 17.15, there are two workers producing four products. The plant works three shifts. The market demand is unlimited and takes all the products that the workers can produce. The only stipulation is that the ratio of products sold cannot exceed 10 to 1 between the maximum

EXHIBIT 17.15

## Production Requirements and Selling Price of Four Products

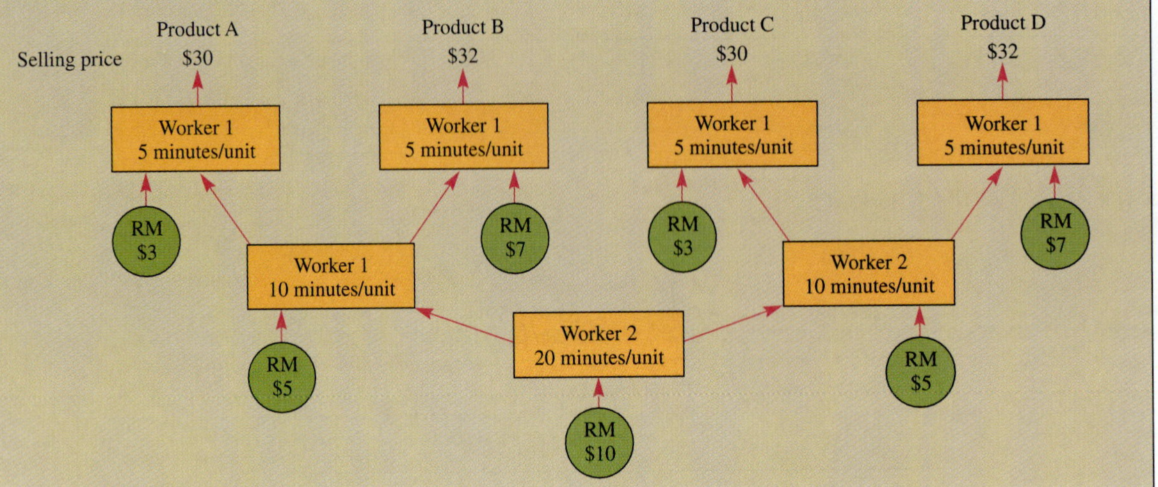


RM = Raw materials

| Product | Selling Price | Processing Time per Unit: Worker 1 | Processing Time per Unit: Worker 2 | Raw Material Cost per Unit |
|---|---|---|---|---|
| A | $30 (each) | 15 min. | 20 min. | $18 |
| B | 32 | 15 | 20 | 22 |
| C | 30 | 5 | 30 | 18 |
| D | 32 | 5 | 30 | 22 |

One Worker 1 and one Worker 2 operate on each shift. Three shifts. Five days per week. Eight hours per shift. Operating expenses $3,000 per week.

sold of any one product and the minimum of another. For example, if the maximum number sold of any one of the products is 100 units, the minimum of any other cannot be fewer than 10 units. Workers 1 and 2, on each shift, are not cross-trained and can work on only their own operations. The time and raw material (RM) costs are shown in the exhibit, and a summary of the costs and times involved is on the lower portion of the exhibit. Weekly operating expenses are $3,000.

What quantities of A, B, C, and D should be produced?

### SOLUTION

As in the previous example, there are three answers to this question, depending on each of the following objectives:

1 Maximize revenue for sales personnel who are paid on commission.
2 Maximize per unit gross profit.
3 Maximize the utilization of the bottleneck resource (leading to maximum gross profit).

*Objective 1: Maximize sales commission on sales revenue.* Sales personnel prefer to sell B and D (selling price $32) rather than A and C (selling price $30). Weekly operating expenses are $3,000.

The ratio of units sold will be: 1A : 10B : 1C : 10D.

Worker 2 on each shift is the bottleneck and therefore determines the output. Note that if this truly is a bottleneck with an unlimited market demand, this should be a seven-day-per-week operation, not just a five-day workweek.

$$5 \text{ days per week} \times 3 \text{ shifts} \times 8 \text{ hours} \times 60 \text{ minutes} = 7{,}200 \text{ minutes per week available}$$

Worker 2 spends these times on each unit:

A 20 minutes B 20 minutes C 30 minutes D 30 minutes

The ratio of output units is 1 : 10 : 1 : 10. Therefore

$$1x(20) + 10x(20) + 1x(30) + 10x(30) = 7,200$$
$$550x = 7,200$$
$$x = 13.09$$

Therefore, the numbers of units produced are

A = 13 B = 131 C = 13 D = 131

Total revenue is

$$13(30) + 131(32) + 13(30) + 131(32) = \$9,164 \text{ per week}$$

For comparison with Objectives 2 and 3, we will compute gross profit per week.
Gross profit per week (selling price less raw material less weekly expenses) is

$$13(30 - 18) + 131(32 - 22) + 13(30 - 18) + 131(32 - 22) - 3,000$$
$$= 156 + 1,310 + 156 + 1,310 - 3,000$$
$$= (\$68) \text{ loss.}$$

*Objective 2: Maximize per unit gross profit.*

| | Gross Profit | = | Selling Price | − | Raw Material Cost |
|---|---|---|---|---|---|
| A | 12 | = | 30 | − | 18 |
| B | 10 | = | 32 | − | 22 |
| C | 12 | = | 30 | − | 18 |
| D | 10 | = | 32 | − | 22 |

A and C have the maximum gross profit so the ratio will be 10 : 1 : 10 : 1 for A, B, C, and D. Worker 2 is the constraint and has

5 days × 3 shifts × 8 hours × 60 minutes = 7,200 minutes available per week

As before, A and B take 20 minutes, while C and D take 30 minutes. Thus

$$10x(20) + 1x(20) + 10x(30) + 1x(30) = 7,200$$
$$550x = 7,200$$
$$x = 13$$

Therefore, the number of units produced is

A = 131 B = 13 C = 31 D = 13

Gross profit (selling price less raw materials less $3,000 weekly expense) is

$$131(30 - 18) + 13(32 - 22) + 131(30 - 18) + 13(32 - 22) - 3,000$$
$$= 1,572 + 130 + 1,572 + 130 - 3,000$$
$$= \$404 \text{ profit}$$

*Objective 3: Maximize the use of the bottleneck resource, Worker 2.* For every hour Worker 2 works, the following numbers of products and gross profits result:

| (1) PRODUCT | (2) PRODUCTION TIME | (3) UNITS PRODUCED PER HOUR | (4) SELLING PRICE EACH | (5) RAW MATERIAL COST PER UNIT | (6) GROSS PROFIT PER HOUR (3) × [(4) − (5)] |
|---|---|---|---|---|---|
| A | 20 minutes | 3 | $30 | $18 | $36 |
| B | 20 | 3 | 32 | 22 | 30 |
| C | 30 | 2 | 30 | 18 | 24 |
| D | 30 | 2 | 32 | 22 | 20 |

Product A generates the greatest gross profit per hour of Worker 2 time, so the ratio is 10 : 1 : 1 : 1 for A, B, C, and D.

Available time for Worker 2 is the same as before:

$$3 \text{ shifts} \times 5 \text{ days} \times 8 \text{ hours} \times 60 \text{ minutes} = 7{,}200 \text{ minutes}$$

Worker 2 should produce 10 As for every 1 B, 1 C, and 1 D. Worker 2's average production rate is

$$10x(20) + 1x(20) + 1x(30) + 1x(30) = 7{,}200$$
$$280x = 7{,}200$$
$$x = 25.7$$

Therefore, the number of units that should be produced is

$$A = 257 \qquad B = 25.7 \qquad C = 25.7 \qquad D = 25.7$$

Gross profit (price less raw materials less $3,000 weekly expenses) is

$$257(30 - 18) + 25.7(32 - 22) + 25.7(30 - 18) + 25.7(32 - 22) - 3{,}000$$
$$= 3{,}084 + 257 + 308.4 + 257 - 3{,}000$$
$$= \$906.40$$

In summary, using three different objectives to decide how many of each product to make gave us three different results:

1 Maximizing sales commission resulted in a $68 loss in gross profit.
2 Maximizing gross profit gave us a profit of $404.
3 Maximizing the use of the capacity-constrained worker gave us the best gross profit, $906.40. ←

Both examples demonstrate that production and marketing need to interact. Marketing should sell the most profitable use of available capacity. However, to plan capacity, production needs to know from marketing what products could be sold.

## CONCLUSION

The measurement system within a firm should encourage the increase of net profits, return on investment, and cash flow. The firm can accomplish this if, at the operations level, it rewards performance based on the amount of throughput, inventory, and operating expense created. This is essential for a firm's success.

To control throughput, inventory, and operating expense, the system must be analyzed to find bottlenecks and capacity-constrained resources. Only then can the company define a drum for control, buffers to ensure throughput, and ropes for communicating the correct information to the correct locations, while minimizing work-in-process everywhere else. Without this focus, problems are not correctly diagnosed and solution procedures are impossible.

Goldratt defined nine rules (Exhibit 17.1) to help guide the logic of an operating system and to identify the important points. These are basic to any operating system and were originally called the Nine Rules of OPT.

The underlying philosophy presented in this chapter—the vital importance of concentrating on system limitations imposed by capacity-constrained resources—has led Goldratt to broaden his view of the importance of system limitations and to develop his five-step "general theory of constraints."[3] (See Exhibit 17.2.)

Although the terms *bottleneck* and *constraint* can mean essentially the same thing, Goldratt uses *constraint* in the broadest sense to mean anything that limits the performance of a system and slows or prevents it from continuing to move toward its goal.

This general theory of constraints directs companies to find what is stopping them from moving toward their goals and find ways to get around this limitation. If, in a manufacturing environment, the limitation is insufficient capacity, then ways to break the constraint might be overtime, specialized tools, supporting equipment, exceptionally skilled workers, subcontracting, redesigning product or process, alternative routings, and so on. Point 5 (Exhibit 17.2) warns against letting biases in thinking prevent the search for further exploitation of constraints. For example, if a search and exploitation of a constraint has been conducted under the limitation of cost, make sure that this cost measure is not carried into the next search. Start clean each time.

One last summary comment on this chapter, which also serves well as a summary comment for this book: The key to competitive advantage through operations is for the firm to operate as a synchronized system, with all parts working in concert. Companies that do this effectively are well on their way to achieving the fundamental goal of the firm—profitability.

Cross Functional

## KEY TERMS

**Synchronous manufacturing** A production process coordinated to work in harmony to achieve the goals of the firm.

**Throughput** The rate at which money is generated by the system through sales (Goldratt's definition).

**Inventory** All the money that the system has invested in purchasing things it intends to sell (Goldratt's definition).

**Operating expenses** All the money that the system spends to turn inventory into throughput (Goldratt's definition).

**Productivity** All the actions that bring a company closer to its goals (Goldratt's definition).

**Bottleneck** Any resource whose capacity is less than the demand placed upon it (Goldratt's definition).

**Nonbottleneck** Any resource whose capacity is greater than the demand placed on it (Goldratt's definition).

**Capacity-constrained resource (CCR)** A resource whose utilization is close to capacity and could be a bottleneck if not scheduled carefully (Goldratt's definition).

## SOLVED PROBLEM

### SOLVED PROBLEM 1

Here is the process flow for Products A, B, and C. Products A, B, and C sell for \$20, \$25, and \$30, respectively. There are only one Resource X and one Resource Y, which are used to produce A, B, and C for the numbers of minutes stated on the diagram. Raw materials are needed at the process steps as shown, with the costs in dollars per unit of raw material. (One unit is used for each product.)

The market will take all that you can produce.

*a.* Which product would you produce to maximize gross margin per unit?

*b.* If sales personnel are paid on commission, which product or products would they sell and how many could they sell?

*c.* Which and how many product or products should you produce to maximize gross profit for one week?

*d.* From *c*, how much gross profit would there be for the week?

## Solution

*a.* Maximizing gross margin per unit:

| | Gross Margin | = | Selling Price | – | Raw Material Cost |
|---|---|---|---|---|---|
| A | 17 | = | 20 | – | 3 |
| B | 18 | = | 25 | – | 7 |
| C | 16 | = | 30 | – | 14 |

Product B will be produced.

*b.* Maximizing sales commission: Sales personnel would sell the highest-priced product, C (unless they knew the market and capacity limitations). If we assume the market will take all that we can make, then we would work 7 days/week, 8 hours/day. Y is the constraint in producing C. The number of C we can make in a week is

$$C = \frac{8 \text{ hours/day} \times 7 \text{ days/week} \times 60 \text{ minutes/hour}}{5 \text{ minutes/part}} = 672 \text{ units}$$

*c.* To maximize profit, we need to compare profits per hour for each product:

| (1) Product | (2) Constraint Resource | (3) Production Time on Resource | (4) Number of Units Output per Hour | (5) Selling Price ($) | (6) RM Cost ($) | (7) Gross Profit per Hour (4) × (5 – 6) |
|---|---|---|---|---|---|---|
| A | Y | 2 | 30 | 20 | 3 | $510 |
| B | X | 4 | 15 | 25 | 7 | 270 |
| C | Y | 5 | 12 | 30 | 14 | 192 |

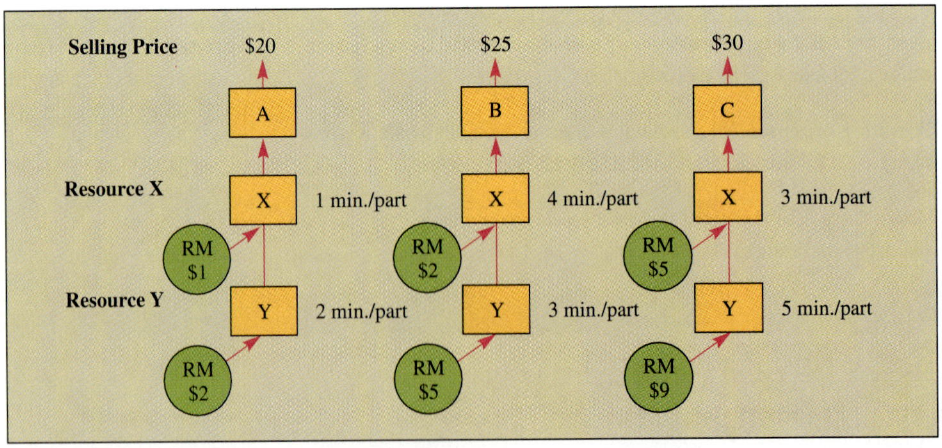


If the constraining resource were the same for all three products, our problem would be solved and the answer would be to produce just A, and as many as possible. However, X is the constraint for B, so the answer could be a combination of A and B. To test this, we can see that the value of each hour of Y while producing B is

$$\frac{60 \text{ minutes/hour}}{3 \text{ minutes/unit}} \times (\$25 - 7) = \$360/\text{hour}$$

This is less than the $510 per hour producing A, so we would produce only A. The number of units of A produced during the week is

$$\frac{60 \text{ minutes/hour} \times 24 \text{ hours/day} \times 7 \text{ days/week}}{2 \text{ minutes/unit}} = 5{,}040$$

*d.* Gross profit for the week is 5,040 × $17 = $85,680.
Solved using profit per hour: $510 × 24 × 7 = $85,680.

## REVIEW AND DISCUSSION QUESTIONS

1 State the global performance measurements and operational performance measurements and briefly define each of them. How do these differ from traditional accounting measurements?
2 Discuss process batches and transfer batches. How might you determine what the sizes should be?
3 Compare and contrast JIT, MRP, and synchronized manufacturing, stating their main features, such as where each is or might be used, amounts of raw materials and work-in-process inventories, production lead times and cycle times, and methods for control.
4 Compare the importance and relevance of quality control in JIT, MRP, and synchronous manufacturing.
5 Discuss what is meant by forward loading and backward loading.
6 Define and explain the cause or causes of a moving bottleneck.
7 Explain how a nonbottleneck can become a bottleneck.
8 What are the functions of inventory in MRP, JIT, and synchronous manufacturing scheduling?
9 Define *process batch* and *transfer batch* and their meaning in each of these applications: MRP, JIT, and bottleneck or constrained resource logic.
10 Discuss how a production system is scheduled using MRP logic, JIT logic, and synchronous manufacturing logic.
11 Discuss the concept of "drum–buffer–rope."
12 From the standpoint of the scheduling process, how are resource limitations treated in an MRP application? How are they treated in a synchronous manufacturing application?
13 What are operations people's primary complaints against the accounting procedures used in most firms? Explain how such procedures can cause poor decisions for the total company.
14 Most manufacturing firms try to balance capacity for their production sequences. Some believe that this is an invalid strategy. Explain why balancing capacity does not work.
15 Discuss why transfer batches and process batches many times may not and should not be equal.

## PROBLEMS

1 For the four basic configurations that follow, assume that the market is demanding product that must be processed by both Resource X and Resource Y for Cases I, II, and III. For Case IV, both resources supply separate but dependent markets; that is, the number of units of output from both X and Y must be equal.

Plans are being made to produce a product that requires 40 minutes on Resource X and 30 minutes on Resource Y. Assume that there is only one of each of these resources, and that market demand is 1,400 units per month.

How many hours of production time would you schedule for X and Y? What would happen if both were scheduled for the same number of hours?

1. Case I:
X used = 933.3 hours
Y used = 700 hours
Case II:
Y = 700 hrs.
X = 933.3 hrs.
Case III:
X = 933.3 hrs.
Y = 700 hrs.
Case IV:
X = 933.3 hrs.
Y = 700 hrs.
Otherwise:
Case I NO problem
Case II Excess work-in-process
Case III Excess spare parts
Case IV Excess finished goods

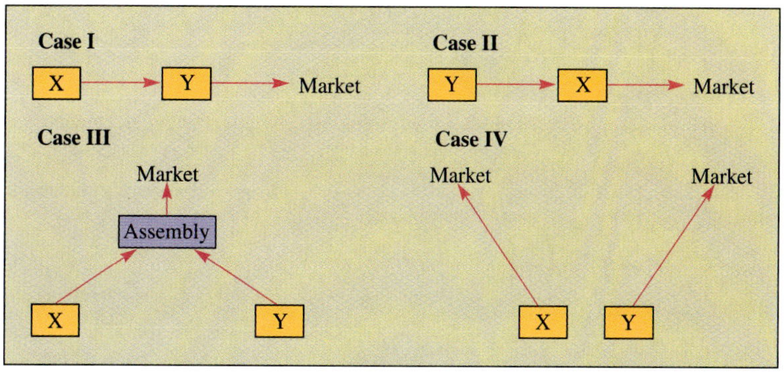


2 Following are the process flow sequences for three products: A, B, and C. There are two bottleneck operations—on the first leg and fourth leg—marked with an X. Boxes represent

2. See ISM.

processes, which may be either machine or manual. Suggest the location of the drum, buffer, and ropes.

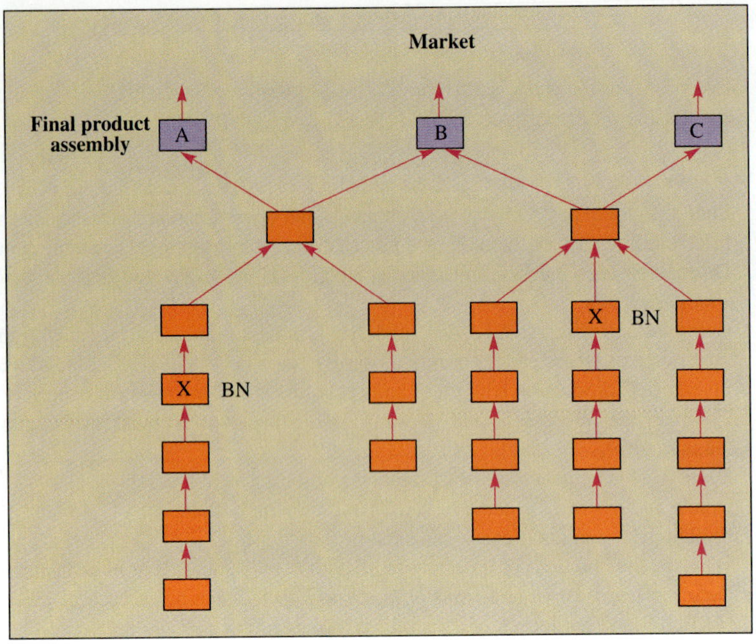


3. See ISM.

3 The accompanying figure shows a production network model with the parts and processing sequences. State clearly on the figure (1) where you would place inventory; (2) where you would perform inspection; and (3) where you would emphasize high-quality output. (Note: Operations may be shown either as rectangles in Problem 2 or as circles in Problem 3.)

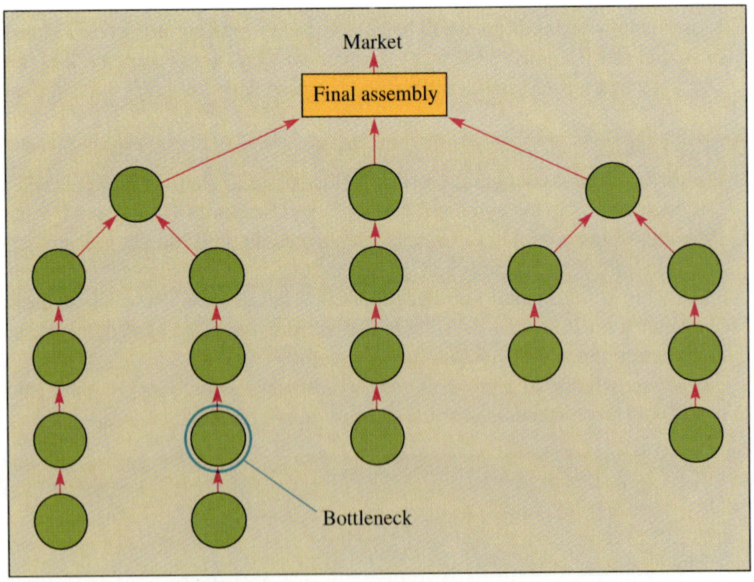


4. See ISM.

4 The following production flow shows Parts E, I, and N; Subassembly O; and final assembly for Product P:

A to B to C to D to E

F to G to H to I

J to K to L to M to N

E and I to O

N and O to P

B involves a bottleneck operation, and M involves a CCR.

*a.* Draw the process flow.
*b.* Where would you locate buffer inventories?
*c.* Where would you place inspection points?
*d.* Where would you stress the importance of quality production?

5 Here are average process cycle times for several work centers. State which are bottlenecks, nonbottlenecks, and capacity-constrained resources. 5. See ISM.

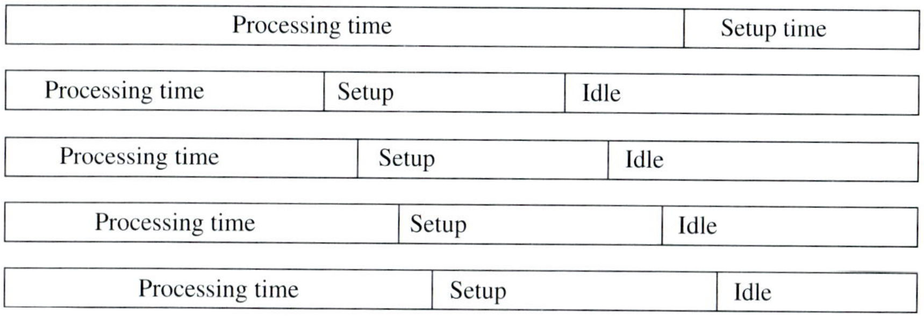


6 The following diagram shows the flow process, raw material costs, and machine processing time for three products: A, B, and C. There are three machines (W, X, and Y) used in the production of these products; the times shown are in required minutes of production per unit. Raw material costs are shown in cost per unit of product. The market will take all that can be produced. 6. *a.* Product C *b.* Product B at $15 *c.* Product A $200/hour

*a.* Assuming that sales personnel are paid on a commission basis, which product should they sell?
*b.* On the basis of maximizing gross profit per unit, which product should be sold?
*c.* To maximize total profit for the firm, which product should be sold?

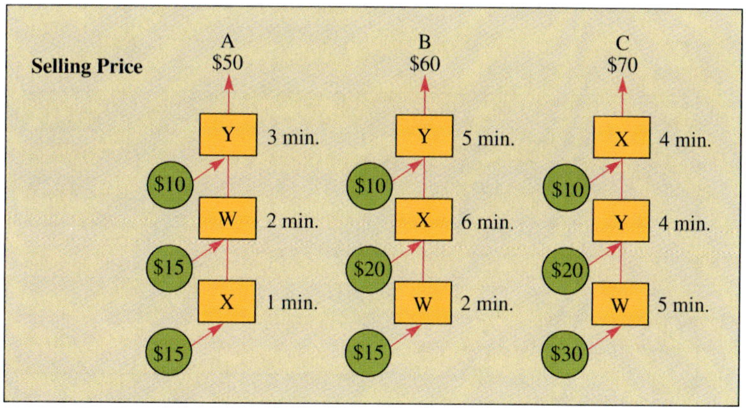


7 Willard Lock Company is losing market share because of horrendous due-date performance and long delivery lead times. The company's inventory level is high and includes many finished goods that do not match the short-term orders. Material control analysis shows that purchasing has ordered on time, the vendors have delivered on time, and the scrap/rework rates have been as expected. However, the buildable mix of components and subassemblies does not generally match the short-term and past-due requirements at final assembly. End-of-month expediting and overtime is the rule, even though there is idle time early in the month. Overall efficiency figures are around 70 percent for the month. These figures are regarded as too low. 7. See ISM.

You have just been hired as a consultant and must come up with recommendations. Help the firm understand its problems. Specifically state some actions that it should take.

8 The M–N plant manufactures two different products: M and N. Selling prices and weekly market demands are shown in the following diagram. Each product uses raw materials with costs as shown. The plant has three different machines: A, B, and C. Each performs different tasks and can work on only one unit of material at a time. 8. *a.* Machine B *b.* All of M and as many of N as possible *c.* $600, 100 M and 30 N

Process times for each task are shown in the diagram. Each machine is available 2,400 minutes per week. There are no "Murphys" (major opportunities for the system to foul up). Setup and transfer times are zero. Demand is constant.

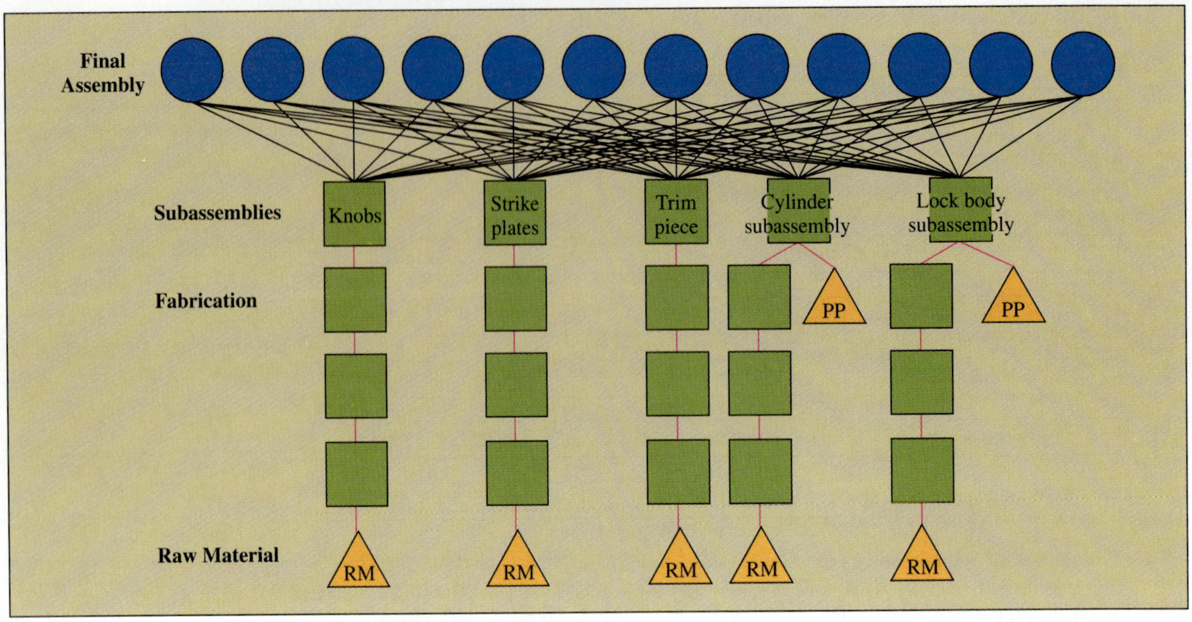


Operating expenses (including labor) total a constant $12,000 per week. Raw materials are not included in weekly operating expenses.

*a.* Where is the constraint in this plant?

*b.* What product mix provides the highest profit?

*c.* What is the maximum weekly profit this plant can earn?

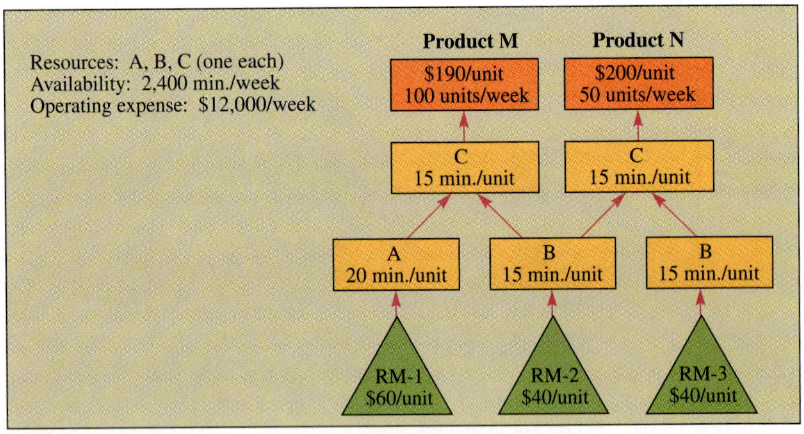


## CASE: SOLVE THE OPT QUIZ—A CHALLENGE IN SCHEDULING

Are you looking for a real scheduling challenge? This is a problem that was proposed by Dr. Eli Goldratt in a promotion for a factory-scheduling package called OPT (Optimized Production Technology). At the time Dr. Goldratt offered a $5,000 prize for the best schedule! See how good a schedule you can develop by applying the concepts described in this chapter to this problem.

### THE TASK

The goal is to ship the most units, given the conditions listed below. Provide schedules on a Gantt chart for each of the three machines for the eight-week period to show how you reached your result.

### CONDITIONS

1. There is one and only one of each of the three machines (A, B, and C).
2. A machine setup of 60 minutes occurs whenever a machine is switched from one operation to another.
3. The eight-week period consists of five-day weeks and 24-hour days with no breaks.

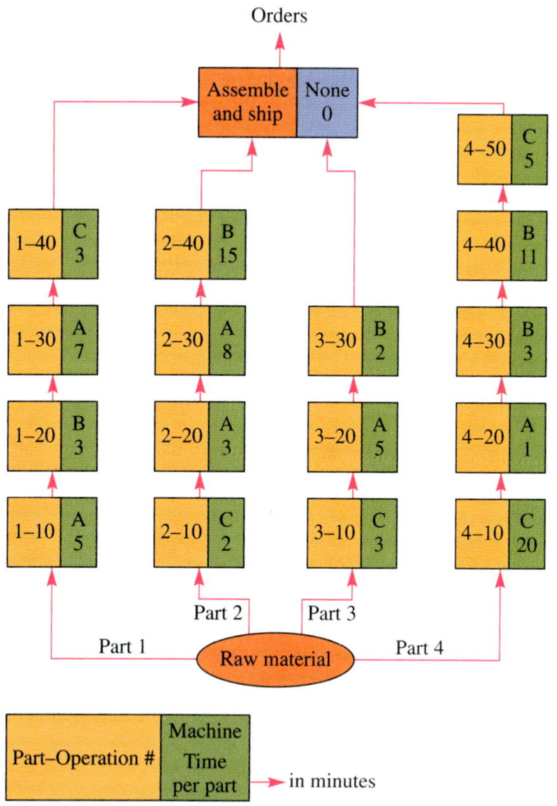


4 There is an unlimited supply of raw materials.
5 There is no inventory in the system at the beginning of the eight-week period.
6 To calculate the value of work-in-process and finished-parts inventory, assume each part has a value of $100 the moment it starts at the first operation. Once a set of four parts reaches assembly, the parts are assembled and shipped immediately. Raw material and completed units should not be included in the inventory calculation.

**Minimum Required for a Solution**

1 The raw material value of work-in-process and finished-parts inventory may not exceed $50,000 at any given time.
2 The minimum shipments of end items must be at least 140 units each week and at least 680 units by the end of the first four-week period.

Good luck!

## Selected Bibliography


Goldratt, E. *Critical Chain.* Croton-on-Hudson, NY: North River Press, 1997.

———. *The Haystack Syndrome: Sifting Information Out of the Data Ocean.* Croton-on-Hudson, NY: North River Press, 1990.

———. *What Is This Thing Called the Theory of Constraints and How Should It Be Implemented?* Croton-on-Hudson, NY: North River Press, 1990.

Goldratt, E. M., and J. Cox. *The Goal: Excellence in Manufacturing.* 2nd rev. ed. Croton-on-Hudson, NY: North River Press, 1992.

Goldratt, E. M., and R. E. Fox. *The Race for a Competitive Edge.* Milford, CT: Creative Output, 1986.

Srikanth, M., and M. Umble. *Synchronous Management: Profit Based Manufacturing for the 21st Century.* Guilford, CT: Spectrum Publishing, 1997.


## Footnotes

1 Most of this chapter is based on the writings and teaching of Dr. Eliyahu M. Goldratt. Dr. Goldratt founded the Avraham Y. Goldratt Institute. The Institute's website is at *http://www.rogo.com.* We thank Dr. Goldratt for his permission to freely use his concepts, definitions, and other material.

2 M. L. Srikanth, *The Drum–Buffer–Rope System of Material Control* (New Haven, CT: Spectrum Management Group, 1987), pp. 25–37.

3 E. M. Goldratt, *The General Theory of Constraints* (New Haven, CT: Avraham Y. Goldratt Institute, 1989).

# LINEAR PROGRAMMING WITH THE EXCEL SOLVER

*Linear programming* (or simply *LP*) refers to several related mathematical techniques that are used to allocate limited resources among competing demands in an optimal way. LP is the most popular of the approaches falling under the general heading of mathematical optimization techniques, and, as can be seen in the box, "Typical Operations Management Applications of Linear Programming," has been applied to myriad operations management problems. Our focus here is on how we can quickly set up and solve these problems using the Solver that comes with Microsoft Excel.

There are five essential conditions in a problem situation for linear programming to pertain. First, there must be *limited resources* (such as a limited number of workers, equipment, finances, and material); otherwise there would be no problem. Second, there must be an *explicit objective* (such as maximize profit or minimize cost). Third, there must be

## Typical Operations Management Applications of Linear Programming

### Applications

*Aggregate production planning:* Finding the minimum-cost production schedule, including production rate change costs, given constraints on size of workforce and inventory levels.

*Service productivity analysis:* Comparing how efficiently different service outlets are using their resources compared to the best-performing unit. (This approach is called data envelopment analysis.)

*Product planning:* Finding the optimal product mix where several products have different costs and resource requirements (for example, finding the optimal blend of constituents for gasolines, paints, human diets, animal feeds).

*Product routing:* Finding the optimal routing for a product that must be processed sequentially through several machine centers, with each machine in a center having its own cost and output characteristics.

*Process control:* Minimizing the amount of scrap material generated by cutting steel, leather, or fabric from a roll or sheet of stock material.

*Inventory control:* Finding the optimal combination of products to stock in a warehouse or store.

*Aggregate production planning:* Finding the minimum-cost production schedule (excluding production rate change costs).

*Distribution scheduling:* Finding the optimal shipping schedule for distributing products between factories and warehouses or warehouses and retailers.

*Plant location studies:* Finding the optimal location of a new plant by evaluating shipping costs between alternative locations and supply and demand sources.

*linearity* (two is twice as much as one; if it takes three hours to make a part, then two parts would take six hours, and three parts would take nine hours). Fourth, there must be *homogeneity* (the products produced on a machine are identical, or all the hours available from a worker are equally productive). Fifth is *divisibility:* Normal linear programming assumes that products and resources can be subdivided into fractions. If this subdivision is not possible (such as flying half an airplane or hiring one-fourth of a person), a modification of linear programming, called *integer programming,* can be used.

When a single objective is to be maximized (like profit) or minimized (like costs), we can use linear programming. When multiple objectives exist, *goal programming* is used. If a problem is best solved in stages or time frames, this is *dynamic programming.* Other restrictions on the nature of the problem may require that it be solved by other variations of the technique, such as *nonlinear programming* or *quadratic programming.*

## THE LINEAR PROGRAMMING MODEL

Stated formally, the linear programming problem entails an optimizing process in which nonnegative values for a set of decision variables $X_1, X_2, \ldots, X_n$ are selected so as to

*Materials handling:* Finding the minimum-cost routings of material handling devices (such as forklift trucks) between departments in a plant and of hauling materials from a supply yard to work sites by trucks, with each truck having different capacity and performance capabilities.

### EXAMPLES

#### AMERICAN RED CROSS BLOOD COLLECTION AND DISTRIBUTION

The blood service of the American Red Cross (ARC) is divided into a number of regions. Each region has responsibility for blood collection, testing, and distribution. The mid-Atlantic region of the American Red Cross (ARC) has responsibility for most of Virginia and northeastern North Carolina. The ARC was concerned with the feasibility and effect of a proposed facility relocation of its permanent blood collection and distribution sites in the mid-Atlantic region. Linear programming models were used to quickly provide insights into its current scheduling of blood collections and distribution as well as the changes imposed by the proposed relocation. As a result of the analysis, ARC decided to postpone its facility relocation and to optimize the operations of its existing facilities.*

#### JUDGING PERFORMANCE APPRAISAL CONSISTENCY

Three researchers used linear programming to determine consistency of performance appraisals of major league baseball players. The model calculated weights for objective performance measures that best fit the subjective ranking assigned to each player. Comparison of the LP results with the appraisal ranking made comparisons within the league possible. Such an application of LP would be equally applicable to evaluating the consistency of business managers' performance appraisals of employees.†

#### VALUING FOREST RESOURCES

When the New Zealand government was privatizing the state-run forest plantations, they needed to value the expected cash flows from the forests to determine a fair selling price. Using linear programming, a forest estate modeling system was developed that calculated renewable harvesting and log allocation of the 14 districts over a 40- to 70-year time horizon. The expected cash flows from these operations were used to help set reserve prices and indicative valuations. The potential buyers also used the system to help develop their bidding strategies.‡

*SOURCE: D. A. JACOBS, M. N. SILAN, AND B. A. CLEMSON, "AN ANALYSIS OF ALTERNATIVE LOCATIONS AND SERVICE AREAS OF AMERICAN RED CROSS BLOOD FACILITIES," *INTERFACES,* MAY–JUNE 1996, PP. 40–50.

†C. ZAPPE, W. WEBSTER, AND I. HOROWITZ, "USING LINEAR PROGRAMMING TO DETERMINE POST-FACTO CONSISTENCY IN PERFORMANCE EVALUATIONS OF MAJOR LEAGUE BASEBALL PLAYERS," *INTERFACES,* NOVEMBER–DECEMBER 1993, PP. 107–13.

‡B. R. MANLEY AND J. A. THREADGILL, "LP USED FOR VALUATION AND PLANNING OF NEW ZEALAND PLANTATION FORESTS," *INTERFACES,* NOVEMBER–DECEMBER 1991, PP. 66–79.

maximize (or minimize) an objective function in the form

$$\text{Maximize (minimize) } Z = C_1X_1 + C_2X_2 + \cdots + C_nX_n$$

subject to resource constraints in the form

$$A_{11}X_1 + A_{12}X_2 + \cdots + A_{1n}X_n \leq B_1$$
$$A_{21}X_1 + A_{22}X_2 + \cdots + A_{2n}X_n \leq B_2$$
$$\vdots$$
$$A_{m1}X_1 + A_{m2}X_2 + \cdots + A_{mn}X_n \leq B_m$$

where $C_n$, $A_{mn}$, and $B_m$ are given constants.

Depending on the problem, the constraints may also be stated with equal signs (=) or greater-than-or-equal-to signs (≥).

## EXAMPLE SA.1: PUCK AND PAWN COMPANY

We describe the steps involved in solving a simple linear programming model in the context of a sample problem, that of the Puck and Pawn Company, which manufactures hockey sticks and chess sets. Each hockey stick yields an incremental profit of $2, and each chess set, $4. A hockey stick requires four hours of processing at Machine Center A and two hours at Machine Center B. A chess set requires six hours at Machine Center A, six hours at Machine Center B, and one hour at Machine Center C. Machine Center A has a maximum of 120 hours of available capacity per day, Machine Center B has 72 hours, and Machine Center C has 10 hours.

If the company wishes to maximize profit, how many hockey sticks and chess sets should be produced per day?

## SOLUTION

Formulate the Problem in Mathematical Terms. If $H$ is the number of hockey sticks and $C$ is the number of chess sets, to maximize profit the objective function may be stated as

$$\text{Maximize } Z = \$2H + \$4C$$

The maximization will be subject to the following constraints:

$$4H + 6C \leq 120 \text{ (Machine Center A constraint)}$$
$$2H + 6C \leq 72 \text{ (Machine Center B constraint)}$$
$$1C \leq 10 \text{ (Machine Center C constraint)}$$
$$H, C \geq 0 \leftarrow$$

This formulation satisfies the five requirements for standard LP stated in the second paragraph of this supplement:

1 There are limited resources (a finite number of hours available at each machine center).
2 There is an explicit objective function (we know what each variable is worth and what the goal is in solving the problem).
3 The equations are linear (no exponents or cross products).
4 The resources are homogeneous (everything is in one unit of measure, machine hours).
5 The decision variables are divisible and nonnegative (we can make a fractional part of a hockey stick or chess set; however, if this were deemed undesirable, we would have to use integer programming).

## GRAPHICAL LINEAR PROGRAMMING

Though limited in application to problems involving two decision variables (or three variables for three-dimensional graphing), **graphical linear programming** provides a quick insight into the nature of linear programming.

Graphical linear programming

We describe the steps involved in the graphical method in the context of the Puck and Pawn Company. The following steps illustrate the graphical approach:

1 **Formulate the Problem in Mathematical Terms** The equations for the problem are given above.

2 **Plot Constraint Equations** The constraint equations are easily plotted by letting one variable equal zero and solving for the axis intercept of the other. (The inequality portions of the restrictions are disregarded for this step.) For the machine center A constraint equation when $H = 0$, $C = 20$, and when $C = 0$, $H = 30$. For the machine center B constraint equation, when $H = 0$, $C = 12$, and when $C = 0$, $H = 36$. For the machine center C constraint equation, $C = 10$ for all values of $H$. These lines are graphed in Exhibit SA.1.

3 **Determine the Area of Feasibility** The direction of inequality signs in each constraint determines the area where a feasible solution is found. In this case, all inequalities are of the less-than-or-equal-to variety, which means that it would be impossible to produce any combination of products that would lie to the right of any constraint line on the graph. The region of feasible solutions is unshaded on the graph and forms a convex polygon. A convex polygon exists when a line drawn between any two points in the polygon stays within the boundaries of that polygon. If this condition of convexity does not exist, the problem is either incorrectly set up or is not amenable to linear programming.

4 **Plot the Objective Function** The objective function may be plotted by assuming some arbitrary total profit figure and then solving for the axis coordinates, as was done for the constraint equations. Other terms for the objective function, when used in this context, are the *iso-profit* or *equal contribution line,* because it shows all possible production combinations for any given profit figure. For example, from the dotted line closest to the origin on the graph, we can determine all possible combinations of hockey sticks and chess sets that yield \$32 by picking a point on the line and reading the number of each product that can be made at that point. The combination yielding \$32 at point $a$ would be 10 hockey

EXHIBIT SA.1

Graph of Hockey Stick and Chess Set Problem

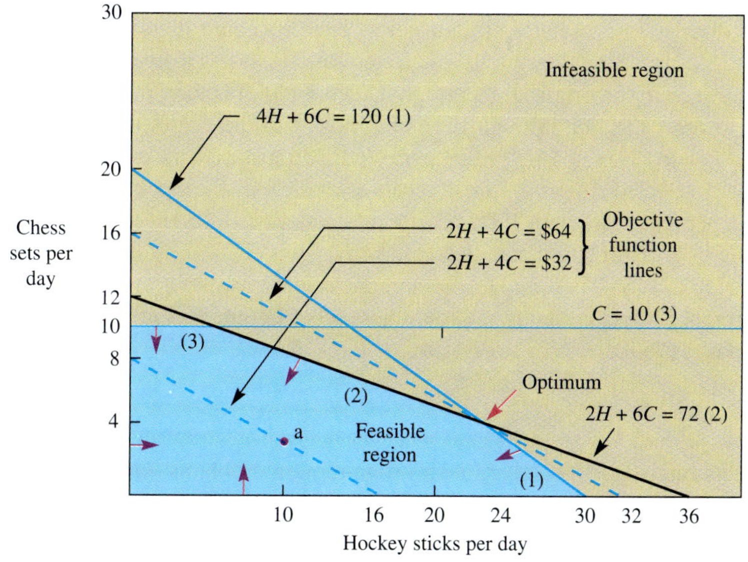

sticks and three chess sets. This can be verified by substituting $H = 10$ and $C = 3$ in the objective function:

$$\$2(10) + \$4(3) = \$20 + \$12 = \$32$$

| *H* | *C* | EXPLANATION |
|---|---|---|
| 0 | 120/6 = 20 | Intersection of Constraint (1) and *C* axis |
| 120/4 = 30 | 0 | Intersection of Constraint (1) and *H* axis |
| 0 | 72/6 = 12 | Intersection of Constraint (2) and *C* axis |
| 72/2 = 36 | 0 | Intersection of Constraint (2) and *H* axis |
| 0 | 10 | Intersection of Constraint (3) and *C* axis |
| 0 | 32/4 = 8 | Intersection of $32 iso-point line (objective function) and *C* axis |
| 32/2 = 16 | 0 | Intersection of $32 iso-profit line and *H* axis |
| 0 | 64/4 = 16 | Intersection of $64 iso-profit line and *C* axis |
| 64/2 = 32 | 0 | Intersection of $64 iso-profit line and *H* axis |

5 **Find the Optimum Point** It can be shown mathematically that the optimal combination of decision variables is always found at an extreme point (corner point) of the convex polygon. In Exhibit SA.1 there are four corner points (excluding the origin), and we can determine which one is the optimum by either of two approaches. The first approach is to find the values of the various corner solutions algebraically. This entails simultaneously solving the equations of various pairs of intersecting lines and substituting the quantities of the resultant variables in the objective function. For example, the calculations for the intersection of $2H + 6C = 72$ and $C = 10$ are as follows:

Substituting $C = 10$ in $2H + 6C = 72$ gives $2H + 6(10) = 72$, $2H = 12$, or $H = 6$. Substituting $H = 6$ and $C = 10$ in the objective function, we get

$$\text{Profit} = \$2H + \$4C = \$2(6) + \$4(10)$$
$$= \$12 + \$40 = \$52$$

A variation of this approach is to read the *H* and *C* quantities directly from the graph and substitute these quantities into the objective function, as shown in the previous calculation. The drawback in this approach is that in problems with a large number of constraint equations, there will be many possible points to evaluate, and the procedure of testing each one mathematically is inefficient.

The second and generally preferred approach entails using the objective function or iso-profit line directly to find the optimum point. The procedure involves simply drawing a straight line *parallel* to any arbitrarily selected initial iso-profit line so that the iso-profit line is farthest from the origin of the graph. (In cost-minimization problems, the objective would be to draw the line through the point closest to the origin.) In Exhibit SA.1, the dashed line labeled $\$2H + \$4C = \$64$ intersects the most extreme point. Note that the initial arbitrarily selected iso-profit line is necessary to display the slope of the objective function for the particular problem.* This is important since a different objective function (try profit $= 3H + 3C$) might indicate that some other point is farthest from the origin. Given that $\$2H + \$4C = \$64$ is optimal, the amount of each variable to produce can be read from the graph: 24 hockey sticks and four chess sets. No other combination of the products yields a greater profit.

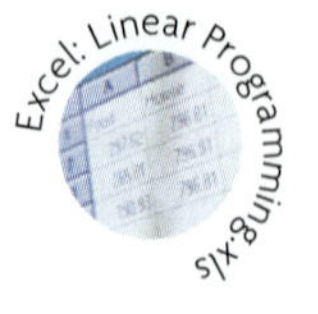


## LINEAR PROGRAMMING USING MICROSOFT EXCEL

Spreadsheets can be used to solve linear programming problems. Most spreadsheets have built-in optimization routines that are very easy to use and understand. Microsoft Excel has

*The slope of the objective function is $-2$. If $P$ = profit, $P = \$2H + \$4C$; $\$2H = P - \$4C$; $H = p/2 - 2C$. Thus the slope is $-2$.

EXHIBIT SA.2

Microsoft Excel Solver Screen

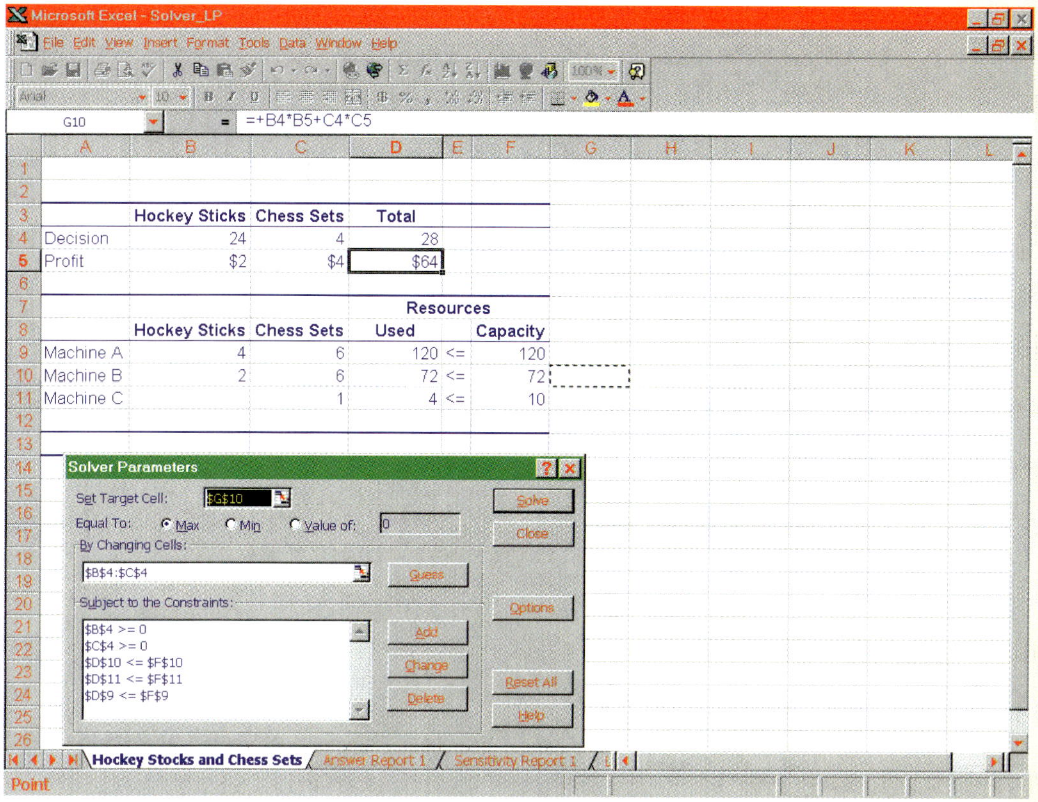


an optimization tool called *Solver* that we will demonstrate by using it to solve the hockey stick and chess problem. We invoke the Solver from the Tools menu. A dialogue box requests information required by the program.

First, we define the problem by identifying a target cell (or objective function), the changing cells (or decision variables), and the constraints that we want in the analysis. Exhibit SA.2 shows a spreadsheet with the information required for the problem. Our "Target Cell" (cell D5) contains a formula that multiplies the quantities of hockey sticks and chess sets produced by their corresponding profit. The "Changing Cells" correspond to the decision variables for the problem. The "Subject to the Constraints" box contains cells that calculate the individual machine requirements for a solution. Note that we must indicate that our solution values must be greater than or equal to zero.

In Exhibit SA.2, we do not show the "Options" dialogue box. If you click on this box, though, you will see a box that allows you to indicate this is a "linear problem." This will speed the solution process for our problem. Many other items can be selected in the "Options" dialogue box that control the solution search mechanism used by Solver. The program can solve problems using search strategies different from the simplex approach.

After we input all of the information in the dialogue boxes, we can press the Solve button to solve the problem. A number of different reports can be obtained. The most interesting reports for our problem are the Answer Report and the Sensitivity Report, both of which are shown in Exhibit SA.3. The Answer Report shows the final answers for the total profit ($64) and the amounts produced (24 hockey sticks and four chess sets). In the constraints section of the Answer Report, the status of each resource is given. All of Machine A and Machine B are used, and there are six units of slack for Machine C.

The Sensitivity Report is divided into two parts. The first part, titled "changing cells," corresponds to objective function coefficients. The profit per unit for the hockey sticks can be either up or down $.67 (between $2.67 and $1.33) without having an impact on the

EXHIBIT SA.3

Microsoft Excel Solver Reports

**Answer Report**

Target Cell (Max)

| Cell | Name | Original Value | Final Value |
|---|---|---|---|
| $D$5 | Profit Total | $64 | $64 |

Adjustable Cells

| Cell | Name | Original Value | Final Value |
|---|---|---|---|
| $B$4 | Decision Hockey Sticks | 24 | 24 |
| $C$4 | Decision Chess Sets | 4 | 4 |

Constraints

| Cell | Name | Cell Value | Formula | Status | Slack |
|---|---|---|---|---|---|
| $D$9 | Machine A Used | 120 | $D$9<=$F$9 | Binding | 0 |
| $D$10 | Machine B Used | 72 | $D$10<=$F$10 | Binding | 0 |
| $D$11 | Machine C Used | 4 | $D$11<=$F$11 | Not Binding | 6 |
| $B$4 | Decision Hockey Sticks | 24 | $B$4>=0 | Not Binding | 24 |
| $C$4 | Decision Chess Sets | 4 | $C$4>=0 | Not Binding | 4 |

**Sensitivity Report**

Changing Cells

| Cell | Name | Final Value | Reduced Cost | Objective Coefficient | Allowable Increase | Allowable Decrease |
|---|---|---|---|---|---|---|
| $B$4 | Decision Hockey Sticks | 24 | 0 | 2 | 0.666666667 | 0.666666667 |
| $C$4 | Decision Chess Sets | 4 | 0 | 4 | 2 | 1 |

Constraints

| Cell | Name | Final Value | Shadow* Price | Constraint R.H. Side | Allowable Increase | Allowable Decrease |
|---|---|---|---|---|---|---|
| $D$9 | Machine A Used | 120 | 0.333333333 | 120 | 24 | 36 |
| $D$10 | Machine B Used | 72 | 0.333333333 | 72 | 18 | 12 |
| $D$11 | Machine C Used | 4 | 0 | 10 | 1E+30 | 6 |

*Shadow price: The monetary value of one more unit of capacity.

solution. Similarly, the profit of the chess sets could be between $6 and $3 without changing the solution. In the case of Machine A, the right-hand side could increase to 144 (120 + 24) or decrease to 84 with a resulting $.33 increase or decrease in the objective function. The right-hand side of Machine B can increase to 90 units or decrease to 60 units with the same $.33 change in the objective function. For Machine C, the right-hand side could increase to infinity (1E + 30 is scientific notation for a very large number) or decrease to four units, with no change in the objective function.

## Genetic Solver Option

On the CD that is packaged with the book, we have included a new product from Frontline Systems called the *Premium Solver.* The package installs on top of Microsoft's Solver and adds many new features to the Microsoft product. All of the old Solver capabilities are retained, but in Premium Solver mode new capabilities include

- A new evolutionary solver for doing genetic searches. This can be very useful for solving problems that are not linear.

- A linearity report for finding where the calculations in a spreadsheet violate the linearity conditions that are needed to use a standard linear programming algorithm.
- A feasibility report to help identify why it is not possible to find a feasible solution to your problem.
- A population report to help explain solutions that are generated with the new genetic search capability.

If you are interested in the latest tricks for solving problems with spreadsheets, install the Premium Solver.

## PROBLEMS

1 Solve the following problem with Excel Solver:

$$\text{Maximize } Z = 3X + Y.$$
$$12X + 14Y \leq 85$$
$$3X + 2Y \leq 18$$
$$Y \leq 4$$

1. $X = 6$
$Y = 0$
$Z = 18$

2 Solve the following problem with Excel Solver:

$$\text{Minimize } Z = 2A + 4B.$$
$$4A + 6B \geq 120$$
$$2A + 6B \geq 72$$
$$B \geq 10$$

2. See ISM; Optimal combination is $B = 10$; $A = 15$. $Z = 70$

3 A manufacturing firm has discontinued production of a certain unprofitable product line. Considerable excess production capacity was created as a result. Management is considering devoting this excess capacity to one or more of three products: $X_1$, $X_2$, and $X_3$.

Machine hours required per unit are

| | Product | | |
|---|---|---|---|
| Machine Type | $X_1$ | $X_2$ | $X_3$ |
| Milling machine | 8 | 2 | 3 |
| Lathe | 4 | 3 | 0 |
| Grinder | 2 | 0 | 1 |

The available time in machine hours per week is

| | Machine Hours per Week |
|---|---|
| Milling machines | 800 |
| Lathes | 480 |
| Grinders | 320 |

The salespeople estimate that they can sell all the units of $X_1$ and $X_2$ that can be made. But the sales potential of $X_3$ is 80 units per week maximum.

Unit profits for the three products are

| | Unit Profits |
|---|---|
| $X_1$ | \$20 |
| $X_2$ | 6 |
| $X_3$ | 8 |

*a.* Set up the equations that can be solved to maximize the profit per week.
*b.* Solve these equations using the Excel Solver.
*c.* What is the optimal solution? How many of each product should be made, and what should the resultant profit be?

3. *a.* See ISM for *a* and *b*.
*c.* $X_1 = 45$; $X_2 = 100$; $X_3 = 80$; $Z = 2140$ (maximum profit)
*d.* Milling machines at capacity; lathes at capacity; grinders have 150 hours slack; $X_3$ is at maximum sales capacity.
*e.* Recommend working 200 hrs. O.T. in milling.

*d.* What is this situation with respect to the machine groups? Would they work at capacity, or would there be unused available time? Will $X_3$ be at maximum sales capacity?

*e.* Suppose that an additional 200 hours per week can be obtained from the milling machines by working overtime. The incremental cost would be $1.50 per hour. Would you recommend doing this? Explain how you arrived at your answer.

4. *a.* $600A + 900B \leq 3{,}600$
$600A + 900B \geq 1{,}800$
$200A + 700B \leq 1{,}400$
$400A + 100B \geq 400$
$A \leq 2$
Minimize $.75A + .15B$
*b.* $A = 0.54$, $B = 1.85$, Obj = 0.68

4 A diet is being prepared for the University of Arizona dorms. The objective is to feed the students at the least cost, but the diet must have between 1,800 and 3,600 calories. No more than 1,400 calories can be starch, and no fewer than 400 can be protein. The varied diet is to be made of two foods: *A* and *B*. Food *A* costs $0.75 per pound and contains 600 calories, 400 of which are protein and 200 starch. No more than two pounds of Food *A* can be used per resident. Food *B* costs $0.15 per pound and contains 900 calories, of which 700 are starch, 100 are protein, and 100 are fat.

*a.* Write the equations representing this information.

*b.* Solve the problem graphically for the amounts of each food that should be used.

5. Cost per student:
$A = 0.75$
$B = 1.5$
Obj = 5.06

5 Do Problem 4 with the added constraint that not more than 150 calories shall be fat, and that the price of food has escalated to $1.75 per pound for food *A* and $2.50 per pound for food *B*.

6. *a.* $A + B \geq 3{,}000$
$A + B \leq 4{,}000$
$A \leq 2{,}000$
$B \leq 4{,}000$
$90A + 75B \geq 80(A + B)$, or
$10A - 5B \geq 0$
*b.* Optimum:
$A = 1{,}000$;
$B = 2{,}000$.

6 Logan Manufacturing wants to mix two fuels (*A* and *B*) for its trucks to minimize cost. It needs no fewer than 3,000 gallons to run its trucks during the next month. It has a maximum fuel storage capacity of 4,000 gallons. There are 2,000 gallons of Fuel *A* and 4,000 gallons of Fuel *B* available. The mixed fuel must have an octane rating of no less than 80.

When mixing fuels, the amount of fuel obtained is just equal to the sum of the amounts put in. The octane rating is the weighted average of the individual octanes, weighted in proportion to the respective volumes.

The following is known: Fuel *A* has an octane of 90 and costs $1.20 per gallon. Fuel *B* has an octane of 75 and costs $0.90 per gallon.

*a.* Write the equations expressing this information.

*b.* Solve the problem using the Excel Solver, giving the amount of each fuel to be used. State any assumptions necessary to solve the problem.

7. Food = $300
Shelter = $700
Entertainment = $300
Satisfaction value = $4,200

7 You are trying to create a budget to optimize the use of a portion of your disposable income. You have a maximum of $1,500 per month to be allocated to food, shelter, and entertainment. The amount spent on food and shelter combined must not exceed $1,000. The amount spent on shelter alone must not exceed $700. Entertainment cannot exceed $300 per month. Each dollar spent on food has a satisfaction value of 2, each dollar spent on shelter has a satisfaction value of 3, and each dollar spent on entertainment has a satisfaction value of 5.

Assuming a linear relationship, use the Excel Solver to determine the optimal allocation of your funds.

## SELECTED BIBLIOGRAPHY

Camm, J. D., and J. R. Evans. *Management Science and Decision Technology.* E. Bridgewater, MA: South-Western College Publishing, 1999.

Winston, W. L., and S. C. Albright. *Practical Management Science: Spreadsheet Modeling and Applications.* Belmont, CA: Duxbury Press, 1997.

# FINANCIAL ANALYSIS

Vol. VI "Valuation of Operations at ABTco"

Cross Functional

In this supplement we review basic concepts and tools of financial analysis for OM. These include the types of cost (fixed, variable, sunk, opportunity, avoidable), risk and expected value, and depreciation (straight line, sum-of-the-years'-digits, declining balance, double-declining balance, and depreciation-by-use). We also discuss activity-based costing and cost-of-capital calculations. Our focus is on capital investment decisions.

## Concepts and Definitions

We begin with some basic definitions.

### Fixed Costs

A *fixed cost* is any expense that remains constant regardless of the level of output. Although no cost is truly fixed, many types of expense are virtually fixed over a wide range of output. Examples are rent, property taxes, most types of depreciation, insurance payments, and salaries of top management.

### Variable Costs

*Variable costs* are expenses that fluctuate directly with changes in the level of output. For example, each additional unit of sheet steel produced by USX requires a specific amount of material and labor. The incremental cost of this additional material and labor can be isolated and assigned to each unit of sheet steel produced. Many overhead expenses are also variable because utility bills, maintenance expense, and so forth vary with the production level.

Exhibit SB.1 illustrates the fixed and variable cost components of total cost. Note that total cost increases at the same rate as variable costs because fixed costs are constant.

### Sunk Costs

*Sunk costs* are past expenses or investments that have no salvage value and therefore should not be taken into account in considering investment alternatives. Sunk costs could also be current costs that are essentially fixed, such as rent on a building. For example, suppose an ice cream manufacturing firm occupies a rented building and is considering making sherbet in the same building. If the company enters sherbet production, its cost accountant will assign some of the rental expense to the sherbet operation. However, the building rent remains unchanged and therefore is not a relevant expense to be considered in making the decision. The rent is *sunk;* that is, it continues to exist and does not change in amount regardless of the decision.

Exhibit SB.1

Fixed and Variable Cost Components of Total Cost

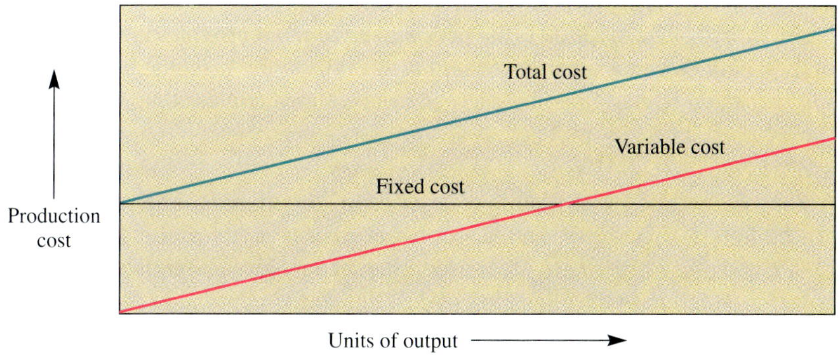

### Opportunity Costs

*Opportunity cost* is the benefit *forgone,* or advantage *lost,* that results from choosing one action over the *best-known alternative* course of action.

Suppose a firm has \$100,000 to invest, and two alternatives of comparable risk present themselves, each requiring a \$100,000 investment. Investment A will net \$25,000; Investment B will net \$23,000. Investment A is clearly the better choice, with a \$25,000 net return. If the decision is made to invest in B instead of A, the opportunity cost of B is \$2,000, which is the benefit forgone.

### Avoidable Costs

*Avoidable costs* include any expense that is *not* incurred if an investment is made but that *must* be incurred if the investment is *not* made. Suppose a company owns a metal lathe that is not in working condition but is needed for the firm's operations. Because the lathe must be repaired or replaced, the repair costs are avoidable if a new lathe is purchased. Avoidable costs reduce the cost of a new investment because they are not incurred if the investment is made. Avoidable costs are an example of how it is possible to "save" money by spending money.

### Expected Value

Risk is inherent in any investment because the future can never by predicted with absolute certainty. To deal with this uncertainty, mathematical techniques such as expected value can help. Expected value is the expected outcome multiplied by the probability of its occurrence. Recall that in the preceding example the expected outcome of Alternative A was \$25,000 and B, \$23,000. Suppose the probability of A's actual outcome is 80 percent while B's probability is 90 percent. The expected values of the alternatives are determined as follows:

$$\text{Expected outcome} \times \text{Probability that actual outcome will be the expected outcome} = \text{Expected value}$$

$$\text{Investment A: } \$25{,}000 \times 0.80 = \$20{,}000$$
$$\text{Investment B: } \$23{,}000 \times 0.90 = \$20{,}700$$

Investment B is now seen to be the better choice, with a net advantage over A of \$700.

### Economic Life and Obsolescence

When a firm invests in an income-producing asset, the productive life of the asset is estimated. For accounting purposes, the asset is depreciated over this period. It is assumed that the asset will perform its function during this time and then be considered obsolete or worn out, and replacement will be required. This view of asset life rarely coincides with reality.

Assume that a machine expected to have a productive life of 10 years is purchased. If at any time during the ensuing 10 years a new machine is developed that can perform the same task more efficiently or economically, the old machine has become obsolete. Whether or not it is "worn out" is irrelevant.

The *economic life* of a machine is the period over which it provides the best method for performing its task. When a superior method is developed, the machine has become obsolete. Thus, the stated *book value* of a machine can be a meaningless figure.

### Depreciation

Depreciation is a method for allocating costs of capital equipment. The value of any capital asset—buildings, machinery, and so forth—decreases as its useful life is expended. *Amortization* and *depreciation* are often used interchangeably. Through convention, however, *depreciation* refers to the allocation of cost due to the physical or functional deterioration of *tangible* (physical) assets, such as buildings or equipment, whereas *amortization* refers to the allocation of cost over the useful life of *intangible* assets, such as patents, leases, franchises, and goodwill.

Depreciation procedures may not reflect an asset's true value at any point in its life because obsolescence may at any time cause a large difference between true value and book value. Also, because depreciation rates significantly affect taxes, a firm may choose a particular method from the several alternatives with more consideration for its effect on taxes than its ability to make the book value of an asset reflect the true resale value.

Next we describe five commonly used methods of depreciation.

### STRAIGHT-LINE METHOD

Under this method, an asset's value is reduced in uniform annual amounts over its estimated useful life. The general formula is

$$\text{Annual amount to be depreciated} = \frac{\text{Cost} - \text{Salvage value}}{\text{Estimated useful life}}$$

A machine costing \$10,000, with an estimated salvage value of \$0 and an estimated life of 10 years, would be depreciated at the rate of \$1,000 per year for each of the 10 years. If its estimated salvage value at the end of the 10 years is \$1,000, the annual depreciation charge is

$$\frac{\$10{,}000 - \$1{,}000}{10} = \$900$$

### SUM-OF-THE-YEARS'-DIGITS (SYD) METHOD

The purpose of the SYD method is to reduce the book value of an asset rapidly in early years and at a lower rate in the later years of its life.

Suppose that the estimated useful life is five years. The numbers add up to 15: $1 + 2 + 3 + 4 + 5 = 15$. Therefore, we depreciate the asset by $5 \div 15$ after the first year, $4 \div 15$ after the second year, and so on, down to $1 \div 15$ in the last year.

### DECLINING-BALANCE METHOD

This method also achieves an accelerated depreciation. The asset's value is decreased by reducing its book value by a constant percentage each year. The percentage rate selected is often the one that just reduces book value to salvage value at the end of the asset's estimated life. In any case, the asset should never be reduced below estimated salvage value. Use of the declining-balance method and allowable rates are controlled by Internal Revenue Service regulations. As a simplified illustration, the preceding example is used in the next table with an arbitrarily selected rate of 40 percent. Note that depreciation is based on full cost, *not* cost minus salvage value.

| YEAR | DEPRECIATION RATE | BEGINNING BOOK VALUE | DEPRECIATION CHARGE | ACCUMULATED DEPRECIATION | ENDING BOOK VALUE |
|---|---|---|---|---|---|
| 1 | 0.40 | \$17,000 | \$6,800 | \$ 6,800 | \$10,200 |
| 2 | 0.40 | 10,200 | 4,080 | 10,880 | 6,120 |
| 3 | 0.40 | 6,120 | 2,448 | 13,328 | 3,672 |
| 4 | 0.40 | 3,672 | 1,469 | 14,797 | 2,203 |
| 5 | | 2,203 | 203 | 15,000 | 2,000 |

In the fifth year, reducing book value by 40 percent would have caused it to drop below salvage value. Consequently, the asset was depreciated by only \$203, which decreased book value to salvage value.

### DOUBLE-DECLINING-BALANCE METHOD

Again, for tax advantages, the double-declining-balance method offers higher depreciation early in the life span. This method uses a percentage twice the straight line for the life span of the item but applies this rate to the undepreciated original cost. The method is the same as the declining-balance method, but the term *double-declining balance* means double the straight-line rate. Thus, equipment with a 10-year life span would have a straight-line depreciation rate of 10 percent per year, and a double-declining-balance rate (applied to the undepreciated amount) of 20 percent per year.

### DEPRECIATION-BY-USE METHOD

The purpose of this method is to depreciate a capital investment in proportion to its use. It is applicable, for example, to a machine that performs the same operation many times. The life of the machine is estimated not in years but rather in the total number of operations it may reasonably be expected to perform before wearing out. Suppose that a metal-stamping press has an estimated life of 1 million stamps and costs $100,000. The charge for depreciation per stamp is then $100,000 ÷ 1,000,000 or $0.10. Assuming a $0 salvage value, the depreciation charges are as shown in the following table:

| YEAR | TOTAL YEARLY STAMPS | COST PER STAMP | YEARLY DEPRECIATION CHARGE | ACCUMULATED DEPRECIATION | ENDING BOOK VALUE |
|---|---|---|---|---|---|
| 1 | 150,000 | 0.10 | $15,000 | $ 15,000 | $85,000 |
| 2 | 300,000 | 0.10 | 30,000 | 45,000 | 55,000 |
| 3 | 200,000 | 0.10 | 20,000 | 65,000 | 35,000 |
| 4 | 200,000 | 0.10 | 20,000 | 85,000 | 15,000 |
| 5 | 100,000 | 0.10 | 10,000 | 95,000 | 5,000 |
| 6 | 50,000 | 0.10 | 5,000 | 100,000 | 0 |

The depreciation-by-use method is an attempt to gear depreciation charges to actual use and thereby coordinate expense charges with productive output more accurately. Also, because a machine's resale value is related to its remaining productive life, it is hoped that book value will approximate resale value. The danger, of course, is that technological improvements will render the machine obsolete, in which case book value will not reflect true value.

## ACTIVITY-BASED COSTING

To know how much it costs to make a certain product or deliver a service, some method of allocating overhead costs to production activities must be applied. The traditional approach is to allocate overhead costs to products on the basis of direct labor dollars or hours. By dividing the total estimated overhead costs by total budgeted direct labor hours, an overhead rate can be established. The problem with this approach is that direct labor as a percentage of total costs has fallen dramatically over the past decade. For example, introduction of advanced manufacturing technology and other productivity improvements has driven direct labor to as low as 7 to 10 percent of total manufacturing costs in many industries. As a result, overhead rates of 600 percent or even 1,000 percent are found in some highly automated plants.

This traditional accounting practice of allocating overhead to direct labor can lead to questionable investment decisions; for example, automated processes may be chosen over labor-intensive processes based on a comparison of projected costs. Unfortunately, overhead does not disappear when the equipment is installed, and overall costs may actually be lower with the labor-intensive process. It can also lead to wasted effort because an inordinate amount of time is spent tracking direct labor hours. For example, one plant spent 65 percent of computer costs tracking information about direct labor transactions even though direct labor accounted for only 4 percent of total production costs.[1]

Activity-based costing techniques have been developed to alleviate these problems by refining the overhead allocation process to more directly reflect actual proportions of overhead consumed by the production activity. Causal factors, known as *cost drivers,* are identified and used as the means for allocating overhead. These factors might include machine hours, beds occupied, computer time, flight hours, or miles driven. The accuracy of overhead allocation, of course, depends on the selection of appropriate cost drivers.

EXHIBIT SB.2

Traditional and Activity-Based Costing

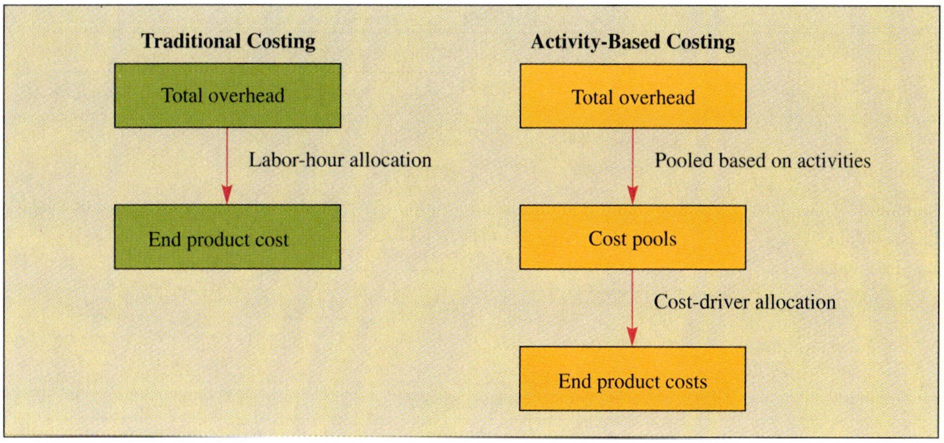


Activity-based costing involves a two-stage allocation process, with the first stage assigning overhead costs to *cost activity pools*. These pools represent activities such as performing machine setups, issuing purchase orders, and inspecting parts. In the second stage, costs are assigned from these pools to activities based on the number or amount of pool-related activity required in their completion. Exhibit SB.2 compares traditional cost accounting and activity-based costing.

Consider the example of activity-based costing in Exhibit SB.3. Two products, A and B, are produced using the same number of direct labor hours. The same number of direct labor hours produces 5,000 units of Product A and 20,000 units of Product B. Applying traditional costing, identical overhead costs would be charged to each product. By applying activity-based costing, traceable costs are assigned to specific activities. Because each product required a different amount of transactions, different overhead amounts are allocated to these products from the pools.

As stated earlier, activity-based costing overcomes the problem of cost distortion by creating a cost pool for each activity or transaction that can be identified as a cost driver, and by assigning overhead cost to products or jobs on a basis of the number of separate activities required for their completion. Thus, in the previous situation, the low-volume product would be assigned the bulk of the costs for machine setup, purchase orders, and quality inspections, thereby showing it to have high unit costs compared to the other product.

Finally, activity-based costing is sometimes referred to as *transactions costing*. This transactions focus gives rise to another major advantage over other costing methods: It improves the traceability of overhead costs and thus results in more accurate unit cost data for management.

## THE EFFECTS OF TAXES

Tax rates and the methods of applying them occasionally change. When analysts evaluate investment proposals, tax considerations often prove to be the deciding factor because depreciation expenses directly affect taxable income and therefore profit. The ability to write off depreciation in early years provides an added source of funds for investment. Before 1986, firms could employ an investment tax credit, which allowed a direct reduction in tax liability. But tax laws change, so it is crucial to stay on top of current tax laws and try to predict future changes that may affect current investments and accounting procedures.

## CHOOSING AMONG INVESTMENT PROPOSALS

The capital investment decision has become highly rationalized, as evidenced by the variety of techniques available for its solution. In contrast to pricing or marketing decisions,

EXHIBIT SB.3

**Overhead Allocations by an Activity Approach**

BASIC DATA

| ACTIVITY | TRACEABLE COSTS | EVENTS OF TRANSACTIONS: TOTAL | PRODUCT A | PRODUCT B |
|---|---|---|---|---|
| Machine setups | $230,000 | 5,000 | 3,000 | 2,000 |
| Quality inspections | 160,000 | 8,000 | 5,000 | 3,000 |
| Production orders | 81,000 | 600 | 200 | 400 |
| Machine-hours worked | 314,000 | 40,000 | 12,000 | 28,000 |
| Material receipts | 90,000 | 750 | 150 | 600 |
| Number of units produced | | 25,000 | 5,000 | 20,000 |
| | $875,000 | | | |

OVERHEAD RATES BY ACTIVITY

| ACTIVITY | (*a*) TRACEABLE COSTS | (*b*) TOTAL EVENTS OR TRANSACTIONS | (*a*) ÷ (*b*) RATE PER EVENT OR TRANSACTION |
|---|---|---|---|
| Machine setups | $230,000 | 5,000 | $46/setups |
| Quality inspections | 160,000 | 8,000 | $20/inspection |
| Production orders | 81,000 | 600 | $135/order |
| Machine-hours worked | 314,000 | 40,000 | $7.85/hour |
| Material receipts | 90,000 | 750 | $120/receipt |

OVERHEAD COST PER UNIT OF PRODUCT

| | PRODUCT A: EVENTS OR TRANSACTIONS | PRODUCT A: AMOUNT | PRODUCT B: EVENTS OR TRANSACTIONS | PRODUCT B: AMOUNT |
|---|---|---|---|---|
| Machine setups, at $46/setup | 3,000 | $138,000 | 2,000 | $ 92,000 |
| Quality inspections, at $20/inspection | 5,000 | 100,000 | 3,000 | 60,000 |
| Product orders, at $135/order | 200 | 27,000 | 400 | 54,000 |
| Machine-hours worked, at $7.85/hour | 12,000 | 94,200 | 28,000 | 219,800 |
| Material receipts, at $120/receipt | 150 | 18,000 | 600 | 72,000 |
| Total overhead cost assigned | | $377,200 | | $497,800 |
| Number of units produced | | 5,000 | | 20,000 |
| Overhead cost per unit, $\frac{\text{Total overhead}}{\text{No. of units}}$ | | $75.44 | | $24.89 |

SOURCE: R. GARRISON, *MANAGERIAL ACCOUNTING*, 6TH ED. (BURR RIDGE, IL: RICHARD D. IRWIN, 1991), P. 94.

the capital investment decision can usually be made with a higher degree of confidence because the variables affecting the decision are relatively well known and can be quantified with fair accuracy.

Investment decisions may be grouped into six general categories:

1 Purchase of new equipment or facilities.
2 Replacement of existing equipment or facilities.
3 Make-or-buy decisions.
4 Lease-or-buy decisions.
5 Temporary shutdowns or plant abandonment decisions.
6 Addition or elimination of a product or product line.

Investment decisions are made with regard to the lowest acceptable rate of return on investment. As a starting point, the lowest acceptable rate of return may be considered to be the cost of investment capital needed to underwrite the expenditure. Certainly an investment will not be made if it does not return at least the cost of capital.

Investments are generally ranked according to the return they yield in excess of their cost of capital. In this way, a business with only limited investment funds can select investment alternatives that yield the highest net returns. (*Net return* is the earnings an investment yields after gross earnings have been reduced by the cost of the funds used to finance the investment.) In general, investments should not be made unless the return in funds exceeds the marginal cost of investment capital. (*Marginal cost* is the incremental cost of each new acquisition of funds from outside sources.)

## DETERMINING THE COST OF CAPITAL

The cost of capital is calculated from a weighted average of debt and equity security costs. This average will vary depending on the financing strategy employed by the company. The most common sources of financing are short-term debt, long-term debt, and equity securities. A bank loan is an example of short-term debt. Bonds normally provide long-term debt. Finally, stock is a common form of equity financing. In the following, we give a short example of each form of financing, and then show how they are combined to find the weighted average cost of capital.

The cost of short-term debt depends on the interest rate on the loan and whether the loan is discounted. Remember that interest is a tax-deductible expense for a company.

$$\text{Cost of short-term debt} = \frac{\text{Interest paid}}{\text{Proceeds received}}$$

If a bank discounts a loan, interest is deducted from the face of the loan to get the proceeds. When a compensating balance is required (that is, a percentage of the face value of the loan is held by the bank as collateral), proceeds are also reduced. In either case, the effective or real interest rate on the loan is higher than the face interest rate owing to the proceeds received from the loan being less than the amount (face value) of the loan.

### EXAMPLE OF SHORT-TERM DEBT

A company takes a \$150,000, one-year, 13 percent loan. The loan is discounted, and a 10 percent compensating balance is required. The effective interest rate is computed as follows:

$$\frac{13\% \times \$150,000}{\$115,500} = \frac{\$19,500}{\$115,000} = 16.89\%$$

Proceeds received equal

| | |
|---|---|
| Face of loan | \$150,000 |
| Less interest | (19,500) |
| Compensating balance (10% × \$150,000) | (15,000) |
| Proceeds | \$115,500 |

Notice how the effective cost of the loan is significantly greater than the stated interest rate.

Long-term debt is normally provided through the sale of corporate bonds. The real cost of bonds is obtained by computing two types of yield: simple (face) yield and yield to maturity (effective interest rate). The first involves an easy approximation, but the second is more accurate. The nominal interest rate equals the interest paid on the face (maturity value) of the bond and is always stated on a per-annum basis. Bonds are generally issued in \$1,000 denominations and may be sold above face value (at a premium) or below (at a discount, termed original issue discount, or OID). A bond is sold at a discount when the interest rate is below the going market rate. In this case, the yield will be higher than the nominal interest rate. The opposite holds for bonds issued at a premium.

The issue price of a bond is the par (or face value) times the premium (or discount).

$$\text{Simple yield} = \frac{\text{Nominal interest}}{\text{Issue price of bond}}$$

$$\text{Yield to maturity} = \frac{\text{Nominal interest} + \dfrac{\text{Discount (or premium)}}{\text{Years}}}{\dfrac{\text{Issue price} + \text{Maturity value}}{2}}$$

**EXAMPLE OF LONG-TERM DEBT**

A company issues a \$400,000, 12 percent, 10-year bond for 97% of face value. Yield computations are as follows:

$$\text{Nominal annual payment} = 12\% \times \$400{,}000 = \$48{,}000$$

$$\text{Bond proceeds} = 97\% \times \$400{,}000 = \$388{,}000$$

$$\text{Bond discount} = 3\% \times \$400{,}000 = \$12{,}000$$

$$\text{Simple yield} = \frac{12\% \times \$400{,}000}{97\% \times \$400{,}000} = \frac{\$48{,}000}{\$388{,}000} = 12.4\%$$

$$\text{Yield to maturity} = \frac{\$48{,}000 + \dfrac{\$12{,}000}{10}}{\dfrac{\$388{,}000 + \$400{,}000}{2}} = \frac{\$48{,}000 + \$1{,}200}{\$394{,}000} = 12.5\%$$

Note that because the bonds were sold at a discount, the yield exceeds the nominal interest rate (12 percent). Bond interest is tax deductible to the corporation.

The actual cost of equity securities (stocks) comes in the form of dividends, which are not tax deductible to the corporation.

$$\text{Cost of common stock} = \frac{\text{Dividends per share}}{\text{Value per share}} + \text{Growth rate of dividends}$$

Here the value per share equals the market price per share minus flotation costs (that is, the cost of issuing securities, such as brokerage fees and printing costs). It should be noted that this valuation does not consider what the investor expects in market price appreciation. This expectation is based on the expected growth in earnings per share and the relative risk taking by purchasing the stock. The capital asset pricing model (CAPM) can be used to capture this impact.[2]

**EXAMPLE OF THE COST OF COMMON STOCK**

A company's dividend per share is \$10, net value is \$70 per share, and the dividend growth rate is 5 percent.

$$\text{Cost of the stock} = \frac{\$10}{\$70} + 0.05 = 19.3\%$$

To compute the weighted average cost of capital, we consider the percentage of the total capital that is being provided by each financing alternative. We then calculate the after-tax cost of each financing alternative. Finally, we weight these costs in proportion to their use.

**EXAMPLE OF CALCULATING THE WEIGHTED AVERAGE COST OF CAPITAL**
Consider a company that shows the following figures in its financial statements:

| | |
|---|---|
| Short-term bank loan (13%) | \$ 1 million |
| Bonds payable (16%) | \$ 4 million |
| Common stock (10%) | \$ 5 million |

For our example, assume that each of the percentages given above represents the cost of the source of capital. In addition to the above, we need to consider the tax rate of the firm because the interest paid on the bonds and on the sort-term loan is tax deductible. Assume a corporate tax rate of 40 percent.

| | PERCENT | AFTER-TAX COST | WEIGHTED AVERAGE COST |
|---|---|---|---|
| Short-term bank loan | 10% | 13% × 60% = 7.8% | .78% |
| Bonds payable | 40% | 16% × 60% = 9.6% | 3.84% |
| Common stock | 50% | 10% | 5% |
| Total | 100% | | 9.62% |

Keep in mind that in developing this section we have made many assumptions in these calculations. When these ideas are applied to a specific company, many of these assumptions may change. The basic concepts, though, are the same; keep in mind that the goal is to simply calculate the after-tax cost of the capital used by the company. We have shown the cost of capital for the entire company, though often only the capital employed for a specific project is used in the calculation.

## INTEREST RATE EFFECTS

There are two basic ways to account for the effects of interest accumulation. One is to compute the total amount created over the time period into the future as the *compound value.* The other is to remove the interest rate effect over time by reducing all future sums to present-day dollars, or the *present value.*

### Compound Value of a Single Amount

Albert Einstein was quoted as saying that compound interest is the eighth wonder of the world. After reviewing this section showing compound interest's dramatic growth effects over a long time, you might wish to propose a new government regulation: On the birth of a child, the parents must put, say, \$1,000 into a retirement fund for that child, available at age 65. This might reduce the pressure on Social Security and other state and federal pension plans. Although inflation would decrease the value significantly, there would still be a lot left over. At 14 percent return on investment, our \$1,000 would increase to \$500,000 after subtracting the \$4.5 million for inflation. That is still a 500-fold increase. (Many mutual funds today have long-term performances in excess of 14 percent per year.)

Spreadsheets and calculators make such computation easy. The box titled "Using a Spreadsheet" shows the most useful financial functions. However, many people still refer to tables for compound values. Using Appendix G, Table G.1 (compound sum of \$1), for example, we see that the value of \$1 at 10 percent interest after three years is \$1.331. Multiplying this figure by \$10 gives \$13.31.

### Compound Value of an Annuity

An *annuity* is the receipt of a constant sum each year for a specified number of years. Usually an annuity is received at the end of a period and does not earn interest during that period. Therefore, an annuity of \$10 for three years would bring in \$10 at the end of the

## USING A SPREADSHEET

We hope that you are all doing these calculations using a spreadsheet program. Even though the computer makes these calculations simple, it is important that you understand what the computer is actually doing. Further, you should check your calculations manually to make sure that you have the formulas set up correctly in your spreadsheet. There are many stories of the terrible consequences of making a wrong decision based on a spreadsheet with errors!

For your quick reference, the following are the financial functions you will find most useful. These are from the Microsoft Excel help screens.

*PV(rate, nper, pmt)*—Returns the present value of an investment. The present value is the total amount that a series of future payments is worth now. For example, when you borrow money, the loan amount is the present value to the lender. Rate is the interest rate per period. For example, if you obtain an automobile loan at a 10 percent annual interest rate and make monthly payments, your interest rate per month is 10%/12, or .83%. You would enter 10%/12, or .83%, or .0083, in the formula as the rate. Nper is the total number of payment periods in an annuity. For example, if you get a four-year car loan and make monthly payments, your loan has 4*12 (or 48) periods. You would enter 48 into the formula for nper. Pmt is the payment made each period and cannot change over the life of the annuity. Typically, this includes principal and interest but no other fees or taxes. For example, the monthly payment on a $10,000, four-year car loan at 12 percent is $263.33. You would enter 263.33 into the formula as pmt.

*FV(rate, nper, pmt)*—Returns the future value of an investment based on periodic, constant payment and a constant interest rate. Rate is the interest rate per period. Nper is the total number of payment periods in an annuity. Pmt is the payment made each period; it cannot change over the life of the annuity. Typically, pmt contains principal and interest but no other fees or taxes.

*NPV(rate, value1, value2, . . . )*—Returns the net present value of an investment based on a series of periodic cash flows and a discount rate. The net present value of an investment is today's value of a series of future payments (negative values) and income (positive values). Rate is the rate of discount over the length of one period. Value1, value2, . . . must be equally spaced in time and occur at the end of each period.

*IRR (values)*—Returns the internal rate of return for a series of cash flows represented by the numbers in values. (Values is defined below.) These cash flows do not have to be even, as they would be for an annuity. The internal rate of return is the interest rate received for an investment consisting of payments (negative values) and income (positive values) that occur at regular periods. Values is an array or a reference to cells that contain numbers for which you want to calculate the internal rate of return. Values must contain at least one positive value and one negative value to calculate the internal rate of return. IRR uses the order of values to interpret the order of cash flows. Be sure to enter your payment and income values in the sequence you want.

SOURCE: MICROSOFT EXCEL, HELP SCREEN FOR FINANCIAL FUNCTIONS.

first year (allowing the $10 to earn interest if invested for the remaining two years), $10 at the end of the second year (allowing the $10 to earn interest for the remaining one year), and $10 at the end of the third year (with no time to earn interest). If the annuity receipts were placed in a bank savings account at 5 percent interest, the total or compound value of the $10 at 5 percent for the three years would be

| YEAR | RECEIPT AT END OF YEAR | | COMPOUND INTEREST FACTOR $(1+i)^n$ | | VALUE AT END OF THIRD YEAR |
|---|---|---|---|---|---|
| 1 | $10.00 | × | $(1 + 0.05)^2$ | = | $11.02 |
| 2 | 10.00 | × | $(1 + 0.05)^1$ | = | 10.50 |
| 3 | 10.00 | × | $(1 + 0.50)^0$ | = | 10.00 |
| | | | | | $31.52 |

The general formula for finding the compound value of an annuity is

$$S_n = R[(1+i)^{n-1} + (1+i)^{n-2} + \cdots + (1+i)^1 + 1]$$

where

$S_n$ = Compound value of an annuity
$R$ = Periodic receipts in dollars
$n$ = Length of the annuity in years

Applying this formula to the preceding example, we get

$$S_n = R[(1+i)^2 + (1+i) + 1]$$
$$= \$10[(1+0.05)^2 + (1+0.05) + 1] = \$31.52$$

In Appendix G, Table G.2 lists the compound value factor of $1 for 5 percent after three years as 3.152. Multiplying this factor by $10 yields $31.52.

In a fashion similar to our previous retirement investment example, consider the beneficial effects of investing $2,000 each year, just starting at the age of 21. Assume investments in AAA-rated bonds are available today yielding 9 percent. From Table G.2 in Appendix G, after 30 years (at age 51) the investment is worth 136.3 times $2,000, or $272,600. Fourteen years later (at age 65) this would be worth $963,044 (using a hand calculator, because the table goes only to 30 years, and assuming the $2,000 is deposited at the end of each year)! But what 21-year-old thinks about retirement?

### Present Value of a Future Single Payment

Compound values are used to determine future value after a specific period has elapsed; present value (PV) procedures accomplish just the reverse. They are used to determine the current value of a sum or stream of receipts expected to be received in the future. Most investment decision techniques use present value concepts rather than compound values. Because decisions affecting the future are made in the present, it is better to convert future returns into their present value at the time the decision is being made. In this way, investment alternatives are placed in better perspective in terms of current dollars.

An example makes this more apparent. If a rich uncle offers to make you a gift of $100 today or $250 after 10 years, which should you choose? You must determine whether the $250 in 10 years will be worth more than the $100 now. Suppose that you base your decision on the rate of inflation in the economy and believe that inflation averages 10 percent per year. By deflating the $250, you can compare its relative purchasing power with $100 received today. Procedurally, this is accomplished by solving the compound formula for the present sum, $P$, where $V$ is the future amount of $250 in 10 years at 10 percent. The compound value formula is

$$V = P(1+i)^n$$

Dividing both sides by $(1 + i)^n$ gives

$$P = \frac{V}{(1+I)^n}$$
$$= \frac{250}{(1+0.10)^{10}} = \$96.39$$

This shows that, at a 10 percent inflation rate, $250 in 10 years will be worth $96.39 today. The rational choice, then, is to take the $100 now.

The use of tables is also standard practice in solving present value problems. With reference to Appendix G, Table G.3, the present value factor for $1 received 10 years hence is 0.386. Multiplying this factor by $250 yields $96.50.

### Present Value of an Annuity

The present value of an annuity is the value of an annual amount to be received over a future period expressed in terms of the present. To find the value of an annuity of $100 for three years at 10 percent, find the factor in the present value table that applies to 10 percent in *each* of the three years in which the amount is received and multiply each receipt by this factor. Then sum the resulting figures. Remember that annuities are usually received at the end of each period.

| Year | Amount Received at End of Year | | Present Value Factor at 10% | | Present Value |
|---|---|---|---|---|---|
| 1 | \$100 | × | 0.909 | = | \$ 90.90 |
| 2 | 100 | × | 0.826 | = | 82.60 |
| 3 | 100 | × | 0.751 | = | 75.10 |
| Total receipts | \$300 | | Total present value | = | \$248.60 |

The general formula used to derive the present value of an annuity is

$$A_n = R\left[\frac{1}{(1+i)} + \frac{1}{(1+i)^2} + \cdots + \frac{1}{(1+i)^n}\right]$$

where

$A_n$ = Present value of an annuity of $n$ years
$R$ = Periodic receipts
$n$ = Length of the annuity in years

Applying the formula to the preceding example gives

$$A_n = \$100\left[\frac{1}{(1+0.10)} + \frac{1}{(1+0.10)^2} + \frac{1}{(1+0.10)^3}\right]$$

$$= \$100(2.487) = \$248.70$$

In Appendix G, Table G.4 contains present values of an annuity for varying maturities. The present value factor for an annuity of \$1 for three years at 10 percent (from Appendix G, Table G.4) is 2.487. Given that our sum is \$100 rather than \$1, we multiply this factor by \$100 to arrive at \$248.70.

When the stream of future receipts is uneven, the present value of each annual receipt must be calculated. The present values of the receipts for all years are then summed to arrive at total present value. This process can sometimes be tedious, but it is unavoidable.

### Discounted Cash Flow

The term *discounted cash flow* refers to the total stream of payments that an asset will generate in the future discounted to the present time. This is simply present value analysis that includes all flows: single payments, annuities, and all others.

## METHODS OF RANKING INVESTMENTS

### Net Present Value

The net present value method is commonly used in business. With this method, decisions are based on the amount by which the present value of a projected income stream exceeds the cost of an investment.

A firm is considering two alternative investments. The first costs \$30,000 and the second, \$50,000. The expected yearly cash income streams are shown in this table:

| | Cash Inflow | |
|---|---|---|
| Year | Alternative A | Alternative B |
| 1 | \$10,000 | \$15,000 |
| 2 | 10,000 | 15,000 |
| 3 | 10,000 | 15,000 |
| 4 | 10,000 | 15,000 |
| 5 | 10,000 | 15,000 |

To choose between Alternatives A and B, find which has the highest net present value. Assume an 8 percent cost of capital.

| **ALTERNATIVE A** | | **ALTERNATIVE B** | |
|---|---|---|---|
| 3.993 (PV factor) × \$10,000 | = \$39,930 | 3.993 (PV factor) × \$15,000 | = \$59,895 |
| Less cost of investment | = 30,000 | Less cost of investment | = 50,000 |
| Net present value | = \$ 9,930 | Net present value | = \$ 9,895 |

Investment A is the better alternative. Its net present value exceeds that of Investment B by \$35 (\$9,930 − \$9,895 = \$35).

### Payback Period

The payback method ranks investments according to the time required for each investment to return earnings equal to the cost of the investment. The rationale is that the sooner the investment capital can be recovered, the sooner it can be reinvested in new revenue-producing projects. Thus, supposedly, a firm will be able to get the most benefit from its available investment funds.

Consider two alternatives requiring a \$1,000 investment each. The first will earn \$200 per year for six years; the second will earn \$300 per year for the first three years and \$100 per year for the next three years.

If the first alternative is selected, the initial investment of \$1,000 will be recovered at the end of the fifth year. The income produced by the second alternative will total \$1,000 after only four years. The second alternative will permit reinvestment of the full \$1,000 in new revenue-producing projects one year sooner than the first.

Though the payback method is declining in popularity as the sole measure in investment decisions, it is still frequently used in conjunction with other methods to indicate the time commitment of funds. The major problems with payback are that it does not consider income beyond the payback period and it ignores the time value of money. A method that ignores the time value of money must be considered questionable.

### Internal Rate of Return

The internal rate of return may be defined as the interest rate that equates the present value of an income stream with the cost of an investment. There is no procedure or formula that may be used directly to compute the internal rate of return—it must be found by interpolation or iterative calculation.

Suppose we wish to find the internal rate of return for an investment costing \$12,000 that will yield a cash inflow of \$4,000 per year for four years. We see that the present value factor sought is

$$\frac{\$12{,}000}{\$4{,}000} = 3.000$$

and we seek the interest rate that will provide this factor over a four-year period. The interest rate must lie between 12 and 14 percent because 3.000 lies between 3.037 and 2.914 (in the fourth row of Appendix G, Table G.4). Linear interpolation between these values, according to the equation

$$\begin{aligned} I &= 12 + (14 - 12)\frac{(3.037 - 3.000)}{(3.037 - 2.914)} \\ &= 12 + 0.602 = 12.602\% \end{aligned}$$

gives a good approximation to the actual internal rate of return.

When the income stream is discounted at 12.6 percent, the resulting present value closely approximates the cost of investment. Thus the internal rate of return for this investment is 12.6 percent. The cost of capital can be compared with the internal rate of return to determine the net rate of return on the investment. If, in this example, the cost of capital were 8 percent, the net rate of return on the investment would be 4.6 percent.

The net present value and internal rate of return methods involve procedures that are essentially the same. They differ in that the net present value method enables investment alternatives to be compared in terms of the dollar value in excess of cost, whereas the internal rate of return method permits comparison of rates of return on alternative investments. Moreover, the internal rate of return method occasionally encounters problems in calculation, as multiple rates frequently appear in the computation.

### Ranking Investments with Uneven Lives

When proposed investments have the same life expectancy, comparison among them, using the preceding methods, will give a reasonable picture of their relative value. When lives are unequal, however, there is the question of how to relate the two different time periods. Should replacements be considered the same as the original? Should productivity for the shorter-term unit that will be replaced earlier be considered higher? How should the cost of future units be estimated?

No estimate dealing with investments unforeseen at the time of decision can be expected to reflect a high degree of accuracy. Still, the problem must be dealt with, and some assumptions must be made in order to determine a ranking.

## SAMPLE PROBLEMS: INVESTMENT DECISIONS

### *EXAMPLE SB.1: AN EXPANSION DECISION*

William J. Wilson Ceramic Products, Inc., leases plant facilities in which firebrick is manufactured. Because of rising demand, Wilson could increase sales by investing in new equipment to expand output. The selling price of $10 per brick will remain unchanged if output and sales increase. Based on engineering and cost estimates, the accounting department provides management with the following cost estimates based on an annual increased output of 100,000 bricks:

| | |
|---|---|
| Cost of new equipment having an expected life of five years | $500,000 |
| Equipment installation cost | 20,000 |
| Expected salvage value | 0 |
| New operation's share of annual lease expense | 40,000 |
| Annual increase in utility expenses | 40,000 |
| Annual increase in labor costs | 160,000 |
| Annual additional cost for raw materials | 400,000 |

The sum-of-the-years'-digits method of depreciation will be used, and taxes are paid at a rate of 40 percent. Wilson's policy is not to invest capital in projects earning less than a 20 percent rate of return. Should the proposed expansion be undertaken?

### *SOLUTION*

Compute the cost of investment:

| | |
|---|---|
| Acquisition cost of equipment | $500,000 |
| Equipment installation costs | 20,000 |
| Total cost of investment | $520,000 |

Determine yearly cash flows throughout the life of the investment.

The lease expense is a sunk cost. It will be incurred whether or not the investment is made and is therefore irrelevant to the decision and should be disregarded. Annual production expenses to be considered are utility, labor, and raw materials. These total $600,000 per year.

Annual sales revenue is $10 × 100,000 units of output, which totals $1,000,000. Yearly income before depreciation and taxes is thus $1,000,000 gross revenue, less $600,000 expenses, or $400,000.

Next, determine the depreciation charges to be deducted from the $400,000 income each year using the SYD method (sum-of-years'-digits = 1 + 2 + 3 + 4 + 5 = 15):

| YEAR | PROPORTION OF $500,000 TO BE DEPRECIATED | | DEPRECIATION CHARGE |
|---|---|---|---|
| 1 | 5/15 × $500,000 | = | $166,667 |
| 2 | 4/15 × 500,000 | = | 133,333 |
| 3 | 3/15 × 500,000 | = | 100,000 |
| 4 | 2/15 × 500,000 | = | 66,667 |
| 5 | 1/15 × 500,000 | = | 33,333 |
| | Accumulated depreciation | | $500,000 |

Find each year's cash flow when taxes are 40 percent. Cash flow for only the first year is illustrated:

| | | |
|---|---|---|
| Earnings before depreciation and taxes | | $400,000 |
| Deduct: Taxes at 40% | $160,000 | |
| (40% × 400,000) Tax benefit of depreciation expense (0.4 × 166,667) | 66,667 | 93,333 |
| Cash flow (first year) | | $306,667 |

Determine the present value of the cash flow. Because Wilson demands at least a 20 percent rate of return on investments, multiply the cash flows by the 20 percent present value factor for each year. The factor for each respective year must be used because the cash flows are not an annuity.

| YEAR | PRESENT VALUE FACTOR | | CASH FLOW | | PRESENT VALUE |
|---|---|---|---|---|---|
| 1 | 0.833 | × | $306,667 | = | $255,454 |
| 2 | 0.694 | × | 293,333 | = | 203,573 |
| 3 | 0.579 | × | 280,000 | = | 162,120 |
| 4 | 0.482 | × | 266,667 | = | 128,533 |
| 5 | 0.402 | × | 253,334 | = | 101,840 |
| | Total present value of cash flows (discounted at 20%) | | | = | $851,520 |

Now find whether net present value is positive or negative:

| | |
|---|---|
| Total present value of cash flows | $851,520 |
| Total cost of investment | 520,000 |
| Net present value | $331,520 |

Net present value is positive when returns are discounted at 20 percent. Wilson will earn an amount in excess of 20 percent on the investment. The proposed expansion should be undertaken.

### *EXAMPLE SB.2: A REPLACEMENT DECISION*

For five years Bennie's Brewery has been using a machine that attaches labels to bottles. The machine was purchased for $4,000 and is being depreciated over 10 years to a $0 salvage value using straight-line depreciation. The machine can be sold now for $2,000. Bennie can buy a new labeling machine for $6,000 that will have a useful life of five years and cut labor costs by $1,200 annually. The old machine will require a major overhaul in the next few months at an estimated cost of $300. If purchased, the new machine will be depreciated over five years to a $500 salvage value using the straight-line method. The company will invest in any project earning more than the 12 percent cost of capital. The tax rate is 40 percent. Should Bennie's Brewery invest in the new machine?

## SOLUTION

Determine the cost of investment:

| | | |
|---|---|---|
| Price of the new machine | | $6,000 |
| Less: Sale of old machine | $2,000 | |
| Avoidable overhaul costs | 300 | 2,300 |
| Effective cost of investment | | $3,700 |

Determine the increase in cash flow resulting from investment in the new machine:

Yearly cost savings = $1,200

Differential depreciation

Annual depreciation on old machine:

$$\frac{\text{Cost} - \text{Salvage}}{\text{Expected life}} = \frac{\$4{,}000 - \$0}{10} = \$400$$

Annual depreciation on new machine:

$$\frac{\text{Cost} - \text{Salvage}}{\text{Expected life}} = \frac{\$6{,}000 - \$500}{5} = \$1{,}100$$

Differential depreciation = $1,100 − $400 = $700

Yearly net increase in cash flow into the firm:

| | | |
|---|---|---|
| Cost savings | | $1,200 |
| Deduct: Taxes at 40% | $480 | |
| Add: advantage of increase in depreciation (0.4 × $700) | 280 | 200 |
| Yearly increase in cash flow | | $1,000 |

Determine total present value of the investment:

The five-year cash flow of $1,000 per year is an annuity.

Discounted at 12 percent, the cost of capital, the present value is

3.605 × $1,000 = $3,605

The present value of the new machine, if sold at its salvage value of $500 at the end of the fifth year, is

0.567 × $500 = $284

Total present value of the expected cash flows is

$3,605 + $284 = $3,889

Determine whether net present value is positive:

| | |
|---|---|
| Total present value | $3,889 |
| Cost of investment | 3,700 |
| Net present value | $189 |

Bennie's Brewery should make the purchase because the investment will return slightly more than the cost of capital.

*Note:* The importance of depreciation has been shown in this example. The present value of the yearly cash flow resulting from operations is

(Cost savings − Taxes) × (Present value factor)

($1,200 − $480) × (3.605) = $2,596

This figure is $1,104 less than the $3,700 cost of the investment. Only a very large depreciation advantage makes this investment worthwhile. The total present value of the advantage is $1,009:

$$(\text{Tax rate} \times \text{Differential depreciation}) \times (\text{PV factor})$$

$$(0.4 \times \$700) \quad \times \quad (3.605) \quad = \$1{,}009$$

## EXAMPLE SB.3: A MAKE-OR-BUY DECISION

The Triple X Company manufactures and sells refrigerators. It makes some of the parts for the refrigerators and purchases others. The engineering department believes it might be possible to cut costs by manufacturing one of the parts currently being purchased for $8.25 each. The firm uses 100,000 of these parts each year. The accounting department compiles the following list of costs based on engineering estimates:

Fixed costs will increase by $50,000.

Labor costs will increase by $125,000.

Factory overhead, currently running $500,000 per year, may be expected to increase 12 percent.

Raw materials used to make the part will cost $600,000.

Given the preceding estimates, should Triple X make the part or continue to buy it?

## SOLUTION

Find the total cost incurred if the part were manufactured:

| | |
|---|---|
| Additional fixed costs | $ 50,000 |
| Additional labor costs | 125,000 |
| Raw materials cost | 600,000 |
| Additional overhead costs = 0.12 × $500,000 | 60,000 |
| Total cost to manufacturer | $835,000 |

Find the cost per unit to manufacture:

$$\frac{\$835{,}000}{100{,}000} = \$8.35 \text{ per unit}$$

Triple X should continue to buy the part. Manufacturing costs exceed the present cost to purchase by $0.10 per unit. ←

## SELECTED BIBLIOGRAPHY

Bodie, Z.; A. Kane; and A. Marcus. *Investments,* 3rd ed. Burr Ridge, IL: Richard D. Irwin, 1996.

Helfert, E. *Techniques of Financial Analysis: A Modern Approach,* 9th ed. Burr Ridge, IL: Irwin/McGraw-Hill, 1997.

Poterba, J. M., and L. H. Summers. "A CEO Survey of U.S. Companies' Time Horizons and Hurdle Rates." *Sloan Management Review,* Fall 1995, pp. 43–53.

## FOOTNOTES

1 T. Johnson and R. Kaplan, *Relevance Lost: The Rise and Fall of Management Accounting* (Boston: Harvard Business School Press, 1987), p. 188.

2 A description of capital asset pricing is included in many finance textbooks; see, for example, Z. Bodie, A. Kane, and A. Marcus, *Investments,* 3rd ed. (Burr Ridge, IL: Richard D. Irwin, 1996), pp. 236–65.

# OPERATIONS TECHNOLOGY

Vol. IV "Quality Product and Process Design at Detroit Diesel"

Much of the recent growth in productivity has come from the application of operations technology. In services this comes primarily from soft technology—information processing. In manufacturing it comes from a combination of soft and hard (machine) technologies. Given that most readers of this book have covered information technologies in services in MIS courses, our focus in this supplement is on manufacturing.

## TECHNOLOGIES IN MANUFACTURING

Although technological changes have occurred in almost every industry, many may be unique to an industry. For instance, a prestressed concrete block is a technological advance unique to the construction industry. Major developments in the design of automobiles will result in cars that are made from recyclable parts. (See Exhibit SC.1 for a description of the materials and process technologies that are being developed.)

Some technological advances in recent decades have had a significant, widespread impact on manufacturing firms in many industries. These advances, which are the topic of this section, can be categorized in two ways: hardware systems and software systems.

Hardware technologies have generally resulted in greater automation of processes; they perform labor-intensive tasks originally performed by humans. Examples of these major types of hardware technologies are numerically controlled machine tools, machining centers, industrial robots, automated materials handling systems, and flexible manufacturing systems. These are all computer-controlled devices that can be used in the manufacturing of

EXHIBIT SC.1

Automobile Recycling

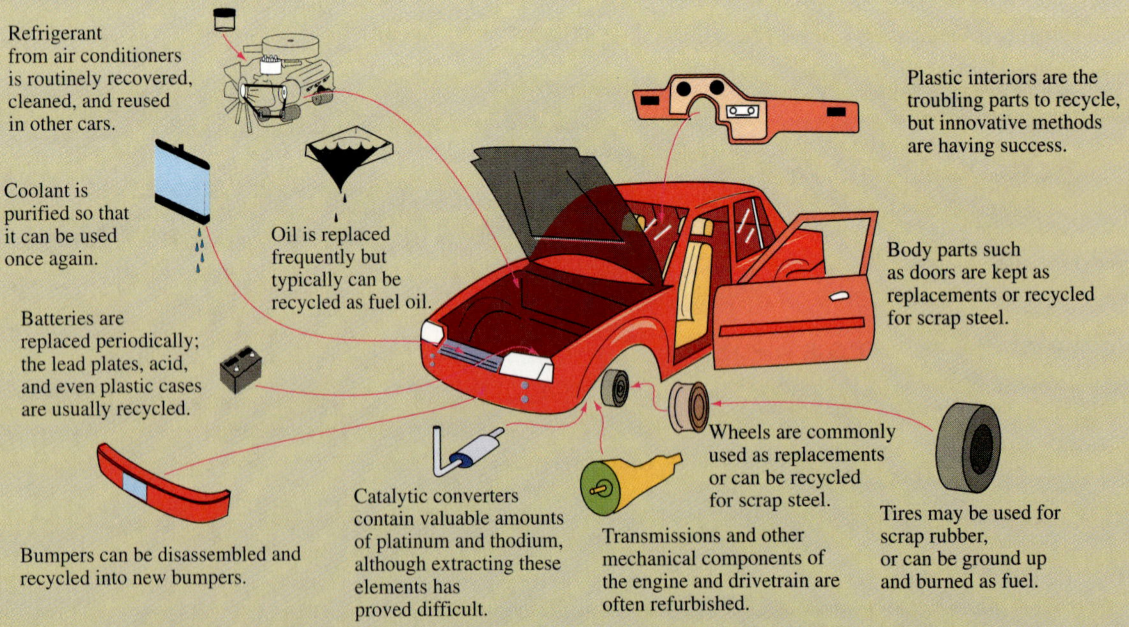


Automobile recycling is one of the most successful examples of reuse of manufactured product. About 75 percent of a typical car can be recycled in the form of refurbished parts, useful fluids and scrap materials. This process can, however, be taken further. New methods to separate and recycle plastic components, for example, offer the possibility of removing even more material from the waste stream and returning it to the manufacturing cycle.

SOURCE: R. A. FROSCH, "THE INDUSTRIAL ECOLOGY," *SCIENTIFIC AMERICAN*, SEPTEMBER 1995, P. 18.

products. Software-based technologies aid in the design of manufactured products and in the analysis and planning of manufacturing activities. These technologies include computer-aided design and automated manufacturing planning and control systems. Each of these technologies will be described in greater detail in the following sections.

## Hardware Systems

*Numerically controlled (NC) machines* are comprised of (1) a typical machine tool used to turn, drill, or grind different types of parts; and (2) a computer that controls the sequence of processes performed by the machine. NC machines were first adopted by U.S. aerospace firms in the 1960s, and they have since proliferated to many other industries. In more recent models, feedback control loops determine the position of the machine tooling during the work, constantly compare the actual location with the programmed location, and correct as needed. This is often called *adaptive control.*

*Machining centers* represent an increased level of automation and complexity relative to NC machines. Machining centers not only provide automatic control of a machine, they may also carry many tools that can be automatically changed depending on the tool required for each operation. In addition, a single machine may be equipped with a shuttle system so that a finished part can be unloaded and an unfinished part loaded while the machine is working on a part. To help you visualize a machining center, we have included a diagram in Exhibit SC.2.

*Industrial robots* are used as substitutes for workers for many repetitive manual activities and tasks that are dangerous, dirty, or dull. A robot is a programmable, multifunctional machine that may be equipped with an end effector. Examples of end effectors include a gripper to pick things up, or a tool such as a wrench, a welder, or a paint sprayer. Exhibit SC.3 examines the human motions a robot can reproduce. Advanced capabilities have been

EXHIBITS SC.2 & 3

### SC.2—The CNC Machining Center

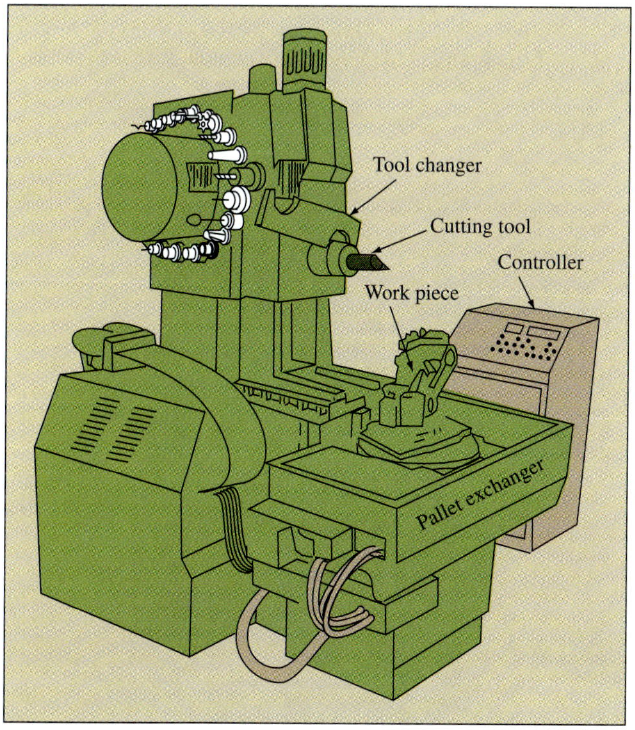


SOURCE: J. T. BLACK, *THE DESIGN OF THE FACTORY WITH A FUTURE* (NEW YORK: MCGRAW-HILL, 1991, P. 39, WITH PERMISSION OF THE MCGRAW-HILL COMPANIES.

### SC.3—Typical Robot Axes of Motion

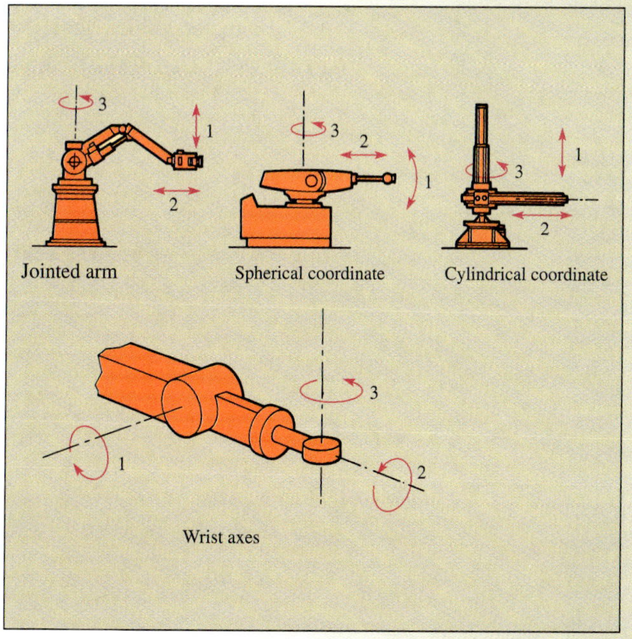


SOURCE: L. V. OTTINGER, "ROBOTICS FOR THE IE: TERMINOLOGY, TYPES OF ROBOTS," *INDUSTRIAL ENGINEERING*, NOVEMBER 1981, P. 30.

designed into robots to allow vision, tactile sensing, and hand-to-hand coordination. In addition, some models can be "taught" a sequence of motions in a three-dimensional pattern. As a worker moves the end of the robot arm through the required motions, the robot records this pattern in its memory and repeats it on command. As shown in the box "Formula for Evaluating a Robot Investment," robots are often justified based on labor savings.

*Automated materials handing (AMH) systems* improve efficiency of transportation, storage, and retrieval of materials. Examples are computerized conveyors, and automated storage and retrieval systems (AS/RS) in which computers direct automatic loaders to pick and place items. Automated guided vehicle (AGV) systems use embedded floor wires to direct driverless vehicles to various locations in the plant. Benefits of AMH systems include quicker material

## Formula for Evaluating a Robot Investment

Many companies use the following modification of the basic payback formula in deciding if a robot should be purchased:

$$P = \frac{I}{L - E + q(L + Z)}$$

where

$P$ = Payback period in years
$I$ = Total capital investment required in robot and accessories
$L$ = Annual labor costs replaced by the robot (wage and benefit costs per worker times the number of shifts per day)
$E$ = Annual maintenance cost for the robot
$q$ = Fractional speedup (or slowdown) factor
$Z$ = Annual depreciation

Example:

$I$ = \$50,000
$L$ = \$60,000 (two workers × \$20,000 each working one of two shifts; overhead is \$10,000 each)
$E$ = \$9,600 (\$2/hour × 4,800 hours/year)
$q$ = 1.5 (robot works 150 percent as fast as a worker)
$Z$ = \$10,000

then

$$P = \frac{\$50{,}000}{\$60{,}000 - \$9{,}600 + 1.5(\$60{,}000 + \$10{,}000)}$$

$$= 1/3 \text{ year.}$$

movement, lower inventories and storage space, reduced product damage, and higher labor productivity.

These individual pieces of automation can be combined to form *manufacturing cells* or even complete *flexible manufacturing systems (FMS).* A manufacturing cell might consist of a robot and a machining center. The robot could be programmed to automatically insert and remove parts from the machining center, thus allowing unattended operation. An FMS is a totally automated manufacturing system that consists of machining centers with automated loading and unloading of parts, an automated guided vehicle system for moving parts between machines, and other automated elements to allow unattended production of parts. In an FMS, a comprehensive computer control system is used to run the entire system.

A good example of an FMS is the Cincinnati Milacron facility in Mt. Orab, Ohio, which has been in operation for over 15 years. Exhibit SC.4 is a layout of this FMS. In this system, parts are loaded onto standardized fixtures (these are called "risers"), which are mounted on pallets that can be moved by the AGVs. Workers load and unload tools and parts onto the standardized fixtures at the workstations shown on the right side of the diagram. Most of this loading and unloading is done during a single shift. The system can operate virtually unattended for the other two shifts each day.

Exhibit SC.4

The Cincinnati Milacron Flexible Manufacturing System

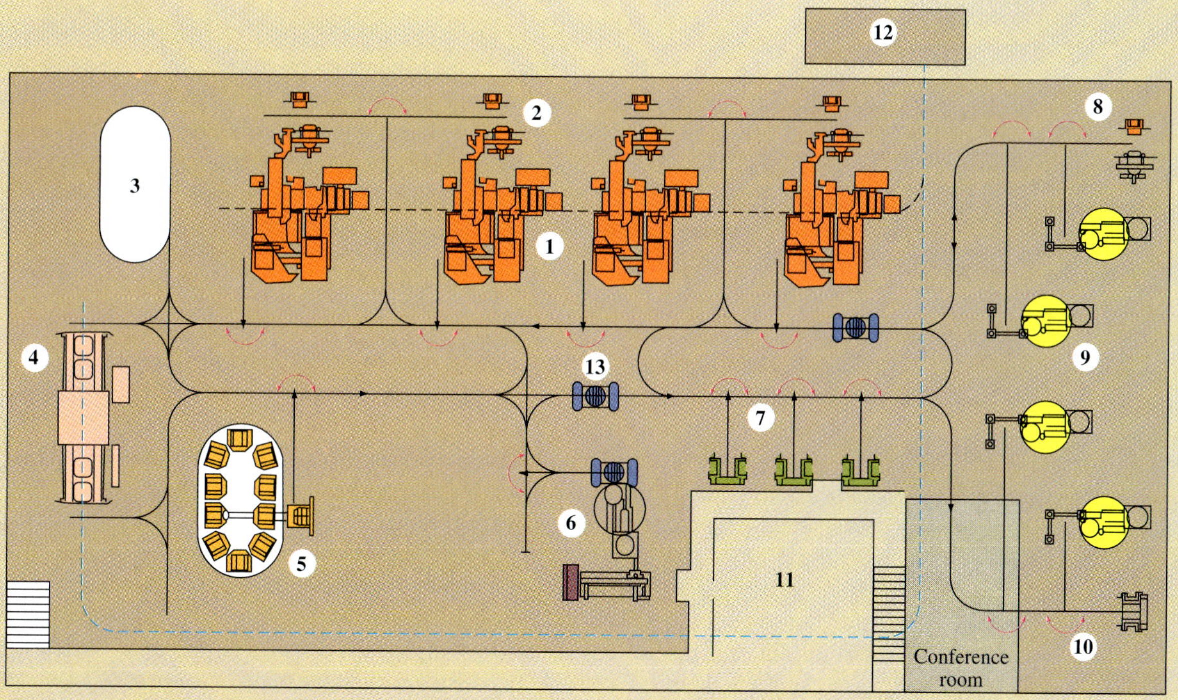


**Key:**

1 Four Milacron T-30 CNC Machining Centers.
2 Four tool interchange stations, one per machine, for tool storage chain delivery via computer-controlled cart.
3 Cart maintenance station. Coolant monitoring and maintenance area.
4 Parts wash station, automatic handling.
5 Automatic Workchanger (10 pallets) for online pallet queue.
6 One inspection module—horizontal type coordinate measuring machine.
7 Three queue stations for tool delivery chains.
8 Tool delivery chain load/unload stations.
9 Four part load/unload stations.
10 Pallet/fixture build station.
11 Control center, computer room (elevated).
12 Centralized chip/coolant collection/recovery system (---flume path).
13 Three computer-controlled carts, with wire-guided path.
Cart turnaround station (up to 360° around its own axis)

Source: Tour brochure from the plant.

ONE OF THE FOUR LARGE MACHINING CENTERS (SEE EXHIBIT SC.4) THAT ARE PART OF THE FLEXIBLE MANUFACTURING SYSTEMS AT CINCINNATI MILACRON'S MT. ORAB, OHIO, PLANT.

Within the system there are areas for the storage of tools (Area 7) and for parts (Area 5). This system is designed to machine large castings used in the production of the machine tools made by Cincinnati Milacron. The machining is done by the four CNC machining centers (Area 1). When the machining has been completed on a part, it is sent to the parts washing station (Area 4), where it is cleaned. The part is then sent to the automated inspection station (Area 6) for a quality check. The system is capable of producing hundreds of different parts.

### Software Systems

*Computer-aided design (CAD)* is an approach to product and process design that utilizes the power of the computer. CAD covers several automated technologies, such as *computer graphics* to examine the visual characteristics of a product, and *computer-aided engineering* (CAE) to evaluate its engineering characteristics. Rubbermaid used CAD to refine dimensions of its ToteWheels to meet airline requirements for checked baggage. CAD also includes technologies associated with the manufacturing process design, referred to as *computer-aided process planning (CAPP).* CAPP is used to design the computer part programs that serve as instructions to computer-controlled machine tools, and to design the programs used to sequence parts through the machine centers and other processes (such as the washing and inspection) needed to complete the part. These programs are referred to as *process plans.* Sophisticated CAD systems are also able to do on-screen tests, replacing the early phases of prototype testing and modification.

CAD has been used to design everything from computer chips to potato chips. Frito-Lay, for example, used CAD to design its O'Grady's double-density, ruffled potato chip. The problem in designing such a chip is that if it is cut improperly, it may be burned on the outside and soggy on the inside, be too brittle (and shatter when placed in the bag), or display other characteristics that make it unworthy for, say, a guacamole dip. However, through the use of CAD, the proper angle and number of ruffles were determined mathematically; the O'Grady's model passed its stress test in the infamous Frito-Lay "crusher" and made it to your grocer's shelf.

CAD is now being used to custom design swimsuits. Measurements of the wearer are fed into the CAD program, along with the style of suit desired. Working with the customer, the designer modifies the suit design as it appears on a human-form drawing on the computer screen. Once the design is decided upon, the computer prints out a pattern, and the suit is cut and sewn on the spot.

*Automated manufacturing planning and control systems (MP&CS)* are simply computer-based information systems that help plan, schedule, and monitor a manufacturing operation. They obtain information from the factory floor continuously about work status, material arrivals, and so on, and they release production and purchase orders. Sophisticated manufacturing and planning control systems include order-entry processing, shop-floor control, purchasing, and cost accounting.

Vol. I "Computer Integrated Manufacturing"

## COMPUTER-INTEGRATED MANUFACTURING (CIM)

All of these automation technologies are brought together under *computer-integrated manufacturing (CIM).* CIM is the automated version of the manufacturing process, where the three major manufacturing functions—product and process design, planning and control, and the manufacturing process itself—are replaced by the automated technologies just described. Further, the traditional integration mechanisms of oral and written communication are replaced by computer technology. Such highly automated and integrated manufacturing also goes under other names: *total factory automation* and the *factory of the future.* The Breakthrough Box "Custom Manufacturing" describes what manufacturing might be like in the future.

All of the CIM technologies are tied together using a network and integrated database. For instance, data integration allows CAD systems to be linked to *computer-aided manufacturing (CAM),* which consists of numerical-control parts programs; and the manufacturing planning and control system can be linked to the automated material handling systems to facilitate parts pick list generation. Thus, in a fully integrated system, the areas of design, testing, fabrication, assembly, inspection, and material handling are not only automated but also integrated with each other and with the manufacturing planning and scheduling function.

## EVALUATION OF TECHNOLOGY INVESTMENTS

Modern technologies such as flexible manufacturing systems or computerized order processing systems represent large capital investments. Hence, a firm has to carefully assess its financial and strategic benefits from a technology before acquiring it. Evaluating such investments is especially hard because the purpose of acquiring new technologies is not just to reduce labor costs but also to increase product quality and variety, to shorten production lead times, and to increase the flexibility of an operation. Some of these benefits are intangible relative to labor cost reduction, so justification becomes difficult. Further, rapid technological change renders new equipment obsolete in just a few years, making the cost–benefit evaluation more complex.

But never assume that new automation technologies are always cost-effective. Even when there is no uncertainty about the benefits of automation, it may not be worthwhile to adopt it. For instance, many analysts predicted that integrated CAD/CAM systems would be the answer to all manufacturing problems. But a number of companies investing in such systems lost money in the process. The idea was to take a lot of skilled labor out of the process of tooling up for new or redesigned products and to speed up the process. However, it can take less time to mill complex, low-volume parts than to program the milling machine, and programmer time is more expensive than the milling operator time. Also, it may not always be easy to transfer all the expert knowledge and experience that a milling operator has gained over the years into a computer program. Only recently has CAD/CAM integration software become available that can be cost-effective even in high-variety, low-volume manufacturing environments.

# BREAKTHROUGH

## Custom Manufacturing

Where can a cross-country bicyclist find a spare derailleur gear for an Italian bicycle when it breaks down in a small town in Nevada? Ten years or so from now, the answer may reside on the floppy disk carried in the rider's backpack. In coming decades, a spare part for a bicycle, automobile, or an array of other consumer goods may be simply "printed" from a computer design file at the corner factory, the futuristic equivalent of the all-night copy shop.

In the case of the gear, a machine tool might receive from a file on the disk a geometric description of the broken part. The program could then tell the tool how to deposit a thin layer of structural material by spraying droplets of liquid metal or by directing the energy of a laser onto a bed of metal powder. Subsequent layers deposited in this manner would fuse together, gradually building up a complete derailleur gear.

This approach to manufacturing has its beginnings in a suite of technologies collectively known as *rapid prototyping*. Today, stereolithography, shape deposition, laser sintering, and other related technologies can construct full-scale models for testing designs, and they can help build a tool for making a part. In years to come, improvements to such processes—and an expected decline in equipment costs—may allow them to be used to manufacture finished parts directly.

As they mature, these techniques may also introduce an unprecedented degree of product customization—a machine that could make a bicycle gear one day might make an automobile carburetor the next. This ability to reduce information about an individual's needs to a series of printable computer files is part of a bigger shift away from mass production of a standardized product, an approach pioneered by auto magnate Henry Ford. Postindustrial manufacturing is evolving toward an era of mass customization: production of substantial quantities of personalized goods.

Customized fabrication, however, would require more than a trip to the corner factory. Manufacturers need to make more than just the odd bicycle gear. For large-scale fabrication, communications networks may link suppliers to an automobile or blue-jeans maker so that they can fill orders speedily. Networks may also connect customers and factories more closely. A postmillennial Gap store might be equipped with optical scanners that take waist, hip, length, and other measurements; send them over a network; and have the custom-tailored pants delivered within a matter of days. Clothing stores have begun to experiment with such tailoring.

SOURCE: EDITORS, "CUSTOM MANUFACTURING," *SCIENTIFIC AMERICAN*, SEPTEMBER 1995, PP. 160–61. REPRINTED WITH PERMISSION. 

# BENEFITS OF TECHNOLOGY INVESTMENTS

The typical benefits from adopting new manufacturing technologies are both tangible and intangible. The tangible benefits can be used in traditional modes of fincancial analysis, such as discounted cash flow, to make sound investment decisions. Specific benefits can be summarized as follows:

### COST REDUCTION

**Labor costs** Replacing people with robots, or enabling fewer workers to run semi-automatic equipment.

**Material costs** Using existing materials more efficiently, or enabling the use of high-tolerance materials.

**Inventory costs** Fast changeover equipment allowing for JIT inventory management.

**Quality costs** Automated inspection and reduced variation in product output.

**Maintenance costs** Self-adjusting equipment.

### OTHER BENEFITS

**Increased product variety** Scope economies due to flexible manufacturing systems.

**Improved product features** Ability to make things that could not be made by hand (e.g., microprocessors).

**Shorter cycle times** Faster setups and change-overs.

**Greater product output**

## Risks in Adopting New Technologies

Although there may be many benefits in acquiring new technologies, several types of risk accompany the acquisition of new technologies. These risks have to be evaluated and traded off against the benefits before the technologies are adopted. Some of these risks are described next.

### TECHNOLOGICAL RISKS

An early adopter of a new technology has the benefit of being ahead of the competition, but he or she also runs the risk of acquiring an untested technology whose problems could disrupt the firm's operations. There is also the risk of obsolescence, especially with electronics-based technologies where change is rapid and when the fixed cost of acquiring new technologies or the cost of upgrades is high. Also, alternative technologies may become more cost-effective in the future, negating the benefits of a technology today.

### OPERATIONAL RISKS

There could also be risks in applying a new technology to a firm's operations. Installation of a new technology generally results in significant disruptions, at least in the short run, in the form of plantwide reorganization, retraining, and so on. Further risks are due to the delays and errors introduced in the production process and the uncertain and sudden demands on various resources.

### ORGANIZATIONAL RISKS

Firms may lack the organizational culture and top management commitment required to absorb the short-term disruptions and uncertainties associated with adopting a new technology. In such organizations, there is a risk that the firm's employees or managers may quickly abandon the technology when there are short-term failures or will avoid major changes by simply automating the firm's old, inefficient process and therefore not obtain the benefits of the new technology.

### ENVIRONMENTAL OR MARKET RISKS

In many cases, a firm may invest in a particular technology only to discover a few years later that changes in some environmental or market factors make the investment worthless. For instance, in environmental issues auto firms have been reluctant to invest in technology for making electric cars because they are uncertain about future emission standards of state and federal governments, the potential for decreasing emissions from gasoline-based cars, and the potential for significant improvements in battery technology. Typical examples of market risks are fluctuations in currency exchange rates and interest rates.

## CONCLUSION

Technology has played the dominant role in the productivity growth of most nations and has provided the competitive edge to firms that have adopted it early and implemented it successfully. Although each of the manufacturing and information technologies described here is a powerful tool by itself and can be adopted separately, their benefits grow exponentially when they are integrated with each other. This is particularly the case with CIM technologies.

With more modern technologies, the benefits are not entirely tangible and many benefits may be realized only on a long-term basis. Thus, typical cost accounting methods and standard financial analysis may not adequately capture all the potential benefits of technologies such as CIM. Hence, we must take into account the strategic benefits in evaluating such investments. Further, because capital costs for many modern technologies are substantial, the various risks associated with such investments have to be carefully assessed.

Implementing flexible manufacturing systems or complex decision support systems requires a significant commitment for most firms. Such investments may even be beyond the reach of small to medium-sized firms. However, as technologies continue to improve and are adopted more widely, their costs may decline and place them within the reach of smaller firms. Given the complex, integrative nature of these technologies, the total commitment of top management and all employees is critical for the successful implementation of these technologies.

## REVIEW AND DISCUSSION QUESTIONS

1. Do robots have to be trained? Explain.
2. How does the axiom used in industrial selling, "You don't sell the product, you sell the company," pertain to manufacturing technology?
3. List three analytical tools (other than financial analysis) covered elsewhere in the book that can be used to evaluate technological alternatives.
4. The Belleville, Ontario, Canada, subsidiary of Atlanta-based Interface Inc., one of the world's largest makers of commercial flooring, credits much of its profitability to "green manufacturing" or "eco-efficiency." What do you believe these terms mean, eh? And how could such practices lead to cost reduction?
5. Give two examples each of recent process and product technology innovations.
6. What is the difference between an NC machine and a machining center?
7. The major auto companies are planning to invest millions of dollars on developing new product and process technologies required to make electric cars. Describe briefly why they are investing in these technologies. Discuss the potential benefits and risks involved in these investments.

## SELECTED BIBLIOGRAPHY


Black, J. T. *The Design of the Factory with a Future.* New York: McGraw-Hill, 1991.

Busby, J. S. *The Value of Advanced Manufacturing Technology.* Oxford, England: Butterworth-Heinemann, 1992.

Chang, T.; R. A. Wysk; and H. Wang. *Computer-Aided Manufacturing.* Upper Saddle Creck, NJ: Prentice Hall, 1997.

Cohen, M., and U. Apte. *Manufacturing Automation.* Burr Ridge, IL: Irwin/McGraw-Hill, 1997.

Flaig, L. S. *Integrative Manufacturing: Transforming the Organization through People, Process, and Technology.* Burr Ridge, IL: Irwin Professional Publishing, 1993.

Gaynor, G. H. *Achieving the Competitive Edge through Integrated Technology Management.* New York: McGraw-Hill, 1991.

Melnyk, S. A., and R. Narasimhan. *Computer Integrated Manufacturing.* Burr Ridge, IL: Irwin Professional Publishing, 1992.

Negroponte, N. *Being Digital.* New York: Vantage Books, 1995.

Tidd, J. *Flexible Manufacturing Technologies and International Competitiveness.* London: Pinter, 1991.

# ANSWERS TO SELECTED PROBLEMS

## Chapter 2

1 Productivity (hours)
  Deluxe 0.20
  Limited 0.20
 Productivity (dollars)
  Deluxe 133.33
  Limited 135.71

## Technical Note 2

3 *LR* labor, 80%
 *LR* parts, 90%
 Labor = 11,556 hours
 Parts = $330,876
7 4,710 hours
11 *a.* 3rd = 35.1 hours
 *b.* Average = 7.9 hours each; well worth it

## Chapter 3

3 *b.* A-C-F-G-I and A-D-F-G-I
 *c.* C: 2 weeks
  D: 2 weeks
  G: 2 weeks
 *d.* Three paths: A-B-E-I; A-C-F-G-I; and A-D-F-G-I; 14 weeks
6 *a.* Critical path is A-E-G-C-D
 *b.* 26 weeks
 *c.* No difference in completion date
8 *a.* Critical path is A-C-D-F-G
 *b.*

| Day | Cost | Activity |
|---|---|---|
| First | $1,000 | A |
| Second | 1,200 | C |
| Third | 1,500 | D (or F) |
| Fourth | 1,500 | F (or D) |
| | $5,200 | |

## Chapter 4

1 Traditional method 20 min. setup + 10 × 2 = 40 min. total scan/retrieve system. 1 min. setup + 10 × 5 = 51 min. total. Traditional method is best.
3 *a.* Market can be served only 3 gals/hr. In 50 hours bathtub will overflow.

## Technical Note 4

3 *a.* 1.35 minutes
 *b.* 1.51 minutes
 *c.* ST = 1.53 minutes. The worker would not make the bonus.
7 *a.* NT = .9286 minute/part
 *b.* ST = 1.0679 minutes/part
 *c.* Daily output = 449.50
  Day's wages = $44.49

## Chapter 5

5 *a.* 5,600 components
 *b.* 8,000; drilling operation

*c.* 9,600; final assembly operation
*d.* \$1.81, \$1.79
9 9,500 miles

## Technical Note 5

3 *b.* 120 seconds
*d.* 87.5%
9 *a.* 33.6 seconds
*b.* 3.51 therefore 4 workstations
*d.* AB, DF, C, EG, H
*e.* Efficiency = 70.2%
*f.* Reduce cycle time to 32 seconds and work $6\frac{2}{3}$ minutes overtime
g. 1.89 hours overtime; may be better to rebalance

## Technical Note 6

5 $\bar{t}_s = 4.125$ minutes
$\bar{n}_l = 4.05$ cars
$\bar{n}_s = 4.95$ car
9 *a.* $L = .22$ waiting
*b.* $W = .466$ hours
*c.* $D = .362$
10 *a.* 2 people
*b.* 6 minutes
*c.* .2964
*d.* 67%
*e.* .03375 hour
17 *a.* 0.833
*b.* 5 documents
*c.* 0.2 hour
*d.* 0.4822
*e.* $\bar{n}_1 =$ tends to infinity

## Technical Note 7

1 *a.* Not inspecting cost = \$20/hr. Cost to inspect = \$9/hr. Therefore, inspect.
*b.* \$.18 each
*c.* \$.22 per unit
6 $\bar{\bar{X}} = 999.1$
$UCL = 1014.965$
$LCL = 983.235$
$\bar{R} = 21.733$
$UCL = 49.551$
$LCL = 0$
Process is in control
9 *a.* $n = 31.3$ (round sample size to 32)
*b.* Random sample 32; reject if more than 8 are defective.
12 $X = .500$
$UCL = .523$
$LCL = .477$
$R = .040$
$UCL = .084$
$LCL = .000$
Process is in control

## Chapter 8

1 2 lbs (\$8,854.90), 3 lbs (\$10,154.30)
4 lbs (\$11,402.60), 5 lbs (\$12,738.50)

6 lbs ($15,337.30), 7 lbs ($15,899.40)
8 lbs ($16,563.70), 9 lbs ($17,147.70)

## Chapter 9

3 No. Must consider demand in fourth year.
5 Expected NPV—Small
$4.8 million
Expected NPV—Large
$2.6 million

## Technical Note 9

1 $C_X = 176.7$
$C_Y = 241.5$
2 $C_X = 374$
$C_Y = 357$

## Chapter 10

1 5 kanban card sets

## Chapter 11

3 *a.* February 84
March 86
April 90
May 88
June 84
*b.* MAD = 15

7

| QUARTER | FORECAST |
|---|---|
| 9 | 232 |
| 10 | 281 |
| 11 | 239 |
| 12 | 231 |

11 *a.* April to September = 130, 150, 160, 170, 160, 150
*b.* April to September = 136, 146, 150, 159, 153, 146
*c.* Exponential smoothing performed better.
15 MAD = 104
TS = 3.1
The high TS value indicates the model is unacceptable.
19 *a.* MAD = 90
TS = −1.67
*b.* Model okay since tracking is −1.67

## Chapter 12

3 Total cost = $413,600
6 Total cost = $413,750

## Chapter 13

3 $q = 713$
6 *a.* $Q = 1{,}225$
$R = 824$
*b.* $q = 390 -$ Inventory on hand
10 *a.* $Q = 89.44$
*b.* $223.61
*c.* $223.61

13 *a.* A (4, 13, 18);
B (2, 5, 8, 10, 11, 14, 16);
C (remainder)
*b.* Classify as A.

16 $q = 691$

25 729 hamburgers

26 5,000 pounds

## Chapter 14

3

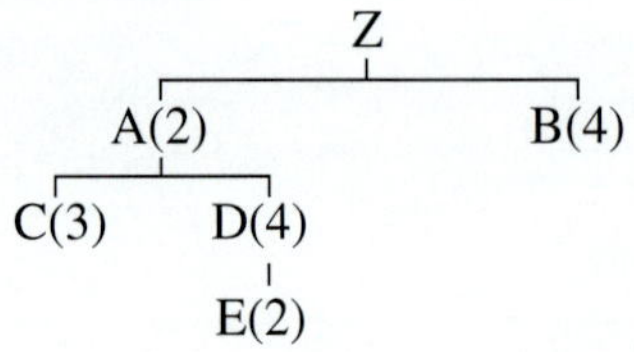


10 Least total cost method: Order 250 units in Period 1 for Periods 1–8;
Least unit cost method: Order 450 units in Period 1 for Periods 1–9.

13 *c.* .A
- .B(2)
  - .E(4)
  - .F(3)
- .C(3)
  - .D(3)
  - .H(2)
    - .E(5)
    - .G(2)
- .D(1)

*d.*

| | |
|---|---|
| Level 0 | 100 units of A |
| Level 1 | 200 units of B |
| | 300 units of C |
| Level 2 | 600 units of F |
| | 600 units of H |
| | 1000 units of D |
| Level 3 | 3800 units of E |
| | 1200 units of G |

## Chapter 15

3 Job order: 5, 6, 7, 3, 1, 2, 4

6 A to 3, B to 1, C to 4, D to 2; cost = $17,000

7 Critical ratio schedule: 5, 3, 2, 4, 1
*Earliest due date,* job priority: 2, 5, 3, 4, 1
*Shortest processing time* (including delay time): 2, 1, 4, 3, 5

9 E, A, B, D, C

14 C, B, D, F, E, A

## Technical Note 15

2 Average customer waiting time = 1/6 minute
Average teller idle time = 4/6 minute

7 *a.*

| Condition 1 | Condition 2 |
|---|---|
| (1) Idle 18 min. | 76 + 134 = 210 min. |
| (2) Delay 87 min. | 0 min. |

*b.*

| Condition 1 | Condition 2 |
|---|---|
| Cost of repairperson | |
| $ 38.80 | $ 77.20 |

Cost of machine down

| | |
|---|---|
| 175.33 | \$117.33 |
| \$214.13 | \$194.53 (Total Cost) |

Lowest cost is Condition 2.

11 One car bypasses.

## Chapter 17

1 Case I: X used = 933.3 hours
Y used = 700 hours
Case II: Y = 700 hours
X = 933.3 hours
Case III: X = 933.3 hours
Y = 700 hours
Case IV: X = 933.3 hours
Y = 700 hours
Otherwise:
Case I: No problem
Case II: Excess WIP
Case III: Excess spare parts
Case IV: Excess finished goods

8 *a.* Machine B is the constraint.
*b.* All of M; as many N as possible
*c.* \$600 (100 M and 30 N)

## Supplement A

2 Optimal combination is $B = 10$, and $A = 15$, and $Z = 70$.

4 *a.* $600A + 900B \leq 3{,}600$
$600A + 900B \geq 1{,}800$
$200A + 700B \leq 1{,}400$
$400A + 100B \geq 400$
$A \leq 2$
Minimize $.75A + .15B$
*b.* $A = 0.54$
$B = 1.85$
Obj = 0.68

APPENDIX B

# UNIFORMLY DISTRIBUTED RANDOM DIGITS

| | | | | | | | | |
|---|---|---|---|---|---|---|---|---|
| 56970 | 10799 | 52098 | 04184 | 54967 | 72938 | 50834 | 23777 | 08392 |
| 83125 | 85077 | 60490 | 44369 | 66130 | 72936 | 69848 | 59973 | 08144 |
| 55503 | 21383 | 02464 | 26141 | 68779 | 66388 | 75242 | 82690 | 74099 |
| 47019 | 06683 | 33203 | 29603 | 54553 | 25971 | 69573 | 83854 | 24715 |
| 84828 | 61152 | 79526 | 29554 | 84580 | 37859 | 28504 | 61980 | 34997 |
| 08021 | 31331 | 79227 | 05748 | 51276 | 57143 | 31926 | 00915 | 45821 |
| 36458 | 28285 | 30424 | 98420 | 72925 | 40729 | 22337 | 48293 | 86847 |
| 05752 | 96045 | 36847 | 87729 | 81679 | 59126 | 59437 | 33225 | 31280 |
| 26768 | 02513 | 58454 | 56958 | 20575 | 76746 | 40878 | 06846 | 32828 |
| 42613 | 72456 | 43030 | 58085 | 06766 | 60227 | 96414 | 32671 | 45587 |
| 95457 | 12176 | 65482 | 25596 | 02678 | 54592 | 63607 | 82096 | 21913 |
| 95276 | 67524 | 63564 | 95958 | 39750 | 64379 | 46059 | 51666 | 10433 |
| 66954 | 53574 | 64776 | 92345 | 95110 | 59448 | 77249 | 54044 | 67942 |
| 17457 | 44151 | 14113 | 02462 | 02798 | 54977 | 48340 | 66738 | 60184 |
| 03704 | 23322 | 83214 | 59337 | 01695 | 60666 | 97410 | 55064 | 17427 |
| 21538 | 16997 | 33210 | 60337 | 27976 | 70661 | 08250 | 69509 | 60264 |
| 57178 | 16730 | 08310 | 70348 | 11317 | 71623 | 55510 | 64750 | 87759 |
| 31048 | 40058 | 94953 | 55866 | 96283 | 40620 | 52087 | 80817 | 74533 |
| 69799 | 83300 | 16498 | 80733 | 96422 | 58078 | 99643 | 39847 | 96884 |
| 90595 | 65017 | 59231 | 17772 | 67831 | 33317 | 00520 | 90401 | 41700 |
| 33570 | 34761 | 08039 | 78784 | 09977 | 29398 | 93896 | 78227 | 90110 |
| 15340 | 82760 | 57477 | 13898 | 48431 | 72936 | 78160 | 87240 | 52710 |
| 64079 | 07733 | 36512 | 56186 | 99098 | 48850 | 72527 | 08486 | 10951 |
| 63491 | 84886 | 67118 | 62063 | 74958 | 20946 | 28147 | 39338 | 32109 |
| 92003 | 76568 | 41034 | 28260 | 79708 | 00770 | 88643 | 21188 | 01850 |
| 52360 | 46658 | 66511 | 04172 | 73085 | 11795 | 52594 | 13287 | 82531 |
| 74622 | 12142 | 68355 | 65635 | 21828 | 39539 | 18988 | 53609 | 04001 |
| 04157 | 50070 | 61343 | 64315 | 70836 | 82857 | 35335 | 87900 | 36194 |
| 86003 | 60070 | 66241 | 32836 | 27573 | 11479 | 94114 | 81641 | 00496 |
| 41208 | 80187 | 20351 | 09630 | 84668 | 42486 | 71303 | 19512 | 50277 |
| 06433 | 80674 | 24520 | 18222 | 10610 | 05794 | 37515 | 48619 | 62866 |
| 39298 | 47829 | 72648 | 37414 | 75755 | 04717 | 29899 | 78817 | 03509 |
| 89884 | 59651 | 67533 | 68123 | 17730 | 95862 | 08034 | 19473 | 63971 |
| 61512 | 32155 | 51906 | 61662 | 64430 | 16688 | 37275 | 51262 | 11569 |
| 99653 | 47635 | 12506 | 88535 | 36553 | 23757 | 34209 | 55803 | 96275 |
| 95913 | 11085 | 13772 | 76638 | 48423 | 25018 | 99041 | 77529 | 81360 |
| 55804 | 44004 | 13122 | 44115 | 01601 | 50541 | 00147 | 77685 | 58788 |
| 35334 | 82410 | 91601 | 40617 | 72876 | 33967 | 73830 | 15405 | 96554 |
| 57729 | 88646 | 76487 | 11622 | 96297 | 24160 | 09903 | 14047 | 22917 |
| 86648 | 89317 | 63677 | 70119 | 94739 | 25875 | 38829 | 68377 | 43918 |
| 30574 | 06039 | 07967 | 32422 | 76791 | 30725 | 53711 | 93385 | 13421 |
| 81307 | 13114 | 83580 | 79974 | 45929 | 85113 | 72268 | 09858 | 52104 |
| 02410 | 96385 | 79067 | 54939 | 21410 | 86980 | 91772 | 93307 | 34116 |
| 18969 | 87444 | 52233 | 62319 | 08598 | 09066 | 95288 | 04794 | 01534 |
| 87863 | 80514 | 66860 | 62297 | 80198 | 19347 | 73234 | 86265 | 49096 |
| 08397 | 10538 | 15438 | 62311 | 72844 | 60203 | 46412 | 65943 | 79232 |
| 28520 | 45247 | 58729 | 10854 | 99058 | 18260 | 38765 | 90038 | 94209 |
| 44285 | 09452 | 15867 | 70418 | 57012 | 72122 | 36634 | 97283 | 95943 |
| 86299 | 22510 | 33571 | 23309 | 57040 | 29285 | 67870 | 21913 | 72958 |
| 84842 | 05748 | 90894 | 61658 | 15001 | 94005 | 36308 | 41161 | 37341 |

# NORMALLY DISTRIBUTED RANDOM DIGITS

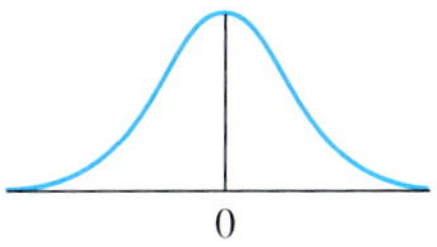


An entry in the table is the value $z$ from a normal distribution with a mean of 0 and a standard deviation of 1.

| | | | | | |
|---|---|---|---|---|---|
| 1.98677 | 1.23481 | −.28360 | .99217 | −.87919 | −.21600 |
| −.59341 | 1.54221 | −.65806 | 1.08372 | 1.68560 | 1.14899 |
| .11340 | .19126 | −.65084 | .12188 | .02338 | −.61545 |
| .89783 | −.54929 | −.03663 | −1.89506 | .15158 | −.20061 |
| −.50790 | 1.14463 | 1.30917 | 1.26528 | .09459 | .16423 |
| −1.63968 | −.63248 | .21482 | −1.16241 | −.60015 | −.55233 |
| 1.14081 | −.29988 | −.48053 | −1.21397 | −.34391 | −1.84881 |
| −.43354 | −.32855 | .67115 | .52289 | −1.42796 | −.14181 |
| .05707 | .35331 | .20470 | .01847 | 1.71086 | −1.44738 |
| .77153 | .72576 | −.29833 | .26139 | 1.25845 | −.35468 |
| −1.38286 | .04406 | −.75499 | .61068 | .61903 | −.96845 |
| 1.60166 | −1.66161 | .70886 | −.20302 | −.28373 | 2.07219 |
| −.48781 | .02629 | −.34306 | 2.00746 | −1.12059 | .07943 |
| −1.10632 | 1.18250 | −.60065 | .09737 | .63297 | 1.00659 |
| .77000 | −.87214 | −.63584 | −.39546 | −.72776 | .45594 |
| −.56882 | −.23153 | −2.03852 | −.28101 | .30384 | −.14246 |
| .27721 | −.04776 | .11740 | −.17211 | 1.63483 | 1.34221 |
| −.40251 | −.31052 | −1.04834 | −.23243 | −1.52224 | .85903 |
| 1.27086 | −.93166 | −.03766 | 1.21016 | .13451 | .81941 |
| 1.14464 | .56176 | .89824 | 1.54670 | 1.48411 | .14422 |
| .04172 | 1.49672 | −.15490 | .77084 | −.29064 | 2.87643 |
| −.36795 | 1.22318 | −1.05084 | −1.05409 | .82052 | .09670 |
| 1.94110 | 1.00826 | −.85411 | −1.31341 | −1.85921 | .74578 |
| .14946 | −2.75470 | −.10830 | 1.02845 | .69291 | −.78579 |

# AREAS OF THE STANDARD NORMAL DISTRIBUTION

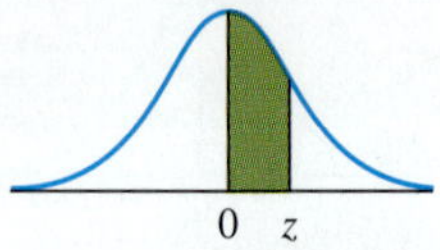


An entry in the table is the proportion under the entire curve that is between $z = 0$ and a positive value of $z$. Areas for negative values of $z$ are obtained by symmetry.

| z | .00 | .01 | .02 | .03 | .04 | .05 | .06 | .07 | .08 | .09 |
|---|---|---|---|---|---|---|---|---|---|---|
| 0.0 | .0000 | .0040 | .0080 | .0120 | .0160 | .0199 | .0239 | .0279 | .0319 | .0359 |
| 0.1 | .0398 | .0438 | .0478 | .0517 | .0557 | .0596 | .0636 | .0675 | .0714 | .0753 |
| 0.2 | .0793 | .0832 | .0871 | .0910 | .0948 | .0987 | .1026 | .1064 | .1103 | .1141 |
| 0.3 | .1179 | .1217 | .1255 | .1293 | .1331 | .1368 | .1406 | .1443 | .1480 | .1517 |
| 0.4 | .1554 | .1591 | .1628 | .1664 | .1700 | .1736 | .1772 | .1808 | .1844 | .1879 |
| 0.5 | .1915 | .1950 | .1985 | .2019 | .2054 | .2088 | .2123 | .2157 | .2190 | .2224 |
| 0.6 | .2257 | .2291 | .2324 | .2357 | .2389 | .2422 | .2454 | .2486 | .2517 | .2549 |
| 0.7 | .2580 | .2611 | .2642 | .2673 | .2703 | .2734 | .2764 | .2794 | .2823 | .2852 |
| 0.8 | .2881 | .2910 | .2939 | .2967 | .2995 | .3023 | .3051 | .3078 | .3106 | .3133 |
| 0.9 | .3159 | .3186 | .3212 | .3238 | .3264 | .3289 | .3315 | .3340 | .3365 | .3389 |
| 1.0 | .3413 | .3438 | .3461 | .3485 | .3508 | .3531 | .3554 | .3577 | .3599 | .3621 |
| 1.1 | .3643 | .3665 | .3686 | .3708 | .3729 | .3749 | .3770 | .3790 | .3810 | .3830 |
| 1.2 | .3849 | .3869 | .3888 | .3907 | .3925 | .3944 | .3962 | .3980 | .3997 | .4015 |
| 1.3 | .4032 | .4049 | .4066 | .4082 | .4099 | .4115 | .4131 | .4147 | .4162 | .4177 |
| 1.4 | .4192 | .4207 | .4222 | .4236 | .4251 | .4265 | .4279 | .4292 | .4306 | .4319 |
| 1.5 | .4332 | .4345 | .4357 | .4370 | .4382 | .4394 | .4406 | .4418 | .4429 | .4441 |
| 1.6 | .4452 | .4463 | .4474 | .4484 | .4495 | .4505 | .4515 | .4525 | .4535 | .4545 |
| 1.7 | .4554 | .4564 | .4573 | .4582 | .4591 | .4599 | .4608 | .4616 | .4625 | .4633 |
| 1.8 | .4641 | .4649 | .4656 | .4664 | .4671 | .4678 | .4686 | .4693 | .4699 | .4706 |
| 1.9 | .4713 | .4719 | .4726 | .4732 | .4738 | .4744 | .4750 | .4756 | .4761 | .4767 |
| 2.0 | .4772 | .4778 | .4783 | .4788 | .4793 | .4798 | .4803 | .4808 | .4812 | .4817 |
| 2.1 | .4821 | .4826 | .4830 | .4834 | .4838 | .4842 | .4846 | .4850 | .4854 | .4857 |
| 2.2 | .4861 | .4864 | .4868 | .4871 | .4875 | .4878 | .4881 | .4884 | .4887 | .4890 |
| 2.3 | .4893 | .4896 | .4898 | .4901 | .4904 | .4906 | .4909 | .4911 | .4913 | .4916 |
| 2.4 | .4918 | .4920 | .4922 | .4925 | .4927 | .4929 | .4931 | .4932 | .4934 | .4936 |
| 2.5 | .4938 | .4940 | .4941 | .4943 | .4945 | .4946 | .4948 | .4949 | .4951 | .4952 |
| 2.6 | .4953 | .4955 | .4956 | .4957 | .4959 | .4960 | .4961 | .4962 | .4963 | .4964 |
| 2.7 | .4965 | .4966 | .4967 | .4968 | .4969 | .4970 | .4971 | .4972 | .4973 | .4974 |
| 2.8 | .4974 | .4975 | .4976 | .4977 | .4977 | .4978 | .4979 | .4979 | .4980 | .4981 |
| 2.9 | .4981 | .4982 | .4982 | .4983 | .4984 | .4984 | .4985 | .4985 | .4986 | .4986 |
| 3.0 | .4987 | .4987 | .4987 | .4988 | .4988 | .4989 | .4989 | .4989 | .4990 | .4990 |

# AREAS OF THE CUMULATIVE STANDARD NORMAL DISTRIBUTION

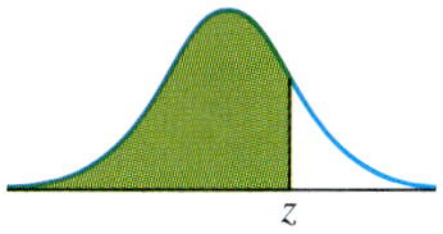


An entry in the table is the proportion under the curve cumulated from the negative tail.

| z | G(z) | z | G(z) | z | G(z) |
|---|---|---|---|---|---|
| −4.00 | 0.00003 | −1.30 | 0.09680 | 1.40 | 0.91924 |
| −3.95 | 0.00004 | −1.25 | 0.10565 | 1.45 | 0.92647 |
| −3.90 | 0.00005 | −1.20 | 0.11507 | 1.50 | 0.93319 |
| −3.85 | 0.00006 | −1.15 | 0.12507 | 1.55 | 0.93943 |
| −3.80 | 0.00007 | −1.10 | 0.13567 | 1.60 | 0.94520 |
| −3.75 | 0.00009 | −1.05 | 0.14686 | 1.65 | 0.95053 |
| −3.70 | 0.00011 | −1.00 | 0.15866 | 1.70 | 0.95543 |
| −3.65 | 0.00013 | −0.95 | 0.17106 | 1.75 | 0.95994 |
| −3.60 | 0.00016 | −0.90 | 0.18406 | 1.80 | 0.96407 |
| −3.55 | 0.00019 | −0.85 | 0.19766 | 1.85 | 0.96784 |
| −3.50 | 0.00023 | −0.80 | 0.21186 | 1.90 | 0.97128 |
| −3.45 | 0.00028 | −0.75 | 0.22663 | 1.95 | 0.97441 |
| −3.40 | 0.00034 | −0.70 | 0.24196 | 2.00 | 0.97725 |
| −3.35 | 0.00040 | −0.65 | 0.25785 | 2.05 | 0.97982 |
| −3.30 | 0.00048 | −0.60 | 0.27425 | 2.10 | 0.98214 |
| −3.25 | 0.00058 | −0.55 | 0.29116 | 2.15 | 0.98422 |
| −3.20 | 0.00069 | −0.50 | 0.30854 | 2.20 | 0.98610 |
| −3.15 | 0.00082 | −0.45 | 0.32636 | 2.25 | 0.98778 |
| −3.10 | 0.00097 | −0.40 | 0.34458 | 2.30 | 0.98928 |
| −3.05 | 0.00114 | −0.35 | 0.36317 | 2.35 | 0.99061 |
| −3.00 | 0.00135 | −0.30 | 0.38209 | 2.40 | 0.99180 |
| −2.95 | 0.00159 | −0.25 | 0.40129 | 2.45 | 0.99286 |
| −2.90 | 0.00187 | −0.20 | 0.42074 | 2.50 | 0.99379 |
| −2.85 | 0.00219 | −0.15 | 0.44038 | 2.55 | 0.99461 |
| −2.80 | 0.00256 | −0.10 | 0.46017 | 2.60 | 0.99534 |
| −2.75 | 0.00298 | −0.05 | 0.48006 | 2.65 | 0.99598 |
| −2.70 | 0.00347 | 0.00 | 0.50000 | 2.70 | 0.99653 |
| −2.65 | 0.00402 | 0.05 | 0.51994 | 2.75 | 0.99702 |
| −2.60 | 0.00466 | 0.10 | 0.53983 | 2.80 | 0.99744 |
| −2.55 | 0.00539 | 0.15 | 0.55962 | 2.85 | 0.99781 |
| −2.50 | 0.00621 | 0.20 | 0.57926 | 2.90 | 0.99813 |
| −2.45 | 0.00714 | 0.25 | 0.59871 | 2.95 | 0.99841 |
| −2.40 | 0.00820 | 0.30 | 0.61791 | 3.00 | 0.99865 |
| −2.35 | 0.00939 | 0.35 | 0.63683 | 3.05 | 0.99886 |
| −2.30 | 0.01072 | 0.40 | 0.65542 | 3.10 | 0.99903 |
| −2.25 | 0.01222 | 0.45 | 0.67364 | 3.15 | 0.99918 |
| −2.20 | 0.01390 | 0.50 | 0.69146 | 3.20 | 0.99931 |
| −2.15 | 0.01578 | 0.55 | 0.70884 | 3.25 | 0.99942 |
| −2.10 | 0.01786 | 0.60 | 0.72575 | 3.30 | 0.99952 |
| −2.05 | 0.02018 | 0.65 | 0.74215 | 3.35 | 0.99960 |
| −2.00 | 0.02275 | 0.70 | 0.75804 | 3.40 | 0.99966 |
| −1.95 | 0.02559 | 0.75 | 0.77337 | 3.45 | 0.99972 |
| −1.90 | 0.02872 | 0.80 | 0.78814 | 3.50 | 0.99977 |
| −1.85 | 0.03216 | 0.85 | 0.80234 | 3.55 | 0.99981 |
| −1.80 | 0.03593 | 0.90 | 0.81594 | 3.60 | 0.99984 |
| −1.75 | 0.04006 | 0.95 | 0.82894 | 3.65 | 0.99987 |
| −1.70 | 0.04457 | 1.00 | 0.84134 | 3.70 | 0.99989 |
| −1.65 | 0.04947 | 1.05 | 0.85314 | 3.75 | 0.99991 |
| −1.60 | 0.05480 | 1.10 | 0.86433 | 3.80 | 0.99993 |
| −1.55 | 0.06057 | 1.15 | 0.87493 | 3.85 | 0.99994 |
| −1.50 | 0.06681 | 1.20 | 0.88493 | 3.90 | 0.99995 |
| −1.45 | 0.07353 | 1.25 | 0.89435 | 3.95 | 0.99996 |
| −1.40 | 0.08076 | 1.30 | 0.90320 | 4.00 | 0.99997 |
| −1.35 | 0.08851 | 1.35 | 0.91149 | | |

APPENDIX F

# NEGATIVE EXPONENTIAL DISTRIBUTION: VALUES OF $e^{-x}$

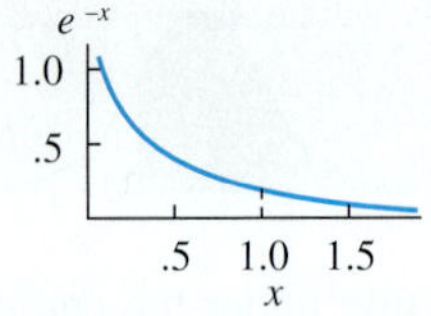


| $x$ | $e^{-x}$ (VALUE) | $x$ | $e^{-x}$ (VALUE) | $x$ | $e^{-x}$ (VALUE) | $x$ | $e^{-x}$ (VALUE) |
|---|---|---|---|---|---|---|---|
| 0.00 | 1.00000 | 0.50 | 0.60653 | 1.00 | 0.36788 | 1.50 | 0.22313 |
| 0.01 | 0.99005 | 0.51 | .60050 | 1.01 | .36422 | 1.51 | .22091 |
| 0.02 | .98020 | 0.52 | .59452 | 1.02 | .36060 | 1.52 | .21871 |
| 0.03 | .97045 | 0.53 | .58860 | 1.03 | .35701 | 1.53 | .21654 |
| 0.04 | .96079 | 0.54 | .58275 | 1.04 | .35345 | 1.54 | .21438 |
| 0.05 | .95123 | 0.55 | .57695 | 1.05 | .34994 | 1.55 | .21225 |
| 0.06 | .94176 | 0.56 | .57121 | 1.06 | .34646 | 1.56 | .21014 |
| 0.07 | .93239 | 0.57 | .56553 | 1.07 | .34301 | 1.57 | .20805 |
| 0.08 | .92312 | 0.58 | .55990 | 1.08 | .33960 | 1.58 | .20598 |
| 0.09 | .91393 | 0.59 | .55433 | 1.09 | .33622 | 1.59 | .20393 |
| 0.10 | .90484 | 0.60 | .54881 | 1.10 | .33287 | 1.60 | .20190 |
| 0.11 | .89583 | 0.61 | .54335 | 1.11 | .32956 | 1.61 | .19989 |
| 0.12 | .88692 | 0.62 | .53794 | 1.12 | .32628 | 1.62 | .19790 |
| 0.13 | .87809 | 0.63 | .53259 | 1.13 | .32303 | 1.63 | .19593 |
| 0.14 | .86936 | 0.64 | .52729 | 1.14 | .31982 | 1.64 | .19398 |
| 0.15 | .86071 | 0.65 | .52205 | 1.15 | .31664 | 1.65 | .19205 |
| 0.16 | .87514 | 0.66 | .51685 | 1.16 | .31349 | 1.66 | .19014 |
| 0.17 | .84366 | 0.67 | .51171 | 1.17 | .31037 | 1.67 | .18825 |
| 0.18 | .83527 | 0.68 | .50662 | 1.18 | .30728 | 1.68 | .18637 |
| 0.19 | .82696 | 0.69 | .50158 | 1.19 | .30422 | 1.69 | .18452 |
| 0.20 | .81873 | 0.70 | .49659 | 1.20 | .30119 | 1.70 | .18268 |
| 0.21 | .81058 | 0.71 | .49164 | 1.21 | .29820 | 1.71 | .18087 |
| 0.22 | .80252 | 0.72 | .48675 | 1.22 | .29523 | 1.72 | .17907 |
| 0.23 | .79453 | 0.73 | .48191 | 1.23 | .29229 | 1.73 | .17728 |
| 0.24 | .78663 | 0.74 | .47711 | 1.24 | .28938 | 1.74 | .17552 |
| 0.25 | .77880 | 0.75 | .47237 | 1.25 | .28650 | 1.75 | .17377 |
| 0.26 | .77105 | 0.76 | .46767 | 1.26 | .28365 | 1.76 | .17204 |
| 0.27 | .76338 | 0.77 | .46301 | 1.27 | .28083 | 1.77 | .17033 |
| 0.28 | .75578 | 0.78 | .45841 | 1.28 | .27804 | 1.78 | .16864 |
| 0.29 | .74826 | 0.79 | .45384 | 1.29 | .27527 | 1.79 | .16696 |
| 0.30 | .74082 | 0.80 | .44933 | 1.30 | .27253 | 1.80 | .16530 |
| 0.31 | .73345 | 0.81 | .44486 | 1.31 | .26982 | 1.81 | .16365 |
| 0.32 | .72615 | 0.82 | .44043 | 1.32 | .26714 | 1.82 | .16203 |
| 0.33 | .71892 | 0.83 | .43605 | 1.33 | .26448 | 1.83 | .16041 |
| 0.34 | .71177 | 0.84 | .43171 | 1.34 | .26185 | 1.84 | .15882 |
| 0.35 | .70469 | 0.85 | .42741 | 1.35 | .25924 | 1.85 | .15724 |
| 0.36 | .69768 | 0.86 | .42316 | 1.36 | .25666 | 1.86 | .15567 |
| 0.37 | .69073 | 0.87 | .41895 | 1.37 | .25411 | 1.87 | .15412 |
| 0.38 | .68386 | 0.88 | .41478 | 1.38 | .25158 | 1.88 | .15259 |
| 0.39 | .67706 | 0.89 | .41066 | 1.39 | .24908 | 1.89 | .15107 |
| 0.40 | .67032 | 0.90 | .40657 | 1.40 | .24660 | 1.90 | .14957 |
| 0.41 | .66365 | 0.91 | .40252 | 1.41 | .24414 | 1.91 | .14808 |
| 0.42 | .65705 | 0.92 | .39852 | 1.42 | .24171 | 1.92 | .14661 |
| 0.43 | .65051 | 0.93 | .39455 | 1.43 | .23931 | 1.93 | .14515 |
| 0.44 | .64404 | 0.94 | .39063 | 1.44 | .23693 | 1.94 | .14370 |
| 0.45 | .63763 | 0.95 | .38674 | 1.45 | .23457 | 1.95 | .14227 |
| 0.46 | .63128 | 0.96 | .38289 | 1.46 | .23224 | 1.96 | .14086 |
| 0.47 | .62500 | 0.97 | .37908 | 1.47 | .22993 | 1.97 | .13946 |
| 0.48 | .61878 | 0.98 | .37531 | 1.48 | .22764 | 1.98 | .13807 |
| 0.49 | .61263 | 0.99 | .37158 | 1.49 | .22537 | 1.99 | .13670 |
| 0.50 | .60653 | 1.00 | .36788 | 1.50 | .22313 | 2.00 | .13534 |

# INTEREST TABLES

TABLE G.1

**Compound Sum of $1**

| YEAR | 1% | 2% | 3% | 4% | 5% | 6% | 7% | 8% | 9% |
|---|---|---|---|---|---|---|---|---|---|
| 1 | 1.010 | 1.020 | 1.030 | 1.040 | 1.050 | 1.060 | 1.070 | 1.080 | 1.090 |
| 2 | 1.020 | 1.040 | 1.061 | 1.082 | 1.102 | 1.124 | 1.145 | 1.166 | 1.188 |
| 3 | 1.030 | 1.061 | 1.093 | 1.125 | 1.158 | 1.191 | 1.225 | 1.260 | 1.295 |
| 4 | 1.041 | 1.082 | 1.126 | 1.170 | 1.216 | 1.262 | 1.311 | 1.360 | 1.412 |
| 5 | 1.051 | 1.104 | 1.159 | 1.217 | 1.276 | 1.338 | 1.403 | 1.469 | 1.539 |
| 6 | 1.062 | 1.126 | 1.194 | 1.265 | 1.340 | 1.419 | 1.501 | 1.587 | 1.677 |
| 7 | 1.072 | 1.149 | 1.230 | 1.316 | 1.407 | 1.504 | 1.606 | 1.714 | 1.828 |
| 8 | 1.083 | 1.172 | 1.267 | 1.369 | 1.477 | 1.594 | 1.718 | 1.851 | 1.993 |
| 9 | 1.094 | 1.195 | 1.305 | 1.423 | 1.551 | 1.689 | 1.838 | 1.999 | 2.172 |
| 10 | 1.105 | 1.219 | 1.344 | 1.480 | 1.629 | 1.791 | 1.967 | 2.159 | 2.367 |
| 11 | 1.116 | 1.243 | 1.384 | 1.539 | 1.710 | 1.898 | 2.105 | 2.332 | 2.580 |
| 12 | 1.127 | 1.268 | 1.426 | 1.601 | 1.796 | 2.012 | 2.252 | 2.518 | 2.813 |
| 13 | 1.138 | 1.294 | 1.469 | 1.665 | 1.886 | 2.133 | 2.410 | 2.720 | 3.066 |
| 14 | 1.149 | 1.319 | 1.513 | 1.732 | 1.980 | 2.261 | 2.579 | 2.937 | 3.342 |
| 15 | 1.161 | 1.346 | 1.558 | 1.801 | 2.079 | 2.397 | 2.759 | 3.172 | 3.642 |
| 16 | 1.173 | 1.373 | 1.605 | 1.873 | 2.183 | 2.540 | 2.952 | 3.426 | 3.970 |
| 17 | 1.184 | 1.400 | 1.653 | 1.948 | 2.292 | 2.693 | 3.159 | 3.700 | 4.328 |
| 18 | 1.196 | 1.428 | 1.702 | 2.026 | 2.407 | 2.854 | 3.380 | 3.996 | 4.717 |
| 19 | 1.208 | 1.457 | 1.754 | 2.107 | 2.527 | 3.026 | 3.617 | 4.316 | 5.142 |
| 20 | 1.220 | 1.486 | 1.806 | 2.191 | 2.653 | 3.207 | 3.870 | 4.661 | 5.604 |
| 25 | 1.282 | 1.641 | 2.094 | 2.666 | 3.386 | 4.292 | 5.427 | 6.848 | 8.623 |
| 30 | 1.348 | 1.811 | 2.427 | 3.243 | 4.322 | 5.743 | 7.612 | 10.063 | 13.268 |

| YEAR | 10% | 12% | 14% | 15% | 16% | 18% | 20% | 24% | 28% |
|---|---|---|---|---|---|---|---|---|---|
| 1 | 1.100 | 1.120 | 1.140 | 1.150 | 1.160 | 1.180 | 1.200 | 1.240 | 1.280 |
| 2 | 1.210 | 1.254 | 1.300 | 1.322 | 1.346 | 1.392 | 1.440 | 1.538 | 1.638 |
| 3 | 1.331 | 1.405 | 1.482 | 1.521 | 1.561 | 1.643 | 1.728 | 1.907 | 2.067 |
| 4 | 1.464 | 1.574 | 1.689 | 1.749 | 1.811 | 1.939 | 2.074 | 2.364 | 2.684 |
| 5 | 1.611 | 1.762 | 1.925 | 2.011 | 2.100 | 2.288 | 2.488 | 2.932 | 3.436 |
| 6 | 1.772 | 1.974 | 2.195 | 2.313 | 2.436 | 2.700 | 2.986 | 3.635 | 4.398 |
| 7 | 1.949 | 2.211 | 2.502 | 2.660 | 2.826 | 3.185 | 3.583 | 4.508 | 5.629 |
| 8 | 2.144 | 2.476 | 2.853 | 3.059 | 3.278 | 3.759 | 4.300 | 5.590 | 7.206 |
| 9 | 2.358 | 2.773 | 3.252 | 3.518 | 3.803 | 4.435 | 5.160 | 6.931 | 9.223 |
| 10 | 2.594 | 3.106 | 3.707 | 4.046 | 4.411 | 5.234 | 6.192 | 8.594 | 11.806 |
| 11 | 2.853 | 3.479 | 4.226 | 4.652 | 5.117 | 6.176 | 7.430 | 10.657 | 15.112 |
| 12 | 3.138 | 3.896 | 4.818 | 5.350 | 5.936 | 7.288 | 8.916 | 13.216 | 19.343 |
| 13 | 3.452 | 4.363 | 5.492 | 6.153 | 6.886 | 8.599 | 10.699 | 16.386 | 24.759 |
| 14 | 3.797 | 4.887 | 6.261 | 7.076 | 7.988 | 10.147 | 12.839 | 20.319 | 31.691 |
| 15 | 4.177 | 5.474 | 7.138 | 8.137 | 9.266 | 11.974 | 15.407 | 25.196 | 40.565 |
| 16 | 4.595 | 6.130 | 8.137 | 9.358 | 10.748 | 14.129 | 18.488 | 31.243 | 51.923 |
| 17 | 5.054 | 6.866 | 9.276 | 10.761 | 12.468 | 16.672 | 22.186 | 38.741 | 66.461 |
| 18 | 5.560 | 7.690 | 10.575 | 12.375 | 14.463 | 19.673 | 26.623 | 48.039 | 85.071 |
| 19 | 6.116 | 8.613 | 12.056 | 14.232 | 16.777 | 23.214 | 31.948 | 59.568 | 108.89 |
| 20 | 6.728 | 9.646 | 13.743 | 16.367 | 19.461 | 27.393 | 38.338 | 73.864 | 139.38 |
| 25 | 10.835 | 17.000 | 26.462 | 32.919 | 40.874 | 62.669 | 95.396 | 216.542 | 478.90 |
| 30 | 17.449 | 29.960 | 50.950 | 66.212 | 85.850 | 143.371 | 237.376 | 634.820 | 1645.5 |

TABLE G.2

## Sum of an Annuity of $1 for *N* Years

| YEAR | 1% | 2% | 3% | 4% | 5% | 6% | 7% | 8% |
|---|---|---|---|---|---|---|---|---|
| 1 | 1.000 | 1.000 | 1.000 | 1.000 | 1.000 | 1.000 | 1.000 | 1.000 |
| 2 | 2.010 | 2.020 | 2.030 | 2.040 | 2.050 | 2.060 | 2.070 | 2.080 |
| 3 | 2.030 | 3.060 | 3.019 | 3.122 | 3.152 | 3.184 | 3.215 | 3.246 |
| 4 | 4.060 | 4.122 | 4.184 | 4.246 | 4.310 | 4.375 | 4.440 | 4.506 |
| 5 | 5.101 | 5.204 | 5.309 | 5.416 | 5.526 | 5.637 | 5.751 | 5.867 |
| 6 | 6.152 | 6.308 | 6.468 | 6.633 | 6.802 | 6.975 | 7.153 | 7.336 |
| 7 | 7.214 | 7.434 | 7.662 | 7.898 | 8.142 | 8.394 | 8.654 | 8.923 |
| 8 | 8.286 | 8.583 | 8.892 | 9.214 | 9.549 | 9.897 | 10.260 | 10.637 |
| 9 | 9.369 | 9.755 | 10.159 | 10.583 | 11.027 | 11.491 | 11.978 | 12.488 |
| 10 | 10.462 | 10.950 | 11.464 | 12.006 | 12.578 | 13.181 | 13.816 | 14.487 |
| 11 | 11.567 | 12.169 | 12.808 | 13.486 | 14.207 | 14.972 | 15.784 | 16.645 |
| 12 | 12.683 | 13.412 | 14.192 | 15.026 | 15.917 | 16.870 | 17.888 | 18.977 |
| 13 | 13.809 | 14.680 | 15.618 | 16.627 | 17.713 | 18.882 | 20.141 | 21.495 |
| 14 | 14.947 | 15.974 | 17.086 | 18.292 | 19.599 | 21.051 | 22.550 | 24.215 |
| 15 | 16.097 | 17.293 | 18.599 | 20.024 | 21.579 | 23.276 | 25.129 | 27.152 |
| 16 | 17.258 | 18.639 | 20.157 | 21.825 | 23.657 | 25.673 | 27.888 | 30.324 |
| 17 | 18.430 | 20.012 | 21.762 | 23.698 | 25.840 | 28.213 | 30.840 | 33.750 |
| 18 | 19.615 | 21.412 | 23.414 | 25.645 | 28.132 | 30.906 | 33.999 | 37.450 |
| 19 | 20.811 | 22.841 | 25.117 | 27.671 | 30.539 | 33.760 | 37.379 | 41.446 |
| 20 | 22.019 | 24.297 | 26.870 | 29.778 | 33.066 | 36.786 | 40.995 | 45.762 |
| 25 | 28.243 | 32.030 | 36.459 | 41.646 | 47.727 | 54.865 | 63.249 | 73.106 |
| 30 | 34.785 | 40.568 | 47.575 | 56.085 | 66.439 | 79.058 | 94.461 | 113.283 |

| YEAR | 9% | 10% | 12% | 14% | 16% | 18% | 20% | 24% |
|---|---|---|---|---|---|---|---|---|
| 1 | 1.000 | 1.000 | 1.000 | 1.000 | 1.000 | 1.000 | 1.000 | 1.000 |
| 2 | 2.090 | 2.100 | 2.120 | 2.140 | 2.160 | 2.180 | 2.200 | 2.240 |
| 3 | 3.278 | 3.310 | 3.374 | 3.440 | 3.506 | 3.572 | 3.640 | 3.778 |
| 4 | 4.573 | 4.641 | 4.770 | 4.921 | 5.066 | 5.215 | 5.368 | 5.684 |
| 5 | 5.985 | 6.105 | 6.353 | 6.610 | 6.877 | 7.154 | 7.442 | 8.048 |
| 6 | 7.523 | 7.716 | 8.115 | 8.536 | 8.977 | 9.442 | 9.930 | 10.980 |
| 7 | 9.200 | 9.487 | 10.089 | 10.730 | 11.414 | 12.142 | 12.916 | 14.615 |
| 8 | 11.028 | 11.436 | 12.300 | 13.233 | 14.240 | 15.327 | 16.499 | 19.123 |
| 9 | 13.021 | 13.579 | 14.776 | 16.085 | 17.518 | 19.086 | 20.799 | 24.712 |
| 10 | 15.193 | 15.937 | 17.549 | 19.337 | 21.321 | 23.521 | 25.959 | 31.643 |
| 11 | 17.560 | 18.531 | 20.655 | 23.044 | 25.733 | 28.755 | 32.150 | 40.238 |
| 12 | 20.141 | 21.384 | 24.133 | 27.271 | 30.850 | 34.931 | 39.580 | 50.985 |
| 13 | 22.953 | 24.523 | 28.029 | 32.089 | 36.786 | 42.219 | 48.497 | 64.110 |
| 14 | 26.019 | 27.975 | 32.393 | 37.581 | 43.672 | 50.818 | 59.196 | 80.496 |
| 15 | 29.361 | 31.772 | 37.280 | 43.842 | 51.660 | 60.965 | 72.035 | 100.815 |
| 16 | 33.003 | 35.950 | 42.753 | 50.980 | 60.925 | 72.939 | 87.442 | 126.011 |
| 17 | 36.974 | 40.545 | 48.884 | 59.118 | 71.673 | 87.068 | 105.931 | 157.253 |
| 18 | 41.301 | 45.599 | 55.750 | 68.394 | 84.141 | 103.740 | 128.117 | 195.994 |
| 19 | 46.018 | 51.159 | 63.440 | 78.969 | 98.603 | 123.414 | 154.740 | 244.033 |
| 20 | 51.160 | 57.275 | 72.052 | 91.025 | 115.380 | 146.628 | 186.688 | 303.601 |
| 25 | 84.701 | 93.347 | 133.334 | 181.871 | 249.214 | 342.603 | 471.981 | 898.092 |
| 30 | 136.308 | 164.494 | 241.333 | 356.787 | 530.312 | 790.948 | 1181.882 | 2640.916 |

TABLE G.3

## Present Value of $1

| YEAR | 1% | 2% | 3% | 4% | 5% | 6% | 7% | 8% | 9% | 10% | 12% | 14% | 15% |
|---|---|---|---|---|---|---|---|---|---|---|---|---|---|
| 1 | .990 | .980 | .971 | .962 | .952 | .943 | .935 | .926 | .917 | .909 | .893 | .877 | .870 |
| 2 | .980 | .961 | .943 | .925 | .907 | .890 | .873 | .857 | .842 | .826 | .797 | .769 | .756 |
| 3 | .971 | .942 | .915 | .889 | .864 | .840 | .816 | .794 | .772 | .751 | .712 | .675 | .658 |
| 4 | .961 | .924 | .889 | .855 | .823 | .792 | .763 | .735 | .708 | .683 | .636 | .592 | .572 |
| 5 | .951 | .906 | .863 | .822 | .784 | .747 | .713 | .681 | .650 | .621 | .567 | .519 | .497 |
| 6 | .942 | .888 | .838 | .790 | .746 | .705 | .666 | .630 | .596 | .564 | .507 | .456 | .432 |
| 7 | .933 | .871 | .813 | .760 | .711 | .665 | .623 | .583 | .547 | .513 | .452 | .400 | .376 |
| 8 | .923 | .853 | .789 | .731 | .677 | .627 | .582 | .540 | .502 | .467 | .404 | .351 | .327 |
| 9 | .914 | .837 | .766 | .703 | .645 | .592 | .544 | .500 | .460 | .424 | .361 | .308 | .284 |
| 10 | .905 | .820 | .744 | .676 | .614 | .558 | .508 | .463 | .422 | .386 | .322 | .270 | .247 |
| 11 | .896 | .804 | .722 | .650 | .585 | .527 | .475 | .429 | .388 | .350 | .287 | .237 | .215 |
| 12 | .887 | .788 | .701 | .625 | .557 | .497 | .444 | .397 | .356 | .319 | .257 | .208 | .187 |
| 13 | .879 | .773 | .681 | .601 | .530 | .469 | .415 | .368 | .326 | .290 | .229 | .182 | .163 |
| 14 | .870 | .758 | .661 | .577 | .505 | .442 | .388 | .340 | .299 | .263 | .205 | .160 | .141 |
| 15 | .861 | .743 | .642 | .555 | .481 | .417 | .362 | .315 | .275 | .239 | .183 | .140 | .123 |
| 16 | .853 | .728 | .623 | .534 | .458 | .394 | .339 | .292 | .252 | .218 | .163 | .123 | .107 |
| 17 | .844 | .714 | .605 | .513 | .436 | .371 | .317 | .270 | .231 | .198 | .146 | .108 | .093 |
| 18 | .836 | .700 | .587 | .494 | .416 | .350 | .296 | .250 | .212 | .180 | .130 | .095 | .081 |
| 19 | .828 | .686 | .570 | .475 | .396 | .331 | .276 | .232 | .194 | .164 | .116 | .083 | .070 |
| 20 | .820 | .673 | .554 | .456 | .377 | .312 | .258 | .215 | .178 | .149 | .104 | .073 | .061 |
| 25 | .780 | .610 | .478 | .375 | .295 | .233 | .184 | .146 | .116 | .092 | .059 | .038 | .030 |
| 30 | .742 | .552 | .412 | .308 | .231 | .174 | .131 | .099 | .075 | .057 | .033 | .020 | .015 |

| YEAR | 16% | 18% | 20% | 24% | 28% | 32% | 36% | 40% | 50% | 60% | 70% | 80% | 90% |
|---|---|---|---|---|---|---|---|---|---|---|---|---|---|
| 1 | .862 | .847 | .833 | .806 | .781 | .758 | .735 | .714 | .667 | .625 | .588 | .556 | .526 |
| 2 | .743 | .718 | .694 | .650 | .610 | .574 | .541 | .510 | .444 | .391 | .346 | .309 | .277 |
| 3 | .641 | .609 | .579 | .524 | .477 | .435 | .398 | .364 | .296 | .244 | .204 | .171 | .146 |
| 4 | .552 | .516 | .482 | .423 | .373 | .329 | .292 | .260 | .198 | .153 | .120 | .095 | .077 |
| 5 | .476 | .437 | .402 | .341 | .291 | .250 | .215 | .186 | .132 | .095 | .070 | .053 | .040 |
| 6 | .410 | .370 | .335 | .275 | .227 | .189 | .158 | .133 | .088 | .060 | .041 | .029 | .021 |
| 7 | .354 | .314 | .279 | .222 | .178 | .143 | .116 | .095 | .059 | .037 | .024 | .016 | .011 |
| 8 | .305 | .266 | .233 | .179 | .139 | .108 | .085 | .068 | .039 | .023 | .014 | .009 | .006 |
| 9 | .263 | .226 | .194 | .144 | .108 | .082 | .063 | .048 | .026 | .015 | .008 | .005 | .003 |
| 10 | .227 | .191 | .162 | .116 | .085 | .062 | .046 | .035 | .017 | .009 | .005 | .003 | .002 |
| 11 | .195 | .162 | .135 | .094 | .066 | .047 | .034 | .025 | .012 | .006 | .003 | .002 | .001 |
| 12 | .168 | .137 | .112 | .076 | .052 | .036 | .025 | .018 | .008 | .004 | .002 | .001 | .001 |
| 13 | .145 | .116 | .093 | .061 | .040 | .027 | .018 | .013 | .005 | .002 | .001 | .001 | .000 |
| 14 | .125 | .099 | .078 | .049 | .032 | .021 | .014 | .009 | .003 | .001 | .001 | .000 | .000 |
| 15 | .108 | .084 | .065 | .040 | .025 | .016 | .010 | .006 | .002 | .001 | .000 | .000 | .000 |
| 16 | .093 | .071 | .054 | .032 | .019 | .012 | .007 | .005 | .002 | .001 | .000 | .000 | |
| 17 | .080 | .060 | .045 | .026 | .015 | .009 | .005 | .003 | .001 | .000 | .000 | | |
| 18 | .069 | .051 | .038 | .021 | .012 | .007 | .004 | .002 | .001 | .000 | .000 | | |
| 19 | .060 | .043 | .031 | .017 | .009 | .005 | .003 | .002 | .000 | .000 | | | |
| 20 | .051 | .037 | .026 | .014 | .007 | .004 | .002 | .001 | .000 | .000 | | | |
| 25 | .024 | .016 | .010 | .005 | .002 | .001 | .000 | .000 | | | | | |
| 30 | .012 | .007 | .004 | .002 | .001 | .000 | .000 | | | | | | |

## TABLE G.4

**Present Value of an Annuity of $1**

| YEAR | 1% | 2% | 3% | 4% | 5% | 6% | 7% | 8% | 9% | 10% |
|---|---|---|---|---|---|---|---|---|---|---|
| 1 | 0.990 | 0.980 | 0.971 | 0.962 | 0.952 | 0.943 | 0.935 | 0.926 | 0.917 | 0.909 |
| 2 | 1.970 | 1.942 | 1.913 | 1.886 | 1.859 | 1.833 | 1.808 | 1.783 | 1.759 | 1.736 |
| 3 | 2.941 | 2.884 | 2.829 | 2.775 | 2.723 | 2.673 | 2.624 | 2.577 | 2.531 | 2.487 |
| 4 | 3.902 | 3.808 | 3.717 | 3.630 | 3.546 | 3.465 | 3.387 | 3.312 | 3.240 | 3.170 |
| 5 | 4.853 | 4.713 | 4.580 | 4.452 | 4.329 | 4.212 | 4.100 | 3.993 | 3.890 | 3.791 |
| 6 | 5.795 | 5.601 | 5.417 | 5.242 | 5.076 | 4.917 | 4.766 | 4.623 | 4.486 | 4.355 |
| 7 | 6.728 | 6.472 | 6.230 | 6.002 | 5.786 | 5.582 | 5.389 | 5.206 | 5.033 | 4.868 |
| 8 | 7.652 | 7.325 | 7.020 | 6.733 | 6.463 | 6.210 | 6.971 | 5.747 | 5.535 | 5.335 |
| 9 | 8.566 | 8.162 | 7.786 | 7.435 | 7.108 | 6.802 | 6.515 | 6.247 | 5.985 | 5.759 |
| 10 | 9.471 | 8.983 | 8.530 | 8.111 | 7.722 | 7.360 | 7.024 | 6.710 | 6.418 | 6.145 |
| 11 | 10.368 | 9.787 | 9.253 | 8.760 | 8.306 | 7.887 | 7.449 | 7.139 | 6.805 | 6.495 |
| 12 | 11.255 | 10.575 | 9.954 | 9.385 | 8.863 | 8.384 | 7.943 | 7.536 | 7.161 | 6.814 |
| 13 | 12.134 | 11.348 | 10.635 | 9.986 | 9.394 | 8.853 | 8.358 | 7.904 | 7.487 | 7.103 |
| 14 | 13.004 | 12.106 | 11.296 | 10.563 | 9.899 | 9.295 | 8.745 | 8.244 | 7.786 | 7.367 |
| 15 | 13.865 | 12.849 | 11.938 | 11.118 | 10.380 | 9.712 | 9.108 | 8.559 | 8.060 | 7.606 |
| 16 | 14.718 | 13.578 | 12.561 | 11.652 | 10.838 | 10.106 | 9.447 | 8.851 | 8.312 | 7.824 |
| 17 | 15.562 | 14.292 | 13.166 | 12.166 | 11.274 | 10.477 | 9.763 | 9.122 | 8.544 | 8.022 |
| 18 | 16.398 | 14.992 | 13.754 | 12.659 | 11.690 | 10.828 | 10.059 | 9.372 | 8.756 | 8.201 |
| 19 | 17.226 | 15.678 | 14.324 | 13.134 | 12.085 | 11.158 | 10.336 | 9.604 | 8.950 | 8.365 |
| 20 | 18.046 | 16.351 | 14.877 | 13.590 | 12.462 | 11.470 | 10.594 | 9.818 | 9.128 | 8.514 |
| 25 | 22.023 | 19.523 | 17.413 | 15.622 | 14.094 | 12.783 | 11.654 | 10.675 | 9.823 | 9.077 |
| 30 | 25.808 | 22.397 | 19.600 | 17.292 | 15.373 | 13.765 | 12.409 | 11.258 | 10.274 | 9.427 |

| YEAR | 12% | 14% | 16% | 18% | 20% | 24% | 28% | 32% | 36% |
|---|---|---|---|---|---|---|---|---|---|
| 1 | 0.893 | 0.877 | 0.862 | 0.847 | 0.833 | 0.806 | 0.781 | 0.758 | 0.735 |
| 2 | 1.690 | 1.647 | 1.605 | 1.566 | 1.528 | 1.457 | 1.392 | 1.332 | 1.276 |
| 3 | 2.402 | 2.322 | 2.246 | 2.174 | 2.106 | 1.981 | 1.868 | 1.766 | 1.674 |
| 4 | 3.037 | 2.914 | 2.798 | 2.690 | 2.589 | 2.404 | 2.241 | 2.096 | 1.966 |
| 5 | 3.605 | 3.433 | 3.274 | 3.127 | 2.991 | 2.745 | 2.532 | 2.345 | 2.181 |
| 6 | 4.111 | 3.889 | 3.685 | 3.498 | 3.326 | 3.020 | 2.759 | 2.534 | 2.339 |
| 7 | 4.564 | 4.288 | 4.039 | 3.812 | 3.605 | 3.242 | 2.937 | 2.678 | 2.455 |
| 8 | 4.968 | 4.639 | 4.344 | 4.078 | 3.837 | 3.421 | 3.076 | 2.786 | 2.540 |
| 9 | 5.328 | 4.946 | 4.607 | 4.303 | 4.031 | 3.566 | 3.184 | 2.868 | 2.603 |
| 10 | 5.650 | 5.216 | 4.833 | 4.494 | 4.193 | 3.682 | 3.269 | 2.930 | 2.650 |
| 11 | 5.988 | 5.453 | 5.029 | 4.656 | 4.327 | 3.776 | 3.335 | 2.978 | 2.683 |
| 12 | 6.194 | 5.660 | 5.197 | 4.793 | 4.439 | 3.851 | 3.387 | 3.013 | 2.708 |
| 13 | 6.424 | 5.842 | 5.342 | 4.910 | 4.533 | 3.912 | 3.427 | 3.040 | 2.727 |
| 14 | 6.628 | 6.002 | 5.468 | 5.008 | 4.611 | 3.962 | 3.459 | 3.061 | 2.740 |
| 15 | 6.811 | 6.142 | 5.575 | 5.092 | 4.675 | 4.001 | 3.483 | 3.076 | 2.750 |
| 16 | 6.974 | 6.265 | 5.669 | 5.162 | 4.730 | 4.033 | 3.503 | 3.088 | 2.758 |
| 17 | 7.120 | 6.373 | 5.749 | 5.222 | 4.775 | 4.059 | 3.518 | 3.097 | 2.763 |
| 18 | 7.250 | 6.467 | 5.818 | 5.273 | 4.812 | 4.080 | 3.529 | 3.104 | 2.767 |
| 19 | 7.366 | 6.550 | 5.877 | 5.316 | 4.844 | 4.097 | 3.539 | 3.109 | 2.770 |
| 20 | 7.469 | 6.623 | 5.929 | 5.353 | 4.870 | 4.110 | 3.546 | 3.113 | 2.772 |
| 25 | 7.843 | 6.873 | 6.097 | 5.467 | 4.948 | 4.147 | 3.564 | 3.122 | 2.776 |
| 30 | 8.055 | 7.003 | 6.177 | 5.517 | 4.979 | 4.160 | 3.569 | 3.124 | 2.778 |

# PHOTO CREDITS

CHAPTER 1—*p. 5,* Courtesy Dell Computer Corporation; *p. 8,* Used with permission of Ben & Jerry's Homemade Holdings, Inc. 2000; *p. 16,* From the Collections of Henry Ford Museum & Greenfield Village; *p. 19,* Louis Psihoyos/Matrix International, Inc.

CHAPTER 2—*p. 23,* Courtesy Southwest Airlines; *p. 25,* Courtesy Federal Express; *p. 28,* Courtesy Southwest Airlines; *p. 32,* Courtesy Wal-Mart.

TECHNICAL NOTE 2—*p. 49,* Courtesy of The University of Chicago.

CHAPTER 3—*p. 57,* Box shot reprinted with permission from Microsoft Corporation; *p. 64,* Courtesy The Boeing Company; *p. 76,* Courtesy of Primavera Systems, Inc. Report created in Primavera Project Planner.

CHAPTER 4—*p. 91,* Courtesy McDonald's Corporation; *p. 92,* © Corbis. All rights reserved. Edward Rozzo, photographer; *p. 93,* © Corbis. All rights reserved; *p. 101,* Seth Resnick/Stock, Boston; *p. 107,* Courtesy of 3D Systems.

TECHNICAL NOTE 4—*p. 118,* Chris Corsmeier; *p. 119,* © Underwood & Underwood/CORBIS; *p. 121,* Bob Sacha; *p. 124,* Courtesy of United Parcel Service.

CHAPTER 5—*p. 143,* Stone/Jeff Corwin; *p. 147,* Courtesy of Hewlett-Packard Company; *p. 152,* Courtesy Solid Concepts Inc.; *p. 156,* Courtesy Miller Brewing Company; *p. 156,* Courtesy Kawasaki Motors Manufacturing Corp. , U.S.A.; *p. 166,* Kraipit Phanyut/ Sipa Press.

TECHNICAL NOTE 5—*p. 175,* Stone/Andy Sacks; *p. 186,* Courtesy of Hewlett-Packard Company; *p. 189,* Bob Daemmrich/The Image Works; *p. 194,* Courtesy Bachman Design Group.

CHAPTER 6—*p. 207,* Reprinted with permission by Lands' End, Inc.; *p. 212,* Courtesy Marriott Corporation; *p. 220,* Courtesy APREX; *p. 221,* John Thoeming.

TECHNICAL NOTE 6—*p. 231,* F. Robert Jacobs; *p. 232,* Courtesy Alexander Ogilvy for Clixnmortar.com.

CHAPTER 7—*p. 259,* Courtesy General Electric Company; *p. 261,* Courtesy of National Institute of Standards & Technology, Office of Quality Programs, Gaithersburg, Maryland, 20899. Photograph by Steuben; *p. 264,* Courtesy European Foundation for Quality Management; *p. 269,* Courtesy Colgate-Palmolive Company.

TECHNICAL NOTE 7—*p. 291,* Courtesy Kawasaki Motors Manufacturing Corp., U.S.A.; *p. 293,* Ad courtesy of Motorola, Inc.; *p. 299,* Richard Pasley; *p. 303,* Courtesy Hershey Foods Corporation.

MANAGERIAL BRIEFING—*p. 324,* © 1999 David Burnett/CONTACT Press Images; *p. 325,* © 1999 David Burnett/CONTACT Press Images; *p. 325,* © 1999 David Burnett/CONTACT Press Images; *p. 325,* © 1999 David Burnett/CONTACT Press Images.

CHAPTER 8—*p. 331,* Stone/Time Davis; *p. 337,* Courtesy of Campbell Soup Company; *p. 343,* William Taufic/The Stock Market; *p. 344,* Photo courtesy of Hewlett-Packard Company.

CHAPTER 9—*p. 353,* © PhotoDisc; *p. 355,* Courtesy AT&T; *p. 359,* Courtesy Xerox Corporation.

TECHNICAL NOTE 9—*p. 374,* Courtesy Archer Daniels Midland Company; *p. 383,* Courtesy of MapInfo Corporation, Copyright 1997.

CHAPTER 10—*p. 393,* Courtesy Toyota Motor Manufacturing, Kentucky, Inc.; *p. 397,* Courtesy Kawasaki Motors Manufacturing Corp., U.S.A.; *p. 400,* Courtesy McDonnell Douglas; *p. 404,* Courtesy Arvin North American Automotive; *p. 404,* Courtesy Arvin North American Automotive; *p. 405,* Courtesy Arvin North American Automotive; *p. 405,* Courtesy Arvin North American Automotive; *p. 405,* Courtesy Arvin North American Automotive; *p. 408,* Courtesy Ford Motor Company; *p. 410,* © Corbis. All rights reserved.

MANAGERIAL BRIEFING—*p. 426,* Courtesy Colgate-Palmolive Company.

CHAPTER 11—*p. 433,* Stone/Jeff Corwin; *p. 435,* Courtesy GTE Corporation; *p. 439,* Courtesy Third Wave Research Group, 1-800-977-9203.

CHAPTER 12—*p. 481,* Stone/Bernard Grilly; *p. 485,* Courtesy Kawasaki Motors Manufacturing Corp., U.S.A.; *p. 485,* Courtesy Kawasaki Motors Manufacturing Corp., U.S.A.; *p. 500,* © Corbis. All rights reserved.

CHAPTER 13—*p. 511,* © Corbis. All rights reserved; *p. 512,* © 1995 GE Information Services, Inc.; *p. 520,* Courtesy of John Deere; *p. 534,* Ovak Arslanian.

CHAPTER 14—*p. 549,* Photo courtesy of IBM Corp.; *p. 550,* © Corbis. All rights reserved. Photography by Edward Rozzo; *p. 557,* Photo courtesy of IBM Corp. and Dassault Systems; *p. 567,* Courtesy Renfro Corporation.

CHAPTER 15—*p. 586,* Courtesy Dana Corporation; *p. 589,* Courtesy Bernard Welding Equipment Company; *p. 600,* David Pollack/The Stock Market.

TECHNICAL NOTE 15—*p. 625,* Courtesy Systems Modeling Corporation. Arena is a registered trademark of Systems Modeling Corporation; *p. 626,* Courtesy Micro Analysis and Design Simulation Software, Inc.

CHAPTER 16—*p. 641,* © Corbis. All rights reserved. Photography by Edward Rozzo; *p. 646,* Courtesy Andersen Consulting; *p. 653,* Courtesy TRW; *p. 657,* John Chiasson/Liasion Agency, Inc.

CHAPTER 17—*p. 663,* Stone/Lori Adamski Peek.

SUPPLEMENT A—*p. 694,* Courtesy APL.

SUPPLEMENT C—*p. 722,* Stone; *p. 724,* Courtesy Cincinnati Milacron; *p. 726,* Courtesy of 3D Systems.

# NAME INDEX

# SUBJECT INDEX

N



O

## Q